the finz
Multistate Method

By

STEVEN R. FINZ

Director
Advance College of Continuing Legal Education
The Sea Ranch, California

Strategies
&Tactics® SERIES

ASPEN
PUBLISHERS

1185 Avenue of the Americas, New York NY 10036
www.aspenpublishers.com

Printed in the United States of America

ISBN 0-7355-4497-2

This book is intended as a general review of a legal subject. It is not intended as a source for advice for the solution of legal matters or problems. For advice on legal matters, the reader should consult an attorney.

Siegel's, Emanuel, the judge logo, Law In A Flash and design, CrunchTime and design, Strategies & Tactics and design, and The Professor Series are registered trademarks of Aspen Publishers.

About Aspen Publishers

Aspen Publishers, headquartered in New York City, is a leading information provider for attorneys, business professionals, and law students. Written by preeminent authorities, our products consist of analytical and practical information covering both U.S. and international topics. We publish in the full range of formats, including updated manuals, books, periodicals, CDs, and online products.

Our proprietary content is complemented by 2,500 legal databases, containing over 11 million documents, available through our Loislaw division. Aspen Publishers also offers a wide range of topical legal and business databases linked to Loislaw's primary material. Our mission is to provide accurate, timely, and authoritative content in easily accessible formats, supported by unmatched customer care.

To order any Aspen Publishers title, go to *www.aspenpublishers.com* or call 1-800-638-8437.

To reinstate your manual update service, call 1-800-638-8437.

For more information on Loislaw products, go to *www.loislaw.com* or call 1-800-364-2512.

For Customer Care issues, e-mail *CustomerCare@aspenpublishers.com*; call 1-800-234-1660; or fax 1-800-901-9075.

Aspen Publishers
A Wolters Kluwer Company

Dedication

To Iris

TABLE OF CONTENTS

How To Use This Book

This book contains a collection of questions (called "items") in the Multistate exam format, accompanied by answers (called "options") and explanations. Each of the explanations is intended to be a mini-dissertation on the topic involved. Every item and explanation was written by a law professor and then checked and rechecked by at least one other law professor who specializes in the subject matter involved.

The chapter entitled **Strategies & Tactics: Playing the MBE Game to Win** (what we call the **Multistate Method**) sets forth a detailed method for approaching and dealing with items in this format. You should study the chapter diligently before beginning to practice on the items which follow it. Then, as you go through the questions, you should return to the appropriate sections of the chapter for help in responding to particular question types. By the time you have worked your way through fifty or sixty items you should have become so familiar with this Multistate Method that its use is second nature.

The questions are divided into the six subject areas tested on the Multistate Bar Examination: Constitutional Law, Contracts, Criminal Law, Evidence, Real Property, and Torts. If you are still in law school, you can use the separate sections to review the material which you are studying in each of the subject areas. Each section is accompanied by a subject matter outline and question index. Using the question index, you can look for questions dealing with the particular topics and subtopics that you wish to review.

The items which appear in this book are similar in content and form to the questions which appear on the Multistate Bar Examination. On the MBE, each item tests only one general subject area, but is likely to cover several topics and subtopics within that area. A Torts question, for example, may test knowledge of intentional torts, negligence, nuisance, and proximate cause all in the same set of answers (options).

For this reason, most questions (items) in this book may be listed in several different places in the question index. If you have just completed your study of intentional torts and wish to field questions which test your newly acquired knowledge, you can find them by looking at the appropriate place in the Torts question index. You may discover, however, that the same questions also test knowledge of topics that you have not yet studied. This need not prevent the questions from being useful to you.

The Multistate Method game plan suggests that in answering Multistate items you treat each option (i.e., proposed answer) as a separate true-false question. Using this approach, you can choose to deal only with the options for which your studies have prepared you. The explanation accompanying each item analyzes why the answer we pick is correct and why each of the incorrect options is incorrect. You can use these analyses to check your responses to the options.

If you are preparing for the MBE, you should work the items in each of the subject areas after completing your review of those areas. If your review has not prepared you for all the options, you will know what areas need further review. The explanations can help you complete your study.

In addition, this book contains a 200 question practice exam in which the items are shuffled, as they are on the MBE, so that the six subjects are tested in random order. The practice exam is accompanied by a question index which indicates which items test which subjects, topics, and subtopics. If you are still in law school, you may use the items contained in the practice exam for further review as you study the subject areas involved.

If you need additional questions to review, or want Strategies & Tactics on each MBE subject, you should purchase a copy of *Strategies & Tactics for the MBE*, also published by Aspen and available at your local bookstore. For each MBE subject, *Strategies & Tactics for the MBE* delivers detailed advice on what to study and what traps to look out for, as well as actual released MBE questions with detailed answers.

For substantive MBE review, you should check out the *Law In A Flash* MBE Set, which contains flashcards on all MBE subjects (Constitutional Law, Contracts, Criminal Law, Criminal Procedure [tested on the MBE as part of Criminal Law], Evidence, Future Interests [tested as part of Property], Real Property, Sales [tested as part of Contracts], and Torts) as well as a copy of *Strategies & Tactics for the MBE*. The MBE Set is available at your local bookstore.

If you are preparing for the bar exam, you should wait until you have completed your review of all six Multistate subjects before taking the practice exam contained in this book. It may be a good idea to simulate examination conditions when taking it. Turn off your phone, lock your door, tell the rest of the world to go away, and give yourself three uninterrupted hours for each half of the exam.

GOOD LUCK!

Steven Finz

Strategies & Tactics® — **Playing the MBE Game to Win**

TERROR AND THE MBE

It's given on the last Wednesday of February and July in almost every one of the fifty states. In the past two decades, it has become a significant factor in the bar admitting standards of most states. It dredges loathing and paranoia from the souls of embryonic attorneys across the land. It's the Multistate Bar Examination (the MBE), an all-day challenge consisting of 200 questions on six important subjects. It scares the devil out of most of us.

The reason it's so frightening to us is that our profession attracts people who learned as they were growing up that they could talk their way into and argue their way out of most situations. I'm one of these people. You probably are, too. Much of the time, people like us treat life as a game. The trouble with the MBE is that it doesn't give us a chance to talk or argue, which is what we believe we do best. We find it too structured, too restrictive. There's not enough game in it. It cramps our style.

When we think that, though, we're forgetting that the people who create the MBE are cut from the same cloth as we are. They are law professors and practitioners who have argued their way into and out of trouble all their lives. They've been playing the same game with their lives that we've been playing with ours. The ideas that appeal to them also appeal to us. The only difference is that they specialize in testing and finding out what other lawyers are made of. Their exam does a pretty good job of it, but we have to approach it the way we approach other problems in our lives — as a game that must be played from a position of strength.

It helps to realize that, by its very nature, the MBE has certain aspects that work in our favor. First, because it is given in most of the states, it can test only general principles of law — no petty details. Second, because its multiple choice format eliminates the options of argument or explanation, each issue must be so precisely drawn that only one of the four possible answers satisfies the requirements of the question. Most important, because it is given to budding lawyers, the most argumentative and litigious people in the world, it must be scrupulously fair and unassailable.

To assure that the exam will be just and to protect it against attack, the creators of the MBE have developed a method for constructing questions. They stick to a policy which requires that there be no trick questions and no trick answers. No problem will be solved on the basis of a subtle turn of word or phrase. They even have rules to assure the effective use of apostrophes and to eliminate the confusing misuse of pronouns. Questions are screened repeatedly before they are used, and then screened again.

After the exam has been given, the answers are analyzed. Questions which proved too tricky to be fair are invalidated, eliminated from further consideration. Questions which show themselves to have no correct answer or more than one correct answer are also invalidated. Applicants are not supposed to be asked to select the best of four bad answers or four good answers. To each question there is only one demonstrably correct answer. The others are clearly incorrect. Clearly, that is, if we follow the right analytical steps.

Since they have a method for creating the exam, we need a method for taking it. This chapter provides a unique Multistate Method. To develop our method, we must begin by understanding theirs.

STRUCTURE OF QUESTIONS

Questions, or "items" as the examiners call them, come in many different shapes and forms. All, however, can be broken into three distinct parts: the root, the stem, and the options.

The *root* is the part of the item containing the underlying facts. Sometimes it's written in the present tense; sometimes it's written in the past tense. Sometimes it's short; sometimes it's long. Sometimes it's followed by one set of options; sometimes it's followed by several sets of options. Sometimes all the facts in the root are significant; sometimes many of the facts are irrelevant.

The *stem* is the part of the item containing the call of the options or assigning a task. Sometimes it is in the form of a question; sometimes it calls for the completion of a sentence. Sometimes it adds facts to those contained in the root; sometimes it requires that an assumption be made. Sometimes it specifies what cause of action or theory a party is advancing; sometimes it doesn't.

The *options* are the choices given as answers. Sometimes they state conclusions and nothing more; sometimes they link a conclusion with a reason to support it. Sometimes two or more of the options seem to be related to each other; sometimes each of the four is independent of the other three. One of them is always the correct option; three of them are always incorrect.

Exhibit A, on the opposite page, shows a typical item.

DISTRACTORS AND *FOILS*

The examiners spend a lot of time and energy creating three wrong options for each item. They call the incorrect options "distractors" or "foils". In using those names, they have unwittingly tipped their hands. According to Webster, a "distractor" is something which compellingly and confusingly attracts in the wrong direction. A "foil" is something which serves to set off another thing to advantage or disadvantage by contrasting with it. By definition, some of the incorrect options are there to make the others look good, and some of them are there to make the correct option seem bad.

Here, again, the nature of the exam works in our favor. The examination is supposed to be a test of knowledge. The correct choice must be somewhere among the four options, but it can't be left exposed for everyone to see; it has to be hidden. According to their own rules, the examiners can't use tricky devices or puzzling language, so they have to hide it behind a

Exhibit A

Construction of an MBE question or "Item"

Root of the question
(Facts)

Congress passes a law providing that no one who has been a member of an organization which uses unlawful means to deprive any group of person of their rights under the United States Constitution is eligible for employment by the federal government.

Stem of the question
("Call" of options)

If the constitutionality of that law is challenged, it should be held

Options
(Answer choices)

(A) unconstitutional because it is an ex post facto law.

(B) unconstitutional because it prohibits members of certain organizations from holding public office whether or not they knew the purpose of the organizations.

(C) constitutional because employment by the federal government is not a right but a privilege.

(D) constitutional because the federal government has the right to protect itself by not employing persons who hold views inconsistent with the United States Constitution.

screen of distractors and foils. Like a magician's banter, these are designed to make us look away from the real action. That's how the game is played.

Many of the people who create the MBE are law professors or former law professors. In creating distractors and foils, they use insight which comes from their experience with law students. After all, the main purpose of the exam is to find out whether we are finished studying the law and ready to start practicing it. Their foils and distractors are usually based on anticipating the errors that law students are likely to make.

Their method gives all the options a look of superficial plausibility. At first glance every option appears to be correct. Our response to their bag of tricks must therefore include a careful reading of the language which they use.

Incomplete definitions and arguments

No one needs to be more precise in the use of language than a lawyer. Learning to communicate precisely is one of the goals of law school education. A first semester law student may define "murder" as the unjustified killing of a human being, but a lawyer knows that an unjustified killing isn't murder unless it's an unjustified killing of **another** human being **with malice aforethought.**

Some of the foils and distractors that appear on the MBE consist of incomplete or imprecise statements, like those made by beginners in the classroom. An option that says, "John is guilty of murder if he committed the unjustified killing of a human being," is wrong because it is based on an incomplete definition. Don't assume that the examiners left out the rest of the definition by mistake, or that they expect you to know what they really mean. Don't allow yourself to complete the argument or definition in your mind and conclude that it is correct.

Dealing with the facts

Lawyers must be very careful with facts. They must assume nothing in addition to what has been established or given. In summing up to a jury, for example, trial counsel may not make reference to any facts which have not been proven. Frequently, distractors and foils are designed to find out whether we have the ability to play the game the way a lawyer plays it. If a prosecutor proved only that John shot Mary and that Mary died an hour later, John's prosecution for murder would have to be dismissed unless the prosecutor had also proven that John's bullet caused Mary's death. If the facts in the root of the item do not say that Mary died as a result of John's bullet, don't assume or infer that she did. Only a medical expert is competent to draw such a conclusion, and you are not a doctor. Without such proof, we must conclude that John's guilt has not been established.

On the other hand, lawyers can't get away with ignoring facts that have been established. In arguing appeals, for example, lawyers may not claim that the facts proven at the trial should be ignored. They are restricted to making arguments about the legal effects of the proven facts. Since examiners are out to determine whether we can do a lawyer's job, they are likely to fill the root with implausible facts in an effort to trick us into rejecting or disbelieving them. Falling for their ploy can be disastrous. In taking the MBE, we must accept the facts that are given to us, no matter how unlikely or implausible they may seem.

We may have been taught, for example, that an intoxicated person is not capable of driving her car in a reasonable manner. If, however, an item's root tells us that after Mary drank two quarts of whiskey, she was driving her car in a reasonable manner when she collided with Paul, we must accept this as true. Since negligence is unreasonable conduct, and since we are told that Mary was driving her car in a reasonable manner, we must conclude that she was not negligent.

Common errors

Some areas of the law are so confusing to law students that they furnish the examiners with a fertile field in which to cultivate foils and distractors. The literature distributed by the examiners indicates that incorrect options contained in MBE items are frequently based on common errors made by law students. Often, these common errors result from misunderstandings about the significance of legal expressions which have different meanings for lawyers than for lay persons.

The doctrine of "last clear chance" is an example of how this common confusion can be used to create an effective foil or distractor. "Last clear chance" is a doctrine that can be raised only by a plaintiff; its only effect is to eliminate the consequence of the plaintiff's contributory negligence. Thus, even in a jurisdiction which applies the "all-or-nothing" rule of contributory negligence, a plaintiff who goes to sleep in the middle of the road and is struck by a defendant who sees her in time but fails to take reasonable steps to avoid striking her, may still win her case. In finding for the plaintiff, the court is likely to say that the plaintiff's negligence does not bar her recovery because the defendant had the "last clear chance" to avoid the accident.

Knowing that many students are confused about this doctrine, the examiners may create a distractor which says, "Defendant wins because plaintiff had the last clear chance to avoid the accident." It sounds logical, but not to someone who understands that "last clear chance" is a doctrine available only to plaintiffs.

Similarly, a foil or distractor may be based on the "dead man's rule" which excludes evidence of certain conversations with a person now deceased. Although the "dead man's rule" sometimes keeps evidence out, it never justifies the admission of evidence. Thus, an option which says, "The evidence is admissible under the dead man's rule" has to be incorrect, even though at first glance it sounds logical.

Overlooking the obvious

Some lawyers lose cases because they overlook the obvious. Perhaps that's why the examiners occasionally create an option which is so obviously correct that there is no rational excuse for missing it. It's amazing how many applicants reject such an option in the belief that nothing so important can possibly be so easy.

Items regarding the sufficiency of a deed description are good examples of this technique. The general rule is that a description in a deed is sufficient if it adequately identifies the realty conveyed. Usually, it is impossible to decide whether a description satisfies this requirement without knowing something about surveying in general and the geographical area involved in particular. Since the MBE is not a test of surveying or geographical knowledge, however, its creators cannot expect us to determine the validity of a particular description. Instead, they are likely to give the language of a deed description, ask whether it is valid, and then create an option which says, "The description is valid if it adequately identifies the realty conveyed." Can anything be more obviously correct? Don't miss a gift like that one.

Plausible creations

Some applicants are so intimidated by the examination process that they are sure the correct options will involve concepts they never heard of before. This not only leads them to reject options which are obviously correct, it causes them to select options which consist of meaningless garbage. Knowing this, the examiners occasionally indulge their sense of whimsy by building foils and distractors around Latin words or phrases which sound momentous but are used in a context which makes them meaningless.

Post hoc ergo propter hoc is an example of a Latin phrase which may be at the core of one of these seemingly plausible creations. The expression translates as "after which, therefore because of which," and is a name given to the error in reasoning which leads people to offer such arguments as, "It always rains after I wash my car, so washing my car makes it rain (i.e., it rains after (and, therefore, because) I wash my car.)" This is likely to show up as a foil or distractor in an option which says something like, "John will win under the doctrine of *post hoc ergo propter hoc.*"

If that kind of bluff fools us, we will end up at the examiners' mercy. In a question which actually appeared on a past Multistate Bar Exam, many applicants were taken in by a double-talk option which stated that a plaintiff could not be the holder of a certain easement because, "an incorporeal hereditament lies only in grant." One way to avoid falling for such seemingly plausible creations is to remember that after passing all your law school finals, taking a bar review course, and cramming for the exam, you probably are familiar with any rule of law that will matter to the examiners. If an option cites a doctrine or rule that you never heard of before, it's probably incorrect.

Unfamiliar phrases

This doesn't mean that all the correct options will use familiar language. One of the goals of the exam is to determine whether we really understand the law we've learned or whether we've just been trained like parrots to spout phrases. To accomplish this goal, the examiners may describe familiar concepts in non-traditional words. Instead of saying, for example, that John owed Mary a duty of reasonable care only if he created a foreseeable risk to her, they may say that "John had no obligation to Mary unless it appeared that John's conduct would injure her." Instead of saying that strict liability is imposed on one who engages in an ultra-hazardous activity, they may say that "a defendant is liable without regard to fault if her occupation is extremely dangerous." Remember that there are many ways of saying anything, and that substance is far more important than form.

PLAYING THE RIGHT ROLE

In the real world, lawyers play various roles. Sometimes they are judges, deciding the outcome of an issue or selecting the winner of a case. Sometimes they are advocates, making the best argument possible for one of the parties, even though there's no telling whether that party is going to win. Sometimes they are scholars, unconcerned about who wins or loses, interested only in seeing the legal significance of a fact or in selecting the most applicable rule of law, without caring whose interest will be served. It is natural that the items appearing in the MBE game should cast us in each of these three roles. This makes knowing how to act in each of the roles an important part of our Multistate Method.

Acting as the judge

[*Typical stem:* If John sues Mary for battery, the court should find in favor of . . .]

In the real world, the judge starts out with no particular result or conclusion in mind. He does not decide questions of fact, but is always alert for misstatements about the facts in lawyers' arguments. If an argument does not accurately characterize the facts, is based on an inference not justified by the facts, or is based on a rule of law which is not correctly stated, the judge rejects it. He rules in favor of the argument in which accurate statements about the facts and law are consistent with the conclusion with which they are coupled.

When you are asked to act as judge, do not decide questions of fact. Do not try to determine who should win or how the issue should be resolved until you have considered all the arguments presented in the options. Examine each option in turn. First, see whether the facts and law are accurately stated. If not, reject the option. See whether the conclusion offered is consistent with the argument advanced. If not, reject the option. There will be only one option in which the argument advanced is based on accurate statements of fact and law and is consistent with the conclusion offered. This is the correct choice. Select it, even though you may not like the result. After all, you're a judge.

Acting as the advocate

[*Typical stem:* "Which of the following is the most effective argument in favor of Mary's position?"]

Unlike the judge, the advocate works toward a particular result, the one she's been paid or assigned to accomplish. It doesn't matter whether she believes that her client will win. As long as there is any question at all for either the judge or jury, she understands that her client is entitled to representation. The advocate assumes that her client can win, and then makes the argument which is most likely to bring about the victory. She doesn't invent facts, but presents and interprets in the light most favorable to her client those facts which have been established.

When an item asks you to be an advocate, examine each of the options in turn to see whether the law is accurately stated and whether the inferences on which it is based are justified by the facts which are given. If not, reject it. See whether the option presented could possibly result in victory for the client the stem has assigned you to represent. If not, reject it. There will be only one option in which the argument advanced is based on accurate statements of law and fact and which supports your client's position. Choose it, even if you don't really believe that your client can win. After all, you're an advocate.

Acting as the scholar

[*Typical stem:* "The interest in Blackacre which John had on the day after Testatrix's death is best described as a . . .]

The scholar doesn't try to decide or influence the outcome of a case. The scholar uses his knowledge of the law to recognize the legal significance of a particular fact or to select the most applicable rule. He sees an intellectual challenge and nothing more. Like a professor asking a question in the classroom, he cares not who wins or loses. He focuses on a specific and limited issue and listens to each of the options chosen by his students. Then he smiles at the student whose choice comes closest to the one he had in mind when he asked the question.

Do the same with an item which casts you in the role of a scholar. Forget about who will win or lose. Don't worry whether the option you select will result in justice. Just focus on the specific issues involved and try to resolve them in your mind. Then examine each of the options carefully and select the one which comes closest to the selection you have already formulated.

TIMING

Our Multistate Method must teach the most efficient possible use of time. Most people barely manage to answer all the items in the allotted time. *You probably will not have an opportunity to go back and check your choices.* It's wise to get them right on the first pass, because that's probably the only chance you will get.

According to the Examiners, six subjects are tested. The test presents 34 questions each on Contracts and Torts, and 33 questions each on Constitutional Law, Criminal Law, Evidence, and Real Property. You should recognize, however, that in reality *nine* law school subjects are tested — the section on Contracts includes questions on Sales, the section on Property includes questions on Future Interests, and the section on Criminal Law includes questions on Criminal Procedure.

There are usually two or more versions of each exam so that, although everyone gets the same questions, the questions are not in the same order. They are randomly shuffled in each version. Therefore, you may see two real property items in a row and then not see another until ten or twenty items later.

Everyone feels stronger in some of the subjects than in others, and there will be a powerful temptation to go looking for those questions that deal with your best subjects. Resist that temptation. ***Answer the questions in the order in which they appear.***

There are three good reasons why you should take this advice. First, the tough ones aren't going to get any easier with the passage of time. If anything, fatigue will make them seem even tougher, so there's no point in putting them off. Second, if you read item #3, for example, and decide not to answer it until later, part of your mind will still be working on it when you try to answer subsequent items. This will keep you from devoting all your energy to the item before you, and may even cause you to base a choice in one question on facts which you still remember from item #3. Third and most important, if you skip item #3, there will be a blank space on your answer sheet, and you may become confused into putting the answer to item #4 in the space for item #3. Once you do that, every choice that follows will be written in the wrong space.

This potential pitfall alone makes it better to guess than to leave a blank space. But there's more. The examiners give you one point for every correct choice and don't subtract any points for a wrong choice. This means that a wrong choice is certainly no worse than a blank space. In most states, you can get 60 or more wrong and still pass the exam. If you can't come up with the correct option, guess and move ahead. You have at least a 25% chance of guessing correctly.

After the exam is over, the examiners usually determine that some of the items — sometimes as many as 10 — were invalid. When this happens, they often give credit for any option chosen. This means that you may receive a point even if you guessed wrong. If you left it blank, you'll get nothing.

You won't really be guessing anyway, because a "guess" is a choice which is based on no real knowledge. By the time you get to the bar exam, your head will be so filled with information that there won't be any item that you don't know at least something about. Even if it's buried deep in the unconscious recesses of your mind, this knowledge will increase the probability that the option you choose is correct.

Time is not on your side. You'll have two three-hour sessions with 100 items in each. That breaks down to 33.3 items per hour, about 17 items per half hour, or 1.8 minutes per item. It is important to stay on schedule. Each item is worth one point. You don't get anything extra for the ones you spend extra time on. Every extra second you spend on one item is a second less that you'll have to spend on the next.

THE TEST BECOMES A GAME

After observing a courtroom proceeding for the first time, the lay person typically scratches his temple and says, "It's a game. Nothing but a game." We tell him it isn't; it's serious business. But when we reflect on the origins of the adversary system, we see knights in armor jousting on a field of battle in the belief that the righteous was assured of winning the contest.

It started out as a game, and we're kidding ourselves if we try to believe that there isn't any game left in it. In a way, the phrase "adversary system" is a euphemism for a complex and exciting game that society plays, with lawyers as its game pieces. It is fitting, therefore, that the bar examination, which tests competency to practice law, is, itself, a kind of game, testing, among other things, the applicant's ability to play.

All games involve a combination of knowledge and strategy. A crap-shooter has no control over the numbers that come up on the dice, but wins or loses by making bets based on his knowledge of the odds. A card-player decides "when to hold 'em and when to fold 'em" by knowing what cards are in the deck and remembering which ones have already been dealt. Trivial Pursuit champions win by moving their game pieces in the most advantageous way, but they don't get to move them at all unless they know the answers to the questions that appear on the game cards.

The MBE is a game that can't be won without knowledge. Knowledge isn't all, though. Given enough time, any decent lawyer who approaches the MBE seriously enough to prepare for it adequately, can get a passing score. But the exam is long and the hours are short. Without an effective strategy, an applicant is likely to be cut down by the clock. Ding dong. Game over.

To avoid running out of time, move through every item as swiftly as possible. To avoid being foiled and distracted, however, read every relevant word patiently and carefully. At first, these goals seem to be inconsistent with each other. By beginning with an orientation, our Multistate Method provides us with a strategy for accomplishing both of them.

ORIENTATION

The fact pattern in an item's root may raise dozens of issues, some of which can be resolved and some of which won't ever be resolved. Usually, however, the stem is more narrowly drawn to eliminate all but one or two of the possible issues. If we waste time answering questions that weren't asked, we won't have a chance of answering the ones that were.

To avoid being drawn in a series of false directions, ***always begin with a quick reading of the stem*** to determine the call of the question. If there are two or more stems, quickly read them all. Look for the role which each stem assigns and the task which it sets before you. It may specify a particular cause of action; it may name a crime; it may point to a clause of the Constitution; it may designate the parties plaintiff and defendant.

After the stem, ***quickly*** read the root. We're still not ready to begin choosing among the options, so we aren't sure what we're looking for, even though the stem gave us a pretty good idea. This first reading of the root is part of our orientation.

Don't struggle too hard at this point to understand all the facts. Don't worry about keeping the chronology straight. Don't begin drawing those little diagrams you learned about in law school or bar review. Some facts in the root may not even be relevant to the options, and attempting to deal with them at this point may turn out to be a waste of time. If necessary, you can always return to the root to check the facts again.

MAKING THE PLAY

Our first reading of the stem and root was an orientation, designed to find out what role we've been assigned to play and what task we've been asked to accomplish. Now it's time to accomplish it. Read the stem again, more carefully this time. Where a single root is followed by two or more stems, deal with one stem at a time, selecting among one set of options before beginning to think about the next.

Basic game plan

Because the examiners' game plan includes options which make us look in the wrong direction, our Multistate Method must adopt a game plan that will keep us from being foiled and distracted. Since the wrong options are supposed to make other options look either good or bad by comparison, don't compare one option to the others. Treat each as a separate option and as if it were the only one before you. Recall, according to the examiners' policy, only one can be correct. To play it safe, even if you have found one which you think is true, don't stop until you have checked all four options.

With pencil in hand, examine each option carefully, returning to the root to confirm facts if necessary. Mark the option with a "T" if it is true, with an "F" if it is false, and with a "?" if you can't make up your mind. When you're done, you should have three "F"s and one "T". As long as you have a good clear "T", count "?"s as "F"s. If you have no "T"s at all, treat a "?" as a "T". The option with the "T" next to it is the correct answer.

Although this basic game plan works for all MBE item-types, there are a few variations which may help us deal more efficiently with particular kinds of items.

Negative response

Occasionally a stem asks for a "reverse" response, like, "Which of the following is LEAST likely to violate the Fourteenth Amendment?" When that happens, restate the stem in the reverse: "Would the following violate the Fourteenth Amendment?" You should end up with three "T"s (yes) and one "F" (no). Choose the one that got the "F".

Overlapping options

Sometimes some of the options contain parts of others. Typical options:

John is guilty of

(A) Burglary only.

(B) Robbery only.

(C) Burglary and Robbery.

(D) Neither Burglary nor Robbery.

Instead of trying to deal with these overlapping options in combination, break them down into the individual components (e.g., Burglary, Robbery). Give each of the individual choices a "T" or "F" and then find the option which contains the correct combination of choices.

Two-tiered options

Sometimes overlapping options are presented in two tiers to make the individual choices easier to spot. A typical question is as follows:

John is guilty of

I. Burglary.
II. Robbery.   **← First Tier**

(A) I only.
(B) II only.
(C) I and II.   **← Second Tier**
(D) Neither I nor II.

Treat two-tiered options in the same way as overlapping options. Assign a "T" or "F" to each statement in the first (Roman numeral) tier, and then select from the second (lettered) tier the option containing the correct combination of choices.

Three-to-one options

In some items, three of the options offer one conclusion coupled with different reasons for it, while the fourth offers the opposite conclusion with no reason at all. A typical question:

John will

(A) lose.
(B) win, because . . . .
(C) win, because . . . .
(D) win, because . . . .

Since the odd option is unaccompanied by a reason, it is impossible to select it without eliminating the other three first. For this reason, when confronted by a three-to-one options item, always consider the odd option last. Then choose it only if all of the others have received "F"s.

What-if options

Sometimes the options offer additional facts, and the stem calls for selection of the fact pattern which would be most likely to bring about a particular result. This kind of item is like the classroom game in which the professor changes the facts in a case under discussion by saying, "Now, what if . . . ."

> [*Typical stem*: Which of the following additional facts or inferences, if it was the only one true, would be most likely to result in a judgment for Mary?]

It is important to remember that this kind of item does not require you to decide whether the additional fact or inference in the "what if" option is true, but directs you to assume that it is. If you encounter one of these, combine the stem with each "what-if" option in turn, accepting as true the facts which it contains. In assigning a "T" or "F", don't ask whether the facts are true or the inference is justified; assume that they are. Then decide whether the existence of these additional facts or inferences would be likely to bring about the particular result. (e.g., In the above item, ask, "If this fact were true or this inference were justified, would it result in a judgment for Mary?")

SELECTING THE CORRECT OPTION

Selecting the correct option is easy once you've placed three "F"s and one "T" next to the given options. The hard part is deciding whether to give an option a "T" or "F". This becomes easier if an appropriate strategy is applied. Although the MBE will present you with 800 options (i.e., four for each question), all options fall into only five categories. Our Multistate Method provides a strategy to use for each of the categories.

Simple options

Some options only state possible conclusions. These are called "simple options." Here's a typical simple-option item:

> Johnson took a diamond ring to a pawnshop and borrowed $20 on it. It was agreed that the loan was to be repaid within 60 days, and if it was not, the pawnshop owner, Defendant, could sell the ring. A week before the expiration of the 60 days, Defendant had an opportunity to sell the ring to a customer for $125. He did so, thinking it was unlikely that Johnson would repay the loan and that if he did, Defendant would be able to handle him somehow, even by paying for the ring if necessary. Two days later, Johnson came in with the money to reclaim his ring. Defendant told him that it had been stolen when his shop was burglarized one night and that therefore he was not responsible for its loss.
>
> Larceny, embezzlement, and false pretenses are separate crimes in the jurisdiction.
>
> Which of the following crimes has the Defendant most likely committed?
>
> (A) Larceny.
> (B) Embezzlement.
> (C) Larceny by trick.
> (D) Obtaining by false pretenses.

These options are "simple" rather than "complex," but not "simple" rather than "difficult." Since nothing is given but a bare conclusion, simple options usually require the most work. In dealing with each simple option, it is necessary to remember the essential elements of whatever rule of law is applicable and to check the root to see whether every one of those elements is satisfied by the facts given.

In the above example, to decide whether to mark option (A) with a "T" or "F", it is first necessary to remember that larceny is the trespassory taking and carrying off of personal property known to be another's with the intent to permanently deprive. Then it is necessary to return to the root to see whether Defendant trespassorily took the ring, whether he carried it off, whether he knew that the ring belonged to another, and whether he had the intent to permanently deprive. The option can receive a "T" only if all the elements of the crime are satisfied by the facts.

In the real world, it is likely that some of these elements will raise questions of fact for a jury to determine or questions of law which ultimately will be decided by an appellate court. Different juries may come up with different answers to the questions of fact, and different appellate courts may come up with different answers to the questions of law. An MBE item must have three options which are clearly incorrect, however, and one which is clearly correct. This means that the facts must be structured so as to make it clear that at least one of the elements of the rule applicable in each option is unsatisfied.

In the above example, Defendant's act cannot be larceny (option A) because there was clearly no trespassory taking. A defendant trespassorily takes when he receives possession contrary to the rights of the owner. Since Defendant received possession of the ring lawfully, with Johnson's consent, and with no improper purpose, he did not trespassorily take it and cannot be guilty of larceny. Larceny by trick (option C) is committed by fraudulently obtaining possession of personal property known to be another's with the intent to permanently deprive. Since Defendant was not planning to steal the ring when he obtained it from Johnson, he did not obtain it fraudulently or with the intent to permanently deprive and cannot be guilty of larceny by trick. Obtaining by false pretenses (option D) is committed by fraudulently inducing another to transfer title to a chattel. Since Johnson never transferred title to the ring, Defendant cannot be guilty of obtaining it by false pretenses. As can be seen, options A, C, and D are clearly incorrect.

At the same time, the facts must establish that all the elements of the rule supporting the correct option are satisfied. Embezzlement (option B) is committed by criminally converting property of which the defendant has lawful custody. Since Johnson delivered the ring to Defendant before Defendant developed the intent to steal it, Defendant's custody was clearly lawful. Because only a person with the right to do so is entitled to sell a chattel, and because Defendant did not have the right to sell it, his sale of the ring was clearly a criminal conversion. Since all the elements of embezzlement are clearly satisfied, (B) must be the correct option.

Complex options

Most of the time, an option will consist of two parts: a conclusion and a reason or condition giving rise to the conclusion. Here's a typical complex-option item:

> Paulsen was eating in a restaurant when he began to choke on a piece of food that had lodged in his throat. Dow, a physician who was dining at a nearby table, did not wish to become involved and did not render any assistance, although prompt medical attention would have been effective in removing the obstruction from Paulsen's throat. Because of the failure to obtain prompt medical attention, Paulsen suffered severe brain injury from lack of oxygen.
>
> If Paulsen asserts a claim against Dow for his injuries, the court should find for
>
> (A) Dow, because Dow did not cause the piece of food to lodge in Paulsen's throat.
> (B) Paulsen, if a reasonably prudent person with Dow's experience, training, and knowledge would have assisted Paulsen.
> (C) Paulsen, but only if the jurisdiction has a statute which relieves physicians of malpractice liability for emergency first aid.
> (D) Dow, unless Dow knew that Paulsen was substantially certain to sustain serious injury.

The strategy to be used for each complex option depends upon the conjunction which joins its parts. Four such conjunctions are commonly used on the MBE, each with a specific meaning of its own. They are "because," "if," "only if," and "unless." Our Multistate Method provides a different approach for each of them.

[**AUTHOR'S NOTE:** Since the following sections deal with complex options, they contain complex explanations. It is recommended that you separately study each of these sections since each deals with a different conjunction. When you work on practice questions containing options built around these four conjunctions, return to the section on each conjunction used and review it.]

"Because" as a conjunction

An option built around the conjunction "because" or its synonym "since" couples a conclusion with a reason for the conclusion. An option of this kind actually makes two statements. If I say, "The street is wet *because* it is raining," my conclusion is "the street is wet," and my reason is "it is raining." If it isn't raining, my whole statement is false. Even if it is raining, my statement is true only if the rain is what is making the street wet.

To decide whether to give the option a "T" or "F", we must first determine whether the reason given is based on an accurate statement. In the real world, we can find out whether it is raining by looking out the window. In an MBE option, if the reason given involves a statement about the facts, we must return to the root to see whether the facts are accurate. If the reason involves a statement about the law, we must search our bank of knowledge to see whether it states the law accurately. If the reason is based on an inaccurate statement of either facts or law, the option gets an "F".

But even if the reason given is based on an accurate statement of the facts or law (i.e., it is actually raining), we can not give the option a "T" unless the reason logically justifies the conclusion. Since rain does make the street wet, the reason given in the above statement (i.e., it is raining) justifies the conclusion (i.e., the street is wet), and the entire statement is correct. If the statement is, "The street is wet because the sun is shining," the statement is incorrect even if the sun is shining, because sunshine does not make the street wet.

Option (A) in the above item says that the court should find for "Dow, because Dow did not cause the piece of food to lodge in Paulsen's throat." Since the reason given (i.e., Dow did not cause the piece of food to lodge in Paulsen's throat) is a statement about the facts, we must return to the root to see whether it is accurate. According to the root, Dow happened to be dining at a nearby table when Paulsen began choking on food. Since there is no fact indicating that Dow had anything to do with the food in Paulsen's throat, the reason is based on an accurate statement about the facts. So far, option A is valid.

Next, we must decide whether the fact that Dow did not cause the food to lodge in Paulsen's throat justifies the conclusion that the court should find for Dow. Here, of course, it is necessary to rely on our knowledge of the law. Under the law of negligence, a defendant is generally not under a duty to assist a plaintiff in peril unless the defendant did something to cause that peril. Since Dow did not cause the food to lodge in Paulsen's throat, Dow had no obligation to help remove it, and his failure to do so cannot result in liability. Since the reason is an accurate statement, and since it logically justifies the conclusion with which it is coupled, option A should receive a "T".

If option A states the reason as follows: "the court should find for Dow *because Paulsen's brain injury resulted from a lack of oxygen*," the option would be incorrect. The root states that Paulsen's brain injury was caused by a lack of oxygen, and this establishes that the reason is based on an accurate statement of the facts. But the medical cause of an injury does not necessarily determine whether a particular defendant is liable. Thus, the reason given does not justify the conclusion to which it is coupled, and the option should receive an "F".

"If" as a conjunction

An option built around the conjunction "if" couples a conclusion with a condition requiring that conclusion. An option of this kind makes only one statement. If I say, "The street is wet *if* it is raining," my conclusion is "the street is wet," and the condition is "if it is raining." It doesn't matter whether it is really raining, because I haven't said that it is. Nor do I need to say that it is. All I've said or need to say is that were it raining, the street would be wet.

To decide whether to give an option a "T" or "F", we don't need to determine whether the "if"-condition is an accurate statement. We don't have to look out the window to see whether it is raining. Use of the word "if" requires that we assume the condition which follows it. In a similar MBE question, we don't have to search through the root to see whether the "if"-condition contains an accurate statement about the facts and we don't have to check our memory to see whether the "if"-condition contains an accurate statement about the law.

All we have to do is assume that the "if"-condition exists and then decide whether it logically justifies the conclusion. If we assume that it is raining, the street will certainly be wet since rain wets everything it touches. The "if"-condition (i.e., it is raining) thus justifies the conclusion (i.e., the street is wet), and the entire option is correct. If the option is "the street is wet if the sun is shining," the statement is incorrect whether or not the sun is shining because sunshine does not make the street wet.

Option (B) in the above item says that the court should find for "Paulsen, if a reasonably prudent person with Dow's experience, training, and knowledge would have assisted Paulsen." Since "if" introduces an assumed condition, we need not decide whether a reasonably prudent person with Dow's experience, training, and knowledge would have assisted Paulsen. We simply assume that this is so. Our job is to decide whether this "if"-condition would be sufficient to make Dow liable.

Although we do not need to search the facts in the root or our memory to decide whether the "if"-condition is based on an accurate statement of fact, it is necessary to rely on our knowledge of the law to determine whether the "if"-condition would justify the conclusion. Since a defendant is generally not under a duty to assist a plaintiff in peril unless the defendant did something to cause the peril in the first place, Dow's liability is not measured by what any other person would have done. Since the "if"-condition (i.e., a reasonably prudent person with Dow's experience, training, and knowledge would have assisted Paulsen) would not justify the conclusion (i.e., the court should find for Paulsen), option (B) should receive an "F".

If the option said that the court should find for "Paulsen if Dow had an obligation to assist him," the statement would be correct. This is so because, once we assume that such an obligation exists, Dow's failure to render aid would be a breach of it, subjecting him to liability. Although no jurisdiction is likely to hold that Dow owed Paulsen such an obligation, the word "if" requires us to assume the existence of the condition (i.e., Dow does owe Paulsen that obligation), and our knowledge of the law tells us that this would make Dow liable. Since the "if"-condition would justify the conclusion, the option would then be correct.

"Only if" as a conjunction

An option built around the conjunctive phrase "only if" couples a conclusion with a different kind of condition--an exclusive condition. An option of this kind makes only one absolute statement. If I say, "The street is wet *only if* it is raining," my conclusion is that "the street is wet," and the condition is "only if it is raining." It doesn't matter whether it is really raining, because I haven't said that it is nor do I need to say that it is. What I've said is that rain is the only thing in the world that can possibly make the street wet.

To decide whether to give the option a "T" or "F", we don't need to ask whether the "only if"-condition is an accurate statement. We don't have to verify that it is raining, because the phrase "only if" requires that we assume the condition which follows it (i.e., that is is raining). Since rain is not the only thing in the world that could possibly make the street wet, the option (i.e., the street is wet only if it is raining) is false in any event.

In an MBE question, we don't have to search the root to see whether the "only if"-condition contains an accurate statement about the facts and we don't have to check our memory to see whether the "only if"-condition contains an accurate statement about the law. As in the "if" option, we must assume that the "only if"-condition exists and ask whether it logically justifies the conclusion. If we assume that it is raining, the street will certainly be wet since rain wets everything it touches.

For our next step, we must decide whether the "only if"-condition (i.e., it is raining) is the only thing in the world that could possibly justify the conclusion (i.e., the street is wet). Since there are many things that can make the street wet, rain is not the only condition which would make the conclusion correct, and the entire option is therefore incorrect. If the option is restated, "The street is wet only if there is liquid on it," the option is correct since, by definition, liquid is the only thing in the world which can make another thing wet.

Option (C) in the above problem states that the court should find for "Paulsen, but only if the jurisdiction has a statute which relieves physicians of malpractice liability for emergency first aid." Since "only if" introduces an assumed condition, the fact that the root says nothing about whether the jurisdiction has such a statute is irrelevant. We must simply assume that it does.

Our job is to decide whether the existence of such a statute is the only thing in the world which would make the court find for Paulsen. Although we do not need to search the root or our memory to decide whether the "only if"-condition is based on an accurate statement of fact, it is necessary to check our knowledge of the law to determine whether the "only if"-condition would justify the conclusion. Where they exist, statutes of the kind described (i.e., Good Samaritan laws) protect a physician who renders aid, but do not require that s/he render aid. For this reason, the existence of such a statute would not impose a duty on Dow and would not be relevant to Dow's liability. Its existence would not make him liable and certainly is not the only thing which could possibly make him liable. For these reasons, this option should receive an "F".

If the option said that the court should find for "Paulsen only if Dow had an obligation to assist him," the option would be correct. This is so because all the other elements of a negligence cause of action are satisfied by facts contained in the root. A defendant is liable for negligence if he breaches a duty of reasonable care and if that breach is a proximate cause of plaintiff's damage. Since the receipt of prompt medical attention would have prevented the injury, Dow's failure to render aid was a cause of Paulsen's damage. If Dow had an obligation to assist Paulsen, his failure to do so would be a breach of his obligation. Thus, the only thing in the world which we make a court find for Paulsen would be a rule imposing on Dow an obligation to ass. him.

"Unless" as a conjunction

An option built around the conjunction "unless" couples a conclusion with still a different kind of condition--a negative exclusive condition. An option of this kind also makes only one statement. If I say, "The street is dry *unless* it is raining," my conclusion is "the street is dry," and the condition is "unless it is raining." It doesn't matter whether it is really raining, because I haven't said that it is. Nor do I need to say that it is. All I've said is that rain is the only thing in the world which would keep the street from being dry.

To decide whether to give the option a "T" or "F", we don't need to determine whether the "unless"-condition is an accurate statement. We don't have to look out the window to see whether it is raining, because the word "unless" requires that we assume the condition which follows it.

In an MBE question, we don't have to search the root to see whether the "unless"-condition contains an accurate statement of fact and we don't have to check our memory to see whether the "unless"-condition contains an accurate statement about the law. We must accept the "unless"-condition as stated and decide whether it is the only condition in the world which would make the conclusion false. If we assume that it is raining, the street will certainly not be dry since rain wets everything it touches. The condition (i.e., it is raining) would thus make the conclusion (i.e., the street is dry), false.

For our next step, we must decide whether the "unless"-condition (i.e., it is raining) is in fact the only condition in the world that would make the conclusion (i.e., the street is dry) false. Since there are many things that can make the street wet, rain is not the only condition which would make the conclusion false. The entire option is, therefore, incorrect.

If the option is "The street is dry unless there is liquid on it," the option will be correct since, by definition, liquid is the only thing in the world which can keep another thing from being dry. "Unless" is the opposite of "only if." "The street is wet only if it is raining" means the same thing as "The street is dry unless it is raining."

Option (D) in the above item says that the court should find for "Dow, unless Dow knew that Paulsen was substantially certain to sustain serious injury." Since "unless" introduces an assumed condition, the fact that the root says nothing about whether Dow knew that Paulsen was substantially certain to sustain serious injury is irrelevant. We must simply assume it.

Our job is to decide whether the state of mind described is the only thing in the world which would prevent the court from finding for Dow. Although we do not need to search the root or our memory to decide whether the "unless"-condition is based on an accurate statement, it is necessary to rely on our knowledge of the law in deciding whether the "unless"-condition would make the option false. A defendant who performs a voluntary act with the knowledge that it is substantially certain to result in injury intends that injury and may be liable for causing it. Intentional tort liability cannot be based on a failure to act, however, unless there was an obligation to act in the first place.

Because of the rule which provides that a defendant has no duty to assist a plaintiff in peril unless the defendant caused that peril, Dow had no obligation to assist Paulsen. Thus, even if he was substantially certain that his failure to do so would result in injury, he is not liable for the injury. For this reason, the "unless"-condition (i.e., Dow knew that Paulsen was substantially certain to sustain injury) would not prevent the court from finding for Dow and, therefore, is not the only thing that would prevent Dow from prevailing. The option thus should receive an "F".

If the option said instead that the court should find for "Dow unless Dow had an obligation to assist Paulsen," the option would be correct. This is so because all the other elements of a negligence cause of action are satisfied by facts contained in the root. Since the receipt of prompt medical attention would have prevented the injury, Dow's failure to render aid would be a cause of Paulsen's damage. If Dow had a duty to assist Paulsen, his failure to do so would be a breach of his duty. Thus, the only thing in the world which would prevent the court from finding for Dow would be a rule imposing an obligation on Dow to assist Paulsen.

PRACTICE MAKES BETTER

Anyone who says that practice makes perfect is telling a tall tale; no one and nothing can be perfect. Practice does lead to improvement, though. No matter how good you are at answering Multistate-type questions now, the more you practice, the better you'll get at it. If you know your law, practicing our Multistate Method will equip you with a strategy for achieving success on the MBE.

People who think that there is a way to get the actual MBE questions in advance are dreaming. It's true that each MBE contains 50 questions that have been used before. But the examiners only publish the ones that they will not use again. So if you have a complilation of released questions, such as *Strategies & Tactics for the MBE*, don't expect to see any of them on your exam.

Some publishers and bar reviewers take the exam every time it is given and tell you that their books contain verbatim copies of all the questions that were on it. This is an empty promise. There's no such thing as a fully photographic memory. Nobody can take a six hour exam and come out of it remembering even a single question word for word. MBE questions are written so precisely that even a slight change of wording alters the effect of the entire question.

Instead of trying to find out what the questions are going to be, concentrate on mastering the Method so that you'll be ready for whatever comes. The questions in this book are similar to those which the Multistate Bar Examiners use. Every one of them was written by a law professor and then reviewed and revised by another law professor. This is how the examiners do it.

Try to deal with the item by using the Method outlined in this chapter. Start by orienting yourself to the item with a quick reading of the stem and root, paying careful attention to the role which each assigns. Then apply the basic game plan, treating each option as a separate true-false choice and marking it with a "T", "F", or "?". In deciding whether to mark a "T" or "F", choose the appropriate strategy for a simple option or a complex option and analyze the use of the conjunctions "because," "if," "only if," or "unless."

The MBE is a very special game because it's a game played only by prospective lawyers. Some will be winners, and some will be losers. Decide in advance which you intend to be and build your whole attitude from that basic decision. When you've learned to think of the MBE as a game, you may even find that you look forward to playing it. Afterwards, you may hear yourself saying that it was fun. Nevertheless, it's a game you don't want to play more than once. So practice, practice, practice.

After you've been sworn in, send me a business card in care of the publisher.

Steven Finz

QUESTIONS
CONSTITUTIONAL LAW

CONSTITUTIONAL LAW
TABLE OF CONTENTS
Numbers refer to Question Numbers

CONSTITUTIONAL LAW QUESTIONS

Questions 1-2 are based on the following fact situation.

The state of New Bedford enacts the Continuing Professional Education Act, which provides that all persons licensed by the state to practice any profession other than medicine are required to complete ten units per year of state-approved continuing education studies as a condition for renewal of their professional licenses.

1. The day after the statute goes into effect, Jude, a law school graduate who has applied for but not yet received a license to practice law, sues in federal court seeking a declaratory judgment that the Continuing Professional Education Act is unconstitutional. Which of the following is the clearest ground for dismissal of this action by the court?

    (A) No substantial federal question is presented.

    (B) The suit presents a non justiciable political controversy.

    (C) Jude lacks standing to attack the statute.

    (D) The validity of the statute has not yet been determined by a state court.

2. An action is brought in a state court by a New Bedford attorney for an injunction prohibiting enforcement of the Continuing Professional Education Act and an order declaring it to be unconstitutional on the ground that it violates the Equal Protection Clause of the Fourteenth Amendment to the United States Constitution. Which one of the following additional facts or inferences, if it were true, would most effectively support a finding that the statute is constitutional?

    (A) Competency in law is based upon knowledge of principles which change more quickly than those upon which competency in medicine is based.

    (B) A license to practice law is a privilege rather than a right.

(C) The power to license professionals is reserved to the states by the Tenth Amendment to the United States Constitution.

(D) The state bar association passed a resolution approving of the requirements contained in the Continuing Professional Education Act.

3. The feral tusker is an unusual species of wild pig which is found in the state of Tuscalona, having evolved from several strains of domestic swine which escaped from the farms of early Tuscalona settlers. A Tuscalona state law declares the feral tusker to be an endangered species, and prohibits the killing or shooting of any feral tusker within the state. The Tusker National Park was established by the federal government in order to preserve plants and animals native to the region, and is located entirely within the state of Tuscalona. The feral tusker is so hardy that it has begun to displace other wildlife in the Tusker National Park. Because the feral tusker is actually descended from European stock, the United States Department of the Interior has contracted with Termine, a resident of another state, to kill all feral tuskers living within Tusker National Park. The contract with Termine is specifically authorized by federal statutes regulating the operation of national parks.

If Termine is prosecuted by the state of Tuscalona for violating the law which prohibits the killing of feral tuskers, which of the following is Termine's strongest argument in defense against that prosecution?

    (A) Only the federal government can declare a species to be endangered.

    (B) As applied, the Tuscalona statute unduly interferes with interstate commerce.

    (C) As applied, the Tuscalona statute violates the Obligation of Contracts Clause of the United States Constitution.

(D) As applied, the Tuscalona statute violates the Supremacy Clause of the United States Constitution.

4. A state statute prohibits the killing of any animal "in a manner which causes unnecessary pain or suffering of said animal." Dobson is prosecuted for violating the statute by strangling a chicken as part of a religious ritual in which he participated. Dobson defends on the ground that the state statute as applied in his case unconstitutionally interferes with his free exercise of religion.

Which of the following may the court **NOT** consider in determining the constitutionality of the statute?

(A) Whether the statute is necessary to protect a compelling state interest.

(B) Whether the religious belief which requires the strangling of a chicken is reasonable.

(C) Whether the religious ritual involving the strangling of chicken has been practiced for a long period of time.

(D) Whether Dobson is sincere in the religious belief which requires the strangling of a chicken.

5. Congress passes a law regulating the wholesale and retail prices of "every purchase of an automobile in the United States." The strongest argument in support of the constitutionality of such a statute is that

(A) taken as a whole, the domestic purchases and sales of such products affect interstate commerce.

(B) the United States Constitution expressly authorizes Congress to pass laws for the general welfare.

(C) Congress has the authority to regulate the prices of products purchased and sold because commerce includes buying and selling.

(D) Congress has the right to regulate interstate transportation and the importation of products from abroad.

Questions 6-7 are based on the following fact situation.

A federal statute directs payment of federal funds to states for use in the improvement and expansion of state hospital facilities. The terms of the statute provide that "No state shall award a contract for hospital improvement or expansion financed in whole or in part by funds received under this section unless said contract requires that the contractor pay its employees a minimum wage of $10.00 per hour."

The state of Calizona contracted with Bilder for the construction of a new wing on the Calizona state Hospital, after receiving funds for that purpose under the federal statute. The contract did not require Bilder to pay its employees a minimum wage of $10.00 per hour. Upon learning this, federal officials demanded that the state of Calizona either modify its contract with Bilder or return the funds received under the statute. When Calizona refused, the federal government sued the state of Calizona in a federal court for return of the money.

6. In the action by the United States against the state of Calizona, the court should find for

(A) the state of Calizona, because fixing the minimum wage of employees is a traditional state function.

(B) the state of Calizona, because the regulation of hospitals and of construction practices are traditional state functions.

(C) the United States, because Congress has the power to regulate the way in which federal funds are spent.

(D) the United States, because some of the materials used in hospital construction are traded in interstate commerce.

7. Assume for the purpose of this question that several employees of Bilder who received less than $10.00 per hour while working on the Calizona State Hospital expansion instituted an action for damages against the state of Calizona in a federal court, and that the state of Calizona moved to dis-

miss their cause of action. Which of the following is the clearest reason for dismissal of the suit?

(A) The state of Calizona is immune from such an action under the Eleventh Amendment to the United States Constitution.

(B) No federal question is involved.

(C) The state of Calizona did not employ the plaintiffs.

(D) The plaintiffs voluntarily accepted the wage which Bilder paid them.

8. The zingbird is a rare species of quail found only in the state of Capricorn. Because its flesh is tasty, it was hunted nearly to extinction until thirty years ago. At that time, the state of Capricorn instituted conservation and game management programs designed to preserve the zingbird. These programs included the establishment of zingbird breeding preserves, the employment of ornithologists to study zingbird habits, the passage of laws restricting the hunting of zingbirds, and the employment of game wardens to enforce those laws. The expense of maintaining the programs was financed in part by the sale of hunting licenses. A recent statute passed by the Capricorn state legislature fixes the fee for a hunting license at $10 per year for Capricorn residents, and $20 per year for non-residents. Gunn, a hunter who resides outside the state of Capricorn, was arrested in Capricorn and prosecuted for hunting without a license in violation of the statute. He defended by asserting that the statute is unconstitutional because the hunting license fee for non-residents is higher than for residents.

Which of the following correctly identifies the clause or clauses of the United states Constitution violated by the Capricorn hunting license statute?

I. The Privileges and Immunities Clause of Article IV.

II. The Privileges and Immunities Clause of the Fourteenth Amendment.

(A) I only.

(B) II only.

(C) I and II.

(D) Neither I nor II.

9. An organization called the National Anarchist Party (NAP) asserts that government should be abolished. NAP's slogan is, "What if they made a law and nobody obeyed?" Its published literature urges all persons to violate laws, no matter how logical they might seem, and in this way to help bring about the abolition of government.

While in law school, Arthur joined the NAP for the purpose of acquiring material for a book which he was writing. Although he had heard that the NAP was a dangerous and subversive organization, Arthur thought its members to be fools, and believed their slogan and literature to be too ridiculous to ever convince anybody of anything. So that he could have access to NAP records, he volunteered to be Party Secretary. In his capacity as such, he frequently typed handbills written by the NAP propaganda Chairperson, and arranged to have them printed for subsequent distribution, although he did not intend for anybody to be convinced by them. All of these handbills contained the NAP slogan and urged the deliberate violation of laws. Eventually, Arthur wrote a book about the NAP entitled "The Lunatic Fringe." When he finished law school and applied for admission to the bar, his application was rejected. The state bar examiners stated that the only reason for the rejection of Arthur's application was a state law which provided that "No person shall be licensed to practice law who has belonged to any organization advocating unlawful activity." If Arthur brings an appropriate judicial proceeding for an order directing the state bar examiners to admit him to practice law, should Arthur win?

(A) Yes, because he joined the NAP for the purpose of gathering information for a book which he was writing.

(B) Yes, because he did not intend for the NAP to succeed in convincing people to violate laws.

(C) No, because he knew that the NAP advocated unlawful conduct when he joined the organization.

(D) No, because he played an active role in the
     NAP's activities.

Questions 10-11 are based on the following fact situation.

A statute of the state of Mammoth requires pay television stations to set aside one hour of air time per week to be made available without charge for the broadcasting of spiritually uplifting programs produced by recognized religious organizations. The statute further provides that air time thereby made available shall be equally divided among Jewish, Roman Catholic, and Protestant organizations. A religious organization known as the American Buddhist League produced a spiritually uplifting program, but was advised by several pay television stations that it could not be broadcast under the statute. The American Buddhist League has instituted a proceeding in federal court challenging the constitutional validity of the Mammoth statute.

10. The clearest reason for finding that the statute is
     unconstitutional is that it violates

     (A) the Free Exercise Clause, in that it treats
          religions unequally.

     (B) the Establishment Clause, in that it is not
          closely fitted to furthering a compelling
          governmental interest.

     (C) the Equal Protection Clause, in that it
          applies only to pay television stations.

     (D) the Supremacy Clause, in that broadcasting
          is an area already subject to extensive federal
          regulation.

11. Assume for the purpose of this question only that
     the state of Mammoth moved to dismiss the proceeding
     on the ground that the American Buddhist
     League lacked standing to challenge the
     constitutional validity of the statute. Should the
     motion be granted?

     (A) Yes, because an intellectual interest in the
          outcome of a constitutional challenge is
          not a sufficient personal stake to confer
          standing.

(B) Yes, unless the American Buddhist League
     is a recognized religious organization.

(C) No, because the American Buddhist League
     produced a spiritually uplifting television
     program which will not be broadcast
     because of the statute's provisions.

(D) No, if the religious sensibilities of the American
     Buddhist League are offended by the
     statute.

12. When revolutionaries seized control of the government
     of Nilezia, a republic on the continent of
     North Antica, they confiscated and nationalized
     several privately owned businesses, including
     some belonging to citizens of the United States.
     The President of the United States ordered the
     Secretary of Defense to prepare to send troops
     into Nilezia to protect American interests there.
     When the Secretary of Defense began giving
     appropriate orders to military leaders, action was
     instituted in a federal court for an injunction prohibiting
     the Secretary of Defense from sending
     troops to Nilezia. The plaintiff in that action
     asserted that the President's order to invade Nilezia
     violated a federal statute which limited the
     President's power to invade the nations of North
     Antica. The Secretary of Defense asked the court
     to dismiss the case, on the ground that it lacked
     jurisdiction.

     Does the federal court have jurisdiction to issue
     the requested injunction?

     (A) No, because the president is commander in
          chief of the Army and Navy.

     (B) No, because the federal courts lack the
          power to review the constitutional validity
          of a Presidential order.

     (C) Yes, because federal officials are subject to
          the jurisdiction of the federal courts even
          when carrying out Presidential orders.

     (D) Yes, because the President lacks the power
          to order the invasion of a foreign nation
          without a declaration of war.

13. A federal statute prohibits male employees of the

United States Census Bureau from wearing beards or moustaches, although no such prohibition exists for employees of other federal agencies. Parsons was discharged from his employment with the U.S. Census Bureau for violating the statute by refusing to remove his moustache. If Parsons asserts a claim on the ground that the statute was invalid, his most effective argument is that the law

(A) denies him a privilege or immunity of national citizenship.

(B) invidiously discriminates against him in violation of the Fifth Amendment to the United States Constitution.

(C) invidiously discriminates against him in violation of the Fourteenth Amendment to the United States Constitution.

(D) deprives him of a property right without just compensation.

Questions 14-15 are based on the following fact situation.

The constitution of the state of Encino contains an equal protection clause identical in language to the Equal Protection Clause in the Fourteenth Amendment to the United States Constitution. The Encino state legislature passed a law empowering insurance companies within the state to charge different rates for males and females where actuarial analysis revealed a relationship between gender and increased risk. Shortly after its passage, Claimant sued in the Encino state court for a judgment declaring that the statute violated the equal protection clause of the Encino constitution. The trial court found the statute to be valid, and Claimant appealed to the Court of Judicial Appeals, the highest court of the state of Encino. The Court of Judicial Appeals affirmed the ruling of the lower court.

14. If Claimant seeks United States Supreme Court review of the Encino Court of Judicial Appeals decision, United States Supreme Court review is available

(A) by appeal only.

(B) by certiorari only.

(C) either by appeal or by certiorari

(D) neither by appeal nor by certiorari.

15. Assume for the purpose of this question only that after the decision by the Encino Court of Judicial Appeals, the owner of an automobile registered in the state of Encino sues in a United States District Court for an injunction prohibiting the Encino state insurance commissioner from authorizing different rates for males and females on the ground that the statute empowering him to do so violates the Equal Protection Clause of the Fourteenth Amendment to the United States Constitution. If the insurance commissioner moves to dismiss the proceeding, the motion to dismiss should be

(A) granted, because adequate state grounds exist for the validity or invalidity of the statute in question.

(B) granted, under the abstention doctrine.

(C) denied, because the United States District Court is empowered to determine the validity of a state statute under the United States Constitution.

(D) granted, because the Eleventh Amendment to the U.S. Constitution prevents a federal court from hearing claims against a state brought by citizens of that state.

16. Congress passes the Federal Humane Act prohibiting the interstate transportation of dogs for use in dogfighting competitions or exhibitions. Kennel is prosecuted in a federal court for violating the Federal Humane Act, and defends by asserting that the statute is not constitutionally valid because it was enacted for purposes which were entirely noncommercial. The most effective argument in support of the constitutionality of the statute is that

(A) Congress is empowered to prohibit cruelty to animals under the federal police power.

(B) the power to regulate interstate commerce includes the power to completely exclude specified items from interstate commerce without regard to Congressional motives.

(C) under the "Cooley Doctrine," the federal and state governments have concurrent power to prohibit cruelty to animals.

(D) acts of Congress are presumptively constitutional.

Questions 17-18 are based on the following fact situation.

Allen, who was not a citizen of the United States, applied for temporary employment with the state of Birch. She was rejected, however, because the Civil Service Law of the state of Birch prohibits temporary state employment of a person who is not a United States citizen. Allen sued in a state court for an order directing the state Civil Service Commission to reconsider her application, on the ground that the section of the Civil Service Law which prohibited the temporary employment of non-citizens was unconstitutional.

17. Assume for the purpose of this question only that Allen asserted that the section in question was invalid under the Supremacy clause. In determining the constitutionality of the section in question, which of the following would be most relevant?

(A) The unemployment rate in the state of Birch.

(B) Federal civil service laws.

(C) The immigration laws and treaties of the United States.

(D) The percentage of persons residing in the state of Birch who are not citizens of the United States.

18. Assume for the purpose of this question only that Allen asserted that the section in question was invalid because it violated the Equal Protection Clause of the Fourteenth Amendment to the United States Constitution. Which of the following would be her most effective argument in support of that position?

(A) The right to earn a living is a fundamental interest.

(B) All state discrimination against aliens is invidious since alienage is a suspect classification.

(C) The section has no rational basis, and is not necessary to serve a compelling state interest.

(D) An alien is not a "person" for purposes of the Equal Protection Clause.

19. Congress enacts the Truth in Selling Act, requiring that certain disclosures be made by sellers in interstate sales transactions, and fixing civil damages for failure to make the requisite disclosures. The Act authorizes parties allegedly damaged by violations of the Truth in Selling Act to sue in either state or federal courts. The act further provides that any decision of a lower state court construing a section of the Truth in Selling Act may be appealed directly to the United States Supreme Court.

The provision of this statute which authorizes appeal of a lower state court decision directly to the United States Supreme Court, is

(A) constitutional, because Congress has the power to regulate interstate commerce.

(B) constitutional, because Congress may establish the manner in which the appellate jurisdiction of the United States Supreme Court is exercised.

(C) unconstitutional, because Article III of the United States Constitution does not authorize the United States Supreme Court to directly review the decisions of lower state courts.

(D) unconstitutional, because it infringes the sovereign right of a state to review decisions of its own lower courts.

20. Congress enacts the Aid to Education Act, which authorizes the direct expenditure of federal tax funds for the purchase of computers and audiovisual equipment which are then to be donated to private schools for educational purposes. The Act makes the equipment available on equal terms to

religiously-oriented and non-religious private schools. However, a provision of the Act states that the equipment so purchased and donated must be used solely for non-religious purposes and non-religious education.

The parents of several students at public schools located in the state of Webster have sued in federal court for an order enjoining the use of federal tax funds for the purchase of equipment to be used by religious schools, on the ground that such expenditure is unconstitutional.

Should the court issue the injunction?

(A) Yes, because expenditures of public funds for the purchase of equipment to be used by religious schools violates the Establishment Clause.

(B) Yes, because regulation of education is solely a function of the states.

(C) No, because the petitioners lack standing to challenge the expenditure of funds by the federal government.

(D) No, because the Aid to Education Act permits such expenditures only for non-religious purposes.

Questions 21-22 are based on the following fact situation.

An ordinance of the city of Lincoln provides for the election of a mayor every four years. The ordinance makes all persons living in the city for one year eligible to vote in mayoral elections. It specifies how a candidate may have his or her name placed on the ballot, and provides that a voter may vote for a person whose name is not on the ballot by writing that person's name onto the ballot at a place provided for that purpose.

Candida was a lawyer active in Lincoln civic affairs. Although she was not associated with any political party, she decided to run for the office of mayor. It was too late for Candida to have her name placed on the ballot, so she campaigned for write-in votes. Because many of the people she regarded as her constituents were not United States citizens and did not read or write English, Candida furnished prospective voters

with self adhesive stickers imprinted with her name, and told them that they could cast a "sticker vote" for her by placing the sticker in the appropriate place on the ballot. Because he feared that stickers would separate from the ballots to which they were attached and attach themselves to other ballots, the City Elections Commissioner advised Candida before the election that sticker votes would not be counted.

21. Assume for the purpose of this question that Candida instituted a judicial proceeding for an order compelling the City Elections Commissioner to count sticker votes on the ground that his refusal to do so violated the constitutional rights of voters. Which of the following would be the City Elections Commissioner's most effective argument in support of the constitutionality of his refusal to count sticker votes?

(A) Candida is not entitled to assert the constitutional rights of others.

(B) The use of sticker votes would interfere with the accuracy and convenience of ballot counts.

(C) Persons who are unable to read and write English should not be permitted to vote.

(D) The use of sticker votes would enable a person to vote who was not familiar with the issues or candidates.

22. Assume for the purpose of this question that the City Elections Commissioner advised Vogt, who is not a citizen of the United States but has been living in the city of Lincoln for ten months, that he will not be permitted to vote in the mayoral election because he fails to meet the one year residency requirement of the city ordinance. Is the one year residency requirement imposed by the ordinance constitutionally valid as applied to Vogt?

(A) Yes, because a municipality has a compelling interest in assuring that voters will be interested in and familiar with the issues.

(B) Yes, because aliens have no constitutional right to vote.

(C) No, because a state may not make durational residency a prerequisite for eligibility to vote.

(D) No, because although a state may establish durational residency requirements for eligibility to vote, a requirement of one year does not serve a compelling state interest.

Questions 23-24 are based on the following fact situation.

The Isles of Pine are a series of islands located in the Wyandango River, which serves as the border between the states of Wyandotte and Durango. Some of the Isles of Pine are part of the state of Wyandotte, and some are part of the state of Durango. Wyandango River Reserve is a state park operated by the state of Durango. The park consists of a thousand acres of land along the Durango shore of the Wyandango River, and includes those islands of the Isles of Pine which belong to the state of Durango. One of the state park's most popular features is the "Wyandango Cruise," a scenic boat ride on the Wyandango River. Wyandango Cruise tour boats, which are operated by employees of the state of Durango, conduct passengers around all of the Isles of Pine, including those which belong to the state of Wyandotte. Wages of the tour boat crew vary from $6.00 to $8.00 per hour, depending on the crewmember's rank in the Durango state civil service system as provided in the state Civil Service Code.

The Federal Interstate Riverboat Act provides that the minimum wage for persons employed on river boats engaged in interstate commerce shall be $6.50 per hour and authorizes the United States Department of Labor to impose sanctions for violations of its provisions.

23. Assume for the purpose of this question only that persons employed by the state of Durango as Wyandango Cruise crewmembers at wages less than $6.50 per hour assert a claim against the state of Durango in a federal court for money damages consisting of the difference between the wages they have been receiving and $6.50 per hour as required under the federal Interstate Riverboat Act. If the state of Durango moves to dismiss the action, should the motion to dismiss be granted?

(A) Yes, under the doctrine of abstention.

(B) Yes, because the Eleventh Amendment to the United States Constitution grants the states immunity from such actions.

(C) No, because the state employs the plaintiffs to engage in the business of tourism, which is not a traditional state function.

(D) No, under the supremacy clause.

24. Assume for the purpose of this question only that persons employed by the state of Durango as Wyandango Cruise crewmembers at wages less than $6.50 per hour assert a claim in a Durango state court for money damages consisting of the difference between the wages they have been receiving and $6.50 per hour as required under the Federal Interstate Riverboat Act. The court should find for

(A) the employees, because as to them, the Durango Civil Service code is superseded by the Federal Interstate Riverboat Act.

(B) the employees, because the federal government has the power to set minimum wages to promote the general welfare.

(C) the state of Durango, because fixing the wages of state employees is a traditional state function

(D) the state of Durango, because the state is immune from wage regulations under the Eleventh Amendment to the United States Constitution.

Questions 25-26 are based on the following fact situation.

X Productions is a distributor of "adult" mail order products. Sumer purchased several pornographic videotapes by mail from X Productions, and showed them to friends who attended a barbecue at his home. Sumer was arrested and charged with presenting an obscene performance in violation of state penal code § 123. X Productions was charged with being an accessory to Sumer's violation.

25. Assume for the purpose of this question only that Sumer pleaded guilty and received a suspended sentence in return for his promise to testify against X Productions in its prosecution for being an accessory to Sumer's violation. In defense against that prosecution, X Productions contended that, as applied, penal code section 123 unconstitutionally violated Sumer's constitutional rights. Does X Productions have standing to assert a violation of Sumer's Constitutional rights in its own defense?

   (A) Yes, because the videotapes which Sumer had been prosecuted for showing were purchased from X Productions.

   (B) Yes, because any person may challenge the validity of a statute regulating freedom of expression.

   (C) No, because Sumer waived his constitutional rights by pleading guilty to the prosecution.

   (D) No, because no person may defend against a criminal charge by asserting the constitutional rights of third persons.

26. Assume for the purpose of this question only that Sumer pleaded not guilty and asserted in his defense that, as applied, the state statute violated his rights under the United States Constitution. Which of the following would be Sumer's most effective argument in support of his position?

   (A) The statute violates Sumer's rights to freedom of speech and the press because the right to hear, see, or read is part of the freedom of expression.

   (B) Application of the statute to Sumer is unconstitutional because it violates the filmmaker's rights to freedom of speech and the press.

   (C) Sumer's constitutional right of privacy was violated because it includes his right to privately possess obscene materials.

   (D) The penal code section which Sumer is charged with violating was intended to punish the publishers rather than the purchase of obscenity.

27. To finance federal aviation services, a federal statute requires the payment of an annual federal tax of $1,000 on every aircraft of a certain size. The state of Agraria Department of Farming owns an airplane which it uses for aerial surveying of agricultural land in the state. Although the size of the airplane makes it subject to the tax, the state of Agraria paid the tax under protest. If the state of Agraria sues in an appropriate federal court for the return of the tax payment which it made to the federal government, the court should find for

   (A) Agraria, because the power to tax is the power to destroy.

   (B) Agraria, under the doctrine of state immunity.

   (C) the federal government, under the doctrine of state subordination.

   (D) the federal government, because the state receives benefit from federal aviation services.

28. A state statute provides that any married persons who engage in certain "unnatural" sex acts as described by the statute are guilty of second degree sodomy, and that unmarried persons who engage in those acts are guilty of first degree sodomy. John and Mary Dalton, a married couple, were prosecuted for second degree sodomy after engaging in the prohibited acts with each other in a friend's home while at a party. In defense, they asserted that the statute was invalid under the United States Constitution.

   The most effective argument in support of the assertion that the statute was unconstitutional is that it violated the Dalton's constitutional right to

   (A) substantive due process.

   (B) procedural due process.

   (C) equal protection.

   (D) freedom of expression.

Questions 29-30 are based on the following fact situation.

The calemone is a shellfish found in waters located several miles off the coast of the state of Kahuna, from which extensive calemone fishing activities are conducted. Because the calemone is regarded as a rare species, a federal law known as the Protected Shellfish Act prescribes the size and number of calemone which may be taken commercially. To enforce the Protected Shellfish Act, the federal government contracts with private enforcement agencies who patrol calemone fishing grounds in unmarked vessels, and who are empowered to make arrests for violation of the Act's requirements. The Protected Shellfish Act provides that contractors hired to enforce the Act shall be exempt from the payment of state income taxes. The state of Kahuna imposes a personal income tax on the income of persons residing within the state. In addition, the state of Kahuna imposes a Building Rental Tax of ten dollars per year on tenants occupying rented commercial space within the state. Hook is a contractor employed by the federal government to enforce the Protected Shellfish Act, and derives his entire income from his contract with the federal government. Under the terms of his contract, Hook rents space for the conduct of his business in a federal office building located in the state of Kahuna at an annual rental of $1.00. Although Hook resides in the state of Kahuna, he has refused to pay the state income tax. In addition, he has refused to pay the state Building Rental Tax.

29. If Hook is prosecuted in a Kahuna state court for failing to pay the state income tax, which of the following would be Hook's most effective argument in defense against the prosecution?

    (A) Income from federal employment is exempt from taxation by the state.

    (B) The state income tax imposes a burden on the federal government, since it is likely to increase the costs of enforcing the Protected Shellfish Act.

    (C) The state does not have the power to tax income derived from activities conducted on the high seas.

    (D) Under the Necessary and Proper Clause, Congress has the power to exempt federal

contractors from the payment of state tax.

30. If Hook is prosecuted in a Kahuna state court for failing to pay the state Building Rental Tax, which of the following would be Hook's most effective argument in defense against the prosecution?

    (A) The Building Rental Tax violates the Equal Protection Clause of the United States Constitution.

    (B) The state may not tax the landlord-tenant relationship with the federal government.

    (C) Hook's tenancy is specifically authorized by the Protected Shellfish Act.

    (D) Hook is a federal contractor.

31. The state of Ascaloosa requires persons applying for state welfare assistance, driving licenses, admission to the state university, or certain other state benefits to list their federal social security numbers as part of their applications. In this connection, Ascaloosa state agencies refer to an applicant's social security number as his or her "Central File Number." Lawrence has brought an action in a federal court against certain specified state officials for an order enjoining them from using social security numbers in this fashion. In support of his position, Lawrence argues that at some time almost all citizens of the state apply for some form of state benefit, and that the compilation of a central file on each citizen of the state is likely to have a chilling effect on the exercise of rights granted by the First Amendment to the United States Constitution.

The clearest reason for the dismissal of Lawrence's suit is that

    (A) the action is unripe.

    (B) the question presented is moot.

    (C) under the Eleventh Amendment to the United States Constitution state officials are immune to lawsuits of this kind.

    (D) the creation of a central file on each person applying for state benefits involves the resolution of political questions.

Questions 32-34 are based on the following fact situation.

Fraser City is located in the state of North Vellum, three miles from its border with the neighboring state of South Vellum. Fraser City hospitals recently treated several persons for food poisoning caused by the consumption of tainted meat. As a result, the Fraser City Council passed an ordinance prohibiting the sale in Fraser City of meat processed at a processing plant not certified by the Fraser City Health Department. Butch, who operated a retail grocery store in Fraser City, was arrested after selling meat to an undercover police officer. Because the meat had been processed at a plant in South Vellum which had not been inspected or certified by the Fraser City Health Department, Butch was charged with violating the ordinance and prosecuted in the Fraser City Municipal Court. Butch admitted violating the ordinance, but argued that the ordinance was not valid under the United States Constitution.

32. Does the Fraser City Municipal Court have jurisdiction to determine the constitutionality of the ordinance?

   (A) No, if determining the constitutionality of the ordinance requires interpretation of the United States Constitution.

   (B) No, because Butch will not have standing to challenge the constitutionality of the ordinance until he has been convicted of violating it.

   (C) Yes, because any court has the power to interpret the United States Constitution.

   (D) Yes, only if the Fraser City Municipal Court is a state court under the laws of North Vellum.

33. Assume for the purpose of this question only that Butch was convicted of violating the ordinance by the Fraser City Municipal Court, and that Butch seeks direct review by the United States Supreme Court. Does the United States Supreme Court have jurisdiction to review the decision of

the Fraser City Municipal Court?

   (A) Yes, because by convicting Butch the Fraser City Municipal Court has, in effect, declared the ordinance to be valid under the United States Constitution.

   (B) Yes, if North Vellum state laws do not permit appeal from judgments of the Fraser City Municipal Court.

   (C) No, unless North Vellum state law specifically authorizes appeal of Fraser City Municipal Court judgments directly to the United States Supreme Court.

   (D) No, because under Article III of the United States Constitution, the United States Supreme Court may only review decisions of federal courts and of the highest state courts.

34. Assume for the purpose of this question only that a person with standing to do so sues in an appropriate federal court for an order enjoining enforcement of the Fraser City ordinance on the ground that it is invalid under the Commerce Clause of the United States Constitution. Which of the following is the best argument in support of granting the injunction?

   (A) As applied, the ordinance interferes with interstate commerce.

   (B) Regulation of the purity of food is not a matter which is of local concern.

   (C) The concurrent power to regulate commerce does not apply to municipalities.

   (D) There are equally effective and less burdensome ways of regulating the purity of food sold in Fraser City.

35. While trying to arrest an unarmed bank robber, Maple City police officer Orville fired a shot which killed an uninvolved bystander. When Orville returned to the police station, Captain, his supervisor, told him that he was suspended from duties without pay effective immediately, and took from him his gun and badge. Orville subsequently instituted an action for an order directing

Captain to restore him to the job of police officer.

Which of the following additional facts or inferences, if it were the only one true, would be most likely to result in a DENIAL of the relief sought by Orville?

(A) A Police Department hearing was scheduled for a future date to determine the propriety of Orville's conduct, and Orville would be restored to his position and compensated for lost pay if he was found to be without fault.

(B) Maple City Police Department policy prohibited police officers from firing their guns in attempting to arrest unarmed persons.

(C) Orville's killing of the bystander amounted to involuntary manslaughter.

(D) The Maple City Police Department Manual of Procedure called for immediate suspension of any police officer whose conduct while attempting to effect an arrest resulted in the death of an uninvolved bystander.

36. In which of the following fact situations has there most clearly been a violation of the plaintiff's rights under the Fourteenth Amendment to the United States Constitution?

(A) Plaintiff is a black person whose application for state employment was rejected because he failed to pass the state Civil Service examination. Statistics reveal that 10% of the black applicants and 60% of the white applicants who have taken the exam have passed it.

(B) Plaintiff is an American of Mexican descent who was denied admission to a privately-owned hospital solely because of her ethnic background, but who received competent professional treatment at a state hospital instead.

(C) Plaintiff is a Jewish person who resided in a federally operated housing project, and who was excluded from a prayer breakfast held by the federal agency which ran the project solely because of his religion.

(D) Plaintiff is a woman whose application for employment as a deputy sheriff was rejected by the county solely because of her sex.

37. The state of Norfolk recently passed a law which prohibits the drivers of trucks over a certain length from driving within the state for more than four hours without stopping to rest for at least 30 minutes. Trucker was prosecuted for violating the law while driving a truck through the state on an interstate run. As part of his defense, he asserted that the Norfolk statute was unconstitutional in that it unduly burdened interstate commerce. The trial court took judicial notice that there is no federal law requiring interstate truck drivers to stop for rest breaks.

In view of the absence of a federal law requiring interstate truck drivers to stop for rest breaks, which of the following is the state's most effective argument in support of the constitutionality of the statute?

(A) The absence of a federal law indicates that Congress does not regard the matter as one requiring national uniformity.

(B) The requirement that truck drivers stop for rest breaks is largely a matter of local concern.

(C) The statute requiring truck drivers to stop for rest breaks is enforceable only within the state of Norfolk.

(D) In the absence of preemptive legislation by Congress, a state is free to impose restrictions on interstate commerce.

Questions 38-39 are based on the following fact situation.

A state statute known as the Unlawful Assembly Law contains the following provisions:

Section I — it shall be a misdemeanor for any group of three or more persons to gather on a public sidewalk and to deliberately conduct themselves in a manner which is offensive to passersby.

Section II — it shall be a misdemeanor for any group of three or more persons to engage in a public demonstration on a public sidewalk in front of any state government office during regular business hours unless said demonstration is related to matters under consideration by officials employed in said government office.

When the governor of the state refused to grant a pardon to a college student who had been convicted of destroying state college property during a campus protest, members of a student organization decided to disrupt state government operations by conducting a loud and boisterous demonstration outside a state government office building which they selected at random. About thirty members gathered on the sidewalk outside the building with noisemakers and musical instruments, and began marching while making a loud and disturbing noise. Several persons who had business inside the building were unable to get past the crowd of demonstrators to enter. Demos, one of the participants, was arrested for marching and shouting obscene words which many passersby found offensive.

38. Assume that Demos is prosecuted for violating Section I of the Unlawful Assembly Law, and that he defends by asserting that the section is overbroad. The court should find him

(A) guilty, because his conduct was in fact offensive to passersby.

(B) guilty, only if the reasonable passerby would have been offended by Demos's conduct.

(C) guilty, only if the reasonable person in Demos's position would have known that his conduct would be offensive to passersby.

(D) not guilty, if some of the conduct which the law prohibited is constitutionally protected.

39. Assume that Demos is prosecuted for violating Section II of the Unlawful Assembly Law, and

that he defends by asserting that the section violates the First Amendment to the United States Constitution. The court should find him

(A) not guilty, because the public sidewalk in front of a government building is traditionally regarded as a public forum.

(B) not guilty, because Section II unlawfully regulates the subject matter of demonstrations conducted outside government offices.

(C) guilty, because the state has a compelling interest in the orderly conduct of governmental affairs.

(D) guilty, because the demonstration in which Demos participated kept persons with lawful business from entering government offices to transact it.

40. Assume that the Hawk Party and the Dove Party are the major American political parties. In a certain presidential election, relations between the United States and the republic of Orinoco were the basis of a substantial disagreement between the candidates, each supporting the view of his political party. Bight, the Hawk Party candidate, had already served one term as president, but was defeated by Gentle, the Dove Party candidate. After taking office, President Gentle communicated with Henderson, who was serving as ambassador to Orinoco by appointment of President Bight with the advice and consent of the Senate. President Gentle demanded that Henderson either agree to support the foreign policy contained in the Dove Party platform or resign. When Henderson refused to do either, President Gentle told him that he was dismissed from the office of ambassador.

Given the facts, did President Gentle have the power to remove Henderson from office?

(A) Yes, because ideological differences constitute cause for dismissal from ambassadorial office.

(B) Yes, because the president has the power to dismiss ambassadors without cause.

(C) No, because an ambassador appointed with the advice and consent of the Senate cannot be dismissed from office without the advice and consent of the Senate.

(D) No, because removal of an ambassador is a *de facto* withdrawal of diplomatic relations with a foreign power.

Questions 41-42 are based on the following fact situation.

The Assembly Appropriations Committee of the State Assembly of the state of Colombia was considering a bill which would appropriate state funds for advertising the availability of abortion to indigent women. Prior to discussion of the bill, the Committee directed the state attorney general to seek an advisory opinion from the state court regarding the validity of the proposed bill under both the state and the federal constitutions. The attorney general made the appropriate ex parte motion pursuant to the state procedure code before the Court of Errors, the highest court in the state. The Court of Errors rendered an advisory opinion in which it stated that the proposed bill did not violate the state constitution, but that it did violate the First Amendment to the United States Constitution.

41. Assume for the purpose of this question that the Assembly Appropriations Committee voted to reject the proposed legislation in reliance on the advisory opinion of the Court of Errors. Does the United States Supreme Court have jurisdiction to review the advisory opinion rendered by the Colombia state Court of Errors?

(A) Yes, because it interpreted a section of the United States Constitution.

(B) Yes, because the decision did not rest on an adequate state ground.

(C) No, because an advisory opinion is not a case or controversy under the United States Constitution.

(D) No, because there has been no opportunity for appellate review by a state court.

42. Assume for the purpose of this question only that

the Assembly Appropriations Committee approved the proposed legislation, and that it was subsequently enacted by the state legislature. Protesse, a state taxpayer and the chairperson of "Save Them," an organization dedicated to campaigning for the rights of unborn children, instituted a proceeding in the federal district court for an injunction prohibiting state officials from disbursing funds under the new law. In support of her petition, Protesse argued that since feelings regarding abortion are related to religious views, state supported advertising for abortion would violate the Establishment Clause of the United States Constitution. Which of the following is the best reason for the court to conclude that Protesse has standing to challenge the statute?

(A) Any person has standing to challenge a statute on the ground that it violates a First Amendment right.

(B) Unborn children are a discrete and insular class which can not be represented in any other way.

(C) The law involves a direct expenditure of state tax funds.

(D) Protesse is chairperson of special interest political group which has a philosophical and moral interest in preventing enforcement of the statute.

Questions 43-44 are based on the following fact situation.

The Young Trailblazers is a youth organization with chapters and members in all fifty states. Concentrating on what it calls "the outdoor experience," the organization attempts to teach its members to love all forms of life. According to the bylaws of the Young Trailblazers, membership is open to all white children between the ages of eight and fourteen years. Penny, a twelve-year-old black child, applied for membership in the Young Trailblazers at the joint request of the Pintada state attorney general and the United States Department of Justice. The Young Trailblazers rejected her application solely on the basis of her race, advising her in writing that membership was open only to white children.

A federal statute makes it a crime for an organization

with members in more than one state to deny membership to any person on the basis of that person's race. A statute of the state of Pintada makes it a crime to violate a right conferred on any person by the Fourteenth Amendment to the United States Constitution.

43. Is the Young Trailblazers guilty of violating the Pintada state statute?

   (A) Yes, because the policy of The Young Trailblazers resulted in a denial of Penny's right to equal protection.

   (B) Yes, because the policy of the Young Trailblazers resulted in a denial of Penny's right to the privileges and immunities of citizenship.

   (C) Yes, because the policy of the Young Trailblazers resulted in a denial of Penny's right to substantive due process.

   (D) No, because the Young Trailblazers is a private organization.

44. Assume that the Young Trailblazers is prosecuted in a federal court for violation of the federal statute, and the Young Trailblazers asserts that the statute is invalid under the United States Constitution. Which of the following would be the prosecutor's most effective argument in supporting the constitutional validity of the federal statute?

   (A) The policy of The Young Trailblazers violates the spirit of the Commerce Clause.

   (B) The policy of The Young Trailblazers establishes a badge of servitude in violation of the spirit of the Thirteenth Amendment.

   (C) The United States Supreme Court has found racial discrimination to violate the United States Constitution.

   (D) Racial discrimination is inimical to the general welfare of the citizens of the United States.

45. In the Mutual Aid Treaty of 1957, the United States and the southeast Asian republic of Curasia agreed to defend each other against aggres-

sion. In connection with a century-old border dispute, one of Curasia's neighbors recently threatened to attack Curasia if Curasia did not relinquish its claim to a certain peninsula. At the request of the Curasian prime minister, the president of the United States has ordered American troops to be flown to Curasia immediately for the purpose of defending Curasia against attack.

If the president's order is challenged in an appropriate proceeding in a federal court, the strongest argument in support of the validity of the order is that the president

   (A) has the power to declare war.

   (B) has the power to commit American armed forces to foreign hostilities to satisfy treaty obligations.

   (C) has the power to make treaties with the advice and consent of the senate.

   (D) is the commander-in-chief of the Army and Navy.

Questions 46-47 are based on the following fact situation.

Sander was a student at Hippocrates University, a privately owned medical college. One weekend during the school semester, Sander was arrested by Hippo City police for participating in a demonstration against the government's position on nuclear disarmament. When Sander was brought before a judge for arraignment, however, the court dismissed the charge with the consent of the public prosecutor. The following day, the dean of Hippocrates University called Sander into her office. The dean referred to the arrest, and said that because his conduct had embarrassed the school, Sander was expelled. Sander subsequently sued Hippocrates University for damages resulting from his dismissal.

46. The most effective argument in support of Sander's claim is that the dismissal violated Sander's right

   (A) to an administrative hearing.

   (B) to due process.

(C) to freedom of expression.

(D) under an implied contract with Hippocrates University.

47. Assume for the purpose of this question only that after Sander instituted the action, Hippocrates University reinstated him, and that he subsequently graduated in good standing. Assume further that Sander passed his state's licensing examination and petitioned the state Board of Medical Licensing Examiners (the Board) for a license to practice medicine, and that solely because of his arrest by Hippo City police and expulsion from Hippocrates University the Board refused to issue him a license. If Sander sues the Board in a federal court for an order directing the Board to license him, the court should find for

(A) the Board, because a license to practice medicine is a privilege rather than a right.

(B) the Board, unless Sander first attempted to sue in a state court and was unsuccessful.

(C) Sander, only of the Board's action is found to be arbitrary and capricious.

(D) Sander, because the Board's decision deprives Sander of property without due process.

48. In which of the following fact situations is the plaintiff most likely to have standing in a federal court to challenge the statute involved on the ground that it is unconstitutional?

(A) Plaintiff is the chairperson of an organization dedicated to preventing cruelty to animals. She sues in that capacity to enjoin the enforcement of a state statute which permits state officials to seize and destroy unlicensed dogs without notice to their owners.

(B) Plaintiff is the state of North Webster in which mining is a major industry. It is suing for a judgment declaring unconstitutional a federal statute which imposes a tax on the mining of certain specified metals, on the ground that the tax invidiously discriminates against members of the mining industry.

(C) Plaintiff is a federal taxpayer. He sues to recover taxes paid by him under protest on the ground that the money so paid is being used to support military activities against a nation with which the United States is not at war, and that the statute authorizing its use for that purpose is therefore unconstitutional.

(D) Plaintiff is a state taxpayer, whose taxes are used, among other purposes, to support the activities of local school districts. Although she has no children of school age, plaintiff is suing to enjoin enforcement of a state law the terms of which permit counselors employed by local school districts to advise students about Acquired Immune Deficiency Syndrome (AIDS).

Questions 49-50 are based on the following fact situation.

After examining the effects of diesel exhaust on the environment, Congress enacts a statute requiring the owners of diesel-powered trucks used in interstate commerce to pay a Diesel-Powered Vehicle Use Tax of $800 per vehicle. Weelco, a trucking company which operates more than one thousand trucks in interstate commerce, refuses to pay the Diesel-Powered Vehicle Use Tax, and sues in a federal court for an injunction prohibiting the enforcement of the tax statute.

49. Which of the following is Weelco's most effective argument in opposition to the tax?

(A) The tax is regulatory in nature.

(B) Imposition of the tax violates Weelco's right to equal protection under the Fifth Amendment to the United States constitution.

(C) The tax is so burdensome as to amount to a taking of private property, for which just compensation is required.

(D) The tax is coercive in nature, since it is likely to discourage the use of diesel powered vehicles in interstate commerce.

50. Which of the following is the federal government's strongest argument in opposition to Weelco's claim that the Diesel-Powered Vehicle Use Tax is invalid?

    (A) The tax protects the general welfare by discouraging the use of diesel powered vehicles in interstate commerce.

    (B) Protection of the environment is part of the federal police power.

    (C) The tax is a valid exercise of the spending power, since it enables Congress to assure that the money which it gives states for the construction of roads will be most efficiently spent.

    (D) Weelco lacks standing since it has not yet paid the tax.

51. Several years ago, the state of Nevorado legalized certain forms of gambling, and began issuing licenses for the operation of gambling casinos. Since then, legal gambling had become the state's most economically significant industry. People travel to Nevorado from all over the United States to visit nearly 2,000 licensed casinos located within the state. All of the casinos discourage the use of cash at gaming tables, and sell chips for gamblers to use when participating in the games which they operate. For this reason, many visitors to the state find themselves to be in possession of chips when returning home. For the convenience of tourists, the Nevorado legislature passed the Casino Chip Law requiring restaurants and retail business located at Nevorado airports, train stations, and bus terminals to accept chips from customers in lieu of cash, at two-thirds the face value of the chips so tendered. The law also requires licensed casinos to redeem the chips at their face value. Mac, the owner of a restaurant located at an airport in Nevorado, was prosecuted in a Nevorado court for violating the state law by refusing to accept casino chips from a customer who attempted to use them to pay for food purchased at Mac's restaurant.

If Mac defends by asserting that the law violates

the United States Constitution, which of the following arguments would most effectively support his position?

    (A) The law denied Mac due process, since it required him to give up merchandise without receiving cash in return.

    (B) By its terms, the law violated the Commerce Clause, since the businesses which were subject to it were all involved in interstate travel.

    (C) The power to coin and fix the value of money is exclusively that of Congress.

    (D) Requiring Mac to accept casino chips in return for merchandise is a taking of private property without just compensation.

52. Mag was prosecuted in the Municipal Court of the city of New Morris for selling an obscene magazine. At his trial, the jury found the following by special verdict:

    (1) Applying standards of the average person residing in the city of New Morris, the magazine taken as a whole appealed to a prurient interest in sex.

    (2) Applying standards of the average person residing in the United States, the magazine taken as a whole did not appeal to a prurient interest in sex.

    (3) The magazine depicted sexual conduct in a way which was offensive to contemporary standards existing in the city of New Morris.

    (4) The magazine did not depict sexual conduct in a way which was offensive to contemporary standards existing in the United States in general.

    (5) Taken as a whole, the magazine had serious literary value.

Based upon the jury's special verdict, Mag was found guilty. If Mag appeals his conviction on the ground that it violates the First Amendment to the United States Constitution, his conviction should be

    (A) reversed, because the magazine was found to have serious literary value.

(B) reversed, because applying a national standard, the magazine did not appeal to a prurient interest in sex.

(C) affirmed, because, applying a contemporary community standard, the magazine depicted sexual conduct in a manner which was offensive

(D) affirmed, because, applying a contemporary community standard, the magazine appealed to a prurient interest in sex.

Questions 53-54 are based on the following fact situation.

In 1979 the United States and the republic of Romania entered into a treaty by which each country agreed not to tax citizens of the other. Pursuant to that treaty, Congress enacted the Romanian National Tax Immunity Act which exempts Romanian nationals residing in the United States from the obligation to pay income tax to the United States. Recently, however, a United States citizen living in Romania was prosecuted by the Romanian government for failing to pay Romanian income tax. Last week, the president of the United States issued an executive order requiring the Internal Revenue Service to begin collecting income tax from Romanian citizens residing in the United States.

53. Which of the following persons would be most likely to have standing to challenge the constitutional validity of the presidential order in a federal court?

(A) An organization known as America's Image which is dedicated to the principle that the United States should keep its promises.

(B) A United States citizen of Romanian descent who owns land both in the United States and in Romania.

(C) A Romanian citizen living in the United States.

(D) A representative of the Romanian government suing on behalf of the republic of Romania.

54. If the constitutional validity of the presidential

order is challenged by a person with standing to do so, the court should find that the order is

(A) valid, since the nation must speak with one voice in matters of foreign affairs.

(B) valid, since the president has broad discretionary powers in matters of foreign affairs.

(C) invalid, since the president may not abrogate foreign treaties without the advice and consent of the Senate.

(D) invalid, since the president lacks the power to suspend enforcement of the Romanian National Tax Immunity Act.

55. In an attempt to reduce air pollution caused by the use of fossil fuels, Congress passes the Fossil Fuel Use Tax Act, which imposes a tax upon the owners of buildings heated by burning fossil fuels. The state of Atlas owns an office building known as the Brill Building, which was once used to house state government offices. Since the state government moved to new quarters, offices in the Brill Building have been rented by the state to tenants engaged in various aspects of private enterprise. Although the Brill Building is heated by fossil fuels, the state of Atlas has refused to pay the tax imposed by the Fossil Fuel Use Tax Act. The federal government has commenced a proceeding against the state of Atlas for taxes due under the Fossil Fuel Use Tax Act as a result of the use of fossil fuel to heat the Brill Building.

Which of the following is the most effective argument in support of the federal government's position?

(A) Under Article I of the United States Constitution, Congress has unlimited power to impose taxes.

(B) Protection of the environment is a legitimate reason for imposing a tax.

(C) The states owe the federal government the obligation of paying those taxes fixed by federal law.

(D) As applied, the Fossil Fuel Use Tax Act

taxes the state of Atlas's activities as a landlord rather than as a state.

56. After examining studies indicating that chewing gum was directly related to the incidence of tooth decay, the legislature of the state of Minnitonka enacted a law prohibiting the advertising of chewing gum in all media. Which of the following is the clearest reason for holding the law to be unconstitutional?

(A) A state may not interfere with commercial speech.

(B) The sale of chewing gum frequently involves interstate commerce.

(C) The law imposes a prior restraint on publication.

(D) There are less restrictive ways of protecting the public against tooth decay which would be equally effective.

57. Assume that Congress enacted a statute making education through the 12th grade compulsory. Which one of the following facts or inferences, if it was the only one true, would be most likely to lead to finding that the statute is constitutionally valid?

(A) The majority of people living in states which have inadequate compulsory education requirements are members of ethnic minorities.

(B) Educational levels in England, France, China, and the Russia are superior to those in several of the states of the United States.

(C) By its terms, the statute is applicable only to residents of the District of Columbia and of United States Military bases.

(D) The majority of American schoolchildren move from one state to another at some time during the first twelve years of their education.

58. While serving a ten year sentence for murder in the Foldora state prison, Dickson was accused of leading a riot which resulted in the death of a prison guard. Without a hearing, the warden ordered Dickson placed in solitary confinement for the remainder of his sentence. Dickson sued in a United States District Court for an order directing his removal from solitary confinement on the grounds that he was deprived of due process, and that solitary confinement for the remainder of his sentence was a cruel and unusual punishment. The District Court rendered judgment against Dickson, who appealed to the United States Court of Appeals. The United States Court of Appeals affirmed, and Dickson petitioned for certiorari to the United States Supreme Court. While Dickson's petition was pending, parole officials voted to release him from prison although it was three years before the end of his sentence, on condition that he meet with a federal probation officer once per month, that he seek gainful employment, that he refrain from consorting with criminals, and that he be returned immediately to prison upon violation of any of the conditions of parole. In opposing Dickson's petition for certiorari, the state's attorney asserted that his release from prison made the issue moot.

Which of the following is the strongest reason for finding that the issues presented by Dickson's petition are NOT moot?

(A) Dickson is no longer a prisoner.

(B) In granting parole, parole officials have acknowledged a violation of Dickson's constitutional rights.

(C) Dickson's claim is capable of repetition if it evades judicial review.

(D) Dickson might be returned to solitary confinement if he is re-incarcerated for violating the conditions of his parole.

Questions 59-60 are based on the following fact situation.

A statute of the state of Eternica provides that no person can be elected to state office who is not a citizen of the United States. The constitutionality of the statute is challenged in an appropriate action by Baker.

59. If the court hearing Baker's challenge takes judicial notice of the treaties and immigration laws of the United States, it will be because they are relevant to the validity of the statute under

   (A) the Supremacy Clause.

   (B) the Privileges and Immunities Clause.

   (C) the due process requirement.

   (D) the doctrine of separation of powers.

60. Assume for the purpose of this question only that Baker's challenge was heard by the highest appellate court of the state of Eternica, and that the court declared the statute to be unconstitutional on the ground that it violated the equal protection clause of the state constitution. If the state of Eternica seeks review by the United States Supreme Court, which of the following statements is most accurate?

   I. The United States Supreme Court may properly review the decision by certiorari.

   II. The United States Supreme Court may properly review the decision by appeal.

   (A) I only.

   (B) II only.

   (C) I and II.

   (D) Neither I nor II.

61. Under which of the following circumstances is a court most likely to uphold the constitutionality of a statute which requires the taking of a loyalty oath by public employees?

   (A) Only persons appointed to state office by the governor are required by law to take the loyalty oath.

   (B) The statute requires that the loyalty oath be taken by all state employees.

   (C) The loyalty oath required by the statute consists entirely of a promise "to uphold the

United States constitution and to oppose the overthrow of the state or federal government by unlawful means."

   (D) The loyalty oath is only required of persons appointed to positions with the state militia which are likely to expose them to classified information.

62. In an attempt to improve air quality, several states pass laws providing that vehicles powered by diesel engines of more than a certain size must be equipped with a specified smog-elimination system in order to be driven on highways within the state. Ace Trucking Company challenges such a law in the state of Baxter on the ground that it unreasonably burdens interstate commerce. Which of the following is the state of Baxter's best argument in support of the law?

   (A) The law applies to intra-state as well as interstate shipments.

   (B) The law applies to all vehicles traveling through the state, including those which are garaged primarily in the state.

   (C) The law is necessary to protect the health and safety of residents of the state.

   (D) Other states have similar requirements.

Questions 63-64 are based on the following fact situation.

The coastal state of Oceania has enacted the Ocean Fishing License Act, which regulates the right to fish in coastal waters. Section 1 of the act provides that no person shall fish in the ocean from a vessel registered in the state of Oceania who has not obtained an ocean fishing license from the state Department of Fish and Game. Section 2 of the act sets the fees for ocean fishing licenses at ten dollars per year for residents of the state of Oceania, and twenty dollars per year for nonresidents. Section 3 of the act provides that if any section of the act is found invalid for any reason, such finding should not affect the validity of any other section of the act.

63. Which of the following would provide the stron-

gest basis for declaring Section 1 of the Ocean Fishing License Act to be INVALID?

(A) A federal law which authorizes a federal agency to issue licenses for fishing in coastal waters of the United States.

(B) The absence of any federal law regulating fishing in coastal waters of the United States.

(C) The Equal Protection Clause of the Fourteenth Amendment to the United States Constitution.

(D) The Due Process Clause of the Fifth Amendment to the United States Constitution.

64. Assume for the purpose of this question only that an action is brought in a federal court by a resident of the state of Oceania for an injunction to prohibit the state of Oceania from enforcing Section 2 of the Ocean Fishing License Act. Which of the following arguments would be LEAST likely to lead to a finding that the provisions of that section are *invalid*?

(A) The act violates the Commerce Clause.

(B) The act violates the Equal Protection Clause.

(C) The act violates the Necessary and Proper Clause.

(D) Section 1 of the act is constitutionally invalid.

Questions 65-66 are based on the following fact situation.

The state of Bostonia enacts legislation appropriating several million dollars of state funds to be spent on conservation of agricultural lands within the state. The statute directs the distribution of such funds to Agricultural Conservation Districts geographically equivalent to the counties of the state, authorizes the creation of such Agricultural Conservation Districts, and empowers them with responsibility for administering funds assigned to them. The statute provides that fiscal decisions of each District shall be made by a Board of Governors to be elected by its residents. The statute also provides that participation in district elections is open

only to persons who are able to pass a simple test of reading and writing in the English language and who own agricultural land within the geographic boundaries of the District, and that voters in such elections may cast one vote for each acre of agricultural land which they own within the district.

65. Assume for the purpose of this question only that the constitutionality of the statute has been challenged by a litigant who claims that it violates the "one person one vote" principle. The best argument in response to that claim is that the principle

(A) applies only to elections for statewide and federal office.

(B) does not apply where property rights are involved.

(C) does not apply because of rights reserved to the states by the Tenth Amendment.

(D) does not apply, because results of District elections will principally affect the owners of agricultural land.

66. Assume for the purpose of this question only that the constitutionality of the statute has been challenged by a litigant who objects to the literacy requirement. If that challenge is successful, it will probably be because the requirement violates

(A) the Equal Protection Clause of the Fourteenth Amendment.

(B) the "race, color, or previous condition of servitude" clause of the Fifteenth Amendment.

(C) freedom of the press under the First Amendment.

(D) the Twenty-Sixth Amendment (granting the right to vote to persons eighteen years of age and above).

67. In a case in which the constitutionality of a state law regulating the sale of birth control devices is in issue, which party will have the burden of persuasion?

(A) The state, because procreation involves a fundamental right, and the law may have a substantial impact on that right.

(B) The state, because the state law is more likely to have a substantial impact on women than on men.

(C) The person challenging the statute, since there is a rebuttable presumption that all state laws are constitutional.

(D) The person challenging the statute, since the regulation on non-expressive sexual conduct is reserved to the states by the Tenth Amendment.

68. A state law makes it a crime to interfere with "any right conferred by the Equal Protection Clause of the Fourteenth Amendment to the United States Constitution." In which one of the following cases is the defendant LEAST likely to be convicted of violating the law?

(A) Defendant, the manager of an apartment building funded and operated by a federal housing agency, refused to rent an apartment to a black family solely because of their race.

(B) Defendant, the commissioner of police of a large city, refused to hire homosexuals as police officers solely because of their sexual preference.

(C) Defendant, threatening violence, induced a school bus driver, employed by a public school district, to refuse Jewish students rides solely because of their religion.

(D) Defendant, the proprietor of a restaurant located in a state office building and rented from the state, refused to serve Vietnamese immigrants solely because of their place of national origin.

69. After the state of Caledonia raised property taxes, Brown became active in an organization called Citizens Opposed to Soaring Taxes (COST). As part of a protest, Brown paraded nude in front of the tax collector's office, carrying a sign which read "Soaring taxes take the clothes off our

backs." Brown was arrested under a statute newly enacted by the Caledonia state legislature. The complete text of the law was, "No person shall behave in a shocking or offensive manner in a public place. Any violation of this section shall be punished by a term not to exceed six months in a county detention facility."

If Brown defends by asserting that the statute is unconstitutional, his most effective argument would be that

(A) under the First and Fourteenth Amendments, expressive conduct may not be punished by the state

(B) the statute is vague.

(C) the reasonable person is not likely to have been shocked or offended by Brown's conduct.

(D) conviction under a newly enacted statute is a violation of due process.

70. A law permitting the payment of public funds as financial aid to schools operated by religious organizations is most likely to be constitutionally valid if it directs payment to

(A) primary schools, for enhancement of the salaries of teachers who do not instruct on religious subjects.

(B) primary schools at which no more than ten percent of the instructional time is spent on religious subjects, for the purchase of laboratory equipment.

(C) secondary schools, for the purchase of textbooks on secular subjects.

(D) colleges, for the purchase of athletic equipment.

71. Because the Oakbranch River is wide, deep and flows through several states, it is an important thoroughfare for interstate commercial cargo ships. The state of Birmingham, through which the Oakbranch flows, has passed a law imposing strict water pollution controls on ships using rivers within the state. Shipco, a transport company

that operates ships on the Oakbranch, has challenged the statute, asserting that it violates the Commerce Clause of the United States Constitution.

Which one of the following facts or inferences, if found to be true, would be most likely to result in a finding that the statute is constitutionally valid?

(A) The Oakbranch is a source of water for agricultural irrigation in all the states through which it passes.

(B) Congress has not prohibited state regulation of water pollution.

(C) Congress has enacted laws regulating water pollution in interstate rivers.

(D) Shipco operates only within the state of Birmingham.

72. Durk was a member of an organization known as The Church of Twelve Gods. Members of this organization worship twelve different deities, each said to be in charge of a different field of worldly activity. Each month of the year, the organization conducts a festival dedicated to a different one of the deities. In March, the festival of Love was held to honor the goddess of love. As part of the festival, members met to engage in activities involving nudity and group sexual intercourse. Along with other members of the organization, Durk, who participated in the festival, was arrested by police from the county vice squad. He was convicted of violating a state law which made it a crime "for any adult to engage in sexual intercourse with another while any third person is present."

If Durk appeals, the conviction

(A) must be overturned, if the group sexual activity was required by a reasonable interpretation of the organization's religious beliefs.

(B) must be overturned, because the conduct was part of the free exercise of a religion.

(C) may be upheld, on the ground that an organization which worships multiple deities is

not a "religion" for First Amendment purposes.

(D) may be upheld, even if the group sexual activity was required by Durk's sincere religious beliefs.

73. The muscovite beetle is an insect pest which threatens the fruit growing industry of the state of New Britain. In an attempt to exterminate the insect, the New Britain Bureau of Agriculture has ordered the aerial spraying of insecticide in all forested regions of the state. A federal law prohibits the use of insecticides in areas designated as national parks. Brittania National Park, owned by the federal government and nearly one million acres in size, is heavily forested, and is located wholly within the state of New Britain.

If an appropriate agency of the United States of America sues in a federal court for an injunction to prevent aerial spraying in Brittania National Park, should the court issue the injunction?

(A) No, because control of the environment is primarily a state function.

(B) No, unless it can be shown that use of the insecticide will be damaging to the park's ecology.

(C) Yes, unless the use of the insecticide can be shown to serve a compelling state interest.

(D) Yes, because Congress has legislative power over federally owned lands.

74. The White People's Socialist Party (WPSP) is a small political organization which advocates racial segregation and which occasionally runs a candidate for election to office in the state of Nevorado. The WPSP planned to hold a campaign rally at the state capitol two weeks prior to the last statewide election. Because anonymous threats of violence were received by the state police, however, a Nevorado court issued an injunction prohibiting the WPSP from conducting any public rallies until after the election. After the election was over, the WPSP sought United States Supreme Court review of the Nevorado court's decision.

The United States Supreme Court should

(A) review the state court's decision if the WPSP desires to hold future rallies in the state of Nevorado.

(B) review the state court's decision because any interference with the right to assemble violates the First Amendment to the United States Constitution.

(C) not review the state court's decision since the question presented has become moot.

(D) not review the state court's decision since the aims of the WPSP violate the Equal Protection Clause of the Fourteenth Amendment to the United States Constitution.

75. In 1980, the state of Corinth enacted the Energy Conservation Tax Rebate Act, creating a state income tax credit for persons who installed solar and/or wind powered generators in residential realty. Homer began to install a solar generator in his home in the state of Corinth in November 1993, but did not complete the installation until February 1994. In December 1993, however, the Corinth legislature repealed the Energy Conservation Tax Rebate Act, effective January 1, 1994.

If Homer challenged the repeal of the Act on the ground that it was constitutionally invalid, his most effective argument would be that repeal of the statute violated the

(A) Obligations of Contracts Clause.

(B) Due Process Clause of the Fifth Amendment.

(C) Privileges and Immunities Clause.

(D) Just Compensation Clause.

76. Congress passes a law requiring all females who are eighteen years of age to register for the draft. A non-profit organization known as Females Against Registration advertises that it will provide an attorney and defend without charge any female prosecuted for failing to register. If the

Bar Association of the state of Tetonic sues to enjoin further publication of the advertisement in that state, the injunction should be

(A) granted, it Tetonic statutes prohibit advertising by attorneys.

(B) granted, since the advertisement could have the effect of encouraging young women to violate the law.

(C) denied, since the advertisement constitutes commercial speech.

(D) denied, under the First Amendment to the United States Constitution.

Questions 77-79 are based on the following fact situation.

Congress passes the Schools Construction Act, providing for grants of federal funds to states to help finance the construction of new school buildings. A section of the Act provides that states which do not alter their building codes to prohibit the use in school construction of certain substances listed as carcinogenic (cancer-causing) are ineligible for federal funds under the law. The state of Forest is the home of an industry which produces one of the materials listed in the federal law as carcinogenic. Its legislature has refused to alter the state building code to conform to the requirements of the Schools Construction Act.

77. In a federal court, which of the following potential plaintiffs is most likely to be able to obtain a judicial determination of the validity of the section of the Schools Construction Act dealing with state building codes?

(A) The parent of a child who currently attends a public school in the state of Forest and who fears that the quality of education in the state will decline if the state does not receive federal funds for school construction.

(B) An organization dedicated to protecting the concept of "states rights" against encroachment by the federal government.

(C) A taxpayer of the United States and the state

of Forest who fears that if Forest does not receive federal funds for school construction, her state taxes will be increased to pay for school construction which would otherwise have been federally funded.

(D) A building contractor who has been hired by the state of Forest to construct a school building, under a contract which is contingent upon receipt by the state of federal school- construction funds to which it would otherwise be entitled.

78. In *defending* the validity of the section, which of the following arguments would be most effective?

(A) The section is a necessary and proper extension of the congressional power to regulate education.

(B) The states surrendered their authority over school construction by accepting federal funds for that purpose in the past.

(C) The federal government can regulate school construction without limitation because the federal government is paying for some of the construction costs.

(D) It was reasonable for Congress to believe that compliance with the section will assure that the federal money spent on school construction will result in greater benefit than harm to the general public.

79. The section is question is probably

I. constitutional on the basis of the federal police power.

II. constitutional on the basis of the spending power.

(A) I only.

(B) II only.

(C) I and II.

(D) Neither I nor II.

Questions 80-81 are based on the following fact situa-

tion.

A law in the state of Atlantis requires any person doing business in that state to obtain a business license from the state's Department of Commerce. A recently enacted amendment to that statute prohibits convicted felons in the state of Atlantis from doing business in that state, and authorizes the state's Department of Commerce to deny a business license to any such person.

Fell, a convicted felon who was released from an Atlantis prison after completion of his sentence, applied for a business license after the passage of the amendment described above. He brings an action in a federal court to enjoin the Atlantis Department of Commerce from enforcing the amendment against him on the ground that it is constitutionally invalid.

80. Fell's strongest argument is that

(A) states are forbidden by the Obligation of Contracts Clause from interfering with the rights of felons to do business.

(B) the statute unreasonably interferes with the right of felons to travel from one state to another.

(C) the statute violates the Equal Protection Clause of the Fourteenth Amendment to the United States Constitution.

(D) he has already paid his debt to society, and should be given the opportunity to make a fresh start in life by engaging in a lawful occupation.

81. A federal court will probably

(A) dismiss the action, because no federal question is involved.

(B) dismiss the action, since Fell is a resident of the state against which the action is being brought.

(C) hear the action, since Fell is a resident of the state against which the action is being brought.

(D) hear the action, since Fell has asserted that

the statute is constitutionally invalid.

82. Congressional legislation abolishing all legal penalties for gambling could most easily be upheld.

    (A) as a regulation of interstate and international commerce.

    (B) under the Supremacy Clause of the United States Constitution.

    (C) if scientific studies showed gambling to be a harmless activity.

    (D) if it applied only to the District of Columbia.

83. Clover, a resident of the state of South Maple, recently lost her job when her employer went out of business. While employed, Clover worked on the night shift and attended college during the day. She applied for unemployment compensation benefits under South Maple's Unemployment Compensation Act. Although she was otherwise entitled to benefits, she was denied them under a provision of the Act which prohibits the payment of benefits to any person who attends school between the hours of 8 a.m. and 6 p.m. After exhausting all administrative remedies, Clover appealed the denial of benefits, asserting that the prohibition against payment of benefits to day students violated the Equal Protection Clause.

    Which of the following is the minimum finding that would result in a ruling that the statute is constitutionally valid?

    (A) The classification is a reasonable way of protecting a compelling state interest.

    (B) The classification has a rational basis.

    (C) The receipt of unemployment benefits is a privilege rather than a right.

    (D) The payment of benefits to day students would result in a clear and present danger.

84. The state of Fargo requires all public and private hospitals to be accredited by the state Department of Health, which is empowered to inspect hospital facilities prior to accreditation and as a condition of continued accreditation. All hospital employees are required to be licensed by the Department of Health. The Department is also responsible for the distribution of funds under a state law that provides financial aid to all accredited hospitals for the purchase of equipment. The state law makes each hospital's share proportional to the number of patients which it treated the previous year.

    Minority Hospital, a privately operated hospital accredited by the state of Fargo, denies admission to Caucasians except under emergency circumstances. An organization known as Patients' Union has brought an action against Minority in a state court for an injunction directing it to discontinue its racially exclusionary policy on the ground that it violates the Equal Protection Clause of the Fourteenth Amendment. Which of the following is the strongest argument in support of the position taken by Patients' Union?

    (A) Under the Fourteenth Amendment no place of public accommodation may discriminate against persons because of their race.

    (B) The licensing of hospital employees by the state requires the hospital to act as the state would act in complying with requirements of the Fourteenth Amendment.

    (C) The Equal Protection Clause of the Fourteenth Amendment requires the state court to eliminate racial discrimination in places of public accommodation.

    (D) The state's involvement in hospital regulation and support makes the Equal Protection Clause of the Fourteenth Amendment applicable to Minority Hospital.

85. In which of the following cases is defendant's conviction most likely to be reversed on constitutional grounds?

    (A) Defendant is convicted of operating a theater showing pornographic films in violation of a zoning ordinance which prohibits such activity from being conducted within 500 feet of a school.

(B) Defendant is convicted of giving weekly parties at his home at which obscene films are shown to persons who pay an entrance fee in violation of a county ordinance which prohibits the display to groups of three or more persons of materials defined by state law as obscene.

(C) Defendant, a professional bookseller, is convicted of selling an obscene book to an undercover police officer, in violation of a state law which provides: "It shall be a misdemeanor for any person to sell or to possess for the purposes of sale any obscene book, magazine, or other publication."

(D) Defendant, a magazine publisher, is convicted of sending obscene materials through the mails in a trial at which the court permitted the introduction of evidence that the defendant advertised his magazine in a way which pandered to the prurient interests of readers.

86. Relations between the United States of America and the Union of Free Republics (UFR) have been strained for the past four decades. In an attempt to improve these relations, the president of the USA and the premier of the UFR enter into a series of executive agreements. One of these agreements requires the government of each country to discourage its press from making derogatory references to the other country. At the president's request and in support of that agreement, Congress enacts the Friendly Nations Publications Act, which prohibits the publication of certain specified disparaging statements about the UFR in any magazine or newspaper published by the armed forces of the United States.

Which of the following would be the strongest argument **against** the constitutionality of the Friendly Nations Publications Act?

(A) The president lacked the power to make an executive agreement requiring the United States to discourage its press from making derogatory references to the UFR.

(B) The executive agreement could have been implemented in a less burdensome manner.

(C) The executive agreement violates the First Amendment to the United States Constitution.

(D) The Friendly Nations Publications Act violates the First Amendment to the United States Constitution.

87. The National Forest Service, an agency of the federal government, leases grazing rights in the national forests to cattle ranchers for a fee. Stock is a cattle rancher who leases grazing rights from the National Forest Service on 1,000 acres of federally owned land in the Woods National Forest. The state of Blue, in which the Woods National Forest is located, had recently enacted a statute imposing a "grazing rights lease tax" on leases of grazing rights within the state. The tax is based on the number of acres leased by the taxpayer for grazing purposes, and approximates one dollar per acre per year.

If Stock seeks an injunction to prevent the state of Blue from collecting the tax, should the court issue the injunction?

(A) Yes, since the power to tax is the power to destroy.

(B) Yes, if the effect of the "grazing rights lease tax" is to increase the cost of leasing grazing land from the National Forest Service.

(C) No, unless the tax discriminates against leases of federal land.

(D) No, because states are immune from taxation by the federal government.

88. Assume that Congress passes a law which provides that whenever the President of the United States delegates any person to travel to a foreign nation for the purpose of negotiating an executive agreement, the President must designate a member of the United States Senate to accompany and advise that person. Assume also that the President vetoes the law, but that the presidential veto is overridden by a two-thirds majority of both

houses of Congress. Assume further that the President subsequently delegates an ambassador to travel to a foreign nation for the purpose of negotiating an executive agreement without appointing a member of the United States Senate to accompany and advise the ambassador.

Which of the following arguments would most effectively justify that action by the president?

(A) The President has sole and exclusive power over foreign affairs.

(B) The law unconstitutionally discriminates against members of the House of Representatives.

(C) The law violates the principle of separation of powers by interfering with the President's power to delegate authority in the field of foreign affairs.

(D) A presidential veto of a law relating to foreign affairs is final, and may not be overridden by Congress.

89. When Candida declared herself to be a candidate for election to the United States Senate from the state of Batavia, the state Commissioner of Elections refused to place her name on the ballot. The commissioner said that his decision was based on the fact that state records indicated that Candida was only twenty-seven years of age. Candida subsequently instituted a proceeding against the commissioner in a state court. After examining state birth records, and after taking the testimony of Candida's mother and of a physician who was present at Candida's birth, the court found that Candida was thirty years of age and directed the commissioner to list her as a candidate. Candida won the election, but after she began her term of office, the Senate expelled her, declaring that she did not meet the constitutional age requirement.

If Candida institutes a proceeding in a federal court for an order reinstating her to her seat in the Senate, which of the following would be the most effective argument in support of a motion to dismiss her proceeding?

(A) Candida should be collaterally estopped

from maintaining the proceeding.

(B) No substantial federal question is presented.

(C) Candida has already had her day in court.

(D) Candida's claim presents a non-justiciable political question.

90. Congress passes the Federal Aid to Scholars Act, providing for grants of federal funds to college and university students who meet certain financial and scholastic standards. A provision of the act restricts such payments, however, to citizens of the United States. Immerson is a foreign national studying at a university located in the United States under an appropriate visa granted by the Department of State. If Immerson challenges the constitutionality of the citizenship requirement of the Federal Aid to Scholars Act, the court should rule that provision

(A) valid, because Congress has plenary power to regulate the rights of aliens.

(B) valid, because resident aliens are not protected by the United States Constitution.

(C) invalid, because it violates the Equal Protection Clause of the Fourteenth Amendment.

(D) invalid, because resident aliens are entitled to the same constitutional protections as citizens.

91. A statute of the state of Penelope permits school districts to determine whether or not they will provide transportation for pupils. The statute provides that school districts electing to furnish such transportation must finance half the resulting costs by taxing the families of students who are so transported, and requires the state to provide "matching funds" upon application by the school district. The Flores School District opted to furnish transportation to pupils. It was considering a policy which would prohibit school buses from traveling on unpaved roads. Parents of school children who reside on unpaved roads in the Flores School District objected to the proposed policy, arguing that it would violate the Equal Protection Clause of the Fourteenth Amendment to the United States Constitution. The school dis-

trict requested an advisory opinion from the state Supreme Court under the state Judicial Code.

If the state Supreme Court issues an advisory opinion determining that the School District's policy is constitutional, and if the parents seek review by the United States Supreme Court, may the United States Supreme Court properly review the state court's decision?

(A) Yes, unless the decision rests on an adequate state ground.

(B) Yes, since the state court found the policy to be valid under the United States Constitution.

(C) No, since a request for an advisory opinion does not satisfy the "case or controversy" requirement of the United States Constitution.

(D) No, unless the state of Penelope receives federal funds for the transportation of pupils.

92. Hauler was in the trucking business, specializing in the transportation of a toxic chemical known as Toxinol within the state of New Brittany. In January 1984, Hauler's truck was involved in an accident which caused a crack in its chemical holding tank. Although he knew about the crack, Hauler continued using the truck to transport Toxinol until January 1985, when he bought a new vehicle. In March 1985 several people who lived in the state became ill. On March 28, after state health investigators determined that the illness resulted from exposure to Toxinol residues on the roadway, the state legislature enacted the Clean Roads Act. The Clean Roads Act authorized the state Department of Transportation to determine without a hearing the identity of persons spilling toxic chemicals on state highways and to order the removal of such chemicals by such persons. The law also provided that failure to comply with such an order within thirty days after receiving it was a crime. On May 1, state investigators submitted a report stating that the leak in Hauler's truck had caused the deposit of Toxinol residues on roads within the state during the period from January 1984 through January 1985. The same

day, the Department of Transportation ordered Hauler to remove all Toxinol residues from the roads of the state of New Brittany. Hauler refused to do so, and on August 15 was convicted of violating the Clean Roads Act by failing to comply with the Department of Transportation order.

If Hauler appeals his conviction, his most effective argument would be that the Clean Roads Act

(A) was an ex post facto law.

(B) was a bill of attainder.

(C) violated the Due Process Clause of the Fifth Amendment to the United States Constitution.

(D) violated the Due Process Clause of the Fourteenth Amendment to the United States Constitution.

Questions 93-94 are based on the following fact situation.

A recently enacted statute of the state of Cantoria provides that no person shall be granted a high school diploma without first passing a series of examinations designed to test minimum competency in reading, writing, mathematics, and American history. The statute requires that the examinations, known as the Regents' Examinations, are to be written by the state Board of Regents and are to be administered on the same day throughout the state. It further provides that each high school in the state may elect to have the Regents' Examinations administered either by its own employees or, without cost, by agents of the state Board of Regents.

93. Assume for the purpose of this question only that Tandy, a taxpayer of the state of Cantoria, has sued in a federal court to enjoin the state from enforcing the statute on the ground that the administration of the Regents' Examinations in religious schools by agents of the state Board of Regents violates the Establishment Clause of the First Amendment to the United States Constitution. Which of the following is the most effective argument in opposition to Tandy's claim?

(A) Tandy lacks standing to challenge the constitutionality of the statute.

(B) The law does not discriminate between religions.

(C) The law has neither the effect nor the primary purpose of advancing religion.

(D) The state has a compelling interest in the competency of high school graduates.

94. Assume for the purpose of this question only that Holy Academy, a religious high school in the state of Cantoria, sues in a federal court to enjoin enforcement of the statute. In support of its petition, Holy Academy asserts that its students belong to a religion which opposes all secular education, and that the statute therefore violates their rights and those of the school under the Free Exercise Clause of the First Amendment to the United States Constitution. Which of the following would be the most effective argument in opposition to that claim?

(A) Holy Academy lacks standing to challenge the constitutionality of the statute.

(B) Opposition to all secular education is not a reasonable religious belief.

(C) The law is not primarily intended to interfere with a religious belief.

(D) The state has a compelling interest in the competency of high school graduates.

Questions 95-96 are based on the following fact situation.

An ordinance of the City of Ortega provides as follows:

Section 1 — No person shall conduct a public speech or demonstration in the City of Ortega without first obtaining an assembly permit from the city mayor, who shall not issue such a permit if, in his opinion, the speech or demonstration is likely to result in a breach of the public peace.

Section 2 — A fee of ten dollars shall accompany every application for an assembly permit, unless the application is for a permit to conduct a political campaign rally, in which case no fee shall be required.

Section 3 — The provisions of this ordinance are severable, and a judicial declaration that one section hereof is unconstitutional shall not affect the validity of any other section.

Speeger desired to hold a rally in the City of Ortega. After submitting his application for an assembly permit, Speeger stated in a radio interview that he planned to lead the people at the rally to raid and burn an abortion clinic operated by the city. Upon hearing the radio broadcast, the mayor of the City of Ortega denied Speeger's application.

95. Assume for the purpose of this question only that Speeger conducted the rally, calling for the immediate destruction by fire of the city abortion clinic; that he passed flaming torches to people in the crowd, saying "Follow me, and we'll burn out that nest of evil"; that he was arrested as the crowd began to follow him towards the abortion clinic, and that he was subsequently convicted of conducting a public rally without an assembly permit in violation of the above ordinance. On appeal, Speeger's conviction should be

(A) reversed, because prior restraint of speech or assembly is inconsistent with the First Amendment to the United States Constitution.

(B) reversed, because although punishment of Speeger's conduct may be constitutionally valid, his conduct cannot be punished under this ordinance.

(C) affirmed, because as a result of Speeger's attempt to incite unlawful action he lacks standing to challenge the constitutionality of the ordinance.

(D) affirmed, because an ordinance which requires a permit for the conduct of a public meeting is constitutionally valid.

96. Which of the following is the LEAST likely reason for holding that Section 2 of the ordinance is *invalid*?

(A) Section 2 violates the Necessary and Proper Clause of the United States Constitution.

(B) Section 2 discriminates against speech on the basis of its content.

(C) Section 2 is vague and/or overbroad.

(D) Section 1 is vague and/or overbroad.

Questions 97-98 are based on the following fact situation.

Statutes in the state of Sartoria provide that:

(1) No producer of unrefined petroleum within the state may sell more than half its annual production to buyers outside the state.

(2) Every carrier transporting unrefined petroleum over roads within the state is required to pay a state highway use tax based upon a formula which combines the quantity transported and the distance over which it is moved within the state.

Petro is a producer of unrefined petroleum within the state of Sartoria and operates a trucking company for the transportation of his product.

97. Assume for the purpose of this question only that there is no federal statute concerning the right of a state to regulate the sale of unrefined petroleum produced within that state. If Petro challenges the constitutionality of statute 1 in an appropriate proceeding, which of the following would be Petro's most effective argument?

(A) The production and sale of unrefined petroleum is a matter of national concern, requiring uniform federal regulation.

(B) The unrefined petroleum sold by Petro remains in its original package until it reaches the ultimate consumer.

(C) The state's attempt to regulate the sale of unrefined petroleum in interstate commerce violates the Full Faith and Credit Clause of the United States Constitution.

(D) Regulation of the sale of unrefined petroleum is preempted by Congressional silence.

98. If Petro challenges the constitutionality of statute 2 in an appropriate proceeding, which of the following additional facts or inferences, if it was the only one true, would be the most likely to result in a finding that statute 2 is unconstitutional?

(A) More than fifty percent of the transportation of unrefined petroleum over roads in the state of Sartoria is connected with interstate commerce.

(B) There is no federal statute concerning the right of a state to tax the transportation of unrefined petroleum within that state.

(C) The state of Sartoria imposes no tax on the transportation of any other product within the state.

(D) The states bordering on Sartoria have indicated an intention to impose similar taxes on transportation over their highways.

Questions 99-100 are based on the following fact situation.

Congress passes the State Highway Subsidy Act which makes matching federal funds available to states for the construction of state highways on condition that states receiving such funds prohibit trucks longer than a specified size from operating on state highways. The state of Carmody has refused to amend its statutes to comply with the Act.

99. Which of the following persons is most likely to have standing to challenge the constitutionality of the State Highway Subsidy Act?

(A) A taxpayer of the state of Carmody who believes that if the state does not receive matching federal funds for the construction of new highways, the state's roads will soon become inadequate for use by its residents.

(B) A federal taxpayer who believes that if the state of Carmody does not receive matching federal funds for the construction of new highways, its roads will soon become inadequate for use in interstate commerce.

(C) A non-partisan political-action membership organization dedicated to the preservation of "states' rights" which believes that the State Highway Subsidy Act interferes with the state's right to regulate the size of trucks using its highways.

(D) A road construction company which has a contract to build a road for the state of Carmody and which believes that without matching federal funds the state will be unable to honor its contract.

100. The State Highway Subsidy Act is most likely to be held constitutional

(A) as an exercise of the general police power of the federal government.

(B) as an exercise of the spending power of Congress.

(C) under the Property Clause of Article IV of the United States Constitution.

(D) under the Eleventh Amendment to the United States Constitution.

101. Dillon was convicted of murder in a state court after a trial in which evidence was admitted over Dillon's objection that it was obtained in violation of his Fourth Amendment rights. On appeal to the highest court in the state, Dillon's conviction was affirmed. After Dillon's petition for certiorari was denied by the United States Supreme Court, he filed a petition for habeas corpus in the appropriate United States district court on the ground that the evidence used to convict him was obtained in violation of his Fourth Amendment rights. Dillon's petition for habeas corpus should be

(A) granted, because the United States district court may consider de novo a constitutional challenge to the admissibility of evidence in a state court.

(B) granted, because Dillon has exhausted all available state remedies.

(C) denied, because the United States Supreme Court did not grant certiorari.

(D) denied, because the state court has already determined that Dillon's Fourth Amendment rights were not violated by admission of the evidence.

Questions 102-04 are based on the following fact situation.

Appleton's application for employment as a state of Moravia police officer was rejected pursuant to a state law which prohibited state employment of "sexual deviates," on the ground that he was a homosexual. Appleton subsequently challenged the validity of the state law in a Moravia state court, asserting that it violated the Equal Protection Clauses of the constitutions of the United States and of the state of Moravia, the language of which is substantially the same. No Moravia court has ever interpreted the phrase "sexual deviates" as used in the state law.

102. Assume for the purpose of this question only that while his state court action was pending, Appleton instituted a proceeding in a United States District Court seeking an order enjoining the Moravia police commissioner from enforcing the law described above on the grounds that it violates the federal constitution's Equal Protection Clause. If the court declines to grant Appleton relief, it will most likely be

(A) based on the abstention doctrine.

(B) based on the Eleventh Amendment to the United States Constitution.

(C) on the ground that the question is moot.

(D) on the ground that Appleton lacks standing.

103. Assume for the purpose of this question that the Moravia court found the law to be valid under the Equal Protection Clause of the United States Constitution but invalid under the Equal Protection Clause of the constitution of the state of Moravia. Assume also that the highest court of the state of Moravia affirmed the judgment. If the commissioner of police of Moravia seeks review

by the United States Supreme Court, such review is

(A) available by certiorari only.

(B) available by appeal only.

(C) available by either certiorari or appeal.

(D) not available because no substantial federal question is presented.

104. Assume for the purpose of this question that the state of Moravia court found the law to be valid under the Equal Protection Clauses of both the federal and state constitutions. Assume further that an intermediate appellate court of Moravia affirmed the ruling, and that Appleton's subsequent petition for certiorari was denied by the highest court in the state. If Appleton seeks judicial review by the United States Supreme Court, can the United States Supreme Court grant such review?

(A) No, because the decision of the Moravia court is based on an adequate state ground.

(B) No, because there has been no determination on the merits by the highest court of the state of Moravia.

(C) No, because sexual preference is not a suspect classification.

(D) Yes.

105. A statute of the state of Lincoln requires hairdressers to be licensed by the State Department of Education. The statute further provides that no person shall qualify for a hairdresser's license who has not completed a prescribed program of study including a two semester-unit course in biology. Benson, who held a valid hairdresser's license from another state, moved to the state of Lincoln and applied to the Lincoln Department of Education for a hairdresser's license. Benson's application was rejected on the ground that, although he had completed all other requirements for a state hairdresser's license, he had never studied biology as required by the state law. If Benson seeks judicial review of the denial of his application, his most effective argument would

be that the law

(A) has no rational basis.

(B) violates the Full Faith and Credit Clause of the United States Constitution.

(C) discriminates against out-of-staters.

(D) violates the Privileges and Immunities Clause of the Fourteenth Amendment to the United States Constitution.

Questions 106-08 are based on the following fact situation.

Pornco placed the following advertisement in a magazine:

STEAMY FORBIDDEN SEX! The United States Supreme Court has said that nobody can interfere with the private possession of pornography for private viewing in the privacy of your own home. SO, NOW, FOR THE FIRST TIME EVER, we are offering films TOO HOT for commercial showing. Fill out this coupon and SEND NOW for porno too sizzling to be legal in theaters or clubs. THIS OFFER AVAILABLE ONLY FOR PRIVATE POSSESSION FOR PRIVATE VIEWING IN THE PRIVACY OF YOUR OWN HOME.

Fenton, a federal police officer, ordered films from Pornco by sending a check to the address given in the advertisement. Fenton signed and enclosed the advertising coupon which stated:

Rush me the films described in this ad. I HEREBY CERTIFY THAT I INTEND TO POSSESS THEM PRIVATELY FOR PRIVATE VIEWING IN THE PRIVACY OF MY OWN HOME.

After Fenton received the films, Pornco was charged in a federal court with violating a federal statute which prohibits sending obscene films through the mail.

106. Assume for the purpose of this question only that at Pornco's trial, an attempt is made by the prosecution to offer into evidence a copy of the advertisement to which Fenton had responded. Upon

timely objection by Pornco, the court should rule the advertisement

(A) admissible because pandering is not protected by the First Amendment.

(B) admissible as evidence that the films sold by Pornco appeal primarily to prurient interest.

(C) inadmissible as constitutionally protected commercial speech.

(D) inadmissible because the advertisement is not, itself, obscene.

107. Which of the following may the court properly consider in determining whether the films sold by Pornco are obscene?

    I. Expert testimony that the films have serious value as works of erotic art.

    II. Expert testimony that activities depicted in the films are likely to appeal to the prurient interest of persons under the age of eighteen years.

(A) I only.

(B) II only.

(C) I and II.

(D) Neither I nor II.

108. Assume for the purpose of this question only that the films are found to be obscene under a constitutionally acceptable definition of obscenity. Can Pornco be properly convicted of sending obscene films through the mail?

(A) No, because the advertisement indicated that the films were being sold only for private possession and use.

(B) No, because Fenton certified that the films were being ordered for private possession and use.

(C) Yes, because although the Constitution permits the private possession of pornography, it does not protect the private possession of obscene films.

(D) Yes, because Pornco sold the films through the mail.

109. Basset was appointed U.S. ambassador to Fredonia by a former President with the advice and consent of the Senate. Three days after taking office, a new President requests Basset's resignation. Upon Basset's refusal to resign, the President issues an order purporting to remove Basset from office as ambassador. Is the presidential order valid?

(A) Yes, but only if there was cause for Basset's removal from office.

(B) Yes, because the President has the power to remove ambassadors without cause.

(C) No, because the President may not remove an ambassador without the advice and consent of the Senate.

(D) No, unless the Senate subsequently ratifies the order by consenting to the appointment of a new ambassador to Fredonia.

Questions 110-111 are based on the following fact situation.

A state law sets the mandatory retirement age for public high school teachers at 65 years for males, 62 years for females, and 60 years for physical education teachers of either gender.

110. Assume for the purpose of this question only that Anderson, a sixty-two-year-old female public high school science teacher, challenges the law, asserting that it violates the Equal Protection Clause of the Fourteenth Amendment to the United States Constitution. Anderson's claim will most likely

(A) succeed, because the classification established by the state law is based on gender.

(B) succeed, unless the state law is substantially related to the achievement of important governmental interests.

(C) not succeed, unless the classification is found to be based on benign sex discrimination.

(D) not succeed, because gender discrimination is not based on a suspect classification.

111. Assume for the purpose of this question only that Bobbins, a sixty-year-old public high school physical education teacher, challenges the law, asserting that it violates the Equal Protection Clause of the Fourteenth Amendment. Which of the following additional facts or inferences, if it were the only one true, would be most likely to result in a finding that the statute is constitutional?

(A) Bobbins is not as vigorous and healthy as he was at the age of fifty years.

(B) Physical education teachers must engage in strenuous physical activities likely to be hazardous to the health of a person over the age of sixty years.

(C) The state has the right to set the retirement age for teachers and other state employees.

(D) State law provides that physical education teachers who reach the age of sixty years must be given first preference in being hired for other teaching positions for which they qualify.

112. A statute of the state of Orlandia provides that no marriage shall be performed without a license, and that no license shall be issued for the marriage of any male person below the age of 19 years or any female person below the age of 17 years. Malcomb, an 18-year-old male, desires to marry Willa, an 18-year-old female. Because of the provisions of the statute, however, Malcomb has not yet asked Willa to marry him. If Malcomb challenges the statute in a state court, asserting that it violates his rights under the U.S. Constitution, which of the following would be the most effective argument in opposition to Malcomb's claim?

(A) Malcomb lacks standing to challenge the statute.

(B) The statute has a rational basis.

(C) Females mature earlier than males.

(D) The right to regulate marriage is reserved to the states by the Tenth Amendment.

113. A policy of the State University of the state of Magnolia prohibits use of campus facilities by persons or organizations without a permit from the University Chancellor. Stuard, a student at Magnolia State University, is president of a student organization known as the Freedom With Responsibility League. On three occasions, Stuard's applications for permits to use a classroom for meetings of the organization were denied by the University Chancellor. The reason given by the Chancellor was that the Freedom With Responsibility League advocates interference with freedom of speech as protected by Magnolia's constitution.

Following the most recent denial of her application, Stuard commenced a proceeding in a U.S. district court seeking an injunction prohibiting denial of permits to the Freedom With Responsibility League on the ground that it violates the organization's constitutional right to freedom of assembly. Before a hearing could be held on Stuard's claim, the University Chancellor reversed his prior decision and granted the Freedom With Responsibility League a permit for the use of campus facilities, declaring that the philosophy embraced by a student organization would no longer be considered in deciding whether that organization would receive a permit for use of campus facilities. If the University attorney moves to dismiss Stuard's claim, the motion should be

(A) denied, if none of the University Chancellor's decisions was based on an adequate state ground.

(B) denied, because Stuard's claim is one which is capable of repetition and likely to evade judicial review.

(C) granted, because the claim is moot.

(D) granted, unless Stuard was damaged by past denials of her application.

114. After archaeologists discovered the fossil

remains of a stone-age society in the state of Caledonia, Congress passed a law establishing "the National Museum of Prehistoric Artifacts for the enjoyment and education of all residents of the United States." Under the statute, the museum was to be built in the state of Caledonia, near the site of the archeological find. It was to be funded entirely by the federal government, using revenues derived from the national income tax. The federal law provided that the museum was to display prehistoric artifacts and fossils gathered from all parts of the United States, in addition to those artifacts which had been discovered in the state of Caledonia. The attorney general of another state instituted a proceeding in a federal district court for an injunction against the use of federal funds to establish the National Museum of Prehistoric Artifacts in the state of Caledonia, asserting that such expenditure would be an unconstitutional disbursal of federal funds. Which of the following is most likely to support a finding in favor of the constitutionality of the federal statute?

(A) The congressional spending power.

(B) The Commerce Clause.

(C) The Eleventh Amendment to the United States Constitution.

(D) The doctrine of state sovereign immunity.

115. The National Preserve Service is a federal agency authorized by Congress to regulate the use of national preserves. The Gatos National Preserve is a tract of land owned by the federal government and located entirely within the state of Los Gatos. Under state and federal law, persons who have obtained fishing licenses from the state of Los Gatos are permitted to fish within the Gatos National Preserve.

Because of a series of destructive forest fires in the state of Los Gatos, the National Preserve Service issues a regulation closing the Gatos National Preserve to public use from dusk to dawn. As a result, there is a reduction in the number of persons applying for fishing licenses and this causes a decline in state revenues. For this reason, the state Department of Fish and Game

institutes a proceeding in a federal court, challenging the constitutionality of the regulation.

Which of the following would provide the National Preserve Service with its strongest argument in support of the constitutionality of its regulation?

(A) The Commerce Clause of Article I of the United States Constitution.

(B) The Property Clause of Article IV of the United States Constitution.

(C) The federal police power.

(D) The federal government's right of eminent domain.

116. After three children residing in the City of Corinth were bitten by poisonous snakes, the City Council passed an ordinance which prohibited keeping poisonous snakes within city limits. Snake Haven, a reptile preserve, was located in the city of Corinth. Prior to passage of the ordinance, Snake Haven engaged in the business of breeding poisonous snakes which it sold to zoos throughout the world. In addition, Snake Haven conducted tours of its facility, charging an admission fee to persons who entered for that purpose. Following passage of the ordinance, Snake Haven instituted a claim against the City of Corinth in a state court, asserting that it was entitled to just compensation under the Fifth Amendment to the United States Constitution.

Will Snake Haven win?

(A) Yes, if the ordinance resulted in a taking of private property for public use.

(B) Yes, unless the City of Corinth can establish that the ordinance serves a compelling interest.

(C) No, because the Just Compensation Clause of the Fifth Amendment is not applicable to takings by a state or municipality.

(D) No, if any person had been bitten by a snake kept by Snake Haven.

117. Because a revolution in the Central American republic of Libertad threatens to topple its government, the President of the United States orders federal troops to invade Libertad. Congress subsequently passes a resolution directing the President to recall the troops. When the President refuses to do so, a proceeding is instituted in a United States District Court seeking an order compelling the President to comply with the congressional directive. Which of the following would be the President's most effective argument in opposition to that proceeding?

    (A) United States District Courts lack power over the President.

    (B) The President is commander-in-chief of the armed forces.

    (C) The matter is a non-justiciable political question.

    (D) The presidential order sending troops to Libertad amounted to a declaration of war.

118. A statute of the State of Ono makes it a felony for a person over the age of 21 years to engage in sexual intercourse with a person under the age of 16 years. The statute further provides that if persons who are unrelated to each other by blood or marriage spend more than three hours in the same hotel room together, they are conclusively presumed to have engaged in sexual intercourse.

    Dow was charged with violating the statute by engaging in sexual intercourse with Young, a person under the age of 16 years. Dow and Young were not related to each other by blood or marriage. In its instructions to the jury, the court said, "If you find that Dow and Young spent more than three hours in the same hotel room, you must find that they engaged in sexual intercourse." The jury found Dow guilty.

    If Dow subsequently challenged the constitutionality of the statute in an appropriate proceeding, Dow's most effective argument would be that the statute violated

    (A) procedural due process requirements.

    (B) substantive due process requirements.

    (C) the Equal Protection Clause of the Fourteenth Amendment.

    (D) the prohibition against bills of attainder.

Questions 119-120 are based on the following fact situation.

Adamson, an alien convicted of murder in a state court, appeals on the ground that aliens were systematically excluded from serving on the jury.

119. Assume for the purpose of this question only that a federal law prohibits aliens from serving on juries in state court proceedings, but that there is no state law creating such a prohibition. If Adamson's appeal results in a reversal of his conviction, it will probably be because the federal law

    (A) violates the Equal Protection Clause of the Fourteenth Amendment.

    (B) violates the Due Process Clause of the Fifth Amendment.

    (C) is invalid under the doctrine of separation of powers.

    (D) is invalid under the Supremacy Clause of Article VI.

120. Assume for the purpose of this question only that a state law prohibits aliens from serving on juries in state court proceedings, but that there is no federal law creating such a prohibition. If Adamson's appeal results in a reversal of his conviction, it will probably be because

    (A) a state law may not discriminate on the basis of alienage.

    (B) the state law violates the Privileges and Immunities Clause of the Fourteenth Amendment.

    (C) the state law violates the prohibition against discrimination on the basis of race, color, or previous condition of servitude contained in the Fifteenth Amendment.

    (D) the state law is invalid under the Supremacy

Clause of Article VI.

Questions 121-123 are based on the following fact situation.

A state law provides that the names of prospective jurors in County Courts shall be drawn from the list of county residents holding state driving licenses. Chandler, a resident of Durban County, is a 22-year old black woman who does not hold a driving license. She has never been called as a prospective juror in the Durban County Court. In a federal court, Chandler challenges the constitutional validity of the state law, claiming that it violates the Equal Protection Clause of the Fourteenth Amendment. In support of her challenge, Chandler offers proof that black women between the ages of 18 and 23 make up a large portion of the population of Durban County, but that no member of this group holds a state driving license or has ever been called as a prospective juror in the Durban County Court.

121. Evidence that no black women between the ages of 18 and 23 who reside in Durban County hold state driving licenses should be

   (A) excluded, because a state law does not violate the Equal Protection Clause on its face unless its purpose is to discriminate.

   (B) excluded, because a state law does not violate the Equal Protection Clause as applied unless it is applied with a discriminatory purpose.

   (C) admitted, because a law which has a discriminatory effect may violate the Equal Protection Clause even if its purpose is not to discriminate and it is not applied with a discriminatory purpose.

   (D) admitted, because the exclusion of black women between the ages of 18 and 23 years may be evidence that the law had a discriminatory purpose or was applied with a discriminatory purpose.

122. Which of the following statements is/are correct?

   I. Chandler's claim of age discrimination should fail if the law has a rational basis.

   II. Chandler's claim of sex discrimination should fail if the law is largely related to an important government interest.

   (A) I only.

   (B) II only.

   (C) Neither I nor II.

   (D) I and II.

123. If a motion is made to dismiss Chandler's claim on the ground that she lacks standing, the motion should be

   (A) granted, because Chandler does not hold a state driving license.

   (B) granted, if Chandler has never been called as a prospective juror.

   (C) denied, if being deprived of the opportunity to serve on a jury is found to be concrete harm.

   (D) denied, because the exclusion of black women between the ages of 18 and 23 could deprive Chandler of due process if she is ever a litigant in the Durban County Court.

124. In an attempt to improve the position of United States companies in the world pleasure-cruise market, Congress voted to sell five former battleships to the Red, White, and Blue Cruise Line for $1 each. If a competitor of the Red, White, and Blue Cruise Line challenges the constitutionality of the congressional action in an appropriate proceeding, the sale will probably be found

   (A) invalid as a denial of equal protection under the Fourteenth Amendment.

   (B) invalid as a bill of attainder.

   (C) valid under the property clause of Article IV.

   (D) valid under the general police powers of Congress.

125. Under authority granted by Congress, the United States Department of Defense awarded a contract to National Munitions Corporation for the production of airborne bomb sights. The contract

called for all work to be performed at a National Munitions Corporation factory located on the banks of Winding River in the State of Tyrol. A clause of the contract prohibited National Munitions Corporation from discharging more than 3 units per day of a pollutant known as Frammisate into Winding River as a result of bomb sight production.

While producing bomb sights pursuant to its contract with the Department of Defense, National Munitions routinely discharged between 2 and 3 units of Frammisate per day into Winding River. Subsequently, the State of Tyrol prosecuted National Munitions Corp. for violating a state statute which prohibits any person or business entity from discharging more than 2 units of Frammisate per day into any river or stream located in the State of Tyrol. In defense, National Munitions Corp. asserted that as a federal contractor it was immune to regulation by the state.

Which one of the following additional facts or inferences, if it were the only one true, would most effectively support the State of Tyrol's argument?

(A) Winding River is located entirely within the State of Tyrol.

(B) Prohibiting the discharge of more than 2 units of Frammisate per day into Winding River would not increase the cost of producing the bomb sights called for by the contract.

(C) Congress has not expressly exempted National Munitions Corporation from compliance with state water pollution statutes.

(D) Winding River is not a navigable river.

126. At the Blue Motel which he operated, Blue equipped all rooms with VCRs and television sets, and rented video-taped movies to guests for viewing in their rooms. After obtaining a video-tape of a film called "Barnyard, The Movie," Blue caused an advertisement to be published which contained the following language: "View outrageous kinky sex with animals in the privacy of your motel room at the Blue Motel. Ask for BARNYARD, THE MOVIE."

Later, an undercover police officer registered at the Blue Motel and rented from Blue a copy of "Barnyard, The Movie." After viewing a portion of the film in his room, the officer arrested Blue for violation of the state's obscenity statute. At Blue's trial, the prosecution attempted to offer Blue's advertisement in evidence. If Blue's attorney objects to the admission of the ad, the objection should be

(A) sustained, because Blue rented the film for private viewing.

(B) sustained, because the film speaks for itself.

(C) overruled, because Blue made the statements contained in the advertisement and should be required to explain them.

(D) overruled, because the language of the advertisement may help establish that the film lacked serious value.

127. Congress passes the Securities and Exchange Court Act establishing the federal Securities and Exchange Court. Under the Act, the new court is to hear civil actions for damages resulting from federal securities and exchange law violations. The Act also provides that there is no right of appeal from decisions of the Securities and Exchange Court, and that the Court's will cease to exist at the end of six years unless Congress specifically authorizes it to continue for an additional period. If a defendant against whom a judgment is rendered by the new court challenges the constitutionality of the Securities and Exchange Court Act, which of the following arguments would be most likely to result in a finding that the Act is unconstitutional?

(A) The Securities and Exchange Court Act does not require that judges be appointed to serve for life.

(B) The provision that there is no right of appeal violates the due process clause of the Fifth Amendment.

(C) The U.S. Constitution does not provide for

the establishment of a federal court to hear prosecutions for federal securities and exchange violations.

(D) The United States Constitution gives the Supreme Court the power of judicial review over all inferior federal courts.

Questions 128-129 are based on the following fact situation.

After negotiation, the president of the United States and that of the Republic of Ruritania reached an executive agreement. Under the terms of the agreement, profits earned by Ruritanian corporations in the United States would not be subject to taxation in the United States, and profits earned by American corporations in Ruritania would not be subject to taxation in Ruritania. Ruricorp is a Ruritanian corporations operating in the state of Athabaska. An Athabaska statute imposes a tax on all income earned within the state and designates the State Revenue Service as the agency which collects it.

128. Assume for the purpose of this question only that the Athabaska State Revenue Service demands that Ruricorp pay income tax as required by state law. If Ruricorp challenges the state law, Ruricorp's most effective argument would be that, as applied to Ruricorp, the law is unconstitutional

(A) because no state may tax imports or exports without the consent of Congress.

(B) under the supremacy clause.

(C) under the necessary and proper clause.

(D) because the power to tax is the power to destroy.

129. Assume for the purpose of this question only that the state of Athabaska commences an appropriate proceeding to challenge the constitutionality of the executive agreement between the United States and Ruritania. Which of the following additional facts or inferences if it was the only one true would be most likely to result in a finding that the executive agreement was unconstitutional?

(A) The executive agreement was self-execut-

ing.

(B) If the state of Athabaska does not collect taxes from Ruritanian corporations doing business in the state, the tax burden imposed on other state residents will be increased.

(C) No federal statute authorizes the president to make executive agreements with Ruritania.

(D) Prior to the agreement, Congress enacted a statute prohibiting the president from agreeing not to tax foreign corporations without the advice and consent of the senate.

130. Following an investigation by a congressional committee, an impeachment proceeding was brought against federal judge Jackson before the United States Senate. Jackson was not permitted to be represented by counsel at the proceeding, although she asked for representation and offered to pay for the services of her own attorney. The Senate found that Jackson engaged in improper acts and entered a judgment of impeachment, removing Jackson from judicial office. Jackson subsequently asked a federal court to set aside the judgment on the grounds that the denial of her request for representation by counsel at the impeachment proceeding was a violation of her constitutional rights. If the federal court refuses to grant the relief requested by Jackson it will probably be

(A) because the Right to Counsel applies only to criminal prosecutions.

(B) under the doctrine of separation of powers.

(C) under the abstention doctrine.

(D) because a judgment of impeachment cannot extend further than to removal and disqualification from office.

131. An ordinance of the City of Elwood requires any person desiring to use public streets for a parade to first obtain a parade permit from the Police Commissioner. The ordinance sets forth procedures and requirements for obtaining such a permit. March challenged these procedures and

requirements in a federal court, and they were found to be constitutional on their face. March subsequently applied to the Police Commissioner for a permit to conduct a street parade. Although March complied with all the requirements contained in the ordinance, the Police Commissioner denied the application, saying "You look like a rebel to me." Two months later, March conducted the parade and was arrested for parading without a permit in violation of the ordinance described above. In defense, March asserted that the ordinance was unconstitutional as applied to him because the Police Commissioner had arbitrarily and capriciously denied his application for a parade permit. Which of the following would be the most effective argument in response to March's assertion?

(A) There was sufficient time for March to seek judicial review of the Police Commissioner's denial of his application.

(B) The constitutionality of the statute is *res judicata.*

(C) The statute imposes a time, place, and manner regulation which is not based on message content.

(D) The street is a traditional public forum.

132. Congress passes a law making it a crime in the District of Columbia to operate any commercial motor vehicle which is not equipped with a specified noise suppression device. If the constitutionality of the law is challenged in an appropriate proceeding, the law should be declared

(A) valid as an exercise of the congressional police power over the District of Columbia.

(B) valid as a reasonable exercise of the Congressional power to protect the environment.

(C) invalid under the Equal Protection Clause of the Fourteenth Amendment.

(D) invalid under the necessary and proper clause.

133. The state of New Bedford enacts a law imposing a one cent tax on each use of any video arcade machine located within the state. All such existing machines are equipped with coin slots which accept only quarters. Since it would be too expensive to convert the coin slots to accept additional one cent coins, the practical effect of the new law will be to require the tax to be paid by video arcade operators. All such machines are manufactured outside the state of New Bedford. Which of the following would be most likely to have standing to challenge the constitutionality of the statute?

(A) A child who regularly plays video arcade amusement machines.

(B) An association of video arcade operators.

(C) An out of state manufacturer of video arcade amusement machines.

(D) A corporation located within the state which is in the business of converting the coin slots on video arcade amusement machines.

134. Congress passes a law imposing a tax on the owners of buildings containing insulating materials made of asbestos. The law provides that funds derived from the tax shall be used to help finance research into the treatment of diseases caused by exposure to asbestos. The constitutional validity of the statute is challenged in an appropriate proceeding on the ground that one of the purposes of the tax is to discourage the use of asbestos insulation in buildings. The statute should be declared

(A) constitutional as a valid exercise of the congressional taxing power.

(B) constitutional under the general federal police power.

(C) unconstitutional because Congress does not have the power to regulate the use of building materials.

(D) unconstitutional if the law was passed for any purpose other than to raise revenue.

Questions 135-136 are based on the following fact situation.

A state law prohibits the ownership of land within three miles of the coast by any person who is not a citizen of the United States.

135. Which of the following is most likely to have standing to challenge the constitutional validity of the state law?

(A) An association of persons owning land in a community located within three miles of the coast which asserts that the statute will prevent the cultural growth of the community.

(B) A citizen who seeks to sell his property to a non-citizen and asserts that the statute will prevent the sale.

(C) A state taxpayer who asserts that the statute will affect the price of real estate, thereby reducing tax revenue.

(D) A real estate broker who asserts that the statute will reduce the number of prospective purchasers of realty.

136. If the constitutionality of the statute is challenged in an appropriate proceeding on the ground that it violates the Equal Protection Clause of the Fourteenth Amendment, a court is most likely to hold that the statute is

(A) constitutional, if the state establishes that the statute has a rational basis.

(B) constitutional, unless the challenger establishes that the statute lacks a rational basis.

(C) unconstitutional, unless the state establishes that the statute is necessary to achieve a compelling state interest.

(D) unconstitutional, only if the challenger establishes that the statute is not substantially related to an important government interest.

137. The publisher of a novel entitled "Devilish Rhymes" was charged with violating a state stat-

ute which made it a crime to publish any obscene work. Prior to trial, the publisher conceded that it published the book and that the book depicted sexual conduct in a way that was patently offensive to contemporary community standards. The prosecution conceded that on the whole the book had serious literary value. The publisher should be found

(A) guilty, because the book depicted sexual conduct in a way which offended contemporary community standards.

(B) guilty, if the average person applying contemporary community standards would find that the book taken as a whole appealed to a prurient interest in sex.

(C) not guilty, but only if the average person applying contemporary standards would not find that the book taken as a whole appealed to a prurient interest in sex.

(D) not guilty, because on the whole the book had serious literary value.

138. Which of the following state laws is LEAST likely to be declared unconstitutional?

(A) A law which imposes a tax on all owners of real property within the state including the federal government.

(B) A law which imposes a registration tax on all vehicles garaged within the state including those owned by the federal government.

(C) A law which imposes a tax on all building contractors operating within the state including those who work exclusively for the federal government.

(D) A law which imposes a tax only on persons who lease grazing land from the federal government.

139. Forty years ago, Congress enacted the Pure Drinking Water Administration Act. By its terms, the Act created an executive agency to be called the Pure Drinking Water Administration (PDWA). The PDWA was empowered to authorize research into the purity of drinking water

throughout the United States and to make its findings known to the states. The act provided that the PDWA was to be headed by a director to be appointed by the president of the United States with the advice and consent of the Senate. Subsequently, with senatorial approval, the president appointed a director. Since that time there have been several PDWA directors, each appointed by the president with senatorial approval to replace a predecessor who had resigned. This year, by presidential order, the president purported to dismiss the present PDWA director.

Is the presidential order constitutional?

(A) Yes.

(B) Yes, but only if the Senate ratifies the removal of the director by the vote of a majority.

(C) No, unless the Senate ratifies the removal of the director by the vote of a two-thirds majority.

(D) No.

140. Because there were limited facilities in the state for disposing of toxic wastes, the state of New Brittany enacted a law prohibiting the disposal within the state of toxic wastes generated outside the state. A manufacturing company located outside the state had previously contracted for the disposal of toxic wastes at a disposal center located inside the state. If the manufacturing company brings an appropriate proceeding challenging the constitutionality of the state law, the argument LEAST likely to result in a finding that the law is invalid is that it violates the

(A) obligations of Contracts Clause.

(B) Commerce Clause.

(C) Equal Protection Clause of the Fourteenth Amendment.

(D) Privileges and Immunities Clause of Article IV.

141. A disastrous earthquake in Mexico resulted in the loss of thousands of lives and the destruction of millions of dollars worth of property. Following the disaster, the president of the United States issued an executive order sending U.S. military troops into Mexico to assist in the evacuation of earthquake victims and in general recovery efforts. Congress was not in session at the time. If the constitutionality of the presidential order is challenged, which of the following arguments is most likely to result in a finding that the president's action was constitutional?

(A) The order was a valid exercise of the president's emergency powers.

(B) The order was required by the humanitarian obligations of the president.

(C) The president is commander-in-chief of the armed forces.

(D) The president has power over foreign affairs.

142. Congress passes a law which grants federal funds to states for the purchase of equipment to be used in public hospitals for the treatment of diseases caused by cigarette smoking. Paragraph 7 of the law provides that "no state shall be eligible to receive such funds unless said state shall have imposed a tax of seven cents on every package of cigarettes sold in such state in addition to whatever cigarette tax is already in existence at the time that this act takes effect." From which of the following does Congress derive the power to enact paragraph 7 of the law?

(A) The congressional taxing power.

(B) The congressional spending power.

(C) The general federal police power.

(D) The congressional power to regulate interstate commerce.

143. Although voters in the state of Metrizona ordinarily cast their votes by going to a specified polling place, a recently enacted state statute makes provision for voting by mail in certain circumstances. The statute provides that in order to vote by mail, a voter must request an absentee ballot from the state's Commissioner of Elections. It further provides that if the applicant for

an absentee ballot is male, his request must be accompanied by satisfactory proof of physical inability to travel to the polling place, but if the applicant is female, no such proof is required. The statute's legislative history indicates that the reason for the differing requirements is that many female voters must care for children, and that this usually makes it more difficult for them to attend the polling place in person. A male voter has challenged the constitutionality of the statute on the ground that it discriminates against males in violation of the equal protection clause of the Fourteenth Amendment.

The court should find that the statute is

(A) constitutional, if it has a rational basis.

(B) constitutional, only if it is substantially related to an important government interest.

(C) constitutional, only if it is necessary to achieve a compelling state interest.

(D) unconstitutional, under the "one person one vote" principal.

144. The Followers of the Holy Flame is a religious organization. According to its religious philosophy, fire is symbolic of the presence of the Creator in all living things. As part of their system of worship, members of the Followers of the Holy Flame attend meetings once per month at which all sit in a circle around a blazing campfire to sing hymns and recite prayers. Usually, they attempt to conduct their meetings on top of the highest mountain in the region, in the belief that such a location is closest to heaven. For the past several years, they have conducted their monthly meetings on a mountain located in Mountain Range National Park, a preserve owned and maintained entirely by the federal government. This year, because of the danger of wildfire, Congress passed a law prohibiting campfires anywhere within Mountain Range National Park. An attorney representing the Followers of the Holy Flame has commenced an appropriate proceeding on behalf of that organization challenging the validity of the law on the ground that it violates the First Amendment to the United States Constitu-

tion by interfering with the free exercise of religion.

Which of the following would be the most effective argument in support of the constitutionality of the law?

(A) The use of fire is not a traditional religious practice.

(B) In view of the danger of wildfire, the use of fire is not a reasonable religious practice.

(C) The prohibition of fires within Mountain Range National Park does not discriminate between religions and has a primarily secular effect.

(D) The law is a valid exercise of the power granted to Congress under the property clause of the Constitution.

Questions 145-146 are based on the following fact situation.

Cheff, who was employed as fire chief by a municipality of the state of Columbia was required to retire under a state of Columbia statute which mandated the retirement of all fire department personnel at the age of 55 years. Two months after his retirement, Cheff obtained employment as director of fire safety with a private corporation at a salary higher than that which he had earned as fire chief.

145. Assume for the purpose of this question only that Cheff institutes a proceeding against the state of Columbia in a federal district court seeking damages resulting from his mandatory retirement. Which of the following would be the most effective argument in opposition to Cheff's claim?

(A) The issues are moot.

(B) Cheff lacks standing to assert the challenge.

(C) The issues are not ripe for determination.

(D) The proceeding is barred by the Eleventh Amendment.

146. Assume for the purpose of this question only that

Cheff institutes a proceeding against the state of Columbia in a federal district court seeking an order enjoining the enforcement of the state's mandatory retirement law on the ground that it violates the equal protection clause of the Fourteenth Amendment. Cheff's application for an injunction should be

(A) denied, because the proceeding is barred by the Eleventh Amendment.

(B) denied, if the law has a rational basis.

(C) granted, unless the law is substantially related to important government interests.

(D) granted, because the statute discriminates against a suspect class.

ANSWERS
CONSTITUTIONAL LAW

ANSWERS TO
CONSTITUTIONAL LAW QUESTIONS

1. **C** The "case or controversy" requirement of the United States Constitution requires a person attacking the constitutionality of a statute in a federal court to satisfy the burden of showing some actual or immediately threatened concrete personal injury which would be prevented if his challenge were sustained. Since Jude has not yet been licensed to practice law, the Continuing Professional Education Act does not affect him; declaring it unconstitutional will not protect him against immediately threatened injury. He, therefore, lacks standing to challenge it.

   A challenge to the validity of a statute on the ground that it violates the United States Constitution is a federal question. **A** is, therefore, incorrect. A claim is said to present a non-justiciable political controversy if its adjudication would unduly interfere with the exercise of powers of co-equal branches of government or with national policy. **B** is, therefore, incorrect. **D** is incorrect because the federal courts are not required to wait until the state courts have acted before determining the constitutionality of a state statute.

2. **A** The Equal Protection Clause of the United States Constitution prohibits classifications based on invidious discrimination. Not all classifications are invidious, however, (e.g., persons licensed as attorneys are not permitted to perform surgery, but persons licensed as physicians are). A system of economic classification is not invidious if it has a rational basis. If it is more important for lawyers to keep up to date on the law than it is for doctors to keep up to date on developments on medicine, then the system of classification adopted by the Continuing Professional Education Act is not invidious, and does not violate the Equal Protection Clause.

   B is incorrect because even where a state has the right to determine conditions for a license, it may not do so in a way which denies equal protection. **C** is incorrect because the states may not exercise their powers in a way which violates constitutionally protected rights. Although the United states Constitution does not specifically protect the right to practice a profession it does protect the right to equal protection. If the statute invidiously discriminates against certain professionals, it violates that right. **D** is incorrect because the state bar association does not have the power to waive the constitutional rights of its members.

3. **D** Under the Supremacy Clause an otherwise valid state statute may be superseded by federal legislation to the extent that the two are inconsistent. The contract to kill feral tuskers in the national park was authorized by federal statutes. Since the Property clause gives Congress the power to control federal property, the federal statutes are valid, and so the state law which prohibits their killing is superseded, at least as to killings within the national park.

   The power to protect the environment is held by both the federal and state governments, so states do have the power to declare a species to be endangered and to enact legislation protecting it. **A** is, therefore, incorrect. Since the Tuscalona statute prohibits the killing of feral tuskers only within the state, and since there is no indication that anyone other than Termine is interested in coming from outside the state to kill them or that killing them is commerce, the statute probably does not unduly interfere with interstate commerce. **B** is, therefore, incorrect. The Obligation of Contracts Clause prevents the state from interfering with rights acquired under existing contracts, but does not prevent the state from prohibiting activities which parties might otherwise contract to perform. **C** is, therefore, incorrect.

4.   **B**   Basic to freedom of religion is the rule that a court may not inquire into the truth or reasonableness of a particular religious belief.

     A is incorrect because in free exercise cases the state's pursuit of a compelling state interest would certainly be sufficient (though not necessary) to lead to the upholding of the statute. In *Wisconsin v. Yoder* 406 U.S. 205 (1972), the United States Supreme Court examined the sincerity of a claimant's religious beliefs in determining whether a state statute as applied violated the free exercise clause. In doing so, the court referred to the fact that the belief involved was of long-standing tradition. **C** and **D** are, therefore, incorrect.

5.   **A**   Under the Commerce Clause, Congress has the power to regulate commerce among the states. The Necessary and Proper Clause permits Congress to do whatever is reasonably necessary to the exercise of its enumerated powers. It has been held that if in the aggregate a particular industry has an impact on interstate commerce, Congress may regulate even those aspects of it which are completely intrastate.

     B is incorrect because no provision of the United States Constitution gives Congress the power to legislate for the general welfare (i.e., federal police power). **C** is incorrect because the congressional power to regulate commerce is limited to interstate commerce, or at least to trade which has an impact on interstate commerce. **D** is a correct statement, but would not furnish an argument in support of the constitutionality of the statute in question since the statute regulates "every purchase of an automobile in the United States," and this may include those which are sold domestically and intrastate.

6.   **C**   Under the Necessary and Proper Clause, Congress has the power to make laws regulating the use of federal money disbursed pursuant to the spending power. This may enable Congress to control functions which are traditionally those of the state.

     A and **B** are, therefore, incorrect. An intrastate activity may be controlled by Congress under the Commerce Clause if its impact on interstate commerce justifies regulation to protect or promote interstate commerce. **D** is incorrect, however, because the fact that some of the materials used are traded in interstate commerce is not, alone, sufficient to establish such an impact.

7.   **A**   The Eleventh Amendment bars action against a state for money damages in a federal court by a resident or non-resident of the state if a judgment in the action would have to be paid out of the state's general treasury.

     B is incorrect because the suit arises under a federal statute. **C** is incorrect because this question does not depend on whom the plaintiff's employer was, since the action by employees of Bilder is for damages resulting from Calizona's failure to require Bilder to pay the $10.00 wage. Unless the employees were aware of their rights, they could not have waived them. **D** is incorrect because there is no indication that the employees knowingly waived their rights.

8. **D**   The Privileges and Immunities Clause of Article 4 requires each state to treat non-residents in the same manner as it treats residents. An exception has been made, however, for a law which makes it more burdensome for non-residents than for residents to exploit a state's natural resources for recreational purposes. See *Baldwin v. Montana Fish and Game*, 436 U.S. 371 (1978), holding that charging non-residents a higher fee than residents for hunting licenses was consistent with the Privileges and Immunities Clause of Article IV. **I** is, therefore, incorrect. The Privileges and Immunities Clause of the Fourteenth Amendment protects only those rights which persons enjoy as citizens of the United States (e.g., the right to travel from state to state, to vote for federal officials, to sue in federal courts, etc.). Since there is no federal right to hunt, **II** is also incorrect.

9. **B**   A person in an organization which advocates illegal conduct can be punished or disqualified for state benefit only when he is an active member of it, knows that it advocates illegal conduct, and has the specific intent to bring about the accomplishment of its illegal goal. Although Arthur was an active member of NAP and knew that it advocated illegal conduct, he did not intend for it to succeed in accomplishing its illegal goal. He, therefore, cannot constitutionally be punished for his membership in it.

C and D are, therefore, incorrect. **A** is incorrect because freedom of the press applies only to the communication of ideas, and not to the conduct involved in acquiring the information to be communicated.

10. **B**   A state law which discriminates among religions violates the Establishment Clause unless it is closely fitted to furthering a compelling governmental interest. It is unlikely that the statute in question would satisfy that test, but, in any event, the argument contained in **B** is the only one listed which could possibly support the challenge. **B** is, therefore, correct.

A statute does not violate the Free Exercise Clause unless it interferes with a practice required by a religious belief. Since there is no indication that the religious beliefs of the American Buddhist League require the broadcasting of their program, **A** is incorrect. Although the statute's discrimination against pay television stations might violate the Equal Protection Clause, **C** is incorrect because only a victim of that discrimination (i.e., a pay television station) would have standing to assert that challenge. **D** is incorrect for two reasons: first, the power to regulate use of the airwaves is, to some extent, shared by the federal and state governments; and second, the Supremacy Clause makes a state law invalid only when it is inconsistent with some valid federal statute affecting the same subject matter. Since there is no indication that there is a federal statute which differs from the state law in question, **D** cannot be the correct answer.

11. **C**   Standing to challenge the constitutional validity of a state statute requires a personal stake in the outcome. The fact that the American Buddhist League's production will not be shown so long as the statute is enforced is a sufficient personal stake to confer standing.

A is incorrect because the personal stake thus created is more than an intellectual interest. **B** is incorrect because a non-recognized organization would be denied benefits under the statute and thus has the necessary personal stake. **D** is incorrect because an affront to religious sensibilities is insufficient to confer standing except in a challenge to the validity of a tax or spending law.

12. **C**   Although there is some question about the court's ability to enforce orders directed at the President, it is clear that the court may exercise control over the conduct of executive officials even when they are carrying out Presidential orders.

        B is, therefore, incorrect. Although the power to commit troops to foreign hostilities without consulting Congress is one of the emergency powers of the president, it may be limited in advance by federal statutes. If the presidential order was, in fact, a violation of the federal statute cited by the plaintiff, it may be held invalid. **A** is, therefore, incorrect. **D** is incorrect because the president may mobilize troops against foreign nations in the protection of the national interest without a declaration of war.

13. **B**   By the process of "reverse incorporation," the Due Process Clause of the Fifth Amendment has been held to require equal protection from the federal government similar to what the Fourteenth Amendment requires of state governments. Parsons may argue that since the statute applies only to employees of the Census Bureau and not to other federal employees who deal with the public, it arbitrarily discriminates against him.

        A is incorrect because the Fourteenth Amendment prohibits states from abridging the privileges or immunities of national citizenship, but does not prohibit the federal government from doing so, and because the right to wear a moustache is probably not protected by the Privileges and Immunities Clause because it is not fundamental. **C** is incorrect because the Fourteenth Amendment prohibits invidious discrimination by the states, but not by the federal government. The Fifth Amendment prohibits the taking of private property for public use without just compensation, but is inapplicable since no property has been taken from Parsons for a public purpose. **D** is therefore, incorrect.

14. **D**   The decision of the Encino Court was based solely on its determination of whether the statute in question violated the state constitution. Since the United States Supreme Court has no jurisdiction to interpret state constitutions, it has no power to review the decision of the state court interpreting its own constitution. **A, B,** and **C** are therefore, incorrect.

15. **C**   Article III of the United States Constitution gives the federal courts the power to decide questions arising under the federal Constitution. Since the action in the United States District Court is for an injunction based on the invalidity of a state statute under the United States Constitution, the United States District Court has jurisdiction.

        A state court decision which rests on an adequate state ground may not be appealed to the United States Supreme Court, but **A** is incorrect because this is a new action, and not an appeal from a state court decision. The abstention doctrine may prevent a federal court from taking a question regarding the constitutionality of a state law when the meaning of the state law is uncertain and may be cleared up by a state court decision. **B** is incorrect because there is no uncertainty about the meaning of the state statute in question, and therefore, no reason to wait for interpretation by a state court. **B** is also incorrect because no relevant state proceeding is pending. **D** is incorrect because although the Eleventh Amendment prohibits a federal court from hearing a claim for damages against a state, it does not prevent a constitutional challenge to a state law.

16.   **B**   The congressional power to regulate interstate commerce has been held to include the power to exclude whatever items Congress wants to exclude from commerce between the states. The courts do not usually examine congressional motives in determining the constitutionality of such a statute.

A is incorrect because there is no federal police power. The "Cooley Doctrine" provides that the commerce power, at least in part, is held concurrently by the state and federal governments. **C** is incorrect because the "Cooley Doctrine" has nothing to do with the prohibition against cruelty to animals. Although acts of Congress are presumptively constitutional, **D** is not an effective argument because the presumption of constitutionality is a rebuttable one.

17.   **C**   Under the Supremacy Clause, an otherwise valid state law is invalid if it is inconsistent with a federal law covering the same subject matter. Since the immigration laws and treaties of the United States might contain provisions which are inconsistent with a state law restricting the employment of aliens, they would be relevant to determining its validity under the Supremacy Clause.

If the state law is invalid under the Supremacy Clause, it is unconstitutional no matter what the unemployment rate in the state of Birch and no matter how many non-citizens reside there. **A** and **D** are, therefore, incorrect. **B** is incorrect because federal civil service laws regulate employment by the federal government, and therefore, do not cover the same subject matter as the Birch Civil Service Law.

18.   **C**   Two tests exist to determine whether a state system of classification violates the Equal Protection Clause, depending on the basis of the classification. The "rational basis" test is applied to economic and social legislation, while the "compelling state interest" test is applied to legislation based on a suspect classification or which interferes with a fundamental interest. Although alienage is ordinarily regarded as a suspect classification requiring application of the compelling state interest test, the rational basis test is applied when the discriminatory legislation involves standards for employment in executing public policy or performing functions which go to the heart of representative government. The argument in **C** is effective in either event.

So far, only voting, marriage, and procreation have been held to be fundamental interests. **A** is, therefore, incorrect. **B** is incorrect because systems of classification which serve a compelling state interest are not invidious even though based on alienage. **D** is an incorrect statement of the law; aliens are "persons" under the Equal Protection Clause. Even if it was a correct statement, however, **D** would not support Allen's position.

19.   **B**   Article III of the United States Constitution gives the Supreme Court appellate jurisdiction over all controversies arising under the laws of the United States, and authorizes Congress to determine the ways in which that jurisdiction shall be exercised. Since the

Truth in Selling Act is a federal law, the court has jurisdiction to hear appeals from decisions construing it, and Congress may authorize appeals directly from lower state courts.

The power to regulate interstate commerce may empower Congress to authorize a statute requiring disclosures in interstate transactions, but **A** is incorrect because the power to regulate interstate commerce is separate from and unrelated to the power to regulate the exercise of appellate jurisdiction by the Supreme Court. **C** is incorrect because Article III gives the Supreme Court jurisdiction over the cases involving federal laws, and empowers Congress to determine how that jurisdiction should be exercised. Although a state has the right to review the decisions of its own courts, the United States Constitution gives the Supreme Court the power to review decisions relating to federal laws. Its exercise of that power is thus constitutionally valid, and not an infringement on the sovereignty of the states. **D** is, therefore, incorrect.

20. **D**   The U.S. Supreme Court upheld such a program against Establishment Clause attack, in *Mitchell v. Helms*, 530 U.S. 793 (2000). A majority of the Court believed that the fact that the program treated religious and non-religious schools identically was enough to avoid Establishment Clause problems, as long as there was no evidence that the equipment was actually being diverted for religious purposes.

A is incorrect for the same reason that D is correct. **B** is incorrect because the power to spend for the general welfare includes the power to subsidize education. Since the use of tax money for religious schools is likely to reduce the amount of tax money available for use by non-religious schools, **C** is incorrect because the petitioners have the necessary standing.

21. **B**   Since the right to vote has been held to be a fundamental interest, state interference with the right to vote is unconstitutional unless it can be shown to serve a compelling state interest. Since the state has a compelling interest in the accuracy and facility of ballot counts, the refusal to count sticker votes will be valid if the City Elections Commissioner shows that it serves that interest. Although it is not certain that this argument will be successful, it is the only one listed which could possibly support the Commissioner's position.

The existence of certain relationships has been held to justify the assertion by one person of another's constitutional rights. **A** is incorrect since the relationship between candidate and voter probably is one of these, and because, as a voter, Candida is asserting her own rights. A federal statute prohibits the use of literacy tests in determining eligibility to vote. Even without it, however, **C** is incorrect because it would not eliminate illiterate voters until after they had cast what they believed to be a vote. **D** is a non-sequitur, since familiarity with issues and candidates does not logically require the ability to write a person's name on a ballot, and because most traditional voting methods (i.e., marking an "X" or flipping a lever) require no more literacy than the sticker vote method.

22. **D**   It has been held that a state may establish durational residency requirements to assure that voters will have sufficient interest in the outcome of an election. It has also been held, however, that overly long durational requirements serve no compelling state inter-

est, and are therefore invalid. The United States Supreme Court has specifically held one year to be too long (*Dunn v. Blumstein*, 405 U.S. 330 (1972)).

A and **C** are therefore incorrect. The United States Constitution sets requirements for determining eligibility to vote in national elections, but is silent about the right of aliens to vote in local elections. **B** is incorrect, however, because the city ordinance extends the right to *all* persons who satisfy the residency requirement.

23. **B** The Eleventh Amendment provision that the judicial power of the federal government shall not be extended to suits brought against a state by residents of another state has been held to prohibit the federal courts from entertaining suits for money damages against a state by its residents, unless authorized by valid federal statute. For this reason, the federal court action against the state of Durango by its employees must be dismissed. **B** is incorrect.

The doctrine of abstention prohibits a federal court from deciding constitutional issues that are premised upon unsettled questions of state law upon which the determination of the action would depend. Since no such unsettled question exists, **A** is incorrect. Tourism is not a traditional state function, and since under the Commerce Clause the federal government has the power to regulate interstate commerce, the Supremacy Clause makes the Federal Interstate Riverboat Act supersede the Durango Civil Service Code. **C** and **D** are incorrect, however, because under the Eleventh Amendment, the federal court lacks jurisdiction to hear an action for damages against a state.

24. **A** Under the Supremacy Clause a state law is invalid to the extent that it is inconsistent with a valid Federal law affecting the same subject matter. Although in paying its employees the state may be immune from federal regulation, this is so only when the state is engaging in a traditional state function. The United States Supreme Court has held, however, that engaging in interstate commerce is not a traditional state function. For this reason, federal law fixing the wages of persons employed in interstate commerce is applicable to state employees, and — under the Supremacy Clause — supersedes inconsistent state law.

B is incorrect because there is no general federal police power (i.e., power to legislate for the general welfare). In determining whether the state is engaging in a traditional state function, and thereby possibly immune from federal regulation, it is necessary to be more specific than the argument in **C** would suggest. Although paying employees is a traditional state function, paying them to operate interstate cruise boats is not. **C** is, therefore, incorrect. **D** is incorrect because the immunity granted to states under the Eleventh Amendment is applicable only in federal courts.

25. **A** Although a party challenging the validity of a statute is not ordinarily permitted to assert the constitutional rights of third persons, X Productions may do so for two reasons: first, if the statute as applied violated Sumer's constitutional rights, Sumer could not be guilty of violating it, and X Productions could not be called an accessory to the commission of a crime; and, second, vendors have been held to have standing to assert the constitutional rights of their customers.

B is incorrect because a person challenging the validity of any statute on any constitutional ground must have standing to do so. **C** is incorrect because although Sumer can waive his own constitutional rights, he cannot waive those of X Productions. If the statute's application to Sumer was unconstitutional, convicting X Productions of being an accessory to it would violate X Productions' constitutional rights. **D** is incorrect because it is overbroad. Several exceptions to this general rule exist, including one which permits a vendor to assert the constitutional right of its customers.

26. **C**   The United States Supreme Court has held (*Stanley v. Georgia*, 394 U.S. 557 (1969)) that there is a constitutional right to privacy which protects the private possession of obscene materials for non-commercial use.

A is incorrect because the First Amendment freedoms of expression protect the rights to speak or print, offering only indirect protection to the rights to see, read, or hear. **B** is incorrect for two reasons: First, one is not ordinarily permitted to assert the constitutional rights of third persons. Although vendors may assert the rights of their customers, no rule has developed which permits vendees to assert the right of their suppliers. Second, freedom of speech and the press does not protect the publication of obscenity. **D**, too, is incorrect for two reasons: first, there is no indication that the statute in question was not designed to punish purchasers of obscenity; and, second, if Sumer presented an obscene performance as charged, he *is* a publisher of obscenity.

27. **D**   Although the doctrine of state immunity prevents Congress from exercising its commerce or taxing power in a way which substantially interferes with traditional state functions, there is no reason why a state should not have to carry its share of the burdens of government by paying taxes for benefits which it receives. Since the federal tax in question is applied to all who derive benefit from federal aviation services, and since it does not interfere with a traditional function of the state, it is valid.

The power to tax may be the power to destroy, and for this reason states may not freely tax the federal government. **A** is incorrect, however because the federal government is not under the same restraint in taxing the states. **B** is incorrect because the doctrine of state immunity does not protect the state against paying its fair share for the federal services which it receives. **C** is a fabrication; there is no "doctrine of state subordination."

28. **A**   The United States Supreme Court has not yet held that the right of privacy protects married persons against all state interference in their sex lives, but it has indicated that, at least to some extent, the right of marital privacy is protected by the substantive Due Process requirement of the Fifth Amendment as extended to the states by the Fourteenth Amendment. Of all the arguments listed, **A** is the only one which could possibly support the Daltons' position.

B is incorrect because procedural Due Process refers to the receipt of notice and the opportunity to be heard before being deprived of life, liberty, or property. Although the statute appears to discriminate between married and unmarried persons, **C** is incorrect because the Daltons are not the victims of this discrimination and will not therefore benefit from a ruling which eliminates the discriminatory effect of the statute. Some public displays of sexual conduct have been held to be expression protected under the First Amendment. **D** is incorrect, however, because there is no indication that the Daltons' activity was intended to be a form of expression.

29. **D** Under the Necessary and Proper Clause, Congress has the right to make whatever laws are necessary and proper in implementing its other powers. This right has been held to include the power to grant immunity from state taxation.

Although the federal government is, itself, immune from state taxation, the immunity is not derivative. For this reason, federal employees and contractors are not automatically immune from state taxation, even though such taxation may indirectly burden the federal government. **A** and **B,** therefore, are incorrect. **C** is an incorrect statement of law, since it has been held that a non-discriminatory state income tax may be imposed on state residents who derive their income from out-of-state activities.

30. **A** The Equal Protection Clause of the Fourteenth Amendment to the United States Constitution provides that no state shall deny to any person within its jurisdiction the equal protection of the laws. Since the Building Rental Tax is imposed on those who occupy rented space, but not on those who occupy space which they own, it is possible to argue that the law denies equal protection. This argument might fail, but it is the only one listed which has any chance at all of success.

Although the federal government is immune from taxation by the states, that immunity is not enjoyed by persons doing business with the federal government, even though their business is specifically authorized by federal statute. **B, C** and **D** are, therefore, incorrect.

31. **A** A controversy is not "ripe" for decision unless the issues are fully developed, clearly defined, and not merely speculative, conjectural, or premature. Usually, this requires a showing that objective harm will occur if the issues are not decided. Mere general allegations of a possible subjective "chill" are not sufficient to satisfy this requirement.

A case is "moot" when no unresolved contested questions essential to the effective disposition of the particular controversy remain for court decision. **B** is incorrect because all the issues raised by the action are unresolved. **C** is incorrect because the Eleventh Amendment does not prevent lawsuits to enjoin state officials from enforcing laws claimed to be invalid. A question is political if its resolution would unduly interfere with the operation of a co-equal branch of the federal government or with national policy. **D** is therefore incorrect.

32. **C** Since the United States Constitution is the supreme law of the land, every court must determine whether the laws which it enforces violate the Constitution either by their terms or by the way in which they are applied. This necessarily involves interpretation of the Constitution.

A is, therefore, incorrect. **B** is incorrect for two reasons: first, the Fraser City Municipal Court determines who has standing to appear or make particular arguments before it; and, second, even if the Municipal Court's rules regarding standing were identical to the federal rules, Butch would have standing because the *possibility* of his conviction is sufficient to give him a personal stake in the outcome of the constitutional argument. **D** is incorrect because every court has the power to interpret the Constitution.

33.   **B**   Federal statutes limit the Supreme Court's review of state court decisions to those of the highest state court to which appeal is possible. If no appeal is possible in North Vellum state courts, then there is no reason why the United States Supreme Court cannot review decisions of the Municipal Court.

         A is incorrect, however, because if appeal to a higher state court were possible, the case would not be ripe for consideration by the Supreme Court until the highest state court decided it. **C** is incorrect because under Article III of the Constitution, the appellate jurisdiction of the Supreme Court is regulated by Congress and not by the states. At present, applicable federal statutes limit Supreme Court review to decisions of federal courts and of the highest state courts. **D** is incorrect, however, because this limitation does not appear in the Constitution.

34.   **D**   Under its police power, a state may enact laws to protect the welfare of its residents even though those laws impose a burden of some kind on interstate commerce, so long as there is no reasonable, less burdensome way of accomplishing that purpose. If, however, the burden which it imposes on interstate commerce is an unreasonable one, the statute will be invalid under the Commerce Clause. Although it is not certain that the argument in **D** would succeed, it is the only one listed which could possibly support granting of the injunction.

         A is incorrect because the fact that a statute interferes in some way with intestate commerce is not, alone, sufficient to make it invalid. Since the state's police power permits it to enact laws for the welfare of its residents, the purity of food is clearly a matter of local concern. **B** is, therefore, incorrect. Powers reserved to the states may be delegated by them to their municipalities and agencies. **C** is incorrect because the state's power to regulate commerce is concurrent with the federal commerce power, and may thus be exercised by municipal governments within the state.

35.   **A**   The concept of due process requires that a person be given a hearing before being deprived by government action of life, liberty, or property. Since termination of government employment is a deprivation of property, Orville is entitled to a hearing before his job, pay, gun, and badge are taken from him. If, however, delaying government action until a hearing would cause threat of serious harm, such emergency situation may justify acting first and holding the hearing later. Since a police officer is armed and has much opportunity to do harm, it may successfully be argued that a suspension pending the hearing was necessary to avoid the obvious threat that would result from allowing an incompetent or unbalanced person to serve as a police officer. If a no-fault finding at the hearing will result in full restoration of job and pay, there has been no deprivation of property interest without Due Process.

         Although the facts assumed in **B** and **C** might justify firing Orville, he is still entitled to due process (i.e., a hearing). **B** and **C** are, therefore, incorrect. **D** is incorrect for the same reason, since putting a procedure in the Procedure Manual does not exempt it from the due process requirement of the United States Constitution.

36.   **D**   The Equal Protection Clause of the Fourteenth Amendment provides that "no state shall … deny to any person within its jurisdiction the equal protection of the laws." Actions of a county or other political subdivision of a state are regarded as state actions. While

there may be valid reasons why certain women should not be employed as deputy sheriffs, the fact that plaintiff's application was rejected solely because of her sex would probably make that rejection invidious, and a violation of her Fourteenth Amendment rights.

In **A**, the disparity between the pass rates of black persons and white persons might be evidence that a law is being applied in a discriminatory manner, but does not establish it conclusively. **A** is therefore, incorrect. Although discrimination based solely on ethnic background may violate the Equal Protection Clause, **B** is incorrect because the Fourteenth Amendment prohibits state action only, and the discrimination in **B** was practiced by a privately-owned hospital. **C** is incorrect for the same reason, since the discrimination was practiced by a federal agency rather than a state one.

37. **B**   Under the Cooley Doctrine, the state's power to regulate commerce is held concurrently with the federal government's commerce power. If an activity is one largely of local concern, the state may regulate it in the absence of a federal statute indicating congressional intention to pre-empt the field. On the other hand, if the activity is one requiring national uniformity, the state may not regulate in it the absence of a federal statute specifically authorizing regulation by the states. For these reasons, the absence of a federal statute would establish that the state regulation is constitutional only if the activity regulated is one largely of local concern. Although it is not certain that the argument in B would succeed, it is the only one that could possibly support the constitutionality of the statute.

A is incorrect because the absence of a federal statute might mean that Congress regards the matter of rest breaks for truck drivers as one requiring national uniformity, but does not consider a statute requiring such breaks to be a good idea. Although the statute is enforceable only within the state of Norfolk, it clearly has an effect on interstate commerce. **C** is, therefore, incorrect. **D** is a correct statement if the activity involved is not one requiring national uniformity. If, however, it does require national uniformity, the states are not free to impose restrictions upon it unless authorized to do so by Congress.

38. **D**   A statute is void for overbreadth if it punishes expression which is constitutionally protected along with expression which can validly be punished. Although certain types of offensive expression (including, perhaps, Demos') may be prohibited by statute, a law which prohibits "offensive" conduct is so vague that it may also end up punishing constitutionally protected speech. Such a law is, therefore, overbroad.

A, B, and C are incorrect because a person whose conduct can be constitutionally punished under a statute has standing to assert the rights of persons whose conduct is unconstitutionally prohibited by the statute. Thus, although it might have been constitutional to punish Demos' conduct, the law is constitutionally invalid because of other conduct which it might reach, and if invalid, cannot be enforced even against Demos.

39. **B**   The state may impose "time, place, and manner" restrictions on expression in protection of its interest in promoting free access to government buildings and the orderly conduct of governmental activities. These restrictions may not, however, be based on message content because such restrictions unconstitutionally interfere with freedom of speech. Since Section II permits demonstrations involving one kind of message and prohibits

demonstrations involving a different kind of message, it violates the First Amendment.

Although the United States Supreme Court has held that a statute may not completely prohibit expression in traditional public forums like streets and parks, **A** is incorrect because this statute is directed only at the sidewalks in front of government office buildings, and does not prevent the use of other parts of the public forum for purposes of expression. The state's compelling interest in the orderly conduct of governmental affairs and in the protection of free access to government buildings would probably justify a law prohibiting noise or demonstrations in front of government office buildings. **C** and **D** are incorrect, however, because Section II imposes restrictions on the message content of such demonstrations.

40.   **B**   Although the Constitution requires the advice and consent of the Senate for ambassadorial appointments, the United States Supreme Court has held that the president may dismiss an ambassador at will and without cause.

A and **C** are, therefore, incorrect. Whether the removal of an ambassador constitutes a withdrawal of diplomatic relations depends on the reason for the ambassador's removal. **D** is incorrect for this reason, and because the president has the power to withdraw diplomatic relations with a foreign government.

41.   **C**   The "case or controversy" requirement of Article III of the United States Constitution prevents the United States Supreme Court from exercising jurisdiction in anything but a concrete dispute in which the Court may effectively remedy damage to a legal right by rendering a judicial decree. Since an advisory opinion does not determine the rights of any person, the opinion of the Colombia Court of Errors is not a case or controversy, and the Supreme Court has no jurisdiction to review it.

A is, therefore, incorrect. If a state court's decision that a state law is invalid rests on an adequate state ground, it is not subject to review by the Supreme Court because such review would be futile. If a state's court's decision in a matter which qualified as a case or controversy were based on its interpretation of the federal Constitution, the United States Supreme Court could review it. **B** is incorrect, however, because the advisory opinion of the Court of Errors was not a case or controversy. Where a constitutional issue is involved, the Supreme Court may review the decision of a state's highest court, even though that decision was based on an exercise of original jurisdiction. **D** is, therefore, incorrect.

42.   **C**   Federal taxpayers are usually regarded as being too remote from the expenditure of federal funds to have standing to challenge them, but state taxpayers are not. If a state law involves a direct expenditure of funds, as this one does, any state taxpayer may have standing to challenge it.

A is incorrect because standing requires a personal stake even if the challenge is based on an alleged violation of the First Amendment. **B** is incorrect for several reasons, but the simplest is that a statute which authorizes the advertising of services that already exist does not threaten the rights of unborn children. **D** is incorrect because philosophical, moral, intellectual, or political interest is insufficient to confer standing on a person challenging a law.

43. **D** Although the Young Trailblazers may have violated a federal law, it did not violate the state statute. The Fourteenth Amendment provides that *no state* shall make or enforce a law which denies the privileges and immunities of citizenship, due process, or equal protection of the laws. Since The Young Trailblazers is not a state, the Fourteenth Amendment does not confer upon Penny a right to be protected against its action. Therefore, **A, B** and **C** are incorrect.

44. **B** The Thirteenth Amendment abolishes slavery, and gives Congress the power to make laws enforcing its provisions. Discrimination based solely on race has been held to involve a "badge" of slavery which the Thirteenth Amendment authorizes Congress to abolish.

The Commerce Clause gives Congress the power to regulate interstate commerce, but imposes no obligations on anyone. The Young Trailblazers' policy could not, therefore, violate "the spirit of the Commerce Clause," so **A** is incorrect. **C** is incorrect because racial discrimination violates the United States Constitution only when practiced by government. **D** is incorrect because there is no federal police power, and thus no congressional power to legislate for the general welfare.

45. **B** The emergency powers of the president have been held to include the power to commit United States military personnel to foreign hostilities in satisfaction of existing treaty obligations.

A is incorrect because Article I of the Constitution grants the power to declare war to Congress rather than the president. **C** is incorrect because the validity of the treaty is not in issue. As commander-in-chief, the president is the ultimate maker of military policy. **D** is incorrect, however, because the decision to send troops to Curasia is a matter not of military policy, but of foreign policy.

46. **D** Constitutional guarantees of due process and freedom of expression protect only against government action. Since Hippocrates University is privately owned, it is not bound to give Sander due process or to avoid interfering with his freedom of expression. Common law and contract rights are thus the only ones which he may hope to enforce against the university.

A, B and **C** are, therefore, incorrect.

47. **D** Whether it is classified as a right or a privilege, a license to practice medicine is an *entitlement* of which a person cannot be deprived without due process. **A** is, therefore, incorrect. Since the denial of this entitlement was based on an arrest and an expulsion, neither of which involved a hearing, it has been accomplished without due process, and thus violates Sander's constitutional right.

B is incorrect because the federal courts have jurisdiction to adjudicate federal questions, and an asserted violation of rights under the United States Constitution obviously raises a federal question. The deprivation of property interest without a hearing violates the due process requirement, even though not arbitrary or capricious. **C** is, therefore, incorrect.

48. **C**   To have standing to litigate the constitutionality of a statute, a plaintiff must show that he has a personal stake in the action. Federal taxpayers do not usually have standing to challenge an expenditure of federal money because their interest in the taxes which they pay into the federal treasury is too remote to be regarded as substantial. If the federal taxpayer is suing to recover taxes paid under protest, however, he has the right to urge any appropriate objections to the validity of the tax — including a constitutional challenge to the law which imposed the tax or directed disbursement of tax money collected.

        A is incorrect because a moral or intellectual interest in the outcome of litigation is not sufficient to satisfy the requirement of a personal stake in the action. **B** is incorrect because a state does not ordinarily have standing to bring an action as a representative of its citizens, since they are said to be protected by their political representation in Congress. State taxpayers have standing to challenge a direct and substantial expenditure of their tax money. But where the activity involved has only a tenuous relationship to an expenditure of funds, it is necessary for the plaintiff to show a direct injury to her financial interest. **D** is incorrect because no such injury is shown to exist.

49. **B**   The Due Process Clause of the Fifth Amendment prohibits arbitrary discrimination by the federal government. Since the law requires the payment of a tax by diesel-powered vehicle users which is not required from non-diesel powered vehicle users, it is possible to argue that the law discriminates against the operators of diesel vehicles. The argument is very likely to fail, since the prohibition falls before an overriding national interest, but it is the only one listed which has any chance of success whatsoever.

        A is incorrect because the fact that the tax has a regulatory effect is not, alone, enough to make it invalid. The argument that a tax is so burdensome as to constitute an unconstitutional taking has been held to be a political question for which appropriate judicial standards of judgment are not available., **C** is, therefore, incorrect. The use of a tax to discourage certain activities has been upheld, if it is imposed to accomplish an objective within the scope of some other delegated power. **D** is incorrect because the tax is probably justified under the Commerce Clause.

50. **A**   If diesel exhaust is harmful to the environment, a tax discouraging the use of the diesel-powered vehicles might be beneficial to the general welfare. Since Article I, Section 8 of the United States Constitution gives Congress the power to impose taxes to provide for the general welfare, **A** is the best argument in support of the tax.

        Although Congress may tax for the general welfare, **B** is incorrect because there is no "federal police power." **C** is incorrect because the tax is not tied to spending, and there is no indication either that it is applicable only in states which have received federal highway funds or that it will result in more efficient use of such funds. A taxpayer has standing to challenge the validity of a tax which, if valid, will require payment from the one challenging it, since he has the necessary personal stake in the outcome of the litigation. **D** is, therefore, incorrect.

51. **C**   Article I, Section 8 of the United States Constitution grants Congress the exclusive right to "coin money and regulate the value thereof." Since the Nevorado statute requires certain businesses to accept casino chips in payment for merchandise and services, in effect

it makes those chips legal tender(i.e., money) thus exercising a function exclusively that of Congress.

Ordinarily, the requirement of due process applies only to governmental deprivations. **A** is incorrect for this reason, and because the Casino Chip Law provides a method for the persons affected to be paid, and even to receive a profit (of one-third) for the handling of the chips. According to the Cooley Doctrine, the commerce power is held concurrently by the state and federal governments. **B** is incorrect because under the Cooley Doctrine the fact that state law affects interstate commerce is not, alone, sufficient to make it invalid. Since the Casino Chips Law requires licensed casinos to redeem the chips at face value, the "taking" (if there is one) is not without compensation. Although Mac might argue that the compensation is not "just," the argument in **D** is not nearly as strong as the one raised by **C**, to which there is really no possible response.

52. **A** In *Miller v California*, 413 U.S. 15 (1973), the United States Supreme Court held that no work may be found obscene unless it appeals to a prurient interest in sex (taken as a whole and applying contemporary community standards), *and* it depicts sexual conduct in a way which is patently offensive according to contemporary community standards, *and* it lacks serious literary, artistic, political, or scientific value. Since the jury found the magazine to have serious literary value, it does not meet all three parts of the definition, and cannot, therefore, be ruled obscene.

In determining whether material appeals to a prurient interest in sex, the standard of the local community (the judicial district or state) is applied. **B** is, therefore, incorrect. There is some question about whether a local or national standard should be applied in determining whether the material depicts sexual conduct in a way which is offensive according to contemporary community standards. **C** is incorrect, however, because no work can be obscene unless it meets all three criteria of the Supreme Courts's definition. **D** is incorrect for the same reason.

53. **C** Standing to challenge the constitutionality of a law or an executive order requires a "personal stake" in the outcome. This requires that the plaintiff be threatened with immediate damage to her rights which can be avoided if the court grants the requested relief. A Romanian citizen living in the United States was immune from taxation until the presidential order was issued, and under that order will be required to pay taxes. Sufficient personal stake thus exists.

A is incorrect because an intellectual or political interest is not sufficient to give a plaintiff the personal stake required. **B** is incorrect because an American citizen was not immune from taxation before the order, and therefore has no personal stake in having it declared unconstitutional. **D** is incorrect because foreign governments have no rights under the United States Constitution, and therefore have no right to seek its enforcement.

54. **D** The president may have the power to abrogate treaties when certain circumstances make such abrogation necessary for protection of the national interest. He does not have the power to suspend enforcement of laws enacted by Congress, however, except in extraordinary circumstances (e.g., wartime emergencies, etc.). Once Congress enacted the Romanian National Tax Immunity Act, the immunity of Romanian nationals was

protected by law, rather than by treaty.

A, B, and **C** are, therefore, incorrect.

55.   **D**   A federal tax on state activities is valid as long as it is non-discriminatory and does not seriously interfere with the functioning of state government as a sovereign entity. If the activity on which a federal tax is imposed is not one unique to the state government, the tax probably does not interfere with the functioning of state government as a sovereign entity. Since the Brill Building is rented to private tenants much as any other commercial office building, the state's activity in operating it is not one which is unique to state government.

A is incorrect because Congress's power to tax is subject to all constitutional limitations. Although protection of the environment is a legitimate reason for imposing a tax, a state will be immune from such a tax if it interferes with the functioning of the state as a sovereign entity. **B** is, therefore, incorrect. **C** is incorrect for the same reason.

56.   **D**   Although the state may interfere with commercial speech to serve a substantial governmental interest, it must not do so in a way which is unnecessarily restrictive. Thus, even though the state may have a substantial interest in protecting the public against tooth decay, the law prohibiting the advertising of chewing gum would be constitutionally invalid if there are less restrictive ways of accomplishing the same objective (e.g., by requiring a warning). Although it is not certain that the argument in **D** would result in a finding that the law is invalid, it is the only one listed which could possibly support such a finding.

A is an incorrect statement of law, since freedom of expression is not absolute and may be interfered with to serve a substantial government interest. The mere fact that a state law will have an effect on interstate commerce is not enough to make that law invalid, unless it imposes an unreasonable burden on interstate commerce. **B** is, therefore, incorrect. Although the United States Supreme Court is wary of laws which impose prior restraint on publication it is far less concerned when those laws affect commercial speech only. **D** is incorrect because the speech involved is commercial, and the fact that the law imposes a prior restraint is, therefore, not alone sufficient to render it constitutionally invalid.

57.   **C**   Congress has the power to make laws regulating conduct on federal property and in the District of Columbia, virtually without limitation.

A is incorrect because the police powers of the states include the power to regulate education. Although states must do so in a way which does not deny equal protection to persons within their jurisdiction, there is no constitutional requirement that each state do so in an identical way. Some highly imaginative argument might lead a court to conclude that if **B** were true the statute would be valid under the war and national defense powers of Congress, or that if **D** were true the statute would be valid under the Commerce Clause. No such stretch of the imagination is necessary in **C**, however, so **B** and **D** are incorrect.

58.   **D**   A question is moot when the issues which it raises have ceased to exist. Although Dick-

son has been released from physical custody, violations of the conditions of his parole would result in his re-incarceration for the remainder of his sentence. Since the warden ordered his confinement to solitary for the rest of his sentence, a return to prison would subject him to enforcement of the warden's order. The issues raised by his petition have, therefore, not ceased to exist.

A is incorrect because although Dickson is no longer in prison, he was paroled on a conditional basis and could be returned to prison for the remainder of his sentence. **B** is incorrect because there are many reasons why parole might be appropriate even if Dickson's rights were not violated. Sometimes the nature of the judicial process makes it impossible for the court to reach a decision in a particular kind of claim before it becomes moot (e.g., challenges to a law prohibiting abortion could never reach the Supreme Court before birth of a petitioner's baby). In such cases, if the claim is one which is capable of being repeated, but likely to evade judicial review, it will not be mooted even though the petitioner is unable to show that specific damage will result from a refusal to hear it. Dickson's petition is not such a case, however, because there is no indication that the warden's order was part of a policy which would lead to repetition of claims like Dickson's; and, even if it were, there is no indication that subsequent claims by other prisoners are likely to become moot before being reached by the court. **C** is, therefore, incorrect.

59. **A**   Under the Supremacy Clause, state legislation is invalid if it is inconsistent with federal law. In a challenge to the constitutionality of a statute excluding non-citizens from public office, the treaties and immigration laws of the United States might be relevant to determine whether federal legislation has already addressed the subject, and, if it has, to determine whether the state law is inconsistent with it.

B is incorrect since the treaties and immigration laws of the United States are not relevant to determine what the privileges and immunities of citizenship are. **C** is incorrect because substantive due process has not been held to include the right to hold public office, and procedural due process does not prevent the enactment of a law. The doctrine of separation of powers refers to the relationship between the three branches of the federal government, not to the relationship of state governments to the federal government, so **D** is also incorrect.

60. **D**   Since the United States Supreme Court does not have jurisdiction to determine whether a statute violates the provisions of a state constitution, it could not overturn the Eternica court's finding that the statute in question violates the Eternica state constitution. Statements **I** and **II** are therefore incorrect.

61. **C**   An oath to uphold the Constitution and to oppose the unlawful overthrow of government is nothing more than a promise to do something which public employees are legally obligated to do.

A, B, and **D** are incorrect because some loyalty oaths (such as those which require a disclaimer of membership in organizations referred to as subversive) have been held to deny the freedom of assembly to public officials who are required by statute to take them.

62.   C   A state law which burdens interstate commerce is valid if the state interest which the law is designed to protect outweighs the burdens which the law imposes on interstate commerce. Although not enough facts are given to allow a determination of whether this is so in the instant case, **C** is the only argument which offers any support at all to the state's argument.

A and B are incorrect because the law is likely to discourage commerce from out of state, even though it applies equally to intra-state shipments and vehicles garaged within the state. If all or most other states have similar requirements, that fact might be relevant in determining that the burden on interstate commerce is not an unreasonable one. But the fact that some other states have such a requirement is not, alone, enough to establish that it is reasonable. **D** is therefore incorrect.

63.   A   Under the Supremacy Clause, a state law which is otherwise valid may be declared invalid if it is inconsistent with a federal law concerning the same subject matter. If there is a federal law like the one described in **A,** the Ocean Fishing License Act may be inconsistent with it. If so, the act will be invalid.

In the absence of any conflicting federal law, the state law might be a valid exercise of police powers or revenue-raising powers. **B** is therefore incorrect. **C** is incorrect because there is no indication that enforcement of Section 1 results in discrimination. **D** is incorrect because the Fifth Amendment imposes restrictions on the federal government, but is irrelevant to state action.

64.   C   The Necessary and Proper Clause permits Congress to do what is necessary and proper in carrying out the powers delegated to it by the Constitution. It is therefore irrelevant to the constitutionality of this state statute.

A might lead to the conclusion that the section is invalid, since it obviously discriminates against interstate commerce. **B** might lead to the same conclusion since the higher license fee imposed on non-residents could constitute invidious discrimination. If Section 1, which requires a license, is constitutionally invalid, Section 2, which sets the fees for such licenses, could not be validly enforced. For this reason, **D** might likewise justify the conclusion that Section 2 is invalid.

65.   D   Because the activities of Agricultural Conservation Districts will only affect owners of agricultural land, and because such owners constitute a narrow class of persons, elections do not have to be conducted according to the "one person, one vote" principle.

A and B are under-inclusive, since the "one person, one vote" principle applies to all elections which affect the general public. **C** is incorrect because states may not exercise their own powers in a manner inconsistent with the requirements of the U.S. Constitution.

66.   A   The Equal Protection Clause prohibits invidious discrimination. Although a literacy requirement in a voting statute is not necessarily invidious, **A** is the only reason listed which could result in a judgment that the statute is unconstitutional.

Literacy tests have sometimes been found to be a tool of racial discrimination, but such a finding generally leads to the conclusion that there has been a denial of equal protection rather than a violation of the somewhat narrower prohibitions of the Fifteenth Amendment. **B** is therefore incorrect. **C** is incorrect because the literacy requirement does not prohibit or otherwise regulate the written use of foreign languages. **D** is incorrect because the Twenty-sixth Amendment only prohibits discrimination in the franchise based on age.

67.   **A**   In a challenge of state interference with a "fundamental right," or to a state law which allegedly discriminates against a "suspect classification," the state has the burden of establishing that the law is necessary to serve a compelling state interest. The United States Supreme Court has characterized marriage and procreation as fundamental rights.

   B is incorrect because although gender-based classification is subject to heightened security, the Supreme Court has not held gender to be a suspect classification. **C** is incorrect because interference with fundamental rights is presumed to be unconstitutional. **D** is incorrect for the same reason, and because state exercises of powers reserved under the Tenth Amendment must be consistent with other requirements of the federal constitution.

68.   **A**   The Equal Protection Clause prohibits *states* from engaging in invidious discrimination. In **A**, the discriminatory action was by a federal rather than by a state officer.

   Convictions in **B** and **C** are likely, since the clause has been held to apply to municipal as well as state action. A conviction in **D** is possible if it is found (and it has been in similar cases) that, because of its location in a state office building, and because of the fact that it is rented from the state, the restaurant is so closely linked to the state that the Equal Protection Clause should apply to its management.

69.   **B**   Statutory language which does not allow the person of ordinary intelligence to know what conduct is prohibited by the statute is vague and, therefore, unconstitutional. Language such as that given has frequently been held to be vague. Although it is not certain that a court would come to that conclusion, **B** is the only argument which could possibly support Brown's position.

   Although it may be expressive, conduct like Brown's can be prohibited as part of "time, place and manner" regulations not aimed at the content of the symbolic speech. **A** is, therefore, incorrect. **C** is incorrect for two reasons: first, it may not be an accurate appraisal of the reasonable person's response to Brown's conduct; and, second, the constitutionality of a statute depends on how the person of ordinary intelligence would understand it without regard to any particular conduct. If the language of a statute can be understood by the person of ordinary intelligence, it is not vague and a conviction under it does not violate due process for the sole reason that the statute has been newly enacted and not yet judicially construed. **D** is, therefore, incorrect.

70.   **D**   The Supreme Court has been permissive of public aid to religious colleges, since the restraint imposed by the academic disciplines of their instructors and the age of their students make it unlikely that they are primarily devoted to religious indoctrination.

   Almost all direct aid to primary and secondary schools operated by religious organizations has been held to violate the Establishment Clause. **A** and **B** are incorrect for this reason, and because investigation and classification of the teachers and curricula of schools seeking such aid would necessarily result in excessive entanglement of the state with religious schools. Although the Supreme Court has approved the loan of textbooks purchased with public funds to students at religious schools, **C** is incorrect since it would involve the payment of public money directly to the school, and this, too, would probably result in excessive entanglement.

71. **B**   Because problems of water pollution tend to vary from place to place, it is generally understood that, in the absence of congressional mandates to the contrary, states are free to exercise inconsistent pollution controls in the interest of local health and safety.

A is incorrect because problems of pollution may differ, even though the water is used for the same purpose in various states. **C** is incorrect because if Congress has enacted laws regulating water pollution in interstate rivers, inconsistent state regulations are likely to be invalid under the Supremacy Clause. **D** is incorrect because the intrastate nature of Shipco's business is not relevant to the effect that the statute may have on interstate commerce.

72. **D**   A state interference with the free exercise of a religious belief is constitutionally valid if it is necessary in light of a compelling state interest. Since a court might find that a prohibition of the kind of activity described by the statute serves a compelling interest of the state, **D** is correct.

A and **B** are therefore incorrect. **C** is incorrect because in considering a challenge to the constitutionality of a state interference with religion, the court may not consider the validity of the religious beliefs in question.

73. **D**   Article I, Section 8, paragraph 17 of the U.S. Constitution, known as the "property clause," grants Congress the power to legislate over federally owned lands.

A is an incorrect statement, since the power to regulate for the protection of the environment is held concurrently by the federal and state governments. **B** is incorrect because the federal government's power to control federal lands can be exercised substantially without limitations other than constitutional ones. The compelling state interest test is ordinarily applied only in cases involving interference with human rights. **C** is therefore incorrect.

74. **A**   The proper means of attacking an injunction is by judicial proceeding. Because of the short time period involved, however, it would have been impossible to obtain judicial review before the election. If the WPSP desires to hold rallies in the future, there is a likelihood that similarly issued injunctions will likewise evade review. Where a problem is capable of repetition, but likely to evade review — even though, as here, the injunction being challenged is no longer in effect — Supreme Court review is available.

B is incorrect because some state interference with the right to assemble is permitted, as in the case of valid time, place, and manner regulations. **C** is incorrect because the possibility that similar future claims will evade review prevents the question from being regarded as moot. **D** is incorrect because the Fourteenth Amendment is not relevant to anything but *state* action, and the WPSP is a private organization.

75. **A** If the Rebate Act was an offer for a unilateral contract, and if Homer's commencement of performance can be regarded as an acceptance of that offer (or as a condition which prevents its withdrawal) then the repeal of the act may be found to impair the obligations of a contract. Although it is unlikely that the act will be found to constitute an offer, this is the only one of the arguments which could possibly benefit Homer.

B is incorrect because the Due Process Clause of the Fifth Amendment applies only to federal action. There are two Privileges and Immunities Clauses, but neither is applicable here. That of Article IV prohibits discrimination against out-of-staters, while that of the Fourteenth Amendment prevents states from denying persons the rights conferred by U.S. citizenship. **C** is therefore incorrect. **D** is incorrect since the Just Compensation Clause requires payment for private property which is taken for public use, and here no private property was taken.

76. **D** It has been held that the First Amendment protects the right of non-profit organizations who use litigation as an instrument of political expression to solicit prospective clients.

A is incorrect, since the Supreme Court has held that non-deceptive advertising of legal services is protected by the First Amendment. **B** is incorrect because the fact that the advertisement "could have the effect" of inciting illegal conduct is not sufficient. In order for an interference with inciting expression to be valid there must be both an intention that the expression will cause illegal conduct and an imminent probability that such illegal conduct will occur. **C** is incorrect for two reasons: first, although commercial speech is entitled to First Amendment protection, the fact that speech is commercial does not alone mean that laws regulating it are invalid; and, second, the communication in this case is more likely to be regarded as political expression rather than commercial speech, since it does not relate solely to economic interests.

77. **D** Since the results of litigation become part of the law, the requirement of standing is designed to assure that the person challenging the constitutionality of a statute has an incentive to litigate all issues fully and vigorously. Ordinarily, this requires that the plaintiff show some actual or imminent concrete personal injury that would be remedied or prevented if his claim were sustained. The building contractor in **D** stands to lose the economic benefits of his contract with the state unless the section in question is invalidated.

A and **C** are incorrect because the damage apprehended is less direct and imminent than that in **D**. **B** is incorrect since it is generally understood that a mere political or intellectual interest does not satisfy the requirement of a personal injury.

78. **D** Since the Constitution grants Congress the power to spend for the general welfare, Congress is entitled to attach conditions to its grants to assure that such spending does, in fact, promote the general welfare. The use of federal funds in a way which is likely to give cancer to school children would not promote the general welfare, and so Congress is empowered to guard against it.

A is incorrect because Congress does not have the power to regulate education. **B** is incorrect because receipt of federal funds does not result in a surrender by the states of the powers reserved to them under the Constitution. **C** is incorrect because Congress' power to regulate by attaching conditions to federal spending programs is limited, at least, to conditions which are themselves constitutionally valid.

79. **B**   **I** is an inaccurate statement since there is no general federal police power. **II** is an accurate statement since the "spending power" entitles the federal government to take steps to assure that its spending benefits the public welfare.

80. **C**   The Equal Protection Clause provides that, "No state shall … deny to any person within its jurisdiction the equal protection of the laws." A statute which invidiously discriminates against members of a particular class violates its requirements. Although some questions might exist as to whether the statute's discrimination against felons is "invidious," there is no need to make a determination since, of the arguments listed, **C** is the only with which Fell stands any chance at all.

A is incorrect because the statute in question did not interfere with rights under a pre-existing contract. Since the statute applies only to persons convicted of felonies within the state, it does not discourage the interstate travel of felons, and **B** is therefore incorrect. **D** is little more than a statement of moral philosophy, and has no basis in constitutional law.

81. **D**   The U.S. Constitution gives the federal courts jurisdiction over all cases arising under the Constitution.

Since Fell's argument is that the statute violates the U.S. Constitution, and thus involves a federal question, **A** is incorrect. The Constitution does not give the federal courts jurisdiction over cases between a state and a citizen of that state, so **C** is incorrect. But because a federal question is involved, **B** is also incorrect.

82. **D**   Since the U.S. Constitution gives Congress the exclusive power of legislation over the District of Columbia, there could be no question about the validity of a federal law applicable only there.

Although legalizing gambling would probably promote certain interstate economic activity, state concerns for the public morals would probably outweigh the federal interest in protecting such commerce. This is especially true since all states now prohibit or regulate gambling. **A** is, therefore, not as effective an argument as **D**. The Supremacy Clause applies only where state legislation conflicts with federal law enacted within the scope of the powers delegated to Congress. Whether a federal gambling law would be within the scope of these powers presents a serious question. **B** is therefore not the best of the four arguments. Since there is no general federal police power, Congress lacks the power to substitute scientific opinion (or congressional opinion) for that of the state regarding the public morality. **C** is therefore incorrect.

83. **B**   In cases of economic regulation, the proper test of constitutional validity is whether there was a rational basis for the law. This means that if any situation can be imagined in which the law would be a reasonable way of accomplishing a legitimate purpose, it is valid.

A is incorrect, since the "compelling state interest" standard is ordinarily applied only in cases involving interference with a "suspect classification" or a "fundamental right." C is incorrect since the distribution of any entitlements, whether they be classified as "privileges" or "rights," must be consistent with the requirements of the Fourteenth Amendment. D is incorrect because the "clear and present danger" test has only been applied to interference with First Amendment rights.

84. **D**   It has been held that significant state involvement in a particular private activity might make the Equal Protection Clause applicable to the private activity. It is possible that the state's licensing, funding, inspection and oversight of the Minority Hospital operation would be sufficient to have this effect. While it is not certain that a court would come to that conclusion, the argument in **D** is the only one listed which could possibly support the position of Patient's Union.

     A is incorrect because the Fourteenth Amendment relates only to state action or to private action in which the state is significantly involved. **B** is incorrect because cases have held that licensing alone is not sufficient state involvement. Although the Equal Protection Clause prevents state courts from enforcing private policies of racial discrimination, it does not require state courts to eliminate privately practiced discrimination. **C** is, therefore, incorrect.

85. **C**   A statute which makes the possession or sale of obscene material by a bookseller a crime without imposing any requirement of scienter is unconstitutional because it is likely to have a chilling effect on booksellers who probably cannot familiarize themselves with all of the books which they sell.

     Statutes like that described in **A** have been declared valid on the ground that they are justified by a municipality's interest in land-use planning. Although the Supreme Court has held that no person may be punished for private possession of materials judged to be obscene unless they involve child pornography, showing films for a fee is not private possession, even when done in the home. **B** is therefore incorrect. **D** is incorrect because the Court has held that evidence of pandering may be relevant to the questions of whether material alleged to be obscene appeals primarily to prurient interest and whether it lacks serious value, two elements of the Supreme Court's definition of obscenity.

86. **D**   Since the First Amendment provides that "Congress shall make no law … abridging the freedom of … the press," a statute that prohibits certain publications probably violates it.

     A is not the strongest argument, since the president's power to make executive agreements is broad, and may cover any area of international concern. **B** is incorrect because there is no constitutional requirement that an executive agreement must be implemented in the least burdensome manner possible. The executive agreement simply calls for the government of each country to "discourage" the press from making certain statements. Since this can be accomplished without violating the First Amendment, **C** is not a correct statement.

87. **C**   Persons dealing with the federal government may be taxed by the states so long as such taxation does not discriminate against them because of their relationship with the federal government.

States are prohibited from taxing the federal government or its agencies because "the power to tax is the power to destroy," but this principle does not prevent the taxation of individuals dealing with the federal government. **A** is therefore incorrect. The state's power to tax will undoubtedly result in increasing costs of engaging in certain businesses, but this, alone, is not sufficient reason to invalidate a non-discriminatory exercise of that power. **B** is therefore incorrect. **D** is incorrect because the facts do not indicate any federal taxation of state activity.

88. **C**   Since the President has broad authority as our chief spokesman in the area of foreign affairs, delegations of authority by him in this field are constitutionally valid. On the other hand, the President's broad powers to delegate authority in this area make interference by Congress with such delegations a violation of the principle of separation of powers.

A is incorrect because the U.S. Constitution specifically gives Congress the power to exercise some control over foreign affairs (e.g., the senatorial power to "advise and consent" in the execution of treaties), thus preventing the President's power in this area from being truly "sole" or "exclusive." **B** is incorrect because the Constitution gives the Senate, not the House of Representatives, power over foreign affairs. Likewise, **D** is inaccurate since any presidential veto can be overridden by a two-thirds vote of Congress.

89. **D**   A case presents a non-justiciable political question when a decision would unduly interfere with the operation of a co-equal branch of government. Article I of the United States Constitution provides that each house of Congress "shall be the Judge of the Elections, Returns, and Qualifications of its own members." Since the order which Candida seeks would interfere with this power of the Senate, her petition might be said to present a non-justiciable political question.

Collateral estoppel prevents the relitigation of an issue identical to one which has already been judicially determined. There is some doubt about whether the doctrine would apply to determinations by non-judicial bodies (such as the Senate). In any event, **A** is incorrect because if the doctrine were applied, it would aid Candida's case rather than lead to its dismissal, since the issue of her age was determined in her favor. Since the qualifications of a United States Senator are established by the United States Constitution, any question about whether a person is qualified to be a United States Senator is a federal one. **B** is, therefore, incorrect. The fact that Candida has already had her day in court might lead to a dismissal of her claim if the Batavia court's decision had been unfavorable to her. Since it found in her favor, however, its decision should not justify a dismissal of her case. **C** is, therefore, incorrect.

90. **A**   Article I, Section 8, clause 4 gives Congress the power to "establish an uniform Rule of Naturalization." This has been held to grant Congress plenary power over aliens which includes the power to treat non-citizens differently from citizens, so long as the discrimination bears some rational relationship to national policy. Since the provision in ques-

tion could have the effect of encouraging naturalization, it is probably justified by the plenary power of Congress over aliens.

B and **D** are incorrect because resident aliens are entitled to many but not all of the protections guaranteed by the United States Constitution. Since the Equal Protection Clause applies only to action by the states and is inapplicable to federal action, **C** is incorrect.

91. **C**   The basic requirements for a "case or controversy" are a concrete dispute in an adversarial context relating to substantive rights threatened with immediate impairment which the court may effectively remedy by a judicial decree. Since the School District has not yet adopted the policy, and since the state court's opinion was advisory only, it does not threaten the immediate impairment of any substantial right.

A and **B** are incorrect for the reasons stated above. **D** is incorrect because the receipt of federal funds would not turn the advisory opinion into a "case or controversy."

92. **D**   The Due Process Clause of the Fourteenth Amendment prevents the states from depriving any person of life, liberty, or property without due process of law. Since the Clean Roads Act made violation of an administrative order a crime, it violated Fourteenth Amendment due process by permitting the order to be issued without giving Hauler an opportunity to be heard.

An ex post facto law is one which punishes as criminal an act which was not prohibited when it was performed. The Clean Roads Act was not an ex post facto law because it did not impose punishment for an act which had already been committed. Instead, it permitted the issuance of an administrative order the *future* violation of which would be a crime. **A** is, therefore, incorrect. A bill of attainder is a law which punishes a person without the benefit of a judicial trial. Since Hauler's conviction was the result of a trial, the Clean Roads Act cannot be called a bill of attainder, making **B** incorrect. **C** is incorrect because the Due Process Clause of the Fifth Amendment applies only to the federal government and has no application to the states.

93. **C**   The United States Supreme Court has held that state aid to religious schools is constitutionally valid if it has a secular purpose, a primarily secular effect, does not result in undue entanglement between state and religion, and does not produce political divisiveness along religious lines. Since the Regents' Examinations are designed to test competence in secular subjects, and are to be given in all high schools, their administration in religious schools by state employees is not likely to result in entanglement or political divisiveness. So, if the law has a purpose and effect which are primarily secular, it does not violate the Establishment Clause.

A is incorrect because the courts have generally held that a state taxpayer has standing to challenge the constitutionality of a statute which will directly result in an expenditure of state funds. **B** is incorrect because even a law which does not discriminate between religions may be found to violate the Establishment Clause if it serves to advance religion in general. If a law violates any of the four prongs of the test outlined above, the fact that it was enacted to serve a compelling state interest does not prevent it from being unconstitutional under the Establishment Clause. **D** is, therefore, incorrect.

94.   **D**   In deciding whether an interference with an activity required by religious belief violates the Free Exercise Clause, the courts apply the compelling-state-interest standard. Thus, if a statute serves a compelling state interest and is sufficiently narrow to be the least burdensome method of achieving that interest, it may be constitutionally valid even though it interferes with a particular religious practice.

A is incorrect for two reasons: first, associations are frequently held to have standing to assert the constitutional rights of their members; and second, since the statute may necessitate a change in the school's curriculum with attendant financial outlays, the school has a personal stake in the outcome. Although the *sincerity* of a professed religious belief may be examined in a free exercise challenge, **B** is incorrect because the Establishment Clause prevents a court from inquiring into the *reasonableness* of a religious belief. Even a law which is not primarily intended to interfere with a religious belief may violate the Free Exercise Clause if it has that effect. **C** is, therefore, incorrect.

95.   **B**   Speeger advocated an act of arson; the fact that the crowd — carrying flaming torches — began following him towards the clinic indicates that unlawful conduct was immediately probable. Speech which advocates illegal conduct may be constitutionally prohibited if it advocates action, and involves incitement of immediate and probably unlawful conduct. Speeger's conduct may, therefore, be constitutionally prohibited. A law which requires a permit for the conduct of a public assembly but provides vague standards for the granting of such permit violates the First Amendment, however. Since this ordinance granted the mayor unfettered discretion in granting permits, it was unconstitutional.

A is incorrect because speech which advocates unlawful action and is probable to immediately incite such unlawful action may be subject to prior restraint which is constitutionally permissible. Although Speeger probably did not have a constitutional right to engage in the conduct described, the requirement of standing is relaxed in a constitutional challenge based on vagueness or overbreadth. Thus, even though Speeger's constitutional rights were not violated by the ordinance, he has standing to challenge it on the ground that its vagueness or overbreadth might result in a violation of the constitutional rights of others. **C** is, therefore, incorrect. **D** is incorrect because it is overinclusive. Some permit requirements (like those which regulate the time, place, and manner of speech) are constitutionally valid. Others (like this one which is based on vague standards) are constitutionally invalid.

96.   **A**   The Necessary and Proper Clause authorizes Congress to do whatever is necessary and proper in carrying out its other powers, and is, therefore, irrelevant to the given facts which involve a municipal ordinance.

Although certain regulations concerning the time, place, and manner of holding public meetings are constitutionally permissible, such regulations may not be directed against or in favor of particular types of message content. **B** might, therefore, be a good argument, since the ordinance requires a fee for a permit to conduct an assembly for some purposes, but not for others. A law is vague or overbroad if the person of reasonable intelligence would not be able to understand its terms. Since Section 2 makes special provision for "political campaign" rallies without defining them, it is possible to argue that it is vague or overbroad. **C** might, therefore, be a valid argument. If Section 1 is vague or overbroad (which it probably is in view of the unfettered discretion which it grants to the mayor) it cannot be enforced. If Section 1 — which requires a permit — cannot be enforced, then, obviously, neither can Section 2 — which fixes a fee for the permit application. Thus, in spite of Section 3 which purports to make Sections 1 and 2 severable, **D** is a good argument.

97.   **A**   Although the Commerce Clause of the United States Constitution gives Congress the power to regulate interstate commerce, it is understood that the states may exercise some regulation as well. If, however, the interstate activity in question is of national concern and requires uniform federal regulation, then the states may not regulate it in the absence of a federal statute specifically authorizing them to do so. Since this question calls for the assumption that there is no such federal statute, Sartoria's attempt to regulate the interstate sale of petroleum produced within the state would be unconstitutional if that activity is of a national concern and requires uniform federal regulation.

Whether an imported product remains in its original package may be relevant to determining a state's right to *tax* it under Article I, Section 10(2) (which prohibits the states from taxing imports or exports). **B** is incorrect, however, because the "original package doctrine" has never been relevant to determining whether a state may regulate a particular activity. Under the Full Faith and Credit Clause, a state is required to enforce judgments and decrees of the courts of other states. Since the facts in this case do not involve an attempt to enforce the judgment or decree of the court of another state, the Full Faith and Credit Clause is inapplicable, and **C** is incorrect. Under the Supremacy Clause, a state law is invalid if it conflicts with a federal law dealing with the same subject matter. In such cases, the field is said to be "preempted" by the existence of a federal statute dealing with the same subject matter. Here, since there is no federal statute, there has been no "preemption," and the Supremacy Clause is inapplicable. **D** is, therefore, incorrect.

98.   **C**   The Equal Protection Clause of the Fourteenth Amendment prohibits invidious discrimination by the state. If Sartoria imposes a tax on the transportation of unrefined petroleum, but not on the transportation of any other product, it is possible to conclude that it is invidiously discriminating against transporters of unrefined petroleum. While it is not certain that a court would come to this conclusion, the argument in **C** is the only one listed which could possibly result in a finding that the section in unconstitutional.

Although the Constitution is silent as to the rights of states to tax interstate commerce, it is generally understood that a state tax is valid if it requires interstate commerce to pay its fair share of the value of state services without discriminating in favor of local commerce. Thus, the fact that the tax is imposed on interstate transporters as well as local ones is not enough to make it invalid, and **A** is, therefore, incorrect. The state's power to tax activities performed within the state does not depend on a statutory grant of authority by the federal government. Thus, unless a federal statute specifically prohibits a particular form of state taxation, it is presumed valid. **B** is, therefore, incorrect. A state tax on interstate commerce is ordinarily valid if it bears a fair relationship to services provided by the state to the taxpayer, and will not readily produce cumulative tax burdens. Since transporters of petroleum receive the benefit of using state roads, a tax based on distance and the quantity of cargo transported bears a fair relationship to that benefit.

Although neighboring states may impose similar taxes, there is no danger of duplicative taxing since the amount of the tax is related to activity actually performed within the state. **D** is, therefore, incorrect.

99.   **D**   Because the determination of any constitutional issue is likely to become an important part of our law, the requirement of standing is designed to assure that persons litigating constitutional issues have incentive to litigate them vigorously and effectively. For this reason, standing requires that a party seeking to assert a constitutional issue must have a personal stake in the outcome. Usually, this takes the form of an actual or immediately threatened concrete injury which would be prevented by a favorable determination of the claim. Since the construction company in **D** will lose profits if the state is unable to honor its contract, it has the necessary personal stake to confer standing.

Although a state taxpayer may have standing to challenge the constitutionality of an outlay of state funds, **A** is incorrect because the challenge in this case is to a federal statute, and not to the expenditure of state funds. The relationship between a federal taxpayer and the federal treasury is regarded as too indirect to confer standing on a federal taxpayer seeking to challenge an outlay of federal funds. **B** is, therefore, incorrect. An interest which is purely intellectual or political is generally not held to be sufficiently "personal" to confer standing, making **C** incorrect.

100.   **B**   Article I, Section 8 of the United States Constitution empowers Congress to spend money for the general welfare. Under the Necessary and Proper Clause, this spending power includes the power to impose conditions designed to assure that Congress will get its money's worth for sums spent. Since the size of the vehicles which use a highway could affect its longevity, the condition contained in the State Highway Subsidy Act is probably a valid exercise of the spending power.

A is incorrect because there is no general federal police power. The "property clause" (Article IV, Section 3) empowers Congress to make needful rules and regulations concerning *federal property*. Since the State Highway Subsidy Act applies to the construction of *state* highways, the "property clause" is inapplicable, and **C** incorrect. The Eleventh Amendment prevents federal courts from hearing certain claims against states. It is, therefore, inapplicable to determining the constitutionality of a federal law. **D** is, therefore, incorrect.

101.   **D**   The primary purpose of the exclusionary rule is to deter police misconduct in gathering evidence. The United States Supreme Court has recently held, however, that after a person has had a full and fair hearing in a state court on his claim that evidence against him was seized illegally, additional review by the federal court would be of minimal use in deterring police misconduct. For this reason, in a habeas corpus proceeding, the federal court is bound by the state court's finding regarding a claimed Fourth Amendment violation.

A is, therefore, incorrect. Although a habeas corpus petition based on an asserted violation of the United States Constitution can be heard in a federal court only after all state court remedies have been exhausted, the exhaustion of state remedies is not, alone, sufficient reason for the federal court to grant the petition. **B** is, therefore, incorrect. **C** is incorrect because a denial of certiorari by the United States Supreme Court indicates only that fewer than four judges wanted to hear the claim. It does not reflect any finding on the merits by the United States Supreme Court, and does not affect the power of any other court — state or federal — to hear the claim.

102.   **A**   The abstention doctrine prevents federal trial courts from deciding constitutional issues which are premised on unsettled questions of state law. Since the constitutionality of the Moravia statute would likely depend on the meaning of the term "sexual deviates," and since the facts say that the Moravia courts have never interpreted that term, the United States district court should refrain from considering the validity of the statute until the state court has had an opportunity to determine the meaning of the term.

Although the Eleventh Amendment prevents federal courts from entertaining damage claims against a state by its citizens or by those of another state, it does not prevent those courts from issuing an injunction ordering a state official not to violate federal law (including the federal constitution). **B** is, therefore, incorrect. A question is said to be moot if there is no longer an issue the judicial determination of which would affect the rights of the parties. Since the rejection of Appleton's application was based on the state law described, an order enjoining the state from enforcing it could result in the hiring of Appleton. The question is, therefore, not moot, and **C** is incorrect. A person has standing to assert a constitutional claim if a judicial determination would prevent a concrete and direct injury to him. Since a favorable decision could result in Appleton's being hired, he does have standing. **D** is, therefore, incorrect.

103.   **D**   Article III, Section 2 of the United States Constitution extends the power of the federal courts to cases arising under the Constitution or laws of the United States (i.e., to federal questions). For this reason, the United States Supreme Court lacks jurisdiction to interpret state constitutions. Since the decision of the Moravia state court was based on its interpretation of the state constitution, the review sought by the commissioner does not present any issue arising under the Constitution or laws of the United States. Because the United States Supreme Court could not grant the commissioner of police the remedy which he seeks, he is not entitled to have it review the state court's decision.

A, B, and **C** are, therefore, incorrect. (**Note:** A recent federal statute has made the distinction between appeal and certiorari virtually obsolete, but the examiners may still use questions like this one to test judicial review.)

104.   **D**   Review by the United States Supreme Court is available when a state court has held a state law valid in the face of a challenge based on the United States Constitution. Since the Moravia court ruled that the state law was valid under the Equal Protection Clause of the United States Constitution, the United States Supreme Court may review that decision.

A law which violates the United States Constitution is invalid. The fact that it does not violate the state constitution could not, therefore, provide an adequate ground for holding it valid. **A** is, therefore, incorrect. Although federal statutes limit Supreme Court review to decisions of the highest state court available, the denial by the highest state court of Appleton's petition for certiorari means that the intermediate appellate court was the highest state court available to him. **B** is, therefore, incorrect. Whether or not a particular system of classification is "suspect" determines the *burdens of proof* to be met in a constitutional challenge to it under the Equal Protection Clause of the Fourteenth Amendment to the United States Constitution, but is not relevant to the *availability* of judicial review. **C** is, therefore, incorrect.

105. **A**   A statutory system of classification is unconstitutional if it lacks a rational basis. Whether or not this statutory requirement has a rational basis is uncertain, but of the arguments listed, **A** is the only one with any possibility of success.

While the Full Faith and Credit Clause requires a state to honor the judgments of the courts of other states, it has never been held to require that states honor professional licenses issued by other states. **B** is, therefore, incorrect. Since biology may be studied anywhere, and since the statute makes the study of biology a requirement for all persons — state residents and non-residents alike — there is no indication that the statute discriminates against out-of-staters. **C** is, therefore, incorrect. The Privileges and Immunities Clause of the Fourteenth Amendment prevents states from interfering with the rights which flow from the relationship between a United States citizen and the federal government. Since the right to be a hairdresser does not arise from that relationship, **D** is incorrect.

106. **B**   Material is obscene if it appeals primarily to prurient interest, depicts sexual activity in a way which offends contemporary community standards, and, on the whole is lacking in serious artistic or scientific value. Although a "pandering" advertisement used to sell allegedly obscene material might not, itself, be obscene, the United States Supreme Court has held that its contents may be admitted as evidence relevant to a determination of whether the material so advertised appeals primarily to prurient interest and whether it is lacking in serious value.

Pornco has not been charged with publishing an obscene advertisement, so it does not matter whether the advertisement is constitutionally protected. Its admissibility depends not on whether the advertisement can be constitutionally punished, but on whether it is relevant to a material issue in the case. **A** and **C** are, therefore, incorrect. **D** is incorrect because, even though not itself obscene, the advertisement may be relevant to determining whether the film is obscene.

107. **A**   Although expert testimony is not necessary to establish that a work does or does not have serious value, it is admissible for that purpose. **I** is, therefore, correct. Unless the material is targeted to a specific group, however, the standards of the *adult* community must be applied. **II** is, therefore, incorrect.

108. **D**   Although the United States Supreme Court has held that the Constitution protects the private possession of obscene material for private use, it does not protect commercial distribution of obscene material for that purpose, or the use of the mails for such distribution.

A and **B** are, therefore, incorrect. **C** is incorrect for two reasons: first, the United States Supreme Court has declared that the private possession and use of obscenity is constitutionally protected; and, second, because Pornco was not charged with privately possessing obscenity, but with sending it through the mails.

109. **B**   Although many presidential appointments are subject to the advice and consent of the Senate, it has been held that the president may remove appointees at will so long as they do not perform judicial or quasi-judicial functions. Since ambassadors perform functions which are strictly executive, the president may remove them at will.

A, C, and **D** are, therefore, incorrect.

110. **B**   Ordinarily, statutory discrimination not based on suspect classifications is valid if it has a rational basis. Although gender has been held not to be a suspect classification, recent decisions of the United States Supreme Court hold that gender discrimination is subject to heightened scrutiny, and is valid only if substantially related to important governmental interests.

A is incorrect because classifications based on gender are constitutionally valid if they are substantially related to important governmental interests. Some gender classifications have been upheld on the ground that they were "benign" (i.e., harmless). Other "benign" gender classifications have been held invalid, however, especially where based on old ideas about sex roles and the dependency of women. **C** is, therefore, incorrect. Whether a classification is "suspect" plays a role in determining which party has the burden of proof in a challenge to its constitutional validity. **D** is incorrect, however, because a statute which discriminates without a rational basis is always unconstitutional.

111. **B**   A statute which discriminates on the basis of age is constitutional if its system of classification has a rational basis (i.e., if facts can be imagined which would make the statute a reasonable means of accomplishing a legitimate purpose). Protection of public health is a legitimate legislative purpose. Thus, if the work of physical education teachers is hazardous to the health of older persons, the statute's age classification is a reasonable means of achieving a legitimate legislative purpose.

A is incorrect because the physical condition of one sixty- year-old person is not sufficient to establish a rational basis for a statute which discriminates against all persons of that age. Even when exercising its legitimate powers, a state must do so in a way which is consistent with requirements of the United States Constitution. **C** is, therefore, incorrect. Since some physical education teachers may be unqualified for other teaching positions, the fact assumed in **D** would leave them no better off than they would be without it. **D** is, therefore, incorrect.

112. **A**   Because the determination of any constitutional issue is likely to become an important part of our law, the requirement of standing is designed to assure that persons litigating constitutional issues have incentive to litigate them vigorously and effectively. For this reason, standing requires that a party seeking to assert a constitutional issue must have a personal stake in the outcome. Usually, this takes the form of an actual or immediately threatened concrete injury which would be prevented by a favorable determination of the claim. Since Willa has not yet consented to marry Malcomb, the state law does not injure or imminently threaten to injure him.

B is incorrect because marriage is a fundamental right, and a statute which interferes with a fundamental right is valid only if it is necessary to serve a compelling state interest. Unless males under the age of 19 are not sufficiently mature for marriage and females over the age of 17 are sufficiently mature for marriage, the fact that females mature earlier than males — even if accurate — is irrelevant. **C** is, therefore, incorrect. **D** is incorrect because the exercise of a power reserved to the state — even a reserved power under the Tenth Amendment — must be consistent with the United States Constitution.

113. **C**   A claim is moot when there are no unresolved questions for the court to determine. Since the injunction which Stuard seeks has been made unnecessary by the change in University policy, there is no longer a need for judicial determination. **C** is, therefore, correct.

Federal courts lack the power to interpret state constitutions. For this reason, a federal court may not review a state court decision which is based on an interpretation of the state constitution. (i.e., based on an adequate state ground). This principle does not prevent a federal court from hearing a challenge to state action, however, if that challenge is based on the federal Constitution. Since Stuard's federal court proceeding asserts that the United States Constitution prohibits the Chancellor's act, the existence or absence of an adequate state ground for the Chancellor's act is irrelevant. **A**, is, therefore, incorrect. A court may hear a claim even though it has become moot if the nature of it is such that the question may come up again and that it is likely to evade judicial review. (For example, the constitutionality of a statute preventing the abortion of a child could not possibly be determined by the United States Supreme Court before the birth of the child.) **B** is incorrect, however, because, in view of the change in University policy, there is no reason to believe that the claim will come up again. Since the Eleventh Amendment prevents federal courts from hearing damage claims against a state, the fact that Stuard had been damaged by past denials of her application would not give the court a reason to hear the claim which is otherwise moot. **D** is, therefore, incorrect.

114. **A**   The spending power authorizes Congress to expend funds to promote the general welfare. Since the museum was intended to serve all residents of the United States, the congressional decision to establish and fund it is probably justified under the spending power.

The Commerce Clause authorizes Congress to regulate the interstate movement of people or commodities. Although the museum is to serve Americans from all states, the statute makes no attempt to regulate their movement or that of the artifacts to be displayed. **B** is, therefore, incorrect. The Eleventh Amendment prevents federal courts from hearing claims against a state. Since this claim is against the United States, and not against any individual state, **C** is incorrect. The doctrine of state immunity relieves states of the obligations imposed by certain federal laws. **D** is incorrect because the statute in question imposes no obligations on a state.

115. **B**   Article IV provides, in part, that Congress shall have the power to make all needful rules and regulations respecting property belonging to the United States. This has been construed to mean that Congress — or an agency authorized by Congress — may exercise power over federal lands substantially without limitation.

The Commerce Clause is inapplicable here, because there is no indication that the Gatos

National Preserve is involved in interstate commerce or movement. **A** is, therefore, incorrect. **C** is incorrect because, although Congress is empowered to spend for the general welfare, there is no general federal police power. The power of eminent domain permits the government to take private property for public use (subject to the Fifth Amendment requirement of "just compensation"). Since there has been no taking of private property, **D** is incorrect.

116.   **A**   The Fifth Amendment provides in part that private property shall not be taken for public use without just compensation. Frequently, a regulation made in furtherance of the police power raises an issue as to whether or not a taking has occurred. Sometimes, a balancing of the importance of the public need against the detriment suffered by an individual leads to the conclusion that the regulation did not result in a "taking." If there was a taking, however, the Fifth Amendment would require just compensation.

This is true even if the taking was required to serve a compelling interest of the government. (The government might, for example, have a compelling need to build a highway over a particular piece of realty. If it took the realty for that purpose, however, it would still be required to pay for it.) **B** is, therefore, incorrect. Although the Fifth Amendment relates primarily to action by the federal government, the Just Compensation Clause has been held to be applicable to the states under the Due Process Clause of the Fourteenth Amendment. **C** is, therefore, incorrect. The fact that a person had been bitten by a Snake Haven reptile might play a role in the balancing used to determine whether the ordinance resulted in a taking. **D** is incorrect, however, because that fact would not, alone, be determinative of the question.

117.   **C**   An issue presents a non-justiciable political question when a decision would unduly interfere with the exercise of powers vested by the Constitution in other co-equal branches of government. Although it is by no means certain that this is such an issue, **C** is the only one of the arguments listed which has any possibility of success.

It is not clear how a federal court could go about enforcing process against the President if he refused to obey a judicial order, but it is generally understood — and was so held in *U.S. v. Nixon*, 418 U.S. 683 (1974) — that the federal courts have jurisdiction over the President. **A** is, therefore, incorrect. **B** is incorrect because, although the President is commander-in-chief of the armed forces, his power as such is subject to limitations imposed by Congress. The United States Constitution gives Congress — and not the President — the power to declare war. Thus, if the presidential order sending troops to Libertad was a declaration of war, it would be constitutionally invalid. **D** is, therefore, incorrect.

118.   **A**   Procedural due process requires, among other things, a jury trial on issues of fact. For this reason, the United States Supreme Court has held that an arbitrary statutory presumption violates procedural due process by depriving the defendant of his right to a jury trial on the issue involved. The State of Ono statute creates an irrebuttable presumption that persons who spent more than three hours together in a hotel room had sexual intercourse. If that presumption is an arbitrary one, it violates the requirements of procedural due process.

Substantive due process requirements are said to be violated when a statute interferes with certain constitutionally protected individual freedoms. This statute forbids sexual intercourse with persons under the age of 16 years. Since there is clearly no constitutionally protected right to engage in sexual intercourse with such persons, **B** is incorrect. The Equal Protection Clause is violated by a state law which invidiously discriminates. Since statutes designed to protect young people against their own lack of mature judgment — particularly with respect to sexual intercourse — have been held not to be invidious, **C** is incorrect. A bill of attainder is a law which has the effect of punishing specific individuals without benefit of a trial. When the law in question does not name the specific individuals to be punished, it is a bill of attainder if it mandates a punishment based on preexisting and unalterable characteristics. Since the State of Ono statute does not impose punishment without a trial, it is not a bill of attainder. **D** is, therefore, incorrect.

119. **B**   The Fifth Amendment provides in part that no person shall be deprived of life, liberty, or property without due process of law. Due process includes the right to a fair trial. Since it is possible to argue that the systematic exclusion of aliens from the jury denied Adamson a fair trial, it is possible that the federal statute excluding aliens from juries violated his due process rights. It is, of course, far from certain that a court would come to this conclusion, but of all the arguments listed, that set forth in **B** is the only one which could possibly lead to a reversal of Adamson's conviction.

    A is incorrect because the equal protection clause of the Fourteenth Amendment only prohibits discrimination by the state and cannot, therefore, be the basis of a decision that a *federal* law is unconstitutional. The doctrine of separation of powers requires that the duties of the federal government be divided among the three branches created by the United States Constitution (i.e., executive, legislative, judicial). It is not applicable here because there is no claim that Congress interfered with any other branch of the federal government by passing the law in question. **C** is, therefore, incorrect. Under the Supremacy Clause, when a state law is inconsistent with a valid federal law, the state law is invalid. For this reason, it could not support a conclusion that a federal statute was unconstitutional. **D** is, therefore, incorrect.

120. **D**   Under the Supremacy Clause of Article VI, a state law is invalid if it is inconsistent with a valid federal law covering the same subject matter. It is easy to decide whether a state law which specifically contradicts a federal law is invalid under the Supremacy Clause. It becomes more difficult when, as here, the state law prohibits something which the federal law does not mention at all. The fact that the federal law is silent about aliens serving on state juries might mean that Congress has permitted aliens to serve on state juries by not prohibiting such service. It could also mean, however, that Congress deliberately left the matter to regulation by the states. In deciding which conclusion to draw, it is necessary to consider the dominance of federal interest. Since Congress has primary authority to determine the legal status of aliens, state legislation which affects aliens is likely to be preempted by congressional silence. While it is not certain that a court would come to this conclusion, the argument set forth in **D** is the only one listed which could support a reversal of Adamson's conviction.

    Although state laws which discriminate on the basis of alienage are unconstitutional unless they are necessary to serve a compelling state interest, they are not per se invalid. (Also, remember that there's an important exception to the general rule that a compelling state interest must be served: where the government job involves a "traditional government function," even just a rational basis is enough to restriction of the job to citizens valid.) **A** is, therefore, incorrect. The privileges and immunities clause of the Fourteenth Amendment prohibits a state from interfering with rights which result from United States citizenship. It is inapplicable to this case since aliens are not United States citizens. **B** is, therefore, incorrect. **C** is incorrect for two reasons: first, discrimination against aliens is not necessarily based on race, color, or previous condition of servitude; and, second, the Fifteenth Amendment only prohibits such discrimination in denying the right to vote.

121. **D**   The Equal Protection Clause prohibits invidious discrimination by the state. Since not all discrimination is invidious, a series of standards have been developed to determine whether a particular form of discrimination is constitutionally valid. If a discriminatory purpose (i.e., a desire to exclude black women between the ages of 18 and 23 from Durban County Court juries) was a motivating factor in enacting the law, or if the law is deliberately applied for that purpose, it is necessary to turn to the standards mentioned above. If, however, a law is neutral on its face and is not purposely applied in a discriminatory way, it does not violate the Equal Protection Clause, even though it may have a discriminatory effect. The fact that a law has a discriminatory effect is, thus, not sufficient to result in its invalidity under the Equal Protection Clause unless it is shown that the law had or was applied with a discriminatory purpose. The fact that the law effectively excluded a particular group may be circumstantial evidence that it was intended — either on its face or in its application — to have that effect.

A and B are, therefore, incorrect. C is incorrect because the fact that an otherwise neutral law had a discriminatory effect is not enough to make it invalid unless there was a discriminatory purpose.

122. **D**   Unless they interfere with fundamental rights (i.e., voting; marriage and procreation) statutory systems of classification are generally valid if they have a rational basis. Systems based on suspect classifications, however, are valid only if they are necessary to achieve a compelling state interest. The United States Supreme Court has held that age is not a suspect classification. Thus, a rational basis would be sufficient to defeat Chandler's claim of age discrimination and **I** is correct. Although the United States Supreme Court has not held gender to be a suspect classification, it has developed a third or middle level of scrutiny for statutory systems of classification based on gender. These are valid if they are substantially related to important government interests. Thus, if the statute is substantially related to important government interests, Chandler's claim of sex discrimination will fail, and **II** is correct.

123. **C**   In order to assure that constitutional challenges will be fully and vigorously prosecuted, the concept of standing requires that a person challenging the constitutionality of a statute have some personal stake in the outcome. Usually this means that the challenger must face some imminent concrete harm which would be avoided if the court grants the relief which she requests. Since Chandler's complaint is that the law effectively prevents her from serving on a jury, she lacks standing unless being deprived of an opportunity to serve on a jury constitutes concrete harm.

Since Chandler does not have a driving license, the existing law makes her ineligible for jury service. Since a declaration that the law is invalid would remove the disability imposed by the statute, Chandler's failure to have a driver's license is more likely to result in a finding that she has standing than a finding that she does not. **A** is, therefore, incorrect. Under the existing law Chandler will not be called as a prospective juror so long as she does not have a driving license. On the other hand, a declaration that the law is invalid would have the effect of making her eligible to be called as a prospective juror. Since this would eliminate the harm which the existing statute causes, the fact that she has never been called is more likely to defeat than to support the motion to dismiss her claim. **B** is, therefore, incorrect. Since there is no fact indicating that Chandler is or is about to become a litigant in the Durban County Court, the possibility that she will be denied due process if she ever does become one is not harm which is imminent or concrete. **D** is, therefore, incorrect.

124. **C**   Article IV Section 3 of the United Constitution provides in part that congress shall have the power "to dispose of ... property belonging to the United States." Since the battleships are property of the United States, Congress has the power to dispose of them under this constitutional provision.

A is incorrect because the Equal Protection Clause of the Fourteenth Amendment prohibits certain discrimination by the states, but is not applicable to the federal government. A bill of attainder is a legislative act punishing an individual or a group of individuals without a judicial trial. Since the sale of battleships did not punish anyone, it could not be a bill of attainder. **B** is, therefore, incorrect. Although Congress has the power to spend for the general welfare, it is generally understood that there is no general federal police power. **D** is, therefore, incorrect.

125. **B**   Under the Supremacy Clause of the U.S. Constitution, a state law is invalid if it conflicts with a valid federal law dealing with the same subject matter. This principle is frequently used to support the conclusion that a state attempt to regulate the federal government or a federal activity is invalid. A state is free to regulate federal contractors, however, so long as such regulations do not interfere with federal purposes or policies. If the state pollution law were likely to have the effect of increasing the cost of producing bomb sights for the Department of Defense, it could successfully be argued that it is invalid under the Supremacy Clause. If, on the other hand, the state pollution law would not significantly increase the costs of the bomb sights, it would probably not interfere with any federal policy, and would, therefore, be valid.

If Winding River is located entirely within the State of Tyrol, it might not be subject to valid congressional regulation under the Commerce Clause. **A** is incorrect, however, because Congress has other powers which might justify federal regulation concerning Winding River. Congress may exempt federal contractors from compliance with a state regulation on the ground that the regulation unduly interferes with a federal activity. Since Congress may create such an exemption impliedly, however, the fact that it has not expressly done so would not be conclusive. **C** is, therefore, incorrect. The question of whether a river is "navigable" is relevant in determining whether the federal courts have admiralty jurisdiction over it. **D** is incorrect, however, because congressional power to regulate activities on the banks of Winding River may come from other sources (e.g., the power to provide for the common defense).

126. **D**   Under the test created by the United States Supreme Court in *Miller v. California*, 413 U.S. 15 (1973), a work may be found to be obscene only if it appeals primarily to prurient interest, depicts sexual conduct in a way which offends community standards, and lacks serious value. Subsequently, the Court held that advertisements used to promote allegedly obscene material might be relevant in determining whether the material was intended to appeal primarily to prurient interest, and in determining whether it lacked serious value. The language of Blue's advertisement may thus be admissible for that purpose.

Although the United States Supreme Court has ruled that a law may not interfere with private possession and use of obscene materials, this rule does not apply to commercial use of obscenity, which obviously includes renting an obscene film for a fee. **A** is, therefore, incorrect. Although a jury may base its decisions about an allegedly obscene film upon a viewing of the film itself, other evidence (e.g., expert opinion) may also be considered. **B** is incorrect because the United States Supreme Court has specifically authorized the admission of advertisements. Since the Fifth Amendment protects against testimonial self- incrimination, Blue cannot be required to explain anything. **C** is, therefore, incorrect.

127. **B**   The Fifth Amendment to the United States Constitution provides in part that no person shall be deprived of life, liberty, or property without due process of law. Although "due process" is an elusive term, it is generally held to include the right of appeal. For this reason, the provision of the Securities and Exchange Court Act which provides that there shall be no right of appeal probably violates the Due Process Clause.

Article III of the United States Constitution provides that federal judges shall hold their offices during good behavior. This has been held to mean that so long as a judge does not act improperly, she may not be removed from office during her lifetime. This does not mean that the office itself may not be abolished, however. **A** is, therefore, incorrect. **C** is incorrect because Article III of the United States Constitution specifically empowers Congress to ordain and establish federal courts inferior to the United States Supreme Court. Although the United States Constitution vests the judicial power of the United States in the United States Supreme Court, it provides that the Court's appellate jurisdiction is subject to such exceptions as Congress shall make. **D** is, therefore, incorrect.

128. **B**   Under the Supremacy Clause of Article VI of the United States Constitution, the statutes and treaties of the United States are the supreme law of the land. This means that a state law which is inconsistent with any valid federal law or treaty is invalid. Although an executive agreement is not a treaty, it has the same effect as a federal law under the supremacy clause. Since the application of Athabaska's state income tax law is inconsistent with the executive agreement which prohibits the taxation of Ruritanian corporations within the United States, the Supremacy Clause may make the state law invalid as applied to Ruricorp.

Although the United States Constitution prohibits the states from taxing imports or exports without congressional consent, **A** is incorrect because the Athabaska income tax is not a tax on imports or exports. The necessary and proper clause gives Congress the power to do whatever is necessary and proper in carrying out its other powers. **C** is incorrect because the constitutionality of an act of Congress is not in question. It has been said that states are prevented from taxing the federal government because "the power to tax is the power to destroy." This argument is not applicable in this case because Athabaska is making no attempt to tax the federal government. **D** is, therefore, incorrect.

129.   **D**   Like treaties, executive agreements are the supreme law of the land. Unlike treaties, however, executive agreements do not stand on the same footing as acts of Congress. Thus, while a treaty supersedes prior inconsistent federal statutes, an executive agreement does not. For this reason, Congress may, by statute, limit the president's power to make executive agreements. If Congress had done so by a prior law which prohibited the president from making this kind of agreement, the agreement may be declared void.

Some executive agreements require subsequent congressional action in order to operate. Others, called "self-executing," require no subsequent act of Congress to become operative. This distinction is related to the effect of an executive agreement, but not to its validity. For this reason, **A** is incorrect. As the Equal Protection Clause of the Fourteenth Amendment prevents invidious discrimination by the states, the Due Process Clause of the Fifth Amendment bars arbitrary discrimination by the federal government. When federal regulation (to which an executive agreement is equivalent) has nationwide impact, however, the existence of overriding national interests may permit regulation that would be forbidden to the states. For this reason, the fact that the executive agreement imposes an increased tax burden on non-Ruritanian corporations is not, alone, sufficient to make it invalid. **B** is, therefore, incorrect. **C** is incorrect because the president's power to make executive agreements is inherent, and, therefore, does not require specific authorization from Congress.

130.   **B**   A federal court may refuse to hear a case because it presents a "non-justiciable political question." An issue is non-justiciable if a decision would unduly interfere with the exercise of powers vested by the constitution in a co-equal branch of government, or if it involves a matter which the text of the constitution commits to one of the other branches of government. Since this concept is designed to keep the judiciary from interfering with the activities of the executive and legislative branches of government, it derives from the doctrine of separation of powers. Since the United States Constitution provides that cases of impeachment shall be tried by the Senate, the doctrine of separation of powers could result in the court's refusal to hear Jackson's challenge.

The Sixth Amendment provides that defendants in criminal proceedings shall enjoy the right to counsel. **A** is incorrect, however, because the Due Process Clause protects the right to counsel at other proceedings as well. The abstention doctrine prevents a federal court from considering a constitutional question based on an unsettled question of state law. Since Jackson's right to counsel at an impeachment proceeding does not depend on state law, **C** is incorrect. Article II, Section 3 of the United States Constitution provides that a judgment of impeachment cannot extend beyond removal and disqualification from office. Federal employment may be a "property" interest, however, to which the Due Process Clause applies. Thus, the fact that the impeachment proceeding results in no more than loss of a job is not, alone, sufficient to prevent the Due Process Clause from requiring the right to counsel.

131.   **A**   If a law requiring a permit for the exercise of First Amendment rights is invalid *on its*

face, its constitutionality may be attacked as a defense against a charge of violating it. If, on the other hand, the law is invalid *as applied,* the unconstitutionality of its application may not be raised as a defense against a charge of violating it. Instead, the appropriate course is to apply for a permit and then seek judicial review of the denial of the application, unless there is no time for such judicial review. Since the law was already held to be valid on its face, and since the only claim made by March is that the law was unconstitutionally *applied,* this claim may not be raised by March as a defense unless two months would not have been sufficient time to obtain judicial review. The facts do not disclose whether this is so, but the argument set forth in **A** is the only one listed which could possibly be an effective response to March's claim.

Although the constitutionality of the ordinance on its face has already been decided by a federal court, and is therefore res judicata, March's claim is that the ordinance is being applied in an unconstitutional manner. Since even a valid ordinance may be applied in an invalid way, **B** is incorrect. To promote the public order or other public good, a law may impose time, place, and manner restrictions on expressive conduct so long as these restrictions are not based on the message content of the expression. Since the ordinance was found to be constitutional on its face, it probably did constitute a valid time, place, and manner restriction. Like **B,** however, **C** is incorrect because the *application* of the ordinance is being challenged. Although laws may regulate expressive conduct even in traditional public forums, **D** is not a good response to March's claim because not all such regulations are valid. [*Note:* Actually, regulations applicable to traditional public forums must face a stricter test than other such regulations.]

132.   **A**   The Constitution gives Congress the exclusive power of legislation over the District of Columbia. Thus, although there is no general federal police power, Congress does have police power over the District of Columbia. **A** is, therefore, correct.

B is incorrect because there is no general federal police power and no specific Congressional power to protect the environment. The Equal Protection clause of the Fourteenth Amendment provides that no state shall deny equal protection of the law to any person within its jurisdiction. Since it applies only to state action and not to action by the federal government, **C** is incorrect. The Necessary and Proper Clause gives Congress the power to do whatever is necessary and proper in exercising its enumerated powers under the U.S. Constitution. Although it may result in a finding that an act of Congress is valid, it cannot be used to justify a finding that an act of Congress is invalid. **D** is, therefore, incorrect.

133.   **B**   The requirement of standing exists to assure that all constitutional issues will be vigorously and thoroughly litigated. In order to have standing to challenge the constitutionality of a statute, it is necessary for the challenger to have a personal stake in the outcome of the challenge. In general, one who is likely to sustain concrete harm which could be avoided by a declaration that the statute is invalid has sufficient personal stake to challenge its validity. Since the statute will have the effect of requiring video arcade operators to pay the tax, and since they will not have to pay the tax if the statute is declared unconstitutional, a video arcade operator would have sufficient personal stake to challenge the statute's validity. Since an association has standing to assert the rights of its members, **B** is correct.

Since the arcade operators would be paying the tax, persons who use video arcade machines will not lose anything if the statute is declared constitutional. For this reason, **A** is incorrect. Since there is no indication that the new statute will have any effect at all on the manufacturers of video arcade amusement machines, the manufacturers of such machines have no personal stake in the outcome of the challenge and, thus, lack standing to assert it. **C**, is therefore, incorrect. If the statute has any effect on a corporation which is in the business of converting coin slots, it would be to increase rather than decrease its earnings. For this reason, **D** is incorrect.

134.   **A**   Under the U.S. Constitution, direct taxes must be allocated among the states in proportion to population, all customs duties and excise taxes must be uniform throughout the United States, and no tax may be imposed on exports from any state. Except for these limitations and prohibitions, the congressional power to tax is plenary. For this reason, **A** is correct.

Although the U.S. Constitution gives Congress the power to *spend* for the general welfare, **B** is incorrect because there is no general federal police power. So long as a tax is within the lawful power of Congress, a court may not inquire into the congressional motive for the imposition of that tax. For this reason, **C** and **D** are incorrect.

135.   **B**   In order to assure that constitutional issues will be thoroughly and vigorously litigated, the requirement of standing makes it necessary for a person challenging the constitutionality of a statute to have a personal stake in the outcome of the challenge. A challenger has sufficient personal stake when it has suffered or is about to suffer some concrete harm which can be remedied or prevented by the court. Since the challenger in **B** asserts that the statute will prevent the sale of his property, he faces imminent concrete harm. Since a declaration that the statute is unconstitutional will permit the sale of his property, thus preventing that harm, he has sufficient personal stake and has standing to assert the challenge.

Although an association may have standing to assert the rights of its members, it is necessary that its members would have standing to sue on their own. **A** is incorrect because the harm faced by the association members is not sufficiently concrete to give any of them standing to challenge the constitutionality of the statute. A state taxpayer lacks standing to challenge any statute except one which provides directly for an expenditure of public funds. **C** is, therefore, incorrect. **D** is incorrect because the harm which the challenger asserts is neither concrete nor imminent.

136.   **C**   Ordinarily, a state classification which regulates economic interests is valid if it has a rational basis. If the classification discriminates against a suspect class, however, it is presumed invalid unless it is shown that the classification is necessary to achieve a compelling state interest. Since alienage has been held to be a suspect class, the statute will be presumed unconstitutional unless the state can satisfy this burden. **C** is, therefore, correct.

A and **B** are incorrect for this reason. **A** is also incorrect because in the case of economic regulation the burden is on the challenger to establish the lack of a rational basis. The language of option **D** suggests the middle level of scrutiny, applied in cases involving classifications which are not suspect but which are close to being suspect (e.g., gender, legitimacy). **D** is incorrect because alienage has been held to be a suspect class.

137. **D**   The United States Supreme Court has held that no work can be declared obscene unless (1) the average person applying contemporary standards would find that taken as a whole it appeals to a prurient interest in sex, *and* (2) it depicts sexual conduct in a way which offends contemporary community standards, *and* (3) on the whole it lacks serious literary, artistic, political or scientific value. Unless all three of these requirements are satisfied, a work cannot constitutionally be declared obscene. Since it conceded that on the whole the work has literary value, the prosecution has failed to meet the third prong of the test and must fail. **D** is, therefore, correct.

   A and **B** are incorrect because all three prongs of the test must be satisfied in order for a work to be declared obscene. **C** is incorrect because since the work is conceded to have literary merit, the prosecution will fail whether or not the book is found to appeal primarily to prurient interest.

138. **C**   Although the federal government is immune from state taxation, that immunity does not shield persons working for the federal government, even where the cost of such taxation will eventually be borne by the federal government. For this reason, a tax on building contractors who work for the federal government is constitutionally valid so long as it does not discriminate against them. **C** is, therefore, correct.

   Because the power to tax is the power to destroy, it has been held that any attempt by a state to impose a tax directly on the federal government or its activities is constitutionally invalid. **A** and **B** are, therefore, incorrect. Although persons doing business with the federal government may be taxed by a state, the state law may not constitutionally discriminate against people doing business with the federal government. **D** is incorrect because the law taxes only those persons leasing land from the federal government.

139. **A**   Although the Constitution is silent on the president's power to remove executive appointees, the United States Supreme Court has held that these appointees can be removed by the president at will. This is true even where the appointment itself required the advice and consent of the Senate. The only exceptions are for officers appointed pursuant to an act which specifies the length of their term of office or who perform a quasi-judicial function. These, too, can be removed by the president, but only for cause. Since the Pure Drinking Water Administration Act did not specify a term of office, the president's order was constitutional.

   B, C, and **D** are, therefore, incorrect.

140. **A**   A state law regulating private contracts violates the obligations of contracts clause only if it is limited to altering contractual rights and remedies. Thus a law, such as this one, which regulates private conduct does not violate the obligations of contracts clause merely because it incidentally reduces the value of existing contracts. Since the statute is not limited to altering contract rights and remedies, it does not violate this clause, and **A** is correct.

   The Commerce Clause has been held to prohibit discrimination by a state against out of staters since this would have the effect of preventing the free movement of persons and things between the states. Since the state law permits the disposal of wastes generated inside the state while prohibiting the disposal of wastes generated outside the state, a court could find that it violates the Commerce Clause. **B** is, therefore, incorrect. The Equal Protection clause prohibits a state from denying to any person within its jurisdiction the equal protection of the laws. Since the state law in question denies to out of staters a benefit which is available to state residents, it could be held to violate equal protection. **C** is, therefore, incorrect. The Privileges and Immunities clause of Article IV requires a state to accord out of staters within a state the same treatment as residents. Since this statute does not, it could be held to violate the Privileges and Immunities clause. **D** is, therefore, incorrect.

141. **C**   Although there are few cases regarding the extent of the president's powers as commander-in-chief, it is clear that they include the command of the military forces of the United States. While it is not certain that this includes the power to send troops into a foreign country in the absence of any military threat to American interests, C is correct because it is the only argument listed which could possibly justify the presidential order.

A is incorrect because the president's emergency powers apply only when there is some threat to the national interest. **B** is incorrect because the U.S. Constitution recognizes no such power or obligation. The president's power over foreign affairs generally is understood to refer only to diplomatic matters such as the negotiation of treaties and executive agreement and the receiving of foreign diplomats. **D** is, therefore, incorrect.

142. **B**   The U.S. Constitution grants to Congress the power to spend for the general welfare. The Necessary and Proper clause adds the power to do whatever is necessary and proper to the execution of Congress's other powers. It has been held that in spending for the general welfare, the Necessary and Proper clause permits Congress to impose conditions to assure that it gets its money's worth. Since the federal funds covered by the law are to be used for the treatment of diseases caused by smoking, it is possible to argue that a required tax which makes cigarettes more expensive and thus discourages people from using them is a necessary and proper way of protecting the investment of federal funds. While it is not certain that a court would come to this conclusion, **B** is the only principle listed which could possibly justify the provision in question.

The taxing power is the power to lay and collect revenues for the federal government. Since the challenged provision would not require any payment to the federal government or result in any federal revenue, **A** is incorrect. **C** is incorrect because there is no general federal police power under the U.S. Constitution. The congressional power to regulate interstate commerce is the power to control the movement of people and things across state lines. Since there is no indication that the addition of a seven cent tax by states would have any effect at all on movement across state lines, **D** is incorrect.

143. **C**   In deciding equal protection cases, the United States Supreme Court has developed three levels of scrutiny. Most statutes which regulate economic or social interests are constitutionally valid if they have a rational basis. Statutes which discriminate against suspect classes or which interfere with a fundamental rights are valid only if they are necessary to achieve a compelling state interest. Statutes which discriminate against classes which are close to being suspect or which interfere with rights which, although not fundamental, are very important, are valid only if they are substantially related to an

important government interest. Since this statute interferes with the right to vote, and since voting has been held to be a fundamental right, it is constitutionally valid only if it is necessary to achieve an important government interest.

For the above reason, **A** is incorrect. Since gender is close to being a suspect class, a statute which discriminates against males would ordinarily be scrutinized under the test indicated in **B**. Since this particular statute interferes with a fundamental right, however, **B** is incorrect. The "one person one vote" principal requires that voting districts be approximately equal in population size so that each voter will receive approximately equal representation. It does not apply in cases involving statutes which might prevent a qualified voter from voting at all. **D** is, therefore, incorrect.

144. **D**   The Property clause gives Congress the power to make laws disposing of and making regulations concerning the use of all property of the federal government. This includes the power to make restrictions for the purpose of preventing injury to federal lands. Since Mountain Range National Park is owned and maintained by the federal government, the Property clause authorizes Congress to prohibit fires within its boundaries. **D** is, therefore, correct.

One of the factors to be considered in freedom of religion cases is whether the challengers are sincere in their religious beliefs. The United States Supreme Court has indicated that the fact that a religious group has engaged in a particular practice for a long period of time is relevant to determining whether the challengers' beliefs are sincerely held. Except for this limited purpose, however, the fact that a particular practice is or is not a traditional one is of no importance. Since no question has been raised regarding the sincerity of the beliefs held by the Followers of the Holy Flame, **A** is incorrect. **B** is incorrect because courts may not inquire into the reasonableness of any religious belief or practice. A law which interferes with the free exercise of religion is valid if necessary to achieve a compelling state interest, considering the weight of the government interest, the degree of interference with a religious practice, and the availability of alternate means of protecting the government interest. Although discrimination between religions and the primarily secular effect of a law are factors to be considered in establishment clause cases, they play no role in free exercise challenges. For this reason, **C** is incorrect.

145. **D**   The Eleventh Amendment prohibits the federal courts from hearing damage claims against a state. For this reason, Cheff's proceeding should be dismissed. **D** is, therefore, correct.

A case is moot when there are no longer any contested issues to be decided by the court. Since Cheff claims to have sustained damage as a result of the enforcement of the mandatory retirement law, at least the issue of damage remains to be decided by the court. For this reason, the case is not moot, and **A** is incorrect. A person has standing to assert a claim if he has sustained or is about to sustain concrete harm which the court could remedy or prevent by granting the relief requested. Since Cheff claims to have sustained damage, and since the court could remedy the harm by awarding a judgment for damages, Cheff has standing to assert his claim. **B** is, therefore, incorrect. A controversy is ripe for decision when the issues are fully developed, defined by concrete facts, and not merely speculative. Since Cheff has been forced to retire and since he was unemployed for a period of two months following his retirement, these requirements are met and the matter is ripe for decision. **C** is, therefore, incorrect.

146. **B**   In deciding equal protection cases, the United States Supreme Court has developed three levels of scrutiny. State regulations of social or economic interests are valid if they have a rational basis. Statutes which discriminate against a suspect class or which interfere with a fundamental right are not valid unless they are necessary to achieve a compelling state interest. Statutes which discriminate against a group which is close to being a suspect class are valid only if they are substantially related to important government interests. It has been held that discrimination based on age does not involve a suspect class or a group which is close to being a suspect class. For this reason, the statute is valid if it has a rational basis.

C is, therefore, incorrect. The Eleventh Amendment prevents the federal courts from hearing damage claims against a state. Since this proceeding is not an action for damages, however, the Eleventh Amendment does not prevent it from being heard. **A** is, therefore, incorrect. **D** is incorrect because age is not a suspect class, and because even a statute which does discriminate against a suspect class may be valid if it is necessary to achieve a compelling state interest.

QUESTIONS
CONTRACTS

CONTRACTS
TABLE OF CONTENTS

Numbers refer to Question Numbers

CONTRACTS QUESTIONS

1. Immediately after his graduation from college in June, Stuart announced his plan to begin law school the following September and to marry Sue in December. Stuart's father, Farrell, was afraid that marriage during Stuart's first year of law school might cause him to fail or drop out of school. He called Stuart on the phone and said that if Stuart postponed his wedding plans until after the completion of his first year of law school, Farrell would give him a cash bonus of $1,000 and would pay Stuart's tuition for the second year of law school. Stuart agreed, and called Sue to tell her that he wanted to postpone the wedding. She became so angry at him that she broke off their engagement. Two months later, Sue married someone else.

Farrell died soon after Stuart began school, but Stuart successfully completed his first year. Although Stuart earned excellent grades, he decided that he was not really interested enough in the law to want to continue his legal education. After failing to register for a second year of law school, he notified Farrell's administrator of his decision. Stuart said that although there would be no tuition expense, he expected to be paid the $1,000 cash bonus which his father had promised him. The administrator refused to pay anything.

If Stuart brought suit against the administrator of Farrell's estate for $1,000, Stuart would probably be

(A) unsuccessful, because his contract with Farrell violated public policy.

(B) unsuccessful, because Stuart failed to register for a second year of law school.

(C) unsuccessful, because Farrell's death terminated his offer.

(D) successful. - unilateral

2. Sorrento, a furniture dealer, had 500 barrel chairs for sale. The chairs had a fair market value of $100 each. The manufacturer had discontinued production of the chairs, however, and they were the last ones Sorrento had. For that reason, Sorrento advertised them at $75 each, even though at that price her profit would only be $10 per chair. Barrie, an interior decorator, had contracted to provide furniture for a new hotel. On May 4, after seeing the barrel chairs advertised, Barrie wired Sorrento, "please ship me 500 barrel chairs as advertised at $75 per chair COD." On May 5, immediately upon receipt of the telegram, Sorrento wired Barrie, "Accept your offer. Will ship 500 barrel chairs tomorrow." Barrie telephoned Sorrento immediately upon receipt of Sorrento's telegram on May 6, saying that after discussing the chairs with his client he had decided to cancel the order. On May 7, Barrie sold all the chairs to Meyers at $75 each. If Sorrento sued Barrie for breach of contract, the court should award Sorrento

(A) $5,000 (500 chairs at $10 profit per chair).

(B) $37,500 (500 chairs at $75 per chair).

(C) $12,500 (fair market value of $100 minus contract price of $75 times 500 chairs).

(D) nothing, since Sorrento sustained no damage.

Questions 3-4 are based on the following fact situation.

On March 12, Homer hired Bilder to construct a three car garage on Homer's realty. After negotiation, they entered into a valid written contract which fixed the price at $8,000. According to the terms of the contract, Homer was to pay $4,000 when the work was half completed on or before April 25, and to pay the balance upon completion. All work was to be completed by June 1. On April 10, when the work was one quarter complete, the partial structure was totally destroyed in a fire which started without fault by either party. The damage done by the fire made it impossible to complete construction on time. Because he was committed to begin construction on a hotel on June 1, Bilder notified Homer on April 12 that he would perform no further work for Homer. Homer subsequently hired Toil, another contractor, to build the garage at a price of $9,000.

3. Assume for the purpose of this question only that Homer instituted an action against Bilder for damages resulting from breach of contract, and that Bilder asserted a defense based on impossibility of performance. The court should find for

    (A) Bilder, because the fire was not his fault.

    (B) Bilder, because he has not yet received any compensation from Homer.

    (C) Homer, because the work was only one-quarter complete when fire destroyed the structure.

    (D) Homer, because Bilder's obligation was to work for Homer until June 1.

4. Assume for the purpose of this question only that Bilder institutes an action against Homer on a quasi-contract theory, seeking compensation for the services which he rendered prior to the fire. Bilder is entitled to receive

    (A) the reasonable value of the work performed by Bilder, less the difference between the price which Homer had agreed to pay Bilder and the price which Homer agreed to pay Toil.

    (B) the reasonable value of the work performed by Bilder.

    (C) one quarter of the price which Homer agreed to pay Bilder for the completed structure.

    (D) nothing, since Homer has received no benefit from Bilder's work.

Questions 5-7 are based on the following fact situation.

Boswell agreed to purchase 250 2" x 4" construction grade wooden studs from Stilton by a written contract which provided that Boswell would make payment prior to inspection. The studs were delivered to Boswell by truck, and were covered with a canvas tarpaulin when they arrived at Boswell's worksite. The driver demanded payment before he would unload or

uncover the studs.

5. Assume for the purpose of this question only that Boswell refused to pay for the studs before inspecting them, and that the driver returned them to Stilton. If Stilton asserts a claim for breach of contract against Boswell, the court should find for

    (A) Stilton, because Boswell's refusal to pay prior to inspection was a breach.

    (B) Stilton, because Boswell's refusal to pay prior to inspection was an anticipatory repudiation.

    (C) Boswell, because the contract provision calling for payment prior to inspection was unconscionable.

    (D) Boswell, because Stilton failed to deliver the studs.

6. Assume that Boswell paid the driver before inspecting the studs. Upon subsequent inspection, however, Boswell discovered that the studs were utility grade instead of construction grade. Assume for the purpose of this question only that he then telephoned Stilton, offering to return the studs and demanding the return of his money, but Stilton refused to take the merchandise back or to return Boswell's money. Which of the following is most correct about the effect of Boswell's payment prior to inspection?

    (A) The terms of the contract required an unconditional acceptance prior to inspection, and payment constituted unconditional acceptance.

    (B) Even if the contract provision calling for payment prior to inspection was invalid, payment resulted in a waiver of the right to inspect prior to acceptance.

    (C) Payment did not impair Boswell's right to inspect the goods prior to acceptance.

    (D) Payment constituted acceptance, but Boswell was entitled to revoke acceptance within a reasonable time thereafter.

7. Assume for the purpose of this question only that after discovering that the studs were utility grade

instead of construction grade, Boswell sent Stilton a letter notifying him that the studs did not conform to the contract. Assume further that Boswell kept and used the studs. If Boswell asserts a claim against Stilton for breach of warranty, the court should enter judgment in favor of

(A) Boswell, for the difference between the value of utility grade studs and the value of construction grade studs.

(B) Boswell, for return of the price which he paid.

(C) Stilton, because Boswell used the studs.

(D) Stilton, because he might have been able to sell the studs elsewhere for a higher price.

Questions 8-9 are based on the following fact situation.

Compinc, a manufacturer of computer hardware and software, was seeking a way to speed up the operation of its Basic Computer Program. On March 1, it posted the following notice in the employees' lounge:

> The stockholders of Compinc are offering a cash prize of $200 to any employee who develops a modification of Compinc's Basic Computer Program which will double its operating speed. Design modification entries should be submitted to the head of the Basic Program Department prior to June 1. In the event that modifications are submitted by more than one employee, the prize will go to the employee who submits the design which, in the opinion of the Basic Program Department, can be used most economically.

Enner, an engineer employed by Compinc, read the notice on March 5, and immediately began working on program modifications in his spare time. On March 8, he wrote and signed a memo which said, "I accept the stockholders' offer of a two hundred dollar prize for redesigning the Basic Computer Program. I am hard at work on the project and expect to submit my modification design within a week or two." Enner sent the note to the head of the Basic Program Department by the interoffice correspondence system, but it was somehow diverted and was never received by the department

head. On March 15, the notice was removed from the employees' lounge, and replaced by a sign which said, "The offer of a cash prize for redesigning the Basic Computer Program is hereby withdrawn." On March 17, Enner submitted a modification design which did double the operating speed and which was eventually adopted for use by the company. No other employees responded to the notice. The company has refused to pay any cash prize to Enner.

8. The notice which was posted on March 1 constituted

(A) an offer for a unilateral contract.

(B) an offer for a bilateral contract.

(C) an offer for a unilateral contract which ripened into a bilateral contract when Enner wrote the memo on March 8 and deposited it in the interoffice correspondence system.

(D) a preliminary invitation to deal, analogous to a newspaper advertisement for the sale of goods.

9. If Enner asserts a claim against Compinc for $200 in a jurisdiction which accepts the view expressed in the *Restatement of Contracts, Second*, Enner's most effective argument will be that

(A) a bilateral contract was formed when Enner submitted the design which the company eventually adopted.

(B) Enner relied on the offer contained in the first notice by working on the design in his spare time prior to March 15.

(C) the promises contained in the first notice could not be withdrawn until June 1.

(D) the company's attempt to withdraw its offer was unconscionable.

10. Corman was the owner of a condominium which consisted of an apartment with a patio and a small backyard. When he moved in, he entered into a written contract with Lansman. Pursuant to its terms, Lansman was to perform certain specified gardening services in the yard of Corman's condominium each week for a period of one year, for

which Corman was to pay the sum of $50 per month. The contract contained a clause which stated, "Corman hereby agrees not to assign this contract without the written permission of Lansman." Three months after entering into the agreement, Corman informed Lansman that he was selling the condominium to Antun, and asked Lansman to consent to Corman's assignment of the contract to Antun. Because the costs of landscaping materials had increased dramatically in the last three months, Lansman was glad for an opportunity to be relieved of his obligations under the contract, and refused to consent to the assignment. Corman assigned the contract to Antun anyway, but Lansman refused to perform any further work on the yard. After formally demanding performance from Lansman, Antun hired another gardener to do the same work for $75 per month which was the best price Antun could negotiate.

In an action by Antun against Lansman for breach of contract, the court should find for

(A) Antun, because Lansman had no right to unreasonably withhold consent to the assignment.

(B) Antun, because the assignment was valid in spite of Lansman's refusal to consent.

(C) Lansman, because the contract prohibited assignment by Corman without Lansman's consent.

(D) Lansman, because the contract was for personal services.

11. On June 1, after arson fires had damaged several city buildings, the City Council of the city of Metro voted to offer a reward to aid in apprehension of the arsonists. On June 2, by order of the City Council, signs were posted in various locations throughout the city. The posters identified the buildings which had been burned, and stated: "$1,000 REWARD is hereby offered by the City of Metro to any person furnishing information leading to the conviction of persons responsible for setting fire to said buildings." Curran, a police officer employed by the City of Metro saw the posters on June 5, and resolved to make a special effort to catch the arsonists. Although he was

not officially assigned to the case, he notified his fellow police officers and his usual underworld informants that he was especially interested in the case. As a result, Marino, a police officer, and Pidgeon, an underworld informant, passed information to Curran which they thought might relate to the arson crimes. The tip which Curran received from Marino proved to be of no assistance, but that which he received from Pidgeon led him to conduct a further investigation. His efforts eventually resulted in the arrest of two men who pleaded guilty to setting fires in public buildings. Curran demanded that the City Council pay him $1,000 but the council refused.

If Curran institutes a lawsuit against the City of Metro for the $1,000 reward offered in the signs posted on June 2, which of the following would be the City's most effective argument in defense?

(A) The reward should go to Pidgeon, since it was his information which eventually led to the arrest of the arsonists.

(B) The reward was not accepted, since the arsonists were not convicted but pleaded guilty.

(C) Curran gave no consideration for the City's promise to pay a reward, since he was already obligated to attempt the apprehension of the arsonists.

(D) There was no enforceable promise by the City, since the offer was for a gratuitous cash award.

12. San Sebastian is an English speaking republic on the continent of Europe. Its unit of currency is the San Sebastian dollar, which is worth about 85 U.S. cents. While on a business trip in the United States, Sella, who owned a glue factory in San Sebastian, entered into a written contract with Belton. According to the contract, Belton was to purchase thirty tons of liquid glue from Sella to be delivered on or before July 10. The contract stated the total price of the glue to be "NINE THOUSAND ($9,000) DOLLARS." After receiving the shipment, Belton sent Sella an international money order for 9,000 San Sebastian dollars. Sella wrote to Belton claiming that the

agreement called for the payment of 9,000 U.S. dollars, but Belton refused to make any further payment. Sella instituted an action against Belton in the United States and offered to testify that, prior to executing the written memorandum, she and Belton agreed that the price expressed in the writing was to be in U.S. dollars.

If Belton objects to the testimony, the objection should be

(A) sustained, since the oral agreement about which Sella is offering to testify was made prior to the execution of the written memorandum of sale.

(B) sustained, only if the written memorandum was prepared by Belton.

(C) overruled, unless the writing is found to be a complete integration of the agreement between Belton and Sella.

(D) overruled, because the evidence which Sella is offering to present does not modify or contradict the terms of the writing.

Questions 13-14 are based on the following fact situation.

Sport was fishing on her boat in Clear Lake, when she heard a call for help. Looking about her, she saw Manfred, who was drowning and flailing his arms over his head. Sport jumped into the water and swam toward Manfred, dropping her fishing gear into the lake and losing it in her effort to aid Manfred. She grabbed Manfred by the hair and swam to the shore, dragging him out of the water. Manfred was unconscious, but she gave him mouth to mouth resuscitation until he regained consciousness. When Manfred opened his eyes, he said, "I know I can never repay you for saving my life, but I promise to pay you $100 the first of next month as a token of my gratitude." A few days later, Manfred died from causes not related to the incident.

The following month Sport made demand upon Manfred's executor for the $100 which Manfred promised her and for an additional $100 which was the value of the fishing gear that she lost in her attempt to rescue Manfred. The executor rejected both demands.

13. If Sport institutes an action for the value of her fishing gear against the executor of Manfred's estate the court should find for

(A) Sport, on a theory of quantum meruit.

(B) Sport, because danger invites rescue.

(C) Sport, because the reasonable person in Manfred's position would have offered to pay for the loss of the fishing gear in exchange for Sport's attempt to rescue Manfred.

(D) the executor of Manfred's estate.

14. If Sport institutes an action against the executor of Manfred's estate for the $100 which Manfred promised to pay her, the court should find for

(A) Sport, if the jurisdiction has a good-samaritan statute.

(B) Sport, because she detrimentally relied on Manfred's promise to pay her one hundred dollars.

(C) Manfred's executor, because Manfred's promise was unsupported by consideration.

(D) Manfred's executor, because it is impossible to calculate the value of Sport's services.

Questions 15-16 are based on the following fact situation.

Honniker's hobby was restoring and collecting antique automobiles. After acquiring a 1919 Bensonhurst Bullet automobile, she contacted Carl's Custom Body Shop about having the car repainted. Carl said that he would paint the Bullet for $700, and would sell Honniker a new bumper for an additional $150. Using an order blank from a pad which he purchased at a stationary store, Carl wrote out all the terms of their agreement. On a printed line marked, "PAYMENT" he wrote, "Paint job -- $700, payable $300 in advance and $400 on completion. Bumper -- $150 payable on delivery." Both Carl and Honniker signed at the bottom of the form.

15. Which of the following statements most correctly describes the obligations set forth in the writing signed by Honniker and Carl?

(A) Payment by Honniker of the initial $300 is a condition precedent to Carl's obligation to paint the car, and Carl's painting of the car is a condition precedent to Honniker's obligation to pay the additional $400.

(B) Payment by Honniker of the initial $300 is a condition precedent in form and substance to Carl's obligation to paint the car, and Carl's painting of the car is a condition precedent in form, but subsequent in substance to Honniker's obligation to pay the additional $400.

(C) Payment by Honniker and painting of the car by Carl are concurrent conditions.

(D) Neither party's obligation to perform is conditioned upon performance by the other party.

16. Assume for the purpose of this question only that Carl notified Honniker that he would not deliver the new bumper as agreed, and that Honniker succeeded in buying one like it in another town for $130, but that her reasonable travel expenses in finding and purchasing it amounted to $20. In an action by Honniker against Carl, the court should find for

(A) Honniker, in the sum of $20.

(B) Honniker, in the sum of $40.

(C) Honniker, in the sum of $170.

(D) Carl.

17. Worthen was employed by Boss as department manager pursuant to a written contract. The contract was for a five year term, and fixed Worthen's compensation at $2,000 per month. Worthen's work was satisfactory, but two years after entering into the contract with him, Boss reorganized the company. As a result of the reorganization, Worthen's department was eliminated, and Boss terminated Worthen's employment. Worthen advertised in the "jobs wanted" section of the newspaper, but did not find a job until six months after his discharge, when he went to work for Newton doing the same general sort of work which he had been doing for Boss and earning the same salary. In an action by Worthen against Boss for damages resulting from breach of the employment contract, the court should give judgment to

(A) Boss, since Worthen's position was eliminated.

(B) Worthen, for severance pay in a sum equivalent to two months salary.

(C) Worthen, in a sum equivalent to the salary which Worthen lost between the time of his discharge and the time he began working for Newton, plus the cost of advertising in the "jobs wanted" section of the newspaper.

(D) Worthen, in a sum equivalent to the salary which Worthen would have received during the balance of the contract term.

18. Cabb was the owner of a fleet of taxis which he leased to independent drivers in return for sixty percent of the fares which they collected. All the leases were scheduled to expire on December 31. Because the cars in his fleet were beginning to look shabby, Cabb decided to have them all painted during the first week of January, before negotiating new leases with the drivers. At the beginning of December, he called Payne, the president of Paint-a- Car Auto Painting company, to inquire about his price for painting all the cars in Cabb's fleet. Payne said the he would do the job for $150 per car.

Cabb said, "I'm talking about sixty cars. That's a lot of business. I'll give you the job if you'll do it for $125 per car."

"I'd really like to have your business," replied Payne.

"See you the first week in January," Cabb said.

On January 3, Cabb brought one of his taxis to the Paint-a- Car shop, and offered to make arrangements for bringing in the rest of the cars to be painted. Payne said that he had just obtained a contract to paint some school buses and that he was too busy to do any work for Cabb. Cabb subsequently asserted a claim for damages against Payne.

Which of the following additional facts or inferences, if it were the only one true, would be most helpful to Cabb in his action against Payne?

(A) Payne's statement, "I'd really like to have your business" implied a promise to paint all the cars in Cabb's fleet at $125 per car.

(B) Cabb relied on Payne's statement by bringing the taxi to the Paint-a-Car shop.

(C) Immediately prior to January 3, Cabb could have had the taxis painted at another shop for $125 each, but immediately after January 3 the lowest price he could find was $150.

(D) On January 3, when Payne told Cabb that he was too busy to do the work, Cabb offered to pay Payne $150 per car, and tendered payment of that sum.

19. When Osteen's uncle died, he left her a ten-story office building which had a motion picture theater on its ground floor. The offices in the building were all occupied when Osteen acquired title to it. The motion picture theater was vacant, however, so she advertised for a tenant. Martin had researched the neighborhood and decided that it was a good location for a pornographic movie theater. When he saw Osteen's advertisement, he contacted her and said that he was interested in leasing the theater. He did not tell her what type of films he intended to show because he thought that she might be unwilling to rent it to him for that purpose. On April 1, they entered into a written rental agreement for the theater, occupancy to begin on May 1. On April 15, the city council passed an ordinance prohibiting the showing of pornographic films in the neighborhood where the theater was located. As a result, Martin advised Osteen that he was canceling the rental agreement.

If Osteen sues Martin for breach of contract, the court should find for

(A) Martin, under the doctrine of frustration of purpose.

(B) Martin, under the doctrine of impossibility of performance.

(C) Martin, because after the contract had been formed, government action made its subject matter unlawful.

(D) Osteen.

20. X-tendo contracted to add a room to Homer's house for $3,000, with the understanding that the materials used by X-tendo were to be included in that price. The day before work was to begin, Homer wired X-tendo, "The deal is off. Do not begin work, Homer." X-tendo subsequently asserted a claim against Homer for breach of contract. Homer raised non-compliance with the Statute of Frauds as a defense. Which of the following statements is most correct about the application of the Statute of Frauds to the contract between Homer and X-tendo?

 I. The contract was required to be in writing if the materials which would have been required had a price in excess of $500.

 II. The contract was required to be in writing if, at the time of contracting, the parties intended that the materials required would have a price in excess of $500.

(A) I only.

(B) II only.

(C) I and II.

(D) Neither I nor II.

21. After Poston said that Dworkin owed him $3,000, Dworkin promised to pay $2,000, which Poston agreed to accept as payment in full. Subsequently, Dworkin refused to make payment, and Poston asserted a claim for $2,000 based on Dworkin's promise. If it was the only one true at the time of Dworkin's promise, which of the following additional facts or inferences would be most likely to result in a judgment for Poston?

(A) Dworkin honestly believed that he owed Poston $3,000, but Poston did not believe that Dworkin owed him the money.

(B) Poston honestly believed that Dworkin owed him $3,000, but Dworkin did not believe that he owed Poston the money.

(C) Poston was threatening to institute a lawsuit against Dworkin for $3,000 plus costs and interest.

(D) Poston had already commenced a lawsuit against Dworkin for $3,000 plus costs and interest.

Questions 22-23 are based on the following fact situation.

Trac's daughter Dot was about to celebrate her twenty-first birthday, and Trac wanted to give her a gift which would express his sentiments for her. Trac was a wealthy and successful building contractor, but had begun his career as an assistant bricklayer. Instead of purchasing something for Dot, he decided to give her a gift with the labor of his hands. Trac entered into a written contract with Smith. According to its terms, Trac agreed to build a brick fireplace for Smith, performing all the labor himself. In return, Smith agreed to pay the sum of $1,000 to Dot on her birthday, February 12, upon completion of the work by Trac to Smith's satisfaction. Dot did not learn of the transaction until February 12. Before signing the writing, Smith and Trac agreed orally that Smith would make a reasonable effort to obtain a loan to pay for the work but that if Smith was unsuccessful in doing so by January 1, the agreement between them would be of no effect.

22. For this question only, assume that Smith made efforts to obtain the loan, but could not do so. Assume further that on January 1, Smith informed Trac that, because he was unable to obtain the loan, he was calling off the deal. In an action for breach of contract brought against Smith by the proper party, will Smith be successful in asserting as a defense his inability to obtain a loan?

(A) Yes, because obtaining a loan was a condition precedent to the existence of an enforceable contract.

(B) Yes, because a modification of a construction contract may be by oral agreement.

(C) No, because Smith is estopped from denying the validity of the written agreement.

(D) No, because the agreement concerning the loan is an oral agreement which was made prior to the writing and which contradicts the terms of the writing.

23. For this question only, assume that Smith obtained the loan, and that Trac completed building the fireplace on February 5. Assume further that because Dot had married a man of whom Trac did not approve, Trac asked Smith to pay the $1,000 to Trac directly, which Smith did on February 6. If, on February 12, Dot learns for the first time of the written agreement between Smith and Trac, and commences a lawsuit against Smith for $1,000, will Dot's lawsuit succeed?

(A) No, because she gave no consideration for Smith's promise to pay her.

(B) No, because the payment by Smith to Trac was the result of an effective oral modification of the written contract.

(C) Yes, because Dot is an intended donee beneficiary of the contract between Trac and Smith.

(D) Yes, because the written contract between Smith and Trac operated as an assignment to Dot of Trac's right to payment.

24. Assume that Defendant in each of the following fact patterns objects to enforcement of the agreement on the ground that it violates the statute of frauds. In which of the following fact patterns is the agreement between Plaintiff and Defendant LEAST likely to be enforced over Defendant's objection?

(A) Defendant orally agreed to purchase a series of porcelain figurines from Plaintiff to be delivered one per week for fifteen weeks at a price of $100 per figurine. Prior to the first delivery, Defendant advised Plaintiff that he was no longer interested in receiving the figurines.

(B) Defendant orally agreed to purchase a hand carved entry door for Defendant's home with Defendant's coat of arms on it for a price of $600. After Plaintiff completed the rough carving of Defendant's coat of arms, Defendant changed her mind and notified Plaintiff that she would not accept delivery of the door.

(C) Defendant's pleadings admitted making an oral agreement to purchase a painting from the Plaintiff for $900, but asserted as an affirmative defense that the agreement was unenforceable under the Statute of Frauds.

(D) Defendant orally agreed to a price of $1,200 for the purchase of 100 lawn-trimmers manufactured by Plaintiff for resale in Defendant's store. Plaintiff then sent Defendant a memorandum signed by Plaintiff and outlining the terms of their agreement. Defendant did not sign the memorandum or respond to it in any way.

25. Margeaux, a minor, purchased a used car from Utrecht Car Sales for $1,200. The reasonable rental value of the car was $150 per month. After she had owned the car for two months, the steering failed while she was driving it, causing it to collide with a tree. Although Margeaux was unhurt, the car sustained $400 worth of damage. Margeaux returned the damaged car to Utrecht and demanded her money back, but Utrecht refused to refund her money. If Margeaux asserts a claim against Utrecht, the court should award her a judgment in the amount of

(A) $1,200 (the full purchase price of the car).

(B) $900 (the purchase price of the car less its reasonable rental value).

(C) $800 (the purchase price of the car less the damage which it sustained).

(D) nothing.

26. Sulton and Brendan were neighbors who owned homes on adjoining parcels of realty. They were both in the business of selling art supplies, each operating an art supply store which engaged in friendly competition with the other. Sulton owned a garden tractor which he used for cultivating vegetables in the backyard of his home. Brendan, who wanted to plant a garden in his own backyard, sent Sulton a note in which he offered to buy the tractor from Sulton for $500. Sulton responded on February 15 by sending Brendan a letter which stated, "I will sell you my garden tractor for six hundred dollars, and not a penny less. To give you time to think it over, I promise to hold this offer open until March 15." On March 5, Brendan noticed a similar garden tractor in the yard of Norton, another neighbor. He called Norton on the phone and offered to buy it for $500, but Norton said, "Are you kidding? I just bought it from Sulton for $600." On March 6, Brendan went to Sulton's store with $600 in cash, and said, "I've decided to buy that tractor from you. Here's the money." Sulton refused the money and told Brendan that he had already sold the tractor to Norton. If Brendan asserts a claim against Sulton for damages resulting from Sulton's refusal to sell the tractor on March 6, the court should find for

(A) Brendan, because Sulton's offer of February 15 was irrevocable until March 15.

(B) Brendan, because Sulton did not notify him that he was withdrawing his offer to sell Brendan the garden tractor until after Brendan accepted it.

(C) Sulton, because Brendan learned of the sale to Norton on March 5.

(D) Sulton, because his letter of February 15 was a rejection of Brendan's original offer to purchase the garden tractor.

27. Seller and Buyer entered into a written contract for the sale of 200 electric power drills. Although they orally agreed on a price, they inadvertently failed to include it among the terms of the written agreement. In an action for breach of the contract, the court should

(A) admit oral testimony to establish the price which the parties intended.

(B) refuse to enforce the contract if it is one

which the Statute of Frauds required to be in writing.

(C) conclude that the contract calls for the payment of a reasonable price.

(D) disregard the writing since it fails to contain all the essential terms of the agreement.

28. On May 15, after negotiation, Payne and Hoser entered into a written agreement for the painting of Hoser's home. The writing stated that the price was to be $300 plus the cost of materials, that the work was to begin on June 2 and to be completed by June 12, that stucco portions of the house were to be painted yellow and that wood trim was to be painted brown, and that the written memorandum was a full and final expression of the agreement between Payne and Hoser. During litigation between Payne and Hoser to enforce the contract, Hoser offered to testify to the following additional facts. Which is the ~~LEAST~~ likely to be [not going] admitted into evidence over timely objection by Payne?

(A) Prior to signing the memorandum, Payne and Hoser orally agreed that the contract would have no legal effect if Hoser sold his house prior to June 2.

(B) Prior to signing the memorandum, Payne and Hoser orally agreed that Hoser would use no paint without first submitting it for Hoser's approval.

(C) While signing the memorandum, Payne and Hoser orally agreed that any promises made by either of them during negotiations were to be enforceable, even if they were omitted from the memorandum.

(D) While signing the memorandum, Payne and Hoser orally agreed that Payne would spend no more than ten dollars per gallon for paint.

Questions 29-30 are based on the following fact situation.

On May 20, on a form provided by Kooler, Bittel agreed to purchase from Kooler 100 described air con-

ditioning units at a price of $250 each, FOB Koolers factory. The contract contained a clause which prohibited either party from assigning its rights or obligations under the contract without the consent of the other party. On June 1, Kooler's employees loaded the units on a truck owned and operated by Carrier, an independent trucking company. When the loading was complete, Kooler phoned Bittel that the shipment was on its way. Later that day, Kooler executed a document which contained the following language: "In consideration of $20,000 to me in hand paid by Abco this date, I hereby assign to Abco all rights under my contract with Bittell dated May 20." On June 2, while en route to Bittell's warehouse, the truck containing the air conditioning units overturned, and the entire shipment was destroyed.

29. Assume for the purpose of this question only that Bittell did not consent to Kooler's assignment of rights to Abco. In an action by Abco against Bittel, Abco will probably recover

(A) the contract price of $25,000 (100 air conditioning units at $250 each).

(B) the difference between the contract price and the market value of the air conditioning units.

(C) nothing, since recovery from Bittell would unjustly enrich Abco.

(D) nothing, since the contract between Bittell and Kooler prohibited assignment.

30. Assume for the purpose of this question only that Bittell did consent to Kooler's assignment of rights to Abco. In an action by Bittell against Kooler for damages resulting from non-delivery of the air conditioning units, which of the following would be Kooler's most effective argument in defense?

(A) There has been a valid assignment to Abco.

(B) The risk of loss passed to Bittell when the air conditioning units were loaded onto Carrier's truck.

(C) The risk of loss passed to Carrier when the air conditioning units were loaded onto

Carrier's truck.

(D) Performance of the contract was made impossible by the destruction of the air conditioning units.

Questions 31-32 are based on the following fact situation.

Paco Toro was a world-renowned artist who painted until he died at the age of 87. His will left a collection of 30 of his paintings to his niece Nan, who was an art dealer. The paintings inherited by Nan were untitled, but were identified by numbers 1 through 30. Nan had a catalog printed containing photographs and descriptions of each in the collection. On August 1 she sent a copy of the catalog to Delia, who was also an art dealer, with the following cover letter:

> Dear Delia: I know how much you like my uncle's work, so I'm giving you an opportunity to buy some of these painting before I offer them to any other dealers. The price is two thousand dollars per painting, no matter how many you buy. Telegraph your order within two weeks, or I'll put them on the market.
>
> (signed) Nan.

On August 2, Delia sent Nan a telegram which said, "I accept your offer to sell Toro painting number 30 for $2,000. I will come to your gallery in two days to pick up the painting, and will pay cash at that time. Delia."

On August 3, after receiving the telegram, Nan telephoned Delia and said that because of favorable publicity which the collection had received, she would not sell painting number 30 for less than $3,000. Delia agreed on the telephone to pay $3,000 for painting number 30.

On August 4, Delia sent and Nan received a telegram which said, "I accept your offer to sell Toro paintings 1 through 29 for $2,000 each. I will pick up the paintings tomorrow, and will pay for them at that time. Delia."

On August 5 Delia presented herself at Nan's gallery and tendered payment of $2000 each for all 30 paintings but Nan refused to sell her any of the paintings

except number 30, for which Nan insisted the agreed price was $3,000. Delia left without buying it, saying that Nan would be hearing from her lawyer.

31. If Nan asserts a claim against Delia for breach of a contract to purchase painting number 30 for $3,000, the court should find for

(A) Delia, because her promise to pay $3,000 for the painting was not in writing.

(B) Delia, unless the fair market value of painting number 30 increased by $1,000 between August 1 and August 3.

(C) Nan, because she relied on Delia's promise to pay $3,000 for painting number 30.

(D) Nan, because she had not received payment from Delia prior to their conversation on August 3.

32. Assume for the purpose if this question only that Delia sued for an order directing Nan to sell Delia the paintings numbered 1 through 29 for two thousand dollars each. Which of the following would be Nan's most effective argument in defense against that action?

(A) Since Delia is an art dealer, there is an adequate remedy at law.

(B) Nan's August 1 promise to keep the offer open for two weeks was unsupported by consideration.

(C) Delia's telegram of August 2 was a rejection of Nan's offer to sell paintings numbered 1 through 29.

(D) The catalog and Nan's cover letter were mere invitations to negotiate.

33. On March 1, Seider, an aluminum siding contractor, entered into a written contract with Forrest for the installation of aluminum siding on the exterior of Forrest's home. The contract called for completion of the job by April 1, and contained a clause which prohibited assignment by either party without the other party's written consent. Seider started work immediately upon the signing

of the contract. On March 15, Forrest sold his house to Byers, assigning to Byers his contract with Seider.

In which of the following fact situations is the plaintiff LEAST likely to succeed in his action against the defendant?

(A) Seider finished the job in a workman-like manner on March 29 and demanded but did not receive payment. Seider instituted an action against Forrest for payment.

(B) Seider finished the job in a workman-like manner on March 29 and demanded but did not receive payment. Seider instituted an action against Byers for payment.

(C) When Seider learned of Forrest's assignment to Byers, he refused to do any further work. Forrest instituted an action against Seider for breach of contract on April 15.

(D) When Seider learned of Forrest's assignment to Byers, he refused to do any further work. Byers instituted an action against Seider for breach of contract on April 15.

34. On August 1, Wells, a wholesaler of office supplies, contracted by telephone to sell 50 cases of typewriter ribbons to Ronson, a business equipment retailer, at a total price of $450. On August 15, Wells telephoned Ronson and told him that because of a shortage of materials, the price which Wells had to pay for typewriter ribbons had increased drastically. Wells said if he delivered the ribbons at the price of $450, he would lose a great deal of money. He asked Ronson to consent to a higher price, suggesting that Ronson pass the increase along to his customers. After further discussion, Ronson and Wells agreed to change the price of the order from $450 to $650. On August 18, Ronson succeeded in purchasing fifty cases of typewriter ribbons from another supplier for $500. On September 1, Wells delivered fifty cases of typewriter ribbons to Ronson together with a bill for $650. Ronson rejected the delivery.

In an action by Wells against Ronson for breach of contract, which of the following would be

Ronson's most effective argument in defense?

(A) Ronson's demand for more money was unconscionable, since typewriter ribbons were available at a lower price.

(B) The August 15 agreement increasing the price was not in writing.

(C) Ronson's promise to pay $650 was unsupported by consideration.

(D) An increase in Well's cost resulting from a shortage of materials was foreseeable on August 1.

Questions 35-36 are based on the following fact situation.

Salas was an importer of arts and crafts products from the Mediterranean countries, selling mainly to large department stores and import shops. To keep his sales force down to a minimum, Salas did most of his selling by sending catalogs describing products and prices to prospective customers and taking orders by mail on forms provided with the catalogs. The phrase "10% discount on COD orders only" appeared on the order form and on each page of the catalog. After receiving one of Salas's catalogs, Bostoria decided to order 1000 Greek coffee pots for sale in her import shop. On April 25, she typed the following across Salas's order form: "Send immediately 1000 Greek coffee pots (Catalog #6047) at ten percent discount. Payment within ten days of receipt and acceptance." Salas received the order on April 27. On April 28, Salas shipped 1000 Greek coffee pots to Bostoria, who received and accepted them on May 2. On April 29, Salas wrote to Bostoria, "I am shipping pursuant to your request and will expect payment within ten days. Since discounts apply only to COD shipments, you are herewith billed at full price." Bostoria received the letter and enclosed bill on May 3. On May 4 Bostoria sent Salas a check in payment of the amount billed, less ten percent.

35. When was a contract for sale of the coffee pots formed?

(A) On April 25, when Bostoria sent the order to Salas.

(B) On April 27, when Salas received the order

from Bostoria.

(C) On April 28, when Salas shipped the coffee pots to Bostoria.

(D) On May 2, when Bostoria received the shipment of coffee pots.

36. If Salas asserts a claim against Bostoria for the balance of the amount billed, the court should find for

(A) Salas, because Bostoria's order was on Salas's order form.

(B) Salas, if Bostoria was aware that Salas's catalog and order form specified that the ten percent discount applied only to COD shipments.

(C) Bostoria, only if she had been doing business with Salas on an "open account" basis.

(D) Bostoria, because Salas accepted her offer to purchase at a ten percent discount.

37. After lengthy negotiations, Beryl purchased a car from Sargent, a car dealer. Beryl was driving it the following day when the brakes failed due to a defect which existed at the time Sargent delivered the car to Beryl. As a result, the car collided with a pole and was damaged. Beryl asserted a claim against Sargent for damages resulting from breach of the implied warranty of merchantability. Which one of the following additional facts, if it were the only one true, would be most likely to result in a judgment for Sargent?

(A) At the time of the sale, both Sargent and Beryl signed a document stating that the car was being sold "as is."

(B) The car which Beryl bought from Sargent was a used car.

(C) The defect which caused the brakes to fail could not have been discovered by reasonable inspection prior to the sale.

(D) Beryl purchased the car in reliance on the advice of a mechanic whom she hired to inspect it prior to making the purchase.

38. Evans, who broke his leg falling from a ladder, was treated by Dr. Drake. At the time treatment began, Evans explained that he was short of cash, but that his treatment was covered by group insurance. Dr. Drake agreed to wait for his fee until the insurance company made payment and offered to bill the insurance company directly for the services which he rendered to Evans. Evans provided Dr. Drake with claim forms from the company which insured Evans's union. Dr. Drake filled out the form, had Evans sign a portion of it authorizing the insurance company to make payment directly to Dr. Drake, and submitted the form to the company. Because of an error by employees of the insurance company, the payment was sent to Evans, who failed to make any payment at all to Dr. Drake.

If Dr. Drake asserts a claim against Evans to recover the amount of the unpaid bill, the court will probably find for

(A) Dr. Drake, because he is a creditor third-party beneficiary of the group insurance policy which covered Evans.

(B) Dr. Drake, because Evans impliedly promised to pay Dr. Drake for his services.

(C) Evans, because Dr. Drake agreed to accept payment from the insurance company.

(D) Evans, because Dr. Drake billed the insurance company directly.

Questions 39-40 are based on the following fact situation.

Marshall wanted to open an amusement park on a parcel of real estate which he owned. After negotiation, Marshall hired Structo to build a roller coaster and several other amusement devices on the land according to specifications furnished by Marshall. Marshall and Structo entered into a written contract by which Structo agreed to begin construction on August 1, to be finished with everything but the roller coaster by November 1, and to complete construction of the roller coaster by December 15. The contract price was $150,000 to be paid as follows: $50,000 on August 1; $50,000 upon completion of everything but the roller coaster; and the balance of $50,000 upon completion of the roller coaster. Structo began work on August 1, after receiving $50,000 from Marshall. By November 1, Structo completed construction of everything but the roller coaster in accordance with the specifications.

39. Assume for the purpose of this question only that on November 1 Structo demanded Marshall pay him $50,000, but that Marshall refused to do so. Which of the following statements is most correct concerning the rights of Structo?

    (A) Structo is entitled to damages limited to the sum of $50,000.

    (B) Structo is entitled to damages in the sum of $100,000.

    (C) Structo may refuse to perform any further work without incurring liability for breach of contract.

    (D) Structo may not sue Marshall for breach of contract until he completes construction of the roller coaster.

40. Assume for the purpose of this question only that Marshall paid $50,000 to Structo on November 1, and that Structo began construction of the roller coaster but before it was completed, Structo informed Marshall that he would not finish the job. Which of the following statements is correct concerning Marshall's rights against Structo?

    I. Marshall may recover all payments which he has made to Structo.

    II. Marshall may recover from Structo the reasonable cost of completing the roller coaster.

    (A) I only.

    (B) II only.

    (C) I and II.

    (D) Neither I nor II.

41. Manna was suffering from a terminal disease and did not expect to live much longer. She was the owner of a parcel of realty known as Mannacre and wanted her son Sokol to have it. Mannacre was worth $500,000, but was subject to a non-assumable mortgage securing a note with a balance of $100,000. For this reason, Manna offered to sell Mannacre to Sokol for $100,000. Sokol said that he would like to buy it, but that it would take him a while to raise the money. Fearful that she would die before the transaction could be completed and that her administratrix would be unwilling to sell the realty to Sokol for that price, Manna wrote and signed a document which said, "In consideration of $20 paid to me by my son Sokol, I hereby promise to convey my realty known as Mannacre to him for the sum of $100,000 if he pays the entire purchase price within one month." Two days later, Manna died. One week after that, Sokol tendered the sum of $100,000 to the administratrix of Manna's estate, demanding that she convey Mannacre to him, but the administratrix refused.

If Sokol instituted a proceeding against Manna's administratrix for an order directing her to sell Mannacre to him for $100,000, the court should find for

(A) Sokol, because the document written and signed by Manna was a valid option contract.

(B) Sokol, because the document written and signed by Manna was intended to be a testamentary substitute.

(C) Manna's administratrix, because $20 is not sufficient consideration for a $100,000 option.

(D) Manna's administratrix, because $100,000 is not sufficient consideration for realty valued at $500,000.

Questions 42-43 are based on the following fact situation.

Morris, a minor who looked older than he was, wished to purchase a motorcycle. Morris went to Dawes's Motorcycle Showroom and looked at some of the models on display. Selecting a Hawk 61, he began negotiating with Dawes. Dawes offered to sell him the Hawk 61 which was on display in the showroom, but Morris said that he wanted a new one. Dawes explained that the display model was the only one she had, but said that she was planning to order some new Hawks from the manufacturer anyway, and would order one for Morris if he agreed to purchase it. Morris and Dawes entered into a written contract for the sale of a new Hawk 61 at a price of $1,000 to be paid on delivery within two weeks. The following day, Dawes ordered ten new Hawk 61 motorcycles from the manufacturer, and Morris purchased materials and began building a storage shed for the motorcycle.

42. Assume for the purpose of this question only that one week after contracting with Morris, Dawes notified Morris that the new Hawk 61 was ready for delivery, but that Dawes would not deliver it to Morris unless Morris either proved himself to be over the age of majority or found an adult to act as co-purchaser of the motorcycle. If Morris immediately commenced an action against Dawes for breach of contract, the court should find for

   (A) Dawes, because if she delivered the motorcycle to Morris, Morris might subsequently disaffirm the contract and demand the return of the purchase price.

   (B) Dawes, because Morris lacked contractual capacity.

   (C) Morris, because he purchased materials for and began construction of a storage shed for the motorcycle in justified reliance on Dawes's promise to deliver it.

   (D) Morris, because one who contracts with a minor is obligated to perform.

43. Assume for the purpose of this question only that one week after contracting with Morris, Dawes notified him that the new Hawk 61 was ready for delivery, and Morris went immediately to Dawes's showroom to take delivery of it. Assume further that Morris tendered his own personal check in payment of the purchase price, but that Dawes refused to accept it. Which of the following most accurately describes the legal rights and obligations of the parties upon such refusal by Dawes?

   (A) Morris's tender of a check discharged

Dawes's obligation under the contract, since an agreement which is silent as to the manner of payment is presumed to call for payment in cash.

   (B) Morris's tender of a check discharged Dawes's obligation under the contract unless Morris tendered payment in cash immediately upon being informed of Dawes's refusal to accept Morris's check.

   (C) Morris's tender of a check did not discharge Dawes's obligation under the contract, but Dawes's obligation will be discharged of Morris fails to tender cash within a reasonable time.

   (D) Dawes's refusal to accept a check discharged Morris's obligation under the contract, since an agreement which is silent as to the manner of payment is presumed to call for payment in any manner current in the ordinary course of business.

44. On March 22, by a written memorandum signed by both parties, Varsey agreed to sell and Pantel agreed to buy a described parcel of realty. The contract called for closing of title on May 30 and fixed all other terms, but did not indicate the price to be paid. On May 30, Pantel tendered $60,000 cash, but Varsey refused to convey the realty. Pantel subsequently instituted an action against Varsey for specific performance of the contract and offered evidence that $60,000 was the fair market value of the realty both on March 22 and on May 30. In defense Varsey asserted that the memorandum failed to satisfy the requirements of the Statute of Frauds. Pantel's suit against Varsey should

   (A) succeed, if Pantel and Varsey are both in the business of buying and selling real estate.

   (B) succeed, because under the Uniform Commercial Code a contract which is silent as to price is presumed to call for payment of fair market value.

   (C) fail, because the written contract did not fix the price to be paid.

   (D) fail, unless the evidence establishes that the

parties orally agreed that the price to be paid was the fair market value of the realty.

Questions 45-46 are based on the following fact situation.

Rusk saved the life of Humbert's wife Welton, who subsequently promised to change her will to leave five hundred dollars to Rusk. Welton later died intestate, however, survived only by Humbert. After Welton's death, Humbert executed a document which read as follows:

> In consideration of my wife's promise to leave Rusk $500, of Rusk's saving my wife's life, and of Rusk's promise not to assert any claim against the estate of my wife, I hereby promise to pay Rusk the sum of five hundred dollars.

Humbert died two months after signing the above agreement. Rusk submitted a claim for $500 to the administrator of Humbert's estate, but the administrator denied the claim.

45. Is the fact that Rusk saved Welton's life sufficient consideration for Humbert's promise to pay him $500?

   (A) Yes, because it is recited as consideration in the document which Humbert signed.

   (B) Yes, because it materially benefitted Humbert.

   (C) No, because Humbert did not ask Rusk to save Welton.

   (D) No, because the value of the service rendered by Rusk to Humbert was speculative.

46. In an action by Rusk against Humbert's administrator, which of the following would be Rusk's most effective argument?

   (A) Rusk and Humbert have made a compromise.

   (B) Humbert's estate would be unjustly enriched if the administrator is permitted to deny Rusk's claim.

   (C) Rusk has detrimentally relied on Humbert's promise to pay him $500.

   (D) Humbert made the promise to pay Rusk voluntarily and of his own free will.

47. Daniels was the owner of a large dock on Lake Waters. Daniels marked three spaces on his dock with paint. The space closest to the shore was numbered 1, the space at the furthest end of the dock was numbered 3, and the middle space was numbered 2. Daniels rented space 1 to Axel, space 2 to Barre, and space 3 to Chula by three separate written agreements. Each of the agreements provided for the use of the designated space by the lessee for one year, and the payment of a monthly dock rent to Daniels. In addition, each lease prohibited assignment. Soon after entering into the agreement, Barre decided to travel on his boat for several months. Without seeking or receiving Daniels's permission, Barre purported to assign his dock rental contract to Newcombe. Newcombe's boat was bigger that Barre's, and Chula feared that if Newcombe docked at space 2, damage to Chula's boat would result. Chula brought an action for a judgment declaring Barre's assignment to Newcombe invalid. In this action, Chula will

   (A) prevail, if he names Daniels as a defendant in the action.

   (B) prevail, because the contract between Daniels and Barre prohibits assignment.

   (C) not prevail, because the non-assignment provision in the contract between Daniels and Barre was not made for the benefit of Chula.

   (D) not prevail, unless he entered into the contract to rent space 3 before Barre entered into the contract to rent space 2.

Questions 48-49 are based on the following fact situation.

In preparation for the annual convention of the Association of Life Insurance Agents which was to be held on January 9, Committee ordered 500 ball point pens from Penco at a total price of $285, paying for them in advance. Because the pens were to be given to conventioneers as souvenirs, they were to be imprinted with the name and slogan of the association and were to be delivered to Committee on or before January 8. Penco and Committee entered into a written contract containing the above terms on November 16. Penco tendered 475 ball point pens to Committee on January 8.

48. Which of the following correctly states the legal relationship between Committee and Penco on January 8?

(A) Committee must accept the tendered delivery of 475 pens, but may successfully sue for damages resulting from breach of contract.

(B) Committee may elect to accept the tendered delivery of 475 pens, but may not successfully sue for breach of contract if it does so.

(C) Committee may reject the tendered delivery of 475 pens, but may successfully sue only for the return of its advance payment if it does so.

(D) Committee may reject the tendered delivery of 475 pens, and may successfully sue for the return of its advance payment and for damages resulting from breach of contract if it does so.

49. Assume for the purpose of this question only that Committee eventually instituted an action against Penco for breach of contract. If only one of the following additional facts were true, which would furnish Penco with its most effective defense to that action?

(A) Penco was unable to obtain necessary materials from its suppliers in time for production of 500 pens by January 8.

(B) Committee failed to serve Penco with notice of its intention to sue before instituting the action.

(C) Only 400 conventioneers attended the convention.

(D) On December 18, Penco advised Committee that it would only be able to deliver 475 pens, and Committee orally agreed to

reduce the order to that number.

50. Ace, a construction contractor, was planning to submit a bid for the renovation of a county office building. Ace called Wire, a subcontractor who had done electrical work for Ace in the past, and described the proposed project. Ace told Wire about the electrical work that would be required, and asked Wire to state the price that Wire would charge to do the electrical work for Ace. Wire inspected the office building on which the work was to be performed, and spent six hours estimating the cost of the job. Wire mailed Ace a letter describing the work to be performed, and containing the following statement: "I will do the work described for a total price of $16,000. This price is not subject to change until one week after the county awards the contract." Wire subsequently purchased materials in anticipation of the job.

Ace submitted a bid for renovating the building, and was awarded the contract. Ace called Wire, offering to pay $12,000 for the electrical work. When Wire refused to accept anything less than $16,000, Ace hired Lectric to do the work instead of Wire.

If Wire sues Ace for the cost of the materials which Wire purchased in anticipation of the job, the court should find for

(A) Wire, if Ace relied on Wire's offer in bidding on the job.

(B) Wire, if the materials which Wire purchased will not otherwise be used in the ordinary course of Wire's business.

(C) Wire, if he purchased the materials in reliance on the belief that Ace would hire him upon receiving the contract from the county.

(D) Ace, because he had no agreement with Wire concerning the electrical work.

Questions 51-53 are based on the following fact situation.

On June 1, Briar, a licensed real estate broker, entered into a written contract with Ostend. According to the contract, Briar was given the exclusive right to sell Ostend's home at a price of $100,000 for a period of three months. Ostend agreed to pay Briar a seven percent commission "upon transfer of title." On July 1, as a result of Briar's efforts, First agreed to purchase Ostend's home at a price of $100,000. According to the terms of the contract, Ostend was to deliver evidence of clear title prior to July 20. At Ostend's request, an abstract company researched the chain of title and delivered an abstract to Ostend on July 15 showing clear title. Ostend did not deliver the abstract to First, however, because his neighbor was unhappy with the prospect of having First move into Ostend's home and asked Ostend to try to get out of the deal. On July 21, First notified Ostend that he would not go through with the transaction because of Ostend's failure to deliver the abstract of title as agreed.

On August 1, Ostend entered into a written contract with Second for the purchase and sale of Ostend's home at a price of $98,000, with title to close on December 1. Briar was unaware of the transaction, and did not participate in it. On November 1, Second informed Ostend that he was retiring because he had suffered a heart attack, and that due to the changes in his financial circumstances, he would not be going through with the deal.

51. Assume for the purpose of this question only that Briar sues Ostend for a seven percent commission based on Ostend's contract with First. Which of the following would be Briar's most effective argument in support of her claim?

    (A) Briar delivered a buyer "ready, willing and able" to purchase Ostend's property.

    (B) But for a willful breach by Ostend, First would have taken title to the realty.

    (C) Ostend and First entered into a contract for the sale of Ostend's realty as a result of Briar's efforts.

    (D) Ostend's refusal to deliver the abstract frustrated the purpose of the contract between Ostend and Briar.

52. Assume for the purpose of this question only that Briar sues Ostend for a seven percent commission based on Ostend's contract with Second. Which of the following would be Ostend's most effective argument in defense against Briar's claim?

    (A) The price which Second agreed to pay for the purchase of Ostend's home was $98,000.

    (B) Transfer of title was not to take place until after the three month period of Briar's exclusive right to sell.

    (C) As a result of Second's conduct, transfer of title never took place.

    (D) Briar did not participate in the formation of Ostend's contract with Second.

53. Assume for the purpose of this question that Ostend instituted an action against Second for breach of contract. Which of the following statements is most correct regarding the legal relationship between Ostend and Second?

    I.   Ostend is entitled to a judgment for damages resulting from Second's refusal to complete the transaction.

    II. Ostend is entitled to a judgment for specific performance, because every parcel of real estate is unique.

    III. Second is excused from performance because of impossibility.

    (A) I only.

    (B) II only.

    (C) I and II only.

    (D) III only.

54. Solder and Brandeis entered into a written contract for the sale of five hundred bicycles at a total price of $50,000. The contract required delivery by Solder prior to June 1, and payment by Brandeis within 30 days after delivery. On May 15, Solder delivered the bicycles to Brandeis, who received and accepted them. On May 21, because Solder was having cash-flow problems, he telephoned Brandeis asking whether

Brandeis could pay for the bicycles immediately. Brandeis said that he would pay by May 25 if Solder was willing to accept $45,000 in cash as payment in full. Solder agreed, but by June 20 Brandeis had made no payment at all. Solder subsequently instituted an action against Brandeis for $50,000. Brandeis admitted the existence of the contract, the delivery of the bicycles, and his non-payment; but asserted that he was liable for only $45,000 because of the agreement which he made with Solder on May 21.

Is Brandeis's assertion correct?

(A) No, because Brandeis did not pay $45,000 by May 25.

(B) No, because a promise to perform a pre-existing obligation is not valuable consideration.

(C) Yes, because there has been a valid novation.

(D) Yes, because there has been a valid agreement of accord.

55. Super was the owner of a grocery store. Because he wanted to expand his business, Super leased the vacant store which was adjacent to his own, planning to combine the two stores into one large supermarket. Super hired Fixer to do the work. On April 1, Super and Fixer entered into a written contract which required Fixer to remove the wall separating the two stores and to perform other specified work, with completion prior to June 1. A series of storms which began on April 3 and continued until April 28 made it impossible for Fixer to do any work on Super's premises during the month of April. On May 1, Fixer advised Super that because the weather had delayed commencement of the work, he would not be able to complete the job by June 1, and that he was, therefore, canceling the contract.

If Super sues Fixer for breach of contract, a court should find for

(A) Fixer, because the delay resulted from an act of God.

(B) Fixer, if on April 1 both knew that it fre-

quently stormed all during the month of April.

(C) Super, if on April 1 both parties knew that it frequently stormed all during the month of April.

(D) Super, only if the parties intended time to be of the essence in their contract of April 1.

Questions 56-57 are based on the following fact situation.

In hopes of improving his hardware store's image in the community and thus improving sales, Hardy advertised that he was running an essay contest. The subject was "The Role of Law in American Society." The contest was open only to persons who had been admitted to but had not yet begun attendance at any law school accredited by the state. The prize, to be called the "Hardy's Hardware Scholarship," was full payment of all law school tuition and registration fees for a period of three years. When Galen's essay won the contest, Hardy delivered to her a document which he had executed, and in which he agreed to make payments for tuition and fees directly to the law school for so long as Galen remained a student in good standing. When Galen showed the document to her mother Monte, Monte was so proud of Galen that she said, "If you successfully complete your first year, I'll buy all your books for the following two years. In addition, I'll give you $250 for every 'A' that you earn in your first year." Monte died while Galen was in her first year of law school, but Galen succeeded in earning two "A"s in her first year, and completed school in two additional years. Galen demanded that Monte's executrix pay her $250 for each of the two "A"s which she received in her first year, and pay for the books which she had purchased in her second and third year, but the executrix refused.

56. If Galen asserts a claim against the executrix for $500 for the two "A"s which she received in her first year of law school, will Galen's claim be successful?

(A) No, because she was already obligated to use her best efforts while in law school.

(B) No, if Monte died before Galen received the

"A" grades.

(C) Yes, if, prior to Monte's death, Galen made extra efforts in an attempt to earn "A"s.

(D) Yes, because Galen's essay won Hardy's contest.

57. If Galen asserts a claim against the executrix for the cost of the books which she purchased in her second and third year of law school, which of the following would be the executrix's most effective argument in defense against Galen's claim?

(A) The agreement between Monte and Galen was divisible.

(B) The agreement between Monte and Galen was not in writing.

(C) Monte's offer was for the payment of a cash bonus.

(D) Monte's promise was unsupported by consideration.

58. In a transaction involving the sale of a bicycle, which of the following persons is NOT a merchant under the Uniform Commercial Code?

(A) The owner of a bicycle store who sells her own personal bicycle after using it for 14 months by placing an advertisement under the heading "Used Merchandise" in the classified section of the newspaper.

(B) The owner of an automobile dealership who buys a bicycle for use by employees of the dealership's parts department in making deliveries.

(C) A bicycle mechanic who buys a new bicycle from a retail store to give as a gift to his nephew.

(D) The owner of a messenger service who employs a full time bicycle mechanic to maintain bicycles used in her business, and who sends the mechanic to inspect a new bicycle before buying it for use by messengers in her employ.

59. Overlook Corporation was the owner and operator of the Overlook Hotel, a summer resort located at a high elevation in the northern part of the country. Because the hotel was only open during the summer, Overlook usually employed a single resident caretaker to live and work at the hotel during the winter months. On August 1, after applying for the job of winter caretaker, Carson entered into a valid written contract with overlook. According to its terms, Carson was to take up residence at the Overlook Hotel on October 1, and to remain in residence until the following April 1, at which time Overlook Corporation was to pay him ten thousand dollars. During Carson's period of residence, he was to receive free room and board, and to perform certain maintenance tasks. On August 15, Carson enlisted in the U.S. Navy, his period of service to begin on September 25 and to continue for three years. Mention of Carson's enlistment appeared in the "Hometown Gossip" section of a local newspaper, and was seen by executives of Overlook Corporation. Overlook immediately began seeking another winter caretaker, and hired Newt on September 15, entering into a valid written contract with him on that date which contained terms identical to those in the contract with Carson.

On September 20, Carson failed the physical examination performed by Navy physicians and was rejected for naval service. Carson reported for work at the Overlook Hotel on October 1, but was advised that his services were not required.

If Carson asserts a claim against Overlook for damages resulting from breach of contract, the court should find for

(A) Carson, since he was ready, willing, and able to perform as agreed on October 1.

(B) Carson, since he never informed Overlook that he would not be reporting to work as agreed.

(C) Overlook, since Carson's enlistment was an anticipatory repudiation of his contract with Overlook.

(D) Overlook, since Overlook hired Newt in reliance on the reasonable belief that Carson would be unable to perform as agreed.

60. On May 1, Ogden hired Sheldon to reshingle the roof of his house at an agreed price of $5,000 to be paid within ten days after completion, and with all work to be completed by July 1. Sheldon began work on May 2 and worked diligently until May 15. At that time, Sheldon had performed services which were worth $1,500 and which increased the value of Ogden's house by $1,500. On May 16, through no fault of either party, the house caught fire and was totally destroyed. Although the proceeds which Ogden received from his fire insurance policy were sufficient to cover the cost of building a new house, Ogden decided to sell the property instead. Sheldon demanded payment under the contract, but Ogden refused to pay.

If Sheldon asserts a claim for payment against Ogden, a court should award judgment to Sheldon in the sum of

(A) $5,000, since it was the price on which Sheldon and Ogden agreed.

(B) $1,500, since it was the value of Sheldon's work.

(C) $0, since Ogden derived no benefit from Sheldon's work.

(D) $5,000, because Ogden could have rebuilt the house with the proceeds from the fire insurance policy.

Questions 61-62 are based on the following fact situation.

Whiz mastered the basics of computer programming by the time he was twelve years old. At the age of 14 he designed a program for a video-computer game which he called "Stump the Hump." He demonstrated the program to Disco, a company in the business of marketing computer software. Disco executives were so impressed by the program designed by Whiz that they hired him as a game program consultant at a salary of $30,000 per year. In addition, they offered to purchase marketing rights to "Stump the Hump" by a separate contract. According to the terms of the contract which

they offered, Disco would have the exclusive rights to copy and market the program for "Stump the Hump" and would pay Whiz 30 percent of all revenues derived from the exercise of those rights. After consulting with his parents and their attorney, Whiz accepted Disco's offer and signed the contract. Three months later, before Disco had begun marketing Whiz's game program, Whiz needed cash to purchase expensive computer equipment. For a large cash payment, he assigned his rights under the contract to Adso. Adso intended to inform Disco of the assignment, but neglected to do so. One month later, Whiz assigned the same rights to Basile as security for a credit purchase of additional computer equipment. Basile was unaware of the assignment to Adso, and never notified Disco that Whiz had assigned the rights to Basile. Two months later, Disco began marketing "Stump the Hump," realizing high profits from its sale. Although Whiz has demanded payment pursuant to the terms of his contract, Disco has refused to make any payments.

61. If Whiz commences an action against Disco for royalties equivalent to 30 percent of the revenues generated by the sale of "Stump the Hump," which of the following would be Disco's most effective argument in defense?

(A) Whiz was a minor at the time he contracted with Disco.

(B) Whiz has made at least one effective assignment of the contract rights.

(C) Neither Adso nor Basile notified Disco about the assignment from Whiz.

(D) An assignment of wages is invalid.

62. Assume for the purpose of this question only that after Whiz commenced the lawsuit, Disco offered to pay Whiz $50,000 for all rights to "Stump the Hump" if Whiz would consent to a mutual rescission of the contract, and that Whiz accepted the offer and received a payment of $50,000. If Adso subsequently institutes an action against Disco for a sum equivalent to 30 percent of the revenues derived from the sale of "Stump the Hump," the court should find for

(A) Disco, because the rights under which Adso

is claiming were subsequently assigned to Basile.

(B) Disco, because Disco was unaware of the assignment to Adso at the time it paid $50,000 to Whiz.

(C) Disco, because the right which Whiz purported to assign to Adso was neither identified nor existing at the time of the purported assignment.

(D) Adso, because he gave value for the right which Whiz assigned to him.

Questions 63-65 are based on the following fact situation.

Mollie and her sister Tia lived together in Mollie's house in the town of Wildwood. On March 1, Mollie called her daughter Susan on the telephone and said that she was beginning to have premonitions of her own death. Mollie said that she was willing to deed her home to Susan while she was alive rather than put Susan through probate expenses. Mollie said, however, that she would only do so if Susan agreed to permit Tia to stay in the house for the rest of her life, and to permit Susan's brother Bob, who resided in another state, to live in the house for as long as he wanted if he should ever decide to come to Wildwood. Susan promised to do so, and on March 15, Mollie deeded the home to her as agreed. At the time, the home had a value of $100,000. Susan called Bob on March 10, and told him that Mollie had deeded her the house but did not tell him about her promise to allow Bob to live there. On March 15, Tia wrote Bob:

"I don't think that either your mother or I have much longer to live, and we both miss you terribly. If you agree to come and live here in Wildwood for as long as either of us lives, I will leave you my entire estate.

Love,
(signed) Aunt Tia."

On March 17, Bob called Susan and told her about the note which he had received from Tia. He said that he was thinking of moving to Wildwood, and that if Susan promised to allow him to live in the house which Mollie had deeded to her until Tia died, he would give her

fifty percent of the inheritance. Susan agreed, and Bob immediately wrote to Tia, telling her that he was moving to Wildwood in response to her offer. Tia received Bob's letter on March 20. Bob made arrangements to move to Wildwood, and did so, at an expense of $800. Both Mollie and Tia died on March 22, but Bob did not learn of their deaths until he arrived in Wildwood on March 24. At that time, Susan refused to allow him to move into the house.

63. Assume for the purpose of this question only that Bob instituted an action against Susan for damages resulting from her refusal to allow him to move into the house, and that the only defense asserted by Susan was that her promises were not in writing. Which of the following would be Susan's most effective argument in support of her position?

(A) Her promises to Mollie and Bob were promises to create an interest in land.

(B) It was possible that the promise which she made to Mollie and Bob would not be performed within a year.

(C) The house had a value in excess of $500.

(D) She received no consideration from Bob for either promise.

64. Assume for the purpose of this question only that Tia's will left her entire estate to Bob, and that Bob refused to share any portion of it with Susan. If Susan asserts a claim against Bob for a share of the inheritance which he received from Tia, a court should find for

(A) Susan, because Bob is estopped from denying the existence of an enforceable contract between him and Susan.

(B) Susan, because Bob promised to share the inheritance with her if she promised to allow him to live in the house until Tia's death.

(C) Bob, because Susan's promise to Mollie created an implied condition precedent to Bob's obligation to share the inheritance with Susan.

(D) Bob, because Bob's promise to Susan was not supported by consideration.

65. Assume for the purpose of this question only that Tia's will left her entire estate to Bob, and that Bob refused to share any portion of it with Susan. If there was an enforceable agreement between Bob and Tia, Susan is most correctly described as an

(A) intended creditor beneficiary of that agreement.

(B) intended donee beneficiary of that agreement.

(C) incidental beneficiary of that agreement.

(D) assignee of 50 percent of whatever rights Bob has under that agreement.

66. Landing owned a parcel of realty which he bought with the intention of building a home, but which he decided to sell instead. On March 10, Vestor, who frequently invested in land, contracted with Landing for the purchase of Landing's realty at a price of $400,000. The state highway department had previously voted to construct an eight lane highway near Landing's realty, as a result of which the value of Landing's property had increased from $400,000 to $4,000,000. Landing was unaware of this on March 10, because the highway department had not yet made its decision public. On March 11, the highway department's plan to construct a highway was announced. When Landing learned of this, he sought rescission of the contract.

Is Landing entitled to rescission of the contract?

(A) Yes, but only if Landing and Vestor were both mistaken about the value of the property at the time that they contracted for its sale.

(B) Yes, if Vestor was aware that the realty was worth substantially more than the contract price at the time that they contracted for its sale.

(C) No, unless the reasonable person in Vestor's position would have been aware that the

realty was worth substantially more than the contract price at the time that they contracted for its sale.

(D) No, because the appropriate remedy is reformation of the contract.

67. Short, a manufacturer of widgets, entered into a valid written contract which called for the sale of 2,000 widgets to Bateman at a price of ten dollars per widget. Several weeks prior to the date set for delivery, Short telephoned Bateman and advised her that because of difficulty in locating a sufficient supply of frammis rods, Short would be unable to deliver more than 1,000 widgets. After discussion, Bateman agreed to accept 1,000 widgets at ten dollars per widget instead of 2,000 as originally agreed. After Short delivered 1,000 widgets, however, Bateman brought an action against him for damages resulting from breach of contract. In adjudicating Bateman's claim, the court should find for

(A) Bateman, because her agreement to accept 1,000 widgets was not in writing.

(B) Bateman, because her promise to accept 1,000 widgets was not supported by consideration.

(C) Short, because Bateman agreed to accept 1,000 widgets.

(D) Short, because there has been an accord and satisfaction.

Questions 68-72 are based on the following fact situation.

Andrews and Bloch were neighbors in a recently created subdivision. Since both wanted to have landscaping work done, they decided to join forces in hopes of getting a better price. They hired Scaper to plant grass and shrubs in their yards, directing him to bill each of them for the labor and materials attributable to his separate realty. After Scaper completed the work, he submitted his bills to Andrews and Bloch, who paid them immediately. The following week, however, Andrews concluded that Scaper had erroneously billed him for some work done on Bloch's land. He showed his calculations to Bloch, asking that Bloch reimburse him for the amounts which he claimed to have paid on Bloch's account. Bloch was certain that Andrews was incorrect, but because he did not want to come to bad terms with his new neighbor, he offered to hire a gardener to keep Andrews's lawn mowed and trimmed for the next two years. Andrews agreed to accept the offered services in lieu of payment.

Bloch hired Mauer to maintain his lawn and Andrews's lawn for the next two years, agreeing to pay him $50 per month for certain specified services. Bloch and Mauer signed a memorandum of agreement, and Bloch gave a photocopy of it to Andrews. Two months later, Bloch sold his house to Purtle. At the closing of title, Bloch handed Purtle the original memorandum of his agreement with Mauer and executed an assignment to Purtle of his rights thereunder. Mauer continued rendering services as agreed for an additional six months, receiving a check for $50 from Purtle each month. Then, Mauer notified Andrews and Purtle that he would no longer be able to work on their lawns. Andrews wrote to Bloch and Purtle demanding that they make arrangements to have his lawn maintained for the remaining 16 months pursuant to his agreement with Bloch, but neither responded.

68. Assume for the purpose of this question only that Bloch sues Mauer for breaching their agreement regarding maintenance of the lawns. Which one of the following facts or inferences, if it were the only one true, would furnish Mauer's most effective argument in defense against Bloch's claim?

(A) There are equally competent gardening services in the area which, for $50 per month, would perform work comparable to that which Mauer agreed to perform.

(B) The value of labor and materials used in lawn maintenance has increased dramatically since the signing of the memo.

(C) The agreement between Andrews and Bloch was oral.

(D) Mauer's inability to work on the lawns was the result of a serious heart attack which led his doctors to advise him against ever working again.

69. Assume for the purpose of this question only that Purtle sues Mauer for breaching the agreement contained in the memorandum. The court should find for

(A) Mauer, unless the payment by Purtle resulted in a novation.

(B) Mauer, because his only agreement was with Bloch.

(C) Mauer, if no consideration flowed from Purtle to Bloch in exchange for the memorandum.

(D) Purtle, as assignee of the agreement between Mauer and Bloch.

70. Assume for the purpose of this question only that Andrews sues Mauer for breaching the agreement contained in the memorandum. The court should find for

(A) Andrews, because Andrews is a creditor third party beneficiary of the contract between Mauer and Bloch.

(B) Andrews, because Andrews is a donee third-party beneficiary of the contract between Mauer and Bloch.

(C) Mauer, because Andrews is only an incidental third- party beneficiary of the contract between Mauer and Bloch.

(D) Mauer because there was no privity between Mauer and Andrews.

71. Assume for the purpose of this question only that after Mauer notified him that he would no longer perform services, Andrews hired a gardener to continue performing the same services on Andrews's lawn for a fee of $25 per month. If Andrews sues Purtle for $400 ($25 per month for the 16 months remaining in the term), the court should find for

(A) Andrews, because Purtle's monthly payments to Mauer resulted in an estoppel-type waiver of his rights to deny liability.

(B) Andrews, because Bloch's promise to provide lawn maintenance services touches and concerns the land.

(C) Purtle, because he did not agree to pay for the maintenance of Andrews's lawn.

(D) Purtle, because the price of $25 per month to maintain Andrews's lawn was equal to one-half the price which Mauer charged for maintaining both lawns.

72. If Andrews sues Bloch for damages resulting from Mauer's failure to provide services, the court should find for

(A) Andrews, only if he is unable to collect from Purtle or Mauer.

(B) Andrews, if Andrews sincerely believed that Bloch owed him money at the time when Bloch promised to pay for lawn maintenance.

(C) Bloch, if in fact there had been no error in Scaper's bill.

(D) Bloch, because his obligation was intended to be conditioned upon continued occupancy by Bloch of the realty.

73. In response to an advertisement which he saw in the newspaper, Huner telephoned Screner and asked him to come to Huner's home to estimate the cost of providing and installing new aluminum screens for all of Huner's window's. After taking measurements, Screner returned to his shop and prepared a written estimate, in which he said that he would do the entire job for $350. When Huner received Screner's written estimate, he wrote across it with a red felt-tipped pen, "I'll pay $300, but not a penny more," and mailed it to Screner. When Screner received the estimate with Huner's statement written on it, he wrote on the estimate, "I'll do it for $325." He sent the estimate back to Huner on September 5, but on September 12, having received no response, he sent Huner a note which said, "All right, you win. I'll do the job for $300. Unless I hear from you to the contrary, I'll be there with the new screens on September 28. Signed, Screner."

Huner received the note on September 14, but made no response. On September 28, without Huner's knowledge and while Huner was at work, Screner went to Huner's home and installed new aluminum window screens.

Which of the following best characterizes the legal relationship between Huner and Screner AFTER installation of the window screens on September 28?

(A) A contract was formed when Huner failed to respond to Screner's letter of September 12 within a reasonable time after he received it.

(B) A contract was formed when Screner began to install the screens on September 28.

(C) A quasi contract was formed when Screner finished installing the screens on September 28, obligating Huner to pay a price equivalent to their reasonable value.

(D) No contractual relationship existed between Huner and Screner.

Questions 74-76 are based on the following fact situation.

When Odyk purchased her home, she obtained a policy of fire insurance from Grail Mutual Insurance Company. The policy provided that if the home was destroyed or seriously damaged by fire, Grail would pay "living expenses necessitated by the loss" until Odyk's house was rebuilt or she acquired another house, but in no event for a period in excess of ninety days. The policy stated that since it was often impracticable to distinguish between normal living expenses and those necessitated by fire-loss, Grail's liability for "living expenses necessitated by the loss" was fixed at $50 per day.

Subsequently Odyk's home was seriously damaged by fire. Odyk moved into a hotel, and entered into a written contract with Recon for repairs to her home. The contract required payment in advance by Odyk and completion of repairs by Recon within sixty days. One of its clauses provided that if Recon failed to complete the job on time, Recon would pay Odyk the sum of $50 per day as liquidated damages.

It took Recon seventy days to complete the job. At the end of that period, Odyk moved back into the house. She furnished Grail with the necessary proof of loss forms, and demanded that Grail pay her $3,500 (70 days at $50 per day). She also sent Recon a notice demanding payment of $500 (10 days at $50 per day) as liquidated damages. Recon refused to pay, asserting that the liquidated damages clause was invalid.

74. Was the liquidated damages clause in the contract between Odyk and Recon valid?

    (A) Yes, if Recon's late performance actually resulted in losses to Odyk which reasonably approximated $50 per day.

    (B) Yes, if at the time Odyk and Recon contracted it reasonably appeared that Odyk would sustain approximately $50 per day in damages in the event of late performance by Recon.

    (C) No, if Odyk was entitled to receive $50 per day from Grail for the same ten days.

    (D) No, if Recon's failure to complete the job on time was reasonable and not caused by any fault of Recon.

75. Assume for the purpose of this question only that Grail paid Odyk $3,000 (60 days at $50 per day), but refused to pay the additional $500 for the ten day period caused by Recon's late performance. If Odyk sues Grail for $500, the court should find for

    (A) Odyk, because Grail agreed to pay $50 per day until Odyk's house was reconstructed.

    (B) Odyk, only if she can establish that her "living expenses necessitated by the loss" exceeded whatever amount she was entitled to receive from Recon.

    (C) Grail, unless at the time the fire insurance policy was issued to Odyk it reasonably appeared that Odyk would expend approximately $50 per day in "living expenses necessitated by the loss" in the event of fire damage to her home.

    (D) Grail, because Odyk is estopped by the liquidated damages clause in her contract with Recon from asserting that her "living expenses necessitated by the loss" exceeded $50 per day.

76. Assume for the purpose of this question only that after Odyk moved back into the house, she discovered that Recon had failed to repair the roof as agreed, and that she hired Shingel to do so at an additional expense of $250, which was the reasonable value of Shingel's services. Assume also for the purpose of this question only that the liquidated damage clause in the contract between Odyk and Recon is held to be valid. If Odyk institutes an action against Recon for the $250 which she paid Shingel, the court should find for

    (A) Odyk, because the additional expense of $250 resulted from Recon's breach.

    (B) Odyk, only if Odyk notified Recon of Recon's failure to repair the roof as agreed, and offered Recon an opportunity to do so prior to hiring Shingel.

    (C) Recon, if Grail compensated Odyk for the additional expense resulting from her hiring Shingel to repair the roof.

    (D) Recon, because the liquidated damages clause took the place of all remedies which would otherwise have been available to Odyk.

77. Hostel Corporation was seeking a contractor to build a hotel on realty which it acquired near the seashore. Hostel sent copies of its plans to several builders with whom it had done business in the past and asked them to submit bids for construction of the building. Coast Construction, one of the builders, assigned an employee, Edwards, to prepare an estimate of the job. Although Hostel's plans called for construction of a twenty-seven story building, Edwards mistakenly believed that the building was to be seven stories. He estimated the costs accordingly and submitted the estimate to Coast, the owner of the company. Based on Edwards's figures, Coast prepared and mailed to Hostel a letter offering to build for $1,000,000

according to Hostel's plans and setting forth all other necessary terms. Hostel had already received four other bids on the job, each for a figure far in excess of $1,000,000. Upon receiving Coast's bid, Hostel immediately telegraphed Coast, "We accept your offer to build according to the plans which we sent you. Entire job to be completed for one million dollars. Hostel." Before Coast began construction, he learned that Hostel's building was to be 27 stories, and that Edwards had calculated in the mistaken belief that it was to be seven stories. Coast wrote to Hostel asking for renegotiation of the contract, but Hostel indicated its intent to hold Coast to his original offer. Coast advised Hostel that he regarded the contract as a nullity and would not perform according to its terms.

In an action by Hostel against Coast for breach of contract, the court should find for

(A) Hostel, if Coast's mistake was the result of negligence by Coast's employee.

(B) Hostel, because Coast's mistake was unilateral.

(C) Coast, because it would be unfair to require Coast to complete construction at the contract price.

(D) Coast, if the reasonable person in Hostel's position would have known that Coast's bid was the result of a mistake.

Questions 78-79 are based on the following fact situation.

Ray, the son of a poor family, grew up on his family's small farm just outside the town of Rural. Despite the handicaps of poverty and lack of education, Ray eventually became the world's heavyweight boxing champion. Proud of Ray's accomplishments, the Rural town Council voted to erect a statue commemorating Ray's victory over his social and economic disadvantages. Pursuant to town ordinances and regulations, bids were accepted from several sculptors, including Chisel. Because Chisel's work was relatively unknown, she attempted to make her bid more attractive to the Council by including a guarantee that her work would be satisfactory. On February 1, the town council entered into

a written contract with Chisel, hiring her to create the statue and agreeing to pay her $5,000 upon its installation on the steps of the town hall on or before June 30. A clause in the contract provided, "It is expressly understood that the personal satisfaction of the mayor of Rural is a condition precedent to the Council's obligation to make payment hereunder. Upon completion of the statue, it shall be made available for inspection by said mayor. If said mayor is unsatisfied with the work, he shall notify Chisel immediately, and the contract shall be canceled without liability of any party."

Chisel sculpted a likeness of Ray in farmer's overalls with his hands in boxing gloves clasped victoriously over his head, which she completed on June 10. Ray had been arrested in another state on May 30, however, and charged with possession of a dangerous drug. His trial was scheduled for September 10. The town council was fearful that Ray would be convicted and that the statue would embarrass the town.

78. Assume for the purpose of this question only that the mayor went to Chisel's studio on June 11 after receiving notice that the statue was ready for inspection. When he arrived, the statue was covered with a canvas tarpaulin. Before Chisel could remove the cover, the mayor said, "It's too small. The deal is off." Chisel subsequently demanded that the town council pay for the statue, but the Council refused. In an action by Chisel against the town council, the court should find for

(A) Chisel, if the reasonable person would have found Chisel's work to be satisfactory.

(B) Chisel, because the mayor was fearful that the statue would embarrass the town if Ray was convicted.

(C) the town council, because the contract gave the mayor the absolute right to reject Chisel's finished work.

(D) the town council, if the mayor actually believed that the statue was too small.

79. Assume for the purpose of this question only that when Chisel finished the statue, an art collector offered to purchase it from her. Fearful that Ray's pending trial would induce the mayor to reject

her statue, Chisel immediately accepted the offer, notifying the town council on June 10 that she would not be submitting a statue for the mayor's approval. In an action by the town council against Chisel, the court should find for

(A) the town council, because Chisel has committed an anticipatory breach.

(B) the town council, only if the statue which Chisel created would have met with the mayor's satisfaction.

(C) Chisel, unless the price which she received from the art collector exceeded $5,000.

(D) Chisel, because the town council's promise under the contract was illusory.

80. On June 1, Sailor was arraigned on a charge of petty larceny. He pleaded not guilty, and told the judge that he was planning to enlist in the U.S. Navy. The judge set July 9 as the date for trial, but told Sailor that she would dismiss the charge if Sailor was accepted into the Navy before then. On June 2, Sailor said to Brady, "I will sell you my motorcycle for $450 cash." Brady said, "I'll need a week to raise the money, but I'll give you $50 now if you promise to hold the offer open until June 10. Then if I buy I'll pay you an additional $400, and if I don't buy you can keep the $50." Sailor agreed to the terms and accepted his check for $50.

On June 5, Sailor's lawyer told him that it was unlikely that Sailor would be convicted on the charge of petty larceny. Upon hearing this, Sailor decided not to enlist in the Navy, and not to sell his motorcycle to Brady for $450. He sent Brady a money order in the sum of $50 with a note stating that he had already sold the motorcycle to someone else. On June 8, Brady went to Sailor's house and handed Sailor the uncashed money order together with $400 in cash, demanding that Sailor sign the motorcycle over to him. Sailor refused.

In an action by Brady against Sailor for breach of contract, Brady will probably

(A) win, because he paid Sailor $50 to keep the

offer open until June 10.

(B) win, unless Sailor had actually sold the motorcycle to someone else.

(C) lose, unless Sailor is found to be a merchant with respect to the sale of the motorcycle.

(D) lose, because the option contract was not in writing.

Questions 81-82 are based on the following fact situation.

By a written contract, Helth, the operator of a natural foods store, agreed to purchase 200 pounds of grade A large gobbus nuts from Gro at a specified price. A term of the contract provided that "payment shall be due immediately on delivery and prior to inspection of the shipment." When a box containing the nuts was delivered, Helth paid the agreed price without inspecting its contents. One hour later, Helth opened the box and discovered that it contained grade A small gobbus nuts instead of grade A large gobbus nuts. When Helth telephoned Gro to ask that Gro exchange the small nuts for large ones, Gro refused. Helth repackaged the nuts and returned them to Gro. Subsequently, Helth asserted a claim against Gro for breach of contract.

81. In considering the contract provision which required payment prior to inspection, a court is most likely to hold that

(A) it is unconscionable, and therefore not subject to enforcement.

(B) it constitutes a waiver of the buyer's right to inspect prior to acceptance.

(C) it does not impair the buyer's right to inspect prior to acceptance.

(D) it was not enforceable when the contract was made, but since Helth did pay before inspecting the goods, he waived his right to a pre-acceptance inspection.

82. If Helth succeeds in an action against Gro for breach of contract, a court is most likely to

(A) issue an order directing Gro to deliver 200

pounds of "grade A large" Gobbus nuts as required by the contract.

(B) award damages consisting of the difference between the value of "grade A large" gobbus nuts and "grade A small" gobbus nuts.

(C) award damages consisting of the purchase price plus the difference between the contract price and the market price for "grade A large" gobbus nuts.

(D) require Gro to return the price which Helth paid.

Questions 83-85 are based on the following fact situation.

Bertrand and Sylvester were members of the graduating class of Tate College. Bertrand, who was planning to go to law school, told sylvester that he might be needing some law books. Sylvester had recently inherited a law library, so he compiled a list of the books in the collection, and mailed it to Bertrand on July 5 with a note that said, "Interested in buying?" Bertrand wrote the following letter on a copy of the booklist and mailed it to Sylvester on Tuesday, July 8:

Dear Sylvester,

I will buy your law library consisting of the books on this list for $2,600 cash if you deliver the books to my home by the time I start law school in mid-September. I promise to hold this offer open until September 1.

Yours Truly,

[signed] Bertrand

Sylvester received the letter on Wednesday, July 9, and immediately responded by writing, "I accept your offer to buy my library, and will deliver it to you as you require." He signed the letter and mailed it properly addressed to Bertrand, but due to a fire in the post office it was never delivered. On August 1, Bertrand decided that he did not want to go to law school after all, and wrote Sylvester a note telling him that he was no longer interested in buying the lawbooks. He was about to go to the post office to mail it, when Sylvester knocked at his door. As soon as Bertrand opened the door Sylvester said, "I'll bring you those law books

tomorrow. I'll just have to borrow a friend's station wagon to transport them." Bertrand said, "Never mind. I don't want them," and handed Sylvester the note which he had written but not mailed.

83. In Bertrand's letter of July 8, what was the legal effect of the statement, "I promise to hold this offer open until September 1"?

(A) The language did not prevent Bertrand from revoking the offer.

(B) At common law, the language creates an irrevocable option in Sylvester's favor.

(C) Under the Uniform Commercial Code, Bertrand was prevented from revoking the offer until September 1.

(D) The language created an option in favor of Sylvester, subject to the condition that Bertrand actually begin law school.

84. If Sylvester instituted an action against Bertrand for breach of contract, which of the following statements is most correct about Sylvester's letter of July 9?

(A) It bound both parties to a unilateral contact when it was mailed.

(B) It formed a bilateral contact when mailed, because Bertrand chose the mail as the medium of communication.

(C) The letter would have constituted an acceptance if it had been received, but because it was not received, no contract was formed.

(D) Sylvester's mailing of the letter did not prevent Bertrand from withdrawing his offer.

85. Sylvester's statement on August 1 that, "I'll be bringing you those law books tomorrow" was probably

(A) an offer.

(B) a ratification of the acceptance which was mailed on July 9 but was never delivered to Bertrand.

(C) an acceptance.

(D) commencement of performance.

86. Which of the following is most likely to be regarded as valid consideration for Brown's oral promise to pay Green $1,000?

(A) The fact that Green had saved Brown's house from a fire the day before Brown's promise was made.

(B) The fact that at the same time Brown made the promise to pay, Green promised to deliver to Brown fire-fighting equipment valued at $1,000.

(C) The fact that after Brown made the promise, Green relied upon it by committing himself to the purchase of fire-fighting equipment at a price of $1,000.

(D) The fact that immediately after Brown made the promise, Green sent Brown a written memorandum of their agreement, to which Brown did not object within thirty days.

87. Bott was the owner of a large yacht which he usually kept moored in Shimmering Bay. On August 15, Fixer agreed to repair Bott's yacht for a fee of $2,000, and to have all work completed by November 1. Because of the yacht's size, it would have been impractical to take it out of the water for repairs, and it was understood that all work would have to be performed while the boat was moored in the bay. There were heavy storms all during the month of October, however, and the waters of the bay were too choppy to permit any work on the yacht. As a result, on October 28, Fixer notified Bott that he would be unable to complete repairs by November 1.

If Bott asserts a claim against Fixer for damages resulting from breach of contract, the court should find for

(A) Fixer, if Fixer's prior commitments made it impossible for him to work on Bott's yacht at any time other than during the month of October.

(B) Fixer, if Bott's prior commitments made it impossible for Bott to use the yacht until the following March.

(C) Bott, if Shimmering Bay was frequently subject to storm conditions and choppy waters in the month of October.

(D) Bott, if Fixer could have completed the work in time by removing the yacht from the water during the month of October.

88. After the commercial success of a rock music group called Porta-Potti, its lead singer, Rocker, entered into a contract with the Groovy Record Company. According to its terms, Rocker, singing alone, was to record a song for Groovy. Groovy was to pay Rocker two thousand dollars thirty days after the record was made, whether or not it was ever commercially released. If the record was released, Rocker was to receive additional compensation depending on the number of copies of the record which were sold.

Rocker made the record required by the contract on March 1. On March 15, Rocker bought a piano from Keys, promising to pay for it when he received payment from Groovy. As security for his promise, Rocker assigned to Keys his right to collect the two thousand dollars which Groovy owed him for making the record. Keys immediately notified Groovy of the assignment. On April 1, Rocker purported to assign the same right to his landlord to induce him to refrain from instituting eviction proceedings based on nonpayment of rent. The landlord immediately notified Groovy of the assignment. On April 20, Rocker sued Groovy for non-payment of the two thousand dollars.

Which of the following additional facts or inferences, if it were the only true, would be most likely to result in a judgment for Groovy?

(A) Rocker was an infant at the time of all of the transactions described above.

(B) Rocker made at least one effective assignment of the right to collect the two thousand dollars.

(C) Rocker's performance at the March 1 recording session was so bad that the record can never be commercially released.

(D) A statute in the jurisdiction prohibited the assignment of future wages by employees.

89. In an agreement made on April 15, Carver agreed to design a coat of arms for Houser and to fabricate a wooden door with the coat of arms carved into it for the front of Houser's home. Houser agreed to pay $650 for the door, but it was understood that if Houser was not completely satisfied with the coat of arms and the door, he would be under no obligation to go through with the deal. Before Carver completed the door, Houser came to the conclusion that he did not really want a coat of arms. When Carver brought the finished door to Houser, Houser took a quick glance at it. Although the coat of arms was properly designed and carved, and although the door had been fabricated in a workmanlike manner, Houser said, "I just don't like it," and refused to accept it.

In an action by Carver against Houser, which of the following would be Houser's best defense?

(A) The agreement was not in writing as required by the Statute of Frauds.

(B) The agreement was an offer for a unilateral contract which Houser rejected by refusing to accept the finished door.

(C) Houser's subjective satisfaction was a condition precedent to his obligation to accept the door.

(D) Since the coat of arms was not yet associated with Houser, it was possible for Carver to find another buyer for it.

90. After they inspected Samson's subdivision together, Brewer and Samson signed an agreement under which Brewer was to buy one of the lots in the subdivision from Samson. The agreement made no mention of purchase price, but contained reference to all the other terms necessary to make the contract enforceable. Samson refused to go through with the sale, and Brewer instituted an action against him for specific per-

formance. At the trial, Brewer offered the testimony of eyewitnesses who were present when the agreement was signed and who heard Samson and Brewer orally agree on a price of $50,000 for the lot. Samson asserted a defense based on the Statute of Frauds.

The court should find for

(A) Samson, unless Brewer can prove that the reasonable market value of the lot was $50,000 at the time the agreement was made.

(B) Samson, because the price agreed upon is an essential part of the contract, and must be specified in a writing signed by the party to be charged.

(C) Brewer, because in a contract for sale, the only term which the Statute of Frauds requires to be included is the quantity.

(D) Brewer, if the testimony of the witness does not contradict any term of the writing.

Questions 91-92 are based on the following fact situation.

When Carter's employer prepared to transfer him to its plant located in Twin Oaks, Carter contracted with Hammond for the purchase of Hammond's home located in Twin Oaks. According to the contract, title was to close and the home was to be vacant and ready for occupancy by Carter no later than April 20. Because Carter was arranging to move his family to Twin Oaks on April 20, at Carter's insistence the contract contained a liquidated damages clause. The clause provided that if the house was not ready for occupancy on April 20, Hammond would pay Carter seventy-five dollars for each day thereafter that it remained unavailable for occupancy. When Carter and his family moved to Twin Oaks on April 20, the home was not ready for occupancy. As a result, Carter and his family had to stay at a motel. On May 1, Hammond advised Carter that he did not intend to go through with the sale of this house. On May 10, Carter instituted an action against Hammond for specific performance and damages.

91. With respect to Carter's demand for specific performance, a court

    (A) may find for Carter, whether or not the liquidated damages clause is held to be enforceable.

    (B) may find for Carter, but only if the liquidation damages clause is held to be unenforceable.

    (C) may find for Carter, but only if the liquidation damages clause is held to be enforceable.

    (D) must find for Hammond.

92. With respect to Carter's demand for damages pursuant to the contract's liquidated damages clause, the court's finding will turn on whether

    (A) the motel at which Carter stayed charged a rate which was commercially reasonable.

    (B) Carter could have avoided staying at a motel by making a reasonable attempt to mitigate damages.

    (C) at the time the contract was formed, the sum of seventy-five dollars a day was reasonably related to what the parties believed Carter's living expenses would be.

    (D) Carter's purpose in insisting on a liquidation damages clause was to encourage Hammond to vacate the premises on time.

93. On June 11, Homer asked Brush, a local handyman, whether Brush would be interested in painting Homer's house. Following their conversation, they entered into the following handwritten agreement, which they wrote on the back of an old envelope and which both signed:

    "Homer and Brush hereby agree that Brush will paint the outside of Homer's house for seven hundred dollars as follows: wood trim brown; doors and window frames green; siding yellow (two coats)."

    Brush painted the siding yellow and gave it two coats of paint. He painted the wood trim brown and the doors and window frames green, but gave them only one coat of paint. Homer refused to pay unless Brush gave the wood trim, doors, and window frames a second coat. Brush instituted an action against Homer for seven hundred dollars. At the trial, Homer attempted to testify that prior to executing the agreement, he and Brush agreed orally that Brush would apply two coats of paint to the wood trim, doors, and window frames, as well as to the siding.

    The trial judge should rule Homer's testimony

    (A) admissible only for the purpose of establishing that the phrase "(two coats)" is ambiguous.

    (B) admissible for the purpose of establishing that the phrase "(two coats)" is ambiguous, and for the additional purpose of explaining the ambiguity.

    (C) inadmissible unless the agreement was written by Brush.

    (D) inadmissible since the writing was a complete expression of the agreement of the parties.

Questions 94-96 are based on the following fact situation.

Wand, who had been studying the writings of various mystical philosophers, decided to sell all his worldly possessions, give the money to charity, and wander about in the desert for a while to seek insight and spiritual fulfillment. After about a month in the desert, Wand became ill and collapsed into unconsciousness. When he woke, he was in the home of Doc, a retired surgeon who now lived like a hermit on the desert, and who had found him in a helpless condition. As Doc fed soup to Wand, Wand said, "I have no money. I can never pay you for any of this." Doc replied, "I'm not doing this for money."

In the next week, Doc fed Wand and gave him medical treatment. When Wand was well enough to travel, Doc borrowed an old pickup truck from a distant neighbor and drove Wand to the house of Wand's mother, Maggie. The following week, after Wand told Maggie what Doc did for him, Maggie wrote Doc: "In gratitude for the services which you rendered my son, I hereby promise to pay you $350.00 when I get my dividend check next month." Before the dividend check arrived, however, both Maggie and Doc died. Ad, Doc's administrator, advised Maggie's husband Harold of the letter which Maggie had sent, and indicated that he intended to make a claim against Maggie's estate for $350.00.

After a discussion with Ad, in which Ad agreed not to assert a claim against Maggie's estate, Harold prepared a document which read, "In consideration of services rendered by Doc to my son, and of Ad's promise to make no claim against the estate of my wife, I hereby agree to pay $350.00 to Doc's estate." After signing the document, Harold handed it to Ad. Harold never paid anything to the estate, however, and Ad instituted suit against him. Harold defended on the ground that his promise to pay $350.00 was not supported by consideration.

94. If Ad's lawsuit against Harold is successful, it will most likely be for which of the following reasons?

   (A) The document which Harold executed was an offer for a unilateral contract which Ad accepted by not making a claim against Maggie's estate.

   (B) A judgment for Harold would result in his being unjustly enriched.

   (C) Harold is estopped from denying the validity of his agreement with Ad.

   (D) Harold's agreement with Ad was a compromise.

95. As to the question of whether services rendered by Doc are sufficient consideration for Harold's promise, a court is most likely to find that

   (A) they are sufficient consideration because they imposed a preexisting moral obligation upon Harold.

   (B) they are not sufficient consideration because they were not requested by Harold.

   (C) the question of whether or not they are suffi-

cient consideration depends upon whether Harold received any material benefit from them.

   (D) the question of whether or not they are sufficient consideration depends upon whether the reasonable value of the services approximated $350.00.

96. If Ad brings an action against Wand for the reasonable value of services rendered by Doc, Ad will most likely

   (A) win, if the state has a "good Samaritan" statute.

   (B) win on a theory of quantum meruit.

   (C) lose, since Doc had no expectation of compensation when he rendered the services.

   (D) lose, since Ad is bound to accept the sum of $350.00 agreed upon by Harold.

Questions 97-99 are based on the following fact situation.

On September 10, Pubco, a well known publisher of law books, posted the following notice on the bulletin board at University Law School:

As an incentive to research and scholastic excellence, Pubco announces the institution of the Pubco Award. The award will consist of a complete set of the Pubco Encyclopedia, and will be presented to the student in each graduating class of the law school who attains the highest overall cumulative Grade Point Average. In the event two or more students graduate with the same Grade Point Average, the dean will be asked to select the winner from among them based on school service and community involvement.

Val, who had just begun her final year at the law school, saw the notice. Her grades already placed her toward the top of her class, but she resolved to work harder than ever before in an attempt to win the Pubco Award. On September 20, she mailed a letter to Pubco saying, "I accept your offer for the Pubco Award, and will do my best to win it." Her letter was received by Pubco, but lost in the mail department before any Pubco officials had an opportunity to see it.

The following May, because of budget cutbacks at Pubco, the following notice was posted at University Law School:

> The Pubco Award program is hereby discontinued. Pubco will be unable to present any prize or award to students of this law school.

The week after the second notice was posted, Val took her final examinations. Her scores on those examinations made her grade point average the highest in the class, and resulted in her being declared Valedictorian at her graduation. She subsequently wrote to Pubco demanding her prize, but Pubco refused to award it.

97. Which of the following statements is most correct about Pubco's first notice

    (A) It was an offer for a unilateral contact.

    (B) It was an offer for bilateral contract.

    (C) It was an offer for either a unilateral contract or a bilateral contract at the offeree's option.

    (D) It was an offer for a unilateral contract which ripened into a bilateral contract when Val achieved the highest grade point average in her class.

98. In a jurisdiction which applies the *Restatement of Contracts, 2nd* rule, a court's decision as to whether Pubco's offer was effectively revoked by the notice posted in May (the second notice) will most likely depend on whether

    (A) Val saw the second notice before taking her final examinations.

    (B) the second notice was as large, and as conspicuously posted as the first.

    (C) Val's letter of September 21 was effective when mailed or when received.

    (D) Val made extra efforts in her studies in reli-

ance on the offer contained in the notice of September 10.

99. In an action by Val against Pubco, a court is most likely to find the promise contained in the September 10 notice

    (A) enforceable, on a theory of promissory estoppel.

    (B) enforceable, because Val's performance was consideration for it.

    (C) unenforceable, since Val was already legally obligated to use her best efforts while in law school.

    (D) unenforceable, since it was a conditional promise to make a future gift.

100. Cohen is the operator of an ice cream parlor where ice cream is sold in cups and cones for consumption on or off the premises. In preparation for Halloween, she ordered fifty gallons of pumpkin-flavored ice cream from her supplier, Darry. Because Darry was sold out of pumpkin-flavored ice cream, he sent fifty gallons of cinnamon-swirl instead. Past experience had taught Cohen that cinnamon-swirl was a poor seller, so she called Darry and told him that she couldn't use it. Darry became offended, told her that if she sent it back he would not accept it, and hung up the phone. The same day, Stand, another ice cream retailer, offered to purchase the cinnamon-swirl ice cream from Cohen at a wholesale price.

Is she entitled to sell it to him?

    (A) Yes, but only if the price which Stand has offered to pay is equal to or greater than the price which Darry was charging Cohen.

    (B) Yes, at any commercially reasonable price, taking into account the fact that because the ice cream is perishable its value is likely to diminish as time goes by.

    (C) No, since under the circumstances, Cohen is not obligated to pay for the ice cream.

    (D) No, unless a public sale is conducted at which Stand is the highest bidder.

101. Sewco was a manufacturer of sewing supplies, including thread, needles, thimbles, and patterns. Pat was an engineer employed by Sewco in its product design department. Working at home on his days off, Pat invented a device which could be used to increase the fuel efficiency of automobile engines. Without telling his employer anything about it, Pat obtained a patent on the device and sold the patent rights for one hundred thousand dollars to General Truck, a motor vehicle manufacturer. Sewco subsequently learned about Pat's invention and demanded the money which Pat had received from General Truck. In support of its demand, Sewco referred to a provision of Pat's employment contract which required him to devote all his working time and energies to his employment. Sewco attorneys argued that because of this provision, the device had been invented on company time, and that the patent rights therefore belonged to Sewco. At a conference with Sewco attorneys, Pat signed a promissory note for fifty thousand dollars payable to Sewco, and Sewco agreed to abandon its claim. When the note came due, Pat refused to pay it.

In an action by Sewco against Pat on the promissory note, which of the following additional facts or inferences, if it was the only one true, would be most helpful to Pat's defense?

(A) The employment contract was oral, although the Statute of Frauds required it to be in writing.

(B) At the time Pat signed the promissory note, Sewco did not honestly believe that it was entitled to the patent rights, but Pat believed that Sewco was entitled to the patent rights.

(C) At the time Pat signed the promissory note, Sewco honestly believed that it was entitled to the patent rights, but Pat did not believe that Sewco was entitled to the patent rights.

(D) Sewco was not entitled to the patent rights under the employment contract.

102. Sally was a manufacturer of wood finishing products with a plant in City. Billy was a manufac-turer of wooden furniture with a factory located in Towne. Pursuant to a written agreement, Billy agreed to purchase fifty gallons of wood stain from Sally at five dollars per gallon "F.O.B. Billy's factory." Sally delivered the wood stain to Carrier Trucking Company which loaded it safely onto a truck at City. While en route to Towne, however, the truck was hijacked by thieves. Its contents were never recovered.

In an action by Sally against Billy for the agreed price of the stain, which of the following comments is most correct?

(A) Sally fulfilled her obligation to Billy when the stain was loaded safely aboard a truck at City.

(B) The risk of loss passed to Billy when Sally delivered the stain to Carrier, although title to the stain never actually passed to Billy.

(C) The risk of loss did not pass to Billy.

(D) The risk of loss was not on Sally, since the loss was the result of action by the public enemy.

Questions 103-104 are based on the following fact situation.

Mut was the owner of an unimproved lot valued at $20,000. Payne was a painting contractor. When Mut's daughter Debra and Payne's son Sal announced that they were getting married, Mut and Payne decided to give them a house as a wedding present. On January 1, Mut and Payne entered into a written agreement with each other, pursuant to which they were to have a house built on Mut's lot, with Mut and Payne each paying half the cost. It was further agreed that after completion of the house Payne would pay Mut $10,000 as his share of the cost of the lot, and Mut would convey the lot to Debra and Sal.

On February 2, Mut and Payne entered into a written contract with Bild, a building contractor. The contract called for payment in installments, each payment being due upon completion of a specified stage of building. In addition to its other terms, the contract contained a clause providing that as each payment came due Bild would bill and collect half of it from Mut and half of it from Payne. In the contract, Bild agreed that neither would be responsible to him for more than half of the price.

On March 3, Payne entered into a separate contract with Bild. Pursuant to this contract, Bild hired Payne as a subcontractor to do all the painting required in connection with the construction of the house. Because the house was being built for his son, Payne agreed to do the job for $3,000 although his work was worth $5,000. The $3,000 was to be deducted from the final payment which Payne would owe Bild for construction of the house.

In April, Payne became ill. Because he could no longer work, he sold his painting business to his son Sal, who was a competent and licensed painting contractor, for about half of what it was actually worth. As one of the terms of the contract of sale, Sal promised to do all the painting work on the house which Bild was constructing. Payne notified Bild of his agreement with Sal. When the house was ready to be painted, however, Sal informed Bild that he would not paint it.

103. Assume for the purpose of this question only that Bild hired another painting subcontractor to do the job at a price of $5,000 and asserted a claim for breach of contract against Sal. If there was an enforceable contract between Payne and Sal, the court should find for

(A) Sal, because there was no privity between Bild and Sal.

(B) Sal, because a contract for personal services is not assignable.

(C) Bild, because Bild was an intended donee-beneficiary of the contract between Payne and Sal.

(D) Bild, because Bild was an intended creditor-beneficiary of the contract between Payne and Sal.

104. Assume for the purpose of this question only that after the house was completed, Mut refused to convey the property to Debra and Sal. In an action by Sal against Mut, which of the following arguments would furnish Mut with her strongest

defense?

(A) Sal did not rely upon or assent to the contract of January 1 between Mut and Payne.

(B) Sal's painting of the house was a condition precedent to Mut's obligation to convey.

(C) Sal was only an incidental beneficiary of the January 1 contract between Mut and Payne, since Mut's primary intention was to benefit her daughter Debra.

(D) The contract which Payne made with Bild on March 3 was a breach of a fiduciary obligation which Payne owed Mut.

Questions 105-106 are based on the following fact situation.

Susan and Barbara had been friends for years. Susan was the owner of a rare antique sports car, which Barbara had offered to buy from her on several occasions, but which Susan had never been willing to sell. On Barbara's birthday, Susan and Barbara went out for dinner and drinks. After dinner, Susan continued drinking until she was somewhat intoxicated. During their conversation, Susan said, "Barbara, as a birthday present, I've decided that I'm going to sell you my sports car for five hundred dollars. And just to make sure that I don't change my mind after I sober up, I'll put it in writing." With that, she wrote on a paper napkin, "We agree to the sale of my sports car to Barbara for five hundred dollars, COD," and signed her name at the bottom. Barbara also signed the napkin and put it in her purse. The following day Barbara tendered five hundred dollars in cash to Susan but Susan refused to sell her the car, claiming that she had been drunk when she made the offer.

105. In an action by Barbara against Susan for breach of contract, which of the following additional facts, if it was the only one true, would be most helpful to Susan's defense?

(A) Susan was so drunk when she wrote on the napkin that she did not know the legal consequences of her act.

(B) Susan would not have offered to sell the car to Barbara for five hundred dollars if she had not been drunk.

(C) The car was worth more than $500.

(D) Susan changed her mind about selling the car before Barbara tendered the cash.

106. If Barbara is successful in her action against Susan, a court is most likely to

(A) issue an order directing Susan to sell her the car for five hundred dollars.

(B) award damages equivalent to the reasonable market value of Susan's sports car.

(C) issue an order directing Susan to sell her car for five hundred dollars, and award damages equivalent to the reasonable market value of Susan's sports car less five hundred dollars.

(D) award damages consisting of five hundred dollars.

Questions 107-108 are based on the following fact situation.

Fether was the owner and operator of a store which sold exotic birds and aviary supplies. Pett was the owner and operator of a pet shop in which dogs, cats, tropical fish, and exotic birds were sold. Fether kept a trained amazon parrot named Ozzie on a perch near the sales counter in his store. The bird had an extensive vocabulary and did tricks on his perch to the great amusement of Fether's customers. Pett wished to have Ozzie for his own personal pet, and had attempted to purchase him from Fether on numerous occasions, but Fether always indicated that he was unwilling to sell. On January 5, Pett again asked Fether if he would sell Ozzie, to which Fether replied, "I'd consider selling him to you, Pett, but I don't even know what a bird with Ozzie's training is worth." Pett said that he would do some research to find out, if Fether would promise to seriously consider selling Ozzie for whatever they found the proper price to be. Based on their conversation, Pett and Fether executed the following document:

Fether hereby agrees to sell to Pett one trained amazon parrot known as Ozzie for a price to be paid in cash and on delivery, said price to be agreed upon after deter-

mining the reasonable value of a bird with Ozzie's training.

Pett contacted five generally acknowledged experts in trained exotic birds, and received opinions from them regarding Ozzie's value which ranged from seven hundred dollars to one thousand dollars. When Pett attempted to buy Ozzie from Fether, however, Fether indicated that he was unwilling to sell Ozzie at any price.

107. In an action by Pett against Fether for specific performance of the agreement made on January 5, Pett will

(A) win, if he offers to pay one thousand dollars for Ozzie.

(B) win, but will be required to pay a price for Ozzie which the trier of the facts finds to be reasonable in light of expert and other evidence presented at the trial.

(C) lose, since the January 5 document does not manifest an intent to be bound.

(D) lose, since specific performance is not available in an action for breach of a contract for the sale of a chattel.

108. Does the Uniform Commercial Code apply to the transaction between Fether and Pett?

(A) Yes, because this was a transaction in goods.

(B) Yes, because only the price and delivery date terms were missing from the agreement.

(C) No, because, unless it is a farm animal, a living thing does not fit the definition of "goods" under the UCC.

(D) No, because Pett was not seeking to purchase Ozzie for resale.

Questions 109-110 are based on the following fact situation.

Ben was the owner of Ben's Air Conditioning Repair Company. His employees did all the repair jobs, but Ben himself did the estimating and made price quotes to customers. Ben maintained a fleet of pickup trucks for use by his employees when traveling to and from repair jobs, but Ben usually drove his own personal station wagon when going out to give a potential customer an estimate.

On February 15, Ben ordered a new Ferris station wagon from Car Sales Inc, a new car dealer. Prior to signing the sales contract, the salesperson who sold him the car explained that the new car could only be obtained by Car Sales Inc from the Ferris Company. For this reason, she said, it might be as long as two weeks before Car Sales Inc could deliver the new car to Ben. Ben said that this would be all right, but that he definitely needed the car by March 10 for use in his business. Based on this discussion, it was agreed that the new car would be ready for him no later than March 5.

Immediately following the signing of the sales contract by Ben and Car Sales Inc, the salesperson contacted the Ferris sales department and placed the order for Ben's car. She explained to the sales representative at Ferris that she had contracted to deliver the car to Ben no later than March 5, and that if she was unable to do so, she would probably lose the sale. The sales representative assured her that the car would be delivered on time.

On March 4, Ben sold his old station wagon, because he believed that he would be receiving the new one the following day. Ferris failed to deliver the new car to Car Sales Inc until March 30, making it impossible for Car Sales to deliver it to Ben on time.

109. Assume for the purpose of this question only that Ben instituted an action for breach of contract against Car Sales Inc, and that he alleged damages which included lost profits resulting from his inability to travel to the premises of potential customers for the purpose of estimating jobs and selling his company's services. Which of the following would be Car Sales most effective argument in response to that allegation?

(A) At the time the contract was formed, it was not foreseeable that late delivery of the automobile would result in business losses.

(B) Late delivery by Ferris made performance of the sales contract by Car Sales Inc impossi-

ble.

(C) Ben could have mitigated damages by renting another vehicle or using one of the company pickup trucks while waiting for delivery of the station wagon.

(D) Consequential damages are not available for the breach of a contract of sale.

110. Assume for the purpose of this question only that on March 5 Car Sales Inc informed Ben that it would be unable to deliver the station wagon as promised, and that Ben thereupon cancelled the contract. In an action by Car Sales Inc against Ferris, Car Sales can recover

(A) nothing, if Ferris's delay in delivery was a reasonable one.

(B) nothing, unless Car Sales Inc is subsequently held liable to Ben for breach of contract.

(C) the profit which Car Sales Inc would have realized on the sale to Ben.

(D) the difference between the price which Car Sales Inc had agreed to pay Ferris and the reasonable wholesale market value of the vehicle ordered.

111. Meder, a licensed physician, was driving home from the hospital where she worked when she saw Hart, a pedestrian, fall unconscious to the pavement. Meder stopped her car, examined Hart, and diagnosed that he was experiencing cardiac arrest. After attempting to render medical treatment, Meder carried Hart to her car and drove him to the hospital. There, she continued attempting to treat him for an hour, after which Hart died without ever having regained consciousness. Meder subsequently sent the administratrix of Hart's estate a bill for medical services, but the administratrix refused to pay it.

If Meder asserts a claim against Hart's administratrix for the reasonable value of her medical services, the court should find for

(A) Meder, if at the time she assisted Hart she reasonably expected to be compensated for her services.

(B) Meder, because a contract was implied-in-fact.

(C) Hart's administratrix, because Hart received no benefit as a result of Meder's services.

(D) Hart's administratrix, if the jurisdiction has a "good Samaritan" statute.

112. Bukke was a professional gambler who made his living by accepting illegal bets on horseraces and other sporting events. Because he suspected that the police had discovered his operation, he began looking for a new location for his illegal activities. Finding an empty store-front building on Main Street, he contacted Opal, its owner. On December 12, they entered into a lease of the premises for a six month period. According to the lease, Bukke's occupancy was to begin on the first of January, at a rent of two hundred dollars per month. Bukke paid the first month's rent upon signing the lease.

On December 17, Bukke was arrested on charges of illegal bookmaking. He pleaded guilty and received a nine month sentence. The following day, his attorney advised Opal that Bukke would not be moving into the leased premises after all. Opal agreed to release Bukke from the lease, and immediately rented the premises to another tenant for three hundred dollars per month, occupancy to begin on December 20. When Bukke was released from prison nine months later, he demanded that Opal return his two hundred dollars. Opal refused, on the ground that the contract which Bukke had made with her had an illegal purpose.

If Bukke institutes an action against Opal, a court should find for

(A) Opal, since the courts will not aid either party to an illegal contract.

(B) Opal, since she and Bukke were not in pari delicto regarding the illegality of the lease agreement.

(C) Bukke, since the lease agreement was not illegal.

(D) Bukke, since his sentence to serve nine months in prison made performance by him impossible as a matter of law.

Questions 113-114 are based on the following fact situation.

On November 19, Maxine, an attorney, hired Consultant to advise her as to how she could derive the benefit of maximum deductions under the tax laws. After examining Maxine's financial condition, Consultant advised her to invest exactly $4,000 in works of art for her office prior to December 31. On December 10 Maxine entered into a written contract with the Gale Gallery for the purchase of a painting known as "Wild Orchids" at a price of $4,000. Pursuant to the contract, Gale was to frame the painting according to Maxine's specifications and to deliver it to her on December 28.

Because of a filing error, the sale to Maxine was not properly noted by Gale employees. As a result, on December 20 Gale sold the painting to Dealer for $3,500. The contract of sale provided that Dealer would not re-sell the painting at any price without first giving Gale an opportunity of repurchasing it at that price. On December 24, when Maxine learned of the sale to Dealer, she purchased a sculpture from a different gallery for $4,000, without saying anything to Gale about it.

On December 26, Gale discovered the clerical error which had led to the sale of "Wild Orchids" to Dealer. Gale employees immediately contacted Dealer, and bought the painting back from him for $4,000. On December 28, when Gale employees delivered the painting to Maxine's office, she refused it, telling them that she had already invested her money in a sculpture.

113. In an action by Gale against Maxine for damages resulting from her refusal to accept delivery of the painting, the court should find for

(A) Maxine, because she justifiably relied on Gale's prospective inability to perform when she purchased the sculpture.

(B) Maxine, if but only if Gale's sale of "Wild Orchids" to Dealer was the result of negligence by Gale's employees.

(C) Gale, since under the contract with Dealer, Gale might have been able to re-acquire the painting prior to December 28.

(D) Gale, because it did not breach its contract with Maxine.

114. Assume for the purpose of this question only that Maxine instituted an action against Gale on December 29 seeking specific performance of the December 10 agreement. With respect to Maxine's demand for specific performance, a court is most likely to find for

(A) Gale, since Maxine refused to accept delivery of the painting on December 28.

(B) Gale, since Maxine has already succeeded in investing $4,000 in art for her office.

(C) Maxine, if the painting known as "Wild Orchids" is found to be a unique chattel.

(D) Maxine, since Gale's sale to Dealer was an anticipatory repudiation of its contract with Maxine.

115. Beatrice received an advertising brochure from Selco in the mail. The brochure contained a photograph of a Peechie 401 computer, and above it the statement, "While they last. All Peechie computers on sale at 25 percent below manufacturer's list price." Beatrice immediately contacted the Peechie Computer Company which manufactured the computer pictured in Selco's brochure, and determined that Peechie's list price for the 410 was $1,000. She then sent her check for $750 ($1000 less 25 percent) to Selco with a covering letter which stated "I hereby accept your offer for the sale of a Peechie 401 computer. My check is enclosed herewith." Selco threw Beatrice's letter and check away.

The brochure which Selco sent Beatrice is best described as

(A) an invitation for offers.

(B) an invitation for offers which ripened into an offer when Beatrice learned the Peechie Computer Company's list price for the 401

computer.

(C) an invitation for offers which ripened into an offer when Beatrice relied on it by sending her check and covering letter.

(D) an offer for the sale of a Peechie 401 computer.

Questions 116-117 are based on the following fact situation.

Muse was a musician who played at weddings and other private parties. As the result of a conversation between Muse and Gru, they entered into a written agreement on February 1. According to the terms of the agreement, Muse was to play at Gru's wedding on June 15 at a hall known as Wedding Plaza for a fee of two hundred dollars. Gru paid half the fee upon the signing of the contract and was to pay the balance in cash immediately after Muse began to perform at the wedding.

On March 10, Gru's fiancee broke their engagement and told Gru that she decided to marry New. She and New planned to marry on June 15 at Wedding Plaza. To show his good will, Gru congratulated her and promised to provide the music as a wedding present. He assigned his February 1 contract with Muse to New and promised that he would attend the wedding and pay Muse the balance of his fee.

Gru said nothing to Muse about the change until the day before the wedding. Then, calling Muse on the phone, Gru informed him that the only change in the plan was that New was to be the groom. Gru assured Muse that he would still be paying the balance of Muse's fee as originally agreed. Because Muse disliked New, he assigned his contract to his brother Bro, who was also a musician. New, who had been looking forward to having Muse play at his wedding, refused to allow Bro to play. Consequently, Gru did not pay the balance of the musician's fee to either Muse or Bro.

116. If Bro brings an action against Gru for breach of contract, a court is most likely to find for

(A) Bro, since Gru's obligation was not assignable.

(B) Bro, if New's credit standing was inferior to Gru's.

(C) Gru, since Gru's assignment of the contract to New relieved Gru of any obligation which he owed thereunder.

(D) Gru, if the February 1 contract called for personal services by Muse.

117. If New brings an action against Muse for breach of contract, a court is most likely to find for

(A) New, if, but only if, the February 1 contract be tween Gru and Muse did not contain a clause prohibiting assignment by Gru.

(B) New, because Gru's assignment of the contract to New resulted in the imposition of different obligations on Muse.

(C) New, if the services of Bro would not have been identical to the services of Muse.

(D) Muse.

Questions 118-120 are based on the following fact situation.

Suzanne was the owner of a lot and building which contained two residential apartments. Suzanne resided in the upstairs apartment, and rented the downstairs apartment to Tenn and his family on a month-to-month basis. Balbo was interested in purchasing the realty from Suzanne. After negotiations, Balbo and Suzanne entered into a written contract which provided that Suzanne would sell the house to Balbo for sixty thousand dollars, and that delivery of title was to occur on or before August 1. Suzanne promised that at the time title was delivered the upstairs apartment would be vacant and that the downstairs apartment would be vacant within three months thereafter. Balbo promised to pay fifty eight thousand dollars upon delivery of title and the balance of $2,000 three months after delivery of title. The contract provided that, "Balbo's obligation to pay $2,000 three months after delivery of title shall be voided if the downstairs apartment has not been vacated by that time."

118. Which of the following statement concerning the order of performances is *least* accurate?

(A) Suzanne's delivery of title on or before August 1, and Balbo's payment of $58,000 are concurrent obligations.

(B) Vacancy of the upstairs apartment is a condition precedent to Balbo's obligation to pay $58,000 upon delivery of title.

(C) Payment by Balbo of $58,000 is a condition precedent to Suzanne's obligation to deliver title to the premises.

(D) Payment by Balbo of $2,000 is a condition subsequent to Suzanne's obligation to have the downstairs apartment vacated within three months after the delivery of title.

119. Assume for the purpose of this question only that Suzanne delivered title to Balbo on August 1, and that as of November 15 the downstairs apartment remained occupied by Tenn and his family. Which of the following statements best describes Balbo's rights?

(A) Balbo is entitled to an order directing Suzanne to commence a legal proceeding against Tenn for the purpose of evicting him from the premises.

(B) Balbo is not required to pay Suzanne the additional two thousand dollars.

(C) Balbo is entitled to rescind his contract with Suzanne, reconveying title to her and receiving the return of his $58,000.

(D) Balbo may bring a legal proceeding for the purpose of evicting Tenn from the premises, and, if successful, is required to pay Suzanne $2,000 less the expenses which he incurred in evicting Tenn.

120. Article 2 of the Uniform Commercial Code applies

(A) only to transactions in goods.

(B) only to transactions involving merchants.

(C) to all commercial transactions.

(D) only to transactions in goods or services.

121. After seeing the small airplane which Pilot was flying go down in stormy seas, Pilot's wife Wanda stood on the shore screaming, "Oh, God, won't somebody please save my husband?" Upon hearing her appeal for help, Robinson went out in his rowboat and succeeded in rescuing Pilot. Robinson subsequently asked Wanda to pay him for his trouble, but Wanda refused.

If Robinson asserts a claim for payment against Wanda on a theory of promissory estoppel, which of the following would be Wanda's most effective argument in defense?

(A) Robinson was an officious intermeddler.

(B) The value of Pilot's life is too speculative.

(C) No promise of payment can be reasonably inferred from Wanda's cry for help.

(D) There was no consideration for Wanda's promise.

Questions 122-124 are based on the following fact situation.

Collard was a collector of antiques who had purchased many expensive pieces from Ansel, an antique dealer. Knowing that Ansel was traveling to Europe, Collard wrote to him on March 11, "Ansel: If you should come across a George IV piece in your travels, please purchase it for me. I don't care about the cost. Collard."

On April 17, Ansel wrote to Collard, "I have found an excellent George IV settee. The price is $15,000, but I think it's a good buy. Are you still interested? If so, let me know if the price is acceptable to you. Ansel."

Collard received Ansel's letter on April 21, and, on that same day, wired Ansel, "Fifteen thousand is OK. Buy the piece on my account. Collard."

Because of negligence by the telegraph company, Collard's telegram was misdirected and therefore delayed. On April 30, not having heard from Collard, Ansel wired Manson as follows: "Will sell you fine George IV settee for $16,000 firm. If interested, respond by

wire. Ansel."

On May 1, Manson received Ansel's telegram, and sent Ansel a telegram stating, "Accept your offer to sell George IV settee for $16,000. Manson." Manson immediately telephoned Collard and boasted about the purchase.

Ansel received Collard's telegram on May 2, and Manson's telegram on May 3. On May 5, Ansel shipped the settee to Manson.

122. In litigation between Collard and Ansel, if a court determines that Ansel's letter of April 17 was not an offer, it will most likely be because that letter

(A) was an acceptance of the offer contained in Collard's letter of March 11.

(B) did not specify the terms of payment.

(C) did not manifest a willingness to be bound.

(D) did not specify a manner of acceptance.

123. In litigation between Collard and Ansel, if a court determines that Ansel's letter of April 17 was an offer, was a contract formed between Collard and Ansel?

(A) Yes, if sending a telegram was a reasonable way for Collard to accept Ansel's offer.

(B) Yes, because, as a merchant, Ansel was obligated to act in good faith.

(C) No, because an offer sent by mail may be accepted only by mail.

(D) No, if Ansel had changed his mind about the price prior to April 21.

124. Assume for the purpose of this question only that no contract was formed between Collard and Ansel. Was a contract formed between Manson and Ansel?

(A) Yes, because after receiving Manson's wire on May 3, Ansel shipped the settee.

(B) Yes, but only if the telegram sent by Manson to Ansel on May 1 was an offer.

(C) No, if the telegram which Ansel sent Manson on April 30 did not manifest Ansel's intention to be bound.

(D) No, unless there was a prior course of dealing between Manson and Ansel.

125. Francis, who resided in the city of Westlake, was the owner of a chain of dry cleaning stores known as Sparkling Frank's. Because his stores had been financially successful, he began selling franchises. By the terms of his franchise agreements, Francis permitted franchisees to use the name Sparkling Frank's in return for an initial fee of $50,000 and ten percent of the gross revenues.

Francis's cousin Amy lived in a distant state. When she heard about the financial success of the Sparkling Frank's stores, she wrote to Francis asking him to sell her a franchise to operate a Sparkling Frank's dry cleaning store in her state. Because Francis had great affection for Amy and wanted her to live near him, he sent her a letter in which he said, "If you will come and live here, I will give you a franchise to operate a Sparkling Frank's in Westlake without any initial fee. All you will have to pay is ten percent of the gross revenues."

Amy immediately wrote Francis to tell him that she was coming to live in Westlake as he requested, and that she was looking forward to operating a Sparkling Frank's store there. After Amy moved to Westlake, however, Francis told her that his contract with another franchisee prevented him from giving her a franchise to operate a Sparkling Frank's store in Westlake.

If Amy asserts a claim against Francis for breach of contract, the court should find for

(A) Amy on a theory of bargained-for exchange.

(B) Amy, because she detrimentally relied on the promise made by Francis.

(C) Francis, because his promise was for a conditional gift.

(D) Francis, because his affection for Amy is not sufficient to support his promise to her.

126. Samson is a manufacturer of wall-coverings which he ordinarily sells to retailers in boxes containing ten packages per box. By a valid written contract, Bixby agreed to purchase and Samson agreed to sell ten boxes of 107-Blue. When the boxes arrived, Bixby inspected them and found that two of the boxes contained 109-Red instead of 107-Blue. Bixby immediately notified Samson, who informed Bixby that he no longer produced #107-Blue, and had sent Bixby his last eight boxes. Samson said that he had sent two boxes of 109-Red as an accommodation, and that Bixby did not have to accept them unless he wanted to.

Which of the following correctly states Bixby's rights regarding the shipment?

I. Bixby may reject the entire shipment.

II. Bixby may accept the eight boxes containing 107-Blue and reject the two boxes containing 109-Red.

III. Bixby may accept the entire shipment, and collect damages resulting from its nonconformity to the terms of the contract.

(A) I only.

(B) I or II only.

(C) II or III only.

(D) I or II or III.

127. By a valid written contract formed on May 7, Bilden agreed to construct a warehouse for Owwens. Pursuant to the terms of the contract, the building was to be completed no later than November 30. The agreed price was $60,000, of which Owwens was to pay $20,000 when the construction was 50 percent complete, and the balance upon completion. Bilden began work on May 11, and had completed 25 percent of the construction by June 5, when the partially finished structure was struck by lightning, and completely destroyed in the resulting fire. No payment had yet been made by Owwens to Bilden. On June 7, Bilden notified Owwens that

he was too busy to rebuild the structure, and that he would not continue to work on the project. Owwens subsequently hired another contractor to build the warehouse at a lower price, and rejected all of Bilden's demands for payment. If Bilden asserts a claim against Owwens, Bilden is entitled to recover

(A) the difference between $60,000 and the price which Owwens paid to have the warehouse built by another contractor.

(B) the reasonable value of work performed by Bilden prior to the destruction of the structure by lightning and fire.

(C) 25 percent of $60,000 ($15,000).

(D) nothing.

128. When Salzburger's employers transferred him to the west coast, they promised to pay all his relocation expenses, including any commission which he might have to pay for the sale of his home. Salzburger contacted Ritchie, a real estate broker, and entered into a written contract with her on September 1. Under its terms, Salzburger agreed that if the house was sold to any buyer who made an offer during the following two months, he would pay Ritchie upon the closing of title a commission equivalent to 6 percent of the actual selling price of the house. In return, Ritchie agreed to make reasonable efforts to find a buyer for the house at a price of $80,000.

On September 15, after Ritchie showed Salzburger's home to Barnaby, Barnaby offered to purchase it for $75,000, on condition that title would close on or before December 1. On September 18, Salzburger accepted Barnaby's offer. On September 19, Barnaby gave Salzburger $10,000 as a deposit.

On November 15, Barnaby notified Salzburger that he had changed his mind, and would not go through with the purchase of the house, agreeing to forfeit the deposit which he had paid in return for Salzburger's agreement not to sue for damages. The following day, Salzburger entered into a contract to sell the house to another buyer for $80,000. Salzburger subsequently rejected

Ritchie's demand for payment.

If Ritchie institutes a claim against Salzburger for her commission, she is entitled to collect

(A) $4,800 (6 percent of $80,000).

(B) $4,500 (6 percent of $75,000).

(C) $600 (6 percent of $10,000).

(D) Nothing.

129. On August 1, Sante said to her friend Crowley, "My brother Burdy needs money. Will you lend it to him for three weeks?"

Crowley said, "Your brother isn't working. I can't lend him money. How do I know he'll pay me back?"

Sante answered, "All right, then. Lend the money to me, but give it to my brother."

Crowley said, "OK. That's good enough for me." Crowley then mailed Burdy a check payable to Burdy for the requested sum.

Three weeks later, when Burdy failed to repay the money, Crowley asked Sante for it. On September 15, not having received payment, Crowley sued both Burdy and Sante. In an appropriate motion to dismiss Crowley's claim against her, Sante asserted that there was no agreement in writing between Crowley and her. Sante's motion should be

(A) granted, if the sum lent by Crowley exceeded $500.

(B) granted, if Sante's statement, "Lend the money to me, but give it to my brother," was a promise to pay Burdy's debt to Crowley.

(C) denied, if Crowley's statement, "That's good enough for me," was an acceptance of Sante's offer to pay Burdy's debt to Crowley.

(D) denied, if Crowley's check was a writing which evidenced the debt.

130. Marilyn and Fred were co-owners of a parcel of realty known as Greenacre. After twenty-five years of marriage, they decided to execute wills. Before executing the wills, they agreed in writing that each would leave a life-estate in his or her share of Greenacre to the other, and that the survivor would leave a fee interest in Greenacre to their son Samuel. After executing their wills, they told Samuel about their agreement. Samuel had recently contracted for the purchase of a residence, but subsequently canceled the contract. Shortly afterwards, Marilyn died, leaving a life estate in her share of Greenacre to Fred. One year later, Fred remarried and changed his will to leave Greenacre to Twylla, his second wife. When Fred died, Samuel learned that Fred's will left Greenacre to Twylla, and sued the executrix of Fred's estate for damages resulting from Fred's breach of his agreement with Marilyn.

The court should find for

(A) Samuel, if he canceled his contract for the purchase of a residence in reliance on the agreement between Marilyn and Fred.

(B) Samuel, because after Marilyn's death, Samuel became a creditor beneficiary of the agreement between Marilyn and Fred.

(C) Fred's executrix, because Samuel is a donee beneficiary of the agreement between Marilyn and Fred.

(D) Fred's executrix, because, by its terms, the agreement between Marilyn and Fred might be capable of being performed within one year.

Questions 131-132 are based on the following fact situation.

When the City of Baden decided to renovate its city hall, it contacted Bilder, a building contractor, and asked him to bid on the job. Since the renovation would require extensive electrical work, Bilder contacted Elco, an electrical subcontractor with whom Bilder had done business in the past. On September 1, after examining plans and specifications for the job, Elco submit-

ted a written bid to Bilder. In the written communication, Elco offered to do all the electrical work on the renovation project for $15,000, and promised to keep its offer open until two weeks after Bilder received the contract from the City of Baden.

Bilder submitted a bid for the renovation project to the City of Baden, and on October 15, the City of Baden awarded the renovation contract to Bilder. On October 16, Wirco, another electrical subcontractor, sent Bilder a written communication in which it offered to do the electrical work on the renovation project for $12,500. Bilder accepted Wirco's offer the following day. On October 18, however, Wirco realized that it had made a mathematical error in calculating its price for the job, and notified Bilder that it would not be able to do the electrical work for less than $18,000. Bilder immediately went to the office of Elco, for the purpose of signing a contract with Elco pursuant to its bid. When Bilder arrived at Elco's office, however, Elco's president informed Bilder that Elco was withdrawing its offer. Bilder subsequently contracted with another electrical subcontractor to do the job at a price of $16,000.

131. If Bilder institutes an action against Wirco for breach of contract, the court should find for

(A) Wirco, because its initial bid was the result of a mathematical error.

(B) Wirco, if Bilder knew or should have known that Wirco's initial bid was the result of an error.

(C) Bilder, unless Wirco's error would permit Bilder to realize a profit which Bilder did not contemplate when bidding on the renovation project.

(D) Bilder, only if Wirco could have done the work for $12,500 without sustaining a loss.

132. If Bilder institutes an action against Elco for breach of contract, the court should find for

(A) Bilder, because of Elco's written promise to keep its offer open until two weeks after Bilder received the contract from the City of Baden.

(B) Bilder, unless Elco was not a merchant.

(C) Elco, if it knew that Bilder had accepted Wirco's offer to do the job for $12,500.

(D) Elco, only if Bilder did not rely on Elco's offer in preparing the bid which he submitted to the City of Baden.

Questions 133-137 are based on the following fact situation.

When they decided to computerize their paperwork, the law firm of Kunkel and Williams contacted Dataflo, a specialist in the application of computer technology to the practice of law. After negotiations, Kunkel and Williams entered into a written contract with Dataflo on June 1. According to the terms of the contract, Dataflo was to immediately deliver and install in the office of Kunkel and Williams a computer and other specified hardware. Dataflo was also required to design and install, by October 15, software consisting of a computer program which would suit the special needs of Kunkel and Williams' practice. In addition, Dataflo agreed to service and maintain the hardware for a period of six years from the date of the contract. In return, the firm of Kunkel and Williams agreed to pay $5,000 within 30 days after delivery of the hardware, $5,000 within 30 days after delivery of the software, and $1,000 on the first day of each year that the contract remained in effect.

The firm also agreed to furnish specifications for the software at least 30 days before the date for its installation. The hardware referred to in the contract was standard equipment, readily available from and serviceable by any reputable computer supplier. The software was not standard, however, and its design required special skill and knowledge regarding the application of computer technology to the practice of law. The contract specified that the price of the hardware was $6,000, the price of the software was $4,000, and the charge for service and maintenance was $1,000 per year. On June 15, Dataflo installed the agreed hardware in the office of Kunkel and Williams. On June 20, in satisfaction of an antecedent debt, Dataflo assigned to Antun her rights to receive payment for hardware already delivered under the contract with Kunkel and Williams. On August 1, before beginning to work on the design for the agreed software, Dataflo sold her business to McOwen, an established and reputable computer dealer. By the terms of the sale, Dataflo assigned to McOwen all her rights under the contract with Kunkel and Williams.

133. Assume for the purpose of this question only that Kunkel and Williams failed to make any payment following the installation of the hardware, and that on August 15, Dataflo instituted a claim against them for $5,000. Which of the following would be Kunkel and Williams' most effective argument in defense against that claim?

(A) Dataflo has not begun work on designing the software required by the contract.

(B) Dataflo has made at least one effective assignment of her rights under the contract.

(C) Kunkel and Williams have no assurance that Dataflo's obligations under the contract will be fulfilled.

(D) The contract between Dataflo and the firm of Kunkel and Williams was divisible.

134. Assume for the purpose of this question only that on August 15 Antun instituted a claim against Kunkel and Williams for $5,000. Which one of the following additional facts or inferences, if it were the only one true, would be most likely to lead to a judgment for Kunkel and Williams?

(A) Antun was not a specialist in the application of computer technology to the practice of law.

(B) The contract between Dataflo and the firm of Kunkel and Williams did not contain a clause permitting assignment.

(C) The contract between Dataflo and the firm of Kunkel and Williams contained language which stated, "This contract may not be modified except by a writing signed by both parties hereto."

(D) Kunkel and Williams paid $5,000 to Dataflo prior to being notified of Dataflo's assignment to Antun.

135. Assume the following facts for the purpose of this question only. On August 15, Dataflo noti-

fied Kunkel and Williams that McOwen had purchased her business, and requested that Kunkel and Williams furnish McOwen with specifications for the software required under the contract. Kunkel and Williams did not furnish specifications, but on August 20 asked McOwen to assure them that he was capable of designing the software called for by the contract. McOwen did not respond until October 10, when he sued Kunkel and Williams for breach of contract. The court should find in favor of

(A) Kunkel and Williams, because McOwen failed to assure them that he was capable of designing the software.

(B) Kunkel and Williams, because they were not in privity with McOwen.

(C) McOwen, because Kunkel and Williams continued to have rights against Dataflo under the contract.

(D) McOwen, because Kunkel and Williams failed to provide specifications as called for by the contract.

136. Assume for the purpose of this question only that on August 16, Dataflo informed Kunkel and Williams of her sale to McOwen, stating that the software called for by the contract would be designed and installed by McOwen and not Dataflo. If Kunkel and Williams institute a claim against Dataflo on August 18, the court should find for

(A) Kunkel and Williams, since Dataflo's statement on August 16 was an anticipatory repudiation.

(B) Kunkel and Williams, since Dataflo's sale to McOwen did not impose on McOwen an obligation to design software.

(C) Dataflo, since design and installation of the software was not required until October 1.

(D) Dataflo, since her sale to McOwen implied a delegation of all her obligations under her contract with Kunkel and Williams.

137. Assume the following facts for the purpose of this question only. McOwen designed the software required by the contract and installed it on October 1 to the complete satisfaction of Kunkel and Williams. Kunkel and Williams paid $5,000 within 30 days and an additional $1,000 on the first day of the following year as required by the contract, but McOwen thereafter failed to service or maintain the hardware. Which statement below correctly completes the following sentence: Kunkel and Williams may succeed in an action for breach of contract against

I. Dataflo, because she continues to be obligated to them under the June 1 contract.

II. McOwen, as third party beneficiaries of the contract between McOwen and Dataflo.

(A) I only.

(B) II only.

(C) I and II.

(D) Neither I nor II.

138. Bildco was a construction company which had been awarded a contract to build a transmission tower for the United States government. Sue Supervisor was a well-known architect and managing partner of S&M Architectural Specialists. On October 20, Bildco wrote to S&M Architectural Specialists indicating that Bildco was interested in retaining the firm to supervise the building project on condition that Sue Supervisor undertake the job personally. On October 28, S&M responded with a letter stating, "Sue Supervisor receives $50,000 for every project which she personally supervises. Our fee for such a project is normally $60,000." Bildco received the letter on October 31. On November 5, after a telephone conversation between Bildco officers and the president of S&M Architectural Specialists, Bildco wrote to S&M, "Terms in your letter of October 28 are acceptable to us."

After Bildco completed the project under the supervision of Sue Supervisor, S&M Architectural Specialists rendered a bill for $110,000, indicating that of this sum $60,000 was the fee charged by S&M, and $50,000 was an additional sum for the personal services of Sue Supervisor. Bildco refused to pay, asserting that the agreement called for a total fee of $60,000, of which $50,000 was to be paid to Sue Supervisor for her services. S&M Architectural Specialists subsequently sued Bildco for breach of contract. At trial S&M's president attempted to testify that in her November 5 conversation with Bildco officers, she had explained that Sue Supervisor's fee was in addition to the $60,000 charged by S&M Architectural Specialists. On timely objection by Bildco's attorney, the testimony of S&M's president should be

(A) excluded, under the parol evidence rule.

(B) excluded, unless it is regarded as evidence of a prior course of dealing between the parties.

(C) admitted, only if S&M's billing arrangement was consistent with customs and procedures normally followed in the construction and architectural industries.

(D) admitted, because it does not contradict a term of any written agreement.

Questions 139-140 are based on the following fact situation.

Victoria was a veterinarian who specialized in the treatment of livestock including pigs, horses, cows, and sheep. Zooloo was a farmer who raised various species of livestock. In addition, Zooloo kept a private collection of exotic animals. Because Zooloo's livestock frequently needed the attention of a veterinarian, he entered into a written contract with Victoria on January 1. Under the terms of the contract, Zooloo was to pay Victoria $250 per month for one year, in return for which Victoria would render whatever treatment Zooloo's livestock required during that period.

On February 10, the local zoo telephoned Victoria, offering to give her a surplus tiger. Although Victoria had no experience with exotic animals, she accepted the tiger and put it in a cage in the back of her office. On February 22, having heard that Victoria had acquired a tiger, Zooloo called her. When he asked Victoria if she was interested in selling the tiger for $450,

she said, "I was hoping to get $1,000 for the tiger, but I'll throw it in under our existing contract without charging you anything at all for it." On March 10, Victoria was at Zooloo's farm for the purpose of inoculating some of his cattle. When Zooloo asked why she had not brought the tiger, Victoria said, "I've changed my mind. If you want the tiger, you'll have to pay $450 for it."

139. Assume for the purpose of this question only that Zooloo asserts a claim against Victoria because of her refusal to deliver the tiger as promised. The court should find for

(A) Zooloo, because although Victoria was not a merchant as to the sale of a tiger, she was a merchant as to the sale of veterinary services.

(B) Zooloo, because his conversation with Victoria on February 22 resulted in a valid modification of the existing contract.

(C) Victoria, because her promise to give Zooloo the tiger was unsupported by consideration.

(D) Victoria, because her promise to give Zooloo the tiger was not in writing.

140. Assume the following facts for the purpose of this question only. On March 10, Victoria and Zooloo agreed that she would sell him the tiger for $450, payment and delivery to be on March 20. On March 15, Zooloo telephoned Victoria and said, "When you deliver the tiger, will you throw in a pig for my daughter Borah without charging me extra for it?" Victoria said, "Yes," but when she delivered the tiger on March 20 she refused to give Borah a pig. If Zooloo asserts a claim against Victoria because of her failure to deliver the pig as promised, the court should find for

(A) Victoria, unless she and Zooloo were merchants with respect to the sale of a pig.

(B) Victoria, unless she and Zooloo were merchants with respect to the sale of a tiger.

(C) Victoria, unless she and Zooloo were merchants with respect to the sale of a tiger and the sale of a pig.

(D) Zooloo.

Questions 141-142 are based on the following fact situation.

On January 3, Benson, a retailer of lumber, ordered from Surly, a lumber wholesaler, 1000 2"x 4" fir boards, each 8 feet in length, for delivery by January 15. When Surly delivered the fir boards on January 15, they were received by Benson's manager, who informed Benson that delivery was made, but that the boards delivered by Surly were only 7 feet long. Benson intended to notify Surly immediately, but was busy and forgot to do so.

141. Assume for the purpose of this question only that Benson failed to notify Surly, and that on February 20, Benson received Surly's bill for the boards, but did not pay the bill or communicate with Surly in any way. Assume further that on May 15, Surly instituted a claim against Benson for the price of the boards and that, in defense, Benson contended that the boards delivered did not conform to the contract of sale. The court should find for

(A) Surly, because Benson failed to inform him that the boards were only 7 feet in length.

(B) Surly, because a merchant buyer who accepts delivery of non-conforming goods is bound to pay for them at the contract price.

(C) Benson, because the boards did not conform to the contract of sale.

(D) Benson, because a merchant seller is not entitled to the price of non-conforming goods if a reasonable inspection prior to shipment would have disclosed the non-conformity.

142. Assume for the purpose of this question only that on January 16 economic conditions caused the price of lumber to double, and that on January 17 Benson notified Surly that the boards were only 7 feet in length, returned them to Surly, and demanded that Surly furnish 8-foot boards at the

contract price. If Surly refuses to do so, and Benson asserts a claim against Surly for breach of contract, the court should find for

(A) Benson in a sum equivalent to the difference between the contract price and the fair market value of 7-foot boards on January 15.

(B) Benson in a sum equivalent to the difference between the contract price and the fair market value of 8-foot boards on January 15.

(C) Benson in a sum equivalent to the difference between the contract price and the fair market value of 8-foot boards on January 17.

(D) Surly.

Questions 143-144 are based on the following fact situation.

Pawnie, a pawnbroker, occasionally sold used jewelry to Johnson, who owned a jewelry store. Each time she did so, she and Johnson entered into a written contract fixing the price of the piece being sold and giving Johnson 30 days to make payment.

On June 1, Pawnie sold Johnson a ring for $2,500, representing the stone in it to be a diamond. Johnson paid the price on June 30. On July 15, Pawnie sold Johnson a pearl necklace, and entered into a contract with him setting the price at $2,200 and requiring payment on or before August 14. On July 16, Johnson learned that the stone in the ring which he had purchased from Pawnie the previous month for $2,500 was not a diamond, but was cubic zirconia, making the ring worth only $300.

On July 17, Pawnie assigned to Ascot, for $1,500 cash, the July 15 contract with Johnson for sale of the pearl necklace. Johnson was immediately notified of the assignment. On August 14, Ascot requested payment from Johnson. Johnson refused, asserting that he was deducting his loss on the cubic zirconia ring from the price of the pearl necklace.

143. Assume for the purpose of this question that Ascot instituted an action against Johnson for $2,200 allegedly due under the July 15 contract between Johnson and Pawnie. Can Johnson successfully assert a defense based upon the fact that

the stone in the ring purchased from Pawnie in June was not a diamond?

(A) Yes, because by the assignment of Pawnie's contract with Johnson, Ascot did not acquire any rights against Johnson which Pawnie did not have.

(B) Yes, but only if Pawnie knew or should have known that the ring was not a diamond.

(C) No, unless Johnson notified Pawnie of his claim to a setoff prior to Pawnie's assignment of the contract to Ascot.

(D) No, because Johnson's claim is a defense which is personal against Pawnie.

144. Assume for the purpose of this question only that Ascot is unsuccessful in her action against Johnson. If Ascot brings an action against Pawnie for damages, the court should find for

(A) Pawnie, because an assignment does not imply a warranty that the obligor will perform.

(B) Pawnie, because the assignment to Ascot caused Ascot to step into Pawnie's shoes with respect to the claim against Johnson.

(C) Ascot, because Johnson's defense existed at the time the assignment was made by Pawnie to Ascot.

(D) Ascot, because an assignment for consideration implies a warranty that the obligor will perform.

Questions 145-148 are based on the following fact situation.

Moto was a manufacturer of engines and motors, including a motor known as the model-614. Tracto, a manufacturer of tractors, had purchased hundreds of model-614 motors from Moto in the past at a price of $5,000 each. In 1984, Moto ceased production of model-614. By April 15, 1985, Moto found that she had only 3 model-614 motors left in her warehouse. Because she wanted to make room for the newer models, Moto signed and sent the following letter to Tracto on April 15, 1985:

Tracto: I have only three model-614 motors left in stock and have stopped manufacturing them. If you are interested, I will sell you any or all of them for $1,000 each, a fraction of their usual price. Because we have done business in the past, I promise to hold this offer open until June 1, 1985.

On May 15 1985, not having heard from Tracto, Moto sold two of the model-614 motors to Second for $1,000 each.

145. Was Moto's statement, "I promise to hold this offer open until June 1" supported by consideration?

(A) Yes, because it was a firm offer under the Uniform Commercial Code.

(B) Yes, if Tracto detrimentally relied upon it by not responding before May 15.

(C) No, unless Tracto subsequently purchased one or more of the model-614 motors from Moto.

(D) No, because Tracto gave nothing in return for the promise.

146. Assume for the purpose of this question only that on June 2, after learning that Moto had sold two of the model-614 motors, Tracto wrote to Moto, "I am enclosing a check for $3,000 as payment in full for all three model-614 motors as per your offer of April 15. My truck will be there next week to pick them up." This letter constituted

(A) an acceptance of Moto's offer to sell three model-614 motors.

(B) an acceptance of Moto's offer to sell one model-614 motor.

(C) an offer to purchase three model-614 motors.

(D) an offer to purchase one model-614 motor.

147. Assume the following facts for the purpose of this question only. On June 2, after learning that Moto had sold two of the model-614 motors to

Second, Tracto wrote to Moto, "I agree to purchase one model-614 as per your letter of April 15." Moto delivered the remaining model-614 motor to Tracto the following day. In a telephone conversation with Moto on June 5, however, Tracto said that he would sue Moto for breach of contract unless Moto agreed to accept $200 as payment in full. Moto agreed to accept that sum, but subsequently rejected Tracto's tender of $200. If Moto sues Tracto for $1,000, the court should find for

(A) Tracto, because the original agreement was modified in the telephone conversation of May 30.

(B) Moto, because her agreement to accept $200 was not evidenced by a writing.

(C) Moto, because her agreement to accept $200 was unsupported by consideration.

(D) Moto, because her agreement to accept $200 was made under duress.

148. Assume the following facts for the purpose of this question only. On May 17, Tracto wrote Moto, "I'll take one model-614 as per your offer." On May 18, Tracto wrote Moto, "Changed mind. Cancel purchase of model-614 motor." On May 19, Moto sold the last model-614 to Second for $1,100. If Moto subsequently asserts a claim against Tracto for breach of contract, the court should find for

(A) Moto, in the sum of $1,000.

(B) Moto, in a sum equivalent to whatever profit Moto would have made if she sold the motor to Tracto for $1,000.

(C) Moto, in a sum equivalent to whatever profit Moto would have made if she sold the motor to Tracto for $1,000, minus $100.

(D) Tracto.

149. Boss and her assistant Edward were working alone late one night when Boss had a heart attack which rendered her unconscious and caused her to fall down an airshaft. Edward believed Boss to be dead, but called for an ambulance and leaped into the airshaft, sustaining serious injury himself. Finding that Boss was still alive, Edward gave her first aid consisting of cardiopulmonary resuscitation. When the ambulance arrived, paramedics used stretchers and pulleys to get Boss and Edward out of the airshaft, and then brought them to the hospital. Several days later while she was still in the hospital, a doctor told Boss that she would probably have died if not for Edward's quick and effective action. Boss wrote Edward a note, which said, "In return for your saving my life, I'm going to pay all your hospital bills. In addition, I'm going to add a bonus of $3,000 per month to your salary for the rest of your life. If you choose to retire right now, I'll pay you $3,000 per month for the rest of your life as a retirement pension." Boss paid Edward's hospital bills, but because her business took an unexpected downturn, she never paid him $3,000, and subsequently informed him that she would not be able to pay him a bonus or a retirement pension. If Edward asserts a claim against Boss for her failure to pay him the bonus of $3,000 per month, which of the following would be Edward's most effective argument in support of his claim?

(A) Boss's promise to pay the bonus was in writing.

(B) Edward detrimentally relied on Boss's promise.

(C) Boss's promise was supported by an underlying moral obligation.

(D) Edward's rescue of Boss resulted in a contract implied-in-fact.

Questions 150-152 are based on the following fact situation.

Gail, an art dealer, employed several agents who traveled throughout the world purchasing art for her to sell in her gallery. One of her agents sent her a painting entitled "Sunset," informing her that it had been painted by Van Gook. Gail had just received the painting and was about to place it on display when Bertrand, a collector of art, came into the gallery. Seeing the new painting, he said, "An interesting Van Gook." Gail replied, "Yes, it is. I'm asking $50,000 for it." Bertrand agreed to the price, and immediately wrote a check for the sum of $50,000 payable to the order of Gail, writing the words "Payment in full for Sunset" on the back of the check. Gail accepted the check and delivered the painting to Bertrand. If the painting had actually been by Van Gook, it would have been worth $50,000. The same day, however, Bertrand discovered that the painting was a forgery, worth only a few hundred dollars, and stopped payment on his check before Gail could cash it.

150. If Gail asserts a claim against Bertrand for breach of contract, which of the following would be Bertrand's most effective defense?

   (A) The contract of sale was not evidenced by a writing signed by both parties.

   (B) At the time of sale, Bertrand and Gail both believed that the painting was by Van Gook.

   (C) It is unconscionable to make Bertrand pay $50,000 for a painting worth only a few hundred dollars.

   (D) The painting known as "Sunset" was not adequate consideration for Bertrand's promise to pay.

151. Assume for the purpose of this question only that when Gail delivered the painting to Bertrand, they both signed a document which said, "Sale of painting entitled 'Sunset' by Gail to Bertrand for the sum of $50,000 paid by check received by Gail subject to collection." Assume further that at the trial of Gail's breach of contract action against Bertrand, Bertrand offered to testify that before purchasing the painting he had a conversation with Gail in which both referred to it as a Van Gook. If Gail objects to the testimony, should it be admitted?

   (A) Yes, but only if offered to establish a willful misrepresentation by Gail.

   (B) Yes, but only if offered for the purpose of establishing that the writing was ambiguous.

   (C) Yes, for the purpose of establishing that the writing was ambiguous and for the purpose

of explaining the ambiguity.

   (D) No, under the parol evidence rule.

152. Assume for the purpose of this question only that Bertrand sues for rescission of the sales contract. The court should find for

   (A) Gail, since the terms of the contract have already been performed.

   (B) Gail, unless she knew with substantial certainty that the painting was not by Van Gook.

   (C) Bertrand, but only if Gail should reasonably have known that the painting was not by Van Gook.

   (D) Bertrand, if Gail knew that Bertrand was not willing to pay $50,000 for a forged Van Gook.

Questions 153-154 are based on the following fact situation.

On February 1, Lawrence and Tennyson entered into a written contract. By its terms, Lawrence was to rent Tennyson a building for use by Tennyson as a "sports book," which is an establishment where bets are made on horse races and other sporting events. Tennyson's tenancy was to commence on April 1 and to continue for a period of two years. Rent was to be $1,000 per month, plus 20% of Tennyson's gross profits. Prior to occupancy by Tennyson, Lawrence was to remodel the building's interior so that it would be suitable for Tennyson's purpose. Specifically, the contract required Lawrence to install a "tote-board" which could instantaneously compute and display gambling odds on specified sporting events, a series of projection-screen televisions with cable connections for the broadcast of sporting events as they happened, and other equipment suitable only for use in a "sports book" establishment. Upon signing the contract on February 1, Tennyson gave Lawrence a deposit of $2,000. At that time, neither party could have reasonably anticipated that existing state law would be changed. On April 1, Lawrence had not made the agreed improvements in the interior of the building, and refused to comply with Tennyson's demand for the return of his deposit.

153. Assume for the purpose of this question only that on February 1, existing state law prohibited the operation of a "sports book," but that on April 1, existing state law permitted the operation of a "sports book." If Tennyson sues Lawrence for the return of his deposit, the court should find for

    (A) Lawrence, because public policy prohibits the enforcement of gambling contracts.

    (B) Lawrence, because the agreement of February 1 had an illegal purpose.

    (C) Tennyson, because he and Lawrence were in pari delicto.

    (D) Tennyson, under the doctrine of frustration of purpose.

154. Assume for the purpose of this question only that on February 1, existing state law permitted the operation of a "sports book," but that on April 1, existing state law prohibited the operation of a "sports book." If Tennyson sues Lawrence for the return of his deposit, the court should find for

    (A) Lawrence, because public policy prohibits the enforcement of gambling contracts.

    (B) Lawrence, because the purpose of the agreement of February 1 has become illegal.

    (C) Tennyson, because he and Lawrence were not in pari delicto.

    (D) Tennyson, under the doctrine of frustration of purpose.

Questions 155-157 are based on the following fact situation.

Kung beans are grown throughout the United States and are harvested at all times of year. Important as a food commodity, kung beans are traded on the American Kung Bean Exchange. Although farmers are free to negotiate prices for the sale of their kung beans, the price received by kung bean farmers on any given day is generally determined by the American Kung Bean Exchange price.

Seeder is a farmer who grows kung beans. In January, she planted a field of kung beans which would be ready for harvest in June. Because she expected the harvest to yield more than 5,000 bushels of kung beans, she entered into a written contract with Amos on March 1, wherein Seeder agreed to sell and Amos agreed to buy 2,000 bushels of kung beans to be delivered during the month of June at the American Kung Bean Exchange price as of June 15. On March 2, Seeder entered into an identical written contract with Barton.

In the first week of April, heavy rains inundated Seeder's field, destroying part of her crop. As a result, she doubted that she would be able to fulfill her contract with Amos and Barton. On April 15, she called Barton and said that because of the storms, she would not be able to deliver more than 1,000 bushels. Barton said "I'll take whatever you deliver, but I intend to hold you to the terms of our contract."

Seeder than called Amos. When she explained the problem to Amos, he said that he would accept 1,000 bushels instead of 2,000 if Seeder would agree to accept the American Kung Bean Exchange price as of May 1 instead of June 15. Seeder said, "Well, you've got me over a barrel. I'll never be able to deliver 2,000 bushels in June, so I accept your terms."

On June 15, Seeder harvested her field. The American Kung Bean Exchange price on both May 1 and June 15 was $2.00 per bushel, and kung beans were readily available on both those days at that price.

155. Assume for the purpose of this question only that Seeder's harvest yielded 2,000 bushels of kung beans, and that on June 15, she delivered 1,000 bushels to Barton. If Barton institutes a claim against her for damages resulting from breach of contract, which of the following would be Seeder's most effective argument in defense?

    (A) Her inability to deliver 2,000 bushels was the result of an act of God.

    (B) She notified Barton on April 15 that she would be unable to deliver more than 1,000 bushels.

    (C) Barton sustained no substantial damage, since the contract price equaled the market price on the day of delivery.

    (D) Her obligation to Amos was greater than her

obligation to Barton, since her contract with Amos was formed before her contract with Barton.

156. Assume for the purpose of this question only that on April 15, immediately after his conversation with Seeder, Barton contracted to purchase 1,000 bushels of kung beans from another supplier with delivery to be on June 15, and price to be the American Kung Bean Exchange price on the day of delivery. Assume further that on June 15 Seeder delivered 2,000 bushels to Barton, but Barton refused to accept any more than 1,000 bushels. If Seeder sues Barton for breach of contract, Barton's most effective defense would be based on the principle of

(A) novation.

(B) anticipatory repudiation.

(C) nudum pactum.

(D) impossibility of performance.

157. Assume the following facts for the purpose of this question only. On June 16 the price of kung beans doubled. Seeder's harvest yielded 4,000 bushels. Seeder delivered 1,000 bushels to Amos on June 20. Amos demanded the right to purchase another 1,000 bushels at $2.00 per bushel, but Seeder refused to sell him an additional 1,000 bushels at that price. If Amos institutes a claim against Seeder for breach of contract, the court should find for

(A) Seeder, because farmers are free to negotiate prices for the sale of their kung beans.

(B) Seeder, because her agreement to accept the American Kung Bean Exchange price as of May 1 was consideration for Amos' agreement to accept 1,000 bushels instead of 2,000 bushels.

(C) Amos, because the agreement to modify his contract with Seeder was not in writing.

(D) Amos, because Seeder's harvest was sufficient to permit her to satisfy her original contractual obligations.

Questions 158-159 are based on the following fact situation.

Homer went into his garage one morning and found that someone had broken in during the night and stolen a hand-carved Bavarian milking stool which had been stored there. The stool did not have much intrinsic worth, but was a family heirloom and had great sentimental value for Homer. Angry, Homer ran into Joe's Bar which was located near his home. Entering the bar, he said in a loud voice, "I'll pay $1,000 to anyone who finds the thief that stole a hand-carved stool out of my garage last night." While Homer was in Joe's Bar, his garage burned down and everything in it was destroyed. Joe, the owner of the bar, heard Homer's statement and said, "I'll catch that thief for you, Homer."

158. Which of the following statements most correctly describes the position of Homer and Joe following the incident in Joe's Bar?

(A) Homer has made an offer for a unilateral contract which became irrevocable when Joe said, "I'll catch that thief for you, Homer."

(B) Homer has made an offer for a unilateral contract which Joe can accept only by catching the thief before Homer makes an effective revocation of the offer.

(C) Homer and Joe are parties to a bilateral contract.

(D) Homer has not made any offer which can be accepted by Joe.

159. Assume the following facts for the purpose of this question only. Two days later, Galen caught the thief and recovered the stool. When Galen returned the stool to Homer and demanded $1,000, Homer refused to pay her. Galen subsequently instituted an action against Homer for $1,000. Which one of the following additional facts or inferences, if it were the only one true, would be most likely to lead to a judgment for Homer?

(A) Homer's statement that he would pay $1,000

to anyone who caught the thief was made in the heat of passion.

(B) If the thief had not stolen the stool, it would have been destroyed in the fire which burned Homer's garage.

(C) Galen was not in Joe's Bar when Homer stated that he would pay $1,000 to anyone who caught the thief, but came in immediately afterwards and heard about it.

(D) Galen was in Joe's Bar when Homer stated that he would pay $1,000 to anyone who caught the thief, but was not aware of Homer's statement until after she had caught the thief and recovered the stool.

160. Owen was the owner of two adjoining parcels of unimproved realty. Although she was interested in improving and selling the realty, she did not have the necessary capital. After negotiation, Owen entered into a written contract with Barksdale, a building contractor. According to the terms of the contract, Barksdale was to provide labor and materials for the construction of a building on one of the parcels according to certain specifications. All construction was to be completed by a certain date, at which time Owen was to convey the other parcel of realty to Barksdale as his sole compensation for the labor and materials supplied. The contract contained a clause providing for liquidated damages in the event of a breach by either party.

After Barksdale completed construction as agreed, Owen refused to convey the other parcel of realty to him. As a result, Barksdale appropriately asserted alternative claims for relief against Owen demanding liquidated damages as provided in the contract, or actual damages, or an order directing Owen to perform as agreed.

Which of the following correctly describes Barksdale's rights against Owen?

I. If the liquidated damages clause established a penalty, the court can properly enter judgment for any actual damages which resulted from Owen's breach.

II. If the liquidated damages clause did not establish a penalty, the court can properly direct Owen to perform as agreed.

(A) I only.

(B) II only.

(C) I and II.

(D) Neither I nor II.

161. Sun Auto was an automobile dealer which sold an expensive line of imported automobiles bearing the name Doppleford. The Doppleford Company, which manufactured the vehicles in Germany, sold them to Sun Auto at the wholesale price for resale by Sun Auto at the retail price.

On January 12, Barlow ordered a new Doppleford automobile from Sun Auto, executing a written contract of purchase and sale at the specified retail price. The car was to be equipped with certain optional equipment, and was to be delivered on or before March 15. Immediately after contracting with Barlow, Sun Auto ordered the car from the Doppleford Company in Germany.

On February 28, Otter ordered from Sun Auto a car identical to that which had been ordered by Barlow at an identical price. The following day, before ordering a car for Otter from the Doppleford Company, Sun Auto received the car ordered by Barlow. When Barlow was notified, however, he said that he had changed his mind and would not go through with the transaction. Sun Auto therefore delivered the car to Otter and did not order a car for Otter from the manufacturer.

If Sun Auto asserts a claim against Barlow for damages resulting from breach of contract, Sun Auto is entitled to recover

(A) nothing, because the car was sold to Otter at the same price which Barlow agreed to pay.

(B) the difference between the wholesale price of the car and its retail price.

(C) the difference, if any, between the price which Barlow agreed to pay for the car and its reasonable market value.

(D) the difference, if any, between the price which Sun Auto paid for the car and its reasonable market value.

Questions 162-164 are based on the following fact situation.

For several years following his graduation from college, Ruskin made no attempt to find employment. During this period, he was usually intoxicated, and spent most of his time drinking alcohol at Barker's tavern. In August 1985, Barker threatened to sue Ruskin for $10,000, claiming that Ruskin owed him that sum for unpaid bar bills. Ruskin asked his mother Lulu to lend him money with which to pay Barker. On September 1, 1985, Lulu stated orally that if Ruskin promised to go to law school and to stop drinking for the rest of his life, she would give him $10,000 on July 1, 1986. Ruskin promised that he would never drink alcohol again, and that he would enroll in law school as soon as possible. On September 3, 1985, Ruskin wrote to Barker describing his agreement with Lulu, and stating that if Barker did not sue him, he would pay Barker the $10,000 as soon as he received it from Lulu.

Ruskin began attending a law school two weeks later. In December 1985, however, he withdrew from the school, deciding that he did not like it.

162. Assume for the purpose of this question only that on July 1, 1986 Lulu refused to pay, and that Ruskin asserted a claim against her for $10,000. Which of the following would be Lulu's most effective argument in response to that claim?

(A) Ruskin's completion of law school was an implied condition precedent to Lulu's promise to pay $10,000.

(B) Ruskin's remaining in law school until July 1, 1986 was an implied condition precedent to Lulu's duty to pay.

(C) Lulu's promise was not supported by consideration.

(D) Lulu's promise was not in writing.

163. Assume the following facts for the purpose of this question only: On July 2, 1986, Barker delivered to Lulu a copy of the letter which Ruskin had sent him on September 3, 1985 asserting that he was an assignee of Ruskin's rights and demanding that Lulu send $10,000 directly to him. Which of the following would be Lulu's most effective argument in opposition to Barker's claim?

(A) Ruskin's letter was not an assignment of Ruskin's rights against Lulu.

(B) Ruskin's assignment to Barker was unsupported by consideration.

(C) Lulu was not notified of Ruskin's assignment to Barker.

(D) Lulu did not consent to Ruskin's assignment to Barker.

164. Assume for the purpose of this question only that on July 1, 1986 Lulu paid Ruskin $10,000, but Ruskin refused to pay Barker, denying that he owed unpaid bar bills. If Barker asserts a claim against Ruskin for breach of the promise contained in Ruskin's letter of September 3, 1985, which of the following additional facts, if it were the only one true, would be most likely to result in a judgment for Barker?

(A) Barker did not respond to Ruskin's letter of September 3, 1985.

(B) On September 3, 1985, Ruskin reasonably believed that he owed Barker $10,000, but Barker did not reasonably believe that Ruskin owed him $10,000.

(C) On September 3, 1985, Barker reasonably believed that Ruskin owed him $10,000, but Ruskin did not reasonably believe that he owed Barker $10,000.

(D) On July 1, 1986, Barker's claim against Ruskin for unpaid bar bills was barred by the statute of limitations.

Questions 165-166 are based on the following fact situation.

Duster's father earned his living as a crop-duster, using an airplane to dust farmers' fields with insecticides for a fee. When he died, he left the business to Duster. Although Duster did not know how to fly an airplane and did not personally participate in crop-dusting, she continued to run the business by hiring pilots to fly the crop-dusting planes. Soon after inheriting the business, Duster entered into a business contract with Flores, a farmer. The terms of the contract required Duster's company to dust Flores' crop four times per year for a period of four years, at a total price of $10,000 which Flores paid upon signing the contract.

Duster's company performed as agreed for two years. At the end of that period, Duster sold the entire business to Airco, assigning to Airco the balance of her contract with Flores. All of Duster's employees agreed to work for Airco.

165. Assume for the purpose of this question only that after being notified of the assignment Flores sued Duster, asserting that Duster's sale of the business to Airco was a breach of Duster's obligation under the contract because crop-dusting involves a personal service. Which of the following would be Duster's most effective argument in response to that claim?

 (A) An assignment of contract rights includes a delegation of contract duties.

 (B) Airco had more expertise at crop dusting than Duster did.

 (C) Duster had never personally participated in dusting Flores' fields.

 (D) Duster's assignment of Flores' contract to Airco did not impose an additional burden on Flores since there was no change in price.

166. Assume for the purpose of this question only that Flores consented to the assignment, but that Airco subsequently failed to perform as required by the contract. If Flores seeks the return of the unearned portion of the money which he paid to Duster on the signing of their contract, he may collect it from

 (A) Duster only.

 (B) Airco only.

 (C) either Duster or Airco.

 (D) neither Duster nor Airco, because Flores' only remedy is a judgment for the difference between the contract price and the price which Flores would have to pay another for the same service.

Questions 167-168 are based on the following fact situation.

Bullion was a major shareholder of Mart Corporation, a retail company. In January, Mart Corporation had cash-flow problems which placed it in danger of insolvency. On January 15, Mart Corporation applied to Trust Bank for a loan, but Trust Bank said that it would lend the money requested only if Bullion agreed to guarantee payment by Mart Corporation. Fearful of losing her investment in Mart Corporation, Bullion promised Trust Bank on January 16 that if Mart Corporation did not repay the loan as agreed, Bullion would do so. On January 17, Trust Bank made the requested loan to Mart Corporation.

On May 1, Mart Corporation defaulted in payment, and Trust Bank threatened to force Mart into bankruptcy. On May 11, in an attempt to save the company, Mart Corporation officials offered to turn some of the corporate assets over to Trust Bank for sale at their market value, with the understanding that if the market value exceeded the amount which Mart Corp. owed Trust Bank, Trust Bank would refund the excess to Mart Corporation.

167. Assume for the purpose of this question only that Trust Bank rejected Mart Corporation's offer of May 11 and asserted a claim against Bullion for repayment of the loan. Which of the following additional facts or inferences, if it were the only one true, would be most likely to lead a court to find in favor of Bullion?

 (A) Bullion's January 16 promise to pay Mart Corporation's debt was induced by the fear that Mart Corporation could not continue to exist without the loan.

(B) Bullion's January 16 promise to pay Mart Corporation's debt was not in writing.

(C) Bullion received nothing of value in return for her January 16 promise to pay Mart Corporation's debt.

(D) The assets which Mart Corporation offered to turn over to Trust Bank on May 11 were sufficient to repay the loan.

168. Assume the following facts for the purpose of this question only: Trust Bank accepted Mart Corporation's offer of May 11 and sold the assets the following day for a sum which was sufficient to repay the loan but which was only half the market value of the assets. Bullion then asserted a claim against Trust Bank, alleging that selling the assets for less than their market value diminished the value of Bullion's stock in Mart Corporation. In deciding Bullion's claim, the court should find for

(A) Bullion, if Bullion was an intended beneficiary of the May 11 agreement between Mart Corporation and Trust Bank.

(B) Bullion, because Mart Corporation was Bullion's fiduciary.

(C) Trust Bank, because Bullion was not a party to the agreement of May 11.

(D) Trust Bank, if the sale of Mart Corporation's assets was made in a commercially reasonable manner.

169. Layton was the owner of a store-front building which she leased to Theobald for a three-year period. Theobald paid the rent for two years, and then assigned the balance of his lease to Su, advising Layton in writing that Su would be paying the rent from that point on. For the following five months, Su paid the rent directly to Layton. Then Su moved out and stopped paying rent. If Layton asserts a claim against Theobald for unpaid rent, which of the following arguments would be most effective in Theobald's defense?

(A) Layton's accepting rent from Su resulted in a novation.

(B) Layton's accepting rent from Su resulted in an accord and satisfaction.

(C) By accepting rent from Su, Layton impliedly consented to Theobald's assignment to Su.

(D) A prohibition against assignment of a leasehold interest is a restraint against alienation.

Questions 170-171 are based on the following fact situation.

Thorn owned a trucking company. His wife Ardiste was a free-lance book illustrator. When Pressley, a book publisher, contacted Thorn to discuss the transportation of his products, Thorn promised Ardiste that he would get Pressley to employ her as a book illustrator for a year. During negotiations with Pressley, Thorn offered Pressley a lower rate if Pressley would do so.

Thorn and Pressley subsequently entered into a written one-year contract for Thorn to transport all of Pressley's products at a specific low rate. At the same time, Pressley orally agreed that in return for the low rate which Thorn was giving him, he would employ Ardiste for a year as his book illustrator starting immediately.

When Ardiste learned of the agreement, she notified all of her clients that she could no longer work for them because illustrating books for Pressley would take all her time. For the next six months, Ardiste did a satisfactory job as Pressley's book illustrator. Then, she and Thorn were divorced. Following the divorce, Thorn told Pressley that he was releasing him from his promise to employ Ardiste and would give him the same low rate even if Pressley did not continue to employ Ardiste for the rest of the year. Pressley thereupon discharged Ardiste from his employ.

170. Assume for the purpose of this question only that Ardiste asserted a claim against Thorn for damages which resulted from his releasing Pressley from the promise to employ Ardiste for a year. If Thorn's only defense is that he received no consideration for promising Ardiste that Pressley would employ her for a year, which of the following would be Ardiste's most effective argument in response to that defense?

(A) Pressley's promise to employ Ardiste for one year was obtained by Thorn as a gift from Thorn to Ardiste.

(B) Thorn made an irrevocable assignment to Ardiste of rights under his contract with Pressley.

(C) No consideration is required to support a promise between husband and wife.

(D) Pressley's promise to hire Ardiste for one year was given in return for the low rate which Thorn gave him.

171. If Ardiste asserts a claim against Pressley for damages resulting from breach of his promise to hire Ardiste for one year, the court should find for

(A) Ardiste.

(B) Pressley, because Ardiste gave nothing in return for his promise.

(C) Pressley, because his promise was not in writing.

(D) Pressley, because he and Thorn mutually rescinded their contract.

172. When Salo inherited a valuable painting, he asked Brantley, an art dealer, if she was interested in buying it. On January 15, after looking at the painting, Brantley said that she would not have enough cash to purchase the painting until February 1. At Brantley's request, Salo signed a document containing a written offer to sell the painting to Brantley for $50,000 and a written promise to hold the offer open until February 2.

On January 20, Salo sold the painting to someone else for $45,000. The following day, after Brantley read about the sale in a newspaper, she went to Salo's home with $50,000 in cash and demanded that Salo sell her the painting for that price. Brantley refused, saying that he was withdrawing his offer.

If Brantley asserts a claim for damages resulting from Salo's sale of the painting to another, the court should find for

(A) Brantley, because she accepted Salo's offer before Salo withdrew it.

(B) Brantley, because Salo promised in writing to hold the offer open until February 2.

(C) Salo, because a judgment for damages is not an appropriate remedy for breach of a contract to sell a unique chattel.

(D) Salo, because when Brantley tendered payment, she knew that Salo had already sold the painting.

173. Beaver operated a grocery store in which he sold fresh fish and other food items. Salley was a wholesaler of fresh fish. By a written contract, Beaver and Salley agreed that Beaver would purchase from Salley 100 kilograms per week of a fish known as "rock lurgid" at a specified price. When Salley made the first delivery under the contract, however, Beaver refused to accept it, complaining that the fish delivered by Salley was scmods, a species unrelated to lurgid.

Salley subsequently asserted a breach of contract claim against Beaver. At the trial, Salley attempted to testify that in the fresh fish industry scmods is frequently referred to as "rock lurgid."

If Beaver objects, this testimony should be

(A) excluded, because it modifies the terms of a written contract which Beaver and Salley intended to be a complete record of their agreement.

(B) excluded, if the price to which Beaver and Salley agreed is higher than the market price of scmods.

(C) admitted, only if Beaver was aware of the fact that scmods is frequently referred to as rock lurgid.

(D) admitted, to explain the meaning of the term "rock lurgid" as used in the contract.

Questions 174-175 are based on the following fact situation.

After serving in the military for ten years, Doris

informed her father Finley that she had gotten married and was retiring from military service. Glad to hear the news, Finley said, "Because that's what I always hoped you would do, I'm going to give you a home as a wedding present." He showed Doris plans for the construction of a house, and promised that he would have it built on a lot which he owned and would deed it to her as soon as it was complete. Doris was so pleased with the plans which Finley showed her that she immediately canceled a contract which she had already made for the purchase of a home.

The following week, Finley contacted Barto, a builder. Finley showed Barto the plans and asked her to build a house according to those plans so that he could give it to his daughter as a wedding present. By a written contract Finley and Barto agreed that Barto would build on Finley's lot according to the plans on a cost-plus-profit basis. Finley immediately sent a copy of the contract and plans to Doris.

Barto subsequently informed Finley that soil conditions would make it necessary to drive piles for the foundation, increasing costs by approximately 600 percent. At Barto's suggestion, Finley and Barto agreed to the construction of a less expensive house instead, to be based on different plans. When Doris learned about the change, she informed Finley and Barto that she was dissatisfied with their new agreement.

174. If Doris asserts a claim against Barto as a third party beneficiary of the original contract between Finley and Barto, Barto's most effective argument in defense would be that

   (A) Doris was a donee beneficiary because the house was being built as a wedding present for her.

   (B) Doris was a creditor beneficiary because the contract between Finley and Barto was made after Finley promised Doris that he would give her the house.

   (C) Doris did not rely to her detriment on Finley's promise to give her a house built according to any particular plans.

   (D) Doris was not an intended third-party beneficiary of the contract between Finley and Barto.

175. If Doris asserts a claim against Finley, which of the following would be the most effective argument in support of her claim?

   (A) The modification of Finley's contract with Barto was unsupported by consideration.

   (B) Doris detrimentally relied on Finley's oral promise by canceling the contract which she had already made to purchase a home.

   (C) The contract between Finley and Barto was a writing signed by Finley.

   (D) Doris' marriage and retirement from military service was consideration for Finley's promise to give her a house built according to the plans which he showed her.

Questions 176-177 are based on the following fact situation.

On January 5, because he needed money to pay the rent on his store, Scott sent copies of the following letter to Asher, to Barrell, to Caper, and to Dodson:

> I need to sell my heart-shaped diamond ring by January 15 for $1,500. I am making this offer to Asher, Barrell, Caper and Dodson because all of you have admired the ring. If interested, please contact me before January 15.

On January 14, Scott received a letter from Asher agreeing to pay $1,500 for the ring. Scott did not respond to Asher's letter. On January 17, Scott received a letter from Barrell agreeing to pay $1,700 for the ring. On January 17, Scott wrote to Barrell saying, "I agree to the terms of your letter."

176. Assume for the purpose of this question only that Asher asserts a claim against Scott on account of Scott's refusal to sell the ring to Asher for $1,500. The court should find for

   (A) Scott, because the offer contained in Scott's letter of January 5 was revoked by his letter to Barrell on January 17.

(B) Scott, because he did not accept the offer contained in Asher's letter.

(C) Asher, because Asher complied with the terms of Scott's offer.

(D) Asher, because Barrell's letter was not received by Scott until after January 15.

177. Assume for the purpose of this question only that Barrell tendered payment immediately after receiving Scott's letter of January 17, but Scott refused to sell him the ring. If Barrell institutes a proceeding for an order directing Scott to sell him the ring for $1,700, is Barrell entitled to the relief requested?

(A) No, because specific performance is not available as a remedy for breach of a contract for the sale of personalty.

(B) No, unless Scott is a merchant with respect to the sale of a diamond ring.

(C) Yes, if the ring is highly unusual.

(D) Yes, because Scott could have obtained specific performance in the event of a breach by Barrell.

Questions 178-179 are based on the following fact situation.

Nursery was a retailer of home gardening supplies. On March 1, Nursery entered into a written contract with Seedco, a wholesaler of seeds. According to the terms, Seedco was to furnish Nursery with ryegrass seeds in 10 pound bags at a specified price. The contract provided that for a period of one year, Nursery would purchase all its ryegrass seeds from Seedco, and that Seedco would furnish all the ryegrass seeds required by Nursery. It provided further that Nursery would advise Seedco of its requirements by the first of each month, and that Seedco would make delivery by the end of that month. The contract was silent about the right to assign or delegate.

Upon signing the contract on March 1, Nursery notified Seedco of its ryegrass seed requirements for that month. Seedco made a delivery to Nursery on March 17. Prior to April 1, Nursery notified Seedco of its

ryegrass requirements for April. On April 20, Seedco sold its entire business to Allgrass, including its contract with Nursery, and notified Nursery of the sale the same day. On April 24, after Nursery received notice of the assignment, Allgrass delivered the seed which Nursery ordered from Seedco.

The next day, Nursery wrote to Allgrass, enclosing a check for the seeds Allgrass had delivered, and demanding that Allgrass assure Nursery that it would be able to meet Nursery's ryegrass seed requirements in the future. On June 1, not having heard from Allgrass, Nursery notified Seedco and Allgrass that it was canceling the contract.

178. If Allgrass asserts a claim against Nursery for breach of contract, the court should find for

(A) Allgrass, because Nursery failed to order seeds as required by contract.

(B) Allgrass, because there was no indication that the terms of the contract would not be performed by Allgrass.

(C) Nursery, because Allgrass failed to furnish assurances as demanded by Nursery.

(D) Nursery, because requirements contracts are not assignable without consent of the purchaser.

179. If Nursery asserts a claim against Seedco for breach of contract, the court should find for

(A) Nursery.

(B) Seedco, because Nursery impliedly consented to the assignment by accepting delivery from Allgrass.

(C) Seedco, because Nursery impliedly consented to the assignment by demanding assurances from Allgrass.

(D) Seedco, because its assignment of rights to Allgrass implied a delegation of duties.

Questions 180-181 are based on the following fact situation.

Otten hired Pullen, a painting contractor, to paint Otten's residence, entering into a valid written contract with Pullen which fixed the price of the job at $5,000 and provided that Pullen would deliver a "satisfactory result." Because Pullen wished to give his daughter Donia the money which he received from the job as a wedding gift, a clause of the contract directed Otten to pay the money directly to Donia. After Pullen finished painting the house, he sent Otten a bill for $5,000. When Otten received the bill, he called Pullen and complained about the paint job, saying that he did not think it was "satisfactory" as required by the contract. He said, "I've got half a mind not to pay you at all, but if you'll take $4,500, I'm willing to call it square." Pullen reluctantly agreed to accept $4,500 payable directly to him, because he needed cash. Otten paid the $4,500 to Pullen, who did not give any part of it to Donia.

180. Assume for the purpose of this question only that Donia learned about the contract between Pullen and Otten after Pullen received payment from Otten. Which of the following most accurately describes the rights of Donia?

   I.   Donia is entitled to collect $5,000 from Otten.

   II. Donia is entitled to collect $4,500 from Pullen.

   (A) I only.

   (B) II only.

   (C) I or II, but not both.

   (D) Neither I nor II.

181. Assume for the purpose of this question that Pullen subsequently brought a claim against Otten for $500 as the balance due on the agreed price of the paint job, asserting that his agreement to accept $4,500 was unsupported by consideration. If Otten defends by claiming that there was an accord and satisfaction, the court should find for

   (A) Otten, if Otten reasonably believed that the result was not "satisfactory" as required by the contract.

   (B) Otten, because no consideration is required for an agreement to modify a contract.

   (C) Pullen, because the agreement to modify the contract was not in writing.

   (D) Pullen, if Pullen did not believe that the result was not "satisfactory" as required by the contract or that Otten was entitled to a reduction in the price.

Questions 182-183 are based on the following fact situation.

When Sinclair decided to sell his home, he entered into a valid written contract with Ruse, a licensed real estate broker. The terms of the contract provided that Ruse would make reasonable efforts to sell the property and that if she succeeded, Sinclair would pay her a commission equivalent to 10% of the selling price. The contract further provided that the commission would be earned when Ruse located a ready, willing, and able buyer, and that payment of the commission would be made upon the closing of title. As a result of Ruse's efforts, Sinclair subsequently entered into a written agreement for sale of the property to Basic at an agreed upon price and under the terms specified in Sinclair's contract with Ruse.

182. Assume for the purpose of this question only that prior to the date set for closing of title, Sinclair notified Basic that he would not go through with the transaction, and that Basic instituted a proceeding for specific performance against Sinclair. If Ruse asserts a claim against Sinclair for her commission, a court should find for

   (A) Sinclair, because closing of title was a condition precedent to Sinclair's obligation to pay Ruse a commission.

   (B) Sinclair, unless his agreement to sell the property to Basic is enforceable by Ruse.

   (C) Ruse, because Sinclair prevented performance of a condition precedent to Sinclair's obligation to pay Ruse a commission.

   (D) Ruse, but only if Basic is successful in obtaining an order directing specific performance by Sinclair.

183. Assume for the purpose of this question only that prior to the date set for closing of title, Basic notified Sinclair that he would not go through with the transaction, and that Sinclair instituted an action for damages against Basic. If Ruse asserts a claim against Sinclair for her commission, a court should find for

    (A) Sinclair, because closing of title was a condition precedent to Sinclair's obligation to pay Ruse a commission.

    (B) Sinclair, but only if Basic's repudiation resulted from some fault by Ruse.

    (C) Ruse, because Ruse found a ready, willing, and able buyer.

    (D) Ruse, but only if Sinclair succeeds in recovering damages from Basic.

184. Otto was the owner of a parcel of realty on which he wished to build a house. After discussion, he entered into a valid written contract with Brosnan, a building contractor. Pursuant to the terms of the contract, Brosnan was to construct a residence on the realty according to attached plans and specifications. The contract required Otto to make periodic payments to Brosnan when the structure was 25%, 50%, and 100% complete, and permitted Brosnan to hire subcontractors at his discretion.

    After entering into the contract with Otto, Brosnan hired Subic, a subcontractor, to do all of the carpentry work. By a written contract, Brosnan agreed to pay Subic a specified price for his labor upon completion of the carpentry work, and, in addition, to "reimburse Subic for all material purchased by Subic for the job". During the course of the work, Subic purchased $5,000 worth of lumber, but actually used only $3,000 worth of it. When the carpentry work was completed, Brosnan paid Subic the agreed price for Subic's labor, but refused to pay more than $3,000 for lumber. Subic asserted a claim against Brosnan for an additional $2,000 for lumber which he purchased for the job but did not use. At the trial, Subic attempted to testify to a conversa-

tion which took place prior to signing of the written contract and in which Brosnan agreed that he would pay for materials purchased but not actually used.

If Brosnan objects to Subic's testimony about the conversation which took place prior to signing the written contract, the court should

    (A) exclude Subic's testimony unless payment for unused materials is customary in the construction industry.

    (B) exclude Subic's testimony because it is prohibited by the parol evidence rule.

    (C) exclude Subic's testimony if the contract between Brosnan and Otto did not provide for Otto to pay for materials purchased for the job but not used.

    (D) permit Subic to testify for the purpose of clarifying any language of the contract with uncertain meaning.

Questions 185-186 are based on the following fact situation.

When Forde's daughter Dale told him that she was getting married, Forde was so happy that he promised to deed her a parcel of realty which he owned and to have a house built on it for her as a wedding present. The following day, Forde entered into a written contract with Boudreau, a building contractor, for the construction of a house on Forde's land. Forde later gave Dale a copy of the contract, and, as a result, Dale canceled a contract into which she had previously entered for the purchase of a home. As a result of an argument between Forde and Boudreau, Boudreau never built the house.

185. Assume for the purpose of this question that Forde later deeds the land to Dale, and that she asserts a claim against Boudreau for failure to fulfill the obligations under his contract with Forde. The court should find for

    (A) Dale, because Forde intended for her to benefit from his contract with Boudreau.

    (B) Boudreau, because the contract called for

personal services.

(C) Boudreau, because Dale is an incidental beneficiary.

(D) Boudreau, because Dale is a donee beneficiary.

186. Assume for the purpose of this question only the Forde refused to deed the realty to Dale, and that Dale institutes a proceeding against him for damages resulting from breach of contract. The court should find for

(A) Dale, because she detrimentally relied on Forde's promise.

(B) Dale, because she is a third party beneficiary of Forde's contract with Boudreau.

(C) Forde, because he received no consideration for his promise to Dale.

(D) Forde, under the doctrine of frustration of purpose.

187. Sandez was an investor who frequently bought and sold real estate on his own account. He had purchased a parcel of realty known as Sandacre for $100,000 and was considering selling it. On September 1, Bethel asked whether Sandez would be willing to accept $125,000 for the property. Sandez said that he would, but only if payment was in cash. When Bethel said that he would need a month or two to raise that kind of money, Sandez wrote the following on a sheet of paper and signed it:

I hereby offer to sell my realty known as Sandacre to Bethel for $125,000 cash. I promise to hold this offer open until November 1, and I further promise that I will not sell the property to anyone else before then. This is a firm offer.

Subsequently, but prior to November 1, Sandez sold the property to Duncan for $110,000 and wrote Bethel a note in which he said, "I hereby withdraw my offer to sell you Sandacre for $125,000." On October 25, Bethel purchased Sandacre from Duncan for $135,000.

If Bethel asserts a claim against Sandez for damages resulting from Sandez's sale of Sandacre to Duncan, the court should find for

(A) Sandez, because he received no consideration for his promise to keep the offer open.

(B) Sandez, only if he sold the realty to Duncan more than 30 days after promising Bethel to keep the offer open.

(C) Bethel, because the document which Sandez signed on September 1 was a firm offer in writing.

(D) Bethel, only if Bethel customarily engaged in buying and selling real estate.

Questions 188-90 are based on the following fact situation.

When he won the state lottery, Hamlin bought a new home and decided to have it landscaped by a well-known landscape architect. After investigating several sources, Hamlin learned that Landsman was one of the most famous landscape architects in the world. Following a series of discussions, Hamlin and Landsman entered into a written contract which called for Landsman to design and execute a landscaping plan for Hamlin's property at a total price of $90,000. Upon completion of the job, Hamlin was to pay $80,000 of this sum directly to Landsman. Hamlin agreed to pay the balance of $10,000 to Crawford because Landsman was indebted to Crawford for that sum. A clause of the contract provided that "there shall be no assignment of rights under this contract."

Landsman's design called for a moat to be dug around Hamlin's house and planted with aquatic plants. Although Landsman completed the rest of the job himself, he hired Digger, an earthmoving subcontractor, to dig the moat, which Digger did in complete conformity with Landsman's plan. When the job was completed, Crawford executed a document purporting to assign his rights under the contract to Anchor. The entire job was completed in a reasonably workmanlike manner, but Hamlin refused to make any payment under the contract.

188. Assume for the purpose of this question only that Crawford asserts a claim against Hamlin for $10,000, which Crawford claims Hamlin owes him under the contract. Which of the following would be Hamlin's most effective argument in defense against that claim?

(A) Crawford has made a valid assignment of his rights under the contract.

(B) Crawford was not a party to the contract.

(C) Crawford was a mere incidental beneficiary of the contract.

(D) There was no mutuality of obligation between Hamlin and Crawford.

189. Assume for the purpose of this question only that Anchor asserts a claim against Hamlin for $10,000. In deciding the claim, a court should find for

(A) Hamlin, because the contract prohibited assignment.

(B) Hamlin, if the contract called for Landsman to perform personal services.

(C) Anchor, because an assignee stands in the shoes of his assignor.

(D) Anchor, but only if Anchor paid consideration for the assignment.

190. Assume for the purpose of this question only that Landsman asserted a claim against Hamlin on account of Hamlin's refusal to pay him for his services, and that Hamlin defended on the ground that Landsman breached the contract by hiring a subcontractor to dig the moat. In deciding the claim, the court should find for

(A) Hamlin, because Landsman hired Digger to dig the moat around Hamlin's house.

(B) Hamlin, because the reason why Hamlin contracted with Landsman was that he wanted the job done by a well-known landscape architect.

(C) Landsman, because the moat was dug in complete conformity with Landsman's

plan.

(D) Landsman, because all contract rights are freely assignable.

Questions 191-192 are based on the following fact situation.

Frost, a manufacturer, needed a new factory and purchased a parcel of realty on which he wished to have it constructed. After negotiation, Frost entered into a valid written contract with Berry, a licensed builder. Pursuant to its terms, Berry was to construct a two story building on Frost's realty according to specifications furnished by Frost, at a total price of $250,000, to be paid in full upon completion of the building.

191. Assume the following facts for the purpose of this question only. Berry completed the building, and Frost paid him $250,000 but subsequently Frost learned that the building failed to conform to the specifications. As a result, it would not serve Frost's purpose. The building had the same value as if constructed in conformity with the specifications, but it would cost Frost $12,000 to make it conform to the specifications. Because of an increase in the costs of construction, it would cost $350,000 to construct a new building in conformity with the specifications.

If Frost asserts a claim against Berry for breach of contract, Frost should recover

(A) nothing, because the building had the same value as if built in conformity with the specifications.

(B) $12,000 (the cost of making the building conform to the specifications).

(C) $100,000 (the difference between the contract price and the cost of having a new building constructed in accordance with the specifications.

(D) $250,000 (the contract price).

192. Assume the following facts for the purpose of this question only. When the structure was partially completed, Frost decided to retire from the

manufacturing business and told Berry to stop work. Berry had already spent $180,000 on material and labor, and would have needed to spend another $35,000 to complete the building in conformity with the specifications. Because of an increase in construction costs, the value of the partially completed structure was $300,000. If Berry asserts a claim against Frost for breach of contract, Berry should recover

(A) $265,000 (the value of the partially completed structure less the cost of completing construction).

(B) $250,000 (the contract price).

(C) $215,000 (the contract price less the cost of completing construction).

(D) $180,000 (the amount which Berry has expended).

Questions 193-94 are based on the following fact situation.

Stubbs wanted to sell his piano. Because Altom, Better, Carrol, and Danton had all expressed interest in it, Stubbs wrote and signed the following letter on May 1, sending a photocopy to each of the persons named:

> Dear Altom, Better, Carrol and Danton:
> I know that you are all interested in buying my piano and I need to sell it. I therefore promise to sell it to whichever of you makes the highest offer prior to June 15.
>   (signed) Stubbs.

Altom, who knew that the piano was worth $1,700, wrote a letter to Stubbs on June 1, in which he said that he would pay that sum for the piano. Stubbs received the letter on June 2. On June 19, Stubbs received a letter from Better which said, "I received your offer of May 1. Will $2,000 buy the piano?"

On June 21, Stubbs wrote to Better, "I accept your offer and will sell you the piano for 2,000. (signed) Stubbs."

193. Stubb's letter of May 1 to Altom, Better, Carrol and Danton is best described as

(A) a firm offer.

(B) an invitation for offers.

(C) an option to purchase which was given to Altom, Better, Carrol and Danton but could only be exercised by the first to respond.

(D) an auction.

194. Stubb's letter of June 21 to Better is best described as

(A) an offer.

(B) an acceptance.

(C) an invitation to negotiate.

(D) an anticipatory repudiation of Stubb's agreement with Altom.

ANSWERS
CONTRACTS

ANSWERS TO
CONTRACTS QUESTIONS

1. **D**   Farrell's offer was for a unilateral contract — his promise to pay in return for Stuart's postponing the wedding. When Stuart postponed the wedding, he accepted Farrell's offer, and a contract was formed.

    Some cases have held that an agreement never to marry violates public policy, but there is no reason why an agreement to postpone a marriage would do so. **A** is, therefore, incorrect. **B** is incorrect because Farrell's promise was to pay if Stuart postponed the wedding. His language did not make payment conditional upon Stuart's registration for a second year. Although an offer terminates upon the death of the offeror, **C** is incorrect because Stuart accepted the offer by postponing the wedding, and, once accepted, an offer is no longer revocable.

2. **D**   Since Sorrento sold the chairs to another buyer at the same price which Barrie had contracted to pay, Sorrento sustained no damage. Where there is no limit to the availability of the items sold, some cases allow a seller to recover lost profits when a buyer cancels, reasoning that even though the seller resold at the same price, she would have made two sales instead of one if the buyer had not breached. Since there were no more barrel chairs to sell, however, Sorrento lost nothing.

    A is, therefore, incorrect. An action for the price might be available where traditional calculation of damages would be inadequate, but **B** is incorrect because Sorrento has suffered no damages. **C** correctly states the remedy which would have been available to Barrie in the event of a breach by Sorrento. Because the fair market value exceeds the contract price, however, the formula expressed in **C** bears no relationship to damages suffered by Sorrento as a result of Barrie's breach. **C** is, therefore, incorrect.

3. **A**   If an event which was not foreseeable to the parties at the time a contract was formed makes performance of the contract impossible, such performance is excused. In the absence of facts which specifically suggest the contrary, destruction of the subject matter of a contract is usually held to have been unforeseeable by the parties at the time of contracting.

    At the time the fire occurred, Homer was not in breach because he was not required to make payment until the garage was half complete, and Bilder was not in breach because he was not required to be half finished until April 25. **B** and **C** are, therefore, incorrect. It is usually held that impossibility excuses performance only to the extent that performance has been made impossible. **D** is incorrect, however, because the contract was not for labor until June 1, but rather for construction of the garage by June 1, and the fire has made completion by that date impossible.

4. **D**   Since quasi-contract remedies are essentially designed to prevent unjust enrichment, they are usually unavailable against a non-breaching defendant who has received no benefits from the plaintiff's work.

    A, **B** and **C** are, therefore, incorrect. In addition, **A** is incorrect because its formula bears no reasonable relationship to the value of either the benefit received by Homer or the detriment suffered by Bilder. **C** is incorrect for the additional reason that quasi-contract recovery is based on reasonable value rather on the contract price.

5. **A** The UCC provides that where there is no agreement to the contrary, a buyer is entitled to inspect the goods prior to making payment or accepting them. It provides further, however, that the parties may agree that payment is required before inspection. If so, failure to make payment upon delivery of the goods is a breach.

Anticipatory repudiation occurs when, *prior to the time when performance is required,* a party indicates by word or deed that he will not perform. **B** is incorrect because Boswell's refusal to pay occurred at the time payment was required, and therefore constituted a breach. The UCC provides that even if payment is made prior to inspection, no acceptance occurs until after the buyer has had a reasonable opportunity to inspect. In view of this provision, a promise to pay prior to inspection is not unconscionable, and **C** is incorrect. Since Stilton tendered delivery in accordance with the terms of the contract, **D** is incorrect.

6. **C** Section 2-606 of the UCC provides that unless the buyer does some act inconsistent with the seller's ownership, acceptance of goods occurs only after the buyer has had a reasonable opportunity to inspect the goods and either notifies the seller of his intention to keep them or fails to reject them. Thus, a payment did not constitute acceptance because it was made before Boswell was given a reasonable opportunity to inspect the studs.

A, **B** and **D** are incorrect because the UCC provides that acceptance does not occur until after there has been a reasonable opportunity to inspect.

7. **A** Under Section 2-313 of the UCC, a warranty is made by any description of the goods which is given by the seller and which is part of the basis of the bargain. Stilton thus warranted that the studs delivered would be construction grade. Under Section 2-714 of the UCC, a buyer who has accepted non-conforming goods and who notifies the seller of the non-conformity within a reasonable time is entitled to damages. The measure of damages for breach of warranty is fixed by Section 2-714 as the difference between the value which the delivered goods had at the time of acceptance and the value which conforming goods would have had at that time.

B is incorrect because it would entitle Boswell to keep the studs without paying anything for them. **C** is incorrect because it would allow Stilton to collect the price of construction grade studs although he delivered utility grade studs. Although Stilton might have been better off selling the utility grade studs to another buyer at a price higher than they were worth, he has breached his warranty that the studs delivered would be construction grade and will be required to compensate Boswell for what Boswell has lost. **D** is, therefore, incorrect.

8. **A** A unilateral contract is a promise to perform in exchange for a specified act by the promisee. Since Compinc promised to make payment to the employee who submitted the winning design, its offer was for a unilateral contract.

A bilateral contract is an exchange of promises, each given in return for the other. Since the company promised to pay only if the modification design was actually submitted, and asked for no promise in return for its promise to pay, **B** is incorrect. Compinc's notice made clear its intention to pay only one prize and its obligation to pay only upon receipt of a design which complied with its requirements. Its promise, therefore, could not have been given in exchange for the promise contained in Enner's March 8 memo, even if that memo had been received. **C** is, therefore, incorrect. The key difference between an offer and an invitation to negotiate is that an offer creates an immediate power of acceptance in the offeree. Since any employee could have accepted the company's offer of a reward by successfully designing and submitting the required program modification, **D** is incorrect.

9. **B** Under the *Restatement of Contracts, Second* an offer for a unilateral contract cannot effectively be withdrawn once the offeree has begun performance. Since Enner began working on the design prior to the company's attempt to withdraw its offer, the company's offer will be held to be irrevocable.

A bilateral contract is an exchange of promises. Since Enner's performance was complete upon his submission of the design, no bilateral contract was created by the submission because no promise by Enner resulted from it. **A** is, therefore, incorrect. **C** is incorrect because an offer for a unilateral contract can be withdrawn at any time prior to the offeree's commencement of performance. **D** is incorrect for the same reason, and because under the UCC "unconscionability" only prevents enforcement of a contract which is found as a matter of law to have been unconscionable at the time that it was made.

10. **B** If a promise not to assign a contract is enforceable, it is like any other promise in that damages may be available as a remedy for its breach. An assignment made in violation of such a promise is usually regarded as valid, however. This means that even though Lansman may be entitled to recover from Corman for damages resulting from Corman's assignment to Antun, Antun may enforce the contract against Lansman.

C is, therefore, incorrect. **A** is incorrect because a promise not to assign without a party's consent does not require that party to act reasonably in deciding whether or not to consent. It is generally understood that a contract involving personal services is not assignable because an assignment of such a contract may increase the obligor's burden. Since the contract between Corman and Lansman specified the tasks which Lansman was to perform, and since a change in obligee (i.e., in the ownership of the condominium) would not alter those tasks, assignment to Antun did not increase Lansman's burden. For this reason, the contract should not be regarded as one calling for personal services, and **D** is incorrect.

11. **C** Consideration is a benefit to the promisor or a detriment to the promisee which was bargained for and given in return for the promisor's promise. For this reason, if Curran did something which he was already obligated to do, his act could not be consideration for the City's promise to pay since no new benefit was given to the City and no detriment was sustained by Curran in return for that promise. A police officer's obligation to his employer includes the duty to attempt to apprehend criminals, so Curran's performance was of a pre-existing duty.

A is incorrect because establishing that Pidgeon is entitled to the reward does not necessarily establish that Curran (or anybody else) is not entitled to it also. **B** is incorrect because a guilty plea is a conviction. Since the City's promise was to pay in return for information leading to a conviction, it was an offer to pay for something of value, not an offer for a gratuitous cash award. **D** is, therefore, incorrect.

12. **D**   The parol evidence rule prohibits the introduction of extrinsic evidence of prior or contemporaneous agreements offered to contradict, vary, or modify an unambiguous writing which the parties intended to be a full and final expression of their agreement (i.e., a "complete integration"). Since the "dollar" is the unit of currency in both the U.S. and San Sebastian, the contract which specifies a price of 9,000 dollars without identifying which country's dollars are intended is probably ambiguous. The evidence offered by Sella would help explain and clarify the ambiguity. It is not barred by the parol evidence rule since it does not contradict, vary, or modify the writing.

         A and **C** are, therefore, incorrect. Ambiguities in a writing are frequently construed against the party who prepared it, but only if they cannot be clarified in some other way. **B** is incorrect because parol evidence may be introduced to explain an ambiguity, no matter who caused it.

13. **D**   Manfred made no express promise to pay for the fishing gear. There was no implied promise because there is no fact indicating that Sport acted with the expectation of compensation or reimbursement for her losses. The executor is, therefore, not bound to pay for her loss.

         Quantum meruit is available to prevent unjust enrichment only where services were rendered under circumstances such that the party from whom payment is sought was aware of the other party's expectation of payment. **A** is, therefore, incorrect. The phrase "danger invites rescue" has been used in tort cases to explain why one who creates a peril owes a duty of care to a person attempting to rescue another from it. **B** is incorrect, however, because the principle has no application in contract problems. Since there is no indication that Manfred promised to pay for the fishing gear, the fact that someone else in his position would have is irrelevant, making **C** incorrect.

14. **C**   Usually, a promise is unenforceable unless it is supported by *consideration*, which requires a bargained-for exchange. Since Manfred's promise was made after Sport rendered a service with no apparent expectation of compensation, the service was not given in exchange for the promise, and the promise is not supported by consideration. For this reason, the majority of jurisdictions would not enforce it. Although some courts might enforce a promise to fulfill a "moral obligation," **C** is the only answer which could be correct in any jurisdiction.

         "Good Samaritan" statutes, where they exist, protect from liability for negligence those who render emergency aid at an accident scene. These statutes do nothing more. **A** is incorrect because they have no application to contract problems. **B** is based on an inaccurate interpretation of the facts: since Sport did not change her position after receiving Manfred's promise, she did not rely on it, detrimentally or otherwise. **D** is incorrect because if something of value has been given in return for a promise, the promise is supported by consideration even though the value of that consideration may be uncertain.

15. **A** Performance of one of a series of mutual promises is a condition precedent to others in the series if the circumstances indicate that it should obviously precede the others. Since the writing called for payment of $300 in advance, it is obvious that the parties intended that it should be paid before the work commenced. Honniker's payment of $300 was thus a condition precedent to Carl's obligation to paint. Since the contract called for the payment of an additional $400 after completion, it is obvious that the parties intended that the paint job should be finished before payment of the additional money was required. Completion of the paint job is thus a condition precedent to Honniker's obligation to pay the additional $400.

A condition subsequent is an event the occurrence or non-occurrence of which operates to discharge a duty which had already become absolute. Since Carl was obligated to paint before receiving the additional $400, and since he could not undo the paint job once it was completed, Honniker's payment of the additional $400 cannot be called a condition subsequent to Carl's obligation to paint the car. **B** is, therefore, incorrect. Concurrent conditions require the parties to exchange performance simultaneously. **C** is incorrect because the language of the contract makes it obvious that the parties intended a consecutive order of performance (i.e., H pays $300, C completes paint job, H pays $400). Since the agreement required part payment in advance, and completion of the job before the balance was due, **D** is incorrect.

16. **A** Upon breach of the sales contract, the non-breaching party is ordinarily entitled to compensatory, incidental, and consequential damages. A buyer's compensatory damages consist of the difference between the contract price and either the fair market value or the "cover" price (i.e., actual cost of replacement, so long as reasonable). If the cover price (or fair market value) is less than the contract price the buyer is not entitled to compensatory damages, but the saving is not credited to the breaching seller. Incidental damages consist of the reasonable costs of repurchasing. Consequential damages are those which foreseeably arise from the special needs or position of the buyer which result from the breach (e.g., seller's non-delivery causes buyer to go out of business). Honniker sustained no consequential losses, and since Honniker's cover price was less than the contract price, she can receive no compensatory damages. Since the repurchase involved $20 in reasonable expenses, she is entitled to $20 as incidental damages.

B is incorrect because it bears no reasonable relation to Honniker's loss. **C** is incorrect because it would award Honniker the entire contract price in addition to incidental damages. **D** is incorrect because it would credit Carl with the savings which resulted from his breach.

17. **C** In an action for breach of an employment contract, a non-breaching employee is entitled to receive the full contract price for the balance of the term plus consequential damages, less damages avoided by mitigation. Since Worthen mitigated damages by taking a job with Newton at the same salary, he is entitled to what he lost between the discharge and the beginning of his new job. His advertising expenses are collectible as consequential damages.

A is incorrect because the reorganization by Boss was voluntary. An employment contract may require payment of severance pay in the event of termination, but absent such agreement, there is no such legal requirement. **B** is, therefore, incorrect. **D** is incorrect because Worthen's work for Newton at the same salary mitigated his damages.

18. **A**   If Payne's statement implied a promise to paint the cars, it was an acceptance of Cabb's offer, thus forming a contract of which Payne's subsequent refusal to paint the cars would be a breach. (*NOTE*: Although Payne's statement probably was not a promise, the question requires this to be assumed as an additional fact.)

             If, on the other hand, he made no promise to paint the cars, there was no contract and could be no breach. This would be true even though Cabb suffered detriment in reliance on his belief that Payne would paint his cars. **B** and **C** are, therefore, incorrect. When Cabb offered $125 per car, he rejected Payne's offer to paint them for $150. It was too late for him to accept that offer on January 3, so **D** is incorrect.

19. **D**   None of the reasons given to justify a victory for Martin are good ones. The doctrine of frustration of purpose may excuse performance of a contract when an unforeseen event destroys its underlying purpose, but only if both parties knew what that purpose was.

             A is incorrect because Osteen did not know Martin's purpose. Impossibility of performance discharges a contractual obligation when an unforeseen event makes performance vitally different from that reasonably contemplated by both parties at the time the contract was formed. **B** is incorrect because Osteen was unaware of the use contemplated by Martin. When government action makes the subject matter of a contract unlawful, it may be unenforceable for illegality, because of frustration of purpose, or under the doctrine of impossibility of performance. **C** is incorrect, however, because the subject matter of the contract between Osteen and Martin was the rental of a motion picture theater, and the showing of motion pictures was not made unlawful by the city council's action.

20. **D**   The Statute of Frauds requires a contract for the sale of goods with a price of $500 or more to be in writing, but does not apply to a contract for services, even if goods are to be provided by the person performing the services. **I** and **II** are, therefore, incorrect.

21. **B**   Usually, a promise is unenforceable unless it is supported by consideration. Consideration is a bargained-for exchange of value given for a promise and may consist of benefit to the promisor or detriment to the promisee. If an alleged debt is invalid, a person who promises to pay a sum in settlement of it receives no benefit in return for his promise. Similarly, if a person who receives such a promise does not honestly believe that the debt is valid, he suffers no detriment by agreeing to accept less in settlement. For this reason, a promise to pay a sum of money to settle a claim for debt is supported by consideration if the debt is valid or the person asserting the claim believes that it is. Thus, if Poston honestly believed that Dworkin owed him $3,000, his agreement to accept $2,000 was consideration for Dworkin's promise, making the promise enforceable.

             On the other hand, if Poston did not believe that Dworkin owed him the money, Poston suffered no detriment and Dworkin received no benefit in return for Dworkin's promise. Since the promise would, thus, be unsupported by consideration, it would be unenforceable. **A** is, therefore, incorrect. **C** and **D** are incorrect because, unless the debt actually existed or Poston believed that it did, his agreement to accept $2,000 would not be consideration for Dworkin's promise to pay it.

22. **A**   Although the parol evidence rule prevents the introduction of extrinsic evidence for the purpose of modifying the terms of certain written memorandums, it does not prevent the admission of such testimony for the purpose of establishing that no contract was ever formed. Since the oral agreement made before execution of the writing establishes a condition precedent to the formation of a contract, it is admissible.

An agreement to modify a contract is one which is made after formation of the contract. **B** is incorrect because the oral agreement regarding the loan was made before execution of the written contract. Since Smith has not asserted that the written agreement is valid, there is no reason why he should be estopped from denying that it is. **C** is, therefore, incorrect. **D** is incorrect because the oral agreement relates to the formation of the contract, and does not modify or contradict its terms.

23. **B**   A donee third party beneficiary of a contract may enforce it. The parties are free to modify that contract, however, any time prior to the donee beneficiary's detrimental reliance on it. Since Dot did not learn of the contract until after it had been modified, she has no right to enforce the terms which existed prior to the modification.

A is incorrect because a third party beneficiary of a contract may enforce it even though she has not, herself, given consideration. **C** is incorrect because the rights of a donee beneficiary do not vest until she learns of or relies upon the contract, and Dot did not learn about or rely on the contract until after it had been modified to exclude her. An assignment of contract rights is ineffective until the assignee learns of and accepts it. **D** is incorrect because even if the written contract between Smith and Trac was an assignment to Dot, Dot did not learn of Trac's intent to create rights in her until after he eliminated those rights by modifying his contract with Smith.

24. **A**   The Statute of Frauds requires a contract for the sale of goods with a price of $500 or more to be in writing. It might be argued that the agreement in **A** was divisible — really 15 separate agreements, each for a single $100 purchase — and therefore not within the Statute of Frauds. (*Note*: Since the agreement was for the purchase of a "series" of figurines, it was probably not a divisible contract, but **A** is the only one of the four fact patterns presented in which the Statute of Frauds *might* prevent enforcement.)

UCC Section 2-201 specifically excludes from application of the statute a contract for the sale of specifically manufactured goods if the seller has made a substantial beginning in their manufacture. The Statute of Frauds would be inapplicable in **B**, since Plaintiff had already completed the rough carving when Defendant attempted to cancel the contract. Since 2-201 specifies that the Statute of Frauds is satisfied by an admission in the pleadings of the existence of a contract, the statute would not prevent enforcement in **C**. Section 2-201 provides that between merchants a written memorandum of a contract which is sufficient to bind the sender binds the receiver also if she fails to object to it within 10 days. Since both parties in **D** are merchants, the writing prepared by plaintiff and not responded to by defendant satisfies the statute.

25. **B**   A minor may disaffirm a contract on the ground of incapacity. If, however, the disaf-

firming minor is the plaintiff in an action for restitution, her recovery will be offset by the reasonable value of the benefit which she had received. Measuring the benefit in terms of reasonable rental value is a common judicial approach.

A is, therefore, incorrect. **C** is incorrect because the damage which the car sustained is not related to the benefit which Margeaux received. **D** is incorrect because it fails to recognize the minor's right to disaffirm the contract.

26.   **C**   An offer may be revoked any time prior to its acceptance, and is effectively revoked when the offeree learns of an act by the offeror which is wholly inconsistent with the offer. Sulton's offer to sell the tractor to Brendan was thus revoked when Brendan learned that Sulton had sold it to Norton.

Sulton's promise to keep the offer open until March 15 was unsupported by consideration, and, therefore, not enforceable. Although UCC §2-205 makes certain firm offers between merchants enforceable without consideration, **A** is incorrect because Sulton and Brendan were not merchants regarding the sale of the tractor. **B** is incorrect because the revocation took effect when Brendan learned of the sale to Norton. **D** is incorrect because the letter of February 15 was an offer to sell the tractor, and could have given rise to a contract if accepted by Brendan before Sulton revoked it.

27.   **A**   A court may reform a contract to reflect the intentions of the parties if as a result of inadvertence the writing does not actually do so. In determining the intentions of the parties, the court may admit whatever evidence is relevant and material.

B is incorrect because UCC Section 2-201 declares that a writing may satisfy the Statute of Frauds even though one or more terms (except the quantity term) are omitted. The UCC provides that parties may conclude a contract for sale even though the price is not settled, and that if they do, the price is to be the reasonable price at the time of delivery. **C** is incorrect, however, because Seller and Buyer did agree on a price. **D** is incorrect because parol evidence may be admitted for the purpose of determining what the parties intended the price to be.

28.   **C**   The parol evidence rule prohibits the introduction of extrinsic evidence of prior or contemporaneous agreements to contradict, vary, or modify an unambiguous writing which the parties intended to be a full and final expression of their agreement. It is generally understood that in the absence of fraud or mistake, a clause in a written contract which states that the writing is intended to be a complete integration of the agreement between the parties establishes that it is. If so, the agreement in **C** would be barred by the parol evidence rule since it was a contemporaneous agreement which contradicts a term of the writing.

The purpose of the parol evidence rule is to discourage litigation by encouraging parties to put their entire agreement in writing. Since this purpose would not be served by prohibiting parol evidence regarding the question of whether or not the obligations created by the writing ever came into being, parol evidence pertaining to a written contract's becoming effective is admissible. **A** is, therefore, incorrect. Since the writing requires Hoser to pay for the paint, the agreements in **B** and **D** do not modify any obligation created by the writing, and so would probably be admitted. **B** and **D** are, therefore, incor-

rect.

29.   **A**   An agreement for the sale of goods FOB a particular place requires the seller to load the goods on board a carrier at that place. Once the seller has done so, the buyer's obligation to pay the seller for the goods becomes complete. Under UCC Section 2-210, a seller who has completely performed may assign its rights even if terms of the contract prohibit assignment. Since the seller's rights have been assigned to Abco, Abco now is entitled to collect the price from Bittell.

B correctly states the remedy usually available to the *buyer* in the event of the seller's failure to deliver, but is incorrect as a statement of the seller's remedy. Payment by Bittell might enrich Abco, but since Abco has given value for the assignment of Kooler's rights, the enrichment would not be unjust. **C** is, therefore, incorrect. So long as assignment does not impose an additional burden on the obligor, an assignment of contract rights is enforceable in spite of a clause prohibiting it. **D** is, therefore, incorrect.

30.   **B**   In an FOB contract, the risk of loss passes to the buyer as soon as the goods are loaded on a carrier at the place specified. This means that once the air conditioner units were loaded onto Carrier's truck, any loss not resulting from the fault of the seller became Bittell's. Bittell is thus not entitled to damages due to non-delivery resulting from such loss.

A is incorrect because assignment does not free the assignor from obligations under the contract, even if the obligee has consented to the assignment. As between parties to a contract, one of them always bears the risk of loss. The fact that a third (i.e., non-contracting) party may also have become liable for such loss does not affect the rights which contracting parties have against each other. **C** is, therefore, incorrect. After a contract is formed, if there occurs a change in circumstances which was not contemplated by the parties at the time of formation and which makes a party's performance impossible, that performance is excused. **D** is incorrect, however, because the destruction of a particular shipment of air conditioning units does not necessarily make it impossible for the seller to deliver other units which would satisfy its obligation under the contract.

31.   **A**   A contract is formed upon acceptance of an offer. An offer is a manifestation of present intent to be bound to specific terms. Since Nan's letter of August 1 clearly expressed her willingness to sell each of the paintings to Delia for $2,000, it was an offer. An acceptance occurs when the offeree communicates to the offeror that she agrees to the terms of the offer. Since Delia's telegram clearly expressed her willingness to pay $2,000 for painting number 30, it was an acceptance. A contract for the sale of painting number 30 at a price of $2,000 was thus formed. For this reason, Nan's action for breach of a contract to purchase the painting for $3,000 must fail unless there has been an enforceable modification of the original contract. Under UCC section 2-209(3) a modification of a contract must be in writing if the contract as modified is within the provisions of the Statute of Frauds. Since, as modified, the oral contract between Nan and Delia calls for the sale of goods with a price in excess of $500, it violates the Statute of Frauds and will not be enforced over Delia's objection. **A** is, therefore, correct.

Since an increase in the fair market value of the painting would not satisfy the requirement of a writing, **B** is incorrect. A promise which is not supported by consideration or one which violates the Statute of Frauds may be enforceable if the promisee *justifiably* relies on it *to her detriment.* **C** is incorrect, however, because reliance alone is insufficient to have this effect and because there is no indication that Nan changed her position (i.e., relied). Since Nan's offer of August 1 called for acceptance by telegraphed order, Delia's telegram on August 2 was an acceptance even though payment had not been made. **D** is, therefore, incorrect.

32.   **C**   Since Nan's offer was for the sale of any or all of the paintings, Delia could accept by promising to purchase any or all of them. Since her telegram specifically agreed to the purchase of only one painting, Nan may successfully argue that it rejected Nan's offer to sell the others.

A is incorrect for several reasons. Specific performance is available as a buyer's remedy when the subject of the contract of sale is unique because no amount of money can replace it. The fact that Delia was an art dealer does not establish that she was buying the paintings for resale. Even if she was, damages might not be an adequate remedy since the uniqueness of each painting makes it impossible to determine what her damages were. **B** is incorrect because Nan and Delia are merchants, and under the UCC a promise between merchants to keep an offer open for a specified period of time may be enforceable even without consideration. Since the language of Nan's letter made it clear that Delia could create a binding contract for the sale of any or all of the paintings simply by telegraphing her order, Nan's letter was an offer, and **D** is incorrect.

33.   **C**   Assignment of a contract transfers all the assignor's rights to the assignee. After the assignment, the assignor has no rights in the contract and cannot sue to enforce it.

A is incorrect because assignment does not discharge the assignor of his obligations under the contract. There is a presumption, however, that an assignment of rights under a contract includes a delegation of duties as well. **B** is, therefore, incorrect because, as assignee, Byers is obligated to make payment as agreed by Forrest. Unless there is a clear agreement to the contrary, a promise not to assign without consent of the other party is usually viewed as a covenant. An obligee who breaches that covenant by assigning may be liable for damages to the obligor, but the assignment is valid in spite of the no-assignment clause so long as it imposes no additional burden on the obligor. Since Seider's obligation after the assignment is identical to his obligation before the assignment (i.e., to install aluminum sliding on the outside of the building), there is no reason to hold the assignment invalid. **D** is, therefore, incorrect.

34.   **B**   The UCC treats a modification of a contract as a new contract. For this reason, if the contract as modified falls within the provisions of the Statute of Frauds, the modification must be in writing. UCC §2-209(3). Since the modification resulted in an agreement to sell goods with a price of $500 or more, the Statute of Frauds requires a written memorandum. The absence of a writing makes the contract unenforceable over the objection of Ronson.

A contract is unconscionable if one party is so deprived of free choice that s/he is forced to make a one-sided bargain which favors the other party. Since the free enterprise system sometimes results in different prices being set by different suppliers of the same commodity, the mere fact that the merchandise was available at a lower price than that requested by Wells is not sufficient to make the agreement to pay Wells' price unconscionable. **A**, is therefore, incorrect. **C** is incorrect because, under UCC §2-209(1), an agreement to modify a contract may be enforceable even though unsupported by consideration. **D** would be relevant if Wells attempted to excuse his own non-performance by asserting impossibility or frustration of purpose. Since Ronson agreed to the modification, however, Wells's reason for requesting it is irrelevant to its enforceability.

35. **C** A contract is formed upon acceptance of an offer. Since Bostoria's order identified the subject of the transaction, specified the quantity, set forth price and terms, and called for shipment, it conferred upon Salas the power to create a contract by accepting, and was, therefore, an offer. Under UCC §2-206(1)(b) an order to purchase goods for prompt shipment calls for acceptance either by prompt shipment or prompt promise to ship. Since Salas shipped (i.e., accepted the offer) on April 28, the contract was formed on that date.

Catalogs of the kind used by Salas are mere invitations to negotiate because they are sent to a large number of buyers and do not refer to specific items for sale, but rather to types of items. For that reason, Bostoria's order could not constitute an acceptance. **A** and **B** are, therefore, incorrect. **D** is incorrect because the contract had already been formed when the goods were shipped.

36. **D** Since Bostoria's order constituted an offer, and the shipment by Salas constituted an acceptance of that offer (see explanation #35), the terms of the offer became the terms of the contract. Bostoria is thus entitled to the discount for which she contracted.

If there is a discrepancy between printed words in a contract form and typed words on that form, the typed words are presumed to control. **A** is, therefore, incorrect. Although Salas's catalog made clear his unwillingness to apply a ten percent discount to any but COD shipments, Bostoria's offer was to purchase at discount with payment within ten days. When Salas accepted by shipping, his pre-offer unwillingness became irrelevant. **B** is, therefore, incorrect. An open account is an arrangement between seller and buyer whereby the buyer regularly purchases on credit without executing notes or security agreements. **C** is incorrect because the existence of an open account, while relevant to credit terms, is not relevant to price terms in a contract.

37. **A** Under UCC Section 2-314 an implied warranty of merchantability accompanies every sale by a merchant unless disclaimed by unequivocal language. UCC Section 2-316(3)(a) specifically provides that the phrase "as is" may be used to disclaim the warranty.

B is incorrect because the implied warranty may accompany the sale of a used product as well as a new one. **C** is incorrect because liability for breach of warranty does not depend on negligence or fault by the seller. Under UCC Section 2-315 an implied warranty that the product is fit for the buyer's particular purpose accompanies a sale only if the seller knows the buyer's purpose, and knows also that the buyer is relying on the seller's judgment in furnishing a product to suit that purpose. **D** is incorrect, however, because the implied warranty of merchantability does not require reliance on the seller's judgment.

38.   **B**   In the absence of an agreement to the contrary, one who seeks the services of another, knowing that the other expects to be paid for those services, impliedly promises to pay for the services by availing himself of them. Although Dr. Drake agreed to wait for payment and to bill Evans's insurance company directly, nothing in the conversation between Dr. Drake and Evans indicates that Drake was willing to look solely to the insurance company for payment.

If the benefit which a contract confers on a non contracting party was intended to satisfy a pre-existing obligation owed by one of the contracting parties, the person on whom the benefit is conferred is called a creditor third party beneficiary. Since Evans's debt to Dr. Drake did not exist at the time the insurance contract was made, Dr. Drake could not have been a creditor beneficiary. **A** is, therefore, incorrect. **C** and **D** are incorrect because, as noted above, nothing in the conversation between Dr. Drake and Evans indicates that Dr. Drake agreed to look solely to the insurance company for payment.

39.   **C**   When either party to a contract breaches it, the other party is excused from further performance. Since Marshall breached by refusing to make payment as required, Structo may refuse to perform any further work.

In addition, the non-breaching party is entitled to damages consisting of the losses which he sustained as a result of the breach. This may include profits which he would have earned if the breach had not occurred. **D** is, therefore, incorrect. Ordinarily, lost profits are measured by the balance of the contract price less whatever it would have cost the builder to complete performance. Since the amounts specified in **A** and **B** are not necessarily based on this measure, **A** and **B** are incorrect.

40.   **D**   When a builder commits an anticipatory repudiation of a building contract, the person who hired him may be entitled to rescind and be free of all obligations under the contract. **I** is incorrect, however, because the builder is then entitled to an offset based on quasi contract (i.e., the reasonable value of his services) for work already performed. If Marshall rescinds, Structo's quasi contract remedy might exceed the amount which he has received from Marshall. If so, Structo is entitled to credit for the excess as a setoff in Marshall's action for the cost of completion. On the other hand, if Marshall does not rescind, but instead sues Structo for the standard remedy, he is entitled to the difference between the contract price and the cost of completion. Since Marshall still holds $50,000 of the contract price, this sum should be deducted from the standard remedy. **II** is, therefore, incorrect.

41.   **A**   An option is a promise to keep a particular offer open for a specified period of time. If it is supported by consideration, it is a separate contract and is enforceable during the specified period. Since the document stated that Manna received $20 in return for her promise to keep the offer open, her promise was supported by consideration and is, therefore, enforceable. Many cases hold that consideration which is cited in a writing but which was never actually given or received is "sham consideration" and that sham consideration does not support a promise. **A** is correct in spite of this, however, because the facts do not indicate that Manna did not receive $20 from Sokol, and because none of the other answers listed could possibly be correct.

An attempted testamentary substitute is an attempt by a person to dispose of her property after death without the formality of a will. Since all jurisdictions have statutes which impose certain formal requirements on wills, a testamentary substitute which fails to satisfy these requirements is ineffective. Thus, if the document signed by Manna is an attempted testamentary substitute, the result would be a judgment for the administratrix. **B** is, therefore, incorrect. To avoid interfering with the freedom of contract, courts do not ordinarily inquire into the adequacy of consideration. This is particularly true where parties to a contract are related to each other or where there is some other reason why one of them might be willing to accept less than actual value from the other. For this reason, **C** and **D** are incorrect.

42. **D** A minor may disaffirm his contract on the ground that he lacked capacity, but the party contracting with him may not.

A and **B** are therefore, incorrect. Detrimental reliance is sometimes given as a reason for enforcing a promise which was unsupported by consideration. **C** is incorrect because Dawes's promise was supported by consideration (i.e., Morris's promise), making Morris's reliance irrelevant.

43. **C** Under UCC Section 2-511, a contract which is silent as to the manner of payment calls for payment in any manner current in the ordinary course of business. The seller is entitled to demand payment in cash, but if she does so the buyer is entitled to a reasonable opportunity to procure it.

A is incorrect for the reason stated above. **B** is incorrect because the buyer is entitled to a reasonable time to procure cash. **D** is incorrect because a seller may demand cash.

44. **C** Under the Statute of Frauds, a contract for the sale of any interest in real estate must be in writing, and the writing must contain all the essential terms. The price is an essential term in a contract for the sale of realty, since the court will be unable to fashion a remedy without it.

Although UCC §2-305(1) makes special provision for contracts between merchants, providing that a contract silent as to price is presumed to be for a reasonable price, these provisions apply only to the sale of goods and not to the sale of realty. **A** and **B** are, therefore, incorrect. Since this contract does not satisfy the requirements of the Statute of Frauds, it is unenforceable over objection, even though oral evidence might establish the intentions of the parties with respect to missing terms. **D** is, therefore, incorrect.

45. **C** Consideration requires a bargained-for exchange. Since Humbert did not ask Rusk to save Welton, Rusk's doing so was neither bargained for nor given in exchange for Humbert's promise.

The fact that a promisor calls something "consideration" for his promise, does not make it so. **A** is incorrect because the service was not given in exchange for the promise. Even though the service rendered by Rusk may have materially benefitted Humbert, it is not consideration for Humbert's promise because it was not performed in exchange for the promise. **B** is, therefore, incorrect. A service given in return for a promise, however, would be consideration for the promise even if the value of the service cannot be specified. **D** is, therefore, incorrect.

46.   **A**   A compromise is made when a party agrees not to assert a cause of action, in exchange for some promise or act by another. It is enforceable if the person agreeing not to assert a cause of action believed in good faith that he had a right to assert it. If Rusk believed in good faith that he was entitled to assert a claim against Welton's estate, his agreement not to do so is consideration for Humbert's promise to pay him, and their agreement is a compromise. Although the facts are silent as to Rusk's belief, the argument in **A** is the only one listed which could possibly support Rusk's position.

Unless Rusk saved Welton with the reasonable expectation that he would be compensated, the enrichment which results from the administrator's failure to pay him is not unjust. **B** is, therefore, incorrect. Sometimes detrimental reliance by a promisee may permit enforcement of an otherwise unenforceable promise, but **C** is incorrect because there is no indication that Rusk relied on Humbert's promise or suffered detriment as a result of such reliance. **D** is incorrect because a promise is not ordinarily enforceable without consideration even though voluntarily and freely made.

47.   **C**   Ordinarily the promises contained in a contract can be enforced only by one in privity. An exception is made when the parties to a contract intend that its benefits shall flow to a third party, but there is no indication that Daniels or Barre had Chula's protection in mind when they included a no-assignment provision in their contract.

A, **B**, and **D** are therefore, incorrect.

48.   **D**   The seller's obligation under a contract of sale is to deliver goods which conform in every way to the terms of the contract. Since the contract called for delivery of 500 pens, delivery of anything less is a breach. Since Penco failed to perform as promised, Committee is entitled to the return of all money already paid. In addition, since Penco breached the contract, Committee is entitled to damages resulting from the breach.

A is incorrect because the buyer is not required to accept a non-conforming tender. If a buyer chooses to accept a non-conforming tender, it must pay at the contract price, but is entitled to sue for damages resulting from the seller's defective performance so long as it notifies the seller of its intention to do so. **B** is, therefore, incorrect. On the other hand, if the tender does not conform to the seller's promise, the buyer may reject it. Having done so, the buyer is entitled to damages which resulted from the seller's breach. **C** is incorrect because return of Committee's advance payment may not be sufficient to compensate Committee for other damages which it sustained. (*Note*: Damages are traditionally measured by the difference between the contract price and the "cover price" or the fair market value of the goods involved.)

49.   **D**   Under UCC §2-209(1), an agreement to modify a contract is enforceable even though unsupported by consideration. Since, as modified, the agreement does not fall within the provisions of the Statute of Frauds, it need not be in writing. Thus, if Committee agreed to accept 475 pens instead of 500, Penco's delivery of 475 pens would not be a breach.

Penco's inability to obtain the necessary materials would not excuse performance unless that inability resulted from circumstances which were not within the reasonable contemplation of the parties at the time the contract was formed. Since there is no indication that this is so, **A** is incorrect. A buyer who accepts a non-conforming tender may recover damages only if it notifies the seller of its intention to sue. **B** is incorrect, however, because no notice is required if the buyer rejects the tender. Since the contract called for delivery of 500 pens, tender of any fewer is a breach in spite of the fact that Committee may not have actually needed 500. **C** is incorrect for this reason (and incidentally, because there is no indication that it was Committee's plan to give only one pen to each conventioneer).

50. **D**   An unaccepted offer binds neither the offeror nor the offeree. There is nothing to indicate that Ace accepted Wire's offer to do the job for $16,000.

Ace's reliance on Wire's offer might entitle Ace to enforce it, but **A** is incorrect because Ace's reliance does not confer any right on Wire. Wire's reliance on the belief that Ace would hire him confers no right on Wire unless that reliance was justified. Since there is no indication that Ace promised the job to Wire, Wire's reliance was not justified. **B** and **C** are, therefore, incorrect.

51. **B**   Under the brokerage contract, transfer of title was a condition precedent to Ostend's obligation to pay a commission. There is always an implied agreement, however, that a party will not willfully prevent the performance of a condition to his obligation. If transfer of title was prevented by Ostend's willful breach of his contract with First, Ostend thus violated the implied agreement with Briar and may be held liable for damages (i.e., the unpaid commission) which resulted.

Although real estate brokerage contracts frequently require payment of the commission when the broker procures a ready, willing and able buyer, **A** and **C** are incorrect because this contract was conditioned on the transfer of title. "Frustration of purpose" may excuse performance of a contract where an unforeseen event destroys the underlying reasons for performing the contract. **D** is incorrect because the doctrine of frustration of purpose never results in liability, but rather excuses a party's failure to perform.

52. **C**   The brokerage contract made transfer of title a condition precedent to Ostend's obligation to pay Briar. Since title was not transferred, the condition had not been met, and Ostend's obligation to pay the commission never came into being.

A is not a good defense because Ostend voluntarily accepted the $98,000 offer, thus waiving the price condition which appeared in the brokerage contract. Since the contract for sale between Ostend and Second was formed on August 1, within the period of Briar's exclusive right to sell, **B** is not a good defense. Since the contract between Briar and Ostend granted Briar the exclusive right to sell Ostend's home, Briar would be entitled to a commission upon the transfer of title even though the sale was made without Briar's participation. **D** is, therefore, not a good defense.

53. **A**   Since Second contracted to purchase Ostend's home, his failure to do so is a breach which entitles Ostend to any damages which result. **I** is, therefore, correct.

A buyer can frequently obtain specific performance of a contract to sell realty because the uniqueness of a given parcel of realty makes money damages an inadequate remedy. **II** is incorrect, however, because there is nothing unique about the money which Ostend was to receive under the contract, making money damages an adequate remedy for the seller. Impossibility excuses performance only if the circumstance which made performance impossible was unforeseeable at the time the contract was formed. The subsequent illness of a party is usually regarded as foreseeable, making **III** incorrect.

54. **A**   An accord is a new obligation intended to take the place of an existing one. To be enforceable, it must be supported by consideration. To discharge the original obligation, it must actually be performed. Performance of the new obligation is known as "satisfaction," and it is the satisfaction rather than the accord which discharges a contractual obligation. The agreement of May 21 constituted an accord, but since Brandeis did not pay $45,000 in cash by May 25 there has been no satisfaction and thus no discharge of his obligation to pay $50,000 as originally agreed.

While a promise to perform a pre-existing obligation is not valuable consideration, **B** is incorrect because Brandeis's original contractual obligation was to pay before June 14, and his May 21 promise was to pay by May 25. A novation is an agreement to substitute a third party for one of the parties to the contract. **C** is, therefore, incorrect. **D** is incorrect because accord without satisfaction does not work to discharge contractual obligations.

55. **C**   Impossibility may excuse performance, but only where the conditions which made performance impossible were unforeseeable to the parties at the time the contract was formed. If on April 1 both parties knew that it frequently stormed all during the month of April, Fixer is deemed to have contemplated that fact when he promised to do the work. The storms would not, therefore, excuse his performance, and he would be held liable for breaching the contract.

A is incorrect because even acts of God may be foreseen, and, if so, do not excuse performance. **B** is incorrect because such knowledge would make the storms foreseeable, and prevent them from excusing performance. **D** might be correct if Fixer performed late, but is incorrect because he cancelled the contract and did not perform at all.

56. **C**   Most jurisdictions agree that an offer for a unilateral contract cannot terminate once the offeree begins performance. Galen's extra efforts to earn "A"s while Monte was alive would thus have prevented Monte's death from terminating the offer. Earning the "A"s constituted acceptance of the offer and entitled Galen to the promised bonus.

A is incorrect because there is no rule of law requiring a law student to use her best efforts while in law school. **B** is incorrect because Galen's efforts would have prevented termination of the offer until she had a reasonable opportunity to complete performance. Since Monte's promise was not made until after Galen's essay had won the contest, and since Galen did not enter the contest with any expectation of compensation from Monte, Galen's essay was not relevant to the enforceability of Monte's promise. **D** is, therefore, incorrect.

57. **B**   Under the Statute of Frauds, a promise which by its terms cannot be performed within a year must be in writing. Since Monte's promise to buy books for a two year period could not be performed within a year, it violated the Statute of Frauds.

Even if the offer made by Monte was divisible, Galen's successful completion of her first year of law school would have been an acceptance of both its parts. **A** is, therefore, incorrect. **C** is incorrect because there is no special rule governing a promise to pay a cash bonus; such a promise is enforceable according to the rules which govern the enforceability of promises in general. Since Monte's offer to pay for Galen's books was an offer for a unilateral contract (a promise for an act), Galen's successful completion of her first year was both an acceptance of the offer and consideration for Monte's promise. **D** is, therefore, incorrect.

58. **B** UCC Section 2-104 defines a merchant as a person who deals in goods of the kind involved in the transaction, or one who by his occupation holds himself out as having knowledge peculiar to the goods involved in the transaction, or one to whom such knowledge may be attributed by his employment of a person who by his occupation holds himself out as having such knowledge. Since the buyer in **B** is not in the bicycle business, does not hold himself out as having special knowledge of bicycles, and does not employ a person who does so, he is not a merchant under UCC §2-104.

The seller in **A** is in the bicycle business, and therefore deals in bicycles. The buyer in **C** is a bicycle mechanic, and as such holds himself out as having special knowledge of bicycles. Special knowledge of bicycles may be attributed to the buyer in **D** because she employed a bicycle mechanic to assist in making the purchase.

59. **D** A prospective inability to perform occurs when a party to a contract has, by his own conduct, divested himself of the ability to perform. A party who justifiably relies to its detriment on another party's prospective inability to perform is discharged form its obligations under the contract. Since Overlook executives learned that Carson had enlisted, and since this would make it impossible for Carson to perform, they were justified in hiring another caretaker. Since Overlook ordinarily employed only one winter caretaker, hiring Newt was sufficiently detrimental to excuse it from performing its contract with Carson.

A and **B** are incorrect because Overlook justifiably relied to its detriment on Carson's prospective inability to perform when it hired Newt upon learning of Carson's enlistment. An anticipatory repudiation occurs when a party refuses to perform even though he is able to do so. **C** is incorrect because Carson never refused to perform.

60. **B** Ordinarily, when unforeseeable circumstances make performance impossible, that performance is excused. When this occurs after performance has begun, the party who has performed is not entitled to contract remedies, since there has been no breach by the other party. In order to avoid injustice, however, a party who has rendered some performance may be entitled to a quasi-contract remedy. Usually, the damages are based on the detriment suffered by the person seeking compensation. In this case, the detriment suffered by Sheldon can be measured by the value of the work which he performed.

A and **D** are incorrect because Sheldon did not fully perform, such performance having become impossible without fault by either party. **C** is incorrect because quasi-contract damages are measured by the value of the plaintiff's detriment rather than by the benefit received by the defendant.

61. **B**   An assignment transfers the assignor's rights to the assignee thus extinguishing the assignor's rights under the contract. Since Whiz has assigned his rights under the contract, he can no longer enforce them.

      A is incorrect for two reasons: first, lack of contractual capacity makes a contract voidable only at the option of the person who lacked it; and, second, a minor has capacity to contract in connection with his own business interests. An assignee's failure to notify the obligor that an assignment has been made may result in a discharge of the obligor's obligation to the assignee to the extent of payments which the obligor made to the assignor. **C** is incorrect, however, because the assignee's failure to notify does not alone discharge any obligation owed by the obligor. In some jurisdictions, an assignment of wages is invalid. **D** is incorrect for two reasons: first, if the assignment is invalid, Disco is liable to Whiz; and, second, the assignment was of royalties, not of wages.

62. **B**   Before the obligor learns of an assignment by the obligee, if an obligor and obligee agree in a commercially reasonable manner to a valid modification of the contract, the modification is effective as to rights which the assignee has acquired against the obligor. Thus, Adso is bound by the modification. An obligor's duty under a contract is discharged to the extent of payment made to the obligee before learning of the obligee's assignment. Thus, Disco should receive credit for any payment which Disco made to Whiz prior to notification of the assignment. Since Disco's payment of $50,000 to Whiz completely discharged Disco's obligation under the contract as modified, and since the modification and payment took place prior to notice of the assignment to Adso, Adso's claim will fail.

      A is incorrect because where the same right has been assigned to two different people, the first in time generally has priority. The right to collect royalties existed and was identified as soon as the contract between Disco and Whiz was made, even though the "Stump the Hump" program had not yet been manufactured or marketed. **C** is, therefore, incorrect. **D** is incorrect because Adso's failure to notify Disco of the assignment resulted in a discharge when Disco satisfied its obligation to Whiz under the contract as modified before receiving notice of the assignment.

63. **A**   The Statute of Frauds requires that a contract to create an interest in land be in writing. Most states agree that this requirement applies to a promise to create a leasehold interest, so it would apply to both promises made by Susan.

      The Statute of Frauds also requires a writing if the contract is one which *by its terms* cannot be performed within one year. The promise which Susan made to Mollie could be performed within one year if Bob died during that period. The promise which Susan made to Bob could be performed within one year if Tia died during that period. **B** is, therefore, incorrect. UCC §2-201(1) requires that a contract for the sale of goods for a price of $500 or more be in writing. **C** is incorrect, however, because a house is realty rather than goods, and because the requirement of a writing is based on the *price* rather than the value of goods sold. Consideration is something of value given in return for a promise, but it is not necessary that the consideration flow from the promisee to the promisor. **D** is incorrect because Mollie's conveyance to Susan was consideration for Susan's promise to Mollie and because Bob's promise to share the inheritance was consideration for Susan's promise to Bob. In addition, **D** is incorrect because the lack of consideration does not relate to the assertion that an oral promise is unenforceable.

64. **D** Ordinarily, no promise is enforceable unless it is supported by consideration. Consideration consists of some legal detriment sustained by the promisee in return for the promisor's promise. Since at the time Susan promised Bob that she would let him live in the house she was already obligated to do so, her promise to him was not a legal detriment to her and so could not be consideration for his promise to share Tia's estate with her. For this reason, **D** is correct.

Even without consideration, a promise many be enforceable under the doctrine of promissory estoppel if the promisee justifiably relied on it to her detriment. **A** is incorrect, however, because there is no indication that Susan relied on Bob's promise to share the estate. **B** is incorrect because Bob's promise was unsupported by consideration. Since Bob was unaware of Susan's promise to Mollie, it could not constitute an implied condition precedent to Bob's obligation. **C** is, therefore, incorrect.

65. **D** An assignment is a transfer of a right to receive the benefits of a contract. If there was an enforceable agreement between Bob and Tia, Bob's promise to share some of the rights which he received under that contract could be called an assignment. Although it is not certain that Bob's conversation with Susan resulted in a valid assignment, **A** is the only answer which could possibly be correct.

The difference between an assignee and a third party beneficiary of a contract is that an assignee's right is transferred to her after a contract has been created, while a third party beneficiary's right (whether an intended or an incidental beneficiary) is created by the contract itself. Since the agreement between Bob and Tia did not require either Bob or Tia to give anything to, or do anything for, Susan, Susan's right was not created by it.

A, **B** and **C** are, therefore, incorrect.

66. **B** Rescission is an equitable remedy granted in the discretion of the court, but is usually available if the parties contracted as the result of fraud by one of them or as the result of a mutual mistake about a basic assumption of the contract. If, at the time they contracted for its sale, Vestor was aware that the realty was worth substantially more than the contract price, his failure to disclose the fact might be fraud which would justify rescission.

A is incorrect for two reasons: first, many courts refuse to grant rescission where the mutual mistake was about market conditions; and, second, because the possibility that the contract will be rescinded on the ground of fraud by Vestor prevents mutual mistake from being the *only* thing which could result in rescission. Negligence by a party is not ordinarily a ground for rescission, or necessary to it. **C** is, therefore, incorrect. Ordinarily, a court will reform a contract only where it is clear that the contract formed does not reflect the true intention of the parties, and where the court can determine what their intention was at the time of contracting. **D** is incorrect because neither of those requirements is established by the given facts.

67. **A** UCC section 2-209(3) provides that an agreement to modify a contract must be in writing if the contract as modified is within the provisions of the statute of frauds. Since the contract as modified calls for the sale of 1,000 widgets at ten dollars per widget for a

total price of $10,000, and since the statute of frauds requires a contract for the sale of goods with a price of $500 or more to be in writing, the contract as modified falls within the provisions of the statute of frauds. Since it is not in writing, it is not enforceable over the objection of Batemen.

C is, therefore, incorrect. **B** is incorrect because UCC section 2-209(1) provides that an agreement to modify an existing contract may be enforceable without consideration. An accord is an agreement to substitute a new obligation for an existing one. In order to be enforceable, an accord, like any other agreement, must be supported by consideration. Since consideration, is a detriment suffered in exchange for a benefit received, and since Short suffered no detriment in return for the reduction in his obligation, the agreement to accept 1,000 widgets instead of 2,000 as originally required by the contract is unsupported by consideration. **D** is, therefore, incorrect.

68.   **A**   Although Mauer breached his contract with Block, he is not liable unless the breach resulted in damage. If there are equally competent gardeners in the area who will perform the same work at the same price, Bloch has sustained no damage as a result of Mauer's failure to perform.

An increase in the costs of labor and materials would not excuse Mauer from performance, since such increases are usually regarded as foreseeable to the parties at the time they contract. **B** is, therefore, incorrect. The agreement between Andrews and Bloch may have motivated Bloch to contract with Mauer, but **C** is incorrect because Mauer's obligation does not depend on the validity of Bloch's motivation. A party's inability to perform does not excuse performance unless the inability was unforeseeable at the time the contract was made. Since the likelihood that one of the parties to a contract will become ill is generally regarded as foreseeable, **D** is incorrect.

69.   **D**   The assignee of a contract rights is entitled to enforce them to the same extent the assignor would have been.

Mauer's breach of his contract with Bloch gives Purtle, as Bloch's assignee, a cause of action against Mauer. **A** and **B** are, therefore, incorrect. Contract rights are ordinarily alienable as are other chattels. Since any chattel or right may be the subject of a gift, the fact that Purtle gave no consideration for the assignment of Bloch's right would not prevent it from having effect. **C** is, therefore, incorrect.

70.   **A**   Although a contract is not usually enforceable except by one in privity, a third-party beneficiary may enforce it if the parties to the contract intended that it should benefit him. This is true whether the intended third-party beneficiary is a creditor beneficiary or a donee beneficiary. A creditor beneficiary is one whom the parties intended to benefit in order to satisfy a preexisting obligation owed by one of them. Andrews is a creditor beneficiary since Bloch made the contract so as to satisfy an obligation that he owed Andrews.

A donee beneficiary is one whom a contracting party intended to benefit even though he owed him no obligation. **B** is incorrect since Bloch owed Andrews an obligation under their previous agreement. An incidental beneficiary is one who derives benefit from a contract not made with the intention of benefiting him. Thus, **C** is incorrect. **D** is incorrect since Andrews was an intended beneficiary of Mauer and Bloch's contract.

71. **C** Since Purtle did not by word or deed express or imply a willingness to pay for the maintenance of Andrews's lawn, he is under no obligation to do so. (*Note:* It is generally understood that an assignment of contract rights includes a delegation of contract obligations. Since Bloch assigned to Purtle his rights under the contract between Bloch and Mauer, Mauer would have been entitled to enforce against Purtle any rights which Mauer had under that contract. Since Bloch did not assign to Purtle any rights under Bloch's contract with Andrews and did not delegate to Purtle any obligations under his contract with Andrews, however, Andrews may not enforce those rights against Purtle.)

A is incorrect because there is no indication that Andrews has suffered any detriment as a result of reliance on the payments made by Purtle to Mauer. A covenant contained in the record of title to realty may be enforceable against subsequent owners of the realty if it touches and concerns the land involved. **B** is incorrect, however, because there is no indication that Bloch's promise was noted in the record of title to his realty. As has been noted above, Purtle is not liable to Andrews because Purtle made no express or implied promise which would be enforceable by Andrews. Although **D** correctly concludes that Purtle is not liable to Andrews, it suggests that the reason is that Andrews sustained no damage. This is incorrect, however, because Andrews is now paying $25 per month while previously he was paying nothing.

72. **B** Ordinarily, a promise is not enforceable unless it was supported by consideration. Consideration is a bargained-for exchange of value given in return for the promise. Usually, it consists of some detriment to the promisee. Andrews gave up his claim for payment in return for Bloch's promise to provide lawn maintenance services. In order for this to serve as consideration, the claim must have been of value. It is generally understood that a promise which is made in return for the promisee's forbearance to assert a claim is supported by consideration (i.e., the forbearance is a thing of value) if the claim was valid or if the person giving it up sincerely believed that it was valid. Thus, if Andrews sincerely believed that Bloch owed him money, then his acceptance of Bloch's offer to satisfy the debt by hiring a gardener was consideration for Bloch's promise to do so.

The fact that Andrews cannot collect from anyone is not, alone, sufficient to give him a right against Bloch, making **A** incorrect. If Andrews sincerely believed that Bloch owed him money, the fact that Bloch actually did not owe it would not prevent the compromise agreement between Bloch and him from being enforceable for the reasons stated above. **C** is, therefore, incorrect. **D** is incorrect because the facts give no indication that such an intention existed.

73. **D** The note which Screner sent on September 5 demanding $325 was a rejection of Huner's offer to pay $300. An offeree who has killed an offer by rejecting it does not have the power to resurrect it by a subsequent acceptance. Screner's note of September 12 was thus no more than a new offer. Since an offer may not make the offeree's silence an acceptance, Screner's offer of September 12 was never accepted because Huner did not respond to it.

A is, therefore, incorrect. Since there was no existing offer which could be accepted by performance, Screner's commencement of performance on September 28 could not have resulted in the formation of a contract, making **B** incorrect. Since Huner did not know that Screner was installing the screens, and since Screner did not have a reasonable expectation of compensation at the time he installed them, Screner has no quasi-contract remedy, and **C** is incorrect.

74.   **B**   The validity of a liquidated damages clause depends not on what damages actually flowed from a contract breach, but on what damages were reasonably contemplated by the parties at the time the contract was formed. Thus, if, at the time they contracted, Odyk and Recon reasonably expected Odyk's damages to approximate $50 per day, the agreement to pay that sum as liquidated damages was valid.

A is, therefore, incorrect. Insurance proceeds are not usually considered in determining the damages sustained by the victim of a breached contract, since doing so would confer on the breaching party a benefit which the insured party bought and paid for. **C** is, therefore, incorrect. **D** is incorrect because liability for breach of contract does not depend on fault, and because the validity of a liquidated damages clause depends on circumstances existing at the time the contract was formed rather than at the time it was breached.

75.   **A**   An insurance contract involves an agreement by the insurer to pay the insured upon the occurrence of an event not within the control of either. The payment agreed upon need not bear any relationship to damage which results from the event (although many policies require that there be such a relationship). Since Grail agreed to pay $50 per day in the event of destruction or substantial damage to the house by fire, it is obligated to do so.

B is, therefore, incorrect. Grail's agreement to pay $50 per day is not a liquidated damages clause, since it does not fix liability in the event of *breach* by Grail. **C** is incorrect because it attempts to apply to an insurance contract the rule which determines the validity of a liquidated damages clause. The insurance policy fixes Grail's liability for Odyk's living expenses at $50 per day without regard to whether or not she actually incurred such expenses. **D** is incorrect for this reason.

76.   **A**   The appropriate remedy for a builder's breach of a construction contract is the cost of making the building conform to the agreed specifications.

Although the UCC Section 2-508 requires that a buyer notify a seller of a delivery's non-conformity before commencing an action, this provision applies only to a sales contract between merchants. **B** is, therefore, incorrect. Since insurance proceeds are not ordinarily considered in determining damages sustained by the victim of a breached contract, **C** is incorrect. If the liquidated damages clause in the contract between Odyk and Recon is valid, it replaces traditional measures of damage. The contract provided it only as a remedy for damages resulting from late performance, however. **D** is incorrect because the subject of Odyk's action is not damage resulting from late performance, but damage resulting from defective performance.

77.   **D**   Ordinarily, a unilateral mistake does not excuse performance and is not grounds for rescission. Where the other party knew or reasonably should have known of the mistake, however, the mistake may be asserted as an excuse for non-performance.

A is incorrect because even though the mistake resulted from negligence by Coast's employee, the difference between Coast's bid and all the others received would probably have led the reasonable person in Hostel's position to realize that an error has been made. **B** is incorrect for the same reason. Unless it is found as a matter of law to have been unconscionable at the time it was formed, a contract may be enforceable even though some unfairness will result. **C** is incorrect because unfairness alone is not sufficient to excuse non-performance.

78.   **D**   Ordinarily, a promise to perform services implies a promise to perform them in a satisfactory manner, judged by an objective standard. A specific agreement that personal satisfaction is required, however, is usually understood to call for subjective satisfaction so long as the party whose satisfaction is required acts in good faith. Thus, if the mayor actually believed that the statue was too small, and he was, therefore, not subjectively satisfied with it, the town is discharged of its obligation under the contract.

       A is, therefore, incorrect. If the mayor liked the statue, but rejected it because he feared embarrassment resulting from a conviction, the town would be in breach because the rejection would not be in good faith. If he genuinely did not like the statue, however, the incidental fact that he feared embarrassment if Ray was convicted would not be relevant. **B** is, therefore, incorrect. Although the clause called for subjective satisfaction, it did not create an absolute right to reject the work, since such an agreement is understood to mean that the decision as to whether or not the work is satisfactory must be made in good faith. **C** is, therefore, incorrect.

79.   **A**   An anticipatory breach occurs when, before performance is required, a party to a contract says or does something which indicates that she will not perform as required. When an anticipatory breach occurs, the other party need not wait until the time for performance is passed, but may immediately avail itself of remedies for breach of contract.

       Since Chisel's obligation under the contract was to submit a statue for approval by the mayor, her failure to do so is a breach whether or not the statue would have met with the mayor's approval when submitted. **B** is, therefore, incorrect. **C** is incorrect because a breach occurs when a party fails to fulfill her contractual obligations, whether or not she profits from such failure. Since a contract calling for a party's personal satisfaction is understood to require good faith, that party's promise to pay if satisfied is not illusory. **D** is, therefore, incorrect.

80.   **A**   Since Sailor's promise to keep the offer open until June 10 was supported by consideration, it is enforceable.

       Refusal to sell the motorcycle to Brady as promised is a breach, whether or not the motorcycle has actually been sold to someone else. **B** is, therefore, incorrect. The UCC provides that a promise to hold an offer open for a specified period of time (i.e., a firm offer) is enforceable without consideration only if it is made between merchants and if it is in writing. **C** and **D** are incorrect, however, because Brady gave consideration for Sailor's promise.

81.   **C**   UCC Section 2-512 (2) specifically provides that where a contract calls for payment prior to inspection, such payment does not constitute acceptance and does not impair the

buyer's right to inspect.

The requirement of payment prior to inspection is not an uncommon one, and therefore not unconscionable, making **A** incorrect. **B** and **D** are incorrect because UCC Section 2-512 (2) prevents pre-inspection payment from having these effects.

82. **C**   Ordinarily, non-delivery by the seller entitles the buyer to damages consisting of the difference between the contract price and either the "cover price" or the reasonable market value of the undelivered goods. Here, because the nuts delivered did not conform to the agreement, Helth was entitled to return them. Since he has already paid the contract price and has received nothing for his money, he is entitled to the return of what he paid in addition to damages.

Specific performance, as suggested by **A**, is available only where the subject of the sales contract is unique or cannot otherwise be obtained. Here there are no facts to suggest that this is so. **B** is incorrect because it is the measure of damages for breach of warranty, and is obviously insufficient to compensate Helth, since the small nuts have been returned, but paid for. **D** is incorrect because it does not permit recovery for damages resulting from Gro's breach.

83. **A**   Since the promise to keep the offer open is unsupported by consideration, it is a gratuitous one, and therefore unenforceable.

Although UCC §2-205 makes certain "firm offers" between merchants enforceable without consideration, at common law an option (i.e., promise to hold an offer open) is not enforceable without consideration. **B** is incorrect because it is, thus, based on an inaccurate statement of the law. **C** is incorrect because UCC provisions relating to "firm offers" apply only when they are made by merchants. **D** is incorrect for these reasons, and also because nothing in the language of Bertrand's letter indicates that Bertrand's beginning law school is a condition for any of the obligations which might result from the transaction. It clearly was not a condition *precedent* because performance was to take place prior to the beginning of law school in mid-September.

84. **D**   Bertrand's offer was for a unilateral contract. According to its terms, it could only be accepted by performance consisting of delivery of the books to Bertrand's home. An offer for a unilateral contract can be withdrawn at any time prior to the offeree's performance or commencement of performance.

A is incorrect because an offer for a unilateral contract binds only one party (the promisor) until accepted by performance. **B** and **C** are incorrect because an offer for a unilateral contract cannot be accepted by any means other than performance.

85. **A**   An offer is an expression of willingness to be bound to specified terms. Since both parties were aware of the price and terms set forth in Bertrand's letter, Sylvester's statement could be construed as an offer to sell the books to Bertrand under those same terms.

B and **C** are incorrect because Bertrand's letter of July 8 bound him to purchase only if the books were delivered to his home, so nothing but delivery could be regarded as acceptance. **D** is incorrect because the performance required is delivery of the books, and Sylvester has, by his statement, made no efforts toward such delivery.

86. **B** Although the Statute of Frauds might require a contract for the sale of goods with a price of $1,000 to be in writing, the question only asks if Green's promise can be viewed as *consideration* for Brown's promise. Consideration is something of value which is bargained for and given in exchange for a promise. Since Green's promise to deliver fire-fighting equipment is of obvious value to Brown, if given in return for Brown's promise of payment, it is consideration for it.

     A is incorrect because Green's prior services were not given in exchange for Brown's promise. **C** is incorrect because the doctrine of promissory estoppel may make a contract enforceable in the *absence* of consideration, but although detrimental reliance may take the place of consideration, it is not consideration unless bargained-for. Although the kind of written memorandum referred to in **D** sometimes satisfies the requirement of a writing, it is not relevant to the question of consideration or the lack of it.

87. **C** Circumstances which make performance of a contractual obligation impossible excuse such performance, but only if the circumstance could not have been foreseen by the contracting parties at the time the contract was formed. If Shimmering Bay was frequently subject to stormy conditions and choppy waters in the month of October, the circumstance which prevented performance was foreseeable and would not excuse Fixer's non performance. **C** is, therefore, correct.

     Since Fixer must have known of his prior commitments at the time he contracted with Bott, **A** is incorrect because the circumstances were, thus, foreseeable. **B** is incorrect because Bott may have been damaged (e.g., by his inability to rent it or lend it to friends) even though he himself was unable to use the yacht until March. Since the parties understood that the work would be performed while the yacht was in the water, Fixer cannot be required to remove it from the water. **D** is, therefore, incorrect.

88. **B** An assignment is only effective if the assignor has given up all rights under the assigned contract. Thus, if Rocker has made an effective assignment, he no longer has any rights against Groovy.

     A is incorrect for several reasons: first, since the contract was for Rocker's business, Rocker's infancy is probably irrelevant; second, even if Rocker's infancy at the time of his contract with Groovy is relevant, it makes the contract voidable at Rocker's option, not Groovy's; third, if Rocker's infancy invalidated the assignments, Groovy would not benefit in Rocker's action against it. **C** is incorrect because the agreement was to pay for the recording session whether or not a record was ever released. **D** is incorrect because Rocker was probably a contractor rather than an employee, and because if the assignments were held invalid, Groovy would have to pay Rocker.

89. **C** A condition precedent is an event which must occur before a party's obligation to perform under a contract becomes absolute. Since the agreement provided that Houser would be under no obligation to pay unless he was satisfied with the product, satisfaction was a condition precedent to his obligation to accept and pay for the door. Ordinarily, a contract making a buyer's satisfaction a condition precedent to his obligation is

held to require that the goods be satisfactory to the reasonable person (i.e., objective satisfaction). Where, as here, however, the agreement calls for the design of something to be personally identified with the buyer, it is more likely that the parties intended the buyer's own personal satisfaction (i.e., subjective satisfaction) to be the standard. If so, Houser's dissatisfaction with the product, so long as it was based on good faith, would prevent Houser from being obligated to purchase the door. While it is not certain that a court would come to this conclusion, the argument set forth in **C** is the only one listed which could possibly support Houser's position.

A is incorrect because the statue of frauds does not apply to goods which are especially designed for the buyer and which, therefore, would not be readily salable in the regular course of business. A unilateral contract is one in which the promisor has agreed to do something in return for a specified act by the promisee (i.e., a promise for an act), and, therefore, one in which only one party is bound to perform. **B** is incorrect because the agreement between Houser and Carver was an exchange of promises, each party's promise being given in exchange for the other party's promise (i.e., a bilateral contract). If Carver were able to sell the door to another buyer, her damages might be mitigated to some extent. **D** is incorrect, however, because the mere possibility that damages might thus be mitigated is not sufficient to defeat Carver's substantive rights.

90. **B**   Under the Statute of Frauds, a contract for the sale of an interest in realty must be in writing, and the writing must contain all essential terms. The price is an essential term in a contract for the sale of realty because, without it, the court could not determine the intentions of the parties or fashion relief in the event of a breach.

A is incorrect, since it suggests that the contract price could be determined by reference to an external standard instead of to the intentions of the parties. Although UCC §2-201(1) provides that a contract for the sale of goods may satisfy the Statute of Frauds even if terms (other than quantity) are omitted. **C** is incorrect because that rule does not apply to a contract for the sale of realty. **D** refers to the parol evidence rule, which excludes certain oral testimony only if it contradicts the terms of a written agreement. Oral testimony is not acceptable, however, to take the place of the writing required by the Statute of Frauds. **D** is, therefore, incorrect.

91. **A**   Specific performance is a remedy which may co-exist with the remedy of damages. Thus, its availability does not depend on the availability of damages — liquidated or otherwise.

B and **C** are, therefore, incorrect. **D** is incorrect, since specific performance is available as a remedy for the seller's breach of a contract for the sale of realty.

92. **C**   A liquidated damages clause is enforceable (and does not constitute a penalty) if the amount specified is reasonable in light of what the parties contemplated at the time the contract was formed, if the actual damages would be difficult to ascertain, and if the liquidated damages agreed to are tailored to the circumstances of the contract. Since living expenses would be difficult to ascertain and since the clause calling for liquidated damages was tailored to the contract, the clause is enforceable if seventy-five dollars per day was reasonable in light of what the parties contemplated at the time the contract was made.

A and B are incorrect since, if the liquidated damages clause is enforceable, Carter need not show that he actually sustained or could not have avoided or mitigated the damage. D is incorrect since a liquidated damages clause does not constitute a penalty just because one of the parties hoped that it would encourage the other to perform on time.

93. B   The parol evidence rule prohibits the admission of extrinsic evidence of a prior or contemporaneous agreement to contradict, vary, or modify the terms of an unambiguous written contract which the parties intended to be a final and complete expression of their agreement. Almost all jurisdictions, however, permit extrinsic evidence to be used to establish that the writing is ambiguous, and, if so, to explain the ambiguity.

A is incorrect since it does not recognize that oral testimony may be used to explain the ambiguity. C is incorrect for the same reason, in spite of a general rule of construction which requires the resolution of *unexplained* ambiguities against the party who drafted the contract. D is incorrect since even if the writing was a complete expression of the parties' agreement, oral testimony is admissible to explain ambiguities.

94. D   A promise to forbear or abandon a civil claim in return for some payment by the promisee is referred to as a compromise. The promise to forbear is sufficient consideration for the promisee's promise to pay if the claim could have been asserted in good faith. Although the facts do not indicate whether Ad believed in good faith that he had a claim against Maggie, D is the only theory listed which might have any prospect of success.

A is incorrect, since Harold's promise was given in exchange for Ad's "promise to make no claim," and a unilateral contract involves a promise which is given in exchange for an act rather than a promise. B is incorrect, since the facts do not indicate any *unjust* enrichment, and since, even if they did, unjust enrichment is not, alone, enough to result in liability. C is incorrect since promissory estoppel requires detrimental reliance by the promisee, and there is no fact indicating detrimental reliance by Ad.

95. B   Although Ad's forbearance might have been consideration for Harold's promise to pay, the question specifically asks whether *Doc's services* are sufficient consideration. Consideration involves a bargained-for exchange, and since Harold did not ask Doc for the services, they cannot be said to have been "bargained-for." (*Note*: Although some cases allow recovery on another theory for services like those rendered by Doc, to the extent necessary to prevent injustice, such services are not "consideration" unless bargained-for.

The services rendered may have imposed a moral obligation upon Harold, but A is incorrect because it is generally understood that a moral obligation is not sufficient consideration for a promise. C is incorrect because even a material benefit is insufficient to serve as consideration unless it was bargained-for. D is incorrect for two reasons: first, courts do not generally inquire into the adequacy of that which was given as consideration; and, second, since there was no bargain, it does not matter whether the services rendered were adequate.

96. C   The law implies a promise to pay reasonable value for services which are rendered with some reasonable expectation of compensation. Here, however, the conversation which

took place between Doc and Wand makes it clear that at the time Doc rendered the services, he had no expectation — reasonable or otherwise — of being compensated.

A "good Samaritan" statute, where it exists, protects a doctor against liability for negligence if he or she voluntarily and without expectation of payment renders emergency aid, but it has no other effect. **A** is, therefore, incorrect. **B** is incorrect since quantum meruit is available only where the services are rendered with a reasonable expectation of payment, and Doc had no such expectation at the time the services were rendered. **D** is incorrect since Wand was not a party to any agreement which may have been made between Ad and Harold. Therefore, although Ad may be bound by that agreement in dealing with Harold, the agreement is not relevant to Ad's rights against Wand.

97. **A**   An offer for a unilateral contract involves an offer to exchange a promise for an act. Since the notice offered a prize to the student achieving the highest GPA and did not ask students to make any promise or agreement that they would do so, it was a promise offered in return for an act.

       B is therefore incorrect. **C** is incorrect, since the offeror has the sole power to decide whether its offer can be accepted by an act or a promise. **D** is incorrect since once Val achieved the highest GPA in her class, there was nothing further for her to do, and so it could not be said that she was now obligated to perform, as she would be under a bilateral contract.

98. **D**   Although an offer can ordinarily be withdrawn by the offeror at any time prior to its acceptance, the *Restatement* Rule is that an offer for a unilateral contract cannot be withdrawn once the offeree has begun to perform. Thus, if Val began making extra efforts in an attempt to win the prize, Pubco was prevented from withdrawing the offer.

       A and **B** are, therefore, incorrect. **C** is incorrect because an offer for a unilateral contract can only be accepted by performance, making Val's letter irrelevant.

99. **B**   Since the promisor in a unilateral contract has called for acceptance by performance of an act, the promisee's performance is consideration for it.

       A is incorrect, since promissory estoppel applies only where there has been no consideration. Since there is no rule of law which requires a law student to use her best efforts while in law school, **C** is incorrect. **D** is incorrect since a gift is something given without consideration, and, here, Val's performance was consideration for Pubco's promise.

100. **B**   Under UCC Section 2-603, after rightful rejection of non-conforming goods in the buyer's possession, a merchant buyer is required to comply with the seller's reasonable instructions. If no such instructions are forthcoming, and if the goods are perishable, the buyer may make attempts to sell the goods on the seller's account in a commercially reasonable manner. Because of the perishable nature of this product, it might be reasonable to accept a price lower than that which the seller ordinarily receives.

       A is therefore incorrect. **C** is incorrect because, even though Cohen was not obligated to pay, she was entitled to sell on Darry's account. **D** is incorrect, since a private sale may be commercially reasonable.

101. **B**   Even if a claim is invalid, a promise to abandon it may be consideration for another's promise of payment if the claim could have been asserted in good faith. If Sewco did not believe that it was entitled to the patent rights, it could not have asserted its claim in good faith, and its promise to abandon the claim would not have been consideration for Pat's promise.

                If Sewco's claim was asserted in good faith, abandonment of the claim was consideration for Pat's promise of payment, regardless of whether the employment contract was enforceable. **A** is therefore incorrect. **C** is incorrect, since it indicates that Sewco's promise to abandon the claim was made in good faith, which would make it good consideration for Pat's promise. **D** is incorrect because abandonment of an invalid claim may be consideration for a promise to pay, so long as the person abandoning the claim believes in good faith that it is a valid one.

102. **C**   The term "F.O.B." requires the seller to deliver the goods on board the carrier at the place specified, and the risk of loss does not pass to the buyer until the seller has done so. Since this contract was "F.O.B. Billy's factory," Sally's obligation was to deliver it there, and the risk of loss did not pass until she did so.

                A and **B** are, therefore, incorrect. **D** is incorrect for two reasons: first, the term "public enemy" refers to a person, group, or nation waging war against the United States; and, second, because while interference by a public enemy might relieve a seller of the obligation to deliver, it does not pass the risk of loss to a buyer.

103. **D**   When a promise is made with the intent that its benefit flow to a third person that person is an *intended* beneficiary of the promise. When that benefit is intended to satisfy an obligation which the promisee owes to the third party, the third party is an intended *creditor* beneficiary. According to the Restatement 2d, a promise is enforceable by an intended creditor beneficiary when he relies upon or assents to the arrangement. Since the beneficiary is presumed to have assented when notified of the contract, and since Payne notified Bild, Bild may enforce Sal's promise, even though there is no privity between them.

                A is, therefore, incorrect. **B** is incorrect for two reasons: first, because non-assignability would prevent the *assignee* from recovering, but could not be raised as a defense by that assignee; and, second, because obligations under a construction contract may generally be assigned to any competent contractor. **C** is incorrect because the pre-existing obligation which Payne owed Bild, and which the Payne-Sal contract was designed to satisfy, made Bild a *creditor* rather than a *donee* beneficiary.

104. **A**   If a contract is made with the intention of benefiting a third party to whom neither of the contracting parties owes any obligation, that third party is referred to as an intended *donee* beneficiary of the contract. Since Mut's intention was to give a wedding gift to Debra and Sal, Sal is an intended donee beneficiary. In some jurisdictions, a donee beneficiary may only enforce a promise on which he has detrimentally relied. In others he may enforce it if he has assented to it. The *Restatement* view is that he may enforce it if he relied *or* assented. But if, as here, he has done neither, he has no right to enforce the agreement.

A condition precedent is an event which must occur before a party's obligation to perform becomes absolute. Ordinarily, it results from an express or implied agreement between the parties. Since Sal's agreement to paint the house was made after Mut's agreement to convey, Sal's performance could not have been intended to be a condition to Mut's obligation. **B** is, therefore, incorrect. **C** is incorrect because when Mut entered into the January 1 contract with Payne, it was for the purpose of giving a wedding gift to Sal as well as Debra. **D** is incorrect for two reasons: first, the agreement between Mut and Payne probably did not create any fiduciary relationship between them; and, second, Payne's agreement with Bild was not inconsistent with any right or benefit to which Mut was entitled.

105.   **A**   Since a contract is a meeting of minds, a person who does not know the legal consequences of her act is incapable of contracting. Where the incapacity results from intoxication, some jurisdictions require proof that the other party was aware of the intoxication and the resulting incapacity. Although it is not clear whether Barbara was sufficiently aware of Susan's incapacity, the additional fact in **A** is the only one listed which could help Susan's defense.

So long as Susan knew the legal consequences of her act, her motivation is irrelevant. **B** is, therefore, incorrect. So long as the consideration given for a promise has value, courts, recognizing that contracting parties may be motivated by factors other than monetary worth, do not usually inquire into the sufficiency of that value. For this reason, **C** is incorrect. Although an offeror may withdraw an offer at any time prior to acceptance, **D** is incorrect for two reasons: first, such withdrawal is not effective until communicated to the offeree; and, second, the facts suggest that a contract was formed when the napkin was signed, making a subsequent attempt at revocation ineffective.

106.   **A**   Specific performance of a sales contract will be granted where money damages which would accurately compensate cannot be measured because the subject of the sale is rare or unique. Since the car was a rare antique, specific performance might be available. Although it is not certain that a court would decide to grant such relief, **A** is the only remedy listed which could possibly be granted.

If a court awarded damages, they would be based on the difference between the contract price and the fair market value of the car. **B** is incorrect because it does not accurately measure the damage. **C** is incorrect because, while Barbara may elect damages or specific performance, she may not receive both. **D** is incorrect since there is no relationship between five hundred dollars and the damage sustained by Barbara.

107.   **C**   Although a court may reform a contract by filling in a missing term in accordance with the manifest intent of the parties, it may not create a contract where the writing fails to indicate that the parties had the intent of creating one. The January 5 document leaves the price term to subsequent agreement after determining reasonable value. It does not indicate that reasonable value will be the price or set forth any method by which the sale price is to be determined. It is an "agreement to agree," and as such does not manifest an intention to be bound to any particular terms.

A and **B** are, therefore, incorrect. Specific performance may be available in an action for breach of a contract for the sale of a chattel if the chattel is unique. Since a trained, talking bird is probably unique, **D** is incorrect.

108. **A**   By its terms the UCC applies to all transactions in "goods," which are defined as any things which are movable at the time of the sale.

           The UCC provides approaches for filling in certain missing terms, but the absence or presence of any particular terms in a contract does not determine whether the UCC applies. **B** is, therefore, incorrect. **C** and **D** are incorrect since nothing in the UCC definition of "goods" excludes living creatures or consumer items (i.e., items purchased for the buyer's own use).

109. **C**   Losses which are normal but not inevitable results of breach of contract (e.g., Ben's claim of lost business resulting from non-delivery of the station wagon) are called "consequential damages" and may be recovered if they were foreseeable to the parties at the time the contract was made, and if they could not have been mitigated by the aggrieved party. If Ben could have traveled to the customers' premises by renting a car or by using one of the company pickup trucks, Car Sales would not be responsible for damages resulting from his failure to mitigate consequential damages by doing so.

           A is incorrect because Ben had advised the sales person that he needed to use the station wagon for his business, making business losses foreseeable. **B** is incorrect because impossibility only excuses performance if it results from factors not within the reasonable contemplation of the parties at the time the contract was formed. Here, both parties knew that Car Sales Inc was planning to order the station wagon from Ferris, and could have anticipated that Ferris might not deliver the car on time. **D** is incorrect since consequential damages are available in actions for breach of a sales contract.

110. **C**   The standard measure of damages for seller's breach of contract consists of the difference between the contract price and the reasonable market value. Based on this measure alone, there might be no damages to Car Sales Inc. But the victim of a seller's breach may also recover consequential damages. These consist of foreseeable losses which could not have been avoided by mitigation, and which resulted from the special position in which the breach placed the buyer. Here, since Ferris knew that the station wagon was being ordered for resale, and that the sale would probably fall through if the car was not delivered on time, Car Sales Inc's loss was a foreseeable one. Since Car Sales Inc could not have gotten the car any other way, it may recover for the profit lost through its inability to complete the sale to Ben.

           A is incorrect because liability for breach of contract does not depend on the reasonableness of the defendant's conduct and may be imposed even if the breach was reasonable. **B** and **D** are incorrect, since they ignore the possibility of consequential damages.

111. **A**   Even though no contract exists, a party can recover from another on a quasi-contract (i.e., contract implied-in-law) theory when she rendered a service to the other with the reasonable expectation of compensation. Thus, if Meder had a reasonable expectation of payment at the time she rendered medical services to Hart, she may recover on a quasi-contract theory.

A contract is implied-in-fact when, although the parties have not expressed agreement, their intent to enter into a mutually binding bargain is evident from their conduct and the surrounding circumstances. Since Hart remained unconscious for the entire period during which Meder rendered services, he could not have acted in a way which manifested the intent to make a binding contract. **B** is, therefore, incorrect. **C** is incorrect because quasi-contract recovery is usually based on the value of the detriment sustained by the plaintiff, rather than that of the benefit received by the defendant. Where they exist, "good Samaritan" statutes protect physicians against negligence liability in connection with treatment which they render without expectation of compensation at accident or other emergency scenes. Although "good Samaritan" statutes do not extend this protection to a physician who charges for her services, they do not prevent her from doing so. **D** is, therefore, incorrect.

112.   **C**   A contract for the lease of realty is not illegal even though the lessee might have an illegal activity in mind when he enters into the lease.

Ordinarily, the courts will not aid either party to an illegal contract, unless the party seeking relief was not equally guilty (i.e., in pari delicto) with the other party. **A** and **B** are incorrect, however, because the contract to lease realty did not have an illegal purpose. **D** is incorrect because impossibility excuses performance only if it is brought about through no fault of the breaching party.

113.   **A**   Prospective inability to perform arises when a party to a contract, by his own conduct, divests himself of the power to perform. Although this is not necessarily a breach which would entitle the other party to damages, all jurisdictions agree that prospective inability to perform excuses the other party's performance if she has justifiably and detrimentally relied on it. Here, Maxine's purpose was to gain a tax advantage which required the investment of exactly $4,000. Since her knowledge that Gale had already sold the painting probably made it reasonable for her to believe that Gale would not be able to deliver it to her as promised, she was justified in relying on Gale's prospective inability by investing the $4,000 in sculpture. Maxine's non-performance is, therefore, excused.

B is incorrect because contract liability in general, and the doctrine of prospective inability in particular, operate regardless of fault. **C** is incorrect because there is no indication that Maxine knew or should have known of the existence of the re-acquisition clause and because, in any event, the uncertainty of Gale's re-acquisition of the painting probably justified Maxine's reliance on the prospective inability. Since Gale delivered the painting to Maxine as promised, it is true that no breach occurred and that Gale might not be liable to Maxine. But **D** is incorrect because Maxine's performance was excused as explained above.

114.   **A**   Although Maxine's refusal to accept the painting is excused by her reinvestment of the money in reliance on of Gale's prospective inability to perform, her refusal of Gale's tender discharges Gale from further obligation to perform.

B is incorrect since Gale's obligation to deliver is not dependent on Maxine's reason for making the purchase. **C** and **D** are incorrect since Maxine's refusal to accept delivery constitutes a waiver of any specific performance rights which she otherwise might have had.

115. **A**   An offer is a manifestation of willingness to be bound to specified terms which gives an offeree the power to create a contract by accepting. Since an advertisement rarely does this, it is usually regarded as a mere invitation rather than as an offer unless the circumstances indicate that the party who published the advertisement did so with the intent of empowering another to turn it into a binding contract simply by accepting it. Usually, such an intent is found only where the advertisement indicates the number of items on sale and contains words indicating an intent to be bound. Here, the phrase "While they last" makes clear that a reader of the advertisement does not have the power to turn it into a binding contract by accepting, and so indicates an intent not to be bound.

   B, **C** and **D** are incorrect because the language used indicates an intent not to be bound to any person who responds.

116. **D**   There have been two assignments: Gru assigned contract benefits to New; Muse assigned contract benefits and delegated contract obligations to Bro. Unless specifically released by the obligee, an assignor remains liable for obligations under the contract. Gru, thus, continues to be obligated under the contract. Bro's right, however, depends upon whether the assignment to him by Muse was valid. Usually an assignment and delegation is invalid if the obligation which it purports to delegate is the performance of personal services. This is because the services performed by the assignee cannot be identical to those of the assignor, and the obligee, therefore, would not be receiving what he had bargained for. (*Note:* Since making music is an art, a contract for a musical performance is generally regarded as one for personal services, and therefore is not assignable.)

   A is incorrect, since it is usually understood that benefits of a contract may be freely assigned. It is true that such an assignment will be regarded as ineffective if it results in the imposition of a burden on the obligor which is heavier than that to which he originally agreed. Here, however, the wedding was at the same place and on the same day, so the burden remained the same. The statement in **B** is irrelevant since Gru assigned only the benefit of the contract, but retained the obligation to pay. **C** contains an incorrect statement since only a novation — requiring consent by the other party — would relieve the assignor of obligations under a contract.

117. **C**   Since Gru's assignment to New did not increase the burden of Muse, it was valid, and New is entitled to the performance to which Gru was entitled. Since the contract called for music to be played by Muse, music played by Bro would not satisfy Muse's obligation unless it was identical to music played by Muse. The contract would, thus, have been breached. Unless he is specifically released by the obligee, an assignor is liable for breach of the contract. For these reasons, Muse would be liable to New under the condition set forth in **C**.

   D is, therefore, incorrect. So long as assignment of a contract benefit does not increase the other party's burden, it is effective in spite of a clause which prohibits assignment. **A** is, therefore, incorrect. **B** is factually inaccurate since the wedding was to take place on the same day and at the same place as originally agreed.

118. **D**   A condition subsequent is an event which, by agreement of the parties, discharges a

duty of performance that had already become absolute. The language of the sales agreement makes it clear that Suzanne's promise to have the downstairs apartment vacated was to be performed prior to payment by Balbo. Since it could not be undone once it was performed, there can be no condition subsequent to it. Thus, **D** is an inaccurate statement.

A, **B**, and **C** are accurate statements since performances which are to be exchanged simultaneously are usually found to be concurrently conditioned on each other.

119. **B**   When a contract calls for performance by one party prior to performance by the other, the first party's performance is generally held to be a condition precedent to the other party's performance. A condition precedent is an event without which a party's obligation does not become absolute. Since the contract provided that Balbo's obligation was void if the downstairs apartment was not vacant within three months after the transfer of title, vacancy of the downstairs apartment was an express condition precedent to Balbo's obligation to pay the additional two thousand dollars. An obligor's obligation is discharged upon failure of a condition precedent to it.

A is incorrect since Suzanne is no longer the owner of the premises and therefore lacks standing to bring a proceeding to evict Tenn. **C** is incorrect because the contract specifies that in the event the apartment remained occupied, Balbo's remedy is to avoid his obligation to pay the additional two thousand dollars. **D** is incorrect because the contract specifically provides that Balbo's obligation to pay the additional two thousand dollars is non-existent if the apartment is not vacant within three months after the passage of title.

120. **A**   UCC Section 2-102 provides that "this Article applies to transactions in goods." Although many of the sections of Article 2 create special rules for transactions involving merchants, many other sections apply to all transactions in goods, whether the parties are merchants or not. Therefore, **B** is incorrect. **C** is incorrect because many commercial transactions (e.g., sales of realty) are not "transactions in goods" and, therefore, are not covered by Article 2. **D** is incorrect because transactions in services are not covered by Article 2.

121. **C**   A promise which is unenforceable for lack of consideration or because it fails to satisfy the requirements of the Statute of Frauds may nevertheless be enforceable under the doctrine of promissory estoppel if the promisee justifiably relied upon it to his detriment. If, however, no express or implied promise was made to the plaintiff, then promissory estoppel is not applicable. Although it is not certain that the trier of the facts would find that no promise was implied, the argument in **C** is the only one listed which could possibly support Wanda's position.

A person who acts without having been asked to and under circumstances such that his action was not called for by the situation is sometimes referred to as an "officious intermeddler" and is prevented from receiving compensation for his performance. **A** is incorrect because Wanda asked for help, and also because the emergency called for Robinson's action. In a claim based on promissory estoppel, the promisee's recovery is not based on the value received by the promisor but on either the promise made by the promisor or the detriment sustained by the promisee. Thus, the value of Pilot's life is not relevant to Robinson's claim and **B** is incorrect. **D** is incorrect because under the doctrine of promissory estoppel a promise may be enforceable without consideration.

122.   **C**   An offer is a manifestation of the offeror's willingness to enter into a contract on the terms specified. It is sometimes said that a communication is an offer if an acceptance is the only thing necessary to turn it into a binding contract. The language used by Ansel — "Are you still interested?" — leaves some doubt about whether the letter expressed a willingness to be bound. Some courts might find that it does; some courts might find that it does not. But if a court held that the letter was not an offer, **C** is the only reason listed which would justify that conclusion.

An acceptance is an unconditional manifestation of willingness to be bound by the terms of an offer, and is, therefore, the last step which must be taken to form a contract. Ansel obviously did not intend his letter to result in a contract since he asked Collard to let him know whether he was still interested and whether the price was acceptable. Thus, even if Collard's letter of March 11 was an offer — which is doubtful — Ansel's letter of April 17 could not have been an acceptance of it. For this reason **A** is incorrect. Under the UCC, the omission of terms in what would otherwise be a contract implies reasonable terms. Specifically, the omission of a payment term implies that full payment is to be made at the time and place of delivery. **B** is, therefore, incorrect. Similarly, an offer which omits to indicate how acceptance should be made implies that acceptance may be made by any reasonable means. **D** is, therefore, incorrect.

123.   **A**   A contract is formed upon acceptance of an offer. Thus, if Ansel's letter of April 17 was an offer, a contract was formed if Collard's acceptance was effective before the offer was revoked. Ordinarily, an acceptance is effective upon dispatch if communicated in a manner authorized by the offer. Since an offer which does not specify a means of communicating acceptance authorizes acceptance in any reasonable manner, a contract was formed on April 21, when Collard dispatched the telegram, if sending a telegram was a reasonable way of communicating acceptance.

Good faith means honesty and fair dealing. **B** is incorrect because there is no indication that Ansel failed to act in good faith. **C** is incorrect because an offer not specifying a means of acceptance authorizes acceptance in any reasonable manner. Revocation of an offer is effective when notice is received by the offeror. Since Ansel did not notify Collard of his change of mind, it could not have effected a revocation. Thus, **D** is incorrect.

124.   **A**   Under UCC Section 2-204, an agreement sufficient to constitute a contract for sale may be found even though the moment of its making is undetermined. Conduct by both parties which recognizes the existence of a contract may be sufficient to establish an agreement. Although it may be difficult to determine which communication was an offer and which communication was an acceptance, the fact is that after receiving a telegram in which Manson agreed to pay $16,000 for the settee, Ansel shipped it to Manson. There is nothing equivocal about Manson's language; its meaning is clear — Manson was willing to pay $16,000 for the piece. Ansel must have intended to be bound by the terms of Manson's telegrams, or he would not have shipped after receiving it. Thus, Ansel's shipment in response to Manson's telegram indicates that a contract existed.

B and **C** are incorrect because the conduct of the parties indicates that a contract was formed, whether or not any particular communication can be regarded as an offer or as an acceptance. Sometimes a prior course of dealing is used to help interpret the language and conduct of the parties. **D** is incorrect, however, because the meaning of their language and conduct is not in doubt.

125.   **A**   Ordinarily, a promise is not enforceable unless it is supported by consideration. Consideration is something which is bargained for and given in exchange for the promise. Although consideration frequently is found in some benefit conferred upon a promisor in exchange for a promise, it is generally understood that a detriment suffered by the promisee is sufficient consideration for a promise if it was bargained for and given in exchange for that promise. Since Francis desired for Amy to be near him, he promised to give her a franchise if she would move to Westlake and live near him. Whether or not Francis gained any benefit from her move, Amy suffered the detriment of moving from her home to Westlake. This detriment, having been bargained for in exchange for Francis's promise, is sufficient to satisfy the requirement of consideration.

A promise which is unsupported by consideration may be enforceable anyway under the doctrine of promissory estoppel if the promisee justifiably relied on it to her detriment. **B** is incorrect, however, because Francis' promise was supported by consideration, and the doctrine of promissory estoppel applies only in the absence of consideration. It is sometimes argued that where a promise is made to confer a benefit on another person in return for some act which is of no benefit to the promisor, the promise is one for a conditional gift, and is therefore unenforceable. This argument does not apply, however, where the detriment suffered by the promisee was something which the promisor wanted and was an inducement for the promisor's promise. Since Francis desired for Amy to live near him in Westlake, and since it was this desire which motivated his promise to her, **C** is incorrect. Affection is not enough to support a promise and cannot serve as consideration, because it is not something bargained for in exchange for a promise. **D** is incorrect, however, because the promise made by Francis was given not merely out of affection for Amy, but to induce Amy to move to Westlake.

126.   **D**   Section 2-601 of the UCC provides that if goods delivered fail in any respect to conform to the contract of sale, the buyer may reject the whole, accept the whole, or accept any commercial units (i.e., quantities which may be sold commercially without substantially impairing their value) and reject the rest. **I** and **II** are, therefore, correct. Section 2-607 provides that acceptance does not of itself impair any other remedy for non-conformity. Since Section 2-714 permits a buyer to recover damages resulting from the non-conformity of accepted goods **III** is also correct.

127.   **D**   If the circumstances which resulted in destruction of the structure excused performance by Bilden, his refusal to continue was not a breach. Since, however, he did not perform as promised, his only remedy would be in quasi-contract. If the circumstances did not excuse performance by Bilden, his refusal to continue was a breach. Even a breaching builder may be entitled to a quasi-contract remedy, however, if the owner of the premises received some benefit as a result of his work. In either event, Bilden's recovery would be limited to the value of the benefit received by Owwens. Since the structure was completely destroyed, Owwens received no benefit from Bilden's work. Bilden is, therefore, not entitled to any recovery.

A seller's damages for the buyer's breach of a contract for the sale of goods may consist of the difference between the contract price and the market value of the goods. The measure of damages expressed in **A** seems to be based on this rule, but is incorrect because it is not an accurate statement of that rule, and because this is not a contract for the sale of goods. **B** and **C** are incorrect because quasi-contract damages are measured by the benefit received by the defendant, and Owwens received no benefit at all.

128. **D**   A condition precedent to a contractual obligation is an event which must occur before a party will be under a duty to perform. Real estate brokerage contracts frequently make the broker's commission due upon her producing a buyer who is "ready, willing, and able" to purchase on the agreed terms. In the contract by which Salzburger agreed to pay a 6 percent commission to Ritchie, however, there were two express conditions precedent to Salzburger's obligation to pay. First, the commission was only due if the house was sold to a buyer who made an offer during a two-month period beginning September 1. Second, the commission was only due upon the closing of title. Although Ritchie found a buyer during the agreed period, the house was not sold to that buyer. In addition, title did not close. Since there was a failure of these conditions precedent, Salzburger's obligation to pay Ritchie's commission never became absolute, and Ritchie is entitled to no recovery from Salzburger.

A, **B**, and **C** are, therefore, incorrect.

129. **B**   Under the Statute of Frauds, a promise to pay the debt of another is unenforceable over objection unless it is written and signed by the party to be charged. Thus, if Sante's statement was a promise to pay Burdy's debt to Crowley, it would be unenforceable under the Statute of Frauds. (*Note:* While it is unlikely that a trier of facts would come to that conclusion, the language of **B** requires the assumption that it would.)

A is incorrect because, although the Statute of Frauds requires an agreement for the sale of goods with a price of $500 or more to be in writing, this provision does not apply to loan agreements. **C** is incorrect because if the offer accepted by Crowley was an offer to pay the debt of another, the Statute of Frauds would require a writing. Although a check may be a writing sufficient to satisfy the requirements of the Statute of Frauds, **D** is incorrect because Crowley's check was not signed by Sante, and Sante is the party whom Crowley seeks to charge.

130. **A**   One who will derive a benefit from a contract to which he is not a party is a third party beneficiary of that contract. If the contracting parties meant for their contract to benefit him, he is an intended third party beneficiary. At some point, an intended third party beneficiary may acquire the right to enforce the contract even though he was not a party to it. Some jurisdictions hold that he acquires that right upon learning of the contract; others hold that he acquires that right upon justifiably and detrimentally relying on the contract; still others hold that he acquires the right either upon relying or upon assenting to the contract. All agree, however, that justified and detrimental reliance by an intended third party beneficiary gives him the right to enforce the contract. If Samuel relied on the agreement between Marilyn and Fred by cancelling his contract to purchase a residence, he is entitled to enforce the agreement against Fred's estate.

If the benefit to a third party was intended to fulfill an obligation which one of the contracting parties owed him, the third party is referred to as a creditor beneficiary. Otherwise the third party is a donee beneficiary. **B** is incorrect because the distinction is based on the intentions of the contracting parties at the time the contract was formed, and because neither Marilyn nor Fred owed Samuel an obligation which was to be satisfied by leaving him the realty. Samuel was, thus, a donee beneficiary of the contract between Marilyn and Fred. **C** is incorrect, however, because a donee beneficiary may enforce a contract if the contracting parties intended to confer a benefit on him (subject to the above rules regarding the rights of intended third party beneficiaries). If, by its terms, an agreement is not capable of being performed within one year, the Statute of Frauds requires a writing. Since the agreement between Marilyn and Fred was in writing, its enforceability does not depend on whether it could be performed within one year. **D** is therefore incorrect.

131.   **B**   Although a *mutual* mistake may prevent the formation of a contract because it may result in a lack of assent, a *unilateral* mistake does not have that effect. In the majority of jurisdictions, a party is not excused from performance because of a unilateral mistake unless the other party knew or should have known of it. Thus, if Bilder knew or should have known of Wirco's mistake, Wirco's performance would be excused.

  A is incorrect because Wirco's unilateral mistake alone would not excuse performance unless Bilder knew or should have known of it. Since the agreement between Bilder and Wirco was made after Bilder had bid on the renovation project, their rights should not be determined by what Bilder contemplated when bidding. **C** is therefore incorrect. If Bilder knew of the mistake made by Wirco in calculating its price, Wirco is excused from performance even though it could have performed without sustaining a loss. If Bilder did not know of the mistake, Wirco's performance would not be excused, even if such performance would result in a loss. The condition expressed in **D** is, therefore, irrelevant, and **D** is incorrect.

132.   **C**   An offer is rejected when the offeror receives notice of the offeree's intent not to accept it. Rejection of an offer terminates the offeree's power of acceptance. Since Elco's offer was to do all the electrical work on the renovation job, Bilder's contract with Wirco was inconsistent with an acceptance by Bilder of Elco's offer. If Elco learned of Bilder's contract with Wirco, it was justified in concluding that Bilder had rejected its offer.

  Although UCC §2-205 makes enforceable without consideration a written promise by a merchant to hold open an offer regarding the sale of goods, that section is inapplicable to a contract for services. **A** and **B** are, therefore, incorrect. Although reliance by Bilder might make enforceable without consideration Elco's promise to hold the offer open, Bilder's failure to rely is not the *only* thing which would relieve Elco of liability (as seen in option **C**). **D** is, therefore, incorrect.

133.   **B**   An effective assignment transfers all of the assignor's rights to the assignee. If Dataflo made an effective assignment of her rights under the contract with Kunkel and Williams, she can no longer enforce those rights, and the court must find against her.

  Since the contract called for payment of $5,000 within 30 days after installation of the hardware, and did not require design of the software until several months later, the parties could not have intended design or its commencement to be conditions precedent to payment. **A** is, therefore, not an effective argument. **C** is incorrect because the contract apportioned $6,000 to the value of the hardware, making the obligation to pay (at least the initial $5,000) unrelated to fulfillment of other obligations under the contract. A divisible contract is one in which separate obligations are regarded as separately enforceable agreements. If this contract was divisible, then the obligation to pay for the hardware already delivered would not be dependent on any other obligation. **D** is incorrect because this argument would hurt, rather than help, Kunkel and Williams' cause.

134. **D** An obligor is discharged of liability to the obligee's assignee to the extent of any payments made to the original obligee prior to notice of the assignment. Thus, if Kunkel and Williams paid $5,000 to Dataflo before being advised that Dataflo had assigned her rights to Antun, they could not be required to pay that sum to Antun.

Since the $5,000 in question was payment for computer hardware which had already been delivered, the fact that Antun might not be capable of carrying out any of the other obligations under the contract is not relevant to her right to collect. **A** is, therefore, incorrect. In general, all rights under a contract are assignable, so a contract which is silent about the right to assign, impliedly permits assignment. **B** is, therefore, incorrect. A modification of a contract occurs when the parties agree to change the performance required. An assignment is a transfer of contract rights. Since assignment of a right does not change the performance required, the right asserted by Antun was not the result of a modification. **C** is, therefore, incorrect.

135. **A** Under UCC Section 2-210, a party to a contract may treat the other party's delegation of duties as a reasonable ground for insecurity, and may demand assurances from the delegatee. Until assurances are furnished in response to that demand, the obligee may suspend his own performance. Having demanded assurances from McOwen, Kunkel and Williams were under no obligation to furnish specifications until they received those assurances.

B is incorrect because the assignee of a contract steps into the shoes of the assignor, receiving whatever rights the assignor had, in spite of the fact that the assignee is not actually in privity with the obligor. Although the delegator of duties under a contract continues to be liable to her obligee, this liability is generally regarded as secondary. For this reason, without losing rights against the delegator, the obligee is entitled to demand assurances from the delegatee as explained above. **C** is, therefore, incorrect. **D** is incorrect because performance of conditions by Kunkel and Williams was suspended pending receipt of assurances from McOwen.

136. **A** An anticipatory repudiation is an unequivocal statement that she will not perform made by a party before performance is due under a contract. Upon a party's anticipatory repudiation, the other party has an immediate right to sue for breach of contract. In general all duties under a contract are delegable, except those which call for personal services or special skills. Since the design of a software program required special skills and knowledge, Dataflo lacked the right to delegate that duty to McOwen, and Dataflo continued to be under an obligation to perform. Her statement on August 16 was, thus, an anticipatory repudiation, giving Kunkel and Williams an immediate right of action against her.

B is incorrect because an assignment of all rights under a contract is generally understood to delegate all duties under that contract. Since anticipatory repudiation results in an immediate right of action, the fact that performance is not yet due does not prevent a suit for breach on that ground. **C** is, therefore, incorrect. **D** is incorrect because the duty to design a program involved personal services and special skills, so even though it was delegated by Dataflo's sale to McOwen, the delegation did not relieve Dataflo of her duties under the contract.

137. **C**   Even after a valid delegation of contractual duties, the delegator is secondarily obligated. **I** is, therefore correct. Persons who will derive a benefit from a contract to which they are not parties are third party beneficiaries of that contract. If the parties to the contract intended for those third party beneficiaries to benefit, they are intended third party beneficiaries. If one of the purposes of the contracting parties was to satisfy an obligation owed by one of them to third party beneficiaries, then they are creditor beneficiaries of the contract. Intended creditor beneficiaries may enforce a contract even though they were not parties to it. The assignment of rights under a contract implies a delegation of duties as well. Since Dataflo assigned her rights (and therefore delegated her duties) under the contract with Kunkel and Williams to McOwen, Kunkel and Williams were intended creditor third party beneficiaries of the agreement between Dataflo and McOwen, and can enforce it against McOwen even without privity. **II** is, therefore, correct.

138. **D**   Under the parol evidence rule, extrinsic evidence of prior or contemporaneous agreements or negotiations is inadmissible if offered to contradict the terms of an unambiguous written contract which was intended by the parties to be the complete expression of their agreement. If, however, the terms of a writing are ambiguous, evidence of prior or contemporaneous discussions may be admissible to clear up the ambiguity. Since the language of this writing could reasonably be understood to mean what each party claims it means, it is ambiguous. Thus, the evidence is offered to explain rather than contradict the terms of the writing, and is admissible for that purpose.

A is, therefore, incorrect. Although the UCC provides that evidence of a prior course of dealing or of usage in the trade may be admitted to explain even an apparently *un*ambiguous contract, **B** and **C** are incorrect because these are not the *only* kinds of evidence which are admissible.

139. **C**   Ordinarily, a promise is unenforceable unless supported by consideration. Since consideration involves a bargained-for exchange, a preexisting obligation cannot serve as consideration for a new promise, since it was not given in exchange for that promise. Except for the $250 per month which Zooloo was already obligated to pay Victoria, Zooloo gave nothing in return for Victoria's promise to deliver the tiger. Thus, Victoria's promise was unsupported by consideration, and is, therefore, unenforceable.

A is incorrect for two reasons: first, the UCC defines "merchant" in terms of the sale of *goods*, not services, so there can be no merchant as to the sale of services; second, the requirement of consideration is not suspended when one of the parties to a promise is a merchant. UCC Section 2-209 provides that an agreement modifying a contract under UCC Article 2 needs no consideration to be binding. **B** is incorrect, however, because under UCC Section 2-102, Article 2 applies only to transactions in goods. Since the original contract between Victoria and Zooloo was for veterinary *services*, it does not come under Article 2. Therefore, Section 2-209 does not apply to the attempted modification. **D** is incorrect because an agreement to modify a contract need not be in writing to be valid unless the contract, as modified, comes within the provisions of the Statute of Frauds. Since the Statute of Frauds requires a contract for the sale of goods with a price of $500 or more to be in writing, and since this agreement — even as modified — called for services, and goods without a price of $500 or more, it does not fall within the provisions of the Statute of Frauds.

140. **D**   Under UCC Section 2-209 an agreement to modify a contract for the sale of goods needs no consideration to be binding. Since a contract for the sale of a tiger is a contract for the sale of goods, the agreement which Victoria made to "throw in a pig" for Borah is binding and may be enforced by Zooloo.

   A, **B**, and **C** are incorrect because the provisions of Section 2-209 do not distinguish contracts between merchants from contracts between non-merchants.

141. **A**   Under UCC Section 2-606, acceptance occurs when the buyer fails to make an effective rejection. Under Section 2-602 rejection must be made within a reasonable time after delivery and is ineffective unless the buyer seasonably notifies the seller. Since Benson was aware of the nonconformity the day the boards were delivered, but failed to notify Surly of the nonconformity until Surly sued him four months later, he accepted the boards. Ordinarily, a buyer who accepts the nonconforming goods may claim damages as a setoff against the contract price. Under UCC Section 2-607, however, a buyer who accepts delivery of nonconforming goods and fails to notify the seller within a reasonable time after discovering the nonconformity is barred from any remedy.

   B is incorrect because a buyer who notifies the seller within a reasonable time may revoke his acceptance or may use damages resulting from nonconformity of the goods as a setoff against the contract price. Although the boards did not conform to the contract of sale, **C** is incorrect because Benson failed to seasonably notify Surly of the nonconformity. **D** is incorrect because it has no basis in existing law. Even if the seller could have avoided the nonconformity by making a reasonable inspection, he is entitled to collect the contract price of goods which the buyer accepts without notifying him of the nonconformity.

142. **B**   A buyer who rightfully rejects nonconforming goods is entitled to damages for non-delivery. Under UCC §2-713(1), these consist of the difference between the contract price and the market price at the time when the buyer learned of the breach. Since Benson learned of the non-conformity on January 15, **B** is correct.

   C is, therefore, incorrect. **A** would be the correct measure of damage if Benson had kept the 7-foot boards, but is incorrect because he returned them to Surly. Rejection of nonconforming goods may be made within a reasonable time after receiving them. Although Benson did not act immediately upon discovering the nonconformity, the return of the goods two days later was probably within a reasonable time. Even if two days was not a reasonable time, however, Surly's agreement to their return would prevent him from making that assertion. **D** is, therefore, incorrect.

143. **A**   An assignment confers upon the assignee whatever rights the assignor had against the

obligor at the moment of the assignment, and only those rights. For this reason, any defense which the obligor could have asserted against the assignor prior to the assignment can be asserted against the assignee. If Johnson's purchase of the ring from Pawnie was based on Pawnie's representation that the stone was a diamond, then — whether or not Pawnie's misrepresentation resulted from fault — Pawnie was liable to Johnson for breach of contract damages. This liability of Pawnie could be asserted by Johnson as a setoff against any subsequent claim which Pawnie might make against Johnson, whether related to the sale of the ring or not. Since Ascot stepped into Pawnie's shoes by receiving the assignment, Johnson's setoff can be asserted against Ascot as well.

Although tort liability for misrepresentation requires fault, **B** is incorrect because liability for breaching a sales contract is based on the delivery of nonconforming goods, whether or not the nonconformity resulted from the seller's fault. No rule of law requires notification prior to the assertion of a setoff. **C** is, therefore, incorrect. Although personal defenses against an assignor which arose subsequent to the assignment cannot ordinarily be asserted against the assignee, all defenses against the assignor (including personal defenses) which existed at the time of the assignment can be raised against the assignee. **D** is, therefore, incorrect.

144. **C**   Although an assignment does not imply a warranty that the obligor will perform, an assignment for consideration does not imply a warranty that at the time of the assignment the obligor has no defenses. Since at the time of Pawnie's assignment to Ascot, Johnson had a defense based on the nonconformity of the ring delivered by Pawnie the previous month, Pawnie's implied warranty to Ascot was breached. Pawnie is, therefore, liable to Ascot.

A and **B** are incorrect because there has been a breach of the implied warranty that the obligor has no defenses. **D** is incorrect because no warranty that the obligor will perform is implied by an assignment, even for consideration.

145. **D**   Consideration usually consists of some legal detriment suffered by the promisee which is given in exchange for the promisor's promise. Since Tracto gave nothing in return for Moto's promise to keep the offer open, her promise was not supported by consideration.

Under UCC Section 2-205 an assurance given by a merchant in a signed writing that an offer regarding the sale of goods will be held open is called a "firm offer," and may be enforced without consideration. **A** is incorrect, however, because although such an offer may be binding without consideration, it is not supported by consideration unless the offeree suffers some detriment in exchange for it. **B** is incorrect for a similar reason. Sometimes justified and detrimental reliance may make a promise enforceable even though it was not supported by consideration, but, although detrimental reliance may serve as a substitute for consideration, it is not consideration. Although a subsequent purchase by Tracto might constitute legal detriment, it could not be consideration for Moto's promise, because Moto did not require it in exchange for her promise. **C** is, therefore, incorrect.

146. **C**   An offer is an expression of the willingness of the offeror to enter into a contract with the offeree on the terms specified. Since Tracto's letter expressed a willingness to enter

into a contract for the purchase of three model #614 motors on the terms specified in Moto's letter of April 15, it was an offer to purchase three model #614 motors on those terms.

An offer cannot be accepted after it has been revoked, and is revoked when the offeree learns that the offeror has performed an act wholly inconsistent with the terms of the offer. Since Moto had only three model #614 motors left, her sale of two of them to Second was wholly inconsistent with her offer to sell all three to Tracto. Thus, when Tracto learned of the sale, Moto's offer to sell all three was revoked and could no longer be accepted by Tracto. Although UCC Section 2-205 (concerning firm offers) might have made Moto's offer irrevocable until June 1, Tracto's knowledge on June 2 that the motors had already been sold to another deprived Tracto of the power to accept it. **A** is, therefore, incorrect. Although Moto's letter of April 15 offered to sell any or all of the remaining three motors, **B** is incorrect because Tracto's letter clearly indicated his intent to be bound only to a contract for the purchase of three motors. Since the offeror is said to be king of the offer (i.e., has the sole right to determine on what terms he is willing to be bound), **D** is incorrect for the same reason. Having said that he would purchase three motors, Tracto could not thereby be bound to a contract for the purchase of one motor.

147. **A**   UCC Section 2-209 provides that the modification of a sales contract is valid, even without consideration. Moto's agreement to accept $200 as payment in full, is, therefore, enforceable as a modification of the original contract.

B is incorrect because a modification need not be in writing unless, as modified, the contract comes under the Statute of Frauds. Since the modification set a purchase price of $200 (i.e., less than $500) the fact that it was not written does not affect its enforceability. **C** is incorrect because Section 2-209 specifically dispenses with the need for consideration. Duress is a compulsion or constraint which deprives a party of the ability to exercise free will, and generally involves physical threats. Economic pressures do not constitute duress unless the one exerting them brings about a desperate economic situation of the other party. Even then, most jurisdictions refuse to call such pressure duress. **D** is, therefore, incorrect.

148. **D**   Upon breach by the buyer, the seller's damages generally consist of the difference between the contract price and the fair market value. If the seller succeeds in reselling the goods, her damages consist of the difference between the contract price and the price which she actually received. Since Moto resold the motor for more than Tracto had agreed to pay, however, she has sustained no damage under this formula. UCC Section 2-708 provides that if this measure of damages is inadequate "to put the seller in as good a position as performance would have done," the seller is entitled to collect the profit which she would have received if the buyer had not breached. This rule, however, is generally understood to apply only when the seller has an unlimited supply of goods for sale. Here, since Moto only had one motor to sell, and since she succeeded in selling it for a price as good as (in fact, better than) that which Tracto had agreed to pay, she has sustained no damage at all, and is not entitled to any recovery.

A, **B**, and **C** are, therefore, incorrect.

149. **C**   Ordinarily a promise is not enforceable unless there was consideration (i.e., something

given in exchange for and to induce the promise) for it. Since Edward's service had already been rendered without expectation of payment, it was not given in exchange for the promise and is not consideration for it. Some cases have held, however, that a promise to do that which the promisor is morally obligated to do should be enforceable. Since this is an infrequently applied exception to the requirement of consideration, it is unlikely that a court would come to this conclusion. **C** is the only one of the arguments listed, however, which could result in a victory for Edward.

A is incorrect, because an otherwise unenforceable promise is not made enforceable simply because it is in writing. Sometimes, a promisee's justified and detrimental reliance makes a promise enforceable, serving as a substitute for consideration. Detrimental reliance means, however, that the promisee changed his position for the worse because he believed that the promise would be kept. **B** is incorrect since there is no fact indicating that Edward relied on her promise by changing his position because of it, or that he was worse off as a result. When a person confers a benefit on another with a reasonable expectation of payment, an implied-in-fact contract may result. **D** is incorrect, however, because there is no fact indicating that Edward had any expectation of payment when he rescued Boss, particularly because he thought Boss was dead when he leaped into the shaft.

150. **B**   If, at the time a contract is formed, the parties to it are operating under a mutual mistake, the resulting lack of mutual agreement excuses non-performance by either party. Thus, if both Bertrand and Gail mistakenly believed that "Sunset" was painted by Van Gook, Bertrand's non-performance would not constitute a breach.

    A is incorrect for two reasons: first, the Statute of Frauds requirement that the writing be signed by the party to be charged may be satisfied by Bertrand's check; and, second, delivery by the seller satisfies the Statute of Frauds. UCC §2-302(1) (and some jurisdictions in non-UCC cases) hold that if a contract was unconscionable at the time it was made, the court may refuse to enforce it. **C** is incorrect, however, because the equality of bargaining positions in a contract between experts (such as an art dealer and an art collector) prevents a voluntary agreement from being unconscionable unless one of them deliberately withholds knowledge from the other. To avoid interfering with the freedom to bargain, courts rarely consider the adequacy of consideration, except in consumer contracts when equitable relief is sought. **D** is, therefore, incorrect.

151. **C**   Under the parol evidence rule, evidence of a prior or contemporaneous oral agreement is inadmissible for the purpose of contradicting or modifying the terms of an unambiguous writing intended to be a complete expression of the agreement between the parties. Oral evidence may be admitted, however, for the purpose of showing an ambiguity in the terms of a writing, and for explaining that ambiguity. Based on his conversation with Gail, Bertrand may successfully argue that the description "a painting entitled 'Sunset'," as used in the writing, was an ambiguous term which was meant to indicate that the painting was by Van Gook.

    A is, therefore, incorrect. **B** is incorrect because if oral testimony shows that there was an ambiguity in the terms of a writing, it may also be used for the purpose of explaining and clearing up that ambiguity. **D** is incorrect because the parol evidence rule permits the use of oral testimony to show and explain ambiguity in a written agreement.

152. **D**   Rescission of a contract is available if the agreement resulted from a willful misrepresentation or from a mutual mistake by the parties. If Gail accepted Bertrand's money, knowing that he was unwilling to pay $50,000 for a forgery, then she either shared his mistake or wilfully misrepresented the identity of the painter. In either event, Bertrand is entitled to rescission.

   A is incorrect because the remedy of rescission may be available even after the terms of the contract have been performed. Although the tort remedy for misrepresentation requires proof of fault (intent or negligence), rescission may be available even in the absence of fault. **B** and **C** are, therefore, incorrect.

153. **B**   A contract which had an illegal purpose when it was made is unenforceable by either party. Of course, the fact that one of the parties had an illegal objective in mind when he entered into an otherwise lawful contract is not enough to make that contract illegal. These facts indicate, however, that both parties knew the illegal purpose for which the premises were to be used, that Lawrence agreed to equip it specifically for that purpose, and that computation of the rent was based on Tennyson's profits from his unlawful activity. Under the circumstances, the contract was an agreement to engage in an unlawful activity. Even though the operation of a "sports book" subsequently became lawful, the illegality of the contract at the time of its formation makes it unenforceable. Although refusing to require the return of Tennyson's deposit is likely to benefit Lawrence, public policy considerations justify such refusal. When asked to enforce a contract with an unlawful purpose, the court will leave the parties as it found them.

   The contract between Lawrence and Tennyson was not a gambling contract, since none of the obligations depended upon the outcome of an event over which neither had control. **A** is, therefore, incorrect, even though public policy does prohibit the enforcement of gambling contracts. Sometimes the courts will come to the aid of one party to a contract with an unlawful purpose, arguing that he was not in pari delicto (i.e., equally guilty) with the other party. **C** is incorrect, however, because the fact that two parties were in pari delicto is never used to justify granting relief to one of them. When an unforeseeable change in circumstances makes a contract fail of its essential purpose, the parties to it may be excused from performance under the doctrine of frustration of purpose. **D** is incorrect because the change in circumstances in this case did not interfere with the essential purpose of the contract, but rather aided it.

154. **D**   When an unforeseeable change in circumstances makes a contract fail of its essential purpose, the parties to it may be excused from performance under the doctrine of frustration of purpose. The essential purpose of the contract between Lawrence and Tennyson was the operation of a "sports book." Since an unforeseeable change in state law made that activity illegal, the contract has failed of the essential purpose contemplated by both parties at the time it was formed. Tennyson is, thus, excused from performance under the doctrine of frustration of purpose. Since his non-performance is, therefore, not a breach, he is entitled to the return of his deposit.

   A is incorrect because the agreement between Lawrence and Tennyson was not a gambling contract. **B** is incorrect because the subsequent and unforeseeable illegality of the contract's purpose makes the doctrine of frustration of purpose applicable. "In pari delicto" means "equally guilty." **C** is incorrect because at the time the contract was formed, neither party was guilty.

155. **C**   Generally, a buyer's damages for a seller's non-delivery consist of the difference between the contract price and the market price on the day of delivery. Since the market price and the contract price are identical, Barton has sustained no real damage as a result of Seeder's non-delivery of 1,000 bushels. (Although Barton may be entitled to *incidental* damages, which include the cost of finding another seller, **C** is still correct because of its emphasis on Barton's lack of "substantial" damage.)

Ordinarily, a circumstance which prevented a party from performing will excuse non-performance only if its occurrence was not foreseeable to the parties at the time of contracting. This is true whether that circumstance is described as an act of God or not. (After all, almost everything a farmer does depends on acts of God.) Since there is no fact indicating that the April storms were unforeseeable, **A** is incorrect. A breach of contract is not excused simply because the breaching party gave notice in advance that there would be a breach. There is a rule that one who treats an anticipatory repudiation as an immediate breach is required to mitigate damages. That rule is inapplicable here, however, because Barton did not treat Seeder's statement as an immediate breach, taking no action until Seeder's non-delivery. **B** is, therefore, incorrect. The rights of contracting parties are not ordinarily relative to the obligations which they may owe under other contracts. Thus, the fact that Seeder owed obligations to Amos under a separate contract would not affect the obligations which she owed to Barton under her contract with him. **D** is, therefore, incorrect.

156. **B**   An anticipatory repudiation occurs when a promisor makes a positive statement to the promisee that she will not perform her contractual duties. An anticipatory repudiation by a promisor may be treated as an immediate breach by the promisee. One who repudiates before the time for performance may withdraw her repudiation unless the other party relied upon it. Since Barton relied on Seeder's repudiation by making other arrangements for the purchase of 1,000 bushels, Seeder is prevented from withdrawing her repudiation, and Barton is relieved of his obligation to her with respect to 1,000 bushels.

Novation is the substitution by mutual consent of a third party for one of the original parties to contract. Since there has been no such substitution, **A** is incorrect. "Nudum pactum" is a phrase which refers to a promise which is not supported by consideration. Since the promises of Seeder and Barton were each given in return for the other, **C** is incorrect. Impossibility of performance excuses performance when an event which was unforeseeable at the time of formation occurs prior to the time of performance, making performance impossible. Its effect is to relieve both parties of their obligations under the contract. The doctrine is inapplicable here because performance was not impossible for either Seeder or Barton. **D** is, therefore, incorrect.

157. **C**   Under UCC Section 2-209 a modification of a contract is valid even though unsupported by consideration. That same section provides, however, that the Statute of Frauds applies to a contract which, as modified, is within its provisions. Since the agreement made on April 15 between Amos and Seeder called for the purchase of 1000 bushels at the American Kung Bean Exchange price as of May 1, and since that price was $2.00

per bushel, the contract called for the sale of goods with a price of $2,000. Since the Statute of Frauds applies to the sale of goods with a price of $500 or more, this oral contract as modified falls within its provisions, and is, therefore, unenforceable over the objection of Amos.

Although farmers are generally free to negotiate prices for the sale of Kung beans, Seeder is bound by the price which she already negotiated. **A** is, therefore, incorrect. **B** is incorrect for two reasons: first, no consideration is required for the modification of a contract under the UCC, so the fact that each promise was consideration for the other is irrelevant; and, second, the Statute of Frauds requires this contract to be in writing, whether it is supported by consideration or not. Since liability for breach of contract is imposed regardless of fault, a party's liability is not dependent on her ability to perform. **D** is, therefore, incorrect.

158.   **B**   A unilateral contract is one in which only the offeror promises to perform, and only if the offeree performs a specified act. Since Homer's offer was to pay $1,000 to the person who "finds the thief," he has made an offer for a unilateral contract. As with any offer, an offer for a unilateral contract does not become binding unless it is accepted before it is effectively revoked. Since an offer for a unilateral contract can only be accepted by performing the required act, Joe could accept Homer's offer only by catching the thief before Homer effectively revoked the offer. (*Note*: Many authorities hold that an offeror may not effectively revoke after substantial performance by the offeree in reliance on the offer.)

Some jurisdictions hold that an offer for a unilateral contract becomes irrevocable after an offeree substantially commences performance. Joe did not commence performance, however, so his statement alone is not sufficient to make Homer's offer irrevocable even in those jurisdictions. **A** is, therefore, incorrect. A bilateral contract is one in which the parties exchange promises, each promise serving as consideration for the other. Although Joe's statement might be construed as a promise, Homer's offer made clear that acceptance could be made only by catching the thief. For this reason, Joe's promise (if it was a promise) could not be an acceptance of Homer's offer, and no bilateral contract could have been formed. **C** is, therefore, incorrect. An offer is a manifestation of the offeror's intention to enter into a contract with the offeree on the terms specified, which raises in the reasonable person an expectation that nothing more than acceptance is required to create a contract. Since Homer's statement expressed an intention to pay the specified amount to any person who performed the specified task, it is an offer. **D** is, therefore, incorrect.

159.   **D**   Acceptance is an unequivocal indication that the offeree agrees to the terms of the offer. For this reason, an offer for a unilateral contract cannot be accepted by a person who was not aware of its existence. Thus, if Galen was not aware of Homer's offer until after she had caught the thief and recovered the stool, her act could not have been an acceptance of the offer.

Under the objective rule of contracts, a statement may be an offer, even though the person making it did not intend to be bound by it, if the reasonable person would have believed that he did intend to be bound by it. Thus, even if Homer's statement was made in the "heat of passion," it is a binding offer, because there is nothing in the facts to indicate that a reasonable person would have known that he did not intend to be bound by it. **A** is, therefore, incorrect. The facts set forth in **B** might raise an interesting causation question in a tort action by Homer against the thief. The reward offered by Homer for the capture of the thief, however, is not related to the question of whether the thief's act caused any damage to Homer. For this reason, **B** is incorrect. In addition to the power to specify the terms of his offer, an offeror has the power to limit the class of persons who may accept his offer. Homer could, therefore, have restricted his offer to persons who were present in Joe's Bar at the time he made it. He did not, however. By its terms, Homer's offer was to pay $1,000 to "anyone" who caught the thief. Thus, so long as Galen knew of the offer when she caught the thief, she accepted it by catching the thief. **C** is, therefore, incorrect.

160. **C**   A liquidated damages clause is a provision in a contract fixing the amount of damages should a breach occur. Courts enforce liquidated damages clauses so long as the amount set is reasonable, the actual damages are difficult to ascertain, and the contract tailors the liquidated damages to the circumstances. If any of these requirements is unfulfilled, the clause is unenforceable as a "penalty." In that event, the parties may collect only the actual damages which resulted from the breach. **I** is, therefore, correct. The purpose of an agreement as to liquidated damages is to eliminate the problems that may arise in establishing or defending against actual damage claims in certain circumstances. For this reason, if the liquidated damages clause is enforceable, it provides the only *damage* remedy. It does not, however, prevent the wronged party from seeking other *non-damage* relief. Thus, even if the liquidated damages clause did not establish a penalty (i.e., was enforceable), Barksdale may be entitled to the equitable remedy of specific performance. **II** is, therefore, correct.

161. **B**   The standard measure of damages for buyer's breach of a sales contract is the difference between the price which the buyer agreed to pay and the reasonable market value or price received by the seller upon resale in a commercially reasonable manner. Under the standard measure for damages, Sun Auto would not be entitled to recover from Barlow, since it sold the car to Otter at the same price which Barlow agreed to pay. UCC section 2-708 provides, however, that where the standard measure of damages "is inadequate to put the seller in as good a position as performance would have done," the seller may recover the profit which it would have made from full performance by the buyer. If Barlow had performed as agreed, Sun Auto would have made one profit from the sale of a car to Barlow and a second profit from the sale of a car to Otter. As a result of Barlow's breach, Sun Auto made only one profit — that derived from its sale to Otter. The standard measure of damages is thus insufficient to put Sun Auto in as good a position as if Barlow had performed as agreed. For this reason, Sun Auto is entitled to the profit which it would have made upon selling the car to Barlow. Since its profit consists of the difference between the wholesale price and the retail price, **B** is correct.

A and C are incorrect for the reason discussed above. In addition to being incorrect for this reason **D** is incorrect because it is not based on any of the existing rules for measuring damages, and also because it bears no logical relationship to damages actually resulting from Barlow's breach.

162. **B**   A contract may make the happening of a particular event a condition precedent to the performance of a contractual duty. If so, the obligation to perform that duty does not

become absolute until the condition precedent is fulfilled. Thus, if Ruskin's remaining in law school was a condition precedent to Lulu's obligation to pay, the fact that Ruskin withdrew in December 1985 would relieve Lulu of that obligation. A condition precedent may be express (i.e., stated in words or a substitute for words) or implied (i.e., not stated but capable of being reasonably inferred from the conduct or language of the parties). The fact that Lulu's promise was not to be performed until July 1, 1986 might justify the inference that Ruskin's remaining in law school until that time was a condition precedent to Lulu's obligation. Although it is not certain that such an inference would be drawn, **B** is the only argument listed which might support Lulu's position.

Since it might take longer than one year to complete law school, and since Lulu promised to pay within one year, it is obvious that completion of law school could not have been a condition precedent to Lulu's obligation. **A** is, therefore, incorrect. Consideration may consist of some legal detriment suffered by a promisee in return for the promisor's obligation. A person suffers a legal detriment when he does or undertakes to do something which he is not already under an obligation to do. Since Ruskin was not legally obligated to stop drinking or to go to law school, his promises and undertakings to do so were legal detriments, and, therefore, may serve as consideration for Lulu's obligation. For this reason, **C** is incorrect. The Statute of Frauds makes an oral contract unenforceable over objection if, by its own terms, it cannot be performed within one year. Although the agreement between Ruskin and Lulu required Ruskin to go to law school and to stop drinking for the rest of his life, these obligations could have been fully performed within one year since Ruskin could have died within that period. **D** is, therefore, incorrect.

163. **A**   An assignment involves the transfer of the assignor's rights to the assignee. Since Ruskin's letter of September 3, 1985 indicated that Ruskin would pay Barker after *Ruskin* received money from Lulu, it was obviously not intended to transfer to Barker the right to receive that money from Lulu. For this reason, it was not an assignment of that right.

Since an assignment is not a promise, but a present transfer of a right, it does not have to be supported by consideration. **B** is, therefore, incorrect. An obligor who has not been notified of the obligee's assignment is discharged from liability to the obligee's assignee to the extent that the obligor has made payment to the obligee (the assignor). **C** is incorrect, however, because Barker's letter to Lulu was notice to Lulu of Barker's claim and was delivered to her prior to any payment by Lulu. **D** is incorrect because, without an agreement to the contrary, rights against an obligor ordinarily may be assigned without the obligor's consent.

164. **C**   Under modern law, forbearance to assert a claim against another party is consideration for the other party's promise to pay money if the party who forbears reasonably believes his claim to be valid. Thus, if Barker reasonably believed his claim for unpaid bar bills to be valid (whether or not Ruskin believed this), his forbearance to assert that claim is valid consideration for the promise to pay which Ruskin made in his letter of September 3, 1985. Under these circumstances, that promise would be enforceable.

A unilateral contract is one in which a party exchanges his promise for the other party's act. An offer for a unilateral contract can only be accepted by performing the act for which the offeror called. Since Ruskin's letter offered to pay if Barker would refrain from suing him (i.e., to exchange Ruskin's promise for Barker's act of forbearance), it was an offer for a unilateral contract. As such, it could only be accepted by Barker's performance (i.e., forbearance to sue). For this reason, Barker's failure to respond to Ruskin's letter would not be relevant to the issue of whether or not Ruskin's offer was accepted. **A** is, therefore, incorrect. If Barker did not reasonably believe that Ruskin owed him $10,000, he suffered no legal detriment by forbearing to assert a claim for that sum. His forbearance could not, therefore, be consideration for Ruskin's promise. Ruskin's promise would thus be unenforceable, and **B** is, therefore, incorrect. Barker's claim is not based on the promises Ruskin made when he incurred the alleged bar bills, but on the promise which Ruskin made in the letter of September 3, 1985. If that promise is enforceable, it is independent of the original claim for unpaid bar bills. For this reason, the enforceability of the claim for unpaid bar bills is not relevant. **D** is, therefore, incorrect.

165.   **C**   A transfer of contract rights is called an assignment; a transfer of contract duties is called a delegation. In general, contract duties are delegable so long as delegation would not prevent the obligee from getting what he bargained for. Duties which involve personal services (i.e., which depend upon the obligor's special skills, training, or expertise) are not delegable, because an obligee who bargained for the obligor's special abilities would not be receiving them if the obligor's duties were performed by another. Whether crop-dusting is an activity which depends on the unique skills of the crop-duster (i.e., calls for personal services) is uncertain. But even if it is, the fact that Duster did not herself participate in the activity would indicate that Flores probably did not bargain for and certainly would not have received her special skills anyway. Thus, the delegation to Airco would not deprive Flores of what he bargained for, and would, therefore, not be a violation of Flores' rights.

Although the statement contained in **A** is an accurate one, it would not provide Duster with an effective response to Flores' claim, because if a contract duty requires personal services it is not delegable. If a contract duty requires the personal services of the obligor, it is generally understood that the obligee bargained for its performance by the obligor herself. **B** is incorrect because such a duty may be non-delegable even if the delegatee possesses skills equal to or greater than those of the delegator. In general, contract rights are assignable so long as the assignment does not increase the burden of the obligor's performance. Although it requires the obligor to pay a different person than the one he agreed to pay, an assignment of the right to collect money usually does not increase his burden since it does not change the amount of money which the obligor must pay. **D** is incorrect, however, because Flores has not objected to Duster's assignment of rights, but rather to Duster's delegation of duties.

166.   **C**   Although an assignment of contract rights divests the assignor of those rights, a delegation of contract duties does not have the same effect, even when consented to by the obligee. For this reason, Duster will remain liable to Flores for any breach of their contract. On the other hand, a delegatee of contract duties also becomes liable to the obligor for breach since the obligor is an intended third-party creditor-beneficiary of the contract of delegation. For this reason, Flores may be entitled to collect from either Duster or Airco.

A and B are, therefore, incorrect. The standard measure of damage for breach of contract is the difference between the contract price and the reasonable market value of the services contracted for. In the event of a major breach, however, the wronged party may elect the remedy of rescission and restitution. Rescission involves cancellation of the contract. Restitution requires the return to the wronged party of any unearned benefit which he conferred on the breaching party. Since Airco's refusal to perform is obviously a major breach, Flores may seek rescission and restitution. D is, therefore, incorrect for this reason and because it fails to account for the fact that Flores has paid Duster.

167. **B**   Ever since 1677, the Statute of Frauds has required a promise to answer for the debt of another to be in writing. Since Bullion's promise was to pay the debt of Mart Corporation, it would be unenforceable over Bullion's objection if it was not in writing.

Although a promise made under duress (i.e., induced by an improper threat) is void, *economic* duress rarely justifies avoidance of a promise. In addition, in order for any duress to make a promise void, the duress must have resulted from some improper threat made by the promisee. Since the economic distress of Mart Corporation did not result from any conduct or threat by Trust Bank, and since Trust Bank's refusal to lend money without a personal guarantee was not improper, the economic fears which induced Bullion's promise will not result in its avoidance. A is, therefore, incorrect. A promise is generally not enforceable unless it is supported by consideration. But consideration may consist of either some benefit conferred upon the promisor or some detriment incurred by the promisee. Since Trust Bank lent money to Mart Corporation in return for Bullion's promise, Trust Bank incurred a detriment which satisfies the requirement of consideration even if Bullion gained no benefit from it. C is, therefore, incorrect. D is incorrect because a surety becomes liable immediately upon default by the principal debtor, and is not entitled to have the creditor proceed first against the principal debtor's assets. (Even without applying this principle, however, D can be eliminated because Bullion promised to pay if Mart Corporation did not, and Mart Corporation did not.)

168. **A**   Ordinarily, contracts may be enforced by parties to them or by intended third-party beneficiaries. Thus, if Bullion was an intended third-party beneficiary of the May 11 contract between Mart Corporation and Trust Bank, she can enforce it. (*Note*: Although it is doubtful that Bullion was an intended beneficiary, use of the word "if" in Option A requires the assumption that she is.) Since the contract required Trust Bank to sell the assets at market value, its sale at less than market value was a breach entitling Mart Corporation and intended third-party beneficiaries to damages.

A fiduciary relationship is one involving trust. For this reason, fiduciaries owe obligations which non-fiduciaries might not owe. B is incorrect, however, because the issues in Bullion's claim against Trust Bank are not dependent on the obligations which Mart Corporation owed to Bullion. Although Bullion was not a party to the May 11 agreement between Mart Corporation and Trust Bank, she may be entitled to enforce it as an intended third-party beneficiary. C is, therefore, incorrect. D is incorrect because the contract called for sale at the market value and not merely in a commercially reasonable manner. (*Note*: Do not be confused by UCC provisions which provide that upon buyer's breach the seller is entitled to resell in a "commercially reasonable manner" goods which were the subject of the contract.)

169.   **A**   Novation is the substitution by mutual consent of a third person for a party to a contract. By assigning to Su, Theobald agreed to substitute Su for himself. It may be argued that by accepting rent from Su with the knowledge that Theobald had assigned to Su, Layton was also consenting to the substitution of Su for Theobald as a party to the contract. Although it is not certain that a court would come to that conclusion, the argument set forth in **A** is the only one which could possibly be effective in Theobald's defense.

An accord is an agreement by which a new obligation is imposed on one of the parties to a contract in place of one which the contract originally created. Satisfaction occurs when the party on whom that obligation was imposed fulfills it. A party who satisfies the new obligation imposed upon him as a result of the accord is discharged from the performance of the original obligation for which the new one was substituted. Since Layton's accepting rent from Su did not result in the imposition of any new obligation on Theobald, it was not an accord. Therefore, there could have been no satisfaction. For this reason, **B** is not an effective argument in Theobald's defense. Consent is willingness. Implied consent is willingness which the reasonable person would gather or infer by observing the conduct of a party. Since Layton accepted rent directly from Su knowing that Theobald had assigned the balance of the lease to Su, the reasonable person might gather or infer that Layton was willing for that assignment to take place. It might, thus, be correct to conclude that Layton impliedly consented to the assignment. **C** is not an effective argument in Theobald's defense, however, because after an assignment, the assignor remains secondarily liable for performance under the contract. This is so even when the other party has consented, expressly or impliedly, to the assignment. The word "alienation" is sometimes used to mean the transfer of an interest in real property, and since an assignment is a transfer, a prohibition against assigning a leasehold interest is a restraint against alienation. Since the courts look with disfavor on restraints against alienation, they are strictly construed. **D** does not present an effective argument in Theobald's defense, however, for two reasons: first, restraints on alienation, if properly drawn, are enforceable; and second, the secondary liability of an assignor as described above makes the question of whether the assignment was a valid one irrelevant (i.e., if the assignment was invalid, Theobald would be primarily liable; if the assignment was valid, Theobald would be secondarily liable).

170.   **A**   A promise is ordinarily not enforceable unless it is supported by consideration. Thus, a promise to make a gift is not usually enforceable. Once a gift has been completed, however, the donee's rights do not depend on the donor's promise. Thus, although a promise to make a gift may be unenforceable, a completed (or executed) gift creates an irrevocable right in the donee. The completion of a gift requires an intent to create a property right coupled with delivery and acceptance of some symbol of that right. It is clear that Thorn intended to create a right in Ardiste. Delivery and acceptance probably occurred when Ardiste was advised of Pressley's promise. While it is not certain that a court would come to that conclusion, **A** is the only argument listed that could possibly provide Ardiste with an effective response to Thorn's defense of no consideration.

An assignment is a transfer from assignor to assignee of the assignor's right to receive performance under a contract. Since Thorn's contract with Pressley did not give Thorn the right to be hired by Pressley as a book illustrator, the benefit which Ardiste received could not have been received by assignment. **B** is, therefore, incorrect. **C** is incorrect because the law of contracts does not recognize any special rule about consideration in agreements between husband and wife. Although **D** addresses consideration which Pressley received for his promise, it is incorrect because it does not address Thorn's defense (i.e., that there was no consideration for Thorn's promise to Ardiste).

171. **A** Contracts frequently benefit persons other than the contracting parties. Such persons are called third-party beneficiaries. If the contracting parties meant for those persons to benefit from the contract, they are intended beneficiaries; otherwise, they are incidental beneficiaries. If a promisor's performance is intended to satisfy a preexisting obligation owed by the promisor to the third-party beneficiary, she is a creditor beneficiary; if not, she is a donee beneficiary. Once an intended third-party beneficiary's rights have *vested*, the contracting parties are no longer free to modify or rescind the portion of their contract which benefits her. Since Thorn and Pressley intended that Ardiste benefit from Pressley's promise to employ her, and since this was not intended to satisfy a preexisting obligation which Thorn owed Ardiste, Ardiste is an intended donee beneficiary. In some jurisdictions the rights of a donee beneficiary vest as soon as she learns of the contract. In other jurisdictions, her rights vest only when she detrimentally relies on the contract. In other jurisdictions, her rights vest when she detrimentally relies or expresses assent. Since Ardiste learned of the contract, assented to it, and detrimentally relied on it by notifying other clients that she could not work for them, her rights have vested in all jurisdictions, and she may succeed in her claim against Pressley.

B is incorrect for two reasons; first, consideration for Pressley's promise was furnished by Thorn's giving him a low rate; and, second, the doctrine of promissory estoppel makes Ardiste's detrimental reliance a substitute for consideration. The Statute of Frauds requires a promise which cannot be performed within a year to be in writing. **C** is incorrect because Pressley's promise was to employ Ardiste for one year, and was, therefore, not required to be in writing. **D** is incorrect because after the donee beneficiary's rights have vested, the contracting parties may not rescind without her consent.

172. **D** An offer can ordinarily be accepted at any time prior to its termination. An offer terminates, however, when the offeree becomes aware that the offeror has acted in a manner inconsistent with the offer. When Brantley learned that Salo had sold the painting to someone else, Salo's offer terminated, depriving Brantley of the power to accept it. This is true, even though Brantley did not learn of the offer's termination directly from Salo.

A is, therefore, incorrect. Since Brantley gave nothing in return for Salo's promise to keep the offer open until February 2, his promise was unsupported by consideration. Ordinarily, a promise to keep an offer open for a specified period of time is unenforceable unless supported by consideration. Under UCC section 2-205 a written promise by a merchant to hold an offer open for a specified period not to exceed three months is a "firm offer," enforceable without consideration. **B** is incorrect, however, because there is no fact indicating that Salo was a merchant. The standard remedy for breach of contract is a judgment for damages. Although specific performance is available in the case of a contract for the sale of a unique chattel, the wronged party may still choose to seek a judgment for damages. **C** is, therefore, incorrect.

173. **D** UCC section 2-202 provides that a writing intended by the parties to be a final expression of their agreement cannot be modified by evidence of a prior or contemporaneous

agreement. It further provides, however, that its terms may be explained by usage of trade. UCC section 1-205 defines "usage of trade" as a practice or method of dealing which is so regularly observed in a trade as to justify the expectation that it will be observed in a particular transaction. Since Salley's testimony would show that calling scmods "rock lurgid" is a usage of trade, it should be admitted to explain the meaning of that term.

A is, therefore, incorrect. Since the law of contracts does not require contracting parties to agree to the market price, **B** is incorrect. A contract is supposed to be interpreted according to the intentions of the parties. For this reason, usage of trade is admissible because it tends to show what members of a particular trade intended by the use of certain language. If one of the parties to a contract was unaware of a particular trade usage, he may attempt to prove this to a court or jury to convince it that the trade usage meaning was not what he intended. Since the trade usage may still be evidence of what the other party intended, however, it should be admitted. **C** is, therefore, incorrect.

174. **D**   Contracts frequently benefit persons other than the contracting parties (i.e., third-party beneficiaries). In general, contracts can only be enforced by parties to them. Under some circumstances, however, intended third-party beneficiaries can enforce contracts to which they are not parties. Whether a third-party beneficiary is an "intended" beneficiary depends in part on whether the contract called for performance to be made directly to that third party. If not, she is merely an "incidental" beneficiary and has no right of enforcement. Although Barto knew that Finley intended to give the house to Doris, Barto may argue that Doris was not an "intended beneficiary" because the contract did not require Barto to perform directly for Doris (i.e., the lot was Finley's). A court might rule differently, but **D** is the only argument listed which might be effective in Barto's defense.

When performance is not designed to satisfy a preexisting obligation to a third-party beneficiary, that third-party beneficiary is a "donee beneficiary." When performance is designed to satisfy a preexisting obligation to a third-party beneficiary, she is a "creditor beneficiary." Because there is some question about whether Finley owed Doris any obligation as a result of his oral promise to her, it is difficult to determine whether she is a donee or creditor beneficiary. **A** and **B** are both incorrect, however, because both donee and creditor beneficiaries may be able to enforce contracts to which they are not parties. **C** is incorrect because the facts indicate that Doris cancelled a contract to buy a house as a result of Finley's promise.

175. **B**   In attempting to enforce Finley's promise, Doris faces two problems. First, the Statute of Frauds requires a writing for a promise to convey an interest in real estate, and Finley's promise was oral. Second, a promise is not ordinarily enforceable if made without consideration, and Doris gave nothing in return for Finley's promise. The doctrine of promissory estoppel might solve both problems, making Doris' detrimental reliance on Finley's promise a substitute for both a writing and consideration. To be more precise, Doris' reliance might cause Finley to be estopped from raising either the lack of a writing or the lack of consideration as a defense. Since Doris' cancellation of the contract which she had already made could subject her to liability and will cause her to lose the benefits of her previous bargain, it could qualify as detrimental reliance. In any event, **B** is the only argument listed which could possibly support Doris' claim.

The argument in **A** is not that modification violated Doris' rights, but that the modification was unenforceable without consideration. It is generally understood, however, that the parties to a fully executory bilateral contract may agree to rescind, the necessary consideration being furnished by each party's giving up the right to the other's performance. The parties are then free to make a new contract by exchanging new promises. Thus the absence of consideration would not invalidate the new agreement between Finley and Barto. **A** is, therefore, incorrect. **C** is incorrect for two reasons: first, the writing did not contain any promise to Doris; and, second, even if the Statute of Frauds is satisfied, the problem of consideration for Finley's promise to Doris remains unsolved. Consideration is something given in return for a promise. Since Doris had married and decided to retire from the military before Finley's promise was made, her marriage and retirement could not be consideration for his promise. **D** is, therefore, incorrect.

176. **B**   An offer is an expression by the offeror of willingness to enter into a contract with the offeree on specified terms. A valid offer creates in the offeree the power of acceptance. In order to determine whether a particular communication qualifies as an offer, it is thus necessary to decide whether the reasonable person in the position of the offeree would believe that nothing more than his acceptance is required in order to form a contract. Although Scott's letter of January 5 used the word "offer" it indicated that it was being made to four different people. Since he had only one diamond ring for sale, it must have been obvious to each of the people who received Scott's letter that someone else might purchase it first. For this reason, none of them could reasonably have believed that his own acceptance was all that was necessary to form a contract. Scott's letter was, therefore, not an offer, but merely an invitation to negotiate. At best, then, Asher's letter was an offer. Since Scott did not accept it, no contract was formed between Scott and Asher.

A is incorrect for two reasons: first, as explained above, Scott's letter to Asher was not an offer; and, second, if it had been an offer it could not have been revoked after Asher accepted it by his letter of January 14. **C** is incorrect because Scott's letter was not an offer. Since Scott was under no obligation to sell the ring to Asher, the date of his negotiation and agreement with Barrell is irrelevant in Asher's case. **D** is, therefore, incorrect.

177. **C**   Although the usual remedy for breach of a sales contract is a judgment for damages, specific performance is available to a buyer if the subject of the contract was unique or highly unusual. This is nearly always true of contracts for the sale of realty, because every piece of realty is regarded as unique. Though not as common in the sale of chattels, specific performance may be granted in the event of a breach by one who has agreed to sell a highly unusual chattel.

A is, therefore, incorrect. **B** is incorrect because the award of specific performance does not depend on whether or not the parties to the sales contract are merchants. Since a seller can usually resell a chattel upon the buyer's breach and recover as damages the difference between the contract price and the resale price, specific performance is not usually available to a seller. **D** is incorrect for this reason, and also because the rule that specific performance should be available to one contracting party whenever it would have been available to the other is now obsolete.

178. **C**   UCC section 2-609 provides that when one party to a contract has reasonable grounds for insecurity about the other's performance, it may demand assurances and suspend its own performance until they are received. The section also provides that failure to furnish such assurances is a repudiation of the contract. Since section 2-210 provides that a delegation of contract duties is a reasonable ground for insecurity, Seedco's sale to Allgrass gave Nursery the right to demand assurances from Allgrass. Since Allgrass failed to provide assurances, Nursery was entitled to suspend performance and did not breach by doing so.

        A is, therefore, incorrect. **B** is incorrect because section 2-210 specifically provides that delegation of contract duties provides the other party with reasonable grounds for insecurity. **D** is incorrect because UCC section 2-210 provides that (except under the special circumstances set forth in that section) a party may perform its contract obligations through a delegate.

179. **A**   Ordinarily, a party to a contract may assign its rights or delegate its duties to another. UCC section 2-210 provides, however, that delegation does not relieve the delegator of contract duties or of liability for breach. Since Seedco delegated its duties to Allgrass, and since Allgrass breached those duties by failing to provide assurances as required [see previous explanation], Seedco (as well as Allgrass) is liable to Nursery for the breach.

        An agreement to substitute the performance of a third person for that of the obligor accompanied by a specific agreement to release the obligor from its contractual duties is a "novation" which relieves the released obligor of any further obligation. Nursery's consent to Seedco's assignment/delegation would not have that effect, however, because Nursery did not specifically agree to release Seedco. **B** and **C** are incorrect for this reason. **C** is also incorrect because UCC 2-210 provides that a party who demands assurances from a delegatee does not thereby prejudice its rights against the original obligor. Although an assignment of rights implies a delegation of duties, **D** is incorrect because the assignor/delegator is secondarily liable upon breach by the delegatee.

180. **D**   When parties to a contract agree that one of the benefits of the contract will flow directly to a non-contracting party, that person is an intended third party beneficiary. If the agreement was made for the purpose of satisfying an obligation which one of the contracting parties owed to the third party beneficiary, she is a creditor beneficiary. Otherwise, she is a donee beneficiary. Once her rights have vested, a donee beneficiary can enforce the contract even though she was not a party to it. Some jurisdictions hold that a donee beneficiary's rights vest when she learns of the contract; others hold that her rights vest when she relies on the contract to her detriment. All agree, however, that until her rights vest, the parties may modify the contract without incurring any liability to the donee beneficiary. Since Donia did not learn of the contract until after the parties had modified it to eliminate the benefit to her, she has no right to enforce it. **I** is, therefore, incorrect. Ordinarily, one to whom a gift has been promised has no right to enforce that promise since it was unsupported by consideration. An exception exists which permits a donee beneficiary to recover from the donor funds which the donor has received under the contract to which the donee had a vested right. **II** is incorrect because the contract between Otten and Pullen was modified before Donia received any vested right to enforce it. Thus, **D** is correct.

181. **A**   An accord is an agreement to substitute a lesser obligation for that which existed under a contract. Like any other agreement, it does not ordinarily have binding effect (i.e., does not discharge the original contract obligation) unless supported by consideration. Consideration usually consists of some legal detriment suffered in return for the benefit received. The benefit received by Otten was a reduction in the price of the paint job. If Otten did not give anything in return (i.e., consideration) for this reduction, Pullen would be entitled to collect the balance due. If Otten did not reasonably believe that Pullen's work was not "satisfactory," he was not entitled to seek damages under the contract and gave up nothing in return for the reduction in price. However, if he did reasonably believe that Pullen's work was not "satisfactory," he had a right to seek damages under the contract. By giving up this right, he has given consideration for the reduction in price.

Although UCC §2-209(1) permits modification of a sales contract without consideration, **B** is incorrect because that provision does not apply to modification of contracts calling for services. The statute of frauds requires that an agreement to modify a contract be in writing if, as modified, the contract falls within the scope of the statute of frauds. Although a contract for the sale of *goods* at a price of $4,500 would be within the scope of the statute of frauds, **C** is incorrect because this was not a contract for goods, but rather for services, and was, therefore, not within the statute of frauds. A contracting party who suffers a legal detriment has given consideration, even if the other party has received no real benefit. If Otten gave up rights which he reasonably believed that he had under the contract, he has suffered a legal detriment. Although Pullen may have received no real benefit from it, Otten's detriment was consideration for the reduction in price even if Pullen did not believe he was receiving anything in return for the reduction. **D** is, therefore, incorrect.

182. **C**   When a contract calls for performance to take place after a specified event, the obligation to perform does not become absolute until the specified event occurs (i.e., the specified event is a condition precedent to the obligation to perform). Since the brokerage contract called for payment of the commission on closing of title, closing was a condition precedent to Sinclair's obligation to pay the commission. In every contract, however, there is an implied agreement that the parties will not interfere with performance of any of the conditions precedent to their own obligations. Breach of this implied agreement excuses performance of the condition precedent. Thus, the obligation of a party who breaches that implied agreement may become absolute even though the condition precedent has not been satisfied. Since Sinclair refused to go through with the transaction, thus preventing the closing of title, his obligation is absolute in spite of the fact that the condition precedent to it (i.e., closing of title) has not been satisfied.

Thus, **A** is incorrect. **B** is incorrect because Ruse is seeking to enforce the agreement between herself and Sinclair rather than the one between Sinclair and Basic. **D** is incorrect because Sinclair's interference with the condition precedent to payment of the commission makes him liable for payment of the commission whether title ever closes or not.

183. **A**   When a contract calls for performance to take place after a specified event, the obligation to perform does not become absolute until the specified event occurs (i.e., the spec-

ified event is a condition precedent to the obligation to perform). Since the brokerage contract called for payment of the commission on closing of title, closing was a condition precedent to Sinclair's obligation to pay the commission. Since title never closed, Sinclair's obligation has not become absolute.

If Basic's repudiation resulted from some fault by Ruse, Sinclair would not be obligated to pay Ruse a commission. **B** is incorrect, however, because, as explained above, Ruse's fault is not the *only* thing which would prevent Sinclair's obligation from becoming absolute. Although the contract indicated that the commission would be earned when Ruse found a ready, willing, and able buyer, it also made closing of title a condition precedent to Sinclair's obligation to pay the commission. Since title did not close, Sinclair's obligation has not become absolute. **C** is, therefore, incorrect. Since the contract made closing of title a condition precedent to payment, Sinclair would not have any obligation to pay Ruse's commission unless title closed. **D** is incorrect because this would be true even if Sinclair succeeded in collecting breach of contract damages from Basic.

184. **D**   Under the parol evidence rule, evidence of prior contemporaneous oral agreements is inadmissible for the purpose of modifying the terms of an unambiguous written contract which the parties intended to be a complete expression of their agreement. The parol evidence rule does not prevent the use of such evidence for other purposes, however. Here, since the language of the contract is ambiguous, parol evidence is admissible to clear up the ambiguity.

B is, therefore incorrect. In construing a contract, the court is primarily concerned with the intentions of the contracting parties. Although custom and usage may help to determine what the parties had in mind when they used particular language, it is not the only way to resolve that question. **A** is, therefore, incorrect. Although Brosnan hired Subic to help him fulfill his obligations under his contract with Otto, the language of that contract does not determine the meaning of Brosnan's contract with Subic. **C** is, therefore, incorrect.

185. **C**   A non-contracting party who will benefit from a contract between two other persons is a third party beneficiary. If the contracting parties intended that the benefit flow to her when they contracted, she is an intended beneficiary. If they did not, she is an incidental beneficiary. Although an intended beneficiary may be entitled, under certain circumstances, to enforce the contract, an incidental beneficiary is not. In determining whether a third party is an intended beneficiary, courts usually consider whether a statement to that effect was made during negotiations or in the contract, and whether performance or payment is to flow directly to the beneficiary. Since the contract between Forde and Boudreau called for the construction of a house on property which belonged to Forde, and since there was no mention made of any contract right flowing to Dale, Dale is probably an incidental beneficiary and not entitled to enforce the contract against Boudreau.

A is, therefore, incorrect. Although a contract calling for personal services is not ordinarily assignable, **B** is incorrect because Forde has made no attempt to assign to Dale his rights under the contract with Boudreau. A donee beneficiary is an intended third party beneficiary to whom neither party was under an obligation at the time the contract between them was formed. Even if Dale were a donee beneficiary, however, **D** would be incorrect because a donee beneficiary may have rights to enforce the contract.

186. **A**   Ordinarily, a promise is not enforceable unless it is supported by consideration. Consideration is some legal detriment suffered by promisee in exchange for the promise. Since Dale did not suffer any legal detriment to induce the Forde's promise, Forde's promise is not supported by consideration. Under the doctrine of promissory estoppel, however, a promise which is unsupported by consideration may be enforceable if the promisee justifiably relied upon it to her detriment. Since Dale canceled a contract which she had already made as a result of Forde's promise, she has relied to her detriment, and may be permitted to enforce Forde's promise.

Although a donee beneficiary of a contract to which she is not party may share the donor's right to enforce the contract against the other party, the fact that the donor has entered into a contract in contemplation of his promise to the beneficiary does not give her any new rights against him. **B** is, therefore, incorrect. **C** is incorrect because Dale's detrimental reliance may take the place of consideration. If an unforeseeable event makes a contract fail of its essential purpose, the doctrine of frustration of purpose might excuse performance by the parties. Since it is still possible for Forde to deed the land to Dale and to have a house built on it by some other contractor, however, the fact that Boudreau has refused to perform does not frustrate the purpose of any agreement which exists between Forde and Dale. **D** is, therefore, incorrect.

187. **A**   Ordinarily, no promise is enforceable without consideration. Consideration consists of some legal detriment suffered by the promisee in return for the promise. Since Bethel suffered no legal detriment in return for Sandez's promise to keep the offer open, Sandez's promise is unenforceable.

UCC section 2-205 provides that a promise to keep an offer open for a specified period of time is binding without consideration if made by a merchant, in a signed writing, and the transaction involves the sale of goods. This kind of offer is known as a "firm offer." The section also provides that the maximum time for which a firm offer is binding is three months. **B**, **C** and **D** are all designed to trap examinees who are confused about section 2-205. All are incorrect because section 2-205 applies only to transactions in goods and has no application to the sale of realty. In addition, **B** is incorrect because the section sets a time limit of three months rather than 30 days. **D** is also incorrect because the section requires only that the offeror be a merchant and fixes no such requirement about the offeree.

188. **A**   An assignment transfers the assignor's rights to the assignee and extinguishes those rights in the assignor. Thus, if Crawford has made a valid assignment of his rights to Anchor, Crawford no longer has those rights and cannot enforce them against Hamlin.

A non-contracting party who will benefit from the contract is a third party beneficiary. If the contracting parties intended him to benefit, he is an intended third party beneficiary; if not he is an incidental beneficiary. If they intended him to benefit to satisfy an obligation which one of the contracting parties owed him, he is a creditor beneficiary; if not, he is a donee beneficiary. Since the agreement between Landsman and Hamlin specified that part of the price was to be paid directly to Crawford, the contracting parties clearly intended that Crawford benefit from the contract. For this reason, he was an intended beneficiary. Since they did so to satisfy a debt which Landsman owed Crawford, Crawford is a creditor beneficiary. **B** and **D** are incorrect because a creditor beneficiary may enforce the contract even though he is not a party to it. **C** is incorrect because Crawford is an intended rather an incidental beneficiary.

189.   **C**   It is frequently said that an assignee stands in the shoes of his assignor. All this means is that the assignee receives whatever rights the assignor had — no more and no less. Thus, if Crawford was entitled to collect $10,000 under the contract, his assignment to Anchor makes Anchor entitled to collect it.

Usually, contract language which provides that there shall be no assignment of rights is held to destroy the right but not the power to assign. This means that an assignment serves as a valid transfer of rights, but that the assignor might be liable for damages resulting from his breach of the covenant not to assign. Since this would have no effect on Anchor's right to collect, **A** is incorrect. An assignment is a transfer of rights under a contract; a delegation is a transfer of obligations. It is generally understood that an obligation to perform personal services cannot be delegated because to do so would deprive the promisee of that for which he has bargained (i.e., the personal services of the promisor). An assignment of the promisor's *rights* would not have that effect, however, since the promisee would still be receiving the services of the promisor. For that reason, the fact that Landsman's obligation was to perform personal services would not prevent an assignment of his right to payment for those services. **B** is, therefore, incorrect. Ordinarily, a promise is not enforceable unless it was given in exchange for consideration. For this reason, a promise to make a future gift (i.e., a promise to make a transfer without consideration) usually is not enforceable. On the other hand, a transfer without consideration which has already been made (i.e., an executed gift) is valid. Since Crawford has already assigned (i.e., transferred) his right to Anchor, the fact that he did or did not receive consideration for the transfer is irrelevant. For this reason, the fact that Anchor gave no consideration for the assignment which he received from Crawford has no effect on Hamlin's obligation to pay. **D** is, therefore, incorrect.

190.   **C**   In general, contract obligations are freely delegable unless the obligee has a special interest in having the obligations performed personally by the obligor. It is usually held that construction contracts are delegable, since any reputable builder can construct whatever was contracted for if provided with the proper plans. Since a moat is simply a hole in the ground, and since Digger completed the moat in complete conformity with Landsman's plans, Landsman's delegation of the digging work was probably not a breach of contract.

A is, therefore, incorrect. **B** is incorrect because Hamlin's interest in having the job done by a well-known architect is probably satisfied by the fact that Landsman designed the plan and executed most of the work himself, coupled with the fact that the moat was dug in complete conformity with Landsman's plan. **D** is incorrect for two reasons: first, contract rights are not freely assignable if the assignment would impose an additional burden on the assignor's obligor; and second, a transfer of contractual obligations is a delegation, not an assignment.

191.   **B**   Ordinarily, the damage remedy is designed to put the parties in the position in which

they would have been had the contract not been breached. If Berry had not breached the contract, Frost would have a building which conformed to his specifications at a price of $250,000. In order to make Frost whole, then, Berry should be required to pay the cost of making the building conform to the specifications.

Although the building has the same value it would have if it conformed to the specifications, it is not the building that Frost contracted for, and it would cost Frost $12,000 to make it so. Since damages should place the parties in the position for which they bargained, **A** is incorrect. Since it would only cost $12,000 to make the building conform to the bargained-for specifications, it would be unjust to permit Frost to receive a windfall by making Berry pay damages based on the difference between the building's value and the value which resulted from an increase in construction costs. **C** is, therefore, incorrect. **D** is incorrect because Frost has received some value, and should not be permitted to keep it without paying for it.

192. **C**   If Frost had not breached his contract, Berry would have collected $250,000 from which he would have had to pay the costs of completing the building. Since the damage remedy should be designed to place the parties in the positions for which they bargained, Berry should receive the contract price less the cost of completing the building.

A is incorrect because Berry did not bargain for and should not receive the benefit of a windfall resulting from increased construction costs. **B** is incorrect because it fails to take into account the expenses which Berry would have had in earning the contract price. A builder who commits a substantial breach may have no remedy other than quasi-contract for the detriment which he has suffered. Since Berry has not committed a breach, however, he should not be restricted to this remedy. **D** is, therefore, incorrect.

193. **B**   An offer is a manifestation of present intent to be bound to specified terms. One of the tests of whether a statement should be construed as an offer is whether a reasonable person in the shoes of a person receiving it would believe that only his expression of assent is necessary to form a binding contract. Since each of the recipients knew that there were three other recipients, and each knew also that his own expression of assent might not result in a contract because it might not be the highest offer, and since Stubb's letter referred to the responses which he expected to receive as "offers," a court would probably hold that it was nothing more than an invitation for offers. While it is not certain that a court would come to that conclusion, **B** is the only option listed which could possibly be correct.

Under UCC section 2-205, a "firm offer" is a written promise by a merchant to hold an offer to buy or sell goods open for a specified period of time. Since there is no indication that Stubbs was a merchant, his letter could not have been a firm offer. **A** is, therefore, incorrect. An option is an agreement to hold an offer open for a specified period of time, and (except for the provisions of UCC section 2-205) is not enforceable without consideration. Since none of the recipients of Stubb's letter gave anything in return for it (i.e., consideration), it could not have been an option. **C** is, therefore, incorrect. An auction is a public sale of property to the highest bidder conducted in the presence of all prospective buyers or their agents. Stubb's letter could not have been an auction because it was not a public sale, and because the bidders were not present. **D** is, therefore, incorrect.

194. **A**   An offer is a manifestation of present intent to be bound to specified terms. Since Stubb's letter expresses an unequivocal intention to sell the piano to Better for $2,000, it is an offer.

C is, therefore, incorrect. An acceptance is an agreement to be bound to the terms of an offer. Stubb's letter could not be an acceptance unless Better's letter was an offer. Since Better's letter did not actually say that he would pay $2,000 (i.e., did not express a willingness to be bound), but rather asked whether Stubbs would accept $2,000, it was not an offer, and Stubb's response could not have been an acceptance. **B** is, therefore, incorrect. Since Stubbs never agreed to sell the piano to Altom, his offer to Better could not be a repudiation of an agreement with Altom. **D** is, therefore, incorrect.

QUESTIONS
CRIMINAL LAW

CRIMINAL LAW
TABLE OF CONTENTS
Numbers refer to Question Numbers

CRIMINAL LAW QUESTIONS

Questions 1-2 are based on the following fact situation.

The public prosecutor had information that unlawful gambling activities were being conducted at a tavern known as the Second Bedroom on Main Street. She obtained a warrant for the search of the Second Bedroom by presenting an affidavit which stated that she had received information regarding the illegal activities from an informant who had observed the reported activities while present at the tavern. The affidavit stated that the informant frequently gave information to the police and prosecutor and that the information received from the informant in the past had always been found to be accurate. It did not give the name of the informant, however, because it stated that his anonymity needed to be preserved both for his own protection and to continue his effectiveness as an informant.

The warrant which was issued authorized the search of "the premises known as the Second Bedroom and located at 481 Chambers Street" and of "all persons in said premises at the time of the execution of the warrant who are found to be in possession of gambling records." There was a furniture store known as the Second Bedroom located at 481 Chambers Street, but the officers assigned to execute the warrant went to the Second Bedroom tavern on Main Street. Upon searching the premises, they found gambling records in a cash drawer located behind the bar. In addition, a customer named Darryl who was in the tavern was searched and found to be in possession of unlawful gambling records.

1. Assume for the purpose of this question only that the owner of the tavern is charged with violating the state's gambling law. Assume further that he moves to suppress the use of gambling records found in the cash drawer. His most effective argument in support of that motion is that

    (A) the affidavit submitted in support of the application for the warrant was based entirely on hearsay.

    (B) the affidavit submitted in support of the

application for the warrant did not identify the informant.

    (C) the information contained in the affidavit submitted in support of the application for the warrant was uncorroborated.

    (D) the information contained in the affidavit submitted in support of the application for the warrant did not properly identify the defendant's premises.

2. Assume for the purpose of this question only that the warrant was properly issued and executed with respect to the tavern. Assume further that Darryl is charged with gambling, and that he moves to suppress the use of gambling records found on his person. The court should

    (A) grant the motion, because the court which issued the warrant did not have probable cause to believe that any customers in the tavern were engaging in unlawful gambling activities.

    (B) grant the motion, because the warrant did not properly identify the persons to be searched.

    (C) deny the motion, because a warrant which authorizes a search of premises may also authorize the search of persons present on those premises.

    (D) deny the motion, because the fact that Darryl was found to be in possession of unlawful gambling records corroborated the information contained in the affidavit which the public prosecutor submitted in support of the application for the warrant.

3. Daniele checked her suitcase when she made a cross country airplane flight. When the plane landed, a police dog which was trained to recognize the smell of marijuana was allowed to sniff all checked baggage as part of a routine inspection procedure. Upon sniffing Daniele's bag, the

dog gave signs which it had been trained to give when it recognized the smell of marijuana. Daniele was allowed to claim the suitcase when she got off the plane. After she claimed it, a police officer arrested her for possession of a dangerous drug as she carried the suitcase through the airport. The arresting officer then searched the suitcase and found a package of marijuana.

Prior to her trial on drug possession charges, Daniele made a timely motion to suppress the use of the marijuana as evidence against her. Should the motion be granted?

(A) Yes, unless the arresting officer had a warrant for Daniele's arrest.

(B) Yes, because allowing the dog to sniff Daniele's luggage was an unreasonable search.

(C) No, because the possibility of airline hijacking makes the routine examination of passengers' luggage necessary to protect the public against a clear and present danger.

(D) No, if when Daniele was arrested the arresting officer had probable cause to believe that she was in possession of marijuana.

Questions 4-5 are based on the following fact situation.

Donnel met Vera in a bar where both were drinking. Because Donnel was too drunk to drive, Vera offered him a ride home. In Vera's car, Donnel put his arms around Vera and attempted to kiss her. Vera told him that she wasn't interested, and tried to push him away, but Donnel overpowered her and succeeded in having sexual intercourse with her. Vera was 17 years old.

4. Assume for the purpose of this question only that Donnel was charged with forcible rape. If only one of the following facts or interferences were true, which would be most likely to lead to Donnel's acquittal on that charge?

(A) Donnel was so drunk that he believed Vera was willing to have sexual intercourse with him.

(B) Donnel was so drunk that he did not realize that he was engaging in sexual intercourse.

(C) Vera was so drunk that she did not realize that Donnel was engaging in sexual intercourse with her.

(D) Vera was so drunk that immediately after intercourse began, she forgot who Donnel was and believed him to be her husband.

5. Assume for the purpose of this question only that Vera consented to the intercourse, but that a statute provided that it was unlawful to engage in sexual intercourse with a female under the age of 18 years. If Donnel believed that Vera was over the age of 18 years, is he guilty of statutory rape?

(A) No, because he believed Vera to be over the age of 18 years.

(B) No, if the reasonable person who was not intoxicated would have believed Vera to be over the age of 18 years.

(C) Yes, unless Vera assured him that she was over the age of 18 years.

(D) Yes, but only if Donnel realized that he was having intercourse.

6. In which of the following fact patterns is Defendant's motion to suppress the evidence most likely to be granted?

(A) Defendant was riding in a car owned by Baxter. Police stopped the car and asked to see Baxter's driver's license. After Baxter showed it to them, they asked his permission to search the car. Baxter said, "Sure, go ahead." Upon searching under the seat in which Defendant had been sitting the police found a package of heroin which was offered at Defendant's trial for illegally possessing narcotics.

(B) Defendant was staying at a hotel, but was two weeks behind on his room charges. The hotel desk clerk permitted the police to search Defendant's room while he was out. Upon doing so, the police found in the room contraband of which Defendant was subsequently charged with possession.

(C) Defendant was arrested for driving while intoxicated. After he was taken to jail, his car was towed to the police auto pound. There, a police officer taking inventory of the car's contents found a weapon in the car which had been used in the commission of a crime with which Defendant was subsequently charged.

(D) While Defendant was driving, police officers stopped him for going through a red light. A routine check of his license through the police department computer indicated that a bench warrant had been issued for his arrest for failing to appear in connection with four parking tickets which had been issued to vehicles registered to him. The officers advised him that he was under arrest. Although they did not handcuff him, they ordered him to empty his pockets onto the hood of the police car. A marijuana cigarette which was in one of his pockets was subsequently offered against him at his trial for possession of a controlled substance.

7. Julie had lost her job and needed to make some money quickly. While visiting a local tavern, she ran into Charlie, an old friend. When Julie told Charlie about her financial problems, Charlie pointed to an expensive-looking coat which was hanging on a coat rack and said, "Why don't you steal that coat. It looks like you should be able to sell it for at least one hundred dollars." Because Julie said that she was afraid the owner of the coat would see her, Charlie agreed to sing in a loud voice to create a diversion so that Julie could steal the coat while everyone was watching Charlie. As soon as Charlie began to sing, Julie took the coat from the coat rack and ran from the tavern. In fact, the coat actually belonged to Charlie, who had been joking when he told Julie to steal it.

Of which of the following crimes may Julie be properly convicted?

(A) Larceny only.

(B) Conspiracy only.

(C) Larceny and conspiracy.

(D) Neither larceny nor conspiracy.

8. Darrel knew that his neighbor Volmer had a weak heart and that Volmer had suffered several heart attacks in the past. Because he was angry at Volmer, Darrel decided to try to frighten him into another heart attack. He watched Volmer's house and when he saw Volmer leaving through the front door, he ran towards him shouting, "Look out. Look out. The sky is falling," Although Darrel was not sure that this would kill Volmer, he hoped it would. When Volmer saw Darrel running toward him, shouting, he became frightened, had a heart attack and died on the spot.

The jurisdiction has statutes which define first degree murder as "the deliberate and premeditated killing of a human being," and second degree murder as "any unlawful killing of a human being with malice aforethought, except for a killing which constitutes first degree murder." In addition, its statutes adopt common law definitions of voluntary and involuntary manslaughter.

Which of the following is the most serious crime of which Darrel can properly be convicted?

(A) First degree murder.

(B) Second degree murder.

(C) Voluntary manslaughter.

(D) Involuntary manslaughter.

9. Dennison was having dinner in a restaurant with his employer Vale, when Vale left the table to go the restroom. As Vale walked away, Dennison noticed that Vale's wristwatch had fallen off Vale's wrist onto the table. Since it looked like a rather valuable watch, Dennison decided to steal it. Picking up the watch, he put it into his pocket. A few moments later, he began to feel guilty about stealing from his employer, so when Vale returned to the table, Dennison handed him the watch and said, "Here, you dropped this, and I

put it into my pocket for safekeeping."

Which is the most serious crime of which Dennison can be properly convicted?

(A) Larceny.

(B) Attempted larceny.

(C) Embezzlement.

(D) No crime.

Questions 10-13 are based on the following fact situation.

One day when Edward's parents were away, Edward, Fanny, and Gerald, who were students at the same high school, cut classes to go to Edward's home and listen to records. Edward was 17 years of age; Fanny and Gerald were each 15. Edward and Fanny knew that Gerald was very shy. Since Fanny had engaged in sexual relations with several other boys at the high school, she and Edward secretly agreed that Fanny would try to seduce Gerald. Fanny had some marijuana in her purse, and she and Gerald smoked some of it. When Gerald was high, Fanny undressed him and attempted to have sexual intercourse with him. Although at first Gerald was unwilling to have intercourse while Edward was in the room, Fanny gave him more marijuana to smoke until he became so intoxicated that he was willing to try. By then, however, his intoxication made him physically unable to perform. Instead, Fanny had intercourse with Edward while Gerald watched. Gerald knew the ages of Edward and Fanny. Gerald knew that it was unlawful to have intercourse with a female under the age of 16. Edward believed that it was lawful to have intercourse with a female over the age of 14.

A statute in the jurisdiction provides that, "A person is guilty of rape in the third degree when, being seventeen years of age or more, he or she engages in sexual intercourse with a person under the age of sixteen years."

10. If Fanny is charged with attempting to commit rape in the third degree as a result of her attempt to have intercourse with Gerald, she should be found

(A) guilty, because she overcame his resistance by the use of an intoxicating substance and would have completed the act of intercourse but for Gerald's physical inability to perform.

(B) guilty, because Gerald was under the legal age of consent.

(C) not guilty, because Fanny was under the age of 17.

(D) not guilty, because Fanny was a female.

11. Assume that the laws in state define a conspiracy as "An agreement to commit a crime between two or more persons with the specific intent to commit a crime." If Edward is charged with conspiracy based on his agreement with Fanny regarding the seduction of Gerald, Edward's most effective argument in defense would be that

(A) the seduction of Gerald would not have been possible without Fanny's participation.

(B) Edward did not commit any overt act which was likely to accomplish the seduction of Gerald.

(C) Fanny was unsuccessful in having intercourse with Gerald.

(D) intercourse between Fanny and Gerald would not have been a crime.

12. If Edward is charged with committing rape in the third degree by having intercourse with Fanny, the Court should find him

(A) guilty, because Edward was over the age of 17 and Fanny was under the age of 16.

(B) guilty, only if he knew that Fanny was under the age of 16.

(C) not guilty, if Fanny instituted the conduct which led to sexual intercourse between them.

(D) not guilty, because Edward believed that it was lawful to have sexual intercourse with a female over the age of fourteen.

13. If Gerald is charged with being an accessory to

third degree rape, he should be found

(A) guilty, because he knew that it was unlawful for a male 17 years of age to have sexual intercourse with a female under 16 years of age.

(B) guilty, only if Edward was first charged with and convicted of the same crime.

(C) not guilty, if sexual intercourse between Edward and Fanny could have been accomplished without Gerald's assistance.

(D) not guilty, because he did not actually aid, abet, or facilitate sexual intercourse between Edward and Fanny.

Questions 14-15 are based on the following fact situation.

Dobson wanted to erect a new storage building so that he could expand his business of selling animal food and veterinary supplies. He was afraid, however, that the building department would not issue him a permit to begin construction. Cook, a building department clerk, said that she would make a false entry in the official records to indicate that a permit had already been issued if Dobson would pay her $500. Dobson agreed, and said that he would bring the money the following day. The next day, however, when Dobson went to Cook's office with $500, he was told that she had been fired.

A statute in the jurisdiction provides that: "Any person who shall give or accept a fee not authorized by law as consideration for the act of any public employee is guilty of bribery, a felony. Any person who shall offer to commit a bribery is guilty of bribery in the second degree, a felony."

14. If the jurisdiction applies the common law definition of conspiracy, of which of the following crimes can Cook properly be convicted?

(A) Bribery in the second degree only.

(B) Conspiracy to commit bribery only.

(C) Bribery in the second degree or conspiracy to commit bribery, but not both.

(D) Bribery in the second degree and conspiracy to commit bribery.

15. If Dobson is prosecuted for attempted bribery in the second degree, the court should find him

(A) not guilty, because bribery in the second degree is an attempt crime, and there can be no liability for attempting to attempt.

(B) not guilty, because it was Cook who made the initial offer.

(C) not guilty, because Dobson committed bribery in the second degree when he agreed to pay Cook for altering the records, and the attempt merged with that crime.

(D) guilty, because attempting to commit bribery in the second degree is a lesser offense included in that crime.

16. Dana called her attorney and asked whether it would be a crime to burn down her own home. The attorney said that arson was defined as the intentional burning of any dwelling and that arson was a serious crime. In fact, Dana's attorney was incorrect because the applicable statute in the jurisdiction defines arson as "the intentional burning of the dwelling of another". Believing what the attorney told her, however, Dana burned down her own home for the purpose of collecting the proceeds of her fire insurance policy. A statute in the jurisdiction defined the crime of insurance fraud as "the intentional destruction of any property for the purpose of obtaining insurance proceeds."

If Dana is charged with attempted arson, she should be found

(A) guilty, because a mistake of fact does not prevent a person from being guilty of a criminal attempt.

(B) guilty, because her mistake of law resulted from reasonable reliance on the advice of an attorney.

(C) not guilty, because Dana did not intend to burn the dwelling of another.

(D) not guilty, because Dana's attempt is sub-
     sumed in the substantive crime of insur-
     ance fraud.

Questions 17-18 are based on the following fact situation.

Angry because her co-worker Ventura had insulted her,
Delman decided to get revenge. Because she worked
for an exterminator, Delman had access to cans of a
poison gas called Terminate which was often used to
kill termites and other insects. She did not want to kill
Ventura, so she carefully read the use manual supplied
by the manufacturer. The manual said that Terminate
was not fatal to human beings, but that exposure to it
could cause serious ailments including blindness and
permanent respiratory irritation. When she was sure
that no one would see her, Delman brought a can of
Terminate to the parking lot and released the poison gas
into Ventura's car. At lunchtime, Ventura and his friend
Alex sat together in Ventura's car. As a result of their
exposure to the Terminate in the car, Alex died and
Ventura became so ill that he was hospitalized for over
a month.

17. If Delman is charged with the murder of Alex,
     she should be found

     (A) guilty, because Alex's death resulted from
          an act which Delman performed with the
          intent to cause great bodily harm to a
          human being.

     (B) guilty, because the use of poison gas is an
          inherently dangerous activity.

     (C) not guilty, because she did not know that
          Alex would be exposed to the poison gas.

     (D) not guilty, because she did not intend to
          cause the death of any person.

18. If Delman is charged with the attempted murder
     of Ventura, she should be found

     (A) guilty, because Ventura suffered a serious ill-
          ness as the result of a criminal act which
          she performed with intent to cause him
          great bodily harm.

     (B) guilty, because her intent to cause great
          bodily harm resulted in the death of Alex.

     (C) not guilty, because she did not intend to
          cause the death of any person.

     (D) not guilty, because the crime of attempted
          murder merges with the crime of murder.

19. Dustin was charged with the attempted murder of
     Volmer. If only one of the following facts or
     inferences were true, which would be most likely
     to result in an acquittal?

     (A) Volmer was already dead when Dustin shot
          him, although Dustin believed him to be
          alive.

     (B) Volmer was alive when Dustin shot him,
          although Dustin believed that Volmer was
          already dead.

     (C) Dustin's gun was unloaded when he aimed it
          at Volmer and pulled the trigger, although
          Dustin believed it to be loaded.

     (D) Intending to poison Volmer, Dustin put a
          harmless substance into Volmer's drink,
          although Dustin believed that the sub-
          stance was lethal.

Questions 20-21 are based on the following fact situation.

Devlin had been arraigned on a charge of burglarizing
the home of Watson. He was assigned a public
defender and pleaded not guilty, but because he was
unable to post bail, was in jail awaiting trial. Ulrich, an
undercover police officer, was ordered by his commanding officer to pose as a prisoner and was placed in
the same cell as Devlin. Ulrich was instructed not to
question Devlin about the charge against him. The day
before Devlin's trial, Devlin and Ulrich were told that
they were to appear in a lineup. Devlin asked for his
lawyer to be present at the lineup, but was told that he
had no right to his lawyer's presence.

After appearing in the lineup, Devlin and Ulrich were
sent back to their cell. While walking through the corridor of the jail, Devlin told Ulrich that he had committed the burglary with which he was charged. He

bragged that he was sure to get away with it because the night of the burglary was too dark for any of the witnesses to identify him.

At Devlin's trial, Watson testified that she had been returning home on the night of the burglary when she saw a man running from her house. She said that she recognized Devlin as the man whom she had identified as the burglar at a lineup the day before. Ulrich testified to the conversation which he had with Devlin in which Devlin admitted his guilt.

20. If Devlin's attorney makes a timely objection to the identification made by Watson, the court should

(A) sustain the objection, because Devlin was entitled to have his attorney present at the lineup.

(B) sustain the objection, unless there were at least five other men in the lineup and all were of approximately the same height, weight, and skin color as Devlin.

(C) overrule the objection, unless Devlin's refusal to participate in the lineup was overcome by force or the threat of force.

(D) overrule the objection, because any taint connected with the lineup procedure has been purged by Watson's subsequent re-identification of Devlin in the courtroom.

21. If Devlin's attorney objects to the testimony of Ulrich regarding the statement which Devlin made to him in the corridor, the objection should be

(A) sustained, because the statement was made to a police officer in the absence of and without the consent of Devlin's attorney.

(B) sustained, because Ulrich entrapped Devlin into making the statement

(C) overruled, only if Ulrich was placed in Devlin's cell pursuant to a warrant.

(D) overruled, because Devlin made the statement voluntarily.

22. "The Heights" was a poor section in the City of Maple. Because many of the residents of The Heights had been complaining about the exploitation of tenants by absentee landlords, and about the lack of law enforcement in their neighborhood, the City Attorney instituted a campaign of neighborhood reform in The Heights. The City Attorney obtained a series of warrants for inspection of buildings in The Heights. He accomplished this by presenting an affidavit which stated that many health and safety violations had been observed in buildings located in The Heights by police and building inspectors traveling through the neighborhood. Pursuant to the warrants, police officers and building inspectors were ordered to inspect certain buildings. As a result, an apartment building owned by Donder was found to have more than twenty violations of the city's building code. Donder was prosecuted under a state law which made it a felony for any landlord to willfully fail to correct health and safety violations in a building which he or she owned.

If Donder moves to suppress the evidence against him which was obtained as a result of the inspection of his building, his motion should be

(A) granted, unless the affidavit which was submitted in support of the request for a warrant specifically stated that violations had been observed in Donder's building.

(B) granted, because the inspections were part of a general scheme to enforce the law in a particular neighborhood only.

(C) denied, because no warrant is needed to inspect buildings for health or safety violations.

(D) denied, if there was probable cause to believe that violations would be found in some of the buildings of The Heights.

23. On Darr's birthday, his friend Mead gave him a new television as a gift. The following day, when Darr opened the box and began using the television, he noticed that there was no warranty document with it. Darr phoned Mead and asked Mead for the missing warranty document. Mead said, "I

can't give it to you because the television was stolen." Darr kept the television and continued using it.

Darr was guilty of

(A) receiving stolen property only.

(B) larceny only.

(C) receiving stolen property and larceny.

(D) no crime.

24. In which of the following fact situations is Dandy most likely to be convicted of the crime charged? Assume that the jurisdiction applies the common law definition of all crimes.

   (A) Dandy offered an acquaintance one thousand dollars to burn down Dandy's factory, but the acquaintance refused. Dandy was charged with solicitation to commit arson.

   (B) Dandy deliberately burned down his home and collected the proceeds of his fire insurance policy. Dandy was charged with larceny by trick.

   (C) Dandy deliberately burned down Vonn's store because he wanted to put Vonn out of business. Dandy was charged with arson.

   (D) Dandy attempted to burn down his neighbor's house because he disliked his neighbor. He poured gasoline on the door of the house and threw a match onto it. The flames had just charred the door when it started to rain and the fire went out. Dandy was charged with arson.

25. In which of the following fact situations is defendant LEAST likely to be convicted of murder?

   (A) At midnight on New Year's Eve, defendant fired his pistol out the window into the street below for the purpose of making a loud noise. One of the bullets ricocheted off a brick wall and struck a passing motorist, killing him.

   (B) At a New Year's Eve party, defendant got so

drunk that she passed out. Unaware of what she was doing, she walked to her car in an unconscious state, got behind the wheel, and started the engine. Because she had left the car parked in gear, it lurched forward, striking a pedestrian who was standing in the roadway. The pedestrian died of his injuries later that night.

   (C) At a New Year's Eve party, defendant was told that his wife was having sexual intercourse with Victor in a bedroom of the house where the party was taking place. Infuriated, defendant ran out to his car and got an iron bar which he kept in the trunk. He slipped it into his pants leg so that no would see it when he re-entered the party. He waited for half an hour outside the room where his wife and Victor were in bed together. Intending to break Victor's collarbone, defendant swung the iron bar at him as Victor exited the bedroom. Defendant aimed at Victor's shoulder, but in attempting to move out of the way, Victor was struck in the head, sustaining a fractured skull. Victor died of his injuries.

   (D) On New Year's Eve, believing Victor to be away at a party, defendant broke into Victor's house for the purpose of stealing cash and other valuables. When he entered the bedroom, Victor and his wife, who had not gone out as planned, jumped out of bed. Taking from his pocket a gun which he knew to be unloaded, defendant grabbed Victor's wife and held the gun to her head, saying, "Don't move or I'll shoot her." Victor took a loaded pistol from under his pillow and shot at defendant. The bullet missed and killed Victor's wife.

26. A small but valuable piece of jewel-encrusted statuary had been stolen from an antique shop, and all foot patrol officers in the area were notified by walkie-talkie to look for the thief. When an officer saw Dinger running down the street away from the direction of the antique shop, she became suspicious of him. The officer stopped Dinger and asked him his name and his reason for running down the street. When Dinger said, "Just

jogging," the officer ordered him to raise his hands, and then frisked him to see if he was in possession of the stolen statue. She felt a hard object in his pocket and, believing it to be the statue, reached inside. The object which she felt turned out to be a pistol for which Dinger did not have a permit as required by law.

Prior to Dinger's trial on the charge of unlawfully possessing a concealed weapon, he moved to suppress the use of the pistol. His motion should be

(A) granted, because it was obtained as the result of an unlawful search.

(B) granted, because it was not the item which the officer was seeking when she frisked him.

(C) denied, because the officer reasonably suspected him of stealing the statue.

(D) denied, because it was discovered as part of a valid pat-down search.

Questions 27-28 are based on the following fact situation.

Tom, John and Sam were teenaged boys staying at a summer camp. One evening Vanney, a camp counselor, ordered Tom and John to go to bed immediately after dinner. Outside the dining hall, Tom and John decided to get even with Vanney. Having seen Vanney take medicine for an asthma condition, they agreed to kill Vanney by finding his medicine and throwing it away. Tom and John did not know whether Vanney would die without the medicine, but they both hoped that he would.

Sam, who disliked Vanney, overheard the conversation between Tom and John and hoped that their plan would succeed. He decided to help them without saying anything about it. Going into Vanney's room, Sam searched through Vanney's possessions until he found the medicine. Then he put it on a night table so that Tom and John would be sure to find it.

As Tom and John were walking towards Vanney's room, John decided not to go through with the plan. Because he was afraid that Tom would make fun of him for chickening out, he said nothing to Tom about his change of mind. Instead, saying that he needed to use the bathroom, he ran away. Tom went into Vanney's room by himself, found the medicine where Sam had left it on the night table, and threw the medicine away. Later that night, Vanney had an asthma attack and died because he was unable to find his medicine.

A statute in the jurisdiction provides that persons the age of Tom, John and Sam are adults for purposes of criminal liability.

27. If Sam is charged with conspiracy, a court will probably find him

(A) guilty, because he knowingly aided and abetted in the commission of a crime.

(B) guilty, because he committed an overt act in furtherance of an agreement to throw away Vanney's medicine.

(C) not guilty, because he did not agree to commit any crime.

(D) not guilty, because John effectively withdrew from any conspiracy which existed.

28. If John is charged with the murder of Vanney, a court will probably find him

(A) guilty, because he and Tom agree to throw away Vanney's medicine in the hope that doing so would cause Vanney's death.

(B) guilty, because he aided and abetted in causing Vanney's death.

(C) not guilty, because he did not physically participate in throwing away Vanney's medicine.

(D) not guilty, because he withdrew from the conspiracy before any overt act was committed.

29. As part of her campaign for re-election, the President of the United States was driving through the main street of a city in the state of Fedora in a car with a bubble-shaped roof made of bullet-proof glass. Intending to shoot the President, Dosset crouched on the roof of a building and aimed a

high-powered rifle at the glass top of her car. He fired three times, striking the glass with each bullet. None of the bullets penetrated the glass, and because of the noise of the cheering crowd the President was unaware that any shots had been fired. A police officer observed Dosset firing at the President, however, and placed him under arrest. Dosset was subsequently charged with violating a federal statute which makes it a crime to attempt to assassinate the President, and was acquitted in a federal court.

If Dosset is prosecuted in a court of the state of Fedora, and charged with criminal assault under the state law, a court should find him

(A) not guilty, because he has already been acquitted in the federal court.

(B) not guilty, because the President was unaware that shots had been fired.

(C) guilty, because Dosset intended to hit the President with the bullets.

(D) guilty, because Dosset's conduct would cause the reasonable person to be placed in fear of her life.

Questions 30-31 are based on the following fact situation.

Conn had just been released from prison after serving a three year term for aggravated assault. In need of money, he called his old friend Delbert and asked whether Delbert would be interested in joining Conn in the robbery of Perry's Pawnshop. Delbert agreed, but only after making Conn promise that there would be no violence. Upon Delbert's insistence, they carried realistic-looking toy guns and when they entered Perry's Pawnshop, they drew their toy guns and ordered Perry to give them all the money in his cash register and all the gems in his safe. Perry took a gun from the safe and shot Conn, killing him. Perry then aimed the pistol at Delbert, who fled from the store. As Perry ran out into the street with his pistol in his hand, Delbert jumped into the car which he and Conn had left parked at the curb. Speeding away from the scene, Delbert accidentally struck Nora, a pedestrian, who died of her injuries. By statute, the jurisdiction has adopted the felony-murder rule.

30. If Delbert is charged with the murder of Conn, Delbert's most effective argument in defense is that

(A) Conn was not a victim of the felony which resulted in his death.

(B) Perry was justified in shooting Conn.

(C) the use of toy guns made it unforeseeable that the robbery would result in the death of any person.

(D) Delbert lacked malice aforethought.

31. If Delbert is charged with the murder of Nora, the court should find him

(A) guilty, because Nora's death resulted from Delbert's attempt to commit a robbery.

(B) guilty, only if he drove the car in a criminally negligent manner.

(C) not guilty, if he was in reasonable fear for his own life when attempting to flee in the automobile.

(D) not guilty, because Nora's death did not occur during the commission of a felony.

32. Although Donnum had been licensed to drive for fifteen years, he allowed his license to expire while he was temporarily out of the country. When he returned, he meant to get it renewed or reinstated, but did not get around to doing so. Although a statute made it a misdemeanor to drive without a license, Donnum continued to drive. One day he accidentally dropped his cigarette while driving his car. He felt around for it while he drove, until his fingers encountered its glowing tip. Taking his eyes off the road for a moment to pick up the still-burning cigarette, he failed to see Vonderhaven who stepped out from between parked cars. Donnum struck Vonderhaven, who died instantly.

If Donnum is charged with homicide as a result of Vonderhaven's death, which of the following would be the prosecutor's most effective argument?

(A) Vonderhaven's death resulted from Donnum's commission of a dangerous misdemeanor.

(B) Donnum's violation of the statute which required a driver's license made him guilty of culpable negligence per se since the statute was designed to protect users of public roads against unqualified drivers.

(C) While mere negligence is insufficient to sustain a murder charge, it is sufficient to sustain a charge of involuntary manslaughter where it results in death.

(D) Donnum created a high and unreasonable risk of death or serious injury when he took his eyes off the road while driving.

Questions 33-34 are based on the following fact situation.

Larraby worked as a lifeguard from 5 P.M. to 10 P.M. every night at a public swimming pool operated by the City of Muni. When she arrived at work Wednesday evening she asked her supervisor Boss whether she could leave early, because she had a date. Since there were only a few people at the pool, Boss said that Larraby could leave at 8 P.M. At 8 P.M., Larraby told Boss she was going and left, although the pool had become quite crowded with adults and young children. At 9 P.M., Susan, a nine-year-old child, fell into the pool, striking her head against its edge. Watcher, one of the adults swimming in the pool, saw Susan fall and realized that the child would drown if someone did not rescue her. Watcher had seen Larraby leave and knew that there was no lifeguard present, but made no effort to rescue Susan although Watcher was a strong swimmer and could easily have done so with no risk to herself. Susan drowned.

33. If Larraby is charged with criminal homicide in the death of Susan, which of the following would be her most effective argument in defense?

(A) She was not present at the time of the drowning.

(B) Her duty to assist people in the swimming

pool terminated when Boss permitted her to leave at 8 P.M.

(C) Susan's death resulted from Watcher's failure to render aid.

(D) She did not intend Susan's death.

34. If Watcher is charged with criminal homicide in the death of Susan, the court should find her

(A) guilty, because she could have saved Susan without any risk to herself.

(B) guilty, if she knew that she was the only person present who was aware of Susans's plight and who was able to rescue her.

(C) not guilty, unless she was related to Susan.

(D) not guilty, because she had no duty to aid susan.

Questions 35-36 are based on the following fact situation.

Vena was addicted to heroin, and frequently committed acts of prostitution to obtain the money she needed to buy drugs. One night she was out looking for customers for prostitution when she was approached by Dorian who asked what her price was. When she told him that she would have intercourse with him for $20, he said that he would get the money from a friend and see her later. When Vena went home several hours later, Dorian was waiting inside her apartment. He said that he wanted to have sex with her, but when Vena repeated her demand for $20, he said that he had no money. She told him to get out or she would call the police. Dorian took a knife from his pocket, saying that if she did not have intercourse with him he would kill her. Silently, Vena took off her clothes and had intercourse with him.

Immediately afterwards, Dorian fell asleep. Vena tied his hands and feet to the four corners of the bed, and woke him. She said, "Now you are going to be punished for what you have done. I should kill you, but I won't because I want to make sure that you suffer for the rest of your life." Using his own knife, she began to cut and jab him with it, planning to torture but not to kill him. She stabbed and blinded him in both eyes, then cut off his sex organs. She also severed the tip of his nose and made a series of cuts across his face and chest.

35. If Dorian is charged with rape, the court should find him

   (A) guilty, because he overcame Vena's refusal to have intercourse with him by threatening to kill her with his knife.

   (B) not guilty, because Vena's demand for twenty dollars made her resistance conditional and therefore less than total.

   (C) not guilty, because Vena offered no resistance and Dorian did not use physical force.

   (D) not guilty, because of the injuries inflicted by Vena.

36. Assume for the purpose of this question only that Dorian dies as a result of the injuries inflicted by Vena. Assume further that she is charged with first degree murder in a jurisdiction which defines that crime as "the unlawful killing of a human being committed intentionally, with deliberation and premeditation." The court should find Vena

   (A) not guilty, because Vena did not intend to cause Dorian's death.

   (B) not guilty, because Vena was acting in self-defense.

   (C) guilty, because Dorian's death resulted from Vena's commission of a dangerous felony.

   (D) guilty, because Dorian's death resulted from torture.

37. Brenda was in her eighth month of pregnancy when her husband left her. Unwilling to face life as a single parent, she asked her doctor to perform an abortion. Her doctor refused, explaining that abortion so late in pregnancy could be dangerous. Brenda's cousin Diedre had graduated from medical school and was waiting for news about whether she had passed the state medical board's licensing exam. Brenda asked Diedre to abort the pregnancy, saying that she would kill herself if Diedre refused. Reluctantly, Diedre agreed to perform the abortion in Brenda's kitchen. Diedre performed a surgical procedure which usually resulted in abortion, but because the pregnancy had advanced as far as it did, the baby was alive when separated from Brenda's body. Diedre held the baby's head under water in an attempt to end his life, but after a short time her conscience bothered her. She pulled the baby from the water and gave him mouth-to- mouth resuscitation, directing Brenda to call an ambulance. When the ambulance arrived, the baby was breathing on his own. He was taken to a hospital where, because of brain damage, he remained in a coma until he died five years later.

If Diedre is charged with murdering the baby, her most effective argument in defense would be that

   (A) Brenda had a constitutional right to an abortion.

   (B) Diedre attempted to save the baby's life by giving him mouth-to-mouth resuscitation.

   (C) the baby's death five years later after Diedre's act was not proximately caused by Diedre's act.

   (D) Diedre lacked the necessary state of mind to be guilty of criminal homicide, because the surgical procedure which she performed usually resulted in abortion.

38. Donnelly shot Vasily to death. She was subsequently charged with voluntary manslaughter. Which of the following additional facts, if true, would lead to an acquittal on that charge?

   (I) At the time of the shooting, Donnelly believed that Vasily was going to stab her, but the reasonable person in her place would not have held that belief.

   (II) At the time of the shooting, the reasonable person in Donnelly's place would have believed that Vasily was going to stab her, but Donnelly did not hold that belief.

   (A) I only.

(B) II only.

(C) Either I or II.

(D) Neither I or II.

Questions 39-41 are based on the following fact situation.

Donald and Denise were law students in Professor Vinton's Contracts class. Knowing that Professor Vinton kept his lecture notes in a cabinet in his office, they planned to break into the office for the purpose of copying his notes. Donald purchased a miniature camera for this purpose, after discussing the purchase with Denise and collecting half the cost from her. When they saw Professor Vinton leave his office at lunch time they went there. Denise opened the locked door by slipping a strip of plastic under its latch. Once inside the office, Donald found Professor Vinton's notes and photographed them with the camera which he had purchased. Denise noticed a gold-plated pen on the Professor's desk and put it into her pocket without telling Donald. She did so with the intention of returning the pen in a week or two, hoping that in the meantime the professor would be so upset about the loss of his pen that he would not notice that his notes had been disturbed. The following day, however, The pen was stolen from Denise's briefcase. The jurisdiction applies the common law definitions of larceny and burglary.

39. Of which of the following crimes may Donald properly be convicted?

   (I) Conspiracy to commit burglary.

   (II) Conspiracy to commit larceny.

  (A) I only.

  (B) II only.

  (C) I and II.

  (D) Neither I nor II.

40. If Denise is charged with larceny as a result of her taking the gold-plated pen, she should be

  (A) acquitted, because theft of the pen from her briefcase was a superseding cause.

  (B) acquitted, because she intended to return the pen in a week or two.

  (C) convicted, because Professor Vinton was permanently deprived of the pen.

  (D) convicted, because theft of the pen from her briefcase was foreseeable.

41. Assume for the purpose of this question only that the jurisdiction has a statute which defines the crime of "larcenous conversion" as "intentionally carrying off property known to belong to another person." If Donald is charged with being an accessory to the larcenous conversion of Professor Vinton's pen, he should be found

  (A) guilty, because Denise committed the larcenous conversion while with Donald.

  (B) guilty, because Denise took the pen to keep Vinton from noticing that his notes had been disturbed.

  (C) not guilty, because Donald did not expect that Denise would take the pen.

  (D) not guilty, because Donald did not know that Denise took Professor Vinton's pen.

Questions 42-43.

Read the summaries of the decisions in the four cases (A-D) below. Then decide which is most applicable as a precedent to each of the cases in the questions that follow, and indicate each choice by marking the corresponding space on the answer sheet.

  (A) Amy was walking on a crowded street with her purse hanging from a strap over her shoulder when Defendant yanked the purse with sufficient force to break the strap, and ran off with it into the crowd. Defendant's conviction for robbery was reversed.

  (B) Defendant took a package of meat from a showcase in a supermarket and slipped it under his shirt. He left the store without paying for it. When Benton, a store cashier, ran after him into the parking lot and stepped in front of him blocking his path, Defendant took a straight razor from his pocket and grabbed another customer. He held the razor to the customer's throat telling Benton to get out of the way. Benton stepped aside, and Defendant ran away, releasing the other customer. Defendant's conviction for robbery was affirmed.

(C) Carrie, a school teacher, took her sixth grade class to visit a display of medieval torture devices at the museum. She sat in a wooden torture-chair and had herself shackled into it to demonstrate its operation to her students. Defendant, who worked at the museum, surreptitiously photographed her with an instant camera. He then went to the office of Carrie's husband Huss, and showed Huss the photograph of Carrie in the torture chair. Defendant said that his confederates would torture her unless he called them on the phone and told them that Huss had given him five hundred dollars. Huss gave him the money. Defendant's conviction for robbery was reversed.

(D) When Edmund purchased a ticket at the airport for his flight, he checked his baggage. Later, Defendant, wearing a mask and carrying a gun, entered the room where checked baggage was stored. Forcing the room attendant to lie face down on the floor, Defendant opened Edmund's suitcase and removed several hundred dollars worth of negotiable securities. Defendant's conviction for robbery was affirmed.

42. Vogt fell asleep on a train, while traveling from one part of the state to another. Defen, who had earlier seen Vogt removing cash from a moneybelt which Vogt wore under his shirt, slipped into the seat beside Vogt. While Vogt slept, Defen used a knife to cut off the buttons of Vogt's shirt, and to cut the moneybelt from Vogt. He then took it to another car of the train where he removed several thousand dollars. Defendant was charged with robbery.

43. Between flights, Veeney set her briefcase down beside her seat in the airport waiting room. Doaks saw this and walked past her in a casual fashion,

picking up the briefcase and walking off with it as he went by. Veeney, believing that he had taken it by mistake, ran to him and said, "Pardon me, sir. You've taken my bag." Doaks drew a realistic-looking toy pistol, pushed her into a seat, and ran away. Doaks was charged with robbery.

44. Herpo earned his living by catching poisonous reptiles for sale to zoos and private collectors. He had been commissioned to capture a rare, highly poisonous species known as the bowsnake. Herpo hired a professional biochemist named Kemo to develop and manufacture a drug which he could take before handling the bowsnake, and which would protect him against the reptile's poison in the event that he was bitten. Although Kemo knew that the bite of the bowsnake was usually fatal and that there was no defense against its venom, she welcomed the opportunity to earn some easy money. She sold Herpo a bottle of tablets telling him that they were based on her secret formula and that they would protect him against the bowsnake's venom. Actually, the tablets were made of nothing more than sugar, but Kemo thought that if Herpo believed strongly enough in their power he would handle the snakes so confidently that he would not be bitten. Herpo caught a bowsnake and took one of Kemo's tablets before handling it, following the instructions which she had given him. While he was handling the bowsnake, it bit him. Because the tablets did not protect him against the venom, Herpo became ill as a result of the snakebite and almost died.

If Kemo is prosecuted for her sale of the tablets to Herpo, she may properly be found guilty of

(A) attempted murder only.

(B) obtaining property by false pretenses only.

(C) attempted murder and obtaining property by false pretenses.

(D) neither attempted murder nor obtaining property by false pretenses.

45. Diller purchased an ounce of cocaine and divided it into fifty packets of about one-half gram each. She was selling them outside the local high

school when Gunn, a cocaine user, noticed her and saw the opportunity to get some free drugs. Gunn stepped up beside her. With his hand in the pocket of his jacket, he thrust his finger forward inside the pocket and jabbed her in the ribs with it. Snarling, he said, "I've got a gun. Give me the dope or I'll blow you away." Diller reached into her purse, drew a small pistol which she kept there, and shot Gunn, killing him.

If Diller is charged with the murder of Gunn, she should be found

(A) guilty, because it was unreasonable for her to use deadly force to protect illegal contraband.

(B) guilty, if Gunn was unarmed.

(C) guilty, because Diller was committing a crime and therefore had no privilege of self-defense.

(D) not guilty, if it was reasonable for her to believe that her life was in danger.

46. In which of the following fact patterns is the evidence offered most likely to be suppressed because it was obtained in violation of the defendant's Fourth Amendment right to be secure against unreasonable search and seizure?

(A) Border officials required Defendant to empty his pockets when he walked across the border from Mexico to the United States. A packet of cocaine which was thus discovered was offered against Defendant.

(B) Defendant called a public official on the telephone several times to offer her a bribe. At the request of the police, the official tape recorded one of her telephone conversations with Defendant. The tape recording was offered in evidence against Defendant.

(C) An undercover police officer trained in lip reading testified that he had observed the Defendant make a telephone call from a public booth, and that he was able to determine what the Defendant was saying by reading the Defendant's lips. He offered to testify to the words used by the Defendant.

(D) While making a series of calls from a public phone Defendant went in search of change, leaving the phone off the hook and leaving her briefcase in the booth. A police officer who had been keeping Defendant under surveillance examined the contents of the briefcase and discovered illegal drugs which were offered in evidence against Defendant.

47. After looking at a car which Samson had advertised for sale, Berrigan agreed to purchase it for three thousand dollars. Berrigan gave Samson one hundred dollars cash, promising to bring the balance and to pick up the car the following day. In fact Samson was a thief who had no intention of selling the car, and had been collecting cash down payments from buyers all over the state. As soon as Berrigan left, Samson ran off with the hundred dollars. One week later, Samson was arrested and charged with embezzlement and larceny by trick. He can properly be convicted of

(A) embezzlement only.

(B) larceny by trick only.

(C) embezzlement and larceny by trick.

(D) neither embezzlement nor larceny by trick.

48. Walton was extremely hot tempered and very possessive of her husband Harris. She frequently flew into a hysterical rage if he even looked at another woman. One evening Walton and Harris were in a bar when they began arguing. Wanting to hurt Walton, and knowing that it would infuriate her, Harris asked Mary, who was sitting at the next table, to dance with him. Mary accepted, but as she and Harris began to dance, Walton became enraged and ran at them, striking Harris over the head with a wine bottle. Later that night, Harris died of a head injury resulting from the blow. Walton was charged with murder, but her lawyer argued that the charge should be reduced to voluntary manslaughter because Walton was acting out of extreme passion when she struck Harris. Is Walton's lawyer correct?

(A) Yes, on the theory of deliberate provocation.

(B) Yes, because of Walton's extreme feelings of possessiveness regarding Harris.

(C) No, if the ordinary person in Walton's situation would not have become violently enraged by Harris's dancing with Mary.

(D) No, on the theory of mistaken justification.

49. Compco was a retailer of computer hardware and software. It frequently sold its products on credit, requiring customers to pay twenty percent down and to sign notes agreeing to pay the balance in monthly installments which included interest at the lawful rate. In addition, credit customers were required to execute security agreements giving Compco in the event of default in payment the right to repossess the goods sold without resort to judicial proceedings. Ritter was employed by Compco as a collection agent. As such, his job was to contact customers whose payments were past due and to repossess computer hardware when necessary.

Viola purchased computer hardware from Compco at a total cost of two thousand dollars, paying four hundred dollars down and executing a note and security agreement as described. She made no monthly payments to Compco for a period of six months, in spite of Ritter's many attempts to collect from her. One night, Ritter went to her home to demand that she either make her payments or return the computer hardware. Although he heard a radio playing inside Viola's apartment, no one answered his knock. Ritter tried the door, thinking that his knock might not have been heard over the sound of the radio. Finding the door unlocked, he opened it and entered the apartment. He called Viola's name as he walked from room to room, but found that nobody was home. He was about to leave when he saw the computer hardware which Viola had purchased from Compco on a table. He left a note which said, "I have repossessed your computer," and which he signed, "Ritter, for Compco," and took the equipment with him.

If Ritter is charged with common law burglary, which of the following would be his most effective argument in defense?

(A) He did not use force to effect an entry.

(B) He did not enter by "breaking," since the door was not locked.

(C) When he opened the door and entered the apartment, he had no intention of committing a crime.

(D) He left a note explaining his actions.

50. Drake suffered a severe head injury in an accident which occurred three years ago. As a result, she experienced eight incidents of sudden unconsciousness, each lasting approximately two minutes. All the incidents occurred within a three month period immediately following the accident, and all occurred while Drake was at home. Last week she was driving her automobile in a lawful manner when she suddenly lost consciousness as a result of the head injury which occurred three years ago. Her car swerved out of control onto the sidewalk, striking and permanently injuring Vincent, a pedestrian. Drake was charged with violating a state statute which defines the crime of "reckless maiming" as "causing permanent injury to another person by acting in knowing disregard of the plain and strong likelihood that death or serious personal injury will result."

Which of the following is Drake's most effective argument in defense against the charge of reckless maiming?

(A) Drake's head injury was not the result of any culpable conduct by Drake.

(B) After losing consciousness while driving, Drake was no longer capable of exercising control over the operation of her vehicle.

(C) Drake reasonably believed that she would not have any further incidents of unconsciousness.

(D) Drake did not know that her driving would lead to death or serious injury.

51. As part of a plan to market a new line of investment securities, Merchant's Bank assigned Veep, one of its vice presidents, to study the accounts of

some of its major depositors. Veep performed a computer analysis to determine at what times of the year the accounts of the depositors in question reflected the most activity. Veep had been reading in the newspaper about a series of unsolved bank robberies in the area. In examining the reports, Veep noticed that Doge had made a substantial deposit on the day following each of the unsolved robberies. Veep telephoned the police to report his discovery. Following the conversation, two police officers went to the Bank to examine with Veep the records of Doge's account. As a result of their findings, the police investigated Doge's whereabouts on the days of the bank robberies and eventually obtained further evidence that he had participated in them. Doge was arrested and prosecuted for the bank robberies.

If Doge makes an appropriate motion to suppress the evidence of his involvement in the robberies, the motion should be

(A) granted, if police examination of Doge's bank account record was the only fact which led the police to suspect and investigate Doge.

(B) granted, unless the prosecution can establish that evidence associating Doge with the bank robberies would have eventually and inevitably surfaced without the facts discovered by examination of Doge's bank account record.

(C) denied, only if police examination of Doge's bank account record disclosed no information in addition to that which the police had already received from Veep.

(D) denied, because it was not reasonable for Doge to expect information contained in his bank account record to be private.

52. Dafton came home from work to find that his wife and two of his children had been slashed and cut and were lying dead in a pool of blood. His third child was also cut and bleeding severely. As Dafton approached, the child said, "Valens hurt Mommy." Dafton said, "I'll kill that son of a bitch." Then he loaded his shotgun and went next door to the home of the Valens. He knocked on

the door, and when Valens opened the door Dafton shot and killed him. State statutes codify the common law definitions of voluntary and involuntary manslaughter, and define first degree murder as "the deliberate and premeditated killing of a human being," and second degree murder as "the killing of a human being with malice aforethought."

If Dafton is charged with voluntary manslaughter, the court should find him

(A) guilty, if he intended the death of Valens because he believed that Valens had killed his wife and children.

(B) guilty, because the killing of Valens was deliberate and premeditated.

(C) not guilty, because the killing of Valens was deliberate and premeditated.

(D) not guilty, if Valens was the killer of Dafton's wife and children.

Questions 53-54 are based on the following fact situation.

Dorner was the chief cashier at a supermarket. As part of her duties, she deposited the day's receipts in the company safe each night. One Friday night when the store was to be closed for the entire weekend, after depositing the day's receipts in the safe, Dorner removed $500 from the safe without permission. She knew that no one would be looking for the money in the safe during the weekend and planned to take it with her on a gambling junket to Las Vegas. Her intentions were to gamble with the money, and, if she won, to return it on Monday morning. If she lost, she planned to alter the store records to hide the fact that the money was missing.

On Monday morning, Dorner returned to the supermarket. Having won a few hundred dollars during her weekend gambling trip, she returned the money which she had taken from the safe. Sears, one of her co-workers, saw her returning the money and questioned her about it until Dorner admitted what she had done. Sears stopped her before she closed the safe and said that unless Dorner gave him $25 of the store's money, he would tell the boss. Dorner knew that she could get away with taking $25 because the store records were frequently off by that much and the boss never worried about it. Thus, she took out $25 from the safe and gave it to Sears.

53. If Dorner is charged with larceny for taking $500 from the safe on Friday night, she should be found

   (A) not guilty, because the owner of the super-market was not deprived of its use.

   (B) not guilty, because when she took the money she intended to return it if she won.

   (C) guilty, because she withheld $25 on Monday morning.

   (D) guilty, because she planned to keep the money if she lost.

54. Of which one of the following crimes is Sears most likely to be guilty as a result of his conduct on Monday morning?

   (A) Robbery, because he obtained money from Dorner by threat and intimidation.

   (B) Larceny, because he obtained money by inciting and encouraging Dorner to steal twenty-five dollars from the safe.

   (C) Embezzlement, because he obtained his employer's money by violating his duty to report Dorner's conduct.

   (D) Fraud, because he obtained money by with-holding information which he had a duty to disclose.

Questions 55-56 are based on the following fact situation.

A statute provides as follows: "Any person who know-ingly sells an intoxicating substance to a person under the age of 18 years shall be guilty of a misdemeanor." Darla, the owner of a cocktail lounge called the Twi-light Bar hired Bart to work as her bartender. Before Bart began working, Darla read him the above statute and explained the need for him to check the identifica-tion of all persons who appeared to be under the age of

18 years. She also told him that if she ever heard of his violating the statute while working at the Twilight Bar she would fire him immediately. Later that night Kidd, a 17-year old who looked like he was 25, ordered a glass of wine. Kidd showed Bart an altered driver's license which falsely stated his age to be twenty. Bart was not sure whether the phrase "intoxicating sub-stance" in the statute included wine, and served it to Kidd. An undercover police officer who was at the bar observed the transaction. Hoping to make an arrest, the officer deliberately waited until after the wine was served. He then showed his badge, demanding to see Kidd's identification. Recognizing the driver's license as a forgery, he arrested Bart.

55. If Bart is charged with violating the statute, his most effective argument in defense is that

   (A) he did not know whether the statutory phrase "intoxicating substance" included wine.

   (B) he reasonably believed Kidd to be over the age of 18 years.

   (C) the undercover police officer entrapped him.

   (D) the wine was not an intoxicating substance because Kidd never got a chance to drink it.

56. Assume that Darla is charged with violating the statute, and that the prosecutor asserts that she should be held vicariously liable for Bart's act. Which of the following would be Darla's most effective argument in defense?

   (A) Darla did not have personal knowledge of the sale to Kidd.

   (B) Darla cautioned Bart against violation of the statute.

   (C) Bart is not guilty of violating the statute.

   (D) Bart was not acting within the scope of his employment when he sold wine to a minor in violation of the statute.

57. A state law requires automobiles to be equipped with a device to reduce the emission of air-pollut-ing substances and provides that any person who

knowingly removes such a device from an automobile shall be guilty of a misdemeanor. Dell was the operator of an automobile service station at which she conducted minor repairs. Velma brought her car to Dell's station and asked whether there was anything that Dell could do to improve the car's fuel economy. Dell said that removing the air-pollution control device would make the car use less fuel, and offered to do so for a fee. Velma paid the fee, and Dell removed the device. Although Dell worked carefully, she accidentally loosened a connection in the exhaust system without knowing she had done so. As a result, when Velma drove away, exhaust gases were leaking from the exhaust system into Velma's car. After driving for a short time, Velma was poisoned by the gases and died.

If Dell is prosecuted for the homicide of Velma, she should be found

(A) guilty of involuntary manslaughter under the unlawful act doctrine, because Velma's death would not have occurred but for Dell's removal of the air-pollution control device.

(B) guilty of voluntary manslaughter, only if she knew there was a possibility that death could result from a leak in the exhaust system.

(C) guilty of involuntary manslaughter, because an automobile is a dangerous instrumentality and Dell was culpably negligent.

(D) not guilty.

Questions 58-60 are based on the following fact situation.

After striking a police officer with a baseball bat, Grover was charged with felonious assault. He was found not guilty by reason of insanity, but the judge directed that he report to a state-employed psychiatrist for weekly psychotherapy treatments. One day, while he was in the waiting room of the doctor's office, Grover drew a knife and waved it at Nelson, a nurse employed there, shouting, "Vader must die. The Empire will be restored." Nelson took a heavy decorative hard plastic replica of a medieval sword from the wall, and held it in front of him. When Grover saw this, he handed his knife to Nelson and knelt before him, crying and saying, "forgive me, Lord of the Galaxy." Although he realized that Grover was no longer trying to kill him, Nelson struck him heavily on the head with the plastic sword, causing a fracture of Grover's skull. Grover grabbed his knife out of Nelson's hand and stabbed Nelson with it, inflicting a slight injury. Grover was arrested and charged with the crime of battery.

58. If Grover asserts that he acted in self-defense, he should be found

(A) not guilty, because the injury which he inflicted upon Nelson was significantly less serious than the injury which Nelson inflicted upon him.

(B) not guilty, if the force which he used against Nelson was reasonable.

(C) guilty, if he knew that the sword in Nelson's hand was made of plastic.

(D) guilty, because he was the initial aggressor.

59. Assume for the purpose of this question only that Grover asserts that he is not guilty by reason of insanity. If the jurisdiction applies the M'Naghten rule, the court should find that Grover is

(A) insane, because a court has already declared him to be insane.

(B) insane, if his delusion made him believe that although his conduct was unlawful, it was not morally wrong.

(C) insane, if he had been suffering from mental illness for a substantial period of time, and if his attack on Nelson resulted from that mental illness.

(D) sane, if he knew that he was stabbing a person and that it was unlawful to do so.

60. Assume for the purpose of this question only that two weeks after the incident, Grover died as a result of the fractured skull which he sustained when Nelson struck him with the plastic sword. If Nelson is prosecuted for criminal homicide, he

may properly be found

(A) guilty of murder, if he knew when he struck Grover that Grover would sustain a serious injury as a result.

(B) guilty of voluntary manslaughter, if he did not intend to inflict a serious injury by his act.

(C) not guilty of involuntary manslaughter, if a reasonable person in his position would have believed that Grover was still trying to kill him

(D) not guilty of any crime, because he acted in self-defense.

61. Davis was a narcotics addict in desperate need of a shot. He offered to permit Randall, a drug dealer, to have sexual intercourse with his wife Wilma in return for drugs. Randall accepted the offer and went home with Davis. When Davis told Wilma about the arrangement, however, she refused to have any contact with Randall. Davis struck her several times, and held her down while Randall had intercourse with her forcibly. Afterwards, Randall handed a packet of heroin to Davis.

Which of the following is the most serious crime of which Davis can be found guilty?

(A) Rape.

(B) Battery.

(C) Procuring for prostitution.

(D) Possession of narcotics.

62. Daner was about to go to his sister's wedding when he remembered that he had inadvertently left his camera at his friend Foster's house. Although he knew that Foster was out of town, Daner went to Foster's house in the hope of finding some way to get the camera so that he could take pictures at the wedding. The door was locked, but when Daner shook the doorknob vigorously with his hand, the door opened. Daner entered and searched for his camera, but could not find it. As he was leaving, he saw a silver candy dish on a shelf with several other items and took it to give his sister as a wedding present. He subsequently changed his mind, however, and returned it to Foster.

Of which of the following crimes may Daner properly be convicted?

(A) Larceny.

(B) Burglary.

(C) Attempted burglary.

(D) No crime.

63. Dutt was a nightclub performer who was billed as "the man with second sight." As part of his nightclub act, he would put on a blindfold and walk between the tables, identifying the contents of pockets and purses of members of the audience. One day, as a publicity stunt, he had himself blindfolded and attempted to drive an automobile in rush-hour traffic. Because he was unable to see the road, he collided with the vehicle in front of him. As a result of the impact, the other vehicle burst into flames and three of its occupants were severely burned, one so badly that he permanently lost the use of his legs. If they had not been rescued by a fire company which happened to be passing by, all three would have died.

On a charge of attempted involuntary manslaughter, Dutt should be found

(A) guilty, since his reckless behavior nearly resulted in the death of another human being.

(B) guilty, since he had completed all steps necessary to result in guilt for involuntary manslaughter, and the deaths of the victims were prevented by an independent agency.

(C) not guilty, since he lacked the requisite state of mind to be liable for an attempt.

(D) not guilty, since the crime of involuntary manslaughter is a lesser offense included in murder.

64. A state statute provides that "any person who

brings about the death of another human being with the intent to cause said death or in the course of committing burglary, rape, robbery, or kidnapping shall be guilty of murder in the first degree." The jurisdiction applies common law definitions for the four enumerated felonies. Dalton was attempting to use dynamite to blow open the door of a warehouse so that he could enter to steal its contents. Williams, his accomplice, was waiting in the getaway car parked at the curb. When Dalton detonated the charge, the resulting explosion damaged the building wall, causing bricks and chunks of mortar to fly through the air. A brick crashed through the windshield of the getaway car, striking Williams in the head and killing him.

If Dalton is charged with murder in the first degree, which of the following arguments would be his most effective defense?

(A) The statute was not intended to protect the accomplice of a felon.

(B) Burglary as defined by common law is not a dangerous felony.

(C) Williams's death was not proximately caused by Dalton's attempt to commit any of the crimes enumerated by the statute.

(D) Williams assumed the risk by participating in the commission of a felony.

65. Wallace, who had applied for employment with the Axtel Corporation, learned that the decision as to whether to hire him would be made by the company's personnel manager, Daniels. Anxious to receive the job, Wallace offered to give Daniels his first week's pay if Daniels would hire him. Daniels accepted Wallace's offer and hired him, later accepting the payment. Subsequently, Wallace and Daniels were both charged with violating a state law which provided that, "it shall be a felony for any person with responsibility for hiring others to solicit, demand, or receive anything of value from persons hired in exchange for hiring said persons." They were tried jointly, Daniels as a principal and Wallace as an accessory.

Wallace's best argument for a dismissal of the

charge against him is that

(A) a person cannot be tried as an accessory until the principal has first been tried and convicted.

(B) he did not assist Daniels in the commission of the crime.

(C) no person can be charged as an accessory if the crime could not have been committed without his participation.

(D) the law was intended to protect people in Wallace's position against people in Daniel's position.

66. Defendant, in need of money, waited in an alley until Vicki walked by on the street. Then, stepping out of the alley, he stuck his hand in his pocket with his finger thrust forward and said, "I've got a gun in this pocket." Snatching Vicki's purse with the other hand, he ran away. Because she thought that he had a gun, Vicki did not attempt to stop him.

Of which of the following offenses would Defendant be most likely to be properly convicted?

(A) Robbery.

(B) Larceny by trick.

(C) Embezzlement.

(D) False pretenses.

67. When Boswell went away on vacation, he left the key to his apartment with his neighbor Crawford, who promised to water Boswell's plants until he returned. One day, as Crawford was watering Boswell's plants, she suspected one of them to be marijuana. She watered the rest of the plants and then went to the public library where she consulted a reference book and found that the suspicious plant was indeed marijuana. She went back to Boswell's apartment and let herself in with the key. Then she pulled the marijuana plant out by its roots and destroyed it by stuffing it into the garbage disposer in her own apartment.

The jurisdiction applies the common law definition of larceny, and has a statute defining burglary as "breaking and entering into the premises of another for the purpose of committing larceny." If charged with larceny and burglary, Crawford should be found guilty of

(A) larceny only.

(B) burglary only.

(C) larceny and burglary.

(D) neither larceny nor burglary.

Questions 68-69 are based on the following fact situation.

In the course of robbing a bank, Siddon pointed a gun at three bank tellers and the bank manager and ordered them to go from the bank lobby to the back room while his confederate attempted to open the safe. Threatening to shoot them if they refused, he then ordered one of the bank tellers to undress, and commanded the bank manager to have sexual intercourse with her. Fearful that they would be killed otherwise, the manager and teller obeyed Siddon's command without protesting.

68. Of which of the following crimes is Siddon guilty?

    I.   Solicitation to commit rape.

    II. Rape.

(A) I only.

(B) II only.

(C) I and II.

(D) Neither I or II.

69. If Siddon is charged with kidnaping the bank manager, his most effective argument in defense would be that

(A) he did not demand a ransom.

(B) he released the bank manager as soon as the robbery was completed.

(C) ordering the bank manager to go from the bank lobby to the back room was incidental and necessary to the commission of the robbery.

(D) the bank manager was an adult.

70. Dana sold a pistol to Wilson. Later Wilson was stopped by police who were routinely checking the licenses of motorists. The officers thoroughly searched Wilson's car and discovered the pistol in the glove compartment. Subsequently, Dana was charged with violating a statute which makes it a crime for any person "to sell or offer for sale any firearm which has not been properly registered pursuant to law."

Dana's motion to prevent introduction of the pistol into evidence will most likely be

(A) denied, since the routine license check was not a violation of Wilson's rights.

(B) denied, because Dana has no standing to object to the search of Wilson's car.

(C) granted, if Wilson objected to the search of his car at the time it took place.

(D) granted, because the search of Wilson's car was excessive in scope.

Questions 71-72 are based on the following case summaries. Read the summaries in the four cases (A-D) below. Then decide which is most applicable as a precedent to each of the cases in the questions that follow, and indicate each choice by marking the corresponding space on the answer sheet.

(A) *People v. Yonson* — Yonson was walking down the street when an intoxicated panhandler began to push and shove him. Yonson pointed a pistol at the panhandler with his finger on the trigger. When the panhandler pushed him again, the pistol went off, killing the panhandler. Yonson testified that he believed the pistol to be unloaded. *Held:* Not guilty of murder.

(B) *State v. Abel* — When Abel became rowdy in a bar, the bouncer asked him to leave. Abel responded by punching the bouncer in the face. The bouncer grabbed Abel's wrist, but Abel picked up a wine bottle with his other hand and struck the bouncer over the head with it, killing him. *Held:* Guilty of voluntary manslaughter.

(C) *Commonwealth v. Karat* — As Karat was leaving the high school where she worked, a student began chasing after her, waving a toy plastic baseball bat and threatening to hit her with it. She ran as fast as she could, but he ran after her. When she felt she could run no further, she took a pistol from her purse and shot him with it, injuring him. Karat testified that she believed the baseball bat to be real. *Held:* Not guilty of battery.

(D) *People v. Harris* — While he was walking her home, Harris's date asked her to have sexual intercourse with him. Offended, Harris slapped his face. When she raised her hand to slap him again, her date knocked her to the ground and began kicking her in the chest and head. As he continued kicking her, she struggled to her feet, and struck him in the head with a rock, killing him with one blow. *Held:* Not guilty of voluntary manslaughter.

71. Ferris made his living by forging endorsements on welfare checks which he stole out of residential mailboxes. Dick was an undercover police officer who suspected that Ferris was the forger he was after. Dressed in plain clothes, Dick surreptitiously followed Ferris in hopes of catching him in the act. Ferris noticed Dick following him and saw the gun which Dick wore in a shoulder holster. Believing that Dick was a thief who wanted to rob him, Ferris ducked into an alley. When Dick followed him into the alley, Ferris threw a steel garbage can at him, striking and killing him with it. Ferris is charged with murder.

72. Prosser, a thief, deliberately bumped into Edwards while trying to pick his pocket. Edwards felt Prosser's hand in his pocket and pushed him away. Then Edwards pulled out a knife and lunged at Prosser with it. Prosser, who had stud-

ied martial arts, struck Edwards in the throat with his clenched fist, killing him. Prosser is charged with third degree murder under a statute which defines that crime as "the killing of a human being committed with the intent to cause bodily harm."

73. Melba belonged to the Sigma Sigma sorority at Rogers College. Members of the sorority who paid a rent of one hundred dollars per semester were entitled to a single-occupancy bedroom in the sorority house. Although house residents shared kitchen and dining room facilities, the bedrooms were not communal and were normally kept locked by their occupants. With the knowledge of its members, the sorority kept duplicates of all keys so that copies could be made in the event that a resident lost her key. Rita, a member of the sorority, suspected that Melba was selling marijuana. One weekend, when she knew that Melba had gone home to visit her parents, Rita called the police and told them of her suspicions. In response to her call, two officers came to the sorority house to interview Rita. During the course of their conversation, Rita stated that she was Melba's roommate, and offered to let them into Melba's room. In fact, Rita was not Melba's roommate. The key which she used to open the door was actually one of the duplicates kept by the sorority. Upon entering, the police officers saw a tobacco pipe containing traces of marijuana residue on a night table. Melba was subsequently prosecuted for possession of marijuana. Prior to trial, she made an appropriate motion to suppress the use of the pipe and its contents as evidence.

Which of the following would be the prosecution's strongest argument in opposition to Melba's motion?

(A) Rita had apparent authority to permit the entry into the room.

(B) Rita had probable cause to believe that the officers would find marijuana in the room.

(C) Melba did not have a reasonable expectation of privacy, since she knew that the sorority kept a duplicate of her room key.

(D) The Fourth Amendment prohibition against

unreasonable search and seizure should not be strictly applied to students at educational institutions.

Questions 74-75 are based on the following fact situation.

Because they were bigots, Allen and Barbara were angry when the Ryders, a black family, moved into a house on their street. Deciding to drive them away and to set an example which would discourage other black people from moving into the neighborhood, they agreed to set fire to the Ryders' home. They went to the Ryders' house, and Allen started pouring gasoline around it. A crowd of onlookers began to gather. Terry, one of the onlookers, shouted, "Burn their house down," intending that Allen and Barbara would do so. Sal, another onlooker, hoped that Allen and Barbara would burn the house down, but said nothing. After Allen finished pouring the gasoline, Barbara lit a match and set it afire, burning the Ryders' house to the ground.

74. On a charge of arson, Terry is

(A) guilty, because he aided and abetted in the crime by his presence coupled with his criminal intent.

(B) guilty, because, intending that Allen and Barbara would burn the house down, he shouted encouragement.

(C) not guilty, because his words did not create a clear and present danger which did not already exist.

(D) not guilty, because words alone are not sufficient to result in criminal liability.

75. On a charge of arson, Sal is

(A) guilty, because she made no attempt to stop the crime from being committed.

(B) guilty, because her hope that Allen and Barbara would burn the house down amounted to criminal intent.

(C) not guilty, because mere presence coupled with silent approval is not sufficient to

result in liability as an accessory.

(D) not guilty, because she was, at most, an accessory after the fact.

76. Anthony was a resident patient at the state mental hospital, where he had been receiving treatment for a mental illness diagnosed as chronic paranoid schizophrenia. As a result of his illness, he believed that the governor of his state was part of a nationwide plot to turn all voting citizens into drug addicts. He felt that the only way to foil the plot was to kill the governor, but realized that the law prohibited such an act. He knew that if he was caught making any attempt on the governor's life he would be punished, but concluded that it would be better to be convicted and punished for a crime than to be turned into a drug addict.

Knowing that the governor visited the hospital every few months, and that when he did he usually ate in the hospital dining room, Anthony volunteered for a job in the hospital kitchen. On the governor's next visit, Anthony placed poison in food he knew would be served to the governor, intending to cause the governor's death. The governor ate the food and died as a result. If Anthony is charged with murder in a jurisdiction which has adopted only the M'Naghten test of insanity, Anthony should be found

(A) guilty, since he knew the nature of his act, and that it was prohibited by law.

(B) guilty, unless Anthony can establish that his mental illness made him unable to resist the impulse to kill the governor.

(C) not guilty, since Anthony's conduct was the result of mental illness.

(D) not guilty, if his delusion was the result of mental disease, and if his conduct was reasonable within the context of that delusion.

77. In which of the following situations is Defendant's claim of intoxication most likely to result in his or her being found not guilty?

(A) In a jurisdiction which applies the common law definition, Defendant is charged with involuntary manslaughter for the death of a pedestrian whom she struck while driving an automobile. Defendant asserts that at the time of the accident, she was so drunk that she did not see the pedestrian in the roadway.

(B) In a jurisdiction in which the statutory age of consent is 18, Defendant is charged with statutory rape after having sexual intercourse with a female who was seventeen years of age. Defendant asserts that he was so intoxicated that he did not realize that he was engaging in sexual intercourse.

(C) In a jurisdiction which applies the common law definition, Defendant is charged with murder for the death of a person whom she struck with her automobile. Defendant asserts that without her knowledge, an unknown person put alcohol in her fruit juice, as a result of which she became so intoxicated that she could not see clearly or control the movements of her hands and feet. She further asserts that, unaware that she was drunk, she believed the visual and physical difficulties to be the result of illness, and was attempting to drive to a hospital when the accident occurred.

(D) In a jurisdiction which applies the common law definition, Defendant is charged with voluntary manslaughter after killing his wife. He asserts that he was so drunk that he imagined that he saw another man in bed with her, and that he killed her in the drunken rage which resulted.

78. In which one of the following situations is Jones *least* likely to be guilty of murder?

(A) Having been hired by a third person to beat Ann severely enough to "put her in the hospital," Jones struck Ann repeatedly with a baseball bat in the knees. Although Jones intended only to break Ann's legs, she died of shock.

(B) Because he suffers from mental disease, Jones believed Basil to be Adolph Hitler. Intending to kill him, Jones shot him to

death.

(C) Believing Carl to be asleep, Jones fired ten bullets into his head. In fact, Carl had died of a heart attack moments before Jones entered the room, and was already dead when Jones shot him.

(D) Jones stole a check from Smith's mailbox and attempted to cash it in a bank by masquerading as Smith. Suspecting forgery, the bank teller signaled to the bank guard. As the guard approached, Jones shot at him. When the guard returned Jones's fire, one of the guard's bullets ricocheted off a wall and struck David, killing him.

Questions 79-80 are based on the following fact situation.

Maggie was the owner of a three dwelling unit residential building. She lived in an apartment on the third floor, her son Derek lived with his wife in an apartment on the second floor, and the ground floor apartment was rented to Paul, a police officer, and his family. One day, while Derek and his wife were out of town, Maggie and Paul were having coffee together in Maggie's apartment. During the course of their conversation, Maggie said that she was worried about Derek because once, while visiting him, she saw a substance in his apartment which she believed to be cocaine. Since she really did not know what cocaine looked like, however, she was not sure. Paul said, "Don't worry, Maggie. For all you know the stuff you saw was talcum powder. I'm a cop, so I know coke when I see it. If you'd like, I'll have a look and let you know whether or not there is anything for you to worry about."

Using her key to open the door to Derek's apartment, Maggie brought Paul inside. Lying on a table in the entrance hall inside the apartment was a plastic pouch containing white powder. Paul sniffed it and said, "That's coke, all right," putting it in his pocket. Then he noticed a television in the living room which looked like one stolen from an appliance store in the neighborhood. Without saying anything about the television to Maggie, Paul obtained a search warrant by submitting an affidavit indicating that he had seen certain items in Derek's apartment which he had probable cause to believe were stolen. Later, he returned, entered, and thoroughly searched the apartment pursuant to the warrant. The television which he had seen on his first visit was not stolen, but during the course of his search, he found several items which were stolen. Eventually Derek was charged with criminal possession of dangerous drugs and with burglary.

79. On the charge of possessing dangerous drugs, if Derek makes an appropriate motion to suppress use of the plastic pouch of cocaine which Paul found in his apartment, his motion should be

    (A) denied, since the plastic pouch was in plain sight when Paul entered the apartment.

    (B) denied, since Maggie, the owner of the building, had given Paul permission to enter.

    (C) denied, since Derek was not under suspicion at the time that Paul entered the apartment.

    (D) granted.

80. On the charge of burglary, if Derek makes an appropriate motion to suppress the use of stolen items found in his apartment, his motion should be

    (A) denied, since the stolen items were obtained as the result of a lawful search.

    (B) denied, since it would not serve the interests of justice to require a police officer to ignore a discovery which he has probable cause to believe is contraband.

    (C) granted, if the search warrant was issued as the result of information obtained in an unlawful search.

    (D) granted, since his possession of stolen items is not necessarily proof that he stole those items.

81. When he was nineteen years old, Dixon pleaded guilty to petty larceny. Because of his age, he was not sentenced to prison, but was required to report to a Youth Supervision Officer every month for one year. At the end of that period he was discharged from supervision. At the time, his attorney advised him that he was pleading guilty to a "Youthful Offense" rather than to a crime, and that because he was assigned to a Youth Supervision Officer he would have no criminal record as a result of the proceeding. Dixon believed this advice, but it was, in fact, false in that the charge to which he pleaded guilty was a criminal one.

Twenty years later, Dixon applied for employment with the state. In his application, he stated under oath that he had never been convicted of a crime.

A state statute reads as follows:

Perjury in the second degree consists of making any statement under oath with the knowledge that such statement is false. Perjury in the second degree is a felony punishable by a term not to exceed five years in the state prison.

If Dixon is charged with perjury in the second degree, the court should find him

    (A) not guilty, because he lacked the mental state required by the statute.

    (B) not guilty, because reliance on the advice of counsel is a complete defense.

    (C) not guilty, because a plea of guilty is not the same as a conviction.

    (D) guilty.

Questions 82-83 are based on the following fact situation.

Maxine was a collector of antique automobiles. One day, she took her infant daughter Mary for a ride in a 1921 Maple, one of the most valuable cars in her collection. On her way, she stopped to buy a newspaper. Because Mary had fallen asleep in the back seat, Maxine left her in the car when she got out. Dover, a professional car thief who happened to be at the newspaper stand, jumped into Maxine's car and drove it away, without noticing Mary in the back seat.

Dover realized that he would not be able to sell a stolen

car as unusual as the Maple, so he parked it in a friend's garage, still unaware of the presence of the sleeping child. Getting Maxine's name and phone number from some papers in the glove compartment of the car, Dover phoned her and left a message on her telephone answering machine telling her that if she did not immediately bring one thousand dollars in cash to a certain location, he would set the Maple on fire.

When Maxine realized that her car, with Mary in the back seat, was gone, she became frantic and rushed home. When she picked up her phone to call the police, her answering machine played Dover's message. Upon hearing it, Maxine brought one thousand dollars to the location specified. Dover, who was waiting for her, took the money and returned the car. Mary was still sleeping quietly in the back seat.

82. If Dover is charged with kidnapping, he should be found

(A) guilty, since he confined and moved Mary without her consent.

(B) guilty, since the asportation of Mary resulted from his commission of a serious felony.

(C) not guilty, since his primary purpose was to steal the car, and the movement of Mary was only incidental to his accomplishing that purpose.

(D) not guilty, since he did not know that Mary was in the car.

83. Which of the following additional facts or inferences if it were the only one true, would be most likely to lead to a conviction of Dover on a charge of robbery of one thousand dollars from Maxine?

(A) The car was in Maxine's possession when Dover took it.

(B) Maxine paid the money to prevent injury to Mary.

(C) Maxine paid the money to prevent damage to her automobile.

(D) By the time Maxine showed up with the money, Dover had discovered Mary sleep-

ing in the back seat.

84. Nichols was appointed to a post as U.S. Customs Inspector at a station located in the state of Aristo on the border separating the U.S. from Mexico. His supervisor Supe, training him in the proper procedure for questioning and searching returning Americans, said, "I'll search the next car that comes through just to give you an idea of how it should be done." At that moment Daryll, who was driving across the border from Mexico, arrived at the border station. Supe asked him to open the trunk of his car and began searching it while Nichols watched. In the course of the search, Supe discovered three pounds of marijuana. Daryll was subsequently charged with the illegal importation of a controlled substance and was tried in a federal court. While his trial was pending, the state of Aristo charged him with violation of a state statute which provided that, "any person in possession of more than one ounce of marijuana shall be guilty of a felony," based on his possession of the marijuana discovered by Supe. While the federal court trial is in progress, if Daryll moves to dismiss the state court prosecution on the ground that it violates the double jeopardy clause of the United States Constitution, his motion should be

(A) granted, since both the prosecutions resulted from the same transaction.

(B) granted, since Supe did not have probable cause for the search.

(C) denied, since he has not yet been placed in jeopardy in the federal court.

(D) denied, since the two prosecutions are not by the same sovereign.

85. Because he was a professional thief, Dudley owned a skeleton key which could be used to open many different locks. One evening, when he knew that Vivian was away on vacation, Dudley went to her home for the purpose of stealing cash which he believed was hidden inside. While he was trying unsuccessfully to use his skeleton key to open Vivian's door, Dudley was arrested by a police officer. In fact, Vivian had placed her cash

in a bank safety deposit box before going on vacation, and her house contained nothing of value.

If charged with violating a statute which makes it a crime to "possess any skeleton key with the intent to use it for the purpose of committing an unlawful entry onto the property of another," he should be found

(A) guilty, because the statute was designed to protect the public against professional thieves.

(B) guilty, because he possessed a skeleton key with the intent to use it for the purpose of committing an unlawful entry.

(C) not guilty, because the crime defined by the statute is merged into the crime of attempted burglary.

(D) not guilty, because to convict him would be to punish him merely for having a guilty mind.

86. A statute provides that, "If the death of any person proximately results from the commission of or attempt to commit any misdemeanor or non-forcible felony, the person committing said misdemeanor or nonforcible felony shall be guilty of third degree manslaughter."

Because he had been convicted three times of driving while under the influence of alcohol, Durban's driving license was revoked. One night, while driving home from a party, Durban lost control of his automobile and collided head-on with a vehicle traveling in the other direction. Two occupants of the other car were killed. Durban was charged with driving without a license, which was a misdemeanor, and with third degree manslaughter under the above statute. Should the court find Durban guilty of third degree manslaughter?

(A) No, unless the deaths were proximately caused by his operation of a motor vehicle without a license.

(B) No, because driving without a license is not

malum in se.

(C) Yes, because driving while intoxicated is a dangerous act.

(D) Yes, if, but only of, he knew or should have known that driving without a license could result in loss of life.

87. Mildred and Bonnie were college students who needed money. One night, Mildred suggested that they hold up a local convenience store. When Bonnie told her that she was afraid to get involved in a robbery, Mildred offered to go into the store alone if Bonnie would wait outside in the car with the engine running so that they could make a getaway after the robbery. Bonnie agreed on condition that they split the take. The following day, they went together to a sporting goods store where Mildred purchased a shotgun. That night, Bonnie drove Mildred to the convenience store and waited in the parking lot with the engine running. Mildred went into the store with the shotgun hidden in a paper bag. Once inside, she pointed it at the store clerk and made him give her the contents of the cash register. Then she ran out to the car. When Bonnie saw Mildred running toward the car, she became frightened and drove away without waiting for Mildred.

Bonnie is guilty of

(A) conspiracy only.

(B) robbery only.

(C) conspiracy and robbery.

(D) either conspiracy or robbery, but not both.

88. In which of the following fact situations is Defendant *least* likely to be properly convicted of murder?

(A) Defendant came home to find his wife lying on the floor of their apartment semi-conscious and severely bruised. When he asked her what happened, she said that their neighbor Fredericks, had raped and beaten her. The following morning, Defendant hid behind some bushes waiting for

Fredericks to leave his home. When Fredericks stepped out of his door, Defendant, intending to kill him, shot him, causing his death.

(B) A state law required every motor vehicle registered within the state to be covered by a valid policy of liability insurance. Defendant was operating a vehicle for which no liability insurance policy had been issued when he struck Norris, who later died of the resulting injuries.

(C) Defendant placed a small quantity of ant poison in a cup of coffee that he was serving to a date. He did not intend to cause any serious injury, but he hoped that the poison would make her slightly ill so that he could induce her to spend the night in his apartment rather than to go home. His date drank the coffee and died as a result.

(D) Defendant's daughter was suffering from a lingering, incurable, fatal disease. One day, while Defendant was visiting her in the hospital, she screamed and writhed in pain. Wanting to end her suffering, Defendant passed a pillow over her face and held it there until she died of suffocation.

89. The flivver is a rare migratory bird which is protected by international treaty. For this reason, hunting of the bird is restricted to seasons fixed by a law known as the Flivver Protection Act. Until recently, the Act permitted hunting of the flivver only during the months of March and April. The law was changed last year, however, to permit flivver hunting during the additional months of May and June.

Dalton did not know that the law fixing the hunting season had been changed. Because he did not like to compete with other hunters, he planned to go flivver hunting in May, believing that the season ended in March. He invited his friend Albert to join him, but Albert refused. Albert, who was also unaware that the law had been changed, informed a game warden about his conversation with Dalton. Dalton went flivver hunting on May 15. He shot at several flivvers and missed, before he succeeded in killing one of them. As soon as he did, the game warden arrested Dalton. If Dalton is charged with attempting to violate the Flivver Protection Act, which of the following would be his most effective argument in defense?

(A) He actually succeeded in killing a flivver prior to his arrest.

(B) The act which he intended to commit was not a crime.

(C) Albert was in pari delicto with Dalton because he was unaware that the law had been changed.

(D) The attempted crime merged with the completed act.

90. Dingle had suspected for some time that his wife Wilma was unfaithful to him. One night when she came home later than usual, Dingle confronted her, demanding to know where she had been. Tearfully, Wilma confessed that she had been out with a male friend, and that she had sexual intercourse with him. Dingle flew into a rage, striking Wilma repeatedly about the face and head with his clenched fist. The following day, Wilma died as a result of the injuries which Dingle had inflicted. Dingle was subsequently charged with murder. At Dingle's trial, his attorney asserted that under the circumstances Dingle should not be convicted of any crime more serious than voluntary manslaughter.

Which of the following would be the prosecuting attorney's most effective argument in response to that assertion?

(A) Dingle's conduct indicated an intent to kill Wilma.

(B) Dingle's conduct indicated an intent to inflict great bodily harm on Wilma.

(C) Dingle did not catch Wilma "in flagrante delicto."

(D) In Dingle's position, a person of ordinary temperament would not have become angry enough to lose normal self-control.

91. Because of a series of early morning burglaries

which had been committed in a suburban neighborhood known as Ashurst, police officers assigned to patrol the area were instructed to stop and question all persons traveling through the neighborhood between the hours of 2 and 5 A.M. One morning at 3:30 A.M., police officer Oswald noticed Damson running along a street in the Ashurst area. Oswald pulled his patrol car against the curb and ordered Damson to stop. Damson said, "What for? Am I under arrest?"

Oswald responded, "No. I just want to talk to you." Oswald got out of the car and opened the back door, pointing his finger at the back seat. When Damson got into the back of the patrol car, Oswald said, "Now, I think you'd better tell me why you're running here at this hour."

Damson said, "I guess you already know. I just broke into a house around the corner."

Oswald arrested Damson, who was subsequently charged with burglary. At the trial, two witnesses testified that they saw Damson leaving the burglarized house shortly before his arrest. In addition, the prosecution offered the testimony of Oswald regarding his conversation with Damson in the back of the patrol car. Damson moved to exclude evidence of his statement.

Which of the following would be the prosecution's most effective argument in response to Damson's motion?

(A) Independent evidence tends to establish that Damson did commit the burglary with which he is charged.

(B) Damson was not in custody at the time of the conversation.

(C) Damson was not a suspect at the time of the conversation.

(D) Oswald's questioning of Damson was part of a routine investigation.

92. Dahle was invited to a party at the home of Hays. Because he wanted to help make the party a success, Dahle purchased fireworks and brought them to the party. A state statute requires that any

person engaging in the use of fireworks have a license and provides that the license may be issued only upon successful completion of a safety course conducted by the fire department. Although Dahle had never completed the safety course and had no license to engage in the use of fireworks, he believed that he was competent to do so without causing any danger. During the party, Dahle set off some of the fireworks in Hays' back yard. Although Dahle acted reasonably, one of them exploded prematurely, causing a fire which completely destroyed Hay's home.

If Dahle is charged with arson, he should be found

(A) guilty, because he violated the statute requiring a license for the use of fireworks.

(B) guilty, because the fire resulted from his conduct.

(C) not guilty, if Hays consented to Dahle's use of the fireworks.

(D) not guilty, because Dahle did not intend damage to Hays' home.

93. Because he was convicted of driving while intoxicated, Durwood's driving license was suspended. One day, he made a series of repairs to the engine of his car. That night, after coming home from a party, Durwood decided to test his car by driving it on State Street, a quiet residential street on the outskirts of town. Traveling north toward the intersection of State Street and Columbia Avenue, he accelerated until he was driving at a speed of 100 miles per hour. Vinson, who was driving west on Columbia Avenue, proceeded across State Street in violation of a red traffic signal light. Durwood saw Vinson's car, but because of the speed at which Durwood was traveling, was unable to avoid striking it. Vinson was killed in the collision. A statute in the jurisdiction provides, "No person shall operate a motor vehicle on any public road or highway in this state unless such person shall be the holder of a valid driving license. Violation of this section shall be punishable by a maximum of 30 days in the county jail."

If Durwood is convicted of the murder of Vinson, it will most likely be because

(A) driving while intoxicated is evidence of culpable negligence.

(B) his speed was evidence of a wanton disregard for human life.

(C) the jurisdiction applies the "misdemeanor manslaughter" rule.

(D) Vinson's death resulted from Durwood's unlicensed operation of a motor vehicle.

94. Victoria was the owner of a hardware store. When she went away on vacation, she left her assistant Askins in charge of the store. One day while Askins was alone in the store, Dennis entered and pointed a realistic-looking toy pistol at Askins, demanding all the money in the cash register. Askins believed that the pistol in Dennis's hand was real, and complied with Dennis's demand because he was afraid that if he did not Dennis would shoot him.

The following day, Victoria returned from her vacation. When Askins told her about the holdup, Victoria became so upset that she suffered a cerebral hemorrhage and died.

The jurisdiction has a statute which provides that "Any person who causes the death of another human being with the intent to cause such death or in the course of committing a dangerous felony shall be guilty of murder." If Dennis is charged with the murder of Victoria, he should be found

(A) guilty, because robbery is a dangerous felony.

(B) guilty, because it was foreseeable that the robbery would result in the death of Victoria.

(C) not guilty, because Victoria's death did not occur while Dennis was committing a dangerous felony.

(D) not guilty, because the toy pistol which Dennis used could not foreseeably have inflicted an injury upon another person.

95. In which of the following fact situations is defendant's claim of intoxication LEAST likely to be an effective defense?

(A) Charged with rape, defendant asserts that immediately before the act he drank a great deal of liquor, and that as a result he was so intoxicated that he believed the victim to be his wife.

(B) Charged with murder, defendant asserts that immediately before she shot the victim, an unknown person put alcohol in her orange juice without her knowledge, and that as a result she was so intoxicated that she believed her gun to be a harmless toy.

(C) Charged with attempted robbery, defendant asserts that at the time she pointed her pistol at the victim and demanded money she was so intoxicated that she thought the victim was a friend of hers and would know that she was joking.

(D) Charged with larceny of an automobile, defendant asserts that after injecting heroin into his bloodstream he was so intoxicated that he believed the automobile to be his own.

96. In which of the following fact situations is Defendant most likely to be convicted of criminally receiving stolen property?

(A) After Harris was arrested for car theft, the district attorney offered to let her plead guilty to a lesser offense in return for her cooperation in the apprehension of Defendant. At the district attorney's request, Harris offered to sell Defendant the car which she had been caught stealing, telling Defendant that it was stolen. Defendant agreed to purchase it for three hundred dollars, and was arrested as he handed the cash to Harris.

(B) Quincy told Defendant that the police were after him for stealing a car, and that he wanted to get rid of the car as soon as possible. When he offered to give the car to

Defendant, Defendant said, "Give it to my brother, but don't tell him it's stolen." Quincy gave the car to Defendant's brother without telling him that it was stolen.

(C) An undercover police officer contacted Defendant, saying, "Are you interested in buying stolen cars?" Defendant said, "If the price is right, I'll take all you can get." Requisitioning a car from the police department's property division, the officer showed it to Defendant, telling him that the car was stolen. Defendant agreed to purchase the car and was arrested as he handed cash to the officer.

(D) Intending to make a fraudulent claim under his automobile theft insurance policy, Baker sold his car to Defendant, telling him that the car was stolen. When Baker was subsequently arrested and charged with insurance fraud, he told the police about the circumstances of his sale to Defendant, who was then charged with receiving stolen property.

97. After observing Deacon for several weeks, police officers concluded that he was engaged in the illegal sale of PLN, a dangerous drug. Officers Axel and Barber obtained a warrant, and searched Deacon's kitchen while Deacon was present. Finding an ounce of the substance, the officers arrested Deacon and advised him of his rights. While driving to the police station, Axel said to Barber, "I'll bet Deacon has the rest of the drugs stashed somewhere. If some kids get their hands on it, it could kill them. Then we'll have the SOB on a murder rap."

Deacon, who overheard Axel's statement from the back of the police car, said, "Wait, I've got ten pounds of the stuff hidden in the tool shed behind my garage." The officers returned to Deacon's house and found the rest of the PLN in the tool shed. Deacon was charged with violating a statute which made it a felony to possess more than eight ounces of PLN. Prior to trial, Deacon moved to suppress the PLN found in his tool shed.

Which of the following additional facts or infer-

ences, if it were the only one true, would provide the prosecution with its most effective opposition to Deacon's motion?

(A) When he told the officers where to find the drugs, Deacon fully understood his Fifth Amendment right to remain silent.

(B) Axel was unaware that Deacon could overhear his conversation with Barber from the back of the police car.

(C) Deacon's statement about the location of the drugs was voluntary.

(D) The search of Deacon's kitchen and the arrest of Deacon for possession of one ounce of PLN were lawful.

98. Dander was employed as store manager by Hardware, a retailer of tools and equipment. One day, as part of her duties, Dander was rearranging merchandise in the storeroom while examining store inventory records. After moving a gasoline-powered lawnmower to a position next to the rear door inside the storeroom, Dander discovered that the lawnmower was not listed in the inventory records. Realizing that the lawnmower would, therefore, not be missed, Dander decided to steal it. She planned to take the mower out onto the loading dock behind the store just before the store closed, and from there to put the mower in her car after the store closed. Before removing it from the storeroom, however, Dander changed her mind, leaving it where she had placed it, and adding it to the store inventory list.

Of which of the following crimes may Dander be properly convicted?

(A) Larceny only.

(B) Embezzlement only.

(C) Larceny and embezzlement.

(D) Neither larceny nor embezzlement.

99. Ventana was a professional basketball player scheduled to play in an important basketball game on Sunday. On Friday, after wagering heavily on the game, Duggan attacked Ventana

with a baseball bat. Duggan's intent was to inflict injuries severe enough to require hospitalization and thus keep Ventana from playing as planned. As a result of the beating, Ventana was taken to a hospital, where he was treated by Dr. Medich. The following day, Dr. Medich injected Ventana with a medicine to relieve his pain. Because of an allergic reaction to the drug, Ventana died within minutes.

If Duggan is charged with the murder of Ventana, he should be found

(A) not guilty, because Ventana's allergic reaction to the drug was an intervening cause of death.

(B) not guilty, if Ventana's death was proximately caused by Dr. Medich's negligence.

(C) guilty, only if Ventana's death was proximately caused by Duggan's attack.

(D) guilty, unless Dr. Medich's conduct is found to be reckless or grossly negligent.

100. Delbert was charged with first degree murder under a statute which defines that crime as "the deliberate and premeditated unjustified killing of a human being." At his trial, Delbert offered the testimony of a psychiatrist who attempted to testify that Delbert had a violent temper, and that at the time of the killing, Delbert was so enraged that he was not in control of his acts.

In a jurisdiction which has adopted only the M'Naghten test of insanity, is the testimony of the psychiatrist admissible?

(A) Yes, because it tends to establish that Delbert was insane at the time of his act.

(B) Yes, because it tends to establish that the killing was not "deliberate and premeditated."

(C) No, because it does not tend to establish insanity under the M'Naghten rule.

(D) No, because in a prosecution for criminal homicide, provocation should be measured by an objective standard.

Questions 101-102 are based on the following fact situation.

Harris, a state police officer, was investigating a series of car thefts. Golden was a federal officer assigned to assist Harris under a federal statute which permits the U.S. Department of Justice to aid local police departments in investigating certain crimes. Because of Martin's criminal record, Harris went to Martin's home and questioned him regarding the recent thefts. She did not inform Golden that she was going to do so. During the course of the questioning, Harris drew her gun and threatened to shoot Martin if Martin did not immediately admit his guilt. Martin confessed to the thefts, identifying his partner as Dellaroche. Harris left Martin, saying, "I'll be back for you later." Then, after obtaining the necessary warrant, Harris arrested Dellaroche.

Unaware of Harris's activity, Golden examined a stolen vehicle which had been recovered by the state police. Golden found fingerprints in locations which indicated that they were made by a person breaking into and starting the car. Using a U.S. Department of Justice computer, Golden identified the fingerprints as Martin's. Golden obtained the necessary warrant and arrested Martin. Dellaroche and Martin were charged in a state court with car theft.

101. Assume for the purpose of this question only that Martin moves to dismiss the prosecution on the ground that his constitutional rights were violated by Harris. His motion should be

(A) granted, because Harris failed to advise him of his *Miranda* rights.

(B) granted, because Harris threatened to shoot him if he did not confess to the crimes.

(C) denied, because Golden and Harris were employed by different sovereigns.

(D) denied, because his arrest resulted from an independent investigation by Golden.

102. Assume for the purpose of this question only that Dellaroche moves to dismiss the prosecution

against him on the ground that his identification was obtained during the course of an unlawful interrogation of Martin. Which of the following would be the prosecution's most effective argument in opposition to Dellaroche's motion?

(A) The discovery of Dellaroche's identity was inevitable.

(B) The discovery of Dellaroche's identity was the result of an independent investigation which purged any taint resulting from the illegality of the interrogation of Martin.

(C) The interrogation of Martin did not violate Dellaroche's constitutional rights.

(D) Dellaroche was not in custody at the time of Martin's interrogation.

Questions 103-105 are based on the following fact situation.

Michael and Norman were roommates at college. Michael heard of someone in a nearby town who bought stolen cars. Because they needed money to pay their rent, Michael proposed to Norman that they steal a car and sell it. Norman agreed, and the two of them went out immediately looking for a car to steal. When they found a late-model convertible parked at the curb, Michael slipped a wire coat hanger under the convertible top and used it to open the door. Then Michael short-circuited the wires under the car's dashboard so that he could start it without a key. Michael got behind the wheel and drove the car while Norman sat beside him. Later, because he felt drowsy, Norman climbed into the back seat and went to sleep.

While Norman was sleeping, Michael thought that he noticed a police car following them. Hoping to avoid contact with the police, he turned off onto a road which led into a neighboring state. Shortly after crossing the state line, Michael and Norman were arrested by federal police. They were subsequently charged in a federal court with violating the Dyer Act, which makes the interstate transportation of stolen vehicles a federal crime, and with conspiracy to violate the Dyer Act.

103. On the charge of violating the Dyer Act, Norman should be found

(A) not guilty, if he could not have anticipated that Michael would drive the car across the state line.

(B) not guilty, if he did not agree to transport the car across a state line.

(C) not guilty, if transportation of the car across the state line was not necessary to the success of the criminal enterprise.

(D) guilty.

104. On the charge of conspiracy to violate the Dyer Act, Norman should be found

(A) guilty, because he agreed to steal the car.

(B) not guilty, if he is convicted of violating the Dyer Act.

(C) not guilty, if he did not agree to transport the vehicle across a state line.

(D) not guilty, because he did not actually participate in the transportation of a stolen vehicle across a state line.

105. Assume for the purpose of this question only that Norman is charged in a state court with larceny for the theft of the car. He should be found

(A) not guilty, unless he is guilty of conspiracy to commit larceny.

(B) guilty, if he was willing to help Michael start the car if necessary.

(C) not guilty, since he did not aid or abet Norman in starting or driving the car.

(D) guilty, unless he is convicted in a federal court of any crime arising from the incident.

Questions 106-107.

Read the summaries of the decisions in the four cases (A-D) below. Then decide which is most applicable as a precedent to each of the cases in the questions that follow, and indicate each choice by marking the corresponding space on the answer sheet.

(A) *People v. Ascot* — After hearing gunshots, police officer Oswald ran toward the sound. Finding Vaca lying dead in a pool of blood, Oswald asked a group of persons who were standing nearby what happened. Ascot, who was among the bystanders, replied, "I shot the son of a bitch." At Ascot's murder trial, the court denied a motion to exclude Oswald's testimony regarding Ascot's statement.

(B) *State v. Binh* — Binh, a recently arrived immigrant from Southeast Asia, was arrested for burglary. After the arresting officer read him his *Miranda* rights, she asked, "Do you understand what I just said?" Binh replied, "Yes, I break in the house for steal." Binh's pretrial motion to exclude evidence of his confession was granted.

(C) *Commonwealth v. Cartier* — Following a series of assaults, police officers went to Cartier's home. The officers told Cartier that she was not under arrest, but that they would appreciate her cooperation in answering their questions. Cartier said, "I'm innocent, and I'm willing to prove it by standing in a lineup." She then accompanied the police officers to the police station where two assault victims picked her out of a lineup. At Cartier's trial on a charge of assault, her motion to exclude evidence of the lineup identification was denied.

(D) *People v. Edwards* — When Edwards was awakened at 3 a.m. by the sound of knocking on his front door, he opened it to find three uniformed police officers. One of them said, "We have reason to believe that there is stolen property in your house. Do you mind if we search?" Edwards let the officers in. During the course of their search they seized a stereo set which had been stolen from a local appliance store. At his trial for criminally receiving stolen property, Edwards's motion to suppress use of the stereo as evidence was granted.

106. Doyle, an attorney, was vice president of PJ Corp, a manufacturer of children's pajamas. After several children were burned to death while wearing PJ Corp's product, both Doyle and the corporation were charged with criminal negligence. After placing Doyle under arrest and informing her of the charge against her, the arresting officer said, "Now your answers may be used against you so you don't have to give any, and you're entitled to an attorney." Doyle said, "I am an attorney," and answered questions which the officer then put to her regarding her corporate duties. At her trial, Doyle moved to exclude evidence of her answers to those questions, although she conceded that her statement was not coerced.

107. After being indicted for violations of a state anti-racketeering statute, Degnan was placed under arrest and brought to the police station where a police officer asked him to appear in a lineup. The officer advised him that he was entitled to have an attorney present during the lineup, but said that if Degnan did not insist on calling his lawyer first, the officer would ask the prosecutor "to go easy on" him. Degnan agreed to participate without contacting a lawyer. At his trial, Degnan moved to exclude the testimony of a witness who identified him at the lineup.

108. After Carpenter was arrested for selling large quantities of illegal substances, he agreed to assist the police in return for a promise that the charges against him would be reduced. In furtherance of their agreement, the police set Carpenter up in the used car business and spread the rumor that Carpenter dealt in stolen vehicles. Subsequently, Tanner came to Carpenter's lot offering to sell Carpenter a stolen car. After conferring with a police officer assigned to the investigation, Carpenter purchased the car from Tanner. When he had done so, the police arrested Tanner and notified the car's owner that it had been recovered. The following day, Dee came to Carpenter's lot and said that he wished to purchase a stolen car. At the direction of an undercover police officer, Carpenter sold Dee the car which he had purchased from Tanner.

If Dee is charged with receiving stolen property, which of the following would be his most effective argument in defense?

(A) Dee was entrapped by an agent of the police.

(B) The car which Dee purchased was not stolen property.

(C) Carpenter's cooperation with the police was coerced.

(D) The police can not bargain away a defendant's rights in an agreement with a third person.

109. Mike and Wanda had been living together and sharing a bedroom for five months, when they began arguing regularly. After one such argument, Mike stormed out of the apartment. Angry at him, Wanda called the police to report that Mike was in possession of nearly a kilogram of marijuana. Two officers came to talk to Wanda in the apartment. When they asked how she knew that Mike had that much marijuana, Wanda said, "I've seen it. Mike keeps it in our closet. Would you like to look?" One of the officers said that they would, and Wanda led them to the closet in the bedroom which she shared with Mike. When Wanda opened the closet door, a plastic bag containing one and one-half pounds of marijuana fell from the shelf. One of the officers took it. Later, Mike was arrested and charged with the unlawful possession of a dangerous drug. If Mike makes a timely motion to suppress use of the marijuana as evidence, which of the following would be the prosecution's most effective argument in opposition to his motion?

(A) Their conversation with Wanda gave the police officers probable cause to believe that there was marijuana in the closet.

(B) Failure to seize the marijuana immediately might have given Mike time to dispose of it before the police officers could obtain a search warrant.

(C) Wanda invited the police officers to search the closet.

(D) The marijuana was in plain view when the closet door was opened.

110. Dobbs was waiting for a bus on a street corner shortly after midnight when three young men approached him and demanded that he give them some money. Fearing that they would attack and injure him, Dobbs drew a pistol from his pocket. The three men began running away, but Dobbs shot each of them in the back, seriously injuring two and killing the third. As a result, Dobbs was charged with two counts of aggravated assault and one count of murder. By the time a grand jury was convened, the incident had received a great deal of media attention, several newspapers referring to Dobbs as "The Vigilante Hero." Dobbs presented no evidence to the grand jury, but after hearing the prosecution's evidence, the grand jury refused to indict. Following the proceeding, the prosecuting attorney stated that she believed that the grand jury's decision resulted from publicity surrounding the incident, and that she intended to bring the matter before another grand jury. Three weeks later, a second grand jury issued an indictment against Dobbs. If Dobbs moves to dismiss the indictment on the ground that it violates his rights under the Double Jeopardy Clause of the United States Constitution, his motion should be

(A) granted, because the first grand jury's failure to indict is res judicata.

(B) granted, if the charges brought before the second grand jury were identical to the charges brought before the first grand jury.

(C) denied, unless the decision of the first grand jury was motivated by sympathy or undue prejudice.

(D) denied, because no trial has begun.

Questions 111-112 are based on the following fact situation.

Deborah, who was a law student, was attempting to study for her final examinations. She was having difficulty concentrating because the people in the apartment above hers were having a loud party, and Deborah found the noise distracting. She telephoned, asking her neighbors to stop making so much noise, but they refused to do so. Finally, Deborah fired a pistol through the ceiling of her apartment. She did not intend to hit anyone with the bullet, but hoped that the shot would frighten her neighbors and chill the atmosphere. After passing through the floor of the apartment above Deborah's, the bullet struck a piece of furniture and ricocheted. It struck Vincent, lodging in his shoulder and injuring him.

111. Assume for the purpose of this question only that an ambulance was called to transport Vincent to a hospital for treatment, and that, because the ambulance driver was driving negligently, the ambulance was involved in a collision which resulted in Vincent's death. If Deborah is acquitted on a charge of murdering Vincent, it will most likely be because the court finds that

   (A) Deborah did not intend to strike anyone with the bullet.

   (B) Vincent's death was proximately caused by the negligence of the ambulance driver.

   (C) Deborah was privileged to abate a nuisance by self-help.

   (D) Deborah's conduct did not show a wanton disregard for human life.

112. Assume for the purpose of this question only that Vincent did not die. Which of the following is the most serious crime of which Deborah may be properly convicted?

   (A) Battery.

   (B) Attempted involuntary manslaughter.

   (C) Attempted voluntary manslaughter.

   (D) Attempted murder.

Questions 113-114 are based on the following fact situation.

Alice and Bonnie were roommates until they began arguing bitterly. During one argument, Alice moved out of the apartment which they shared. As she left, she said, "I'm going to get even with you for all the grief you've caused me." The following day, Bonnie's friend Frieda told Bonnie that Alice had purchased a gun. Frieda also said that Alice told her that she was going to shoot Bonnie the next time she saw her. As a result, Bonnie began carrying a loaded pistol. Several days later, realizing that she still had the key to Bonnie's apartment, Alice went back to return it. Bonnie was leaving her apartment when she saw Alice walking toward her. As Alice reached into her pocket for the apartment key, Bonnie drew her pistol and shot Alice, aiming to hit her in the chest. The bullet grazed Alice's shoulder, inflicting a minor injury. Alice immediately drew her own pistol and shot Bonnie with it, striking her in the thigh, and inflicting a serious injury.

113. If Bonnie is charged with attempted murder, which of the following would be her most effective argument in defense?

   (A) Alice's injury was not serious enough to result in death.

   (B) Bonnie did not succeed in striking Alice in the chest as she intended.

   (C) It was reasonable for Bonnie to believe that Alice was reaching into her pocket for a gun.

   (D) The force which Bonnie used was not deadly.

114. Assume that Alice is charged with attempted murder. If Alice asserts the privilege of self-defense, she will most probably be found

   (A) guilty, if it was reasonable for Bonnie to believe that Alice was reaching into her pocket for a gun.

   (B) guilty, because Alice's injury was not serious enough to result in death.

   (C) guilty, because the fact that Alice was carrying a pistol is evidence of premeditation.

   (D) not guilty.

Questions 115-116 are based on the following fact situation.

Sal and Terry were members of a militant political group known as the Environmental Protection Army. As a protest against the use of harmful agricultural chemicals, they planned to burn down a factory which produced such chemicals. To be certain that no persons would be injured in the explosion, they chose a time when they knew that the factory was closed. At 10 p.m. they broke into the factory and wired a fire bomb to a timer which was set to detonate at 11 p.m. At 10:45 p.m., they telephoned the local police and told them that the factory would be bombed in 15 minutes, warning them to evacuate any persons who might happen to be in the area. At 11 p.m. the bomb detonated, causing flames which totally destroyed the factory. Two transients who had broken into the factory at 10:30 p.m. in search of a place to sleep were killed by the blast.

115. If Sal and Terry are charged with murder, they should be found

    (A) not guilty, because they did not desire or know that their act would result in the death of a human being.

    (B) not guilty, because the deaths of the transients were totally independent of their purpose in blowing up the factory.

    (C) guilty, because it was not reasonable to believe that the police could successfully evacuate the area in fifteen minutes.

    (D) guilty, because the deaths resulted from their commission of a dangerous felony.

116. Assume for the purpose of this question only that the jurisdiction had a statute which extends the common law definition of arson to buildings other than dwellings. Of which of the following crimes may Sal and Terry be properly convicted?

    I. Arson.

    II. Conspiracy.

    (A) I only.

    (B) II only.

    (C) I or II, but not both.

    (D) I and II.

117. There were three employees and three customers in the Smalltown Bank when Dart entered and drew a pistol from his pocket. Waving the pistol in the air, Dart shouted, "Freeze. This is a holdup." Threatening to shoot him if he did not obey, Dart ordered one of the tellers to open the vault. After the teller had done so, Dart directed everyone present to lie down on the floor. Dart then removed all the cash from the vault and left the bank, forcing one of the customers at gunpoint to accompany him into his car as a hostage. After driving for about fifteen minutes, Dart opened the car door and permitted the hostage to get out.

Of how many kidnappings may Dart properly be convicted?

    (A) 0.

    (B) 1.

    (C) 2.

    (D) 6.

Questions 118-120 are based on the following fact situation.

Agsten and Bates, who were undercover police officers, received an anonymous tip that Dake was engaged in buying and selling stolen cars. They decided to catch Dake by pretending to be criminals. Bates arranged to meet Dake, telling Dake that his friend Agsten was looking for a buyer for stolen cars. When Dake said that he might be interested in purchasing one for resale, Bates offered to put up half the money and to buy it with him as a partner. Dake agreed, and Bates gave him $1,000 in cash as his share. Bates had requisitioned the money from the police department for that purpose and had it marked in a way which would permit its subsequent identification. Bates then introduced Dake to Agsten, saying that Agsten was a car thief. Agsten offered to sell Dake a car which he said he had stolen, but which he had actually requisitioned from the police department for that purpose. After agreeing on a price for the car, Dake paid Agsten with the marked money which Bates had given him. Agsten immediately placed Dake under arrest.

118. Assume for the purpose of this question only that Dake is charged with criminally receiving stolen property. Which of the following would be his most effective argument in defense against that charge?

(A) The car which Dake purchased from Agsten had been requisitioned from the police department.

(B) The money which Dake used to purchase the car from Dake had been requisitioned from the police department.

(C) Bates and Agsten entrapped Dake into purchasing the car.

(D) The anonymous tip received by Bates and Agsten was not sufficient to give them probable cause to believe that Dake was guilty of a crime.

119. Assume for the purpose of this question only that Dake is charged with attempting to criminally receive stolen property. The court should find him

(A) guilty, if he is convicted of criminally receiving stolen property.

(B) guilty, only if he is not convicted of criminally receiving stolen property.

(C) not guilty, because he was operating under a mistake of law at the time he agreed to purchase the car from Agsten.

(D) not guilty, because he was operating under a mistake of fact at the time he agreed to purchase the car from Agsten.

120. Assume for the purpose of this question only that Dake is charged with conspiracy to criminally receive stolen property. The court should find him

(A) guilty.

(B) guilty, unless he is convicted of attempting to criminally receive stolen property.

(C) not guilty, because neither Agsten nor Bates

actually intended to participate in the purchase or sale of a stolen vehicle.

(D) not guilty, because the car which he agreed to purchase from Agsten was not actually stolen.

Questions 121-122 are based on the following fact situation.

Four weeks after breaking her engagement with Goss, Dealy was angry because Goss still had not returned a stereo set which he borrowed from her. She went to his house one night to demand its immediate return. When she got there, Goss was not at home and his door was unlocked. Dealy entered to look for her stereo, but could not find it. While searching, she noticed that Goss had a new couch. Thinking that the couch was worth as much as her stereo, she tore open one of its cushions and set it on fire before leaving. The fire destroyed the couch completely, and charred the walls and ceiling of the room, although the house itself was not seriously damaged. Dealy was subsequently prosecuted. Statutes in the jurisdiction adopt the common law definitions of burglary, larceny, and arson.

121. If Dealy is charged with burglary and arson, she can properly be convicted of

(A) burglary only.

(B) arson only.

(C) burglary and arson.

(D) neither burglary nor arson.

122. If Dealy is charged with larceny as a result of the destruction of the couch, which of the following would be her most effective defense against that charge?

(A) Goss' door was unlocked when she entered.

(B) She believed the couch to be equal in value to her stereo set.

(C) She did not physically move the couch.

(D) She did not intend to benefit from the destruction of the couch.

123. After being arrested and charged with bribery, Dalke spent one night in a detention cell at the county jail. Cecil, who had been arrested on a charge unrelated to Dalke's case, was assigned to the same detention cell as Dalke. The following morning, Dalke and Cecil were released on bail. Leaving the jail together, they stopped for breakfast and chatted about the charges against them. During the course of their conversation, Dalke told Cecil that he was in fact guilty of bribery, and that he had paid unlawful fees to several public officials. At Dalke's trial, Cecil was called as a prosecution witness. Cecil stated that he spoke to Dalke about the bribery case because the police had offered to drop charges against him in return for help in getting evidence against Dalke. Cecil then attempted to testify to the conversation in which Dalke admitted his guilt. If Dalke's attorney objected and moved to exclude the testimony on the ground that Dalke was not warned that anything he said to Cecil might be used against him, should Cecil's testimony regarding Dalke's admission of guilt be excluded on that ground?

    (A) Yes, if the police asked for Cecil's help before putting him in a cell with Dalke.

    (B) Yes, because at the time of Cecil's conversation with Dalke, Cecil was acting as an agent of the police.

    (C) No, because the prosecution may not bargain away the rights of one defendant in a deal with another.

    (D) No, if Dalke was not in police custody when he admitted his guilt to Cecil.

124. As a result of mental illness, Dominguez was obsessed with the delusion that his wife Viola was building a bomb in the basement of their house, and that she was going to use it to blow up the world. Because he twice tried to kill Viola, he had been confined to a state mental hospital on two occasions. After his most recent release from confinement, Dominguez discussed his belief with the police, but they did not take him seriously. Although he knew that he would be imprisoned for murder if he was caught, he pushed Viola down a flight of stairs, thinking that he would save the world by killing her. Viola died of

injuries which she sustained in the fall.

If Dominguez is prosecuted for the murder of Viola, his most effective argument in defense would be that as a result of mental illness,

    (A) he did not know that his act was wrong.

    (B) he lacked criminal intent.

    (C) he was unable to control his conduct.

    (D) he did not appreciate the nature and quality of his act.

125. Thomas, a teacher at a privately operated high school, found an anonymous note on his desk stating that the writer had heard through the grapevine that Donell, one of Thomas' students, was unlawfully selling drugs to other students. Thomas immediately showed the note to the school administrator, Adams, who ordered Donell to report to her office. When Donell did so, Adams reached into Donell's trouser pocket where she found 23 capsules containing drugs. Donell was subsequently prosecuted for unlawful possession of a controlled substance. In an appropriate proceeding, Donell moved to suppress evidence of the capsules found by Adams on the ground that she had violated his Fourth Amendment rights by searching him.

Which of the following is the most effective argument in opposition to Donell's motion?

    (A) Adams was not working for the government.

    (B) The special relationship between a high school administrator and a student implies the student's consent to a search by the administrator.

    (C) Special concern for the well-being of young people justifies a warrantless search of a student suspected of selling drugs to other students.

    (D) Adams had probable cause to believe that Donell was in possession of dangerous drugs.

Questions 126-127 are based on the following fact situation.

Okner was the owner of a department store. One day, Okner asked Shafer, who was employed in the store's shoe department, to temporarily replace a sporting goods salesman who did not show up for work. Yule, who was 15 years of age, subsequently entered the sporting goods department and asked Shafer to sell her ammunition for a pistol. Shafer placed a box of ammunition on the counter and said, "That'll be nine dollars, please." Realizing that she did not have any money with her, Yule left the store without the ammunition, saying that she would return for it later. A statute in the jurisdiction provides as follows: "Any person who sells ammunition for a firearm to a person below the age of 16 years shall be guilty of a felony. The employer of any person who violates this section during the course of such employment shall be guilty of a misdemeanor punishable by a fine not to exceed $250. It shall not be a defense to a violation of this section that the defendant had no knowledge of the age of the person to whom the sale was made."

126. Assume for the purpose of this question only that Yule did not return to the store. If Shafer is charged with attempting to violate the above statute, which of the following would be Shafer's most effective argument in defense against that charge?

(A) Shafer did not know of the statute or its provisions.

(B) Shafer did not know that Yule was below the age of 16 years.

(C) Okner should be prosecuted under the statute, since she was Shafer's employer.

(D) Shafer is customarily employed in the shoe department, and should not be held to the same standard as a person in the business of selling firearms and ammunition.

127. Assume for the purpose of this question only that Yule subsequently returned to the store with money and that Shafer sold her the ammunition. If Okner is prosecuted under the statute, Okner should be found

(A) guilty, because her employee sold ammunition to a person under the age of 16 years.

(B) guilty, only if it was unreasonable for Okner to assign Shafer to the sporting goods department without properly instructing him regarding the statute.

(C) not guilty, unless Okner was present when Shafer made the sale to Yule.

(D) not guilty, because holding one person vicariously liable for the crime of another violates the constitutional right to due process of law.

128. DeLong and Verona had hated each other for years. One day, DeLong waited outside Verona's office building with a loaded pistol, planning to kill Verona. When DeLong saw Ralston leave the building, she believed Ralston was Verona and shot at her, aiming to kill her. Ralston was struck by the bullet, and died of the bullet wound. If DeLong is charged with Ralston's murder in a jurisdiction which applies the common law definition, DeLong should be found

(A) guilty, but only if the jurisdiction applies the doctrine of transferred intent.

(B) guilty, because DeLong intended to bring about the death of the person at whom she shot.

(C) not guilty.

(D) guilty, because DeLong created an unreasonable risk that a human being would die.

129. Federal agents arrested Delta and others in the state of Columbus pursuant to a warrant issued by a federal court. At the time of the arrest, federal officers seized one quarter ounce of heroin which was in Delta's possession. As a result, Delta was convicted of violating a federal statute which prohibits the possession of heroin with the intent to engage in interstate distribution thereof. Following her conviction in the federal court, federal officials offered to permit the state of Columbus to use the seized heroin as evidence in a state prosecution of Delta. Delta was subsequently charged in a state court with conspiracy to sell a controlled substance in violation of a state of

Columbus statute. If Delta moves to dismiss the state prosecution on the sole ground that it violates her rights under the double jeopardy clause of the United States Constitution, her motion should be

(A) granted, if the same evidence that was used to convict her in the federal prosecution will be used to convict her in the state prosecution.

(B) granted, because the crime of conspiracy is a lesser offense which was constructively included in the federal prosecution.

(C) denied, because she is being charged in the state of Columbus court with the violation of a different statute than that which she was convicted of violating in the federal court.

(D) granted, because a person may not be prosecuted by different sovereigns for the same offense.

130. After Dane entered a tavern and sat on a stool at the bar, a friend sitting beside him said, "Did you ever have a Russian bomber?" Dane ordered one, although he had never heard of a Russian bomber. Although he realized that it had some alcohol in it, he was unaware that it was 90% alcohol. When the bartender placed the drink in front of Dane, Dane drank it quickly. A few moments later, Dane fell off his bar stool because he was overcome by the alcohol in the Russian bomber which he had drunk. He fell against an elderly man named Thatcher, knocking him against the wall and causing Thatcher to fracture several ribs. If Dane is charged with committing a criminal battery against Thatcher, which of the following additional facts or inferences, if it was the only one true, would provide Dane with his most effective argument in defense?

(A) Dane did not intend to become intoxicated by drinking the Russian bomber.

(B) Dane did not know that drinking the Russian bomber would cause him to fall off the bar stool.

(C) Dane did not intend to make contact with Thatcher.

(D) Dane had never before been overcome by the alcohol in one drink.

Questions 131-132 are based on the following fact situation.

Balin was the owner of a tavern. On two occasions in the recent past, thieves entered Balin's tavern after closing time and stole several thousand dollars worth of liquor. In an attempt to protect himself against further thefts, Balin began sleeping in the tavern at night with a loaded pistol by his side. Oden was a police officer assigned to patrol the street on which Balin's tavern was located. One night while on his rounds, Oden noticed that one of Balin's windows was open and climbed through the window to investigate. Hearing the sound of someone moving about his tavern, Balin stood up and cocked his pistol. When Oden heard the sound and saw the outline of a person standing by the bar with a pistol in his hand, Oden shouted, "Drop that gun or I'll shoot." Balin and Oden fired their pistols at each other. Each was struck by the other's bullet.

131. If Balin is charged with attempted murder because of his shooting of Oden, the court should find him

(A) not guilty, if Balin reasonably believed that his life was in danger.

(B) guilty, because deadly force is not permitted in defense of property.

(C) guilty, because the intent to kill or inflict great bodily harm can be inferred from Balin's conduct.

(D) guilty, because at the time of the shooting Oden was a police officer acting within the scope of his official duties as such.

132. If Oden is charged with attempted murder because of his shooting of Balin, his most effective defense would be that

(A) at the time of the shooting, Oden was a police officer acting within the scope of his official duties as such.

(B) the circumstances gave Oden probable cause to believe that a crime was in progress in

Balin's tavern.

(C) deadly force may be used by a police officer who reasonably believes that his life is in danger.

(D) it was unreasonable for Balin to fire without taking steps to determine the identity of the person at whom he was firing.

Questions 133-134 are based on the following fact situation.

Dailey and Reavis had been in the same cell together while serving time in prison. Soon after their release, Reavis asked Dailey to join with him in robbing a bank. Dailey refused, stating that he did not want to go back to prison. Reavis then said that he would rob the bank himself if Dailey would provide him with a place to hide afterwards. Dailey agreed that Reavis could hide in Dailey's apartment following the robbery in return for one fourth of the proceeds of the robbery. The following day, Reavis robbed the bank. While he was attempting to leave the bank, a security guard began shooting at him, and Reavis fired back, killing a bystander. One week later, Reavis was arrested at Dailey's apartment where he had been hiding, and was charged with robbery and felony murder.

133. Assume for the purpose of this question only that Daily was subsequently charged with felony murder on the ground that he was an accomplice to the robbery committed by Reavis which resulted in the death of a bystander. The court should find Dailey

(A) not guilty, because he was an accessory after the fact.

(B) not guilty, if he did not know that Reavis was going to use deadly force to accomplish the robbery.

(C) guilty, only if it was foreseeable that someone would be shot during the course of the robbery.

(D) guilty, because an accomplice is responsible for all crimes committed in furtherance of the crime to which he is an accomplice.

134. Assume for the purpose of this question only that Dailey was charged with conspiracy to commit robbery. The court should find Dailey

(A) not guilty, because he did not agree to participate in the actual perpetration of the robbery.

(B) not guilty, because Dailey's agreement to permit Reavis to stay at his apartment following the robbery was not per se unlawful.

(C) guilty, because he was an accessory to the robbery.

(D) guilty, because he agreed to furnish Reavis with a place to hide in return for a portion of the proceeds of the robbery.

Questions 135-136 are based on the following fact situation.

After being advised by an informant that Dage was growing marijuana in a large field, two police officers flew over the field in an airplane and observed marijuana growing there. Because of particularly dense cloud formations, it was necessary for them to use special equipment to photograph the field. The following day, the officers drove to the field and looked through the barbed wire fence which surrounded it. Although nothing was growing in the field, they observed that something had recently been harvested. They also observed a series of footprints leading to a barn located in the field. After obtaining a search warrant, the officers entered the field and searched the barn, where they found two suitcases containing marijuana.

The officers arrested Dage and advised him of his *Miranda* rights. Dage asked to have his attorney present and telephoned her office, leaving a message that he had been arrested. When the attorney received the message, she telephoned the county sheriff, asking where Dage was being held. The sheriff said that he did not know. As a result, it took the attorney several hours to find Dage. While waiting for the attorney, one of the officers said to Dage, "Why don't you tell us about it?" whereupon dage admitted growing the marijuana. Dage was subsequently charged with violating a state law which prohibits growing marijuana.

135. Assume for the purpose of this question only that Dage's attorney made an appropriate motion to exclude the marijuana contained in the suitcases. Should the evidence be excluded?

    (A) Yes, because the police used special equipment to photograph the field.

    (B) No, if the reliability of the informant can be established.

    (C) Yes, if it was reasonable for Dage to believe that nobody would look into his field.

    (D) No, because the officers had a warrant to search the barn.

136. Assume for the purpose of this question only that Dage's attorney made an appropriate motion to prevent the use of Dage's statement as evidence against him. The motion should be

    (A) granted, because Dage asserted his right to have an attorney present.

    (B) granted, only if the sheriff actually knew Dage's whereabouts when he said that he did not.

    (D) denied, if the sheriff actually did not know Dage's whereabouts when he said that he did not.

    (D) denied, because Dage waived his right to remain silent when he admitted growing the marijuana.

137. A statute prohibited the sale of liquor between the hours of midnight and 8 A.M. When a customer came into Donohue's liquor store and asked to buy a bottle of liquor, Donohue looked at the clock and saw that it said five minutes past eleven, so he sold the liquor to the customer. Donohue believed that the clock was correct and did not realize that the previous day the state had changed from standard time to daylight savings time. In fact, the correct time was five minutes past midnight.

    If Donohue is charged with attempting to violate the statute, he should be found

    (A) guilty, because he sold liquor between midnight and 8 A.M.

    (B) guilty, if he should have known the actual time.

    (C) not guilty, unless the statute did not require specific intent.

    (D) not guilty, because he believed that the time was five minutes past eleven.

138. Vinton borrowed fifty dollars and a watch worth an additional fifty dollars from Dover. Although Dover repeatedly requested that Vinton return the watch and the money, Vinton refused to do so. Dover and Vinton belonged to the same exercise club. One day while Vinton was in the shower, Dover opened Vinton's locker and took $100 from Vinton's wallet, returning the wallet to the locker. It was Dover's intention to keep $50 of the money to pay himself back for the money he had loaned Vinton, and to keep the other $50 to pay himself for the watch which Vinton had refused to return. A statute in the jurisdiction adopts the common law definition of larceny and provides that a larceny of $50 or less is a misdemeanor while a larceny of more than $50 is a felony. Dover is guilty of

    (A) one misdemeanor only.

    (B) two misdemeanors only.

    (C) a felony.

    (D) no crime.

139. In which of the following cases is a charge of murder most likely to be reduced to a charge of voluntary manslaughter?

    (A) People in a neighboring apartment were having a noisy party. Intending to frighten them so that they would stop making so much noise, Defendant knocked on the door of the apartment where the party was being held and, when the door was opened, fired a pistol into the room. Defendant did not intend to strike anyone, but the bullet struck a person, killing her.

(B) After repairing the transmission of his auto-mobile, Defendant drove the automobile on a street in a residential neighborhood at a speed of 110 miles per hour to test the transmission. The vehicle struck a child, killing him.

(C) After learning that Victor had raped Defendant's daughter, Defendant shot Victor with the intention of killing him. Victor died as a result of the bullet wound.

(D) After stealing a car, Defendant robbed a bank and was driving the stolen car away from the robbery in a reasonable manner when he collided with a pedestrian who was jaywalking. The pedestrian was killed by the impact.

140. Joe, Al and Bob met while in prison and decided that when they were released they would rob a bank together. Soon after their release, they planned the robbery, agreeing that Al would steal and drive the getaway car and that Joe and Bob would commit the actual robbery. Al stole a car for the robbery and brought it to Joe's house, but the day before the robbery was to be committed, Al was arrested for violating the conditions of his parole and was returned to prison. The following day, Joe and Bob went ahead with the plan, entering the bank and threatening to shoot the cashiers if they did not hand over all available cash. A teller pushed a button which alerted the police, and Joe and Bob were arrested before leaving the bank.

Of which of the following crimes is Al guilty?

I. Attempted robbery.

II. Conspiracy to commit robbery.

(A) I only.

(B) II only.

(C) I and II.

(D) II or II, but not both.

ANSWERS
CRIMINAL LAW

ANSWERS TO
CRIMINAL LAW QUESTIONS

1. **D**   An officer executing a warrant for the search of premises is limited to a search of the place described in the warrant. A misidentification will invalidate the search unless the officer could not mistake the place to be searched. The officer executing the warrant could not have been certain whether it was a tavern known as the Second Bedroom (which was located on Main Street) or for premises known as the Second Bedroom and located at 481 Chambers Street (but which contained a furniture store rather than a tavern). It may, therefore, be successfully argued that the warrant did not properly identify the defendant's premises, and the search was invalid. While it is not certain that a court would come to this conclusion, **D** is the only argument listed which could possibly support the motion to suppress.

   A is incorrect because an affidavit submitted to establish probable cause may be based entirely on hearsay. If it establishes the credibility of the informant and the reliability of his information, it may serve as the basis for the warrant, even though it does not name the informant. **B** is incorrect because the affidavit indicated that the informant had given information in the past which had always proved to be accurate (thus establishing his credibility), and that he had observed the activities himself (thus establishing the reliability of his information). Even without establishing credibility and reliability, an affidavit which fails to identify the informant could support the issuance of a warrant if the information which it contains is corroborated by other independent evidence. **C** is incorrect, however, because if credibility and reliability are established, corroboration is unnecessary.

2. **B**   A warrant authorizing the search of persons must clearly identify the particular persons to be searched, although it is not necessary that they be identified by name. This warrant identified them in terms of a fact which could not be determined until they had been searched, however (i.e., "all persons … who are found to be in possession of unlawful gambling records"). It therefore lacked the required particularity. If there was probable cause to arrest a person, a search performed incident to that arrest would be valid. While it is uncertain whether a court would find that there was probable cause to arrest Darryl, **B** is the only answer listed which could possibly be correct.

   Probable cause means that facts are known which would lead the reasonable person to believe that a crime was being committed. If the reasonable person would believe that gambling activities were being conducted in the tavern, he would certainly be justified in believing that some of the people present were engaging in them. **A** is, therefore incorrect. Although a warrant which authorizes the search of premises may also authorize search of persons present on said premises, **C** is incorrect because this warrant does not identify the people to be searched with sufficient particularity. **D** is, incorrect because if corroboration is required, it must exist prior to the issuance of the warrant, not after its execution.

3. **D**   A police officer who has probable cause to believe that the defendant is in the process of committing a crime may arrest the defendant without a warrant. Upon making a lawful arrest, the police officer may search the defendant's person and packages within the

defendant's control to prevent the loss of evidence and to protect the officer.

A is incorrect because if probable cause existed, the arrest was lawful even without a warrant. Some courts have held that one who ships baggage on an airline has no reasonable expectation of privacy with respect to the contents of the baggage; other courts hold that sniffing of baggage by a dog does not violate the reasonable expectation of privacy because it is non-intrusive. Either way, most agree that such an inspection is not an unreasonable search. **B** is, therefore incorrect. Since the dog sniffed the baggage after the plane had landed, and since it was sniffing for marijuana rather than weapons, **C** is a non sequitur, and, therefore, is incorrect.

4. **B**   Rape is a "general intent" crime, which means that a conviction may be had even though the defendant did not intend to engage in intercourse without the female's consent if he acted recklessly or was criminally negligent in determining whether or not she consented. It is necessary, however, that the defendant intend to engage in intercourse. If Donnel did not intend to have intercourse, he cannot be convicted.

   A is incorrect because it may have been reckless or criminally negligent for Donnel to believe that Vera consented. Since Vera initially attempted to resist Donnel's advances, it may be found that the intercourse was without her consent even though she was so drunk that she was unaware that it took place or unaware of Donnel's identity. **C** and **D** are, therefore, incorrect. **C** is also incorrect since most courts agree that sexual intercourse with a woman lacks the capacity to consent because she is unconscious or intoxicated is without her consent and, therefore, is rape. In addition, **D** is, incorrect because a rape takes place when penetration occurs without consent, and is not undone if the victim subsequently consents.

5. **D**   Some courts say that statutory rape is a strict liability crime, requiring no intent at all; other courts say that it is a general intent crime requiring only the intent to have sexual intercourse. Under either view, this means that a defendant who has sexual intercourse with a female who is too young to consent is guilty if he was aware that he was engaging in intercourse. This is so even though he did not know that she was underage, even though the reasonable person would not have known it, and even though she told him that she was over the age of consent.

   A,B and **C** are, therefore incorrect.

6. **B**   Although a warrantless search is usually invalid, it may be valid if consented to by one with authority to consent. Since a guest in a hotel is entitled to exclusive possession of the room which he occupies, the hotel keeper does not have the power to consent to the search of a guest's room, even if the guest is overdue in his payments. The motion in **B** would probably be granted for this reason.

   On the other hand, the owner of an automobile does have the power to consent to a search of it, so the motion in **A** would fail. After a defendant's automobile has been impounded by the police, they have the right to search it for the purpose of making an inventory of its contents. Although the reason for the inventory search is to protect the police against possible subsequent claims that contents of the impounded vehicle were taken or converted while the vehicle was in police custody, evidence which is incidentally discovered during the course of such a search is admissible against the defendant. The motion in **C** would, therefore, fail. In **D**, the search did not take place until the defendant was placed under arrest. A search of the defendant's person conducted incidentally to a lawful arrest is not a violation of his Fourth Amendment right to be secure against unreasonable search and seizure, so the motion in **D** would fail.

7. **D**   Larceny is defined as a trespassory taking and carrying off of personal property known to be another's with the intent to permanently deprive the owner thereof. A taking is trespassory if it violates the rights of the owner. Since the coat was Charlie's and since Charlie told Julie to take it, the taking did not violate Charlie's rights and was, therefore, not trespassory. **A** and **C** are, therefore, incorrect.

A criminal conspiracy is committed when two or more persons with the specific intent to commit a crime agree to commit that crime. Since Charlie knew that the coat was his, he did not have the specific intent to commit a crime when he agreed to help Julie take it. **B** and **C** are, therefore, incorrect.

8. **A**   A killing is intentional if the defendant desired or knew to a substantial degree of certainty that it would result from his act. A killing is deliberate and premeditated if the defendant was capable of reflecting upon it with a cool mind and did in fact do so. Since Darrel hoped for (i.e., desired) Volmer's death, the killing was intentional. Since he reflected on it in advance with a cool mind, it was deliberate and premeditated.

Since first degree murder is the most serious crime listed, **B**, **C** and **D** are incorrect. Voluntary manslaughter is an intentional killing resulting from extreme emotional disturbance or in the mistaken belief that it is justified. **C** is also incorrect because there is no indication that Darrel was emotionally disturbed or mistakenly believed that his act was justified. Involuntary manslaughter is an unintended killing which results from criminal negligence. **D** is also incorrect because Darrel intended the death of Volmer.

9. **A**   Larceny is defined as a trespassory taking and carrying off of personal property known to be another's with the intent to permanently deprive the owner thereof. A trespassory taking is an acquisition of possession contrary to the rights of the owner and without the owner's consent. Since Dennison acquired possession without Vale's permission, he committed a trespassory taking. A carrying off occurs when the defendant moves the property, even slightly, with the intention of exercising dominion over it. Since Dennison moved the watch from the table to his pocket with the intention of keeping it, he carried it off. Since he knew that the watch belonged to Vale and intended to keep it for himself, he had knowledge that the property was another's and intended to deprive the owner of it. He, therefore, committed a larceny, making **A** correct.

A person is guilty of a criminal attempt when with the specific intent to bring about a criminally prohibited result, he comes substantially close to bringing it about. Although Dennison is probably guilty of attempted larceny, **B** is incorrect because larceny is a more serious crime. Embezzlement is defined as a criminal conversion of personal property by one in lawful custody of that property. Employees who steal property from their employers while in custody of it because of the employment relationship may be guilty of embezzlement. **C** is incorrect, however, because Dennison did not come into possession of the watch as a result of his employment relationship with Vale. **D** is incorrect because Dennison is guilty of larceny for the reasons stated above.

10.   **C**   At common law, rape can be committed by using intoxicants to overcome the victim's resistance. Under the given statute, however, third degree rape is committed only when a person over the age of seventeen has sexual intercourse with a person under the age of sixteen. Since Fanny was only fifteen, she cannot be guilty of committing it.

A and **B** are, therefore incorrect. **D** is incorrect because the statute specifically provides that the crime can be committed by a female.

11.   **D**   Under the state's definition, conspiracy requires an agreement to commit a crime with the specific intent to commit a crime. If the act which Edward and Fanny agreed to commit was not a crime, Edward lacked the specific intent required. Since neither the common law nor the statute given prohibit sexual intercourse between persons of Gerald's and Fanny's age, intercourse between them would not have been a crime, and the agreement between Edward and Fanny was not a conspiracy.

Wharton's Rule provides that there can be no conviction for conspiracy unless one of the parties to the agreement was not logically essential to the commission of the act which they agreed to commit. **A** is incorrect, however, because although Fanny's participation was essential to the seduction of Gerald, Edward's participation was not. Conspiracy is a separate crime and is committed when the conspiratorial agreement is made. Some jurisdictions also require that there have been an overt act in furtherance of the conspiracy. **B** is incorrect, however, because such an act need only be committed by one of the co-conspirators, and Fanny's acts would suffice. Since the crime is committed when the agreement is made, the fact that the act which parties agreed to commit never actually took place is not a defense. **C** is, thus, incorrect.

12.   **A**   Statutory rape is a crime for which no intent is required other than the intent to have sexual intercourse. The given statute defines it as sexual intercourse between a person 17 or older and a person under 16. Since Edward engaged in sexual intercourse with Fanny while he was 17 and she was 15, he is guilty of violating the statute.

Since the crime charged is a strict liability crime, **B** and **C** are incorrect because it is not necessary for the defendant to have knowledge of the "victim's" age, or to be the one who instituted the intercourse. **D** is incorrect because ignorance of the law ordinarily is not a defense.

13.   **D**   A person may be guilty as an accessory or accomplice if he intentionally aids, abets, or facilitates the commission of a crime. Standing by in silent acquiescence, however, does not constitute aiding, abetting, or facilitating unless the defendant is ready, willing, and able to render assistance in its commission if needed. Here there is no indication that this was so.

Since mere knowledge that a crime is being committed is not enough to result in liability, **A** is incorrect. **B** is incorrect because in the majority of jurisdictions it is no longer necessary for the principal to be convicted before an accomplice can be tried. A person who intentionally aided, abetted or facilitated the commission of a crime may be convicted even though his participation was not essential to its commission. **C** is, therefore, incorrect.

14. **A** Cook is obviously guilty of bribery in the second degree because she offered to alter the official records for five hundred dollars. She cannot be guilty of conspiracy, however, because of Wharton's Rule, which provides that there can be no conspiracy unless the agreement involves at least one person who is not essential to the commission of the crime to which the conspirators agreed. Since the crime of bribery could not have been committed by either Cook or Dobson acting alone, neither can be found guilty of conspiring with the other to commit it.

B, C and **D** are, therefore, incorrect. **C** is additionally incorrect because conspiracy is a separate crime which does not merge with the crime which the conspirators agreed to commit.

15. **D** A lesser included offense is an offense the elements of which are completely included among the elements of a more serious crime. Attempting to commit a crime is always a lesser included offense, since its elements are always included among the elements of the completed crime. One who commits a crime is guilty of all lesser included offenses. Since Dobson offered to commit bribery (as explained below), he is guilty of bribery in the second degree, and since the attempt is included in the completed crime, he is guilty of attempting to commit bribery in the second degree.

A person is guilty of attempting to commit a crime when, with the specific intent to commit that crime she comes substantially close to committing it. **A** is incorrect because bribery in the second degree is not an "attempt" crime. It is statutorily defined as offering to commit bribery and is committed when the offer is made. **B** is incorrect because, although Cook first offered to accept the money, Dobson's subsequent agreement was also an offer to pay the money. In addition, Dobson's trip to Cook's office the following day was for the purpose of offering to pay the money. **C** is based on a misinterpretation of the law. A lesser included crime is said to "merge" with the more serious one, but this means only that a defendant cannot be convicted of both. There is no reason why he cannot be convicted of the lesser one only.

16. **C** A person is guilty of a criminal attempt when, with the specific intent to bring about a result which is criminally prohibited, she comes substantially close to bringing about that result. Since, under the applicable statute, burning down one's own house is not arson, the result which Dana specifically intended to bring about was not criminally prohibited by the arson statute. For this reason, Dana could not be guilty of attempted arson. **C** is, therefore, correct.

Even though it was factually impossible for a defendant to commit a particular crime, she may be convicted of an attempt if the crime would have been committed had the facts been as the defendant thought them to be. For example, if Dana burned her own house believing it to be the dwelling of another, she could be convicted of attempted arson. Thus, **A** is an accurate statement of the law. **A** is incorrect, however, because Dana did not make a mistake of fact (i.e., she knew that the dwelling was her own). Since guilt for attempt requires the specific intent to accomplish a purpose which is criminally prohibited, a person cannot be guilty if what she intended to accomplish was not criminally prohibited. This is true even if she believes that it is criminally prohibited, no matter how that mistaken belief was formed. **B** is, therefore, incorrect. **D** is incorrect for two reasons: first, while a defendant cannot be convicted of both a substantive crime and an attempt to commit that substantive crime, she can be convicted of the attempt instead of the substantive crime; and, second, Dana is charged with attempted arson, not attempted insurance fraud.

17. **A**   Murder is the unjustified killing of a human being with malice aforethought. Malice aforethought includes the intent to cause great bodily harm to a human being. A defendant "intends" a particular consequence if she desires or knows to a substantial degree of certainty that it will occur. Since Delman desired and/or knew that exposure to Terminate was likely to result in great bodily harm to Ventura, she intended to cause great bodily harm to a human being. Since Alex died, Delman may be found guilty of his murder. **A** is, therefore, correct.

B is incorrect because engaging in an inherently dangerous activity is not equivalent to malice aforethought. **C** is incorrect because Delman's intent to cause great bodily harm to any human being is sufficient to make her guilty of murder in causing the death of Alex. Although the intent to kill is a form of malice aforethought, **D** is incorrect because the intent to cause great bodily harm is also a form of malice aforethought.

18. **C**   A person is guilty of a criminal attempt when, with the specific intent to bring about a prohibited result, she comes substantially close to doing so. Thus, all attempts are "specific intent" crimes. This means that although murder does not require a specific intent to cause the death of a person, attempted murder does. Since Delman did not intend to cause the death of a human being, she lacks the intent required to make her guilty of attempted murder.

A is, therefore, incorrect. The death of Alex does not satisfy the specific intent requirement unless Delman intended to bring it about. For this reason, **B** is also incorrect. Although the attempt to murder a person may merge with the actual murder of the person, **D** is incorrect because Ventura did not die, and so could not have been murdered.

19. **B**   A person is guilty of a criminal intent when, with the specific intent to bring about a criminally prohibited result, he comes substantially close to achieving that result. Thus, all attempts are "specific intent" crimes. This means that, although murder may be committed without the intent to kill, attempted murder may not. If Dustin believed that Volmer was already dead, he could not have intended to kill him, and so could not be guilty of attempted murder.

A defendant with the specific intent to commit a particular crime may be guilty of attempting it even though accomplishing the intended result was factually impossible. **A** is incorrect because Dustin's intent to kill Volmer could make him guilty of attempted murder even though the fact that Volmer was already dead made murder factually impossible. **C** is incorrect because Dustin's belief that the gun was loaded could establish that he had the specific intent to kill Volmer, even though the fact that the gun was unloaded made it factually impossible for him to accomplish the result which he intended. **D** is incorrect because Dustin's belief that the substance was a poison could help establish that he had the specific intent to kill Volmer, even though the fact that the substance was harmless made it impossible for him to accomplish the intended result.

20. **A**   Because of the possibility that manipulation of the circumstances of a lineup will result in a likelihood of inaccurate identification, the United States Supreme Court has held that after the filing of formal charges against him, a prisoner is entitled to the presence of counsel at a lineup.

B is incorrect because requirements as to lineup procedures are more flexible than those listed. It has even been held that a one-person "showup" may be valid if it is conducted properly. Since all prisoners are expected to obey the commands of their jailors, no prisoner is required to resist violations of his constitutional rights by those in apparent legal authority. **C** is incorrect because it suggests that failure to resist results in waiver. The taint of an improper lineup procedure may be purged by evidence that the in-court identification was arrived at by means distinguishable from the lineup. **D** is incorrect, however, because Watson's courtroom identification of Devlin was nothing more than a repetition of the lineup identification.

21. **A**   Under the *Massiah* rule, a criminal suspect may not be interrogated in the absence of his attorney once formal charges have been brought. It has been held that placing a secret police agent to elicit incriminating statements violates this rule even though the officer asks no questions.

B is incorrect because "entrapment" refers only to conduct by a police officer which induced the defendant to commit a crime which he was not otherwise inclined to commit. **C** is incorrect because a warrant does not justify a police interrogation in violation of the *Massiah* rule. **D** is incorrect because even a voluntary statement violates the *Massiah* rule if made as a result of a police interrogation conducted without the presence or consent of the defendant's attorney.

22. **D**   Even in the absence of probable cause to believe that health and safety violations exist in a particular building, a warrant to search it for such violations may be issued upon probable cause to believe that such violations exist in buildings in the neighborhood.

A is, therefore, incorrect. **B** is incorrect because such a scheme justifies the issuance of warrants like those issued here, rather than invalidating it. Although the courts have considerable leeway in issuing warrants for health and safety inspections, **C** is incorrect because warrants are required by the Fourth Amendment to the United States Constitution.

23. **D**   The crime of receiving stolen property consists of acquiring stolen property with the knowledge that it was stolen and the intent to permanently deprive the owner thereof. Since Darr did not know that the television was stolen when he acquired possession of it, he cannot be guilty of receiving stolen property. **A** and **C** are, therefore, incorrect.

The crime of larceny consists of the trespassory taking and carrying off of personal property known to be another's with the intent to permanently deprive the owner thereof. Since Darr did not know that the television was the property of another when he took it (i.e., received it from Mead), he cannot be guilty of larceny. **B** and **C** are, therefore, incorrect.

24.　**D**　At common law, arson is defined as the intentional or malicious burning of the dwelling of another. Any burning which chars some actual part of the structure is sufficient to result in a conviction. Since the door was charred, there was sufficient burning to establish Dandy's guilt.

Although modern statutes prohibit the acts described in **A**, **B**, and **C**, the question specifies that the jurisdiction applies common law definitions of all crimes. Since common law arson involves a burning of the dwelling of another, and since the structure which Dandy attempted to burn was not a dwelling and was his own, **A** is incorrect. At common law, larceny by trick is committed when the defendant defrauds another into parting with temporary possession of personal property. Since the insurance company gave Dandy title to rather than temporary possession of the policy proceeds, **B** is incorrect. Since the building which Dandy burned in **C** was not a dwelling, **C** is incorrect.

25.　**B**　Murder is the unlawful killing of a human being with malice aforethought. Malice aforethought may consist of intent to kill, intent to cause great bodily harm, wanton reckless disregard for human life, intent to commit a felony, or intent to resist a lawful arrest. Since defendant was unconscious, she lacked any of the requisite intents. Since she did not know that she was starting her car, she did not act with a wanton reckless disregard for human life.

In **A**, defendant's conduct might show wanton reckless disregard for human life. In **C**, defendant clearly had the intent to cause great bodily harm. Although it might be found that defendant acted in the heat of passion, reducing his crime to voluntary manslaughter, a conviction for murder is likely because he had sufficient opportunity to cool off before attacking Victor. The defendant in **D** could be convicted because his threat — even with an empty pistol — might constitute a wanton reckless disregard for human life in view of the fact that some people are likely to react to such a threat with violence, and because a death which occurs in the course of a burglary may be murder under the felony-murder rule.

26.　**A**　An officer who reasonably suspects a person of a crime may be justified in questioning that person about his identity and activity. If during the course of the conversation, she has reason to suspect that he may be armed, she is justified in frisking him for weapons. If during the course of a legitimate frisk for weapons, she discovers contraband in his possession, it may be seized and used as evidence against him. Dinger was not frisked for weapons, however, but for the stolen statue. In the absence of a warrant or valid arrest, such a search violates the Fourth Amendment guarantee against unreasonable search and seizure.

B is incorrect because if a frisk is valid, items discovered during its course may be seized and used as evidence, even though they were not what the officer was seeking. **C** is incorrect because there is no fact to indicate that the officer's suspicion was reasonable, and because even a reasonable suspicion does not justify any warrantless search other than a frisk for weapons. **D** is incorrect because the search was for contraband, and not for a weapon, so it was not a valid pat-down search.

27.　**C**　A criminal conspiracy is an agreement to commit a crime and is complete when two or more persons make such an agreement. Although Sam privately decided to assist Tom and John in the commission of a crime, he did not agree with them that he would do so. He is, therefore, not guilty of conspiracy, and **C** is correct.

One who knowingly aids and abets in the commission of a crime is guilty of that crime as an accessory. For this reason, Sam might be guilty of murder. **A** is incorrect, however, because Sam is charged not with murder but with conspiracy. Some jurisdictions hold that to convict for conspiracy it is necessary to prove an overt act in addition to an agreement to commit a crime. Even in these jurisdictions, however, Sam would not be guilty of conspiracy because he did not agree to commit a crime. **B** is, therefore, incorrect. Co-conspirators are guilty of the crime of conspiracy when their agreement is made and are not rendered innocent by the withdrawal of one or more of them from the conspiracy. **D** is incorrect for this reason, and because Sam was never part of the conspiracy in the first place.

28. **A** Murder is the unjustified killing of a human being with malice aforethought. Malice aforethought includes the intent to kill, which means the desire or knowledge that the defendant's act will bring about the death of another person. Since Tom threw away Vanney's medicine with the desire that doing so would bring about the death of Vanney and since Vanney died as a result, Vanney was murdered. A criminal conspiracy is an agreement to commit a crime. Since Tom and John agreed to kill Vanney, they were involved in a criminal conspiracy. Co-conspirators are vicariously liable for any crimes committed in furtherance of the conspiracy. Since the murder of Vanney was committed by Tom in furtherance of his agreement with John, John is vicariously liable for it. **A** is, therefore, correct.

Since John did no physical act which enabled Tom to bring about Vanney's death, he did not aid or abet him in bringing it about. **B** is, therefore, incorrect. **C** is incorrect because the principle of vicarious liability as explained above makes it unnecessary for John to physically participate in the commission of the crime with which he is charged. One who effectively withdraws from a conspiracy before its goal is accomplished may avoid vicarious guilt for the substantive crime, although not for the crime of conspiracy. In order for a withdrawal to be effective, however, the withdrawing conspirator must at least do something which places his co-conspirator on notice of his withdrawal. Since John did not do so, he has not effectively withdrawn from the conspiracy, and **D** is incorrect.

29. **C** There are two different forms of criminal assault — conduct which intentionally induces fear, and attempted battery. Criminal battery is the intentional or reckless application of force to the body of another. A person is guilty of a criminal attempt when, with the specific intent to bring about a criminally prohibited result, he comes substantially close to achieving that result. Since Dosset shot at the President with the intention of hitting her, he attempted a battery. Since he did not succeed, his crime was assault.

A is incorrect because the crime of which he was acquitted in the federal court was not the same crime with which he is charged in the state court. It is generally held that the constitutional protection against double jeopardy is not offended by separate prosecutions for violating the laws of two different sovereigns (i.e., federal and state governments) even though both arise from the same act. Assault based on intentionally inducing fear requires that the victim was aware of the defendant's conduct and that as a result the victim experienced reasonable apprehension of contact. **B** and **D** are incorrect, however, because assault based on attempted battery requires no such awareness or apprehension.

30. **B**   Many jurisdictions hold that the defendant will not be guilty of the murder of a co-felon under the felony murder rule if the co-felon's death resulted from a justifiable attempt by the crime-victim to prevent the crime. Although this is not the law in all jurisdictions, it is the only argument listed which would provide Delbert with any defense at all.

A is incorrect because the felony murder rule is applied to deaths which occur during the commission of a felony, even though the person killed is not the intended crime-victim. **C** is incorrect because the normal reactions of victims, bystanders, and police, make violence a foreseeable result of any robbery. **D** is incorrect because jurisdictions which apply the felony murder rule regard the intent to commit a felony as a form of malice aforethought.

31. **A**   The felony murder rule provides that the intent to commit a felony is malice aforethought, and that a death which results from the perpetration of a felony is, therefore, murder. For this purpose, the perpetration of a felony continues during the defendant's attempt to escape to a place of seeming safety. Nora's death thus occurred during the perpetration of a robbery, and Delbert could be convicted of murder even if he was driving carefully at the time it occurred.

B, **C**, and **D** are, therefore, incorrect.

32. **D**   Involuntary manslaughter is an unintended killing which results from conduct which created a high and unreasonable risk of death or serious injury, or from the commission of a malum in se misdemeanor. If Donnum's conduct created such risk, he could thus be guilty of involuntary manslaughter. While it is not certain that a court would come to this conclusion, **D** is the only argument listed which could possible support the prosecution.

The unlawful act doctrine (also called the misdemeanor-manslaughter rule) might make a death resulting from the commission of a misdemeanor involuntary manslaughter, but only if the misdemeanor involved is inherently dangerous or malum in se. Since driving without a license is neither, **A** is incorrect. **B** is incorrect because it is based on a perversion of a rule of tort law which provides that the violation of a statute which was designed to protect a class of persons to which the plaintiff belongs from the risk which resulted in harm may be described as negligence per se. There is no counterpart in the criminal law, however. **C** is not an accurate statement since mere negligence will not result in a criminal conviction.

33. **B**   Ordinarily, an omission (i.e., failure to act) does not lead to criminal responsibility unless it violated a legal duty to act. Larraby's duty to aid people at the swimming pool existed only because she was employed as lifeguard and, therefore, only during her hours of employment. Since her supervisor allowed her to leave at 8 p.m., her hours of employment ended at that time. For this reason, she may successfully argue that she had no duty to rescue someone who came into peril after she left the pool.

If she did have a legal duty to render aid, her absence could be a violation of that duty. **A** is, therefore, incorrect. Since any death may have more than one cause, the fact that Watcher's inaction was a cause of Susan's death does not establish that criminal conduct by Larraby was not also a cause. **C** is, therefore, incorrect. **D** is incorrect because at common law and under statutes there are many forms of criminal homicide which can be committed without the intent to cause the death of a person.

34.   **D**   In the absence of special circumstances, no person is under a legal duty to render aid to another. Since a failure to act can lead to criminal responsibility only in the face of a duty to act, Watcher's failure to rescue Susan was not a crime.

This is true even though she could have saved Susan without risk to herself, even though she knew that there was no one else who could rescue the child, and even if she was related to Susan. **A**, **B** and **C** are, therefore, incorrect.

35.   **A**   Rape is committed when the defendant intentionally has sexual intercourse with a female not his wife without consent. Although it is necessary that the victim be unwilling, it is not necessary for her to put up a fight if it would be futile for her to do so or if she reasonably believes that resisting will cause her to sustain serious injury. Since Vena's refusal was overcome by a threat which would have led a reasonable person in her place to fear for her life, the intercourse was without her consent.

If her resistance had been overcome by payment, the intercourse would not have been against her will. But the fact that she was willing to accept payment does not mean that she consented to intercourse with one who did not offer payment, or even with one who did. **B** is, therefore, incorrect. **C** is incorrect because Vena's resistance was overcome by Dorian's threat of physical force. Since Vena inflicted the injuries after the intercourse occurred, her conduct in inflicting them could not possibly relate to whether she consented to the intercourse. **D** is, therefore, incorrect.

36.   **A**   Since the statute requires intent, and since Vena did not intend Dorian's death, she is not guilty of first degree murder under the statute.

B is incorrect because once Dorian was asleep (and certainly once he was tied to the bed), Vena was no longer in danger and therefore not privileged to use force in self-defense. Although some first degree murder statutes include deaths resulting from the commission of dangerous felonies, this particular statute does not. **C** is, therefore, incorrect. Many first degree murder statutes include death resulting from torture, but this one does not. **D** is, therefore, incorrect.

37.   **C**   Murder is the unjustified killing of a human being with malice aforethought. Since malice aforethought includes the intent to kill, and since Diedre held the baby's head under water in an attempt to end his life, Diedre had the necessary mental state and committed the necessary act to make her criminally responsible for murder. It is also necessary, however, for the prosecution to show that her act was a proximate cause of the baby's death. Since there is no clear indication that this is so, it is possible that Diedre may be acquitted of murder. In addition, many states have rules which fix a period of time (usually one to three years) following a defendant's act and provide that no death occurring after that time is proximately caused by the act. Although it is not certain that her argu-

ment will succeed, it is the only one listed which could possibly provide her with an effective defense.

A is incorrect because no constitutional right to an abortion has been found to exist in the last three months of pregnancy, and because the baby was born alive. Diedre's attempt to save the baby's life after she tried to kill him is not sufficient to relieve her of criminal liability for his death if his death was proximately caused by her previous conduct. **B** is, therefore, incorrect. Even though the surgical procedure which Diedre performed did not usually result in the death of a human being, her attempt to kill the baby after he was born makes **D** incorrect.

38. **D** One who intentionally kills another under the mistaken but reasonable belief that she was defending herself against imminent bodily harm may be protected by the privilege of self-defense, and therefore not guilty of any criminal homicide. If her belief was unreasonable, however, she is still guilty of voluntary manslaughter, although not of murder. *I* is incorrect because if the reasonable person would not have had held the belief, Donnelly is guilty of voluntary manslaughter. *II* is incorrect because if Donnelly did not hold the belief, she is not only guilty of voluntary manslaughter, but of murder as well.

39. **D** Persons are guilty of conspiracy to commit a particular crime when they agree to commit it. At common law, burglary is defined as breaking and entering into a dwelling at night for the purpose of committing a larceny or any felony therein. Since the agreement was to break into an office rather than a dwelling and to do so at lunchtime rather than nighttime, it was not a conspiracy to commit burglary. At common law larceny is defined as intentionally taking and carrying off the personal property of another with the intent to permanently deprive the owner of it. Since the agreement was to copy but not carry off the notes of Professor Vinton, it was not a conspiracy to commit larceny.

40. **B** At common law, larceny is defined as intentionally taking and carrying off the personal property of another with the intent to permanently deprive the owner of it. Since Denise planned to return the pen to the professor in a week or two, she lacked the intent to permanently deprive him of it.

A is incorrect because if she had the requisite intent at the time she took the pen, the fact that it was later taken from her would not undo the crime which she had already committed. **C** is incorrect because Denise lacked the requisite intent. There are no facts justifying the inference on which **D** is based, but even if there were, Denise's taking would not be a larceny unless she intended (i.e., was substantially certain) that Vinton would be permanently deprived of the pen.

41. **B** Co-conspirators are vicariously liable for crimes committed by members of the conspiracy in furtherance of its goals. Since one of the goals of Donald's and Denise's agreement was to avoid Vinton's notice, and since Denise's taking of the pen was an attempt to accomplish that goal, Donald is vicariously liable for it.

A is incorrect because mere presence during the commission of a crime is not enough to result in guilt. **C** and **D** are incorrect because a co-conspirator's vicarious liability does not depend on whether he knew or foresaw that the crime would occur, but simply on whether it was in furtherance of the conspiratorial goal.

42. **A** In order to be applicable as a precedent, a previously decided case must resolve an issue similar to the one which appears in the subject case. In the fact pattern which appears in item 42, Defen was charged with robbery after accomplishing the theft of Vogt's money belt by the use of physical force directed against the property itself. Robbery is a larceny committed by the use of force or the threat of force. Although Defen clearly committed a larceny (i.e., the trespassory taking and carrying off of personal property known to be another's with the intent to permanently deprive), an issue arises as to whether force directed against the victim's property rather than his person satisfies the force requirement. Since the same issue arose in **A**, where Defendant used force to break the strap of Amy's handbag, **A** is most likely to be applicable as a precedent.

In **B**, although force was used to retain the property after a larceny had been committed, no force whatsoever was used in acquiring it. For this reason, the issue is not sufficiently similar to make the case applicable as a precedent to the facts in item 42. In **C**, Defendant acquired the property of the victim by threatening the victim with force to be directed at another person. In **D**, the victim's property was acquired by using or threatening force against the person in custody of it. Since the facts in item 42 did not involve the use or threat of force against any person, **C** and **D** are not likely to be applicable.

43. **B** Robbery is larceny accomplished by physical force or threat. Doaks clearly committed a larceny. Although he acquired possession and carried off the briefcase without the use of force, the issue is whether his subsequent use of force to retain possession was sufficient to make him guilty of robbery. **B** is the only case in which this issue arose.

In **A,** no force was used after acquisition of the purse. In **C** and **D,** although force was used to acquire the stolen property, none was used thereafter.

44. **B** Obtaining property by false pretenses is committed when, with the intent to cause the victim to transfer title to personal property, the defendant makes a fraudulent misrepresentation which causes the victim to do so. Since Kemo told Herpo that the pills were made from a secret formula which would protect him against the venom when she knew that statement to be false, and since she did so for the purpose of obtaining money from him and succeeded in doing so, she is guilty of "false pretenses."

Attempted murder requires a specific intent to cause the death of a human being. Intent to cause death requires either the desire or substantial certainly that death will result. Since Kemo believed that Herpo would not be bitten if he took the sugar pills, she lacked the intent necessary to make her liable for attempted murder. **A**, **C**, and **D** are, therefore, incorrect.

45. **D** Self defense is a privilege to use reasonable force to protect oneself against aggression. In determining whether force was reasonable, courts usually balance the danger likely to result from its use against the benefit of using it. If the benefit which would be apparent to the reasonable person in the defendant's situation outweighs the danger which would be apparent to the reasonable person in defendant's situation, the force which the defendant used was reasonable. Since it is generally understood that the reasonable person would consider the benefit of saving her own life to be of greater weight than the

danger of killing an assailant, it is usually held that lethal force (i.e., force likely to kill or do serious bodily harm) is reasonable if used by a person who reasonably believes that she is being attacked with lethal force. Thus, if it was reasonable for Diller to believe that her life was in danger, it was probably reasonable for her to use lethal force to protect it.

A is incorrect because Diller was attempting to protect herself rather than the cocaine. Even if Gunn was actually unarmed, Diller's reasonable belief that he had a pistol might have privileged her use of lethal force in self defense. **B** is, therefore, incorrect. A person who is committing a crime has no right to defend herself against a lawful arrest. Since Gunn was not attempting to arrest Diller, however, the fact that she was committing a crime at the time of his attack is irrelevant. **C** is, therefore, incorrect.

46. **D**   Ordinarily, a search violates a defendant's Fourth Amendment rights unless it is conducted pursuant to a warrant or as an incident to a lawful arrest. Since the examination of Defendant's briefcase did not comply with either, it violated Defendant's rights if it was a search. A search occurs when a defendant's effects are inspected under circumstances which violate the defendant's reasonable expectation of privacy. Since people do not ordinarily look into the briefcases of others, a person may reasonably expect the contents of her briefcase to remain private. This is not true if it has been abandoned. Since the defendant left the phone off the hook when she left her briefcase in the booth to go in search of change, however, she would probably not be held to have abandoned it or to have given up the expectation that its contents would remain private.

The United States Supreme Court has held that border guards may reasonably search persons crossing the border without violating their Fourth Amendment rights. **A** is, therefore, incorrect. Since each party to a conversation knows that the other has a right to repeat a conversation to others, it is generally held that a person's expectation of privacy is not defeated when one to whom he voluntarily speaks records or repeats the conversation. **B** is, therefore, incorrect. Since the user of a public phone knows that others may be visually observing him, his reasonable expectation of privacy is not violated by evidence of such visual observation. **C** is, therefore, also incorrect.

47. **D**   Embezzlement is the conversion of personal property known to be another's with the intent to defraud, by a person in lawful possession of the property. Since Samson's possession was the result of fraud and therefore not lawful, he is not guilty of embezzlement. **A** and **C** are, therefore, incorrect. Larceny by trick is committed when the defendant fraudulently induces the victim to deliver *temporary possession* of personal property to the defendant. If the victim transfers title to the property involved, the crime of larceny by trick has not been committed. Since Berrigan's intention was to make Samson the owner of the money, he transferred title to the money, and **B** and **C** are incorrect.

48. **C**   Although killing with the intent, at least, to cause great bodily harm is ordinarily classified as murder, it may be reduced to voluntary manslaughter if the defendant was acting in the heat of passion. This is only so, however, if the provocation which produced the passion would have done so in the person of ordinary temperament.

A is a fabrication; there is no "theory of deliberate provocation." **B** is incorrect because the objective standard described above (i.e., the person of ordinary temperament) makes Walton's emotional peculiarities irrelevant. **D** is based on a misinterpretation of the law. An intentional killing may be reduced from murder to manslaughter if the defendant was acting under the mistaken belief that the killing was justified. This is known as the theory of mistaken justification. **D** is incorrect because Walton did not act in the mistaken belief that she was justified, and because **D** would erroneously apply the theory to *prevent* reduction to manslaughter.

49. **C** At common law, burglary is defined as breaking and entering into a dwelling at night with the intent to commit a larceny or felony therein. If at the time Ritter entered he did not intend to commit an act which would amount to a crime, he cannot be guilty of burglary.

A "breaking" occurs when the defendant creates the opening through which he enters, even though no force is used. **A** and **B** are incorrect because by opening the door to Viola's apartment, Ritter created the opening through which he entered, thus committing the necessary "breaking." The crime of burglary is committed, if at all, at the time the unlawful entry takes place with the requisite state of mind. Conduct performed subsequently (i.e., leaving a note), does not undo a crime which has already been committed. **D** is, therefore, incorrect.

50. **C** Since all the incidents of unconsciousness occurred within three months after the accident and nearly three years ago, it was probably reasonable for Drake to believe that they would not occur again. If she entertained that belief, and if it was reasonable, she cannot be said to have knowingly disregarded the plain and strong likelihood of harm as required by the statute. Although it is not certain that a court would come to that conclusion, **C** contains the only argument listed which could possibly support Drake's defense.

A is incorrect because if Drake did knowingly disregard the plain and strong likelihood of further blackouts, it would not matter what caused them. **B** is incorrect because the crime, if any, took place when Drake drove in knowing disregard (etc.), and so would have already been committed by the time Drake passed out. **D** is incorrect because the statute does not require knowledge that death or serious injury will result, but only knowledge that there is strong likelihood that it will.

51. **D** Ordinarily, a search violates a defendant's Fourth Amendment rights unless it is conducted pursuant to a warrant or as an incident to a lawful arrest. Since the examination of Defendant's bank records conformed to neither, it violated Defendant's rights if it was a search. A search occurs when a defendant's effects are inspected under circumstances which violate the defendant's reasonable expectation of privacy. Since bank records are commercial instruments, the United State Supreme Court has held that they are not confidential communications, and that a depositor has no reasonable expectation that they will remain private. Thus their inspection, even by police, does not constitute a search and, therefore, does not violate the depositor's Fourth Amendment rights. Since the examination did not violate Doge's rights, his motion should not be granted.

A, **B**, and **C** are, therefore, incorrect.

52. **A** Voluntary manslaughter is committed when the defendant, with the intent to cause death

or great bodily harm, causes the death of a human being under circumstances such that the defendant is acting in the "heat of passion." The belief that Valens brutally murdered his family probably is sufficient to furnish the heat of passion which reduces the crime from murder to manslaughter.

B is incorrect for two reasons: first, deliberation and premeditation require a mind which is capable of thinking coolly and rationally, and under the circumstances Dafton's probably wasn't and, second, deliberation and premeditation are not elements of voluntary manslaughter. Since voluntary manslaughter is a lesser offense included in first degree murder, Dafton could be convicted of voluntary manslaughter even if he were guilty of first degree murder. **C** is incorrect because it suggests that guilt of first degree murder would prevent a conviction for voluntary manslaughter. Convicting and sentencing for crime are functions of the court, not of the family of the crime's victim. **D** is incorrect because it suggests a law of vendetta (i.e., that if Valens was the killer Dafton could punish him without incurring criminal responsibility).

53. **D** Larceny is a trespassory taking and carrying off of personal property known to be another's with the intent to permanently deprive the owner of it. Although Dorner planned to return the money in the event of one contingency, she planned not to return it in the event of another. This contingent intent to permanently deprive is sufficient to make her guilty of larceny when she took and carried off the money on Friday night.

A is incorrect because she took the money with the intent (contingent at least) to permanently deprive the owner. **B** is incorrect because she intended not to return it if she lost. Since the crime was committed when she took the money, the fact that she did or did not return it all on Monday morning is irrelevant. **C** is, therefore, incorrect.

54. **B** One who incites and encourages another to commit a crime may be guilty as an accomplice or accessory, especially when he derives some direct benefit from the crime. Since Sears demanded $25 to cover up Dorner's crime while they were standing in front of the open safe, then watched as Dorner reached into the safe and handed it to him, he can be found guilty as an accessory to larceny.

Robbery is larceny committed by force or threat of force. **A** is incorrect because the threat which Sears made was not of force. Embezzlement is the fraudulent taking of property which is lawfully in the defendant's possession. Since the $25 which Sears took from Dorner was not in Sear's possession to begin with, he did not embezzle it. **C** is, therefore, incorrect. Crimes characterized by the term "fraud" involve takings which are committed by making misrepresentations which induce the owner to willingly part with possession or title. **D** is incorrect because the owner of the supermarket was not induced to part with the money by reliance on a misrepresentation.

55. **B** Although most statutes which forbid the sale of alcohol to minors impose strict liability (i.e., defendant's knowledge is not an element), this one does not because it only prohibits the *knowing* sale. If Bart reasonably believed that Kidd was over the age of 18, he lacked the knowledge which is requisite to a conviction.

Not knowing whether wine was an intoxicating substance under the statute would not be a defense because all persons are conclusively presumed to know the law. Ignorance of the law is not a defense. **A** is, therefore, incorrect. Entrapment is available as a defense only when a police officer induced the defendant to commit a crime which he was not already disposed to commit. **C** is incorrect because the police officer did nothing to encourage the sale. The statute prohibits the sale of intoxicating substances, without regard to whether or not anyone becomes intoxicated by them. **D** is therefore, incorrect.

56. **C** Vicarious liability refers to responsibility which is imposed on one person for a crime committed by another. If Bart was not guilty of violating the statute, there has been no crime for which Darla can be held vicariously liable. Although it is not certain that this argument will succeed, it is the only one listed which could possibly support Darla's defense.

      A is incorrect because when vicarious liability is imposed, the fault (or lack of fault) of the person on whom it is imposed is irrelevant. **B** is similarly incorrect because vicarious liability may be imposed for the crime committed by an agent even though the agent violated specific instructions in committing it. **D** is incorrect because a bartender selling drinks to a bar customer is acting in the scope of employment, since his conduct is designed to benefit his employer, and since he is subject to the employer's right of control while doing so.

57. **D** Under the "unlawful act doctrine" (also known as the "misdemeanor-manslaughter rule") a person may be guilty of involuntary manslaughter if a death results from her commission of a crime which is malum in se or inherently dangerous. Neither of these factors exists here. Therefore, **A** is incorrect. **B** is incorrect because voluntary manslaughter requires the intent to kill or cause great bodily harm, and the knowledge that death is "possible" is not sufficient to constitute such intent. Most jurisdictions hold that criminal or culpable negligence which results in death may support a conviction for involuntary manslaughter. In some of those jurisdictions, culpable negligence is defined as unreasonable conduct in the face of a foreseeable risk. In others, more is required: either that the defendant knew of the risk and wilfully disregarded it, or that under the circumstances known to defendant, her conduct created a high degree of risk of death or serious bodily injury. Since the facts do not indicate that Dell engaged in unreasonable conduct in the face of a foreseeable risk, that she wilfully disregarded a known risk, or that under the circumstances which she knew her conduct created a high degree of death or serious bodily injury, **C** is incorrect because there is no evidence of criminal negligence.

58. **B** Self-defense involves a privilege to use reasonable force to prevent what is reasonably perceived as a threat of imminent bodily harm. Since Nelson had already struck Grover hard enough and with an object heavy enough to fracture Grover's skull, and since Nelson still had the weapon in his hand, the perception that Grover was in danger of imminent bodily harm was probably reasonable. Thus, if the force which he used to protect himself against it was reasonable, its use was privileged.

      The difference between the seriousness of the injuries inflicted by Nelson and Grover does not, alone, establish that the force used by Grover was reasonable, making **A** incorrect. Since the plastic sword was not only heavy enough to cause a serious injury, but in fact did cause such an injury, the fact that Grover knew that it was plastic would not alone make his response to its threatened use unreasonable. **C** is, therefore, incorrect. A person against whom force is initiated is privileged to use reasonable force to defend himself against it. Thus, one who initiates aggression is not ordinarily privileged to use force in response to reasonable force which his adversary is using in self-defense. **D** is incorrect, however, because when Grover surrendered his knife and fell to his knees, his initial act of aggression had ended. Since Nelson's use of force was not privileged, Grover was privileged to defend himself against it.

59.   **D**   Under the M'Naghten rule a person is insane if, at the time the otherwise criminal act was committed, as a result of mental illness he did not understand the nature and quality of his act or that it was wrong. For this purpose, knowledge that an act is unlawful is knowledge that it is wrong. If Grover knew that he was stabbing a person, he knew the nature and quality of his act; if he knew his act was unlawful, he knew it was wrong.

  A is incorrect because the finding that Grover was not guilty of felonious assault by reason of insanity meant only that he did not know the nature and quality of his act or that it was wrong at the time he struck the police officer. **B** is incorrect because a person who knows his conduct to be unlawful knows it to be "wrong" under the M'Naghten rule. Mental illness does not result in insanity under the M'Naghten rule unless it deprives the defendant of the ability to know the nature and quality of his act or that it is wrong. **C** is, therefore, incorrect.

60.   **A**   Murder is the unlawful killing of a human being with malice aforethought. Malice aforethought may consist of intent to cause great bodily harm. A defendant has intent to cause great bodily harm when he desires or knows that his act will result in serious injury. Thus, if Nelson knew that his act would inflict a serious injury, he may be found to have acted with malice aforethought.

  Voluntary manslaughter is the unlawful killing of a human being with the intent to cause death or great bodily harm, but under circumstances of great emotional distress or mistaken justification. **B** is incorrect because if Nelson did not intend serious injury, he lacked the intent necessary to make him guilty of voluntary manslaughter. Self defense is a privilege to use reasonable force to protect oneself against a threatened contact. Even if no contact is actually threatened, a defendant who uses force to protect himself against an apparent threat may be privileged if he reasonably believed that a contact would occur. If a defendant actually believed that contact was threatened, deciding whether that belief was reasonable requires determining what the reasonable person in his position would have believed. If the defendant did not actually believe that contact was threatened, however, he had no privilege to use force even if the reasonable person in his position would have believed that such force was necessary. **C** and **D** are incorrect because the facts indicate that when Nelson struck Grover, he was aware that the threat was over.

61.   **A**   A person is guilty as an accessory to a crime when he aids and abets in its perpetration. At common law, a defendant commits rape when he has sexual intercourse with a woman who is not his wife without the woman's consent. Although under this definition a husband cannot be guilty as a principal of raping his wife, he can be guilty as an accessory if he aids and abets another to have sexual intercourse with her without her consent. Since Davis assisted Randall in committing rape (i.e., having intercourse with Wilma without her consent), he is guilty of rape as an accessory.

Depending on the statutory definitions of procuring for prostitution and possession of narcotics, Davis may be guilty of all the crimes listed. **B**, **C** and **D** are incorrect, however, because rape is clearly the most serious of them.

62. **A**   Larceny is defined as the trespassory taking and carrying off of personal property known to be another's with the intent to permanently deprive the owner thereof. Since Daner's taking and carrying off of the candy dish was inconsistent with Foster's rights, it was trespassory. Since Daner knew that the candy dish was Foster's and since giving it to his sister as a wedding present would permanently deprive Foster of it, he committed larceny, and **A** is correct.

Burglary is the breaking and entering into a dwelling house for the purpose of committing a felony therein. Since Daner entered to recover his own camera, his purpose was not to commit a felony and he is not guilty of burglary, B is, therefore, incorrect. A person is guilty of a criminal attempt when, with the specific intent to bring about a result which is criminally prohibited, he comes substantially close to bringing about that result. Since Daner did not have the purpose of committing a felony inside Foster's home, he lacked the intent necessary to burglary, and, therefore, could not be convicted of attempted burglary. **C** is, therefore, incorrect. **D** is incorrect because Daner is guilty of larceny as explained above. The larceny was committed at the moment that Daner carried off the candy dish with the requisite intent, and was not uncommitted when he returned it.

63. **C**   A person is guilty of attempting to commit a crime when, *with the specific intent* to bring about a criminally prohibited result, he comes substantially close to achieving that result. Since involuntary manslaughter is *unintended* homicide, there can be no attempt to commit it because the requisite state of mind cannot exist.

A and **B** are therefore incorrect. Since there is no requirement that a person be prosecuted for the highest possible crime which he committed, **D** is incorrect.

64. **C**   Dalton obviously did not have the intent to cause the death of Williams, and was obviously not engaged in committing rape, robbery, or kidnapping at the time that Williams was killed. Under the common law definition, burglary is a breaking and entering into a dwelling at night for the purpose of committing a felony therein. Since Dalton was not attempting to enter a dwelling house, he was not committing a burglary either.

A is incorrect because most jurisdictions apply the felony murder rule to the killing of one felon by another. **B** is incorrect because the statute does not require that the felony being committed is a dangerous one. While assumption of the risk is a defense in tort actions, it is not in criminal prosecutions. **D** is therefore incorrect.

65. **D**   The victim of a crime does not share the guilt of the perpetrator, even though the victim's participation was necessary to the crime's commission. If the law was designed to protect people in Wallace's position against people in Daniel's position, Wallace can be regarded as the victim of Daniel's act, and thus escape criminal liability. While it is not certain that a court would be persuaded by this argument, it is the only one listed which could possibly result in dismissal.

Although the statement contained in **A** was correct at early common law, it is no longer true in a majority of jurisdictions. **B** is factually incorrect, since Daniels could not have committed the crime if Wallace had not paid him the money. Under Wharton's Rule, persons who agree to commit a crime cannot be convicted of conspiracy unless at least one of them was not essential to the commission of that crime. Since the crime created by the statute could not have been committed by one person alone, Wharton's Rule would prevent the conviction of Daniels and Wallace for conspiracy to commit it. **C** is incorrect, however, because Wallace is not being charged with conspiracy but with being an accessory to the substantive crime, and because accessories frequently are people without whom the crime could not have been committed.

66. **A**   Robbery is larceny accomplished by force or a threat of force directed at the lawful possessor of the property taken. Defendant's snatching of the purse was accomplished by force, and the hand in his pocket coupled with his words constituted a threat of force.

Larceny by trick requires that the victim give up the property in reliance on the defendant's fraud. Since Vicki's purse was taken by force, **B** is incorrect. Embezzlement is criminal conversion of personal property by one in lawful possession. **C** is incorrect because Defendant did not obtain possession of the property lawfully. Larceny by false pretenses involves a misrepresentation of fact which is intended to and does in fact cause the victim to transfer title to property. **D** is incorrect because Vicki did not transfer title to Defendant.

67. **A**   Larceny is a trespassory taking and carrying off of property known to be another's with the intent to permanently deprive. There is no requirement that the victim's possession of the property be lawful. Crawford's taking of the plant was trespassory, and therefore a larceny, because she had been authorized to water it, not to carry it off. Therefore, it was a larceny. Crawford could not be guilty of burglary since her use of the key which Boswell gave her prevents her entry from constituting a "breaking" which requires force against the premises.

68. **B**   Rape is sexual intercourse without consent of the female. Since the bank teller's resistance was overcome by Siddon's threat and her resulting fear of death, the intercourse occurred without her consent. One who commands another to do an act is responsible for the criminal consequences thereof. Although Siddon did not himself have sexual intercourse with the teller, he is guilty of rape because he commanded the bank manager to do so. **II** is, therefore, correct. Solicitation is committed by encouraging, ordering, or commanding another to commit a crime. If the person solicited actually commits the crime, however, solicitation merges with the substantive crime and is not subject to separate prosecution. **I** is, therefore, incorrect.

69. **C**   Kidnapping is the intentional asportation and confinement of a person against the person's will by means of force or threat and without lawful authority. Although it is obvious that Siddon intentionally confined the bank manager against his will by means of force and threat and without lawful authority, there is some question as to whether there was an asportation. Ordinarily, any moving of the victim satisfies the requirement of asportation. Many jurisdictions now hold, however, that there is no asportation if the movement of the victim was incidental to and a necessary part of the commission of

some other substantive crime. Although it is not certain that a court would accept that view, the argument in **C** is the only one listed which could possibly support Siddon's defense.

In some jurisdictions, a ransom demand makes the defendant guilty of a more serious degree of the crime, but no jurisdiction requires a ransom demand as an essential element of kidnaping. **A** is, therefore, incorrect. **B** is incorrect because, once committed, a crime cannot be uncommitted. **D** is incorrect because the crime of kidnaping can be committed against an adult as well as a child.

70.   **B**   Ordinarily, no person has standing to assert the constitutional rights of another. For this reason, a defendant who seeks to suppress evidence seized as the result of the search of another person may not successfully argue that the search and seizure were unconstitutional unless he had a sufficient possessory or proprietary interest in the thing searched to give him a reasonable expectation of privacy which was violated by the search. Since the car and the pistol were both Wilson's, and since Dana thus could not have a reasonable expectation of privacy, Dana has no standing to object to the search, and his motion should be denied.

For the reasons stated above, **C** and **D** are incorrect. Usually, a search without a warrant violates the rights of the person searched unless it is incidental to a lawful arrest. Since the facts do not indicate that Wilson was arrested prior to the search of his glove compartment, the search probably did violate his rights. **A** is, therefore, incorrect.

71.   **C**   A person is justified by the privilege of self-defense to use such force as reasonably appears necessary to protect himself from what he reasonably believes to be an imminent threat of bodily harm. Although there was no real threat of harm to Ferris, he believed there was and used force to prevent it. Since Karat also used force in the mistaken belief that she was under attack, her case is probably applicable as a precedent.

In **A,** the mistake made by the defendant related to the degree of force he was using, not to the danger which he faced, so **C** is a better choice. **B** and **D** are not applicable because there the issue was whether the violence against which the defendants sought to protect themselves was a reasonable response to their own unprivileged aggression.

72.   **D**   Although the privilege of self-defense may justify the use of force against one who threatens the defendant with imminent bodily harm, it does not justify the use of force if the harm threatened was a reasonable response to the defendant's own unprivileged aggression. Since Prosser first made unprivileged contact with Edwards, the issue is whether Edward's response was excessive and, if so, whether the force used by Prosser was a reasonable response to it. The same issues are resolved in **B** and **D**, but since the bouncer's response to Abel's punch in **B** was obviously not excessive, **D** is a better choice.

A and **C** are inapplicable since they do not involve force used by the victim in response to initial aggression by the defendant.

73.   **A**   A search may be lawful if consent is given by one in apparent authority to do so. If Rita actually was Melba's roommate, she would have had authority to consent to a search of

common areas of their room. Since she told the police that she was, and since she had a key to the room, it was probably reasonable for them to believe her. Her apparent authority might, thus, justify the search. While a court might not find it to be so, the argument in **A** is the only one listed which could possibly result in denial of Melba's motion.

B is incorrect because although information received from an informant might furnish probable cause sufficient to permit the issuance of a warrant, the informant's belief is not sufficient to justify a warrantless search. **C** is incorrect because Melba had no expectation that any other person would enter the room in her absence. Although she knew that the sorority retained a copy of her room key, she knew also that this was done to facilitate duplication in the event a resident lost her key. **D** is incorrect because even though there are some cases indicating that a primary or secondary school administrator can consent to a search of a locker used by a student, this view has not been applied to college students or to searches of a student's room, and Rita was not a school administrator.

74. **B**   One who, with the intent that a crime will be committed, encourages another to commit that crime, is liable for it as an accessory.

A is incorrect because mere presence at the scene of a crime is not sufficient, even if the defendant intended or was willing for the crime to be committed. **C** is incorrect because the words of encouragement need not create a new danger in order for liability to be imposed. **D** is incorrect for two reasons: first, under some circumstances words alone might be sufficient; and, second, here the words were coupled with intent.

75. **C**   Unless a defendant was ready, willing, and able to give affirmative assistance in the commission of the crime, her presence and silent acquiescence are not sufficient to result in criminal liability.

Ordinarily, one is not under any obligation to attempt to prevent a crime from being committed. **A** is therefore incorrect. **B** is incorrect because, even with criminal intent, mere presence at the scene of a crime is not sufficient to satisfy the requirement of *actus reus*. Sal was not an accessory at all since her presence was not sufficient participation, but in any event she could not have been an accessory *after* the fact, since the crime was committed after her involvement began. **D** is therefore, incorrect.

76. **A**   Under the M'Naghten test, a person may be found not guilty by reason of insanity only if mental illness prevented him from knowing the nature and quality of his act or from knowing that the act was legally wrong. Since Anthony knew what he was doing (i.e., that he was poisoning the Governor) and knew that it was against the law, he was not insane.

B refers to the irresistible impulse supplement, and is incorrect because the facts indicate that the jurisdiction has adopted only the M'Naghten test. **C** is incorrect because it refers to the Durham rule, which is no longer applied in any jurisdiction. In some jurisdictions, a defendant is insane under the M'Naghten rule if mental disease caused him/her to suffer from a delusion within the context of which the defendant's act would be lawful. **D** is incorrect, however, because even within the context of Anthony's delusion,

Anthony knew that killing the governor was an unlawful act.

77. **B**   Although statutory rape is sometimes called a strict liability crime, this means only that liability can be imposed even though the defendant was not aware that the female with whom he was having intercourse was under age. No liability can be imposed, however, unless the defendant had intent to engage in intercourse.

A is incorrect because liability for involuntary manslaughter may be imposed if the victim's death resulted from reckless conduct by the defendant. Driving while drunk may be sufficiently reckless to result in liability. **C** is incorrect because even if the defendant did not know that she was drunk, it may have been reckless for her to drive while she knew that her vision and motor abilities were impaired. Since voluntary manslaughter is the killing of a human being with the intent to kill or to cause great bodily harm under circumstances of great emotional distress, **D** is incorrect because the facts asserted by Defendant would inculpate rather than exculpate him.

78. **C**   Murder is defined as criminal homicide with malice aforethought. Since homicide involves an act which causes the death of human being, and since Carl's death did not result from Jones' act, Jones could not be guilty of murdering Carl.

Malice aforethought consists of the intent to kill, to cause great bodily harm, to commit a felony, to escape from lawful custody, or of wanton disregard for human life. **A** is incorrect because Jones's desire to cause Ann great bodily harm might constitute malice aforethought. **B** is incorrect because knowledge of the victim's identity is not a material element of either murder or of malice aforethought. Since Jones did intend to cause Basil's death, he had the requisite *mens rea*, even though he believed Basil to be someone else. **D** is incorrect for two reasons: first, shooting at the bank guard was a felony, and the intent to commit a felony may constitute malice aforethought in a prosecution for the death of any person killed during the course of that felony; and, second, starting a gun battle in a bank can be regarded as wanton disregard for human life, which may also constitute malice aforethought.

79. **D**   An examination of a defendant's effects is a search if it is conducted under circumstances which violate the defendant's reasonable expectation of privacy. Ordinarily, a person has a reasonable expectation that an apartment which s/he has the exclusive right to occupy will remain private. For this reason, the inspection of Derek's apartment probably violated his reasonable expectation of privacy and, therefore, was a search. Ordinarily, a search of a defendant's effects violates his/her Fourth Amendment rights unless it is conducted pursuant to a warrant. Since the examination of Derek's apartment was conducted without a warrant, it violated Derek's rights. Evidence seized in violation of a defendant's Fourth Amendment rights is inadmissible under the exclusionary rule.

A is incorrect because the plastic pouch was not in plain sight until Paul entered, and the entry itself violated Derek's rights. **B** is incorrect because a landlord does not have the power to waive her tenant's constitutional rights — even if she is the tenant's mother. At one time, *Miranda* warnings were not required until a person became a suspect. No such qualification ever applied to the right to be secure against unreasonable search and seizure however. **C** is therefore incorrect.

80.   C   Since one purpose of the exclusionary rule is to deter police officers from violating the Fourth Amendment, information obtained as a result of an unlawful search may not be used to justify the issuance of a warrant authorizing further search.

             Such a warrant is invalid, and anything found pursuant to it is excluded as one of the fruits of the original unlawful search. **A** is therefore incorrect. **B** is incorrect for the same reason, even though it sounds philosophically sound. Although possession of stolen items is not, alone, sufficient to permit the conclusion that the possessor was the thief, it is certainly acceptable as circumstantial evidence to be considered by a jury. **D** is therefore incorrect.

81.   A   Since the statute requires knowledge that the statement is false, and since Dixon believed the statement to be true, he lacked the required mental state to be guilty of perjury.

             D is therefore, incorrect. If, as the result of his attorney's advice, Dixon believed that he had not been convicted of a crime, he lacked the knowledge necessary to make him guilty under the statute. However, Dixon's reliance on the advice of counsel would not, alone, have prevented him from being guilty unless he actually believed that advice, so **B** is incorrect. Since a guilty plea is equivalent to a conviction, **C** is incorrect.

82.   D   Kidnapping is defined as the intentional asportation and confinement of a person against that person's will, by force or threat, and without lawful authority. Since Dover did not know that Mary was in the car when he drove it away, he lacked the requisite intent.

             A is therefore incorrect. **B** is incorrect because kidnapping has no equivalent of the felony murder rule. **C** is incorrect, since if he knew that Mary was in the car, Dover could be guilty of kidnapping even if the asportation of Mary was secondary to his stealing of the car.

83.   D   Robbery is a larceny which is committed by force or threat to use force against the lawful possessor of the property taken or any other person. If Maxine gave Dover one thousand dollars because he knowingly threatened to injure Mary if she did not, his taking of the money was robbery. Although he did not know that Mary was in the car when he first made the threat, it could be found that the threat was continued by his conduct. Thus, if he knew that Mary was in the car when he received the money from Maxine, it might be concluded that he obtained the money by a threat to burn Mary.

             A is incorrect for two reasons: first, he did not take the car by force; and, second, he is charged with robbery of the cash, not of the car. **B** would not make him guilty of robbery, unless he knew that Mary was in the car when he threatened to burn it. **C** is incorrect since for robbery most jurisdictions require that the threat be directed against a person.

84.   D   The double jeopardy clause prevents a person from being placed twice in jeopardy for the same offense. This does not prevent prosecution by two separate sovereigns for crimes arising out of the same transaction, however, because a different offense has been committed against each sovereign. In addition, the two crimes with which Darryl is charged are not identical. (The federal prosecution is for illegal importation; the state

prosecution is for illegal possession.)

A is therefore incorrect. **B** is incorrect since it has been held that customs agents have probable cause to search the car of any person entering the U.S. **C** is incorrect because it is generally understood that jeopardy begins as soon as a trial commences.

85. **B** Since the statute prohibits possession of a skeleton key with the intent to commit an unlawful entry, and since Dudley was, in fact, attempting to effect an unlawful entry with his skeleton key, he is guilty of violating the statute.

A is incorrect because the fact that Dudley was a professional thief is not enough to make him guilty of violating any law, even one designed to protect the public against professional thieves. The crime defined by the statute would merge into the crime of attempted burglary if Dudley was charged with or convicted of attempted burglary. But in the absence of an attempted burglary charge, there is no reason why the lesser crime cannot be prosecuted. **C** is therefore incorrect. A careful reading of the statute discloses that it punishes conduct (i.e., possession of a skeleton key) coupled with a guilty mind. **D** is therefore incorrect.

86. **A** Since the statute defines as third degree manslaughter any death which proximately results from the commission of a crime, Durban cannot be found guilty under the statute unless the victim's death proximately resulted from his crime.

Although the common law misdemeanor-manslaughter rule is applied only to deaths resulting from the commission of misdemeanors which are *mala in se*, the statute given makes no such requirement. **B** is therefore incorrect. **C** is incorrect for the same reason, and because there is no indication that Durban was driving while intoxicated at the time the accident occurred. **D** is incorrect because neither the common law rule nor the statute requires that the risk be a foreseeable one.

87. **C** One who intentionally aids or facilitates the commission of a crime is guilty of the crime as an accessory. Robbery is larceny committed by force or threat of force. Although Bonnie did not point a gun and demand money, she aided and abetted Mildred by operating the getaway car. She is thus guilty as an accessory. Conspiracy is an agreement to commit a crime made by two or more people who have specific intent. Bonnie and Mildred committed the crime of conspiracy when they agreed on the commission of the robbery.

A, **B** and **D** are incorrect because the crime of conspiracy is separate from and does not merge into the substantive crime which the conspirators agreed to commit.

88. **B** A defendant is guilty of murder when he proximately causes the death of another human being unlawfully and with malice aforethought. Malice aforethought consists of the intent to kill, the intent to cause great bodily harm, escape from lawful custody, the commission of a felony, or reckless disregard for human life. Since there are no facts indicating that the defendant in **B** intended to kill or cause harm, was escaping from lawful custody, or engaged in conduct demonstrating a reckless disregard for human life, the only way he could be convicted of murder would be if Norris's death proximately resulted from the commission of a felony. There is no fact indicating that viola-

tion of the insurance statute was a felony. Even if it was, the violation was not causally related to Norris's death since the death would have occurred whether or not the vehicle was insured. For this reason, the defendant could not be convicted of murder.

An unlawful killing committed with the intent to kill or inflict great bodily harm might be voluntary manslaughter if the defendant was acting under extreme emotional distress or mistaken justification. The defendant in **A** might still be convicted of murder, however, because the lapse of time between his discovery of the atrocity which Fredericks committed and his killing of Fredericks could prevent a court from finding that he was acting under extreme emotional distress. **A** is, therefore, incorrect. Although the defendant in **C** did not have an intent to kill, his conduct might be regarded as sufficiently reckless to result in a conviction for murder. Although it is possible that the defendant in **D** was acting under sufficient emotional distress for the killing to be regarded as voluntary manslaughter rather than murder, courts rarely make special allowances for "mercy" killings. **D** is, therefore, incorrect.

89. **B**   A person is guilty of a criminal attempt when, with the specific intent to bring about a criminally prohibited result, she performs some act which comes substantially close to achieving that result. Many jurisdictions hold that if the result which the defendant specifically intended to bring about was not a crime the defendant cannot be guilty of a criminal attempt. This is sometimes known as the doctrine of legal impossibility. Although not all jurisdictions recognize this defense, it is the only argument listed which could furnish Dalton with an effective defense in any jurisdiction.

Since the elements of criminal attempt are often included among the elements of the substantive crime which was attempted, criminal attempts are often lesser included offenses of the substantive crimes. Lesser offenses are said to merge with the crime in which they are included, which means that a person who is convicted of a substantive crime cannot also be convicted of attempting it. There is no requirement that a defendant be prosecuted for the highest or most serious crime resulting from his act, however. This means that a prosecutor may choose to charge a defendant with attempting a crime, even if a conviction for the substantive crime could have been obtained. For this reason, the fact that Dalton actually succeeded in killing a flivver would not prevent his conviction for attempting to do so, and **A** *and* **D** are incorrect. A person is in pari delicto with another when they are equally guilty. Since Albert did not commit or attempt to commit a crime, he is not guilty of anything and, therefore, not in pari delicto with Dalton. **C** is, therefore, incorrect.

90. **D**   Voluntary manslaughter is the killing of a human being with the intent to kill or inflict great bodily harm, under circumstances of extreme emotional distress (or mistaken justification). Frequently, the rage which accompanies a discovery of infidelity by a spouse has been held to be sufficient emotional distress to reduce an intentional homicide from murder to voluntary manslaughter. Most jurisdictions apply an objective standard, however, in judging a defendant's emotional distress. Thus, if a person of ordinary temperament would not have lost self-control, Dingle's emotional distress would not have been sufficient to result in a reduction of his crime from murder to manslaughter.

A and **B** are incorrect because although a killing with the intent to kill or inflict great bodily harm *may* be murder, extreme emotional distress may reduce it to voluntary manslaughter even though the defendant intended to kill or inflict great bodily harm. Although anger which results from the defendant's catching his spouse in *flagrante delicto* (i.e., in the act) may justify reducing a murder charge to one of manslaughter, **C** is incorrect because there is no requirement that defendant's emotional distress result from this particular circumstance.

91. **B** Evidence obtained in violation of a defendant's constitutional rights may not be used against him. The United States Supreme Court has held that *Miranda* warnings must be given before questioning a person in custody. An interrogation conducted without giving the required *Miranda* warnings thus violates a defendant's rights, making confessions so obtained inadmissible. The warnings are required only when the person being questioned is in custody, however. Thus, if Damson was not in custody at the time his statement was made, his rights have not been violated, and his statement should not be excluded. A person is in custody when the police deprive him of his freedom of action in any significant way. It is possible that a court would find that Oswald's pointing toward the back seat of the patrol car was an order coupled with an implied threat sufficient to deprive Damson of his freedom, and that he was therefore in custody. It is also possible, however, that Damson's entry into the police car was voluntary, and that it did not, therefore, amount to custody. Of all the arguments listed, this is the only one with any possibility of success.

Even if a defendant's confession is excluded because of a failure to give the required *Miranda* warnings, he may be convicted on the basis of other evidence. The existence of such independent evidence, although it may convict the defendant, does not make admissible the confession which was obtained in violation of his rights. **A** is, therefore, incorrect. Prior to the *Miranda* decision, the Supreme Court's *Escobedo* decision required that a suspect be given certain warnings as soon as he became the *focus* of a police investigation. **C** is incorrect, however, because *Miranda* subsequently changed the "focus" test to a "custody" test, requiring that warnings be given only after the suspect was in custody. Whether or not the investigation was routine, *Miranda* warnings are required whenever the person interrogated is in custody. **D** is therefore, incorrect.

92. **D** Arson is the intentional or reckless burning of the dwelling of another. Although Dahle caused the burning of Hay's dwelling, he did not do so intentionally since he believed that there would be no damage. [***Note:*** Although some jurisdictions hold that a reckless burning may be arson, the facts indicate that Dahle acted reasonably.]

Although violation of a statute may be *evidence* of negligence or even of recklessness, a statutory violation is not alone sufficient to satisfy the *mens rea* requirement for arson. **A** is, therefore, incorrect. **B** is incorrect because it would impose criminal liability without the necessary *mens rea*. **C** is incorrect because consent by Hays to Dahle's use of fireworks is not equivalent to consent to the burning of his home.

93. **B** Murder is a killing with malice aforethought. Malice aforethought includes wanton disregard for human life, which means acting in deliberate disregard of the plain and strong likelihood that death or great bodily harm would result. Operating a motor vehicle at a speed of 100 miles per hour might or might not be found to constitute wanton disregard for human life, but of the reasons listed, **B** is the only one which could result in a conviction for murder.

A is incorrect for two reasons: first, culpable negligence is insufficient to constitute malice aforethought; and, second, the facts do not indicate that Durwood was intoxicated at the time the accident occurred. Under the "misdemeanor-manslaughter" rule, a death resulting from the commission of a misdemeanor might be classified as *manslaughter*. Since driving without a license carries a maximum sentence of less than one year (i.e., 30 days) it is properly classified as a misdemeanor. **C** and **D** are incorrect, however, because the misdemeanor-manslaughter rule cannot lead to a conviction for *murder*.

94. **C**   All jurisdictions which recognize a felony murder rule apply it only when the victim's death (or the injury which leads to it) occurs during the commission of a felony. Since the stroke which caused Victoria's death did not occur until the day after Dennis robbed the store, it did not occur during the perpetration of a felony by Dennis, and the felony murder rule does not apply.

             A and **B** are, therefore, incorrect. **D** is incorrect because many cases have held that since the victim of a robbery is likely to respond with force, even a robbery with a toy gun is a dangerous felony.

95. **A**   "Specific intent" crimes are those which require a state of mind amounting to a desire or knowledge by the defendant that his conduct will result in a consequence which is criminally proscribed. "General intent" crimes are those for which conviction may be based on recklessness or criminal negligence. Voluntary intoxication may provide a defense to crimes requiring specific intent since it may prevent its formation. Awareness of the effect which alcohol is likely to have on the capacity to assess risks, however, prevents voluntary intoxication from serving as a defense to crimes involving general intent. Since rape may consist of recklessly having intercourse without the victim's consent, it is a general intent crime, and voluntary intoxication is not a defense to it.

             Involuntary intoxication, on the other hand, may be a defense to crimes involving recklessness as well as to specific intent crimes. Defendant's assertion in **B,** might, therefore, provide her with an effective defense. Since attempted robbery requires the specific intent to commit a larceny by force or threat of force, defendant's intoxication in **C** may have prevented her from having the intent required and may thus provide her with an effective defense. In **D**, defendant's assertion is that he lacked the intent to deprive the rightful owner of possession of the automobile. Since this specific intent is an essential element of larceny, his intoxication may provide him with an effective defense.

96. **B**   Receiving stolen property consists of the acquisition of stolen property with the knowledge that it has been stolen and with the intent to permanently deprive its owner of it. Acquisition occurs when the defendant takes possession of the property himself, or when he directs that possession be delivered to another. Thus although Defendant did not personally take possession of the car which Quincy stole, he "received" it when he directed that it be delivered to his brother.

             In **A,** the car which Defendant received had already been recovered by the police, and was, therefore, not stolen at the time of the sale. In **C** and **D,** there is no indication that the cars sold to Defendant ever had been stolen. **A, C,** and **D** are, therefore, incorrect.

97. **B**   After being advised of his *Miranda* rights, a suspect in custody cannot be subjected to police interrogation unless he voluntarily and intelligently waives those rights. If Axel was unaware that Deacon could overhear his conversation with Barber, Axel's comment was not an interrogation of Deacon, and Deacon's statement was not obtained in violation of his rights.

      If Deacon's statement was the result of an interrogation, it violated his rights unless he waived them voluntarily and intelligently. **A** is incorrect because it would make Deacon's waiver intelligent but not necessarily voluntary (e.g., he may have been intimidated by the presence of police). **C** is incorrect because it would make Deacon's waiver voluntary, but not necessarily intelligent (e.g., he might not have understood his rights). The Constitution protects Deacon against custodial interrogations, even if the custody itself is lawful. **D** is, therefore, incorrect.

98. **D**   Larceny is the trespassory taking and carrying off of personal property known to be another's with the intent to permanently deprive. In this definition, "trespassory" means without the consent of the owner. Since rearranging the merchandise in the storeroom was part of Dander's duties and therefore done with Hardware's consent, her moving of the lawn mower was not trespassory. "Taking" means acquiring possession. Since Dander did not transfer the lawn mower from her employer's possession to her own, she did not take it. Although any exercise of dominion accompanied by even a slight movement may constitute a "carrying off," Dander moved the lawn mower as part of her duties and without any intention — at that time — of making it her own. She, therefore, did not carry it off. In order for a person to be guilty of larceny, the intent to permanently deprive must exist at the time she took and carried off the chattel involved. Although Dander did decide to permanently deprive Hardware of the lawn mower, she did not perform any act which might be taking or carrying off after making that decision. For these reasons, Dander is not guilty of larceny. Embezzlement is a criminal conversion of personal property by one in lawful custody of it. Conversion takes place when the defendant seriously interferes with the rights of the owner, usually by exercising dominion or control over the chattel. Because Dander never did anything inconsistent with Hardware's rights in the lawn mower, and never exercised dominion or control over it, she cannot be said to have converted it. She is not, therefore, guilty of embezzlement.

99. **C**   Murder involves malice aforethought coupled with an act which proximately results in the unlawful killing of a human being. Since malice aforethought includes the intent to inflict great bodily harm, and since it was Duggan's intention to severely injure Ventana, the only issue to be resolved in determining Duggan's guilt is whether Duggan's act was a proximate cause of Ventana's death. If it was, then Duggan is guilty of murder.

      Intervening proximate causes of Ventana's death would not prevent Duggan's act from also being a proximate cause, unless those intervening causes could be characterized as unforeseeable or independent. Although Ventana's allergic reaction to the drug was an intervening cause of harm, there is no indication that such an allergic reaction was unforeseeable. Since the drug was given to relieve pain which resulted from the beating, neither its administration nor the patient's allergic reaction to it can be termed independent. **A** is, therefore, incorrect. **B** is incorrect because Ventana's death may have had several proximate causes. The fact that Dr. Medich's conduct was one of them does not mean that Duggan's conduct was not also one of them. Since Ventana's death would not have occurred without Dr. Medich's conduct, Dr. Medich's conduct was a *factual* cause of death. Since Dr. Medich's conduct occurred after Duggan's, Dr. Medich's conduct was an *intervening* cause of that death. But an intervening cause does not break the chain of proximate causation, unless that intervention was unforeseeable. Sometimes gross negligence or recklessness by an intervenor is held to be unforeseeable. This is not an inflexible rule, however. Under some circumstances, even reckless conduct or gross negligence has been held foreseeable. For this reason, a finding that Dr. Medich's conduct was reckless or grossly negligent — without an additional finding that it was unforeseeable — would not be sufficient to result in the conclusion that Duggan's conduct was not one of the proximate causes of Ventana's death. **D** is, therefore, incorrect.

100.   **B**   When the words "deliberate and premeditated" appear in a murder statute, "deliberate" means that the defendant was possessed of a cool mind capable of reflection, and "premeditated" means that the defendant actually did reflect on his act before committing it. Since the psychiatrist's testimony indicates that Delbert may have been incapable of cool reflection at the time of his act, it may be admitted for the purpose of showing that the killing was not "deliberate and premeditated."

           A is incorrect because under the M'Naghten test, a defendant is insane only if mental disease made him incapable of knowing the nature and quality of his act, or that it was wrong. **C** is incorrect because the testimony may be admitted to establish lack of deliberation and premeditation, even though it does not establish that Delbert was insane. An intentional killing may be reduced from murder to voluntary manslaughter if the defendant was acting in the heat of passion caused by sufficient provocation. for this purpose, the provocation and defendant's response to it are usually judged by an objective standard. **D** is incorrect, however, because, as explained above, psychiatric evidence of Delbert's state of mind may be relevant to the elements of deliberation and premeditation.

101.   **D**   If the only evidence against Martin was excluded because it was obtained by coercing his confession, his motion to dismiss might be granted. But although a coerced confession cannot be used in a criminal prosecution against the person who made it, evidence which was obtained independently of the coerced confession can be used. Since Golden obtained evidence of Martin's identity without knowledge of Martin's statement, Martin's motion must be denied.

           A and **B** are, therefore, incorrect. **C** is incorrect because if Golden's discovery of the evidence against Martin resulted from a violation of Martin's constitutional rights, it might be excluded in spite of the fact that Golden was employed by the federal government and Harris by the state.

102.   **C**   Statements obtained from a suspect in violation of his constitutional rights (and, some authorities suggest, the fruits of such statements) cannot be used against him. Only the person from whom the statement was obtained, however, has standing to assert the constitutional violation. Since the interrogation of Martin did not violate Dallaroche's rights, Dellaroche lacks the necessary standing to assert its unconstitutionality.

           A and **B** are incorrect because there are no facts indicating that Dellaroche's complicity would have been discovered without Martin's statement. Since the interrogation of Martin did not violate the constitutional rights of Dellaroche, it does not matter whether Dellaroche was in custody at the time it took place. **D** is, therefore, incorrect.

103. **D**   A conspiracy is an agreement to commit a crime. Conspirators are vicariously liable for crimes committed in furtherance of the conspiratorial goal by other members of the conspiracy. This is so even if those crimes were unforeseeable, not included in the original plan, or unnecessary to the success of the conspiracy, so long as they were committed in furtherance of the conspiratorial goal. Since Michael transported the car across a state line for the purpose of aiding their escape it was in furtherance of the conspiratorial goal. **A, B,** and **C** are, therefore, incorrect.

104. **C**   A conspiracy is an agreement to commit a crime. Since the Dyer Act prohibits the interstate transportation of stolen vehicles, a person can be guilty of conspiring to violate it only if he agrees to transport a stolen vehicle across a state line. Thus, although Norman may be guilty of violating the act, he could not be guilty of conspiring to violate it unless he expressly or impliedly agreed to do so.

A is incorrect because an agreement to steal a car is not necessarily an agreement to transport it across a state line. **B** is incorrect because a substantive crime does not merge with the crime of conspiring to commit it. Thus, conviction of the substantive crime does not prevent conviction for conspiracy. **D** is incorrect because the crime of conspiracy is committed when parties agree to commit a crime, and is complete before the substantive crime is committed (or even if it is never committed).

105. **B**   A person is guilty as an accessory if, with criminal intent, he aided and abetted in the commission of a crime, or if he stood by ready and willing to give aid in its commission. Thus if Norman was willing to help Michael steal the car, he is guilty of larceny as an accessory.

Although a co-conspirator is vicariously liable for crimes committed in furtherance of the conspiracy, this is not the only way that Norman might be found guilty of larceny. As explained above, he may have been guilty as an accessory. **A** is, therefore, incorrect. **C** is incorrect because a person may aid and abet in the commission of a crime by making himself available to assist in its perpetration if necessary. **D** is incorrect because the Double Jeopardy Clause of the United States Constitution does not apply to prosecutions by different sovereigns (such as by the United States and a state).

106. **B**   A statement made in response to a custodial interrogation of a suspect is admissible against her only if, after being advised of her *Miranda* rights, she makes a voluntary and intelligent waiver. Since Doyle concedes that her statements were voluntary, the only remaining issue is whether she had sufficient knowledge and understanding of her rights to intelligently waive them. The same issue was resolved in **B,** in which Binh's response to the officer's question made it doubtful that Binh understood his constitutional rights.

In **A,** since Ascot was not in custody at the time he answered the officer's questions (and since the question was probably not an "interrogation"), the issue of waiver did not arise. Although a person who has been formally charged with a crime is entitled to counsel at a lineup, **C** is not applicable since Cartier had not been formally charged with any crime, and since, therefore, she was not entitled to counsel, no issue of waiver arose in her case. The Fourth Amendment protects against warrantless search, but this protection may be waived by a person who voluntarily and intelligently consents to such a search. Waiver was, therefore, an issue in **D**. Although the officer's statement might not have been sufficient to make Edward's waiver intelligent, the circumstances — an unexpected, middle-of-the-night visit by three uniformed police officers — also raise serious doubts about its voluntariness. For this reason, **B** (in which the only issue was the intelligence of the waiver) is more applicable as a precedent. [*Note:* Case-summary-analysis questions are usually as uncertain as this one. Fortunately, they are no longer common on the MBE.]

107. **D**   After being formally charged with a crime, a suspect is entitled to counsel at a lineup. The lineup in which Degnan participated may have been valid, however, if Degnan voluntarily and intelligently waived his right to counsel. The officer's statement — which suggested that Degnan's reliance on his constitutional rights would keep the prosecutor from going easy on him — raises doubts about both the voluntariness and intelligence of his waiver. In **D**, the middle-of-the-night appearance of the police at Edward's door raised the same doubts.

In **B** there was an obvious issue relating to the intelligence of Binh's waiver. In addition, it could be argued that the presence of a police officer was coercive enough to raise an issue of voluntariness. Since the conduct of the officers in **D** was more obviously coercive, however, **D** is a better precedent [*Note:* Case-summary-analysis questions are usually as uncertain as this one. Fortunately, they are no longer common on the MBE.] In **A,** since Ascot was not in custody at the time he answered the officer's question (and since the question was probably not an "interrogation"), the issue of waiver did not arise. Although a person who has been formally charged with a crime is entitled to counsel at a lineup, **C** is not applicable since Cartier had not been formally charged with any crime. Because Cartier was not entitled to counsel, no issue of waiver arose in her case.

108. **B**   The crime of receiving stolen property is committed when the defendant receives stolen property with the knowledge that it is stolen and with the intent to permanently deprive the owner of it. Since the car which Dee purchased was in the lawful custody of the police, it could be argued that it was no longer stolen. Although it is not certain that this argument would succeed, it is the only one listed which could possibly be effective in Dee's defense. **B** is, therefore, correct.

Since the police are supposed to prevent crime rather than instigate it, many jurisdictions hold that a defendant who was induced by the police or an agent of the police to commit a crime which he was not otherwise disposed to commit is entrapped and has a valid affirmative defense to the crime charged. **A** is incorrect, however, because Dee came looking for a stolen car and was, therefore, already disposed to commit the crime with which he was charged. Ordinarily, a defense may not be based on the assertion of another's rights. If Carpenter's cooperation was coerced, Carpenter's rights may have been violated. **C** is incorrect, however, because Dee may not base his defense on the invasion of Carpenter's rights. **D** is incorrect because no right of Dee's was bargained away.

109. **C**   If a warrantless search violates a reasonable expectation of privacy held by the person whose property is searched, it violates that person's Fourth Amendment rights. Since each person who shares property with another knows that the other has access to it, neither of them has a reasonable expectation that the property will remain private. For this reason, a search is generally valid if authorized by one of the persons who shares the property which is searched. Since Wanda shared the apartment, the bedroom, and the closet with Mike, Mike could have no reasonable expectation that these areas would remain private, and Wanda's consent to the search made it valid.

Although a search warrant may not be issued without probable cause, probable cause does not justify a search without a warrant. **A** is, therefore, incorrect. If police discover contraband during hot pursuit of a suspect, they may be permitted to seize it without a warrant if necessary to prevent disposal or destruction. **B** is incorrect, however, because the police were not in hot pursuit of Mike when they discovered the marijuana. The seizure of contraband "in plain view" might be valid because its discovery was not the result of a search. **D** is incorrect, however, because the police officers had already begun their search (i.e., by having Wanda open the closet door for them to look inside it) when the marijuana fell into view.

110. **D**   The Double Jeopardy Clause provides that no person shall for the same offense be placed twice in jeopardy. It is generally understood, however, that jeopardy does not begin until the commencement of a trial, which occurs when a jury is empaneled. Since a grand jury proceeding is not "jeopardy", there is no constitutional reason why a matter should not be brought before a grand jury several times.

A and **B** are, therefore, incorrect. In addition, **A** is incorrect because the term "res judicata" is applied only to a final determination by a court. **C** is incorrect because jeopardy has not yet begun, so the motion must be denied whether or not the first grand jury's decision was motivated by prejudice.

111. **D**   Murder is the unjustified killing of a human being with malice aforethought. Malice aforethought means a wanton disregard for human life, or an intent to kill, inflict great bodily harm, commit a felony, or resist a lawful arrest. Since it is clear that Deborah did not intend to commit a felony, to resist a lawful arrest, or to strike anyone with the bullet, she can be found guilty of murder only if her conduct showed a wanton disregard for human life. Thus, if she is acquitted, it can only be because the court found that her conduct did not show a wanton disregard.

A is incorrect because malice aforethought may exist without an intent to kill. Since any result may have many proximate causes, the fact that the ambulance driver's conduct was a proximate cause of Vincent's death does not establish that Deborah's conduct was not also a proximate cause of that death. **B** is, therefore, incorrect. The privilege to abate a nuisance permits the use of reasonable force only. Although the conduct of Deborah's neighbors may have constituted a nuisance, it is obvious that the use of a deadly weapon was not a reasonable response to it. **C** is, therefore, incorrect.

112. **A**   Criminal battery consists of the intentional, reckless, or criminally negligent application of force to the body of another. Deborah's act of shooting through the ceiling into an apartment in which she knew there were people probably was, at least, criminally negli-

gent, and so probably constituted a battery.

A person is guilty of attempting to commit a crime when, with the specific intent to bring about a criminally proscribed result, she comes substantially close to accomplishing that result. Since involuntary manslaughter is an unintended homicide, no person can have the specific intent to commit it. Thus, there can be no attempt to commit it. **B** is, therefore, incorrect. Attempted murder and attempted voluntary manslaughter both require an intent to kill. Since Deborah did not intend to strike anyone with the bullet, **C** and **D** are incorrect.

113. **C**   A person is privileged to use reasonable force to protect herself from what she reasonably believes to be a threat of imminent bodily harm. Potentially lethal force is reasonable when used in response to what the defendant reasonably perceives to be a threat of potentially lethal force. Thus, if Bonnie reasonably believed that Alice was reaching for a gun, her use of a gun in response may have been reasonable, and therefore privileged. While it is not certain that a court would come to this conclusion, the argument in **C** is the only one listed which could possibly provide Bonnie with an effective defense.

A person is guilty of a criminal attempt when, with the intent to bring about a criminally prohibited result, she comes substantially close to achieving it. **A** is incorrect because the fact that a death did not actually occur will not prevent a conviction for attempting to cause one. If Bonnie had the intent to kill Alice when she aimed her pistol at Alice's chest, she would be guilty of attempted murder if she came subsequently close to causing Alice's death. this might be so even if she did not strike Alice in the chest, or even if she did not strike Alice at all. for this reason, **B** is incorrect. **D** is incorrect because deadly force is force which is likely to result in death or great bodily harm. The use of a pistol thus constitutes deadly force even though the harm which it actually causes happens to be slight.

114. **D**   A person is privileged to use reasonable force to protect herself from what she reasonably believes to be a threat of imminent bodily harm. Since Bonnie fired a pistol at Alice, and was (or appeared to be) capable of firing it again, it was reasonable for Alice to believe herself threatened with imminent bodily harm, and was probably reasonable for her to respond with deadly force.

If Bonnie's belief that Alice was about to shoot her was a reasonable one, Bonnie's use of force may have been privileged. **A** is incorrect, however, because, although an aggressor has no right of self-defense against a reasonable response to her initial aggression, Alice committed no act of aggression until after Bonnie fired at her. Self-defense may privilege the use of deadly force in response to what is reasonably perceived as deadly force. Even though the force used by Bonnie had not yet caused death or serious injury, it was capable of doing so, and can, therefore, be regarded as deadly force. **B** is, therefore, incorrect. **C** is incorrect because even a premeditated killing may be privileged by self-defense.

115. **D**   Murder is the unjustified killing of a human being with malice aforethought. In addition to reckless disregard for human life, and the intent to kill, to cause great bodily harm, or to resist a lawful arrest, malice aforethought includes the intent to commit a felony. Since arson is a dangerous felony, **D** is correct.

A is incorrect because malice aforethought may exist even though the defendants did not intend to kill. Some jurisdictions have held that the felony murder rule cannot be applied *unless* the deaths were totally independent of the defendants' purpose in committing a felony. **B** is a misstatement of this rule, and is, therefore, incorrect. **C** is incorrect because unreasonable conduct is not sufficient to constitute malice aforethought.

116. **D**   At common law, arson was defined as the intentional burning of another's dwelling. Under the statute given, the definition includes buildings other than dwellings as well. Since Sal and Terry desired to burn down the factory, they had the necessary intent. Since they succeeded in doing so, they are guilty of arson. **I** is, therefore, correct. Conspiracy consists of an agreement to commit a crime. Since Sal and Terry agreed to commit arson, they are guilty of conspiracy. **II** is, therefore, correct. Conspiracy does not merge with the substantive crime and may be the basis of separate prosecution and conviction. **D** is, therefore, correct.

117. **B**   Kidnapping consists of intentionally transporting and confining a person against that person's will by force or threat and without legal authority. The essential difference between kidnapping and criminal false imprisonment is the requirement of asportation: unless the defendant has moved the victim to the place of confinement, there is no kidnapping. Since Dart forced the hostage to accompany him to his car where he confined her for a period of fifteen minutes, he has kidnapped her. Because he did not move any of the other victims to the place of their confinement, he did not kidnap them.

A, **C**, and **D** are, therefore, incorrect.

118. **A**   A defendant is guilty of criminally receiving stolen property when he acquires stolen personal property with knowledge that it is stolen and with the intent to permanently deprive its owner. Since the car which Dake purchased from Agsten had been requisitioned from the police department, it was not stolen property. Since Dake never received stolen property, he cannot be guilty of this crime.

B is incorrect because guilt does not require that the defendant pay for stolen property with his own money (or that he pay for it at all). Police officers are supposed to prevent crime, not to cause it. For this reason, many jurisdictions hold that a defendant who was entrapped (i.e., induced by a police officer to commit a crime which he was not otherwise inclined to commit), cannot be convicted of committing it. Agsten and Bates did not entrap Dake because Dake indicated his inclination to purchase a stolen car before either Agsten or Bates suggested that he do so. **C** is, therefore incorrect. A search or arrest warrant may not be issued without a showing of probable cause, but no such showing is required before beginning an investigation. For this reason, **D** is incorrect.

119. **B**   A person is guilty of a criminal attempt when with the intent to bring about a criminally prohibited result he comes substantially close to achieving it. Since Dake intended to receive property in the belief that it was stolen and with the intent to permanently deprive the owner, and would have done so had the facts been as he believed them to be, he is guilty of attempting to receive stolen property. Since the elements of criminally receiving stolen property include all the elements of attempting to criminally receive stolen property, however, the attempt is a lesser offense included in the substantive

crime. For this reason, Dake cannot be convicted of both receiving and attempting to receive. Thus, he can be found guilty of the attempt only if he is not convicted of criminally receiving stolen property.

A is, therefore, incorrect. In many jurisdictions, a person who performs a lawful act in the mistaken belief that it is prohibited (i.e., while operating under a mistake of law) cannot be guilty of a criminal attempt, since the result which he intended to achieve was not criminally prohibited. **C** is incorrect, however, because Dake was not operating under a mistake of law; the result which he intended to accomplish — the purchase of a stolen car — was actually unlawful, as he believed it to be. On the other hand, if the defendant intends to accomplish an unlawful result, but his mistake *about the facts* prevents the result of his act from actually being unlawful, he can be convicted of a criminal attempt. Here, Dake's intent was to purchase a stolen car. Since the car was not stolen, he could not be guilty of receiving stolen property. But since he believed it to be stolen, and would have been guilty of receiving stolen property if the facts were as he believed them to be (i.e., if it was stolen), he can be convicted of the attempt. **D** is, therefore, incorrect.

120. **C**   A criminal conspiracy is an agreement between two or more persons to commit a crime. Without such an agreement, there can be no conspiracy. Since neither Agsten nor Bates actually intended to commit a crime, Dake never made such an agreement with either of them, even though he believed he did. For this reason, he cannot be guilty of conspiracy.

A is, therefore, incorrect. **B** is incorrect for this reason, and because conspiracy is a separate crime which does not merge with the substantive crime which the conspirators agreed to commit. Thus, if there had been an agreement to receive stolen property, Dake could be convicted of conspiracy in addition to being convicted of attempting to receive stolen property. Since the crime of conspiracy is complete when the conspirators agree to commit a crime, the fact that they never actually accomplished the purpose of their conspiracy does not prevent a conspiracy conviction. **D** is, therefore, incorrect.

121. **B**   Arson is the intentional or malicious burning of the dwelling of another. Since even the slightest charring of the walls or ceiling is regarded as a burning, there was a burning of Goss' dwelling. Since malice includes recklessness, and since it was clearly reckless to set fire to a couch while it was inside the house, the necessary state of mind is present. Dealy is, therefore, guilty of arson.

Burglary is the trespassory breaking and entering of the dwelling of another at night with the intent to commit a larceny or any felony therein. Dealy entered Goss' dwelling at night. The unauthorized opening of a closed door can constitute a breaking, and any unauthorized entry is trespassory. Although Dealy did commit a felony inside (i.e., arson), she cannot be guilty of burglary unless she intended to do so when she entered. Since at the time Dealy entered Goss' house she meant only to retrieve her own property, she did not have the requisite intent to make her guilty of burglary. **A** and **C** are, therefore, incorrect. **D** is incorrect because Dealy is guilty of arson as explained above.

122. **C**   Larceny is a trespassory taking and carrying off of personal property known to be another's with the intent to permanently deprive the owner. Since Dealy did not physically move the couch, she may successfully argue that because there was no asportation

(i.e., carrying off), there was no larceny.

It is sometimes argued that one who enters through an unlocked door committed no breaking and, therefore, is not guilty of burglary. **A** is incorrect, however, because "breaking" is not an element of larceny. If a defendant carried off personal property which actually was her own, she could not be guilty of larceny because she did not take the property of another. If she mistakenly believed that it was her own, she still would not be guilty of larceny, because she did not carry off property known to be another's. The couch was not Dealy's, however, and she knew that it was not hers. The fact that it was equal in value to her stereo would not, therefore, justify her taking or carrying it off. **B** is, therefore, incorrect. A person who takes and carries off personal property known to be another's with the intent to permanently deprive is guilty of larceny without regard to whether or not she intended to benefit by doing so. **D** is, therefore, incorrect.

123. **D**   Because of the inherently coercive nature of police custody, the United States Supreme Court held (in *Miranda*) that inculpatory statements resulting from custodial interrogation of a defendant are inadmissible unless the defendant received certain warnings prior to making the statements. Among the required warnings is a caution that anything which the defendant says may be used against him. Because Cecil was working for the police, it is possible that his conversation with Dalke amounted to a police interrogation. Thus, if Dalke was in custody at the time, his statement might be inadmissible because he had not received *Miranda* warnings. The *Miranda* rule applies only to custodial interrogations, however. So if Dalke was not in custody at the time of his conversation with Cecil, the lack of *Miranda* warnings would not make his statement to Cecil inadmissible.

A is incorrect because even though Cecil might have been an agent of the police at the time he and Dalke shared a cell (i.e., while Dalke was clearly in custody), the statements in question were not made at that time. **B** is incorrect because *Miranda* warnings are required for custodial interrogations only. The issue to be determined is whether the conversation between Cecil and Dalke was a custodial interrogation, and therefore a violation of Dalke's rights. **C** assumes that Dalke's rights were violated and uses that assumption to prove that Dalke's rights were violated. This is circular reasoning and is, therefore, incorrect.

124. **C**   Under the "irresistible impulse" test, a person is not guilty by reason of insanity if mental disease made him incapable of controlling his conduct at the time of the alleged criminal act. Although not all jurisdictions accept this definition of insanity, under the facts given **C** is the only argument listed which would serve as an effective defense in any jurisdiction.

The M'Naghten rule provides that a person is not guilty of insanity if, at the time of the allegedly criminal act, mental disease prevented him from knowing either the nature and quality of his act or that it was wrong. A defendant is said to know that his act is "wrong," however, if he is aware that it is prohibited by law. Since Dominguez knew that if he was caught he would be imprisoned for murder, he had sufficient understanding that his act was wrong to make him sane under this rule. **A** is, therefore, incorrect. The concept of "intent" relates to the defendant's state of mind regarding the immediate consequences of his act, quite apart from the concept of "motive" which refers to a defendant's purpose in bringing that consequence about. Since Dominguez desired to kill Viola, he had the necessary intent to make him guilty of murder, in spite of his noble motive (i.e., to save the world). **B** is therefore, incorrect. A person who, by reason of mental illness, is incapable of understanding the nature and quality of his act is insane under the M'Naghten rule discussed above. The phrase "nature and quality of the act," however, refers to the physical character of the act and to its physical consequences. Since Dominguez understood that he was pushing Viola down the stairs and that this could result in her death, he did understand the nature and quality of his act. **D** is, therefore, incorrect.

125.   **A**   The Fourth Amendment to the United States Constitution protects against unreasonable search and seizure. Ordinarily, a warrantless search is regarded as unreasonable and, therefore, unlawful under this clause. This constitutional provision applies only to searches conducted by the police or by other *government officials*, however. For this reason, the fact that Adams was not a government employee — and was not working in conjunction with any government employee — would make the Fourth Amendment protection absolutely inapplicable here.

As to Choice **B**, there is some Supreme Court support for the proposition that a student's consent to an administrative search may sometimes be implied from the special relationship between students and administrators. But that consent would be unlikely to extend to something as intrusive as a bodily search (which is what occurred here when Adams reached into Donell's pocket) on only the weak hearsay evidence that was present here. And in any evident, this explanation is not as good as Choice A, which resolves the issue automatically. Therefore Choice B is wrong. Similarly, Choice **C**'s "special concern for the well-being of young people" rationale might support certain types of searches, but wouldn't support a bodily search with the much-less-than-probable-cause hearsay-type evidence here; Choice C, too, is thus clearly worse than Choice A.

D is incorrect for three reasons: first, an anonymous note does not ordinarily give anyone probable cause to believe its contents, especially where the note is itself based on hearsay; second, probable cause does not justify a warrantless search by a government official; and, third, Adams' search of Donell did not violate his Fourth Amendment rights even if she did not have probable cause, because as explained in Choice A Donell was not a government actor.

126.   **B**   A person is guilty of a criminal attempt when, with the specific intent to bring about a criminally prohibited result, he comes substantially close to bringing about that result. Thus, while certain crimes may be committed without intending the prohibited consequences, criminal attempt always requires the specific intent to bring about the prohibited result. Although Shafer could be convicted of violating the statute if he actually sold ammunition to Yule who was under the age of 16, he could not be convicted of attempting to violate the statute unless he knew that Yule was under the age of 16 and intended to sell her the ammunition.

For obvious practical reasons, there is usually an irrebuttable presumption that all persons know the law. Ignorance of the law, therefore, would not provide Shafer with a defense. **A** is, therefore, incorrect. The fact that Okner is vicariously liable under the statute would not furnish Shafer with a defense, since the statute imposes liability on both employee and employer. **C** is incorrect for this reason, and because the statute imposes vicarious liability on the employer only if the employee actually makes a sale, which Shafer did not do. **D** is incorrect because the statute does not make knowledge or experience an element of guilt.

127. **A**   Some cases have held that the imposition of a prison term on the basis of vicarious liability for a strict-liability crime committed by a defendant's employee is a violation of due process. It is generally understood, however, that the imposition of a fine on this basis is constitutionally valid. Since this statute makes an employer vicariously liable for the payment of a fine if an employee sells ammunition to a minor, and since Okner's employee sold ammunition to a minor, Okner may be convicted.

         B and **C** are incorrect because of the specific language of the given statute: **B** because the statute imposes strict liability, and does not make negligence or unreasonable behavior a basis of guilt; and **C** because the statute does not make the employer's presence an element of guilt. **D** is incorrect because it is overinclusive: there are many situations in which the criminal law may validly impose vicarious liability for the crime of another (e.g., co-conspirators are vicariously liable for each other's crimes committed in furtherance of the conspiracy).

128. **B**   At common law, murder is the unlawful killing of a human being with malice aforethought. One state of mind which constitutes malice aforethought is the intent to kill a human being. Since knowledge of the victim's identity is not an essential element of murder, the fact that DeLong was mistaken about the identity of the person at whom she was shooting does not prevent her from having the necessary state of mind (i.e., intent to kill). For this reason, DeLong may be convicted even without application of the doctrine of transferred intent.

         A is, therefore, incorrect. **C** is incorrect because DeLong unlawfully killed Ralston with the intent to kill a human being, and is, therefore, guilty of murder. Although a wanton disregard for human life may constitute malice aforethought, mere negligence does not. Since the creation of an unreasonable risk is merely negligent, this fact is not sufficient to justify a finding that DeLong had malice aforethought, which is necessary to a conviction for murder. **D** is, therefore, incorrect.

129. **C**   The Fifth Amendment to the United States Constitution provides, in part, that "no person shall ... be subject for the same offense to be twice put in jeopardy of life or limb." This prevents a defendant from being charged twice with the same crime. The charge against Delta in the state court involves the violation of a statute which is different from the one which she was convicted of violating in the federal court, however. The state prosecution is, thus, not for the same offense. For this reason, the double jeopardy clause does not require its dismissal even though the same evidence will be used in both prosecutions.

         A is, therefore, incorrect. A criminal conspiracy consists of an agreement between two or more persons to commit a crime, and is complete when the agreement is made. It is a crime separate from the substantive crime which the conspirators agreed to commit, and does not merge with that substantive crime. **B** is incorrect for this reason, and because prosecutions for violating state and federal statutes are not for the same offense, even though based on a single act by the defendant. **D** contains an incorrect statement since violations of the statutes of different sovereigns constitute different offenses; therefore, separate prosecutions are not barred by the double jeopardy clause.

130. **D**   Criminal battery consists of the intentional, reckless, or criminally negligent application of force to the body of another. Since it is, thus, a general intent crime, it may be committed without the intent to make contact with the victim. While voluntary intoxication is no defense to a general intent crime, involuntary intoxication ordinarily is. A person has become involuntarily intoxicated when his intoxication was the result of an unpredictable and grossly excessive reaction to an intoxicating substance. Thus, if Dane had never before been overcome by the alcohol in one drink, it may be that his intoxication was involuntary, and that it will provide him with a defense to the charge of criminal battery. It is not certain that this defense would be successful, since a court might find that although the response was unpredictable, it was not grossly excessive. The fact set forth in **D,** however, is the only one listed which might possibly provide Dane with an effective defense.

A person may become "voluntarily" intoxicated even without the intent to become drunk so long as he is aware that the substance which he is taking has an intoxicating potential. Since Dane was aware that the Russian bomber had some alcohol in it, his intoxication may be called voluntary even if he did not intend to become drunk. **A** is, therefore, incorrect. If Dane's conduct in drinking the Russian bomber was reckless or criminally negligent he could have the necessary *mens rea* to be guilty of battery (i.e., general intent), even though he did not specifically know what risk he was creating (i.e., that he would fall off the bar stool). **B** is, therefore, incorrect. **C** is incorrect because battery is a general intent crime, and, therefore, does not require the intent to make contact with another human being.

131. **A**   A person is privileged by self-defense to use reasonable force to protect himself against what reasonably appears to be an imminent threat of bodily harm. In this connection, reasonable force is the force which would appear necessary to the reasonable person. Even deadly force is reasonable if the person using it reasonably believes that he is being threatened with deadly force. Thus, if Balin reasonably believed that his life was in danger, the force which he used in self-defense was probably reasonable, making Balin not guilty of attempted murder.

Although deadly force is not ordinarily considered reasonable in defense of mere property, **B** is incorrect because Balin's shot was probably fired in response to a threat against his person, and may have been justified by self-defense. Although the intent to kill or inflict serious injury can be inferred from the fact that Balin fired at Oden, **C** is incorrect because, if reasonable, his conduct was privileged by self-defense. Since Balin had no way of knowing that the person threatening him was a police officer, Oden's status as such can have no bearing on the reasonableness of Balin's actions. **D** is, therefore, incorrect.

132. **C**   Police officers, like private citizens, are privileged to use reasonable force to protect themselves against attack. This privilege does not permit the application of deadly force by a police officer unless he is confronted by what reasonably appears to be deadly force against him. When Oden heard the sound of a pistol being cocked and saw the out-

line of a person with a pistol in his hand, it may have been reasonable for him to believe that deadly force was about to be used against him. Although it is not certain that a court would find Oden's belief to be reasonable, **C** is the only argument listed which could possibly provide Oden with an effective defense.

Although police officers may be entitled to use more force than private citizens under certain circumstances, **A** is incorrect because the fact that a defendant was a police officer is never, alone, sufficient to privilege his conduct. An officer who has probable cause to believe that a crime is being committed may be privileged to make an arrest. **B** is incorrect, however, because deadly force is not privileged in effecting that arrest, unless the crime is an "atrocious" one. Since Oden's shot was not fired in response to Balin's shot [**Note:** Read the facts again if you think that it was], the reasonableness of Balin's conduct cannot be relevant to the reasonableness of Oden's. **D** is, therefore, incorrect.

133. **C**   One who intentionally aids, abets, or facilitates the commission of a crime is criminally responsible for the crime as an accomplice. In addition, an accomplice is criminally responsible for all the foreseeable consequences of the crime which he facilitated. Since the use of Dailey's apartment to escape detection was part of Reavis' plan in preparing for the robbery, Dailey's agreement to permit Reavis to use it facilitated the robbery, making Dailey an accomplice to it. As such, Dailey may be guilty of felony murder in the death which resulted from the robbery, but only if it was foreseeable that such a death would occur.

One who becomes an accessory after a crime has been committed (i.e., accessory after the fact) by knowingly harboring the person who committed it is not criminally responsible for prior acts committed by the person harbored. A person who facilitates the commission of a crime by agreeing in advance that he will harbor the perpetrator after the crime is committed is guilty as an accomplice (i.e., accessory before the fact), however. As such he is criminally responsible for all foreseeable consequences of the crime to which he was an accomplice. **A** is, therefore, incorrect. Since an accomplice is criminally responsible for those consequences which were foreseeable, the fact that Dailey did not actually know that Reavis would use a gun does not protect him from liability if Reavis' use of a gun was foreseeable. **B** is, therefore, incorrect. A conspirator is criminally responsible for all crimes committed by co-conspirators in furtherance of the subject of the conspiracy. **D** is incorrect, however, because an accessory is criminally responsible only for consequences which were foreseeable.

134. **D**   A conspiracy is an agreement by two or more persons to commit a crime. Ordinarily, one who agrees to furnish services to another which the other will use in committing a crime is not guilty of conspiracy merely because he knows the purpose to which the services will be put. Where, however, the supplier has a stake in the criminal enterprise, his agreement to furnish services may constitute a conspiracy to commit the crime. Since Dailey knew that Reavis would be using his apartment as a hideout following the robbery, and since Reavis' promise to compensate Dailey by paying him a percentage of the loot gave Dailey a stake in the criminal enterprise, Dailey may be guilty of conspiracy.

A is, therefore, incorrect. **B** is incorrect for two reasons: first, Dailey's agreement probably was per se unlawful, since he knew that Reavis would be hiding in his apartment to escape detection (i.e., that he would be harboring a felon); and, second, Dailey had a personal stake in Reavis' crime. The crime of conspiracy to commit robbery is complete when the defendant agrees with another to commit the robbery, and is a separate crime from the robbery itself. Thus, the fact that a defendant is guilty of robbery is not relevant to the issue of whether he conspired (i.e., agreed) to commit it. For this reason, **C** is incorrect.

135. **C** The United States Constitution protects criminal defendants against unreasonable search and seizure. To give this protection meaning, the courts exclude evidence obtained as the result of an unreasonable search. Not every observation or inspection by police officers is properly classified as a search, however. In general, it is understood that a search occurs only when the police inspect a place in which the defendant has a reasonable expectation of privacy. If the field was such a place, the overflight and subsequent visit by police constituted searches, and, since they were performed without a warrant, the evidence obtained as a result of those searches should be excluded. On the other hand, if the field was not a place in which Dage had a reasonable expectation of privacy, the overflight and visit were not searches and the evidence should not be excluded.

A is incorrect because if Dage had no reasonable expectation of privacy, the use of special equipment to photograph what the police observed would not be a search. The Constitution provides that a warrant may be issued only upon a showing of probable cause. For this reason, a warrant obtained solely on the basis of information received from an informant may be invalid unless the reliability of the informant can be properly established. **B** is incorrect, however, because the warrant in this case might have been issued on the basis of the police officers' observations. The constitutional protection against unreasonable search and seizure prevents the use of evidence obtained directly or indirectly as a result of an improper search (i.e., "fruit of the poisonous tree"). Thus, if the warrant was issued as the result of observations which the officers made in violation of Dage's constitutional rights, the evidence will be excluded even though it was discovered after the warrant was issued. **D** is, therefore, incorrect.

136. **A** Once a criminal defendant has asserted his right to have an attorney present, further interrogation in the absence of the attorney makes any incriminating statements by the defendant inadmissible. Since Dage was questioned after asserting his right to counsel, the statement which he made in response to that questioning should be excluded.

B and **C** are, therefore, incorrect. Even after asserting his right to counsel, a defendant may waive that right by making incriminating statements during a discussion which he himself initiates. Since Dage's statement was made in response to a question by the police officer, however, it does not constitute a waiver of his rights and is, therefore, inadmissible. **D** is, therefore, incorrect.

137. **D** A person is guilty of a criminal attempt when, with the specific intent to bring about a result which is criminally prohibited, he comes substantially close to accomplishing that result. Since Donohue believed that the time was five minutes past eleven, and since it would have been lawful to sell liquor at that time, he did not have the specific intent to bring about a result which was criminally prohibited. For this reason, he could not be

guilty of attempting to violate the statute.

A and **B** are, therefore, incorrect. Attempt always requires specific intent, even where the substantive crime does not. Thus, even if the statute did not require specific intent, Donohue could not be guilty of *attempting* to violate it without specifically intending to sell liquor after midnight. **C** is, therefore, incorrect.

138. **A**   At common law, larceny is defined as a trespassory taking and carrying off of personal property known to be another's with the intent to permanently deprive the owner thereof. A person who is reclaiming his own property is not committing larceny since he is not carrying off the property of another. Thus, Dover's taking of $50 to pay himself back for the money which Vinton owed him was not a larceny. Except in the case of fungible goods, however, this rule does not protect a defendant who takes something which is not his own, even though it is equivalent in value to the property which he seeks to reclaim. Thus, Dover's taking of $50 cash to pay himself for the watch which Vinton refused to return is a larceny.

Since the statute provides that a larceny of $50 or less is a misdemeanor, **A** is correct, and **B**, **C** and **D** are incorrect.

139. **C**   A defendant is guilty of voluntary manslaughter when, with the intent to kill or cause great bodily harm, the defendant causes the death of a human being under circumstances of extreme emotional distress or mistaken justification. Many cases have held that the emotional distress which results from learning that a close relative has been raped or otherwise injured is sufficiently extreme to justify the reduction of a charge of murder to a charge of voluntary manslaughter where the defendant kills the rapist. Although it is not certain that a court would reduce it, **C** is the only fact pattern listed in which the murder charge could possibly be reduced to voluntary manslaughter.

Since the defendants in **A**, **B** and **D** did not have the intent to kill or inflict great bodily harm, the defendants in these cases could not have committed voluntary manslaughter. **A**, **B** and **D** are, therefore, incorrect.

140. **C**   A criminal conspiracy is an agreement to commit a crime and is complete when the agreement is made. Since Al agreed to commit a robbery with Joe and Bob, he is guilty of conspiracy. **II** is, therefore, correct. A person is guilty of a criminal attempt when, with the specific intent to bring about a result which is criminally prohibited he comes substantially close to bringing about that result. Since Joe and Bob intended to rob the bank and came substantially close to doing so, they are guilty of attempted robbery. Co-conspirators are vicariously liable for crimes committed in furtherance of the agreement. Since the attempted robbery was committed in furtherance of the agreement between Joe, Al and Bob, Al is criminally liable for the attempt even though he did not physically participate in it. **I** is, therefore, incorrect.

QUESTIONS
EVIDENCE

EVIDENCE
TABLE OF CONTENTS
Numbers refer to Question Numbers

EVIDENCE QUESTIONS

1. Finney operated a chain of fast food restaurants which specialized in fried fish. Finney entered into a valid written contract with C-Foods, for the purchase of "six thousand pounds of frozen pinktail fish filets of frying quality," to be delivered by C-Foods over a period of six months. One week after C-Foods made its first delivery pursuant to the contract, however, Finney notified C-Foods that the product delivered was unacceptable because the filets delivered weighed only eight ounces each, and that they were cut from Grade B pinktail fish. Finney offered to return the unused portion of the delivery, and refused to make payment.

   C-Foods subsequently brought an action against Finney for breach of contract. At the trial of that action C-Foods offered the testimony of Cooke. Cooke testified that he was the head chef at a leading hotel, and that he had been employed as a chef in fine restaurants for more than thirty years. He testified further that in that time he had purchased large quantities of fish on numerous occasions, and was familiar with the terminology used in the wholesale fish industry. Cooke stated that when the phrase "pinktail fish filets of frying quality" is used in the wholesale fish business, it means boneless pieces from six to nine ounces in weight and cut from Grade A or B pinktail fish. Upon proper objection by Finney's attorney, Cooke's testimony as to the meaning of the phrase should be

   (A) admitted as evidence of trade terminology.

   (B) admitted, only if Cooke qualifies as an expert on the preparation of fried fish in fast food restaurants.

   (C) excluded, since it is an opinion.

   (D) excluded, unless the parties specifically agreed to be bound by the terminology of the wholesale fish industry.

Questions 2-3 are based on the following fact situation.

While visiting the United States from the Central American Republic of Platano, Perez purchased a sweater at Alfred's Department Store and paid for it at the appropriate cash register. In ringing up the sale, however, the store employee neglected to remove a security tag which was still affixed to the sweater to prevent theft. As a result, the tag caused an electronic security alarm to ring as Perez attempted to exit the store with the purchased merchandise. Security guards immediately accosted her and placed her under citizen's arrest. Eventually, the police were called, and a more thorough investigation was instituted. As a result, it was determined that Perez had paid for the merchandise. Authorities of Alfred's Department Store apologized to Perez, and permitted her to leave. Subsequently, *Today* magazine erroneously reported that Perez had been arrested, charged with shoplifting at Alfred's Department Store, and taken into police custody. Because Perez was a candidate for political office in the Republic of Platano, newspapers in that country reprinted the *Today* magazine article. Perez lost the election, and instituted an action against *Today* magazine for damages resulting from defamation.

2. At the trial of Perez's action, *Today* called as a witness Colombo, who resided in the Republic of Platano and who testified that he was familiar with Perez's reputation in that country. He stated that in Platano, Perez was generally known as a thieving and corrupt politician. If Perez's attorney moves to strike that testimony, the motion should be

   (A) granted, since reputation evidence is not admissible for the purpose of establishing a party's conduct at any particular time.

   (B) granted, since evidence of a party's character is admissible only in criminal cases.

   (C) denied, since evidence of the plaintiff's reputation is relevant to her claim for damage resulting from defamation.

(D) denied, since the evidence is relevant to the truth or falsity of the statements made in the *Today* magazine article.

3. Assume the following facts for the purpose of this question only: On cross-examination Perez's attorney asked Colombo whether he and Perez were political rivals, and Colombo answered that they were not. Perez's attorney subsequently offered the testimony of Macias, a Platano public official, who stated that in a recent election Colombo ran against Perez for political office, and that Colombo won the election by engaging in a campaign of false accusations against Perez. Upon appropriate motion of *Today's* attorney, the testimony of Macias should be

(A) admitted, since it tends to attack Colombo's credibility by showing bias.

(B) admitted, since *Today* opened the door by bringing Perez's reputation into question.

(C) admitted, since it is evidence of an admission.

(D) excluded.

4. At the trial of an action by Purco against Venco for breach of contract, Purco alleged that Venco failed to deliver three thousand filters as agreed. Purco asserted further that, as a result, it was required to purchase filters on the open market at a price substantially higher than that agreed upon in its contract with Venco. As part of its case, Purco offered the testimony of Waller who stated that she was Purco's purchasing agent. She said that when Venco breached its contract with Purco, she had been assigned to purchase filters elsewhere. In answer to a question, she said, "I recall buying three thousand filters at a price of twenty-three dollars per hundred." Purco's attorney then showed her a paper which Waller identified as a photocopy which she personally had made of Purco's file on that purchase, explaining that the original was kept in Purco's home office which was located in another state. Upon objection by Venco's attorney, which of the following should the court admit into evidence?

I. Waller's testimony as to her recollection of the purchase price.

II. The copy which Waller authenticated.

(A) I only.

(B) II only.

(C) I and II.

(D) Neither I nor II.

5. Investigating a hold-up of the First Bank, state police obtained descriptions of the robbers from bank employees. A warrant for the arrest of Abel was issued on the basis of one of those descriptions. After his arrest, Abel was identified by Tella, a bank employee who picked him out of a police line-up. Abel was charged with armed robbery in the state court. A federal prosecutor learned of the arrest and subpoenaed Abel to appear before a federal grand jury investigating the robberies of federally insured banks. After being granted use immunity by the federal prosecutor, Able admitted that he had participated in the robbery of the First Bank and identified Bell and Charles as his co-felons. As a result, indictments were issued against Bell and Charles for the violation of a federal law which prohibited the robbery of any federally insured bank. At his trial in the state court on the robbery charge, Abel was convicted solely on Tella's testimony. Abel's attorney moved to set the conviction aside on the ground that Abel had been granted immunity by the federal prosecutor. The motion should be

(A) denied, since a state court is not bound by a federal prosecutor's grant of use immunity.

(B) denied, since the testimony which Abel gave at the grand jury proceeding was not used against him.

(C) granted, since the state court proceeding had been instituted prior to the grant of use immunity.

(D) granted, since the state court is bound by the federal prosecutor's grant of use immunity.

Questions 6-7 are based on the following fact situation.

At the trial of a personal injury action, the plaintiff claimed that he had sustained a shattered elbow when he was knocked from his bicycle by the defendant's car. Dr. Withey testified for the plaintiff, stating that she examined him for the first time on the morning of trial and that her examination was made specifically in preparation for her testimony.

6. Dr. Withey stated that during the course of the examination the plaintiff said, "My arm hurts so much, I don't see how I'll ever be able to go back to work." Which of the following would be the defendant's strongest argument in support of a motion to strike the testimony?

   (A) The plaintiff's statement was made in contemplation of litigation.

   (B) The doctor was not examining the plaintiff for the purpose of treatment.

   (C) The plaintiff's statement was self-serving.

   (D) Evidence of the plaintiff's statement is more prejudicial than probative.

7. Dr. Withey then stated that during the course of the examination the plaintiff also said, "When I was struck by the car my right elbow struck the ground so hard that I heard a sound like a gunshot." If the defendant objects to this testimony, the court should

   (A) sustain the objection, since the statement is hearsay.

   (B) sustain the objection, since the examination was not performed for the purpose of diagnosis or treatment.

   (C) overrule the objection, since the statement was part of a pertinent medical history.

   (D) overrule the objection, since the statement described a former sense impression.

Questions 8-9 are based on the following fact situation.

After a minor impact caused a Wildflight automobile to explode, killing all its occupants, the Wildbird Motor Corporation which manufactured the car was charged with criminal negligence and prosecuted by the state of Madlington. At the trial, Neer, an automobile safety design expert, testified under oath on behalf of the prosecution. He stated that in his opinion the Wildflight was poorly designed, and that because of the construction of its engine, an explosion was inevitable if the front end of a Wildflight collided with any object at an impact speed in excess of thirty-five miles per hour.

Subsequently, Pennet was injured when the Wildflight which he was driving exploded after striking another vehicle in the rear. Pennet brought an action in the state of Richmond against Wildbird Motor Corporation for personal injuries.

8. At the trial of Pennet's action against Wildbird, Pennet offers a properly authenticated transcript of Neer's testimony at Wildbird's criminal negligence trial in the state of Madlington. Upon objection by Wildbird's attorney, the transcript should be

   (A) admitted, if Neer is unavailable to testify at the trial of Pennet's action.

   (B) admitted, if Wildbird was convicted of criminal negligence at the trial in the state of Madlington.

   (C) excluded, if Wildbird's attorney did not cross-examine Neer at the criminal negligence trial.

   (D) excluded, if Neer is unavailable for cross-examination at the trial of Pennet's action.

9. Pursuant to a subpoena which had been served on Wildbird, Pennet's attorney called upon Wildbird to produce records of tests which it had performed on the Wildflight before marketing it. Wildbird's attorney objected, on the ground that Wildbird had turned the test records over to its attorney in preparation for trial. Should the trial court require production of the records?

   (A) No, since they are privileged as an attorney's work product.

(B) No, since they are privileged as materials prepared for litigation.

(C) No, since they are privileged as a confidential communication to an attorney.

(D) Yes, since they are relevant to the issues and not protected by privilege.

10. In an action by Percy against the city of Muni, Percy alleged that he sustained injury as a result of the negligence of a Muni employee in the operation of a bus. As part of Percy's case, Dr. Treet testified that she had been consulted by Percy shortly after the accident. She stated that she had examined him clinically and by X-ray, and that she had diagnosed his injury as a fractured collarbone. On cross-examination, Muni's attorney asked Dr. Treet whether she had brought Percy's X-ray with her. She answered that she had given it to Percy's attorney several months ago, and had not seen it since.

As part of the defendant's case, Dr. Radell testified that he had been consulted by Muni's attorney prior to trial. He stated that at his request the X-ray taken by Dr. Treet had been sent to him by Percy's attorney, and that he had studied it carefully. He stated that it was his opinion that the X-ray did not disclose a fracture of the collarbone. If the X-ray is neither produced in court nor shown to be unavailable, on appropriate motions by counsel, which of the following statements is most correct?

(A) The testimony of Dr. Treet should be admitted, but the testimony of Dr. Radell should be excluded.

(B) The testimony of Dr. Radell should be admitted, but the testimony of Dr. Treet should be excluded.

(C) The testimony of Drs. Treet and Radell should be admitted.

(D) The testimony of Drs. Treet and Radell should be excluded.

11. Welch was the mother of a four-year-old girl named Child. One day, because Welch had an appointment, she left Child in the care of Welch's friends Dole and Smith. While in their custody, Child began to cry. In an attempt to quiet her, Dole beat her severely, striking her repeatedly across the back and raising a series of welts and bruises. Soon afterwards, Welch returned and took Child home. As Welch was undressing Child to prepare her for bed, she noticed the marks on Child's body and asked, "What happened?" Child responded by saying, "Dole spanked me." Dole was subsequently arrested and charged with child abuse. At Dole's trial on that charge, Welch was called as a witness by the prosecution on the presentation of its direct case. When Welch attempted to testify to the above conversation between herself and Child, Dole's attorney objected on the ground that Child's statement was hearsay.

The prosecutor's most effective argument in opposition to the objection would be that the statement is admissible as

(A) a present sense impression.

(B) an excited utterance.

(C) a statement of present physical condition.

(D) an identification.

12. At the trial of Darien for receiving stolen property, the prosecution called Wescott to the witness stand. Wescott testified that in a conversation which he had with Darien in jail shortly after Darien's arrest, Darien admitted that he knew that the car which he had been driving was stolen. Which of the following facts or inferences would best support Darien's motion to exclude Wescott's testimony?

(A) At the time of their conversation, Wescott told Darien that he was an attorney.

(B) At the time of their conversation, Darien reasonably believed that Wescott was employed as an investigator for Darien's attorney.

(C) Wescott had offered to recommend an attorney to Darien, and had asked Darien to tell him the facts of the case.

(D) Wescott had been charged with a crime, and on the day of Darien's trial had negotiated a favorable plea-bargain in return for his testimony.

Questions 13-14 are based on the following fact situation.

Packer was injured when she fell down a flight of steps at the Robinson Bartending School. She subsequently sued Robinson for damages, asserting that the accident resulted from Robinson's negligence in allowing parts of the stairway to become loose. At the trial, Dr. Won testified that he had examined and treated Packer following the accident. On direct examination he stated that, in his opinion, Packer had sustained a herniated spinal braggis as a result of her fall. He also stated that in making the diagnosis he did not take a spinal braggigram, because he regarded it as a dangerous procedure.

13. On cross-examination, Robinson's attorney asked Dr. Won whether he had ever read the work of a specialist in spinal injuries named Dr. Martha Tue. Dr. Won replied that he had heard of Dr. Tue, but that he had never read any of her work. Robinson's attorney then opened a book by Dr. Tue entitled *Injuries of the Spine,* and said, "In this book, Dr. Tue says that it is impossible to diagnose herniation of the spinal braggis without taking a braggigram. How do you justify your diagnosis in view of that statement?" If Packer's attorney objected to the question, the court should

(A) sustain the objection, since Dr. Tue has not testified in the proceeding.

(B) sustain the objection, since no proper foundation has been laid.

(C) overrule the objection, since an expert may be cross-examined regarding the works of other experts in the field.

(D) overrule the objection, since Dr. Won admitted having heard of Dr. Tue.

14. On the defendant's case, Robinson's attorney called Dr. Martha Tue to the stand. After establishing that she was an expert in the field of spi-

nal injuries, Robinson's attorney asked her whether, in her opinion, it was possible for a person to sustain a herniation of the spinal braggis in a fall down a flight of steps. Dr. Tue stated that in her opinion it was not possible to sustain such an injury in that way. On cross-examination, Packer's attorney asked Dr. Tue whether she had ever examined or treated Packer. Dr. Tue answered, "I have never even met Ms. Packer." Packer's attorney then moved to strike the testimony which Dr. Tue had given on direct examination. The motion should be

(A) granted, since Dr. Tue's opinion is not based on matters within her personal knowledge.

(B) granted, since Dr. Tue's opinion is based on matters not in evidence.

(C) denied, since Dr. Tue was testifying in response to a hypothetical question.

(D) denied, since an expert's testimony may be based on observations made in the courtroom.

15. At the trial of *People v. Morgan,* Wellesley, testifying on behalf of the prosecution, stated that he saw Morgan shoot the victim three times in the back. During the defendant's case, Morgan's attorney offered two properly authenticated judgments of conviction. One showed that Wellesley had been convicted two years ago of attempted murder, which was a felony. The other showed that Wellesley had been convicted one year ago of knowingly making false statements in an application for a business license, which was a misdemeanor. Over objection by the prosecution, the court should admit the judgment(s) of conviction of

(A) attempted murder only.

(B) knowingly making false statements in an application for a business license only.

(C) both crimes.

(D) neither crime.

16. Specker, an inspector employed by the State Aeronautics Bureau, was assigned to investigate

the crash of a Jetco Airlines flight. During the course of his investigation, Specker questioned Renich, a Jetco mechanic who had worked on the plane just before it took off on its last flight. Renich said that while going over the plane, he had discovered some dangerous cracks in its engine parts, but that when he called them to the attention of his supervisor, he was told to forget them. He stated also that after the crash, he was fired as part of a cover-up. Specker included a verbatim transcript of Renich's statement in the report which he filed as required by Bureau procedure. In an action brought against Jetco under the state's wrongful death statute by the surviving spouse of a passenger who died in the crash, the plaintiff offered Specker's written report into evidence. Upon objection by Jetco, the portion of the report containing the transcript of Renich's statement should be

(A) admitted, if Specker is dead or legally unavailable.

(B) admitted, if Renich is dead or legally unavailable.

(C) admitted, as a vicarious admission by Jetco.

(D) excluded, since it is hearsay.

Questions 17-18 are based on the following fact situation.

Fritz, a house painter, was charged with stealing three valuable figurines from the home of Valens while painting the interior of that home.

17. At Fritz's trial, Valens testified that he first noticed that the figurines were missing about an hour after Fritz left his home. He stated that he looked Fritz's number up in the telephone book and properly dialed the number listed therein. Over objection by Fritz's attorney, Valens stated that a man answered the phone by saying, "Fritz speaking." Valens stated that he then said, "Fritz, where are the figurines?" and that the person at the other end of the line said, "I'm sorry. I took them." The objection by Fritz's attorney should be

(A) sustained, unless independent evidence establishes that Fritz was the person to whom Valens was speaking.

(B) sustained, since Valens did not actually see the person to whom he was speaking.

(C) sustained, since the statement is hearsay.

(D) overruled.

18. Assume for the purpose of this question only that Valens stated that the man on the phone spoke with a heavy German accent like Fritz's. If Fritz's attorney makes a proper objection to this testimony, the testimony should be

(A) admitted, if Valens testifies that he recognized the voice as that of Fritz.

(B) admitted, only if Valens qualifies as an expert on voice identification.

(C) excluded, unless Valens can establish that Fritz was the only person in the household called who speaks with a German accent.

(D) excluded, since the probative value of such evidenced is outweighed by its prejudicial effect.

19. A statute provides that the owner of a motor vehicle is vicariously liable for the negligence of any person driving with said owner's permission. In an action for personal injuries brought by Prudence against Olivia, Prudence alleges that she was injured as a result of the negligent driving of Martha, who was operating Olivia's car with Olivia's permission at the time of the accident. Olivia denies ownership of the vehicle in question. Over the objection of Olivia's attorney, Prudence offers into evidence an insurance policy issued by the Grail Mutual Insurance Company. The policy is authenticated by the testimony of an officer of Grail who states that the policy was purchased by and issued to Olivia, and that on the day of the accident the policy was in force on the vehicle in question. The policy and authenticating testimony should be

(A) admitted, since it tends to establish that Olivia was the owner of the vehicle at the time of the accident.

(B) admitted, since it is relevant to Olivia's ability to pay a judgment rendered against her.

(C) excluded, because policy prohibits the introduction of evidence that a party did or did not have liability insurance on the day of an accident.

(D) excluded, because it has no probative value relative to the issues in the case.

20. Bonnie and Clyde were charged with committing an armed robbery which occurred on a Saturday. Although they were being tried together, Bonnie and Clyde were represented by different attorneys. Both asserted that they were together at a rock concert in another state on the day of the robbery. At the trial, Wellington testified on behalf of the defendants. On direct examination, Bonnie's attorney asked Wellington about a conversation he had with Bonnie on the Thursday before the robbery. Wellington stated that during that conversation, Bonnie told him that she and Clyde were planning to leave for the rock concert together on Friday morning and would not be back in town until some time Monday. upon timely objection by the prosecution, the testimony of Wellington should be

(A) admitted, only in so far as it refers to Bonnie.

(B) admitted, only in so far as it refers to Clyde.

(C) admitted, in so far as it refers to both Bonnie and Clyde.

(D) excluded as hearsay.

Questions 21-23 arc based on the following fact situation.

Brasi was charged with murdering Laber, a prominent union leader, by throwing him off the roof of an office building. At Brasi's trial, the prosecution offered the testimony of Onder, a police officer who arrived at the scene moments after Laber's death.

21. Onder testified that as he was getting out of his cruiser, he heard an unidentified person in the crowd shout, "A tall man pushed him off the roof." Brasi's objection to the statement should be

(A) overruled, since it does not establish with certainty that Brasi was the person referred to in the declarant's statement.

(B) overruled, if the person making the statement did so while in a state of excitement resulting from what he had just observed.

(C) sustained, since the identify of the person making the statement is unknown.

(D) sustained, unless there are no eyewitnesses available to testify in court.

22. The prosecuting attorney asked Onder whether he interviewed any of the people in the crowd. Onder replied that he interviewed an eyewitness, but that he no longer remembered her name or what she told him. He then said that he had accurately recorded the contents of the eyewitness's statement in his notebook as she was making it and that he had brought the notebook to court with him. The prosecuting attorney asked Onder to read the contents of the statement to the jury. If Brasi's attorney objected, the court should

(A) sustain the objection, since the statement of the eyewitness is hearsay, not within any exception to the hearsay rule.

(B) overrule the objection, since the statement is a past recollection recorded.

(C) overrule the objection, since the statement is part of the res gestae.

(D) overrule the objection, since the officer's notebook is a business record.

23. The prosecuting attorney then asked Onder whether he knew the defendant Brasi. Onder said that prior to the death of Laber he had arrested Brasi three times for aggravated assault, and that Brasi had been convicted each time. The prosecu-

tor offered properly authenticated court records of the convictions. Upon timely objection by Brasi's attorney, the court should admit into evidence

(A) Onder's testimony only.

(B) the court records only.

(C) both Onder's testimony and the court records.

(D) neither Onder's testimony nor the court records.

Questions 24-26 are based on the following fact situation.

Pastor was the spiritual leader of the First Drive-in Church of the Lord and conducted religious services in a drive-in theater every Sunday morning, with members of the congregation remaining in their cars during the entire service. Occasionally the services were televised. Pastor was a frequent guest on television talk shows, where he was known as a witty and entertaining speaker. Pastor usually spoke about what he termed "popular religion," entreating television viewers to "Go to church for the fun of it!" which was the slogan of his congregation. Tribune, the publisher of a large daily newspaper, printed an article by Wright, a journalist in its employ. The article accused Pastor of misusing church funds. Pastor commenced a defamation action against Tribune. In its answer, Tribune affirmatively pleaded that Pastor was a public figure, asserting a constitutional privilege to print defamatory statements about him in the absence of malice. As a separate defense, Tribune asserted Pastor's non-compliance with a state law which limited damages for defamation unless a demand for retraction is made.

24. At the trial of the defamation action, Tribune's attorney called Tender, who worked in a bar near the Tribune office. Tender stated that on the day after Wright's article appeared in the Tribune, Wright told him, "When I wrote that piece on Pastor, I believed every word of it." On objection by Pastor's attorney, Tender's testimony should be

(A) admitted as evidence that the article was

published without malice.

(B) admitted as a declaration of Wright's state of mind.

(C) admitted as a self-serving declaration.

(D) excluded as hearsay.

25. Tribune's attorney next offered the testimony of Ed, an editor employed by Tribune. Ed testified that it was his job to note retraction demands in an office file, and that as a matter of company policy and practice all such demands were promptly reported to him for that purpose and promptly noted by him. He said that on the morning of trial, he had searched the file for note of any retraction demand made by Pastor, and found none. If Tribune's attorney offers the file in evidence, Pastor's objection should be

(A) sustained, since the absence of a notation cannot be used as evidence that an event did not occur.

(B) sustained, since the file is self-serving.

(C) overruled, if the file itself is admissible as a business record.

(D) overruled, since Ed used the file to refresh his recollection.

26. Tribune's attorney subsequently called Member, who said that she had belonged to Pastor's congregation for several years, was active in church affairs, and knew most of the other members. She then stated that long before the Tribune article appeared it had been rumored among church members that Pastor was misusing church funds. If Pastor's attorney objects, the court should

(A) sustain the objection, since rumor evidence is hearsay not within any exception to the hearsay rule.

(B) sustain the objection, since character evidence is not admissible in a civil proceeding.

(C) overrule the objection, since Pastor's reputation is in issue.

(D) overrule the objection, only if Pastor testified in his own behalf.

27. Doltum was an orderly employed by the hospital in which Trolley died. Ad, the administrator of Trolley's estate, sued Doltum, seeking the return of a watch which he claimed that Doltum had taken from Trolley's hospital room after Trolley died. At the trial, Doltum testified that about one week prior to Trolley's death, Trolley called him into his room and handed him the watch, saying "Doltum, you've been kind to me. This is for you." If Ad objects to the testimony, the court should

(A) overrule the objection, since the statement is an admission.

(B) overrule the objection under the applicable Dead Man's Act.

(C) overrule the objection, since Trolley's statement had a direct legal effect on Doltum's right to possess the watch.

(D) sustain the objection, since the statement is hearsay, not within any exception to the hearsay rule.

Questions 28-29 are based on the following fact situation.

Following his arrest on New Year's Eve, Dunk was charged with reckless driving and driving while under the influence of intoxicating liquor. Arrow, the arresting officer, testified at Dunk's trial on those charges.

28. Arrow stated that she was a highway patrol officer, that she was familiar with the stretch of state highway on which Dunk was arrested, and that she had extensive experience observing and estimating the speed of moving vehicles. She said that she was in her patrol car observing traffic from behind some bushes when she saw Dunk drive by at what appeared to be an excessive rate of speed. When asked by the prosecuting attorney whether she formed an opinion of Dunk's speed at that time, she replied that she had. When the prosecutor asked her to state that opinion, Dunk's

attorney objected. The objection should be

(A) sustained, unless Arrow qualifies as an expert on the speed of moving vehicles.

(B) sustained, since no proper foundation was laid.

(C) overruled, since a police officer is regarded as an expert on the speeds of moving vehicles.

(D) overruled, since a lay person may express an opinion regarding the speed of a moving vehicle.

29. Arrow then stated that she chased Dunk in her patrol car, apprehended him, and ordered him out of his car. The prosecutor asked, "Did you notice anything in particular about his breath at that time?" Arrow answered, "Yes, it smelled like alcohol." Dunk's attorney objected to the question and moved to strike the answer. The motion should be

(A) granted, because the question was leading.

(B) granted, since Arrow's answer was a conclusion.

(C) granted, since Arrow's statement went to an ultimate issue in the case.

(D) denied.

30. Charged with forcible rape, Derby relied on a defense of alibi. At the trial, Vonda testified that Derby was the man who accosted her on the street, dragged her into the basement of an apartment building, and forced her to submit to sexual intercourse. During the case, Derby's attorney offered the testimony of Mary, who stated that she was familiar with Vonda's reputation in the community and that Vonda was thought of as a prostitute. Derby's attorney also offered into evidence a certified court record indicating that Vonda had been convicted of prostitution, a misdemeanor, two months prior to the alleged rape.

Upon proper objection by the prosecution, which of the following should the court admit?

(A) Mary's testimony only.

(B) The court record only.

(C) Mary's testimony and the court record.

(D) Neither Mary's testimony nor the court record.

Questions 31-32 are based on the following fact situation.

Telink was a small retail store which sold televisions, video-cassette recorders, and blank videotapes. On January 15, after receiving a brochure from Vidco advertising a sale of blank video-tapes at an especially reduced price, Telink ordered two thousand blank videotapes from Vidco for resale. When the tapes were delivered, however, Telink's manager Layton refused to accept delivery, asserting that she had expected the tapes to be packaged in plastic cases, but that those delivered were packaged in paper boxes. Vidco sued Telink for breach of contract.

31. At the trial of *Vidco v. Telink*, Layton testified that it is easier to sell videotapes when they are packaged in plastic cases. She attempted to testify further that she had ordered blank videotapes from Vidco on three previous occasions, and that the tapes received in response to each order had been packaged in plastic cases. If Vidco's attorney objects to this testimony, which of the following would be Vidco's most effective argument in support of the objection?

(A) Evidence of past conduct is not admissible for the purpose of establishing a party's conduct on any particular occasion.

(B) The order was in writing, and made no mention of the way in which the products were to be packaged.

(C) The videotapes were being sold at an especially reduced price to permit resale at a lower price.

(D) Videotapes are commonly packaged in paper boxes like those in which the blank videotapes had been delivered to Telink.

32. Vidco offered the testimony of Schipper, who stated that he was Vidco's shipping manager and in charge of filling orders for blank videotapes received by Vidco. Schipper testified that Telink had not ordered any videotapes from Vidco for a period of six months prior to the January 15 order. He stated further that until four months ago, Vidco had packaged its product in plastic cases, but that the rising cost of plastics had made it impractical to continue doing so. Over objection by Telink's attorney, Schipper stated that in the past four months, it had shipped videotapes packaged in paper boxes to twenty other customers, and that none had rejected them. The objection should have been

(A) overruled, since evidence of previous dealings is usually admissible for the purpose of establishing the parties' state of mind at the time the contract was formed.

(B) overruled, since Telink opened the door by offering the testimony of Layton.

(C) sustained, unless the twenty customers to which Schipper referred were of the same general size and class as Telink.

(D) sustained, since such transactions are not relevant to the agreement between Vidco and Telink.

33. A statute provides that "No person shall operate a motor vehicle on the public roads of this state who is not covered by a policy of automobile liability insurance with a limit of no less than fifteen thousand dollars. Any person in violation of this section shall be guilty of a felony." Following an automobile accident in which a vehicle driven by Dirkson collided with a vehicle driven by Peterson, Dirkson was charged with operating an uninsured vehicle in violation of the statute. After trial, Dirkson was found guilty of violating the section, and sentenced to a term of imprisonment. Subsequently Dirkson died, and Peterson commenced an action against Dirkson's estate for personal injuries sustained in the collision. In selecting the jury, Peterson's attorney asked each of the prospective jurors whether he or she owned stock in any automobile liability insurance carrier. During the trial of the action, Dirkson's

attorney offered into evidence a judgment of Dirkson's conviction for driving an uninsured vehicle. Upon objection by Peterson's attorney, the judgment should be

(A) admitted, since Peterson's attorney has falsely suggested that Dirkson was insured at the time of the accident.

(B) excluded, since evidence that a party is or is not covered by liability insurance is inadmissible to establish fault or freedom from fault.

(C) excluded, since it is self-serving.

(D) excluded, since it is hearsay, not within any exception to the hearsay rule.

34. During the trial of a personal injury claim arising from an automobile accident, the defendant offered a videotape into evidence after properly marking it for identification and testifying that it was an accurate representation of the accident scene. On voir dire examination by the plaintiff's attorney, the defendant stated that he hired Vido to make a videotape of the place where the accident occurred and that the tape which had been offered in evidence was a copy of the tape made by Vido. He stated further that after Vido gave the copy to him, he mislaid it for several months, and that his wife found it only a few days before the trial. When asked about the location of the original videotape, the defendant said that he did not know where it was or even whether it still existed.

Upon objection by the plaintiff's attorney, the court should rule that the videotape copy is

(A) inadmissible, because the original videotape has not been shown to be unavailable.

(B) inadmissible, because there is a period of time during which custody of the videotape cannot be established.

(C) admissible.

(D) inadmissible, because Vido has not authenticated it.

Questions 35-36 are based on the following fact situation.

After his vehicle collided with Pringle's on March 1, Dicton retained Addie, an attorney, to represent him in any possible litigation which might develop. Addie hired Vesto, a private investigator, to interview Pringle regarding the facts of the accident. On March 5, Vesto followed Pringle into a bar, sat next to him, and engaged him in conversation. During the conversation, Pringle described the accident which he had with Dicton, and said, "Just between you and me, I drank a six-pack of beer just before the accident happened. It's a good thing nobody smelled my breath." Eventually Pringle commenced a personal injury action against Dicton. At the trial of the action, Pringle testified on direct examination that he had been driving at a slow rate of speed when Dicton's vehicle suddenly pulled out of a driveway into his path.

35. On cross-examination, Dicton's attorney asked Pringle whether he had drunk alcohol during the hour prior to the accident. Pringle answered that he had not. Dicton's attorney then asked, "Didn't you tell an investigator from my office that you had consumed an entire six-pack of beer just before the accident?" If Pringle's attorney objects to the question, the court should

(A) sustain the objection, since Pringle's prior statement was not made under oath.

(B) sustain the objection, since it was unethical for Dicton's attorney to make contact with Pringle through an investigator.

(C) sustain the objection, since the statement is hearsay not within any exception to the hearsay rule.

(D) overrule the objection.

36. During presentation of the defendant's case, Dicton's attorney called Vesto to the stand. Over objection by Pringle's attorney, Vesto described the conversation which he had with Pringle in the bar on March 5, and stated that Pringle told him that he had consumed a six-pack of beer just prior to the accident. Vesto's testimony was

(A) admissible for impeachment purposes only.

(B) admissible as substantive evidence only.

(C) admissible for impeachment purposes and as substantive evidence.

(D) inadmissible.

Questions 37-38 are based on the following fact situation.

In an action by Sellco against Buyco for breach of contract, Sellco's manager Manny testified that after Buyco refused to accept delivery of merchandise as agreed, he personally arranged for the resale of the goods at a price which was three thousand dollars less than that which Buyco had agreed to pay.

37. On cross-examination, Buyco's attorney asked, "Didn't you once plead guilty to violating Penal Code section 22.9(a)?" Which of the following additional facts or inferences, if it were the only one true, would most effectively support Sellco's objection to the question?

(A) Manny's plea of guilty was the result of a plea bargain after he had originally been charged with a more serious crime.

(B) Manny subsequently withdrew the guilty plea.

(C) Penal Code section 22.9(a) prohibits operating an automobile without proper liability insurance coverage.

(D) Manny was not in the employ of Sellco at the time of his guilty plea.

38. Assume for the purpose of this question only that the court overruled the objection, and that Manny denied ever pleading guilty to the code section. Buyco's attorney subsequently offered a transcript of Manny's conviction for violating the code section. If only one of the following facts or inferences were true, which would most effectively support Sellco's objection to its admission into evidence?

(A) Manny's violation of the code section is

unrelated to his duties as an employee of Sellco.

(B) Manny's conviction was subsequently reversed on the ground that the evidence used against him was obtained in violation of the Fourth Amendment to the United States Constitution.

(C) The crime of which Manny was convicted was a misdemeanor.

(D) The crime of which Manny was convicted was a malum prohibitum felony.

39. Plant was a student at the Drysdale Academy, a private high school. One day, while leaving the school building in the rain, Plant slipped on the wooden steps which led from the school to the street. He immediately experienced pain in his elbow, but got up and went home. Later, the pain became so severe that he went to see a doctor who X-rayed the elbow and told him that it was fractured. Eventually, Plant commenced an action for negligence against Drysdale, claiming that the paint which had been used on the wooden steps became extremely slippery when wet with rain, and that Drysdale was negligent in using it.

At the trial, Plant subpoenaed Manny, the school's maintenance manager. Manny testified that he stripped the old paint from the wooden steps the day after Plant's accident, and repainted the steps with a paint which did not become slippery when wet with rain. Upon objection by Drysdale's attorney, Manny's testimony should be

(A) admitted, since it is an admission.

(B) admitted, if the steps were stripped and repainted before Drysdale learned about Plant's accident.

(C) excluded, if it is offered for the purpose of proving that the steps were in a dangerous condition at the time of the accident.

(D) excluded, since evidence of subsequent repair is not admissible in an action for negligence.

Questions 40-41 are based on the following fact situation.

Postum was crossing the street on foot when she was struck by a delivery van driven by Currier, a Daxco employee in the process of making a delivery. Following the accident, Currier was charged with reckless driving and pleaded not guilty. At the trial on the charge of reckless driving, Currier testified in his own defense. He stated that at the time of the accident, he had taken his eyes off the road to look for the address of the place to which he had to make his delivery, and that as a result he didn't see Postum crossing the street.

40. Postum subsequently brought an action against Daxco under the theory of *respondeat superior* for personal injuries resulting from Currier's negligence. At the trial of *Postum v. Daxco*, Postum proved that Currier remained in Daxco's employ until Currier died from causes not related to the accident. Postum then offered a transcript of Currier's testimony at the reckless driving trial. Upon objection by Daxco's attorney, the transcript should be

(A) admitted, under the prior testimony exception to the hearsay rule.

(B) admitted, under the past recollection recorded exception to the hearsay rule.

(C) admitted as a vicarious admission, under the public record exception to the hearsay rule.

(D) excluded as hearsay, not within any exception to the hearsay rule.

41. Assume for the purpose of this question only that the court refused to admit the transcript of Currier's testimony. Upon presentation of Daxco's case, Daxco's attorney offered into evidence a properly certified transcript of a court record indicating that Currier had been acquitted after trial on the charge of reckless driving. Upon objection by Postum's attorney, the transcript should be

(A) admitted as an official record.

(B) admitted, to raise a conclusive presumption that Currier was not driving recklessly at the time of the accident.

(C) excluded, since Currier is not available for cross-examination regarding his guilt or innocence of the charge of reckless driving.

(D) excluded, since it is not relevant to the issues on trial.

Questions 42-43 are based on the following fact situation.

Alicia and Benton, both attorneys, had been dating for several months. Benton was driving Alicia home from a party which they had attended together, when his car collided with a car operated by Pentel. Police who arrived at the scene of the accident moments later arrested Benton and charged him with driving while intoxicated. Alicia immediately advised the arresting officers that she was Benton's attorney, accompanied them to the police station, and arranged for Benton's bail. Benton was eventually tried and acquitted, with Alicia representing him at the trial. Several months after the trial, Pentel instituted an action against Benton for personal injuries resulting from the accident. Benton retained a different attorney to defend him in the civil action.

42. At the trial of *Pentel v. Benton,* Pentel's attorney called Alicia as a witness. After Alicia testified that she had been in the car with Benton at the time of the accident, Pentel's attorney asked her whether Benton appeared to be intoxicated immediately following the accident. Benton's attorney objected on the ground of attorney-client privilege. The objection should be

(A) sustained, since Alicia defended Benton against the charge of driving while intoxicated.

(B) sustained, unless Alicia qualifies as an expert on intoxication.

(C) overruled, unless Alicia objects and asserts the privilege.

(D) overruled, since the question does not require Alicia to testify to a confidential communication.

43. Assume for the purpose of this question only that Alicia and Benton married after the criminal trial, but divorced before the civil trial. If Pentel's attorney asked her to state how much alcohol she had observed Benton consume at the party, Benton's objection should be

    (A) sustained, since Alicia's testimony would involve a confidential marital communication.

    (B) sustained, under the spousal privilege.

    (C) sustained, since a rule of policy prevents the testimony of a former spouse from being used against a party.

    (D) overruled.

44. Vason was found dead in his garage, hanging by the neck from a rope tied to a roof beam. His widow Alma brought an action against Vason's psychiatrist Si under the state's wrongful death statute. In her complaint, Alma alleged that Si was negligent in his treatment of Vason, whom he knew or should have known to be suicidal. In his answer, Si denied that he knew Vason to be suicidal, denied that he had treated him negligently, and denied that Vason's death was a suicide. At the trial of the wrongful death action, Nina, a nurse employed by Si, testified that the day before Vason's death, she heard Vason say to Si, "I think suicide is the only way out." Upon objection by Si's counsel, which of the following statements is most correct?

    I. The statement should be admitted for the purpose of establishing that Vason's death was a suicide.

    II. The statement should be admitted for the purpose of establishing that Si knew or should have known that Vason was suicidal.

    (A) I only.

    (B) II only.

    (C) Both I and II.

    (D) Neither I nor II.

Questions 45-46 are based on the following fact situation.

Dally, a police officer who had recently joined the police department, was charged with the murder of his wife under a statute which defined the crime as "the unlawful killing of a human being with the intent to bring about the death of said human being." At the trial, the prosecution claimed that while on a visit to the country, Dally's wife was walking across a meadow when Dally shot her from three-quarters of a mile away with a Firetag 401 rifle equipped with a telescopic sight. Dally admitted firing the rifle, but maintained that his wife's death was an accident. On the presentation of Dally's case, his attorney called Gunn, a firearms expert, who testified that the Firetag 401 was not reliably accurate at any distance in excess of one-half mile.

45. On direct examination, Dally's attorney showed Gunn a treatise entitled *Rating the Weapons,* and asked him whether he had ever heard of it. Gunn said that he had, that the treatise was a recognized authority in the field of firearms and ballistics, and that he used it in forming his own opinion regarding the capabilities of the Firetag 401. Over objection by the prosecutor, Dally's attorney read Gunn a passage of the treatise which stated that the accurate range of the Firetag 401 was one-half mile, and asked whether Gunn agreed with that statement. When Gunn said that he did, Dally's attorney offered the treatise in evidence. The trial court will most likely

    (A) sustain the objection, since direct examination of an expert regarding the materials which he used in forming his opinion is not permitted.

    (B) sustain the objection, since although the questioning was proper, the treatise itself is not admissible in evidence.

    (C) overrule the objection, since Gunn's testimony that the treatise was a reliable authority laid a proper foundation for admission of the treatise in evidence.

    (D) overrule the objection, since Gunn's testimony that he relied on the treatise in forming his opinion laid a proper foundation for admission of the treatise in evidence.

46. In rebuttal, the prosecutor called Rookie, a police officer who joined the police force at the same time as Dally. Rookie testified that he and Dally had attended firearms classes together at the police academy, and that Dally had been with him in a firearms class when their instructor said that the Firetag 401 rifle was capable of remarkable accuracy at distances of up to two miles if fired by a good marksman. On objection by Dally's attorney the testimony of Rookie should be

(A) admitted, only for the purpose of proving that Dally believed the rifle to be accurate at the distance involved.

(B) admitted, only for the purpose of proving that the rifle was accurate at the distance involved.

(C) admitted for the purpose of proving that Dally believed the rifle to be accurate at the distance involved, and for the purpose of proving that it was accurate at that distance.

(D) excluded as hearsay.

47. Angel was insured by Innco Insurance Company under a policy which required Innco to pay the total value of any damage to Angel's motorcycle resulting from collision. After Angel's motorcycle was totally destroyed in a highway accident, Angel submitted a claim to Innco as required by the terms of her policy. Innco offered only two thousand dollars, although Angel claimed that the motorcycle was worth twice that amount. Angel subsequently instituted an action against Innco for benefits under the policy. At the trial of Angel's action against Innco, which of the following is LEAST likely to be admitted as evidence of the motorcycle's value?

(A) Angel's testimony that it was worth four thousand dollars.

(B) Angel's testimony that two days before the accident she had received an offer of four

thousand dollars from someone who wanted to purchase the motorcycle.

(C) The testimony of a used motorcycle dealer who had never seen Angel's motorcycle, but who, after examining a photograph of it, stated that motorcycles like it were regularly bought and sold for prices ranging from three thousand five hundred to four thousand two hundred dollars.

(D) The testimony of an amateur motorcycle collector, who had bought and sold many motorcycles like Angel's, that two days before the accident he had looked at Angel's motorcycle because he was interested in buying it, and that in his opinion the motorcycle had been worth four thousand dollars.

48. At the trial of the case of *Stanley v. Gardiner,* which of the following is LEAST likely to be admitted into evidence for the purpose of determining whether a certain letter was written by Gardiner?

(A) A sample of Gardiner's signature, together with the testimony of a handwriting expert that the letter was signed by the same person who created the sample.

(B) A sample of Gardiner's signature submitted to the jury together with the letter in question.

(C) The testimony of a layperson who stated that he saw Gardiner sign the letter in question.

(D) Testimony that the letterhead on the letter in question was Gardiner's.

Questions 49-50 are based on the following fact situation.

Lanham was the owner of a three-story professional building. The entire second floor of Lanham's building was rented to Dr. View, an optometrist. Persons visiting the office of Dr. View either rode in an elevator located inside the building or climbed a stairway which was fastened to the outside of the building and which led from the street level to the second floor only. Priller was a patient of Dr. View's. One day upon leaving Dr. View's office and descending the stairway on the outside of the building, Priller fell, sustaining serious injuries. She commenced an action against Lanham, alleging that the stairway was dangerous in that it was too steep, it lacked a handrail, and the stair treads were too narrow. Lanham denied that the stairway was dangerous. In addition, as an affirmative defense, he denied control over the stairway, asserting that it had been leased to Dr. View as part of the second-floor office.

49. At the trial, Priller called Walker, who had been employed by Lanham as building manager at the time of the accident, but who was presently unemployed. Walker testified that two days after the accident Lanham instructed him to install a handrail on the stairway, and to post a sign which read, "CAUTION: Steep and narrow stairway!" Lanham's attorney objected to the testimony and moved that it be stricken. Which of the following would be Priller's most effective argument in response to the objection and in opposition to the motion to strike?

(A) Walker is no longer in Lanham's employ.

(B) The testimony is relevant to establish that the stairway was dangerous.

(C) The testimony is relevant to establish that Lanham was aware that the stairway was dangerous.

(D) The testimony is relevant to establish that Lanham was in control of the stairway.

50. On cross-examination by Lanham's attorney, Walker testified that he had been employed by Lanham as building manager for a period of three years prior to the accident. He stated that the condition of the stairway was substantially the same during that period as it was on the day of Priller's accident, and that although many people used the stairway every day, Walker had never before heard of anyone falling while using it. Priller's attorney objected to this testimony. Should the court sustain Priller's objection?

(A) Yes, since evidence that no accident had

occurred in the past is not relevant to the issues on trial.

(B) Yes, unless there is evidence that Walker would have heard of such accidents had they occurred.

(C) No, if Lanham raised a defense of contributory negligence.

(D) No, since Walker was called as Priller's witness.

51. Alex and Bailey, who were employed as clerks in the law office of Counsel, disliked each other intensely. On February 6, they argued bitterly, almost coming to blows. Later, Alex went to the company parking lot and discovered that the tires and canvas top on his car had been slashed with a knife. Angrily, he returned to the office and accused Bailey of the vandalism in the presence of Counsel, saying "I dare you to deny it, Bailey." Alex subsequently instituted a tort action against Bailey for damage to his auto. At the trial, Counsel testified on behalf of Alex. After describing the events which took place in his office on February 6, he stated that when Alex dared Bailey to deny damaging his car, Bailey said nothing. Counsel stated that he, Counsel, then said, "Bailey, if I thought you did this, I'd have to fire you. Now did you?" and that Bailey still said nothing. Counsel testified further that he gave Bailey another opportunity to deny Alex's accusation, and that after Bailey refused once again to answer, Counsel fired him. If Bailey's attorney objected to the testimony, the court should

(A) overrule the objection, if the reasonable person in Bailey's situation would have denied slashing the tires and canvas top.

(B) overrule the objection, since Bailey is a party to the action and will have an opportunity to deny making the statement.

(C) sustain the objection, since silence cannot be used as an admission or form the basis for civil liability.

(D) sustain the objection, since answering Counsel's question might have tended to incriminate Bailey.

52. In an action by Pillow Products against Daphne, Pillow alleged that it had entered into a written contract with Daphne for the purchase of satin material which Pillow intended to use in manufacturing its products, and that Daphne failed to deliver the material as promised. At the trial, Legg testified that he worked in the Pillow Products legal department, and that he had negotiated the contract in question. He stated further that, although the original and all copies of the contract had been destroyed in an office fire, he knew the substance of its contents. When Pillow's attorney began to question Legg about the contents of the contract, Daphne objected. The trial court should

   (A) sustain the objection, since Legg's testimony would violate the parol evidence rule.

   (B) sustain the objection, since Legg's testimony would violate the best evidence rule.

   (C) overrule the objection, since the absence of the original document has been explained.

   (D) overrule the objection, since the Statute of Frauds is satisfied by the fact that a written memorandum of agreement was made.

53. At the trial of Draper on a charge of criminal homicide, the prosecution alleged that Draper, Wellum, Robins, and Victor had been quarreling in the cabin of Victor's boat, and that Draper had stabbed Victor to death in a battle which ensued. Draper asserted that Robins stabbed Victor and Draper, and then shot Wellum and himself. The prosecution offered the testimony of a sheriff's deputy, who stated that he had boarded the drifting boat after it smashed against a rock. He said that after ascertaining that Robins and Victor were dead, and that Draper's wounds were not serious, he attempted to attend to Wellum. He testified that Wellum stared at him and said, "Don't bother. It's too late. I shot Robins, and now I'm dying," and that Wellum then died. If Draper objects to this testimony, it should be

   (A) admitted as Wellum's dying declaration.

   (B) admitted as a declaration against Wellum's

interest.

   (C) admitted as a self-inculpating statement exculpating another.

   (D) excluded as hearsay.

54. Suspecting that some students at State College were trafficking in illegal drugs, the college chancellor requested assistance from the state police in apprehending the traffickers. In response to the request, Mark, an undercover police officer, registered at State College as a student. While attending classes, Mark became friendly with Drummond, who was rumored to be involved in the illicit drug traffic. One day, while chatting with Drummond, Mark said, "Hey, Drummond, how about selling me some heroin?" Drummond responded by saying, "I don't know what you're talking about." But Mark said, "Come on, everybody knows about it. And I really need the stuff." Drummond again denied knowing anything about drugs, but Mark insisted, displaying a fifty dollar bill. "I'm really strung out," Mark said. "I'll give you fifty for twenty-five dollars' worth. Come on. How about it?" At this, Drummond handed Mark a packet of heroin and took the fifty dollar bill. Drummond was subsequently arrested and charged with the unauthorized sale of a dangerous drug. At his trial, he asserted the defense of entrapment. The prosecution offered the testimony of several other students who stated that on various occasions in the past they had purchased heroin from Drummond. Drummond's attorney objected to the introduction of the testimony of the students. The objection should have been

   (A) sustained, since character evidence is not admissible against a defendant in a criminal proceeding.

   (B) sustained, since proof of unconvicted bad acts is not admissible for the purpose of establishing a person's character.

   (C) overruled, since such evidence would tend to prove that Drummond was predisposed to commit the crime with which he has been charged.

   (D) overruled, since evidence of past conduct is relevant to establish that a defendant

engaged in criminal behavior on a particular occasion.

55. Pleasance slipped on a wet spot on the floor of
the produce department in Key Supermarket. He
commenced an action for damages two years and
eleven months later, just before the three year
statute of limitations would have run. In her
opening statement at the trial of the action, Key's
attorney said that it was her client's contention
that the delay in instituting action indicated that
Pleasance had not sustained any real injury, and
that the damage claimed by Pleasance was fabricated.

Pleasance testified in his own behalf. During
cross- examination, Key's attorney asked him
when he consulted for the first time with an attorney regarding the accident. Pleasance answered,
"Not until a few months ago, because a man from
Key offered to settle for three thousand dollars,
and I was trying to get a better offer."

If Key's attorney moved to strike that part of the
answer which referred to settlement negotiations,
the motion to strike should be

(A) denied, since evidence of the settlement
negotiations is admissible to explain the
plaintiff's delay in instituting the action.

(B) denied, since the settlement offer is relevant
to establish that Key believed itself to be at
fault.

(C) granted, since a rule of policy prevents evidence of settlement negotiations from
being admitted.

(D) granted, since that portion of the answer was
not responsive to the question asked.

Questions 56-58 are based on the following fact situation.

Executing a valid warrant, police raided the Cinem-
adult Theater, lawfully arresting Schauer, its proprietor,
and lawfully seizing a copy of "Nude Awakening," the
film he was showing. Schauer was subsequently
charged with "conducting an obscene film perfor-

mance" in violation of a state law.

56. At the trial of *People v. Schauer*, the prosecution
called Proffer to the stand. Proffer testified that
she was a professor of film arts and the author of
several books on the art of erotic filmmaking.
She said that although she believed the erotic film
to be a valid art form, she found "Nude Awakening" to be devoid of any literary or artistic merit.
She stated further that in her opinion, it was
obscene. In objecting to this testimony, which of
the following would be Schauer's most effective
argument?

(A) Proffer's opinion relates to an ultimate issue
in the prosecution.

(B) Proffer's opinion is stated in legal terms.

(C) Proffer does not qualify as an expert.

(D) Since the matter at issue is a subjective one,
expert testimony is inadmissible.

57. Assume for the purpose of this question only that
without offering the film itself in evidence, the
prosecution offered the testimony of Sanders,
who stated that he viewed "Nude Awakening" at
the prosecutor's request. The prosecutor asked
Sanders to describe the subject matter of the film
and to summarize the content of scenes depicting
explicit sexual conduct. If Schauer's attorney
objected, the court would most likely

(A) admit the testimony, since it is relevant to
contemporary community standards.

(B) admit the testimony, only to the extent that
Sander's descriptions are factual rather
than statements of his opinions.

(C) exclude the testimony, unless the court
determines independently that it would be
scandalous to display the film to a jury.

(D) exclude the testimony, if the film is not
shown to be unavailable.

58. Assume for the purpose of this question only that
the prosecution offered the film of "Nude Awakening" in evidence. Which of the following state-

ments is most correct about whether or not the film should be admitted?

I. The court may prevent the showing of the film if it determines that its probative value would be outweighed by its prejudicial effect.

II. The court must view the film in camera for the purpose of determining whether it is suitable for viewing by the jury before allowing it to be shown to the jury.

(A) I only.

(B) II only.

(C) I and II.

(D) Neither I nor II.

59. After bonds which Pettigrew purchased from Danzig proved to be worthless, Pettigrew instituted an action against Danzig for breach of contract and misrepresentation. At the trial, Pettigrew's attorney subpoenaed West, Danzig's chief bookkeeper. West appeared in court in response to the subpoena, but refused to take the stand. The trial judge told West that unless he took the stand, he would be held in contempt of court. West continued to refuse, asserting his privilege against self-incrimination under the Fifth Amendment to the United States Constitution. Should West be held in contempt?

(A) Yes, since the privilege against self-incrimination applies only to testimony at criminal proceedings.

(B) Yes, since West was not a party to the proceeding.

(C) Yes, since the privilege against self-incrimination does not justify a refusal to take the stand in a civil proceeding.

(D) No, if West reasonably believed that his testimony could tend to incriminate him.

60. After Damon was arrested and charged with selling a dangerous drug, a trial was held at which Wolfe testified that he was present when Damon sold an ounce of cocaine to an unidentified person. Damon's attorney was given an opportunity to cross-examine Wolfe, but did not do so. A jury found Damon not guilty. Subsequently, Damon's employer fired him. Damon asserted a tort claim against his employer for wrongful termination. At the trial of Damon's claim, the attorney for his former employer offered into evidence a transcript of the testimony which Wolfe gave at the criminal trial.

If Damon's attorney objects, the court should hold that the transcript is

(A) admissible as prior testimony.

(B) admissible, but only if Wolfe is unavailable to testify at the trial.

(C) inadmissible, unless Wolfe testifies at the trial.

(D) inadmissible, because Damon's attorney did not cross examine Wolfe at the preliminary hearing.

61. Darnell, who was charged with armed robbery, retained Ames as his attorney. In preparing the defense of his client, Ames interviewed Willis. Willis told Ames that he and Darnell had been together at a baseball game at the time of the robbery. At Darnell's trial, Ames called Willis to the witness stand and asked if he had seen Darnell on the day of the robbery. Willis said that he had not. Ames subsequently called Sutcliffe, to testify that he had seen Willis and Darnell together at the baseball stadium at the time of the robbery. The trial judge should rule that Sutcliffe's testimony is

(A) inadmissible, because Ames cannot impeach his own witness.

(B) inadmissible, because Ames is bound by the testimony of his own witness.

(C) admissible, because Willis is a hostile witness.

(D) admissible, because Sutcliffe's testimony is relevant to material issues.

62. Rider, an investigative reporter for the *Daily Globe,* wrote a series of articles exposing corruption in city government. In the articles, he said that "a building permit can be obtained for just about anything in this town if bribes are given to the right city officials." As a result of the series, a grand jury began investigating the allegations of corruption. When Rider was called to testify, however, he refused to divulge the sources of his information, claiming reportorial privilege. Rider was charged with contempt. While his prosecution on that charge was pending, the grand jury continued with its investigation by causing the city's mayor, Mayo, to be served with a subpoena. When asked whether she knew of any city official accepting bribes for the issuance of building permits Mayo refused to answer, invoking her Fifth Amendment privilege against self-incrimination. After being granted use immunity, however, she testified that Cooms, the city's building commissioner, regularly accepted bribes for the issuance of permits, and that Cooms regularly shared the bribe money with Mayo. After Mayo's testimony, both Mayo and Cooms were indicted by the grand jury on charges of bribery. Because there was no other evidence against Mayo, prior to the trial, the prosecutor agreed to accept a plea to a lesser offense from Cooms if he would testify against Mayo. At Mayo's trial, if Mayo objects to the testimony of Cooms, the objection should be

    (A) sustained, if the prosecutor had no evidence against Cooms other than Mayo's testimony.

    (B) sustained, since a prosecutor may not bargain away the rights of one co-defendant in a deal with another.

    (C) overruled, because the proceeding was instituted as a result of the statements made in the articles by Rider, not as a result of the testimony of Mayo at the grand jury hearing.

    (D) overruled, if the testimony of Cooms was voluntary and not the result of coercion.

63. Pelton sued Transport Inc. for damage which resulted from a collision between Pelton's motorcycle and one of Transport's trucks. After receiv-

ing the summons, Thomas, the president and sole stockholder of Transport Inc., notified Lottie, the company attorney. Lottie said that she wanted to meet with Thomas and the driver of the truck. At Lottie's request, Thomas went to Lottie's office with Darla, who had been driving the truck at the time of the accident. While discussing the case with Lottie in the presence of Darla, Thomas said that on the day before the accident he was aware that the truck's brakes were not working properly, but that because of a heavy work load he postponed making the necessary repairs.

At the trial of Pelton's suit against Transport, Pelton attempted to have Darla testify to the statement which Thomas made to Lottie about the brakes. Transport's attorney objected on the ground of the attorney-client privilege.

Should Darla be permitted to testify to Thomas's statement?

(A) Yes, because the attorney-client privilege does not apply to testimony by one who does not stand in a confidential relationship with the person against whom the evidence is offered.

(B) Yes, because it is presumed that a communication made in the presence of third persons is not confidential.

(C) Yes, because communications made by or on behalf of corporations are not privileged.

(D) No.

Questions 64-65 are based on the following fact situation.

At the trial of *People v. Hobbs*, Munson testified that on the day of the incident she looked up Hobbs's number in the phone book and dialed it, and that a male voice answered, "Hobbs speaking." Munson stated further that she then asked, "Are you the animal that exposed his privates to my daughter?" to which the voice replied, "Yes, I couldn't help myself."

64. If Hobbs's attorney objects to Munson's testimony regarding the identification of Hobbs's voice, the judge should rule this testimony

(A) admissible, since the usual accuracy of the telephone directory coupled with the self-identification of the person who answered makes it likely that the person who answered was Hobbs.

(B) admissible, since there is a presumption that a person who gratuitously identifies himself when answering a telephone will do so accurately.

(C) inadmissible, unless Munson testifies that she was familiar with Hobbs's voice, and recognized it when speaking to him on the phone.

(D) inadmissible as a violation of Hobbs's privilege against self-incrimination.

65. Assume for the purpose of this question only that Munson testified further that she knew it was Hobbs on the phone because she had once chatted with him outside the grocery store and recognized his voice. If Hobbs moves to strike this testimony, the motion should be

(A) granted, since one conversation is not sufficient to justify testimony as to voice identification.

(B) granted, since expert testimony is required for the identification of a voice.

(C) denied, since a voice may be identified by a layperson who testifies that she recognized it because she had heard it before under circumstances connecting it with the alleged speaker.

(D) denied, if but only if Munson testifies to some distinctive characteristic about Hobbs's voice which permitted her to recognize it.

66. At the trial of an automobile accident case, for the purpose of showing the relationship and directions of the streets involved, the plaintiff offered into evidence a photograph of the intersection where the accident occurred. The plaintiff testified that on the day of the accident the intersection looked exactly as depicted in the photo-graph, except that on the day of the accident some of the trees on the street had small Christmas ornaments on them. Upon objection, should the photograph be admitted in evidence?

(A) Yes, if the absence of Christmas tree ornaments did not prevent the photograph from being a fair representation of the intersection at the time of the accident.

(B) Yes, but only if the photograph was taken within a reasonable time following the accident.

(C) No, unless the photographer who made the photograph testifies to its authenticity.

(D) No, not under any circumstances.

67. Peterson was sitting in his car at a dead stop waiting for a traffic light to change color, when his vehicle was struck in the rear by a car operated by Dodge, rendering Peterson unconscious. Police were called to the accident scene and as a result of their investigation Dodge was charged with "operating an unregistered vehicle," a misdemeanor. The following day, Dodge pleaded guilty to the charge and was sentenced to five days in jail.

Peterson subsequently asserted a claim for damages resulting from Dodge's negligence. Because of admissions which were made in the pleadings, a hearing was held on the sole questions of whether Dodge was negligent. At the hearing, a transcript of Dodge's conviction for operating an unregistered vehicle should be

(A) admitted.

(B) excluded, because it is not relevant to the question of negligence.

(C) excluded, because it was not the result of a trial.

(D) excluded, because it is hearsay, not within any exception.

Questions 68-69 are based on the following fact situation.

In a personal injury action by Piersall against Dockery, Piersall claimed that the accident occurred because Dockery, who was operating a blue Ford sedan, was driving at an excessive rate of speed. At the trial, Piersall's attorney called Wilcox as a witness on Piersall's direct case. Wilcox testified that after hearing a broadcast on a police radio on the day of the accident, she looked out of her window and saw Dockery's blue Ford sedan strike Piersall's red convertible on Main Street. Wilcox said that she did not have a present recollection of what she had heard on the police radio, but that she made a written note of it immediately following the broadcast. Piersall's attorney showed her a piece of paper which had been marked for identification, and Wilcox said that she now remembered that she had heard a police dispatcher saying that officers were in pursuit of a blue Ford sedan which was traveling down Main Street at an excessive rate of speed.

68. If Dockery's attorney objects to the testimony of Wilcox regarding what she heard on the police radio, the court should hold that her testimony is

(A) inadmissible as hearsay, not within any exception.

(B) admissible as a sense impression.

(C) admissible as a past recollection recorded.

(D) admissible as present recollection refreshed.

69. Assume for the purpose of this question only that Piersall's attorney next called Willham who testified that she was walking on Main Street at the time the accident occurred and that, although she did not see the vehicles before the collision, she knew that Dockery's vehicle was traveling at a high rate of speed because of the screeching sound made by his tires immediately before the impact. If Dockery's attorney objects to this testimony, the court should

(A) permit Willham to testify, but should give the jury a cautionary instruction regarding lay opinions.

(B) permit Willham to testify, because a lay person is competent to form an opinion regarding the speed of a moving automobile.

(C) exclude Willham's testimony, because a lay person is not competent to form an opinion as to the speed of a moving automobile.

(D) exclude Willham's testimony, because Willham did not have an adequate opportunity to form an opinion regarding the speed of Dockery's automobile.

70. At the trial of a personal injury action instituted by Pearson against Danick, Danick testified on his own behalf as part of his direct case. In response to a question by his attorney, Danick stated that shortly after the accident he told a police officer that the traffic signal light had been red against Pearson. Upon objection by Pearson's attorney, the court should hold that Danick's testimony regarding his statement to the police officer is

(A) inadmissible hearsay.

(B) admissible, because Danick's testimony was based on first-hand knowledge.

(C) admissible as a prior consistent statement.

(D) admissible, because Danick was on the witness stand and available for cross examination.

71. Charged with the rape of Ellen, Randall claimed that he and Ellen had frequently engaged in sexual intercourse in the past, and that they sometimes played a game in which Ellen pretended to resist him and he pretended to overcome her resistance by force. He asserted that on the day of the alleged rape, either Ellen consented to the intercourse or her conduct led him to reasonably believe that she consented. At his trial, Ellen testified that Randall forced her to have sexual intercourse with him on the day in question. On cross-examination, Randall's attorney asked Ellen whether she ever had sexual intercourse with Randall willingly before the alleged rape. If the prosecutor objects to this question, the objection should be

(A) sustained, since past sexual behavior of the complainant is not material to the allegations of a rape prosecution.

(B) sustained, since the probative value of her answer is likely to be outweighed by its prejudicial effect.

(C) overruled, in the absence of a statute prohibiting the inquiry, since the complainant's past sexual behavior is logically relevant to the elements of a rape prosecution.

(D) overruled, since the question and the testimony which it will elicit are relevant to Randall's defense of consent.

72. A state statute provides that the owner of any motor vehicle operated on the public roads of the state is liable for damage resulting from the negligence of any person driving the vehicle with the owner's permission. Pavlov was injured when a vehicle operated by Dawson struck her while she was walking across the street. At the scene of the accident, Dawson apologized to Pavlov, saying, "I'm sorry. It isn't my car. I didn't know that the brakes were bad." Pavlov subsequently instituted an action against Oster for her damages, asserting that Oster owned the vehicle. She alleged that Oster was negligent in permitting the vehicle to be driven while he knew that the brakes were in need of repair, and that he was vicariously liable under the statute for the negligence of Dawson. Oster denied ownership of the vehicle. At the trial, Pavlov offered testimony by Mecco, a mechanic, that on the day after the accident Oster hired him to completely overhaul the brakes. Upon objection by Oster, the evidence is

(A) admissible, to show that Oster was the owner of the vehicle.

(B) admissible, to show that the brakes were in need of repair on the day of the accident.

(C) inadmissible, because the condition of the vehicle on any day other than that of the accident is irrelevant to show its condition at the time the accident occurred.

(D) inadmissible, under a policy which encourages safety precautions.

73. A hidden videotape camera at the office of the Friendly Finance Company routinely records all transactions taking place during business hours. At the trial of Dabney, a black man charged with robbing the Friendly Finance Company, the prosecution offers a videotape made by the hidden camera at the time the robbery occurred. Dabney's attorney objects to introduction of the videotape on the ground that, while it is clear from the tape that the robber was a black man, there is no certainty that the man pictured was Dabney. Should the objection be sustained?

(A) Yes, since use of the tape violates Dabney's privilege against self-incrimination.

(B) Yes, because the tape's value is outweighed by unfair prejudice.

(C) No, since if Dabney is pictured in the tape, it is admissible as an admission.

(D) No, if the tape would tend to prove that Dabney was the robber.

74. Avery sued Lavell for defamation after being defeated by him in a statewide election. In his complaint, Avery alleged that Lavell's campaign literature accused Avery of dishonesty and corruption. At the trial of the action, Avery offered the testimony of several witnesses who stated that they had received printed brochures from Lavell which stated that Avery was dishonest and corrupt. Lavell moved to strike their testimony. Lavell's motion to strike the testimony should be

(A) denied, since a defamatory communication is one which would tend to injure the plaintiff's reputation in the minds of any substantial group of respectable people.

(B) denied, since an action for defamation may be based on statements which were not made in writing.

(C) granted, unless Avery produces the brochures or shows that they are unavailable.

(D) granted, unless the witnesses testify to the exact language of the brochures.

75. At Mable's trial for murder, Winston testified that he heard three gunshots immediately after hearing Mable shout, "I'll kill you." Mable's attorney

asked no questions on cross-examination, but reserved the right to call Winston back to the stand at a later time. Subsequently, Mable's attorney offered the testimony of a police officer who stated that in an interview at the scene of the shooting Winston said that he did not hear any gunshots. The police officer's testimony is

(A) admissible for impeachment purposes only.

(B) admissible as substantive evidence only.

(C) admissible for impeachment purposes and as substantive evidence.

(D) inadmissible, since it is hearsay not within any exception.

76. After derailment of a Webster Railroad passenger train, the Webster Railroad Corporation was charged with criminal negligence under a statute which made corporations criminally liable for the criminal negligence of their employees. At the trial of *People v. Webster Railroad Corporation*, Phillips, a state railroad inspector, testified that on the day of the derailment, the driver of the derailed train was operating the train while intoxicated. The jury found Webster Railroad Corporation not guilty of criminal negligence. Taylor, a passenger on the derailed train, subsequently instituted an action against Webster Railroad Corporation for personal injuries which he sustained as a result of the derailment. Although Taylor's attorney properly served Phillips with a subpoena, he failed to appear at the trial. If Taylor's attorney offers evidence of the testimony which Phillips gave at the criminal proceeding, the evidence is most likely to be admissible as

(A) an admission.

(B) past recollection recorded.

(C) former testimony.

(D) a sense impression.

77. Keller had been a member of a professional crime organization for twenty years, and had participated in many crimes during that period of time. Because Keller's testimony was crucial to the district attorney's attempt to break the crime

organization, Keller was offered immunity if he would testify against other members of the organization. He did so, and his testimony resulted in several convictions. Keller subsequently wrote and published a book entitled *Contract Killer*, in which he described in detail many of the crimes which he committed, including the shotgun murder of Vicuna. Following the publication of *Contract Killer*, Vicuna's wife commenced an action against Keller for damages resulting from the wrongful death of her husband. At the trial, a police officer who had been called to the scene of Vicuna's shooting testified that just before Vicuna died he heard him say, "I saw Keller pull the trigger on me." If Keller moves to strike the police officer's testimony, his motion should be

(A) granted, since a dying declaration is admissible only in a trial for criminal homicide.

(B) granted, if Keller received transactional immunity.

(C) denied, if Vicuna believed himself to be dying when he made the statement.

(D) denied, if the jurisdiction has a "dead man's statute."

Questions 78-79 are based on the following fact situation.

After the crash of Wing Airlines Flight 123, an action for wrongful death was brought by the husband of a passenger killed in the crash. During the trial, the plaintiff called Weston, an employee of the State Aviation Agency which investigated the circumstances surrounding the crash.

78. Weston testified that during the course of his investigation he questioned a mechanic named Marshall on the day of the crash. He said that Marshall stated that he and a mechanic named Stevens had been assigned by the Wing Airlines airport supervisor to inspect Flight 123 before take-off, but that they did not inspect the plane as directed. If Weston's testimony is objected to, the judge should rule it admissible

(A) if Weston testifies that Marshall claimed to

be an employee of Wing.

(B) only if independent evidence indicates that Marshall was employed by Wing at the time the statement was made.

(C) only if independent evidence indicates that at the time the statement was made, Marshall was authorized to speak for Wing.

(D) if Marshall is unavailable to testify.

79. Weston also read aloud from an investigation report which quoted an unidentified witness to the crash as stating that she heard an explosion several seconds before she saw the plane burst into flames. He testified that the report from which he was reading was one kept in the regular course of business by the State Aviation Agency, that the entry from which he was reading had been made by another investigator who worked for the Agency, that the investigator who made the entry was sworn to investigate airplane crashes and to keep honest and accurate records of the results of those investigations, and that the investigator who made the entry was now dead. Upon appropriate objection, the evidence should be ruled

(A) admissible as a business record.

(B) admissible as an official written statement.

(C) admissible as past recollection recorded.

(D) inadmissible as hearsay not within any exception.

Questions 80-81 are based on the following fact situation.

Hiert was injured when the ladder on which she was standing collapsed without warning. Immediately following the accident, Hiert was taken to County Hospital where she remained for approximately six hours. At the trial of Hiert's action against the manufacturer of the ladder, Nathan, a nurse employed by County Hospital, was called to the stand by Hiert's counsel.

80. Nathan testified that he was on duty when Hiert was brought into the hospital, and that Hiert com-

plained of pain almost continually from the time she arrived until the time she left. Upon proper objection by the defendant, this testimony should be

(A) admitted as a part of a pertinent medical history.

(B) admitted as a statement of present physical sensation.

(C) not admitted, since pain is a purely subjective matter, and not a proper subject of testimony by anyone but the injured party.

(D) not admitted, since it is hearsay.

81. Hiert's attorney next offered a properly authenticated County Hospital record. After examining the record, the defendant's attorney, outside the presence of the jury, moved to exclude a portion of the record which read: "History: Ladder collapsed. Patient fell." The motion to exclude that portion of the record should be

(A) granted, if, but only if, it can be excluded without causing any physical damage to the record.

(B) granted, because it has no bearing on the plaintiff's medical condition.

(C) denied, if the history was taken for the purpose of diagnosis or treatment.

(D) granted, since hospital personnel are not experts in determining the causes of accidents.

Questions 82-83 are based on the following fact situation.

Kane's dog frequently dug holes in the lawn of Kane's neighbor Nixon, who had telephoned Kane to complain in a loud voice on several occasions. One day, after the dog dug up Nixon's prize rosebush, Nixon ran to Kane's house and banged on Kane's front door. When Kane opened the door, Nixon shouted, "You dirty son of a bitch." Kane struck him in the face with his fist, and closed the door. Nixon later sued Kane for battery, and Kane asserted the privilege of self-defense. At the trial Kane offered the testimony of a local shopkeeper who stated that he knew Nixon's reputation in the neighborhood, and that Nixon was known as "a bad actor who will fight at the drop of a hat." He also offered the testimony of the local parish priest who stated that he had known Kane for years, and that everyone in the community thought of him as a peaceable man who would never resort to violence except in self-protection.

82. If Nixon's attorney objects to the testimony of the shopkeeper, the objection should be

(A) sustained, since evidence of Nixon's character is not relevant to his action for battery.

(B) sustained, since Nixon is not the defendant.

(C) overruled, since the testimony is relevant to Kane's assertion of the privilege of self-defense.

(D) overruled, since Nixon placed his character in issue by bringing the lawsuit.

83. If Nixon's attorney objects to the testimony of the parish priest, the testimony should be

(A) excluded, if it is offered as circumstantial evidence to prove that Kane did not strike Nixon without justification.

(B) excluded, unless the priest testified that his own opinion of Kane coincided with what the community thought about him.

(C) admitted, because Kane is the defendant.

(D) admitted, for the limited purpose of establishing Kane's state of mind at the time of the occurrence.

84. At the trial of a negligence action, Dr. Ortho testified that she was the orthopedic surgeon who treated the plaintiff. She stated that, at her direction, technicians in her office X-rayed the plaintiff's left leg. She stated further that based upon her examination of the plaintiff's leg and upon her study of the X-ray, it was her opinion that the plaintiff had suffered a fracture of the tibia (a bone in the leg). The X-ray was not produced in court or offered in evidence. Upon proper objec-

tion by the defendant, Dr. Ortho's opinion should be

(A) excluded, because the X-ray was hearsay, and she stated that her opinion was based on it.

(B) excluded, unless the X-ray is unavailable.

(C) admitted, if but only if, she testifies that she would have formed the same opinion without inspection of the X-ray.

(D) admitted, since the opinion of an expert may be based on matters not in evidence.

Questions 85-86 are based on the following fact situation.

While walking down a stairway which led to the women's restroom at the Biloxi theater, Prell fell and sustained serious injuries to her shoulder. She sued Biloxi for damages, alleging that it had negligently permitted the stairway to be littered with scraps of paper, and that she had slipped on one of them.

85. At the trial, Manny testified that he had been employed as Biloxi's theater manager for a period of three weeks prior to the accident, that as such he was the person to whom accidents would ordinarily be reported, and that in the three-week period preceding the accident he had received no reports of accident or injury occurring on those particular stairs. The judge should rule this testimony

(A) admissible, because it tends to prove that Prell did not use the care which would have been exercised by a reasonable person.

(B) admissible, because it tends to prove that Biloxi was generally careful about maintaining the stairway.

(C) inadmissible, because it is self-serving.

(D) inadmissible, because it is not probative of Biloxi's exercise of due care on this particular occasion.

86. Manny testified further that immediately following the accident, a crowd formed around the fallen Prell, and he heard someone in the crowd shout, "She was taking the stairs three at a time and she missed one." The judge should rule this testimony

   (A) admissible as an excited utterance.

   (B) admissible if, but only if, Manny can identify the person who made the statement.

   (C) inadmissible, unless the person who made the statement testifies to it him-or herself.

   (D) inadmissible as hearsay.

87. A state's code of civil procedure provides that no appeal may be prosecuted unless a notice of such appeal is mailed within twenty days after the entry of the final judgment which is being appealed. An appellee moves to dismiss an appeal on the ground that the notice of appeal was not timely served. At a hearing on the motion to dismiss, a secretary in the office of the appellant's attorney testifies that he personally enclosed the notice of appeal in a properly addressed envelope which he then sealed. He states further that he placed the envelope in a basket marked "outgoing mail" in the office conference room at 2 p.m. on the eighteenth day after the judgment appealed from was entered. He states that as a matter of office routine the "outgoing mail" basket is emptied and its contents taken to the post office every day at 4 p.m. by another employee, although he does not personally know whether it was done on that particular day. The testimony should be

   (A) excluded, since evidence of past conduct is not relevant to what was done on any particular day.

   (B) excluded, unless some evidence is offered that the envelope which was deposited in the basket was actually mailed that day.

   (C) admitted, only if the office employee who usually mails the contents of the "outgoing mail" basket testifies to what is customarily done.

   (D) admitted, to prove that the notice of appeal was actually mailed on that day.

88. At the trial of an action for personal injuries resulting from an automobile accident which occurred in Treeville, Wagner testified for the defendant. He stated that he was standing on a street corner at the time of the accident and observed the plaintiff's car go through a red light. The plaintiff's attorney had information indicating that Wagner was not even in Treeville on the day of the accident, and had been observed on that day committing an armed robbery in Green City located at the other end of the state. On cross-examination, she asked, "Weren't you actually robbing a store in Green City on the day this accident occurred?" Wagner refused to answer, invoking the privilege against self-incrimination under the Fifth Amendment to the United States Constitution. Over objection by the defendant's attorney the judge ordered that Wagner's entire testimony be stricken. Subsequently, the defendant appealed from a judgment for the plaintiff, asserting that the trial court erred in striking Wagner's testimony. Which of the following would be the plaintiff's most effective argument in response to the defendant's assertion?

   (A) The privilege against self-incrimination is effective only in criminal proceedings.

   (B) The trial record, independent of Wagner's testimony, does not indicate that Wagner's answer would incriminate him.

   (C) Since the trial determined the rights of persons other than Wagner, the requirement of due process outweighed Wagner's privilege against self-incrimination.

   (D) Wagner's refusal to answer prevented adequate cross-examination.

89. Dessel, a college student, was charged with the attempted murder of Victorio, a fellow student, outside of one of the college classrooms. At the trial, Dessel's attorney called Fran, the school's dean of students, to the witness stand. Fran testified that immediately following the stabbing which led to the prosecution, she interviewed

Dessel, and that he stated that when Victorio insulted him, he stabbed Victorio in anger. She testified further that she had taken notes of the conversation, which she then placed in Dessel's student file. If the prosecutor offered Dessel's student file in evidence as a business record, which of the following would be Dessel's most effective argument in support of an objection to the admission of the file?

(A) Fran had an independent recollection of the events and was present in court to testify.

(B) The investigation of crimes is not a regularly conducted business activity for the college.

(C) The business record exception to the hearsay rule does not apply in criminal trials.

(D) Dessel's statement is second level hearsay.

90. In a challenge to the will of Tilsit, opponents of the will called Tilsit's next-door neighbor Nolan to the stand. Nolan testified that she had observed Tilsit acting strangely for several months before and after the date on which his will had been executed. When asked to specify in what way his behavior was strange, she said that he frequently appeared in his front yard wearing nothing but a towel and a football helmet, turning his face to the sky and shouting, "Bring on the saucers. I'm ready to do battle." She said that there were also times when she found him wandering about the street in a daze, and that on several occasions she had to take him home because he told her that he didn't know where he was. In rebuttal, proponents of the will called Dr. Medich to the stand. Dr. Medich testified that he had seen Tilsit only three days before the execution of the will for his semi-annual medical checkup, and that he did not observe any strange behavior at that or any other time. If opponents of the will seek to exclude Dr. Medich's statement from evidence, the statement should be

(A) excluded, since evidence that abnormal behavior was not observed is inadmissible to establish the sanity or competence of a decedent.

(B) excluded, because Dr. Medich's testimony

does not indicate a sufficient opportunity to observe Tilsit's behavior.

(C) admitted, because the opponents of the will opened the door by introducing the testimony of Nolan.

(D) admitted, since a medical doctor may qualify as an expert on the sanity of a patient.

91. At the trial of Pattel's personal injury action against Daumier, Wechsler was called as a witness on Pattel's direct case. Wechsler, a police officer, testified that he arrived at the scene of the accident about ten minutes after it occurred. He stated that when he got there he had a conversation with Koppel, another police officer who was already on the scene. When Wechsler said that he had no independent recollection regarding the nature of their conversation, Pattel's attorney showed him a copy of an official police report, and asked whether he recognized it. Wechsler identified it as the report which he filed following his investigation of the accident. Pattel's attorney offered the report in evidence. Daumier's attorney objected to its admission on the ground that it contained the following statement:

> Officer Koppel reports that an unidentified witness told him that Daumier went through a red light without stopping.

Should the police report be admitted into evidence?

(A) Yes, because Wechsler used it to refresh his recollection while testifying.

(B) Yes, because it is a business record.

(C) No, because a police report is not a record kept in the usual course of business.

(D) No, because neither Wechsler nor Koppel saw the accident.

92. Bolter, an American importer, contracted with VanderHaag, a Dutch manufacturer, for the purchase of trivets to be manufactured in Holland by VanderHaag. When VanderHaag delivered the trivets, however, Bolter refused to accept them, asserting that he had contracted for genuine porcelain, and that the trivets delivered by Vander-

Haag were imitation porcelain. Bolter died shortly afterwards. VanderHaag sued Bolter's estate in the United States for breach of contract, claiming that he explained to Bolter during negotiations that the trivets would be made of imitation porcelain.

At the trial, the attorney for Bolter's estate called Bolter's brother Worden as a witness. Worden testified that he spoke some Dutch, and had been present at the negotiations between Bolter and VanderHaag. He said that VanderHaag and Bolter asked him to assist by translating when necessary, because neither spoke the other's language very well. He stated further that when the trivets were being discussed, VanderHaag said something in Dutch which Bolter said he did not understand. Bolter then asked Worden to translate, and Worden replied, "He says that the trivets will be genuine porcelain." VanderHaag's attorney objected to Worden's last statement and asked the court to exclude it from the record.

Worden's statement should be

(A) admitted, because it is relevant to Bolter's intention at the time the contract was formed.

(B) admitted, only if the jurisdiction has a "dead man's statute."

(C) excluded, unless Worden qualifies as an expert on the Dutch language.

(D) excluded, because it is hearsay not within any exception.

93. After receiving a tip, police officers stopped a car being driven by Davidson, and forced him to open the trunk. In it, the officers discovered a canvas bag containing seven pounds of cocaine. They seized the car and the cocaine as evidence, and placed Davidson under arrest. Without advising him of his rights to remain silent and to consult with an attorney, they questioned him about the cocaine. During the questioning, Davidson said, "I don't know anything about it. It isn't even my car."

Davidson was charged with illegal possession of a controlled substance. Subsequently, Davidson's motion to suppress the use of the cocaine as evidence was granted, and the charges against him were dismissed. Davidson thereupon commenced an appropriate proceeding against the police department for recovery of his automobile. On presentation of his direct case, Davidson testified that he owned the seized automobile, but had registered it to a friend for purposes of convenience. On cross-examination, the attorney representing the police department asked, "After your arrest, did you tell the arresting officers that it wasn't your car?"

If Davidson's attorney objects to this question, the objection should be

(A) sustained, because Davidson's interrogation was in violation of his *Miranda* rights.

(B) sustained, because Davidson's motion to suppress was granted.

(C) overruled, because the automobile in which the cocaine was transported is "fruit of the poisonous tree."

(D) overruled, because his denial that he owned the car was a prior inconsistent statement.

94. In an action by Prussian Dyes against Dyeco for breach of contract, the attorney for Prussian Dyes called Wilmington as a witness. Wilmington testified that she was the employee of Prussian Dyes in charge of the Dyeco account. She said that on May 17, she had supervised a shipment of dyes to Dyeco. She stated that she did not personally inspect the shipment, but that immediately after the company shipping clerk inspected the shipment he told her its contents and she listed them on an invoice and signed it. A copy of the invoice was then sent to Dyeco in accordance with standard company practice. She said that she no longer had any independent recollection of what the shipment contained, but that the original invoice was now in the hands of the company attorney. When the attorney representing Prussian Dyes showed her a document and asked her to identify it, she said that it was the invoice to which she had referred, and that the signature on it was her own. When the attorney for Prussian

Dyes offered it in evidence, the attorney for Dyeco objected.

If the court admits the invoice into evidence, it will most probably be as

(A) past recollection recorded.

(B) a record kept in the usual course of business.

(C) an original document under the best evidence rule.

(D) present recollection refreshed.

Questions 95-96 are based on the following fact situation.

Finishco was a commercial furniture-finisher. Varilac was a manufacturer of commercial furniture finishing supplies. In an action by Finishco against Varilac for breach of contract, a dispute arose as to the meaning of the term "unit of lacquer" which appeared in a contract between the parties. Worley, an officer of Finishco, testified on her company's direct case.

95. Assume for the purpose of this question only that Worley testified that in the furniture finishing industry the term "unit of lacquer" means 55 gallons of lacquer. If Varilac's attorney objects, Worley's testimony should be

(A) excluded as a self-serving statement.

(B) excluded as hearsay, not within any exception to the hearsay rule.

(C) admitted as evidence of business habit.

(D) admitted, because it serves to establish a trade usage.

96. Assume for the purpose of this question only that Finishco's attorney then asked Worley whether Finishco and Varilac had ever done business in the past. In response, Worley said, "Definitely. In fact, before coming to court today, I refreshed my recollection by looking at company files. Then, based on my own knowledge, I prepared a chart, which accurately indicates the dates of the occasions we have done business together." After

Worley testified to those dates, Finischco's attorney offered the chart which Worley had prepared into evidence. Should the chart be admitted into evidence over the objection of Varilac's attorney?

(A) Yes, as a summary of a business record.

(B) Yes, as an illustration of Worley's testimony.

(C) No, because it is not the best evidence of the contents of Finishco's files.

(D) No, because a witness may not refresh her recollection by reference to materials unless they are in court and marked for identification.

97. At Doane's trial on a charge of rape, Ventura testified that after meeting him in a bar, she accompanied Doane to his apartment where he forced her to have sexual intercourse with him against her will. Doane's attorney did not cross-examine Ventura.

In his opening statement, Doane's attorney said that although his client admitted to having sexual intercourse with Ventura shortly after they first met on the night in question, he intended to prove that Ventura consented to the intercourse. Then, on direct presentation of Doane's case, his attorney attempted to offer evidence of Ventura's prior sexual conduct with other men.

Upon objection by the prosecution, this evidence should be

(A) admitted for the purpose of impeachment only.

(B) admitted as substantive evidence only.

(C) admitted as substantive evidence and for the purpose of impeachment.

(D) excluded.

98. In the trial of a tort action in a United States District Court, if the substantive law of the state is being applied, which of the following statements is correct regarding confidential communications between psychotherapist and patient?

I. The United States District Court MUST recognize the psychotherapist-patient privilege if it is recognized by the law of the state.

II. The United States District Court MAY recognize the psychotherapist-patient privilege even if it is not recognized by the law of the state.

(A) I only.

(B) II only.

(C) I and II.

(D) Neither I nor II.

99. In an action by Peterson against Docker for personal injuries resulting from negligence, Peterson's attorney called Melba as a witness on Peterson's direct case. Melba's testimony was offered to prove that Peterson suffered physical pain from his injuries. Melba testified that she was Peterson's mother and that during the weeks following the accident, she observed Peterson taking pink pills on several occasions. Peterson's attorney then asked Melba if she knew why Peterson was taking the pink pills. When Docker's attorney objected, Peterson's attorney withdrew the question and asked whether Melba was present when Dr. Treat examined Peterson the day after the accident. Melba responded that she heard Peterson say, "My neck hurts," and that Dr. Treat handed Peterson the pink pills and said, "These pink pills are very effective for pain."

If Docker's attorney moves to exclude Melba's testimony about what Dr. Treat said, that testimony should be

(A) admitted as a declaration of present physical sensation.

(B) admitted as a declaration of past physical sensation.

(C) excluded as hearsay, not within any exception to the hearsay rule.

(D) admitted as evidence of a medical history.

Questions 100-101 are based on the following fact situation.

Dustin pleaded not guilty to a charge of committing an armed robbery of Lendco. When Dustin appeared in court on the day of trial, his head was completely bald.

100. The prosecuting attorney called Verona as a witness on the prosecution's direct case. Verona testified that she was employed by Lendco, and that she was present when the robbery was committed. She stated that the robber had bushy red hair. When asked whether Dustin was the robber, she looked at him sitting in the courtroom and said that she was not sure. The prosecuting attorney then asked her whether she had identified Dustin as the robber at a lineup conducted on the day of the robbery. If Dustin's attorney objects to that question, the objection should be

(A) sustained, since her statement is hearsay not within any exception.

(B) sustained, since the prosecuting attorney may not impeach his own witness.

(C) overruled, since Verona is on the witness stand and available for cross-examination.

(D) overruled, since Verona is a disinterested witness.

101. The prosecuting attorney next called Warder as a witness. Warder testified that she was employed as a guard in the county house of detention where Dustin had been in custody since the day of his arrest. She stated that when she saw Dustin on the day of his arrest, he had bushy red hair. She stated further that, at Dustin's request, she provided Dustin with shaving articles on the morning of trial and remained outside his cell where she watched while he shaved his head. If Dustin's attorney objects to this testimony, the testimony should be

(A) excluded, as extrinsic evidence of a collateral matter.

(B) excluded, under Dustin's privilege against self-incrimination.

(C) admitted, to explain why Dustin no longer

has bushy red hair.

(D) admitted, as evidence of an admission by conduct.

102. Derringer was charged with violating a federal law which prohibits the unlicensed transportation of specified toxic wastes across a state line. At his trial in a federal district court, the prosecution proved that Derringer had transported certain toxic wastes from Detroit, Michigan to Chicago, Illinois. The prosecuting attorney then moved that the court take judicial notice that it is impossible to travel between those two cities without crossing a state line. Upon proper objection by Derringer's attorney, the prosecution's motion should be

(A) granted, if it is generally known within the territorial jurisdiction of the court that it is impossible to travel from Detroit to Chicago without crossing a state line.

(B) granted, but only if the prosecution presents the court with a reputable map or other reference work indicating that a state line lies between the cities of Detroit and Chicago.

(C) denied, but only if Derringer's attorney demands an offer of proof for the record.

(D) denied, if the fact that Derringer traveled across a state line concerns an ultimate issue of fact.

Questions 103-104 are based on the following fact situation.

Soon after his election as labor union president, Danziger raised his presidential salary from $35,000 to $60,000 per year. As a result, he was subsequently charged with violating a state law making it a felony for union officials to knowingly misappropriate union funds. Danziger admitted granting himself the pay raise, but claimed as a defense that when he did so he believed the union rules authorized such action. At Danziger's trial, his attorney called Wesley, the union secretary, as a witness. On direct examination, she testified that before Danziger ordered the pay raise, Wesley told him that the union constitution gave the president the power to raise his own salary whenever

he thought it necessary.

103. If the prosecuting attorney objects to Wesley's testimony on the ground that it violates the best evidence rule, the objection should be

(A) sustained, unless Danziger proves that the original or a qualified duplicate of the union constitution is unavailable.

(B) sustained, unless Wesley's knowledge of the union rules was obtained from some source other than the union constitution.

(C) overruled, unless Wesley's statement is offered to prove the contents of the union constitution.

(D) overruled, unless the prosecuting attorney proves that the original or a qualified duplicate of the union constitution is available.

104. Danziger's attorney then called Forman, the former president of the union. Forman testified to a conversation which took place between him and Danziger before Danziger ordered the pay raise. Forman stated that when Danziger asked him whether the union president was permitted to raise his own salary, Forman told him that the president could do so whenever he deemed it necessary. If the prosecuting attorney objects to Forman's testimony on the ground that it is hearsay, Forman's testimony should be

(A) admitted as evidence of Danziger's state of mind.

(B) excluded as hearsay, not within any exception.

(C) excluded, unless Forman qualifies as an expert on the union's rules.

(D) admitted, because the out of court assertion was made by the witness himself.

105. Draper was charged with the second degree murder of Valle under a statute which defined that crime as "the unlawful killing of a human being with malice aforethought, but without premedita-

tion." Draper's attorney asserted a defense of insanity, and called Draper as a witness in his own behalf. After Draper testified on direct and cross-examination, his attorney called Dr. Wendell to the witness stand. Dr. Wendell stated that he was a psychiatrist, had practiced for thirty years, had treated thousands of patients with illnesses like Draper's, and had testified as an expert in hundreds of criminal homicide trials. He testified, "After listening to Draper's testimony, I am of the opinion that Draper did not have malice aforethought as our law defines it on the day of Valle's death." On cross-examination, Dr. Wendell admitted that he had never spoken to or seen Draper before, and that his opinion was based entirely on his observations of Draper's testimony.

Which of the following would be the prosecuting attorney's most effective argument in support of a motion to exclude Dr. Wendell's statement?

(A) Dr. Wendell's testimony embraces the ultimate issue.

(B) Dr. Wendell's opinions were based entirely upon courtroom observations.

(C) Dr. Wendell had insufficient opportunity to examine Draper.

(D) Whether Draper had "malice aforethought" is a question to be decided by the jury.

Questions 106-107 are based on the following fact situation.

At the trial of her negligence action against Deventer, Pasadena exhibited her leg to the jury and testified that following the accident her leg was so badly mangled that she believed that she was going to die. Pasadena's attorney then called Winton who testified that he arrived at the scene of the accident moments after it occurred, and found Pasadena lying in the roadway in a pool of blood. Winton stated that he heard Pasadena scream, "Oh, God, I had the green light in my favor and now I'm dying." Deventer's attorney made timely objection to Winton's testimony.

106. Which of the following is the best reason for con-

cluding that Pasadena's statement was NOT a dying declaration?

(A) Pasadena's statement did not identify the person who she believed to be responsible for her death.

(B) Pasadena was in court when Winton testified to her statement.

(C) The proceeding was a civil one.

(D) Pasadena was not dying at the time her statement was made.

107. Winton's testimony is

(A) admissible as evidence of an excited utterance.

(B) inadmissible as hearsay, not within any exception.

(C) admissible as evidence of a declaration of present state of mind.

(D) admissible as evidence of a declaration of past state of mind.

108. Callahan retained Lewis, an attorney, to represent him in connection with a boundary dispute between Callahan and his neighbor. Subsequently, Callahan sued Lewis for malpractice, alleging that Lewis negligently failed to institute an action to quiet title before such action was barred by the statute of limitations. At the trial, Lewis testified that he advised Callahan to commence an action to quiet title, but that Callahan instructed Lewis not to do so, stating that he feared that because of the litigation his neighbor might find out that Callahan had once been convicted of a felony. Callahan objected on the ground that his communication with Lewis was confidential. In a jurisdiction which recognizes the common law attorney-client privilege, Callahan's objection should be

(A) sustained, because Callahan's statement was related to the reason for his consultation with Lewis.

(B) sustained, only if Callahan's statement was

necessary to his consultation with Lewis.

(C) overruled, if Lewis' testimony is relevant to the issue of Lewis' negligence.

(D) overruled, because an adversary proceeding between attorney and client terminates the confidential relationship between them.

109. In a negligence action brought by Pauling against Davidson, Pauling alleged that Davidson failed to signal before making a left turn onto Front Street. During the presentation of Davidson's direct case, Weigand was called as a witness. Weigand testified that she was Davidson's secretary and that Davidson drove her to work every morning. She said that she was in Davidson's car on the morning of the accident, but did not see him signal because she was reading a magazine at the time. She added, however, that she had seen Davidson turn at that intersection many times, and that he always signaled before doing so. If Pauling's attorney objects to this testimony by Weigand, her testimony should be

(A) excluded, unless there were no eyewitnesses to Davidson's behavior on the morning in question.

(B) excluded, because evidence of past behavior is inadmissible for the purpose of proving reasonable care on a particular occasion.

(C) admitted, as circumstantial evidence that Davidson signaled on the morning of the accident.

(D) admitted, but only if it is corroborated by Davidson's testimony.

110. Dorah, a sixteen-year-old child, was involved in an accident while driving a friend's car. At the request of Prawley, who was injured in the accident, a court designated Dorah's father Felton as Dorah's legal guardian for the purpose of defending Prawley's lawsuit against Dorah. Prawley then sued Dorah, joining Felton as a defendant as required by state law. Dorah and Felton consulted Watt, an attorney, about the lawsuit. Felton was present when Dorah told Watt that she had been driving over the speed limit at the time of the

accident. Watt refused to represent Dorah, and Felton thereafter retained another attorney. At the trial of Prawley's action against Dorah and Felton, Watt was called as a witness on Prawley's direct case. When Prawley's attorney attempted to question him regarding the conversation which he had with Dorah, Dorah's attorney objected on the ground that the conversation was privileged. In a jurisdiction which recognizes the common law attorney-client privilege, should the objection to Watt's testimony be sustained?

(A) Yes, because Felton's designation as Dorah's legal guardian made his presence at the consultation necessary.

(B) Yes, because all communications made by a client to an attorney while seeking advice are privileged.

(C) No, because Dorah and Felton are joint defendants.

(D) No, because Watt never agreed to represent Dorah and Felton.

Questions 111-112 are based on the following fact situation.

Dempsey was charged in a state court with third degree arson on the allegation that he set fire to his own house for the purpose of collecting benefits under a fire insurance policy. At his trial, Dempsey called Wrangler as a witness in his favor. On direct examination by Dempsey's attorney, Wrangler testified that at the time of the fire he and Dempsey were together at a baseball game fifty miles away from Dempsey's home.

111. On rebuttal the prosecuting attorney offered evidence that two years earlier Wrangler was released from custody after serving a five -year sentence in a federal prison following his conviction for perjury. If Dempsey's attorney objects to the introduction of this evidence, the objection should be

(A) overruled, but only if Wrangler is given a subsequent opportunity to explain the conviction.

(B) overruled, because perjury is a crime involving dishonesty.

(C) sustained, because the conviction was not more than ten years old.

(D) sustained, unless the prosecuting attorney asked Wrangler on cross-examination whether he had ever been convicted of a crime.

112. The prosecuting attorney then offered proof that Wrangler had been arrested as an accessory to the burning of Dempsey's house, and that the charge against him was still pending. If Dempsey's attorney objects to this evidence, the objection should be

(A) sustained, because evidence of unconvicted bad acts is inadmissible to extrinsically impeach a witness.

(B) sustained, because the arrest of Wrangler is not material to the charge against Dempsey.

(C) overruled, because the pending charge against Wrangler is evidence that Wrangler is a biased witness.

(D) overruled, because the arrest is evidence that Wrangler has a bad reputation for honesty and truthfulness.

113. Section 481 of the City of Hawthorne Code of Municipal Ordinances provides in part, "In any municipal parking lot operated by the City of Hawthorne, it shall be a misdemeanor for any person to park a vehicle more than seventeen feet in length in a space marked 'Compact Car Only'." At Darling's trial on a charge of violating that section, the public prosecutor rested after proving that Darling's car was more than seventeen feet in length, and that it had been parked in a municipal parking lot operated by the City of Hawthorne in a space marked "Compact Car Only." Without offering any evidence, Darling moved to dismiss on the ground that the public prosecutor had failed to prove the contents of Section 481 of the City of Hawthorne Code of Municipal Ordinances. In response to Darling's motion, the public prosecutor asked the court to

take judicial notice of that section. Darling's motion to dismiss should be

(A) granted, unless the jurisdiction permits a court to take judicial notice of municipal ordinances.

(B) granted, because the alleged violation of Section 481 of the Code of Municipal Ordinances is an ultimate issue to be determined by the trier of fact.

(C) denied, because the contents of local law need not be proven in a criminal prosecution.

(D) denied, unless the court qualifies as an expert on the contents of the City of Hawthorne Code of Municipal Ordinances.

114. Purcell and Danton were running against each other for the office of mayor of their city. One month before the election, Danton was interviewed on a television program called "Meet the Candidate." After the program appeared on television, Purcell sued Danton, claiming that Danton made defamatory statements about him during the interview. At the trial, Purcell called Wellman as a witness. Wellman testified that he was employed as a video engineer by the producers of "Meet the Candidate" and that he was present in the studio when Danton was interviewed. He stated that he heard Danton say, "Purcell is as crooked as any thief in the USA" in response to a question by the interviewer. On timely objection and motion by Danton's attorney, Wellman's testimony should be

(A) admitted.

(B) excluded, if a videotape of the interview is available.

(C) excluded, because it is hearsay.

(D) excluded, unless Danton admits making the statement.

Questions 115-116 are based on the following fact situation.

State Police Commissioner Watkins was subpoenaed to

appear before a state grand jury investigating corruption in state law enforcement agencies. After being sworn, Watkins refused to answer any questions, asserting his privilege against self-incrimination under the Fifth Amendment to the United States Constitution. After the state prosecutor granted him use immunity, however, Watkins testified that for years he had been aware that his assistant Dacey and certain other members of his department were receiving bribes from members of nationwide organized crime syndicates. Dacey was subsequently charged in a state court with receiving bribes. At Dacey's trial, Watkins was called as a witness for the defense. On direct examination, Watkins testified that he had never heard of Dacey or any other member of his department engaging in corrupt acts.

115. On cross-examination the prosecuting attorney asked Watkins, "Didn't you testify at a grand jury proceeding that you had been aware for years that Dacey had been taking bribes?" Watkins refused to answer on the ground that he had received immunity before testifying at the grand jury proceeding. Should the court compel Watkins to answer the question?

    (A) Yes, but the answer is admissible only for the purpose of impeaching Watkins' credibility.

    (B) Yes, but the answer is admissible only as substantive evidence against Dacey.

    (C) Yes, and the answer is admissible for the purpose of impeaching Watkins' credibility and as substantive evidence against Dacey.

    (D) No.

116. Watkins was subsequently charged in a federal court with violation of a federal statute which made it a crime for state law enforcement officials to knowingly permit members of their departments to accept bribes from interstate crime syndicates. Prior to trial, Watkins moved to dismiss on the ground that he had been granted use immunity by the state prosecutor. Watkins' motion should be

    (A) granted, because state grants of use immunity must be honored in federal courts.

    (B) granted, under the Double Jeopardy Clause of the United Stated Constitution.

    (C) denied, because use immunity does not prevent prosecution in any jurisdiction.

    (D) denied, because federal courts are not required to honor use immunity granted by a state prosecutor.

117. While crossing Marshal Boulevard in the City of Burg, Proust was struck by a northbound hit and run motorist and severely injured. In a subsequent negligence action against the City of Burg, Proust asserted that there was a dangerous curve on Marshal Boulevard just south of the place where the accident occurred, and that the City of Burg was negligent in failing to post signs warning pedestrians and motorists of the danger.

As part of its defense, the City of Burg called Wenzel as a witness. Wenzel testified that she had been the City of Burg traffic commissioner for the past 20 years. Wenzel stated that because of her official position, all reported traffic accidents in the City of Burg were brought to her attention whether or not they resulted in lawsuits. She stated further that although Marshal Boulevard was a busy thoroughfare, she had never heard of an accident on Marshal Boulevard prior to Proust's injury.

Upon proper motion by Proust's attorney, the testimony of Wenzel should be

    (A) admitted, only if Marshal Boulevard south of the accident location was substantially unchanged during the period of Wenzel's employment.

    (B) admitted, only if the court issues a special instruction to the jury regarding the dangers of negative evidence.

    (C) excluded, because it is possible that accidents occurred which were not reported.

    (D) excluded, because of the inherent unreliability of negative evidence.

118. In a negligence action against the Dixie Hotel, Poulter asserted that while she was a guest at the Dixie Hotel she slipped on wet pigeon droppings in an alley located next to the hotel, sustaining injury. In defense, the Dixie Hotel denied that it was negligent, and denied ownership and control of the alley in which the accident occurred. At the trial, Poulter called Wells, a hotel maintenance employee, as a witness. Wells testified that although employees of the Dixie Hotel had never before cleaned pigeon droppings from the alley, they began doing so after Poulter commenced her lawsuit against the hotel. If the Dixie Hotel objects to the testimony of Wells, the testimony should be

    (A) admitted.

    (B) excluded, because subsequent cleaning of pigeon droppings may have been nothing more than a response to the litigation.

    (C) excluded, because of a policy which encourages the taking of remedial measures following an accident.

    (D) excluded, because the Dixie Hotel denied that it was negligent.

119. At the trial of a personal injury action, Dr. Watson testified that she examined the plaintiff on the day of trial, and that at that time the plaintiff told her that she felt pain in her knee. On cross-examination, the defendant's attorney asked Dr. Watson whether she had ever met the plaintiff before the day of trial. Dr. Watson responded that she had not, and that her sole purpose in examining the plaintiff was to prepare for testifying at the trial. The defendant's attorney then moved to strike that portion of Dr. Watson's testimony which referred to the plaintiff's complaint of pain. In a jurisdiction which applies the common-law rule regarding confidential communications between patient and physician, should the defendant's motion be granted?

    (A) Yes, because the examination was solely for the purpose of litigation.

    (B) Yes, because the probative value of the state-

    ment is outweighed by the possibility of prejudice.

    (C) Yes, because statements made to a physician are privileged.

    (D) No, because the statement described what the plaintiff was feeling at the time.

120. In an action against DelMonte, Praxton asserted that as a result of DelMonte's negligent driving, Praxton's car was damaged. In defense, DelMonte denied that there was any damage to Praxton's car and denied that she was negligent. At the trial, Praxton testified that following the accident DelMonte said, "I'm sure my insurance company would give you $500 if you agree not to sue me for damages." DelMonte's attorney immediately moved to strike that portion of Praxton's testimony from the record.

    Should the motion of DelMonte's attorney be granted?

    (A) Yes, but only if the statement is offered to prove that DelMonte was negligent.

    (B) Yes, if the statement is offered to prove that there was damage to Praxton's car.

    (C) No, because the statement is an implied admission.

    (D) No, because DelMonte opened the door by denying that there was damage to Praxton's car.

Questions 121-123 are based on the following fact situation.

At George's trial on a charge of criminal battery, the prosecutor called Vinson as a witness. Vinson testified that he had argued with George in a bar shortly before he was struck in the head from behind. He said that he did not see who struck him, but that a moment before the blow he heard a voice which he did not recognize shout, "Watch out for George."

121. If George's attorney objects to Vinson's statement about what he heard, that statement should be

(A) excluded, because Vinson could not identify the person who shouted.

(B) excluded, because Vinson's testimony is self-serving.

(C) admitted.

(D) excluded, because there was no proof that the person shouting had personal knowledge of the assailant's identity.

122. The prosecutor next called Bierman, who testified that he was working as bartender at the time and place where Vinson was attacked. In answer to a question by the prosecutor, Bierman said that he did not remember whether he shouted anything immediately before the attack. The prosecutor showed George's attorney a written report of a conversation between Bierman and an investigator, and had it marked for identification. Then the prosecutor showed the report to Bierman and asked whether it refreshed his recollection. If George's attorney objects to this procedure, the objection should be

(A) sustained, unless the report has been admitted into evidence.

.(B) sustained, because the report is inadmissible hearsay.

(C) overruled, because Bierman testified that he did not remember whether or not he shouted anything prior to the attack.

(D) overruled, but only if the prosecutor offers the report into evidence.

123. Assume for the purpose of this question only that, without looking at the written report, Bierman said, "I remember now. I shouted, 'Watch out for George.' " If George's attorney moves to strike this testimony on the ground that it is hearsay, the prosecutor's most effective argument in opposition to that motion would be that

(A) the shout was an excited utterance.

(B) the shout was not an out-of-court statement because Bierman testified to it in court.

(C) Bierman is permitted to corroborate the hearsay by testifying independently to what he observed prior to shouting.

(D) Bierman's testimony qualifies as a present recollection refreshed.

124. Procedural delays caused five years to pass before Poe's personal injury claim against Del-Monte was ready for trial. At the trial, Poe's attorney called Wolf, an eyewitness to the accident. Wolf testified that before coming to court, she had refreshed her recollection by looking at written notes of her interview with Poe's attorney which took place the week after the accident. On proper motion by DelMonte's attorney, the court

(A) should strike Wolf's testimony, unless it is shown that the notes themselves are unavailable.

(B) may direct that the notes be brought into court for inspection by DelMonte's attorney.

(C) may not properly direct that the notes be brought into court because they have not been offered into evidence.

(D) should admit the notes into evidence as an admission of a party.

Questions 125-126 are based on the following fact situation.

During the presentation of plaintiff's direct case in a personal injury action, the plaintiff's attorney called Dr. Wallace to the stand for the purpose of establishing that the plaintiff had sustained an injury to her epiglammis gland.

125. When the plaintiff's attorney began to question Dr. Wallace about her qualifications, the defendant's attorney conceded on the record and in the presence of the jury that Dr. Wallace was an expert on injuries of the epiglammis gland and objected to any further questions regarding the qualifications of Dr. Wallace. Should the plaintiff's attorney be permitted to continue questioning Dr. Wallace regarding her qualifications?

(A) No, because the qualifications of Dr. Wallace are no longer in issue.

(B) No, if the court is satisfied that Dr. Wallace qualifies as an expert on diseases and injuries of the epiglammis gland.

(C) Yes, because the court must determine for itself whether a witness qualifies as an expert, and cannot allow the matter to be determined by stipulation of the parties.

(D) Yes, because the jury may consider an expert's qualifications in determining her credibility.

126. On direct examination, Dr. Wallace testified that after receiving a positive result in a test known as a glandular arviogram she concluded that the plaintiff had sustained an injury to her epiglammis gland. On cross-examination, the defendant's attorney showed Dr. Wallace a book entitled "Glandular Arviography" and asked whether she relied on it in forming her diagnosis. Dr. Wallace stated that she did not, but admitted that it was a well-respected work in the field. The defendant's attorney then asked Dr. Wallace to read aloud a passage from the book which stated that a positive result in a glandular arviogram almost always indicated that there was no injury to the patient's epiglammis gland. If the plaintiff's attorney objects, can that passage be read to the jury?

(A) Yes, for the purpose of impeachment only.

(B) Yes, as substantive evidence only.

(C) Yes, for the purpose of impeachment and as substantive evidence.

(D) No.

Questions 127-128 are based on the following fact situation.

Padilla brought a negligence action against Daggett for personal injuries which Padilla sustained when she was struck by Daggett's car while she was a pedestrian. In defense, Daggett asserted that he was not negligent, and that Padilla was contributorily negligent in that she was not in the area designated as a crosswalk at the time of the accident. Padilla's attorney called Wagner as a witness on Padilla's behalf.

127. Wagner testified that she and Padilla were close friends, that they walked over that intersection together almost every day for three years prior to the accident, and that when doing so, Padilla always walked in the area designated as a crosswalk. If Daggett's attorney objects to Wagner's statement, the objection should be

(A) sustained, unless Wagner has a specific recollection of whether Padilla was in the crosswalk at the time of the accident.

(B) sustained, because Padilla's practice at any time other than that of the accident is a collateral matter.

(C) overruled, but only if Padilla corroborates Wagner's testimony by stating that she was in the crosswalk at the time of the accident.

(D) overruled, since evidence of Padilla's habit is relevant to her conduct at the time of the accident.

128. Wagner then testified that she held a valid driver's license, that she had been driving an automobile for forty years, that she had seen Daggett's car just before it struck Padilla, and that in her opinion it was moving at a speed in excess of the thirty-five miles per hour speed limit. If Daggett's attorney objects to Wagner's testimony regarding the speed of Daggett's vehicle, which of the following would be the most effective argument in support of that objection?

(A) Wagner did not qualify as an expert on the speed of a moving automobile.

(B) Wagner's statement of opinion concerned an ultimate fact in the litigation.

(C) Wagner did not have sufficient opportunity to form an opinion regarding the speed of Daggett's vehicle.

(D) The speed of Daggett's vehicle was a fact, and therefore cannot be established by opinion evidence.

Questions 129-130 are based on the following fact situation.

Pasko was a passenger in a car driven by Dooley when the car struck a pole. Pasko subsequently asserted a claim against Dooley, alleging that injuries which resulted from Dooley's negligent driving caused Pasko to be hospitalized for more than a month. At trial, on the presentation of Pasko's direct case Pasko testified that immediately after the accident, while Dooley was extremely nervous and upset, Dooley said, "Don't worry, I've got plenty of insurance."

129. Upon objection by Dooley's attorney, that portion of Pasko's testimony should be

   (A) excluded, because it is not relevant to a material issue.

   (B) excluded, because it relates to a compromise offer.

   (C) admitted as evidence of an admission of a party.

   (D) admitted as evidence of an excited utterance.

130. Assume for the purpose of this question only that Pasko then testified that following his release from the hospital, Dooley's insurance company paid Pasko's hospital bill of $20,000. Upon objection by Dooley's attorney, this portion of Pasko's testimony should be

   (A) admitted, unless the payment of Pasko's hospital bill is found to be an offer of compromise.

   (B) excluded.

   (C) admitted, only if reference to the fact the Dooley was insured can be severed from the rest of Pasko's statement.

   (D) admitted as circumstantial evidence that Dooley regarded himself to be at fault in causing the accident.

Questions 131-132 are based on the following fact situation.

At the trial of an action brought by Pallas against Dalbey for breach of contract, Waite was called as a witness by Pallas's attorney. Waite identified the signature on a document as Dalbey's, testifying that he knew Dalbey's signature because he and Dalbey had once been partners, and that he had seen Dalbey's signature many times during the course of their partnership.

131. Upon proper motion by Dalbey's attorney, Waite's testimony regarding the signature should be

   (A) excluded, unless Waite is found to be an expert on handwriting.

   (B) excluded, unless Waite is found to be an expert on Dalbey's handwriting.

   (C) admitted.

   (D) excluded, because it is the jury's function to decide whether the signature was Dalbey's.

132. Assume for the purpose of this question only that Waite testified to other matters, and that on cross-examination Dalbey's attorney asked Waite, "Didn't the partnership between you and Dalbey break up because Dalbey accused you of dishonesty?" If Pallas's attorney objects to that question, the objection should be

   (A) sustained, because the question seeks to elicit hearsay not within any exception to the hearsay rule.

   (B) overruled, because the question seeks to elicit an admission.

   (C) overruled, because the question seeks to elicit evidence which is admissible for purposes of extrinsic impeachment.

   (D) overruled, because the question seeks to elicit evidence which would tend to establish that Waite is a biased witness.

133. At Danek's trial on charges of criminal assault and battery, Weary was called by the prosecutor

as a witness. Weary testified that while he was walking through a parking lot at night, Danek attacked and beat him. Weary stated further that although there were no artificial lights of any kind in the vicinity of the parking lot, he was able to see Danek clearly in the light of the full moon. After direct examination of Weary by the prosecutor, Danek's attorney waived cross-examination, and Weary left the courtroom.

Danek's attorney subsequently called an expert witness to testify that there was no moon at all on the night of the alleged crime. The prosecutor conceded the expert's qualifications.

Upon timely objection by the prosecutor, the expert's testimony should be

(A) admitted to show that Weary's testimony is not worthy of belief.

(B) admitted, because it is part of the *res gestae*.

(C) excluded, because Weary was not given an opportunity to explain his testimony in view of the additional evidence.

(D) excluded as extrinsic evidence of a collateral matter.

134. Danfield was arrested after she used a credit card bearing the name of Timothy Nolan to pay for a purchase. Danfield was subsequently charged with fraudulent use of a credit card. At her trial, a police officer testified that when she arrested Danfield, she found her to be in possession of 5 credit cards bearing the name of Timothy Nolan and 36 other credit cards bearing a total of 36 different names. In addition, the officer stated that Danfield's wallet contained driver's licenses to match each of the various names on the credit cards.

If Danfield's attorney moves to exclude evidence that Danfield possessed credit cards or driver's licenses other than that which she was charged with fraudulently using, which of the following would be the prosecutor's most effective argument in opposition to that motion?

(A) The number of credit cards and driver's

licenses in Danfield's possession tends to establish a criminal plan.

(B) The number of credit cards in Danfield's possession makes it likely that she had stolen them.

(C) Danfield should be required to explain why she possessed so many credit cards belonging to other people.

(D) Danfield's possession of 41 credit cards bearing names other than her own is an admission by conduct.

Questions 135-136 are based on the following fact situation.

Handel, a federal officer, had been informed that a person arriving from Europe on a particular airline flight would be carrying cocaine in his baggage. Handel went to the airport and stood at the arrival gate with Findo, a dog which had been specially trained to recognize the scent of cocaine. When Dodd walked by carrying his bag, Findo began barking and scratching the floor in front of him with his right paw. Handel stopped Dodd and searched his bag. In it, he found a small brass statue with a false bottom. Upon removing the false bottom, Handel found one ounce of cocaine. Dodd, who was arrested and charged with the illegal importation of a controlled substance, claimed he had purchased the statue as a souvenir and was unaware that there was cocaine hidden it its base.

135. Assume for the purpose of this question only that Dodd's attorney moved for an order excluding the use of the cocaine as evidence at Dodd's trial. At a hearing on that motion, Handel testified that he was an expert dog trainer and handler, that he had personally trained Findo to signal by barking and scratching the floor in front of him with his right paw whenever he sniffed cocaine, that Findo had successfully found and signaled the presence of cocaine on several previous occasions, and that Findo had given the signal when Dodd walked away. If Dodd's attorney moves to exclude Handel's testimony regarding the way Findo acted when Dodd walked by, that testimony should be

(A) excluded, because the sounds and movements made by Findo are hearsay and not within any exception.

(B) excluded, unless Findo is dead or otherwise unavailable.

(C) admitted, but only if Findo's effectiveness is established by an in-court demonstration.

(D) admitted, because a proper foundation has been laid.

136. Assume for the purpose of this question only that at Dodd's trial the prosecution offers to prove that Dodd had been convicted fifteen years earlier of illegally importing cocaine by hiding it in the base of a brass statue. If Dodd's attorney objects, the court should rule that proof of Dodd's prior conviction is

(A) admissible, as evidence of habit.

(B) admissible, because it is evidence of a distinctive method of operation.

(C) inadmissible, because evidence of previous conduct by a defendant may not be used against him.

(D) inadmissible, because the prior conviction occurred more than ten years before the trial.

Questions 137-138 are based on the following situation.

Packard brought a negligence action against Danesh for damages resulting from personal injuries sustained in an automobile accident. Prior to trial, the parties and their attorneys attended a settlement conference in the judge's chambers. During the course of the settlement conference, the judge asked Danesh how fast she was going at the time of the accident, to which Danesh replied, "I really don't know, your honor." Danesh was not under oath.

At the trial, Danesh testified on her own behalf. In response to a question by her attorney, Danesh said, "When the accident occurred, I was definitely not exceeding the speed limit." On cross examination, Packard's attorney asked Danesh, "Did you ever say

that you didn't know how fast you were going at the time of the accident?" Danesh's attorney objected to the question.

137. The objection of Danesh's attorney should be

(A) sustained, because a proper foundation was not laid.

(B) sustained, because Danesh was not under oath at the settlement conference.

(C) overruled, because the statement which Danesh made at the settlement conference tends to establish that Danesh is not worthy of belief.

(D) sustained, because Packard's attorney failed to confront Danesh prior to asking her about the statement.

138. Assume for the purpose of this question only that Packard's attorney subsequently called as a rebuttal witness Westcott, a law clerk who was present in the judge's chambers during the settlement conference, and that Packard's attorney asked Westcott whether he had heard Danesh say that she did not know how fast she was going at the time of the accident. If Danesh's attorney objects to the question, the objection should be

(A) sustained, because Danesh was not given an opportunity to explain the inconsistency while she was on the witness stand.

(B) sustained, unless Danesh is given a subsequent opportunity to explain the inconsistency.

(C) overruled, because the statement is admissible for the purpose of extrinsic impeachment.

(D) overruled, under the collateral witness rule.

139. Decco was arrested for driving under the influence of alcohol while operating a car which he borrowed from a friend earlier that day. After the arrest, the police conducted an inventory search of the vehicle and found a container of marijuana in the trunk. As a result, Decco was charged with violating a state law which made it a crime to

knowingly possess marijuana. Testifying on his own behalf at the trial, Decco stated that he was not aware there was marijuana in the trunk. On cross examination, after properly marking it for identification, the prosecutor showed Decco a letter which had been taken from his coat pocket following his arrest, and asked whether he recognized it. When Decco said that it was a note from his wife, the prosecutor showed it to Decco's attorney and offered it in evidence. Among other things, the note said, "We sure got high on that stuff we smoked last night."

If Decco's attorney objects to admission of the letter, his objection should be

(A) sustained, because the letter is hearsay not within any exception to the hearsay rule.

(B) sustained, because the letter is not relevant to a material issue.

(C) overruled, because the letter is a declaration against the penal interest of Decco's wife.

(D) overruled, unless the jurisdiction recognizes the common law spousal privilege.

140. At the trial of an action for breach of contract brought by Pacetti against Decker, Pacetti's attorney called Pacetti as a witness in her own behalf. On direct examination, Pacetti's attorney asked, "Do you own a German shepherd with a white forepaw?" Pacetti said that she did. No other questions were asked on direct examination. On cross examination, Decker's attorney asked Pacetti, "Your dog is generally known to be gentle, isn't that correct?"

If Pacetti's attorney objects to the question, the objection should be

(A) sustained, if the question went beyond the scope of cross examination.

(B) sustained, because the question is leading.

(C) overruled, because Pacetti is a hostile witness.

(D) overruled, if Pacetti is an expert in dog behavior.

141. Which of the following is NOT self authenticating?

(A) A will with the attestation of witnesses affixed to it.

(B) A newspaper.

(C) A directory of public service telephone numbers issued by the state civil services administration.

(D) A copy of a divorce decree prepared by the attorney for one of the divorced spouses and certified correct by the clerk of the court.

Questions 142-43 are based on the following fact situation.

Peterson was riding a motorcycle manufactured by Byko when he collided with an automobile, sustaining serious personal injuries. Following the accident, examination of the motorcycle revealed that its fork was severely bent. Peterson claimed the fork bent when he drove the motorcycle over a bump in the road, and the bending of the fork caused him to lose control and strike the automobile. Peterson asserted a personal injury claim against Byko on the ground that the motorcycle was equipped with a fork which was not strong enough to withstand the pressures of normal operation and was, therefore, defective in design. Byko denied that the motorcycle was defective and claimed that the accident resulted from Peterson's negligent operation of the motorcycle and that the fork did not bend until the motorcycle collided with the automobile.

142. Assume for the purpose of this question only that Byko called as a witness Walters, who was employed by Byko as vice president in charge of safety. Walters testified that he had held that position for six years, that in that time the company had sold more than 10,000 motorcycles identical to the one ridden by Peterson, and that Walters had never heard about a fork bending in normal operation. If Peterson's attorney objects, Walter's testimony should be

(A) admitted, but only if the judge gives the jury a special instruction regarding the uncertainty of negative evidence.

(B) admitted, if Walters was the person to whom all complaints of product failure would be reported.

(C) excluded, because it is possible that accidents occurred which were never reported to the company.

(D) excluded, because negative evidence is inherently unreliable.

143. Assume for the purpose of this question only that Byko's attorney attempted to offer a film into evidence. The film showed a test being conducted on a motorcycle fork identical to the one on Peterson's motorcycle. In the test, the fork was subjected to the application of more than 15,000 pounds of pressure and did not bend. If Peterson's attorney objects, the film should be

(A) excluded, unless it is properly authenticated by the photographer who made the film.

(B) excluded, because it is not the best evidence of the test which was performed.

(C) excluded, if the test conditions were not identical to the conditions which Peterson claims existed at the time of the accident.

(D) admitted.

ANSWERS
EVIDENCE

ANSWERS TO
EVIDENCE QUESTIONS

1.   **A**   Under both common law and the UCC, evidence of trade terminology is admissible for the purpose of establishing the meaning of a particular term in a contract between parties in the trade. Since the contract calls for the sale of fish at wholesale, evidence of trade terminology used in the wholesale fish industry is relevant to establish the meaning of the term in question.

        Ordinarily, a witness is not permitted to testify to her opinion. A witness who qualifies as an expert in a particular field, however, may be permitted to testify to an opinion regarding her field of expertise. Since Cooke is not offering an opinion regarding the preparation of fried fish in fast food restaurants, he need not qualify as an expert in that particular field. **B** is, therefore, incorrect. **C** is incorrect because an expert may offer an opinion regarding her field of expertise. **D** is incorrect because even if parties have not specifically agreed to be bound by the terminology of a particular industry, that terminology may be relevant in determining the meaning of unexplained terms in a contract so long as both parties are likely to have been aware of the meaning of the trade terminology.

2.   **C**   Damages in a defamation action are supposed to compensate the plaintiff for an injury to her reputation. Since the injury would be less severe if the plaintiff's reputation was not a good one to begin with, evidence of Perez's reputation in Platano is relevant to the issue of damages, and is, therefore, admissible.

        A is incorrect because the evidence was not offered for the purpose of proving that Perez engaged in any particular conduct. If proper, character evidence may, with some limitations, be used in any litigation, whether civil or criminal. **B** is, therefore, incorrect. **D** is incorrect because evidence of reputation is not usually admissible for the purpose of establishing that the person in question did or did not act in a particular way on a particular occasion.

3.   **A**   Evidence which tends to impeach a witness' credibility by showing bias is admissible. The fact that Columbo and Perez were political rivals, and that Columbo had used smear tactics in campaigning against Perez in the past would tend to show bias, and is therefore likely to be admitted.

        B is incorrect because the fact that *Today* brought Perez's reputation into issue is not, alone, sufficient to require the admission of evidence of a type which would otherwise be inadmissible. An admission is a statement by a party which is offered against that party. Since Macias is not a party, nothing said by him could be regarded as an admission. **C** is, therefore, incorrect. **D** is incorrect, since the evidence was admissible to show bias.

4.   **C**   The best evidence rule requires production of an original or qualified duplicate when the terms of a writing are in dispute or when a writing is offered as evidence of a fact, and when the writing is not shown to be unavailable. **I** is correct because Waller's testimony was based on her own recollection and is not dependent on Purco's file on the purchase.

II is correct because a photocopy is admissible as a qualified duplicate.

5.　**B**　　A grant of use immunity prevents testimony given under such immunity, or its fruits, from being used against the person who gave it, but does not prevent prosecutions from being based on evidence which was obtained without reference to such testimony.

A grant of use immunity would prevent use of the testimony in any criminal proceeding against the witness in any state or federal court in the United States. **A** and **C** are, therefore, incorrect. **D** is also incorrect, however, since the grant of use immunity would not prevent prosecution of the witness or the use of testimony, like that of Tella's, which was not obtained as a result of the testimony given under the grant of immunity.

6.　**D**　　Hearsay is an out of court assertion offered for the purpose of proving the truth of the matter asserted. Thus, if the plaintiff's statement to Dr. Withey is being offered to prove that the plaintiff was experiencing pain in his arm, the statement would be hearsay. An exception to the hearsay rule, however, permits the admission of statements made as part of a medical history given in connection with a medical examination made for the purpose of treatment or diagnosis. Since Dr. Withey's examination was being made for the purpose of diagnosis, the patient's statement should be admissible. Under FRE 803(4), the circumstances surrounding the medical examination in which a patient's statement was made go to the weight rather than to the admissibility of that statement. Thus the fact that the examination was not made for the purpose of treatment or that it was made in contemplation of litigation is not, alone, sufficient to prevent admission unless the prejudicial effect of the statement is likely to outweigh its probative value. While a court might not come to that conclusion, the argument in **D** is the only one listed which could possibly support the motion to strike.

A and **B** are incorrect because, unless the probative value is likely to be outweighed by the prejudicial effect, the fact that the examination was not being made for the purpose of treatment or that it was being made in contemplation of litigation would not be sufficient to result in its exclusion. **C** is incorrect because there is no rule which prevents the admission of self-serving statements.

7.　**C**　　Under FRE 803(4), statements purporting to describe the way in which a physical condition came about are admissible as part of a medical history if made for the purpose of diagnosis, and if pertinent to diagnosis. "Diagnosis" refers to the nature and origin of an injury. Even though Dr. Withey's examination was performed to enable her to testify, she was attempting to form a diagnosis. Since the sound made by the plaintiff's elbow striking the pavement might be pertinent to a determination of the nature and origin of plaintiff's injury, (i.e., diagnosis) the statement is admissible.

A is incorrect because a statement made as part of a medical history is admissible as an exception to the hearsay rule. **B** is incorrect because even though the examination was performed in contemplation of Dr. Withey's testimony, one of its purposes was to allow Dr. Withey to diagnose (i.e., determine the nature of) the plaintiff's injury. Although a witness might be permitted to testify to his own former sense impression, there is no exception to the hearsay rule for a witness's repetition of a declarant's former sense impression. **D** is, therefore, incorrect.

8. **A** Under FRE 804(b)(1), prior testimony is admissible as an exception to the hearsay rule if it was given under oath by a presently unavailable declarant and is offered against a party which had the opportunity and incentive to cross-examine when the testimony was given. Since Neer testified under oath at a proceeding in which Wildbird had the right to cross-examine, the prior testimony is admissible if Neer is unavailable.

B is incorrect because the admissibility of prior testimony does not depend on the disposition of the proceeding in which it was given. If the party against which the prior testimony is offered had the opportunity and incentive to cross-examine, the fact that it chose not to do so is not relevant. **C** is, therefore, incorrect. **D** is incorrect because Neer's unavailability would make the prior testimony admissible, not inadmissible.

9. **D** The records are relevant to the issues since they would tend to establish what knowledge Wildbird had regarding the effects of the Wildflight's design. They are not privileged for the following reasons.

They are not an attorney's work product because they do not contain mental impressions formed by an attorney. **A** is, therefore, incorrect. They are not materials prepared for litigation since they were made before the car was even marketed. **B** is, therefore, incorrect. They were not prepared for the purpose of communicating with Wildbird's attorney, so **C** is incorrect.

10. **A** When the terms of a writing are in issue, the best evidence rule requires production of the original unless it is shown to be unavailable. For this purpose, an X-ray is regarded as a writing. Oral testimony as to its contents is not permitted unless the X-ray is either produced or shown to be unavailable. An expert may testify to an opinion based on matters not in evidence. Since Dr. Treet's opinion was formed as the result of various factors, of which the X-ray was only one, her testimony is not about the contents of a document, so her opinion is admissible even without production of the X-ray. On the other hand, Dr. Radell's opinion was based entirely upon the X-ray. In effect, his testimony was nothing more than a description of the X-ray's contents. For this reason, the best evidence rule would require either that the X-ray be produced or that it be shown to be unavailable. Without such a showing, Dr. Radell's testimony is inadmissible. **A** is therefore correct, and **B**, **C**, and **D** are, therefore, incorrect.

11. **B** Since hearsay is an out of court statement offered for the purpose of proving the matter asserted in that statement, and since Child's statement that Dole struck her is offered for the purpose of proving that Dole struck her, the statement is hearsay. FRE 803(2) provides, however, that an excited utterance may be admissible as an exception to the hearsay rule. An excited utterance is a statement made about a startling event while the declarant is under stress caused by the event. The common law equivalent — spontaneous declaration — could not ordinarily be applied if the statement was made in response to a question. The FRE have eliminated that condition however. While the passage of time might lead a court to conclude that the Child was no longer under stress produced by the beating and hold that the statement is not admissible, **B** is the only argument listed which could possibly be effective in response to the objection.

Although a witness is permitted to make statements regarding her own sense impressions, and these statements may include identification of other persons, there is no hearsay exception for such statements when they are made out of court. **A** and **D** are, therefore, incorrect. Similarly, while a witness may make statements regarding her own physical condition including explanations of the causes for that condition, **C** is incorrect because Child's statement was made out of court, and was not given in connection with a medical examination done for the purpose of treatment or diagnosis.

12. **B**   The attorney-client privilege applies to communications made to an attorney by a person seeking legal advice.Generally, the privilege of confidential communication with an attorney extends also to the employees or agents of that attorney who are acting in furtherance of the attorney-client relationship. Some jurisdictions hold that where one mistakenly confides in another believing the other to be an attorney, there is a privileged relationship so long as that mistaken belief was reasonable. Thus, if Darien reasonably believed that he was communicating with an agent of his attorney, the conversation may have been privileged. While it is not certain that a court would come to that conclusion, the argument in **B** is the only one listed which could possibly support the motion.

            A is incorrect because Wescott's statement would not result in a privilege unless Darien was speaking with Wescott for the purpose of obtaining legal advice. **C** is incorrect because Wescott's offer would not make disclosure of the facts to him essential to the relationship between Darien and his attorney. Police interrogation of a person in custody might violate the prisoner's constitutional rights. Unless Wescott had been sent by the police for the purpose of obtaining a statement from Darien, however, the fact that he negotiated a plea-bargain on the day that his testimony was given would not violate Darien's rights, and would not prevent Westcott's testimony from being admissible as an admission. **D** is, therefore, incorrect.

13. **B**   In many jurisdictions, an expert witness may be cross-examined in reference to a text not in evidence only if his opinion was based upon it. Under FRE 803(18) it is not necessary to show that the witness relied on the text involved, but it is necessary to establish that it is a reliable authority. **B** is correct because neither of these two foundations has been laid.

            A is incorrect because there is no requirement that the author of a text used on cross-examination be a witness at the proceeding. **C** is only partially correct, since it is first necessary to show such works to be reliable authorities before they can be used in cross-examination. Since Dr. Won's admission that he has heard of Dr. Tue is not sufficient to establish that her work is a reliable authority, **D** is incorrect.

14. **C**   An expert may testify in answer to a hypothetical question so long as the facts assumed in that hypothetical have been established (or will be established) by evidence offered. Since Packer's case involves the assertion that her fall down the stairs resulted in her injury, it was proper for Robinson's attorney to ask for Dr. Tue's opinion as to whether such an injury was possible in such facts.

            The expert's answer may be based on the facts assumed in the hypothetical and need not be based on facts actually in evidence or known by her. **A** and **B** are, therefore, incorrect. Although an expert's opinion may be based on observations made in the courtroom, **D** is incorrect because Dr. Tue's was not.

15. **C** Under FRE 609, convictions may be used to impeach the credibility of a witness. A court may not exclude proof of such convictions if they are for felonies or for misdemeanors involving dishonesty. Since attempted murder is a felony, and since the other crime was a misdemeanor involving dishonesty, evidence of both was admissible.

16. **D** Hearsay is an out-of-court assertion offered to prove the truth of the matter asserted. Since Renich's statement was made out of court and is offered to prove the truth of what it asserts, it is inadmissible as hearsay.

    Although the record filed by Specker might qualify as either a business record or an official document, the transcript which it contains of a statement made by Renich makes this a multiple hearsay problem. While the record itself might be admissible under one of the two named exceptions to the hearsay rule, only that information which was within Specker's personal knowledge may be admitted. The fact that either the declarant or the person who made the record is dead is not, alone, sufficient to make the statement admissible. **A** and **B** are, therefore, incorrect. Under both the common law and FRE 801(d)(2)(D), a statement by an employee may be admissible as a vicarious admission of the employer only if the statement was made within the scope of employment and while the employment relationship existed. Since Renich had been discharged before making the statement in question, **C** is incorrect.

17. **D** Under FRE 901(5), voice identification can be made by a witness who testifies that he properly dialed a number listed in the telephone book, and that circumstances including self-identification show that the person listed was the one who answered.

    A and **B** are, therefore, incorrect. Since Fritz's statement is contrary to his interests, it is an admission, which is not hearsay under the FRE and is admissible as an exception to the hearsay rule under common law. **C** is, therefore, incorrect.

18. **A** The identity of a speaker may be established by evidence that the speaker's voice or manner of speaking had a distinctive characteristic.

    B is incorrect because any person can testify to the identity of a speaker if he had experience with the voice sufficient to allow him to identify it. **C** and **D** are incorrect since evidence is relevant if it tends to establish the fact which it offered to prove, even though it is not, alone, sufficient to establish that fact.

19. **A** Although evidence of insurance is not admissible for the purpose of showing fault or wrongful conduct, it is admissible for other purposes if relevant to them. Evidence is logically relevant if it tends to prove or disprove a fact of consequence. Since a person would probably not purchase liability insurance on a vehicle which she does not own, the fact that Olivia purchased the policy and that it was in force on the day of the accident tends to establish that she was the owner of the vehicle on that day. It is thus relevant to the issue of ownership, and therefore, admissible.

    B is incorrect, since a defendant's ability to pay a judgment against her is not relevant to either liability or damages in a negligence case. **C** is incorrect because the policy mentioned prevents such evidence only if offered to establish fault or wrongful conduct. **D** is incorrect because the evidence tends to establish ownership, which has been disputed by Olivia.

20.   **A**   Under FRE 803(3), declarations of a declarant's then-existing intentions are described as statements of present state of mind and are admissible as exceptions to the hearsay rule. They may be relevant to establish that the declarant acted in a way which was consistent with those stated intentions; however, such evidence is relevant only to establish the conduct of the declarant herself. The view taken by the majority and by the FRE is that they are not relevant to establish the conduct of others. Courts generally admit such statements with limiting instructions directing the jury to consider the only on the issue of the declarant's actions.

            B, **C** and **D** are, therefore, incorrect.

21.   **B**   Under FRE 803(2), a statement relating to a startling event which was made while the declarant was under the stress of excitement from that event is admissible as an (excited utterance) exception to the hearsay rule.

            A is incorrect because the uncertainty of the identification goes to the weight of the evidence rather than to its admissibility. **C** is incorrect because a statement may be admissible as an excited utterance even though the identity of the person making it is unknown. An excited utterance is admissible as an exception to the hearsay rule whether or not other evidence is available. **D** is, therefore, incorrect.

22.   **A**   The statement of the eyewitness fits the classic definition of hearsay: an out-of-court statement offered to prove the truth of the matter asserted in that statement.

            Exceptions to the hearsay rule are made for past recollection recorded and business records, but only if the person recording the information knew it to be true of his own knowledge when the record was made. Since Onder could not have known of his own knowledge whether the statement of the eyewitness was true, **B** and **D** are incorrect. *Res gestae* is sometimes used as a synonym for excited utterance, but **C** is incorrect because the fact that the statement resulted from an interview would probably prevent it from being an excited utterance and because there is no indication that the witness made the statement under stress.

23.   **D**   Evidence of past crimes might be admissible to impeach a witness' credibility, but never solely for the purpose of showing that a criminal defendant had a disposition to commit a particular kind of crime. Since there is no indication that Brasi testified, there is no reason to impeach his credibility.

            A, **B** and **C** are, therefore, incorrect.

24.   **D**   Hearsay is defined as an out-of-court statement offered to prove the truth of the matter asserted in that statement. Since Tribune can only be offering Wright's statement to prove that he believed the statement, it is hearsay.

            A is, therefore, incorrect. **B** is incorrect because under FRE 803(3), a statement of declarant's past state of mind is admissible only in a will contest. That a statement is self-serving may keep it from being admitted under certain exceptions to the hearsay rule, but is never grounds for its admission. **C** is, therefore, incorrect.

25. **C**   Under both FRE 803(7) and the majority rule, if a business record is otherwise admissible, the absence of entries in it may be used to establish non-occurrence of a particular event if it was the practice of the business to promptly record all such events.

A is, therefore, incorrect. **B** is incorrect because the fact that evidence is self-serving is not, alone, sufficient to make it inadmissible. Although almost anything may be used by a witness to refresh his recollection, the fact that a document was so used is not sufficient to permit its admission into evidence. **D** is, therefore, incorrect.

26. **C**   Since a defamation action seeks damages for injury to the plaintiff's reputation, evidence that the plaintiff's reputation was already tarnished is relevant to the issue of damages.

Evidence of the rumor is not hearsay since it is offered not to prove the truth of the rumor, but to establish the quality of Pastor's reputation. **A** is, therefore, incorrect. **B** is based on an inaccurate statement of law, since character evidence — if properly presented — may be admitted in a civil as well as a criminal case. **D** is incorrect because evidence of a defamation plaintiff's reputation is admissible whether he testifies or not, since his reputation is in issue.

27. **C**   Hearsay is an out of court statement offered to prove the truth of the matter asserted in that statement. If offered for any other purpose it is not hearsay. If an out-of-court statement has a direct legal effect apart from its communicative effect, it is not hearsay, since it is offered not to prove the truth of any matter asserted, but to prove its direct legal effect. Since Doltum is attempting to establish that the watch was a gift to him, and since Trolley's words coupled with delivery by handling Doltum the watch would have the legal effect of creating an executed gift, the statement is admissible.

An admission is a statement made by a party and offered against that party. Since Trolley is not a party to the proceeding, his statement cannot be termed an admission. **A** is, therefore, incorrect. The Dead Man's Act, where it exists, prevents evidence of a conversation with a decedent from being offered against the interests of that decedent. **B** is incorrect, since the Dead Man's Act, if it existed, would require that the objection be sustained, not overruled. Trolley's statement was not hearsay, since it is offered to establish its direct legal effect apart from its communicative effect. **D** is, therefore, incorrect.

28. **D**   Most modern courts, and FRE 701, allow lay persons to give opinions regarding matters within the competence of the ordinary person so long as a proper foundation is laid. This foundation requires a showing that the witness had experience which would enable them to form an opinion, that she had an opportunity to perceive, and that she formed an opinion based on that perception. Since Arrow has so testified, her testimony regarding Dunk's speed should be admitted as a lay opinion.

A and **B** are, therefore, incorrect. Although some police officers might qualify as experts on the speeds of moving vehicles, **C** is incorrect for two reasons: first, a witness to the speed of a vehicle need not be an expert; and, second, not all police officers qualify as experts.

29.　**D**　Lay persons may testify to their sense impressions in terms of opinion when there is no other practical way to describe these sense impressions. The only possible way of describing the smell of alcohol is to say that it smells like alcohol, and testimony so describing it is admissible.

A leading question is one which would cause the reasonable person to believe that the questioner was seeking one specific answer rather than another. **A** is incorrect because the question did not indicate what answer it sought. **B** is incorrect because under the circumstances, a conclusion was the only possible way of describing Arrow's sense impression. Although it was once held that opinion testimony was not admissible if it went to an ultimate issue in the case, the prohibition has been abandoned under the FRE and in a majority of common law jurisdictions. **C** is, therefore, incorrect.

30.　**D**　Under FRE 412, reputation evidence of the past sexual behavior of the victim is not admissible in a trial for rape under any circumstances. Evidence of the victim's past is not admissible except for conduct with the defendant offered to support a defense of consent, or conduct with others offered to show that the defendant was not the source of semen or the victim's injury. Since the court record is not offered for these purposes, it is not admissible.

A and **C** are, therefore, incorrect. Under the FRE, evidence of conviction for a crime is admissible for the purpose of impeaching a witness's credibility if the crime was a felony or a misdemeanor involving dishonesty. Since prostitution is neither, the conviction is not admissible to impeach Vonda's credibility. **B** is, therefore, incorrect.

31.　**C**　Evidence of past dealings between the parties to a contract is usually admissible to prove the intentions of the parties at the time the contract was formed. This is only so, however, if conditions at the time the previous dealings took place are substantially the same as conditions which existed at the time the contract was formed. If the videotapes were being sold at an especially low price, evidence of past sales at the regular price might not be relevant in determining the intentions of the parties.

A is incorrect because the evidence is not being offered for the purpose of establishing Vidco's conduct, but rather for the purpose of establishing Telink's intentions. The parol evidence rule prohibits the introduction of oral testimony of prior or contemporaneous agreements for the purpose of contradicting the terms of an unambiguous written contract. **B** is incorrect, however, since the absence of any reference to the way in which the product was to be packaged would make the contract ambiguous, and oral evidence could be offered to explain the ambiguity. **D** is incorrect because the common practice would not, alone, be sufficient to overcome the expectations which might have resulted from past transactions between the parties.

32.　**D**　In interpreting terms in a contract, courts attempt to determine what the parties had in mind when they agreed to those terms. Since evidence of prior transactions between the same parties may be relevant indications of what they were thinking or expecting when they formed the agreement, such evidence is ordinarily admissible. However, evidence of transactions which did not involve Telink would not give any indication of Telink's state of mind unless Telink was aware of those transactions. Since the facts do not show that Telink was aware of the transactions in question, **D** is correct.

A is incorrect because such evidence is only admissible if it involved the same parties. **B** is incorrect because Schipper's statement is not directly relevant to any statement made by Layton. Even if the twenty customers were of the same general size and class as Telink, evidence of their responses does not tend to establish anything at all about Telink's intentions or expectations at the time the contract was formed. **C** is, therefore, incorrect.

33.   **A**   Evidence that a party is insured is inadmissible to establish fault or damage, because insurance coverage or the lack of it is not logically or legally relevant to those issues. For this reason, it is ordinarily improper for either party to comment on insurance or the lack of it during the trial of a negligence action. If a plaintiff falsely suggests that the defendant is insured, however, a defendant may be permitted to counter the suggestion by proving that he lacked insurance. Since the plaintiff's attorney asked jurors whether they owned stock in an automobile liability insurance carrier, a court might conclude that a false suggestion of insurance coverage has been made and that the defendant should therefore be permitted to prove that he had none. While it is not certain that a court would come to this conclusion, **A** is the only option which could possibly be correct.

B is incorrect because the evidence involved was not offered for the purpose of establishing fault or freedom from it. **C** is incorrect because there is no prohibition against the offer of evidence which is self-serving (a party's evidence almost always is). The FRE specifically authorize the admission of a judgment of conviction when it is relevant. **D** is, therefore, incorrect.

34.   **C**   If relevant, photographs and films are admissible if a witness testifies that they are accurate representations of what they purport to be. Since the defendant has identified the videotape copy as a fair and accurate representation of the accident scene, and since the appearance of the accident scene is relevant in the trial of an accident claim, the videotape is admissible and **C** is correct.

Under the best evidence (i.e., original document) rule, where the contents of a document are in issue, secondary evidence of its contents is inadmissible unless the original or a qualified duplicate are shown to be unavailable. Although a videotape could be regarded as a document for this purpose, **A** is incorrect because the contents of the videotape are not in issue; the tape is offered to show what the accident scene looked like. Since the defendant testified that the tape is an accurate representation of the accident scene, it is admissible without regard to its custody and whereabouts since made. **B** is, therefore, incorrect. **D** is incorrect because any witness may authenticate a pictorial representation by testifying that it is an accurate representation of what it purports to be.

35.   **D**   Since a person who makes statements which contradict each other might not be worthy of belief, a witness may be impeached on cross-examination by inquiry regarding prior inconsistent statements.

If a prior inconsistent statement is offered as substantive evidence, it must have been made under oath and at a trial. But a prior inconsistent statement used merely to impeach does not need to fulfill those requirement. Since only impeachment use is being made here, **A** is incorrect. Although it may be unethical for an attorney to make contact directly with an adversary known to be represented by counsel, information obtained by such a contact is not necessarily inadmissible. In any event, **B** is incorrect because there is no reason to believe that Pringle was represented by counsel at the time of his conversation with Vesto, or, if he was, that Addie knew him to be. A statement of a party offered against that party is admissible as an admission. Under FRE 801(d)(2), an admission is not hearsay; under the common law, an admission is an exception to the hearsay rule. **C** is, therefore, incorrect.

36.   **C**   Hearsay is an out-of-court statement offered to prove the truth of the matter asserted in that statement. If Pringle's statement is offered to impeach Pringle by showing that he is not worthy of belief because he tells different stories on different days, it is not hearsay. His statement is, therefore, admissible for impeachment. At common law, a statement of a party offered against that party (i.e., an admission) is hearsay but is admissible under an exception to the hearsay rule. Under FRE 801(d)(2), an admission is not hearsay at all. Either way, Pringle's statement would be admissible as substantive evidence. **C** is, therefore, correct.

37.   **B**   Under FRE 410(4), a withdrawn guilty plea cannot be used in any subsequent action or proceeding, so if the plea was withdrawn, Buyco's attorney can properly be prevented from asking about it.

            A and **C** are incorrect because the circumstances in which and the crime to which the plea was given go to the weight rather than to the admissibility of the evidence. **D** is incorrect because the impeachment of Sellco's witness does not depend on Sellco's employment of that witness.

38.   **B**   Proof that a witness was convicted of a felony or a misdemeanor involving dishonesty may be admissible for the purpose of extrinsically impeaching the credibility of the witness, but not if the conviction was subsequently reversed for any reason.

            A is incorrect because the evidence is offered to impeach Manny's credibility as a witness, and this is not related to his employment by Sellco. The fact that the conviction was for a misdemeanor would not prevent its admission if the misdemeanor was one which involved dishonesty. **C** is, therefore, incorrect. **D** is incorrect because if the crime of which the witness was convicted was a felony, it may be admissible without regard to the nature of the felony.

39.   **C**   Because of a policy to encourage repairs of dangerous conditions, evidence that a defendant repaired a condition subsequent to the occurrence of an accident is inadmissible for the purpose of establishing negligence or that the condition was dangerous at the time of the accident.

            A is incorrect for that reason, and because the term "admission" ordinarily describes an *out-of-court* statement made by a party. **B** is incorrect because the rule of policy applies whether or not the defendant has received notice of the accident and pending lawsuit. **D** is incorrect because it is overinclusive. Such evidence is admissible for some purposes (like establishing ownership or control).

40.   **C**   Since an employer is vicariously liable for the negligence of an employee committed within the scope of employment, statements tending to establish that the accident resulted from Currier's negligence are relevant in Postum's action against Daxco. The evidence should, thus, be admitted unless excluded under the hearsay rule. Hearsay is an out of court statement offered to prove the truth of the matter asserted. These facts raise what is sometimes called a multiple level hearsay problem (i.e., a problem involving an out of court statement which contains another out of court statement). This is so because Currier's testimony at the reckless driving trial was not made during the negligence trial and so is an "out of court" statement, and because the evidence of his statement is contained in a transcript which was also not made as part of the negligence trial and so is an "out of court" statement. In order for multiple level hearsay (i.e., the transcript containing Currier's statement) to be admissible each level must be separately admissible. The first level of hearsay is the testimony by Currier at the reckless driving trial. Under the common law, statements by an employee are admissible against the employer only if the employee had the authority to make them. But FRE 801(d)(2)(D) requires only that the employee's statement concerned a matter within the scope of his employment, and was made while the employment relationship existed. Currier's statement is therefore a vicarious admission which is an exception to the hearsay rule at common law, and is not hearsay at all under the FRE. The second level of hearsay is the transcript. Since it was made by a public official (the court reporter), regarding "matters observed pursuant to duty imposed by law as to which matters there was a duty to report" (that Currier made the admission), the transcript qualifies as a public record or report under FRE 803(8). **C** is, therefore, correct.

Under FRE 804(b)(1), prior testimony is admissible as an exception to the hearsay rule only if the party against whom it is offered had an incentive and an opportunity to cross-examine when the testimony was first given. Since Daxco was not a party to the proceeding at which Currier's testimony was given, the testimony does not qualify for admission under this exception. **A** is, therefore, incorrect. The past recollection recorded exception requires that the record was made from the recorder's own knowledge and requires the recorder to authenticate the record in court. **B** is incorrect because Currier's statement was not authenticated or recorded by Currier. **D** is incorrect for the reasons stated above.

41.   **D**   A plaintiff in a negligence action is not required to prove that the defendant or its employee acted recklessly or committed any crime. Currier's acquittal on the criminal charge or reckless driving is therefore irrelevant to the issues in Postum's action.

Thus, even though a court record might be admissible as an official written statement, **A** is incorrect because this record is not relevant. **B** is incorrect for two reasons: first, the fact that Currier was not driving recklessly is not relevant to Postum's claim; and, second, since the burden of proof in a criminal case differs from the burden of proof in a civil case, acquittal in the criminal court cannot determine the issues in a civil case. If a court record were covered under an exception to the hearsay rule, the unavailability of the person who was the subject of the proceeding from which the record emanated would not prevent its admission. **C** is, therefore, incorrect.

42.   **D**   Although Alicia and Benton may have been in an attorney-client relationship at the time

Alicia made the observations under examination, the attorney-client privilege only protects confidential communications. Although a communication may be non-verbal as well as verbal, Benton's appearance can not be regarded as any communication at all, and is therefore not privileged.

A is, therefore, incorrect. **B** is incorrect because a lay person may be competent to testify to appearances commonly observed by lay persons including the appearance of intoxication. **C** is incorrect because the attorney-client privilege belongs to the client, and need not be raised by the attorney.

43. **D**   **A** is incorrect for two reasons. First, a confidential marital communication is one which takes place during the course of the marriage, and Alicia and Benton were not married at the time of the party. Second, the privilege only protects confidential communications, and Benton's consumption of alcohol at the party would not be determined to be a confidential communication. Although the common law spousal privilege might prevent adverse testimony by a party's spouse even though it concerns events which preceded the marriage, **B** is incorrect because the privilege does not survive the marriage and would have terminated with Alicia's and Benton's divorce. **C** is a fabrication, with no basis in law. **D** is, therefore, correct.

44. **C**   Under FRE 803(3), statements of a declarant's then-existing state of mind are admissible as an exception to the hearsay rule. Since it is likely that a suicidal state of mind such as that indicated by Vason's statement to Si would continue until the following day, and since it is likely that a person with that state of mind would commit suicide, the fact that Vason was of a suicidal state of mind on the day before his death is relevant to the question of whether his death was a suicide. **I** is, therefore a correct statement. Hearsay is an out-of-court statement offered to prove the truth of the matter asserted in that statement. If Vason's statement to Si is offered for the purpose of establishing that Si knew or should have known that Vason was suicidal, it is not hearsay, since it is not offered to prove the truth of the matter asserted (i.e., that suicide is the only way out). **II** is, therefore, a correct statement.

45. **B**   Under FRE 803(18), statements contained in a published treatise may be called to the attention of an expert on direct or cross-examination, and, if the treatise is established to be a reliable authority, may be read into the record. To prevent the jury from misunderstanding and misapplying a work written by and for experts, however, the treatise itself is not admissible.

         A, C and **D** are, therefore, incorrect.

46. **A**   Hearsay is defined as an out-of-court statement offered to prove the truth of the matter asserted in that statement. The statement of the firearms instructor is relevant to establish what Dally believed, since Dally was present when he said it, and it is likely that he believed what his instructors said. If offered to prove Dally's state of mind rather than the range of the rifle, it is not hearsay because it is not offered to prove the truth of what was asserted (i.e., that the rifle is accurate at 2 miles).

         On the other hand, if offered to prove the range of the Firetag 401 (i.e., the matter asserted in the statement) it would be inadmissible as hearsay. **B** and **C** are, therefore, incorrect. **D** is incorrect because the statement is not hearsay if used to prove Dally's state of mind.

47.   **B**   Since a statement as to the value of a chattel is a statement of opinion, and since lay opinions are not usually admissible, some qualification is necessary to demonstrate the competence of a person stating an opinion regarding the value of a chattel. Since an unaccepted offer to purchase a chattel suggests the offeror's opinion as to its value, an unaccepted offer to purchase is not usually admissible to establish the value of the subject chattel because the offeror is not necessarily an expert in the value of such chattels, and because even if the offeror were an expert, his out of court statement as to its value would be hearsay. For this reason, evidence of an offer to purchase the motorcycle is probably inadmissible, and **B** is the correct answer.

In the belief that the owner of a chattel has some special knowledge about his property, courts usually allow a chattel's owner to give an opinion regarding its value. **A** is, therefore, likely to be admitted. In **C**, the motorcycle dealer would probably qualify as an expert on the value of motorcycles. An expert may testify to an opinion in response to a hypothetical question, even though he has no personal knowledge of the facts in a particular case. Thus, if the photograph can be shown to be a fair and accurate representation of the motorcycle immediately prior to the accident, the motorcycle dealer's opinion of its value may be admissible. **D** would be admissible since an expert's qualifications may be based on experience with the matter in issue, and the amateur motorcycle collector's previous purchases and sales might qualify him as such.

48.   **D**   Under common law, self-identifying statements are not sufficient to establish the source of a writing. FRE 902 creates some exceptions to this rule, but letterheads are not among them.

A is admissible since an expert may state an opinion concerning the authorship of a particular writing based upon a comparison of the writing in question with an exemplar of the defendant's writing. **B** is admissible because the trier of the facts may form a conclusion about the authorship of a particular writing based upon its own comparison of that writing with an exemplar of the defendant's handwriting. **C** is admissible, since any person may testify to what he has seen if it is relevant to the facts in issue.

49.   **D**   Although evidence of subsequent repairs is inadmissible to establish that a condition was dangerous or that the defendant was negligent, it may be admitted if relevant to some other issue. Since it is not likely that Lanham would have taken the action indicated if he were not in control of the stairway, the evidence may be admitted for the purpose of establishing control.

A is incorrect because it suggests that some rule of privilege prevents testimony by the defendant's employee, when no such rule exists. The admissibility of Walker's testimony does not, therefore, depend on his employment status. **B** and **C** are incorrect because of the rule of policy which prohibits evidence of subsequent repairs to establish fault.

50.   **B**   Testimony that a witness never heard of similar accidents in the past may be admitted as circumstantial evidence that the condition was not dangerous if a proper foundation is

laid. This requires showing that the condition was substantially the same on the day of plaintiff's accident as it was during the period described by defendant, that there was sufficient traffic over the condition and sufficient time to provide an opportunity for such accidents to have occurred, and that the witness was likely to have heard of such accidents had they occurred. Since Walker testified that the stairs were in substantially the same condition throughout the period described, that many people used them every day for three years, and that he never heard of such an accident, the only element of the necessary foundation which is lacking is evidence that he probably would have heard of such an accident if it had occurred. His testimony is thus admissible if this can be shown, but is not admissible otherwise. **B** is, therefore, correct.

A is incorrect because the fact that no accident had previously occurred would tend to establish that the condition was not a dangerous one. Evidence of the non-occurrence of similar accidents in the past might tend to prove that the plaintiff did not use the care exercised by ordinary persons in encountering the situation. **C** is incorrect, however, because without evidence that Walker would have heard of such accidents had they occurred, the assertion of contributory negligence is not, alone, sufficient to make Walker's statement probative. **D** is incorrect because there is no rule which prevents a party from objecting to improper testimony elicited by cross-examination of its own witness.

51. **A**   Silence may be regarded as a tacit admission of a fact asserted in the presence of the person remaining silent under circumstances such that the reasonable person would have denied the assertion. Evidence of Bailey's refusal to answer Alex's assertion, is, therefore, admissible as an admission so long as the reasonable person would have denied the assertion.

If it were not otherwise admissible, however, the mere fact that Bailey was a party and able to deny it would not be sufficient to make the testimony admissible. **B** is, therefore, incorrect. **C** is incorrect because silence may constitute an admission as stated above. The Fifth Amendment privilege against self-incrimination might prevent an inference of guilt from being drawn in a criminal case from the silence of a defendant, but does not prevent such an inference from being drawn in a civil case. **D** is, therefore, incorrect.

52. **C**   Under the best evidence rule, where the terms of a writing are in issue, the writing itself must be offered into evidence unless the writing is shown to be unavailable through no action in bad faith. Since the original and all copies of the contract were destroyed in a fire, oral testimony as to its contents is admissible.

The parol evidence rule prohibits oral testimony of prior or contemporaneous agreements to alter the terms of a contract intended to be a complete integration of the parties, but does not prevent oral testimony regarding the contents of a written agreement. **A** is, therefore, incorrect. **B** is incorrect because the writing has been shown to be unavailable. The Statute of Frauds provides that certain contracts are unenforceable unless in writing, but does not relate to the evidence used to establish the existence of a contract. **D** is, therefore, incorrect.

53. **D**   Hearsay is defined as an out-of-court statement offered to prove the truth of the matter asserted in that statement. Since Wellum's statement that he killed Robins is being

offered to prove that Wellum did kill Robins (thus discrediting Draper's assertion that Robins killed himself), it is hearsay, and should be excluded unless admissible under an exception to the hearsay rule. Wellum's statement is not an exception for the following reasons.

A dying declaration is admissible as a hearsay exception if it was made from his own knowledge and with a sense of his own impending death by a presently unavailable declarant concerning the cause and circumstances of his own death. Since Wellum's statement did not concern the cause of his own death, it is not admissible as a dying declaration. **A** is, therefore, incorrect. Under FRE 804(b)(3), a statement is admissible as a declaration against interest in two ways. A statement may be admitted if it is so contrary to the declarant's financial interests that a reasonable person in his position would not have made it unless it was true. The rationale for this exception to the hearsay rule is that a person is not likely to make false statements if he knows that they will probably damage his financial interests. When a person believes himself to be dying, however, he is not likely to worry about damage to his financial interests, and, for this reason, a statement made by a person who believes he is dying will probably not qualify under this exception. **B** is, therefore, incorrect. A statement may also be admitted if it is contrary to the declarant's penal interest in that it inculpates him. Such a statement may be admissible only if offered to exculpate the accused and only if independent evidence corroborates its trustworthiness. **C** is incorrect for two reasons: first, there is no independent evidence to corroborate Wellum's declaration; and, second, since Draper's prosecution is for murdering Victor, Wellum's statement that Wellum killed Robins does not exculpate Draper.

54. **C**   The defense of entrapment applies if the police were responsible for inducing the defendant to commit a crime which he was not otherwise likely to commit, and does not apply if the defendant was predisposed to commit the crime charged. Since Drummond has raised the defense of entrapment, evidence that he had previously sold heroin is relevant to establish his predisposition to do so at the time when Mark made the purchase.

Although character evidence is not admissible for the purpose of showing that a criminal defendant committed a certain act, it may be admissible against him for other purposes. **A** is, therefore, incorrect. **B** is incorrect because the evidence was being offered not to establish Drummond's character, but to establish that Mark provided the opportunity for the crime (which is not entrapment) rather than that he induced Drummond to commit it (which would have been entrapment). **D** is incorrect because character evidence may not be used for that purpose.

55. **D**   Since an attorney is entitled to control the direction of his examination, an answer which is otherwise admissible may be stricken if it is not responsive to the question asked. Since Key's attorney did not ask why Pleasance delayed consulting with counsel, Pleasance's explanation is unresponsive to the question and may be stricken. **D** is, therefore, correct.

Although policy prevents admission of settlement negotiations to prove damage, the rule of limited admissibility permits admission of such evidence if it is offered for some other purpose, such as to explain the delay in instituting an action. **A** is incorrect, however, because, although otherwise admissible, that portion of the answer may be stricken as unresponsive. **B** is incorrect because the rule of policy specifically prohibits the admission of settlement negotiations for the purpose of establishing fault. **C** is incorrect because the policy rule does not apply if the evidence is offered for a proper purpose.

56. **B**   At one time, the courts recognized a prohibition against opinion testimony relating to an ultimate issue in the case on trial. Now, however, it is recognized that such testimony may be admitted in evidence so long as the opinion is not couched in legal terms. Since the word "obscene" has special legal significance, Proffer may not state an opinion that the film was obscene.

A is incorrect for the reason stated above. **C** is not the best argument. Since a witness may qualify as an expert by a showing of her knowledge, skill, experience, training, or education in a particular area, the fact that Proffer is a professor of film arts and an author of several books on the topic of erotic filmmaking would probably be sufficient to qualify her as an expert. **D** is incorrect because FRE 702 abandons the requirement of strict necessity for expert testimony, and permits it whenever the witness's specialized knowledge will assist the jury to understand the evidence or to determine a fact in issue.

57. **D**   When the terms of a writing or the contents of a film are in issue, the best evidence rule requires production of the original, unless the original is shown to be unavailable. Since the question of whether "Nude Awakening" is obscene depends on its specific content, the best evidence rule applies.

A and **B** are, therefore, incorrect. **C** is incorrect because even a finding that it would be scandalous to show the film to the jury would not justify admitting descriptions of its contents when the film itself is available.

58. **A**   So long as it does not abuse its discretion, a court may exclude evidence if it finds that the probative value would be outweighed by prejudicial effect. Thus, the court may prevent the showing of the film if its prejudicial effect would outweigh its probative value. **I** is, therefore, correct.

II is incorrect, because although the court may first view the film in camera to determine whether its probative value will be outweighed by its prejudicial effect, it is not required to do so.

59. **C**   Although the Fifth Amendment privilege against self-incrimination protects a witness in a civil or criminal case against being required to give testimony which might tend to incriminate him, it does not justify a complete refusal to take the stand, except by a defendant in a criminal prosecution.

The privilege applies to any testimony anywhere if it might subsequently be used in a criminal proceeding against the person who gave it. **A** and **B** are, therefore, incorrect. **D** is incorrect because West's belief would justify his refusal to answer certain questions, but not his complete refusal to take the stand.

60. **B**   Under FRE 801(d)(1), prior testimony is admissible as substantive evidence if it was given under oath by a presently unavailable declarant in a proceeding in which the party against whom it is now offered had an opportunity to cross examine. Since Wolf's testi-

mony was given under oath at a hearing in which Damon had an opportunity to cross examine, it is admissible if Wolfe is presently unavailable.

A and **C** are incorrect because the prior testimony is not admissible unless Wolfe is unavailable. So long as the party against whom prior testimony is offered was given an opportunity to cross examine when the testimony was first given, the testimony is admissible without regard to whether he availed himself of that opportunity. **D** is, therefore, incorrect.

61. **D**   Evidence is admissible if relevant, and relevant if it tends to prove or disprove a fact of consequence. Since Darnell could not have committed the crime if he was elsewhere at the time, evidence of his whereabouts tends to establish his guilt or innocence and is, therefore, relevant.

A and **B** are incorrect statements because FRE 607 expressly permits a party to impeach his own witness. A hostile witness is one who manifests hostility to the attorney questioning him, not just one who gives unexpected answers. Since Willis did not manifest hostility, **C** is incorrect.

62. **A**   Although use immunity does not prevent prosecution relating to the transaction which was the subject of the testimony for which the immunity was granted, it does prevent the subsequent use of that testimony *or its fruits. The "fruits" include all evidence gained as a direct or indirect result of the testimony.* If the prosecutor had no evidence against Cooms other than Mayo's testimony, then Cooms' testimony was one of the "fruits" of Mayo's, and should be excluded.

B is incorrect because it is based on a distorted view of the facts. By making a deal for the testimony of Cooms, the prosecutor has not bargained away any "rights" of Mayo. **C** is incorrect because the articles by Rider did not identify Cooms. Cooms's evidence must, therefore, be seen as one of the fruits of Mayo's testimony. **D** is incorrect because the use immunity granted Mayo makes Cooms' testimony inadmissible. The fact that it was given voluntarily and without coercion is not, alone, enough to make it admissible.

63. **D**   A client is privileged to prevent another from disclosing the contents of a confidential communication with his attorney. Although the presence of third persons usually results in a finding that the communication was not intended to be confidential, this is not so if the presence of those persons was essential to the communications with the attorney. Darla's presence does not prevent Thomas's communication with Lottie from being confidential since, as the driver of the truck, she was essential to the conference between Thomas and Lottie.

A is incorrect since, if the communication was confidential, the client's privilege applies to any attempt to disclose it. **B** is incorrect because Darla's presence was essential to the purpose of the conference. **C** is incorrect because corporations are entitled to the privilege, which clearly applies to communications between lawyers and high-ranking officers of the corporation.

64. **A**   Under FRE 901(b)(6), voice identification can be made if the witness testifies that she properly dialed a number listed in the directory and circumstances, including self-iden-

tification, show the person answering to be the one listed and called.

B is a fabrication; there is no such presumption. Although the combination of a listing in the telephone directory and self identification by the person answering the phone may result in an inference regarding that person's identity, there is no presumption that the person who answered identified himself accurately. **C** is incorrect since the FRE make independent recognition unnecessary under the circumstances described above. The privilege against self-incrimination protects against "testimonial communications," but does not prevent testimony by others than the defendant concerning admissions made by the defendant. **D** is, therefore, incorrect.

65. **C** Any person who recognizes a voice because of experience which she has had with that voice may testify as to the identification of the speaker. Since Munson had experience with Hobbs's voice in a face-to-face conversation and claims to recognize it as a result, her testimony identifying Hobbs as the speaker is admissible.

A is incorrect because the extent of the experience which a witness had with the voice she is identifying goes to the weight of the evidence rather than to its admissibility. **B** is incorrect because everyday experience with speech places the identification of a voice within the capacity of a layperson who has experience with the voice sufficient to recognize it. Although a witness may testify to a distinctive characteristic which helped her to recognize a voice, **D** is incorrect because she is not required to do so.

66. **A** If relevant, a photograph or pictorial representation is admissible if a witness identifies it as a fair and accurate representation of what it purports to be. Since the directions and relationship of the streets which were the scene of an accident are relevant to the way in which the accident occurred, a photograph which fairly and accurately depicts them is admissible. Thus, even though the absence of Christmas tree ornaments in the photograph prevents it from showing all aspects of the accident scene exactly as they appeared on the day of the accident, it is admissible if it fairly and accurately represents the directions and relationship of the streets. Since the plaintiff testified that it does, the photograph should be admitted.

B is incorrect because a photograph which fairly and accurately represents what it purports to represent is admissible without regard to when it was taken. **C** is incorrect because the authentication of a photograph may be made by any competent witness who is familiar with what the photograph purports to represent, and need not be made by the photographer herself. **D** is incorrect for the reasons stated above.

67. **B** Evidence is relevant if it tends to prove or disprove a fact of consequence. Since the hearing is being held on the sole question of whether Dodge was driving negligently, the only facts of consequence relate to that question. Dodge was driving negligently if he was driving in a way in which the reasonable person would not. Since the fact that the vehicle was unregistered is not related to how it was being driven, the conviction for operating an unregistered vehicle is not relevant to the question of negligence.

A is, therefore, incorrect. An admission is a statement made by a party and offered against that party. **C** is incorrect because, if it is relevant, a guilty plea may be admissible as an admission. At common law, admissions fall under an exception to the hearsay rule. Under FRE 801(d)(2), an admission is not hearsay. Either way, **D** is incorrect.

68.   **A**   Hearsay is an out of court statement offered to prove the truth of the matter asserted in that statement. Since the statement that a blue sedan was traveling at an excessive speed was made out of court, and since it was offered to prove that Dockery's blue sedan was traveling at an excessive speed, it is hearsay. **A** is, therefore, correct.

A witness may testify to her sense impression, even though that testimony is stated as an opinion. Since Wilcox is not testifying to her own sense impression, but rather to something that she heard another person say, **B** is incorrect. Under the hearsay exception known as "past recollection recorded", a witness may read from a written note if she made it herself based on information which she knew of her own knowledge while the information was fresh in her mind. The note which Wilcox read does not qualify, however, because it was not based on something which she knew of her own knowledge, but rather on something she had heard another person say. **C** is, therefore, incorrect. A witness may refresh her recollection while testifying by examining almost anything which will have that effect. She may then testify from her refreshed recollection, but only if her testimony is otherwise admissible. Since the statement to which Wilcox is attempting to testify is hearsay, it is inadmissible, and is not made admissible by the fact that she refreshed her recollection by looking at a writing. **D** is, therefore, incorrect.

69.   **D**   A lay witness may be permitted to testify to opinions if those opinions are rationally based on the personal perceptions of the witness. This requires, of course, that the witness have an adequate opportunity to perceive that on which her opinion is based. Since Willham did not see Dockery's car before the accident, and since tires may screech even when vehicles are being operated at reasonable speeds, Willham's opinion as to the speed of Dockery's car is probably not based on sufficient opportunity to perceive, and should be excluded.

A and **B** are, therefore, incorrect. **C** is incorrect because if she had sufficient opportunity to perceive and form an opinion, a layperson is competent to form and testify to some opinions.

70.   **A**   Hearsay is defined as an out of court statement offered to prove the truth of the matter asserted in that statement. Since Danick's statement that the light was red was made out of court, and since it apparently offered to prove that the light was red, it is hearsay, and therefore, inadmissible. Although Danick may testify to facts which he knows of his own knowledge (i.e., that the light was red against Pearson) he may not testify to an out of court statement for the purpose of proving the truth of the matter asserted in that statement (i.e., hearsay).

Since his testimony is not that the light was red but rather that he told the police officer it was red, **B** is incorrect. Evidence of a prior consistent statement may be admissible to rebut a claim of recent fabrication. **C** is incorrect, however, because there is no indication that Pearson has claimed that Danick's statement about the color of the light is a recent fabrication. Hearsay is inadmissible even though the declarant is present in court and available for cross examination. **D** is, therefore, incorrect.

71.   **D**   Under FRE 412, a rape victim's past sexual conduct is generally not admissible in a

prosecution for her rape. An exception is made, however, for evidence of past sexual conduct between the defendant and the complainant if offered to support the defense of consent. Since evidence regarding past sexual conduct between Randall and Ellen might tend to support Randall's assertion that he reasonably believed that Ellen consented, it should be admitted.

A and **B** are therefore incorrect. **C** is incorrect because the complainant's past sexual conduct does not ordinarily tend to establish that defendant did or did not have sexual intercourse with her against her will on the occasion in question.

72. **A**   The law seeks to encourage safety precautions by prohibiting evidence of subsequent remedial measures from being used for the purpose of showing fault. Such evidence may be admissible for other purposes, however. Here, Oster had denied ownership of the vehicle. Since it is unlikely that anyone other than the owner would arrange to have the brakes overhauled, the testimony of Mecco is relevant to establish Oster's ownership and should, therefore, be admitted.

B is incorrect because of the above stated rule of policy. **C** is incorrect because the evidence is being used to establish that Oster was the owner of the vehicle, not to establish the condition of the brakes. **D** is incorrect since the evidence is admissible to establish ownership.

73. **D**   Evidence is relevant if it would tend to establish a fact in issue. If the tape would tend to prove that Dabney was the robber, it is logically relevant. It should, therefore, be excluded only if it violates some other rule of evidence, or if its probative value is substantially outweighed by its prejudicial impact.

A is incorrect because the privilege against self-incrimination applies only to "testimonial communications," and does not prevent evidence based on observations of the defendant. Whether or not it is certain that the person pictured in the videotape was the defendant is a question for the jury. The robber's skin-coloring (like his height, weight, and walk) is relevant to his identification. Since there are many people with the same skin color, the fact that the robber's was the same as the defendant's is not, alone, enough to result in prejudice which outweighs the probative value of the videotape. **B** is, therefore, incorrect. An admission by conduct is an act by a defendant from which the logical inference may be drawn that he believes himself to be criminally liable. Usually, it refers to flight, the use of an assumed name, fabrication of evidence, or some other act committed after the crime. **C** is, therefore, incorrect.

74. **C**   Under the best evidence rule, where the terms of a writing are in issue, the writing itself must be offered unless it is unavailable. In a defamation action, the precise words used by the defendant are essential to a determination of whether they were defamatory. Since the defamatory statements were contained in a writing, the best evidence rule applies.

A accurately states the definition of defamation but is incorrect since the question concerns itself with proof that a defamatory statement was made. Although an oral statement may be the basis of defamation liability, **B** is incorrect because this action is founded upon a written statement. The oral testimony suggested by **D** is inadmissible under the best evidence rule, making **D** incorrect for the reason stated above.

75. **A**   Hearsay is defined as an out-of-court assertion offered for the purpose of proving the truth of the matter asserted. The fact that a witness made a prior contradictory statement is relevant to his credibility as a witness, whether or not the prior statement was actually true, since people who tell different stories on different days may not be worthy of belief. If offered for that purpose, and not to prove the absence of gunshots, the officer's testimony is not hearsay. If offered to prove that there were no gunshots (i.e., as substantive evidence), however, it is hearsay.

B and **C** are, therefore, incorrect. **D** is incorrect since for purposes of impeachment the statement is not hearsay because it is not offered to prove the truth of what it asserted.

76. **C**   Former testimony is admissible if it was given under oath by a presently-unavailable declarant in a proceeding where the party against which it is now offered had an opportunity and incentive to cross-examine. Since Phillips did not respond to the subpoena, he is presently unavailable. Since his testimony was given at a criminal prosecution of Webster at which Webster had opportunity and incentive to cross examine, the former testimony is admissible. Although the facts do not indicate how Phillips knew that the driver was intoxicated or why he was permitted to so testify at the criminal negligence trial, **C** is the only reason listed which could result in the admission of his statement.

An admission is a statement made by a party which is offered against that party. Since Phillips is not a party, **A** is incorrect. A past recollection recorded must have been prepared by the witness while the information was fresh in his mind, and requires the witness to testify that the record was true when made. Since Phillips did not record the statement and is not present to testify, **B** is incorrect. A sense impression is a statement describing an event which was made while or soon after the declarant perceived the event. Since there is no indication that Phillips perceived the event, **D** is incorrect.

77. **C**   Under FRE 804(b)(2), a statement is admissible as a dying declaration in a civil or criminal case if it was made by a person now unavailable, about the cause of his death, upon personal knowledge, and under a sense of immediately impending death. Since Vicuna is presently unavailable and said that he saw Keller shoot him, his statement is admissible if he made it with a sense of impending death.

Although the common law made such statements admissible in cases of criminal homicide only, **A** is incorrect because the FRE extend the exception to civil litigation as well. Transactional immunity prevents criminal prosecution, but does not prevent civil litigation. **B** is, therefore, incorrect. Where it exists, the effect of the "dead man's statute" is to exclude certain evidence, not to make it admissible. **D** is, therefore, incorrect.

78. **B**   Hearsay is an out of court statement offered to prove the truth of the matter asserted in that statement. An admission is an out of court statement made by a party which is offered against that party. Under the common law, admissions are admissible as exceptions to the hearsay rule. Under FRE 801(d)(2), admissions are admissible because they are not hearsay. If an employee of a party makes a statement which is offered against the employer, the statement may be admissible as a vicarious admission of the employer if it was made while the employment relationship existed and concerned a matter within

the scope of the declarant's employment. If Marshall was employed by Wing as a mechanic, his statement that he failed to inspect Flight 123 does concern a matter within the scope of his employment. It would not be admissible as a vicarious admission of Wing, however, unless it can be established that Marshall was so employed. If Marshall made an out of court statement that he was so employed, it would be hearsay if offered to prove his employment by Wing. For this reason, independent evidence of the employment relationship is required.

A is, therefore, incorrect. Although the common law requires that the declarant be one authorized to speak for the party, **C** is incorrect because the FRE has abolished that requirement. **D** is incorrect because the unavailability of a declarant is not, alone, sufficient to make his out-of-court assertion admissible.

79. **D**   Hearsay is defined as an out-of-court assertion offered for the purpose of proving the truth of the matter asserted. Since there appears to be no reason for offering the statement of the unidentified witness except to prove the truth of the matter which it asserts, it is hearsay. A business record may be admitted under an exception to the hearsay rule only if it was made by one who had personal knowledge of the information recorded or received it from an inherently reliable source. Since the investigator did not have personal knowledge and there is no indication that the witness interviewed by the deceased investigator was an inherently reliable source, **A** is incorrect. An official written statement may be admitted as an exception to the hearsay rule only as to information which the public official who recorded it knew of his own knowledge. Since the quote from the unidentified witness concerns information which the investigator did not know of his own knowledge, **B** is incorrect. Past recollection recorded is also admissible only if the record was made from the recorder's own knowledge and if the recorder is present in court to authenticate it. **C** is incorrect for these reasons, and because even if it were admissible, past recollection recorded can be read to the jury but not physically introduced into evidence.

80. **B**   Under FRE 803(3), an assertion of a declarant's then-existing physical sensation is admissible as an exception to the hearsay rule.

Statements made as part of a medical history may be admissible if made for purposes of diagnosis or treatment. Ordinarily, "medical history" refers to statements made by a declarant about physical sensations and events in the past. **A** is incorrect for this reason, and because Nathan's testimony does not indicate that Hiert's complaints were made for the purpose of facilitating a diagnosis or treatment. **C** is incorrect because others than the injured party may testify to objective signs of pain, or to the injured party's statements about the pain if they fit into exceptions to the hearsay rule. **D** is incorrect because of the present physical sensation exception.

81. **C**   FRE 803(4) and (6) permit the introduction of hospital records containing statements made by the patient for purposes of diagnosis. Since the circumstances which led to the injury are relevant to a diagnosis of the injury, they may be included in the record offered in evidence.

A and **B** are, therefore, incorrect.**D** is incorrect since the statements in the record were not of opinion and, therefore, do not require the testimony of experts.

82. **C**   Evidence is relevant if it tends to prove or disprove a fact of consequence. Relevant evidence is ordinarily admissible. Self-defense is a privilege to use force which the reasonable person in Kane's shoes would have considered necessary to prevent an attack upon himself. Evidence of Nixon's reputation for unprovoked violence is relevant because it tends to establish whether the reasonable person in Kane's shoes would have believed himself to be under attack.

            A and **B** are incorrect because the evidence is relevant to the reasonableness of Kane's fear. **D** is incorrect because the plaintiff's character is not related to the essential elements of a battery action.

83. **A**   Character evidence is not ordinarily admissible for the purpose of proving a person's conduct on a particular occasion. Thus, if evidence of Kane's character is offered to prove anything about his conduct on the occasion of the incident in question, it is not admissible.

            B is incorrect because a witness who testifies to a person's reputation is not required to know that person or to have any personal opinion about him. The "mercy" rule which permits a defendant to offer evidence of his own character as circumstantial evidence of his innocence applies only to criminal prosecutions. **C** is, therefore, incorrect. If the evidence were allowed for the purpose stated in **D**, it would be to prove that Kane did not strike Nixon without justification. **D** is, therefore, incorrect for the same reasons that make **A** correct.

84. **D**   An expert may testify to an opinion based upon material not in evidence so long as it is material upon which the reasonable expert would have based an opinion, even if the material itself would be inadmissible.

            A is, therefore, incorrect. An X-ray is regarded as a writing, and if a witness is testifying only to its contents, it may be covered by the best evidence rule. If so, such testimony may be excluded unless it can be shown that the X-ray itself is not available. In this case, however, the witness was not testifying solely to the contents of the X-ray, but to an opinion which she formed based upon examination of the plaintiff's leg in addition to study of the X-ray. **B** is, therefore, incorrect. **C** is incorrect because an expert may base her opinion testimony on material not in evidence.

85. **D**   Evidence of the non-occurrence of similar accidents might be admissible to prove that the area was not dangerous, but only if the condition during the period testified to was substantially the same at the time of the accident. Since there is no indication that the stairs were littered with paper during the period described by Manny, the fact that no similar accidents occurred does not prove that the condition was not unsafe when Prell fell.

            A and **B** are, therefore, incorrect. **C** is incorrect because it is perfectly permissible and proper for witnesses to give self-serving testimony (That they often do is illustrated by the fact that criminal defendants frequently say, "I didn't do it," when taking the stand.)

86. **A**   Under FRE 803(2), a statement is admissible under the excited utterance exception to

the hearsay rule if it was about a startling event and made while under the stress of excitement resulting from that event. The FRE further provides that the statement may be admissible even if the identity of the declarant is unknown.

B and **C** are, therefore, incorrect. **D** is incorrect because an excited utterance is admissible as a hearsay exception.

87. **D**   Under FRE 406, evidence of an established business practice is admissible as circumstantial proof that it was followed on a particular day.

A is, therefore, incorrect. **B** is incorrect because the evidence offered establishes circumstantially that the notice was mailed. **C** is incorrect because any office employee who knows about the practice of his own knowledge may testify to it.

88. **D**   Since cross-examination about Wagner's whereabouts is directly relevant to impeachment of his direct testimony, his refusal to answer makes meaningful cross-examination impossible. When a witness cannot be subjected to full cross-examination, his direct testimony should be stricken.

A is incorrect because the privilege is available whenever testimony of the witness might lead to criminal prosecution of the witness, even though the matter in which the testimony is elicited is not a criminal proceeding. The privilege against self-incrimination would offer little protection if it was necessary for the person invoking it to show how the statement might be incriminating. Thus, unless it is impossible to conceive of circumstances in which the answer called for would be incriminating, the witness may invoke the privilege. **B** is, therefore, incorrect. **C** is a fabrication without any basis in law; in any event, it is patently incorrect since the issue is not whether Wagner should have been allowed to invoke the privilege, but whether his direct testimony should have been stricken.

89. **B**   A writing may be admitted under the business record exception to the hearsay rule if it was made in the course of a regularly conducted business activity from the recorder's own knowledge or from an inherently reliable source and was accurate when made. If the investigation of crimes is not a regularly conducted business activity for the college, its record of such an investigation would not be admissible as a business record. Although it is not certain that a court would come to that conclusion, the argument in **B** is the only one listed which could possibly support Dessel's objection.

A is incorrect because a business record may be admissible even though the person who made it is available and has testified. **C** is incorrect because it is an inaccurate statement of law; the exception applies in all trials. Hearsay is an out-of-court statement offered to prove the truth of the matter asserted in that statement. The phrase "second level hearsay" is sometimes used to describe a hearsay which is included in another statement which is also hearsay. Here, for example, Dessel's statement was made out of court and is offered to prove that Dessel stabbed Victorio (i.e., the matter asserted). The file which includes the statement is also an out-of-court statement which is offered to prove the truth of what it asserts (i.e., that Dessel said he stabbed Victorio). **D** is incorrect, however, because Dessel's statement is an admission, which FRE 801(d)(2) defines as a statement made by a party and offered against that party, and which that rule specifically provides is not hearsay.

90. **B**   Evidence that the witness never observed strange behavior in a testator is admissible to prove he was competent, but only if the nature of the witness' experience with the testator is such that he is likely to have observed such behavior if it occurred. Semi-annual examinations of the testator probably are not frequent enough to permit the inference that behavior which did not occur on those visits did not occur at other times.

A is incorrect since, if a witness does have sufficient opportunity to observe, the testimony will be admitted. **C** is incorrect since the door is thus opened only to testimony which is not otherwise inadmissible. **D** is incorrect because Dr. Medich is not testifying to his opinion but to his observations.

91. **D**   The FRE recognizes an exception to the hearsay rule for business records. Some courts interpret the FRE in a way which makes police records inadmissible under this exception to the hearsay rule. Other courts interpret the FRE in a way which makes police records admissible under this exception. Under FRE 803(6), a written report is admissible as a business record if it was made in the regular course of business, while the transaction recorded was fresh in the entrant's mind, regarding facts within his own knowledge or from an inherently reliable source. The statement contained in the police record filed by Wechsler was not based on a fact known by Wechsler of his own knowledge. It might still be admissible, however, if it had been received from an inherently reliable source. Although officer Koppel may be regarded as such a source, he did not have personal knowledge either. Since the source of the recorded fact was an unidentified witness, and since an unidentified witness is not an inherently reliable source, the record is not admissible.

Although a testifying witness may refresh his recollection by reference to documents which are not in evidence, his doing so does not make those documents admissible. **A** is, therefore, incorrect. **B** is incorrect for the reason given above. Since the police are in the business — among other things — of investigating accidents, a police report may be regarded as a record kept in the usual course of business, and may be admissible as such if all the other requirements are met. **C** is, therefore, incorrect.

92. **A**   Unless it is excluded by some rule of law, evidence is admissible if it is relevant to a material issue. Since contracts are interpreted in accordance with the intentions of the parties, Bolter's intentions are material to VanderHaag's action for breach of contract. Since Bolter did not understand VanderHaag's statement, Worden's translation of that statement would tend to establish (i.e., is relevant to) Bolter's intentions. It should, therefore, be admitted.

In jurisdictions which have a "dead man's statute," that law may prohibit the admission of evidence regarding a transaction with a decedent. **B** is incorrect because although the "dead man's statute" may result in the exclusion of evidence, it is never used as a justification for its admission. If Worden were testifying to the meaning of a Dutch word or expression, his testimony would not be admissible unless he qualified as an expert on the Dutch language. **C** is incorrect, however, because Worden's testimony is not offered for the purpose of explaining the meaning of VanderHaag's language, but for the purpose of showing what Bolter believed it to mean. Hearsay is an out-of-court statement offered for the purpose of proving the truth of the matter asserted in that statement. Since Worden's statement to Bolter was made out-of-court, it would be hearsay if offered for the purpose of proving the truth of anything which it asserted. **D** is incorrect, however, because the statement is offered not to prove the truth of what was asserted by either VanderHaag or Worden, but to establish Bolter's state of mind at the time of the negotiation. It is, therefore, not hearsay.

93. **D**   The fact that a witness made prior statements which were inconsistent with his testimony indicates that he may not be a credible witness, or at least that his testimony may not be worthy of belief. Thus, for the purpose of impeachment, a witness may be cross-examined about prior inconsistent statements. Since Davidson's statement to the arresting officers was inconsistent with his statement on the witness stand, he may be cross-examined about it.

The purpose of the exclusionary rule which prohibits the use of illegally obtained evidence or confessions is to remove police incentive for violating the constitutional rights of suspects. For this reason, statements obtained in violation of a prisoner's *Miranda* rights cannot be used against him in a criminal prosecution. Because use of such statements for impeachment in a civil proceeding is not ordinarily contemplated by the police, prohibiting such use is not likely to affect police conduct. For this reason, it has been held that statements obtained in violation of a prisoner's *Miranda* rights may be used for purposes of impeachment in civil proceedings. **A** is, therefore, incorrect. **B** is incorrect for two reasons: first, Davidson's motion was to suppress the use of the physical evidence, rather than the use of statements made during the interrogation; and, second, even an order suppressing the use of his statements in the criminal prosecution would not prevent their use in this civil proceeding. If statements are obtained from a prisoner in violation of his constitutional rights, the same policy which prohibits their use as evidence prohibits also the use of leads obtained as a result of those statements. This is the "fruit of the poisonous tree" doctrine. Although this doctrine may result in the exclusion of evidence, it never is used to justify the admission of evidence. **C** is, therefore, incorrect.

94. **B**   Under FRE 803(6), a properly authenticated written record qualifies as an exception to the hearsay rule if it was made as part of the regular course of business while the transaction recorded was fresh in the entrant's mind regarding facts within her personal knowledge or from an inherently reliable source. This invoice was kept in the regular course of business, and has been authenticated by Wilmington. Although Wilmington did not personally know the contents of the shipment, the shipping clerk's business duty to report accurately makes him an inherently reliable source, and Wilmington made the entries immediately upon receiving the information from him.

A is incorrect because the past recollection recorded exception applies only if the record was prepared from the witness' own knowledge, and permits it to be read to the jury but not admitted into evidence. The best evidence rule provides that where the contents of a writing are in issue, secondary evidence of the writing is inadmissible unless the original is shown to be unavailable. **C** is incorrect because the effect of the best evidence rule is to exclude certain classes of evidence, and not to make admissible evidence which would otherwise be inadmissible. A witness whose present recollection has been refreshed by reference to a document may testify from her refreshed recollection. **D** is incorrect because Wilmington stated that she had no present recollection, and because the attorney for Prussian Dyes sought to introduce the document itself.

95.   **D**   Under the UCC, evidence of the usage of trade terminology is admissible to prove the meaning of such terms in a contract between parties in the trade. Since both Finishco and Varilac are in commercial industry, Worley's evidence of trade usage should be admissible.

Witnesses frequently make self-serving statements. In fact, almost anything said by a party-witness is likely to be self-serving (e.g., a criminal defendant's testimony that she is "not guilty," or a personal injury plaintiff's testimony that the defendant went through a red light). **A** is incorrect because there is no rule of law which excludes self-serving statements from evidence. Hearsay is defined as an out-of-court statement offered for the purpose of proving the truth of the matter asserted in that statement. Since Worley's testimony is not of an out-of-court statement, it cannot be hearsay. **B** is, therefore, incorrect. Although proof of an established business custom may be offered as evidence that it was followed on a particular occasion, **C** is incorrect, because Worley has not testified to any particular custom of her company.

96.   **B**   Physical illustrations of a witness's testimony are admissible to illustrate that testimony if the witness testifies from personal knowledge that the illustration is a fair representation of what it purports to be. Since Worley testified from her own knowledge that the chart was an accurate representation of the dates on which her company had done business with Varilac, it may be admitted for that purpose.

FRE 803(6) permits the admission of business records if they were kept in the regular course of business and made while the transaction recorded was fresh in the entrant's mind regarding facts within her personal knowledge or from an inherently reliable source. This exception to the hearsay rule applies only to the record itself, however, and not to any summary of it. **A** is, therefore, incorrect. Under the "best evidence rule," secondary evidence of a writing is not admissible to prove the terms of the writing unless the original or a qualified duplicate is shown to be unavailable. This rule is only applicable, however, when the terms of the writing are in dispute. Since the contents of Finishco's files are not in dispute, the best evidence rule is inapplicable. Introduction of the chart might be said to place the contents of the chart in issue. Since the chart is an original, however, the best evidence rule does not exclude it. **C** is incorrect for these reasons. Materials used by a witness to refresh her recollection while she is testifying *must* be shown to opposing counsel and marked for identification. The court *may* also require the production of materials that were used to refresh a witness' recollection before trial. **D** is incorrect, however, because FRE 612 leave this requirement to the court's discretion.

97.   **D**   Under FRE 412, evidence of specific acts involving the victim's past sexual behavior is admissible in a rape trial only if it is relevant to an issue regarding the source of semen, or if it involves past sexual behavior between the victim and the defendant, and is offered for the purpose of establishing the defense of consent. Since Doane admits to having sexual intercourse with Ventura, there is no issue regarding the source of semen. Although Doane has asserted a defense of consent, the evidence offered by his attorney does not relate to prior sexual contact between Doane and Ventura. The evidence is,

thus, inadmissible.

A, B and **C** are, therefore, incorrect.

98.   **A**   FRE 501 provides that in the trial of a civil proceeding in which state law provides the rule of decision, the rules of privilege shall be determined in accordance with state law. Thus, if a civil action is being tried in a federal court under the substantive law of a state, the federal court must apply the state law of privilege. If the state law recognizes a psychotherapist-patient privilege, the federal court must recognize it as well. **I** is, therefore, correct. If the state law does not recognize a psychotherapist-patient privilege, the federal court may not. **II** is, therefore, incorrect.

99.   **C**   Hearsay is an out-of-court assertion offered for the purpose of proving the truth of the matter asserted. Since Melba's testimony referred to Dr. Treat's assertion that the pink pills were for pain, and was offered for the purpose of proving that Peterson took them for pain, that assertion is hearsay.

A declaration of the *declarant's* present physical sensation is admissible as an exception to the hearsay rule. Peterson's statement, "My neck hurts," might thus be admissible. **A** is incorrect, however, because Dr. Treat's statement did not declare anything about his own physical state. **B** is incorrect for the same reason. Statements of a declarant's past physical sensation are admissible under the medical history exception if made to a doctor for the purpose of diagnosis and treatment. **D** is incorrect, however, because the objection was to testimony regarding a statement by Dr. Treat.

100. **C**   Under FRE 801(d)(1)(C), evidence of prior identification is not hearsay, if the declarant is on the witness stand and available for cross-examination.

A is, therefore, incorrect. **B** is incorrect for two reasons: first, a party is permitted to impeach his own witness; and second, to impeach means to attack the witness' credibility, which the prosecuting attorney has not attempted to do to Verona. **D** is incorrect because although a jury may consider the fact that a witness is interested or disinterested in weighing the value of her testimony, the interest of a witness does not affect the admissibility of her testimony.

101. **C**   Unless excluded by a rule of law, all evidence is admissible which tends to prove or disprove a fact in issue. The robber's identification is obviously a fact in issue. Since Warder's testimony tends to establish that at the time of his arrest Dustin's physical appearance fit the description of the robber given by witnesses, her testimony is admissible for the purpose of explaining why Dustin no longer has bushy red hair.

A rule of evidence prohibits impeachment of a witness by extrinsic evidence of a collateral matter. **A** is incorrect, however, because Warder's testimony is not offered for the purpose of impeaching Dustin, and because the identity of the robber is not a collateral matter. The Fifth Amendment privilege against self-incrimination protects a person from being compelled to give evidence which might be used against him in a criminal proceeding. **B** is incorrect, however, because the privilege relates only to testimonial evidence, and does not prevent another from testifying to what she has seen the defendant do. An admission by conduct occurs when a defendant does some act which logi-

ANSWERS TO EVIDENCE QUESTIONS

cally indicates that he believes himself to be guilty. Although Dustin's attempt to change his appearance might suggest such a conclusion, the fact that there are many other legitimate reasons for Dustin to shave his head makes this a weak argument in this case. **D** is, therefore, incorrect.

102. **A** To save time and expense in proving facts which cannot reasonably be disputed, and to avoid the embarrassment which might result from a judicial finding which is contrary to well-known fact, a court may take judicial notice of certain facts without requiring evidence to establish them. Courts will take judicial notice of facts which are either generally known within the territorial jurisdiction of the trial court or capable of accurate and ready determination by resort to sources whose accuracy cannot reasonably be questioned. Thus, if it is generally known within the territorial jurisdiction of the court that it is impossible to travel from Detroit to Chicago without crossing a state line, the court may judicially notice that fact, making proof of it unnecessary.

Although the presentation of a map or other reputable reference would permit the court to take judicial notice, **B** is incorrect because this is not the only way; in the case of facts which are generally known, such references are not required. If the fact in question is one which qualifies for judicial notice, the objection of a party or the fact that it bears on an ultimate issue in the case will not prevent the court from judicially noticing it. **C** and **D** are, therefore, incorrect.

103. **C** Where the terms of a writing are in issue, the best evidence rule prohibits secondary evidence to prove its contents unless the original or a qualified duplicate of the writing is shown to be unavailable. Since Danziger's guilt may depend on the terms of the union constitution, Wesley's testimony would violate the best evidence rule if it was offered for the purpose of proving the constitution's contents. If it is offered for any other purpose, however, the best evidence rule would be inapplicable.

Since the statute which Danziger is charged with violating requires the "knowing" misappropriation of funds, Danziger's state of mind is relevant. Danziger's state of mind may be related to what he heard from Wesley, even if what Wesley told him was not actually correct. Wesley's testimony is thus offered to prove Danziger's state of mind, and not to prove the contents of the union constitution. **A** and **B** are, therefore, incorrect. **D** is incorrect for this reason, and because if the best evidence rule were applicable, the burden of proving the unavailability of the original or a qualified duplicate would be on Danziger, the party offering the secondary evidence.

104. **A** Hearsay is an out-of-court statement offered to prove the truth of the matter asserted in that statement. If Forman's statement was offered to prove that the president was permitted to raise his own salary (i.e., the matter asserted), it would, thus, be hearsay. Since Danziger's defense is that he believed the union rules permitted him to act as he did, evidence of his state of mind is material. Since what he heard from the former president is likely to have affected his state of mind, Forman's testimony is relevant to Danziger's state of mind. Thus, it is not hearsay if offered to prove what Danziger thought, rather than to prove the truth of Forman's statement (i.e., that Danziger was entitled to raise his own salary).

B is, therefore, incorrect. **C** is incorrect because Forman is not telling the jury his opinion, but rather testifying that he stated that opinion in a conversation which he had with Danziger. This is offered not to prove that his opinion was correct, but to establish Danziger's state of mind as a result of hearing Forman's opinion. An out-of-court statement offered to prove the truth of the matter asserted in that statement is inadmissible as hearsay even if the person who made that statement testifies to it himself. **D** is, therefore, incorrect.

105. **D**   It is the jury's job to determine whether the evidence proves facts sufficient to satisfy the requirements of law as charged by the court. Expert opinion may be admitted to *assist* the trier of fact to understand the evidence or to determine a fact in issue, but it may not be stated in a way which would deprive the jury of its power to determine facts. Since the jury must decide whether Draper had malice aforethought, expert testimony regarding Draper's mental capacity would be admissible. Dr. Wendell's statement, however, did not express an opinion regarding Draper's mental condition, but rather his opinion whether Draper had malice aforethought.

Although the common law once prohibited expert testimony which "embraced the ultimate issue," **A** is incorrect because FRE 704 (and many states) have eliminated this restriction. The opinions of an expert may be based solely on courtroom observations (or may even be based on assumed facts contained in a hypothetical question). The fact that a testifying psychiatrist has never spoken to the subject or even seen him outside a courtroom may reflect on the weight (i.e., persuasive value) of his testimony, but not on its admissibility. **B** and **C** are, therefore, incorrect.

106. **B**   Under FRE 804(b)(2), a statement qualifies for the dying declaration exception to the hearsay rule if it was made by a presently unavailable person under a sense of immediately impending death upon personal knowledge respecting the cause and circumstances of death, and is offered in a criminal homicide trial or a civil action. Since Pasadena was in court, she is not presently unavailable, and her statement does not qualify as a dying declaration.

A is incorrect because it is sufficient that the statement concerned a cause or circumstance of what Pasadena believed was her impending death. Although the common law restricted the use of dying declarations to criminal homicide trials, **C** is incorrect because the FRE specifically authorize their admission in civil proceedings. The FRE do not require that the declarant actually be dying in order to qualify her statement as a dying declaration, so long as she believed herself to be dying at the time she made it. **D** alone is, therefore, not sufficient reason to prevent Pasadena's statement from being admissible as a dying declaration.

107. **A**   Under FRE 803(2), an excited utterance is a statement relating to a startling event made while the declarant was under the stress of excitement caused by that event, and is admissible as an exception to the hearsay rule.

B is, therefore, incorrect. Statements of a declarant's then-existing state of mind also fall under FRE 803(3)'s hearsay exception for descriptions of the declarant's intention, attitude, emotional condition, or mental feeling. **C** is incorrect, however, because although "I'm dying" might qualify as a declaration of Pasadena's state of mind, "I had the green light in my favor" does not, since it does not describe her mental state. **D** is incorrect for two reasons: first, Pasadena's statement said nothing about her past mental state; and, second, FRE 803(3) permits declarations of past state of mind to be admitted only in certain will cases.

108. **C** In general, evidence is admissible if it is relevant to a material issue. Since Lewis' negligence is a material issue in a malpractice action against him, testimony which is relevant to Lewis' negligence is admissible unless excluded under one of the rules of evidence. The common law attorney-client privilege prevents an attorney from testifying, over his client's objection, to confidential communications by the client which were related to the professional relationship. The privilege does not prevent such testimony, however, in litigation relating to a breach of duty arising from the relationship.

Thus, **A** is incorrect. **B** is incorrect for the above reason and because even unnecessary statements may be privileged if they relate to the purpose of the consultation. Ordinarily, the attorney-client privilege survives the relationship, protecting the confidentiality even after the attorney-client relationship ceases to exist. Thus, **D** is incorrect.

109. **C** Circumstantial evidence is proof of one fact from which another can be inferred. The fact that Davidson always signals at that intersection may permit the inference that he did so on this particular occasion, if it is logically relevant to that conclusion. FRE 406 provides that evidence of a person's habit "whether corroborated or not and regardless of the presence of eyewitnesses" is relevant to prove that his conduct on a particular occasion was consistent with that habit. Weigand's testimony should, therefore, be admitted as circumstantial evidence of that fact.

A is incorrect because the FRE specifically dispenses with the requirement that there were no eyewitnesses. **B** is incorrect because the above section authorizes the use of such evidence for that purpose. **D** is incorrect because the language of the cited section makes corroboration unnecessary.

110. **A** At common law, a confidential communication made to an attorney by a person seeking legal advice is generally privileged. If the communication is made in the presence of a third person, an inference may be drawn that the person speaking did not intend for the communication to be confidential. But, if the presence of the third person was necessary, such an inference cannot be drawn, and the communication remains privileged. Since state law provided for the designation of Felton as Dorah's legal guardian and required his joinder as a defendant in an action against her, his presence at the consultation with Watt was necessary so that he could assure that Dorah's rights were protected.

B is incorrect because it is over-inclusive; only those communications which the client intended to be confidential are privileged. Where two or more clients have consulted an attorney together on a matter of common interest, their communications are not privileged if one client seeks to offer them as evidence against the other. **C** is incorrect, however, because unless Felton is seeking to offer Watt's testimony against Dorah (or vice-versa), the mere fact that Dorah and Felton are joint defendants is not sufficient to destroy the privilege. A confidential communication made to an attorney while seeking legal advice is privileged at common law, whether or not the attorney actually gives advice or agrees to represent the person who made the communication. **D** is, therefore, incorrect.

111. **B**   Under FRE 609, conviction for a crime punishable by imprisonment for one year or more or by death is admissible for the purpose of impeaching a witness. If either the conviction or the termination of incarceration occurred within the past ten years, the trial judge has discretion to exclude such a conviction only if it was not for a crime involving dishonesty. Since Wrangler's perjury was punished by five years in prison, since his period of incarceration terminated within the past ten years, and since perjury is obviously a crime involving dishonesty, the trial judge is without discretion to exclude evidence of Wrangler's conviction.

Although the common law requires confrontation prior to the use of certain evidence offered for the purpose of impeachment, **A** is incorrect because the FRE completely dispense with that requirement. The FRE provide that if more than ten years have elapsed since the conviction or termination of incarceration (whichever is *later*), the conviction is inadmissible unless the trial court finds that its probative value substantially outweighs its prejudicial effect. **C** is incorrect because if, as here, fewer than ten years elapsed, the conviction is admissible. Under the FRE, extrinsic evidence of prior inconsistent statements by a witness is admissible for the purpose of impeachment, but only if the witness is given a subsequent opportunity to explain the inconsistency. **D** is incorrect, however, because no such requirement exists regarding the use of convictions.

112. **C**   Although evidence of unconvicted bad acts is inadmissible for the purpose of proving bad character, if relevant it may be admissible for the purpose of attacking a witness' credibility by showing bias. An acquittal of Dempsey would affect the prosecution of Wrangler on the charge of being his accessory. Thus, the pending prosecution against Wrangler is relevant evidence of bias, and is admissible for impeachment purposes.

A is, therefore, incorrect. The bias of a witness is always material to his credibility. For this reason, evidence of such bias is admissible, even though it may relate to a matter which is not material to the charge against the person on trial. **B** is, therefore, incorrect. **D** is incorrect because, although it may be used to establish bias, extrinsic evidence of unconvicted bad acts is not admissible for the purpose of proving that a witness has a bad or dishonest character.

113. **A**   Judicial notice is a doctrine which permits courts to accept as true facts or propositions of law without specific evidence. A fact which has been judicially noticed becomes part of the record and requires no further proof. Although judicial notice is commonly taken of the statutes of the state in which a particular court is sitting, most jurisdictions do not permit municipal ordinances to be judicially noticed, requiring that their contents be proven as facts. Thus, unless the jurisdiction permits a court to take judicial notice of municipal ordinances, the prosecution has failed to make out a case against Darling. On the other hand, if the jurisdiction permits judicial notice of municipal ordinances, the court could judicially notice the section in question and deny Darling's motion for dismissal.

In determining whether there has been a violation, the trier of fact may consider facts which have been judicially noticed by the court. **B** is, therefore, incorrect. The contents of relevant law must be proven unless they are judicially noticed by the court. Since courts frequently refuse to take judicial notice of municipal ordinances, **C** is over-inclusive, and, therefore, incorrect. Ordinarily, judicial notice is taken of facts which are commonly known. This may include the contents of laws, since all are presumed to know them. **D** is incorrect for two reasons: first, the judge's personal expertise or knowledge of particular facts is not sufficient to justify his judicially noticing them; and, second, judicial notice may be taken of commonly known or readily verifiable facts, even though the judge lacks personal expertise.

114. **A** Unless it is excluded by some rule of law, evidence is admissible if it is relevant to a material issue. In a defamation action, the contents of defendant's statement are relevant to a material issue, since the essence of the plaintiff's claim is that the statement was a defamatory communication. Wellman's testimony is, therefore, admissible unless a rule of law excludes it. For the following reasons, none of the statements listed would exclude the testimony.

If the contents of a videotape are in issue, the best evidence rule might prohibit secondary evidence of those contents unless the videotape is shown to be unavailable. If Purcell claimed damage resulting from the broadcast, the contents of the videotape would be in issue. The facts do not indicate that he did, however. Since defamation liability can be based on the publication of a defamatory communication about the plaintiff to any third person, (e.g., to persons in the studio when the statement was made), Danton's statement could be the basis of a defamation action whether or not it actually appeared in a videotape of the broadcast. The contents of the videotape are thus not in issue, and **B** is, therefore, incorrect. Hearsay is an out-of-court statement offered to prove the truth of the matter asserted in the statement. If Wellman's testimony regarding Danton's out-of-court statement was offered to prove that Purcell really was a crook, it would be hearsay. In a defamation action, it is necessary for the plaintiff to prove that the defendant made a defamatory statement. For this reason, the words of the defendant are operative facts having independent legal significance. Evidence of Danton's statement was not offered to prove that Purcell was a crook (i.e., the matter asserted in that statement), but to prove that Danton made a defamatory statement. It is, therefore, not hearsay, and **C** is incorrect. If Danton admits making the statement, there would be no issue as to whether he made it. Wellman's testimony might then be excluded because it would not be relevant to a material issue. **D** is incorrect because it argues that such an admission by Danton would make Wellman's testimony admissible, rather than inadmissible.

115. **C** A witness who testifies under a grant of use immunity is protected against use of that testimony in any subsequent criminal proceeding against him. Since Watkins was not a defendant in the prosecution, use immunity did not prevent the use of his statement. FRE 613 permits the admission of prior inconsistent statements of a witness for the purpose of intrinsically or extrinsically impeaching the credibility of that witness. Evidence of Watkins' prior statement is, thus, admissible for the purpose of impeachment. FRE 801 permits the use of a witness's prior inconsistent statement as substantive evidence if it was given under oath subject to the penalty of perjury at a trial, hearing, or other proceeding. Since Watkins' statement was made under oath at a grand jury proceeding, it is admissible as substantive evidence as well.

A, B, and **D** are, therefore, incorrect.

116. **C** A witness who testifies under a grant of use immunity is protected against use of that

testimony or its fruits in any subsequent criminal proceeding against him. He is not immune from prosecution, however, so long as the prosecutor does not attempt to use the testimony which had been obtained under the grant of use immunity or the fruits of that testimony.

Although a state grant of use immunity must be honored by the federal courts, **A** is incorrect because use immunity does not prevent prosecution. The Double Jeopardy Clause protects a person against being prosecuted twice for the same offense. It is inapplicable to these facts, however, because Watkins was never before prosecuted for the crime with which he is charged in the federal court. **B** is, therefore, incorrect. Although Watkins' motion should be denied, **D** is incorrect because federal courts are required to honor state grants of use immunity.

117.   **A**   If a proper foundation is laid, evidence that a place has been used over a period of time without any accident is logically relevant to prove that the place was not dangerous. The foundation for such negative evidence requires proof, however, that the place was used a substantial number of times under substantially similar conditions. Wenzel's testimony that Marshal Boulevard was a busy thoroughfare is probably sufficient to establish its use a substantial number of times. Unless, however, it is established that Marshal Boulevard was substantially unchanged, proof that there were no prior accidents is irrelevant to Proust's claim that there was a dangerous curve in the road.

B is incorrect because if a proper foundation is laid for the introduction of negative evidence, there is no requirement that the court issue a special instruction to the jury. The argument in **C** is one which Proust's attorney may make to the jury in an attempt to persuade it not to draw from Wenzel's testimony an inference that Marshal Boulevard is safe. **C** is incorrect, however, because if a proper foundation for the evidence is laid, that argument goes to its weight rather than to its admissibility. Although negative evidence presents severe relevancy problems, the laying of a proper foundation resolves them, making such evidence admissible. **D** is, therefore, incorrect.

118.   **A**   Unless otherwise provided by law, all evidence is admissible which has a tendency to prove or disprove a fact of consequence (i.e., which is relevant). Since the Dixie Hotel has denied ownership and control of the alley, evidence relevant to ownership or control is, therefore, admissible. The testimony of Wells is relevant to ownership or control, since it is unlikely that hotel employees would clean the alley if the hotel did not own or control it. His testimony is, therefore, admissible.

Hotel employees might have begun cleaning the alley even though the hotel did not own or control it, and the hotel attorney may try to convince a jury not to infer ownership or control from the remedial measure. **B** is incorrect, however, because the argument which it states goes to the weight rather than the admissibility of the evidence. Although a policy seeks to encourage safety by prohibiting evidence of subsequent remedial measures for the purpose of proving fault, **C** and **D** are incorrect because the testimony of Wells is admissible for the limited purpose of proving ownership or control.

119.   **D**   Under FRE 803(3), an assertion of the declarant's then-existing physical sensation is admissible as an exception to the hearsay rule. The common law makes a distinction which prohibits the admission of such statements if they were made in contemplation of

litigation. The FRE does not make such a distinction, however, allowing the circumstances under which the statement was made to go to the weight rather than the admissibility of the evidence.

A and **B** are, therefore, incorrect. Where it is recognized, the physician-patient privilege may prevent the admission of testimony by a doctor regarding confidential communications with the patient over objection by the *patient*. **C** is incorrect because an objection based on the privilege would not be available to anyone but the patient.

120. **B**   Because of a rule of policy which encourages out-of-court settlements, evidence of settlement offers is inadmissible for the purpose of establishing liability or the value of a claim. If the statement is offered to prove that there was damage to Praxton's car, it is inadmissible because it would thus be evidence of the claim's value.

A is incorrect because it is too restrictive. Evidence of a settlement offer is inadmissible not only if offered to prove negligence, but also if offered to prove the value of a claim. Whether or not a settlement offer is an implied admission is doubtful, since people sometimes settle cases just for the purpose of avoiding vexatious litigation. **C** is incorrect in any event, however, since public policy prevents the admission of such evidence. **D** is incorrect for the same reason.

121. **C**   Under FRE 803(2), a statement relating to a startling event made while the declarant was under the stress of excitement caused by the event is admissible as an excited utterance. This is so even if the declarant's identity is unknown.

A is, therefore, incorrect. The term "self-serving declaration" usually refers to an out-of-court statement made by a party and which is offered by that party to prove an element of his case. Like any other hearsay, it is inadmissible unless it falls into one of the exceptions to the hearsay rule. (For example, a document containing self-serving declarations might be admissible as a business record.) Since Vinson is not a party to the prosecution, it is probably not correct to call his testimony self-serving. More important, although self-serving declarations made *out-of-court* may be excluded from evidence as hearsay, there is no rule prohibiting self-serving *testimony*. For these reasons, **B** is incorrect. Although an excited utterance is admissible only if made by a declarant with personal knowledge, such knowledge is presumed. **D** is, therefore, incorrect.

122. **C**   In order to get the whole story, a direct or cross examiner may attempt to refresh a witness's present recollection by showing the witness's physical objects or writings. If the purpose is to refresh the witness's recollection (rather then to expose the item to the jury) any item may be used, so long as it is first shown to opposing counsel and marked as an exhibit (i.e, for identification). Before refreshing items can be used, however, the witness must have exhausted his unrefreshed memory. Since Bierman stated that he could not remember whether he shouted (i.e., that his present memory was exhausted), the prosecutor was permitted to attempt to refresh his recollection in the manner described.

Since the report was used only to refresh Vinson's recollection, but was not itself being used to prove anything, it need not be admitted, admissible, or offered into evidence. **A, B,** and **D** are, therefore, incorrect.

123.   **A**   Under FRE 803(2), a statement relating to a startling event made while the declarant was under the stress of excitement caused by the event is admissible as an excited utterance. Since the shout described the imminent attack on Vinson and was made by a person who was excited by that attack, it was an excited utterance.

Except in connection with the authentication of written statements, the admissibility of a hearsay declaration does not depend on who testifies to it. Thus, Bierman may testify to his own excited utterance. It is important to recognize that the shout is hearsay (i.e., an out-of-court statement offered to prove the truth of the matter asserted in that statement), but is admissible under the "excited utterance" exception to the hearsay rule. The fact that a declarant testifies that he made a certain statement out of court does not, alone, prevent that statement from being hearsay or make it admissible. **B** is, therefore, incorrect. Using independent evidence to establish the truth of an assertion contained in a hearsay declaration does not make the hearsay admissible. **C** is, therefore, incorrect. Although a witness who refreshes his recollection while testifying may testify from his refreshed recollection, the fact that he has refreshed his recollection does not by itself make his testimony any more admissible than it would have been if he had not needed the refresher. **D** is, therefore, incorrect.

124.   **B**   A witness is permitted to refresh her recollection before testifying by reviewing past notes, depositions and other statements. FRE 612 gives the trial court discretion to require the production at trial of any writings that were used to refresh a witness's recollection before trial.

Secondary evidence to prove the contents of a writing is inadmissible under the best evidence rule unless the original or a qualified duplicate is shown to be unavailable. Thus, if Wolf were testifying to the contents of the notes, her testimony would be inadmissible unless the notes were shown to be unavailable. She is not testifying to the contents of the notes, however, but from her memory after refreshing it by looking at the notes. For this reason, the best evidence rule is inapplicable, and **A** is incorrect. Although the notes have not been offered into evidence, they have been used to refresh Wolf's recollection before trial. For this reason, the court may require their production under FRE 612. **C** is, therefore, incorrect. An admission is a statement by a party which is offered against that party. Since Wolf is not a party to the proceeding, her statements cannot be admissions. **D** is, therefore, incorrect.

125.   **D**   Although the court decides whether evidence is admissible and whether a witness is competent to testify, it is for the jury to decide what weight to give testimony which the court has admitted. In doing so, the jury must determine how credible it finds a particular witness to be. If that witness is an expert testifying to her opinions, it would be impossible for the jury to make that determination without knowing the witness' qualifications. The concession by the defendant's attorney is not sufficient, since it is very likely that the jury will hear contrary opinions given by other experts. To decide which of the experts it believes, the jury must be able to compare their qualifications. For this reason, the details of Dr. Wallace's qualifications remain an issue even though the defendant's attorney concedes that she is sufficiently qualified to testify to her opinions.

A and **B** are, therefore, incorrect. If all parties agree to a fact, a court may accept it as true without requiring further proof. Thus, if all parties agree that a particular witness qualifies as an expert, the court may — on the basis of that stipulation — dispense with the *requirement* of further proof (although it may not prevent the party offering the testimony of that witness from questioning her about her qualifications). **C** is, therefore, incorrect.

126. **C** In some jurisdictions, a learned treatise can be used on the cross-examination of an expert witness only if the witness relied upon that treatise in forming her opinion. FRE 803(18) dispenses with that requirement, however, making the contents of a learned treatise an exception to the hearsay rule to the extent that they are called to the attention of a witness during cross-examination. This provision makes portions of learned treatises on medicine admissible both for impeachment and as substantive evidence. (**Note:** Such portions may be read aloud, but a copy may not be physically admitted into evidence.)

A and B are, incorrect because they are under-inclusive. **D** is incorrect because the above section makes the contents of a learned treatise an exception to the hearsay rule.

127. **D** FRE 406 provides that evidence of the habit of a person, *whether corroborated or not*, is relevant to prove that her conduct on a particular occasion was in conformity with the habit. **A**, **B**, and **C** are, therefore, incorrect.

128. **C** It is generally understood that a lay witness may testify to opinions regarding matters within the contemplation of the ordinary person so long as the opinion is rationally based on the witness' personal perception. In order for an opinion to be rationally based on the witness' personal perception, however, it is necessary to show that the witness had sufficient opportunity to perceive the matter about which she formed an opinion. Since Wagner testified that she first saw Daggett's car just before it struck Padilla, her opportunity to perceive was probably not adequate to support her opinion. While it is not certain that a court would sustain the objection, the argument in **C** is the only one listed which could possibly support the objection.

A is incorrect because the ordinary driver is competent to form an opinion regarding the speed of a moving vehicle. FRE 704 specifically provides that if opinion testimony is otherwise not objectionable, it is not objectionable simply because it concerns an ultimate issue to be determined by the trier of the facts. **B** is, therefore, incorrect. It is sometimes said that witnesses must testify to facts, and inferences are to be drawn by the jury. For this reason, lay opinions are usually not admissible if it would be reasonably practical for the witness to state the separate facts which caused her to form that opinion so that the jury could draw whatever inferences it deems proper. On the other hand, if it is not reasonably practical to express the separate factors that caused the witness to form a particular opinion, the witness may be permitted to state the opinion which she formed. Since the factors which go into an opinion regarding the speed of a moving vehicle cannot ordinarily be expressed as separate facts, a witness who is competent to form an opinion as to that speed will be permitted to express that opinion. **D** is, therefore, incorrect.

129. **A** In general, evidence is admissible if it is relevant to a material issue (i.e., tends to establish some fact of consequence) in the litigation. Since liability for negligence does not

depend on whether the defendant was insured, the fact that Dooley was or was not insured is not of consequence (i.e., not relevant to a material issue) in the litigation. It is, therefore, not admissible.

A compromise consists of a payment or a promise to pay given in return for a promise to discontinue or not to assert a claim. Since Dooley was not offering anything in return for a promise not to assert a claim, his statement was not a compromise offer. **B** is, therefore, incorrect. Admissions are words or acts of a party offered against that party. Under the common law, admissions of a party may be admissible as exceptions to the hearsay rule; under FRE 801(d)(2), admissions of a party are not hearsay at all. Like all other evidence, however, admissions may be admitted only if relevant to a material issue. Since the fact that Dooley was or was not insured is not material, his statement — even if it could be regarded as an admission — is inadmissible. (***Note:*** It might be argued that Dooley's statement implies that he knew himself to be at fault. This argument would not make the statement admissible, however, because FRE 411 specifically provides that evidence that a party was insured is not admissible for the purpose of establishing that party's fault or liability.) FRE 803(2) provides that an excited utterance may be admissible as an exception to the hearsay rule, and defines an excited utterance as a statement relating to a startling event or condition which is made while the declarant is under stress or excitement caused by that event or condition. **D** is incorrect for two reasons: First, Dooley's statement that he had plenty of insurance is not related to the accident which produced his excitement; and, second, like any other evidence, an excited utterance is not admissible unless it is relevant to a material issue.

130. **B**   Under FRE 409, offers to pay or actual payments of medical or hospital bills are inadmissible for the purposes of proving negligence, liability, or the value of a claim. Although there are purposes for which such evidence might be admissible, none are listed among the options.

        A is incorrect because FRE 409 excludes evidence of payment of hospital bills, whether or not such payments are part of an offer of compromise. **C** is incorrect for this reason and because a statement which is otherwise admissible may remain admissible even though it is inseparable from a statement about insurance. **D** is incorrect because FRE 409 specifically excludes such evidence if it is offered for the purpose of establishing fault.

131. **C**   Although lay witnesses are usually permitted to testify only to facts, a lay opinion may be admissible if it would be helpful to a clear understanding of the witness's testimony and if it is rationally based on the witness's perceptions. For this reason, any person who is familiar with the handwriting of another may offer an opinion regarding its identification.

        A and **B** are, therefore, incorrect. Although it is the jury's function to determine the identity of the signature, opinion evidence is admissible to help the jury do so. **D** is, therefore, incorrect.

132. **D**   A cross-examiner is given broad leeway in attempting to impeach a witness intrinsically (i.e., by eliciting testimony from that very witness). In general, a cross-examination question is proper if it has a logical tendency to discredit the testimony of the witness

being cross-examined. A witness thus may be questioned about any facts which tend to show that the nature of his relationship to a party gives him a bias (i.e., motive to be less than objective in his testimony). Since Dalbey's accusation that Waite was dishonest would be likely to result in making Waite angry at Dalbey and therefore biased, the question is proper and the objection should be overruled.

Hearsay is an out-of-court statement offered to prove the truth of the matter asserted in that statement. If Dalbey's statement that Waite was dishonest were offered to prove that Waite was dishonest, it would be hearsay. Since it is offered for another purpose (i.e., to show that Waite is biased), however, it is not hearsay. **A** is, therefore, incorrect. An admission is a declaration by a party which is offered against that party. Since Dalbey's declaration that Waite was dishonest would be offered in favor of Dalbey, it is not an admission. **B** is, therefore, incorrect. "Extrinsic" impeachment is evidence tending to impeach a witness which does not come from that witness's own testimony. Since the evidence which would tend to impeach Waite is sought from Waite himself, it cannot be called "extrinsic". **C** is, therefore, incorrect.

133. **A**   The credibility of a witness may be impeached extrinsically (i.e., by evidence which does not come from the witness's own mouth) by evidence which tends to show that his testimony is not worthy of belief because he was incapable of perceiving accurately. Since Weary stated that his identification of Danek was by the light of the full moon, evidence that there was no moon that night would tend to show that Weary's identification is unworthy of belief because he was incapable of making accurate observations.

The phrase "res gestae" was formerly used to refer to statements made under stress resulting from a startling event. Its use has largely been replaced by the "excited utterance" concept. **B** is incorrect because the testimony of the expert did not refer to any statement made while under stress or excitement. Except for evidence of prior statements, the FRE does not require confrontation as a foundation for the introduction of extrinsic evidence offered to impeach a witness. **C** is, therefore, incorrect. A matter is described as "collateral" if it is not material to issues in a case. **D** is incorrect because a witness's ability to perceive or remember is always regarded as material.

134. **A**   Although evidence of unconvicted bad acts is generally inadmissible to extrinsically impeach a witness, FRE 404 provides that it may be admissible for other purposes. One of the most common permissible uses of such evidence is to create an inference that the defendant is guilty of the crime charged by showing that it was part of a general criminal plan or scheme. Since Danfield's possession of 41 different credit cards bearing 36 different names suggests that she planned to make fraudulent use of them all, evidence of that fact may be admissible. Such circumstantial evidence must be subjected to close examination to determine whether its probative value is outweighed by its prejudicial effect, so it is not certain that a court would admit the evidence. Of all the arguments set forth, however, **A** is the only one which could possibly provide the prosecutor with an effective argument in opposition to the motion to exclude.

Since Danfield is not charged with stealing credit cards, an inference that she did so is not relevant to any fact of consequence in the prosecution. For this reason, **B** is incorrect. (***Note:*** It might be logical to argue that such an inference is relevant because a person who would steal credit cards is probably disposed to make fraudulent use of them.

Such an argument would fail, however, because evidence of unconvicted acts is inadmissible for the purpose of proving a mere criminal disposition.) Under the Fifth Amendment privilege against self-incrimination, a criminal defendant cannot be required to explain her conduct. **C** is, therefore, incorrect. An admission by conduct occurs when a party engages in conduct which indicates her own belief that she is guilty of the crime charged (e.g., attempting to bribe an arresting officer to let the defendant go free or attempting to flee after being charged with a crime). Since possession of credit cards bearing other names does not indicate that Danfield believed herself to be guilty of fraudulently using the card bearing the name of Timothy Nolan, it is not an admission by conduct. **D** is, therefore, incorrect.

135. **D**   Ordinarily, evidence of the behavior of a trained dog is admissible if a foundation is laid similar to the foundation required for any other kind of scientific evidence. This means that it must be shown that the dog was competent to do the job which it was doing and that its handler was competent to interpret the result. Since Handel was an expert dog trainer and handler, and since Findo successfully detected cocaine on several prior occasions, the proper foundation has been laid, and the evidence is admissible.

Hearsay is an out of court statement offered for the purpose of proving the truth of the matter asserted in that statement. Although our society tends to personify dogs, dogs are not persons and are not capable of making statements. For this reason, the behavior of a dog cannot be hearsay (Since a primary reason for the hearsay rule is that out of court declarants are not subject to cross examination and since a dog could not be cross examined in any event, it would not be logical to apply the hearsay rule to a dog's behavior.) **A** is therefore, incorrect. **B** is incorrect because, since the dog could not testify, its availability is irrelevant to the admissibility of its behavior. Although a court might permit demonstration of a scientific method, there is no requirement that it do so. **C** is, therefore, incorrect.

136. **B**   In general, evidence of a defendant's character or disposition is inadmissible for the purpose of proving that he acted in a particular way on a particular occasion. An exception is made, however, for evidence which shows a definite, particular, and strong inference that the defendant did the precise act charged. Included in this exception is evidence tending to establish that the defendant uses a distinctive *modus operandus* (MO), or method of operation. For this reason, the fact that Dodd previously smuggled cocaine using a brass statue with a false bottom could be admissible. Although it is not certain that a court would admit the evidence for this purpose, **B** is the only answer listed which could possibly be correct.

FRE 406 permits evidence of habit to be used as circumstantial evidence that on a particular occasion the defendant's conduct was consistent with his habit. **A** is incorrect, however, because habit evidence requires a showing that the actor in question consistently acts in a particular way, and one prior experience is not sufficient to establish a habit. Although evidence of a defendant's previous conduct is inadmissible if offered against him for some purposes, it may be admissible if offered against him for others. **C** is thus incorrect because it is overinclusive. Evidence of a prior conviction is not usually admissible for the purpose of impeaching a witness if the conviction occurred more than ten years prior to the trial at which it is offered. **D** is incorrect, however, because Dodd's prior conviction is not being offered to impeach his credibility, but rather to establish a distinctive MO.

137. **C**   The fact that a witness has previously made a statement which is inconsistent with her testimony indicates the she is not always honest and that, therefore, her testimony is not worthy of belief. For this reason, a witness may be cross-examined about prior inconsistent statements. Although the common law requires that the witness first be told when and to whom the statement was made, the FRE has dispensed with this requirement.

For the above reason, **A** and **D** are incorrect. Under some circumstances, former testimony given under oath may be admissible as substantive evidence, but prior inconsistent statements are admissible for purposes of impeachment even if not made under oath. **B** is, therefore, incorrect.

138. **B**   Under certain circumstances a witness may be impeached by extrinsic (i.e., not from the witness's own mouth) evidence that she made a prior inconsistent statement. Although the common law requires that the witness be confronted with and given an opportunity to explain the inconsistency before the extrinsic evidence is offered, FRE 613 provides that extrinsic evidence of prior inconsistent statements by a witness is admissible if the witness is given a prior *or subsequent* opportunity to explain the inconsistency. For this reason, the objection should be sustained unless Danesh is given a subsequent opportunity to explain the inconsistency.

A and **C** are, therefore, incorrect. The "collateral matter rule" provides that extrinsic evidence is not admissible for purposes of impeachment unless it relates to a substantive issue in the case. **D** is incorrect, however, because there is no principle of law known as the "collateral witness rule."

139. **B**   In general, evidence is admissible only if it is relevant to a material issue. Evidence is relevant to a material issue if it tends to establish some fact of consequence. Since Decco is charged with knowingly possessing the marijuana found in the trunk, the only material issue is whether Decco knew it was there. The note from his wife may indicate that they smoked marijuana together on some other occasion (although her use of the word "stuff" makes even this questionable), but it does not tend to establish anything about Decco's knowledge of what was in the trunk of the borrowed car. For that reason, it is not relevant to a material issue and should be excluded.

Hearsay is an out of court statement offered to prove the truth of the matter asserted in that statement. There is some doubt about the reason for offering the note from Decco's wife. If it is offered for any reason other than to prove that they "got high on the stuff [they] smoked last night" it is not hearsay. Even if it is offered for that purpose, however, it probably falls under an exception to the hearsay rule since it is a declaration against the penal interests of Decco's wife. Although declarations against the penal interest are not exceptions to the hearsay rule at common law (which makes exception only for declarations against financial interest), they are exceptions under FRE 804(b)(3). **A** is, therefore, incorrect. Although the statement contained in the note from Decco's wife is a declaration against her interest and, therefore, an exception to the hearsay rule, it is not admissible because, as explained above, it is not relevant to a material issue. **C** is, therefore, incorrect. Under the common law spousal privilege one spouse may not give evidence against another in a criminal case. Thus, if the jurisdiction recognizes the common law spousal privilege, it would probably result in the exclusion of the note from Decco's wife. **D** is incorrect, however, because its language indicates that this would be the only reason for excluding the note, and, as explained above, the note would be excluded even if the jurisdiction did not recognize this privilege.

140. **A**   Most jurisdictions hold that cross examination should be limited to inquiry into matters to which the witness testified on direct examination. Some jurisdictions grant broader latitude. All agree, however, that questions which go beyond the scope of cross examination are improper. Thus, if the question went beyond the scope of cross examination, the objection should be sustained.

B is incorrect because leading questions are permitted on cross examination. A hostile witness is one who has demonstrated anger or hostility to the attorney questioning her. **C** is incorrect because there is no indication that Pacetti has done so. Since the question is not whether the dog is gentle, but whether the dog is generally known to be gentle, Pacetti's expertise (or lack of it) on the subject of dog behavior is irrelevant. **D** is, therefore, incorrect.

141. **A**   Ordinarily a will must be authenticated by witnesses who testify to its execution. **A** is, therefore, correct. FRE 902 provides that periodicals, publications issued by public authorities, and certified copies of public records are self authenticating. **B**, **C**, and **D** are, therefore, incorrect.

142. **B**   If a proper foundation is laid, evidence that a particular product has been used many times without accident is admissible as circumstantial evidence that its condition is not dangerous. The required foundation includes evidence that the conditions under which the product was used were identical to those which existed at the time of the accident and that the witness would have heard if there had been any accidents. Since Walters testified that more than 10,000 of the motorcycles were sold, and since presumably they were used on roads, and since most of the roads have bumps, the requirement of use in identical conditions has probably been satisfied. To complete the required foundation, it is thus necessary only to show that Walters was the person to whom all complaints of product failure would have been made.

A is incorrect because although a judge may choose to give a special instruction regarding the uncertainty of negative evidence, there is no rule of law requiring such an instruction. **C** is incorrect because the objection that it raises goes to the weight rather than the admissibility of the evidence. **D** is incorrect because under conditions such as those described above, negative evidence is admissible.

143. **C**   Evidence of a scientific test or experiment is admissible only if a foundation is laid which indicates the substantial identity of material conditions. Thus, if the test conditions were not substantially the same as the conditions which existed at the time of the accident, evidence of the test and its results should be excluded.

A is incorrect because a film may be authenticated by anyone who knows it to be an accurate representation of what it purports to be. The best evidence rule provides that when the contents of a document are in dispute, secondary evidence is not admissible in the absence of a showing that the original or a qualified duplicate is not available. Since there is no dispute about the contents of any document, the best evidence rule is not applicable, and **B** is incorrect. **D** is incorrect for the reasons given above.

QUESTIONS
PROPERTY

PROPERTY
TABLE OF CONTENTS
Numbers refer to Question Numbers

PROPERTY QUESTIONS

1. Sosa owned a five acre tract of realty known as Greenacre in fee simple. In desperate need of money, Sosa prepared a deed purporting to convey Greenacre in fee simple to "Bearer," and took it to the office of Bell, a real estate investor. For a cash payment of five hundred dollars which Bell paid him on the spot, Sosa signed the deed and handed it to Bell saying, "You own it now."

A statute in the jurisdiction provides that no document purporting to convey any interest in real property shall be recorded unless it is in writing, clearly identifies the grantor, the grantee, and the interest conveyed, and is signed and acknowledged by the grantor.

Bell subsequently instituted a proceeding to eject Sosa from Greenacre. Sosa defended by asserting that he held a fee simple in Greenacre and was therefore entitled to possess it. Which of the following arguments would most effectively support Sosa's assertion?

(A) The deed was unrecordable.

(B) The deed failed to identify the grantee.

(C) Five hundred dollars was inadequate consideration.

(D) Sosa acted under economic duress in selling Greenacre to Bell.

2. Twenty-two years ago, Fowl built a chicken coop near the edge of his yard. In fact, about one-third of the structure was built on Nearacre, the neighboring parcel of real estate. Polsky, the present owner of Nearacre, has demanded that Fowl remove the part of his chicken coop which encroaches upon Nearacre. Fowl has refused to do so, claiming that he has become the owner of that part of Nearacre by adverse possession. A statute in the jurisdiction fixes the period of time for acquiring title to land by adverse possession at twenty years. Polsky has instituted legal proceedings against Fowl for an order directing Fowl

to remove the encroachment, and Fowl has filed a counterclaim, requesting a judgment declaring him to be the owner of the portion of Nearacre on which his chicken coop encroaches.

Which of the following additional facts, if it were the only one true, would be LEAST likely to result in a judgment for Polsky?

(A) Ever since he built the chicken coop, Fowl has given the owner of Nearacre one dozen eggs per week in return for permission to encroach on the land.

(B) After a portion of the chicken coop had been built on Nearacre, the owner of Nearacre told Fowl that it could remain there so long as Fowl used it to house chickens.

(C) Soon after building the chicken coop Fowl told the owner of Nearacre that he realized that he was encroaching, and that he would remove the encroachment whenever the owner of Nearacre asked him to.

(D) Polsky purchased Nearacre from the prior owner fifteen years after the chicken coop was built, and commenced the action against Fowl six years after acquiring title.

3. On March 1, Sharp owned a tract of realty called Stoneacre, and on that date sold it to Uno for ten thousand dollars. Uno paid two thousand dollars cash to Sharp when the deed was delivered and executed a note for the balance secured by a mortgage on the realty. Neither the deed nor the mortgage was recorded. On April 1, Sharp again purported to sell Stoneacre, this time to Dewey for eight thousand dollars. Dewey paid cash upon receiving a deed to the property. Although Uno's note called for monthly payments to Sharp beginning on April 1, Uno made no payments until September. Then, when Sharp threatened to foreclose on the mortgage, Uno reconveyed the property to Sharp. In November, Dewey learned about Sharp's sale to Uno and Uno's reconveyance to

Sharp. If Dewey institutes an action against Sharp to quiet title to Stoneacre, the court should find for

(A) Dewey, since Sharp is estopped from denying Dewey's title

(B) Dewey, if Sharp's sale to him on April 1 was fraudulent.

(C) Sharp, unless Dewey recorded Sharp's deed to him.

(D) Sharp, because at the time of his conveyance to Dewey, Sharp did not hold title to Stoneacre.

4. Maria, who was ill, executed a deed to her home naming her sons Arnold and Benton as joint tenants. Because Benton was on an extended trip out of the country, she handed the deed to Arnold saying that she wanted him to let Benton know about it as soon as possible. She told Arnold that she was conveying the property while she was alive because she did not want her sons to be responsible for inheritance tax, but that she wished to continue living in the house until her death. Arnold had the deed duly recorded, and then returned it to Maria, asking that she keep it for him in her safe-deposit box. Maria continued living in the home until the time of her death one month later. Arnold died the following week without occupying the realty and without telling Benton about the conveyance. Maria's will left all her property to her sister Sissy. Arnold's will left all his property to his friend Fred. Who is entitled to the realty?

(A) Fred, because Maria delivered the deed only to Arnold, and Arnold devised the property to Fred.

(B) Sissy, because Maria delivered the deed to Arnold in an attempt to avoid tax liability while making a testamentary disposition.

(C) Sissy, because Arnold never occupied the realty and the deed was in Maria's possession at the time of her death.

(D) Benton, because Arnold received the deed as Benton's agent and Benton succeeded to

Arnold's interest on Arnold's death.

5. Gebhart sued to quiet title to a certain parcel of realty, seeking judgment declaring her as its owner. Bosco opposed her claim, asserting that she had delivered to Bosco a deed purporting to convey all of her interest in the realty. Which of the following additional facts or inferences, if it was the only one true, would provide Gebhart with the most effective argument in response to Bosco's assertion?

(A) Bosco gave no consideration for the conveyance.

(B) The deed did not indicate what interest was being conveyed.

(C) The deed was not signed by Gebhart or her agent.

(D) The deed was not recorded.

Questions 6-7 are based on the following fact situation.

After looking at most of the real estate in the county, Clubb decided that Landsman's ranch, The Flying L, would be ideal for the golf course and country club which he wanted to build. Since the two-story ranch residence building was in good condition, Clubb planned to renovate and convert it into the club restaurant. The other buildings on the Flying L were old and run-down and it was Clubb's intention to tear them down. After negotiations, Clubb and Landsman entered into a contract for the sale of the farm, describing it as follows: "All that realty known as The Flying L Ranch, and identified as Tract 14, Lot 249, Parcel 61 in the Tract Index maintained by the office of the Recorder of the County of Parsons; said realty consisting of 240 acres more or less, one two-story residential building, one 60-foot by 140-foot cattle barn, and nine small wooden sheds measuring approximately 50 square feet each." The contract set the purchase price at $240,000, with title to close two months from the date that the contract was signed. Two weeks after signing the contract, Clubb experienced a drastic change in his financial position, and decided not to go through with the purchase of The Flying L.

6. Assume for the purpose of this question only that before Clubb had a chance to contact Landsman about his change in plan, a severe windstorm blew down two of the small wooden sheds on the property. Assume further that immediately after the destruction of the two sheds, Clubb notified Landsman that he would not purchase The Flying L on the ground that part of the realty had been destroyed. In a jurisdiction which has rejected the doctrine of equitable conversion, if Landsman sued Clubb for damages resulting from Clubb's refusal to conclude the sale, the court should find for

(A) Clubb, because the realty no longer conforms to the description of it in the contract of sale.

(B) Clubb, because the risk of loss from causes not the fault of either party remained with Landsman until the closing of title.

(C) Landsman, because the risk of loss from causes not the fault of either party passed to Clubb immediately upon execution of the contract.

(D) Landsman, because the sheds were not essential parts of the realty and abatement of the purchase price would have been a suitable remedy.

7. Assume for the purpose of this question only that the realty was not damaged, and that Clubb did not notify Landsman of his change in plan. Assume further that at the time and place of closing Landsman tendered a deed containing a description of the realty which was identical to that which appeared in the contract of sale, but that Clubb refused to accept it. In a subsequent action by Landsman against Clubb for damages resulting from breach of contract, the court should find for

(A) Landsman, if his land was the only realty in the county which was known as The Flying L, and the only parcel identified by the Tract, Lot and Parcel numbers used in the contract description.

(B) Landsman, because Clubb has waived any

objection to the validity of the description by signing a contract containing an identical description.

(C) Clubb, because the contract and deed lacked a metes and bounds description.

(D) Clubb, unless it was standard practice in the area to use descriptions like the one contained in the contract and deed.

8. Sanderson entered into a valid written contract with Barberi for the sale of a parcel of real estate known as Sandy Woods. The contract provided that Sanderson was to deliver marketable title. Prior to the date of closing, Barberi learned that Planchet had been in possession of Sandy Woods for a period in excess of that required for adverse possession, and that he had paid no rent and entered into no agreement with Sanderson. On the day title was to close, Barberi refused to accept the deed tendered by Sanderson on the ground that Sanderson's title was not marketable, and demanded the return of his deposit. Sanderson refused to return the deposit, and demanded that Barberi accept the tendered deed. In litigation between Barberi and Sanderson, who will win?

(A) Sanderson, unless Planchet is successful in an action to quiet title to Sandy Woods.

(B) Sanderson, if he was ready, willing and able to furnish Barberi with a policy of title insurance which specifically insured against claims of adverse possessors.

(C) Barberi, but only if Planchet has complied with all the requirements for acquiring title by adverse possession.

(D) Barberi, if there is doubt about whether Planchet has acquired title by adverse possession.

Questions 9-10 are based on the following fact situation.

Devel was the owner of a tract of realty which she divided into 40 lots in accordance with the state's subdivision statute. When Devel prepared deeds to all the lots in the subdivision, the deeds to all lots numbered 21 through 40 contained language restricting the use of the land to one-story single family residences, but the deeds to lots numbered 1 through 20 contained no such restriction. Devel sold lot 1 to Yarrow, conveying it by a deed which contained no restrictions. Albert subsequently purchased lots numbered 25 through 30 from Devel for investment purposes, receiving deeds containing the above restriction. Before construction began on any of the lots in the subdivision, Albert sold lot 25 to Barbara, conveying it by a deed which contained no restrictions. Lots 1 and 25 were located across the street from each other, each visible from the other.

9. Assume for the purpose of this question only that Barbara began construction of a three-story, three- family residence on lot 25, and that Yarrow sued for an injunction to prevent its construction. Which of the following would be Barbara's most effective argument in defense?

    (A) The deed which she received did not mention any restriction in the use of lot 25.

    (B) The deed which Yarrow received did not mention any restriction in the use of lot 25.

    (C) Yarrow was not aware of the restriction contained in the deed to lot 25, and did not rely on it in purchasing lot 1.

    (D) The restriction in the deed to lot 25 did not touch and concern the land.

10. Assume for the purpose of this question only that Yarrow began construction of a gas station on Lot 1. If Barbara institutes an action for an injunction prohibiting Yarrow from building anything other than a one-story single family residence, will she win?

    (A) Yes, on the theory of implied reciprocal servitudes.

    (B) Yes, if lot 25 is held to be restricted to use for one-story single family residence.

    (C) No, unless Yarrow was aware of the restriction in the deeds to lots 21 through 40 when he purchased lot 1.

    (D) No, if such a restriction was not part of the subdivision plan.

Questions 11-12 are based on the following fact situation.

Ossie was the owner of six acres of land, the northern boundary of which fronted on Country Road, and the southern boundary of which fronted on Quiet Lake. Ossie's house was located in the middle of the property, about half way between the road and the lake. Pursuant to the laws of the jurisdiction, he divided the land into three lots. Lot 1, the northernmost lot, fronted on Country Road; Lot 3, the southernmost lot, fronted on Quiet Lake. Lot 2, which contained Ossie's house, was located between Lots 1 and 3, with no frontage on either Country Road or Quiet Lake. The only ingress and egress to Lot 2 was over a clearly marked and graded dirt driveway which crossed Lot 1, connecting Lot 2 with Country Road.

Ossie continued to live in his house on Lot 2, but sold Lot 1 to Rhodes, and Lot 3 to Laker. The deed to Rhodes reserved an easement over the dirt driveway which connected Lot 2 with Country Road. Ossie had never used the lake, and there was no clearly marked road or path to it across Lot 3. The deed to Laker, however, reserved an easement described by metes and bounds across Lot 3 for the purpose of access to Quiet Lake from Lot 2.

11. Assume for the purpose of this question only that five years after Ossie's conveyance to Rhodes, the county constructed New Road along the westernmost boundary of Lots 1, 2, and 3, and that New Road led from Country Road to Quiet Lake. Assume further that Ossie began using New Road for ingress and egress to his property, maintaining but not using the dirt driveway which crossed Lot 1. If Rhodes, desiring to sell Lot 1, brought an action to enjoin Ossie from further use of the right of way across Lot 1, the court should find for

    (A) Ossie, because his easement was created by express reservation.

    (B) Ossie, because an implied easement by necessity does not terminate upon the termination of the necessity.

(C) Rhodes, because an implied easement by necessity terminates upon termination of the necessity.

(D) Rhodes, because continued use of the easement by Ossie will unreasonably reduce the value of Lot 1.

12. Assume for the purpose of this question only that two years after Ossie's conveyance to Laker, Laker sold Lot 3 back to Ossie. Assume further that one month later, Ossie conveyed Lot 3 to Waters by a deed which made no mention of any easement over Lot 3. Ossie subsequently sold his home and Lot 2 to Middel, executing a deed which granted Middel a right-of-way over Lot 3 for access to the lake, identical to the easement described in the original grant from Ossie to Laker. When Middel attempted to cross Lot 3, however, Waters refused to permit him to do so. If Middel institutes an action for an injunction directing Waters to refrain from interfering with Middel's right of way over Lot 3, the court should find for

(A) Middel, because the right to cross Lot 3 was expressly granted by Ossie in the deed to Lot 2.

(B) Middel, because the easement to cross Lot 3 was created by the deed which conveyed Lot 3 to Laker.

(C) Waters, because Ossie's non-use of the easement across Lot 3 resulted in its termination.

(D) Waters, because the easement to cross Lot 3 terminated when Ossie repurchased Lot 3 from Laker.

13. Fred was the owner in fee simple absolute of a parcel of realty known as The Heights. He executed a valid will in which he devised The Heights to "those of my children who survive me, to hold equally, share and share alike, as joint tenants." Fred's son Bob and daughter Susan, both adults, were his only living children at the time his will was executed. Three months later, Bob borrowed money from Loanco, a financial institution, executing a note secured by a mortgage on

The Heights. Soon afterwards, Bob committed suicide without repaying the loan. The following year, Fred died, survived only by his daughter Susan.

Assuming that the jurisdiction has a statute which provides that a mortgagee of realty holds equitable title to the realty, which of the following statements best describes Susan's interest in The Heights following the death of Fred?

(A) Susan holds The Heights as a joint tenant with Loanco.

(B) Susan holds The Heights as a tenant in common with Loanco.

(C) Susan is the sole owner of The Heights, subject to Loanco's lien for the amount owing by Bob.

(D) Susan is the sole owner of The Heights, and her interest is not subject to any lien on behalf of Loanco.

14. Tona was the owner of a parcel of undeveloped realty known as Tonacre. When she died, her will devised the realty to her husband Hernando "for life, remainder to such person as Hernando shall designate by his will." Three months after Tona's death, Hernando married Walley. As a wedding present, he executed a deed purporting to convey Tonacre to Walley in fee simple absolute. The day after executing the deed, Hernando died intestate survived only by Walley. Walley subsequently agreed to sell Tonacre to Benton by a contract which required the conveyance of marketable title. On the day set for closing, Benton refused to accept the deed tendered by Walley and demanded the return of his deposit. In litigation between Walley and Benton, a court should find for

(A) Benton, unless the deed tendered by Walley contained a covenant of general warranty.

(B) Benton, because Tonacre reverted to Tona's estate upon the death of Hernando.

(C) Walley, because Hernando's conveyance to Walley was a valid exercise of the power of appointment which he received under

Tona's will.

(D) Walley, if she was the only person qualified to inherit from Hernando under the laws of intestacy.

Questions 15-16 are based on the following fact situation.

Givers executed a deed to his realty known as Givacre, which contained the following clause:

> "To Senior Center, for so long as the realty shall be used as a home for the elderly, but if racial discrimination is practiced in the admission of residents to said home, to Senior Life for so long as the realty shall be used as a home for the elderly."

Senior Center and Senior Life were both charitable institutions devoted to the needs of indigent elderly persons.

15. On the day after the deed was executed, Givers' interest in Givacre is best described as

(A) a valid reversion.

(B) a valid possibility of reverter.

(C) a valid right of re-entry.

(D) void under the Rule Against Perpetuities.

16. On the day after the deed was executed, Senior Life's interest in Givacre is best described as a

(A) valid contingent remainder.

(B) valid executory interest.

(C) void contingent remainder.

(D) void executory interest.

Questions 17-18 are based on the following fact situation.

Roland sold a parcel of realty known as Rolling Hills to Telly. The realty consisted of one hundred acres, of which thirty acres were wooded and the balance was in livestock pasture. The purchase price was $100,000 of which Telly paid $50,000 in cash. The balance of $50,000 was to be paid in full ten years after the closing of title, with interest of eight percent per annum to be paid on a monthly basis until then. After receiving title to Rolling Hills, Telly entered into possession and paid the interest to Roland as agreed. In addition, Telly paid real estate taxes of $1,000 per year as they came due. After occupying the realty with his wife Wilma for nine years, Telly died. His will devised Rolling Hills to Wilma for life, remainder to Telly's brother Bertrand. After Telly's death, Wilma remained on Rolling Hills, making monthly interest payments to Roland. The next year, the balance of the purchase price became due, and Wilma received a tax bill from the county assessor for $1,000.

17. As between Wilma and Bertrand, which of the following correctly states their respective obligations regarding payment of the real estate taxes and principal balance owed by Telly?

(A) Wilma is obligated to pay the real estate taxes and to pay $50,000 to Roland.

(B) Wilma is obligated to pay the real estate taxes, but Bertrand is obligated to pay $50,000 to Roland.

(C) Bertrand is obligated to pay the real estate taxes, but Wilma is obligated to pay $50,000 to Roland.

(D) Bertrand is obligated to pay the real estate taxes and to pay $50,000 to Roland.

18. Assume for the purpose of this question only that the fences surrounding the livestock pastures on the realty were in decaying condition, and that Wilma made arrangements to have some of the trees cut down for use in repairing the fences. When Bertrand learned of Wilma's plan, he brought a proceeding for an injunction to prevent her from doing so. In response to Bertrand's petition, a court should find for

(A) Wilma, if the cutting of trees on the land was a reasonable way of maintaining the fences.

(B) Wilma, because a life tenant has an unlimited right to make use of natural resources of the realty.

(C) Bertrand, because destruction of trees on a parcel of realty constitutes ameliorating waste.

(D) Bertrand, if the fences were permitted to decay during Telly's lifetime.

Questions 19-20 are based on the following fact situation.

Tess willed her realty "to my nephew Ned for twenty years, remainder to my niece Nellie if she is living at that time; but if Nellie is not living at the termination of Ned's estate, to the oldest child of Nellie who is living at the time of my death." Tess died in January 1961, survived by Ned, Nellie, and Nellie's two children -- Paul, who was fourteen, and Eddie, who was seven. In January 1962, Adder moved onto the realty, living in a shack which he constructed from discarded packing crates. Nellie died in 1970. In January 1981, twenty years after the death of Tess, Paul discovered that Adder had been in possession of the realty for nineteen years. He made no attempt to have Adder removed from the realty until January 1983, when Adder had been in possession for twenty-one years. A statute in the jurisdiction fixes the period for acquisition of title by adverse possession at twenty years. Another statute fixes the age of majority at eighteen years.

19. If Paul sued to have Adder removed from the realty in January of 1983, the court should find for

(A) Paul, because the period of adverse possession began running against him when he became the owner of the realty in 1981.

(B) Paul, because the period of adverse possession began running against him when Nellie died in 1970.

(C) Paul, because the period of adverse possession began running against him when he was no longer an infant under the laws of the jurisdiction.

(D) Adder.

20. Which of the following correctly describes the interest which Eddie had in the realty on the day after the death of Tess?

(A) Vested remainder subject to complete divestment on the happening of a condition subsequent.

(B) contingent remainder.

(C) Springing executory interest.

(D) No valid interest in the realty.

Questions 21-22 are based on the following fact situation.

On March 1, Marcel conveyed a tract of realty to her daughters Andrea and Bessie as joint tenants. On April 1, Marcel purported to sell that same tract to Parton by general warranty deed. Parton paid cash for the property and was unaware of the prior conveyance to Marcel's daughters. Andrea and Bessie recorded their deed on April 3. Parton recorded his deed on April 5. Andrea died on April 7.

21. Assume for the purpose of this question only that the jurisdiction has ONE of the following statutes:

I. "No conveyance of real property is effective against a subsequent purchaser for value and without notice unless the same be recorded."

II. "Every conveyance of real estate is void as against any subsequent purchaser in good faith and for value whose conveyance is first duly recorded."

Is Bessie's right superior to Parton's on April 8?

(A) Yes, only if the jurisdiction has Statute I.

(B) Yes, only if the jurisdiction has Statute II.

(C) Yes, if the jurisdiction has Statute I or Statute II.

(D) No.

22. Assume for the purpose of this question only that the jurisdiction has a statute which provides, "In determining the priority of conflicting interests in land, the first such interest to have been recorded shall have priority." Who has priority on April 8?

   (A) Bessie, because the conveyance to Andrea and Bessie was recorded before the conveyance to Parton was recorded.

   (B) Bessie, because the realty was conveyed to Andrea and Bessie before the conveyance to Parton was recorded.

   (C) Parton, because Bessie's interest did not ripen until after Parton's interest was recorded.

   (D) Parton, because Marcel conveyed to him by general warranty deed.

Questions 23-24 are based on the following fact situation.

Derry was the owner of a dairy farm known as Bovine Acres. The farm consisted of 300 acres of land, 200 dairy cows, and a series of buildings. Among the buildings was a "processing plant" in which fresh milk was filtered, chilled, and stored until the next daily pickup. About five years ago, Derry decided to build a new barn for his animals and borrowed thirty thousand dollars for that purpose from Dairyman's Bank. At the time he made the loan, Derry executed a note requiring monthly payments of a specified sum and secured by a mortgage on Bovine Acres. The following year, Derry sold the farm to Furth, conveying it by a deed which stated, "Grantee expressly assumes the note and mortgage previously executed by Grantor to Dairyman's Bank." The deed was signed by Furth as well as by Derry. The year after that, Furth sold the farm to Seckin, conveying it by a deed which stated, "The realty described herein is conveyed subject to an existing note and mortgage held by Dairyman's Bank."

Several months after buying Bovine Acres, Seckin purchased a new cooling tank for the processing plant. The tank had a five-thousand-gallon capacity and weighed several tons when empty. In installing the cooling tank, Seckin had the wooden floor of the processing plant torn out and replaced with concrete. Brackets were placed in the wet concrete so that when it hardened

they could not be removed. The new tank was then permanently fastened to the brackets. Seckin made several monthly payments to Dairyman's Bank on the mortgage note, but then missed three consecutive payments.

23. If Dairyman's Bank sues for the amount of the missed payments, who may be held personally liable to Dairyman's Bank for the amount owing?

   (A) Derry only.

   (B) Furth only.

   (C) Derry and/or Furth.

   (D) Neither Derry nor Furth.

24. Assume for the purpose of this question only that Dairyman's Bank was unsuccessful at collecting on the note, that it instituted foreclosure proceedings, and that as a result an appropriate court directed the sale of all property subject to the mortgage. Should the cooling tank purchased and installed by Seckin be included in the foreclosure sale?

   (A) Yes, if installation of the tank converted it to a fixture.

   (B) Yes, because Seckin made several of the monthly payments.

   (C) No, because the cooling tank was brought onto the realty after the execution of the note and mortgage.

   (D) No, because Seckin took the property "subject to" the mortgage.

25. On January 3, Vender and Purcher entered into a written contract for the sale of Vender's realty located in the state of Columbia. At the time the contract was signed, Purcher handed Vender a check drawn on a foreign bank in payment of the entire purchase price. Pursuant to the contract, Vender executed a deed to the realty and deposited it with a commercial escrow company, with instructions to deliver the deed to Purcher as soon as Purcher's check cleared the bank. Purcher's check cleared the bank on January 15, but because of a strike by certain bank employees,

the escrow company did not learn that the check had cleared until January 21, and did not deliver the deed to Purcher until January 22. On January 17, Purcher executed a deed purporting to convey the realty to Jackson. A statute in the state of Columbia makes it a misdemeanor for any person "to execute any document purporting to convey an interest in real estate which the person executing said document did not actually hold at the time the document was executed, regardless of whether the person executing said document was aware that s/he did not hold the interest which the document purported to convey." If Purcher is charged with violating the above statute by executing a deed to Jackson on January 17, he should be

(A) convicted, because he did not become the owner of the realty until the deed was delivered on January 22.

(B) convicted, because he did not become the owner of the realty until January 21, when the escrow company learned that the check had cleared.

(C) acquitted, because his title to the property relates back to January 15 when his check cleared the bank.

(D) acquitted, because when his check cleared the bank his title to the property related back to January 3 when the contract of sale was executed.

26. After working twenty years for the People's Trust Company, Singer was promoted from assistant manager of the Twin Oaks branch to manager of a branch located in another state. When he learned that Bryant was moving to Twin Oaks to replace him as assistant manager, he offered to sell Bryant his home in Twin Oaks for $60,000. After inspecting the premises, Bryant accepted the offer. They entered into a written contract of sale calling for closing of title six weeks after the signing of the contract. Because their employer was eager to have them both start at their new positions as soon as possible, the contract contained a clause permitting Bryant to move into the house immediately. Bryant did so a few days after signing the contract of sale. Singer kept the

fire insurance policy on the house in effect, planning to cancel it upon conveying title to Bryant. In addition, Bryant purchased a policy of fire insurance on the house immediately after contracting for purchase of the house. Two weeks after Bryant moved in, a fire of unknown origin partially destroyed a portion of the roof, the entire kitchen, and parts of the exterior of the house. Bryant immediately notified Singer that he was unwilling to complete the transaction at the price originally agreed upon, but that he would be willing to renegotiate to determine a new price based on the diminished value of the real estate as the result of the fire.

If Singer sues for damages based upon Bryant's anticipatory repudiation of the contract of sale, Singer's most effective argument would be that the court should find for him because

(A) the risk of loss passed to Bryant when he took possession of the premises pursuant to the contract.

(B) Bryant purchased a policy of fire insurance covering the premises prior to the contract.

(C) Singer had a policy of insurance insuring him against fire damage to the house.

(D) a fire is presumed to be the fault of the person who is in possession at the time it occurs.

27. Sollen was the owner of a 40-acre tract of land. Complying with the state's subdivision law, he subdivided the tract, creating 20 building lots in addition to the necessary public areas. Sollen retained five acres on which he installed a well and water-purifying equipment. He laid pipes from his water-purifying plant to all of the other lots in the subdivision. Every conveyance of land in his subdivision contained a restriction requiring the grantee to purchase from Sollen all water used on the realty. Bangor contracted to purchase a lot in the subdivision from Sollen by a written agreement in which Bangor agreed that after the closing of title he would purchase all water used on the realty from Sollen at a specified price for a period of ten years. At the closing, Sollen delivered a deed with the aforementioned restriction,

but Bangor did not sign it. Three years after closing, Bangor installed his own well and stopped buying water from Sollen. If Sollen asserts a claim for damages against Bangor, the court should find for

(A) Sollen, because Bangor contracted to purchase water from Sollen for a period of ten years.

(B) Sollen, because a discrepancy between a contract for the sale of realty and a conveyance is resolved by looking to the contract.

(C) Bangor, because the agreement to purchase water did not touch and concern the land of Sollen.

(D) Bangor, because Bangor did not sign the deed.

Questions 28-29 are based on the following fact situation.

Onner owned a parcel of real estate which fronted on a major road. At the other end of the property, the Ragged Mountains rose majestically toward the sky. Onner divided the parcel into Lot I which fronted on the road, and Lot II which did not. He sold Lot I to Servo, conveying title by a deed which reserved a thirty-foot-wide ingress and egress easement for the benefit of Lot II. Servo immediately constructed a house on Lot I, taking advantage of the spectacular view of the Ragged Mountains by installing a picture window in his living room on the wall facing Lot II. Dom then purchased Lot II from Onner, receiving a deed which included the aforementioned easement over Lot I. After purchasing Lot II, Dom visited Servo, admiring the view from Servo's picture window. Several years later, Dom began construction of a home on Lot II.

28. Assume for the purpose of this question only that Dom executed a deed to Powerco, the electric company, granting it the right to erect poles on and string wires over his right-of-way across Lot I for the purpose of bringing power to Lot II. If Servo sues for an injunction preventing Powerco from erecting poles on or stringing wires over Lot I, the court should find for

(A) Servo, since an appurtenant easement is not alienable.

(B) Servo, since Powerco's proposed activity is outside the scope of the easement.

(C) Dom, since an appurtenant easement may be divisible for purposes incidental to its contemplated use.

(D) Dom, since every appurtenant easement contains and includes an easement in gross.

29. Assume for the purpose of this question only that the house which Dom was constructing on Lot I was to be three stories tall and would block the view from Servo's picture window of the Ragged Mountains. If Servo seeks an injunction to prevent the construction of Dom's house in a manner likely to obstruct Servo's view, the court should find for

(A) Servo, because Servo's house was built before Don began construction.

(B) Servo, because the construction of Dom's house as planned, will interfere with Servo's natural easement for air, light, and view.

(C) Dom, because Servo has no right to an undisturbed view of Ragged Mountains.

(D) Dom, unless he was aware of the view from Servo's picture window when he purchased the property from Onner.

30. Benefactor inherited from her grandfather an old building located in the City of Magnolia and known as the Benefactor Theater. Upon her death, she willed it "to the City of Magnolia for as long as the building is used as a theater for the presentation of dance, drama, and the arts." Subsequently, the Magnolia city council passed a valid resolution empowering the mayor to authorize temporary use of the theater building by an appropriate production company. The mayor orally authorized the Magnolia Ballet to occupy the theater without charge, and to use it for the presentation of dance productions. Three months

after moving into the Benefactor Theater, the director of the Magnolia Ballet advertised for bids from contractors for the renovation of the building. In requesting the bids, the director announced that it was his intention to remove all interior walls from the building, thus converting the Benefactor Theater into a "theater-in-the-round." The City of Magnolia instituted a proceeding in which it sought an injunction to prevent the Magnolia Ballet from permitting any permanent alteration in the structure of the Benefactor Theater. If the City of Magnolia is successful, it will probably be because the Magnolia Ballet

(A) paid no rent to the city.

(B) has not entered into any lease with the city.

(C) was a tenant at sufferance.

(D) was guilty of ameliorating waste.

31. Lawson was the owner of a two bedroom house which he rented to Tanner pursuant to a three-year lease which provided, "Tenant agrees that he will not assign or sublet the premises without the written permission of the landlord." Seven months after taking possession under the lease, Tanner asked Lawson's permission to sublet the house for a period of three months. Although Tanner offered to submit the names of potential subtenants to Lawson for approval, Lawson said that he would not approve the sublease to any person under any circumstances. Tanner thereafter sublet the premises to Subtor. Which of the following statements is most correct regarding the rights of Lawson?

   I. Lawson may elect to terminate the lease and evict Subtor.

   II. Lawson may successfully assert a claim against Tanner for breach of covenant.

(A) I only,

(B) II only.

(C) I and II.

(D) Neither I nor II.

Questions 32-33 are based on the following fact situation.

Grande died leaving a will which, among others, contained the following clauses:

> CLAUSE X — I hereby devise my realty located on Main Avenue to my wife for life, remainder to those of my children who achieve the age of twenty-one years. If any child of mine shall predecease me, or if any child of mine shall survive me but shall die before achieving the age of twenty-one years, that child's share shall be distributed equally among any of that child's children who shall marry, but if such child of mine shall die without issue, then his or her share shall be distributed among my children who achieve the age of twenty-one years.

> CLAUSE XI — I further direct that my realty located on Barret Drive be sold, and that the proceeds of such sale be given to a charity to be selected by my executor from among those to which I made contributions during the year immediately prior to my death, provided, however, that out of said proceeds two thousand dollars shall first be given to each of my children and grandchildren who survive to the age of twenty-two years.

At the time of Grande's death, he had no grandchildren, and was survived by three children: Alice who was eighteen years of age, Burton who was nineteen years of age, and Carrie who was twenty-two years of age. Two years after Grande's death, Alice gave birth to a child whom she named Gretchen. One week after Gretchen's birth, Alice died at the age of twenty. At the time of Alice's death, Burton was twenty-one years of age, and Carrie was twenty-four.

32. If Gretchen marries at the age of eighteen, will she be entitled to share in the Main Avenue property?

(A) Yes, because her interest vested within twenty-one years after the death of Grande.

(B) Yes, because her interest vested within

twenty-one years after the death of Alice.

(C) No, because at the time of Grande's death it was possible that Gretchen's interest would not vest until more than twenty-one years after the deaths of Alice, Burton, and Carrie.

(D) No, because at the time of Alice's death it was possible that a grandchild would subsequently be born who would marry more than twenty-one years after the deaths of Alice, Burton, and Carrie.

33. Assume for the purpose of this question only that Grande's realty on Barret Drive was sold by the executor of Grande's will for a price in excess of one million dollars, that Carrie demanded the executor pay her two thousand dollars under CLAUSE XI of Grande's will, and that the executor refused to pay, asserting that Carrie's interest was void under the Rule Against Perpetuities. Carrie should

(A) lose, because the interests of a charity cannot be made to depend upon the happening of an event which might occur after expiration of the period of perpetuities.

(B) lose, because it is possible that a grandchild will be born whose interest will not vest until more than twenty-one years after the death of all persons in being at the time of Grande's death.

(C) win, because Carrie's interest vested upon Grande's death, and is not dependent upon the number of children or grandchildren who survive to the age of twenty-two years.

(D) win, because Carrie is the first person who can possibly qualify to take under CLAUSE XI.

34. When Wendy married Herman, he had a child named Alba from a previous marriage, and had acknowledged himself to be the father of an illegitimate child named Barco. Together, Wendy and Herman had a child named Calli, and legally adopted another child named Delta. When Wendy

died, her will left a parcel of realty "to all children of my husband Herman, including those children not born of our marriage, and whether legitimate or illegitimate." At the time of Wendy's death, Calli's interest in the realty can be described as

(A) vested subject to partial divestment, since Herman may have more children in his lifetime.

(B) absolutely vested, since the class of persons to whom the realty was devised closed immediately upon Wendy's death.

(C) contingent, since Herman may subsequently acknowledge his paternity of other illegitimate children in being at the time of Wanda's death.

(D) void, since the birth of a person not in being at the time the interest was created may affect Calli's right in the realty.

35. As part of a divorce settlement between Wanda and Harold, Wanda conveyed a parcel of realty "to Harold for life; remainder to the children of Wanda who survive Harold." Which of the following interests does Harold have the power to convey to Bart?

(A) The right to possess the realty until Harold's death.

(B) The right to possess the realty until Wanda's death.

(C) The right to possess the realty until Bart's death.

(D) No right to possess the realty.

36. Forty years ago, the city of Rock Hill built a dam on Rock Creek for improvement of the city water supply. The city already owned the realty on which the dam was to be built, but before commencing construction it obtained from all downstream owners grants of the right to interfere with the creek water. Each of these grants included a conveyance of the right to completely stop the flow of Rock Creek by erecting the dam and of the right to release water from the dam into Rock

Creek when necessary in the city's discretion for proper management of the dam. All such grants were properly recorded. Since construction of the dam, the city has not released water from the dam into Rock Creek. As a result, Rock Creek has been completely dry for the past forty years. This year, because of an extremely wet winter, city hydrologists in charge of dam management have decided to release water from the dam into Rock Creek. Rogers is the owner of a 250 acre parcel of realty downstream from the dam and crossed by Rock Creek.

If Rogers institutes an action for an injunction to prevent the city of Rock Hill from releasing water into the creek, the court should find for

(A) Rogers, because no easement is valid which purports to authorize the maintenance of a private nuisance.

(B) Rogers, because the right to release water in the creek was terminated by the city's non-use of it for forty years.

(C) the city, because an incorporeal hereditament lies only in grant.

(D) the city, because it obtained the right to release water into the creek from all down-stream owners before constructing the dam.

37. Vestor owned a large tract of realty in a wooded and undeveloped region of the state. Holden, knowing that Vestor rarely visited his realty, built a cabin on it and began to occupy it on January 1, 1964, in hopes that Vestor would not discover his presence. Five years later in January 1969, Vestor learned that Holden was occupying the realty, and had him removed. In February 1969, however, Holden moved back in without Vestor's knowledge, and remained in possession for an additional sixteen years until March 1984. The law in the jurisdiction provides that one who openly, notoriously, hostilely, and continuously occupies realty for a period of twenty years acquires title to it by adverse possession. If Vestor instituted an action in April 1984 to eject Holden from the land, the court should find for

(A) Vestor, only if the removal of Holden in January 1969 was by court order.

(B) Vestor, only if the removal of Holden in January 1969 was by self-help without a court order.

(C) Vestor, whether the removal of Holden in January 1969 was by self-help or by court order.

(D) Holden, because his removal in January 1969 was temporary and therefore consistent with his claim of right.

38. Sercer and Bardel entered into a written contract for the sale of Sercer's realty. The contract was complete in all other respects, but failed to indicate the quality of title to be conveyed or the type of deed to be used. If the other party failed to perform, who could successfully sue for breach of contract?

(A) Sercer only, because the contract is clear as to Bardel's obligations.

(B) Either Sercer or Bardel, because the contract requires conveyance of marketable title by whatever deed is customarily used in the area.

(C) Either Sercer or Bardel, but only if parol evidence is available as to the intentions of the parties regarding the quality of title to be conveyed and the type of deed to be used.

(D) Neither Sercer nor Bardel, because of lack of mutuality of obligation.

Questions 39-41 are based on the following fact situation.

Several years ago, the Johnson Chemical Company developed a plan to use underground pipes for the purpose of transporting non-poisonous chemical wastes to a waste storage center located several miles away from its plant. At that time, it began negotiating for the right to lay an underground pipeline for that purpose across several tracts of realty. In return for a cash payment, the owner of Westacre executed a right-of-way deed for the installation and maintenance of the pipeline across his land. The right-of-way deed to Johnson Chemical Company was properly recorded. Westacre passed through several intermediate conveyances until it was conveyed to Sofield about fifteen years after the right-of-way deed was recorded. The intermediate deeds were recorded, but none mentioned the right-of-way.

Two years later, Sofield agreed to sell Westacre to Belden, by a written contract in which, among other things, Sofield agreed to furnish Belden with an abstract of title. Sofield hired Titleco, a reputable abstract company, to prepare the abstract. Titleco prepared an abstract and delivered it to Sofield. The abstract omitted any mention of the right-of-way deed. Sofield delivered the abstract of title to Belden. After examining the abstract, Beldon paid the full purchase price to Sofield who conveyed Westacre to Belden by a deed which included covenants of general warranty and against encumbrances. At the time of closing, Sofield, Belden, and Titleco were all unaware of the existence of the right-of-way deed. After possessing Westacre for nearly a year, Belden was notified by the Johnson Chemical Company that it planned to begin installation of an underground pipeline on its right-of-way across Westacre.

39. Assume for the purpose of this question only that Belden subsequently asserted a claim against Titleco for damages which Belden sustained as a result of the existence of the right-of-way. The court should find for

   (A) Titleco, because it was unaware of the existence of the right-of-way deed.

   (B) Titleco, because the right-of-way deed was outside the chain of title.

   (C) Belden, because Belden was a third party beneficiary of the contract between Sofield and Titleco.

   (D) Belden, because the deed executed by Sofield contained a covenant against encumbrances.

40. If Belden sues Sofield because of the presence of the right-of-way, the most likely result will be a decision for

   (A) Sofield, because Belden relied on the abstract of title prepared by Titleco in purchasing Westacre.

   (B) Sofield, because Sofield was without knowledge of any defects in the title to Westacre.

   (C) Belden, because the covenants in Sofield's deed to Belden were breached.

   (D) Belden, because Sofield negligently misrepresented the condition of title to Westacre.

41. Assume for the purpose of this question only that Belden sued for an injunction prohibiting the installation of the underground pipeline across Westacre. Which one of the following additional facts or inferences, if it was the only one true, would be most likely to lead the court to issue the injunction?

   (A) The Johnson Chemical Company sold its entire business to another company which was planning to continue operating the business exactly as Johnson had operated it, and it was the new company which was attempting to install the underground pipeline.

   (B) The Johnson Chemical Company's operation had changed since the conveyance of the right-of-way, and it was now planning to use the pipeline for the transportation of poisonous wastes.

   (C) No use of the right-of-way has been made since the conveyance eighteen years ago, and the law of the jurisdiction sets a ten year period for acquiring title by adverse possession or acquiring an easement by prescription.

   (D) In purchasing Westacre Belden detrimentally relied on the absence of any visible encumbrances, and the installation of an underground pipeline will result in substantial reduction in the value of the realty.

42. Immediately after World War II, the return of thousands of servicemen to the City of Pleasantville resulted in a severe housing shortage. To ease the problem, an area at the east end of town

which had been used primarily for agriculture was rezoned for residential use. As soon as the change in zoning took place, Buldin purchased a 200 acre farm located in that part of Pleasantville and subdivided it in accordance with applicable laws, naming the subdivision Pleasant Estates. Setting aside space for public streets, a public school, drainage, and utility easements, he created 500 building lots. He constructed a single family residence on each lot, and sold them all. Every deed contained a covenant restricting the land to single family residential use. In addition, a subdivision plan containing a description of the subdivision and of the deed restrictions was filed and a copy furnished to all buyers. Many of the residences in Pleasant Estates have since changed ownership, but all conveyances have contained restrictions similar to those originally used. Because Buldin was primarily interested in a quick profit, he built the houses cheaply. As a result, most of them are now in decaying condition. Several of the owners have reconstructed their homes. A few have torn them down completely and replaced them with new single-family dwellings. Commers is the owner of a lot in Pleasant Estates, having inherited it from his father who was one of the original purchasers from Buldin. Commers has torn down his house, and is about to begin construction of a three-story professional building in which he is planning to rent office space to doctors, lawyers, and dentists. If a group of homeowners in Pleasant Estates sue for an injunction to prevent Commers from building the office building, are they entitled to the injunction?

(A) Yes, because of the restrictions contained in the deeds.

(B) Yes, if the majority of homeowners oppose any change in the development.

(C) No, if most of the buildings in the subdivision are in a state of decay and therefore require reconstruction.

(D) No, because of the changing character of the neighborhood.

43. Lance Industries completed construction of a new office building and rented the entire ground floor to Tollup, an attorney, under a three year lease which fixed rent at six hundred dollars per month. Lance was unable to obtain a tenant to rent any other space in the building. Six months later, Tollup vacated the premises. In a claim by Lance against Tollup for rent for the balance of the term, which one of the following additional facts, if it were the only one true, would be most likely to result in a judgement for Tollup?

(A) The day after Tollup vacated, Lance rented the ground floor to another attorney on a month-to-month basis at a rent of five hundred dollars per month.

(B) The day after Tollup vacated, Lance began using the ground floor as a management office for the building.

(C) The reason Tollup vacated was that the building was located in a part of town not easily accessible by public transportation, and as a result many of Tollup's clients refused to travel to see him there.

(D) The reason Tollup vacated was that he had been disbarred and was disqualified from the practice of law.

44. Sorrel agreed to sell Blenheim a tract of realty known as Newacre by a written contract which said nothing about the interest to be conveyed. Sorrel subsequently delivered a deed which was complete in all other respects, but failed to indicate the interest conveyed. Blenheim received the deed and had it duly recorded. Which of the following statements is most correct about the effect of the deed?

(A) It conveys a fee simple absolute, resulting in liability for damages if Sorrel did not, in fact, hold such an interest at the time the deed was delivered.

(B) It conveys whatever interest Sorrel had at the time the deed was delivered.

(C) It conveys whatever interest Sorrel had at the time the contract of sale was formed.

(D) It does not effectively convey any interest in the realty.

Questions 45-48 are based on the following fact situation.

When Dado died, he was the owner of two hundred acres of undeveloped land. His will devised the land to his three daughters, Ada, Beatrix, and Connie as joint tenants. All three of them lived in a distant state, but after Dado's death Ada moved onto the land and began cultivating it. She grew grain and beans, realizing substantial profits from these farming activities almost immediately.

45. Assume for the purpose of this question only that shortly after Dado's death Ada became ill and died. Assume further that Ada's will devised her entire interest in the realty to Connie. Which of the following most correctly states the proportional interests which Beatrix and Connie would hold as a result?

   (A) Connie and Beatrix would be tenants in common with equal interests in the realty.

   (B) Connie and Beatrix would be joint tenants with equal interests in the realty.

   (C) Connie and Beatrix would be tenants in common, with Connie holding a two-thirds interest and Beatrix holding a one-third interest in the realty.

   (D) Connie and Beatrix would be joint tenants, with Connie holding a one-third interest and Beatrix holding two-thirds interest in the realty.

46. Assume that Ada recovered from her illness. Assume for the purpose of this question only that Beatrix subsequently sold her share of the land to Nuco by a valid deed containing covenants of general warranty. Which of the following statements would correctly describe the relationships between the parties?

   (A) Ada, Nuco, and Connie hold the land as joint tenants.

   (B) Ada, Nuco, and Connie hold the land as tenants in common.

   (C) Ada, Nuco, and Connie hold the land as tenants in common, but Ada and Connie have rights of survivorship as to each other's interests.

   (D) Ada and Connie hold equal shares of a two-thirds interest in the land as joint tenants, and Nuco holds a one third interest in the land as a tenant in common.

47. Assume for the purpose of this question only that the land had a reasonable rental value of $12,000 per year. Assume further that after Ada began realizing a profit from her farming enterprise, Connie asserted a claim against Ada for $4,000 per year, equivalent to one-third of the reasonable rental value. Which of the following facts or inferences, if it were the only one true, would be most likely to result in a judgment for Connie?

   (A) Farming was the best and highest use of the land.

   (B) A real estate developer had offered to purchase the land for substantially more than its reasonable market value, but Ada refused to sell her interest.

   (C) Connie had attempted to move onto the land, but Ada prevented her from doing so.

   (D) Ada erected permanent structures on land which she occupied for residential and agricultural purposes.

48. Assume for the purpose of this question only that three years after Dado's death Connie executed a quitclaim deed which purported to convey her interest in the farm to Pearl. If Pearl asserts a claim against Ada for a share of the profits which result from Ada's operation of the farm, which of the following would be Ada's most effective argument in defense against Pearl's claim?

   (A) A quitclaim deed is not sufficient to convey a joint tenant's interest in realty.

   (B) A quitclaim deed conveys only the interest held by the grantor.

   (C) A quitclaim deed is not sufficient to convey the grantor's right of survivorship.

(D) Joint tenancy requires unity of title.

49. Oliphant purchased a ten acre tract of realty known as Sellacre from Sella, paying one-half the purchase price upon closing, and giving Sella a note for the balance secured by a purchase money mortgage. Although Oliphant never missed a payment on the note, Sella foreclosed on Sellacre six months later by falsely certifying that Oliphant was in default, and by falsely swearing that notice of the foreclosure proceeding had been given to Oliphant as required by statute. Poser purchased Sellacre at the resulting foreclosure sale, receiving a sheriff's deed. Poser immediately recorded the deed and took possession of the realty. He constructed a residence on the land, and put a fence up around the building and a small area surrounding it. Since then he has openly and continuously occupied the land enclosed by the fence, but made no use of the land outside it.

Oliphant continued making payments to Sella according to the terms of his note. Because he lived in a distant part of the state, he was unaware of the foreclosure sale until eleven years later when he attempted to sell the realty. Then, when an abstract company informed him of the sale, he sued for an order setting aside the sheriff's deed to Poser and ejecting Poser from Sellacre. Poser counterclaimed for a judgment declaring him to be the owner of Sellacre by adverse possession.

A statute in the jurisdiction sets the period for acquiring title to realty by adverse possession at ten years. If the court decides that the sheriff's deed should be set aside, which of the following comments is most correct about Poser's interest in Sellacre?

(A) Poser has no lawful interest in Sellacre since he possessed it under color of a title which proved to be defective.

(B) Poser is the owner of the area surrounded by his fence, but has no lawful interest in the land outside the fence since he did not occupy or possess it.

(C) Poser is the owner of all of Sellacre, since

adverse possession cannot result in a subdivision of realty.

(D) Poser is the owner of all of Sellacre, since he occupied part of it under color of title to the entire tract.

50. Several years ago Ostend conveyed realty called Leafacre to Apple. Apple immediately resold Leafacre to her partner Banner, without recording the deed which she had received from Ostend. Banner duly recorded the deed which he received from Apple, and resold Leafacre two years later to Compton, who immediately recorded his deed. One year after Compton's purchase of Leafacre, Ostend purported to convey it to Zieman who immediately recorded his deed. The jurisdiction has a statute which provides that no conveyance of real estate is effective against a subsequent purchaser for value without notice unless it shall have been recorded. The official recording office does not maintain a tract index.

If Zieman asserts that his title is superior to Compton's, and sues Compton to quiet title to Leafacre, which of the following would be Zieman's most effective argument?

(A) The deed from Apple to Banner was recorded outside the chain of title.

(B) Apple did not have the power to convey Leafacre.

(C) Ostend was guilty of intentional misrepresentation in the sale of Leafacre to Zieman.

(D) Banner had constructive notice that Apple had not recorded the deed which she received from Ostend.

51. Docker owned a small parcel of real estate which fronted on Blue Lake, with a dock providing access to the lake. Because his friend Fischer owned a boat and enjoyed fishing on Blue Lake, Docker told him orally that he could launch his boat from the dock whenever he wanted to. Docker subsequently sold the realty to Ballantine, advising him that Fischer had permission to launch his boat from the dock. When he took title, Ballantine assured Docker that he would

continue to permit Fischer to use the dock. The next time Fischer attempted to do so, however, Ballantine ordered him off the realty and told him not to enter it again.

If Fischer sues for an order directing Ballantine to permit him to continue using the dock for launching his boat, the court should find for

(A) Fischer, because Ballantine purchased the realty with knowledge of Fischer's right.

(B) Fischer, because an easement in gross survives the sale of the servient estate.

(C) Ballantine, because Fischer's right to use the dock terminated or was revoked.

(D) Ballantine, because an easement appurtenant does not survive the sale of the servient estate.

52. In January, Torrey executed a will leaving a tract of realty known as Torrey Pines to "my brother Bob for life, remainder to be divided equally among Bob's children, share and share alike." At the time of the will's execution, Bob had two daughters, Donnie and Deborah. In March, Donnie and Deborah were killed in a boating accident. The following June, Torrey died. Fifteen years later, Bob executed a deed to Pomme purporting to convey "all my right, title, and interest in Torrey Pines." A year after he executed that deed, Bob died without a will. Bob was survived by his six year old son, Sol.

Which of the following correctly describes Sol's interest in Torrey Pines immediately BEFORE the death of Bob?

(A) Vested remainder subject to complete divestment.

(B) Vested remainder subject to partial divestment.

(C) Contingent remainder

(D) No valid interest.

53. Lardner rented a warehouse to Torrelson pursuant to a lease which fixed the rent at five hundred

dollars payable at the beginning of each month. The lease contained a provision stating that in the event Torrelson failed to pay rent as agreed, Lardner had the right to terminate the tenancy and re-enter the premises. After Torrelson missed two rent payments, Lardner threatened to institute an eviction proceeding unless the unpaid rent was paid immediately. The following day, Torrelson moved out, sending Lardner a check for one thousand dollars in payment of rent already owing. Also enclosed was an additional check for five hundred dollars in payment of the following month's rent and a letter which stated that it was Torrelson's intention to surrender the premises immediately. Lardner made no attempt to re-rent the warehouse, and it remained vacant for the balance of the term of Torrelson's lease. Upon its expiration, Lardner asserted a claim against Torrelson for unpaid rent from the date Torrelson vacated until the end of the lease term.

In deciding Lardner's claim against Torrelson, the court should find for

(A) Lardner, since Torrelson failed to pay the rent as agreed.

(B) Lardner, since the lease reserved a right of re-entry.

(C) Torrelson, since the lease reserved Lardner's right of re-entry.

(D) Torrelson, since, in effect, he gave Lardner a month's notice of his intention to vacate.

54. Older lived on 40 acres of land in a remote area. He split the land into two twenty-acre parcels. Lot 1 which contained his house, and Lot 2 on which there were no buildings. He subsequently negotiated for the sale of Lot 2 to Benedict. During the course of their discussions, Benedict told Older that he planned to build a small cannery on the land for the commercial processing of locally grown produce. They subsequently entered into a written contract for the sale of Lot 2, which contract contained no mention of restrictions regarding the use of the subject land.

Older thereafter realized that the construction of a commercial cannery on land adjacent to his home might disturb his peace and quiet, and reduce the value of his property. At the time scheduled for the closing of title, Older delivered a deed which stated: "Grantee does hereby covenant for himself, his successors and assigns that the realty conveyed herein shall not be used for any purpose other than the construction of a single story residential building." Benedict read the deed and accepted it, paying the full purchase price as agreed, but when Older asked him to sign the deed, Benedict refused to do so. The following day, Benedict had the deed recorded in accordance with law. Several months later Benedict completed construction of a commercial cannery on the land.

If Older sues Benedict for damages resulting from Benedict's construction of the cannery on the land adjacent to Older's, the court should find for

(A) Older, because the operation of a commercial cannery adjacent to a private residence constitutes a private nuisance.

(B) Older, because of the restrictive covenant contained in the deed.

(C) Benedict, because at the time the contract was made Older knew that Benedict intended to use the land for the construction of a commercial cannery.

(D) Benedict, because he did not sign the deed containing the restrictive covenant.

55. Farmcorp was a holding company which owned controlling interests in several agricultural enterprises. Because many of Farmcorp's holdings were expanding rapidly, Farmcorp retained a consultant to project and predict Farmcorp's real estate needs for the next fifty years. Based on advice which it received from its consultant, Farmcorp began looking for more land. Because Opus owned a 400 acre farm in the vicinity of one of Farmcorp's holdings, Farmcorp offered to purchase the land from him. Opus refused to sell, saying that he planned to work the land until he retired from farming. Instead, Opus and Farmcorp entered into a written option agreement pursuant to which, for an immediate cash payment,

Opus granted Farmcorp the right to purchase the land at a fixed price thirty years from the date the agreement was executed. The following year, Opus had a heart attack and sold the land to Pommard.

In subsequent litigation, a court should declare that Farmcorp's interest under the option agreement was

(A) invalid, unless Farmcorp recorded the option agreement.

(B) invalid under the Rule Against Perpetuities.

(C) valid only if Pommard had actual notice of the option when he purchased the land from Opus.

(D) valid because Farmcorp gave consideration for the option.

56. Sculpin was a sculptor who had created several well-known statues using a rare stone known as webbed granite which she purchased in Europe. While visiting the home of her friend, Patron, in the United States, she discovered a rich deposit of webbed granite on his land. When she told Patron how much money she had to pay for the stone in Europe, he told her that she could take as much webbed granite as she wanted from his land without charge for as long as he owned the land. Sculpin purchased a machine called a stone surfacer for use in processing and removing the stone from Patron's land. The stone surfacer weighed 40,000 pounds and was approximately 20 feet long by 20 feet wide by 20 feet tall. It was delivered in sections and assembled after delivery, but was not fastened to the ground in any way.

Two years later, Patron entered into a written contract to sell the land to Bannister. The contract referred to the subject of the sale as "all the realty located at... " followed by a metes and bounds description which adequately identified Patron's land. Prior to the closing, Sculpin dismantled and removed the stone surfacer. A statute in the jurisdiction provides that if part of the realty which is subject to a contract of sale is removed or destroyed prior to closing of title, the buyer may elect to take title subject to appropriate abatement of the purchase price. On the date set for closing, Bannister discovered that the stone surfacer had been removed and demanded that the selling price of the realty be abated under the above statute.

Should the selling price be abated?

(A) Yes, because the size and weight of the stone surfacer made it non-movable.

(B) Yes, if the stone surfacer was a fixture which became part of the realty.

(C) No, if Patron gave Sculpin permission to remove the stone surfacer.

(D) No, because the stone surfacer was not fastened to the ground.

Questions 57-58 are based on the following fact situation.

Several years ago, Owen sold a one acre parcel of realty called Streamside to Prospect, who immediately moved onto the land, built a cabin, and set up a mechanical apparatus for removing gold from the stream which flowed across the realty. Prospect never recorded the deed because he heard that he could save money on taxes that way. Two years later Owen, who was aware that Prospect had not recorded the deed, purported to sell Streamside to Arthur by a deed which Arthur immediately recorded. As a gift, Arthur subsequently conveyed the land to Bostoria, who recorded the conveyance. Neither Arthur nor Bostoria ever saw or inspected the land. Last month Bostoria sold Streamside to Campbell, delivering a quitclaim deed which Campbell immediately recorded. The jurisdiction has a statute providing in essence that no conveyance is valid against a subsequent purchaser for value without notice unless it is recorded.

57. Is Campbell's interest in Streamside superior to Prospect's?

(A) Yes, unless Prospect filed a claim under the

Federal Mining Act.

(B) Yes, unless Prospect has been in open and notorious possession of the land long enough to acquire title by adverse possession.

(C) No, if a reasonable inspection of the realty at the time of Campbell's purchase would have disclosed that Prospect was in possession.

(D) No, if at the time Bostoria conveyed Streamside to Campbell Bostoria was aware that Prospect was in possession to Streamside.

58. Assume for the purpose of this question only that a court declared Campbell's interest to be inferior to Prospect's. If Campbell instituted an action against Bostoria for damages, the court should find for

(A) Bostoria, unless at the time Bostoria conveyed Streamside to Campbell, Bostoria was aware that Prospect was in possession of Streamside.

(B) Bostoria, since his conveyance to Campbell contained no covenants of title.

(C) Campbell, since Bostoria did not give value for Streamside.

(D) Campbell, if a reasonable inspection by Bostoria would have revealed that Prospect was in possession of Streamside.

59. When Olivera died, among her personal effects was found a deed by which she purported to convey an interest in the Olive Vista Ranch to her nephew, Niles. Based on the deed, Niles claimed to have an interest in the realty, but the administratrix of Olivera's estate denied the claim. Which of the following facts or inferences, if it was the only one true, would provide Niles with his most effective argument in support of his claim?

(A) Before she died, Olivera told Niles that he would become the owner of the Olive Vista Ranch after she was gone.

(B) Niles was out of the country on the day that

Olivera executed the deed.

(C) The deed names as grantees, "Olivera and Niles as tenants in common."

(D) Olivera signed the deed two hours prior to her death.

60. Because it was her niece Nancy's birthday, Sandra duly executed a deed by which she conveyed her realty known as Sandy Acres to Nancy. Sandra was elderly and had been chronically ill for several years. On days when she did not feel well enough to go out, she frequently sent Chapel, her chauffeur, to run errands for her. One morning, she called Chapel into her room and handed him an envelope. "I want you to give this deed to my niece Nancy," she said. "I also want you to go to the bank and the grocery store. Be sure and call me before you come home." Chapel went first to the bank, and then to the grocery store. Then, before going to Nancy's house, he called Sandra to ask whether there was anything else she wanted him to do. He was advised on the telephone that Sandra had died soon after he left the house. Upon hearing this news, he returned immediately, without giving the deed to Nancy. Eventually, Nancy learned about the deed, and claimed title to Sandy Acres.

Which of the following is the most effective argument in opposition to Nancy's claim?

(A) Title does not pass until there is a physical delivery to the grantee or her agent.

(B) Sandra died before the deed could be recorded.

(C) The deed remained in Sandra's control until her death.

(D) The deed was an attempted testamentary substitute.

61. In 1954 Oola died, leaving a will which devised The Gables, a tract of real estate, "to Linville for life, and then to Roberts." Linville, who lived in a distant state, never took possession of The Gables. In 1956 Benson, who was Linville's brother, moved onto The Gables without informing Linville or obtaining his permission. Benson fenced most of the land, paid the real estate taxes as they came due, and lived in a house which he constructed on The Gables. He continued to occupy the realty until 1982, when Linville died without ever having learned of his brother's possession of The Gables. Under the jurisdiction's applicable statute of limitations, title by adverse possession may be acquired after ten years of continuous, open notorious, and hostile possession of realty. In 1982 Roberts discovered that Benson was in possession of The Gables, and commenced an action to eject him. Benson counterclaimed, seeking a judicial decree that he had acquired title by adverse possession.

Which of the following arguments is most likely to result in a victory for Roberts?

(A) Benson's possession of The Gables was not hostile, since he was Linville's brother.

(B) Benson's possession of The Gables was not open and notorious, since Linville did not know that he was occupying it.

(C) The period of limitations did not begin running against Roberts until Linville's death in 1982.

(D) Absent a unity of possessory right, no tacking of successive periods of adverse possession is permitted.

62. In 1982 Tillie died, leaving a will which in pertinent part read as follows: "I hereby give, devise, and bequeath my realty known as Whitehall to my husband for life, remainder to my children. If, however, any of my children shall predecease my husband, said child's share shall pass to said child's children to be distributed equally among them, share and share alike." When the will was executed in 1976, Tillie was married to Fred, and they had two children, Arthur and Belle. Fred died in 1977, in an automobile accident which also killed Arthur. Arthur had no children. The following year, Tillie married Sam. At the time of her death in 1982, Tillie was survived by Sam, Belle, and Charles. Charles, who had been born in 1981, was her child by Sam.

474 FINZ MULTISTATE METHOD

In a jurisdiction which has abolished the Rule in Shelley's Case, but which applies the common law Rule Against Perpetuities, which of the following most accurately describes the interests held by Tillie's children and grandchildren?

(A) The remainder to Tillie's children is valid, but the substitutionary gift to her grandchildren is void since the size of the class was not determinable at the time the interest was created.

(B) The remainder to Tillie's children and the substitutionary gift to her grandchildren are void since it was possible for Tillie to marry a person who was unborn at the time their interests were created.

(C) The remainder to Belle is valid, but the remainder to Charles and the substitutionary gift to his children are void since their lives were not in being at the time the interest was created.

(D) The remainder to Tillie's children and substitutionary gift to her grandchildren are valid.

63. Monty conveyed Blackacre to Wilson by a deed which contained the following provisions:

Monty hereby conveys the described realty to Wilson in fee simple, in return for Wilson's agreement that he shall use the land for residential purposes only, and that he will require any person to whom he grants an estate in said land to make the same promise.

Wilson used Blackacre for residential purposes for a period of twenty-two years, after which he commenced construction of a supermarket on the land. If Monty institutes an appropriate action in which he seeks a judgment declaring that Blackacre has reverted to him because of the change in use, Monty should

(A) win, because the language of the deed created a fee simple subject to an executory limitation.

(B) win, because Wilson has violated a covenant

contained in the deed by which Monty conveyed the property to him.

(C) lose, because the restrictive language of the deed violated the Rule Against Perpetuities.

(D) lose, because the language of the deed created no more than a contractual obligation.

64. In a will which is offered for probate today, realty is devised "to my children, but if my friend Morris is still alive thirty years after my death, to Morris." The interest of Morris is

(A) a valid contingent remainder.

(B) a valid executory interest.

(C) an invalid contingent remainder.

(D) an invalid executory interest.

Questions 65-66 are based on the following fact situation.

Owen was the owner of a 200 acre parcel of unimproved realty located on the edge of the town of Treewood. In 1978, when the area was largely uninhabited, she platted and obtained government approval for a subdivision of 100 acres to be known as Towne Estates. It was divided into 200 building lots, with necessary streets, and utilities and drainage easements. All lots in Towne Estates were conveyed during 1978, every deed containing provisions restricting use of the lots to single-family, one-story residences. Each deed contained the following language:

The restrictions contained herein are binding on the grantee, her heirs and assigns, and may be enforced by the owner or lawful occupant of any lot in the Towne Estates development.

The second parcel, known as Towne Heights, remained undeveloped. When the subdivision was created in 1978, applicable zoning ordinances permitted the use of land in the area for any purpose other than agriculture or heavy industry. In 1980, however, the opening of an airplane factory six miles from Treewood resulted in a population expansion. In 1981, the zoning laws were changed to restrict the use of land in the areas known as Towne Estates and Towne Heights to residential use for one, two or three family dwellings.

65. Assume for the purpose of this question only that Zevon purchased a lot in Towne Estates in 1978 and sold it to Feldman, who built a one-story single family residence thereon in 1979. Assume further that the house burned down in 1983, and that Feldman applied for a building permit for the construction of a three family dwelling on the same site. If a resident of Town Estates brings an appropriate action to prevent the construction of a multiple family dwelling, the court will most probably

(A) not prevent the construction, since zoning laws supersede restrictions contained in deeds.

(B) not prevent the construction, unless Zevon's deed to Feldman contained a restriction like that contained in Owen's deed to Zevon.

(C) prevent the construction, because the restriction contained in the deeds to the lots in Towne Estates runs with the land.

(D) prevent the construction, since a building destroyed by fire must be replaced, if at all, by a building of the same general character and use.

66. Assume for the purpose of this question only that Owen now seeks to develop the parcel known as Towne Heights as a residential subdivision of 75 lots. She wishes to place restrictions in the deeds limiting the use of lots in the subdivision to residential, and wants to make the restrictions enforceable by residents of Towne Estates. Under which of the following circumstances would her scheme be most likely to succeed?

(A) Restrictions in deeds to lots in Towne Heights limit their use to one, two, or three family dwellings.

(B) Restrictions in deeds to lots in Towne Heights are consented to by all purchasers of lots contained therein.

(C) All deeds to lots in Towne Heights contain a clause providing that the restrictions contained therein can be enforced by any resident of either Towne Heights or Towne Estates.

(D) Towne Heights is regarded as a part of a common development scheme which includes the land known as Towne Estates.

67. Oliver held a tract of land known as Rolling Hills in fee simple absolute. On March 1, she sold it to Garland for thirty thousand dollars cash, executing and delivering a deed of general warranty. On April 1, discovering that Garland had never recorded his deed, Oliver purported to sell the realty to Harriet, who was unaware that it had been previously sold to Garland. Harriet recorded her deed on April 13, after conducting a title search. Ira, who knew of the previous sale to Garland, told Harriet about it on April 15, offering her twenty-eight thousand dollars if she would quitclaim the property to him. Fearful that she might lose the property to Garland, Harriet accepted the offer, executing and delivering to Ira a quitclaim deed that same day. Garland recorded on April 16. Ira recorded on April 17.

The jurisdiction has a recording statute which provides that, "No conveyance of an interest in realty shall be good against subsequent purchasers unless it shall have been recorded." Whose interest is superior?

(A) Garland's, since his recording of April 16 placed Ira on constructive notice of his right.

(B) Garland's, since Ira had actual notice of the sale to Garland.

(C) Ira's, since Ira purchased for value before Garland recorded his deed.

(D) Ira's since Garland acquired no rights in Rolling Hills until April 16, which was after Ira's purchase from Harriet.

68. Oren was the owner of a 100 acre tract of land. After obtaining the necessary government approval, he platted a 75 acre subdivision consist-

ing of 135 building lots, with streets and utilities easements. He then sold the subdivision to a developer, retaining the other 25 acres for his own residential use. After the developer began building houses on the subdivision, the Jingle Telephone Company asked Oren to grant it an easement across a corner of his land so that it could bring service to the lots in the subdivision. Oren agreed and, by an appropriate written document which Jingle duly recorded, granted Jingle an easement over a described strip of his land "for the erection of such poles, and the placement of such wires, as Jingle shall require for the purpose of providing telephone service."

Two years later, Cable Television Company entered into a contract with Jingle pursuant to which it was licensed by Jingle to transmit cable television signals through Jingle's wires, in return for which it agreed to pay Jingle a substantial fee. The cable television signals sent through the wires were similar to telephone signals, and neither increased the wear and tear on Jingle's wires nor increased the burden on Oren's land.

If Oren brings an action against Jingle for an order enjoining it from permitting Cable's use of the wires, which of the following statements most accurately explains why Oren will lose?

(A) All easements appurtenant are freely alienable.

(B) All easements in gross are freely alienable.

(C) Although non-commercial easements in gross are not alienable, commercial easements in gross are alienable.

(D) Oren derived commercial benefit from the easement which he granted Jingle.

Questions 69-70 are based on the following fact situation.

On January 1, 1995, Olive borrowed $15,000 from Loner, signing a note secured by a mortgage on Olive View, her farm. The following August 1, Olive entered into a valid written contract to sell Olive View to Penny. The contract contained a provision by which Olive promised to deliver title free from encumbrances

on or before October 10. On October 10, 1995, Olive executed and delivered to Penny a deed which contained a covenant against encumbrances. On October 11, 1995, Loner duly recorded his mortgage on Olive View. On October 14, 1995, Penny recorded her deed.

A statute in the jurisdiction states: "In the event of a dispute between parties claiming conflicting interests in realty, the interest which shall first have been recorded shall have priority."

69. Assume for the purpose of this question only that, using funds which she had received from Penny upon the sale of the farm, Olive paid her debt to Loner in full on October 16, 1995, receiving and duly filing a satisfaction of mortgage. If Penny institutes an appropriate action against Olive for breach of the covenant against encumbrances, Penny is entitled to

(A) rescission of the deed, since the covenant was breached at the time the deed was delivered.

(B) damages for breach of contract, since the covenant was breached at the time the contract was made.

(C) nominal damages only, since Penny sustained no actual damages as a result of the existence of Loner's interest.

(D) nothing, since there has been no breach of the covenant.

70. Assume for the purpose of this question only that Olive did not pay Loner; that two years later Penny conveyed Olive View to Quentin by a deed dated October 30, 1997 which contained a covenant against encumbrances; that Loner instituted foreclosure proceedings one month after Quentin took title to the land; and that Quentin satisfied Loner's mortgage on December 10, 1997 by paying the debt contracted by Olive. Assume further that the statutory period of limitations on actions for breach of any covenant contained in a deed is one year. If Quentin instituted an action against Olive on December 20, 1997 for breach of the covenant against encumbrances, which of the following would be Olive's LEAST effective argu-

ment in defense?

(A) Quentin has an adequate remedy against Penny.

(B) An action for breach of a covenant contained in a deed can only be brought by the grantee named in that deed.

(C) Quentin had constructive notice of the mortgage.

(D) The statute of limitations bars Quentin's action against Olive.

71. Asa was in the business of manufacturing furniture and occupied a factory building which he rented for that purpose from Lawrence. When Lawrence told Asa that he was thinking of selling the building, Asa discussed with his brothers Bill and Carlo the possibility of purchasing it as an investment. After negotiation, they bought the building from Lawrence, who conveyed it by a deed which referred to the grantees simply as "Asa, Bill, and Carlo," but did not specify the tenancy created. The purchase price was one hundred thousand dollars, of which the three brothers paid half in cash at the time the deed was delivered. At the same time, the three brothers executed and delivered a deed of trust to secure a note for the balance of the purchase price. It was the intention of the three brothers to hold the building until rising real estate prices made it possible for them to sell it at a profit. Until then, it was understood that Asa would continue to occupy and use it for his business.

Subsequently, after requesting but not receiving contributions from his brothers, Asa spent six thousand dollars to improve the building by adding another bathroom, and three thousand dollars to preserve the building by repairing the roof which had begun to leak. In addition, Asa alone paid principal and interest on the outstanding trust deed obligation, and all real estate taxes on the property.

If Asa does not sue for partition, but brings an appropriate action for contributions against Bill and Carlo, which of the following statements most accurately describes the rights of the par-

ties?

I. Bill and Carlo must pay a portion of the sum which Asa spent on improving the property.

II. Bill and Carlo must pay a portion of the sum which Asa spent to pay principal, interest, and taxes on the property.

III. Any right which Asa has against Bill and Carlo is subject to a setoff for the reasonable rental value of the premises.

(A) I only.

(B) II only.

(C) II and III only.

(D) I, II, and III.

72. In January, Samuels bought a parcel of realty as an investment. In February, Brewer approached Samuels about purchasing the property, offering to pay substantially more than Samuels had paid for it. After negotiation, they entered into a contract for the purchase and sale of the property. The contract was complete in all other respects, but made no mention of the quality of title to be conveyed. Is the contract enforceable?

(A) No.

(B) Yes, and Samuels will be required to convey whatever title he held on the date the contract was signed.

(C) Yes, and Samuels will be required to convey whatever title he holds on the date title passes to Brewer, but will be liable for damages if such title is inferior to the title he held on the date the contract was signed.

(D) Yes, and Samuels will be required to convey marketable title.

73. Ona conveyed a tract of land known as Whiteacre to Bob and Carole. In which of the following circumstances are Bob and Carole most likely to

hold Whiteacre as tenants by the entirety?

(A) Bob and Carole were not married, but Ona, believing them to be married, executed a deed "to Bob and Carole as tenants by the entirety."

(B) Bob and Carole had been living together for twenty years, but were not married. Ona knowing that they were not married, executed a deed "to Bob and Carole as tenants by the entirety."

(C) Bob and Carole were not married, but believed themselves to be married. After Ona executed a deed "to Bob and Carole as joint tenants," Bob and Carole reconveyed Whiteacre to themselves "as tenants by the entirety."

(D) Bob and Carole were married, and Ona executed a deed "to Bob and Carole."

74. In 1970 Ollie, who owned a tract of land known as Oldacre in fee simple absolute, executed and delivered a valid deed which conveyed Oldacre "to my sisters Frances and Gala as joint tenants." Frances died in 1974, leaving a will which devised "all my interest in Oldacre to my daughter Dotty for life, then to Dotty's daughters Alice and Babs for life, then to all children of Alice and Babs whenever born." Gala died in 1976, leaving a will which devised "all my interest in Oldacre to my friend Mary." In 1977, Mary quitclaimed Oldacre to Iris in return for payment of $20,000.

In 1983 Iris contracted to sell Oldacre to Presley, promising to convey marketable title. When she tendered a general warranty deed on the date that title was to close, Presley refused to accept it on the ground that Iris's title was unmarketable.

In an appropriate action by Iris against Presley for damages resulting from his breach of contract, the court should find for

(A) Iris since Gala became the sole owner of Oldacre upon the death of Frances in 1974.

(B) Iris since her tender of a general warranty deed gave Presley sufficient protection,

even if her title was unmarketable.

(C) Presley, since a title granted by quitclaim deed is unmarketable.

(D) Presley since the devise contained in the will of Frances gave interests in Oldacre to Dotty, Alice, Babs, and the children of Alice and Babs.

75. When Tallen graduated from business college, he decided to go into the retail shoe business. He leased a small store for this purpose from Larson for a period of three years. The written lease contained a clause which prohibited subletting without the written permission of the landlord. After six months, Tallen found the shoe business unsatisfactory. He asked Larson to release him from the lease, but Larson refused to do so. One month later, Tallen assigned the balance of the lease to Anne, who moved in immediately. When Larson learned of the assignment, he demanded that Anne vacate the premises.

If Larson commences an appropriate proceeding to remove Anne from the premises on the ground that the assignment to her was void Larson should

(A) win, since the lease prohibited alienation of the leasehold interest.

(B) win, since in the absence of a specific agreement to the contrary, a tenant may not assign without the landlord's express permission.

(C) lose, unless the lease contains an express reservation of the landlord's right to terminate the leasehold in the event of a breach.

(D) lose, since restraints on alienation of estates in land are strictly construed.

76. Bilder constructed an office building and leased it to Tennyson for a period of twenty years. A clause of the lease provided that, "nothing herein shall be construed to prevent the assignment of rights or obligations hereunder by either the landlord or the tenant." Three years later, Tennyson assigned his interest under the lease to Acme

Investments, notifying Bilder of the assignment. The assignment agreement was signed by both Tennyson and Acme, and contained a promise by Acme to make rent payments directly to Bilder.

If Acme defaults in rent payments, which of the following statements is most correct about the rights of Bilder?

I. Bilder *can* recover from Acme as a third party beneficiary of the assignment agreement.

II. Bilder *cannot* recover from Tennyson under the lease.

(A) I only.

(B) II only.

(C) I and II.

(D) Neither I nor II.

77. Assume that a life tenant is in possession of realty the reasonable rental value of which exceeds the sum necessary to pay principal and interest on an obligation secured by an encumbrance on the realty. Which of the following correctly states the rule regarding the obligations of the life tenant and remainderman with respect to payment of an obligation secured by an encumbrance on the realty?

(A) The life tenant must pay both principal and interest.

(B) The life tenant must pay interest, and the remainderman must pay principal.

(C) The life tenant must pay principal, and the remainderman must pay interest.

(D) The remainderman must pay both principal and interest.

Questions 78-79 are based on the following fact situation.

Ogden was the owner of a three acre parcel of undeveloped land on Barrett Road. This was the only land which he owned on Barrett Road. He also owned a rectangular two hundred acre parcel known as Ogden's Retreat located outside of town. On his son Edward's birthday, Ogden executed a deed naming Edward as grantee, and containing the following descriptions:

(1) All of my property located on Barrett Road, consisting of four acres of undeveloped land.

(2) Five acres of Ogdens' Retreat, being those five acres which lie at the northeast corner of said realty, and constituting a square with its northernmost and easternmost sides lying on the north and east boundaries of Ogden's Retreat respectively.

As soon as he finished executing the deed, Ogden handed it to Edward, saying "Consider this a birthday present." Edward examined the deed, thanked his father, and handed it back to him asking that Ogden hold the deed for safekeeping. Ogden took it and locked it in the drawer of his desk. The following day, Ogden died. The executor of Ogden's estate has refused to deliver the deed to Edward and claims that there has been no valid conveyance of any land by Ogden to Edward.

78. If Edward commences an action to quiet title to the realty on Barrett Road, Edward should

(A) lose, since a deed which purports to convey more land than the grantor owns is void.

(B) lose, since there has been no delivery of the deed.

(C) lose, since there was no consideration for the transfer.

(D) win.

79. Is the description identified as (2) legally sufficient to result in a conveyance if all other requirements are found to have been satisfied?

(A) Yes, if it adequately identifies the realty described.

(B) Yes, but all that it can convey is an unidentified fractional portion of the land known as

Ogden's Retreat.

(C) No, since it lacks either metes and bounds or reference to existing government surveys.

(D) No, since a deed cannot convey less than the entire parcel of realty to which it refers.

Questions 80-81 are based on the following fact situation.

A state statute provides that:

> No fire insurance proceeds shall be payable under any policy issued in this state except to a person who holds an insurable interest in the insured property at the time a fire loss occurs. For purposes of this section, an insurable interest in realty is held only by the person suffering the risk of loss.

On May 10, Osgood contracted with Bennet for the sale of Osgood's home, title to close on or about July 1. According to the terms of the contract, Bennet was to move into the house on June 1, and to pay rent of $350 per month until title closed. On May 11, Bennet purchased a policy of fire insurance on the house from Mutual Insurance Company. Bennet moved in as planned on June 1. On June 10, Bennet fell asleep while smoking in bed. His cigarette ignited the bedclothing, causing a fire which severely damaged the house.

80. Assume for the purpose of this question only that Bennet filed the appropriate proof of loss with Mutual Insurance Company, but that Mutual refused to pay on the ground that Bennet lacked the necessary insurable interest. Assume further that Bennet sued Mutual for breach of contract. If the jurisdiction recognizes the doctrine of equitable conversion, a court should find for

(A) Bennet, since the risk of loss passed to him as soon as he contracted to purchase the house.

(B) Bennet, if, but only if, the fire resulted from his negligence.

(C) Mutual, if Osgood was the legal owner of the realty.

(D) Mutual, since at the time Bennet purchased the policy of insurance, he had no insurable interest in the realty.

81. Assume for the purpose of this question only that the jurisdiction does not recognize the doctrine of equitable conversion. Which of the following correctly states the rights of Bennet and Osgood?

(A) Bennet is not required to purchase the property, and Osgood must return any monies already received from Bennet in connection with the purchase.

(B) Bennet is not required to purchase the property, but Osgood may retain any monies already received from Bennet in connection with the purchase.

(C) Bennet is required to purchase the property, and must pay the full price agreed upon in the contract of sale.

(D) Bennet is required to purchase the property, but the purchase price should be abated to the extent of the damage.

82. When Oliphant was seventy-eight years of age, her doctors advised her that she had a terminal disease. She immediately arranged to have a will prepared in which she devised her realty "to my twin brother Michael for life, remainder to his children in fee simple." At the time of Oliphant's death, Michael was alive, and had two living children: Alvin, aged fifty-five, and Betty, aged fifty-three. The jurisdiction has a statute permitting the alienation of all future interests in land.

Which of the following most correctly describes the interest held by Alvin and Betty at the time of Oliphant's death?

(A) Contingent.

(B) Indefeasibly vested.

(C) Vested subject to complete defeasance.

(D) Vested subject to partial defeasance.

Questions 83-84 are based on the following fact situation.

Ohner was the owner in fee simple of a rectangular parcel of real estate, the north edge of which fronted on Joseph Street. He subdivided it into three lots, identified as Lots 1, 2, and 3. Lot 1 was the northernmost lot, and fronted on Joseph Street. Lot 3 was the southernmost lot, with Lot 2 located between the other two. After the subdivision, Ohner conveyed Lot 1 to Allen and Lot 2 to Benson, and retained Lot 3 for himself. Since there was no access to Lots 2 and 3, the deed to Allen created an easement across Lot 1 for access in favor of the occupants of Lots 2 and 3, and the deed to Benson created an easement across Lot 2 for access in favor of the occupants of Lot 3.

As soon as she received title, Allen constructed a residence on Lot 1. When it was completed, she sold the property to Johnson. Benson subsequently built a residence on Lot 2 with a large picture window facing south. Because the view from the window was unspoiled, the existence of the window increased the value of Benson's property.

Twenty-five years after Benson constructed the house, Primrose Lane, a public road, was dedicated and built along the westernmost boundary of Lots 1, 2, and 3, providing convenient access to all three parcels. When Primrose Lane was completed, Johnson informed Benson and Ohner that he would no longer allow them to cross his land to get to theirs, and erected a barrier across the access road which they had been using.

Ohner then began construction of a three-story, one family residence on his lot. If the building is completed, it will substantially interfere with the view from the picture window in Benson's house, reducing its value.

83. In an action by Ohner to enjoin Johnson from interfering with his continued use of the right of way across lot 1, the court should find for

(A) Ohner, since the removal of the need for the easement did not affect the right to the easement.

(B) Ohner, since to hold otherwise would adversely affect the rights of the occupants

of lot 2.

(C) Johnson, since an easement by necessity terminates when the need for it ceases to exist.

(D) Johnson, since the construction of a three-story building by Ohner will increase the burden of the servient estate.

84. In an action by Benson to enjoin Ohner from completing construction of the three-story building in such a way as to obstruct the view from Benson's picture window, the court should find for

(A) Benson, because upon purchasing lot 2 from Ohner, he received an implied easement for light, air and view.

(B) Benson, because he acquired by prescription an easement to an unobstructed view from the picture window.

(C) Benson, if, but only if, he notified Ohner of his intention to build the picture window at the time of his purchase of Lot 2 from Ohner.

(D) Ohner.

85. Oxford's employer transferred him to a branch of the firm located in another state, so Oxford listed his home for sale with Agee, a licensed real estate broker. Since the house had not been sold by the time Oxford was to move, he signed and delivered to Agee a power of attorney which stated, "I hereby appoint Agee as my attorney-in-fact, and authorize her to contract for the sale of my home on Baker Street." Three weeks later, Perk offered to buy Oxford's home. After showing Perk the power of attorney which Oxford had given her, and after negotiations, Agee prepared a contract for the sale of Oxford's home. The contract was complete in every other respect, but said nothing about the kind of deed which was to be executed. Perk and Agee both signed the contract, Agee signing, "Oxford, by Agee, his agent and attorney-in-fact." At the time when title was to pass, Oxford executed and tendered a quitclaim deed to the realty, but Perk refused to accept it. If Oxford

institutes an action against Perk for breach of contract, a court should find for

(A) Oxford, since the power of attorney was silent as to the type of deed which Oxford was willing to execute.

(B) Oxford, if the title which he held at the time the deed was tendered was, in fact, marketable.

(C) Perk, if the use of general warranty deeds is customary in the area.

(D) Perk, since a quitclaim deed does not convey valid title to realty.

Questions 86-87 are based on the following fact situation.

On March 1, Ogilvie and Baxton entered into a valid written contract for the sale of Ogilvie's home to Baxton at a price of $80,000, with title to close on June 15. It was further agreed that Baxton could move into and occupy the premises until title passed, at a rent of $500 per month to be added onto the purchase price and paid to Ogilvie at the time of closing. On April 15, before the closing, a fire completely destroyed the house. The fire was not the result of fault by either party.

86. Assume for the purpose of this question only that the jurisdiction applies the doctrine of equitable conversion. In litigation between the parties, which of the following statements best describes the rights of the parties?

(A) Baxton is obligated to purchase the premises at the price agreed in the contract.

(B) Baxton is obligated to purchase the premises, with the price reduced by the value of the house which was destroyed.

(C) Baxton may choose either to purchase the premises with the price reduced by the value of the house which was destroyed, or to cancel the contract and receive a refund of any monies paid by him to Ogilvie.

(D) The sales contract is canceled by operation of law, and Baxton is entitled to the return of any monies paid by him to Ogilvie.

87. Assume for the purpose of this question only that the jurisdiction does not apply the doctrine of equitable conversion. In litigation between the parties, which of the following additional facts, if it was the only one true, would be most likely to result in a finding that Baxton is obligated to purchase the premises at the price agreed upon in the contract of March 1?

(A) On March 1, Baxton purchased a policy of fire insurance on the premises which was in force on the day that the house was destroyed by fire.

(B) In accordance with an agreement between the parties, Baxton was in possession of the house on the day of the fire.

(C) On March 1 it was foreseeable to the parties that fire could damage the realty prior to the closing of title.

(D) Destruction of the house resulted in a relatively minor reduction in the value of the realty.

88. By a will executed in 1983, Ogden devised a parcel of commercial realty known as Greenacre "to my niece Agnes and her heirs for as long as the property is not used for the sale of alcohol; but if the property is ever used for the sale of alcohol, to the National Cancer Association, a charitable organization." Ogden died on July 7, 1985.

In a jurisdiction which applies the common law Rule Against Perpetuities, which permits the alienation of all future interests in land, and which has abolished the destructibility rule, which of the following most correctly describes the interest of the National Cancer Association in Greenacre on July 8, 1985?

(A) Valid contingent remainder.

(B) Valid executory interest.

(C) Void executory interest.

(D) Void contingent remainder.

89. On January 15, 1985, Olly executed a deed conveying a parcel of realty "to Antoine and his heirs until the United States goes to war with the Republic of Platano, and in that event to Borsell and her heirs." On January 17, 1985, members of the armed forces of the Republic of Platano placed the president of that country under arrest, and declared themselves to be "The Revolutionary Government of the Republic of Platano." The following day, the President of the United States ordered the United States Marine Corps to invade the Republic of Platano for the purpose of protecting American university students who were studying there.

On January 16, 1985, Antoine's interest in the realty is best described as

(A) a fee simple absolute.

(B) a fee simple determinable on special limitation.

(C) a quasi-life estate subject to a condition subsequent.

(D) void under the Rule Against Perpetuities.

90. Ossie was the owner of a forty-acre tract of realty the northern boundary of which lay along the shore of Lake Hammer, and the southern boundary of which lay along Carpenter Road. Twenty years ago, Ossie split the tract into two equal parcels. Parcel 1 fronted on Lake Hammer, and Parcel 2 fronted on Carpenter Road. Ten years later, Ossie sold a lot consisting of a three-acre portion of Parcel 1 to Arcturo. Arcturo's lot fronted on the lake, and was surrounded on its other three sides by the balance of Parcel 1. Because ingress and egress to the lot without crossing Ossie's land was impossible, Ossie granted Arcturo an easement from Carpenter Road to the lot. The easement crossed Parcels 1 and 2 at a location which was described by metes and bounds in the grant deed. Arcturo built a cabin on the lot, and constructed a driveway leading from the cabin to his easement.

Five years later, Ossie sold the remaining land to Devo.

Devo subdivided it into 60 building sites, dedicating roads and drainage easements as required by state law. None of the roads in Devo's subdivision followed the path of Arcturo's easement, but two paved roads led from Carpenter Road to Arcturo's driveway. Arcturo began using the paved roads as soon as they were completed to gain ingress and egress to his property. Two months later Devo began building a house on the site of Arcturo's easement.

If Arcturo asks a court to stop Devo from building over his easement, the court should find for

(A) Devo, because the dedication and construction of roads leading to Arcturo's driveway removed the strict necessity for the initial right-of-way.

(B) Devo, because unity of ownership resulted in a destruction by merger of the easement.

(C) Arcturo, because he did not consent to relocation of his easement.

(D) Arcturo, because an easement in gross is freely alienable by the holder of the dominant estate.

Questions 91-92 are based on the following fact situation.

Olsen was the owner in fee simple of a parcel of realty known as Oldacre. On May 1, Olsen executed two deeds. Deed #1 purported to grant an undivided one-quarter interest in Oldacre to Olsen's chauffeur Callender. Deed #2 purported to grant an undivided one-quarter interest in Oldacre to Olsen's nephew Norton.

On May 1, Olsen handed Callender Deed #1, saying, "Because you have been a good and faithful chauffeur for all these years, I'm giving you this deed. But it isn't to take effect until after my death." Callender thanked Olsen and took the deed.

On May 2, Olsen sent for her nephew Norton. She said, "I was planning to leave you an interest in Oldacre in my will, but I see no reason why you should have to pay inheritance tax. So I'll give it to you while I'm still alive if you promise to move in here with me some time during the next year." Norton promised that he would do so, and Olsen gave him Deed #2, saying, "Then it's yours." Norton read the deed, thanked Olsen, and handed the deed back to Olsen for safekeeping. Olsen placed it in a drawer of her desk.

On May 7, Olsen argued with Norton. Angry, Olsen tore Deed #2 into eight pieces and returned them to her desk drawer. On May 10, Olsen died, leaving no will. Following Olsen's death, Callender and Norton each claimed a right to an undivided one-quarter interest in Oldacre. The administrator of Olsen's estate denied both claims.

91. If Callender seeks a judicial declaration that he held a possessory interest in Oldacre on Olsen's death which would be his most effective argument

   (A) Callender's possession of Deed #1 raises an irrebuttable presumption that the conveyance was effective at the time the deed was delivered.

   (B) On May 1 Callender received a remainder interest in Oldacre.

   (C) The deed was a testamentary substitute.

   (D) Olsen's death completed delivery of the deed.

92. In an appropriate proceeding, should a court find that Norton held a possessory interest in Oldacre on Olsen's death?

   (A) No, because Deed #2 was an attempted testamentary substitute.

   (B) No, because Olsen's possession of the deed raises an irrebuttable presumption that there was no effective delivery.

   (C) Yes, because there was an effective conveyance to Norton on May 2.

   (D) Yes, because Norton detrimentally relied by promising to move in with Olsen.

93. The City of Hampshire owned land known as Hampshire Heights which was located outside the city limits, east of the city itself. Because the Hampshire River ran along the western edge of Hampshire Heights, the City of Hampshire built a bridge across the river more than fifty years ago. The eastern part of Hampshire Heights had once been used as a storage yard for city maintenance equipment, and was surrounded by an eight foot chain link fence. The part of Hampshire Heights between the fenced yard and the bridge had been used primarily as a dirt road connecting the bridge to the storage yard.

Due to periodic flooding of the Hampshire River, the City of Hampshire stopped using the Hampshire Heights storage yard and bridge thirty years ago. At that time, Adpo built a wooden shack on that portion of Hampshire Heights which had formerly been used as a dirt road between the storage yard and the bridge. Since then, Adpo has been living in the shack and has been raising donkeys on the land formerly used as a dirt road. In addition, he planted a vegetable garden which produced food for himself and his donkeys.

Earlier this year, the City of Hampshire decided to begin using the Hampshire Heights storage yard again and demanded that Adpo remove himself and his possessions. Adpo refused, asserting that by adverse possession he had become the owner of the land which he occupied. A statute in the jurisdiction conditions ownership by adverse possession on twenty years' continuous, hostile, open and notorious possession.

If the City of Hampshire institutes a proceeding to eject Adpo from Hampshire Heights, the outcome is most likely to turn on whether

   (A) the City of Hampshire had knowledge that Adpo was in possession of part of Hampshire Heights.

   (B) the jurisdiction permits the acquisition of city property by adverse possession.

   (C) Adpo paid taxes on the land which he occupied.

   (D) Adpo occupied Hampshire Heights under color of title.

94. Soon after Harold and Wilhemina married, they

became interested in the purchase of a home with a price of $75,000. Because neither of them had been employed for very long, they were unable to find a bank to lend them money for the purchase. The seller indicated that he would be willing to accept a note for part of the purchase price if Harold and Wilhemina could obtain an acceptable co-signor.

Wilhemina's mother Marion said that she would give them the money for the down payment and co-sign the note if Wilhemina and Harold promised to make all payments on the note as they came due, and if the three of them took title to the property as joint tenants. All agreed. On the day title closed, Marion paid $25,000 cash to the seller, and she, Harold, and Wilhemina all signed a note promising to pay the balance, secured by a mortgage on the realty which they all executed. The seller executed a deed conveying the realty to Harold, Wilhemina, and Marion as joint tenants.

Harold and Wilhemina moved into the house, but Marion never did. The following year Marion died, leaving a will purporting to devise her interest in the realty to her husband Allan. The year after that, Wilhemina and Harold were divorced. Wilhemina subsequently executed a deed purporting to convey her interest in the realty to Bernard. Harold subsequently executed a deed purporting to convey his interest in the realty to Charles.

Which of the following best describes the interests of Allan, Bernard, and Charles in the realty?

(A) Allan, Bernard, and Charles are tenants in common, each holding a one-third interest.

(B) Bernard and Charles are tenants in common, each holding a one-half interest.

(C) Bernard and Charles are joint tenants as to a two-thirds interest, and tenants in common as to a one-third interest.

(D) Allan, Bernard and Charles are joint tenants, each holding a one-third interest.

Questions 95-96 are based on the following fact situation.

Folger was the owner in fee simple absolute of a tract of land known as Flying Acres. On January 10, 1983, Folger borrowed $20,000 from Lender, and executed a note secured by a mortgage on Flying Acres. On April 30, 1983, as a twenty-first birthday present, Folger executed a grant deed conveying Flying Acres to his son Santor. The deed made no mention of the mortgage held by Lender. On May 15, 1983, Lender duly recorded his mortgage. On May 17, 1983, Santor duly recorded his deed. Neither Folger nor Santor ever made any payments to Lender.

95. Assume for the purpose of this question only that the jurisdiction has a statute which provides that "No conveyance, transfer, or mortgage of real property shall be good and effectual in law or equity against creditors or subsequent purchasers for value and without notice, unless the same be recorded." If Lender attempts to foreclose on the mortgage, will he succeed?

(A) Yes, because Folger executed the mortgage to Lender before executing the deed to Santor.

(B) Yes, because Lender recorded his mortgage before Santor recorded his deed.

(C) No, because Santor did not take Flying Acres "subject to" Lender's mortgage.

(D) No, because Lender is not a purchaser for value.

96. Assume for the purpose of this question only that the jurisdiction has a statute which provides that "Every conveyance of an interest in real estate which shall not be recorded shall be void against any subsequent grantee in good faith of the same real estate or any portion thereof whose conveyance shall be first duly recorded." If Lender attempts to foreclose the mortgage, will he succeed?

(A) No, because Lender's mortgage was

recorded outside the chain of title.

(B) No, because Santor did not have actual or constructive knowledge of Lender's interest at the time Flying Acres was conveyed to him.

(C) Yes, because Lender's interest was recorded prior to Santor's interest.

(D) Yes, because Santor did not give consideration for the conveyance from Folger.

Questions 97-98 are based on the following fact situation.

On April 1, Onda's grandmother died, leaving a will which purported to devise to Onda a 90 acre parcel of realty known as Southacre and an adjoining 10 acre parcel known as Northacre.

On May 1, Onda executed a general warranty deed containing covenants of title and quiet enjoyment, which purported to convey to Alton "a 100 acre tract of land consisting of a 90 acre parcel known as Southacre and a 10 acre parcel known as Northacre."

On June 15, Alton sold Northacre and Southacre to Berkley, executing a general warranty deed describing both parcels, and containing covenants of title.

On July 1, Onda learned that just before her death, his grandmother had sold Northacre to Naylen. Unaware of Alton's conveyance to Berkley, Onda offered Naylen $10,000 to convey Northacre to Alton. On July 2, Naylen accepted Onda's offer, and conveyed Northacre to Alton, by general warranty deed containing covenants of title.

97. Assume for the purpose of this question only that Berkley institutes an action against Onda for breach of covenant. The court should find for

(A) Onda because he cured the breach by procuring a conveyance of Northacre to Alton.

(B) Onda because Onda did not purport to convey the realty to Berkley.

(C) Berkley because the covenant of quiet

enjoyment runs with the land.

(D) Berkley because Onda's covenant was breached when Alton purported to convey Northacre to Berkley.

98. Assume for the purpose of this question only that Berkley institutes an appropriate proceeding for an order declaring himself to be the owner of Northacre. Which of the following would be Berkley's most effective argument in support of his claim?

(A) Naylen's conveyance of Northacre to Alton was the result of an attempt by Onda to conform the title to the covenant.

(B) Alton has an effective remedy against Onda.

(C) Alton's intention was to convey Northacre to Berkley on July 1.

(D) Alton's conveyance to Berkley on June 15 estops Alton from asserting his title to Northacre.

Questions 99-100 are based on the following fact situation.

Orr was the owner of two parcels of land, one known as Greenacre, and the other known as Redacre. By a deed dated January 1, she granted Greenacre "to First Foundation for as long as the realty is used as a home for the elderly, but if said realty shall ever cease to be used as a home for the elderly, to Second Foundation." By a deed dated January 2, she granted Redacre "to Nephew for life, remainder to Niece, but if the realty shall ever be used for any purpose other than residential, to Second Foundation." First Foundation and Second Foundation are both charitable organizations. Nephew and Niece are relatives of Orr.

99. Second Foundation has a valid future interest in

(A) Greenacre only.

(B) Redacre only.

(C) Greenacre and Redacre.

(D) Neither Greenacre nor Redacre.

100. Assuming that Second Foundation's interest in Redacre is valid, it is best described as a

   (A) vested remainder subject to divestment upon a condition subsequent.

   (B) contingent remainder.

   (C) shifting executory interest.

   (D) springing executory interest.

Questions 101-102 are based on the following fact situation.

Lattimer leased an office to Torry for a period of five years by an agreement which prohibited assignment by the tenant without the landlord's written permission. Two years after taking occupancy, Torry requested Lattimer's permission to assign the balance of his leasehold to Antun. After checking Antun's credit, Lattimer wrote Torry that the assignment was acceptable to him so long as Antun personally assumed all obligations of the lease. Torry's attorney prepared an agreement by which Torry assigned all his rights under the lease to Antun and Antun agreed to personally assume all obligations under the lease. After the agreement was signed by Torry and Antun, Torry's attorney sent a copy of it to Lattimer. Antun moved into the premises and began paying rent to Lattimer.

101. Assume for the purpose of this question only that after paying rent for six months, Antun abandoned the premises and made no further payment. If Lattimer asserts a claim against Torry for damages resulting from Antun's non-payment of rent, the court should find for

   (A) Torry, because Lattimer consented to Torry's assignment to Antun.

   (B) Torry, because there was a novation.

   (C) Torry, because Antun personally assumed all obligations under the lease.

   (D) Lattimer.

102. Assume the following facts for the purpose of this question only: After paying rent for six months, Antun assigned the balance of the lease-

hold to Bates. Bates paid rent directly to Lattimer for two additional months and then stopped paying rent and abandoned the premises. In an action by Lattimer against Antun for unpaid rent, the court should find for

   (A) Lattimer.

   (B) Antun, because Bates paid rent directly to Lattimer for two months.

   (C) Antun, because there was no privity of contract between Lattimer and Antun.

   (D) Antun, because Antun was only obligated to pay rent so long as he remained in possession of the premises.

103. Pursuant to a written lease, Tolliver rented a two acre parcel of realty from Lockett for a period of two years. During the period of his tenancy, Tolliver made substantial and valuable improvements to the realty. Prior to the termination of the lease period, Tolliver told Lockett that he intended to remove the improvements. Lockett objected, asserting that the improvements had become part of the realty and threatening to sue Tolliver if he made any attempts to remove the improvements. Tolliver thereupon sued for a judicial declaration that he was entitled to remove the improvements.

   Which of the following additional facts or inferences, if it was the only one true, would be most likely to result in a judgment for Tolliver?

   (A) The value of the improvements made by Tolliver exceeded $20,000.

   (B) The improvements made by Tolliver were not of a kind which the reasonable landlord would have expected a tenant to make.

   (C) The written lease was silent regarding the tenant's right to make or remove improvements.

   (D) The improvements made by Tolliver could be removed without causing any damage to the realty.

104. Ocie was the owner in fee simple of a rectangular parcel of realty which was five hundred feet deep

with one hundred feet of frontage on Cameron Avenue. He divided it into two building lots, each forty-five feet wide by five hundred feet deep, with a strip ten feet wide and five hundred feet deep between them. He sold one lot to Anthony and the other to Bernice, deeding the ten foot strip between the lots to Anthony and Bernice as tenants in common. Anthony and Bernice both wish to construct commercial buildings toward the rear of their lots, and plan to use the ten-foot strip between the lots as a driveway for access to the buildings in the rear. Each fears, however, that the other will sell, and that the new owner will sue to partition the ten foot strip, cutting off access to the rear of the lot.

If Anthony and Bernice seek your advice as to how best to prevent this from happening, you should suggest that they

(A) enter into a contract not to partition, inserting language which specifically makes the agreement binding on the heirs, assigns, and successors of each.

(B) convey the property to themselves as joint tenants.

(C) take no legal action, since tenants in common have no right of partition.

(D) partition the strip into two five-foot wide strips, each granting the other an easement over his/her strip and recording the right-of-way deeds.

Questions 105-107 are based on the following fact situation.

In 1976, Testor executed a will by which he devised his realty known as Testacre "to Agatha for life; and upon the death of Agatha as follows: a one-third interest to the children of Agatha, a one-third interest to the children of Brooke, and a one-third interest to the children of Carmody, but if any of Carmody's children should fail to survive to the age of 25 years, then the interest of such child or children of Carmody shall pass to all grandchildren of Carmody equally, share and share alike."

At the time the will was signed, Agatha had a son

named Albert. In 1980, Albert was heavily in debt to Koppell who was threatening to commence an involuntary insolvency proceeding against him. To induce Koppell to refrain from commencing the proceeding, Albert executed a quitclaim deed conveying his interest in Testacre to Koppell.

When Testor died in 1982, Brooke had a twenty-two year old daughter named Babs. In 1983, Babs sold her interest in Testacre to Lincoln, executing a quitclaim deed which named him as grantee.

In January 1985, Carmody gave birth to a baby boy whom she named Carrera. In June 1985, Agatha died. Her only surviving child was Albert. At the time of Agatha's death, Brooke's only living child was Babs and Carmody's only living child was Carrera.

Statutes in the jurisdiction abolish the Rule in Shelley's Case and permit the alienation of future interests in land.

105. Assume the following facts for the purpose of this question only: In August 1985, Albert contracted to sell a one-third interest in Testacre to Purch, agreeing to convey marketable title. On the day title was to pass, Albert tendered a general warranty deed, but Purch refused to accept it, asserting that the quitclaim which Albert had executed in 1980 was a cloud on the title. If Albert sues Purch for breach of contract, the court should find for

(A) Purch, since a quitclaim deed conveys whatever interest the grantor possesses at the time of its execution.

(B) Purch, since Albert received no valid interest in Testacre.

(C) Albert, since even if title was not marketable, his tender of a general warranty deed gave Purch sufficient protection.

(D) Albert, since he held marketable title to a one-third interest in Testacre.

106. Which of the following best describes Lincoln's interests in Testacre on the day AFTER Agatha's death?

(A) An indefeasible one-third interest.

(B) A one-third interest subject to partial defeasance should Brooke have any subsequent children.

(C) A one-third interest subject to complete defeasance should Brooke have any subsequent children.

(D) No valid interest.

107. Which of the following best describes Carrera's interest in Testacre on the day BEFORE Agatha's death?

(A) Valid contingent remainder.

(B) Contingent remainder, void under the Rule Against Perpetuities.

(C) Valid vested remainder subject to a condition subsequent.

(D) Vested remainder subject to a condition subsequent, void under the Rule Against Perpetuities.

Questions 108-109 are based on the following fact situation.

By grant deed, Oldham conveyed a parcel of realty "to the Church of the Lord so long as the property is used for church purposes, but if the grantee permits the property to be used for any purpose other than a church purpose, the property shall revert to the grantor." Two weeks after receiving title, the Church of the Lord filed an application with the county Building Department for a permit to construct a house of worship on the parcel. Prior to issuing the permit, the Building Department published notice of the Church's application as required by state law. Upon seeing the notice, Nabor, who owned an adjacent parcel, advised Church officials that he had been driving across the parcel to gain access to his land for more than thirty years. He claimed that he had thus acquired an easement by prescription and threatened to commence an action to quiet title to the realty for the purpose of having his easement judicially recognized. The county Building Department informed officials of the Church of the Lord that no building permit could be issued while an

action to quiet title was pending. Because it could take several years for such an action to reach conclusion and because the easement claimed by Nabor would not significantly interfere with building plans, the church attorney advised granting him the easement which he claimed to hold. Church officials subsequently executed a deed granting Nabor the easement which he claimed.

108. Which of the following best describes the interest held by Oldham in the realty on the day after his grant to the Church of the Lord?

(A) Contingent remainder.

(B) Reversion.

(C) Possibility of reverter.

(D) Shifting executory interest.

109. Assume for the purpose of this question only that on the day after the Church of the Lord granted an easement to Nabor, Oldham asserted that Nabor's use of the premises was other than for church purposes, and instituted an action for an order declaring that he was the owner of the realty. Which of the following would be the Church of the Lord's most effective argument in opposition to Oldham's claim?

(A) The Church of the Lord acted in good faith on the advice of its attorney.

(B) The language of the deed created a fee simple determinable.

(C) Nabor's easement pre-existed Oldham's grant to the Church of the Lord.

(D) Oldham's interest violated the Rule Against Perpetuities.

Questions 110-112 are based on the following fact situation.

When Oliphant purchased her home, she borrowed part of the purchase price from National Bank. Simultaneously with receipt of title to the realty, she executed a note payable to National Bank and secured by a mortgage on the realty. Subsequently, Oliphant sold the realty to April who took it subject to the mortgage and assumed the mortgage. Two years later, April sold the property to Beryl who also took it subject to the mortgage and assumed the mortgage. The following year, Beryl sold the property to Carrol, who took it subject to the mortgage, but did not assume the mortgage.

For two years, Carrol made payments on the note to National Bank. Then, because of changes in the area, the property decreased sharply in value, and Carrol stopped making payments.

110. Assume for the purpose of this question only that National Bank sued Carrol on the note. The court should find for

   (A) National Bank, because it is a third party beneficiary of the agreement between Carrol and Beryl.

   (B) National Bank, only if the mortgage executed by Oliphant contained a "due on sale" clause.

   (C) Carrol, only if the mortgage executed by Oliphant contained a clause permitting buyers of the realty to take it "subject to" the mortgage.

   (D) Carrol, because she did not agree to pay the note.

111. Assume for the purpose of this question only that the mortgage executed by Oliphant contained a clause which specifically permitted buyers of the premises to take them "subject to the mortgage" and/or to "assume the mortgage." If National Bank sues Oliphant, April and Beryl on the note, from which of them is it entitled to recover?

   (A) Oliphant only.

   (B) Beryl only.

   (C) Oliphant and Beryl only.

   (D) Oliphant, April, and Beryl.

112. Assume for the purpose of this question that National Bank assigned the mortgage to Investco, and that Investco instituted a foreclosure action

against Carrol. If Carrol opposes the foreclosure, the court should find for

   (A) Investco, but only if the mortgage executed by Oliphant contained a clause permitting assignment by National Bank.

   (B) Investco, if payments due under the note executed by Oliphant continue to be unpaid.

   (C) Investco, but only if the value of the realty exceeds the unpaid balance on the note.

   (D) Carrol, because she did not assume the mortgage.

113. Ostendigger was the owner of a parcel of realty which was 600 feet deep with 100 feet of frontage on the north side of Public Road. After complying with all his state's legal requirements, he subdivided the parcel into three lots, each 100 feet by 200 feet in size. Lot 1 was the only one which fronted on Public Road. Lot 2 was north of Lot 1, and Lot 3 was north of Lot 2. In order to assure that the occupants of Lots 2 and 3 would have access to their property, the deeds created a 12-foot-wide easement from Public Road across Lot 1 for the benefit of Lots 2 and 3, and across Lot 2 for the benefit of Lot 3. Ostendigger sold Lot 1 to Aggie, Lot 2 to Bolton, and Lot 3 to Corfu. Bolton and Corfu used the easement for three years, creating by their use a bare dirt road across Lots 1 and 2. They found, however, that whenever there were heavy rains, the dirt road became muddy and passage became difficult. Because Corfu was in the construction business, he offered to construct a 24-foot-wide paved road across Lots 1 and 2, at his own expense, for use by all persons with a legal right to the easement. Aggie consented to its construction across Lot 1, but Bolton stated that he would not permit Corfu to construct such a road on Lot 2. If Corfu institutes a proceeding for an order compelling Bolton to permit the construction across Lot 2, the court should find for

   (A) Corfu, if the construction is necessary to prevent the road from becoming muddy after heavy rains.

(B) Corfu, because he is willing to construct the road at his own expense.

(C) Bolton, because the construction of such a road would impose an additional burden on the servient estate.

(D) Bolton, unless construction of a paved road would improve the values of Lots 2 and 3.

114. When Bridey and Gallon married, Gallon's mother decided to give them a parcel of realty known as Whiteacre as a wedding present. She executed a deed conveying Whiteacre "to Gallon and Bridey, husband and wife, as joint tenants" and handed it to them at the wedding reception. Two years later, Bridey left Gallon. Although she and Gallon did not divorce, Bridey began living with a man named Thomas. At Thomas' request, Bridey executed a quitclaim purporting to convey her interest in Whiteacre to Thomas. In a jurisdiction which recognizes tenancy by the entirety, which of the following statements is most correct about the interest which Thomas received as a result of the quitclaim executed by Bridey?

(A) Thomas received no valid interest, since a quitclaim extinguishes the rights of the person executing it, but does not necessarily confer any rights on the person receiving it.

(B) Thomas became a joint tenant with Gallon, since a quitclaim conveys whatever title the grantor held at the time of its execution.

(C) Thomas became a tenant by the entirety with Gallon, since a quitclaim conveys whatever title the grantor held at the time of its execution.

(D) Thomas became a tenant in common with Gallon, since conveyance by a joint tenant severs the joint tenancy.

Questions 115-116 are based on the following fact situation.

Orsican was the owner of a two hundred acre parcel of realty known as Westacre. Because he knew that he

was dying, Orsican executed a deed purporting to convey a portion of Westacre to his sister Geriardy, who lived in another state. The deed described the realty conveyed as, "A portion of Westacre two hundred feet by two hundred feet in size, with its northeastern corner located at the eastern end of the northern border of Westacre." On Sunday, Orsican placed the deed in an envelope with the proper postage affixed, addressed it to Geriardy, and placed it on his dining-room table with the intention of mailing it the following day. That night Orsican died. The following morning, unaware that his father had died, Orsican's son Sal found the envelope on the table and mailed it. Geriardy died on Tuesday. The letter carrier delivered the envelope containing the deed to Geriardy's house on Wednesday. Without opening the envelope, Geriardy's daughter Dot wrote the word "deceased" across it and handed it back to the letter carrier, asking him to return it to the sender. The envelope reached Orsican's house on Friday. When it did, Sal opened the envelope and tore up the deed which it contained. Orsican's will left everything he owned to Sal. Geriardy's will left everything she owned to Dot. Subsequently, both Sal and Dot asserted ownership of the realty described in the deed.

115. Assume for the purpose of this question only that the description was sufficient. In litigation between Dot and Sal regarding title to the realty described in the deed, the court should find for

(A) Sal, because Geriardy died before the envelope containing the deed reached her house.

(B) Sal, because Orsican died before the envelope containing the deed was mailed to Geriardy.

(C) Dot, because she did not know that the envelope contained a deed when she asked the letter carrier to return it to the sender.

(D) Dot, because when the deed was mailed to Geriardy, the sender relinquished control over it.

116. If the deed were enforceable in all other respects, would the description which it contains be sufficient to effect a conveyance?

(A) No, because it does not set forth metes and bounds.

(B) No, unless there is a man-made or natural monument at the eastern end of the northern border of Westacre.

(C) Yes, if it identifies the realty conveyed with reasonable clarity.

(D) Yes, but only if there are no government survey markers in the area.

117. Lessee leased a parcel of realty from Lord for a term of five years. During that term, the entire parcel was taken by eminent domain. Which of the following statements is correct about the rights of Lessee?

    I. Lessee may continue to occupy the premises for the balance of the term unless the leasehold interest was specifically mentioned in the condemnation award.

    II. Lessee is freed of the obligation to pay rent for the balance of the term.

    III. Lessee is entitled to a share of the condemnation award based on the value of the unexpired term of the leasehold less rent which would have become due during that term.

(A) I only.

(B) II only.

(C) III only.

(D) II and III only.

118. In 1970, without Odette's permission, Altman moved onto Odette's realty and constructed a dwelling. Since then, she has lived there continuously, openly, and notoriously. In 1977, Odette died, leaving the realty to his 2-year-old son Stephen. At that time Grayson was appointed as Stephen's legal guardian. In 1980, Grayson became aware that Altman was in possession of the realty which Stephen had inherited from Odette. In 1986, after Altman had been in posses-sion of the realty for 16 years, Grayson sued on Stephen's behalf to eject Altman. In her defense, Altman asserted that she had become the owner of the realty by adverse possession.

A statute in the jurisdiction fixes the time for acquiring title by adverse possession at 15 years.

Has Altman become the owner of the realty by adverse possession?

(A) No, because the statutory period will not begin to run against Stephen until he achieves majority at the age of 18 years.

(B) No, because the statutory period began to run against Stephen when he inherited the realty in 1977.

(C) No, because the statutory period began to run against Stephen when Grayson became aware that Altman was in possession of the realty in 1980.

(D) Yes.

119. Statler was an architect and interior designer. She lived in a house which she had designed, and frequently invited potential clients to her home so that she could show them the quality of her work. The house was located on a 20-acre parcel of realty which Statler had inherited from her grandmother. Because the land had once been part of a farm, there were many old farm buildings on it, most of which were in a badly deteriorated condition. Statler used one of these old buildings as a barn for a horse which she kept as a hobby.

When Statler was offered a position working for a real estate developer in another state, she decided to sell her realty. She entered into a valid contract to sell the property to Buchanan for $250,000. She also offered to sell Buchanan her horse, but Buchanan said that he was not interested in keeping any animals. Since Statler needed to relocate to her new job location immediately, she gave Buchanan permission to move onto the realty before the closing of title. After Buchanan had done so and prior to the closing, the building which Statler had used for a barn burned down as the result of a fire which did no other damage.

Prior to the date set for closing, Buchanan claimed that the purchase price should be reduced by a sum equivalent to the value of the barn.

If Statler consults you regarding Buchanan's claim, you should advise her that she is entitled to collect the full $250,000

(A) because the barn was not an essential part of the realty.

(B) because Buchanan's possession of the realty when the barn burned down raises a presumption that he was at fault.

(C) if the jurisdiction applies the doctrine of equitable conversion.

(D) unless the barn burned without any fault by Buchanan.

Questions 120-121 are based on the following fact situation.

Obie was the owner of two adjacent parcels of realty known as Lot A and Lot B. The northern boundary of Lot A was the southern boundary of Lot B. An old dirt road crossed both parcels, providing access to a river which flowed along the southern boundary of Lot A. Obie sold Lot B to Boylan by a grant deed containing a river access easement permitting the holder of Lot B to use the dirt road which crossed Lot A. Subsequently, Obie divided Lot A in half. He retained the southern portion, conveying the northern portion to Atkins. The deed to Atkins contained no mention of an easement for river access over the property which Obie retained. At the closing, however, Obie told Atkins that she was welcome to use the dirt road across his property for river access.

During the next ten years, Boylan and Atkins frequently used the dirt road across Obie's property for gaining access to the river. Then, because weather conditions made it necessary, Boylan paved that portion of the road.

A statute in the jurisdiction fixes ten years as the period for obtaining an interest in realty by prescription or adverse possession. Another statute provides that all holders of an easement shall share equally the expenses of maintaining it.

120. Assume for the purpose of this question only that when Boylan asked Atkins to contribute to the cost of paving the dirt road, Atkins refused on the ground that she was not the holder of an easement. If Boylan asserts a claim against Atkins under the above statute, Boylan's most effective argument would be that Atkins held an easement by

(A) dedication.

(B) implication.

(C) express reservation.

(D) express grant.

121. Assume for the purpose of this question only that after Boylan paved the road, Obie told Atkins that she could no longer use it to cross his property for river access. If Atkins claims that she has acquired a prescriptive easement, which of the following would be Obie's most effective argument in response to that claim?

(A) Atkins had been using the road with Obie's permission, and Obie had a right to withdraw his permission.

(B) The road was no longer in the same condition as when Obie told Atkins that she could use it.

(C) Atkins' deed made no mention of an easement across Obie's property.

(D) The road was no longer in the same condition as it was during the ten-year period of use by Atkins.

Questions 122-123 are based on the following fact situation.

Upton is the owner of a hillside parcel of realty known as Slopeacre, on which he grows apples for sale to a company which makes juice from them. For several years, Upton has been irrigating his apple trees with water from a stream which flows across Slopeacre. After flowing across Slopeacre, the stream flows through Flatacre, a parcel of realty located in the valley below Slopeacre. Downey, who owns Flatacre, lives there with his family. Downey's family uses water from the stream for household purposes. This year, Upton informed Downey that he was planning to build a small dam across the stream so that he would be able to pump water out of it more easily for irrigating his apple trees. Downey immediately instituted a proceeding to prevent Upton from constructing the dam.

The jurisdiction determines water rights by applying the common law.

122. If it were the only one true, which of the following additional facts or inferences would be most likely to cause a court to grant the relief requested by Downey?

(A) Construction of a dam will increase Upton's consumption of water from the stream.

(B) Construction of a dam will change the natural flow of the stream.

(C) Construction of a dam will cause Upton to consume more water from the stream than is reasonably necessary for the enjoyment of Slopeacre.

(D) Upton can continue to pump water from the stream without constructing a dam.

123. Assume for the purpose of this question only that because of a drought there is enough water in the stream to satisfy the needs of either Flatacre or Slopeacre, but not both, and that there are no other riparian owners. Who is entitled to use the water?

(A) Upton, because he is the upstream owner.

(B) Upton, because he needs the water for agricultural use.

(C) Downey, because he needs the water for household use.

(D) Downey, because he is the downstream owner.

124. Larrick executed a document purporting to lease a parcel of real estate to Teeter for fifty years at

an annual rent of $1,000. Twenty years before the scheduled expiration of the lease, the entire parcel was taken by the state for the construction of a reservoir. At a condemnation proceeding, the trier of the facts found that the balance of Teeter's leasehold was valued at $30,000. Of the total condemnation award, Teeter should receive

(A) $30,000, but Teeter will be required to pay Larrick a sum equivalent to the rent for the balance of the lease term.

(B) nothing, because Teeter's interest violates the Rule Against Perpetuities.

(C) $30,000, and Teeter will have no further obligation to Larrick.

(D) $30,000 minus a sum equivalent to the rent for the balance of the lease term, and Teeter will have no further obligation to Larrick.

125. Oster purchased a parcel of realty, borrowing $50,000 for that purpose from Bank and executing a note and mortgage on the realty for that amount in favor of Bank. Bank did not record the mortgage. Five years later, because he needed money to go into business, Oster borrowed $20,000 from Finance, executing a note and trust deed on his realty for that amount in favor of Finance. Finance recorded the trust deed immediately. Two years later, Oster defaulted on both notes. As a result of a foreclosure proceeding brought jointly by Bank and Finance, a court approved the sale of Oster's realty for $50,000.

The jurisdiction has a recording statute which provides, "No transfer of an interest in real property shall be good against subsequent transferees for consideration and without notice unless it is recorded."

If Bank and Finance both claim a right to the proceeds of the foreclosure sale, whose claim should receive priority?

(A) Finance, because the mortgage held by Bank was not recorded.

(B) Finance, because Bank had constructive

notice of the trust deed in favor of Finance.

   (C) Bank, because the priority of security interests is not governed by recording statutes.

   (D) Bank, because the mortgage held by Bank was a purchase-money mortgage.

126. Soon after they were married, Wendy and Hal purchased a house, taking title as tenants by the entirety. They made a $20,000 down payment and executed a note and mortgage for the balance, agreeing to make payments of $600 per month. Three months later, realizing that it would be difficult for them to make the payments, Wendy offered to make her grandmother Claire a part owner if she would help them pay for the house. Claire agreed to contribute $300 per month toward the payments, and at Claire's request Wendy and Hal executed a deed reconveying the property to themselves and Claire as joint tenants. A statute in the jurisdiction permitted a joint tenancy to be created in this manner. Wendy subsequently died, leaving a will which named Hal as her sole distributee.

Which of the following most correctly describes the relationship between Hal and Claire following the death of Wendy?

   (A) Joint tenants, with each holding a one-half interest in the realty.

   (B) Joint tenants, with each holding a one-third interest in the realty, and tenants in common as to the other third.

   (C) Tenants in common, with Hal holding a two-thirds interest in the realty, and Claire holding a one-third interest in the realty.

   (D) Tenants in common, with each holding a one-half interest in the realty.

Questions 127-128 are based on the following fact situation.

Farmer was the owner of a large tract of land on which he grew crops. Because his income was declining, he decided to subdivide and sell his land. With government approval, he platted a subdivision called Farmer's

Green consisting of 50 parcels of land with necessary access and utility easements. Soon afterwards, he conveyed one of the parcels to Amador by a properly recorded deed which they both signed, and which contained the following language:

> The parties hereto hereby covenant for themselves, their heirs, successors, and assigns that the realty herein conveyed shall not be used for any purpose other than residential, and that all conveyances of realty in the subdivision known as Farmer's Green shall contain this covenant.

Amador subsequently sold half of his parcel to Berge, conveying it by a deed which contained no covenants or restrictions. Six months later, because he was unable to sell any of the other parcels, Farmer resumed agricultural activities on his remaining land. At the same time, Berge began construction of a gas station on the realty which he had purchased from Amador.

127. Assume for the purpose of this question only that Berge commences a proceeding to prevent Farmer from engaging in agricultural activities on the land in Farmer's Green, on the ground that such activities are not for residential purposes. Which of the following would be Farmer's most effective argument in opposition to Berge's proceeding?

   (A) Berge's deed contained no language of covenant or restriction.

   (B) Farmer did not covenant to refrain from using the land for agricultural purposes.

   (C) Berge and Farmer were not in privity.

   (D) The covenant in Farmer's deed to Amador did not touch and concern the land.

128. Assume for the purpose of this question only that Farmer commences a proceeding to prevent Berge from constructing a gas station on the realty. Should the court grant the relief requested by Farmer?

   (A) No, because Farmer did not sell any of the other land in Farmer's Green.

(B) No, because Berge did not agree to refrain from non-residential use of the land.

(C) Yes, because the covenant in Farmer's deed to Amador ran with the land.

(D) Yes, because the construction of a gas station by Berge was likely to inhibit sale of the remaining parcels in Farmer's Green.

Questions 129-130 are based on the following fact situation.

On January 1, Lawson and Thaler entered into a written agreement by which Thaler rented a furnished apartment from Lawson. According to their agreement, Thaler was to occupy the apartment for one month at a rental of $250 payable in advance. The agreement further provided that its terms were to be automatically renewed at the end of each month unless either party terminated it by giving 20 days written notice to the other. Upon signing the agreement and pursuant to its terms, Thaler paid Lawson $150 as a security deposit, with the understanding that Lawson could elect to apply it to any unpaid rent upon termination of the agreement.

Thaler occupied the apartment for six months during which time he complained to various government agencies about building and health code violations which he believed existed in the premises. Although the government agencies investigated Thaler's complaints, Lawson was never charged with code violations.

129. Which of the following best describes Thaler's interest in the realty after executing the written agreement on January 1?

(A) Tenancy for years.

(B) Tenancy at will.

(C) Periodic tenancy.

(D) Tenancy at sufferance.

130. Assume for the purpose of this question only that ten days after receiving Thaler's rent for the seventh month, Lawson served Thaler with a written notice purporting to terminate Thaler's tenancy when the month ended twenty days later. If Thaler refused to vacate the premises at the end of that time and Lawson instituted a judicial proceeding to evict Thaler, the court should find for

(A) Lawson because the written agreement of January 1 specified that either party could terminate on 20 days written notice.

(B) Lawson only if Lawson can prove that Thaler violated a covenant contained in the written agreement of January 1.

(C) Thaler only if Lawson breached an express covenant contained in the written agreement of January 1.

(D) Thaler because the written agreement of January 1 implied a covenant of fair dealing.

131. When Fletcher died he left his farm to his son Sam for life with remainder to Unity Church. Because Fletcher had been a farmer, Sam tried farming the land for a while, but found the work unpleasant. Although gravel had never before been mined or removed from the land, Sam learned that he could derive a substantial income by doing so. He therefore dug a deep and extensive pit on the land from which he began removing gravel for sale to builders and other commercial purchasers.

If Unity Church asserts a claim against Sam because of his removal of gravel the court should

(A) grant Unity Church a proportionate share of any profits derived from the sale of gravel removed from the land.

(B) issue an injunction against further removal of gravel and order Sam to account to Unity Church for profits already derived from the sale of gravel removed from the land.

(C) deny relief to Unity Church, because no right of action will accrue until Unity Church's interest becomes possessory at the termination of Sam's estate.

(D) deny relief to Unity Church, because a life tenant is entitled to remove minerals from an open pit.

132. Orr's will devised a parcel of realty "to all the children of my son Seth equally, share and share alike." At the time of Orr's death, Seth had two children named Judy and Pete. One year after Orr's death, Seth's third child, Ella, was born. Because Seth's estate was sizable, probate court procedures were not completed until several months after Ella's birth.

    Who received a valid interest in the realty under Orr's will?

    (A) Judy and Pete only.

    (B) Judy, Pete, and Ella only.

    (C) Judy, Pete, Ella, and any other children of Seth born subsequently.

    (D) Neither Judy, Pete, nor Ella because the devise of an interest to them is void under the Rule Against Perpetuities.

Questions 133-134 are based on the following fact situation.

Lawrence, who was the owner of a commercial office building, leased an office in the building to Arthur pursuant to a 10 year lease calling for rent in the sum of $1,000 per month. Arthur occupied the premises for a period of two years, paying the rent as it became due each month. At the end of that period, he assigned the balance of the leasehold to Burton by a document in which Burton agreed to be personally liable for all obligations under the lease and which was signed by Arthur and Burton. Immediately following execution of the assignment, Arthur sent a copy of it to Lawrence. Burton occupied the premises for several years, paying the rent as it came due. When seven months of the lease period remained, Burton assigned the balance of the leasehold to Calloway. Calloway did not agree to be personally liable for all obligations under the lease, and Lawrence was not informed of the assignment. Calloway occupied the premises for two months, but did not pay rent. At the end of that period, Calloway assigned the balance of the lease to Daniel. Daniel occupied the premises for five months without paying rent, abandoning the premises when the lease expired. When the premises were vacated, a total of seven months rent remained unpaid.

133. Assume for the purpose of this question only that Lawrence asserts a claim against Arthur for unpaid rent. The court should award judgment for Lawrence in the sum of

    (A) nothing, since Burton agreed to be personally liable.

    (B) $2,000, the rent which accrued while Calloway occupied the premises.

    (C) $5,000, the rent which accrued while Daniel occupied the premises.

    (D) $7,000, all unpaid rent.

134. Assume for the purpose of this question only that Lawrence asserts a claim against Calloway for unpaid rent. The court should award judgment for Lawrence in the sum of

    (A) nothing, since Calloway did not agree to be personally liable.

    (B) nothing, since Calloway and Lawrence are not in privity of contract.

    (C) $2,000, the amount of rent which remains unpaid for the period during which Calloway occupied the premises.

    (D) $7,000, the amount of rent which remains unpaid for the period during which Calloway and his assignee Daniel occupied the premises.

135. In January 1987, Alvarez, Barnum, and Curtis took title to a parcel of realty as joint tenants. In March of that year, after obtaining the written consent of Barnum and Curtis, Alvarez purported to convey her interest in the realty to her daughter Dot. In January 1988, Barnum died, leaving a will in which he purported to leave his interest in the realty to his son Sonny.

    Which of the following most accurately states the interests of the parties in the realty?

(A) Curtis, Dot, and Sonny are tenants in common, each holding an undivided one third interest.

(B) Curtis and Dot are joint tenants and Sonny is a tenant in common, each holding an undivided one third interest.

(C) Curtis and Dot are joint tenants, each holding an undivided one half interest.

(D) Curtis and Dot are tenants in common, with Curtis holding an undivided two thirds interest, and Dot holding an undivided one third interest.

136. Oscar, the owner of a summer beach cabin, conveyed it to his daughter Debra as a gift for her sixteenth birthday. Two years later, on her eighteenth birthday, Debra went to the cabin for the first time and found Adamo in possession of it. When she asked what he was doing there, Adamo said, "Anyone who lives around here can tell you that I've been coming here every summer." In fact, Adamo had occupied the beach cabin every summer for the past ten years, but had not occupied the cabin during other seasons. Debra instituted a proceeding to evict Adamo. In defense, Adamo claimed that he had acquired title to the cabin by adverse possession. Statutes in the jurisdiction fix the period for acquiring title to realty by adverse possession at 10 years and the age of majority at 18 years.

Has Adamo acquired title by adverse possession?

(A) No, because computation of the period of adverse possession begins anew each time there is a change in ownership of the realty.

(B) No, because for the past two years the owner of the cabin was under a legal disability.

(C) Yes, if occupancy only during the summer was consistent with the appropriate use of the cabin.

(D) Yes, if Adamo had Oscar's permission to occupy the cabin during the summers.

137. Oyler was the owner of a parcel of realty known as Oylacre. On January 11, Oyler borrowed

money from Morgan, executing a note secured by a mortgage on Oylacre. The following March, Oyler conveyed Oylacre to his niece Norwood as a gift by a deed which made no mention of Morgan's mortgage. Norwood recorded the deed on March 15. Morgan recorded the mortgage on March 18. The jurisdiction has a recording statute which provides that "no interest in realty shall be good against a subsequent purchaser for value and without notice unless it shall first have been recorded." Payment to Morgan was not made as required by the note, and Morgan attempted to foreclose on Oylacre.

When Norwood received notice of the foreclosure proceeding, she opposed it on the ground that her interest was superior to Morgan's. Is Norwood correct?

(A) No, because Oyler executed the mortgage to Morgan before executing the conveyance to Norwood.

(B) No, because a mortgage is not regarded as an interest in realty under recording statutes.

(C) Yes, because Norwood recorded the deed before Morgan recorded the mortgage.

(D) Yes, because the conveyance to Norwood made no mention of the mortgage.

138. Owings conveyed a parcel of land "to Agar for life, but if Agar should ever use liquor on the premises to Chevalier for life; then to Baretto. Baretto's interest is best described as

(A) a reversion.

(B) a contingent remainder.

(C) a vested remainder.

(D) void under the rule against perpetuities.

139. Anderson and Bradshaw own adjacent parcels of realty. In 1985, Anderson constructed ten houses on his realty and a well which tapped the underground aquifer to supply water to the houses. Since that time, Anderson has been renting the houses to tenants. Recently, Bradshaw began

construction of a house and well on his realty. Bradshaw's well will tap into the same aquifer as Anderson's and will reduce the water available to Anderson's tenants. If Anderson institutes a proceeding against Bradshaw asking the court to issue an order directing Bradshaw to cease construction of the well, the court should find for

(A) Anderson, because Anderson's well supplies water to more users than Bradshaw's will.

(B) Anderson, only if Anderson's use of the water is found to be reasonable.

(C) Bradshaw, because Anderson is deriving a profit from use of the water.

(D) Bradshaw, if Bradshaw's planned use of the water is found to be reasonable.

140. Lenox was the owner of a commercial building which he leased to Ashdown for use as a retail shoe store for a period of five years. In the lease, Ashdown covenanted not to assign the premises without Lenox's written consent. A clause of the lease reserved Lenox's right to terminate the lease in the event of a breach of this covenant. Two years after Ashdown began occupancy, he sold the business to Boyer, his store manager. After obtaining Lenox's written consent, Ashdown assigned the balance of the lease to Boyer. Boyer operated the shoe store for several months and then sold it to Cole. As part of the sale, Boyer executed a document purporting to transfer to Cole all remaining rights under the lease. Boyer did not obtain Lenox's permission for this transfer. When Lenox learned of this transfer to Cole, he instituted a proceeding in which he sought Cole's eviction on the ground that the covenant not to assign had been violated.

Which of the following would be Cole's most effective argument in opposition to Lenox's claim?

(A) The covenant against assignment is void as a restraint against alienation.

(B) Lenox's only remedy is an action against Boyer for damages resulting from breach of the covenant.

(C) Lenox waived his rights under the covenant by consenting to the assignment by Ashdown to Boyer.

(D) The transfer by Boyer to Cole was not an assignment but a sublease.

Questions 141-142 are based on the following fact situation.

Owsley was the owner of a large tract of realty with its southernmost boundary fronting on a public road. Owsley divided the tract into two parcels, one to the north of the other. Owsley named the southernmost parcel, which fronted on the public road, Southacre. He named the northernmost parcel Northacre, and sold it to Archer. Northacre did not have road frontage, and was accessible only by a visible dirt road which crossed Southacre. The deed by which Owsley conveyed Northacre to Archer contained language granting a right-of-way easement over the dirt road. Several years after purchasing Northacre, Archer purchased Southacre from Owsley. Archer never occupied Northacre and never used the dirt road which crossed Southacre.

141. Assume for the purposes of this question only that Archer subsequently sold Northacre to Barnhart by a deed which made no mention of a right-of-way easement across Southacre. If Barnhart claims that he received a right-of-way easement over Southacre, which of the following would be Barnhart's best argument in support of that claim?

(A) The visible dirt road across Southacre which provided access to Northacre was a quasi-easement.

(B) Since there was no other access to Northacre, Barnhart received an easement by implied reservation.

(C) Since there was no other access to Northacre, Barnhart received an easement by necessity.

(D) The grant of a right-of-way easement across Southacre contained in the deed by which

Owsley conveyed Northacre to Archer benefits all subsequent purchasers of Northacre.

142. Assume for the purpose of this question only that Coates subsequently contracted to purchase Southacre from Archer after Coates inspected Southacre and saw the dirt road which crossed it prior to contracting, and that the purchase contract made no mention of an easement or of the quality of title to be conveyed. Assume further that prior to closing of title, Coates refused to go through with the transaction on the ground that the existence of an easement across Southacre made Archer's title unmarketable. If Archer asserts a claim against Coates for breach of contract, which of the following would be Archer's most effective argument in support of his claim?

(A) A contract to purchase real property merges with the deed by which the title is conveyed.

(B) Coates had notice of the easement at the time he entered into the contract to purchase Southacre.

(C) The existence of an easement does not make title unmarketable.

(D) The purchase contract did not specify the quality of title to be conveyed.

Questions 143-145 are based on the following fact situation.

Zoning laws in Green City provided that all land on the north side of Main Street was restricted to residential use, and that commercial use was permitted on all land on the south side of Main Street. The zoning laws also provided that up two horses could be kept on any land zoned for residential use, but that no business could be operated on land zoned for residential use. Although all the other realty on the south side of Main Street was being put to commercial use, Homer owned and resided in a one story house located on the south side of Main Street.

Green Hills was a housing development located on the north side of Main Street. All deeds to realty in Green

Hills contained language prohibiting the keeping of horses anywhere within the subdivision. The subdivision plan which had been filed when Green Hills was created provided that persons occupying realty in Green Hills were permitted to operate small businesses in their homes so long as such operation did not interfere with or annoy other residents in the subdivision.

143. Assume for the purposes of this question only that Typer operated a typing service from an office in her home in Green Hills, and that Foley entered into a contract to buy Typer's typing service and home. After entering into the contract of sale, however, Foley learned of the zoning law which prohibited the operation of any business in a residential zone. He immediately informed Typer that he would not go through with the purchase of Typer's home because of the zoning violation. If Typer asserts a claim against Foley for breach of contract, the court should find for

(A) Foley, because the purchaser of realty cannot be forced to buy potential litigation.

(B) Foley, but only if he could not have discovered the zoning violation by reasonable inquiry prior to entering into the contract of sale.

(C) Typer, because the zoning law which prohibited the operation of Typer's business existed before the contract of sale was formed.

(D) Typer, because her business was permitted by provisions of the Green Hills subdivision plan.

144. Assume for the purpose of this question only that Graves purchased the land owned by Homer, tore down the existing house, and began construction of a three story office building. Kaham, who operated a business known as a water slide on the adjacent realty, objected on the ground that the building which Graves was constructing would block off Kaham's air and light, thus diminishing the value of his realty. If Kaham commences an appropriate proceeding against Graves seeking an order which would prohibit construction of the building, the court should find for

(A) Graves if the construction of a three story office building is permitted by the zoning law.

(B) Graves because commercial use of the realty is the highest and best use.

(C) Kaham, because previous use by Homer created an implied easement for air, light, and view.

(D) Kaham, if residential use by Homer was a continuing non-conforming use.

145. Assume for the purpose of this question only that Equis, a resident of Green Hills, began keeping horses in his yard. If his neighbor, Ralph, commences a proceeding in which he seeks an order preventing Equis from keeping horses, the court should find for

(A) Equis because the zoning law permits the keeping of horses.

(B) Equis only if keeping horses is part of ordinary residential use.

(C) Ralph because of the language in Equis's deed which prohibits the keeping of horses.

(D) Ralph only if keeping horses is a nuisance.

Questions 146-147 are based on the following fact situation.

Olsen conveyed a parcel of realty "to Geller so long as liquor is not sold on the premises, but if liquor is sold on the premises, to the Foundation for Hereditary Diseases." Two years later, Geller began selling liquor on the premises.

146. Which of the following best describes Geller's interest in the realty on the day before he began selling liquor on the premises?

(A) void, since the interest of the Foundation for Hereditary Diseases could have vested more than 21 years after the death of all persons who were in being at the time of the conveyance.

(B) fee simple absolute.

(C) fee simple determinable, since Geller's interest will terminate if liquor is ever sold on the premises.

(D) fee simple subject to a condition subsequent, which will ripen into a fee simple absolute if liquor is not sold during a period measured by a life or lives in being plus twenty-one years.

147. Which of the following best describes the interest of the Foundation for Hereditary Diseases in the realty on the day after Geller began selling liquor on the premises?

(A) fee simple absolute if the Foundation for Hereditary Diseases is a charity.

(B) right of re-entry.

(C) no interest, since at the time of the conveyance it was possible that the interest which the deed purported to grant to Foundation would not vest within a period measured by a life or lives in being plus twenty-one years.

(D) valid shifting executory interest which will not become possessory until the Foundation for Hereditary Diseases takes some step to exercise its right.

148. When Suzanne said that she was interested in selling her home and the lot on which it stood, Balbo expressed interest in purchasing it. After negotiations, Balbo and Suzanne entered into a written contract which provided that Suzanne would sell the realty to Balbo for $60,000, and that delivery of title was to occur on or before August 1. Suzanne further promised that at the time title was delivered the house would be vacant. A clause in the contract provided that "The risk of loss from non-negligent causes shall remain with the seller until delivery of title." On July 15, through no fault of Suzanne or Balbo, the house burned down. Suzanne had not yet moved out of the house, and title had not yet been transferred to Balbo.

Following the destruction of the house, if Balbo seeks to rescind the contract, he

(A) can, since the parties agreed that the risk of loss would not shift to Balbo until passage of title.

(B) can, if, but only if, the jurisdiction has rejected the doctrine of equitable conversion.

(C) cannot, unless the jurisdiction recognizes the doctrine of equitable conversion.

(D) cannot, because the risk of loss passed to Balbo immediately upon execution of the contract to purchase.

ANSWERS
PROPERTY

ANSWERS TO
PROPERTY QUESTIONS

1. **B**   Under common law, a conveyance of real estate is not valid unless it identifies the grantor, the grantee, and the property conveyed. The statute simply codified this rule. Realty cannot be conveyed by the use of negotiable paper (i.e., to bearer). For this reason, the document conveyed no interest.

   A is incorrect because even an unrecordable deed may affect the rights of grantor and grantee as against each other. **C** is incorrect for two reasons: first, consideration is not required to make a deed effective; and, second, courts do not generally inquire into the adequacy of consideration. Although a claim of economic duress has occasionally been used to avoid the legal effect of documents which are otherwise valid, it is not applied consistently enough to make **D** the correct answer and is not applied unless the duress was created by the party against whom it is asserted.

2. **D**   So long as the adverse possessor has remained openly, notoriously, hostilely and continuously in possession for the statutory period, he may acquire title to the land even though it changed ownership during the period of his adverse possession. Thus, the fact that Polsky bought the land from a prior owner during the period of Fowl's possession would not result in a judgment for Polsky.

   Possession of realty is hostile if it is contrary to the rights of the owner. Since occupying realty which has been rented from the owner is not contrary to his rights, the payment of rent would have prevented Fowl's possession from being hostile. Since a dozen eggs per week could be construed as rent, **A** might result in a judgment for Polsky and is, therefore incorrect. Permission from the owner of Nearacre would have had the same effect, making **B** incorrect. If Fowl said that he would remove the chicken coop whenever the owner of Nearacre asked him to, and the owner of Nearacre did not, it might likewise be concluded that the chicken coop remained by permission of the owner of Nearacre. Fowl's possession would not, therefore, be hostile, making **C** incorrect.

3. **A**   Under the doctrine of estoppel by deed, one who conveys realty in which he has no interest is estopped from denying the validity of the conveyance if he then acquires the realty.

   A fraudulent transaction might result in liability for damages, but fraud is not alone sufficient to result in a finding that title has passed. **B** is, therefore, incorrect. Compliance or non-compliance with recording statutes may affect the rights of a grantee as against future grantees, but does not relate to his rights as against the grantor. **C** is, therefore, incorrect. **D** is incorrect because of the estoppel doctrine described above.

4. **D**   A deed is effective upon delivery to and acceptance by the grantee or his agent. Delivery of a deed to one co-tenant is usually viewed as delivery to all co-tenants. Thus, the delivery to Arnold was a delivery to Benton as well. If a conveyance is beneficial to a named grantee, acceptance by that grantee is presumed. Since the transfer was beneficial to Benton, it is presumed that Benton accepted delivery of the deed. These facts, coupled with recording by Benton's co-tenant, are sufficient to result in an effective

conveyance to Benton of a joint tenancy in the land. Since joint tenants have the right of survivorship, Arnold's interest passed to Benton upon Arnold's death.

A is incorrect because the delivery to Arnold was a delivery to his co-tenant as well, and because Benton's right of survivorship made Arnold's devise to Fred ineffective. A testamentary disposition is a transfer made by will. Since Maria conveyed the realty *inter vivos* (i.e., while alive), **B** is incorrect. **C** is incorrect because occupancy by a grantee is not necessary to make the grant effective, and because the conveyance was effective upon delivery and acceptance of the deed and was not undone by the grantee's return of the deed to the grantor for safekeeping.

5. **C**   Unless a deed is signed by the grantor or the grantor's agent, it does not effectively convey an interest in realty.

A gift is a transfer without consideration. **A** is incorrect because an interest in realty may be conveyed as a gift, and such a conveyance is valid even though no consideration was given for it. **B** is incorrect because a deed which is silent as to the interest being conveyed is presumed to convey whatever interest the grantor holds. Recording a deed gives the world constructive notice of the grantee's interest, but does not affect the validity of the deed. **D** is incorrect because an unrecorded deed is effective at least against the grantor.

6. **D**   Under the doctrine of equitable conversion, the risk of loss of realty passes to the buyer as soon as a contract of sale is executed. In jurisdictions which have rejected the doctrine of equitable conversion, the risk of loss of realty subject to a contract for sale remains with the seller until the transfer of either title or possession to the buyer. Most jurisdictions agree, however, that if destruction of an *immaterial* part of the realty occurs prior to that time, the seller may enforce the contract after the price is abated to account for the damage. Since the facts make it clear that the sheds were inconsequential and that Clubb intended to demolish them after taking title to the realty, they may be regarded as immaterial parts of the realty.

A is, therefore, incorrect. **B** is incorrect because the sheds were not material parts of the realty. In jurisdictions which have rejected the doctrine of equitable conversion, **C** is an inaccurate statement of the law.

7. **A**   A contract for the sale of realty is unenforceable unless it adequately describes the subject realty. Similarly, a deed is ineffective unless it adequately describes the realty conveyed. For these purposes, any description of realty is adequate if it clearly identifies the property being conveyed. There can be no doubt that the description would be adequate if Landsman's was the only realty in the county known as the Flying L and identified by the Tract, Lot, and Parcel numbers given. (*Note:* So long as it clearly identified the property involved, the description in the deed tendered by Landsman would have been adequate even if the property was not the only parcel in the county known as the Flying L, or was not the only parcel known by the Tract, Lot, and Parcel numbers given.) If the description is adequate, the contract of sale is enforceable, and Landsman has fulfilled his obligation under it by tendering the deed. Clubb's refusal to accept the deed would, thus, be a breach which would entitle Landsman to damages.

A contract for the sale of realty, like any other contract of sale, must identify the subject of the agreement. If it does not, it is unenforceable because the court would be unable to fashion a remedy for its breach. **B** is incorrect because it suggests that a contract which is not sufficiently specific to be enforced becomes enforceable simply because the parties entered into it. **C** and **D** are incorrect because any description which clearly identifies the realty is sufficient even if it is not expressed in metes and bounds or the standard form.

8. **D**   Marketable title is title which the well-informed, reasonably prudent buyer would be willing to accept. Since the reasonably prudent buyer is not usually willing to buy a lawsuit, any doubt about the title held by Sanderson (i.e., about the rights acquired by Planchet) would make the title unmarketable. Since the contract of sale required Sanderson to deliver marketable title, he would thus be in breach.

This is so even if Planchet might ultimately lose his claim for title by adverse possession. **A** and **C** are, therefore, incorrect. Although a policy of title insurance might protect against economic losses resulting from Sanderson's failure to deliver good title, delivery of such a policy would not make the title marketable. **B** is, therefore, incorrect.

9. **C**   Ordinarily, restrictions contained in a conveyance cannot be enforced to benefit realty in which the grantor has no interest. Since Devel had already conveyed Lot 1, he had no interest in it when he conveyed Lot 25 to Albert. For this reason, restrictions contained in the deed for Lot 25 can not be enforced for the benefit of Lot 1. An exception is sometimes made in the case of a subdivision if it can be shown that a prior purchaser bought in reliance on restrictions to be contained in deeds to subsequent purchasers. Since there is no indication that Yarrow was aware that the deed to Lot 25 would contain a restriction, however, he could not have relied on it when purchasing Lot 1 and cannot enforce it. **C** is, therefore, correct.

A is incorrect because a restriction may be enforced against a covenantor's successor, even though the deed by which the covenantor conveyed to his successor did not mention it. Thus, the fact that Barbara's deed did not mention the restriction is not sufficient to prevent the issuance of the injunction. **B** is incorrect because, as explained above, if Yarrow knew that the restriction would be contained in the deed to Lot 25 and relied upon that restriction, he may have acquired the right to enforce it even though it was not mentioned in his deed. A covenant is said to "touch and concern" the burdened land if only the possessor of that land may perform it, and is said to "touch and concern" the benefitted land if the resulting benefit is tied to possession of that land. Since only the possessor of Lot 25 can comply with the use restriction, it touches and concerns Lot 25. Since Lot 1 is in close physical proximity and in full view of Lot 25, its value will be affected by the use to which Lot 25 is put. The restriction, therefore, touches and concerns Lot 1. For these reasons, **D** is incorrect.

10. **D**   Ordinarily, realty is not subject to restrictions unless they appear in the chain of title or in the deed which conveys it. Exceptions might be made for restrictions which appear in a general subdivision plan, if a purchaser of realty in that subdivision is aware that such restrictions exist. Since there were no restrictions in the chain of title to Lot 1 or in the deed by which it was conveyed to Yarrow, there are no restrictions on the use of Lot 1 which can be enforced by Barbara unless restrictions on Lot 1 were part of the general

subdivision plan. Thus, if such a restriction was not part of the general subdivision plan, Barbara will not win.

If a purchaser buys realty in a subdivision with knowledge that there are restrictions in the deeds to other parcels in the subdivision and with knowledge that restrictions which appear in the general subdivision plan apply to the lot which he purchases, that lot might be subject to the restrictions under a theory of implied reciprocal servitudes, even if they do not appear in the purchaser's deed. **A**, **B**, and **C** are incorrect, however, because there is no fact indicating that restrictions applicable to Yarrow's lot appear in the general subdivision plan, or that when Yarrow purchased Lot 1 he was aware of any restrictions in the deeds to Lots 21 through 40.

11. **A**   An easement by express reservation is one for the benefit of the grantor which he creates by language contained in the deed by which he conveys the servient estate. It does not terminate with non-use, unless there is a clear manifestation of the intention to abandon it by the easement-holder. Ossie's maintenance of the right-of-way across Lot 1 indicates that it was not his intention to abandon it.

An implied easement by necessity terminates when the strict necessity ceases to exist. **B** and **C** are both incorrect, however, because the easement across Lot 1 was by *express* reservation. The existence of an easement generally does diminish the value of the servient estate. **D** is incorrect because this reduction in value, even if unreasonable, is not alone sufficient to invalidate the easement.

12. **D**   An appurtenant easement is terminated by merger if the dominant and servient estates come into common ownership, and does not automatically revive if they are severed. Thus, when Laker sold Lot 3 back to Ossie, the easement terminated. When Waters received Lot 3 from Ossie by a grant which did not mention the right-of-way, he took it free of the right-of-way.

Since waters received title to Lot 3 free of the easement, Ossie could not unilaterally revive it. **A** is, therefore, incorrect. **B** is incorrect because the easement terminated by merger when Ossie re-acquired Lot 3. **C** is incorrect because non-use is not, alone, sufficient to terminate an easement which was created by express reservation or grant.

13. **D**   Fred's will did not speak until Fred's death and devised an interest in the realty only to those children who survived Fred. Since Bob predeceased Fred, Bob never received an interest in the realty; his purported mortgage to Loanco did not give Loanco any interest. For this reason, Fred's interest was unaffected by the mortgage and was absolute. As Fred's only surviving child, Susan received Fred's interest upon Fred's death.

Since Loanco held no interest in the realty, **A**, **B**, and **C** are incorrect.

14. **B**   Tona has given Hernando a power of appointment. A power of appointment is the legal right to designate subsequent transferees of realty. It may only be exercised in the manner specified by the donor of the power. If the donee of the power fails to exercise it, the realty subject to the power of appointment reverts to the estate of the donor. Since Tona specified that Hernando's power of appointment could only be exercised by will, and since Hernando failed to exercise it by his will, Tonacre reverted to the estate of Tona

upon Hernando's death. Marketable title is title which is free from claims which would lead a reasonable person to doubt its validity. Since the realty reverted to Tona's estate, Walley had no interest in it subsequent to the death of Hernando. Her inability to deliver marketable title is a breach of her contract with Benton, entitling Benton to the relief which he seeks.

Covenants for title in the deed might have given Benton a lawsuit against Walley if the title which the deed purported to convey proved to be defective, but they would not have made the title marketable. **A** is, therefore, incorrect. Since Tona specified that Hernando's power could only be exercised by will, his *inter vivos* conveyance to Walley was without effect. **C** is, therefore, incorrect. Tonacre did not pass to Hernando's heirs under the laws of intestacy, because Hernando's failure to exercise the power by will resulted in reversion of Tonacre to the estate of Tona. **D** is, therefore, incorrect.

15. **B**   A reversion is a future interest of the grantor which will automatically follow a prior estate which will inevitably terminate (e.g., a life estate; a leasehold). A possibility of reverter is a future interest of the grantor which will automatically follow a prior estate which will not inevitably terminate (e.g., fee simple determinable). A right of re-entry is a future interest of the grantor which does not revert automatically, but which requires some act by the grantor in order for him to re-acquire a possessory right, and which follows an estate which will not inevitably terminate. Since the property was conveyed only for so long as it is used as a home for the elderly, it will automatically revert to the grantor if that use is ever discontinued. It is, thus, either a reversion or a possibility of reverter. Since it is not certain that it ever will cease to be used as a home for the elderly, however, the prior estate is not one which will inevitably terminate. For this reason, the grantor's interest is a possibility of reverter.

A is, therefore, incorrect. **C** is incorrect because if the property ever ceases to be used as a home for the elderly, no act of the grantor is necessary to make his interest possessory. **D** is incorrect because the Rule against Perpetuities does not apply to a grantor's interest.

16. **B**   A remainder is a future interest in a grantee which will automatically become possessory following a prior estate which will terminate inevitably (e.g., a life estate). An executory interest is a future interest in a grantee which will not automatically become possessory and which follows a prior estate which will not terminate inevitably. Since the interest of Senior Life will only become possessory if racial discrimination is practiced by Senior Center, and since this may never happen, the interest of Senior Life is best classified as an executory interest. Under the Rule Against Perpetuities, no interest is good unless it must vest, if at all, during a period measured by a life or lives in being plus 21 years. Since Senior Center might begin practicing racial discrimination after the period proscribed by the Rule, the interest of Senior Life seems to violate the Rule. Because of an exception, however, the Rule Against Perpetuities does not apply to the interest of a charity which follows the interest of a charity. Since Senior Center and Senior Life are both charitable institutions, the Rule Against Perpetuities does not apply, and the interest of Senior Life is valid.

D is, therefore, incorrect. **A** and **C** are incorrect because it is not inevitable that the interest of Senior Center will terminate, and the interest of Senior Life, therefore, can not be a remainder.

17. **B**   A life tenant is required to pay real estate taxes which become due during the term of her life tenancy. Although a life tenant is required to pay interest on outstanding encumbrances, the remainderman is under an obligation to pay principal.

A is incorrect because as life tenant, Wilma should not be required to pay principal. **C** is incorrect for this reason, and because as remainderman, Bertrand should not be required to pay the real estate taxes. **D** is incorrect for the latter reason.

18. **A**   A life tenant is entitled to make reasonable use of natural resources for the purpose of maintaining the realty.

B is incorrect, however, because this right is limited to reasonable use. The term "waste" is used to describe any substantial change in realty which occurs while it is in the possession of a person holding less than a fee interest. If the change is beneficial to the value of the realty, it is known as "ameliorating waste." **C** is incorrect for two reasons: first, the destruction of trees on a parcel of realty is not necessarily ameliorating waste, since that term would be used only if such destruction benefits the value of the realty; and, second, since ameliorating waste benefits the realty, a court is not likely to enjoin it. **D** is incorrect because a life tenant is not required to permit decay to continue simply because it began while the realty was possessed by a prior tenant.

19. **A**   Acquisition of title by adverse possession results from application of a statute of limitations which prevents the record owner from enforcing any rights which he might have against the adverse possessor. For this reason, the period does not begin to run until a cause of action by the record owner accrues. Thus, it does not begin running against an infant owner until he achieves majority; it does not begin running against a remainderman until the preceding estate terminates. (**Note**: If the realty was held in fee simple when the period of adverse possession began, it may continue in spite of changes in ownership of the fee.) Until Ned's estate terminated, Paul had no right to sue Adder. (After all, Adder may have been a tenant of Ned's.) For this reason, the period of adverse possession did not begin running until Paul became the owner of the realty in 1981.

B is incorrect because Paul's right was not possessory until the termination of Ned's estate. **C** is incorrect because even after achieving majority (circa 1964), Paul's interest in the realty was not possessory. **D** is incorrect because Adder's period of adverse possession against Paul did not begin until Paul's interest became possessory. Another way of looking at the problem is to recognize that the adverse possessor acquires no greater interest than is held by the person against whom his possession is adverse. Thus, Adder's possession during Ned's term could not have resulted in more than his acquisition of a 20 year term (i.e., Ned's interest) by adverse possession.

20. **D**   Tess's will devised a contingent remainder to Nellie and an alternate contingent remainder to the oldest child of Nellie living at the time of Tess's death. Since Eddie was not the oldest child living at the time of Tess's death, he received no interest.

He did not receive a vested remainder since he had no right at all to take the realty. **A** is, therefore, incorrect. He did not receive a contingent remainder because there was no condition which would result in his taking the realty. **B** is, therefore, incorrect. He did not receive an executory interest because there was no condition which would entitle him to divest a previous estate and assert an interest in the realty. **C** is, therefore, incorrect.

21. **B**   Under Statute I (a pure notice type statute), Parton's interest would be superior to Bessie's because while Bessie's interest was unrecorded, he purchased for value and without notice of the prior conveyance. Under Statute II (a race-notice type statute) Bessie's interest would be superior even though Parton purchased for value and in good faith (i.e., without notice of the prior conveyance), because Parton's interest was not recorded before Bessie's.

22. **A**   Under this recording statute (a pure race type statute), the first interest recorded is superior. Bessie's interest derives from the deed which was recorded on April 3. Since Parton's deed was not recorded until April 5, Bessie's interest had priority.

          B is incorrect because under a race type statute, all that matters is the order in which the interests were recorded. **C** is incorrect because Bessie's interest derives from the deed which was recorded on April 3. The general warranty deed by which Marcel conveyed to Parton will determine Parton's rights against Marcel. But **D** is incorrect because the recording statute determines the rights of Parton and Bessie as against each other.

23. **C**   One who assumes a mortgage when purchasing realty agrees to pay the note which the mortgage secures and becomes personally liable for such payments. Furth is, therefore, liable. Neither a subsequent assumption nor a subsequent taking subject to a mortgage, will release from personal liability the original mortgagor or one who previously assumed the mortgage. Derry is, therefore, liable.

          A, **B** and **D** are, therefore, incorrect.

24. **A**   A mortgage given as a security interest in realty covers all of the realty at the place described therein, including parts which are affixed after the mortgage is created. A fixture is a former chattel which has become part of realty. Once it becomes part of the realty, it is subject to a security interest created by a mortgage on that realty even if the mortgage was given before the fixture became part of the realty. Thus, if the cooling tank was a fixture, the mortgage which Derry gave Dairyman's Bank includes a security interest in it. (A chattel becomes a fixture when it is permanently affixed to the realty or, even if it is not permanently affixed, when its installation is essential to the use of a particular building. Since both of these conditions were met by the installation of the cooling tank, it was probably a fixture. It is unnecessary to make this decision, however, since the language of option **A** [i.e., the word "if"] requires the assumption that the tank was a fixture.)

          The question of whether a chattel has become a fixture does not depend on whether the person installing it made payments on a note, so **B** is incorrect. **C** is incorrect because a fixture is subject to a mortgage on the realty even if affixed to the realty after the mortgage was created. Seckin is not personally liable for payment of the note because the property was conveyed "subject to" the mortgage, but the realty — including fixtures —

is subject to enforcement of the mortgagee's rights. **D** is, therefore, incorrect.

25.   **C**   When a deed is deposited with a commercial escrow agent with instructions to deliver it to the grantee upon the happening of a condition outside the grantor's control, title passes automatically upon the happening of the specified condition. Purcher thus owned the realty as soon as his check cleared on January 15, and is not guilty of violating the statute.

A and B are, therefore, incorrect. In some jurisdictions the risk of loss passes to the buyer upon execution of a contract for the sale of realty. **D** is incorrect, however, because the passage of title does not relate back to the execution of the contract.

26.   **A**   Whether they apply the doctrine of equitable conversion, the Uniform Vendor and Purchaser Risk Act, or some other system for apportioning the risk of loss under a real estate sales contract, most jurisdictions agree that the risk of loss from causes other than the fault of the vendor passes to the vendee when he takes possession of the realty prior to closing. Although a small minority of jurisdictions disagree, **A** is the only argument listed which could possibly support Singer's position.

B and C are incorrect because passage of the risk of loss does not depend on the purchase of fire insurance by either party. **D** is incorrect because no jurisdiction recognizes such a presumption.

27.   **A**   No reason appears in the fact situation why the contract between Sollen and Bangor is not enforceable. Since the contract contains Bangor's promise to purchase water from Sollen, he will be liable to Sollen for damages resulting from his breach.

B is incorrect because there is no discrepancy between the contract and the deed, and because — at least in determining what estate the grantee has received — discrepancies between a deed and a contract for sale are resolved by looking to the deed. Since only the possessor of the land on which the well and water-purifying plant were located could benefit from the covenant to purchase water, and since only the possessor of the land granted by Sollen could comply with it, both the benefit and the burden resulting from the covenant touched and concerned the land. Although this is not relevant to Bangor's obligations under the contract, the inaccuracy of the statements makes **C** incorrect. **D** is incorrect for two reasons: first, acceptance of a deed containing restrictions may bind the grantee to those restrictions even though he did not sign the deed; and second, Bangor agreed to purchase water in the contract of sale.

28.   **B**   The holder of an easement may not use it in a way which goes beyond the scope of use contemplated at the time of its creation. Since the easement across Lot I was created for ingress and egress to Lot II, its use for the purpose of erecting poles and stringing power lines exceeds its scope.

A is incorrect because an appurtenant easement is ordinarily transferred by conveyance of the dominant estate, and is, therefore, alienable. In addition to the fact that calling an easement "divisible" says nothing about it, **C** is incorrect because the stringing of wires was not incidental to the contemplated use of the ingress-egress easement. An easement is appurtenant if it is designed to benefit the holder of a particular piece of realty. An easement in gross is not designed to benefit the holder of a particular piece of realty. Since this easement was for access to Lot II, it was appurtenant. **D** is incorrect because it is a meaningless and incorrect statement of the law.

29.   **C**   Ordinarily, no person has a right to an unspoiled view. Thus, in the absence of special circumstances (such as those making the interference a nuisance), interference with the view is not actionable even if the person complaining was there first, or if the newcomer knew that his building would obstruct a view.

A, **B** and **D** are, therefore, incorrect.

30.   **B**   A tenancy with no fixed duration is a tenancy at will and can be terminated by either party. Since the mayor's authorization did not specify a duration, it created a tenancy at will. Since the city can terminate the occupancy, it has the right to prevent occupancy other than under conditions which it sets, and, therefore, to obtain an injunction against violations of those conditions.

Since the Ballet's agreement with the city did not obligate it to pay rent, its non-payment of rent is not a breach which would give the city any rights which it would not have had otherwise. **A** is, therefore, incorrect. **C** is incorrect because a tenant at sufferance is one who entered under a valid lease which has since expired or terminated. Ameliorating waste is the name given to substantial alterations made by the tenant of leased premises which do not diminish the value of the real estate. **D** is incorrect because the fact that there was no lease probably makes the term an inappropriate one, because there is no indication that the proposed changes would not diminish the value of the realty, and because courts are not always willing to enjoin ameliorating waste.

31.   **B**   A tenant's violation of a lease provision prohibiting sublet or assignment of a leasehold is usually regarded as a breach of covenant for which the tenant may be liable for damages. II is therefore a correct statement. Because courts favor the alienability of estates in land, however, the violation does not ordinarily result in a finding that the assignment or sublease is void. A lease may expressly reserve the landlord's right to terminate the lease if the covenant against alienation is breached. If so, the landlord may elect to evict the subtenant or assignee as a holdover. I is incorrect, however, because the lease between Lawson and Tanner did not expressly reserve that right.

32.   **C**   Under the Rule Against Perpetuities, no interest is good unless it must vest, if at all, during a period measured by lives in being plus twenty-one years. Since Gretchen's marriage might have taken place more than twenty-one years after the deaths of Alice, Burton and Carrie, her interest might not have vested until after the period prescribed by the Rule expired, and thus violates the Rule.

A and **B** are incorrect because the interest *might* have vested after the period expired; the fact that it actually did not does not make it valid. The birth of other grandchildren would not affect the interests of Gretchen, since the will provided that the share of a prematurely deceased child should be divided among issue *of that child,* and Alice could not possibly have any children after her own death. **D** is, therefore, incorrect.

33.   **C**   Grande's will specified the amount to be paid to each child and grandchild who reached

twenty-two, so Carrie's share does not depend on the number of children and grandchildren who will meet that condition. Since she was twenty-two at the time of Grande's death, she already met the condition, and her interest vested immediately without any possibility of defeasance.

A is incorrect for two reasons: first, there are situations in which the interest of a charity might be valid although it does not vest until after the period of perpetuities (as when its executory interest is to vest following termination of the interest of another charity); and, second, because the effect which the vesting of her interest has on that of the charity is immediate. **B** is incorrect because Carrie's share is specific, and, therefore, does not depend on the number of people in the class. The validity of Carrie's interest depends on whether it must vest, if at all, before the expiration of the period of perpetuities. **D** is incorrect because there is no reason why this should depend on whether or not she is the first person to qualify.

34. **B**   If a gift is made to a class of persons some of whom are in being and ascertained at the time the gift is made, the class opens and closes immediately. Since the gift was made in Wendy's will, it became effective at her death. Since some of Herman's children were in being and ascertained at that time, the class closed immediately.

A is incorrect because, as explained above, the class closed upon the death of Wendy. An interest is contingent if its vesting is subject to a condition precedent. Calli's right to take a share of the realty does not depend on the happening of a condition precedent, and so it is not contingent. **C** is, therefore, incorrect. **D** is incorrect because the class closed immediately upon the death of Wendy, and because even if it had not, Calli's right would be vested subject to partial divestment, and, therefore, not void.

35. **A**   Harold may convey the interest which he holds. Since his interest is a life estate (i.e., the right to possess for a period measured by his own life), **A** is correct.

Since Wanda or Bart might outlive him, **B** and **C** are incorrect. Since life estates are alienable, **D** is also incorrect.

36. **D**   An easement by express grant does not terminate by non-use unless there is a clearly manifested intent to abandon it. Since there is nothing to indicate that the city intended to abandon the right to empty water into the creek which crossed Rogers' land, it may exercise that right even though it has not done so for forty years.

A private nuisance is a tortious interference with the plaintiff's right to use and enjoy realty. Since the easement privileged the city to dump water into the creek, its conduct in doing so is not a violation of any right held by Rogers. **A** is, therefore, incorrect. **B** is incorrect because there was no manifestation of an intent to abandon the easement. **C** is a fabrication which has no meaning at all.

37. **C**   In order for a possessor to acquire title by adverse possession, he must possess openly, notoriously, hostilely (i.e., under claim of right), and continuously for the statutory period. Temporary absences do not necessarily break the continuity of the possession if they are consistent with the adverse possessor's claim of right. If the possessor's absence is the result of either a court order directing eviction or self-help by the true

owner, however, such absence is not consistent with the possessor's claim of right (i.e., not hostile), and breaks the continuity of his possession.

D is, therefore, incorrect. **A** is incorrect because the removal would have interrupted the continuity of Holden's possession even if it had been without a court order. **B** is incorrect because the removal would have interrupted the continuity of Holden's possession even if it had been by a court order.

38. **B**   In the absence of language to the contrary, a contract for the sale of realty is presumed to call for conveyance of marketable title by whatever form of deed is customarily used in the area. Thus, the contract is complete, valid, and enforceable, even though silent about these two requirements.

A and **D** are incorrect because the contract so construed is enforceable by either party. Although parol evidence may be admitted for the purpose of determining the intentions of the parties to a contract, this contract can be enforced without it, based upon the presumption described above. **C** is, therefore, incorrect.

39. **C**   Some jurisdictions hold that an abstractor of title impliedly warrants the abstract to be accurate; all jurisdictions agree that there is at least an implied warranty that the service will be performed in a reasonable manner. Since the right-of-way deed was properly recorded, Titleco's failure to include it in the abstract which it furnished was a breach of either the promise to perform reasonably or the implied warranty of accuracy. In either event, since Belden was an intended creditor beneficiary of the contract between Sofield and Titleco, Belden can enforce it.

If there was an implied warranty of accuracy, **A** is incorrect because liability is imposed without fault for its breach. If there was no implied warranty of accuracy, **A** is incorrect because liability may be imposed if Titleco's lack of awareness of the right-of-way resulted from its failure to act reasonably. Since the right-of-way deed from the owner of Westacre to Johnson Chemical Company was properly recorded before any of the grants of Westacre took place, it was not outside the chain of title, and **B** is incorrect. **D** is incorrect because the liability of Titleco does not depend on covenants made by Sofield.

40. **C**   The covenant against encumbrances is a representation that there are no easements or liens burdening the realty. If the realty is, in fact, burdened by such an encumbrance, the covenant is breached and liability is imposed on the covenantor.

This is so even though the purchaser relied on assurances in addition to the covenant, and even though the grantor was unaware of the existence of the encumbrance at the time he executed the covenant. **A** and **B** are, therefore, incorrect. **D** is incorrect because there is no indication that Sofield failed to act reasonably (i.e., was "negligent").

41. **B**   The holder of an easement may not unreasonably burden the servient estate by using it in a way not contemplated when the easement was created. Since the dangers incident to the possible leakage of poisonous materials are much greater than those incident to the possible leakage of non-poisonous materials, the change in Johnson's intended use would unreasonably burden the estate of Belden.

An easement the benefit of which is directly tied to a particular parcel of realty (e.g., an easement across the servient estate for ingress and egress to the dominant estate) is known as an easement appurtenant. An easement the benefit of which is not directly tied to a particular parcel of realty (e.g., an easement held by the power company to erect poles and string wires across the servient estate) is known as an easement in gross. An easement in gross is commercial if its benefit is designed to result in a profit to its holder. Johnson's easement may have been an easement appurtenant since it directly benefitted the realty on which the chemical plant was located. On the other hand, it may have been an easement in gross since its use did not require ownership of the realty on which the chemical plant was located. Since most jurisdictions agree that, so long as alienation does not increase the burden on the servient estate, easements appurtenant and commercial easements in gross are freely alienable, **A** is incorrect. Non-use of an easement created by express grant is not sufficient to terminate it unless the holder of the easement manifests a clear intention to abandon it. Since there is no indication that Johnson manifested such an intention, **C** is incorrect. Since the easement was created by deed which was properly recorded, Belden had constructive notice of it when he purchased, and would not have been justified in relying on the absence of visible encumbrances. **D** is, therefore, incorrect.

42.   **A**   If a deed contains a restriction or covenant prohibiting the grantee from using the realty in a particular way, that restriction may be equitably enforced (i.e., by injunction) by a successor to the grantor's interest against a successor to the grantee's interest if the restriction constitutes an equitable servitude. A restriction may be held to constitute an equitable servitude if it creates a burden which touches and concerns the land of the original grantor and a benefit which touches the land of the original grantee, if the original parties intended it to run with the land, and if the person against whom enforcement is sought had actual or constructive notice of the burden when s/he received her/his interest. The restriction touches and concerns the land of Commers (against whom enforcement is sought) because only the occupant of Commers's land can comply with it. The restriction touches the land of the other residents of the subdivision (who seek to enforce it) because the value of their realty will be affected by the use to which Commers's lot and other realty in the subdivision are put. The fact that the subdivision plan which was filed contained a description of the deed restrictions indicates that the original parties intended it to be enforceable by all residents of the subdivision and also serves to give successors to original grantees constructive knowledge of the restriction. Thus, the restriction is enforceable as an equitable servitude against Commers by other residents of the subdivision.

      B is incorrect because the enforcement of restrictive covenants in the deeds to lots in a subdivision does not depend on the will of other members of the subdivision. Restrictions which touch and concern the land outlive buildings which are on the land, and do not cease to be enforceable simply because those buildings have ceased to be operative. **C** is, therefore, incorrect. Changes in the community may result in a decision to stop enforcing deed restrictions only where the changes are such that it is no longer substantially possible to secure the benefits which the restrictions were intended to create. **D** is incorrect because no facts indicate that such a change has occurred.

43.   **B**   Ordinarily, a tenant who abandons the premises before the expiration of the lease is lia-

ble for rent for the balance of the term. If, however, the landlord *surrenders* its rights under the lease, the tenant will be free from liability for the balance of the term. A surrender generally takes place when the landlord occupies the premises for its own purposes.

Reletting the premises for the balance of the term might be a surrender of the landlord's rights or might be performed on the defaulting tenant's account to mitigate damages, depending on the intent of the landlord. Where, as here, there is much other vacant space in the building, and the landlord has relet the premises for rent lower than provided in the lease, and on a month-to-month basis, it is not likely that its intent was to surrender its rights but rather to mitigate damages. **A** is, therefore, incorrect. The agreement between Lance and Tollup did not restrict use of the premises to any particular activity. For this reason, the fact that the premises are not well suited to the activity which Tollup had in mind, or that Tollup is no longer licensed in the practice for which he planned to use them, is irrelevant to his liability under the lease. **C** and **D** are, therefore, incorrect.

44. **B** If a conveyance of realty is complete in all other respects but silent as to the interest which is being conveyed, it is presumed to convey whatever interest the grantor holds at the time the conveyance is executed.

Thus, **A** and **C** are incorrect. Although a deed to realty should expressly identify the parties, the realty, and the interest conveyed, **D** is incorrect because, without language to the contrary, the deed is presumed to convey whatever interest the grantor held.

45. **B** The distinguishing feature of joint tenancy is that it includes the right of survivorship. This means that, although a joint tenant may sever a joint tenancy during her/his lifetime, if s/he dies without doing so, her/his interest passes to surviving joint tenants. The result is that unless the joint tenancy is severed by one of the joint tenants, the joint tenant who lives the longest will become the holder of the combined interests of all the original joint tenants. In order to give effect to this principle, it is understood that upon the death of one of the joint tenants, her/his share passes to the remaining joint tenants, increasing the fractional shares which they hold in joint tenancy. Since a will speaks only upon the death of the testatrix, Ada's purported devise to Connie did not occur during Ada's life and, therefore, could not sever the joint tenancy. As a result, Beatrix and Connie continue to be joint tenants, the share of each being increased from one third to one half.

A and **C** are incorrect because Beatrix and Connie continue to be joint tenants for the reason given above. **D** is incorrect because Ada could not sever the joint tenancy by will, and her interest, therefore, will be divided equally between Beatrix and Connie, the surviving joint tenants.

46. **D** If a joint tenant sells her interest, she severs the joint tenancy as to her interest, but not as to the interests of the other joint tenants. Nuco, therefore, acquired a one-third interest in the realty, but as a tenant in common. Ada and Connie continued to be joint tenants as to their two one-third interests.

A is incorrect because Nuco is a tenant in common. **B** and **C** are incorrect because Beatrix and Connie are joint tenants.

47.　**C**　　Ordinarily, a co-tenant has a right to occupy and possess the premises without being required to account to other co-tenants for rent. A co-tenant who has *ousted* another co-tenant or prevented her from occupying the premises may be required to account for profits and the reasonable value of rent, however.

A contains a familiar phrase, but is not related in any way to the rights and obligations which arise from co-tenancy. **B** is incorrect because a co-tenant is not obligated to sell her interest, and no new obligations arise from her failure to do so. The construction of permanent buildings on the land may increase the value of the interests of other co-tenants, but does not obligate the co-tenant who builds them to account for rent. **D** is, therefore, incorrect.

48.　**B**　　Ordinarily, a co-tenant is not required to account to other co-tenants for profits taken from the realty. Connie, therefore, did not have a right to a share of Ada's profits from farming the land. Since a quitclaim conveys only the right which the grantor held, Pearl did not acquire such a right.

A is incorrect because a quitclaim does transfer the grantor's right (except that the grantee of a joint tenant takes as a tenant in common). Sale by a joint tenant of her interest severs the joint tenancy, so **C** is a correct statement of the law — a joint tenant's right of survivorship is not alienable. **C** is not a correct answer, however, because the right of survivorship is not related to the right to a share of the profits earned by a co-tenant. Since the law regarding the right to a share is the same for joint tenants as for tenants in common, **D** is also incorrect.

49.　**D**　　Ordinarily an adverse possessor of realty acquires title only to that portion of the realty which he actually occupied and possessed. One who occupies any portion of a parcel of realty under "color of title" (i.e., pursuant to a written instrument which appears to convey title), however, is said to occupy it all. Since Poser openly, notoriously, hostilely, and continuously occupied a portion of Sellacre for the statutory period under color of the title conveyed by the sheriff's deed, he has acquired title to that entire parcel of realty by adverse possession.

Although the document under which Poser believed himself to have title proved to be defective, **A** is incorrect because of the interest which he acquired by adverse possession. **B** is incorrect because he occupied a portion of the realty under color of title. Although possession of part of the premises under color of title may result in acquisition of title to the whole, the *general* rule is that the adverse possessor may only acquire title to that portion of the premises which he has actually occupied. **C** is, therefore, incorrect.

50.　**A**　　A conveyance is recorded outside the chain of title if a reasonable search of the chain of title to the realty conveyed would not disclose that it occurred. A tract index identifies parcels of realty by number and enables a title searcher to trace the chain of title by searching for transactions involving realty identified by the appropriate number. By using a tract index to search for transactions involving Leafacre's parcel number, a title searcher would discover that Leafacre had been conveyed by Apple to Banner and by Banner to Compton. Without a tract index, a title searcher traces the chain of title by searching for transactions involving appropriate grantees and grantors. Without a tract index, a title searcher would have no way of determining that the realty conveyed by Apple to Banner and by Banner to Compton was Leafacre, because Ostend's conveyance of Leafacre to Apple had never been recorded, and so there was nothing in the record to connect Apple with Leafacre. Thus, the conveyance from Apple to Banner was recorded outside the chain of title. For the purpose of determining priorities under a recording statute, a conveyance outside the chain of title is treated as an unrecorded conveyance. Under the statute, no conveyance of realty is effective against a subsequent purchaser without notice of it unless it was recorded. Since the deed from Apple to Banner is treated as unrecorded, neither it nor the subsequent deed from Banner to Compton (which is also out of the chain of title) is effective against Zieman, who purchased without notice.

Recording statutes determine the priority of interests. Under the statute given, Apple's conveyance to Banner and Banner's conveyance to Compton are not effective against Zieman for the reasons given above, and, as a result, Zieman's interest takes priority over Compton's. This does not mean, however, that Apple did not have the power to convey the realty. If Ostend purported to sell to a purchaser who had notice of Ostend's previous conveyance to Apple, for example, Apple's conveyance to Banner would have been effective against that purchaser. For this reason, **B** is incorrect. Intentional misrepresentation by Ostend might make Ostend liable in tort for damages, but does not affect the rights of Compton and Zieman as against each other. **C** is, therefore, incorrect. Since Zieman is seeking to establish that his title is superior to Compton's, knowledge by Compton's predecessor is not relevant. **D** is, therefore, incorrect.

51. **C** An easement is an interest in realty. A license is permission to use realty. An interest in realty cannot be conveyed except by written instrument. Thus, the oral permission which Docker gave Fischer could not have created an easement, and must have created a license. Unless consideration is given for it, a license to use realty is revokable at will by the licensor or his successor. In most jurisdictions, a license automatically terminates when the realty is sold by the licensor. In those jurisdictions, Fischer's license terminated upon Docker's sale to Ballantine. In a few jurisdictions, a license survives the sale of the realty, but if it was a revokable license, it remains revokable. Since Fischer did not give consideration for the license, it was revokable, and if it survived the sale to Ballantine, it was effectively revoked when Ballantine ordered Fischer off the property.

A is incorrect because knowledge by a grantee that the grantor created a license to use the realty does not cause the license to survive the sale. **B** and **D** are incorrect because the oral permission could not have resulted in any easement. **D** is also incorrect because an easement appurtenant does survive the sale of the servient estate.

52. **B** A remainder is a grantee's future interest which will become possessory upon the termination of a prior estate which is certain to terminate. If the remainder is not subject to any conditions precedent other than the event which terminates the prior estate, it is said to be vested. If it is subject to an additional condition precedent, it is said to be contingent. Since Bob will surely die, the termination of Bob's life estate is inevitable, and Sol's interest is a remainder. Since there are no other conditions precedent to Sol's interest becoming possessory, it is a vested remainder. Since the gift is to be shared by all of Bob's children, however, the interest which Sol receives will be diminished if Bob has

any more children before his death. It is thus subject to partial divestment.

A is incorrect because there is no condition which would result in complete divestment of Sol's interest. A gift to an unborn person is usually regarded as contingent (i.e., upon her birth). For this reason, Sol's interest at the time of Torrey's death could be described as a contingent remainder. When Sol was born, however, the contingency was satisfied, and his interest became vested (subject to partial divestment). **C** is, therefore, incorrect. **D** is incorrect because Sol had a vested remainder subject to partial divestment.

53. **A**   Ordinarily, a tenant who abandons the premises before the expiration of the lease is liable for rent for the balance of the term.

The lease may reserve to the landlord the right to terminate the tenancy and re-enter in the event of non-payment, but **B** is incorrect because this is alternative to the right to collect rent, not the source of it. A landlord who elects to terminate the tenancy, will not be entitled to collect rent for the balance of the term. **C** is incorrect, however, because a landlord may elect not to terminate, as did Lardner, and hold the tenant for rent. **D** is incorrect because neither party to a lease may avoid obligations under it merely by giving notice, unless the lease so provides.

54. **B**   In determining the extent of the estate conveyed and the restrictions to which it is subject, the courts look to the deed which conveyed it. If there is a disagreement between the contract of sale and the conveyance, the language of the conveyance prevails. Although the Statute of Frauds requires the transfer of an interest in realty to be in writing and signed by the party to be charged, most courts hold that accepting and recording a conveyance containing restrictions in the use of the land conveyed binds the grantee to those restrictions even though he did not sign the deed in which they appeared or agree to them in the contract of sale.

The operation of a commercial cannery next to a residence might constitute a private nuisance, depending on the character of the neighborhood and the way in which the cannery is operated. **A** is incorrect, however, because such an operation is not necessarily a nuisance. **C** is incorrect because the restriction in the deed is controlling. **D** is incorrect because Benedict accepted and recorded the deed.

55. **B**   Under the Rule Against Perpetuities, no interest is good unless it must vest, if at all, within a period measured by a life or lives in being plus twenty-one years. Options to purchase realty are required to meet the requirements of the Rule Against Perpetuities unless they are attached to a lease or other interest in the realty held by the optionee. Since the option purports to convey a right to purchase at a time beyond the period prescribed by the Rule, it is void.

A and **C** are incorrect because notice, whether actual or constructive (i.e., by recording), does not make valid an interest which violated the Rule. **D** is incorrect because the option violates the Rule Against Perpetuities.

56. **B**   The contract called for delivery of "all the realty." The statute provides for abatement of the price if any of the realty subject to a contract of sale is removed prior to closing. Since the stone surfacer was removed prior to closing, Bannister is entitled to abatement

of the price if the stone surfacer was realty. Realty is generally defined as land or anything permanently attached to the land. According to another definition, realty is non-movable property. A fixture is a chattel which has become part of the realty. In deciding whether a chattel has become part of the realty, the phrases "permanently attached" and "non-movable" are not always helpful, because, with the right equipment just about anything can be moved. For this reason, in deciding whether a chattel is a fixture which has become part of the realty, courts usually look to the intentions of the parties. Since the permission which Patron gave Sculpin was oral and not in return for consideration, it was probably a revocable license. It is doubtful that the holder of a revocable license would bring an expensive piece of equipment onto the licensor's realty with the intention that it would become a permanent part of the realty. For this reason, a court is likely to hold that the stone surfacer was not a fixture and therefore not part of the realty. It is clear, however, that if it *was* found to be part of the realty, Bannister would be entitled to abatement of the price under the statute. **B** is, therefore, correct.

A is incorrect because if it was not Sculpin's intention that the stone surfacer become part of the realty, the fact that its weight made it difficult to move would not make it a fixture. **C** is incorrect because if the stone surfacer was realty, Bannister is entitled to abatement under the statute even though Sculpin's removal of it was not wrongful. **D** is incorrect because if Sculpin intended the stone surfacer to be part of the realty, the fact that it was not physically fastened to the ground would not prevent it from being a fixture.

57. **C**   Under the recording statute given, Campbell's interest is superior to Prospect's only if Campbell was without notice of Prospect's interest. While Campbell lacked actual notice or constructive notice that would have resulted from a recording of Prospect's interest, he is said to be on "inquiry notice" (i.e., constructive notice) of the interests of any person whose possession would have been disclosed by a reasonable inspection of the realty.

A is pure fabrication, offered as bait for those who so doubt their own knowledge that they are tempted to select the unfamiliar. It is incorrect because there is no Federal Mining Act which is relevant to determining the rights of those who hold unrecorded interests in realty. In **B**, the word "unless" indicates that the only way prospect's interest could possibly be superior to Campbell's would be if he acquired title by adverse possession. **B** is incorrect because Campbell's "inquiry notice" is enough to make Prospect's interest superior to Campbell's even without adverse possession. **D** is incorrect because Bostoria's knowledge is not relevant to the rights of Campbell and Prospect as against each other.

58. **B**   A quitclaim deed resembles a release, since it purports to convey only the interest which the grantor holds at the time of its execution. It includes no implied warranties for title, so the grantor incurs no liability if the title that he held proves less than perfect.

This is true even if the grantor knew that this title was defective at the time the quitclaim was executed, **A** is, therefore, incorrect. Whether or not Bostoria gave value for the realty is not relevant in determining the effect of Bostoria's conveyance to Campbell, since an interest in realty may be acquired without payment of consideration. **C** is, therefore, incorrect. **D** is incorrect because a quitclaim does not imply a promise by the grantor to act reasonably.

59. **C**   A deed does not effectively convey an interest in realty until it has been "delivered" to the grantee. Delivery to one tenant in common is usually regarded as delivery to all. If the deed named Olivera and Niles as tenants in common, it can be successfully argued that possession by Olivera indicates delivery to her as a grantee, which would satisfy the requirement of delivery to Niles, her co-tenant. While it is not certain that a court would come to this conclusion, **C** is the only one of the additional facts listed which could possibly support Niles's claim.

Delivery of a deed may occur even though the deed is not physically placed in the grantee's hands, but only if there is some act by which the grantor manifests the intention to make the deed presently effective. In **A**, Olivera's words simply indicate her intention that the transfer not take effect until her death. **A** is therefore incorrect. **B** is incorrect because the fact that Niles was out of the country on the day Olivera executed the deed does not indicate anything about her state of mind when she executed it. **D** is incorrect because when the deed was signed is irrelevant in determining the intent of the grantor.

60. **C**   Title to realty does not pass by deed unless the deed is delivered to the grantee while the grantor is alive. In order for delivery to occur, the grantor must perform some act which manifests an intention for the conveyance to be presently effective. Usually, this is done by physically placing the deed in the grantee's hands. Although this is not the only available method of delivery, it is apparently the one which Sandra chose, since she instructed her chauffeur Chapel to bring the deed to Nancy. Since Chapel was Sandra's employee, however, Sandra retained the right and power to change her mind and instruct him not to give the deed to Nancy, or even to tear it up. Since she retained this control over the deed, it might be concluded that she never manifested an intention to make a presently effective transfer. While it is not certain that a court would come to this conclusion, **C** is the only argument listed which could possibly be effective in opposition to Nancy's claim.

Although physical delivery to the grantee is a common way of manifesting the intention to make a presently effective transfer, **A** is incorrect because it is not the only way. Recording statutes determine the priority of interests in realty, but do not determine the validity of those interests. For this reason, a valid transfer of realty can occur without recording. **B** is, therefore, incorrect. An attempted testamentary substitute is a living person's attempt to make a disposition of property after her death without complying with the statutory formalities required for wills. The law regards these formalities as so important that an attempt to make a testamentary disposition without them is usually invalid. **D** is incorrect, however, because if the deed had been delivered to Nancy prior to Sandra's death, it would have been effective immediately, and would thus have been an inter vivos transfer rather than a testamentary disposition.

61. **C**   Title by adverse possession results from the operation of a statute of limitations which prevents an action to recover possession from being brought after a specified period of time. But the statute does not begin to run against a potential plaintiff until he has a possessory right in the realty. Since Roberts had no right to possession during the life of Linville, the statute did not begin running against him until Linville's death. Since Lin-

ville did have a possessory interest at the time Benson's occupancy began, the statutory period ran against Linville. As a result, Benson had probably acquired Linville's interest by adverse possession. Since Linville's interest was a life estate, however, Benson's interest terminated upon Linville's death.

A is incorrect, since "hostile" means against the right of the owner. Possession without the owner's permission is hostile. **B** is incorrect because "open and notorious" means in full view of the world, and does not require that the owner have actual knowledge. **D** is a fabrication which lacks any meaning at all. In any event, "tacking" refers to one adverse possessor's getting credit for a previous adverse possessor's time.

62. **D** Depending on the law of the jurisdiction, the "husband" to whom Tillie's will refers is either Fred, to whom she was married when the will was executed, or Sam, to whom she was married when she died. Under the Rule Against Perpetuities, no interest is good unless it must vest, if at all, within a period measured by a life or lives in being plus twenty-one years. A will is effective upon the death of the testatrix. If the will gave a life estate to Fred, the rights of the children and grandchildren vested immediately upon Tillie's death, since Fred is already dead. Since this is within the period described by the Rule Against Perpetuities, their interests are valid. If the will gave a life estate to Sam, the interests of the children and grandchildren will vest upon the death of Sam. Since this is within the period described by the Rule Against Perpetuities, their interests are valid.

If a class to which an interest in realty is given can be determined at the time the interest vests, the interest is valid even though the class could not be determined when the interest was created. If the will left a life estate to Fred, **A** is obviously incorrect since the size of the class was already determined when the interest was created (i.e., on the death of Tillie). If the will left a life estate to Sam the only grandchildren who will take are those born to a child of Tillie's who dies before Sam. Since the deceased child could not have any children after his/her own death, the class of grandchildren who will receive the substitutionary gift can be determined at the time the interest vests. **A**, therefore, would still be incorrect. Since a will is effective upon the death of the testatrix, the interests devised by Tillie's will were created when Tillie died. Since she could not marry after her death, **B** is incorrect. If the will left a life estate to Sam, the interests of Charles's children will vest only if Charles dies before Sam. Since Charles's life and Sam's life were both in being when the interest was created (i.e., when Tillie died), the interests will vest, if at all, during a period measured by a life or lives in being. **C** is, therefore, incorrect.

63. **D** Frequently deeds contain language restricting the way the realty conveyed may be used. Such language may help to define the estate conveyed by imposing a condition which limits the possessory right of the grantee, or it may simply create a contractual obligation between the grantor and the grantee. A conveyance of realty in fee simple transfers absolute ownership, subject to any limitations which appear in the conveyance. A fee simple may be restricted by language which makes it determinable, or which subjects it to defeasance upon the happening of a condition subsequent, or which subjects it to an executory limitation. If the language indicates that the grantor will automatically get the realty back upon the happening of a stated event, it creates a fee simple determinable. If the language indicates that the grantor has a right to do something to get the realty back

upon the happening of a stated event, it creates a fee simple subject to defeasance upon the happening of a condition subsequent. On the other hand, restrictive language in a deed may simply create a contract between the grantor and the grantee, which, if breached by the grantee entitles the grantor to damages. Usually, courts hold that the restrictive language creates nothing more than a contract unless it specifically provides for termination of the grantee's estate in the event the restrictions are violated. Since the language of the restriction in Monty's deed to Wilson does not specifically provide for the termination of Wilson's estate in the event that the realty is used for purposes other than residential, it probably created no more than a contractual obligation. While it is not certain that a court would come to this conclusion, **D** is the only answer listed which could possibly be correct.

An executory limitation gives a future interest to someone other than the grantor, and so if the language in the deed created an executory limitation it would not result in judgment for Monty. **B** is incorrect because the violation of a covenant contained in a deed is not sufficient to divest the grantee of the realty. **C** is incorrect because the Rule Against Perpetuities is not applicable to the interest of a grantor.

64. **B**   A grantee's future interest which will become possessory upon the termination of a prior estate is either a remainder or an executory interest. If termination of the prior estate is inevitable, the interest which follows it is a remainder. The remainder is contingent if there is a condition precedent to it other than termination of the prior estate. If termination of the prior estate is not inevitable, the interest which follows it is an executory interest. Under the language of the will, the estate of "my children" will not terminate unless Morris lives another thirty years. Since this is not inevitable, Morris's interest is executory. Under the Rule Against Perpetuities, no interest is good unless it must vest, if at all, within a period measured by a life or lives in being plus twenty-one years. Since Morris's interest will vest, if at all, during Morris's lifetime, his executory interest is valid.

D is, therefore, incorrect. Morris's interest is not a remainder since the prior estate will not terminate unless Morris lives another thirty years, and this is not inevitable. **A** and **C** are, therefore, incorrect.

65. **C**   In order for a burden imposed by a deed restriction to be applied to the grantee's (covenantor's) successor, it must be one which runs with the land. A burden runs with the land if it touches and concerns the land, and if there is privity of estate between the covenantor and his successor as well as between the covenantor and the covenantee (the original grantor) and if the parties so intended. A restriction touches and concerns the burdened land if only the possessor of that land can comply with it. It touches and concerns the benefitted land if the benefit of the restriction is directly tied to the land. In this case, the building restriction touches and concerns the land because it affects the value of the lot in question and of the surrounding land, and because only the holder of the burdened land can comply with it. The necessary privity exists because Feldman purchased from Zevon, and because Zevon purchased from Owen. The language indicates that the parties intended the covenant to run. It, therefore, may be enforced against Feldman.

A is incorrect because zoning laws only supersede deed restrictions when those zoning laws are more restrictive than the deed restrictions. **B** is incorrect because if the burden runs with the land, a successor to the covenantor is bound by the covenantor's promise. **D** is a fabrication, with no basis in law.

66. **D**   Ordinarily, a covenant cannot be used to benefit lands owned by third persons. Since the land in Towne Estates is no longer owned by Owen, the restrictions contained in deeds to lots in Towne Heights would not, therefore, be enforceable by residents of Towne Estates. If, however, it can be shown that when residents of Towne Estates purchased their lots it was with the expectation that similar restrictions would be imposed on subsequent purchasers of lots in Towne Heights, they will be permitted to enforce the covenants made by Towne Heights purchasers on a theory of implied reciprocal servitudes. The best way of establishing this expectation is by showing that Towne Estates was part of a common development scheme with Towne Heights.

A is incorrect, since the lack of privity between residents in Towne Heights and those in Towne Estates would prevent the restriction from being enforceable by residents of Towne Estates. Although **B** might result in burdens being imposed on purchasers of lots in Towne Heights, it would not make the restrictions enforceable by residents of Towne Estates. **B** is, therefore, incorrect. **C** is incorrect because such a clause would only bind the grantees of the deeds, but would not burden successors to those grantees, since there will be no privity between them and the residents of Town Estates.

67. **C**   The recording statute provides that a conveyance which has not yet been recorded is not effective against a subsequent purchaser for value. Since Harriet purchased before Garland recorded, Garland's title was inferior to Harriet's. Since Harriet's quitclaim to Ira conveyed whatever interest Harriet had, the interest which Ira received (i.e., Harriet's) was superior to Garland's. Since Ira's purchase occurred before Garland recorded, the conveyance from Oliver to Garland is not effective against Ira.

The effect of the recording statute is that a conveyance is not effective against a subsequent purchaser unless it was recorded prior to that purchase. Since Ira purchased on April 15 and Garland did not record until April 16, Garland's deed is not effective against Ira. **A** is, therefore, incorrect. **B** is incorrect because the statute does not require that the subsequent purchaser be without notice. Although recording statutes determine the priority of interests to realty, they do not determine the rights which exist between a grantor and grantee. It is not accurate to say that Garland received no rights until he recorded, because the conveyance by Oliver gave him rights at least against Oliver. **D** is, therefore, incorrect.

68. **C**   An easement is in gross if it is created for the benefit of a grantee in a status other than that of an owner of a specific piece of realty. Since this easement was created for the benefit of the phone company rather than for the owner of a specific parcel of realty, it was in gross. It is generally understood that commercial easements in gross may be alienated, so long as such alienation does not increase the burden on the servient estate.

Although the statement in **A** is accurate, it is inapplicable and therefore incorrect because an easement appurtenant is one which is created for the benefit of a grantee in a status as owner of a specific piece of land. **B** is incorrect because non-commercial easements in gross are generally held to be inalienable. Even if it were an accurate statement, **D** would not result in Oren's defeat. It is not an accurate statement since Oren sold the subdivision before he created the easement.

69.   **C**   A covenant against encumbrances is a grantor's promise that the title conveyed is free from liens. If a lien exists when the covenant is made (i.e., on delivery of the deed), there is a breach which entitles the grantee to damages. Olive's satisfaction of the mortgage cut off any rights to the realty which Loner had. Thus, although there has been a breach of covenant, Penny has sustained no actual damages. Most jurisdictions would allow recovery of nominal damages, however.

       A is incorrect because the appropriate remedy for breach of the covenant against encumbrances is an action for damages. **B** is incorrect because the covenant which was contained in the deed was not breached until the deed was delivered. There was a breach, though, because the encumbrance existed at the time when Olive delivered the deed. **D** is, therefore, incorrect.

70.   **A**   The fact that a plaintiff has an adequate remedy against a third person is no defense for a defendant against whom the plaintiff has an otherwise enforceable right.

       B might be an effective defense because most jurisdictions hold that the requirement of privity makes a covenant against encumbrances enforceable only by the grantee of the deed containing that covenant. In many jurisdictions, the existence of an encumbrance which is known to the grantee is not a breach of the covenant against encumbrances. **C** might be an effective defense since Loner's mortgage was recorded prior to Penny's interest. Quentin was, therefore, on notice of it. **D** is an effective defense since a statute of limitations on actions for breach of covenant contained in a deed begins to run upon delivery of the deed containing the covenant.

71.   **B**   Unless a contrary intention is shown, a conveyance to two or more persons is presumed to create a tenancy in common. Tenants in common are obligated to share in the payment of principal, interest, and real estate taxes. **II** is, therefore, correct.

       Although co-tenants are required to share in the costs of maintenance, I is an inaccurate statement because in the absence of a specific agreement they are not required to share in the costs of improvements. III is an inaccurate statement because, unless he has ousted (i.e., denied possession to) his co-tenants, a tenant in possession is not required to account to co-tenants for the rental value of the property occupied.

72.   **D**   In the absence of an agreement to the contrary, the seller of realty is required to deliver marketable title. **A**, **B**, and **C** are, therefore, incorrect.

73.   **D**   In jurisdictions which recognize tenancy by the entirety, a conveyance to a husband and wife is presumed to create a tenancy by the entirety in the absence of a contrary intention.

       A, **B**, and **C** are incorrect because only persons who are validly married to each other may hold land as tenants by the entirety.

74.   **A**   Marketable title is generally a title that a reasonable buyer, fully informed of the facts

and their legal significance, would be willing to accept. It is often impossible to tell in advance whether a third person's claim to an interest in realty will be successful. Since the reasonable buyer is not usually willing to purchase an interest which s/he may lose in later litigation, title is not marketable if anything could give a third person a reasonable chance of successfully asserting a claim to an interest in the realty. Thus, the title tendered by Iris was marketable only if there was no reasonable doubt about the success or validity of a claim which might then be asserted by persons claiming under Dotty, Dotty's children, or Dotty's grandchildren. Frances and Gala were joint tenants, who have the right of survivorship. Thus, Gala received Frances's interest upon Frances's death, and Frances's attempt to will her interest was ineffective. As a result, Mary received an unclouded title from Gala, and since a quitclaim conveys the grantor's interest, Iris received an unclouded title from Mary. While there is nothing to prevent the assertion of a lawsuit by Dotty, her children, her grandchildren, or persons claiming under them, there is no reasonable chance of success for such a lawsuit. The title which Iris tendered to Presley is, thus, marketable, and Presley's refusal to accept it was a breach.

B is incorrect, since if the title was unmarketable, Presley would not be required to buy a lawsuit by accepting any deed at all from Iris. A quitclaim conveys whatever interest the grantor holds. **C** is, therefore, incorrect. **D** is incorrect because the effect of a joint tenant's right of survivorship is that the interest of a joint tenant cannot be devised by will.

75. **D** Assignment of a leasehold interest occurs when the holder of the interest transfers to another all that remains of her/his interest. Sublease of a leasehold interest occurs when the holder of the interest transfers part but not all of her/his remaining interest. Since Tallen transferred all of his remaining interest to Anne, he made an assignment. The lease prohibited subletting. Because courts favor the free alienation of interests in land, contractual restraints on alienation are strictly construed. For this reason, a clause which prohibits subletting does not prohibit assignment.

A is, therefore, incorrect. **B** is an incorrect statement of the rule; assignment of a lease is *permitted* in the absence of an agreement to the contrary. Even if the lease contained an express reservation of the landlord's right to terminate in the event of a breach, Larson could not terminate Anne's leasehold since Tallen's assignment did not breach his agreement not to sublet. **C** is, therefore, incorrect.

76. **A** Since the parties to the assignment agreement intended that payments be made by Acme to Bilder, Bilder was a third party beneficiary of the assignment agreement, and can enforce it against Acme. **I** is, therefore, correct. Unless released by the obligee, a party to a lease, like a party to any other contract, continues to be responsible for performance of the obligations thereunder even after assigning rights or delegating duties which exist under the lease. This is true even if the lease permits assignment and even if the obligee consents to the assignment. **II** is incorrect because Bilder has not released Tennyson from his obligations under the lease and, therefore, can still collect from Tennyson.

77. **B** Although all of the statements might be logical ways of solving this problem, the law is clear that a life tenant is required to pay interest — to the extent of the reasonable rental value of the realty — and a remainderman is required to pay principle.

A, C, and **D** are, therefore, incorrect.

78.   **D**   So long as a description is sufficient to identify the realty conveyed, it is legally adequate, even though it contains some error with respect to the size of the parcel. Since Ogden owned only one parcel of realty on Barrett Road, description (1) can only identify one parcel, and is, thus adequate.

A is, therefore, incorrect. **B** is incorrect because delivery occurred when Ogden handed the deed to Edward, telling him that it was a birthday present. The fact that Edward returned it to Ogden is not relevant, since he only asked Ogden to hold it for safe-keeping. **C** is incorrect because there is no requirement that a deed be supported by consideration, and because once the deed was delivered, there was an executed gift.

79.   **A**   A description in a deed is legally sufficient if it adequately identifies the realty being conveyed. Thus, although the description used by Ogden is not in the traditional form, it is legally sufficient if it adequately identifies the subject realty.

Where a deed purports to convey a portion of a parcel of realty by a description which clearly states the amount of land conveyed but does not adequately describe it, it is sometimes held that the deed conveys an unidentified fractional portion of the parcel. **B** is incorrect, however, if the description adequately identifies the realty being conveyed. Although metes and bounds and reference to government survey markers are the most commonly used forms of description, **C** is incorrect because they are not the only acceptable forms. **D** is a fabrication with no basis in existing law and is, therefore, incorrect.

80.   **A**   Under the doctrine of equitable conversion, the risk of loss passes to the buyer of real estate as soon as the contract is made. On the day of the loss, Bennet thus had an insurable interest as defined by the statute.

Although various jurisdictions disagree about when the risk of loss passes in a sale of realty, all agree that if a party causes a loss, he bears the risks which result from it. For this reason, if the fire resulted from Bennet's negligence, he probably bore the risk of loss. **B** is incorrect, however, because it indicates that this is the only way Bennet would bear the risk of loss, and, under the doctrine of equitable conversion the risk of loss fell upon him as soon as the contract of sale was formed. Under the doctrine of equitable conversion, as soon as the contract of sale is formed, the risk of loss passes to the purchaser, despite the fact that the seller continues to be the legal owner until the closing of title. **C** is, therefore, incorrect. **D** is incorrect because the statute recognizes that an insurable interest is held by the person suffering the risk of loss, and the doctrine of equitable conversion passes the risk to the buyer when the contract is formed.

81.   **C**   All jurisdictions agree that a party who damages realty bears the risk of the resulting loss. This means that since the destruction of the premises resulted from Bennet's negligence, he will not be relieved of his obligations under the contract.

A and **B** are, therefore, incorrect. **D** might be correct if the damage did not result from the fault of either party, but is incorrect because the damage resulted from Bennet's negligence.

82. **D**   A remainder interest is vested if there are no conditions precedent to its becoming possessory other than the termination of the prior estate. If there are additional conditions precedent, the remainder is contingent. Since it is inevitable that Michael will die, and since there are no conditions precedent to the interests of Alvin and Betty, their interests are vested. It is possible, however, that Michael will have additional children. If so, Alvin and Betty will share in the realty, but their shares will be diminished. Their interests are therefore subject to partial divestment.

          A is incorrect, since there are no conditions precedent to the vesting of their interests. **B** is incorrect because of the possible partial defeasance described above. **C** is incorrect, because although their shares may be diminished, they will receive some share.

83. **A**   An easement created by express grant is not affected by the fact that the reason for its creation no longer exists.

          B is incorrect because the rights of third persons are not relevant in the consideration of easement disputes between landholders. **C** is based on an accurate statement of the law about implied easements by necessity, but is incorrect because the easement in question was created by grant, and was, therefore, not an implied easement by necessity. Since the three-story building is to be a one-family residence, its existence will not appreciably increase the burden on the servient estate. **D** is, therefore, incorrect.

84. **D**   The law does not recognize an easement for light, air, or view, unless it was created by express grant.

          A and **B** are, therefore, incorrect. **C** suggests an estoppel theory, but an easement by estoppel exists only where there is evidence of an attempt to create an express easement which attempt failed for formal reasons. Since the facts indicate no attempt to create an express easement for light, air, or view, **C** is incorrect.

85. **C**   Absent an agreement to the contrary, a contract for the sale of realty calls for the execution and delivery of whatever deed is customarily used in the area. Thus, if the use of general warranty deeds is customary, Oxford's tender of a quitclaim was a breach which would excuse Perk from performance.

          A is incorrect because the creation of a power of attorney to sell realty implies the power to contract for whatever deeds are customarily used in the area. Quitclaims are not customarily used anywhere, except under special circumstances. A quitclaim conveys whatever title the grantor held at the time it was executed, and thus conveys marketable title if the grantor held same. **B** is incorrect, however, because even if title is marketable, a quitclaim does not give a grantee recourse against the grantor if problems should develop, and because the contract implied a promise to deliver the kind of deed customarily in the area. **D** is incorrect because a quitclaim conveys valid title if the grantor held valid title.

86. **A**   Under the doctrine of equitable conversion a purchaser of realty becomes its equitable owner as soon as the sales contract is formed, and suffers the risk of loss resulting from

damage to the premises prior to the passage of title. Thus, in a jurisdiction which applies the doctrine of equitable conversion, the loss would be suffered by Baxton. He is, therefore, obligated to pay the full contract price in spite of the fact that the value of the realty has been diminished through no fault of his own.

B, C, and **D** are, therefore, incorrect.

87.   **B**   In most jurisdictions which do not apply the doctrine of equitable conversion, the risk of loss remains with the vendor until the transfer of either title to or possession of the premises. If Baxton was living in the house at the time of the fire, his possession would, therefore, result in passage of the risk of loss to him. Although a minority of jurisdictions disagree, **B** is the only additional fact listed which could result in that finding in any jurisdiction.

Although some states hold that a purchaser of realty acquires an insurable interest as soon as the sales contract is formed, his purchase of insurance does not cause the risk of loss to pass to him. **A** is, therefore, incorrect. If destruction of the house was foreseeable when the contract was formed, a party might be prevented from asserting a defense based on impossibility of performance. If the risk of loss did not pass to the buyer, however, the fact that such loss was foreseeable would not affect his right to cancel the contract or to abate the purchase price in proportion to the damage. **C** is, therefore, incorrect. Even if the risk of loss has not passed to the purchaser, the vendor in a contract for the sale of real property is entitled to enforce it against the purchaser so long as damage to the premises does not materially affect its value. **D** is incorrect, however, because even under those circumstances, the purchaser is entitled to a proportional abatement of the contract price.

88.   **C**   A remainder is a grantee's future interest which is to become possessory after the termination of a prior interest which will inevitably terminate. An executory interest is a grantee's future interest which follows an interest which will not inevitably terminate. Since the interest of the National Cancer Association was to become possessory only if Greenacre was used for the sale of alcohol, and since this event is not inevitable, the interest of the National Cancer Association must be executory. **A** and **D** are, therefore, incorrect. Under the Rule Against Perpetuities no interest is good unless it must vest, if at all, within a period measured by a life or lives in being plus twenty-one years. Since Greenacre might not be used for the sale of alcohol until after the expiration of the period of perpetuities, and since the interest of the National Cancer Association will not vest until that time, its interest is void under the Rule Against Perpetuities. [***Note:*** An exception to the Rule Against Perpetuities is made for a shift from one charity to another. This exception does not apply in this case since Agnes is not a charity.] **C** is, therefore, correct, and **A** is, therefore, incorrect. [***Note:*** The common law "destructibility rule" resulted in a merger of a present possessory interest and a future interest held by the same person, even if there were intervening contingent remainders. Although the question indicates that the jurisdiction has abolished the destructibility rule, its existence or non- existence has no application to these facts.]

89.   **B**   A grant to a named grantee "and his heirs" traditionally conveys a fee interest. A fee simple determinable on special limitation is a fee interest which will terminate automatically upon the happening of a specified contingency. The grant of a fee followed by the

word "until" is usually held to create a fee simple determinable, because the language indicates that the grantee's interest will not continue beyond the happening of the specified contingency.

A fee simple absolute is a possessory interest which includes all present and future interests in the realty. **A** is incorrect because the grant limits the interest of Antoine, making it terminate upon the happening of a specified event. A life estate is a possessory interest in realty which will terminate at the end of a specified life. Since the interest conveyed to Antoine by the deed will not terminate at the end of a specified life, it is not a life estate. The law does not recognize any interest known as a "quasi life estate." **C** is, therefore, incorrect. Under the Rule Against Perpetuities no interest is good unless it must vest if at all within a period of time measured by a life or lives in being plus twenty-one years. Since the interest of Borsell would not vest until the United States went to war with the Republic of Platano, and since this could have occurred hundreds of years after the conveyance was made, Borsell's interest was void under the Rule Against Perpetuities. The fact that a portion of a grant is void under the Rule Against Perpetuities, however, does not affect the validity of other interests created by that grant. For this reason, and because Antoine's interest vested immediately, **D** is incorrect.

90. **C**   If the location of an easement is precisely indicated by a written instrument such as the deed which created it, neither the holder of the dominant estate nor the holder of the servient estate may relocate it without the consent of the other. Sometimes, the fact that the holder of an easement has stopped using it for a substantial period of time justifies the conclusion that he has abandoned it. This always requires some additional evidence of an intent to abandon, however. Ordinarily, two months is not a sufficient length of time to indicate abandonment, and, since there is no additional evidence of Arcturo's intent to abandon the easement, his use of the paved road for two months does not imply consent to a relocation. Since this easement was described by metes and bounds in the deed which created it, and since Arcturo has not consented to its relocation, it continues to exist in its original location. Since the holder of the servient estate is not permitted to interfere with the easement holder's use of the easement, Arcturo is entitled to the relief which he seeks.

Although an implied easement by necessity terminates when the strict necessity for it terminates, an easement created by express grant does not terminate without abandonment, consent, or condemnation. **A** is incorrect because Arcturo's easement was created not by implication, but by grant. When the dominant and servient estates come to be owned by the same person, there is said to be a merger, and preexisting easements which the dominant estate held over the servient estate are extinguished. **B** is incorrect, however, because after Arcturo's easement was created, Arcturo's lot was the dominant estate and Parcels 1 and 2 were the servient estates, and the dominant and servient estates were not owned by the same person. An easement which directly benefits another parcel of realty (e.g., a right-of-way for ingress and egress) is an easement appurtenant. An easement which benefits an individual regardless of his relationship to another parcel of realty (e.g., a power company's right to install power lines) is an easement in gross. Easements appurtenant are freely alienable; easements in gross are not. **D** is incorrect for three reasons: first, Arcturo's easement was an easement appurtenant; second, easements in gross are not freely alienable; and, third, the case raises no issue regarding alienability.

91.   **B**   A deed does not operate to convey any interest in land until it has been delivered. Phys-
                ical transfer of a deed which is absolute on its face constitutes a delivery only if the
                grantor intended to make a presently effective transfer of an interest. When Olsen
                handed Callender a deed and said that it was not to take effect until his death, his intent
                may have been to make a present transfer to Callender of a future interest which would
                become possessory upon his death. Such an interest is a remainder. While it is not cer-
                tain that a court would come to this conclusion, **B** is the only argument listed which
                could possibly support Callender's position.

                Although possession by a grantee raises a presumption that there has been a valid and
                effective delivery, **A** is incorrect because the presumption is not irrebuttable; it may be
                rebutted by proof that the grantor did not intend to effect a present transfer. A testamen-
                tary substitute is an attempt by a living person to dispose of property after his death
                without complying with the formalities which statutes require of valid wills. **C** is incor-
                rect because an attempted testamentary substitute is ineffective. Delivery is complete
                when the grantor does some voluntary act which manifests his intention to make a pres-
                ently effective transfer. Since there is no indication that Olsen's death was voluntary, it
                could not have completed delivery. **D** is, therefore, incorrect.

92.   **C**   An otherwise valid conveyance is effective upon delivery. Delivery occurs when the
                grantor, by words or conduct, manifests an intention that the deed have a present opera-
                tive effect. Transfer of physical possession of the deed to the grantee raises a presump-
                tion that the grantor had such intent. In this case, Olsen's statement, "Then it's yours"
                supports that presumption.

                An attempt to make a gift which is to become effective only after the donor's death may
                fail because it is essentially a testamentary gift which does not meet the formal require-
                ments for wills. **A** is incorrect, however, because Olsen's language indicated that she
                intended the transfer of an interest to Norton to take effect immediately. A grantor's
                possession of a deed may raise a presumption that there has been no effective delivery.
                B is incorrect, however, because the presumption may be rebutted by proof that there
                was a delivery, and that the grantee thereafter returned the deed to the grantor for safe-
                keeping only. When consideration is an issue, detrimental reliance may take the place of
                the required consideration. **D** is incorrect, however, since a deed may be valid without
                consideration.

93.   **B**   Adpo has been in continuous possession for more than twenty years. His possession was
                hostile, because it was contrary to the rights of the City of Hampshire, the land's true
                owner. It was open and notorious because it was not hidden, and knowledge of his pos-
                session could have been obtained by anyone who looked. Having fulfilled all the statu-
                tory requirements, he would ordinarily be correct in his assertion that he has acquired
                title by adverse possession. Most jurisdictions, however, prohibit the acquisition of city
                or state property by adverse possession. This being the only legal obstacle to Adpo's
                assertion, the outcome will most likely depend on whether the jurisdiction permits the
                acquisition of city property by adverse possession.

                A is incorrect because if the possession was open and notorious as described above, it
                does not matter whether the actual owner ever really knew of it. Some adverse posses-

sion statutes establish a condition that the adverse possessor pay taxes on the realty during the period of his adverse possession. **C** is incorrect, however, because this statute did not contain such a requirement. An adverse possessor who occupies land under color of title may become the owner of all the land which he believed he owned, including that which he did not actually occupy. Since Adpo asserts ownership only of the land which he occupied, however, color of title is irrelevant, and **D** is incorrect.

94. **B**   Joint tenancy is a form of co-ownership in which the joint tenants have the right of survivorship. This means that upon the death of one joint tenant, the others receive equal shares in her interest. When Marion died, Harold and Wilhemina received equal shares of her interest. The joint tenancy of Harold and Wilhemina continued, but each held a one-half interest in the whole instead of a one-third interest. Joint tenants may convey their interests inter vivos without each other's consent, but a joint tenant's grantee takes as a tenant in common with the remaining owners. Thus, upon Wilhemina's conveyance to Bernard, Bernard and Harold were tenants in common, each with a one-half interest. Upon Harold's conveyance to Charles, Charles and Bernard became tenants in common, each with a one-half interest.

A is incorrect because as a joint tenant, Marion could not effectively pass her interest by will. Since a conveyance by a joint tenant makes the grantee a tenant in common, neither Bernard nor Charles received a joint tenancy in any part of the estate. **C** is, therefore, incorrect. **D** is incorrect for this reason, and because Allan received no interest at all under Marion's will.

95. **A**   Today, all jurisdictions have recording statutes which determine priorities. In cases not covered by the recording statutes, however, common law rules of priority apply. The statute in this question determined the priority of interests in cases in which the subsequent taker was a purchaser for value and without notice. Since Santor received the conveyance as a gift, he gave nothing in return for it, and was, therefore, not a purchaser for value. As a result, the statute does not apply, and common law rules of priorities do. At common law, priorities between successive transferees of interests in real property are determined simply on the basis of chronology — "first in time, first in right." Thus, since Lender received his interest before Santor received his interest, Lender's is superior.

If the statute was applicable, Lender's interest would have been superior to Santor's only if Lender's mortgage was recorded before Flying Acres was conveyed to Santor. If the mortgage was not recorded before the conveyance occurred, the fact that the mortgage was recorded before the conveyance was recorded would not give priority to the mortgage. **B** is, therefore, incorrect. Unless an applicable recording statute has a contrary effect, a grantee of mortgaged realty takes subject to the mortgage, whether or not the existence of the mortgage is mentioned in the grantee's deed. Since the recording statute is not applicable to Santor's interest, Santor took the realty subject to Lender's mortgage. **C** is, therefore, incorrect. **D** is incorrect for two reasons: first, the statute imposes the requirement of value on junior claimants, and Lender is the senior claimant; and, second, Lender was a purchaser for value since he gave consideration (i.e., a loan of $20,000) in return for an interest in realty (i.e., the mortgage).

96. **C**   The given statute is a "race-notice" type statute, in that it makes good faith and prior

recording conditions for a subsequent grantee's priority. Although Santor took the realty in good faith, he did not record before Lender. Lender's interest is, therefore, superior to Santor's.

An interest is said to be recorded outside the chain of title when it was recorded in a way which would have prevented the reasonable title searcher from discovering it. In most jurisdictions, an interest recorded outside the chain of title is regarded as not having been recorded at all. Under the given statute, however, the first interest has priority so long as it was recorded before the subsequent interest was recorded. Since Santor's interest was recorded two days after Lender's, and since there was no reason why a title searcher would not have discovered Lender's interest at that time, **A** is incorrect. Although the statute's "good faith" requirement is probably satisfied by the fact that Santor lacked actual or constructive notice of Lender's interest at the time Flying Acres was conveyed to him, **B** is incorrect because the statute imposes the additional requirement that the subsequent interest be recorded before the earlier one. Most "notice" and "race-notice" statutes establish the payment of value as a condition of the junior claimant's priority. A careful reading of this statute will show that it does not, however. **D** is, therefore, incorrect.

97. **B**   Warranties of title contained in a deed are representations that the grantor has a right to convey the title which he purports to convey. If those warranties are breached, it is by the delivery of a deed which purports to convey title which the grantor does not have a right to convey. The warranties can thus be breached only at the time that the deed is delivered. For that reason, most jurisdictions hold that only the grantee can maintain an action for damages resulting from the breach. Since Berkley was not Onda's grantee, Berkley will not succeed in his action against Onda.

Since the breach occurs upon delivery of the deed, it is not "cured" by any subsequent act of the grantor. **A** is, therefore, incorrect. The covenant of quiet enjoyment is a warranty that the grantee shall peaceably and quietly enjoy possession without interference by anyone with a lawful claim of title. It is breached only by some interference with the right of possession, not merely by the existence of superior interests. Although the covenant of quiet enjoyment can be enforced by successors to the grantee's interest, **C** is incorrect because there has been no interference with Berkley's possession. Because covenants of title can be breached only upon the covenantor's delivery of the deed, Onda's covenant could not be breached by Alton's conveyance. **D** is, therefore, incorrect.

98. **D**   If a person without ownership purports to convey an estate which he does not have and he subsequently acquires title to that estate, the doctrine of estoppel prevents the grantor from asserting his title against his grantee and causes the after-acquired title to pass directly to the grantee by operation of law.

Since the covenants made by Onda were breached only by Onda's delivery of a deed purporting to convey title which he did not have, and since only his grantee could sue for damages resulting from such breach, Onda's covenants to Alton are not relevant in Berkley's action. **A** is, therefore, incorrect. **B** is incorrect because Berkley's rights against Alton are independent of any rights which Alton may have against Onda. Thus, the existence of an effective remedy which Alton can exercise against Onda is not, alone, sufficient to entitle Berkley to the relief he seeks from Alton. Although Alton's intention may have been to convey Northacre to Berkley on June 15, he was incapable of doing so at that time since he had not received title to Northacre from Onda. For this reason, Alton's conveyance to Berkley could not have conveyed an interest in Northacre, no matter what Alton intended. **C** is, therefore, incorrect.

99. **A**   Under the Rule Against Perpetuities, no interest is good unless it must vest, if at all, during a period measured by a life or lives in being plus 21 years. Since it is possible that the change in use would occur after the end of this period, both grants to Second Foundation would appear to violate the Rule. The Rule Against Perpetuities is not applied, however, to shifts from one charity to another, so Second Foundation's interest in Greenacre is valid. Since Nephew and Niece are not charities, Second Foundation's interest in Redacre is invalid. **B**, **C**, and **D** are, therefore, incorrect.

100. **C**   An executory interest is a grantee's future interest in land which will become possessory upon the termination of a prior estate, which termination is not inevitable. If the executory interest replaces the interest of another grantee, it is a shifting interest. Since the termination of Nephew's and Niece's interests in Redacre is not inevitable, Second Foundation holds an executory interest. Since its interest will replace that of Nephew or Niece, it is a shifting executory interest.

A and **B** are incorrect because a remainder is a future interest which will become possessory upon the termination of a prior estate, which termination is inevitable, and the termination of Nephew's and Niece's interests in Redacre is not inevitable. **D** is incorrect because a springing interest is one which will cut off the possessory right of the *grantor.*

101. **D**   While a tenant who vacates after an assignment is no longer in privity of estate with the landlord, he continues to be in privity of contract under the initial lease and continues to be liable for rent. The assignor's liability is secondary while the assignee's liability is primary. Thus, if Lattimer is successful in collecting from Torry, Torry may seek indemnity from Antun. This does not, however, protect Torry from liability to Lattimer.

The lease required Torry to obtain Lattimer's permission before assigning. If he had not done so, some jurisdictions might permit Lattimer to avoid the assignment, although the majority would not. In any event, however, Lattimer's consent does not operate to destroy his contract rights against Torry. **A** is, therefore, incorrect. A novation is an agreement by which parties to a contract substitute a new party for one of the original parties. In order for a novation to occur, there must be an agreement by the new party to assume the contractual obligations of the party whom he is replacing, *and* an agreement by the original obligee to extinguish the contractual obligations of the party who is being replaced. Although Antun agreed to personally assume Torry's obligations under the lease, Lattimer did not agree to relieve Torry of those obligations. Thus, there was no novation, and **B** is incorrect. Usually, an assignee of a tenant's rights under a lease is liable to the landlord only for rent which accrued during the assignment period. An assignee who personally assumes obligations under the lease may also be liable for rent accrued before the assignment took place or after reassignment. The assumption of obligations by an assignee might, thus, impose additional duties on that assignee. It does not, however, relieve the assignor of any of his initial obligations to the landlord. **C** is, therefore, incorrect.

102. **A**   An assignee of a tenant's rights under a lease is in privity of estate with the landlord, and is, therefore, liable for rent accrued during the period of his possession. If he personally assumes the obligations of the lease he is also liable for rent accrued before the assignment went into effect and after it terminates. Since in his agreement with Torry, Antun personally assumed the obligations of the lease, he is personally liable for rent accrued throughout the entire duration of the lease. Although Lattimer was not a party to this agreement, he can enforce it as an intended, creditor, third party beneficiary.

      By collecting from subsequent assignees, a landlord does not waive the right to collect rent from an assignor who is obligated to pay it. **B** is, therefore, incorrect. **C** is incorrect because Lattimer was a third party beneficiary of the contract between Antun and Torry, and can therefore enforce the promise made by Antun. Because Antun agreed to personally assume the obligations of the lease, he was obligated to pay all sums due under it. Since the obligation to pay rent under a lease does not depend on whether or not the lessee is in possession of the premises, Antun is liable for all rent which accrued throughout the duration of the lease whether he was in possession of the premises or not. **D** is, therefore, incorrect.

103. **D**   A fixture is a former chattel, which, by reason of its annexation to realty, has become part of the realty. A tenant is entitled to use leased realty, but not to remove parts of it when he leaves. Thus, if the improvements made by Tolliver were fixtures (i.e., became part of the realty), Tolliver would not be entitled to the judgment which he seeks. One of the factors considered in determining whether an improvement made by the tenant was so annexed to the realty as to be a fixture is whether it can be removed without causing any substantial damage to the realty. If so, the improvement may be regarded as a *chattel* which belongs to the tenant, and which he is, therefore, entitled to remove, rather than as a *fixture* which has become part of the realty. Although this factor alone might not be sufficient to keep the improvements from being regarded as fixtures, it is the only one listed which could support the conclusion that they are not.

      The value of the improvements is not relevant, since even a valuable improvement may be a fixture if it became part of the realty, and if so, it belongs to the landlord. **A** is, therefore, incorrect. **B** is incorrect because an improvement is a fixture if it has become part of the realty, and this does not logically depend on whether it was foreseeable that the tenant would make it. The general rule is that the tenant may not remove fixtures, unless the parties agreed to the contrary. Absent such an agreement, the general rule applies. **C** is, therefore, incorrect.

104. **D**   An easement is the right to use realty of another. The realty subject to the easement is called the servient estate. If the benefit which the holder of an easement receives is associated with her/his ownership of a particular parcel of realty, the easement is appurtenant, and the realty benefitted by that easement is called the dominant estate. Easements appurtenant are freely alienable, usually transferred with a conveyance of the dominant estate. If an easement is recorded, subsequent grantees of the servient estate have constructive notice of its existence and take the servient estate subject to the easement. Since according to the advice in option **D** the easements which Anthony and Bernice would grant each other would be for access to their own parcels of realty, they would be

easements appurtenant. The effect of the transaction would be that Anthony and Bernice each would own half of the driveway and hold an easement over the other's half. Since the easements would be appurtenant, they would be transferable to any transferees of the dominant estates. Since they would be recorded, they would bind any transferees of the servient estates. Thus, each property owner would have the right to use the entire driveway (i.e., the half which s/he owns and the half over which s/he has an easement), and neither would have the right to interfere with the other's use.

A is incorrect because such a contract would only bind the parties to it. If the successor to either were to partition, the only remedy would be an action for damages against the original promisor. **B** is incorrect since a joint tenant may sell her interest, the grantee becoming a tenant in common with the remaining party. This would leave the remaining party in the same position in which she was in the beginning. **C** is based on an inaccurate statement of the law, since tenants in common do have the right to partition.

105. **D**   Valid title is not necessarily marketable. Since no one should be required to purchase a lawsuit, marketable title means title about which there is no reasonable doubt of validity. To decide whether Albert held marketable title in August 1985, it is necessary to determine whether the quitclaim which he executed in 1980 could possibly have affected his title to the realty. A will speaks on the death of the testator. This means that no devise of an interest in realty created by Testor's will was of legal effect until Testor's death in 1982. Albert, thus, had no interest at all in Testacre in 1980 when he executed the quitclaim to Koppell. Since a quitclaim conveys only the interest which the grantor holds at the time of its execution, Albert gave up no interest in the realty as a result of the 1980 quitclaim. Under Testor's will, Albert received a remainder in a one-third interest in Testacre which became possessory upon the death of Agatha in June 1985. His title was, therefore, marketable on the day he tendered the deed to Koppell.

Although a quitclaim conveys whatever interest the grantor possesses at the time of its execution, **A** is incorrect because Albert held no interest in Testacre when he executed the quitclaim to Koppell in 1980. A remainder is a future interest which will become possessory upon the termination of a prior estate the termination of which is inevitable. Since Agatha's death was inevitable, Albert received on the death of Testor a remainder which became possessory on the death of Agatha. Albert's interest was, therefore, valid, making **B** incorrect. A general warranty deed ordinarily contains a grantor's warranty that he holds the interest which is conveyed. But no one is required to buy a lawsuit. A warranty of title provides a remedy against the grantor, but it does not make the title marketable. Were title unmarketable at the time Albert tendered the deed, Albert would be failing to fulfill his obligation under the contract of sale, and Purch could not be required to go through with the transaction. **C** is, therefore, incorrect.

106. **A**   A "class gift" is a gift to a group of persons undefined in number when the gift is made, to be ascertained at a time subsequent to the making of the gift, the share of each being dependent on the ultimate number of persons within the group. Since Testor's devise of a one-third interest following Agatha's death was to "the children of Brooke," the share received by each child of Brooke was dependent on the total number of Brooke's children. Since Testor's will spoke upon his death, and since Brooke could continue having children after Testor's death, this number was undetermined at the time the gift was made. The gift to the children of Brooke was, thus, a class gift. Since Babs was a mem-

ber of that class (i.e., the children of Brooke) at the time the gift was made (i.e., on the death of Testor) she received a vested interest immediately upon Testor's death. But since enjoyment of her interest was postponed until the death of Agatha, and since it was possible for Brooke to have more children (thus enlarging the size of the class, and diminishing the share of each of its members) before Agatha died, the interest of Babs was subject to partial defeasance until Agatha's death. So, when Babs conveyed to Lincoln, he received an interest which was subject to partial defeasance for as long as the class remained open. When enjoyment of a class gift is postponed until the happening of a specified event (here, the death of Agatha), the class closes upon the happening of that event, so long as there are class members at that time. Since Babs was in existence at the time of Agatha's death, the class closed at that time. No new members could be added to the class, and Babs' interest, which had by then been conveyed to Lincoln, was no longer subject to partial defeasance. Thus, on the day after Agatha's death, Lincoln held an indefeasible one-third interest.

B is incorrect because even if Brooke had more children, they could not take, since the class closed on the death of Agatha. **C** is incorrect for that reason, and because even if the class remained open, the addition of new members would decrease the share of each old member, but would not completely displace that share. Since Testor's will imposed no conditions on Babs' interest except the death of Agatha, and since the death of Agatha was inevitable, Babs' interest was vested (subject to partial defeasance) when she conveyed it to Lincoln. **D** is, therefore, incorrect.

107. **C**   A remainder is a future interest which will become possessory upon the termination of a prior estate the termination of which is inevitable. If some further condition must be met BEFORE the remainder will become possessory (i.e., a condition precedent) it is contingent. If no further condition must be met before the remainder will become possessory (i.e., if it will automatically become possessory upon the termination of the prior estate), it is vested. If some condition exists which could destroy the interest AFTER it becomes possessory, the remainder is subject to a condition subsequent. Since the devise in Testor's will provided that a one-third interest would go to the children of Carmody "upon the death of Agatha" and imposed no other conditions *precedent,* Carrera's interest was a vested remainder. Since, however, the interest would pass to another if Carrera failed to survive to the age of 25, Carrera's vested remainder was subject to a condition subsequent.

Under the Rule Against Perpetuities, no interest is good unless it must vest, if at all, within a period of time measured by a life or lives in being plus 21 years. Since Carrera's interest was already vested, the Rule Against Perpetuities does not apply to it. **B** and **D** are, therefore, incorrect. Since there was no condition precedent to Carrera's remainder's becoming possessory, it was not contingent. **A** and **B** are, therefore, incorrect.

108. **C**   After granting an interest in realty, a grantor may continue to hold one of three future interests in the realty. If the grantor has conveyed any interest which is less than that which s/he holds, her/his future interest is a reversion (e.g., Grantor, who holds a fee simple absolute, conveys only a life estate or an estate for years. Grantor retains a reversion.) If the grantor conveys her/his interest in a way which may result in the grantee's eventual loss of the interest conveyed, the grantor's possible future interest is either a

possibility of reverter or a right of re-entry. If the grantee's interest is to terminate automatically upon the happening of a specified event, the grantee's interest is determinable, and the grantor's future interest is called a possibility of reverter (e.g., Grantor, who holds a fee simple absolute, conveys "to Grantee for so long as the premises are used for residential purposes." If the premises ever cease to be used for residential purposes, Grantee's estate will terminate automatically and the fee will revert to Grantor. The conveyance has given Grantee a fee determinable, and Grantor retains a possibility of reverter.) On the other hand, if the grantee's interest will not terminate automatically, but the grantor retains the right to terminate the grantee's interest on the happening of a specific event, the grantee's interest is subject to a condition subsequent, and the grantor's future interest is a right of re-entry (e.g., Grantor, who holds a fee simple absolute, conveys "to Grantee, but if the premises ever cease to be used for residential purposes, Grantor may re-enter." The conveyance has given Grantee a fee subject to a condition subsequent, and Grantor retains a right of re-entry.)

Although the conveyance executed by Oldham contains language which may result in the Church's loss of its interest, it does not convey an interest less than that held by Oldham. For this reason, the future interest retained by Oldham cannot be a reversion and must be either a possibility of reverter or a right of re-entry. The deed makes use of the realty for non-church purposes an event which could result in the Church's loss of its interest. From the language of the deed, however, it is difficult to tell whether the Church's interest is one which will terminate automatically (i.e., a fee determinable) or which can be terminated by some act of Oldham (i.e., a fee subject to a condition subsequent). It is thus difficult to determine whether Oldham's future interest is a possibility of reverter or a right of re-entry. Since right of re-entry is not listed among the options, however, **C** is the correct answer.

A remainder is a future interest held by a **grantee** which will become possessory following the inevitable termination of a prior estate. Since Oldham was the grantor rather than a grantee, his interest cannot be a remainder. **A** is, therefore, incorrect. **B** is incorrect because Oldham did not convey less than his entire interest. An executory interest is a future interest held by a **grantee** which will become possessory following the termination of the prior estate when termination is not inevitable. Since Oldham was the grantor rather than a grantee, his interest cannot be executory. **D** is, therefore, incorrect.

109.　**C**　Nabor asserted that his easement pre-existed the grant by Oldham. If it did, it could not be said that the Church of the Lord permitted a use other than for church purposes, since it had no power to do otherwise. Since Oldham's right was to become possessory only if the church permitted use other than for church purposes, this argument might defeat Oldham's claim. While it is not certain that a court would come to this conclusion, **C** is the only argument listed which might support the Church's position.

A is incorrect because if the church permitted use of the property for other than church purposes, thus violating the limitation (or fulfilling the condition subsequent) contained in the grant, then the interest of the Church of the Lord would terminate, even though there may have been sound motivation for its conduct. It may be true that the language of the deed created a fee simple determinable. **B** is incorrect, however, because this conclusion would result in the termination of the Church of the Lord's interest. Although Oldham's interest under the deed will not necessarily vest within the period prescribed by the Rule Against Perpetuities, **D** is incorrect because the Rule Against Perpetuities does not apply to a future interest of the grantor.

110. **D**   One who "assumes" an existing mortgage when purchasing realty personally undertakes to pay the note which the mortgage secures and is thus personally liable for payments on the note. On the other hand, one who merely takes "subject to" the mortgage does not undertake to satisfy any personal obligations. Since Carrol took the realty subject to the mortgage, without agreeing to personally undertake obligations under the note, National Bank cannot collect from her under the note.

If Carrol made an enforceable promise to Beryl to pay the note, National Bank would be a third party beneficiary of that promise and would be entitled to enforce it. **A** is incorrect, however, because by taking "subject to the mortgage," Carrol did not promise to pay the note. A "due on sale" clause makes the entire debt under a mortgage note payable when the mortgaged realty is sold, thus effectively prohibiting a purchaser from taking subject to or from assuming the mortgage. **B** is incorrect, however, because a "due on sale" clause does not impose any personal obligations on a purchaser. Because courts favor the alienability of interests in real property, a purchaser of realty may take "subject to" or "assume" an existing mortgage unless a clause of the mortgage specifically prohibits such a transaction. **C** is incorrect for this reason and because one who merely takes "subject to" a mortgage does not thereby undertake any personal obligation.

111. **D**   One who assumes an existing mortgage when purchasing realty personally undertakes to pay the note which the mortgage secures and is thus personally liable for payments on the note. Subsequent sales of the realty, even to other purchasers who "assume" the mortgage, do not relieve prior obligors of personal obligations which they agreed to assume. Since Oliphant promised to pay (by executing the initial note) she continues to be personally liable. Since April and Beryl promised to pay (by assuming the mortgage) they continue to be personally liable.

A, B, and **C** are, therefore, incorrect.

112. **B**   So long as payments due under a mortgage note remain unpaid, the mortgagee, or its assignee, is entitled to foreclose.

In the absence of a specific agreement to the contrary, rights under a contract in general, and a mortgage in particular, are assignable, so long as the assignment does not impose any additional burden on the obligor. Since the assignment by National Bank to Investco imposed no additional burden on anyone obligated to make payments under the mortgage note, it was valid. **A** is, therefore, incorrect. Some jurisdictions require a mortgagee to elect a remedy upon default, offering a choice of foreclosure or an action on the note, but not both. Although the value of the realty relative to the amount due under the note might make one choice strategically better than another, **C** is incorrect because the mortgagee is always free to choose foreclosure. One who takes property "subject to" a mortgage is not personally liable for payments on the mortgage note. **D** is incorrect, however, because the mortgagee's right to foreclose is not extinguished by a sale of the premises. [*Note:* An obvious meaning of the phrase "subject to" is "affected by," and should make it clear that the rights of one who takes subject to a mortgage may be affected by that mortgage.]

113.   **C**   An easement is a right to use, but not to possess, the land of another. The land which is subject to an easement is known as the servient tenement or estate. The holder of an easement may not overburden the servient estate. This means that the easement holder may not change the easement or use it in a way which was not contemplated when it was created. An easement holder has the right and the duty to maintain the easement, but may not do so in a way which would overburden the servient estate. Some cases have held that paving an easement which has long existed as a dirt road overburdens the servient estate. Whether or not a court would so hold in this case is unknown. The easement created by the deeds was only 12 feet wide, however, and Corfu now seeks to widen it to 24 feet. This would undoubtedly overburden the servient estate, since it would increase the portion of that estate which is subject to use by the easement holder and reduce the portion available for unlimited use by its owner.

Sometimes a change in circumstance may justify a change in use of an easement. The fact that the road becomes muddy after a heavy rain for example, might justify paving it. **A** is incorrect, however, because doubling the width of the easement is a change substantial enough to result in an overburdening of the servient estate. The holder of a servient estate has no obligation to maintain an easement running across it, while the user of such easement is required and is entitled to maintain it at his own expense. This does not give the easement holder the unilateral right to make changes in the easement, however, simply because he is willing to pay for them himself. **B** is, therefore, incorrect. Even if the construction of the road which Corfu proposes to build would improve the value of the lots affected, Bolton is free to reject the improvement in value, choosing to keep his land the way it is. **D** is, therefore, incorrect.

114.   **D**   Some jurisdictions recognize a special co-tenancy known as tenancy by the entirety which can be held only by a husband and wife. Where it exists, tenancy by the entirety is like joint tenancy in that it gives each co-tenant the right of survivorship, but is unlike joint tenancy in that neither co-tenant may sever it without the consent of the other. In those jurisdictions which recognize tenancy by the entirety, it is presumed that any conveyance to a husband and wife creates a tenancy by entirety. Most such jurisdictions hold that the presumption may be rebutted by evidence that some other form of ownership was contemplated by the parties to the conveyance. The conveyance to Bridey and Gallon "as joint tenants" rebuts the presumption and results in a joint tenancy. Although a joint tenant may convey her interest without the consent of the other joint tenant, such a conveyance severs the joint tenancy as to the interest conveyed and makes the grantee a tenant in common. (Note: In some jurisdictions, there is an **irrebuttable** presumption that a conveyance to husband and wife creates a tenancy by the entirety. In these jurisdictions, Bridey's purported transfer to Thomas would be void unless Gallon consented to it. Of the answers listed, however, **D** is the only one which could possibly be correct.)

A quitclaim extinguishes the rights of the person executing it by conveying those rights to the person receiving it, although it does not specify what those rights are or warrant that they exist. **A** is, therefore, incorrect. Although a quitclaim ordinarily transfers whatever interest is held by the person executing it, any transfer by a joint tenant severs the joint tenancy. For this reason, Bridey's conveyance to Thomas severed the joint tenancy, and **B** is incorrect. **C** is incorrect because only a husband and wife may hold title as tenants by the entirety.

115. **B**   A deed does not effectively convey realty until it is delivered. Although delivery does not always require a transfer of physical possession of the deed by the grantor to the grantee, it does require some word or act by the grantor which manifests his intent that the conveyance shall have a present operative effect. When Orsican placed the envelope on the dining-room table, it was with the intention of mailing it the following morning. Since it was always possible for him to change his mind before mailing it, the fact that he planned to mail it is not sufficient to manifest an intent that it would be presently operative. Since he died without doing anything which would manifest such an intent, there was no delivery.

Conveyance by deed is not effective unless the deed is accepted by the grantee, but if the grant is beneficial, the grantee's acceptance is presumed. Thus, if Orsican had manifested the necessary intent (e.g., by mailing the deed), a delivery might have taken place even though Geriardy died before she became aware of the conveyance. **A** is, therefore, incorrect. The presumption that a grantee has accepted a deed can be rebutted by proof that she rejected it. Such a rejection could not take place, however, unless the grantee knew about the deed. For this reason, if Geriardy had sent back the envelope containing the deed without knowing its contents, she would not have rejected it by so doing. **C** is incorrect, however, because Dot was not the grantee, and because there was no delivery to Geriardy. Ordinarily, a grantor's delivery of a deed to a third person with instructions to deliver it to the grantee is a delivery to the grantee so long as the grantor relinquished all control. It may be that mailing a deed has that effect, since the sender ordinarily loses control over an envelope once it is delivered to the postal authorities. **D** is incorrect, however, because Orsican did not relinquish control over the envelope before his death.

116. **C**   Although the most common forms of description involve reference to metes and bounds, manmade and natural markers, government survey markers, or property address, any method of description is sufficient if it establishes the identity of the realty conveyed with reasonable clarity. Under the facts, it cannot be determined whether the description identifies the realty conveyed with reasonable clarity. If it does, however, the description is adequate.

A, **B**, and **D** are, therefore, incorrect.

117. **D**   The taking of an entire parcel of realty by eminent domain results in acquisition by the taker of all present and future interests in the realty. For this reason, the leasehold interest passes with the rest of the property whether or not it is specifically mentioned in the judicial decree. **I** is, therefore, incorrect. Since the lessee thus loses his right to occupy the property, he is freed from the obligation of paying rent due under the balance of the lease. **II** is, therefore, correct. A leasehold interest is a non-freehold but possessory interest in real property. As with any property interest, if it is taken for public use, its holder is entitled to "just compensation" under the Fifth Amendment to the United States Constitution. Since taking the realty by eminent domain results in a condemnation of the leasehold as well as the landlord's reversion, the lessee is entitled to a proportionate share of the condemnation award. Since he is entitled to be compensated for what he has lost, his share should be based on the value of the unexpired balance of his term. Since he is no longer obligated to pay rent, however, the rent which he would have

otherwise had to pay should be deducted from the value. **III** is, therefore, correct.

118. **D**   A person may acquire title to realty by adverse possession if she occupies it without its owner's permission openly, notoriously, and continuously for the statutory period of time. This occurs because the running of a statute of limitations then makes it impossible for the adverse possessor to be judicially ejected. Since a new owner acquires the old owner's right to eject an unlawful possessor, the statutory period of limitations continues to run in spite of changes in ownership. Since Altman has adversely possessed the realty for more than 15 years, she has acquired title by adverse possession.

For the above reason, the fact that Stephen became the owner in 1977 did not restart the period. If the owner of the realty is under a legal disability (e.g., infancy) at the time the adverse possession begins, commencement of the statutory period is delayed until the legal disability has terminated. If the owner is not under a legal disability at the time the possession begins, however, the fact that he subsequently suffers a legal disability or that title subsequently passes to a person who is under a legal disability will have no effect on the running of the statutory period. Since there is no fact indicating that Odette was under any legal disability in 1970 when Altman began her possession of the realty, the running of the statutory period commenced at that time, and continued without interruption upon the passage of title to Stephen. **A** is, therefore, incorrect. Since only a person with a right of possession can sue to eject an unlawful possessor, the statute of limitations cannot work against the holder of a future interest. Thus, an adverse possessor acquires only the possessory interest which existed at the time of her possession. If, for example, Odette had been the holder of a life estate with a remainder in Stephen, Altman's adverse possession during Odette's life could have led only to Altman's acquisition of a life estate by adverse possession. Then, upon Odette's death in 1977, a new period of possession would have begun against Stephen's fee interest. The will by which Stephen received title spoke only upon Odette's death, however. This means that when Altman began possession in 1970, Stephen had no future interest at all. Since there is no fact to the contrary, Odette's interest must have been a fee when Altman moved on, and it was this fee which Altman acquired by adverse possession. For this reason, **B** is incorrect. **C** is incorrect for the reasons given above, because at the time Altman's adverse possession began, the holder of the fee interest (Odette) was under no disability, and because if the possession is open and notorious, it does not matter whether the owner is aware of it.

119. **C**   Under the doctrine of equitable conversion, the risk of loss passes to a buyer of realty as soon as a contract of sale is formed. Thus, if the jurisdictions applies this doctrine, Buchanan must sustain the loss resulting from destruction of the barn.

If an essential part of the realty is destroyed prior to passage of the risk of loss, a buyer might be excused from performing his obligations under the contract of sale. On the other hand, if a non-essential part of the realty is destroyed, the buyer might be required to go through with the purchase with an abatement of the price to compensate for the loss. Thus, if the risk of loss had not passed to Buchanan, the fact that the barn was not an essential part of the realty might prevent him from withdrawing from the transaction, but would not permit Statler to collect the full price. **A** is, therefore, incorrect. Although many jurisdictions hold that the risk of loss passes to a buyer as soon as he takes possession of the realty, there is no principal of law by which possession creates a presumption of fault. **B** is, therefore, incorrect. Once a risk of loss passes to a party, that party suffers the consequence of such a loss even if it did not result from his fault. Since there are various theories which might have passed the risk of loss to Buchanan (e.g., the doctrine of equitable conversion; possession), the fact that he was without fault would not, alone, be sufficient to prevent him from bearing the loss. **D** is, therefore, incorrect.

120.   **B**   Under the facts given, it is possible that the conveyance to Atkins created an "easement implied by prior use" (similar to "easement by necessity"). This may arise when a grantor conveys a portion of his land, retaining a part over which an apparent previous use existed which was reasonably necessary to the enjoyment of the portion conveyed and could have been the subject of an easement. Since the existence of a dirt road made previous use across Obie's land apparent, and since river access might be reasonably necessary to the use and enjoyment of Atkins' land, the deed to Atkins may thus have created an easement by implication. Although it is not certain that a court would come to this conclusion, **B** is the only argument listed which might be effective for Boylan.

An easement by dedication is a use granted to the public either by deed or by operation of law. Since there is no indication that the dirt road ever became a public right-of-way, **A** is incorrect. An easement by express reservation is created by a deed in which the grantor retains a right to use the realty conveyed. Since Atkins was a grantee, she could not have obtained an easement by express reservation. **C** is, therefore, incorrect. An easement by express grant is created by a deed which specifically conveys to a grantee the right to use the property of another. Since Obie's deed to Atkins did not mention the easement, and since there is no fact indicating that Atkins ever received it by conveyance, there was no easement by express grant. **D** is, therefore, incorrect.

121.   **A**   An easement by prescription (similar to title by adverse possession) may be acquired by hostile, continuous, open, and notorious use of another's realty for the statutory period of time. In order to be hostile, the use must be inconsistent with the rights of the owner. Since the owner of realty has the right to permit use of his realty, use with his permission is not inconsistent with his rights (i.e., hostile). Since Atkins was using the road with Obie's permission, she could not have acquired rights by prescription.

B and **D** are incorrect because changes in conditions of the realty do not affect the acquisition of prescriptive rights to use it. **C** is incorrect because prescriptive easements do not require express grants.

122.   **C**   Those who own land adjacent to a flowing body of water (i.e., riparian owners) have some rights to use that water. Under modern common law, each riparian owner has the right to make reasonable use of the water. If construction of a dam would result in the consumption of more water than is reasonably necessary, a court might hold that Upton has no right to build the dam.

A is incorrect because Upton's increased use of the water might still be reasonable. At one time it was said that no riparian owner was permitted a use which altered the natural flow of the stream. If "natural flow" is given a literal meaning, this would make it virtually impossible for anyone but the furthest downstream owner to use the water. For this reason, the natural flow rule has given way to a rule which bases riparian rights on reasonable use. Thus, even if the dam altered the natural flow, Upton would have a right to construct it so long as his use was reasonable. **B** is, therefore, incorrect. Under the reasonable use test, Upton may dam the stream so long as doing so would not make his water use unreasonable. **D** is incorrect because this would be so even if he could accomplish the same without damming the stream.

123. **C**   Under the existing reasonable use doctrine, when it is necessary to determine which riparian owner is entitled to water which is in limited supply, the courts consider many factors. Most important, however, is the use to which each owner puts the water. Although agricultural use is considered "higher" than most other uses, domestic or household use is universally acknowledged to be the "highest" use of all, entitling it to priority over all other uses. Since the choice to be made is between Upton's agricultural use and Downey's household use, Downey's rights will prevail.

A is incorrect because upstream owners do not ordinarily have greater rights than downstream owners. **B** is incorrect because household use is a higher use than agricultural use. **D** is incorrect because with the retreat from the natural flow doctrine, downstream owners do not have greater rights than upstream owners.

124. **D**   If leased realty is taken by eminent domain, the leasehold and the reversion merge in the taker, the leasehold is terminated, and the obligation to pay rent ceases. Since both the lessor and the lessee have had something of value taken for public use, each is entitled to receive just compensation for what she has lost. The lessor is entitled to receive the value of the leased premises (including the value of rent to be received) minus the value of the leasehold interest which he has already conveyed. The lessee is entitled to receive the value of the leasehold. If not for the condemnation, however, the lessee would have been required to pay rent in order to enjoy the benefits of her leasehold. Since the condemnation terminates that obligation, the rent which the lessee otherwise would have been required to pay should be deducted from the value of her leasehold.

A is incorrect because the taking terminates the leasehold, and with it, the obligation to pay rent. The Rule Against Perpetuities provides that no interest is good unless it must vest if at all within a period of time measured by a life or lives in being plus twenty-one years. Since a lessee's interest in leased premises vests at the moment the lease is executed, the Rule Against Perpetuities is inapplicable to it. **B** is, therefore, incorrect. Since the condemnation terminates Teeter's obligation to pay rent for the balance of the lease term, allowing her to keep the entire $30,000 would result in her receiving more than she has actually lost. For this reason, **C** is incorrect.

125. **A**   Proceeds of a foreclosure sale are taken by holders of security interests in the order of the priority of their respective interests. Since mortgages and trust deeds create security interests in realty, the priority of the conflicting claims will be determined in accordance with the recording statute. The statute given is a typical notice statute. According to its terms, the interest held by Bank cannot take priority over the interest held by Finance because Bank's mortgage had not been recorded when Finance received its interest, Finance gave value for its interest, and there is no fact indicating that Finance was aware of Bank's mortgage when Finance received its interest.

Since neither the statute nor the common law makes priority depend on whether any person has notice of the interests of **subsequent** takers, **B** is incorrect. Recording statutes generally do apply to security interests in realty. In addition, this statute specifically refers to the transfer of "an interest in realty," and so, by its terms, applies to security interests. **C** is, therefore, incorrect. **D** is incorrect because in determining priorities of interests in real property, purchase-money mortgages do not receive any greater priority than other mortgages.

126. **A**   Probably the best-known characteristic of the joint tenancy is the right of survivorship. Under it, when a joint tenant dies, her interest is not inherited by her heirs and distributees, but passes to the remaining joint tenants. At common law, a joint tenancy could not exist unless the shares and possessory rights of the joint tenants were equal, and unless the interests of the joint tenants were created at the same time, and by the same document. (These are known as the four unities — unity of interest, possession, time, and title.) Many states have modified these common law requirements by statute, but even in those states the shares of joint tenants are presumed equal unless there is an agreement to the contrary. For this reason, the reconveyance by Wendy and Hal created a joint tenancy, with Wendy, Hal, and Claire each holding a one-third interest. Upon Wendy's death, her third passed to Hal and Claire in equal shares, continuing them in joint tenancy with each holding a one-half interest in the realty.

B, **C**, and **D** are incorrect because upon the death of a joint tenant, the surviving joint tenants continue in joint tenancy. In addition, **B** and **C** are incorrect because upon a joint tenant's death, her share passes equally to the surviving joint tenants.

127. **B**   The language of the covenant in Farmer's deed to Amador contained two parts. The first part restricted the use of the land conveyed by that deed. Since Farmer was not engaging in any activity on that land, this part of the covenant does not burden him at all. The second part required all further deeds to land in Farmer's Green to bear the same covenant. Since Farmer has not yet conveyed any of the other land in Farmer's Green, none of it is burdened by the covenant.

A covenant which runs with the land benefits successors to the original covenantee, and burdens successors to the original covenantor. Thus, a covenantee's successor may enforce it even though it was not mentioned in his deed, and even though he was not in privity with the covenantor. For this reason, **A** and **C** are incorrect. In order for a covenant to run, it must touch and concern the land. A covenant restricting the use of land in a subdivision touches and concerns the covenantor's estate because it affects the value of the burdened estate, and because only the person in possession of that estate can possibly be burdened by it. Such a covenant touches and concerns the covenantee's estate because the permitted uses of land in a subdivision necessarily affect the value of other land in the subdivision. For these reasons, **D** is incorrect.

128. **C**   Ordinarily, if a covenant would have been enforceable as between the covenanting parties, it is enforceable by and against their successors if it runs with the land. A covenant is said to run with the land if the covenanting parties intended that it would bind their successors, if the covenant touches and concerns the land involved, and if the necessary privity exists between the covenanting parties, and between the parties by and against whom enforcement is sought. The language of the covenant, "for themselves, their heirs, successors, and assigns," is the language traditionally used to indicate that the parties intended that their successors be bound. The covenant touches and concerns the

land for the reasons given in the explanation for Option **D** in the previous question. The necessary privity existed between Farmer and Amador because they were grantor and grantee. The necessary privity exists between Farmer and Berge because Berge succeeded to Amador's interest. For these reasons, the covenant contained in Farmer's deed to Amador runs with the land, thus binding Berge. Although covenants running with the land are usually enforceable only at law (i.e., by a judgment for damages), they may be enforceable as equitable servitudes (i.e., by injunction) if money damages would not be an adequate remedy. Since it was Farmer's intention to create a residential community, since the presence of a gas station would probably interfere with the residential character of the community, and since money damages would not prevent this from happening, the remedy at law is probably not adequate and the covenant is probably enforceable by injunction as an equitable servitude.

This is true whether or not Farmer succeeds in selling the rest of the subdivision. Some cases hold that when passage of time and change of circumstances make restrictive covenants fail of their initial purpose, they may cease to be of effect. Perhaps this could eventually lead a court to find that the restriction, obviously designed to protect the residential nature of the subdivision, is unenforceable because the neighborhood is not really residential in nature. **A** is incorrect, however, because six months is not a sufficiently long period of time to justify such a conclusion. Equitable servitudes may be enforced against successors to the covenantor even though they did not agree to be bound by them. This is particularly so where recording of the deed gives those successors constructive notice of the existence of the restriction. **B** is, therefore, incorrect. If the covenant runs with the land, it is enforceable against Berge whether or not his violation of it will result in actual damage. If the covenant does not run with the land, it is not enforceable against Berge, even if its violation would result in actual damage. For this reason, **D** is incorrect.

129. **C** A periodic tenancy is a tenancy which will continue for a stated period and for repeated similar periods unless terminated by proper notice from one of the parties. Since the written agreement created a tenancy for one month which was to automatically renew each month unless terminated as provided, it created a periodic tenancy.

A tenancy for years is an estate for a fixed determinable period of time (not necessarily measured in years). Since the written agreement did not fix a time for the expiration of Thaler's tenancy, it did not create a tenancy for years. **A** is, therefore, incorrect. A tenancy at will is an estate without a fixed duration which will continue until terminated by either party. By its nature, it is continuous until affirmatively terminated. Unlike the periodic tenancy, its continuation does not depend on the automatic renewal of an agreement for a stated period. Since the written agreement of January 1 was for one month subject to automatic renewal, **B** is incorrect. When a tenant fails to vacate at the expiration of his leasehold, he becomes a tenant at sufferance. **C** is incorrect because a tenancy at sufferance is not created by written agreement.

130. **A** One of the features of a periodic tenancy is that at the end of the period it can be terminated by either party on notice and without cause. At common law, one month was required to terminate a month-to-month periodic tenancy. Today, however, it is understood that the parties are free to negotiate their own terms including the notice required for termination. Since the written agreement specified that either party could terminate

on 20 days notice, and since Lawson gave 20 days notice, the court should find for Lawson.

Since a periodic tenancy can be terminated on notice without cause, it is not necessary for Lawson to show that Thaler has violated any covenant. **B** is, therefore, incorrect. Although a breach of covenant by Lawson might entitle Thaler to damages or give him the right to terminate, it would not prevent Lawson from terminating. Thus, even if Lawson did violate some express covenant of the agreement, the court should find for Lawson in this eviction proceeding. **C** is, therefore, incorrect. Some jurisdictions have held that implicit in a lease is a covenant of good faith and fair dealing. **D** is incorrect, however, because, even if such a covenant was implied by the agreement, there is no evidence that Lawson was not acting in good faith or dealing fairly. [**Note:** Although the facts state that Thaler made complaints, there is no indication that the complaints motivated the eviction. Although some jurisdictions presume that an eviction is retaliatory if it occurs within 90 days after complaints by a tenant, there is no indication that Lawson's notice was served within 90 days after Thaler's complaints. Thus, even if the jurisdiction forbids "retaliatory eviction," Thaler cannot prevail on this theory.]

131. **B**   Voluntary waste consists of some act by a possessory tenant which diminishes the value of the realty or otherwise "injures the inheritance." One of the ways in which it is committed is by removing minerals from the land. Ordinarily, when a life tenant commits voluntary waste, the holder of a vested remainder is entitled to bring an immediate action at law for damages. In the alternative, the remainderman may be entitled to the equitable remedies of injunction and an accounting for profits already derived from the sale of such minerals. [**Note**: Although it is understood that a possessory tenant may remove minerals from realty which is good for no other purpose, or may continue removing minerals from a mine which was open when his tenancy began, neither of these exceptions applies under the facts in this case.]

A possessory tenant who commits voluntary waste is not entitled to retain any of the profits from his activity. For this reason, Unity Church is entitled to all profits derived from the sale of gravel, rather than merely to a proportionate share. **A** is, therefore, incorrect. It is sometimes held that the holder of a contingent remainder or a remainder subject to defeasance has no right to sue for waste until its interest vests indefeasibly. Since the remainder interest held by Unity Church is already vested, however, **C** is incorrect. The rule which permits a possessory tenant to continue removing minerals from a mine which was open when he began his tenancy is sometimes known as the "open pit" doctrine. **D** is incorrect, however, because the facts indicate that gravel had never before been mined or removed from the land.

132. **A**   A class gift is a gift to a group of persons undefined in number when the gift is made. Orr's will created a class gift, since it devised the realty to all children of Seth without specifying their names or their number. A class gift passes to all persons who are in the class at the time the class opens or who enter the class prior to its closing. Ordinarily a class opens at the time the gift is created. Since Orr's will spoke at the time of Orr's death, and since Judy and Pete were already in existence at that time, they are obviously within the class and entitled to an interest in the realty. In determining whether Ella received an interest, it is necessary to decide when the class closed. If there are members of the class in existence at the time the class gift is created, the class opens and closes

immediately upon creation of the gift. Since Judy and Pete were in existence at the time of Orr's death, the class closed immediately upon Orr's death. For this reason, Ella did not enter the class before its closing, and, therefore, received no interest in the realty.

B and **C** are incorrect for the above reason. Under the Rule Against Perpetuities, no interest is good unless it must vest, if at all, within a period of time measured by a life or lives in being plus twenty-one years. Since Seth was in being at the time Orr's will spoke, and since Seth could not have children after his own death, no interest created by Orr's will could possibly vest after a period measured by the life of Seth. **D** is, therefore, incorrect.

133. **D** In the contract between Lawrence and Arthur (i.e., the lease), Arthur agreed to pay rent of $1,000 per month for the entire term of the lease. Arthur cannot unilaterally change this obligation by assigning the lease to another. Thus, although the assignment to Burton might make Burton responsible for rent, it does not free Arthur of such liability. For this reason, Lawrence is entitled to collect from Arthur all unpaid rent.

 A is incorrect because Burton's liability is additional to Arthur's and does not free Arthur from liability. **B** and **C** are incorrect because Arthur agreed to pay rent for the entire lease period.

134. **C** An assignee of a leasehold interest is under an obligation to pay rent accruing under the lease so long as he is in possession of the premises. For this reason, Calloway is responsible for the rent which was unpaid during his occupancy.

 If the assignee agrees to be personally liable for all obligations under the lease, he may be responsible for unpaid rent which accrued before or after his period of occupancy as well. One who does not agree to be personally liable is not responsible for rent which accrued before and after his occupancy. **A** is incorrect, however, because even if he does not agree to be personally liable for all obligations, he is required to pay rent accrued during his occupancy. Although Calloway and Lawrence are not in privity of contract, Lawrence may collect from Calloway on two theories: first, as an occupant of the premises, Calloway was in privity of estate with Lawrence which at least allows Lawrence to collect rent from him for that period; and second, an assignment of rights includes an implied delegation of obligations, which Lawrence may enforce directly against Calloway as an intended creditor third party beneficiary of the agreement between Calloway and Burton. **B** is, therefore, incorrect. Since Calloway did not agree to be personally liable for all obligations under the lease, he is not responsible for rent which accrued after his assignment of the leasehold to Daniel. **D** is, therefore, incorrect.

135. **D** Probably the best known attribute of joint tenancy is the right of survivorship. This means that when one joint tenant dies, the remaining joint tenant(s) inherit(s) the interest of the deceased. Sale of an interest by a joint tenant destroys the joint tenancy as to the seller's interest, and the buyer takes as a tenant in common. The other joint tenants continue to be joint tenants, however. This means that when Alvarez conveyed her interest to Dot, Dot became a tenant in common with a one third interest, while Barnum and Curtis continued to be joint tenants as to the remaining two thirds. Because of the right of survivorship, Barnum's attempt to transfer his interest by will was ineffective. As a result, upon Barnum's death, Curtis (as Barnum's joint tenant) survived to Barnum's

interest, and Sonny received no interest at all. Since Curtis already held a one third interest and since he inherited Barnum's interest, Curtis ended up with a two thirds interest.

A is incorrect because, as a result of Curtis's right of survivorship, Barnum's will could not pass an interest to Sonny. **B** is incorrect for the same reason, and because sale by a joint tenant breaks the joint tenancy as to the seller's interest, which means that Dot took as a tenant in common. **C** is incorrect because Dot took as a tenant in common and, therefore, did not receive any share of Barnum's interest upon Barnum's death.

136.　**C**　Title to property may be acquired by adverse possession if the person claiming such title occupies the realty openly, notoriously, hostilely, and continuously for the statutory period. Possession is "open and notorious" if the possessor has, in general, behaved as an owner. Since Adamo occupied the premises every summer, his possession was open and notorious. Possession is "hostile" if it is contrary to the rights of the owner. Since the facts do not indicate that Adamo had the owner's permission to occupy the cabin, his occupancy was hostile. While possession must be "continuous," it need not be without interruptions if the interruptions are consistent with the appropriate use of the realty. Since this was a summer cabin, occupancy only during the summers might have been consistent with its appropriate use. If it was, Adamo has acquired title by adverse possession.

Once the period of possession has begun, it continues to run in spite of conveyances or other changes in ownership. Thus, **A** is an inaccurate statement and is, therefore, incorrect. If the owner of realty is under a legal disability at the time adverse possession begins, computation of the period of possession does not start until the disability ends. If, however, the owner is not under a legal disability at the time adverse possession begins, subsequent legal disability or legal disability of a subsequent owner does not interrupt the running of the period. **B** is, therefore, incorrect. Because of the requirement that adverse possession be hostile to the rights of the owner, one who occupies with permission of the owner cannot acquire title by adverse possession. **D** is, therefore, incorrect.

137.　**A**　By its terms, the given recording statute applies only where the subsequent taker is a "purchaser for value." Since Norwood received the realty as a gift, she is not a purchaser for value. The recording statute, therefore, does not apply, In the absence of an applicable recording statute, the common law rule of "first in time — first in right" prevails. Since Morgan received his interest before Norwood received hers (i.e., Morgan is first in time), Morgan's interest is superior to Norwood's.

By definition, a mortgage is a security interest in realty. **B** is, therefore, an inaccurate statement and is incorrect. As explained above, the absence of an applicable recording statute makes Norwood's interest inferior to Morgan's because it was created after Morgan's. **C** is, therefore, incorrect. Since the conveyance to Norwood made no mention of Morgan's mortgage, Norwood is without notice of its existence. The statute only protects a person without notice, however, if she is a purchaser for value. **D** is, therefore, incorrect.

138.　**C**　A grantee's future interest is a remainder if it follows an estate which is certain to terminate. If there are no conditions precedent to the remainder's becoming possessory other than termination of the prior estate, the remainder is vested. If there are additional conditions precedent, the remainder is contingent. Since Baretto's estate becomes possessory on the death of either Agar or Chevalier, and since these deaths are certain to occur, Baretto's interest is a vested remainder.

A is incorrect because only a grantor can hold a reversion. **C** is incorrect because, except for the death of the life tenant, there is no condition precedent to Baretto's interest becoming possessory. Under the rule against perpetuities, no interest is good unless it must vest, if at all, during a period measured by a life or lives in being plus twenty-one years. Since Baretto's interest is vested, it does not violate the rule against perpetuities. **D** is, therefore, incorrect.

139. **D**   Most jurisdictions in the United States apply the doctrine of "reasonable use" to disputes involving underground percolating waters. This means that owners of realty are permitted to make whatever use of the aquifer is reasonable, even if it adversely affects their neighbors. Thus, if Bradshaw's planned use of water tapped from the aquifer is found to be reasonable, the court will not enjoin him from using it. Although a minority of jurisdictions disagree, **D** is the only answer listed which could be correct in any jurisdiction.

A is incorrect because the number of persons using a well is not relevant in determining the rights of other users of the aquifer. Since both Anderson and Bradshaw are entitled to make reasonable use of water taken from the aquifer, **B** is incorrect. **C** is incorrect because a court could find Anderson's use of the water reasonable even though he derives a profit from it.

140. **C**   Under the "Rule in Dumpor's Case," many jurisdictions hold that if a landlord consents to an assignment by the tenant, the covenant against assignment is thereafter waived and the assignee may in turn assign to another without being bound by the covenant. Although it is not certain that the court in this jurisdiction would apply the rule, **C** is the only option listed which could possibly be effective in Cole's defense.

Courts strictly construe restraints against the alienation of leasehold interests. This means that a covenant against assignments does not prevent subleases, and vice versa. **A** is incorrect, however, because although such covenants are strictly construed, they are not void. Ordinarily, an assignment made in violation of a covenant not to assign is valid, and the landlord has no remedy other than an action for damages resulting from the breach. Where, as here, however, the landlord reserves the right to terminate the lease in the event of a violation of the covenant, the assignment is voidable at the landlord's election. **B** is, therefore, incorrect. An assignment is a transfer of all remaining rights under a lease; a sublease is a transfer of less than all remaining rights. Since Boyer transferred all remaining rights to Cole, the transfer was an assignment, and **D** is incorrect.

141. **C**   An easement is a right to use the land of another. If the right benefits a parcel of realty, that parcel is known as the dominant estate and the one burdened by the easement is known as the servient estate. If both the dominant and servient estates were owned by the same person, and if a right-of-way easement across the servient estate is necessary

to provide access to the dominant estate, the sale of either parcel results in an implied easement by necessity. Northacre and Southacre were both owned by Archer, and since the only access to Northacre was over the dirt road which crossed Southacre, Barnhart received an implied easement by necessity over Southacre when he purchased it.

When the common owner of two parcels uses one of them for the benefit of the other, and when signs of that use are visible, a quasi-easement may exist which passes by implication to the buyer of the parcel which received the benefit of such use. **A** is incorrect, however, because Archer never actually used Northacre or the dirt road which crossed Southacre. A grantor of realty may reserve for himself an easement to use it, and under some circumstances (e.g., strict necessity), such a reservation may be implied. **B** is incorrect, however, because only a grantor can receive an easement by reservation. Ordinarily, an easement of record benefits subsequent owners of the dominant estate even if it is not mentioned in the deeds by which the dominant estate was conveyed to them. When the dominant estate and the servient estate merge (i.e., are owned by the same person), however, all existing easements terminate. **D** is, therefore, incorrect.

142. **B**   Although the existence of an easement may make title to realty unmarketable, most courts hold that this is not so where the buyer was aware of the easement at the time he contracted to purchase the realty. Since Coates saw the dirt road prior to contracting, it is likely that a court would hold that its existence does not prevent the title from being marketable. While it is not certain that a court would come to this conclusion, the argument in **B** is the only one listed which could possibly provide support for Archer's claim.

If a buyer accepts a deed which does not conform to the requirements of the purchase contract, he has waived his rights under the contract because the contract is said to merge with the deed. **A** is incorrect, however, because Coates did not accept the deed and so is still protected by the terms of the contract. Marketable title means title that is reasonably secure against attack. Since the existence of an easement would provide the holder of a dominant estate with a ground to attack the rights of the holder of the servient estate, an undisclosed easement is usually sufficient to render title to the servient estate unmarketable. **C** is, therefore, incorrect. A covenant to deliver marketable title is implied in a contract for the sale of realty unless some other quality of title is specified. Since the contract between Archer and Coates did not specify the quality of title to be conveyed, Archer is required to convey marketable title. **D** is, therefore, incorrect.

143. **A**   Every contract for the sale of realty contains an implied covenant by the seller that he will deliver marketable title. Marketable title means title which is reasonably secure against attack. It is generally understood that title to property which is being used in violation of a zoning law is not marketable. If a seller is unable to deliver marketable title, the buyer is not required to complete the transaction because no person should be required to purchase potential litigation. Since Foley's agreement to purchase the house was connected with his purchase of the business, it is likely that a court would find that the zoning violation constitutes a defect which excuses Foley from going through with the purchase. Although it is not certain that a court would come to this conclusion, **A** is the only option which could possibly be correct.

B and **C** are incorrect because the courts usually hold that an existing zoning violation makes title unmarketable. **D** is incorrect because a public law which prohibits a particular activity takes precedence over a private rule which permits it.

144.   **A**   Ordinarily zoning laws determine the use to which land may be put. Thus, if the zoning law permits the construction of a three story office building, Graves may construct it.

B is incorrect because there is no rule which requires a court to permit the highest and best use of realty. Although an easement for air, light, and view may be created by express grant, **C** is incorrect because courts do not recognize an implied easement for air, light, or view. If land was being used in a way which violates a zoning law passed after the use began, the non-conforming use is permitted to continue. **D** is incorrect, however, because the non-conforming use is never *required* to continue.

145.   **C**   Developers are permitted to create conditions on the use of land in their subdivisions which are more restrictive than public laws. Thus, even where zoning law permits a particular activity, deed restrictions may validly prohibit it. Since restrictions contained in all the deeds to land in Green Hills prohibit the keeping of horses, a court will enforce these restrictions, and Ralph should receive the relief which he seeks.

A is, therefore, incorrect. Where a zoning law restricts land to residential use but does not define that use, the resolution of a dispute about whether a particular activity can be conducted there will depend on whether that activity is part of ordinary residential use. **B** is incorrect, however, because the deed restrictions in Green Hills clearly prohibit the keeping of horses. Although a court may enjoin a nuisance, **D** is incorrect because a court may enforce the deed restrictions without regard to whether keeping horses is a nuisance.

146.   **C**   A fee simple determinable is a fee interest which will terminate automatically upon the happening of a specified event. Courts almost always hold that a grant to a particular grantee "so long as" something does not happen creates this interest. Although the phrase "but if" makes it uncertain that a court will come to this conclusion, **C** is the only answer listed which could possibly be correct.

Although an interest which might vest after a period measured by a life or lives in being plus twenty one years is void under the rule against perpetuities, this does not affect the validity of any prior estate. For this reason, even if the interest of the Foundation for Hereditary Diseases violates this rule against perpetuities, that has no effect on the validity of Geller's interest. **A** is, therefore, incorrect. A fee simple absolute is complete ownership which is not subject to defeasance. **B** is incorrect because of the special limitation created by the phrase "so long as." A fee simple subject to a condition subsequent is an interest which is subject to defeasance on the happening of a specified event, but which does not terminate until the holder of the future interest takes some step to make his interest possessory. Courts frequently hold that the phrase "but if" creates a condition subsequent which allows the holder of a future interest to take action to terminate the estate upon the happening of that condition. **D** is incorrect, however, for two reasons. First, the phrase "so long as" probably results in a fee simple determinable. The second reason relates to application of the Rule Against Perpetuities. Although the Rule may prevent interests which violate it from vesting, this does not affect the validity or character of interests which become possessory during the period prescribed by the Rule. This means that even if the interest of the Foundation is void under the Rule, the character of Geller's interest does not change.

147. **C**   Under the rule against perpetuities, no interest is good unless it must vest, if at all, during a period measured by a life or lives in being plus twenty one years. Since liquor might be sold on the premises after the expiration of this period, it is possible that the interest of the Foundation for Hereditary diseases would vest beyond the period of perpetuities. For this reason, it received no valid interest.

The future interest of a charity is not subject to the rule against perpetuities if it follows the estate of another charity. Otherwise, the rule against perpetuities applies as it would to any other grantee. **A** is incorrect because there is no indication that Geller is a charity. **B** is incorrect because only a grantor can hold a right of re-entry. An executory interest is a future interest which follows an estate which is not certain to terminate. If it follows the estate of a grantor, it is a springing executory interest. **D** is incorrect, however, because the interest of the Foundation for Hereditary Diseases is void as explained above.

148. **A**   In those jurisdictions which apply the doctrine of equitable conversion, a purchaser under a real estate sales contract becomes the equitable owner of the realty and bears the risk of loss as soon as the contract is formed. In those jurisdictions which have adopted the Uniform Vendor and Purchaser Risk Act, the risk of loss does not pass to the buyer until either title or possession has passed. But both these rules apply only when the parties have not agreed to the contrary. Parties to a contract are free to agree as to when the risk of loss is to pass. In this contract, the parties agreed that the risk of loss would not pass until title was conveyed.

B, **C**, and **D** are incorrect because they ignore the agreement of the parties.

QUESTIONS
TORTS

TORTS
TABLE OF CONTENTS
Numbers refer to Question Numbers

TORTS QUESTIONS

Questions 1-3 are based on the following fact situation.

Delphi was the manufacturer of a product known as Delphi's Follicle, which was sold over the counter for the treatment of dandruff and dry scalp conditions. Patrick purchased a bottle of Delphi's Follicle at Farma's drugstore. A statement on the label read, "This product will not harm normal scalp or hair." Patrick used the product as directed. Because of a scalp condition making him allergic to one of the ingredients, the product irritated his scalp, causing him much pain and discomfort.

1. In an action for negligence by Patrick against Delphi, which of the following additional facts or inferences, if it was the only one true, would be most effective in Delphi's defense?

   (A) Patrick did not read the statement on the label.

   (B) The reasonable person in Delphi's position would not have foreseen that the product would injure persons with Patrick's allergy.

   (C) The product was manufactured for Delphi by another company.

   (D) Delphi was unaware that an allergy existed like that suffered by Patrick.

2. In an action by Patrick against Delphi on the theory of strict liability in tort, which of the following additional facts or inferences, if it was the only one true, would be most helpful to Patrick's case?

   (A) Injuries of the kind sustained by Patrick do not ordinarily result from the use of a product like Delphi's Follicle unless the manufacturer was negligent.

   (B) Prior to Patrick's purchase of the product, an article regarding the allergy from which he suffered had appeared in a widely-read journal of the hair-care industry.

   (C) The reasonable person would not have expected the use of Delphi's Follicle to result in an irritation of the scalp of someone with Patrick's allergy.

   (D) At the time it manufactured the product purchased by Patrick, Delphi was aware that its ingredients could irritate the scalp of persons with allergies like Patrick's.

3. In an action by Patrick against Farma, which of the following would be Patrick's most effective argument?

   (A) Any negligence by Delphi is imputed to Farma.

   (B) The product was defective as labeled.

   (C) Farma breached an express warranty.

   (D) A drugstore is under a special duty to be aware of possible allergic reactions to products which it sells.

4. Drake lived in a neighborhood in which the incidence of violent crime had been increasing. Poll and Drake were having tea together in Drake's kitchen, when there was a knock at the door of Drake's home. Although the door was equipped with a peephole which would have enabled Drake to see who was outside before opening, Drake opened the door without looking. As soon as the door was opened, Thug, an armed robber, entered with a gun. Thug struck Poll several times with the barrel of his pistol before robbing her of her money and leaving. Poll subsequently asserted a negligence claim against Drake for injuries resulting from the attack, alleging that it was negligent for Drake to open the door without looking to see who was there.

   Which of the following additional facts if it was the only one true, would be most helpful to Poll's claim against Drake?

(A) Drake was aware of the high incidence of crime in the neighborhood.

(B) Poll was aware of the high incidence of crime in the neighborhood.

(C) Drake had invited Poll for tea because she hoped to sell Poll her used living room furniture.

(D) One of Drake's neighbors had been robbed and attacked by Thug in a similar manner the previous day.

5. Homsted had been living on the family farm most of his life. Because he was ready to retire, he advertised his farm for sale. Devel, a real estate investor and developer, had been secretly advised by a friend in the state highway department that a major highway would soon be built adjacent to Homsted's land. Knowing that this would increase the value of the property, Devel contacted Homsted and offered to purchase the farm. Devel said that she would be willing to pay the fair market value as determined by any licensed real estate appraiser selected by Homsted. Homsted hired Prays, a licensed real estate appraiser, who determined the fair market value to be $400,000. Devel purchased the land, paying that price.

Three weeks after the closing of title, the state announced plans to build a highway adjacent to the land. This announcement increased the value of the land to $4,000,000. If Homsted institutes an action for misrepresentation against Devel, the court should find for

(A) Devel, if Homsted knew her to be a real estate investor.

(B) Devel, because she allowed Homsted's appraiser to determine the fair market value of the land.

(C) Homsted, because Devel's failure to disclose the coming of the highway was a breach of a fiduciary obligation.

(D) Homsted, if Devel had an obligation to disclose that the state would be building a highway adjacent to the land.

6. Patton was injured when a robber shot her with a pistol manufactured by Gunco. She asserted a claim against Gunco, alleging that the pistol with which she had been shot was meant to be sold for a price under $50. Which of the following arguments is most likely to lead to a judgment for Patton?

(A) Gunco is vicariously liable for battery, since it was foreseeable that a purchaser of the pistol would shoot another person with it.

(B) Gunco breached an implied warranty that the gun was merchantable, since a pistol which is meant to be sold for under $50 is unfit for ordinary use.

(C) Gunco is liable for negligence, since the criminal law is designed to protect persons like Patton from becoming the victims of robbers.

(D) Gunco is liable for negligence, since the low selling price of the pistol made it foreseeable that it would be used in connection with a crime.

Questions 7-8 are based on the following fact situation.

Sippy was already intoxicated when he entered Barr's Tavern. At first, Barr refused to serve him any more alcohol. Sippy insisted, however, and at his insistence, Barr served him three more drinks. When Sippy left the bar he was unable to start his car. He asked Helper, who was driving by, to assist him. Helper, who realized that Sippy was drunk, determined that Sippy's battery was weak, and started Sippy's car by connecting a cable to her own battery. Later, while driving, Sippy struck Pedex, who was walking across the street.

7. Assume for the purpose of this question only that Pedex asserted a claim for his personal injuries against Helper. Which one of the following facts or inferences, if it was the only one true, would provide Helper with the most effective defense?

(A) The state had a statute making a barkeeper liable for damage done by a person who purchased alcohol from the barkeeper after already being intoxicated.

(B) Helper was in the business of rendering road service to motorists having trouble with their cars.

(C) Sippy drove 200 miles before striking Pedex.

(D) Sippy would not have struck Pedex if he had not been intoxicated.

8. Assume for the purpose of this question only that Pedex asserted a claim for his personal injuries against Barr. Which of the following would be Barr's most effective argument in defense?

(A) Sippy was already intoxicated when he came into the bar.

(B) The accident would not have occurred if Helper did not help Sippy get his car started.

(C) The reasonable person would not have expected Sippy to drive when he left the bar.

(D) Persons outside Barr's tavern were not in privity with Barr.

9. Danvers was driving down Main Street at an unreasonably fast rate of speed when, as a result, he collided with Parker's car which was standing unattended against the curb. The impact caused a loaded rifle which Parker had left in the back seat of the car to fire. The bullet went through the car window and traveled four blocks before striking Blandings, who was leaving the Rainbow paint factory after work. Although Blandings had lost the sight in his left eye in an accident which occurred when he was a child, he was employed by the Rainbow Paint Company as a color coordinator. As a result of his being struck by the bullet from Parker's rifle, Blandings lost the sight in his right eye. This rendered him totally blind, causing him to lose his job. Blandings subsequently asserted a negligence claim against Danvers, alleging permanent loss of earning capacity in addition to other items of damage.

Which of the following is Danvers's most effective argument in defense against Blandings's claim for permanent loss of earning capacity?

(A) Blandings was a super-sensitive plaintiff, since he was already blind in one eye.

(B) Parker acted unreasonably by leaving a loaded rifle in the back seat of his car.

(C) Blandings was outside the foreseeable zone of danger.

(D) The reasonable person would not have expected that Danvers's conduct would cause any person to be rendered blind.

10. Burg broke into Gro's grocery store in the middle of the night. After stealing all the money that was in the cash register, she blew open the door of the safe with nitroglycerin and stole its contents as well. Then, as she was leaving, she stole a six-pack of Three Star Beer. Because of poor quality control at the Three Star brewery where it was made, the beer contained a toxic ingredient. Later that night, Burg drank three cans of the beer and was made seriously ill by the toxic ingredient which it contained. In an action by Burg against Three Star, the court will most likely find for

(A) Burg, if her injury was proximately caused by the negligence of Three Star.

(B) Burg, since Three Star breached an express warranty.

(C) Three Star, since Burg does not come into court with "clean hands."

(D) Three Star, if Burg's theft of the beer is regarded as unforeseeable.

11. Global Studios was filming part of a motion picture at a large residential apartment building with the permission of the building owner. To avoid interference by curious onlookers, Global's security agents set up a command post in the lobby of the building. No persons were allowed to enter the building without identifying themselves and explaining their reasons for being there. Rezzie, who lived in an apartment in the building, was returning from a fishing trip late one night.

Unaware of Global's activities, he was stopped by Global employees as he attempted to enter. Because he was not carrying identification, Rezzie was unable to establish his identity. For this reason, the employees refused to allow him to enter. After trying unsuccessfully to convince them that he lived there, Rezzie stayed with his sister who lived a block away. The following morning, he contacted the building owner who spoke to Global officials and arranged to have them allow Rezzie to enter.

If Rezzie asserts a claim against Global for false imprisonment, which of the following would be Global's most effective argument in defense?

(A) Global employees did not know that Rezzie was entitled to enter the building.

(B) The conduct of Global employees was not unreasonable.

(C) Rezzie was not imprisoned.

(D) Rezzie sustained no damage as a result of the conduct of Global employees.

12. Prescott, who owned an appliance repair shop, was at a cocktail party when he saw Dresden, one of his competitors. Approaching Dresden, Prescott said, "I'm glad to run into you. I was hoping that we could discuss the possibility of going into partnership instead of competing with each other." Dresden responded, "I wouldn't go into business with you because you're the most incompetent person I've ever known."Audit, a customer of Prescott's, overheard the conversation. As a result, the following day, Audit cancelled a contract which he had with Prescott.

If Prescott asserts a claim against Dresden for defamation, Prescott will be successful if

(A) Dresden knew or should have known that the statement was defamatory when he made it.

(B) Dresden knew or should have known that the statement was false when he made it.

(C) Dresden knew or should have known that the statement would be overheard when he

made it.

(D) Dresden knew or should have known that harm would result from the statement.

Questions 13-14 are based on the following fact situation.

Farmer owned 500 acres of land on which she grew wheat. By a valid written contract, she agreed to deliver all her wheat to Bredco to be used by that company in the production of bread for sale to the general public. While harvesting the crop, she realized that a blade on her harvesting machine was broken, and that fine slivers of metal were becoming mixed with the wheat. She said nothing about this when she delivered the wheat to Bredco, since she knew that Bredco ordinarily cleaned its wheat before using it. The harvesting machine had been manufactured and sold by Tracto.

Bredco used the wheat which it purchased from Farmer to manufacture a loaf of bread which it sold to Deli, who operated a sandwich shop. Deli used the bread to make a sandwich. Because the bread contained slivers of the blade from Farmer's harvesting machine, Pawnie lacerated the lining of his throat when he swallowed a bite of the sandwich.

13. Which of the following additional facts or inferences, if it was the only one true, would be most helpful to Farmer in defense against an action brought by Pawnie on a theory of strict liability in tort?

(A) If Bredco acted reasonably, the slivers of metal would have been removed from the wheat before it was baked into bread.

(B) The sandwich which contained the slivers of metal had been purchased by one of Pawnie's co-workers who gave it to Pawnie after changing his mind about eating it.

(C) Bredco made substantial changes in the wheat before it reached Pawnie.

(D) The blade on Farmer's harvesting machine was defective when she purchased it from Tracto.

14. In an action by Pawnie against Bredco, can Pawnie successfully rely on the doctrine of res ipsa loquitur?

   (A) Yes, if the exercise of reasonable care in the baking process would ordinarily have eliminated all metal slivers from the wheat.

   (B) Yes, if the presence of metal slivers made the bread defective.

   (C) No, if the presence of the metal slivers in the wheat resulted from Farmer's failure to use reasonable care.

   (D) No, if it was unforeseeable that a broken blade on Farmer's harvesting machine would result in the presence of metal slivers in the wheat.

15. Purtle and Delfin were drinking at the same bar when Purtle began insulting Delfin by calling him names which were ethnically offensive. When they started to argue with each other, the bartender asked them both to leave. Purtle got into his car and drove away. Angry, Delfin began chasing him in his own car. When he caught up with Purtle, Delfin began passing Purtle's car on the left. As he did so, he swerved his car towards Purtle's for the purpose of frightening Purtle. Purtle did not know that the car swerving toward him was Delfin's but he became frightened that it would hit him and steered away from it, striking a fire hydrant and sustaining injury.

   If Purtle institutes an action against Delfin, a court should hold Delfin liable for

   (A) battery only.

   (B) assault only.

   (C) both battery and assault.

   (D) neither battery nor assault.

16. Bender was interested in purchasing Solet's house. Because Bender knew that some of the houses in the area were infested with termites, he asked Solet whether there were any termites in his house. Solet said that there were none, believ-ing this statement to be true. Bender purchased the house from Solet and moved into it. Three months later, Bender discovered that the framework of the house had been damaged by termites, and that the termites had been damaging the framework for several years. He subsequently asserted a claim against Solet on a theory of negligent misrepresentation.

   Which of the following is Solet's most effective argument in defense against Bender's claim?

   (A) Solet did not know that there were termites in the house.

   (B) Solet had no duty to tell Bender whether there were termites in the house.

   (C) Solet's statement that there were no termites in the house was an expression of opinion.

   (D) Solet's belief that there were no termites in the house was reasonable.

17. Preston purchased a box labeled "Generic Breakfast Cereal" from Riteway Supermarket. While he was eating it, he broke a tooth on a stone which the product contained. The product sold by Riteway and labeled "Generic Breakfast Cereal" is furnished by three different companies: Acme, Birdco, and Cullen. Each sells an approximately equal quantity to Riteway. In addition, all package their product in identical wrappers, so that it is impossible to tell which of them furnished any given box of breakfast cereal. Although the companies compete with each other, at Riteway's request they worked together to design the product wrapper.

   If Preston is successful in an action for damages against Riteway, it will probably be because

   (A) Riteway, Acme, Birdco, and Cullen were involved in a concerted action in the manufacture and marketing of the product.

   (B) Riteway, Acme, Birdco, and Cullen established standards on an industry-wide basis, which standards made identification of the product's manufacturer impossible.

   (C) the negligence of either Acme, Birdco, or

Cullen resulted in harm to Preston under circumstances such that it was impossible to tell which of them caused the harm; and Riteway is vicariously liable for that negligence.

(D) either Acme, Birdco, or Cullen manufactured a defective product, and Riteway sold that product while it was in a defective condition.

Questions 18-19 are based on the following fact situation.

Dot, a thirteen-year-old girl, was a member of Survival Scouts, a national young people's organization. As part of a Survival Scout project, she planned to spend an entire weekend camping alone in the woods. Napper, who knew about the project, phoned Dot's mother Mabe the day after Dot left home. Napper said, "We have your daughter. We've already beaten her up once, just to hear her scream. Next time, we might kill her." Napper instructed Mabe to deliver a cash ransom to a specified location within one hour. Since there was no way to locate Dot's campsite in the woods, Mabe could not find out whether Napper was telling the truth. Horrified that her daughter might be beaten and injured or killed, she delivered the ransom as instructed. She remained in a hysterical state until Dot returned from her camping trip, and Mabe realized that the ransom demand had been a hoax. Mabe, who already suffered from a heart ailment, had a heart attack the day after Dot's return.

18. If Mabe asserts a claim against Napper for assault, the court should find for

(A) Mabe, because Napper was aware that his conduct would frighten her.

(B) Mabe, because the court will transfer Napper's intent.

(C) Napper, because Mabe did not perceive injury being inflicted upon Dot.

(D) Napper, because Mabe had no reason to expect to be touched by Napper.

19. If Mabe asserts a claim against Napper for dam-

ages resulting from her heart attack on a theory of intentional infliction of mental distress, the court should find for

(A) Napper, because the heart attack occurred the day after Dot's return.

(B) Napper, if Mabe's pre-existing condition made her especially susceptible to heart attack.

(C) Mabe, if the heart attack was caused by Napper's outrageous conduct.

(D) Mabe, because Napper should have foreseen that his conduct would result in harm.

20. Starr was a retired motion picture actor whose career had consisted primarily of a series of small roles in films about the jungle. Starr owned a leopard named Spots, which Starr had trained and which had appeared with him in motion pictures. Spots had always been tame and gentle, even when young. When Starr retired, Spots was old, almost blind, somewhat slow moving, and the size of a large dog. Starr brought the animal to live with him, keeping it in the fenced yard alongside his house. Paston was a thirteen-year-old girl who delivered newspapers to Starr. One day, she came to Starr's home to collect for the past week's deliveries. Since she knew Spots, Paston opened the gate and called the animal so that she could pet him. Spots bounded toward the place from which the sound had come, but because he was almost blind, he bumped into Paston. Paston fell to the ground, fracturing her ankle.

If Paston asserts a claim against Starr on a theory of strict liability, the court should find for

(A) Starr, because the injury did not result from a trait which made it dangerous to keep a leopard.

(B) Starr, because Spots was not a wild animal.

(C) Paston, because it was unreasonable for Starr to keep Spots in his yard.

(D) Paston, because Starr should have anticipated that a child would attempt to pet

Spots.

Questions 21-22 are based on the following fact situation.

While Primm was visiting her daughter, the two of them decided to go swimming at a nearby public pool. Since she had not brought a bathing suit along on her visit, Primm went to Depp's store to purchase one. While looking at the suits on the bargain counter, she found one which had been manufactured by Sutter. The package which contained it bore a label which read, "Disposable Bathing Suit. This garment is made completely from recycled paper. Although it is strong enough to be worn several times and is even washable, it's inexpensive enough to be thrown away after one use. Buy several, and take them with you on trips to the beach." Primm bought the bathing suit and wore it at the public swimming pool. After swimming for a few minutes, she climbed up to the diving board. She was preparing to dive into the pool when the wet paper bathing suit suddenly dissolved and fell from her in shreds, leaving her completely naked. Horrified, Primm climbed down from the diving board as quickly as she could, calling to her daughter who ran over and wrapped her in a towel.

21. If Primm asserts a claim against Sutter for damages resulting from her embarrassment, Sutter's best argument in defense is that

(A) Sutter made no representations to Primm.

(B) Primm sustained no physical injury or symptoms.

(C) Primm purchased the suit from Depp.

(D) Sutter acted reasonably in manufacturing and labeling the bathing suit.

22. Which of the following additional facts or inferences, if it was the only one true, would be most helpful to Depp's defense in an action by Primm against Depp?

(A) Depp had sold Sutter's products for several years, and had never heard of any problem like the one experienced by Primm.

(B) A sign on the bargain counter where Primm found the suit said, "Sale Merchandise. All sales final."

(C) Primm knew that paper bathing suits like the one she had purchased sometimes dissolved when they became wet.

(D) Depp could not implead Sutter into the action because Sutter had gone out of business.

23. Mater needed butter for the cookies which she was baking, so she asked her seven-year-old son Sammy to go to the store on Main Street. Because traffic on Main Street was sometimes heavy, Sammy was not usually permitted to ride his bicycle on the roadway there. Mater needed the butter right away, however, so she told him that he could ride in the roadway if he was sure to stay on the left side so that he could see cars coming towards him. Danzing was driving his car on Main Street when he was momentarily blinded by the sun. He did not see Sammy, who was riding toward him in the roadway, and struck him, causing Sammy to sustain serious injuries. Sammy subsequently asserted a claim for negligence against Danzing. Danzing raised a defense based on contributory negligence. In a jurisdiction which applies the "all or nothing" rule of contributory negligence, Danzing's defense will succeed only if

(A) Sammy acted unreasonably.

(B) Mater acted unreasonably.

(C) Either Mater or Sammy acted unreasonably.

(D) Both Mater and Sammy acted unreasonably.

Questions 24-25 are based on the following fact situation.

Leadco manufactured a device called the Leadco Trainer, for training dogs. The Leadco Trainer consisted of a leather strap fastened to a collar made of metal links. The links were connected to each other in such a way that a pull on the leather strap would cause the collar to tighten painfully around the neck of the dog wearing it. In this way, the dog being trained could be disciplined immediately upon performing improperly. Doughty, a professional dog trainer, was working with a dog known as Rommel in her unfenced front yard and was using a brand new Leadco Trainer. Passer was walking past the yard when Rommel began to snarl and lunge at him. When Doughty yanked on the leather strap of the Leadco Trainer it suddenly broke, freeing Rommel. The dog sprang forward, biting Passer.

24. If Passer asserts a claim against Leadco alleging that the Leadco Trainer used by Doughty was defective, the court should find for

    (A) Leadco, because Passer was not a purchaser or consumer of the product.

    (B) Leadco, if the Leadco Trainer had been submitted to all reasonable tests and inspections before being marketed.

    (C) Passer, if Rommel was a dog of average size and strength.

    (D) Passer, because it was foreseeable that a leather lead would eventually weaken and break when used as the Leadco Trainer was meant to be used.

25. If Passer asserts a claim against Doughty, Passer's most effective argument in support of his claim would be that

    (A) Doughty is strictly liable for damage resulting from her use of a defective product.

    (B) it was unreasonable for Doughty to work the dog in her front yard.

    (C) Doughty's conduct was a concurring cause of harm.

    (D) Doughty was a professional dog trainer.

26. On Sonny's first birthday, his aunt Annie bought him a rag doll as a gift. The toy was made of plush material with buttons sewn on for eyes. While playing with the toy, Sonny pulled one of the buttons off, put it in his mouth, and choked to death on it. Sonny's father Preston commenced an action against Annie under the state's wrong-

ful death statute.

If Preston is successful in his action against Annie, it will probably be because

    (A) Annie was negligent in giving the rag doll to Sonny.

    (B) the rag doll was unfit for ordinary use.

    (C) the rag doll was defective when Annie gave it to Sonny.

    (D) the rag doll was unreasonably dangerous when Annie gave it to Sonny.

Questions 27-28 are based on the following fact situation.

Because Pauling had a headache, he took two headache tablets from a bottle which had been purchased by his wife at the Mart grocery store. The tablets had been manufactured by Tabco which sold them to Mart in sealed bottles for resale. Because of a toxic ingredient which the tablets contained, Pauling became ill as a result of taking them.

27. If Pauling asserts a claim based on negligence against Mart for his damages, the court should find for

    (A) Pauling, because Tabco's negligence is imputed to Mart.

    (B) Pauling, because a retailer has an absolute duty to provide safe products.

    (C) Mart, because the bottle containing the tablets was sealed when Mart received it.

    (D) Mart, because the tablets had been purchased by Pauling's wife.

28. If Pauling asserts a claim against Tabco based on a theory of strict liability in tort, the ruling should turn on the question of whether

    (A) Tabco knew that the tablets contained a toxic ingredient.

    (B) headache tablets which contain a toxic ingredient are inherently dangerous.

(C) it was reasonable for Tabco to market the tablets.

(D) the reasonable consumer would expect headache tablets to contain a toxic ingredient.

Questions 29-30 are based on the following fact situation.

Danton was looking for an address as he drove down the street, and was not watching the road in front of him. As a result, he did not see Peri crossing the street in front of him, and struck her with his car, knocking her down. Danton immediately got out of her car to help Peri. When he saw that she was unconscious, he became afraid to move her, and left her in the roadway while he ran to a nearby phone. While Danton was gone, Secon drove down the same street. Because he was intoxicated by the drug PCP, Secon did not see Peri in the roadway, and drove over her, fracturing her leg.

29. If Peri brings an action against Secon for damages resulting from her fractured leg, Secon's liability will most probably turn on whether it was foreseeable that

→ address negligence

(A) Danton would drive negligently and would leave Peri lying in the roadway after striking her.

(B) a person struck by an automobile would be involved in a second accident within a short period of time.

(C) a person would be in the roadway.

(D) Secon would drive while intoxicated by the drug PCP.

30. In an action by Peri against Danton for damages resulting from her fractured leg, a court is most likely to find for

(A) Peri, if Danton's negligence was a factual and legal cause of Peri's fractured leg.

(B) Peri, since the negligence of Secon is imputed to Danton.

(C) Danton, since his conduct was a legal cause but not a factual cause of Peri's fractured

leg.

(D) Danton, if Peri would not have been injured but for Secon's striking her.

31. Nuke operated a nuclear power plant on the seashore just outside the city of Columbia and sold electricity generated by its operations to Columbia residents. To cool its equipment, Nuke drew water from the ocean and piped it through portions of its plant. Because this operation made the water highly radioactive, Nuke stored used water in a series of large concrete holding ponds. The water stored in this fashion was subjected to a series of procedures designed to "neutralize" it by removing the radioactivity before it was returned to the ocean. Because of an earthquake, one of the concrete holding ponds cracked, permitting several million gallons of neutralized water to escape. Although the escaping water was not radioactive, it caused substantial damage to the fields of Farmer as it passed over them.

If Farmer asserts a claim against Nuke for damage to his realty, the court should find for

(A) Farmer, because operating a nuclear power plant is an abnormally dangerous activity.

(B) Farmer, because water is a substance which is likely to do great harm if it should escape from captivity.

(C) Farmer, because it was unreasonable to operate a nuclear power plant in an area where an earthquake could occur.

(D) Nuke, because the damage resulted from an act of God.

32. Blowco was a manufacturer of explosives used in mining for gold and silver. Its warehouse, which contained large quantities of explosives, was located a short distance from the town of Mastiff. A group of political extremists known as the Holy Terrors were planning to set off a series of bombs in public places in Mastiff. Several members broke into the Blowco warehouse for the purpose of stealing explosives to use in making bombs. Their entry set off an alarm which brought the police. Rather than surrender to the

police, the terrorists committed suicide by detonating the explosives which they had stolen. The blast caused the entire warehouse to explode. A house owned by Parbal and located a half mile away was damaged by the explosion.

If Parbal asserts a claim for damages against Blowco on the ground that storing explosives was an abnormally dangerous activity, which of the following would be Blowco's most effective argument in defense?

(A) The explosion did not result from unreasonable conduct by Blowco.

(B) The damage did not result from a physical invasion of Parbal's realty by any tangible object in the control of Blowco.

(C) The conduct of the terrorists was an intervening cause of harm.

(D) It was not foreseeable that terrorists would deliberately detonate explosives in the warehouse.

33. Sanders kept an antique hay wagon in front of her house as a yard ornament. On several occasions, she offered to sell the hay wagon to her neighbor Berry for $500. Although Berry admired it, he had always been unwilling to pay Sanders' price. After reading a magazine article about the increasing popularity of farm antiques, Berry concluded that the value of Sanders' hay wagon was likely to increase, and that it would therefore be a good investment. One day he approached her, saying, "If you're still interested in selling that hay wagon, I'll pay $500." Sanders was surprised that he had changed his mind, but did not ask him why because she was afraid that he would change it back again. Instead, she said, "I'll take your offer," and sold him the wagon. Two months later, an antique dealer who saw the wagon in Berry's yard bought it from him for $2,000.

If Sanders' asserts a misrepresentation claim against Berry, the court should find for

(A) Sanders, if Berry knew more about the value of antique hay wagons than Sanders did.

(B) Sanders, because Berry purchased the hay wagon for the undisclosed purpose of profiting from his investment.

(C) Berry, because he was not required to disclose his purpose in purchasing the hay wagon.

(D) Berry, if Sanders was initially satisfied with the price which Berry paid her for the hay wagon.

Questions 34-35 are based on the following fact situation.

A state statute provides that no person shall transport passengers for hire in an airplane unless that person shall be licensed as a commercial airplane pilot. Wing owned a small private airplane, but did not have a commercial pilot's license. Rider, who had a business engagement in the city of Atlantis, offered Wing $200 to fly him there in Wing's plane. Wing agreed, after informing Rider that he did not have a commercial pilot's license as required by law. While the were flying over the city of Byzantine, Wing realized that he had miscalculated the amount of fuel which he needed for the trip. As a result, he was forced to land at the Byzantine Airport. After landing and while waiting to be refueled, Wing's plane was struck by a plane which was being negligently operated by Delbert. Wing and Rider were both injured in the collision. The jurisdiction applies the "all-or-nothing" rule of contributory negligence.

34. Assume for the purpose of this question only that Rider asserts a claim against Wing, alleging that Wing was negligent in miscalculating the quantity of fuel needed to make the trip to Atlantis. Which of the following arguments would be Wing's most effective argument in defense?

(A) Rider assumed the risk, because he knew that Wing did not have a commercial pilot's license.

(B) Rider was contributorily negligent in accepting a ride with Wing whom he knew to be unlicensed.

(C) Wing's miscalculation was not a legal cause of the injury sustained by Rider, because

Wing's plane was safely on the ground when struck by the plane operated by Delbert.

(D) Wing's miscalculation was not a factual cause of the injury sustained by Rider, because the harm would not have occurred if Delbert had not been negligent.

35. Assume for the purpose of this question only that Wing asserted a claim against Delbert for damages resulting from personal injuries which he received in the collision. A court is most likely to find for

(A) Wing, because the accident resulted from the negligence of Delbert in the operation of his airplane.

(B) Delbert, because Wing's transportation of a passenger for hire in violation of the statute was negligence per se.

(C) Delbert, because Wing's original flight plan did not include a stop at Byzantine Airport.

(D) Delbert, under the doctrine of necessity.

36. Medco was the manufacturer of various products used by physicians engaged in practice and research. One of its products was Medihol, a colorless alcohol used by physicians for cleaning the skin of patients before administering injections. Another of its products was Slid-Kleen, a red liquid for cleaning glass microscope slides used in medical and research laboratories.

Because Slid-Kleen contained a strong solvent which was damaging to human skin, the label normally affixed to bottles in which it was sold contained language advising users to wear rubber gloves while handling the product.

As a result of an oversight at the Medco plant, Medihol labels were erroneously placed on several bottles of Slid-Kleen. One of the mislabeled bottles was delivered to Dr. Daley's office. In giving an injection to Patient, Dr. Daley used the Slid-Kleen, believing it to be Medihol. As a result, Patient sustained damage to his skin.

In a negligence action by Patient against Medco, if one of the following facts or inferences were true, which would provide Medco with its strongest argument in defense?

(A) It was unforeseeable that a doctor with Dr. Daley's training and experience would mistake Slid-Kleen for Medihol, since they were two different colors.

(B) If Dr. Daley had been acting reasonably, she would have realized that the product which she was using was not Medihol, since it was red instead of colorless.

(C) Dr. Daley's failure to notice that the product which she was using was red, and therefore was not Medihol, amounted to gross negligence.

(D) Dr. Daley's conduct was an intervening cause of Patient's injury.

37. Which of the following persons is most likely to recover in an action against the manufacturer of a hypodermic needle?

(A) A doctor's child who found the needle in the doctor's medical bag and was injured when a defect caused it to break while the child was playing with it.

(B) The patient of a doctor who was injured when a defect caused the needle to break while the doctor was injecting him with it.

(C) A dentist who lost profits when she was unable to inject a patient with the needle because a defect caused it to break.

(D) A narcotics addict who contracted hepatitis because the needle was infected with the microbe which caused that disease.

38. Dusty was a "crop duster," an occupation which required her to spray insecticides onto growing crops from an airplane which she flew within fifteen feet of the ground. In locating the fields of her customers, she used a map which the county published for that purpose, and on which every parcel of real estate in the area was identified by a parcel number. Arrow, a farmer, hired Dusty to

spray his fields with insecticide. Arrow knew that his farm was identified on the county map as parcel 612, but by mistake told Dusty that it was parcel 621. As a result, Dusty sprayed the farm which the county map identified as parcel 621. That farm belonged to Plower, who had contracted to grow his crop without chemical insecticides and to sell it to an organic produce distributor. As a result of Dusty's spraying, Plower was unable to fulfill his contract and sustained serious economic losses.

If Plower asserts a claim against Dusty for damages resulting from trespass to land, the court should find for

(A) Plower, because crop dusting is an abnormally dangerous activity.

(B) Plower, because Dusty intentionally flew through the air space above his land.

(C) Dusty, because she reasonably believed that the farm which she was spraying belonged to Arrow.

(D) Dusty, because there was no damage to Plower's land.

39. Semble, a member of the state senate, was chair of the Senate Investigations Committee which was looking into accusations of corruption in the Governor's office. Because reports of committee agents were beginning to indicate that there was a sound basis for the accusations, Semble kept them locked in her office safe to prevent them from becoming public knowledge before the investigation could be completed. Raker was an investigative journalist who specialized in exposing dishonesty in government. One night he broke into Semble's office, picked the lock on her safe, and photographed the documents which it contained. The following day, realizing that the security of the documents had been compromised, Semble conducted a press conference in which she made their contents known. Before she had completed the conference, however, newspapers containing Raker's story about the papers in Semble's safe were being sold.

If Semble instituted an action against Raker for

invasion of privacy, the court should find for

(A) Raker, since the documents in Semble's safe were newsworthy.

(B) Raker, since he was protected by the First Amendment to the United States Constitution.

(C) Raker, since Semble made the documents a matter of public record at the press conference.

(D) Semble, since Raker entered her office without her permission and broke into her safe.

40. Nichol, who was 11 years of age, was playing with Paul, who was ten years of age. While they were playing together, Nichol offered to show Paul his new air rifle. The air rifle was manufactured by the Loly Company. Nichol purchased it from Storr, with money which he earned by mowing the lawns of several of his neighbors. While demonstrating the air rifle to Paul, Nichol accidentally shot him with it, severely injuring Paul's eye. Paul subsequently asserted a negligence claim against Storr.

If Paul is successful in his claim against Storr, it will be because a jury finds that

(A) any negligence by Loly Company in the design of the air rifle should be imputed to Storr.

(B) the air rifle was defectively designed.

(C) the air rifle was defectively manufactured.

(D) it was unreasonable for Storr to sell the air rifle to Nichol.

41. Carrent was in the auto rental business, under the name "Rent-A-Lemon." His rates were low because the cars in his inventory were all at least six years old, and many of them were in poor condition. In order to keep his expenses as low as possible, he had his cars serviced by Fixer, a 17 year old student at the High School of Automotive Trades. Fixer worked on Carrent's cars in his parents' garage after school and on weekends, charging fees which were lower than any of the

professional repair shops in town. Sometimes Carrent found it necessary to send a car back to Fixer three or four times before Fixer finally succeeded in repairing it correctly, but since Fixer did not charge for the return trips Carrent did not mind doing so. One of Carrent's cars had a leaking frammis in the carburetor, which Carrent knew made it unsafe to drive. He had the frammis repaired by Fixer and then rented the car to Pommel. One hour later while Pommel was driving the car, the frammis began leaking again. As a result, the car exploded, injuring Pommel.

If Pommel asserts a claim against Carrent, Pommel's most effective argument in support of her claim would be that

(A) Carrant is vicariously liable for the negligence of his employee.

(B) the duty to maintain a safe car was non-delegable.

(C) Fixer was an independent contractor.

(D) it was unreasonable for Carrent to hire Fixer to repair the car.

42. Which statement most correctly completes the following sentence? A retailer owes its customers

(A) no duty to inspect products furnished by reputable manufacturers.

(B) a duty to inspect the packages of all products sold, but no duty to inspect the contents of those packages.

(C) a duty to inspect only those products which are furnished by manufacturers whose products are not well-known to the retailer.

(D) a duty to make a reasonable inspection of all products which are sold by that retailer.

Questions 43-44 are based on the following fact situation.

Pellum was employed by Denner as chief field mechanic. When he received his salary, Pellum noticed that he had not been paid for the overtime which he had worked the previous month. When he complained to

Denner about it, Denner said that all company employees were expected to put in extra time when necessary, and that he had no intention of compensating Pellum for the excess hours. Pellum resigned immediately and advised Denner that he would hold the tools which Denner had issued to him until he received payment.

43. Assume for the purpose of this question only that after Pellum's resignation, Denner wrote him a letter in which he said, "You were never any good as a mechanic, and in addition you were the most dishonest employee this company ever had," and that these statements were false. Pellum's mother, who lived with Pellum and frequently opened his mail, read the letter as soon as it arrived. In an action by Pellum against Denner for defamation, a court should find for

(A) Pellum, because Denner's statements were published to Pellum's mother.

(B) Pellum, only if Denner had reason to know that someone other than Denner would open and read the letter.

(C) Denner, because the statements contained in the letter were communicated only to Pellum.

(D) Denner, because of the employer's privilege.

44. Assume for the purpose of this question only that Pellum applied for a job with Nuco, and that Nuco wrote to Denner asking for an evaluation of Pellum's honesty and ability. Denner wrote a letter to Nuco which stated, "When Pellum left my company a valuable set of tools left with him. This disappearance has never been properly explained or straightened out." As a result, Nuco did not hire Pellum. If Pellum asserts a claim against Denner for defamation, Pellum should

(A) lose, if Pellum did not return the tools which he took when he left Denner's employ.

(B) lose, because Denner's statement was made in response to a specific request by Pellum's prospective employer.

(C) win, because Denner's statement could not have benefitted Denner's own business interests.

(D) win, if Denner's statement accused Pellum of stealing tools.

Questions 45-46 are based on the following fact situation.

Flier was injured when the helicopter which he was flying ran out of fuel and fell from the air, crashing into the roof of Homer's house. Flier purchased the helicopter from its manufacturer, Kopto, two months before the accident occurred. The helicopter came equipped with a fuel gauge which was manufactured by Instruments, Inc. The day after Flier purchased the helicopter, he noticed that the fuel gauge gave incorrect readings. He complained to an officer of Kopto who told him to have it fixed and to send Kopto the bill. A week before the accident Flier hired an independent airplane mechanic named Max to repair the fuel gauge. Max worked on the gauge, but failed to repair it properly. The day before the accident Flier's partner, Pard, flew the helicopter, using most of the fuel in the tank. Although Pard noticed that the fuel gauge continued to indicate that the tank was full, he neither mentioned it to Flier nor replaced the fuel in the tank. On the day of the accident, the fuel gauge indicated that the tank was full, although it was actually almost empty.

45. If Flier wishes to assert a claim for damages on a theory of strict liability in tort, he is most likely to recover against

(A) Kopto only.

(B) Kopto and Pard only.

(C) Kopto and Max only.

(D) Kopto, Pard, and Max.

46. If Homer institutes an action for damage to his house against Kopto on a theory of strict liability in tort, the court should find for

(A) Homer, since the doctrine of res ipsa loquitur applies to aircraft accidents.

(B) Homer, if the accident proximately resulted from a defect in the fuel gauge which existed when Flier purchased the helicop-

ter.

(C) Kopto, since Homer was not a user of the helicopter.

(D) Kopto, if the accident proximately resulted from the conduct of either Max or Pard.

47. Grav was the owner of a gravel pit in the northern part of the state. Because the land on which the pit was located was usually covered by a thick layer of snow during the winter months, Grav did not conduct operations at the pit during the winter, and the land remained unoccupied during that season. Grav was aware of the fact that neighborhood children used a steep slope on his realty for sledding during the snow season, and feared that one of the children would be injured by sledding onto the public road adjacent to the property. Although he could have prevented this from happening by erecting a small fence at a cost of under $200, Grav was unwilling to expend that sum. Instead, he posted a sign which read, "No Sledding, Keep Out." Three weeks later, Childer, an eight year old boy, was sledding down the hill on Grav's property when his sled coasted onto the adjacent public road into the path of a vehicle driven by Carrol. Childer sustained serious injuries when he was struck by Carrol's vehicle.

If Childer asserts a negligence claim against Grav, the court should find for

(A) Childer, because danger invites rescue.

(B) Childer, if Grav's failure to erect a fence to prevent the accident was unreasonable.

(C) Grav, because Carrol had the last clear chance to avoid injuring Childer.

(D) Grav, if Carrol's conduct was an intervening cause of harm.

Questions 48-49 are based on the following fact situation.

Samuels knew that the zoobie of his car's engine was cracked. Because he wanted to sell the car, he filled the crack with putty and painted it so that the crack would not show. Then he brought the car to Barton, a used car dealer, and offered to sell it for $1,000 cash. Barton placed the car on a lift so that he could inspect it from underneath and noticed the filled crack, but thought that he would be able to resell the car in spite of it. Barton offered $500, which Samuels accepted. The next day, Barton was showing the car to Poynter, a customer, when the crack in the zoobie caused the engine to explode, necessitating $500 in repairs and injuring Poynter.

48. If Barton institutes an action against Samuels for misrepresentation, which of the following would be Samuels's most effective argument in defense?

(A) Samuels made no representation concerning the zoobie.

(B) Barton did not rely on Samuels's representations concerning the zoobie.

(C) Barton was not justified in relying on Samuels's representations concerning the zoobie.

(D) Barton did not sustain damage.

49. If Poynter asserts a claim against Samuels for injuries which he sustained when the engine exploded, which of the following would be Poynter's most effective theory?

(A) Battery, because Samuels knew that the zoobie was cracked.

(B) Intentional misrepresentation, because Samuels knew that the zoobie was cracked.

(C) Negligent misrepresentation, because Samuels had a duty to disclose that the zoobie was cracked.

(D) Negligence, because Samuels should have anticipated that a customer of Barton would be injured as a result of the cracked zoobie.

50. Arnold was driving north on Canal Street. As he approached the intersection of First Avenue, he noticed that the traffic light was red against him. Preparing to stop, he stepped on his brake pedal. Because the brakes were not working properly, he could not stop, and continued into the intersection. Burger, who was driving east on First Avenue, saw Arnold go through the red light. Because the light was green in his favor, however, Burger did not stop, but continued into the intersection, believing that he could avoid striking Arnold by steering around him. The two vehicles collided in the intersection. Although damage to Arnold's car was minimal, Burger's car was totally destroyed. The jurisdiction has a statute which prohibits entering an intersection against a red traffic signal light and another statute which adopts the all or nothing rule of contributory negligence.

In an action by Burger against Arnold, the court should find for

(A) Arnold, since Burger had the last clear chance to avoid the accident.

(B) Arnold, if it was unreasonable for Burger to enter the intersection when he did.

(C) Burger, if Arnold's violation of statute was a substantial factor in producing the damage.

(D) Burger, since Arnold's conduct was negligence per se.

51. Fridge was the operator of an appliance store. Once, while testing a refrigerator prior to selling it, she discovered a defect in its wiring. Realizing that the defect would make it dangerous for a person to touch the refrigerator while it was plugged in, she resolved not to sell it. Instead, she placed it on the sidewalk in front of her store to attract the attention of passersby. After two years, the refrigerator became so dirty that she decided to get rid of it. In crayon, Fridge wrote "AS IS - $25" on its door. Pally, who was building a food smoker, needed the body of a refrigerator. When he saw the one in front of Fridge's store, he bought it. As she was loading it onto Pally's pickup truck, Fridge said, "I hope you know that this refrigerator doesn't work." Pally said that he did. When Pally got the refrigerator home he plugged it in, and received a severe electrical shock while attempting to open its door.

In an action by Pally against Fridge for damages

resulting from his injury, the court will probably find for

(A) Pally, if it was unreasonable for Fridge to sell the refrigerator without warning him about the wiring defect.

(B) Pally, since the refrigerator was unfit for ordinary use.

(C) Fridge, since Pally purchased the refrigerator "AS IS."

(D) Fridge, if it is found that Pally had the "last clear chance" to avoid being injured.

52. Danker was hunting rattlesnakes on his land with a pistol when he saw Hunt carrying a shotgun and attempting to enter Danker's land by crawling under the barbed wire fence which surrounded it. He waited until Hunt had gotten past the fence and approached him, telling him that he was trespassing and ordering him to leave. Hunt said, "I only want to shoot some birds. I got a right to do that if I want to, don't I?" After Hunt said this, Danker placed his hand on Hunt's chest and pushed him gently backward, repeating his demand that Hunt leave. Hunt shoved Danker away from him and pointed his shotgun at Danker, saying "Nobody pushes me, Mister." Danker immediately drew his pistol from the holster on his belt and fired at Hunt, striking him in the arm and causing him to drop his shotgun.

If Hunt asserts a claim against Danker for battery, the court should find for

(A) Danker, if he fired at Hunt to defend his realty against a trespass.

(B) Danker, if he fired at Hunt to defend himself against Hunt's threat with the shotgun.

(C) Hunt, because Danker struck the first blow.

(D) Hunt, because Danker did not use force against him until his entry onto the realty was complete.

53. The felicet is a species of wild cat which inhabits the Island of Langoa in the Creolic Ocean. Although the wild felicet is ferocious, natives of Langoa frequently capture young felicets and, after taming them, keep them as house pets. Doggel grew up on the Island of Langoa where he obtained his pet felicet. When he immigrated to the United States five years ago, he was permitted to bring his felicet with him after submitting it to a six week period of quarantine. The cat had been gentle ever since Doggel tamed it eight years before leaving Langoa. Recently, Doggel's neighbor Pruitt was walking past Doggel's house when the felicet tore through a window screen, jumped into the street, and attacked Pruitt, seriously injuring him. Pruitt subsequently asserted a claim against Doggel for his damages.

If Pruitt is successful in his claim against Doggel, it will probably be because

(A) Pruitt's damage resulted from Doggel's keeping of a wild animal.

(B) it was foreseeable that the felicet would do something unforeseeable.

(C) the thing speaks for itself (*res ipsa loquitur*).

(D) Pruitt's keeping of the felicet amounted to a private nuisance.

54. Helmco manufactured a safety helmet in hopes of selling it to the United States Marine Corps for general utility purposes, but was unsuccessful in doing so. Instead, it sold the helmets to the general public under the name Head Shields. Head Shields were packaged in boxes which showed pictures of three persons wearing the helmet: one riding a horse, one riding a motorcycle, and one doing construction work. Post found a Head Shield which someone had discarded in its original box. He wore it the next day while riding his motorcycle and sustained a severe head injury when he fell from his motorcycle.

Post asserted a claim against Helmco for his injuries in a jurisdiction which has adopted a rule of "pure comparative negligence." At the trial, Post proved that the Head Shield was not suitable for use as a motorcycle helmet and that if it had been he would not have sustained injury.

The court should find for

(A) Helmco, because Post found the Head Shield.

(B) Helmco, if Head Shields were not designed or intended for use as motorcycle helmets.

(C) Post, unless his fall from the motorcycle resulted from his own unreasonable conduct.

(D) Post, because the box in which the Head Shield was sold contained a picture of a person wearing the Head Shield while riding a motorcycle.

55. When Ocie brought his car to Meck's Fixit Shop for repairs, Meck told him that he would test drive the car after repairing it. While Meck was test driving the car, he struck Walker, a pedestrian. A statute in the jurisdiction provides that "The owner of any motor vehicle operated on the roads of this state shall be vicariously liable for the negligence of any person operating said motor vehicle with said owner's permission." Walker instituted an action against Ocie and Meck, and obtained a judgment against both of them for $10,000.

If Ocie pays the judgment in full, which of the following is correct regarding Ocie's rights against Meck?

(A) Ocie may recover $10,000 from Meck.

(B) Ocie may recover $5,000 from Meck.

(C) Ocie may recover $7,500 from Meck.

(D) Ocie may not recover from Meck.

Questions 56-58 are based on the following fact situation.

Mayflower seeds are a common ingredient in bird food. Although they are sometimes processed for use as cooking oil, they are not usually eaten raw by human beings because they have a bitter oily taste. Quill was a breeder of exotic birds. Since he had studied bird nutrition, he preferred to mix feed for his birds according to his own formula instead of using commercially available mixes. For this purpose, he purchased a sealed fifty-pound package labeled "Mayflower Seeds" from Deal, who was in the business of selling supplies for bird and livestock breeders. Deal had bought the sealed package from Miller, a wholesaler of seed and grain. Because of negligence at Miller's plant, the seeds in the package were poisonous. Quill ate some of the mayflower seeds while he was mixing the bird food, and became ill several hours later as a result. Before becoming ill, Quill fed the seeds to several of his birds, which died as a result.

56. If Quill brings an action against Miller for the value of the birds which died, a court is most likely to find for

(A) Quill, if it was foreseeable that poisonous seeds would kill birds.

(B) Quill, but only if it was reasonable for Deal to resell the seeds without inspection.

(C) Miller, since Miller had no contractual relationship with Quill.

(D) Miller, unless Quill is unable to recover damages from Deal.

57. If Quill institutes a personal injury action against Deal for damages resulting from his illness, Quill's most effective theory of recovery would be

(A) negligence, since the unreasonable conduct of Miller is imputed to Deal.

(B) negligence, if the contents of a sack of mayflower seeds would not ordinarily be poisonous unless they were defective when sold.

(C) breach of express warranty, since the label "Mayflower Seeds" implies that the ingredients are fit for human consumption.

(D) strict liability in tort, if it was reasonable for Quill to believe that he could eat the seeds without being made ill.

58. Assume for the purpose of this question only that Quill is successful in his action against Deal. If Deal subsequently asserts a claim against Miller

for total indemnification, the court will probably find for

(A) Miller, since Deal is a joint tortfeasor.

(B) Miller, unless Quill named Miller in the original action.

(C) Deal, if Deal was free from fault.

(D) Deal, but only if a statute in the jurisdiction creates such a right.

59. Although he had been warned that swimming within one hour after eating was likely to cause a cramp, Sal went swimming in the lake immediately after lunch. He had been swimming for a few minutes when he developed severe cramps. Finding himself unable to swim any further, he began calling for help. Sal's cries attracted the attention of Ralph, who happened to be walking near the lake. Ralph jumped into the water, swam to Sal's side, and, grabbing Sal by the hair, towed him to safety. In getting out of the lake, however, Ralph cut his leg on a fragment of glass which was embedded in the lake bottom.

If Ralph asserts an action against Sal for personal injuries, the court should find for

(A) Ralph, if it was negligent for Sal to swim so soon after eating.

(B) Ralph, because his injury occurred while he was attempting to rescue Sal.

(C) Sal, because danger invites rescue.

(D) Sal, if the glass fragment is an intervening cause of Ralph's injury.

60. Thurston was a manufacturer of computer hardware. Dentin was a retailer who purchased products from Thurston. At an industrial convention, Dentin told Thurston that he heard that their mutual friend Prann was about to go into personal bankruptcy. Thurston did not believe what Dentin was telling him, and resolved to mention it to Prann as soon as the opportunity presented itself. The following day, Prann called Thurston to discuss computer hardware. Thurston told Prann what Dentin had said at the party. Prann laughed,

assured Thurston that he was in excellent financial condition, and they both laughed at the rumor.

If Prann asserts a defamation claim against Dentin, which of the following would be Dentin's most effective argument in defense?

(A) Prann did not experience mental suffering.

(B) Prann did not sustain damage to his reputation as a result of the statement.

(C) Dentin was only repeating what he had heard.

(D) Dentin did not publish any statement about Prann.

61. Pullo was employed as an insulation installer by various builders and general contractors for a period of thirty-five years. During that time, he was repeatedly exposed to an insulating material known as plastic wool which was manufactured by Woolco. Last year it was discovered for the first time that exposure to plastic wool is a cause of cancer, and that Pullo had contracted cancer as a result of his contact with the product.

In a jurisdiction which applies the "all-or-nothing" rule of contributory negligence, if Pullo asserts a negligence claim against Woolco for damages resulting from Pullo's exposure to plastic wool, Woolco's most effective defense would be based on the argument that

(A) Pullo assumed the risk.

(B) Woolco did not know that contact with plastic wool would result in cancer.

(C) The reasonable person in Woolco's situation would not have anticipated that exposure to plastic wool would result in cancer.

(D) Pullo's only remedy is that created by workers' compensation statutes.

Questions 62-63 are based on the following fact situation.

The Chemco insecticide factory was located on the

edge of the city of Pinetree. When the wind blew from the east, foul-smelling waste gases from Chemco factory chimneys were blown over Pinetree, causing most of the residents to experience a burning of the eyes and throat.

62. Assume the following additional facts for the purpose of this question only: Gro's flower and plant shop was located across the street from the Chemco factory in a building which Gro rented from Laird. Gases from the Chemco factory caused some of the potted plants which Gro had for sale in his shop to die. One of Gro's employees, Edwards, suffered from allergies. As a result, he found the gases so irritating to his eyes that he was unable to continue working at Gro's shop, and had to quit his job. Who may successfully assert a private nuisance claim against Chemco?

   (A) Laird only.

   (B) Laird and Gro only.

   (C) Gro and Edwards only.

   (D) Laird, Gro, and Edwards.

63. Assume the following additional facts for the purpose of this question only. Packer was a resident of Pinetree. On several occasions, she attempted to persuade the City Attorney to seek an injunction against Chemco. The City Attorney refused, however, because the City Council was afraid that doing so would drive Chemco from the area. If Packer seeks an injunction by asserting a claim against Chemco on a theory of public nuisance, which of the following would be Chemco's most effective argument in defense?

   (A) The City Attorney's decision is binding.

   (B) Packer has not sustained harm different from that of the general public.

   (C) A private citizen may not seek an injunction against environmental polluters.

   (D) A private citizen may not sue on a theory of public nuisance.

64. When Darren entered a restaurant for lunch, she hung her coat on the coat rack. When she was leaving, she removed from the rack a coat which looked like hers, but which actually belonged to Perdu. At the time she took it, Darran believed it to be her coat, but when she had driven two miles from the restaurant, she realized that it was not hers. She turned around and was driving back to the restaurant when she was involved in an automobile accident. Perdu's coat was completely destroyed in the accident.

If Perdu asserts a claim against Darran for trespass to chattel, the court should find for

   (A) Perdu, because the coat was completely destroyed after Darran took it.

   (B) Perdu, unless the automobile accident in which the coat was destroyed occurred without fault by Darran.

   (C) Darran, because she believed the coat to be her own when she took it.

   (D) Darran, if she was making a reasonable effort to return the coat when it was destroyed.

Questions 65-66 are based on the following fact situation.

Penler was eating cherry pie in Joe's Restaurant when a cherry pit contained in the pie stuck in his throat. Unable to breathe, Penler began choking. Doc, a physician who was eating in the restaurant, ran to Penler's aid and performed an operation known as an emergency tracheotomy. She did this by cutting the skin of Penler's throat with a pocket knife and creating an opening in his windpipe through which Penler was able to breath. Then, at Doc's direction, Penler walked across the street to Mercy Hospital so that the opening which Doc created could be cleaned and bandaged. Because hospital employees negligently failed to enter Penler's name in the emergency room register, he sat in the emergency room for six hours without further attention. At that time, an earthquake caused a portion of the hospital's structure to fall, striking Pember in the head and fracturing his skull.

65. In an action by Penler against Mercy Hospital for

damages resulting from his fractured skull, the court is most likely to find for

(A) Mercy, but only if the state has a "good Samaritan" statute.

(B) Mercy, unless Doc's conduct was found to be foreseeable.

(C) Mercy, unless it was foreseeable that Penler would be injured by an earthquake if left waiting for six hours.

(D) Penler, since a hospital owes its patients a duty to protect them against natural disasters.

66. Assume for the purpose of this question only that Doc's conduct in performing the emergency tracheotomy was unreasonable, and that if Doc had acted reasonably, Penler would have coughed up the pit without any injury. In an action by Penler against Doc for damages resulting from his fractured skull, will Penler win?

(A) Yes, since he would not have been in Mercy Hospital if Doc had not performed the tracheotomy.

(B) Yes, if it was foreseeable that Penler would be required to wait six hours in the hospital's emergency room.

(C) No, since he would not have been injured were it not for the cherry pit contained in the pie.

(D) No, if the earthquake was an independent intervening cause of Penler's injury.

67. Hume went to Green's Garden Supply Store to purchase fertilizer for the apple trees which grew in his backyard. Since he did not know what brand was best for his purposes, he asked the store's proprietor Green to recommend a fertilizer which was especially good for apple trees. Green suggested Fedem, a product which he said was good for all fruit trees. Hume purchased the product, and applied it as the label directed. While doing so, he got some of the Fedem on his hands. Because of an allergy which he had, the product irritated his skin, causing him considerable pain,

and disabling him for a period of time.

In an action by Hume against Green for damages resulting from breach of warranty, which of the following comments is most correct?

I. There was no implied warranty that the product was fit for Hume's particular purpose, because his purpose was the same as the product's ordinary use.

II. There was no implied warranty of merchantability since Hume relied on Green's recommendation in purchasing the product.

(A) I only.

(B) II only.

(C) I and II.

(D) Neither I nor II.

68. Comcorp is a supplier of telephone service to the City of Burg. Many of the wooden poles from which Comcorp's wires are strung have been standing for more than forty years and are in rotted condition. Driver lost control of his automobile because he was driving while intoxicated, and collided with one of Comcorp's rotted poles. As a result of the collision, the pole fell over, striking a parked car and injuring Pessel, who was sitting in it.

In an action by Pessel against Comcorp, the court should find for

(A) Pessel, if it was unreasonable for Comcorp to permit its poles to become rotted.

(B) Pessel, since it was foreseeable that if a pole fell it would injure a person sitting in a parked car.

(C) Comcorp, since Driver's conduct either amounted to gross negligence or was criminal.

(D) Comcorp, if the force of the collision would have caused even a reasonably good pole to fall.

Questions 69-71 are based on the following fact situation.

Automobiles driven by Andrews and Zell collided in an intersection. Andrews and Zell asserted negligence claims against each other for damage to their vehicles. In addition, Petro, who was a passenger in Andrews's car at the time of the accident, asserted a negligence claim against both of them for her personal injuries. The claims were all consolidated and tried together. In answer to specific questions posed by the court, the jury found that the accident was 60 percent the fault of Andrews and 40 percent the fault of Zell. In addition, the jury found that damage to Andrews' car amounted to $1,000, that damage to Zell's car amounted to $10,000, and that damage to Petro amounted to $100,000. The court ruled that Andrews and Zell were jointly and severally liable for Petro's injuries.

69. Assume for the purpose of this question only that the jurisdiction had a statute which provided that "In any negligence action, a plaintiff's recovery shall not be barred by that plaintiff's fault, but the recovery of said plaintiff shall be diminished in proportion to that plaintiff's fault." Which of the following correctly states the sum to which Zell is entitled?

   (A) $6,000 ($10,000 less 40%).

   (B) $4,000 ($10,000 less 60%).

   (C) $10,000.

   (D) 0.

70. Assume for the purpose of this question only that the jurisdiction had a statute which provided that "In any negligence action, a plaintiff's recovery shall not be barred by that plaintiff's fault, but the recovery of said plaintiff shall be diminished in proportion to such plaintiff's fault, unless that plaintiff's fault shall be greater than that of the defendant, and in such event the plaintiff's recovery shall be barred." Which of the following correctly states the sum to which Andrews is entitled?

   (A) $600 ($1,000 less 40%).

   (B) $400 ($1,000 less 60%).

   (C) $1,000.

   (D) 0.

71. Assume for the purpose of this question only that the jurisdiction had a statute which provided that "In any negligence action, a plaintiff's recovery shall not be barred by that plaintiff's fault, but the recovery of said plaintiff shall be diminished in proportion to such plaintiff's fault unless that plaintiff's fault shall be greater than that of the defendant, and in such event the plaintiff's recovery shall be barred." Which of the following correctly states the sum which Petro is entitled to receive from Zell?

   (A) $60,000 (60% of $100,000).

   (B) $40,000 (40% of $100,000).

   (C) $100,000.

   (D) 0.

72. Michael, who was eleven years old, received a sled manufactured by Rosebud from his uncle as a Christmas present. Since he already had a better sled, Michael sold the Rosebud to his neighbor Petey. Petey was riding the Rosebud sled down a snow-covered hill when one of the bolts which held it together broke, causing the sled to overturn and injure Petey severely. The bolt broke because of a crack which existed when the sled left the Rosebud factory, but which was too minute to be discovered by reasonable inspection. If Petey brings an action against Rosebud, the court should find for

   (A) Petey, if the cracked bolt was a defect.

   (B) Petey, but only if Michael did not use the sled before selling it to Petey.

   (C) Rosebud, since the sale by Michael was outside the regular course of business.

   (D) Rosebud, because the crack was too minute to be discovered upon reasonable inspection.

Questions 73-74 are based on the following fact situation.

Lord was the owner of a four-story office building. The entire second floor of the building was leased to Less, an attorney, and the other floors were divided into offices and leased to various other tenants. Pursuant to the lease between Lord and Less, a building manager employed by Lord was to be on duty daily between the hours of 8 a.m. and 6 p.m. The building was to be open to the public during those hours. At other times Less was free to enter by using his key. On April 1, Less was riding in the building elevator when it suddenly and without warning plunged swiftly downward, shaking Less up severely. Less immediately notified Lord, who promised to fix it. Lord did nothing about it, however. On April 2, Clyde called to make an appointment to consult with Less for legal advice. Because Clyde was unable to come to Less's office during regular business hours, Less told Clyde to come the following morning at 6:30 a.m. On April 3, Less met Clyde at the entrance to the building, let them both in with his key, and led Clyde to the elevator. While they were riding in the elevator to Less's office, the elevator suddenly plunged swiftly downward, stopping short when it reached the bottom of the elevator shaft. Clyde was severely injured in the fall.

73. Assume for the purpose of this question only that Clyde asserted a negligence claim against Less for damages resulting from the elevator accident. The court should find for

    (A) Clyde, if Less knew or should have known that the elevator might not be working properly.

    (B) Clyde, because the entire second floor had been leased to Less.

    (C) Less, if the lease required Lord to keep the elevator in good repair.

    (D) Less, because he was only a tenant in the building.

74. Assume for the purpose of this question only that Clyde asserts a claim against Lord for damages resulting from his injuries, alleging that Lord was negligent in failing to fix the elevator or warn

Clyde about it. Which of the following would be Lord's most effective argument in defense?

    (A) Lord did not owe Clyde a duty to repair the elevator, since Lord's promise was not made to Clyde.

    (B) Clyde was a mere licensee, since his presence did not confer a benefit on Lord.

    (C) It was not foreseeable that Less would permit Clyde to use the elevator, since Less knew it was not working properly.

    (D) It was unreasonable for Less to permit Clyde to use the elevator, since Less knew that it was not working properly.

75. Trokker was driving a truckload of gravel over a highway in a rural part of the state, when through no fault of her own, one of the tires on her truck blew out, causing the truck to go out of control. The truck overturned, spilling the gravel onto the land of Owner, which was adjacent to the road. Trokker, who was unhurt, returned later with another truck and a tractor equipped with a power shovel. Using the power shovel, Trokker scooped up the spilled gravel and loaded it onto the other truck.

    If Owner asserts a claim against Trokker for trespass to land, the court should award Owner a judgment for

    (A) nominal damage only.

    (B) all damage resulting from the spilling of gravel onto Owner's land.

    (C) only the damage caused by Trokker's removal of the gravel from Owner's land.

    (D) no damage.

76. Stabel owned and bred horses, and was an excellent rider. He purchased a horse known as Thunder even though he had heard that Thunder was wild and dangerous, because he hoped that he would be able to "break" or train him. Each time Stabel attempted to approach the horse, however, Thunder reared and kicked at him. Finally, Stabel hired a professional horse trainer named Parte to

break Thunder. After explaining that Thunder had repeatedly attacked him, Stabel showed Parte to Thunder's corral. While Stabel stood outside watching, Parte entered the corral holding out his hand and making soft murmuring noises to attract Thunder's attention. When Thunder saw Parte, the horse kicked him, fracturing Parte's leg.

If Parte asserts a claim for damages against Stabel, the court should find for

(A) Parte, since Stabel knew that Thunder had a propensity to attack human beings.

(B) Parte, since Thunder was a wild animal.

(C) Parte, since Stabel acted unreasonably in permitting Parte to enter the corral under the circumstances.

(D) Stabel, since Parte knew that Thunder was dangerous when he entered the corral.

77. Harold bought a used car from Dann's Car Sales. Although Dann assured Harold that he believed the car to be in good condition, the contract of sale signed by both Harold and Dann contained the phrase "This Vehicle Sold AS IS" in large black letters. Harold was driving the car the following day when the steering jammed, causing the car to collide with a power pole. Harold's wife Wanda, who was sitting beside him in the car, was injured in the crash.

If Wanda asserts a claim for damages against Dann, on the grounds that Dann breached the implied warranty of merchantability, the court should find for

(A) Dann, because the contract of sale contained the phrase "This Vehicle Sold AS IS."

(B) Dann, because he did not enter into any contractual relationship with Wanda.

(C) Wanda, because the vehicle was unfit for ordinary use.

(D) Wanda, because Dann said that he believed the car to be in good condition.

78. Percy brought her car to Doane, a used-car dealer, asking him to sell it for her. Doane said that he would attempt to do so on consignment, at a commission consisting of twenty percent of the sale price. Percy said that the terms were acceptable to her, but that because she had recently spent $800 for a custom two-tone black and silver paint job, she wanted the car kept out of the sun. Doane agreed, and Percy left the car with him.

Doane left the car in the sun, which caused its paint to fade. Believing that a new paint job would make the car easier to sell, Doane had it painted red without consulting Percy. Before it was repainted, Doane drove Percy's car 4,000 miles on his own personal business. After it was painted, Doane's customers drove it an additional 1,000 miles while deciding whether to purchase it. Although the value of Percy's car did not change while it was in Doane's possession, Doane was unable to sell the car. Percy subsequently asserted a conversion claim against Doane.

If Percy is successful in her conversion action, she will be entitled to recover

(A) the value which the car had at the time Percy delivered it to Doane.

(B) the value which the car had at the time Percy delivered it to Doane, plus the cost of restoring its paint to the condition which existed at the time she delivered it to Doane.

(C) the value which the car had at the time Percy delivered it to Doane, plus the cost of restoring its paint to the condition which existed at the time she delivered it to Doane, plus the reasonable value of the car's use for 4,000 miles.

(D) the value which the car had at the time Percy delivered it to Doane, plus the cost of restoring its paint to the condition which existed at the time she delivered it to Doane, plus the reasonable value of the car's use for 5,000 miles.

Questions 79-80 are based on the following fact situation.

Drubb manufactures a product called Term-Aid, consisting of chemical pellets which emit fumes that are poisonous to termites and their eggs. Because Term-Aid fumes are poisonous to human beings as well, Drubb sells the product to professional exterminators only, requiring that each purchaser show his or her state exterminator's license when making a purchase. Mato, a licensed exterminator, bought a large container of Term-Aid from Drubb for use in his business. The container bore a label which read: "Term-Aid. For killing termites. Caution: This product is intended for use by professional exterminators only. Unauthorized use by any other persons may be dangerous." Mato placed the container on a shelf in his shop where it was discovered by Clener, an independent contractor whom Mato periodically hired to clean his shop. Since Clener thought there were termites in his house, he opened the container and poured some of the chemical pellets into a plastic bag which he then brought home. The next day, Clener's three-year-old daughter Puella found the plastic bag containing the Term-Aid pellets and ate some of them, becoming seriously ill as a result. A statute in the jurisdiction adopted the all-or-nothing rule of contributory negligence.

79. In a negligence action by Puella against Drubb, Drubb's most effective argument in defense would be that

(A) Clener was contributorily negligent.

(B) Mato's conduct was an intervening cause of harm.

(C) Clener's conduct was an intervening cause of harm.

(D) Drubb did not act unreasonably.

80. In an action by Puella against Mato, which of the following would be Puella's most effective argument?

(A) Mato should have foreseen that the Term-Aid would cause injury to someone in Puella's position if left on an exposed shelf in his shop.

(B) The Term-Aid was defective since its label did not adequately warn of the dangers connected with its use.

(C) Term-Aid is an inherently dangerous product.

(D) Clener's theft of the Term-Aid pellets was a concurring cause of Puella's harm.

81. Houser was the owner of a warehouse which was usually unattended at night. As a result, burglars had broken in on several occasions and had stolen valuable merchandise from the warehouse. Houser looked into the possibility of hiring a security guard, but decided that it would be too expensive. Instead, he installed an explosive device in the doorway, rigging it to explode if anyone opened the door without first inserting a key in a specially constructed slot. Burg was attempting to break into Houser's warehouse for the purpose of stealing, when the explosive device detonated while he was trying to open the door. Burg was seriously injured in the explosion.

If Burg is successful in an action against Houser, it will most probably be because the court finds that

(A) it was negligent for Houser to install the explosive device, since it was foreseeable that a person entering on legitimate business might be injured by it.

(B) Houser used excessive force to defend his property, since the explosive device was liable to inflict serious or deadly injury.

(C) the use of a mechanical device is not permitted in defense of property.

(D) the explosive device was just as likely to injure an innocent bystander as a thief.

Questions 82-83 are based on the following fact situation.

After living together for several months, Mike and Wanda began to argue frequently. On Monday, after an argument, Mike left their apartment in anger, saying that he didn't know when he was coming back. On

Tuesday, Wanda changed the lock on the front door and began advertising for a roommate. The following Saturday, Wanda took all of Mike's possessions, including his television set which was valued at six hundred dollars, to a swap meet in hopes of selling them. At the swap meet, she put up a sign which said, "Moving. Everything Must be Sold Today."

Ina was browsing at the swap meet when she saw the television set at Wanda's booth. She asked whether it was in good condition, and when Wanda said that it was, she asked the price. Wanda said, "Fifty dollars." Ina immediately handed Wanda the cash, placed the television in her station wagon, and hurried home.

82. In an action by Mike against Ina for conversion, a court should find for

(A) Mike, since Ina desired to make the television her own, and did so.

(B) Mike, since the price of fifty dollars should have made Ina aware that there was something suspicious about the sale.

(C) Ina, since it was reasonable for her to believe that Wanda owned the television set and that the price was low because Wanda needed to sell it in a hurry.

(D) Ina, since the television was not in Mike's possession when she acquired it.

83. If Mike instituted an action against Wanda for trespass to chattel, which one of the following additional facts or inferences, if it was the only one true, would be most helpful to Wanda's defense?

(A) Mike's leaving the apartment constituted implied consent to Wanda's sale of his possessions.

(B) Wanda's interference with Mike's right to the television was serious enough to justify a forced sale.

(C) Ina committed a conversion by purchasing the television set at the swap meet.

(D) At the time Mike's action against her was

instituted, Wanda could not re-acquire possession of the television set from Ina.

Questions 84-85 are based on the following fact situation.

Packs and Draiv lived on the same street and worked in the same office so they formed a car pool, each driving his own car on alternate days. One day while Draiv was driving, the car in front of his stopped suddenly and without warning. Since Draiv had taken his eyes off the road for a moment to look at Packs, he was unable to stop in time and collided with the rear of the stopped car. Packs was injured as a result of the collision.

84. Assume for the purpose of this question only that a statute in the jurisdiction provides that "No person shall maintain an action for damages resulting from negligence in the operation or ownership of an automobile if said person was a guest in said automobile at the time said damages allegedly occurred." In an action by Packs against Draiv for damages resulting from his injuries, which of the following arguments is most likely to result in a judgment for Packs?

(A) The fact that most drivers have insurance makes the statute obsolete.

(B) Packs was not a guest, since his driving on alternate days was consideration for the ride.

(C) Draiv's conduct was reckless, and therefore constituted aggravated negligence, a lawsuit for which is not prohibited by the statute.

(D) Enforcement of the statute will leave Packs without a remedy.

85. Assume for the purpose of this question only that there was no automobile guest statute in the jurisdiction. In an action by Packs against Draiv, which of the following would be Draiv's most effective argument in defense?

(A) Packs assumed the risk since he knew that it was possible that Draiv's car would be involved in an accident while traveling to work.

(B) Draiv's conduct was not a cause-in-fact of harm, since the accident would not have occurred if the car in front of his had not stopped suddenly.

(C) Draiv did not owe Packs a duty of reasonable care, since Packs was a licensee.

(D) It was not negligent for Draiv to take his eyes off the road for a moment.

Questions 86-87 are based on the following fact situation.

Respro is the manufacturer of a device known as the Res-Nibbler, which was designed for use by professional rescuers in removing accident victims who have become pinned in automobiles. The Res-Nibbler consists of power- scissors which, when connected to a portable power-pack, are strong enough to rapidly cut through the metal of a car body. Because the Res-Nibbler is heavy and powerful, improper use of it could result in serious harm to the user as well as to the person being rescued. For this reason, Respro sells it only to fire, police, and other rescue agencies, and offers a free training course to members of any such agencies which purchase it.

The Town of Mayberry fire department purchased a Res-Nibbler from Respro, and Charles, its fire chief, attended the Respro training course on its use. Subsequently, the Mayberry fire department was called to the scene of an accident in which Ponder was trapped in her car. Charles directed Fred, a volunteer fire-fighter, to use the Res-Nibbler to free Ponder from her car, although he knew that Fred had not been trained in its use. Then, while Fred attempted to do so, Charles began spraying the road with foam to prevent gasoline which had been spilled in the accident from catching fire.

Fred, who had never heard of the Res-Nibbler before, used it improperly, injuring both himself and Ponder.

86. If Fred instituted an action against Respro, alleging that the Res-Nibbler was defective because it lacked attached warnings regarding the dangers

incident to its use, Respro's most effective argument in defense would be that

(A) it had acted reasonably in its marketing and sale of the Res-Nibbler.

(B) it was unforeseeable that a person with Charles' training would direct someone whom he knew to be untrained to use the Res-Nibbler.

(C) Fred assumed the risk, since he attempted to use the device without proper training.

(D) Fred's attempt to use the machine without training was an independent intervening cause of harm, which broke the chain of proximate causation.

87. If Ponder instituted an action against Charles, Ponder's best theory would be

(A) negligence.

(B) battery.

(C) strict products liability.

(D) res ipsa loquitur.

Questions 88-89 are based on the following fact situation.

As a result of Nancy's negligence, Polly's shoulder and eye were both injured. Polly went immediately to Dr. Glass, her eye doctor. Dr. Glass treated the injury to Polly's eye, but suggested that she see an orthopedist for treatment of her shoulder. The following day, Polly visited Dr. Bonz, an orthopedist who treated Polly's shoulder.

Because of negligent treatment by Dr. Glass, Polly's nose became infected and because of negligent treatment by Dr. Bonz, she lost the use of her elbow.

88. In an action by Polly against Dr. Glass, a court is most likely to hold Dr. Glass liable for

(A) nothing, since all of the injuries were caused by the negligence of Nancy.

(B) the injury to Polly's nose, since it is the only

one of her injuries which was caused by his negligence.

(C) the injury to Polly's nose and the injury to Polly's elbow, since both were caused by his negligence.

(D) the injuries to Polly's nose, shoulder, and elbow, since all were caused by his negligence.

89. In an action by Polly against Nancy, which of the following parts of Polly's body is a court most likely to find were injured as a proximate result of Nancy's negligence?

   I. Nose.

   II. Elbow.

   (A) I only.

   (B) II only.

   (C) I and II.

   (D) Neither I nor II.

90. After taking and failing the state bar exam on twelve different occasions, Lipp decided to practice law without a license. Moving to a small town, he hung out a shingle which proclaimed him to be an attorney and ran advertisements in the local newspaper referring to himself as an attorney. Having seen one of the advertisements, Tippel retained Lipp to defend him against a charge of driving while intoxicated. Lipp attempted to negotiate a plea to a lesser charge, but because he was unable to do so, a trial was held. Lipp appeared on behalf of Tippel, but Tippel was convicted. During the course of the trial, the district attorney became suspicious of Lipp's credentials. Following an investigation which the district attorney instituted, Lipp was charged with violation of a state law which made it a crime to practice law without a license. He pleaded guilty and was sentenced to six months in jail.

If Tippel brings an action against Lipp for negligence in the way Lipp handled his defense, a court should find for

(A) Tippel, if but only if Lipp failed to defend him the way a reasonable attorney would have done.

(B) Tippel, since it was unreasonable for Lipp to practice law without a license.

(C) Tippel, since the law which prohibited practicing law without a license was designed to keep unqualified persons from practicing law.

(D) Lipp, since not even a licensed attorney guarantees results.

91. Penny was attending a nightclub at which Dr. Hypno was performing. Before the show began, a request was made for a volunteer to assist Dr. Hypno with his act, and Penny volunteered. She was taken backstage to Dr. Hypno's dressing room where she and Dr. Hypno had a conversation. Following their conversation, Penny agreed to participate in Dr. Hypno's show. During the course of the performance, Dr. Hypno attempted to hypnotize Penny on stage. He then touched her skin with an electric cattle-prod (a device which produces an electric shock and is used for handling stubborn cattle) causing her great pain and discomfort.

Penny subsequently instituted an action against Dr. Hypno. In it, she alleged that he committed various intentional torts against her by touching her with the cattle prod. If one of the following facts were established at the trial, which would be most helpful to Penny in responding to Dr. Hypno's defense of consent?

(A) During the conversation in Dr. Hypno's dressing room, Dr. Hypno stated that he was going to attempt to hypnotize Penny on stage, stated that he was usually successful in hypnotizing volunteers, and stated further that if he was successful, the cattle prod would cause her no discomfort.

(B) During the conversation in Dr. Hypno's dressing room, Dr. Hypno promised to pay her $100 for participating in the show; he never did pay her; and, in fact, when he promised that he would pay her, he did not intend to do so.

(C) During the conversation in Dr. Hypno's dressing room, Dr. Hypno stated that the electric cattle-prod produced a mild electric shock which would cause no real discomfort, when he knew that this was not true.

(D) When Penny consented to participating in Dr. Hypno's act, she did not know that contact with the electric cattle-prod would result in great pain and discomfort.

92. Speeger, a professor at City University, has publicly stated her opposition to the consumption of alcohol. As a result, she is much in demand as a lecturer on the evils of intoxication. One of her slogans is, "When you drink, make it fruit juice." Sweetapple Corporation, a producer of packaged apple juice, invited Speeger to participate in a promotional apple- juice-drinking contest which it was holding. Speeger, who succeeded in drinking one and one-half quarts of chilled apple juice without stopping for a breath, was declared the winner.

The *Bugle,* the City University student newspaper, ran a photo of Speeger holding the winner's trophy over a caption which read, "City U Prof. Speeger drinks them all under the table, winning first prize at the Sweetapple Corporation's drinking contest." A story which described the fruit-juice drinking contest in detail appeared on the same page as the photo, but some distance from it. The day after the photo and story appeared, an organization which had hired Speeger to lecture on the evils of alcohol canceled its contract with Speeger because, after seeing the photo and caption in the *Bugle,* some members believed that Speeger was a drinker of alcohol.

If Speeger sues the *Bugle* for defamation, the court should instruct the jury that the statements made by the *Bugle* in the photo and caption were *not* defamatory if

(A) the reasonable person would have read the story.

(B) the organization members who saw the

photo and caption did not read the story.

(C) a substantial group of respectable persons would have read the story.

(D) the reasonable person would not have read the story.

93. Strong, a member of the USA's 2002 Olympic team, and a multiple gold medal winner, appeared in a television commercial. While films of his medal- winning performances showed in the background, Strong ate a Power candy bar. He said that he had been eating Power candy for energy ever since he was a child. He ended the commercial by smiling, and saying, "Who knows? Maybe Power candy gave me the power to win."

Purlie purchased a case of twenty-four Power candy bars after seeing the commercial several times on television. After tasting one, however, he found he did not like the flavor. If Purlie brings an action against Strong for misrepresentation, which of the following arguments will be most helpful in Strong's defense?

(A) Strong is not in the business of selling Power candy.

(B) The script for the commercial was not written by Strong.

(C) Purlie was not in privity with Strong.

(D) Purlie has not sustained damage as the result of a false assertion by Strong.

94. Horace was a breeder of valuable thoroughbred race horses. Blass was a demolition contractor who had been hired by Constructo to demolish a large office building located one-half mile from Horace's farm. Blass was using dynamite for that purpose. On Thursday, Horace telephoned Blass to complain that the sounds of the explosions were frightening his animals. He said, "If anything happens to my horses, I'm planning to hold you personally responsible." On Friday, sounds of the explosions so frightened one of Horace's horses that she tried to jump over a fence, injuring herself in the process.

If Horace institutes an action against Blass on a strict liability theory, which of the following would be Blass' most effective argument in defense?

(A) Horace's farm was not within the foreseeable zone of danger.

(B) The possibility that noise will frighten animals is not one of the risks which makes blasting an ultra-hazardous activity.

(C) Blass used reasonable care in setting off the blast.

(D) Blass was working under contract to Constructo.

95. Landers was the owner of a small office building. Her own office was located on the ground floor of the building, the second floor was leased to Boss, and the third and fourth floors were divided into smaller offices which were rented to various tenants on a month-to-month basis. Although the building was equipped with an elevator, occupants of the building frequently used a stairway over which Landers retained control. Hirt was employed by Boss on the second floor of the building. One day, while Hirt was walking down the stairs from the second floor, she cut her hand on a jagged part of the handrail which ran alongside the stairs. She commenced an action against Landers, alleging that the handrail was jagged because of negligence by Landers.

Which of the following is an accurate statement about the case of *Hirt v. Landers?*

I. Hirt was an invitee, since she was an employee of one of Landers' tenants.

II. Hirt was contributorily (or comparatively) negligent if the reasonable person in her situation would have noticed the jagged condition of the handrail and would have avoided being injured by it.

(A) I only.

(B) II only.

(C) I and II.

(D) Neither I nor II.

96. Spec was a building inspector employed by City to conduct periodic inspections of business premises located in a territory to which she was assigned. The instruction manual which City furnished to its inspectors contained instructions on testing draperies for fire-retardant properties. In large bold-face letters, the manual stated, "NEVER EXPOSE DRAPERIES TO FLAME WHILE THEY ARE HANGING IN PLACE."

One of the businesses in Spec's territory was a nightclub known as The Spot. On one of her inspections of The Spot, Spec asked the manager of the business whether the window draperies were fire- retardant as required by City's building code. The manager responded that they were. Although Spec was familiar with the instructions in the manual, she was in a hurry. Taking a cigarette lighter from her pocket, she held its flame under one of the draperies where it was hanging. The drapery caught fire, which spread, completely destroying the building. Paulette, a passerby, was injured in the fire.

If Paulette brings an action for damages against City on a theory of respondeat superior, Paulette will

(A) lose, since Spec was acting in violation of specific instructions from her employer

(B) lose, if a building inspector's duties involve the exercise of unsupervised discretion

(C) win, if Spec was negligent

(D) win, whether or not Spec was negligent

97. A statute provides that every motor vehicle must be equipped with an ignition lock, and that it shall be a misdemeanor for any person to park a motor vehicle without locking it and removing the ignition key. David left his car parked on a public street with the ignition key in it in violation of the statute. Kidd, a fourteen year old child, saw the key in the ignition and stole the car. While driving it, he struck and injured Pell. In an

action by Pell against David, Pell will

(A) win, if but only if it was unreasonable for David to leave his keys in the ignition.

(B) win, if, but only if, the statute was designed to prevent accidents involving stolen cars.

(C) lose, unless Kidd's intervention is held to have been foreseeable.

(D) lose, if Kidd's conduct is found to be an intervention which proximately caused the injury.

98. The state governor was attending a major league baseball game when a member of the home team hit a home run. The governor jumped to his feet and cheered loudly, along with the rest of the crowd. Frank, a freelance photographer, took his picture while he was cheering. When the photograph was developed, Frank had it imprinted on targets. With toy plastic darts, Frank marketed them under the name of "The Cheering Governor Dart Board Game" and sold several thousand. The governor sued Frank for invasion of privacy.

On which of the following theories is the governor most likely to be successful in his action against Frank?

(A) Appropriation of identity.

(B) Public disclosure.

(C) Intrusion.

(D) False light.

99. Professor Hardy was disturbed by the fact that students frequently left the room during her lectures, so she instructed Tay, a teaching assistant, to lock the door of her classroom ten minutes after the class began, and not to unlock it again until ten minutes before the class was scheduled to end. On Thursday Peter attended Professor Hardy's four o'clock class. By five minutes past four, Peter was sound asleep in his seat. At ten minutes past four, Tay locked the classroom door as instructed by Professor Hardy, unlocking it at ten minutes to five. When the class ended at five, Peter who had slept through the class, was awak-

ened by a classmate, and left the room. The classroom had been painted the previous day with a paint to which Peter was allergic, although neither Professor Hardy, Tay, nor Peter knew about it. As a result of his exposure to the paint in the room, Peter developed allergic symptoms later that day which required hospitalization.

If Peter institutes an action for false imprisonment against Professor Hardy, who will win?

(A) Peter, because his illness resulted from Hardy's intentional confinement of him.

(B) Peter, since a professor owes her students a duty to refrain from exposing them to unreasonable risks of foreseeable harm.

(C) Hardy, since she did not know with substantial certainty that harm would result from locking the door.

(D) Hardy, since she did not confine Peter against his will.

Questions 100-102 are based on the following fact situation.

The Lovers of the Lord (LOL) is a small religious sect which had its origins in colonial America. Originally, members of the sect believed that physical acts of love were holy. During the Nineteenth Century, they were prosecuted for engaging in religious rituals which involved public nudity and group sex. At the start of the Twentieth Century, the leaders of the sect revised its philosophy and prohibited the sex acts that they had formerly encouraged. Some non-members of the sect continue to associate it with illicit sex, and continue to call its members "Makers," a term coined by Nineteenth Century journalists who campaigned against the LOL.

Preech is a minister ordained in the Church of Love, a religious organization which is not associated in any way with the Lovers of the Lord. Preech delivered the benediction at the year's first meeting of the Town Council of Smallville. The following day, the *Smallville Globe,* a daily newspaper, printed an article about the meeting. The article referred to Preech as "a minister of the Church of Love, better known as the Makers (LOL)." Preech instituted an action against the *Small-*

ville Globe, alleging that the reference to him as a minister of "the Makers (LOL)" was defamatory.

100. In his lawsuit, Preech must prove that the *Smallville Globe*

    (A) knew, or that the reasonable publisher would have known, that Preech was not affiliated with the Lovers of the Lord.

    (B) entertained serious doubts about whether or not Preech was affiliated with the Lovers of the Lord.

    (C) knew that "the Makers (LOL)" were associated with shame or disgrace in the minds of some readers.

    (D) made the statement, but Preech is not required to prove fault since Preech is not a public person.

101. Which of the following is a court most likely to find about the statement which appeared in the *Smallville Globe*?

    (A) The statement is not defamatory if the Makers (LOL) can be classified as a religion under the First Amendment to the United States Constitution.

    (B) The statement is not defamatory if members of the Lovers of the Lord do not currently engage in improper activities.

    (C) The statement is not defamatory if a substantial group of right-thinking people know that members of the organization known as the Makers no longer engage in improper activities.

    (D) The statement is defamatory if many people continue to believe that members of the organization known as "the Makers" engage in improper activities.

102. Assume for the purpose of this question only that the *Smallville Globe* moved to dismiss Preech's action on the grounds that his complaint contained no allegation of damage. Which of the following additional facts or inferences, if it was the

only one true, would be most helpful to Preech in opposing the motion to dismiss?

    (A) Editors of the *Smallville Globe* knew that Preech was not a member of the organization known as the Makers when they published the statement.

    (B) Preech was so upset upon reading the *Smallville Globe's* statement about him that he became physically ill.

    (C) Editors of the *Smallville Globe* disliked Preech, and wanted to injure his reputation.

    (D) Preech is neither a public official nor a public figure.

Questions 103-104 are based on the following fact situation.

Mashco was in the business of developing and manufacturing machinery used in other industries. Having developed a zoobie machine for shaping and stamping widgets, Mashco manufactured and sold seven of them to widget companies throughout the United States. One of the zoobie machines manufactured by Maschco was sold to the Johnson Widget Company, which used it without problems for three years. At the end of that time, however, Johnson redesigned its widgets. Since the zoobie machine that it had purchased from Maschco was inadequate for the production of Johnson's improved widget, Johnson sold the machine to Discount, a company specializing in selling products which, since they were slightly out of date, could be produced and sold at low prices.

Mashco learned that the finnegan pins in its zoobie machines tended to wear out after three or four years, making the machines dangerous. It contacted the Johnson Widget Company, offering to replace the worn part for one thousand dollars, which was what the repair would cost Mashco to make. When Johnson advised Mashco that the machine had been sold to Discount, Mashco contacted Discount and made the same offer. Because Discount did not want to spend the money, however, it refused Mashco's offer. Two months later, Worker, a Discount employee, was injured when the worn part in the zoobie machine caused it to explode.

103. Assume for the purpose of this question only that Worker instituted an action against Mashco on a theory of strict liability in tort. Assume further that the jury specifically found that the finnegan pin made the zoobie machine defective when sold by Mashco to Johnson and, that it had not been substantially changed since then. The jury should find in favor of

    (A) Worker, only if workers' compensation statutes prevent her from suing her employer.

    (B) Worker, if the defect in the zoobie machine was a proximate cause of her injury.

    (C) Mashco, if the machine had been removed from the stream of commerce when sold by Johnson to Discount.

    (D) Mashco, only if Discount's refusal to spend one thousand dollars to repair the machine was unreasonable.

104. Assume for the purpose of this question only that Worker instituted a negligence action against Mashco, and that Mashco's defense was based on the assertion that prior to the accident, Mashco neither knew nor reasonably could have known that the finnegan pin would wear out. If the jury believes this assertion, Worker will

    (A) win, since Mashco is deemed to be an expert in its field, and has a duty to know all relevant facts about the product which it makes.

    (B) win, since it is foreseeable that if the finnegan pin did wear out someone would be hurt.

    (C) win, since a manufacturer is strictly liable for defects in its product, whether or not it could have prevented those defects.

    (D) lose.

Questions 105-106 are based on the following fact situation.

Alice was driving her automobile on Country Road in the rain when she rounded a bend and saw a cow standing directly in her path. She immediately jammed on her brakes and pulled the steering wheel to the right in an attempt to avoid striking the cow. As a result, she lost control of her car, which skidded off the road and into Basil's yard. Basil, who was in the process of installing an automatic watering system, had dug a trench across the yard for pipes. When the wheels of Alice's car hit the trench, the car stopped abruptly, throwing Alice forward into the windshield, and causing her to be injured.

105. In an action by Alice against Basil for negligence, will a court decide that Basil owed Alice a duty of reasonable care?

    (A) Yes, if it was foreseeable that persons driving on Country Road might lose control of their vehicles and skid into Basil's yard.

    (B) Yes, if, but only if, the cow was in the road because of some conduct by Basil.

    (C) No, because it was not unreasonable for Basil to dig a trench on his own land.

    (D) No, because Alice was a trespasser.

106. In an action by Basil against Alice for negligence, which of the following arguments would be most effective as a defense for Alice?

    (A) Her conduct did not result in damage.

    (B) She was not required to act reasonably because she was confronted by an emergency.

    (C) She was privileged by the doctrine of necessity.

    (D) It was foreseeable that users of Country Road would deviate onto adjacent private land in connection with their use of the road.

Questions 107-110 are based on the following fact situation.

Carp, who was building a house on his own property, had posted a sign which said, "No Trespassing." He was working on the framework of his roof when he found that he had brought the wrong hammer onto the roof with him. Without looking to see if anyone was around, he tossed the hammer to the ground, shouting, "Heads up!"

Truck was a truck driver assigned to deliver lumber on the street where Carp was building a house. Carp had not ordered lumber, but when Truck saw Carp working on the roof of an unfinished house, he incorrectly assumed that Carp was the person to whom he was supposed to deliver the lumber. He parked his truck at the curb and was walking across Carp's property toward the unfinished house to talk to Carp about the delivery, when he was struck in the head by the hammer thrown by Carp. Truck cried out in pain, and then fell to the ground, unconscious and bleeding. Carp saw it happen, but merely shrugged and continued working.

A moment later a passerby who had seen what happened called an ambulance. When it arrived, Truck was still unconscious. The driver, Ann, loaded Truck into the ambulance and began driving to the hospital. Because of Ann's negligent driving, the ambulance struck a pole. Truck was killed in the crash.

107. Assume for the purpose of this question only that the representative of Truck's estate instituted an appropriate action against Carp, alleging that Carp's failure to call for medical assistance after he saw the hammer strike Truck was negligence. Which of the following comments is most accurate regarding that allegation?

(A) Carp owed Truck no duty to call for help if Truck was a trespasser.

(B) Truck's estate is entitled to punitive (exemplary) damages if Carp was substantially certain that there was a possibility of harm resulting from his failure to act.

(C) Carp's failure to call for medical aid was not a factual cause of harm to Truck, since someone did call a moment later.

(D) Truck was an invitee since he was a user of the public street who had entered upon adjacent private land.

108. Assume for the purpose of this question only that the representative of Truck's estate instituted an appropriate action against Carp, in a jurisdiction which applies the "all or nothing" rule of contributory negligence, alleging that Carp's throwing of the hammer without looking was negligence. If it was the only one true, which of the following additional facts or inferences would be most effective in Carp's defense against that allegation?

(A) It was reasonable for Carp to believe that no one would be struck by the hammer.

(B) It is customary in the construction industry for people working on a roof to toss unwanted tools and objects to the ground without looking, so long as they shout, "Heads up!"

(C) Truck could have avoided being struck by the hammer if he had seen it coming.

(D) The blow of his hammer would not have caused a serious injury to a normal person, but seriously injured Truck because his head was extraordinarily sensitive.

109. In a negligence action by the representative of Truck's estate against Carp, a court will most probably find Carp

(A) liable for Truck's death only if Carp's negligence was a proximate cause of Truck's head injury.

(B) liable for Truck's head injury if Carp's negligence was a proximate cause of it, but not liable for Truck's death since the negligence of Ann was an intervening cause.

(C) liable for Truck's head injury if Carp's negligence was a proximate cause of it, but not liable for Truck's death since the ambulance accident was an intervening cause of it.

(D) not liable for Truck's death, since Carp's conduct was not a factual cause of Truck's death.

110. If the representative of Truck's estate instituted

an appropriate action against Ann under the state's "wrongful death" statute, the court would be most likely to find for

(A) Ann, if Carp's conduct was foreseeable

(B) Ann, since a rescuer is not under an obligation to use reasonable care in the face of an emergency

(C) Truck's estate, since Ann's negligence was a proximate cause of Truck's death

(D) Truck's estate, unless Carp is found to be liable for Truck's death

111. Rend had been operating a soap factory in Travis County for fifty years. When the factory was first opened, the nearest residential settlement was Growtown, six miles away. Because the factory has been in existence for fifty years, Travis County zoning ordinances were drafted to allow its continued operation. In the past fifty years, however, Growtown has expanded in size. Now the edge of town is only a quarter of a mile from Rend's factory. On days when the wind is blowing from the direction of the factory, residents of the town are annoyed by the obnoxious odor emanating from the factory chimneys. Cooke, who moved to Growtown three years ago, has asked the Growtown Town Attorney to seek an injunction to prohibit Rend from emitting foul odors, but the Town Attorney has refused.

If Cooke sues Rend for damages resulting from the odors on a theory of public nuisance, which of the following will be Rend's most effective argument in defense?

(A) Rend's operation preceded the growth of Growtown.

(B) Cooke came to the nuisance.

(C) Cooke's damages are no different from those of other residents of Growtown.

(D) A lawful activity cannot constitute a public nuisance.

112. Trik and Vik had been friends for years, and worked in the same office. Ever since they were children, they had enjoyed playing "practical jokes" on each other. Frequently, they would spend hours together, laughing about the tricks they had played on each other. One day, planning to have some fun with Vik, Trik bought a large rubber spider from a toy store. Knowing that Vik was horrified of spiders, Trik came into work early, and placed the toy spider in the top drawer of Vik's desk. Later, when Vik arrived at work, he opened his top drawer to get out a letter opener and saw the rubber spider. Believing it to be real, and terrified that it would bite him, Vik screamed in fear, fainted, and fell to the floor. As he fell, he struck his head on the corner of his desk, sustaining a serious fracture of the skull.

If Vik asserts a claim for assault against Trik for the injury which he sustained in the fall, which of the following arguments would be most effective in Trik's defense?

(A) Vik's fear of being bitten by a spider was not apprehension of a battery.

(B) The reasonable person in Vik's position would not have become apprehensive at the sight of a spider.

(C) Vik impliedly consented to the prank by engaging in a course of practical joking with Trik.

(D) Trik was not substantially certain that Vik would be injured as a result of the joke.

113. Pierre commenced an action against Marc, and proved the following:

Marc and Mary were both slingshot enthusiasts known for the accuracy of their aim. They were planning to compete against each other in a slingshot tournament to be held on Sunday. On Saturday, without consulting the other, each went independently to the woods outside of town to practice his/her skill. Since not many people frequented the area, Marc and Mary were both somewhat casual about their targets, each shooting at anything that moved without properly checking to make sure of what they were shooting at. Pierre, who had gone to the woods to read in solitude, was struck by a steel ball shot from one of the slingshots. Since Marc and Mary were using the same kind of ammunition, it is impossible to determine which of them fired the ball which struck Pierre, but it is certain that one of them did.

If the court finds for Marc, it will probably be for which one of the following reasons?

(A) Marc did not owe Pierre a duty of reasonable care, since not many people frequented the area.

(B) There is no evidence that Marc acted unreasonably.

(C) The evidence does not establish that Marc's conduct was a factual cause of the injury.

(D) Even if Marc's conduct was a factual cause of the injury, it is impossible to tell whether it was a legal cause of the injury.

114. Statutes in the state of Avery provide that persons under the age of twenty years are incompetent to enter into contracts, may not marry without the written consent of their parents, may not lawfully purchase alcoholic beverages, and are subject to local curfew regulations. Melanie, a nineteen-year old, was fishing for pleasure from a pier in the state of Avery when she accidentally struck Pearson in the eye with a fish hook on the end of her line. Pearson commenced a negligence action against Melanie. The trial court should find that Melanie was negligent

(A) if she failed to act like the reasonable nineteen- year old with her experience and intelligence, because under the laws of Avery she is still a child.

(B) if she failed to act like the reasonable adult, because fishing is an adult activity.

(C) if she failed to act like the reasonable adult, because at nineteen she is old enough to be treated as an adult by the law of torts.

(D) because the risk of injury by being struck with a fish hook outweighs the utility of fishing for pleasure.

Questions 115-117 are based on the following fact situation.

Fruitco manufactures several kinds of cooked-fruit desserts, which are marketed in packages labeled, "Person Pleasers." Each such package consists of an aluminum can containing cooked fruit packed in syrup, and a plastic spoon. The aluminum can is equipped with an "easy- open" lid which can be removed by pulling an aluminum ring fastened to the top of the can.

One morning on his way to work, Pederson purchased a package of Person Pleasers from Gordon's Grocery Store. Later that day, while eating lunch, Pederson opened the package, removed the lid from the aluminum can, and began eating the contents with a spoon. After consuming more than half of the product, Pederson noticed parts of a rat's tail mixed with the cooked fruit.

115. If Pederson asserts a claim against Fruitco on the theory of strict liability in tort, which of the following would be Pederson's most effective argument?

(A) The presence of a rat's tail was a defect which made the product unreasonably dangerous.

(B) Pederson was in horizontal privity with Gordon's Grocery Store, and there is no need for vertical privity.

(C) The labeling and packaging of Person Pleasers implied a promise that the contents of the package purchased by Pederson was fit for human consumption.

(D) The doctrine of *res ipsa loquitur* applies, since the product was sold in a sealed package.

116. If Pederson asserts a claim for negligence against Gordon's, the court should find for

(A) Pederson, because any negligence by the manufacturer of a product is imputed to a retailer selling that product.

(B) Pederson, if the product was defective when Pederson purchased it from Gordon's Grocery Store.

(C) Gordon's, unless Gordon's failed to act reasonably in selling the product to Pederson.

(D) Gordon's, because a retailer is under no duty of reasonable care when selling products packaged in sealed containers.

117. In an action by Pederson against Fruitco, which of the following additional facts or inferences, if it were the only one true, would provide Fruitco with its most effective defense?

(A) Fruitco did not act unreasonably in manufacturing, packaging, or marketing the product purchased by Pederson.

(B) Pederson sustained no injury as a result of the presence of parts of a rat's tail in the product.

(C) Fruitco complied with all statutory requirements for quality control in the production of Person Pleasers.

(D) Pederson purchased the product on the recommendation of a sales clerk at Gordon's Grocery Store.

Questions 118-119 are based on the following fact situation.

Denton was driving her car north on Ocean Boulevard when the car in front of hers stopped suddenly to avoid striking a cat which had run into the roadway. Since there were no cars coming toward her, Denton swerved over the centerline and into the southbound lane. When she did so, she struck and injured Sal, a nine-year-old boy who was walking a bicycle south in the southbound lane. Because the sun was in her eyes, Denton did not see Sal until her car struck him.

Half an hour before the accident, Sal's mother Mona told Sal that she did not want him riding his bicycle on Ocean Boulevard because it was a heavily travelled roadway with no sidewalks. She gave him permission, however, to walk his bicycle carefully along the road shoulder.

As a result of the accident, Sal sustained brain damage

which will make it impossible for him to support, feed, or care for himself for the rest of his life. The jurisdiction applies the all-or-nothing rule of contributory negligence.

118. If Mona asserts a negligence claim against Denton for the medical bills which she incurred as a result of Sal's injury, which of the following may Denton assert in defense?

I. The accident resulted from Sal's negligence.

II. The accident resulted from Mona's negligence.

(A) I only.

(B) II only.

(C) I and II.

(D) Neither I nor II.

119. Assume for the purpose of this question only that Denton was acting unreasonably when her car struck Sal. If Sal asserts a negligence claim against Denton for his injuries, the court should find for

(A) Sal, unless the accident resulted from his own unreasonable conduct.

(B) Sal, because a nine-year-old is presumed incapable of contributory negligence.

(C) Sal, under the doctrine of res ipsa loquitur.

(D) Denton, if it was unreasonable for Mona to give Sal permission to walk his bicycle along the roadway.

120. Darby was towing a small travel-trailer with his automobile when the hitch which attached the trailer to the car broke, causing the trailer to collide with the vehicle of Venden which was parked at the curb. A statute in the jurisdiction provides that "No person shall operate a motor vehicle or trailer on the roads of this state unless said motor vehicle or trailer is covered by a valid policy of liability insurance." Darby was in violation of that statute in that he knew that his trailer was not covered by a valid policy of liability insurance at

the time of the accident. Is his violation of statute relevant to the issue of negligence in an action brought against him by Venden?

(A) Yes, because the statute was designed to protect the victims of automobile and trailer accidents.

(B) Yes, because the reasonable person does not knowingly violate a statute.

(C) No, because the law encourages the purchase of automobile insurance, and therefore absolutely prohibits disclosure to the jury about whether or not a defendant was insured.

(D) No, because compliance with the statute does not prevent automobile or trailer accidents.

Questions 121-123 are based on the following fact situation.

One night police officers Axel and Barber received a message that a burglary was in progress at the Super Grocery Store. Rushing to the location, they discovered that the back door of the store was open. Entering cautiously, they saw two burglars hiding in the storage room. In the ensuing attempt to effect an arrest in the dark, Axel and Barber knocked over several stacks of merchandise, including cases of bottled soda-pop manufactured by Popco. This caused minute cracks in all the bottles. The following day, store employees cleaned up the mess, restacking the cases of soda-pop. Approximately one week later, six of the cases were placed on display in the store. Frieda purchased one of the bottles from these six cases but did not notice the minute crack in it.

That evening Frieda was placing the bottle on the dinner table when the bottle exploded because of the crack in it, sending fragments of glass flying in all directions. Both Frieda and her daughter Tanya were cut by the flying glass.

121. In an action by Frieda against Popco, may she successfully rely on the doctrine of res ipsa loquitur?

(A) Yes, because it applies in exploding bottle cases.

(B) Yes, because Popco was in exclusive control of the bottling process.

(C) No, because the bottles were knocked over by Officers Axel and Barber.

(D) No, because the bottles were not in Popco's possession at the time Frieda's injury occurred.

122. In an action by Tanya against Super, a court is most likely to find for

(A) Tanya, because she could not have done anything to protect herself against the kind of injury which occurred.

(B) Tanya, if Super's conduct in restacking and selling the bottles was unreasonable under the circumstances.

(C) Super, if the conduct of Officers Axel and Barber is found to be a proximate cause of the injury sustained by Tanya.

(D) Super, because Tanya and Super were not in privity.

123. Assume for the purpose of this question only that when the stacked groceries fell over during the chase in the storage room, a bottle broke, and a fragment of flying glass struck Officer Axel, injuring him. If Axel institutes an action against Super, Axel will

(A) win, since the fact that he was attempting to apprehend a criminal who was burglarizing Super's store made him an invitee.

(B) win, if but only if Super's conduct was a physical cause of the harm.

(C) lose, since he was a bare licensee at the time the injury occurred.

(D) lose, if it was unforeseeable that persons would be chasing around the storeroom in the dark.

124. After several neighboring stores had been bur-

glarized, Keeper decided to take steps to protect her own grocery store against burglars. She purchased an alarm bell and wired it to the store cash register so that it would make a loud noise if the register was forced open. In addition, she connected a canister of X-Eleven gas to the system so that as the alarm went off, the gas would be discharged into the area around the cash register. Keeper had read a government report which indicated that X-Eleven had no harmful effects, but that a person exposed to it would become temporarily disoriented. She hoped that if a burglar attempted to steal from her cash register, the combination of disorientation produced by the gas and the loud noise produced by the bell would frighten the burglar away. That night, Baron broke into Keeper's store. When he attempted to open her cash register, the alarm bell began to sound and the canister discharged X-Eleven gas into the area. Baron became frightened, and ran away, but because he was unusually sensitive to the ingredients of X-Eleven gas, exposure to it permanently damaged his vision.

If Baron asserts a claim against Keeper for his damages, the court should find for

(A) Baron, if the alarm system created by Keeper constituted a trap.

(B) Baron, because a human being's vision is of greater value than mere property.

(C) Keeper, because no duty is owed to a trespasser who enters for the purpose of committing a crime.

(D) Keeper, if she used reasonable force to defend her property.

Questions 125-126 are based on the following fact situation.

Collins was a well-known collector of art. Dillon was an art dealer who operated a gallery in which she sold paintings and other works of art. One day, while Collins was visiting Dillon's gallery, Dillon showed him a new painting called "The Petticoats" which she had received that day.

"The artist didn't sign it," Dillon said. "But I'm sure it was painted by Degas. That would make it worth at least $250,000."

Collins answered, "It's by Degas, all right. It's worth every cent you're asking. But I already have several paintings by Degas in my collection, and I don't need another."

Barton, who was browsing in Dillon's gallery, overheard the conversation between Collins and Dillon. Barton knew very little about art, but had just inherited a large sum of money. Because he knew that Collins and Dillon were art experts, he believed what he heard them saying. After Collins left the gallery, Barton asked Dillon if she would accept $200,000 for "The Petticoats." Dillon said that she would not take anything less than $250,000. After negotiation, Barton purchased it for $225,000. Barton subsequently learned that "The Petticoats" had not been painted by Degas, and was worth only $600.

125. If Barton asserts a tort claim for misrepresentation against Dillon, which of the following would be Dillon's most effective argument in defense?

(A) A statement of opinion cannot be construed as a misrepresentation, since there is no such thing as a false idea.

(B) Barton did not sustain damage as a result of his reliance on a statement by Dillon.

(C) Dillon did not know that Barton would rely on the statements which she made to Collins.

(D) The value of any work of art is a matter of opinion.

126. If Barton is successful in a tort action for misrepresentation, the court is likely to award him a judgment for

(A) $250,000 (the value which Dillon stated).

(B) $250,000 (the value which Dillon stated), on condition that Barton return "The Petticoats" to Dillon.

(C) $225,000 (the price which Barton paid to Dillon).

(D) $224,400 (the price which Barton paid to Dillon less the value of "The Petticoats").

127. As a joke, Jason knocked on Pamela's door, wearing a police officer's uniform which he had rented from a costume shop. When Pamela came to the door, Jason told her that her husband had just been killed in a highway accident, and that she would have to come with him to claim the body. Pamela, who recognized Jason and knew that he was not a police officer, slammed the door in his face and told him to leave her alone. She was outraged at his attempt to play such a joke on her, but sustained no physical or mental injury.

If Pamela asserts a claim against Jason for intentional infliction of emotional distress, the court should find for

(A) Pamela, because Jason's conduct exceeded all bounds normally tolerated by decent society.

(B) Pamela, because Jason's conduct was calculated to cause severe mental suffering.

(C) Jason, because his intention was merely to play a joke on Pamela.

(D) Jason, because Pamela sustained no physical or mental injury as a result of Jason's conduct.

128. Which of the following most correctly states the duty owed to customers by a druggist who dispenses prescription drugs?

(A) To know all the harmful side effects of the drugs being dispensed.

(B) To warn of all the harmful side effects of the drugs being dispensed.

(C) To sell only those drugs which are not defective.

(D) To make whatever inspection of the drugs is reasonable before dispensing them.

129. Anson and Baker were members of the same golf club and frequently played golf together. One day, after meeting in the club's cocktail lounge, they argued about which of them could hit a golf ball farthest. To settle the dispute, they agreed to a contest and wager. Each handed one hundred dollars to Carter, who offered to hold the stakes. Their understanding was that each would hit a single golf ball, and that the one whose ball traveled the greatest distance would win the bet. Anson and Baker went together to the club's driving range. Both struck their golf balls at the same time. A moment later, they heard a shout coming from the far end of the driving range. Upon investigating, they found Pauling, another member of the club, lying unconscious on the ground with a single lump on his head. Lying beside him were the balls driven by Anson and Baker. Pauling subsequently asserted a claim for damages against Anson and Baker. He succeeded in proving that the ball which struck him had been driven by one of them, but was unable to show which. The court found that both Anson and Baker had acted negligently, and that they were involved in a concert of action.

Which of the following statements is most correct about the relationship of the parties?

(A) Either Anson or Baker may avoid liability by proving that his ball was not the one which struck Pauling.

(B) Neither Anson's nor Baker's conduct was a factual cause of harm, because each induced the other's conduct to be a substantial factor in producing Pauling's injury.

(C) Anson's conduct and Baker's conduct were legal causes of harm, but neither was a factual cause of harm.

(D) Anson and Baker may each be held vicariously liable for the other's conduct.

130. Medco is the manufacturer of a drug known as HLP, which is used in the treatment of certain cancers. Because HLP induces an allergic reaction in about ten percent of the people treated with it, Medco has sent every doctor in the United States a brochure describing the possible side-effects, and suggesting methods for deter-

mining in advance whether a patient is allergic to the drug. In addition, Medco has published warnings about the drug in *The Physician's Medical Guide,* a book which describes the effects of all prescription drugs sold in the United States and which is part of the library of virtually every practicing physician. Pattie was being treated by Dr. Oncol for cancer of the epiframmis gland. In the course of treatment, Dr. Oncol prescribed the use of HLP. Although Dr. Oncol had read the Medco brochure, and was aware of the possibility of an allergic reaction, she did not take any steps to determine whether Pattie was allergic to the drug. Because Pattie was allergic to HLP, its use caused her to lose the sight of one of her eyes.

Pattie subsequently retained Laird, an attorney, to commence a malpractice action against Dr. Oncol for the damages which resulted from her allergic reaction to HLP. Although the statute of limitations on such an action fixed a period of one year, more than one year passed before Laird commenced an action against Dr. Oncol. As a result, no such action could ever be brought. Pattie eventually sued Laird, alleging that Laird's failure to bring the action on time was negligent.

Which one of the following additional facts or inferences, if it was the only one true, would be most effective as part of Laird's defense?

(A) Laird had been admitted to the bar only three weeks before being retained by Pattie.

(B) Laird honestly believed that the statutory period of limitations for the commencement of medical malpractice actions was two years.

(C) After discussing the case with Dr. Oncol's attorney, Laird came to the conclusion that Pattie's case against Dr. Oncol was weak.

(D) Cancer of the epiframmis gland would have led to Pattie's death within a few months if left untreated, and HLP was the only drug available for its treatment.

131. Dalton was an elderly man who lived in a house with a swimming pool in the back yard. Although Dalton enjoyed swimming in the pool, his age

and physical infirmity made him unable to clean or maintain the pool himself. Instead, he agreed to allow his fourteen-year-old neighbor Nellie to swim in the pool anytime she wanted to without notifying Dalton or asking his permission, in exchange for Nellie's services in cleaning and maintaining the pool.

On Friday morning, Nellie thoroughly cleaned Dalton's pool. Later that day, Dalton drained all the water from the pool and did not refill it. Saturday morning, Nellie woke up early and decided to go swimming in Dalton's pool. She put on her bathing suit and went into Dalton's yard, running onto the diving board of his swimming pool and diving in without looking first. Nellie was severely injured when she fell to the concrete bottom of the empty swimming pool.

If Nellie asserts a negligence claim for her injuries against Dalton in a jurisdiction which has a pure comparative negligence statute, the court should find for

(A) Nellie, because the pool constituted an attractive nuisance.

(B) Dalton, because Nellie was a trespasser.

(C) Nellie, if it was unreasonable for Dalton to drain the pool without warning her.

(D) Dalton, if the reasonable person in Nellie's position would have known the risk of diving into an empty swimming pool.

132. Power and Light Company (PALCO) was the owner of electrical generating equipment located on a parcel of real estate in the City of Haven. Electrical power lines ran from the equipment to a sixty-foot power pole, also located on the realty. Spikes had been driven into the pole every twelve inches, for use as steps by persons climbing the pole to service the wires fastened to it. Twelve feet above the ground, a wooden platform was mounted on the pole, with a hole in its center so that a person climbing up the pole could climb through the hole onto the platform.

The playground of Haven Grammar School was directly adjacent to the PALCO property, separated from it by a six-foot wire mesh fence. PALCO officials were aware that a large gaping hole in this fence had existed for approximately one year, and that children frequently crept through the hole to play on PALCO property.

One morning, Paulette, a twelve-year-old student at the Haven Grammar School, entered the PALCO property through the hole in the fence. Paulette began climbing the spikes which had been driven into the pole. When she reached the wooden platform located twelve feet above ground, she put her head through the hole in its center to see what was above it. Her head came into contact with a high-voltage wire which had been strung over the platform, causing her to sustain serious injuries.

In a negligence action by Paulette against PALCO, which one of the following additional facts or inferences, if it were the only one true, would provide PALCO with its most effective argument in defense?

(A) Paulette entered the premises without PALCO's permission.

(B) To PALCO's knowledge, no child had ever before attempted to climb the pole.

(C) Paulette was old enough to comprehend the dangers associated with an attempt to climb the pole.

(D) The fence which separated the PALCO property from the school yard was located completely on realty occupied by the Haven Grammar School.

133. Explo was a manufacturer of explosives. Several cases of explosives which Explo had shipped to a buyer in another state were being stored by Warehouse pending delivery. While the explosives were there, the Warehouse facility was struck by lightning, causing the explosives to explode. The cases containing the explosives did not bear any description of their contents. If Warehouse employees knew that the cases contained explosives, they would have stored them in a way which would have prevented the explosion. Praxton, who sustained property damage as a result of the explosion, has asserted a claim against Explo.

Which of the following facts or inferences, if it were the only one true, would provide Explo with its most effective argument in defense?

(A) Explo did not do anything unreasonable or irresponsible in manufacturing, packaging, or labeling its product.

(B) When Explo shipped the cases of explosives, they had been properly labeled with firmly affixed labels identifying their contents, but the labels had somehow come off in transit.

(C) Explo had assigned an employee to make sure that all cases of explosives shipped by Explo were properly labeled, but the employee had forgotten to inspect this shipment.

(D) The storage of explosives by Warehouse was an ultra-hazardous activity.

134. In which one of the following cases is the defendant LEAST likely to be held liable for battery?

(A) Defendant is a six-year-old boy who shot plaintiff with a bow and arrow, because he wanted to see if she would shout when the arrow hit her.

(B) Defendant is an insane woman who struck the plaintiff because she believed the plaintiff to be a horse which was attacking her.

(C) Defendant is a man who was on a date with the plaintiff, and who suddenly took her into his arms and kissed her because he believed that she wanted to be overwhelmed by his passion.

(D) Defendant is a mentally retarded adult who threw a stone at the plaintiff and struck her with it, because he believed that the plaintiff was going to hurt him.

135. Fred Fredericks was a comedian who continued performing until he was ninety years old. During his seventy-year career in the entertainment busi-

ness, his trademark was always a cigar which he clenched between his teeth or held in his hand while delivering his jokes. As part of an interview on the Bill Ball television show, Ball asked Fredericks whether he really smoked cigars. Fredericks replied, "Sure. I always smoke Georgia Cigars. They're the best cigars made."

The following day, Georgia Cigar Company, the manufacturer of Georgia Cigars, placed several advertisements in newspapers. All of the advertisements said, "Fred Fredericks says Georgia Cigars are the best cigars made. He always smokes Georgia Cigars, and you should too."

If Fredericks asserts a claim against Georgia Cigar Company for invasion of privacy by misappropriation of identity, the court should find for

(A) Georgia Cigar Company, because Fredericks had in fact made the statement which appeared in the advertisement.

(B) Georgia Cigar Company, because the advertisement constituted a constitutionally protected form of commercial expression.

(C) Fredericks, because when he made the statement on the Bill Ball television show, it was unforeseeable that Georgia Cigar Company would use it in its advertising.

(D) Fredericks, because Georgia Cigar Company used his name to sell its product without his permission.

136. Fennel grew fruit trees on her farm outside of Village. In addition, she operated a fruit store in Village. Every day during the harvest season, in a trailer which she towed with her pickup truck, she hauled fresh fruit from her orchards to her store. One day, as she was towing the trailer filled with fruit up a hill on her way to village, the hitch which fastened the trailer to the pickup truck failed, permitting the trailer to break loose and roll down the hill, striking and damaging the home of Perlman. Subsequent investigation revealed that the hitch failed because one of its parts was made of defective steel.

If Perlman asserts a claim against Fennel for

damage to his house, the court's decision is most likely to turn on whether

(A) Fennel acted reasonably.

(B) the hitch was defective in manufacture or in design.

(C) Fennel was a merchant.

(D) Perlman could have foreseen the damage.

137. Flier was a helicopter pilot employed by a radio station as a traffic reporter. One day, while flying in his helicopter, he hovered over the home of Pauline. Using powerful binoculars, he looked into her window to watch her while she was exercising in the nude. If Pauline institutes an action against him, which of the following facts or inferences must she establish in order to make out a prima facie case of trespass to land?

(A) The altitude at which Flier hovered over her house.

(B) Damage to her land, or to her right to enjoy it, which resulted from Flier's conduct.

(C) That she had a reasonable expectation of privacy while exercising nude in her own home.

(D) That she was in lawful possession of the premises at the time that Flier hovered over her house.

138. When Chevan discovered that her car had been stolen, she reported the theft to the police. Then, while she was walking home from the police station, she saw her car in Homer's driveway where the person who stole it had abandoned it after using it in a bank robbery. When she began walking toward the automobile, Homer ran out of his house, shouting, "Hey, you. Where do you think you're going?" Chevan explained that she was attempting to retrieve her car, but Homer pushed her, saying, "Get off my land." Chevan, who sustained no physical or mental injury as a result of Homer's contact with her, got into her car and drove it away. Chevan subsequently commenced a battery action against Homer. If, in response to Chevan's claim, Homer asserts the privilege to

defend realty, the court should find for

(A) Homer, because Chevan was not in hot pursuit of her car when she entered Homer's realty.

(B) Homer, because Chevan was not injured as a result of his contact with her.

(C) Chevan, because force is never permitted in defense of realty.

(D) Chevan, because she was privileged to enter and retake her automobile.

Questions 139-140 are based on the following fact situation.

Hudson asserted a claim against Adjust, alleging that statements made by Adjust were misrepresentations. Attorneys for both parties agreed on the following facts:

Hudson's wife died when she jumped in front of a train operated by the X & L Railroad Corporation. Two weeks later, Adjust, a representative of X & L, contacted Hudson. Adjust said that although X & L was not legally responsible for the death of Hudson's wife, X & L was willing to pay $1,000 in full settlement of all claims arising from the death of Hudson's wife. When Hudson said that he wanted to discuss the matter with an attorney, Adjust said, "If a lawyer gets involved, we won't pay you anything. You haven't got a legal leg to stand on anyway. You couldn't possibly win a suit against X & L." Hudson doubted that Adjust was telling him the truth, so he consulted with Laird, an attorney. After interviewing Hudson, Laird said that she did not think Hudson would win an action against X & L under the state's wrongful death statute, and refused to represent Hudson in such action. Hudson thereafter accepted Adjust's offer to settle all claims for $1,000, and executed a general release in return for X & L's payment in that amount. Subsequently, Hudson -- represented by a different attorney -- instituted a wrongful death action against X & L. Upon motion by X & L, the court dismissed that action on the ground that Hudson had released X & L of all liability as part of the settlement.

139. Which of the following additional facts must

Hudson prove in order to establish a cause of action for misrepresentation against Adjust?

I. If Hudson's wrongful death action against X & L was not dismissed, it would have resulted in a judgment for Hudson in excess of $1,000.

II. When Adjust made the statements to Hudson, Adjust knew or should have known that the statements were false.

(A) I only.

(B) II only.

(C) Both I and II.

(D) Neither I nor II.

140. Which of the following would be Adjust's LEAST effective argument in defense against Hudson's claim?

(A) Liability should not be imposed on Adjust, because he was acting within the scope of his employment when he made the statements to Hudson.

(B) Statements regarding the law are statements of opinion, because all persons are presumed to know the law.

(C) Hudson did not rely on the statements made by Adjust, because he consulted with an attorney before accepting Adjust's offer.

(D) Hudson was not justified in relying on the statements made by Adjust, because Hudson knew that Adjust represented X & L.

141. Tweeter was a manufacturer of dog-whistles, and operated a factory for that purpose. The whistles manufactured by Tweeter issued a sound so high-pitched that it could not be heard by human ears; only dogs could hear it. For this reason, before leaving the assembly line, each whistle was tested by a machine which blew air through it and metered the sound which it made. After Tweeter's factory had been in operation for fifteen years, Ken moved onto the adjoining realty and began operating a kennel. Ken bred and raised pedigreed dogs and boarded customers'

dogs as part of his business. Two weeks after moving onto the realty, Ken discovered that the dogs in his kennel were being disturbed by the testing of dog-whistles in Tweeter's factory. He wrote Tweeter a letter advising him that Tweeter's operation was making it impossible for Ken to remain in business, and demanding that Tweeter change his methods so that the sounds of the whistles would not upset Ken's dogs. When Tweeter refused, Ken commenced a private nuisance action against him. Which of the following would be Tweeter's most effective argument in defense against Ken's claim?

(A) The operation of a dog-whistle factory is a lawful business.

(B) Ken came to the nuisance.

(C) Tweeter did not intend to cause harm to Ken or to Ken's business.

(D) Ken's damage resulted from the fact that Ken was making an ultra-sensitive use of the land.

Questions 142-143 are based on the following fact situation.

Perry purchased a bottle of Feather dishwashing detergent from Clubmart, a self-service supermarket. Perry selected the product from the Clubmart store shelves, carried it to a checkout counter, and paid the cashier. Perry then placed the bottle in a bag furnished by Clubmart and carried it home. The product purchased by Perry was manufactured by Feather. After using the product for washing dishes, Perry experienced a serious rash on his hands and wrists as the result of an allergic reaction to a chemical in the product.

142. If Perry asserts a claim against Clubmart for breach of express warranty, a court should find for

(A) Perry, if the label stated that the product would not harm the skin of a user.

(B) Perry, if the product was unfit for ordinary use.

(C) Clubmart, if Perry's injury resulted from

reliance on a statement which Feather caused to be printed on the label of its product.

(D) Clubmart, if no Clubmart employee knew what statements were contained on the Feather detergent label.

143. If Perry asserts a claim against Feather on the ground that the product was not merchantable, which of the following additional facts or inferences, if it were the only one true, would provide Feather with its most effective defense?

(A) Perry's allergic reaction was the only such reaction which ever occurred.

(B) Clubmart purchased the product from an independent wholesaler which purchased it from Feather.

(C) Before marketing the product, Feather made a reasonable effort to determine whether the product would be harmful to normal skin.

(D) Prior to manufacturing and marketing the product, Feather received approval for its sale from the federal Food and Drug Administration.

144. Hubert bought a new sailboat, although he had never been on one before. When he purchased the boat, the salesman told him to be sure and receive boating instruction before attempting to use the boat, because this particular model required considerable skill to operate. Although Hubert had not received any instruction at all, and although he heard a weather report which warned of severe storms, he decided to take the boat out for a test sail by himself. A few minutes after he left the dock with his boat, the storm struck, causing high and dangerous waves. Fearful that Hubert would be killed at sea, his wife Wanda stood crying on the shore. Sam, an experienced sailor who knew Hubert and Wanda, heard Wanda crying for her husband's safety. Without saying anything to Wanda, Sam went out in his own boat to look for Hubert. Hubert returned unhurt an hour later, but Sam's boat capsized in the storm, severely damaging his boat, and causing Sam to sustain injury.

If Sam asserts a claim against Hubert for the damage which he sustained, the court should find for

(A) Sam, if his damage resulted from Hubert's failure to act reasonably.

(B) Sam, because a rescuer is entitled to indemnity from the person whom he was attempting to rescue.

(C) Hubert, because Sam was an officious intermeddler.

(D) Hubert, unless Hubert was aware that Sam would attempt to rescue him.

145. Carolyn was driving to visit her fiancee who was staying in Smallville, about fifty miles away. Before she left, her friend Frieda asked her to deliver a small package to someone in Smallville. The package contained a bottle of caustic chemical. Because she was afraid that Carolyn would refuse to carry it if she knew its contents, Frieda wrapped the package in brown paper and did not tell Carolyn what was in it. Carolyn placed the package in the glove compartment of her car and began driving to Smallville. Along the way, Carolyn saw Harold hitchhiking by the side of the road. Since they had gone to high school together, Carolyn offered Harold a ride. While Harold was sitting in the front seat beside Carolyn, the package in the glove compartment began to leak, dripping liquid onto Harold's trousers. Without saying anything to Carolyn, Harold opened the glove compartment and removed the wet package. As soon as the caustic liquid touched Harold's hand, it burned his skin severely.

If Harold commences a negligence action against Carolyn in a jurisdiction which has no automobile guest statute and which applies the all-or-nothing rule of contributory negligence, which of the following would be Carolyn's most effective argument in defense?

(A) Harold was a mere licensee, and was only entitled to a warning of those conditions which Carolyn knew were dangerous.

(B) Carolyn could not have known or antici-

pated that the contents of the package would cause harm to a passenger in her car.

(C) Harold was contributorily negligent in touching the wet package.

(D) Harold assumed the risk of injury resulting from contact with the wet package.

146. Preston, a photographer's model, decided to have a rosebud tattooed on her shoulder in the hope that it would increase the demand for and the value of her modeling services. She went to Tolliver, a tattoo artist, for that purpose. After Tolliver explained that tattooing involved the insertion of needles into the skin and was therefore a painful process, Preston selected the tattoo which she wanted and told Tolliver to proceed. While Tolliver was tattooing Preston's shoulder, the tattoo needle broke off in Preston's skin, injuring Preston. If Preston asserts a strict liability claim against Tolliver on the ground that the tattoo needle which Tolliver used was defective, Tolliver's most effective argument in defense would be that

(A) Tolliver did not sell the needle to Preston.

(B) Tolliver was not the manufacturer of the needle, and therefore had no control over its quality.

(C) Preston assumed the risk of injury.

(D) A tattoo needle is not an inherently dangerous product.

147. Stroll enjoyed walking vigorously in the hours before sunrise, and was doing so when Osman, a police officer, drove by in a patrol car. When Osman saw Stroll hurrying down the street in the early morning darkness, he pulled his car over to the curb and ordered Stroll to stop and identify himself. Stroll showed Osman his driving license, told him that he lived only a few blocks away, and explained that he was just taking a walk. When Osman told Stroll to get into the back of the patrol car, Stroll asked whether he was under arrest. Osman replied, "No, but if you know what's good for you, you'll get into the car and

shut up while I decide what to do with you."
Stroll got into the car and sat quietly in the back
seat with the door open, while Osman called
Stroll's description in to police headquarters over
the radio. About fifteen minutes later, satisfied
that Stroll was not wanted for violating any law,
Osman told him that he could go. If Stroll asserts
a claim against Osman for false imprisonment,
the court should find for

(A) Osman, if the rear door of Osman's patrol
car remained open all the time that Stroll
sat in the car.

(B) Osman, because Stroll did not object to sitting in the patrol car.

(C) Stroll, if the language used by Osman
induced Stroll to obey Osman's order.

(D) Stroll, only if he sustained damage as a
result of his detention by Osman.

148. Because he was driving in an unreasonable manner, Carter's truck collided with a power pole on
Main Street. The power pole fell down as a result
of the impact, causing electrical power to fail in
the operating room of Merced Hospital on Broad
Street, two blocks away. At the time of the power
failure, Pirtle was undergoing facial surgery in
the Merced Hospital operating room. The hospital's emergency generator went on automatically,
supplying enough electrical power to dimly light
the operating room. Dr. Hoffman, the surgeon
who was operating on Pirtle, was able to complete the surgery on Pirtle's face, but the operation left Pirtle with permanent and disfiguring
scars. If the power had not failed, Dr. Hoffman
would have been able to prevent the scarring. If
Pirtle asserts a claim for negligence against
Carter, which of the following additional facts or
inferences, if it were the only one true, would
provide Carter with his most effective defense?

(A) The reasonable surgeon in Dr. Hoffman's
position would not have proceeded with
the operation while the operating room
was dimly lit by the hospital's emergency
generator.

(B) The reasonable person in Carter's position

would not have anticipated that driving a
truck on Main Street would affect any person at Merced Hospital.

(C) Dr. Hoffman was guilty of aggravated negligence in continuing to operate on Pirtle
under the circumstances then existing.

(D) Pirtle's scarring was caused by the conduct
of Dr. Hoffman.

149. The Leopards and the Sharks were major league
baseball teams headquartered in the city of York.
Shea and Murphy were sportswriters who wrote
for competing newspapers in York. Because most
of Shea's articles praised the Leopards, and most
of Murphy's articles praised the Sharks, a rivalry
developed between Shea and Murphy. One of
Murphy's recent columns contained the following statement:

> Shea's team can't play ball, and Shea can't
> write his way out of a paper bag. The only
> thing more boring than reading Shea's stuff is
> reading it while watching the Leopards play.

If Shea commences an action for defamation
against Murphy, which of the following would be
Murphy's most effective argument in defense?

(A) Shea is a public figure.

(B) The statements made by Murphy were
expressions of opinion.

(C) Murphy's occupation makes him a media
defendant.

(D) Murphy's statements were privileged by the
defense of competition.

Questions 150-152 are based on the following fact situation.

Patterson was a commercial pilot, who operated a
package air-delivery service. Having been hired to
deliver a parcel to an airport located 300 miles away, he
had his plane filled with fuel supplied by Marvelco Oil
Refining Company. The fuel which was put into Patterson's fuel tank had been contaminated before leaving
the Marvelco refinery, but neither Patterson nor Marvelco knew about the contamination. After Patterson

had flown one hundred miles from the airport, the contaminants in the fuel caused his engine to fail. Patterson looked for a place to make an emergency landing and chose the parking lot of the Contemporary Art Museum, because it was the only level land in the vicinity. The Contemporary Art Museum housed a rare and valuable collection of art.

150. Assume for the purpose of this question only that Patterson succeeded in landing in the parking lot without causing any damage. If the Contemporary Art Museum asserts a claim against Patterson for trespass to land, which of the following arguments would be most effective for Patterson's defense?

(A) The engine failure which resulted from contaminated fuel was unforeseeable.

(B) Patterson did not intend to enter the realty of the Contemporary Art Museum.

(C) Landing on the parking lot of the Contemporary Art Museum was reasonable, considering the risk to Patterson and his airplane.

(D) The accident was caused by a defect in the product furnished by Marvelco.

151. Assume for the purpose of this question only that the building of Contemporary Art museum was damaged by Patterson's landing. If the Contemporary Art Museum asserts a claim against Marvelco on the theory of strict liability in tort, the court should find for

(A) the Contemporary Art Museum, if the contaminants in the fuel supplied to Patterson made the fuel defective.

(B) the Contemporary Art Museum, unless Marvelco acted unreasonably.

(C) Marvelco, only if the contamination of fuel before it left the Marvelco refinery was unforeseeable.

(D) Marvelco, because it had no business relationship with the Contemporary Art Museum.

152. Assume for the purpose of this question only that Patterson was injured in the emergency landing and that he asserted a negligence claim against Marvelco for his injuries. If it were the only one true, which of the following additional facts would be most likely to result in a judgment for Patterson?

(A) The contaminated fuel furnished by Marvelco was unreasonably dangerous.

(B) The reasonable oil refining company would not sell fuel which it knew to be contaminated.

(C) A reasonable inspection of the fuel before it left the Marvelco refinery would have revealed that it was contaminated.

(D) Contaminated airplane fuel defeats the reasonable expectations of the reasonable consumer.

Questions 153-154 are based on the following fact situation.

At 9 a.m., Ansel parked his car on Village Road in front of the play yard of Village Elementary School. At the time he parked the car, Ansel knew that he was violating a statute which prohibited parking within two blocks of any elementary school. At 10 a.m. on the same day, because she was driving at an unreasonably fast rate of speed, Baker lost control of her car and struck Ansel's parked vehicle. The impact caused Pringle, a passenger in Baker's car, to be thrown against the windshield, severely cutting her face, and rendering her unconscious. If Ansel's car had not been parked where it was, Baker would have collided with a six- foot concrete wall which surrounded the school play yard.

153. If Pringle asserts a negligence claim against Ansel, which of the following additional facts or inferences, if it was the only one true, would be most likely to lead to a judgment for Ansel.

(A) The statute which prohibited parking within two blocks of any elementary school was designed to protect schoolchildren.

(B) The accident would not have occurred if Baker had not been operating her vehicle in an unreasonable manner.

(C) If Baker's car had hit the concrete wall, Pringle would have sustained injuries as serious as those sustained in the collision with Ansel's car.

(D) Baker's unreasonable driving was an intervening cause of harm.

154. If Pringle asserts a negligence claim against Baker, the court should find for

(A) Baker, unless it was foreseeable that a car would be illegally parked in front of an elementary school play yard.

(B) Baker, if Ansel's conduct can be regarded as gross and willful misconduct.

(C) Pringle, if it was likely that collision with a stationary object would result in injury to a passenger in Baker's car.

(D) Pringle, unless there were other causes of harm.

Questions 155-156 are based on the following fact situation.

At the trial of *Preston v. Wonder and Tudor*, the jury found that Preston was damaged to the extent of $100,000. The jury further found that Preston's damage was caused 20 percent by Preston's negligence, 40 percent by Wonder's negligence, and 40 percent by Tudor's negligence. The jurisdiction had a statute which read as follows:
In a negligence action, no plaintiff shall be barred from recovery because of that plaintiff's contributory negligence, but such plaintiff's recovery shall be diminished in proportion to plaintiff's own fault.

The court held that Wonder and Tudor were jointly and severally liable for Preston's damage, and entered judgment for Preston consistent with the jury's verdict.

155. Assume for the purpose of this question only that Wonder became insolvent following the entry of judgment. How much money is Preston entitled to collect from Tudor?

(A) $100,000.

(B) $80,000 ($100,000 less 20%).

(C) $40,000 (40% of $100,000).

(D) None.

156. Assume for the purpose of this question only that prior to the entry of judgment, Preston collected $10,000 from an insurance company under a policy in which it agreed to pay any medical bills which Preston might incur as the result of an automobile accident. Which of the following correctly reflects the sum which Preston is entitled to collect from Wonder and Tudor?

(A) $90,000, because Preston's damage of $100,000 should be diminished by a sum proportional to Preston's own fault, less any loss against which Preston has insured himself.

(B) $80,000, because Preston's damage of $100,000 should be diminished by a sum proportional to Preston's own fault, without regard to sums which Preston has received under the insurance policy.

(C) $70,000, because Preston's damage of $100,000 should be diminished by a sum proportional to Preston's own fault, and further diminished by the sum which Preston received under the insurance policy.

(D) $60,000, because Preston's damage of $100,000 should be diminished by a sum proportional to Preston's own fault, and Wonder's and Tudor's proportional shares should each be further diminished by the sum which Preston received under the insurance policy.

Questions 157-159 are based on the following fact situation.

While waiting for a bus, Barrera decided to go into Joe's Bar to use the public phone. Capewell, one of Barrera's neighbors, was seated at the bar when Barrera entered. Although Barrera realized that Capewell was drunk, Barrera asked Capewell for a ride home. Capewell agreed and left with Barrera at once. Because he was drunk, Capewell lost control of his car and collided with a car driven by Austin, injuring Austin and Barrera, and damaging Austin's car.

157. Assume for the purpose of this question only that Austin asserts a negligence claim against Barrera for damages resulting from the accident. The court should find for

   (A) Austin, if Barrera's negligence was a proximate cause of Austin's injuries.

   (B) Austin, unless Barrera's conduct was a superseding cause of Austin's injuries.

   (C) Barrera, only if Barrera's conduct was a concurring cause of Austin's injuries.

   (D) Barrera, because a passenger in an automobile is under no obligation to control the conduct of its driver.

158. Assume for the purpose of this question only that Barrera asserts a negligence claim for his injuries against Capewell in a jurisdiction which applies the all-or-nothing rule of contributory negligence. Which of the following arguments would be likely to provide Capewell with an effective defense to that claim?

   I. Barrera was contributorily negligent in accepting a ride from Capewell when he knew Capewell to be drunk.

   II. Barrera assumed the risk by accepting a ride from Capewell when he knew Capewell to be drunk.

   (A) I only.

   (B) II only.

   (C) Neither I nor II.

   (D) I and II.

159. Assume for the purpose of this question only that Austin asserts a trespass to chattel claim against Capewell for damage to his car. The court should find for Austin

   (A) if the possibility that Capewell would collide with another vehicle would have been apparent to the reasonable sober person.

   (B) only if the possibility that Capewell would collide with another vehicle was apparent to Capewell.

   (C) because Capewell intended to drive his car, and an unauthorized interference with Austin's chattel resulted.

   (D) only if Capewell wanted to collide with another car or knew that he would do so.

Questions 160-161 are based on the following fact situation.

The Historic Investor is a monthly publication of interest primarily to persons who deal in the purchase and sale of historic buildings as an investment. It is read by approximately 1,000 subscribers each month. An issue of the Historic Investor contained an article about the recent sale of Montebello, an old house which had once been owned by a United States president. The article stated that Montebello had been purchased by Paulette Pepin for $450,000. It described Pepin as a bank president earning a salary of $100,000 per year, and stated that she had purchased Montebello with part of the one million dollar fortune which she inherited from her mother.

Writers of the article had obtained information about the sale of Montebello from public records of the Office of the County Recorder. Information about Pepin's employment and salary had been obtained from public records of the state Department of Banks, and information about her inheritance from public records of the state Probate Court. All statements made in the article were accurate.

160. Assume for the purpose of this question only that Pepin asserts a claim for invasion of privacy against The Historic Investor on the ground that the article publicly disclosed facts about her salary and inheritance. The court should find for

   (A) Pepin, if most members of the general public were unfamiliar with records of the state Department of Banks and the state Probate Court.

   (B) Pepin, because there is no right to publish

information regarding the personal wealth of a person who is not a public employee.

(C) The Historic Investor, because liability cannot be imposed for publication of the truth.

(D) The Historic Investor, because Pepin's salary and inheritance were a matter of public record.

161. Assume for the purpose of this question only that Pepin asserts a claim for invasion of privacy against The Historic Investor on the ground that The Historic Investor appropriated her identity by publishing the article about her without her permission. Which of the following would be The Historic Investor's most effective argument in defense?

(A) Information about the purchaser of Montebello was of interest to readers of The Historic Investor.

(B) The article about Pepin did not enrich The Historic Investor because Pepin was not a celebrity.

(C) The sale of Montebello to Pepin was a matter of public record.

(D) Publication of the article was not the result of "actual malice" as defined by the United States Supreme Court.

Questions 162-163 are based on the following fact situation.

Blocko operated a factory in Harris Valley. For many years, powdered cement used by Blocko in its factory was delivered in ninety pounds sacks. Recently, however, Blocko officials determined that it would be considerably less expensive to purchase unbagged cement. Since then, Blocko has maintained a huge bin containing unbagged powdered cement in a yard outside its factory building. As a result of Blocko's change to unbagged cement, the amount of cement dust in the air around its factory has increased substantially.

Perkins lived in a cabin in Harris Valley. After Blocko began using unbagged cement, cement dust from Blocko's operation continually settled on the cabin

which Perkins occupied. Although the dust did no physical harm to the cabin or to Perkins, Perkins complained to officials of Blocko that the dust annoyed her. Because Blocko received no other complaints from Harris Valley residents, however, it continued using unbagged cement.

162. If Perkins wishes to assert a tort claim against Blocko on account of the cement dust which continually settles on the cabin, which of the following would be her most effective theory?

(A) Invasion of Privacy.

(B) Public nuisance.

(C) Trespass to land.

(D) Strict liability for engaging in ultra-hazardous activity.

163. Assume for the purpose of this question only that Perkins asserts a negligence claim against Blocko. Which of the following would be Blocko's most effective argument in defense?

(A) Changing from bagged cement to unbagged cement resulted in substantial financial savings to Blocko.

(B) Blocko's conduct was not a factual cause of Perkin's discomfort because no other residents of Harris Valley complained about the dust.

(C) Perkins assumed the risk by continuing to live in Harris Valley.

(D) Perkins sustained no damage as a result of Blocko's conduct.

Questions 164-165 are based on the following fact situation.

Allen was driving a pickup truck owned by Company when he collided with an automobile owned and operated by Boren. Pachter, a passenger in Boren's car, subsequently asserted a claim against Company, Allen, and Boren for injuries sustained in the accident. At trial the jury fixed the amount of Pachter's damages and found that Allen was 40% at fault, Boren was 60% at fault, and Pachter was not at fault. It was also found that Allen was acting within the scope if his duties as an employee of Company when the accident occurred. In issuing a judgment for Pachter, the court held that Allen and Boren were jointly and severally liable for Pachter's injuries, and that Company was vicariously liable for Allen's tort. The jurisdiction had statutes which adopted pure comparative negligence and recognized a right of contribution between joint tortfeasors.

164. In enforcing the judgment, what portion of her damages is Pachter entitled to collect from Allen?

   (A) 0%

   (B) 40%

   (C) 50%

   (D) 100%

165. Assume for the purpose of this question only that in enforcing the judgment Pachter succeeded in collecting $100,000 from Company. If Company asserts a claim against Allen seeking compensation for Company's payment to Pachter, Company is entitled to recover

   (A) nothing, because Company was found to be vicariously liable for allen's tort.

   (B) $40,000 as partial indemnity.

   (C) $50,000 as contribution.

   (D) $100,000 as complete indemnity.

Questions 166-167 are based on the following fact situation.

In a negligence action by Peckham against Aspen and Botkin, the court found that Peckham's injuries were proximately caused by the combined negligence of Aspen and Botkin, and that Aspen and Botkin were jointly and severally liable to Peckham in the sum of $100,000. The court also found that in producing Peckham's injury, Aspen was 40% at fault, and Botkin was 60% at fault. The jurisdiction has a statute recognizing the right of contribution between joint tortfeasors, and that contribution shall be based on apportionment of fault.

166. Assume for the purpose of this question only that after the entry of judgment, Peckham succeeded in collecting $10,000 from Aspen. Which of the following correctly states the amount which Peckham is entitled to collect from Botkin?

   (A) $50,000 (60% of $100,000 minus $10,000 already collected).

   (B) $60,000 (60% of $100,000).

   (C) $90,000 ($100,000 minus $10,000 already collected).

   (D) $100,000.

167. Assume for the purpose of this question only that after the entry of judgment, Peckham succeeded in collecting $100,000 from Aspen. In an action for contribution by Aspen against Botkin, which of the following correctly states the amount which Aspen is entitled to collect from Botkin?

   (A) 0.

   (B) $40,000 (40% of $100,000).

   (C) $50,000 (50% of $100,000).

   (D) $60,000 (60% of $100,000).

Questions 168-169 are based on the following fact situation.

Baker was riding her bicycle in a reasonable manner when she was struck by a car negligently driven by Foy. As a result, Baker was thrown to the ground, breaking her left leg. A moment later, while lying in the road, Baker was struck by a car negligently driven by Salmi, breaking Baker's right Leg.

168. If Baker asserts a claim against Foy, will Foy be held liable for damages resulting from Baker's broken RIGHT leg?

   (A) No, because Salmi was required to take Baker as he found her.

   (B) No, if Baker's right leg would not have been

broken but for Salmi's negligence.

(C) Yes, if it was foreseeable that a person lying in the roadway with a broken leg would be struck by a second car.

(D) Yes, because Baker's right leg would not have been broken but for Foy's negligence.

169. If Baker asserts a claim against Salmi, Salmi will be held liable for damages resulting from Baker's

   I. broken left leg.

   II. broken right leg.

(A) II only.

(B) I and II.

(C) I and II, but only if Foy's conduct was foreseeable.

(D) Neither I nor II.

170. During the course of an argument about politics, Darrell slapped Pack in the face. Angry, Pack pointed an unloaded pistol at Darrell. Darrell immediately drew a knife and stabbed Pack with it, injuring him severely. Pack subsequently asserted a battery claim against Darrell. The only defense raised by Darrell was self-defense.

In determining Darrell's liability to Pack, the most important issue that must be decided is whether

(A) the use of a knife by Darrell constituted deadly force.

(B) Darrell knew or should have known that he could safely and easily retreat without sustaining harm.

(C) Darrell was the initial aggressor.

(D) Pack knew that his pistol was unloaded.

Questions 171-173 are based on the following fact situation.

As a result of a minor earthquake, the framework of a building which Castle was erecting on Third Street col-

lapsed. When Castle began the building, he knew that the steel which he was using for that purpose was of poor quality, but decided to use it anyway. If the steel had not been of poor quality, the earthquake would not have caused the building to collapse.

Dacy was employed by Gasco to operate a gasoline truck. She had parked the truck on Third Street in front of the Castle construction site moments before the earthquake. When the building collapsed, falling debris struck the truck, causing it to rupture and causing its cargo of gasoline to leak. A stream of gasoline which leaked from the truck flowed for three blocks until it reached Sixth Street. There, unaware of the presence of gasoline, Hankin tossed a lit cigarette into the street. The cigarette caused the gasoline to explode, injuring Page.

171. If Page asserts a claim against Castle, alleging that Castle's use of poor quality steel in the construction of a building on Third Street was negligent, the court should find for

(A) Castle, if the presence of the gasoline truck was an intervening cause of Page's harm.

(B) Castle, because an earthquake is an "Act of God".

(C) Page, because the earthquake was a minor one.

(D) Page, if the use of poor quality steel in the construction of a building on Third Street created an apparent danger to persons on Sixth Street.

172. If Page asserts a claim against Dacy, alleging that it was negligent for Dacy to park a gasoline truck in front of a construction site, which of the following would be Dacy's most effective argument in defense against Page's claim?

(A) Castle's use of poor quality steel was a superseding cause of Page's injury.

(B) The explosion would not have occurred if Hankin did not throw a lit cigarette into the street.

(C) Dacy could not have anticipated that falling

debris from the construction site would cause the truck to rupture and leak.

(D) The explosion which injured Page was proximately caused by the earthquake.

173. If Page asserts a claim against Gasco, alleging that Gasco is liable for the negligence of Dacy, which one of the following additional facts or inferences, if it was the only one true, would be most likely to result in a judgment for Gasco?

(A) Dacy parked the truck on Third Street so that she could keep an appointment with her personal physician.

(B) A statute in the jurisdiction prohibited parking gasoline trucks on Third Street.

(C) A Gasco company rule prohibited parking any Gasco truck on a public street while the truck was loaded with gasoline.

(D) The person employed by Gasco to supervise Dacy had specifically instructed Dacy not to park on Third Street.

Questions 174-176 are based on the following fact situation.

Mart, the operator of a supermarket, purchased an automatic door-opener from Stepco, its manufacturer. The device included rubber step-plates which were to be installed on the floor on both sides of the door. When a person stepped on one of the step-plates, the machine was designed to swing the door away from him or her. Stepco furnished detailed installation instructions which contained the following warning:

> "After installing step-plates, test by stepping on one of them. If the door swings toward you instead of away from you, disconnect the automatic door-opener at once and make no further use of it until you have called our hotline for further directions."

Mart hired Ingram to install the automatic door-opener while the store was closed for the night. Ingram read the instructions furnished by Stepco, but disregarded the above warning. When he finished installing the device, he did not test it by stepping on one of the step-plates, but advised the store's night manager that the job was complete. The following morning when the store opened, Parker entered to purchase a particular brand of soft drink. When he was attempting to leave, he stepped on the step-plate which Ingram had installed. Because of a short-circuit in the step-plate, the door swung toward him, striking and injuring his face.

174. Assume for the purpose of this question only that Parker asserts a claim for his injuries against Mart. Which one of the following additional facts or inferences, if it was the only one true, would be most likely to result in a judgment for Parker?

(A) Parker's injury resulted from a defect in the step-plate.

(B) Ingram was not negligent in his installation of the automatic door-opener.

(C) A reasonable inspection by Mart would have disclosed that the door opened improperly.

(D) Parker made a purchase from Mart before being struck by the door.

175. Assume for the purpose of this question only that Parker asserts a claim against Stepco on the ground that the step-plate was defective when sold by Stepco. Which of the following would be Stepco's most effective argument in defense?

(A) It was not foreseeable that a person installing the automatic door-opener would disregard the warning contained in the instructions.

(B) Stepco did not act unreasonably in designing or manufacturing the automatic door-opener, or in furnishing the instructions which came with them.

(C) Parker was not a purchaser of the automatic door-opener.

(D) Mart was negligent in selecting Ingram to install the automatic door-opener.

176. In a claim by Parker against Ingram, which of the following would be Parker's most effective argu-

ment?

(A) Ingram's liability is established by res ipsa loquitur.

(B) It was unreasonable for Ingram to disregard the warning contained in the instructions furnished by Stepco.

(C) The automatic door-opener was installed in a way which made it unfit for ordinary use.

(D) The short circuit in the step-plate made the automatic door-opener defective.

177. Pagan, an adult, took his neighbor's 7 year old son Johnnie to see Cirque's circus. During the show, many children left their seats to watch the performance from the edge of the area on which it took place. Johnnie did so with Pagan's permission. When Cirque's trained lions were performing, one of the animals got away from its enclosure and struck Johnnie with its paw, injuring him. Horrified, Pagan ran from his seat and chased the lion away from Johnnie. Pagan was not touched by the lion, but became highly nervous as a result of the incident.

If Pagan asserts a claim for battery against Cirque, the court should find for

(A) Pagan, but only if the jurisdiction applies the doctrine of transferred intent.

(B) Pagan, because Pagan experienced mental suffering as a result of harmful contract inflicted upon Johnnie.

(C) Cirque, because Pagan was not touched by the lion.

(D) Cirque, unless Cirque knew that the lions would attack a member of the audience when Cirque exhibited them.

Questions 178-179 are based on the following fact situation.

When Moira was divorced from her husband Farnham, the court awarded custody of their 4 year old son David to Moira. Moira frequently permitted David to spend weekends with Farnham at the home of Farnham's

father Giles, however. One weekend, while David was visiting with Farnham, a friend of Moira's phoned her. The friend said that she heard that Farnham was planning to remove David from the state permanently.

Panicked, Moira ran to the home of Giles and pounded on the door. When Giles came to the door, Moira demanded, in a loud voice, that Giles tell here where Farnham and David were. Giles knew that Farnham had taken David to the movies and would soon be returning. Because Moira's manner frightened him, however, Giles said that he had no idea where they were or when they were coming back and refused to talk to Moira any further.

As a result, Moira became highly upset. She visited her physician, who prescribed a mild tranquilizer, but she remained nervous until Farnham brought David to her home that evening.

178. Assume for the purpose of this question only that Moira asserts a claim against Giles for false imprisonment. The court should find for

(A) Giles, because Moira sustained no physical injury as a result of the incident.

(B) Giles, if he did not prevent Moira from leaving his home.

(C) Moira, only if she was legally entitled to custody of David.

(D) Moira, because Giles prevented her from seeing or communicating with David.

179. Assume for the purpose of this question only that Moira asserts a claim against Giles for intentional infliction of emotional distress. The court should find for Moira

(A) because Moira was treated by a physician for mental suffering which resulted from Giles' refusal to tell her where Farnham and David were.

(B) if it was unreasonable for Giles to refuse to tell Moira where Farnham and David were.

(C) only if Giles was certain that refusing to tell Moira where Farnham and David were would cause Moira to experience mental suffering.

(D) only if the reasonable person would have known that refusing to tell Moira where Farnham and David were would cause Moira to experience mental suffering.

180. Daly was driving down a residential street when he saw Chase, a 5 year old child, riding a tricycle in the roadway in front of him. Daly attempted to stop his car, but was unable to do so because he was traveling at an excessive rate of speed. Daly's car struck and killed Chase, flinging the child and tricycle through the air.

Pagel was standing in her living room when she heard the screech of Daly's brakes. Glancing out through her window, she saw Chase's bloody body fly through the air and land on her front lawn. Pagel was so shocked by what she saw that she suffered a heart attack and needed to be hospitalized for several weeks.

If Pagel asserts a claim against Daly for damages resulting from mental distress which she experienced because of the incident, which one of the following additional facts or interferences, if it was the only one true, would be most likely to result in a judgment for Pagel?

(A) The reasonable person would have expected someone to be in Pagel's position and to experience mental suffering as a result of the incident.

(B) The jurisdiction applies the doctrine of transferred intent.

(C) The jurisdiction applies the doctrine of transferred consequences.

(D) The reasonable person would regard Daly's speed as outrageous.

Questions 181-182 are based on the following fact situation.

Owen hired Paynter to paint the outside of Owen's house. About two hours after Paynter had finished the job and left, Owen noticed Paynter's ladder lying across Owen's front lawn. Owen immediately phoned

Paynter, asking him to remove the ladder. Paynter said he would come back for the ladder, but did not do so.

Two days later, Lewis, a government employee, was walking across Owen's lawn while delivering mail. On several occasions in the past, Owen had asked her to use the sidewalk and not to walk on his lawn. Owen saw Lewis walking towards Paynter's ladder on his lawn, but did not warn Lewis because he believed that she saw it. Although the lawn had recently been mowed and the ladder was in plain view, Lewis did not see the ladder and tripped over it, injuring her knee.

The jurisdiction applies the all-or-nothing rule of contributory negligence.

181. If Lewis asserts a negligence claim against Owen for damages resulting from her injury, which of the following would be Owen's most effective argument in defense?

(A) Owen did not know with certainty that Lewis would be injured.

(B) The dangerous condition was created by Paynter.

(C) Owen believed that Lewis knew that the ladder was there.

(D) A landowner owes no duty to government employees entering on official business.

182. If Lewis asserts a negligence claim against Paynter for damages resulting from her injury, which of the following would be Paynter's most effective argument in defense?

(A) The ladder was in plain view.

(B) Lewis was trespassing at the time the accident occurred.

(C) Paynter owed no duty to licensees of Owens.

(D) Owens was negligent in not warning Lewis about the ladder.

183. Six months after Dr. Danh performed surgery on her, Peck was x-rayed by another doctor. The x-ray disclosed a surgical instrument inside Peck's

chest. Danh was the only person who had ever performed surgery on Peck. Peck subsequently asserted a medical malpractice claim against Danh, alleging that Danh had negligently left the surgical instrument inside her while operating on her.

If an expert testifies that surgeons do not usually leave instruments inside a patient's body unless they are acting unreasonably, may Peck rely on res ipsa loquitur in her claim against Danh?

(A) No, because the doctrine of res ipsa loquitur is not applicable to a claim for professional malpractice.

(B) No, because a jury of laypersons is not competent to infer that a physician was negligent.

(C) Yes, because a surgeon is under an absolute duty not to leave instruments inside a patient's body.

(D) Yes, because Danh was the only person who had ever performed surgery on Peck.

184. Ashby and Bloomfield were driving their vehicles in an unreasonable manner when they collided. The collision caused Ashby's vehicle to strike and injure Walker, a pedestrian who was crossing the street in the middle of the block. Walker was hospitalized as a result of the accident, but had hospitalization insurance which paid $10,000 towards his hospital bill.

Walker subsequently asserted a claim against Ashby and Bloomfield. At the trial, in response to the judge's instructions, the jury found that Walker sustained damage of $100,000, and that the accident resulted 40% from the negligence of Ashby, 40% from the negligence of Bloomfield, and 20% from the negligence of Walker. The judge ruled that Ashby and Bloomfield were jointly and severally liable to Walker, and entered judgment in accordance with the jury's verdict.

Which of the following statements correctly describes the amount which Walker is entitled to collect from Ashby in a jurisdiction which has a pure comparative negligence statute?

(A) $100,000 reduced by 20%.

(B) $100,000 reduced by $10,000 and further reduced by 20%.

(C) 40% of $100,000.

(D) 40% of the amount derived by subtracting $10,000 from $100,000.

185. When Perl, a law student, told her cousin Joe that she needed a place to study, Joe gave her the key to his mountain cabin and said that she could use it. Because Perl had never been there before, Joe drew a map and wrote instructions on how to find it. Perl followed the map and instructions, but when she arrived she found five identical cabins in a row and did not know which one was Joe's. She tried the key which Joe had given her. When it opened the door of one of the cabins, she went inside, believing the cabin to be Joe's.

Actually, the cabin which Perl entered did not belong to Joe, but to his neighbor Darrin. Joe knew that his key fit the doors of all five of the cabins, but had forgotten to mention it to Perl. While Perl was inside the cabin, she attempted to turn on the gas stove. Because of a defect in the stove, it exploded, injuring Perl.

If Perl asserts a claim against Darrin for her injuries, the court should find for

(A) Perl because the stove was defective.

(B) Perl if Darrin should have anticipated that a person would enter his cabin by mistake.

(C) Darrin only if Perl was a trespasser at the time of the explosion.

(D) Darrin unless Darrin knew or should have known that someone would be injured by the stove.

Questions 186-187 are based on the following fact situation.

One evening in Alfred's tavern, Yeong, who was 17 years old, drank alcoholic beverages which Alfred sold her. Yeong then left and went to Barney's tavern where she drank alcoholic beverages which Barney sold her.

When Yeong left Barney's tavern, she attempted to ride home on her motorcycle. Because Yeong was intoxicated, she struck and injured Palco, a pedestrian. Palco subsequently asserted claims against Alfred and Barney under a state law which provides as follows: "If a minor under the age of 20 years injures another while intoxicated, any person who sold said minor the alcohol which resulted in said minor's intoxication shall be liable to the injured person."

186. Assume for the purpose of this question only that Alfred did not sell Yeong enough alcohol to make Yeong intoxicated, and that the alcohol which Barney sold Yeong would have made Yeong intoxicated even if Alfred had sold Yeong no alcohol at all. In determining Palco's claim against Barney, the court should find that

(A) Barney's conduct was not the cause of Yeong's intoxication because Alfred's conduct was a substantial factor in making Yeong intoxicated.

(B) Barney is liable under the statute even if Barney's conduct did not cause Yeong to become intoxicated.

(C) Barney's conduct was a cause of Palco's injury because Yeong would not have become intoxicated if Barney did not sell Yeong alcoholic beverages.

(D) Barney's conduct was a cause of Yeong's intoxication, but was not a cause of Palco's injury because Yeong's driving superseded it.

187. Assume for the purpose of this question only that the amount of alcohol which Alfred sold Yeong would have made Yeong intoxicated even if Barney sold Yeong no alcohol at all, and that the amount of alcohol which Barney sold Yeong would have made Yeong intoxicated even if Alfred sold Yeong no alcohol at all. Which of the following statements is/are most correct?

I. Alfred did not cause Palco's injury because Barney subsequently sold Yeong enough alcohol to make her intoxicated.

II. Barney did not cause Palco's injury

because Alfred had previously sold Yeong enough alcohol to make her intoxicated.

(A) I only.

(B) II only.

(C) I and II.

(D) Neither I nor II.

Questions 188-189 are based on the following fact situation.

Ocampo hired Anderman, a professional architect, to draw plans for a two story residence to be constructed on Ocampo's realty. The plans which Anderman prepared called for a staircase to be supported by a single concrete pillar. Ocampo then hired Brown, a licensed building contractor, to construct a house in accordance with Anderman's design. Upon examining the plans, Brown told Ocampo that she did not think that one pillar would provide sufficient support for the staircase. When Ocampo discussed Brown's objection with Anderman, however, Anderman insisted that one pillar would be sufficient. Ocampo told this to Brown and convinced Brown to rely on Anderman's plan.

Brown completed the building as agreed and turned it over to Ocampo on April 1. Two weeks later, Ocampo hired Myers to move a piano onto the second floor of the house. While Myers was carrying the piano up the staircase, the staircase collapsed causing Myers to sustain injury. If the staircase had been supported by two columns, it would not have collapsed.

188. If Myers asserts a negligence claim against Brown, the court should declare that

(A) Brown assumed the risk because she supported the stairway with only one pillar even though she was aware of the danger of doing so.

(B) Brown is not liable because she had turned the building over to Ocampo prior to the accident.

(C) Brown is not liable if it was reasonable for her to rely on Anderman's instructions in constructing the stairway.

(D) Brown absolved herself of the risk by objecting to supporting the stairway with only one pillar.

189. If Myers asserts a negligence claim against Anderman, which of the following would be Anderman's most effective argument in defense?

   (A) It was reasonable to support the stairway with only one pillar.

   (B) Anderman owed Myers no duty since Anderman was employed by Ocampo.

   (C) Brown had the last clear chance to avoid the accident.

   (D) The use of a single pillar to support the stairway was a matter exclusively within Anderman's professional judgment as an architect.

Questions 190-191 are based on the following fact situation.

Drinker was obviously intoxicated when he entered Barr's tavern one night and ordered a drink of Old Wheatstraw alcoholic liquor. A statute in the jurisdiction prohibits serving alcoholic liquor to any intoxicated person. Barr knew that Drinker was intoxicated, but because Drinker was a good customer, Barr opened a new bottle of Old Wheatstraw and poured him some of it. After drinking the liquor, Drinker left the tavern and began driving home.

The liquor which Barr served Drinker was manufactured by Wheatstraw. Before the liquor left Wheatstraw's factory, Fuller, an angry employee, added a poison to it which could not have been discovered by reasonable inspection. While Drinker was driving in a reasonable manner, the poison caused him to die. As a result, Drinker's car struck Prill, injuring her.

190. If Prill asserts a claim against Wheatstraw, the court should find for

   (A) Wheatstraw, because Fuller deliberately poisoned the liquor before it left the factory.

   (B) Wheatstraw, because Prill did not purchase

or consume Wheatstraw's product.

   (C) Prill, because the liquor contained poison when it left Wheatstraw's factory.

   (D) Wheatstraw, because the poison could not have been detected by reasonable inspection.

191. If Prill asserts a claim against Barr based on Barr's violation of the above statute, which of the following would be Barr's most effective argument in defense against that claim?

   (A) Barr did not serve Drinker enough liquor to make him intoxicated.

   (B) The statute was not meant to prevent people from drinking liquor which had been poisoned.

   (C) Serving Old Wheatstraw alcoholic liquor to Drinker was not a cause of Prill's injuries.

   (D) Fuller's conduct was a superseding cause of Prill's injuries.

192. Pursuant to a contract with the federal government, Rocketcorp manufactured and launched rockets used for placing communications satellites into space. Shortly after Rocketcorp launched one of its rockets, the rocket exploded in the air. It then crashed into a storage building owned by Medco which contained antibiotics with a value of $180 million, totally destroying the building and its contents. No one could determine the cause of the explosion. Although Rocketcorp used reasonable care in all aspects of the manufacturing and launching process, a few of Rocketcorp's rockets had exploded in the past shortly after launch. Each time this happened, the rocket involved was completely destroyed while in the air and caused no damage on the ground.

If Medco asserts a claim against Rocketcorp for the loss of its building and contents, the courts should find for

   (A) Medco, if the construction and launching of rockets is an extremely hazardous activity.

   (B) Medco, under the doctrine of res ipsa loquitur.

(C) Rocketcorp, if the reasonable person would not expect antibiotics worth 180 million dollars to be stored in one building.

(D) Rocketcorp, because none of Rocketcorp's rockets caused any damage on the ground in the past.

Questions 193-194 are based on the following situation.

Beltco manufactures belt trucks, which are small, open motor vehicles equipped with conveyor belts and used by airlines for handling baggage. Beltco officials are aware that persons who maintain belt trucks frequently set the belt idle above 15. They are also aware that this can cause the belt truck to lurch forward when the belt is activated, unless it is equipped with an acceleration suppressor. For this reason, Beltco's design calls for every belt truck to be equipped with an acceleration suppressor.

Several months ago Beltco learned that, because of a factory error, it had sold to Treetop Airlines a belt truck which was not equipped with an acceleration suppressor. Beltco officials immediately notified Treetop, offering to install the acceleration suppressor without charge. Treetop never responded to the notice.

Two months later, Treetop went out of business and sold the belt truck to Cloud Airlines. McCann, an independent contractor hired by Cloud to maintain Cloud's equipment, set the belt idle above 15. Subsequently Plum, an employee of Cloud, attempted to activate the belt while standing beside the belt truck. She was injured when the belt truck lurched forward and struck her.

193. Assume for the purpose of this question only that Plum asserts a claim against Beltco on the ground that the absence of an acceleration suppressor made the belt truck defective. The court should find for

(A) Beltco, because it was unreasonable for

Treetop to sell the belt truck after learning that it was not equipped with an acceleration suppressor.

(B) Beltco, because if McCann had acted reasonably in setting the belt idle, Plum would not have been injured.

(C) Plum, because persons who maintain belt trucks frequently set the belt idle above 15.

(D) Plum, because the negligence of McCann is imputed to Beltco.

194. Assume for the purpose of this question only that Plum asserts a negligence claim against McCann. Which one of the following additional facts or inferences, if it was the only one true, would be most likely to result in a judgment for McCann in a jurisdiction which applies the "all-or-nothing" rule of contributory negligence?

(A) Belt trucks are usually equipped with acceleration suppressors.

(B) If Plum had been in the driver's seat when she started the belt truck she would not have been injured.

(C) The omission of an acceleration suppressor was a manufacturing defect in the belt truck.

(D) Treetop failed to notify Cloud about the need for an acceleration suppressor.

Questions 195-196 are based on the following fact situation.

Kemco operated a manufacturing plant just outside the city of Town. Breezes frequently carried fumes from Kemco's plant into Town. Although the fumes did not violate state air pollution laws, they caused many buildings in Town to need frequent repainting, and led many homeowners to complain about it to Kemco. Kemco did nothing about it, however, because the cost of eliminating the fumes was extremely high.

Fox who owned a house in Town in which he resided with his son Sal, had to repaint his house several times because of the fumes. In addition Fox's son Sal developed a respiratory illness as the result of an unusual reaction to the fumes. Fox did not notify Kemco about the damage to his paint, but did complain to Kemco about Sal's illness. When Kemco responded by offering to buy Fox's house, Fox refused.

195. Assume for the purpose of this question only that Fox asserts a private nuisance claim against Kemco for the damage to his paint, asserting that Kemco was negligent in failing to eliminate the fumes. Which of the following would be Kemco's most effective argument in defense against Fox's claim?

   (A) The operation of Kemco's plant did not result in a physical invasion of Fox's realty.

   (B) The fumes affected others in substantially the same way as they affected Fox.

   (C) Kemco officials did not know that the fumes would affect the paint of Fox's house.

   (D) The cost of eliminating the fumes would have driven Kemco out of business.

196. Assume for the purpose of this question only that Fox asserts a public nuisance claim on behalf of Sal in which he seeks an order directing Kemco to eliminate the fumes. Which of the following would be Kemco's most effective argument in response to this claim?

   (A) The claim is not for special damages.

   (B) Sal's illness was the result of an unusually sensitive reaction to the fumes.

   (C) Fox assumed the risk by refusing to sell the property to Kemco.

   (D) The fumes did not violate state pollution laws.

ANSWERS
TORTS

ANSWERS TO
TORTS QUESTIONS

1. **B**   If the risk of injury to Patrick was not foreseeable, then Delphi could not be said to have acted unreasonably in the face of a foreseeable risk. Since negligence is usually defined as failure to act reasonably in the face of a foreseeable risk, this would mean that Delphi was not negligent.

    Conduct is a cause of harm if the harm would not have occurred without it. Thus, if the label contained a warning which Patrick disregarded or failed to read, his conduct could be contributory or comparative negligence which helped cause his injury. Since the label did not contain any warning, however, his injury would have occurred whether he read it or not. For this reason, his failure to read it was not causally related to the harm he suffered and does not provide Delphi with a defense. If Patrick sued for breach of warranty, he might be required to show that he relied on some statement contained on the label, and his failure to read it might prevent him from establishing such reliance. Since his lawsuit is based on negligence, however, **A** is incorrect. Even if the product was manufactured by another, Delphi would be under a duty to use reasonable care in marketing it, so that fact alone would not protect Delphi against liability to Patrick. **C** is, therefore, incorrect. **D** is incorrect because Delphi's lack of awareness might have been negligent if the reasonable person in Delphi's shoes would have been aware.

2. **C**   Strict liability in tort is imposed, regardless of fault, on a professional supplier who sells a product while it is in a defective condition. Courts usually define a product as defective if its condition would defeat the reasonable expectation of the reasonable consumer or of the reasonable manufacturer. If the reasonable person would not have expected the product to irritate the scalp of a person with Patrick's allergy, then the product's condition would defeat the reasonable expectation of the reasonable consumer and was defective.

    Under the doctrine of *res ipsa loquitur*, an inference of negligence can be drawn from the fact that a particular kind of accident does not usually occur without negligence. **A** is incorrect, however, because Patrick's theory is strict liability in tort, and since strict liability is imposed without regard to fault, an inference that the defendant was negligent is not relevant to it. The facts in **B** and **D** would suggest that Delphi knew or should have known about Patrick's allergy. This knowledge is not sufficient, however, to establish that the product's condition would have defeated the reasonable expectation of either the reasonable consumer or the reasonable manufacturer (i.e., that the product was defective). For this reason, **B** and **D** are incorrect.

3. **B**   A seller of a product which is defective at the time it was sold is held strictly liable for damages which result. Thus, if the product was defective when Farma sold it, Farma would be strictly liable to Patrick. A product is "defective as labeled" if its condition would defeat the expectations which the reasonable person would form upon reading its label. While it is not certain that a court would come to this conclusion about Delphi's Follicle, the argument in **A** is the only one listed which could possibly support Patrick's claim.

A is incorrect because the negligence of a manufacturer is not ordinarily imputed to a retailer. C is incorrect because any express warranty which was made referred to "normal hair and scalp," and would therefore be inapplicable to Patrick. Although a drug store might be under the type of duty set forth in D, there is no indication that Farma failed to act reasonably in pursuance of such a duty. D is, therefore, incorrect.

4. A   Negligence is unreasonable conduct in the face of a foreseeable risk. Drake's awareness of the high incidence of crime in the neighborhood would make the risk foreseeable, and might result in a finding that it was unreasonable for her to open the door under the circumstances. While it is not certain that a court would come to this conclusion, the fact in A is the only one listed which would help support Poll's case.

Poll's knowledge would not impose any duty on Drake, so B is incorrect. Although Drake's intention to sell furniture to Poll might make Poll an invitee, and thereby impose upon Drake a duty to act reasonably, the duty would not be breached unless Drake had some reason to know that there was a danger in opening the door. C is, therefore, incorrect. D is incorrect because unless Drake knew or should have known of the incident, it would have no relevance to the reasonableness of Drake's conduct.

5. D   A misrepresentation is a false assertion of material fact made with the intent to induce the plaintiff's reliance. If the defendant knew that the statement was false, and if the plaintiff justifiably relied upon it, the defendant is liable for damage which results. If a party to a transaction is under a legal obligation to disclose a fact, non-disclosure may be an assertion that the fact does not exist. Thus, although Devel said nothing about the coming of the highway, if she had an obligation to disclose that it was coming, her silence was an assertion that there was no highway coming. Since she knew this assertion to be false, she is liable for misrepresentation if Homested's reliance on it was justified. While it is not certain that a court would conclude that such reliance was justified, D is the only answer which could possibly be correct.

Since real estate investors are usually experts in determining the value of real estate, the fact that Homested knew Devel to be a real estate investor might have justified his reliance on her misrepresentation. A is incorrect because this would be likely to result in a victory for Homested rather than Devel. If Devel's non-disclosure was a misrepresentation, she probably repeated the misrepresentation by permitting an appraiser to determine value without disclosing the coming of the highway. B is, therefore, incorrect. A fiduciary relationship is one based on trust. Since buyer and seller are adversaries, neither is the other's fiduciary. C is, therefore, incorrect.

6. D   Negligence is the failure to act reasonably in the face of a foreseeable risk. If selling a pistol for less than $50 created a foreseeable risk to Patton, it might be found that Gunco's conduct in doing so was unreasonable and that Gunco is liable to Patton for negligence. While it is not certain that a court would come to this conclusion, the argument in D is the only one listed which could possibly support Patton's claim.

Intent is an essential element of battery. In a battery case, intent means that the defendant desired (or knew with substantial certainty) that harmful or offensive contact with the plaintiff would occur. A is incorrect because the fact that harm is foreseeable (rather than substantially certain) is not sufficient to result in liability for battery. In every sale by a merchant, there is an implied warranty that the product sold is merchantable, or fit for ordinary use. There is no indication, however, that the pistol did not function as a pistol ordinarily functions. **B** is, therefore, incorrect. It is sometimes said that violation of a criminal statute establishes negligence if the statute was designed to protect a class of persons to which the plaintiff belongs against risks like the one which led to harm. **C** is incorrect, however, because there is no indication that Gunco violated a criminal statute.

7. **C** One whose conduct creates a foreseeable risk to any person owes that person a duty of reasonable care. One who helps an intoxicated person get his car started is creating a foreseeable risk to all who are likely to be endangered by that person's driving. If the injury to Pedex occurred two hundred miles away from the place where Helper assisted Sippy, however, it may successfully be argued that the reasonable person in Sippy's situation would not have anticipated harm to him, because Sippy could be expected to sober up in the time it took to drive that distance. While it is not certain that a court would come to this conclusion, the argument in **C** is the only one listed which could possibly support Helper's defense.

Although a statute like the one mentioned in **A** might impose liability on Barr, it would not have the effect of relieving any other person of liability, making **A** incorrect. **B** is incorrect because being in the road service business does not exempt any person from her common law duty to act reasonably in the face of a foreseeable risk. **D** would establish that Sippy's intoxication was a cause of the accident, but would not establish that Helper's was not. If anything, it would prove the cause and effect relationship between Helper's conduct and the accident. **D** is, therefore, incorrect.

8. **C** Negligence is a breach of the duty of reasonable care. Ordinarily, a defendant owes a plaintiff a duty of reasonable care only if the defendant's conduct creates a foreseeable risk to the plaintiff. A risk is foreseeable if it is one which the reasonable person would anticipate or expect. Thus, if the reasonable person would not have expected Sippy to drive upon leaving the bar, the risk which led to Pedex's injury was not a foreseeable one, Barr owed Pedex no duty to act reasonably to protect against it, and Barr could not have been negligent. Negligence does not lead to liability unless it is a proximate cause of damage. Courts usually hold that conduct is not a proximate cause of a particular injury unless the injury was a foreseeable result of that conduct. If the reasonable person would not have expected Sippy to drive upon leaving the bar, the accident which resulted from his driving was unforeseeable, and Barr's conduct was not a proximate cause of it. While it is not certain that a court would come to these conclusions, the argument listed in **C** is the only one which could possibly support Barr's defense.

A is incorrect because serving three drinks to Sippy may have increased the risk by making him even more intoxicated. Although the argument in **B** establishes that Helper's conduct was a cause in fact of the accident, it does not provide Barr with a defense, since any accident may have more than one cause, and Barr's negligence also may have been a cause. **D** is incorrect since liability for negligence does not depend on the existence of a contractual relationship (i.e., privity) between the plaintiff and defendant.

9. **C** Negligence liability requires a breach of the duty of reasonable care which is a proxi-

mate cause of the plaintiff's damage. To say that the plaintiff was outside the foreseeable zone of danger is simply another way of saying that because of where the plaintiff was located the injury to him was not foreseeable. This argument could help support Danver's defense in two ways. First, if harm to Blandings was not foreseeable, Danvers did not owe him a duty of reasonable care. This would mean that, although Danver's conduct might have been negligent as to Parker, it could not have been negligent as to Blandings. Second, unless some injury to Blandings was a foreseeable result of Danver's conduct, that conduct was not a proximate cause of it. Although a court might not agree that Blandings was outside the foreseeable zone of danger, the argument in **C** is the only one listed which could possibly support Danver's defense.

It is generally understood that if an injury to the plaintiff was foreseeable, all its complications are foreseeable too, no matter how improbable those complications actually were. For this reason, **A** and **D** are incorrect. Joint tortfeasors are two or more persons whose torts proximately caused the same injury. In most jurisdictions, they are jointly and severally liable for the full extent of the plaintiff's injury. The argument in **B** would establish that Parker was negligent, but this would not provide Denver with a defense, since he and Parker might be found to be joint tortfeasors.

10. **A**   All persons are liable for the harm which proximately results from their negligence. Thus, if Burg's injury was proximately caused by Three Star's negligence, Three Star is liable to her.

An express warranty is an assertion of fact which becomes part of the basis of the bargain. **B** is incorrect because there is no indication that an express warranty was made. **C** is incorrect because the "clean hands" doctrine, which is relevant in equity proceedings, is not applicable to an action for money damages. If it is foreseeable that Burg would obtain the beer in some manner, the precise manner in which Burg obtained the beer is immaterial. **D** is, therefore, incorrect.

11. **C**   False imprisonment occurs when the defendant intentionally confines the plaintiff. The plaintiff is confined when his will to leave a place with fixed boundaries is overcome in a way which would similarly overcome the will of the reasonable person in the plaintiff's situation. Since Rezzie was not prevented from leaving, he was not confined (i.e., imprisoned).

In a false imprisonment case, "intent" means a desire or knowledge that the defendant's act will result in a confinement of the plaintiff, and does not depend on whether the defendant knew that the plaintiff's rights were being violated. Thus, if the acts of Global's employees had resulted in a confinement of Rezzie, the fact that they did not know they were violating Rezzie's rights would not provide them with an effective defense. **A** is, therefore, incorrect. **B** is incorrect because false imprisonment is an intentional tort of which unreasonable conduct is not an essential element. **D** is incorrect because damage is not an essential element of liability for false imprisonment.

12. **C**   Although liability ordinarily results from the publication of false defamatory statements about the plaintiff, the courts have always required that publication be either intentional or the result of negligence. Dresden's statement to Prescott was not a publication, since Prescott is the plaintiff. The fact that it was overheard by Audit does not satisfy the

requirement of publication unless either Dresden intended that Audit hear it or Audit heard it as a result of Dresden's unreasonable conduct in the face of the foreseeable risk that Audit would hear it. If Dresden knew that Audit would hear it, he intended the publication. If he should have known that Audit would hear it, he acted unreasonably in saying it.

The courts have never required proof that the defendant knew the statement to be defamatory, so **A** is incorrect. The United States Supreme Court has held that in some defamation cases the plaintiff must prove that the defendant knew or should have known that the statement was false when he made it. **B** is incorrect, however, because the requirement has not been applied to a defamation action brought by a private person against a non-media defendant. **D** is incorrect because knowledge that harm will result is not an essential element of any defamation case.

13. **C**   Strict liability is imposed on the seller of a product which is in a defective condition when sold and which reaches the consumer in a condition which is substantially unchanged. If the wheat was substantially changed before reaching Pawnie, Farmer could not be held strictly liable for damages which resulted from a defect in it.

A is incorrect because intervening negligence, unless it was unforeseeable, is not sufficient to relieve the supplier of a defective product from liability. Although privity or some substitute is relevant to warranty liability, strict liability in tort may be applied to benefit any plaintiff whose contact with the product was foreseeable. **B** is, therefore, incorrect. Since strict liability is not based on fault, proof that the defect resulted from some circumstance beyond the defendant's control is not sufficient to free that defendant from liability. **D** is, therefore, incorrect.

14. **A**   *Res ipsa loquitur* permits an inference of unreasonable conduct to be drawn where the accident is one which would not ordinarily have occurred without negligence, and the defendant was in exclusive control of the circumstances which produced the harm. Since Bredco was in exclusive control of the baking process, *res ipsa loquitur* would apply if reasonable care in baking would ordinarily have eliminated the slivers (i.e., if the accident would not ordinarily have occurred without negligence).

B is incorrect because liability for negligence (which is the only theory to which *res ipsa loquitur* applies) does not depend on whether a product is defective. Pawnie's harm was caused by the presence of the metal slivers in the bread. **C** is incorrect because even if Farmer's negligence caused them to be in the wheat, Bredco may be liable for the harm if its negligence caused them to be in the bread. If reasonable care would have prevented the slivers from getting in the bread, it does not matter how they got into the wheat. Thus, even if the breaking of Farmer's blade was unforeseeable, Bredco might be liable to Pawnie for its negligence in failing to keep the slivers out of the bread. **D** is, therefore, incorrect.

15. **C**   Assault results when the defendant, with the intention of causing either offensive contact or apprehension of offensive contact, induces apprehension of such contact in the plaintiff. Battery results when the defendant, with the intention of causing either offensive contact or apprehension of offensive contact, causes offensive contact with the plaintiff. Delfin, intending to cause apprehension of offensive contact, induced such

apprehension, making him liable for assault. With intent to induce apprehension, he also caused offensive contact, making him liable for battery.

16. **D**   A negligent misrepresentation is a false assertion of fact which is made without knowledge of its falsity but under circumstances such that a reasonable person in the defendant's situation would have had such knowledge. Thus, if Solet's belief that there were no termites in the house was reasonable, his misrepresentation was not negligent. Although there are not enough facts to determine whether a court would come to this conclusion, **D** is the only argument listed which could possibly support Solet's position.

     A is incorrect because lack of such knowledge would be negligent if the reasonable person would have known. Whether or not Solet had a duty to disclose the presence of termites, when he discussed termites, he had a duty to do so honestly and reasonably. **B** is, therefore, incorrect. A statement is of opinion if it concerns a subjective matter or contains an expression of doubt. Since Solet's statement was neither, it was not of opinion. **C** is, therefore, correct.

17. **D**   Strict liability is imposed on the seller of a product which is in a defective condition when sold. Thus, if Riteway sold the product while it was defective, Riteway would be held strictly liable no matter who manufactured it.

     Parties who work together to accomplish a particular result are involved in a concert of action which may make any one of them vicariously liable for torts committed by the others. **A** is incorrect, however, because the facts indicate that the manufacturers and retailer did not work together on manufacturing or marketing the product. It has been held that where there are a small number of manufacturers in a particular industry, where all belong to an industry-wide association which establishes industry standards, where those standards result in their products' being defective, and where all members of the industry and the association are named as defendants, liability may be imposed on an industry-wide basis. **B** is incorrect, however, because there is no indication that the number of cereal manufacturers is small or that they belong to an industry-wide association which sets standards or that their standards made the product defective or that all members of the industry and their association have been named as defendants. Under the alternate liability theory, where two or more defendants commit identical acts of negligence under circumstances which make it impossible to tell which one injured the plaintiff, it will be presumed that all of them factually caused the plaintiff's injury. **C** is incorrect, however, because there is no indication that all of the parties named committed identical acts of negligence or that any of them was negligent at all.

18. **D**   Assault occurs when, with the intent to induce such apprehension, the defendant induces in the plaintiff a reasonable apprehension that a harmful or offensive contact with the plaintiff will occur. Since Mabe did not fear contact with herself, she was not assaulted.

     A and **B** are incorrect because Napper's conduct did not induce Mabe to apprehend contact with herself. If Napper's conduct did give Mabe reason to apprehend contact with herself, it would not matter whether she had perceived contact with Dot. **C** is, therefore, incorrect.

19. **C**   A defendant is liable for intentional infliction of mental distress if, with the intent to

cause mental distress, he engages in outrageous conduct which causes serious mental suffering. The defendant intends the plaintiff's mental distress if he desires or knows that it will result from his conduct. Because of the affection normally associated with the mother-daughter relationship, Napper probably knew (i.e., intended) that his threats to injure or kill Dot would cause her mother to experience mental distress. If his conduct was outrageous and caused her to experience mental distress, Napper is liable to her for the mental distress and any physical manifestations of it.

A is incorrect because the passage of time is not sufficient to prevent liability for an injury which was caused by the defendant's tortious conduct. If the reasonable person would not have experienced any suffering as a result of Napper's conduct, then a plaintiff who did experience suffering might not be permitted to recover for it because the law does not seek to benefit a supersensitive plaintiff. If the reasonable person would have experienced some suffering, however, the plaintiff will be permitted to recover for her suffering even if a pre-existing condition makes it unusually severe. (This rule sometimes leads courts to exclaim, "The defendant takes the plaintiff as he finds her.") **B** is, therefore, incorrect. **D** is incorrect because liability for intentional infliction of mental distress requires intent, not merely a foreseeable risk.

20. **A** Strict liability is imposed on the keeper of a wild animal, but only for harm which proximately results from an aspect of the animal which made keeping it dangerous. Leopards are dangerous because they bite or attack. The risk that they may clumsily knock someone over is not one which makes them more dangerous than a dog or other domestic animal.

B is incorrect because an animal is "wild" if it comes from a species which cannot ordinarily be safely kept without special training or restraint. Since this is true with leopards, Spot's tameness does not prevent it from being so classified. **C** and **D** are incorrect because strict liability does not depend on the reasonableness of a defendant's conduct.

21. **B** A claim for damages resulting from contact with a product manufactured or sold by the defendant may be based on several theories, including negligence, misrepresentation, breach of warranty, and strict liability in tort. In most jurisdictions, however, mental suffering is not a recoverable item of damage in a claim based on any of these theories unless the mental suffering is the result of a physical injury or has a physical manifestation. Although a few jurisdictions permit recovery even in the absence of physical injuries, the argument in **B** is the only one listed which could possibly support Sutter's defense.

A is incorrect for two reasons: first, even without a representation, Sutter could be held liable on negligence, implied warranty, or strict liability theories; and second, the statement that the suit was "strong enough to be worn several times" was probably a representation. **C** is incorrect because none of the theories requires that the plaintiff be in privity with the manufacturer. Although the argument in **D** might provide an effective defense to a negligence claim, **D** is incorrect because the other theories which are available do not depend on unreasonable conduct by the defendant.

22. **C** Assumption of the risk is a defense in all approaches to products liability (although some jurisdictions have merged it with the concept of comparative fault), and occurs

when the plaintiff voluntarily encounters a known risk. If Primm knew that the paper suit was likely to dissolve when wet and wore it anyway, she voluntarily encountered (and therefore assumed) a known risk.

A is incorrect because Depp may be held liable without fault for selling a defective product. **B** is incorrect because a sign like the one described is not sufficient to apprise the buyer that the product is being sold without any warranty of merchantability, or to prevent the reasonable consumer from expecting the bathing suit to hold together when wet. Although a product retailer who is held liable for selling a defective product has a right to be indemnified by the product's manufacturer, the right of the injured plaintiff to recover does not depend on this right of the retailer. **D** is, therefore, incorrect.

23. **A**   Under the all-or-nothing rule of contributory negligence, unreasonable conduct by the plaintiff which contributes to the happening of an accident is a complete bar to recovery by the plaintiff. Thus, if Sammy's conduct was unreasonable, Danzig's defense of contributory negligence will succeed.

B, **C**, and **D** are incorrect because the negligence of a parent in supervising a child is not imputed to the child. The reasonableness of Mater's conduct is, therefore, not in issue.

24. **C**   Strict liability is imposed on the seller of a product which is in a defective condition when sold. A product is defective if its condition would defeat the reasonable expectations of the reasonable consumer. Since the reasonable consumer probably would not expect a brand new training leash to break when used on a dog of average size and strength, one which did was probably defective.

Strict liability may be applied to benefit any person whose contact with the defective product was foreseeable, so **A** is incorrect. **B** is incorrect because strict liability does not depend on the reasonableness of the defendant's conduct. **D** is incorrect because the risk which it describes as foreseeable is not the one which led to the harm in this case since the Trainer was brand new when it broke.

25. **B**   Negligence is a failure to act reasonably. Thus, if it was unreasonable for Doughty to work the dog in her front yard, her conduct was negligent and could result in liability. While it is not certain that a court would come to this conclusion, the argument in **B** is the only one listed which could possibly support Passer's claim.

Strict liability for damage resulting from a product defect is imposed only against a professional supplier who placed the product in the stream of commerce. Since Doughty was a user of the Trainer rather than a supplier of it, **A** is incorrect. Conduct which causes damage can result in tort liability only if the damage was intended or resulted from negligence or an activity for which strict liability is imposed. Without establishing one of these bases of liability, calling Doughty's conduct a cause of harm would not be sufficient to result in liability. For this reason, the argument in **C** is incomplete, making **C** incorrect. Although some special standard of care might be imposed because of Doughty's profession, **D** is incorrect because there is no indication that the standard was breached.

26. **A**   A person is liable for all harm which proximately results from her negligence. Thus, if

Annie was negligent in giving the doll to Sonny, she may be held liable for the injury which resulted. It is possible that a court would come to this conclusion, since it may have been foreseeable that a child of Sonny's age would swallow the button and be injured. Although the result is not certain, the argument in **A** is the only one listed which could possibly result in a judgment for Preston.

In every sale by a merchant, there is an implied warranty that the product sold is fit for ordinary use. If the product is unfit, breach of warranty liability is imposed without regard to fault. Similarly, if a product is defective or unreasonably dangerous, strict tort liability may be imposed on the supplier. **B**, **C**, and **D** are incorrect, however, because these theories are available only against a defendant who is a professional supplier of products, which Annie was not.

27. **C**   Since negligence is a breach of the duty to act reasonably, Mart could only be held liable under that theory if it acted unreasonably. Since the tablets were delivered in a sealed bottle, and since the reasonable merchant does not ordinarily open sealed products before selling them, Mart probably did not breach the duty which it owed to Pauling.

A is incorrect because a manufacturer's negligence is not imputed to a retailer. **B** is based on an incorrect statement of the law. A retailer's duty is *to use reasonable care*. The breach of this duty is negligence. Although a retailer may be held liable without fault under a theory of strict liability, this liability is based not on the breach of "an absolute duty," but on a policy which attempts to distribute the risks of being injured by defective products. **D** is incorrect because negligence liability depends on the foreseeability of the risk, not upon the existence of any contractual relationship.

28. **D**   Strict liability is imposed on the seller of a product which is in a defective condition when sold. A product is defective if its condition would defeat the reasonable expectations of the reasonable consumer. Thus, if the reasonable consumer would not have expected the tablets to contain a toxic ingredient, the presence of one makes them defective.

A is incorrect because strict liability is imposed regardless of fault or knowledge by the defendant. Although the classification of a product as "inherently dangerous" was significant during a certain historical period in the development of the law of torts, decisions which followed *McPherson v. Buick* have deprived it of significance. **B** is, therefore, incorrect. **C** is incorrect because strict liability in tort does not depend on the reasonableness of the defendant's conduct.

29. **C**   A defendant owes a plaintiff a duty of reasonable care if the defendant's conduct creates a foreseeable risk to the plaintiff. Thus, if it was foreseeable that a person would be in the roadway, Secon owed that person a duty to drive as the reasonable person. Once it is established that such a duty existed, its breach by driving while intoxicated is obvious.

Since Peri's presence in the roadway was part of the set stage (i.e., pre-existed the defendant's tortious act), it does not matter whether the circumstances which put her there were foreseeable. **A** and **B** are, therefore, incorrect. Although a plaintiff must establish that her injury was a foreseeable result of the defendant's negligent conduct, she is never required to establish that the defendant's negligence was foreseeable. **D** is, therefore, incorrect.

30.   A   A person whose conduct is negligent is liable for damage which is proximately caused by that negligence. Conduct is a proximate cause of harm if it is a factual and legal cause of that harm. Thus, if Danton's negligence was a factual and legal cause of Peri's broken leg, Danton is liable for it.

B is incorrect because there was no relationship between Danton and Secon which would result in such an imputation. C is an impossibility, since nothing can be regarded as a legal cause of harm unless it was a factual cause of that harm. The reasoning of D establishes that Secon's conduct was a cause of harm, but does not establish that Danton's conduct was not. D is, therefore, incorrect.

31.   B   Strict liability is often imposed on one who uses his land in a non-natural manner for the storage of a substance which is likely to do harm upon its escape from storage. The storage of water frequently leads to the application of this principle.

Although strict liability is imposed on one who engages in an abnormally dangerous activity, it is imposed only for damage which results from the dangerous nature of the activity. Although the operation of a nuclear power plant may be an abnormally dangerous activity, A is incorrect because harm in this case did not result from any of the aspects of operating a nuclear power plant which make it abnormally dangerous. If Nuke knew or should have known that an earthquake might occur in the area of the nuclear power plant, it might have been unreasonable to operate it there. But absent such actual or constructive knowledge, Nuke's conduct cannot be presumed to be unreasonable. C is, therefore, incorrect. The intervention of an act of God does not free an antecedent wrongdoer from liability unless that intervention was unforeseeable. D is, therefore, incorrect.

32.   D   Strict liability may be imposed for damage resulting from participation in abnormally dangerous activities such as the manufacture and storage of explosives. Even under a theory of strict liability, however, a defendant is not liable for harm unless it was proximately caused by the defendant's activity. Conduct which is a factual cause of harm is a proximate cause of that harm if the harm was a foreseeable result and was not brought about by unforeseeable intervention. Thus, if the intervening conduct of the terrorists was not foreseeable, the harm sustained by Parbal was not proximately caused by the conduct of Blowco. While it is not certain that a court would come to this conclusion, D is the only argument listed which could possibly support Blowco's defense.

A is incorrect because strict liability may be imposed regardless of fault and regardless of whether the defendant's conduct was reasonable. Most jurisdictions hold that there can be no liability for trespass to land unless there was a physical invasion of the plaintiff's realty. B is incorrect, however, because Blowco may be held liable on a strict liability theory, which does not require a physical invasion. Even though a defendant's conduct was a factual cause of harm, that defendant will not be held liable if there was an unforeseeable intervening cause of the harm. C is incorrect, however, because the intervening cause will not prevent such liability unless the intervention was unforeseeable.

33.   **C**   Non-disclosure of a fact is not an assertion (i.e., representation) unless the fact is one which is essential to the transaction and the circumstances are such that the other party is reasonably entitled to expect disclosure of it. Since Berry had no special expertise, his reason for purchasing the hay wagon was not a fact essential to the transaction, and there were no circumstances which entitled Sanders to expect disclosure of his hope of making a profit.

A and **B** are incorrect because slight differences in knowledge concerning the subject of a particular transaction are not sufficient to impose a duty of disclosure. **D** is incorrect because Sanders' initial satisfaction would not prevent her from recovering if it had been induced by a misrepresentation by Berry.

34.   **C**   A defendant's conduct is not a proximate cause of harm if the harm was brought about by an independent intervening cause. An intervening cause is "independent" if it did not result from one of the normal risks resulting from defendant's conduct. Since Wing's plane was safely on the ground at an airport when struck by Delbert's plane, it can be argued that the collision was independent of the risks created by Wing's miscalculation. While it is not certain that a court would come to this conclusion, the argument in **C** is the only one listed which could possibly be effective in Wing's defense.

A plaintiff may be barred from recovery by assumption of the risk when the harm results from a danger of which the plaintiff was aware and which he voluntarily encountered. Since there is no indication that Wing's miscalculation resulted from his lack of a commercial pilot's license, the harm did not result from a risk of which Rider knew. **A** is, therefore, incorrect.Under the "all or nothing" rule, a plaintiff's negligence may prevent recovery if it was causally related to the harm which he sustained. Since there is no indication that Wing's miscalculation resulted from his lack of a commercial pilot's license, any negligence by Rider in accepting a ride from him was not causally related to the accident. **B** is, therefore, incorrect. Conduct is a factual cause of harm if the harm would not have occurred without it. The argument in **D** states that the harm would not have occurred if Delbert had not been negligent. This is obviously true and establishes that Delbert's negligence was a factual cause of the accident. The argument also states, however, that Wing's miscalculation was, therefore, not a factual cause of the accident. Since the accident would not have occurred if Wing's plane had not been on the ground, and since Wing's plane would not have been on the ground had Wing not miscalculated, Wing's miscalculation was also a factual cause of the accident. **D** is, therefore, incorrect.

35.   **A**   A person is liable for the proximate results of his negligence. Since Delbert was negligent and since his negligence was a proximate cause of Wing's harm, Delbert is liable for it.

Although violation of a statute may be negligence per se, **B** is incorrect because there is no causal relation between Wing's violation and the accident since the accident might have happened even if Wing had a license. (***Note:*** Violation of a licensing statute is usually held to be unrelated to the happening of an accident.) Since Wing was on the ground and at a stop when Delbert struck him, it does not matter how he got there. Thus, Wing's original flight plan is of no relevance, and **C** is incorrect. The doctrine of necessity privileges intentional and reasonable invasion of property rights in the face of an emergency. It has no application to the facts in this case since Delbert's conduct was neither intentional nor reasonable and there is no indication that Delbert was faced with an emergency. **D** is, therefore, incorrect.

36.   **A**   Patient's injury would not have occurred without Medco's negligence, so Medco's negligence was a cause of it. Since Patient's injury would not have occurred without Dr. Daley's error, and since Dr. Daley's error came between Medco's conduct and Patient's injury, Dr. Daley's error was an intervening cause of Patient's injury. If negligence which is a cause of harm is followed by an intervening cause of harm which was not foreseeable, the intervention is regarded as a superseding cause which relieves the antecedent wrongdoer of liability. Thus, if Dr. Daley's error was unforeseeable, Medco would not be liable to Patient.

If Dr. Daley's conduct was foreseeable, it would constitute a concurring cause of harm and, as such, would not shield the antecedent wrongdoer from liability. This is true whether that intervention was reasonable or not, and whether it is classified as gross negligence or not. **B, C,** and **D** are, therefore, incorrect.

37.   **B**   All theories of products liability (with the exception of misrepresentation under Restatement (2d) §402B) require that the plaintiff's contact with the product be foreseeable. Since hypodermic needles are commonly used by doctors to give injections to patients, the patient's contact with the needle is foreseeable.

It is less foreseeable, if it is foreseeable at all, that a three-year-old would play with a hypodermic needle, so **A** is incorrect. **C** is incorrect because none of the products liability theories permit the recovery of losses which are unrelated to personal injury or property damage. **D** is incorrect because there is no indication that the needle was infected when sold by the manufacturer or that the infection resulted from the manufacturer's negligent conduct.

38.   **B**   Trespass to land is defined as intentional entry on the plaintiff's realty without authorization. Since realty includes the air space immediately above the land, Dusty entered Plower's realty when she flew through the air fifteen feet above his land. Although she believed that she had authority to do so, she did not have such authority. Her overflight was, thus, a trespass if her entry onto the realty was intentional. A defendant has the necessary intent to be liable for trespass to land if s/he desires or knows that her/his act will result in an entry onto the realty which s/he entered. This is so regardless of whether s/he knows whose realty s/he is entering or that the entry is unauthorized. Since Dusty did desire to fly over parcel 621, she had the necessary intent and will be liable for trespass to the land of Plower.

Without intent, there is no trespass liability. **A** is incorrect because participation in an abnormally dangerous activity does not satisfy the requirement of intent. **C** is incorrect because intent means a desire to enter the land or air space above it (without regard to knowledge of the plaintiff's right). **D** is incorrect because damage to the realty is not an essential element of trespass to land.

39.   **D**   The tort known as invasion of privacy can be committed in various ways. One, called "intrusion," is committed by intentionally invading the plaintiff's right to solitude in a manner which would offend the reasonable person. An invasion of plaintiff's solitude

occurs when the defendant causes a physical entry into the plaintiff's private space. Since Raker deliberately entered Semble's private office, opened Semble's private file, and copied Semble's private documents, there is no doubt that Raker intentionally invaded Semble's solitude. Although it can never be certain that a court or jury will decide that the reasonable person would have been offended by any particular conduct, **D** is the only answer listed which could possibly be correct.

A and **B** are incorrect because freedom of the press under the First Amendment does not privilege invasions of privacy for the purpose of obtaining documents, even if they are newsworthy. **C** is incorrect for two reasons: first, the documents were not made public until after Raker invaded Semble's privacy by obtaining them; and, second, the privilege to publish facts which are matters of public records does not include a privilege to invade privacy for the purpose of obtaining them.

40. **D**   The facts specify that Paul's claim is for negligence. Negligence is unreasonable conduct. It may be unreasonable to sell a device as dangerous as an air rifle to an eleven-year-old, because the risk that he will use it to shoot another child is foreseeable. In any event, **D** is the only finding listed which could result in a judgment for Paul.

A is incorrect because negligence of a manufacturer is not imputed to a retailer. **B** and **C** are incorrect for two reasons. First, there is no indication that the air rifle was defective. Second, negligence liability requires unreasonable conduct, and there is no indication that Storr acted unreasonably. Thus, even if the air rifle was defective, there would be no reason to impose negligence liability on Storr.

41. **D**   Since Carrent knew that Fixer's repairs were frequently not successful until the third or fourth attempt, it was probably unreasonable for Carrent to trust him with the repair of a condition which Carrent knew made the car unsafe to drive. While it is not certain that a court would come to this conclusion, the argument in **D** is the only one listed which could possibly result in a judgment for Pommel.

Under the doctrine of respondeat superior, an employer is vicariously liable for torts of an employee committed within the scope of employment. In determining whether one who renders services to the defendant is an employee, courts generally hold that if the employer has a right to control the details of performance, the worker is an employee, while if the employer does not have a right to control the details of performance, the worker is an independent contractor. Since Carrent did not control the details of Fixer's performance, Fixer probably was not an employee. **A** is, therefore, incorrect. Statutory duties are sometimes held to be "non-delegable," but **B** is incorrect because no statute is given. Since employers of independent contractors are not ordinarily held vicariously liable for the torts of those contractors, **C** is incorrect.

42. **D**   Like other suppliers of products, a retailer owes its customers a duty to act reasonably. This includes a duty to make whatever inspection is reasonable. Sometimes the circumstances make it reasonable for a retailer to make no inspection at all, but in such a case no inspection constitutes a reasonable inspection.

A, B, and **C** are incorrect because under some circumstances the conduct specified would not be reasonable. (***Note:*** Beware of slogans and shibboleths which are overly broad or general. For example, some writers and judges have stated that "a retailer owes the customer no duty to inspect products furnished by reputable manufacturers." Do you think that this statement would be true if the retailer knew that a shipment of glassware furnished by a reputable manufacturer was dropped by the delivery company, or that many customers had found dead rats in the jars of peanut butter which were furnished by a reputable manufacturer? It is safer to recognize that a retailer, like any other supplier of products, owes customers a duty to act reasonably, and that under some circumstances failure to inspect merchandise furnished by reputable manufacturers is reasonable, while under other circumstances it is not.)

43. **B**   There can be no liability for defamation unless the defendant intentionally or negligently communicated the defamatory statement to a person other than the plaintiff. Communication of the accusation to Pellum's mother would satisfy this requirement only if Denner knew or should have known that she would see the letter that contained them.

A is, therefore, incorrect. **C** is incorrect because the statements actually were communicated to Pellum's mother, who read the letter. Courts have sometimes held that an employer who defames a former employee in a communication with a prospective employer of that former employee is privileged if he believes reasonably and in good faith that his statements are true. This reasoning does not apply to the facts given, however, because Denner's statements were not being made to a prospective employer of Pellum. **D** is, therefore, incorrect.

44. **D**   A statement is defamatory if it would tend to hold the plaintiff up to shame, disgrace, or ridicule in the minds of a substantial group of respectable people. Since most respectable people believe that theft is disgraceful, an accusation that the plaintiff is a thief is probably defamatory. In a defamation action, a statement means what the reasonable person reading it would think it means. The reasonable person reading Denner's statement might believe that it accuses Pellum of stealing tools. Whether this is so is a question for the jury, but it is clear that *if* Denner's statement accused Pellum of stealing tools, it was defamatory and might lead to liability.

If Pellum did not return the tools, Denner's statement is literally true. Since a statement means what the reasonable person hearing it thinks it means, and since the reasonable person might think that Denner's statement accused Pellum of theft, the literal truth of the statement would not prevent Denner from being liable. **A** is, therefore, incorrect. A defendant may be privileged to make defamatory statements in a reasonable and good faith attempt to protect a legitimate interest. In deciding whether a former employer was acting in good faith when making a defamatory statement to a plaintiff's prospective employer, courts frequently look to whether the former employer made the statement gratuitously (making it less likely that she was acting in good faith) or in response to a request for information (making it more likely that she was acting in good faith). **B** is incorrect, however, because this fact alone is not sufficient to privilege a defendant's publication. **C** is incorrect because if the defendant was acting reasonably and in good faith, the interest which a former employer has in common with a prospective employer might be sufficiently legitimate to make the privilege apply.

45. **A**   Strict liability is imposed on the professional seller of a product which is in defective

condition when sold. Neither Pard nor Max sold the helicopter, so **B**, **C**, and **D** are incorrect.

46. **B**   If it was foreseeable that the plaintiff would be affected by a product, the seller of the product is strictly liable for injuries which the plaintiff sustained as the result of a defect in the product which existed when the seller placed it in the stream of commerce. Since aircraft fly over the ground, it is foreseeable that a defective aircraft will affect people on the ground. For this reason, the fact that Homer would be affected by the helicopter was foreseeable, and Kopto will be strictly liable to Homer if the helicopter was defective when Kopto sold it. A product is defective if its condition would defeat the reasonable expectation of the reasonable consumer. Since the reasonable consumer generally expects all the parts of a finished product to function properly, a defect in the fuel gauge which prevents it from functioning properly will make the helicopter defective. Thus, if the accident proximately resulted from a defect in the fuel gauge which existed when Flier purchased the helicopter from Kopto, Kopto would be strictly liable for the damage to Homer.

A is incorrect for two reasons: first, res ipsa has no application to cases based on strict liability; second, although res ipsa may be applied to airplane accidents, it is commonly applied only against the pilot, since he is the one in exclusive control of the circumstances which produce the harm. **C** is incorrect because any person whose contact with the product is foreseeable may benefit from the application of strict liability in tort. Since any harm might have several proximate causes, **D** is incorrect.

47. **B**   A trespassing child is entitled to reasonable care if it was foreseeable that a child would trespass and be injured, and if the child's age made it likely that he would fail to recognize the danger. Thus, although Childer was a trespasser, the fact that Grav could foresee his presence and foresee that he would be injured by the proximity of the hill to the road, imposed upon Grav the duty to act reasonably and to keep the premises reasonably safe. If Grav's failure to erect a fence was unreasonable, Grav was negligent and probably is liable to Childer.

The phrase "danger invites rescue" is usually used to explain why a person who created a danger to another owed a duty of reasonable care to a rescuer who came to the aid of that other. **A** is incorrect because it has no application to these facts. Last clear chance is a doctrine which accomplishes only one thing: under the proper circumstances it negates the effect of a plaintiff's contributory negligence. Only the plaintiff raises it, and only for the purpose of negating the effect of his own negligence. **C** is incorrect because it would put the argument at the disposal of a defendant. An intervening cause does not free an antecedent wrongdoer from liability unless its occurrence was unforeseeable. Thus, the mere fact that Carrol's conduct was an intervening cause would not lead to a judgment for Grav. **D**, is therefore, incorrect.

48. **B**   A misrepresentation is a false assertion of material fact made for the purpose of inducing the plaintiff's reliance. If the defendant knows that the assertion is false, and damages result from the plaintiff's justified reliance on it, the defendant may be held liable. It may be argued successfully that by concealing the crack, Samuels falsely asserted that it did not exist. No liability will result from that assertion, however, unless Barton relied on it. A plaintiff relies on a misrepresentation when it is a significant factor in the plain-

tiff's decision. Since Barton discovered the crack, the assertion that it did not exist could not have been a factor in his decision to buy the car. For that reason, he did not rely on it, and is not entitled to recover damages.

A is incorrect because a court would probably hold that the affirmative act of concealing the crack was an assertion that it did not exist. Since Barton did not rely on Samuels's representation, it does not matter whether such reliance would have been justified. **C** is, therefore, incorrect. Since the facts indicate that Barton was required to spend $500 on repairs, **D** is an inaccurate statement of fact and is, therefore, incorrect.

49. **D**   Negligence is the failure to act reasonably in the face of a foreseeable risk created by defendant's conduct. Since it probably was foreseeable that Barton would show a customer the car after buying it for resale, Samuels owed such customers a duty of reasonable care which probably was breached by his failure to disclose the crack. Although it is not certain that a court would come to this conclusion, **D** is the only argument listed which could possibly lead to recovery by Poynter.

Battery is committed by intentionally causing the harmful or offensive contact with the plaintiff. In a battery case, intent means a desire or knowledge that there will be harmful or offensive contact with the plaintiff or that the plaintiff will become apprehensive of such contact. Although Samuels knew that the zoobie was cracked, there is no indication that he desired or knew that the crack would result in harmful or offensive contact with any person or that it would cause apprehension of such contact. Although these risks may have been foreseeable, battery liability cannot be imposed without intent. For this reason, **A** is incorrect. Misrepresentation liability is imposed only for the benefit of a plaintiff who justifiably relied on the defendant's false representation. Since Poynter did not rely on any express or implied statement made by Samuels, **B** and **C** are incorrect.

50. **B**   Under the all-or-nothing rule of contributory negligence, a plaintiff is completely barred from recovering damages if his own unreasonable conduct contributed to the occurrence. Since Burger saw Arnold in the intersection, it was probably unreasonable, and therefore contributorily negligent for him to enter the intersection when he did. It is unnecessary to decide whether this is so, however, because the use of the word "if" in option **B** requires the assumption that Burger acted unreasonably. Assuming that he did, his contributory negligence would provide Arnold with a complete defense.

The doctrine of last clear chance does no more than negate the effect of a plaintiff's contributory negligence. If a defendant had "the last clear chance" to avoid injuring the plaintiff, the defendant might be held liable in spite of the plaintiff's negligence. The plaintiff never loses a case, however, simply because that plaintiff had "the last clear chance" to avoid being injured. **A** is, therefore, incorrect. **C** and **D** are incorrect for two reasons: first, the presumption which results from a defendant's violation of a statute (sometimes called negligence per se) may ordinarily be rebutted by proof that the violation resulted from circumstances beyond the defendant's control; and, second, even if Arnold could not rebut the presumption that he was negligent, Burger's contributory negligence is still available to him as a defense.

51. **A**   Although the phrase "AS IS" disclaims implied warranties of merchantability or fitness

for a particular purpose, it does not free a seller from the duty of acting reasonably. Since it probably was foreseeable that the purchaser of a refrigerator would plug it in even after being advised that it did not work, Fridge had a duty to take reasonable precautions against the harm which might result therefrom. If her failure to warn Pally was unreasonable, it was negligence which was a proximate cause of harm and would result in liability.

B is incorrect because the phrase "AS IS" is an effective disclaimer of the implied warranty of merchantability (i.e., fitness for ordinary use). **C** is incorrect because Fridge is still liable under a negligence theory. **D** is based on a misinterpretation of the doctrine of "last clear chance" which accomplishes nothing more than undoing the effect of a plaintiff's contributory negligence. (If a defendant had "the last clear chance" to avoid injuring the plaintiff, the defendant might be liable in spite of the plaintiff's negligence. The plaintiff never loses a case, however, simply because that plaintiff had "the last clear chance" to avoid being injured.)

52. **B**   Self defense is a privilege to use reasonable force to defend oneself against a threatened contact. Reasonable force is that force which would appear necessary to the reasonable person. Courts generally hold that it is reasonable to use deadly force in defense against what reasonably appears to be a threat of deadly force.

A is incorrect because it is never reasonable to use deadly force for the sole purpose of preventing a trespass to land or chattel. **C** is incorrect because Danker's initial use of gentle force was privileged in defense of property, making Hunt's response to it a threatened battery. Hunt's trespass did not end when he completed his entry, but continued so long as he refused to leave in response to Danker's demand. **D** is, therefore, incorrect.

53. **A**   One who keeps a wild animal is strictly liable for harm which proximately results from his keeping of it. An animal is "wild" if it comes from a species which cannot ordinarily be kept safely without special training or restraint. For this purpose, the felicet was a wild animal even though it had been tamed.

The terms "foreseeable" and "unforeseeable" are mutually exclusive. Thus if the cat's behavior was unforeseeable, it could not have been foreseeable. **B** is incorrect for this reason, and because the foreseeability of harm is not, alone, sufficient to result in liability. **C** is incorrect for several reasons: first, res ipsa does not apply in strict liability cases; second, there is no reason to believe that the injury would not ordinarily have occurred without negligence; third, res ipsa does not apply when there is direct evidence of the defendant's conduct. **D** is incorrect because private nuisance is an interference with plaintiff's right to use and enjoy realty and there was no interference with Pruitt's right to use or enjoy realty.

54. **D**   If a product fails to live up to an express assertion of fact which a supplier made about it, the supplier may be liable without regard to fault on theories of breach of express warranty and misrepresentation (under section 402B of the Restatement (2d) of Torts). For this purpose, an assertion of fact may be made by the use of models or pictures. The photo on the box probably was an express assertion that the helmet was suitable for use as a motorcycle helmet. Since it was not suitable for such use, Helmco is liable for breach of express warranty and misrepresentation. In addition, strict product liability

may be imposed for damage which results from a defect in a product supplied by defendant. For this purpose, a product is defective if its condition would defeat the reasonable expectations of the reasonable consumer. Since the photo on the box showed the helmet being used as a motorcycle helmet, the reasonable person probably would have expected it to be suitable for such use. Since it was not, Helmco is strictly liable for damage.

A is incorrect because the misrepresentation and strict product liability theories discussed above do not require privity between defendant and plaintiff, and because under the express warranty theory, it has been held that the necessary privity exists between anyone who made the express assertion and anyone who relied on it. **B** is incorrect because even if the product was not intended for use as a motorcycle helmet, the photo on the box probably was an assertion that it was suitable for such use. **C** is incorrect for three reasons. First, the jurisdiction's "pure comparative negligence" system would diminish the plaintiff's recovery in proportion to his own fault, but would not completely bar that recovery. Second, since the purpose of a motorcycle helmet is to protect the user in an accident, the defendant's assertion and the reasonable person's expectation might have been that the helmet would be effective even if the accident was the wearer's own fault. Third, most jurisdictions hold that comparative negligence is not a defense to actions which are not based on fault (i.e., breach of warranty, misrepresentation, strict product liability).

55. **A**   The statute given is typical of the "owner-consent" statute which exists in a number of jurisdictions. It requires the owner to pay for the tort committed by the driver. Whenever the law imposes vicarious liability on one for damage which another has caused, the one who pays is entitled to complete indemnity from the one who should have paid.

B would be correct if the accident resulted from some fault by Ocie in addition to that of Meck, but is incorrect because there is no indication that Ocie acted unreasonably. **C** is incorrect because there is no factual basis for determining that Ocie is himself responsible for any portion of the loss. **D** is incorrect because of Ocie's right of indemnity.

56. **A**   Negligence is a proximate cause of harm if it is a factual cause of it and if the harm was a foreseeable result. Miller's negligence is given. It was a factual cause of harm since the birds would not have died without it. Thus, if the death of the birds was a foreseeable result, Miller's negligence was a proximate cause.

Since Deal sold the seeds in the same package in which they came, Deal's failure to inspect them was foreseeable whether or not it was reasonable. **B** is incorrect because a foreseeable intervention, even if unreasonable, does not free an antecedent wrongdoer from liability. Although liability for breach of warranty may require privity, the theories of negligence and strict liability in tort do not. **C** is, therefore, incorrect. **D** is incorrect because strict liability is imposed on the seller of a product which is in a defective condition when sold, without regard to the possibility that some other seller of the same product might be liable. Thus a manufacturer and retailer of a defective product may be jointly and severally liable as joint tortfeasors.

57. **D**   Strict liability is imposed on the seller of a product which is in a defective condition when sold. A product is defective if its condition would defeat the reasonable expectations of the reasonable consumer. If it was reasonable for Quill to believe that he could

eat the seeds without being made ill, then the fact that the seeds were poisonous made them defective.

A is incorrect because the negligence of a manufacturer is not imputed to a retailer. Proof that the product was defective when sold is not proof that the seller acted unreasonably in selling it. Since negligence liability is imposed only for unreasonable conduct, **B** is incorrect. An express warranty is an assertion of fact which is made in words. All that the phrase "Mayflower Seeds" expresses is that the contents are "Mayflower Seeds." Any assertion that they are fit for consumption is made *impliedly* rather than expressly. **C** is, therefore, incorrect.

58. **C**   Although strict liability is liability without fault, most jurisdictions agree that any loss which results from the sale of a defective product should ultimately be borne by the manufacturer of that product. Thus, even though Deal may be held liable for furnishing a defective product, he should be entitled to receive full indemnification from Miller so long as he was, himself, free from fault in causing the loss.

     A is, therefore, incorrect. **B** is incorrect because the right to indemnification does not depend on whom the injured party chooses to sue. **D** is incorrect because unlike contribution, indemnification is a right recognized by the common law.

59. **A**   Since the coming of a rescuer is generally viewed as a foreseeable result of peril, negligence which causes peril is often held to be a breach of a duty owed to a rescuer. Thus, if Sal's negligence caused the need for Ralph to rescue him, it was a breach of duty owed to Ralph.

     B is incorrect because if Sal had not acted negligently, there would be no basis for holding him liable to Ralph. The phrase "danger invites rescue" is often used to explain why one who imperils another owes a duty of reasonable care to a rescuer attracted by that peril. If that principle had any application to these facts, it would be to establish liability, not to free Sal from such liability. **C** is, therefore, incorrect. An intervening cause does not prevent an antecedent wrongdoer from being liable unless the intervention was unforeseeable. **D** is, therefore, incorrect.

60. **B**   There is some question about whether it is defamatory to say that a person is impoverished or on the verge of bankruptcy. But even if Dentin's statement was defamatory, it was oral and, therefore, classified as slander. Ordinarily, there is no liability for slander unless the plaintiff establishes actual damage to his reputation. Since Thurston did not believe what Dentin told him, there was no damage to Prann's reputation, and Dentin will not be held liable for saying it.

     A is incorrect because mental suffering is not an essential element of defamation. Since liability for defamation is imposed on the publisher of a defamatory statement, the fact that Dentin was only repeating what he heard would not, alone, protect him against liability. **C** is, therefore, incorrect. Since publication is defined as communication to any person other than the plaintiff, **D** is incorrect.

61. **C**   Since negligence is defined as a failure to act reasonably in the face of a foreseeable risk, Woolco cannot be called negligent if the reasonable person in its situation would

not have acted any differently than it did.

Assumption of the risk requires that the plaintiff have knowledge of the risk which he is voluntarily encountering. Since there is no indication that Pullo knew of the risks associated with exposure to plastic wool, **A** is incorrect. **B** is incorrect because Woolco's lack of knowledge would not prevent liability if the reasonable person in Woolco's situation would have known. Workers' compensation may be the exclusive remedy against an injured party's employer, but since Pullo did not work for Woolco, **D** is incorrect.

62.　**B**　　A claim for private nuisance can be asserted only by a plaintiff who claims that the defendant's conduct interfered with his use and enjoyment of realty in which he has a present or future possessory interest. Since Gro held a leasehold interest and Laird a reversion, they can successfully assert a private nuisance claim.

　　　　　A is incorrect because as a tenant, Gro had sufficient interest in the realty. **C** and **D** are incorrect because since Edwards was only an employee of Gro's, he lacked the property interest necessary to the assertion of the claim.

63.　**B**　　A private individual can successfully assert a claim for public nuisance only if the harm which she sustained was different from that sustained by the general public (i.e., "particular" harm). Since no fact indicates this to be so of Packer, she may not assert the public nuisance claim.

　　　　　A is incorrect because if Packer had sustained "particular" harm, the decision of the City Attorney would not prevent her from suing for damages. Although it is generally held that a private individual may not seek an injunction on a public nuisance theory, **C** is incorrect because there are other theories on which a private individual may receive an injunction against environmental polluters. **D** is incorrect because a private individual who sustains particular harm as result of a public nuisance may sue for damages.

64.　**A**　　Trespass to chattel is intentional interference with the plaintiff's chattel resulting in damage. For this purpose, intent consists of a desire or knowledge that the chattel will be involved, without regard to whether the defendant knows that the chattel is the plaintiff's or that the plaintiff's rights are being violated. Interference can consist of any act regarding the chattel which only its rightful possessor is entitled to perform. Since Darren desired to take that particular coat, she had the necessary intent, regardless of her belief that the coat was her own. Since only Perdu was entitled to take the coat, Darren interfered with it. Since the coat was destroyed while Darren possessed it, her interference resulted in damage to Perdu. Darren is, therefore, liable to Perdu for trespass to chattel.

　　　　　B is incorrect because the tort was committed when Darren took the coat and the tort led to the coat's destruction. In trespass to chattel, intent does not require knowledge that the chattel belongs to another or that the defendant's act will affect the rights of another. **C** is, therefore, incorrect. Trespass to chattel was committed when Darren took the coat. If she had succeeded in returning the coat, damages might have been mitigated (i.e., reduced), but the tort would not have been undone. **D** is incorrect because her unsuccessful attempt to return the coat could not even mitigate damages.

65.   **C**   Liability is imposed on a defendant for damage which was proximately caused by defendant's negligence. Since it is given that Mercy was negligent in keeping Penler waiting 6 hours, it is necessary to determine whether that negligence was a proximate cause of his injury in the earthquake. Conduct is a proximate cause of harm if it was a factual and legal cause of that harm. Conduct is a factual cause of harm if the harm would not have occurred without it. Since Penler would not have been struck by the debris which fell in the earthquake if he had not been present, the delay occasioned by Mercy's negligence was a factual cause of his injury. If conduct is a factual cause of harm, it is a legal cause if the harm was foreseeable. Thus, if it was foreseeable that Penler would be injured by an earthquake, Mercy's negligence was a legal cause of that injury and Mercy is liable for it. Otherwise, Mercy is not liable.

"Good Samaritan" statutes, where they exist, only protect doctors who voluntarily render emergency aid at the scenes of accidents. **A** is, therefore, incorrect. Although the liability of an antecedent wrongdoer might depend on whether subsequent intervention was foreseeable, since Doc's conduct preceded Mercy's, Mercy's liability does not depend on whether Doc's conduct was foreseeable. **B** is, therefore, incorrect. **D** is too absolute a statement to be correct. Even if a hospital owes its patients some duty with respect to natural disasters, that duty is only to act reasonably in the face of them.

66.   **D**   It is given that Doc's conduct was negligent. Even if a defendant's conduct was negligent, however, the defendant is not liable for the plaintiff's injuries unless they were proximately caused by that conduct. Conduct is a proximate cause of an injury if it is a factual and legal cause of the injury. Conduct is a factual cause of injury if the injury would not have occurred without it. Since Penler would not have been in the hospital and injured by the falling of the hospital structure except for Doc's conduct, Doc's conduct was a factual cause of Penler's injury. If conduct was a factual cause of harm, it was a legal cause of that harm if the harm was foreseeable and not brought about by superseding intervening causes. An intervening cause of harm is superseding if it was unforeseeable or independent of the risks created by the defendant's conduct. Thus, if the earthquake was an independent intervening cause of Penler's fractured skull, it was a superseding cause which prevented Doc's negligence from being a legal or proximate cause of the fractured skull.

A establishes that Doc's conduct was a factual cause of the fractured skull, but is incorrect because it does not deal with the problem of legal cause. Doc's conduct was not a legal cause of the fractured skull unless the **fractured skull** was a foreseeable result of it. The fact that the wait might have been foreseeable does not make the fractured skull foreseeable. **B** is therefore incorrect. **C** establishes that the presence of the cherry pit was a factual cause of Penler's injury, but does not establish that Doc's conduct was not also a cause of it. **C** is, therefore, incorrect.

67.   **D**   If the seller of a product knows the buyer's purpose in buying it, and knows also that the buyer is relying on the seller's skill in selecting a product to suit that purpose, the sale is accompanied by an implied warranty that the product is fit for the buyer's particular purpose (UCC §2-315), even where that purpose is identical to the ordinary use of such a product. **I** is, therefore, incorrect. Similarly, even where the implied warranty of fitness for the buyer's particular purpose is present, the implied warranty of merchantability accompanies every sale by a merchant (UCC §2-314) unless it is effectively disclaimed.

II is therefore incorrect.

68. **D**   Comcorp is not liable for harm unless its conduct was a factual and legal cause of it. Its conduct was a factual cause of harm only if the harm would not have occurred without it. If the force of the collision would have caused a good pole to fall, then the fact that the pole was rotten is not a factual cause of its falling.

      A and **B** are incorrect because they do not establish that Comcorp's conduct was a factual cause of harm, and liability cannot be imposed unless it was. If Comcorp's conduct was a factual cause of harm, Driver's intervention might be a superseding cause which protects Comcorp from liability, but only if the intervention was unforeseeable. This does not necessarily depend on whether it was criminal or grossly negligent. **C** is, therefore, incorrect.

69. **A**   The statute given is typical of the "pure comparative negligence" approach. Since Zell's loss amounted to $10,000, and since it was 40% by his own fault, 40% of $10,000 (or $4,000) must be deducted from his recovery. The balance which he is entitled to collect is $6,000.

70. **D**   The statute given is typical of the "modified" comparative negligence approach. A deduction is made from the plaintiff's recovery based on the percentage of fault which was the plaintiff's. But if the plaintiff's fault exceeds the defendant's, the plaintiff receives nothing. Since the jury found Andrews to be 60% at fault, he can recover nothing.

71. **C**   The statute given is typical of the "modified" comparative negligence approach. Since Petro was not at fault at all, however, it has no relevance to her rights. No matter what approach a jurisdiction takes to contributory or comparative negligence, most agree that joint tortfeasors are jointly and severally liable to the injured plaintiff. In this case, the court specifically held that Andrews and Zell are jointly and severally liable. This means that Petro can collect all her damage from Andrews, or Zell, or the two of them in any combination.

72. **A**   Strict liability is imposed on the seller of a product which is in a defective condition when sold. Since the bolt was cracked when the sled left the Rosebud factory, Rosebud would be held liable if the crack constituted a defect.

      B and **C** are incorrect because the use and/or sale by Michael would not prevent the imposition of strict liability if the sled was defective when it left Rosebud's factory, so long as such use or sale did not substantially change its condition. **D** is incorrect because strict liability in tort does not depend on unreasonable conduct by the defendant.

73. **A**   Negligence is the failure to act as the reasonable person would act in the face of risks which are foreseeable or known to exist. Since the reasonable person would not ordinarily subject others to unnecessary risks, it would probably have been unreasonable (i.e., negligent) for Less to subject Clyde to the danger of a defective elevator if Less knew or should have known of the danger.

      However, if Less did not act unreasonably, he would not be negligent even though he occupied the entire second floor. Thus, **B** is incorrect. Ordinarily obligations in a lease flow only between parties to that lease. Some jurisdictions hold that a landlord's lease obligation to keep premises in good repair may impose on the landlord a duty to invitees of tenants. **C** is incorrect, however, because Less continues to be liable for the proximate results of his own negligence even though Lord might also be liable. While a tenant might not have an obligation to repair the leased premises, **D** is incorrect because Less might be liable for his negligence in allowing Clyde to use the elevator.

74.　**C**　Even if a defendant's conduct is negligent, the defendant is not liable for the plaintiff's injuries unless they were proximately caused by that conduct. Conduct is a proximate cause of harm if it was a factual and legal cause of the harm. Conduct is a factual cause of harm if the harm would not have occurred without it. Since Clyde would not have been hurt if Lord had fixed or warned him about the elevator, Lord's failure to do so was a factual cause of Clyde's injuries. Conduct which is a factual cause of harm is a legal cause if the harm was a foreseeable result of it and not brought about by an unforeseeable intervening cause (i.e., a superseding cause). Since Clyde would not have been hurt if Less had not permitted him to use the elevator, Less's conduct was also a cause of Clyde's injury. Thus, if it was not foreseeable that Less would permit Clyde to use the elevator, Less's conduct was a superseding cause of Clyde's injury, and Lord's failure to repair or warn Clyde about it was not. While it is not certain that a court would come to this conclusion, **C** is the only argument listed which could possibly support Lord's defense.

Although Lord's promise to repair the elevator might not be enforceable by Clyde, **A** is not an effective argument because, apart from the promise, one who holds realty owes a duty of reasonable care to invitees. An invitee is a person whose presence confers an economic benefit on the landholder. Clyde was Less's client, and Less would not have rented space in the building unless his clients could come to see him there. For this reason, Clyde's presence did confer an economic benefit on Lord, and Clyde was Lord's invitee. (*Note:* It is usually held that invitees of a tenant are also invitees of the landlord.) **B** is, therefore, incorrect. Although an *unforeseeable* intervening cause may be superseding (i.e., prevent the antecedent wrongdoer from being liable), the fact that it was *unreasonable* is not sufficient to make it superseding. **D** is, therefore, incorrect.

75.　**C**　One who enters the realty of another to retrieve a chattel which got there through no fault of her own has a qualified privilege to do so, but must compensate the landholder for any actual damage which results.

A and **D** are, therefore, incorrect. Unless damage to the realty of another results from participation in an abnormally dangerous activity, liability for it is imposed only if the entry resulted from fault (i.e., was intentional or negligent). Since transporting gravel is not an abnormally dangerous activity, and since the gravel was spilled without any fault on the part of Trokker, Trokker is not liable for damage resulting from spilling the gravel. **B** is, therefore, incorrect.

76.　**D**　One who voluntarily encounters a known risk assumes that risk, and is not entitled to damages resulting from it.

A, B, and **C** are all incorrect since assumption of risk is available as a defense in claims based on negligence or strict liability. In addition, **B** is incorrect because horses are not regarded as wild animals, and **C** is incorrect because the fact that Parte, a professional horse trainer, had been warned of the animal's propensity indicates that Stabel's conduct was reasonable.

77.　**A**　The phrase "AS IS" disclaims the implied warranty of merchantability. In addition, it may be argued that it modifies any express warranties or representations which resulted from Dann's assurance that he believed the car to be in good condition, and that it would have placed the reasonable consumer on notice that the car might not be in good condition. In any event, **A** contains the only combination of conclusion and reason which are reasonably related to each other.

　　　　B is incorrect because all jurisdictions permit an action for breach of the implied warranty of merchantability to be brought by any member of the purchaser's household. **C** and **D** are incorrect because the phrase "AS IS" disclaimed the implied warranty that the car was fit for ordinary use.

78.　**A**　A judgment for conversion effects a forced sale, requiring the defendant to pay plaintiff the value which the chattel had at the time it was converted, and making the defendant the owner of it upon satisfying the judgment. A court might find that Doane converted the car by leaving it in the sun, by driving it 4,000 miles on his own personal business, or by painting it a different color without Percy's permission. If so, Percy would be entitled to recover from Doane the value which the car had immediately prior to the act which constituted a conversion. Since the car's value did not change while in Doane's possession, the value which it had at the time it was delivered to him would be the correct measure of damage no matter which of his acts is found to have been a conversion.

　　　　Because a judgment for conversion effects a forced sale as of the time the act of conversion was committed, the plaintiff is not entitled to collect additional sums for damage done to the chattel or for benefits received by the defendant as a result of the conversion. **B, C,** and **D** are, therefore, incorrect.

79.　**D**　Negligence is unreasonable conduct. If Drubb did not act unreasonably, it could not have been negligent. Although a court might not come to this conclusion, the argument in **D** is the only one listed which could possibly support Drubb's defense.

　　　　A is incorrect because contributory negligence is unreasonable conduct by a *plaintiff.* In this case the plaintiff is Puella, not Clener. **B** and **C** are incorrect because an intervening cause of harm does not cut off a wrongdoer's liability unless that intervening cause was unforeseeable.

80.　**A**　If the harm to Puella was foreseeable, then Mato had a duty to act reasonably in the face of it. His failure to do so would constitute negligence, for which he may be liable to Puella. Although a court might not come to this conclusion, the argument in **A** is the only one listed which could possibly support Puella's claim.

　　　　Strict liability is imposed on the seller of a defective product, but since Mato did not sell the Term-Aid pellets to Clener, **B** is incorrect. Although in the absence of privity a manufacturer's duty to act reasonably in designing or producing a product once existed only if the product was an inherently dangerous one, the courts now impose that duty on the manufacturers of all products. For this reason, the question of whether a product is inherently dangerous is no longer of any importance, and **C** is incorrect. Unless Mato was negligent, questions of causation are irrelevant. **D** is, therefore, incorrect.

81. **B** A landholder is entitled to use reasonable force to prevent a trespass. Serious or deadly force is not regarded as reasonable, however, since human life is so much more valuable than mere property. The use of such force is therefore a battery.

Negligence is the breach of a duty of reasonable care owed by the defendant to the plaintiff. Ordinarily, a defendant owes a plaintiff a duty of reasonable care if the defendant's conduct creates a foreseeable risk to the plaintiff. Thus, if the risk to persons entering on legitimate business was foreseeable, Houser owed a duty of reasonable care to such persons. This does not mean that he owed such a duty to everyone, however, or that he owed it to Burg. **A** is incorrect for this reason, and because of a rule applied by most jurisdictions that a landholder owes no duty of reasonable care to trespassers. **C** is incorrect because no rule of law prohibits the use of mechanical devices unless they inflict excessive force. Although courts have made statements like that in **D,** it is irrelevant here since the device did not injure an innocent bystander. **D** is, therefore, incorrect.

82. **A** An intentional exercise of dominion and control over a chattel by defendant is a conversion if the plaintiff was lawfully entitled to possession of the chattel, and if he was thereby damaged. In a conversion case, "intent" means a desire (or knowledge with certainty) that the defendant's act will affect the particular chattel involved. In this case, Ina's desire to make the television hers and to carry it off satisfies the intent requirement even though it was reasonable for her to believe that the sale was legitimate.

B and **C** are, therefore, incorrect. **D** is incorrect since the plaintiff need not be in possession of the chattel at the time of conversion, so long as he had a right to possess it.

83. **A** Consent (i.e., willingness) is a defense to all intentional torts. While it is not likely that this inference would be drawn, it would give Wanda a complete privilege if it was.

B is incorrect because the plaintiff has a right to elect whether to sue for conversion or trespass to chattel. **C** is incorrect because Ina's liability would not prevent Wanda from being liable as well. The remedy for trespass to chattel is money damage. **D** is therefore incorrect.

84. **B** A guest rides free. If something of value — like rides on alternate days — is given in return for passage, courts will conclude that the passenger was not a guest for purposes of the automobile guest statute.

In a negligence claim, the existence of insurance coverage is not relevant in determining liability. **A** is incorrect for this reason, and because the "guest" statute was originally created to protect insurance companies against collusive claims. Recklessness or aggravated negligence is usually held to be actionable in the face of a statute which prohibits actions for negligence. **C** is incorrect, however, because the facts do not indicate the conscious disregard of an obvious and serious risk which aggravated negligence requires. **D** is probably an accurate statement. It is incorrect, however, because it does not justify non-enforcement of the statute.

85.   **D**   Negligence means failing to act like the reasonable person. If Draiv can convince the trier of the facts that the reasonable person occasionally takes his eyes off the road while driving, and that his conduct was therefore not negligent. Pack's negligence action against him will fail. While a court might not come to this conclusion, **D** is the only argument listed which might be effective in Draiv's defense.

A is incorrect because assumption of the risk requires a voluntary encounter with a known risk. For this purpose, a risk is "known" if the plaintiff is substantially certain that harm will probably occur. Recognition of a possibility of harm is not sufficient. **B** is incorrect because, although it establishes that the other car's sudden stop was a cause of the accident, that does not mean that Draiv's conduct was not also a cause. **C** is incorrect since the special rules about duties owed to licensees applies only to accidents which occur on a defendant's land.

86.   **B**   If the defect in a product was a factual case of harm, it was a legal cause of that harm if the harm was foreseeable and not brought about by unforeseeable intervening causes. Thus, if it was unforeseeable that a person with Charles's training would direct an untrained person to use the Res-Nibbler, Charles's intervention would prevent any defect in the product from being regarded as a proximate cause of the harm to Fred. Although a court might not conclude that Charles's conduct was unforeseeable, the argument in **B** is the only one listed which could possibly be effective in Respro's defense.

Strict liability may be imposed regardless of whether the defendant was negligent. Since the basis of Fred's action is a claim that the product was defective (i.e., strict liability in tort), the fact that Respro acted reasonably would not furnish it with an effective defense. **A** is, therefore, incorrect. A plaintiff assumes the risk when he knows of it and voluntarily encounters it. Since Fred had never heard of the Res-Nibbler before, he could not have known of the risk or assumed it. **C** is, therefore, incorrect. An intervening cause of harm is one which came between the defendant's conduct and the plaintiff. It is "independent" if it is not related to the risk created by the defendant. **D** is incorrect for two reasons: First, a plaintiff's own conduct is not usually regarded as an intervening cause of harm; and second, since Fred's assertion is that the device was defective because it failed to carry a warning, the risk that an untrained person would use it is not an independent one.

87.   **A**   It was probably unreasonable for Charles (who knew the dangers connected with the use of the product by an untrained person) to permit Fred (whom he knew to be untrained) to use the product. Although a court might not find that Charles was negligent, **A** is the only theory listed which could result in a judgment for Ponder.

Unless Charles had a substantial certainty that harm would result, he lacked the intent to make him liable for battery. **B** is, therefore, incorrect. Strict products liability is imposed only on a professional supplier of a defective product. Since Charles was not in the business of supplying Res-Nibblers, **C** is incorrect. **D** is incorrect because res ipsa only permits an inference of negligence to be drawn from the circumstances when there is no direct evidence of the defendant's conduct.

88.   **B**   Since it is given that the injury to Polly's nose resulted from Dr. Glass's negligence, Dr. Glass is liable for it.

It is, of course, possible for harm to have more than one proximate cause. Thus, even if Nancy's conduct was a proximate cause of the injury, Dr. Glass's conduct may also be a cause of it, making Dr. Glass liable as a joint tortfeasor. (In most jurisdictions, joint tortfeasors are jointly and severally liable.) **A** is, therefore, incorrect. Conduct is a factual cause of harm if the harm would not have occurred without it. Since the injuries to Polly's elbow and shoulder would have occurred even without the negligence of Dr. Glass, his conduct was not a factual cause of those injuries, and Dr. Glass could not be held liable for them. **C** and **D** are, therefore, incorrect.

89.   **C**   A defendant is liable for damage which was proximately caused by her negligence. A defendant's conduct is a proximate cause of harm if it is a factual and legal cause of that harm. Conduct is a factual cause of harm if the harm would not have occurred without it. Since Polly would not have sustained any injuries at all were it not for Nancy's negligence, Nancy's negligence is a factual cause of all her injuries. Conduct which is a factual cause of harm is a legal cause of that harm if the harm was foreseeable and not brought about by unforeseeable or independent interventions. Courts usually hold that in treating injuries inflicted by a defendant, the malpractice of a physician is neither unforeseeable nor independent of the conduct which caused the initial injuries. For this reason, all complications caused by the malpractice of Drs. Glass and Bonz were proximately caused by Nancy, making Nancy liable for them. **C** is, therefore, correct. (Note: The negligent doctors may also be held liable as joint tortfeasors.)

90.   **A**   One who holds himself out to be an attorney, even if unlicensed, is required to act like the reasonable attorney. If Lipp did not, he will be held liable for damages which proximately resulted.

Negligence does not lead to liability unless it is a cause of damage. Thus, although violation of a statute sometimes results in a presumption of negligence, it does not result in liability unless it was a cause of the plaintiff's damage. Negligence is not a cause of damage which would have occurred without it. Since licensed attorneys sometimes lose cases, it cannot be said that Lipp would not have lost the case if he had had a license. **B** and **C** are incorrect for this reason, and because courts usually hold that violation of a licensing statute does not result in a presumption of negligence. **D** is incorrect because even though an attorney does not guarantee results, he is liable for damages which result from his negligence.

91.   **C**   Consent means willingness, and the affirmative defense of consent is effective because of the rule that a plaintiff who is willing for a particular thing to happen to her has no right to complain when it does. For this reason, a defendant does not commit a tort when he does something to which the plaintiff has consented. If the defendant induces her consent by fraud, however, the consent does not have this effect, and does not privilege the defendant's conduct. A defendant induces consent by fraud when he knowingly misrepresents the nature of the act to which the plaintiff is consenting. Thus, if Dr. Hypno told Penny that the cattle prod would produce no real discomfort when he knew that this was false, he fraudulently induced her consent to contact with it, and was not privileged

by her consent.

In **A**, Penny consented to the contact even though she was aware that Dr. Hypno was not always successful in hypnotizing volunteers and that if he was not successful in hypnotizing her, the cattle prod might cause discomfort. Since she knew the nature of the act to which she was consenting, her consent would furnish Dr. Hypno with a privilege. **A** is, therefore, incorrect. In **B**, although Dr. Hypno defrauded Penny by promising money which he did not intend to pay, the fraud did not relate to the nature of the act to which she was consenting. He would, therefore, be privileged by her consent, and **B** is, therefore, incorrect. A mistake which induces consent does not destroy the effect of that consent unless the defendant is aware of the mistake. Since there is no indication in **D** that Dr. Hypno was aware of Penny's mistake regarding the effect of a cattle prod, her consent privileged him, and **D** is, therefore, incorrect.

92. **A**   A statement is defamatory if it is likely to cause a substantial group of respectable people to lose respect for the person about whom it is made. A statement that Speeger drank a large quantity of alcohol might be defamatory because many people regard such conduct as disreputable, and because it implies that Speeger's public statements were dishonest. A statement that she drank a large quantity of fruit juice clearly would not be defamatory. If an allegedly defamatory statement is ambiguous (i.e., has two possible meanings) it is held to mean what the reasonable person would think it means. Thus, the statements made in the photo and caption would not have been defamatory if the reasonable person wold have believed them to mean that Speeger drank fruit juice. If the reasonable person would have read the story, she or he would have known that this was what the statements in the photo and caption meant.

B and C are incorrect because the standard used to determine the meaning of an ambiguous statement is objective, and does not depend on what any particular group of persons thought. **D** is incorrect because if the reasonable person would not have read the story, the photo and caption might mean that Speeger had drunk a large quantity of alcohol, and thus might be a defamatory statement.

93. **D**   Liability for misrepresentation may be imposed upon a defendant who makes an intentionally (or, in some jurisdictions, negligently) false assertion of fact upon which the plaintiff justifiably relies to his detriment. Strong's only assertion of fact was that he ate Power candy bars for energy. There is no indication, however, that this assertion was false. Strong made no assertion about the flavor of the candy bar, so even if Purlie's dislike of the flavor can be regarded as damage, it is not damage which proximately resulted from his reliance on an assertion by Strong.

A is incorrect because misrepresentation liability can be imposed on anyone who makes a misrepresentation, and also because the facts indicate that Strong is in the business of selling Power candy. If Strong's statements were misrepresentations, the fact that he said them could result in liability even though they were written by someone else. **B** is, therefore, incorrect. **C** is incorrect because liability for intentional misrepresentation may be imposed to benefit anyone who was damaged by his justified reliance on the misrepresentation, regardless of privity.

94. **B**   Although blasting is generally recognized to be an ultra-hazardous activity, strict liabil-

ity applies only to harm which resulted from the risks which made the activity ultra-hazardous. The possibility of noise frightening animals accompanies a great many activities which are not ultra-hazardous, so it is probably not one of the risks which makes blasting ultra-hazardous.

A is incorrect because Horace's phone call announcing that harm was occurring on his farm made it foreseeable that harm would continue to occur there if the activity was continued. **C** is incorrect because strict liability may be imposed even though the defendant acted reasonably. While Blass' relationship with Constructo might impose liability on Constructo as well, it would not relieve Blass from liability for his acts. **D** is, therefore, incorrect.

95. **C**   An invitee is one whose presence confers an economic benefit on the landholder. That which enables a tenant to do business on the premises confers economic benefit on the landholder by making the premises attractive to the tenant. This applies to the presence of tenant's employees, and makes them invitees of the landlord. **I** is therefore an accurate statement. Contributory (comparative) negligence is unreasonable conduct by the plaintiff. If the reasonable person in Hirt's shoes would have seen and avoided the dangerous condition, then Hirt's failure to do so was negligent. **II** is, therefore, an accurate statement.

96. **C**   Under the doctrine of respondeat superior, an employer is vicariously liable for the negligence of an employee committed within the scope of employment. An employee is acting within the scope of employment if her conduct is intended to further the interests of her employer and if her employer has a right to control her conduct. Since Spec was attempting to find out whether the drapes were fire retardant, which was part of what City hired her to do, and since City had the right to tell her how to test drapes, she was acting within the scope of her employment even if she was violating specific instructions which she received from City.

A is, therefore, incorrect. **B** is a fabrication with no basis in law, since even when an employee's conduct is unsupervised, respondeat superior may result in the imposition of vicarious liability on her employer. **D** is incorrect because under respondeat superior an employer is only vicariously liable for that for which the employee is liable.

97. **C**   It may have been unreasonable for David to leave his keys in the ignition. If so, he was negligent. Even if his conduct was not unreasonable, his violation of the ignition key statute may result in a presumption of negligence if the statute was designed to prevent accidents involving stolen cars. Negligence does not result in liability, however, unless it is a proximate (i.e., factual and legal) cause of harm. Conduct is a factual cause of harm if the harm would not have occurred without it. Since Kidd probably would not have stolen David's car and struck Pell with it had David not left his key in the ignition, David's conduct was a factual cause of Pell's injury. A factual cause of harm is a legal cause if the harm was foreseeable and not brought about by an unforeseeable intervening cause (i.e., a superseding cause). Since the accident would not have occurred without Kidd's conduct and since Kidd's conduct came between David's conduct and Pell's injury, it was an intervening cause. If it was unforeseeable, it was a superseding cause of Pell's harm, and David's conduct was not a proximate cause of it. Thus, Pell will lose his case against David unless it is found that Kidd's intervention was foreseeable.

Even if David's conduct was reasonable, his violation of statute might result in a presumption of negligence. **A** is, therefore, incorrect. Even if the violation of statute does not result in a presumption of negligence, David's conduct might have been unreasonable and, therefore, negligent. **B** is, therefore, incorrect. **D** is incorrect because an intervening cause of harm is not superseding unless it was unforeseeable.

98. **A**   Appropriation of identity is committed when the defendant, without the plaintiff's permission, uses the plaintiff's identity for a commercial purpose. Since Frank sold games which were imprinted with the governor's likeness, a court could conclude that he is liable for appropriation.

Public disclosure is committed when the defendant publicly discloses a private fact about the plaintiff, the disclosure of which would offend the reasonable person in the plaintiff's position. Since a photo of the governor's face as it appeared in a public place is obviously not a private fact, **B** is incorrect. Intrusion is committed by intentionally invading the plaintiff's private space in a manner which would offend the reasonable person in the plaintiff's position. Since Frank snapped the photo in a public place, he did not invade the governor's private space, and **C** is incorrect. False light is committed by publishing false statements about the plaintiff which, although not defamatory, are in some way embarrassing or damaging. Since Frank did not publish any statements about the governor, **D** is incorrect.

99. **D**   False imprisonment requires intentional confinement, which is an overcoming of the plaintiff's will to leave. Since a sleeping person has no will to leave, Peter was not confined by the locked door.

A is, therefore, incorrect. **B** is based on an inaccurate statement since the risk probably was not a foreseeable one, but is incorrect in any event because false imprisonment requires intent. If Hardy intentionally confined Peter, she would be held liable for all the harm which foreseeably resulted. **C** is incorrect, however, because she did not confine him.

100. **A**   In a defamation action by a private person against a professional publisher (media defendant) the plaintiff must prove either actual malice or negligence. If the *Globe* knew the statement to be false, it had actual malice. If the reasonable publisher would have known the statement to be false, the *Globe* acted negligently.

B describes actual malice and is incorrect because a plaintiff who is not a public person is not required to prove actual malice. **C** is incorrect because no liability can be imposed unless the *Globe* knew or reasonably should have known that the statement was false. **D** is incorrect since the Supreme Court has specifically indicated that liability without fault cannot be imposed in an action for defamation against a professional (media defendant) publisher.

101. **D**   A statement is defamatory if it would lead a substantial group of respectable people to associate the person about whom it is said with shame or disgrace.

A is incorrect since a judgment for Preech will not violate either the Establishment

Clause or the Free Exercise Clause. **B** is incorrect because what matters is what a substantial group of respectable people would believe about the plaintiff as a result of the statement. The fact that a substantial group of right-thinking people would not associate the plaintiff with shame or disgrace does not prevent the statement from being defamatory if there is also a substantial group of respectable people who would. **C** is, therefore, incorrect.

102. **A**   Most states permit a plaintiff to succeed in an action for libel without proof of actual damage, but the United States Supreme Court has indicated that unless malice is shown, actual damage must be proved. If editors of the *Globe* knew that the statement was false, they had the requisite malice.

When a plaintiff in a defamation case is required to plead and prove actual damage, he must show harm to his reputation. Since "reputation" involves the opinion that other people have of the plaintiff, proof that he became ill upon reading the statement which was made about him does not satisfy that requirement. **B** is incorrect for this reason, and because even if Preech did sustain the necessary harm, it was not pleaded in his complaint. **C** would establish "malice" in its traditional sense, but would not satisfy the Supreme Court's requirement because in defamation actions "actual malice" means either that the defendant knew the statement was false, or that it entertained serious doubts about whether the statement was true. **D** is incorrect because actual damage must always be proved in the absence of malice (or at least negligence) in the case of a private person suing a media defendant.

103. **B**   A professional supplier who sells a product in a defective condition is strictly liable for harm which proximately results from the defect. Thus, if the defect in the machine was a proximate cause of Worker's injury, Mashco is strictly liable for it.

A is incorrect because Worker's rights against Mashco are independent of any rights she might have against her employer. **C** is incorrect because the machine was defective when Mashco placed it in the stream of commerce, and nothing happened to change its condition thereafter. The unreasonable conduct of an intervenor is not a superseding cause of harm unless it is unforeseeable. **D** is, therefore, incorrect.

104. **D**   Negligence is the failure to act reasonably in the face of a foreseeable risk. If the risk was not foreseeable, Mashco's failure to guard against it was not negligence.

A is incorrect since an expert is only expected to know that which the reasonable expert would know. If the risk that it will wear out was not foreseeable, knowledge that harm would occur if it did wear out does not result in a duty to protect against its wearing out. **B** is, therefore, incorrect. **C** is incorrect because Worker's action is based on negligence.

105. **A**   Holders of land owe a duty of reasonable care to travelers who foreseeably deviate onto the land for reasons related to their use of the adjacent public way.

B is, therefore, incorrect. **C** is incorrect because although the reason given explains why Basil's conduct was not negligent, it fails to explain why he had no duty. Although a landholder generally owes no duty of reasonable care to a trespasser, **D** is incorrect because a strayed traveler as described above is entitled to reasonable care as an exception to the general rule.

106. **A**   Although damage is not an essential element of an action for trespass to land, it is an essential element of a negligence action. Since there is no indication that Basil was damaged, **A** is correct.

B is incorrect because even in an emergency a person is expected to act as the reasonable person would under the circumstances (although conduct which would ordinarily be regarded as unreasonable might be reasonable in an emergency). While necessity is a defense to actions for intentional tort, it is not a defense to actions founded in negligence. **C** is, therefore, incorrect. **D** is probably an accurate statement, but its effect is to impose a duty of reasonable care on Basil, not to relieve Alice of liability for negligence.

107. **C**   Conduct is a factual cause of harm if the harm would not have occurred without it. Since medical assistance was summoned just a moment later, and since the facts do not indicate that Truck was worse off for the momentary delay, Carp's failure to summon aid was not a cause of harm.

Most jurisdictions agree that a landholder owes no duty of reasonable care to a trespasser. When the landholder knows of the trespasser's presence, however, and knows that the trespasser has been imperiled by some affirmative act of the landholder, the landholder does have a duty to act reasonably to protect the trespasser from that act. Since Carp knew that his act of throwing the hammer created the need for aid, he probably did owe Truck a duty to act reasonably in summoning it. **A** is, therefore, incorrect. Punitive damages may be available against a defendant who intended harm by his act. Intent requires a substantial certainty that the harm will probably occur, however. Knowledge that harm is *possible* is not intent, and is not sufficient to result in liability for punitive damages. **B** is, therefore, incorrect. A user of the public way who enters upon private land foreseeably and in connection with his use of the public way is entitled to some measure of reasonable care. **D** is incorrect, however, because he does not thereby become an invitee, and, further, because Truck's entry onto Carp's realty was not connected with Truck's use of the public way.

108. **A**   Negligence is a breach of the duty of reasonable care. Most cases hold that a defendant does not owe a duty of reasonable care unless it is foreseeable (i.e., the reasonable person would anticipate) that his act will cause harm. If it was reasonable for Carp to believe that his act would cause no harm, he owed no duty of reasonable care. If Carp owed no duty of reasonable care, Carp could not have been negligent.

B is incorrect because custom does not determine what reasonable care is. Although Truck's contributory negligence might prevent him from recovering, there is no indication that Truck's failure to see the hammer was negligent. **C** is, therefore, incorrect. **D** is incorrect because of the rule that a defendant takes the plaintiff as he finds him. (Note: What this means is that if an injury to the plaintiff is foreseeable, the full extent of that injury is foreseeable even though some special sensitivity of the plaintiff was a contributing factor to its extent.)

109. **A**   A defendant is liable for harm which is proximately (i.e., factually and legally) caused

by his negligence. Conduct is a factual cause of harm if the harm would not have occurred without it. Since Truck would not have been killed in an ambulance accident if Carp had not thrown the hammer, Carp's conduct was a factual cause of Truck's death. A factual cause of harm is a legal cause if the harm was foreseeable and was not brought about by an unforeseeable intervening cause. Since motorists are frequently negligent, courts usually hold that the negligence of any driver is foreseeable. For this reason, it probably was foreseeable that the ambulance in which Truck was riding would be involved in an accident and that further injuries would occur. Thus, if Carp's negligence was a proximate cause of the injury which required Truck's transportation in the ambulance, it probably was a proximate cause of the injury which occurred in the ambulance accident. While it is not certain that a court would come to this conclusion, **A** is the only answer listed which is logically correct.

B and **C** are incorrect because, unless it was unforeseeable, an intervening cause does not prevent an antecedent wrongdoer from being held liable. **D** is incorrect because, as explained above, Carp's conduct was a factual cause of Truck's death.

110. **C**   Since the death would not have occurred without Ann's negligence, her negligence factually caused it. Since it is obviously foreseeable that an automobile accident will result in the death of a passenger, Ann's negligence was also a legal cause of the harm.

Since Carp's conduct preceded Ann's, it was not an intervening cause. For this reason, the foreseeability of Carp's conduct is not relevant, and **A** is incorrect. Although "reasonable care" may require less in an emergency than it does under ordinary circumstances, one faced with an emergency is still required to act as a reasonable person would under similar circumstances. **B** is, therefore, incorrect. Even if Carp is liable for Truck's death, Ann would be liable also if her negligence proximately caused it. **D** is, therefore, incorrect.

111. **C**   A private individual may sue for public nuisance only if his damages were different in kind from those sustained by the general public.

A and **B** are incorrect because the fact that the defendant's conduct pre-existed the plaintiff's presence is not, by itself, a defense to nuisance unless it can be shown that the plaintiff came to the nuisance specifically for the purpose of instituting litigation. **D** is an incorrect statement of the law; even a lawful activity may constitute a public nuisance if it is conducted in a way which unreasonably interferes with the rights of the public.

112. **C**   Consent — plaintiff's willingness — is a complete defense to most intentional tort actions. Consent is implied if the reasonable person would infer from the plaintiff's conduct and the surrounding circumstances that the plaintiff is willing for the defendant's act to occur. The fact that Trik and Vik have been enjoying each other's jokes for years could result in the inference that Vik was willing to have a joke played upon him. Although it is not certain that a court would come to this conclusion, the argument in **C** is the only one listed which could support Trik's defense.

A is incorrect because assault requires apprehension of harmful contact, but not necessarily of battery. Ordinarily, the apprehension experienced by plaintiff must be such as a reasonable person in his shoes would experience. **B** is incorrect, however, because an exception to this objective standard is made when the plaintiff has a special sensitivity about which the defendant knows, and because Trik knew that Vik was horrified of spiders. **D** is incorrect because assault requires an intent to cause apprehension, not necessarily an intent to cause injury.

113. **C**   Conduct is a factual cause of harm if the harm would not have occurred without the conduct. Since there is no way of knowing whether Marc's shot struck Pierre, it cannot be established that Pierre's harm was factually caused by Marc's conduct. (Note: Do not confuse these facts with the rule of *Summers v. Tice* in which **both** negligent persons were named as defendants.)

Marc's duty of reasonable care might not require the same vigilance that would be required in an urban area, but **A** is incorrect because the possibility that someone would come by required some vigilance. Since it is likely that a person struck by a pellet shot from a slingshot would be seriously injured, it is probably unreasonable to shoot a slingshot without taking some precaution against hitting other persons. **B** is, therefore, incorrect. If Marc's conduct was a factual cause of the harm it was a legal cause if the harm was foreseeable. Since it is clearly foreseeable that a person struck by a slingshot pellet will sustain an injury, **D** is incorrect.

114. **C**   Although the law recognizes a special standard for judging the negligence of children, it is applied only when the youth of the defendant is likely to prevent her from exercising the same mature judgment as an adult. When a child is old enough to have acquired the judgment of an adult with respect to a particular activity, the child standard no longer applies. It is rare for a court to apply the child standard to persons over the age of fourteen years.

A is, therefore, incorrect. An adult activity is one which is substantially more likely to be dangerous when performed by a child than by an adult or one in which only adults traditionally engage. **B** is incorrect because fishing is neither. The balancing test which is sometimes used to determine whether conduct is negligent weighs the risks which foreseeably result from acting a certain way against the utility of acting that particular way. **D** is incorrect because it distorts that rule by weighing the risk of handling a fish hook in whatever way Melanie was handling it against the utility of fishing in general.

115. **A**   Strict liability in tort is imposed on the supplier of a product for damages which result from a defect in the product which existed at the time it left that supplier's hands and which made the product unreasonably dangerous. Since a defect is a condition which would defeat the reasonable expectations of the reasonable consumer, and since the reasonable consumer probably does not expect to find a rat's tail in food products, the presence of a rat's tail was probably a defect. Since a product is unreasonably dangerous if the benefits of its condition are outweighed by its disadvantages, and since the presence of a rat's tail has no advantage and is likely to be a source of disease and disgust in a person eating it, the presence of a rat's tail in a food product probably makes that product unreasonably dangerous.

B is incorrect because strict liability in tort may be imposed for the benefit of any plaintiff whose contact with the product was foreseeable, without regard to the existence of a contractual relationship (i.e., privity). Although the sale of a product by a merchant implies a warranty that the product is merchantable (i.e., fit for ordinary use) **C** is incorrect because the question stem specifies the theory of strict liability in tort, and this theory does not depend on the existence of an implied promise. The doctrine of res ipsa loquitur is applied to establish circumstantially an inference that the defendant acted unreasonably. Since the reasonableness of the defendant's conduct is not relevant to the imposition of strict liability, **D** is incorrect.

116. **C**   Negligence consists of a failure to act reasonably. Since the question stem specifies an action for negligence, Pederson cannot win without establishing that Gordon's was negligent (i.e., acted unreasonably).

   A is incorrect because it is based on an inaccurate statement of law: the negligence of a manufacturer is not ordinarily imputed to a retailer selling products made by that manufacturer. Although a retailer may be held strictly liable for damages resulting from a defect which existed when the product was sold by that retailer. **B** is incorrect because *negligence* liability is not imposed unless the defendant acted unreasonably. **D** is incorrect because it is based on an inaccurate statement of law; a retailer owes its customers a duty of acting reasonably, which may require the inspection of products packaged in sealed containers.

117. **B**   All of the products liability theories require proof that the plaintiff sustained damage as a result of his contact with the product. If Pederson did not, he cannot succeed against Fruitco on any theory.

   A is incorrect because some of the approaches to products liability (i.e., strict liability in tort and breach of warranty) do not depend on the unreasonableness of the defendant's conduct. **C** is incorrect because compliance with statute is not a defense to any products liability theory. A seller who recommends a particular product knowing why the purchaser wants it and that the purchaser is relying on the seller's judgment may be held liable for breach of warranty if the product is unfit for the buyer's particular purpose. **D** is incorrect, however, because imposing liability on Gordon's would not prevent its being imposed on Fruitco.

118. **C**   A parent's claim for medical bills incurred as a result of injuries negligently inflicted on a child is a derivative one, subject to any defenses which could have been raised in response to an action by the child. Since Sal's negligence could be asserted by Denton in response to a claim by Sal, **I** is correct. Since a plaintiff's contributory negligence may be asserted in defense, and since Mona is the plaintiff, **II** is also correct.

119. **A**   Negligence is unreasonable conduct. Thus, if Denton was acting unreasonably, she was negligent, and should be liable for Sal's injuries. Under the "all-or-nothing" rule of contributory negligence, however, a plaintiff is completely barred from recovery if his/her own negligence contributed to the happening of the accident. Contributory negligence is unreasonable conduct by a plaintiff. Thus, if Sal's injury resulted from his own unreasonable conduct (i.e., contributory negligence), he will not recover, in spite of the fact that Denton was also negligent.

   A child is said to have been negligent if he failed to act like the reasonable child of the same age, experience, and intelligence. **B** is, therefore, incorrect. Res ipsa loquitur permits an inference that the defendant was negligent to be drawn from certain circumstantial evidence. Since Denton's negligence is given (in the stem of the question) res ipsa loquitur is inapplicable, and **C** is incorrect. Unreasonable conduct by a third person is no longer imputed to a plaintiff as contributory negligence, even when the third person is the plaintiff's parent. **D** is, therefore, incorrect.

120. **D**   Violation of statute is relevant to the question of negligence only if the statute violated was designed to protect a class of persons to which the plaintiff belongs against risks like the one which resulted in harm to the plaintiff. Since insurance would not have prevented the trailer hitch from failing, the statute was not designed to protect against the risk that it would. Its violation is, therefore, not relevant.

A is, therefore, incorrect. **B** is incorrect because the violation is not relevant unless the statute was designed to protect against the risk involved. Public policy generally prohibits disclosing to a jury that a defendant was or was not insured. Such disclosure is not *absolutely* prohibited, however, since there are circumstances under which such disclosure could be made to a jury (e.g., to establish ownership of a vehicle). **C** is, thus, based on an overinclusive statement of the law, and is, therefore, incorrect.

121. **C**   An inference of negligence may be established under the doctrine of res ipsa loquitur when the accident was one which would not ordinarily have occurred without negligence, and the circumstances eliminate the probability that the negligence was anyone's but the defendant's. Bottles don't *usually* explode unless the company which was in exclusive control of the bottling process acted negligently, so res ipsa frequently is applied in exploding bottle cases. But where, as here, some other event was as likely a cause of the explosion, res ipsa cannot be applied.

A and **B** are, therefore, incorrect. **D** is incorrect because the fact that the bottles were not in the defendant's possession when the accident occurred is not, alone, sufficient to eliminate the probability that the negligence was anyone's other than the defendant.

122. **B**   A defendant's conduct is a proximate cause of harm if it was a factual and legal cause of that harm. Conduct is a factual cause of harm if the harm would not have occurred without it. Since Tanya would not have been injured by the bottle if Super had not restacked and sold the bottles, Super's conduct was a factual cause of Tanya's injury. Conduct which is a factual cause of harm is a legal cause of that harm if the harm was a foreseeable result of it. Since the contents of bottles of soda-pop are under pressure, it is probably foreseeable that a crack in the bottle will result in an explosion and injury. Super's conduct was thus a proximate cause of Tanya's injury. A defendant is liable for the proximate results of its negligence. For this reason, if Super's conduct was negligent, Tanya is likely to win her lawsuit against it.

A is incorrect because the plaintiff's helplessness is not, alone, a basis of the defendant's liability. **C** is incorrect because harm may have more than one proximate cause. The fact that the conduct of the officers was a proximate cause of the plaintiff's harm does not mean that the negligence of Super was not. Since privity is not an essential element of a negligence action, **D** is also incorrect.

123. **D**   Negligence is the breach of a duty of reasonable care. A defendant owes a plaintiff a duty of reasonable care when the defendant's conduct creates a foreseeable risk to the plaintiff. If it was unforeseeable that persons would be running about the storeroom in the dark, the stacked groceries did not pose a foreseeable risk to the plaintiff. There would, therefore, be no duty to protect him against them and no negligence.

   A is incorrect because an invitee is only entitled to reasonable care, and unless Super's conduct was unreasonable, the duty to Axel was not breached. **B** is incorrect for the same reason, since unless the conduct was negligent there is no liability. The fact, alone, that Axel was a licensee would not be sufficient to defeat his case, since even a licensee is entitled to reasonable warnings about known hidden dangers on the premises. **C** is therefore incorrect.

124. **D**   The privilege to defend property permits the use of reasonable force to prevent a trespass to realty. Thus, if the force used by Keeper was reasonable, it was privileged, and would not be the basis of liability to Baron.

   A is incorrect because the use of a trap to defend realty might be privileged, if the force which resulted from the use of the trap was reasonable. Reasonable force is the force which would appear necessary to the reasonable person. If the reasonable person would have believed that X-Eleven gas was harmless, its use might have been reasonable, even though in fact it resulted in damage to Baron's vision. **B** is, therefore, incorrect. **C** is incorrect, because it is over-inclusive: a landholder owes trespassers at least a duty to refrain from using excessive force against them.

125. **C**   An essential element of tort liability for misrepresentation is the defendant's intent to induce the plaintiff's reliance on the defendant's statement. If Dillon did not know that Barton would rely on the statements which she made to Collins, she could not have intended to induce Barton's reliance on those statements. Since there is no indication that Dillon was aware that Barton had overhead her conversation with Collins, **C** is correct.

   A is overinclusive, and, therefore, incorrect: statements of opinion, especially when made by experts, may be regarded as assertions of fact (i.e., the fact that the speaker actually held that particular opinion). Since Barton paid $250,000 for something worth only $600, based on his belief in what he had overheard Dillon saying, he did sustain damage as a result of his reliance on Dillon's statement. **B** is, therefore, incorrect. **D** is incorrect for two reasons. First, as indicated above, an expert may incur misrepresentation liability by stating that she holds an opinion which she doesn't actually hold. Second, Dillon's statement was not only an evaluation of the painting's value, but included a statement about who had painted it.

126. **D**   Since Barton received something for his money, the measure of his damage must consider the value which he has received. In some jurisdictions, damage for misrepresentation is measured by the difference between what the plaintiff received and what the defendant told him he would be receiving (benefit of the bargain theory). In this case, that would be $250,000 less $600, or $249,400. In other jurisdictions, the damage is measured by the difference between what the plaintiff paid and what he actually received (out of pocket theory). In this case, that would be $225,000 less $600 or

$224,400. **D** is, therefore, correct.

A and **C** are incorrect because they ignore the value of what Barton actually received. **B** is incorrect because it describes a rescission remedy, which may be available in a claim for breach of contract, but is not available in this tort claim for damages.

127.   **D**   Intentional infliction of emotional distress requires intentional, outrageous conduct which results in severe mental suffering. Since Pamela did not experience any mental injury, Jason is not liable to her for this tort.

Conduct is "outrageous" if it exceeds all bounds normally tolerated by decent society and is calculated to cause mental suffering. Conduct is "calculated to cause mental suffering" if suffering in the mind of a reasonable person is an almost inevitable result. Jason's conduct probably was both. **A** and **B** are incorrect, however, because Pamela sustained no mental injury. Outrageous conduct is "intentional" if the defendant desired or knew with substantial certainty that it would result in mental suffering in the plaintiff. **C** is incorrect because Jason might have had such a desire or knowledge, even though his motive was to play a joke.

128.   **D**   A seller of products owes her customers the duty to act reasonably. If it would be reasonable to inspect a product before selling it, then the druggist owes his customers a duty of doing so.

A, B, and **C** are overinclusive statements. Since some of the harmful side effects or defects associated with a particular drug might be unknown even to the reasonable druggist, a druggist cannot be said to have a duty to know them all. [*Note:* A druggist who sells a defective drug may be held strictly liable for damages which result. This is because strict liability is not based on fault, however, and does not justify the conclusion set forth in **C**.]

129.   **D**   Persons engaged in a concert of action are regarded as members of a joint enterprise. As such, they are vicariously liable for torts committed by other members of the enterprise. Thus, Anson and Baker may each be held liable for the other's tort.

To recover against either or both of them, Pauling need prove only that his injury was caused by the negligence of some member of the enterprise. **A** is, therefore, incorrect. **B** suggests that one thing cannot be a cause of harm if some other thing is. Since any effect may have more than one cause, **B** is incorrect. **C** is incorrect because nothing can be a legal cause of harm unless it is a factual cause of that harm.

130.   **D**   Negligence does not result in liability unless it was a proximate cause of damage. Although Laird's failure to commence Pattie's action against Dr. Oncol was probably negligent, no liability will result unless Laird's negligence was a proximate cause of damage. If Pattie would have lost her lawsuit against Dr. Oncol anyway, Laird's failure to institute it did not result in damage, since Pattie lost nothing as a result. If Dr. Oncol's use of HLP did not result in damage to Pattie, Dr. Oncol would not have been liable to her even if her conduct was negligent. If HLP saved Pattie's life at the expense of her eye, it probably did not result in damage, since what Pattie gained from its use exceeded what she lost. This means that Pattie would have lost her lawsuit against Dr. Oncol, and

that Laird's failure to assert it did not result in damage.

A is incorrect because even an inexperienced lawyer is required to act as the reasonable attorney. Laird's honest belief is no defense unless the reasonable attorney would have held it. **B** and **C** are therefore incorrect.

131.　**C**　　Under pure comparative negligence statutes, a plaintiff's recovery in a negligence action is diminished in proportion to the plaintiff's fault, but is not barred by the plaintiff's own negligence. Thus, Nellie would be entitled to recover part of any damages which she sustained as a result of Dalton's conduct if Dalton's conduct was unreasonable.

In most jurisdictions, a landholder owes a duty of reasonable care to an invitee, but owes no duty of reasonable care to a trespasser. For this purpose, an invitee is one whose presence confers an economic benefit on the landholder, and a trespasser is one who enters without permission. Since Nellie's use of Dalton's pool was consideration for valuable services which she rendered, she was an invitee. Under the "attractive nuisance" doctrine, a trespassing child may be entitled to reasonable care, but it is inapplicable here because Nellie was an invitee rather than a trespasser. **A** and **B** are, therefore, incorrect. If Nellie's conduct was unreasonable, the amount of her damages would be diminished accordingly. The language of option **D** may suggest defenses based on comparative negligence and on assumption of the risk. If it suggests a comparative negligence defense, it is incorrect because in a pure comparative negligence system the plaintiff's recovery is diminished in proportion to her own fault but is not barred completely. In most jurisdictions, assumption of the risk is a complete bar to recovery by the plaintiff. A plaintiff assumes the risk when s/he voluntarily encounters a risk of which she knows. The knowledge requirement is subjective, meaning that unless the plaintiff herself was aware of the risk, the fact that the reasonable person would have been is irrelevant. **D** is also incorrect for this reason, and because the facts indicate that Nellie dove in without looking and was, thus, unaware that the pool was empty.

132.　**C**　　Since Paulette entered without PALCO's permission, she was a trespasser. Ordinarily, a landholder owes trespassers, even if they are children, no duty of reasonable care with respect to dangerous conditions of the premises. A trespassing child may be entitled to reasonable care, however, if it was foreseeable that children would trespass, and it was foreseeable that a child who trespassed would be injured, and if the child was too young to comprehend the danger. Thus, if Paulette was old enough to comprehend the danger associated with an attempt to climb the pole, PALCO owed no duty of reasonable care to protect her against it. Although a minority of jurisdictions holds that a landholder owes a duty of reasonable care to all who enter, **C** is correct because it is the only argument listed which could provide PALCO with an effective defense in any jurisdiction.

A is incorrect because under the rule stated above, a duty of reasonable care may be owed to a trespassing child. The fact that no child had ever before attempted to climb the pole would not prevent the rule from being applied if it was foreseeable that a child would do so in the future. **B** is, therefore, incorrect. **D** is incorrect because even if PALCO could not repair the fence, there may have been other steps which the reasonable person in PALCO's position would have taken to prevent the danger which resulted in Paulette's injury.

133.   **B**   Praxton's lawsuit may be founded either on negligence or upon strict products liability. Negligence involves unreasonable conduct. If the explosives were properly labeled, Explo's conduct was not unreasonable. Strict liability is imposed only if the product which caused harm left the defendant in a defective condition. A product may be defective because of the way in which it is labeled, but if the labels were properly affixed when the cases left the Explo plant, the product was not defective at the time it left Explo's hands.

                  A is incorrect because strict liability may be imposed even though the defendant acted reasonably. **C** is incorrect because the negligence of an Explo employee would be imputed to Explo. Although the storage of explosives is usually regarded as an ultra-hazardous activity, resulting in the imposition of strict liability upon one storing it, **D** would not furnish Explo with a defense, since the imposition of liability on Warehouse would not prevent liability from being imposed on Explo.

134.   **B**   Battery requires the intent to make a harmful or offensive contact *with another person.* If defendant believed plaintiff to be a horse, she lacked the requisite intent. **B** is therefore the scenario in which the defendant is LEAST likely to be liable.

                  A is incorrect since a child who intends to make an offensive (i.e., unauthorized) contact will be held liable if an offensive or harmful contact occurs as a result. If the child desired to strike plaintiff with the arrow, he intended an offensive contact. Since he struck her, an offensive contact occurred. If the belief of the defendant in **C** was reasonable, he would be privileged by consent. There is no fact indicating that such belief was reasonable, however. If the belief of the defendant in **D** was reasonable, he would be privileged by self-defense. There is no fact indicating that such belief was reasonable, however.

135.   **D**   Misappropriation of identity is an invasion of privacy which consists of the unauthorized use of the plaintiff's identity for a commercial purpose. Since Georgia used Frederick's name without his permission for the purpose of selling its product, it has committed this tort against Fredericks.

                  Although the truth of the statement made in the advertisements might justify its publication for some purposes, its use for a commercial purpose is not privileged. **A** is, therefore, incorrect. Although the protection of the First Amendment to the United States Constitution has been extended to commercial expression, it has not been extended to the unauthorized use of another's identity for a commercial purpose. **B** is, therefore, incorrect. **C** is incorrect because liability for misappropriation of identity does not depend on the foreseeability of the defendant's conduct.

136.   **A**   Tort liability may be imposed only for harm which resulted from intent, negligence, or any activity for which strict liability may be imposed. Since there is no indication that Fennel intended the harm, and since her activity was not an abnormally dangerous one, the only theory available to Perlman is negligence. Negligence is a breach of the duty of reasonable care. The duty exists if defendant's conduct creates a foreseeable risk to the plaintiff. Since the operation of a motor vehicle on a roadway creates foreseeable risks to persons owning property along the roadway, the operator of a vehicle owes a duty of reasonable care to such persons. The question of whether Fennel breached that duty

depends on whether Fennel acted reasonably.

A professional seller of products (i.e., a merchant) may be held liable for damage resulting from a defect in a product which s/he supplied, on theories of strict liability in tort or breach of the implied warranty of merchantability. Since Fennel did not supply the trailer, however, neither of these theories can be applied to her. Thus, the questions of whether the hitch was defective or Fennel was a merchant are not relevant. **B** and **C** are, therefore, incorrect. Although negligence liability is often made to depend on whether the reasonable person in the position of the **defendant** would have foreseen the harm, **D** is incorrect because it is never necessary that the harm be foreseeable to the **plaintiff**.

137. **A**   The old rule that "she who holds the land holds upward unto heaven" is no longer true. All jurisdictions agree that a flight over land is a trespass to the land only if it was below a certain altitude (although they frequently disagree about what that altitude is). Thus, unless Pauline can prove the altitude at which Flier hovered, she cannot establish a trespass.

B is incorrect because damage is not an essential element of an action for trespass to land. **C** is incorrect since an action for trespass is not one for invasion of privacy, but rather for invasion of the right to exclusive possession of realty. **D** is incorrect because even one whose possession is unlawful may sue for trespass.

138. **D**   A person entitled to possess a chattel who enters the realty of another for the purpose of recovering that chattel is privileged to make such entry, provided that she does so in a reasonable manner (and provided further that the chattel did not get onto the realty through any fault of her own). Chevan's entry onto Homer's realty was therefore privileged. Since Chevan's entry was privileged, Homer was not entitled to use force against her to defend his realty, and his use of such force constituted a battery.

A privilege to use force *against the wrongful dispossessor* of a chattel exists only when that force is used in hot pursuit of the dispossessor. **A** is incorrect, however, because hot pursuit is not a prerequisite to the privilege *to enter realty* to recover a chattel. **B** is incorrect because injury is not an essential element of battery. **C** is incorrect because a possessor of realty is privileged to use reasonable force to prevent a trespass to that realty.

139. **C**   An action for misrepresentation requires proof that the defendant made a statement which he knew was false, or (in some jurisdictions) which he should have known was false, for the purpose of inducing plaintiff's reliance, and that the plaintiff was damaged by his justified reliance on the statement. The facts given establish that Adjust made statements to Hudson for the purpose of inducing him to settle his claim. Hudson's independent consultation with Laird would at least create a jury question about whether Hudson was acting in reliance on Adjust's statements. The fact described in **I** would have to be proved, however, to establish that Adjust's statements were false, and to establish that Hudson's reliance on them led to damage. The fact described in **II** would have to be proved to show that Adjust had the necessary fault (i.e., that he knew or should have known that the statements were false).

140. **A**   [Warning: This question calls for the "LEAST" effective argument. In effect, this means

the one argument which could not be effective at all.] The fact that a tortfeasor was acting within the scope of employment might result in the imposition of vicarious liability upon the tortfeasor's employer, but would not relieve the tortfeasor himself of liability.

Misrepresentation liability requires that the plaintiff was damaged by his justified reliance on false assertions of fact made by the defendant. **B** might be an effective defense, because the irrebuttable presumption that everyone knows the law usually results in the conclusion that statements regarding the law are statements of opinion rather than assertions of fact. That the plaintiff "relied" on the defendant's statements means that the statements were a significant factor in the plaintiff's decision. Since Hudson did not believe Adjust, and did not decide to accept the settlement offer until Laird advised him that she did not think he would win, a jury could conclude that Adjust's statements were not significant factors in Hudson's decision to settle for $1,000. **C** might, therefore, be an effective defense. A plaintiff's reliance on defendant's statements is only justified if the reasonable person in plaintiff's position would have believed and relied upon those statements. Since settlement negotiations are adversarial in nature, there is some doubt about whether the reasonable person would have believed statements that his claim was not a valid one when made by a representative of his adversary. **D** might, therefore, be an effective defense.

141. **D**   Private nuisance may consist of an intentional and unreasonable interference with the plaintiff's right to use and enjoy his realty. Interference is intentional if the defendant is substantially certain that it will occur. Since Tweeter continued testing dog-whistles after Ken notified him that the testing procedure was interfering with Ken's business, the interference with Ken's use and enjoyment of land was intentional. The interference was not unreasonable, however, unless Tweeter's conduct would have interfered with ordinary use or enjoyment of Ken's realty. So, if Ken's damage resulted from an ultra-sensitive use of Ken's land, it would not be the result of an unreasonable interference. Since only dogs could hear the sound, and since most people are not in the business of keeping dogs, the argument in **D** might be successful. Of the arguments listed, it is the only one which could possibly be successful.

A is incorrect because even a lawful business may constitute a private nuisance if it is operated in a way which unreasonably interferes with the use and enjoyment of plaintiff's realty. **B** is incorrect because if a defendant's activity unreasonably interferes with plaintiff's use and enjoyment of his realty, the fact that the defendant was engaging in it before the plaintiff arrived is not alone sufficient to prevent that activity from being characterized as a nuisance. Since the intent requirement is satisfied by Tweeter's knowledge that his activity was interfering with Ken's use of his land, **C** is also incorrect.

142. **A**   An express warranty is a representation regarding a condition of the product sold. Liability for breach of express warranty is imposed on the warrantor, regardless of fault, if the product's failure to be what it was represented to be results in damage. If the label said that the product would not harm the skin, the fact that it harmed Perry's skin would be a breach of warranty.

Although liability may be imposed for the breach of an implied warranty of fitness for ordinary use (i.e., merchantability), express warranty liability requires some assertion of fact about the product. **B** is, therefore, incorrect. Liability for breach of express warranty is imposed on whoever made the warranty which was breached. A retailer who delivers a product makes whatever warranties are printed on its label. **C** is, therefore, incorrect. **D** is incorrect because liability for breach of express warranty is imposed without regard to fault.

143.   **A**   "Merchantable" means fit for ordinary use. Proof that Perry's allergic reaction was the only one which ever occurred indicates that it was an unusual one. If Perry's allergy was unusual enough to be regarded as extraordinary, the product may have been fit for ordinary use (i.e., by ordinary persons) although unfit for use by Perry. While a court might not come to this conclusion, **A** is the only fact listed which could possibly support Feather's defense.

Most jurisdictions hold all members of the chain of commercial product distribution liable for a condition of the product which breaches the implied warranty of merchantability. **B** is, therefore, incorrect. Although reasonable inspection may have revealed that the product was safe for persons with "normal" skin, **C** is incorrect for two reasons. First, warranty liability does not depend on unreasonable conduct by defendant; and, second, ordinary use may include use by persons with skin which is not normal. **D** is incorrect because government approval or compliance with government requirements does not prevent common law liability.

144.   **A**   As a general rule, the courts hold that the coming of a rescuer is foreseeable. This is what is meant by the well-known phrase, "Danger invites rescue." For this reason, one who unreasonably creates a danger to any human being — including himself — creates a risk to a potential rescuer as well, and owes a potential rescuer a duty of reasonable care. Thus, if Hubert's conduct was unreasonable, it was a breach of a duty he owed Sam.

B is based on an over-inclusive statement of law; a rescuer's right to collect from the person whom he rescued must be based either on the breach of duty to act reasonably, or on an implied contract, but is otherwise non-existent. An officious intermeddler is a person who acts without a legitimate reason. **C** is incorrect because a human life was at stake, giving Sam a legitimate reason to act. The rule which is characterized by the phrase "Danger invites rescue" makes **D** incorrect, because Sam's attempt to rescue Hubert is regarded as foreseeable for the reason given.

145.   **B**   Negligence is a failure to act reasonably in the face of a foreseeable risk. If it was not foreseeable that the contents of the package would cause harm to a passenger in her car, Carolyn's conduct with respect to the package could not have been negligent. Although it is not certain that a court would come to this conclusion, the argument in **B** is the only one listed which is supported by the facts.

A is incorrect because the rule limiting the duty owed to a licensee applies only to conditions of realty occupied by a defendant. Contributory negligence is unreasonable conduct by plaintiff which contributes to the happening of the accident. Since Harold could not have known that the contents of the package were caustic, there is no reason to conclude that his conduct was unreasonable. **C** is, therefore, incorrect. A plaintiff is said to have assumed the risk when he voluntarily encounters a known risk. **D** is incorrect because Harold did not know that the contents of the package were caustic, and touching it did not, therefore, constitute an encounter with a known risk.

146.   **A**   Strict liability in tort may be imposed upon a professional supplier of products who places a defective product into the stream of commerce. Since a tattoo artist does not sell tattoo needles to his customers, he does not place them in the stream of commerce, and cannot be held strictly liable for damage which results from his customer's contact with them.

B is incorrect because strict liability is imposed regardless of fault and therefore may be imposed on a defendant although s/he did not exercise any control over the quality of the product. A plaintiff assumes a risk when she knows of it and voluntarily encounters it. Although Tolliver informed Preston that the process was likely to be a painful one, there is no indication that Preston knew that the needle would break off in her skin. **C** is, therefore, incorrect. Strict liability may be imposed upon the supplier of defective products, without regard to whether those products would be dangerous without the defect (i.e., inherently dangerous). **D** is, therefore, incorrect.

147.   **C**   False imprisonment consists of the intentional confinement of plaintiff. Confinement is an overcoming of the plaintiff's will to leave in a manner which would overcome the reasonable person's will to leave. Since the reasonable person usually obeys the directions of a police officer, Osman's words would have been sufficient to overcome the reasonable person's will to leave. For this reason, if Osman's language overcame Stroll's will to leave, it confined him.

A is incorrect because if it was reasonable for Stroll to believe that an attempt to leave would result in some harm to him, then he was confined even though no physical barriers prevented him from getting out of the police car. **B** is incorrect because Osman's assertion of legal authority and threatening language would have made any protest by Stroll a futile — and thus unnecessary — gesture. **D** is incorrect because damage is not an essential element of false imprisonment.

148.   **B**   A defendant owes a duty of reasonable care to a plaintiff if the defendant's conduct creates a foreseeable risk to that plaintiff. A foreseeable risk is a danger that the reasonable person would anticipate. If Carter's conduct created no foreseeable risks to persons in Merced Hospital, Carter did not owe such persons a duty of reasonable care and could not be held liable to them for negligence.

The intervening act of a third person may be a superseding cause of harm, relieving the original wrongdoer of liability for plaintiff's injuries. This is so, however, only if the intervention was unforeseeable. **A** is incorrect because the negligence of a surgeon is usually regarded as foreseeable. **C** is similarly incorrect because even aggravated negligence may be foreseeable. Since any result may have several causes, the fact that the scars were caused by the conduct of Dr. Hoffman does not establish that they were not also caused by the negligence of Carter. **D** is, therefore, incorrect.

149.   **B**   There can be no liability for making defamatory statements unless those statements are false. The United States Supreme Court has held that statements of opinion cannot be false because there is no such thing as a false idea. Statements which are expressions of

the writer's feelings regarding subjective matters are statements of opinion. Since the quality of Shea's writing is a subjective matter, Murphy's statements are opinions.

A media defendant may be held liable for defaming a public figure if the defamatory statements were made with actual malice. **A** and **C** are, therefore, incorrect. Although a business person may be privileged to compete by making unflattering reference to his competitor's products, **D** is incorrect because the privilege is qualified by the requirement of good faith.

150. **C**   Under the doctrine of private necessity, a defendant is privileged reasonably to invade the property rights of another in the face of an emergency which threatens life or property and requires immediate action. Since Patterson was obviously faced with such an emergency, his landing was privileged if it was reasonable. In determining whether an entry onto the land of another was reasonable, courts usually compare the importance of what the defendant was trying to protect with the importance of the right which the defendant invaded to protect it. Since Patterson was trying to protect his life and since his entry caused no damage, the landing was probably a reasonable invasion of Contemporary's rights and privileged by private necessity. Although a defendant whose entry is privileged by private necessity is required to pay for any actual damage which resulted from his entry, Patterson will not be required to pay damages since his entry caused no harm. **C** is correct for this reason and because it is the only argument listed which could possibly provide Patterson with an effective defense.

A is incorrect because the reasonableness of the entry depends on the above comparison, and not on the foreseeability of the emergency which required it. **B** is incorrect because it is based on an inaccurate interpretation of the facts. Since Patterson deliberately chose to land his plane on the parking lot, he "intended" his entry. Although D would show that Marvelco is liable for damages, it is incorrect because Marvelco's liability would not free Patterson from responsibility.

151. **A**   One who supplies a product is strictly liable for damage which results from a defect in the product which existed at the time the product left that supplier's hands. Since the fuel was contaminated before it left the Marvelco refinery, a finding that the contaminants made the fuel defective would result in the imposition of strict liability upon Marvelco. Strict liability in tort may be imposed for the benefit of any plaintiff on whom the effect of defendant's product was foreseeable. Since an airplane which falls from the sky might damage any person under it, the Contemporary Art Museum falls into this category.

B and **C** are incorrect because strict liability does not depend on whether the defendant's conduct was reasonable. **D** is incorrect because privity is not an essential element of strict products liability.

152. **C**   Marvelco owed Patterson a duty of reasonable care since it was foreseeable that he would be affected by their product. Since negligence is a breach of the duty of reasonable care, Marvelco's failure to discover what would have been revealed by a reasonable inspection is negligence.

Conversely, if Marvelco did not act unreasonably, the fact that its product was unreasonably dangerous would not result in liability for negligence. **A** is, therefore, incorrect. **B** is incorrect because the sale of contaminated fuel is not unreasonable unless the seller knows or should know that the fuel is contaminated. A product which defeats the reasonable expectations of the reasonable consumer is defective. **D** is incorrect, however, because negligence liability is not imposed unless the defendant acted unreasonably.

153.   **C**   A defendant is liable only for harm caused by his conduct. Conduct is a cause of harm only if the harm would not have occurred without that conduct. If Pringle's harm would have occurred without Ansel's conduct, Ansel's conduct could not have been a cause of Pringle's harm.

Although the violation of statute is relevant to the issue of negligence if the statute was designed to protect persons like plaintiff against risks like that which produced plaintiff's harm, **A** would not be an effective defense for two reasons. First, the fact that the statute was designed to protect schoolchildren does not prove that it was not also designed to protect automobile passengers. Second, even if the statutory violation is not relevant to the issue of negligence, Pringle might succeed in establishing common law negligence (i.e., that Ansel failed to act reasonably). An intervening cause of harm may be a superseding cause which shifts responsibility from the original wrongdoer to the intervenor, but only if the conduct of the intervenor was unforeseeable. Since the negligence of motorists is a common occurrence, Baker's negligence was probably foreseeable. **B** and **D** are, therefore, incorrect.

154.   **C**   Negligence is a breach of the duty to act reasonably. Since it is given that Baker was driving unreasonably, the question of whether Baker's unreasonable conduct was *negligence* depends on whether she owed Pringle a duty to drive reasonably. A defendant owes a plaintiff a duty of reasonable care if defendant's conduct creates a foreseeable risk to the plaintiff. If it was likely that collision with a stationary object would result in injury to Pringle, then Baker owed Pringle a duty to act reasonably to avoid such a collision.

Since a collision with any stationary object was likely to have the same result, it is not necessary that the presence of Ansel's parked car specifically could have been anticipated. **A** is, therefore, incorrect. Since any harm can have several causes, and since each person whose negligence proximately caused harm may be held liable for the full amount of the damage, neither **B** nor **D** would affect the outcome of Pringle's claim against Baker. **B** and **D** are, therefore, incorrect.

155.   **B**   Since Wonder and Tudor were found to be jointly and severally liable, the plaintiff can collect the entire amount of his judgment from either of them, or from both of them in any combination. Under the pure comparative negligence statute which existed in the jurisdiction, Preston's judgment should be for the amount of his damages, diminished in proportion to his own fault. Since Preston's injury was found to have resulted 20 percent from Preston's own negligence, his judgment should be for $100,000 less 20 percent, or $80,000.

A is incorrect because it does not diminish Preston's recovery in proportion to his fault. **C** is incorrect because joint tortfeasors are jointly and severally liable. In an "all or nothing" contributory negligence jurisdiction, a plaintiff who was contributorily negligent will receive nothing, even though the defendant may have been negligent as well. Under the "pure comparative negligence" statute given, however, Preston's recovery is not completely barred by his negligence. **D** is, therefore, incorrect.

156. **B** Under the given "pure comparative negligence" statute, Preston's damage should be diminished by 20 percent, since 20 percent of his injury resulted from his own negligence. Under the collateral sources rule, applied in most jurisdictions, money which the plaintiff has received from collateral sources (i.e., those other than tortfeasors) is not relevant to his rights against tortfeasors who caused his injury. The insurance money which Preston received was from a collateral source, and should, therefore, not play any role in determining the damages.

A, C, and **D** are, therefore, incorrect.

157. **A** A person is liable for damage which was proximately caused by his negligence. Negligence is the breach of a duty of reasonable care which the defendant owes the plaintiff. A defendant owes a plaintiff a duty of reasonable care if the defendant's conduct creates a foreseeable risk to the plaintiff. A court might find that Barrera created a foreseeable risk to other users of the road by encouraging Capewell to drive when he knew Capewell was drunk, and that encouraging Capewell to drive was unreasonable in view of Barrera's knowledge that Capewell was drunk. If a court came to this conclusion, it would find that Barrera was negligent. While it is not certain that a court would so conclude, it is clear that *if* Barrera's negligence was a proximate cause of Austin's injuries, Barrera would be held liable for the resulting damage.

An intervening cause of harm is a causal force which occurred after the defendant's conduct. Some intervening causes are classified as superseding causes, others as concurring causes. Neither expression can be applied to the defendant's conduct, however, since by definition the defendant's own conduct could not be an intervening cause. For this reason, both **B** and **C** are incorrect. People are not ordinarily under any duty to control the conduct of other persons. **D** is incorrect, however, since Barrera could be liable for his own negligence in encouraging Capewell to drive while drunk.

158. **D** Contributory negligence is unreasonable conduct by the plaintiff without which his injury would not have occurred. Since Barrera would not have been injured if he had not accepted a ride from Capewell, and since doing so was obviously unreasonable, Barrera was contributorily negligent. **I** is, therefore, an effective argument in Capewell's defense. Assumption of the risk occurs when plaintiff voluntarily encounters a known risk. Since Barrera knew that Capewell was drunk and voluntarily rode with him, Barrera assumed all the risks which normally accompany riding in a car driven by a person who is drunk. **II** is, therefore, an effective argument in Capewell's defense.

159. **D** Trespass to chattel occurs when the defendant intentionally interferes with plaintiff's possessory interest in a chattel, causing damage. Although Capewell damaged Austin's car by colliding with it, he cannot be held liable for trespass to chattel unless he had the necessary intent. In a trespass to chattel case, intent means a desire or knowledge that the particular chattel involved would be affected by the defendant's volitional act. Thus, unless Capewell wanted (i.e., desired) to collide with another car or knew that such a collision would occur, he could not have had the intent necessary to make him liable for

trespass to chattel.

While the foreseeability of a risk is relevant to negligence liability, it does not satisfy the requirements of intent. **A** and **B** are, therefore, incorrect. The intentional torts require desire or knowledge that a particular consequence will result from the defendant's act. **C** is incorrect because a desire to perform the act which happened to lead to a particular consequence is not enough to satisfy this requirement.

160. **D**   Invasion of privacy by public disclosure of private facts consists of publishing offensive and previously unknown facts about the plaintiff. The United States Supreme Court has held, however, that First Amendment guarantees of free expression prohibit imposing liability for the publication of facts which are already matters of public record. The Court said that this rule applies even to facts which are not commonly known, since the press often serves as eyes and ears for a public too busy to search public records for itself.

A and **B** are incorrect for the above reason. **B** is also incorrect because a privilege to publish information about one who is involved in a matter of public interest may exist even though that person is not a public employee. **C** is incorrect because virtually all of the cases imposing liability for this tort have involved publication of the truth. Although publication of the truth cannot lead to liability for defamation, publication of private facts which are not newsworthy may result in liability when it would offend the reasonable person, even if those facts are true.

161. **A**   Tortious appropriation of identity is committed by making commercial use of plaintiff's name, likeness, or identity without her permission. It has been repeatedly held, however, that newsworthy publications about the plaintiff do not constitute commercial use, and therefore cannot result in liability for this tort. It has also been held that information may be regarded as "newsworthy" for this purpose, even though the group to which it is of interest is a limited one.

Since the use of a non-celebrity's identity might be put to commercial gain (e.g., the photograph of an unknown but muscular person in an advertisement for exercise equipment), it is not necessary that the plaintiff be a public figure. Many of the cases imposing liability for this tort have involved plaintiffs who were not celebrities. **B** is incorrect for this reason, and because every article of interest to a publication's readers enriches the publisher by increasing the demand for its product. Although the publication of facts which are contained in public records is protected by the First Amendment, the *commercial* use of such information is not necessarily protected. For this reason, although **C** would be an effective defense against a claim of public disclosure, it is not necessarily an effective defense against a claim of appropriation. The United States Supreme Court has indicated that liability for false light privacy invasions cannot be imposed without a showing of actual malice, but no such requirement exists for the tort of appropriation. **D** is, therefore, incorrect.

162. **C**   Trespass to land consists of intentional unauthorized entry on realty possessed by the plaintiff. There is no requirement of damage. Since Perkins' complaint gave Blocko knowledge that dust from its operation was settling on the cabin, and since Blocko thereafter continued operating as it had been, the necessary intent is present (i.e., Blocko

was substantially certain that entry would occur). Some cases have held that the settling of dust constitutes a tangible entry on affected realty; other cases have held that it does not. For this reason, it is not certain that a court would find that a trespass occurred. Of all the theories listed, however, trespass to land is the only one which might possibly result in a judgment for Perkins.

Invasion of privacy by intrusion involves an interference with the plaintiff's interest in solitude, and requires some kind of prying into plaintiff's affairs or private life. This did not occur here. Other privacy theories — appropriation, public disclosure, false light — are not even remotely applicable. **A** is, therefore, incorrect. Unlike trespass which requires no damage, nuisance liability is imposed only where the plaintiff has sustained some substantial harm. An individual may assert a *public* nuisance claim only if the harm which she sustained differed from that sustained by the general public. **B** is incorrect for these reasons. An ultra-hazardous activity is one which necessarily involves a serious risk of harm which cannot be eliminated by acting reasonably. Since there are no facts indicating that the use of unbagged cement is such an activity, **D** is incorrect.

163. **D** Damage is an essential element of a negligence action. There are circumstances under which a plaintiff's mental suffering, although unrelated to physical injury, may be regarded as damage. Mere annoyance, however, is probably not damage sufficient to justify recovery for negligence. While it is not certain that this argument would defeat the claim of Perkins, **D** is the only argument listed which could possibly lead to a judgment for Blocko.

The reasonableness of a defendant's conduct is ordinarily determined by weighing the risks which it creates against the benefits which it confers. The argument set forth in **A** is not an effective defense, however, because it considers only the benefit resulting from the use of unbagged concrete without balancing it against the resulting risks. **A** is, therefore, incorrect. Conduct is a factual cause of any result which would not have occurred without it. Since Perkins would not have experienced annoyance if Blocko had not used unbagged cement, the use of unbagged cement was a factual cause of Perkins' annoyance. **B** is, therefore, incorrect. A plaintiff assumes a risk when she knows of it and voluntarily encounters it. **C** is incorrect because there is no indication that Perkins' encounter with the dust was voluntary.

164. **D** When tortfeasors are jointly and severally liable, a plaintiff is entitled to collect all her damages from any one of them (i.e., "severally"), or to collect her damages from them together (i.e., "jointly") in any combination whatsoever. Since the court held Company, Allen, and Boren to be jointly and severally liable to her, Pachter is entitled to collect 100 percent of her damages from Allen if she chooses to do so.

A, B, and **C** are, therefore, incorrect. (*Note:* Comparative negligence statutes determine the effect of the plaintiff's fault. Since the jury found the plaintiff to be free of fault, the existence of a comparative negligence statute is irrelevant. Statutory and common-law contribution systems give joint tortfeasors certain rights against each other but do not affect a plaintiff's right to collect from them jointly and/or severally.)

165. **D** The doctrine of "respondeat superior" makes an employer vicariously liable to a plaintiff for torts committed by an employee acting within the scope of employment. But the

concept of indemnity may shift the burden of payment from the one who actually did pay to the one who should have paid. Therefore, an employer who has been required to pay for a tort committed by an employee is entitled to complete indemnity (i.e., repayment) from the employee.

The concept of vicarious liability determines a plaintiff's rights against a tortfeasor's employer, but does not determine the rights of that employer against its employee. **A** is, therefore, incorrect. When parties are found to be jointly and severally liable to a plaintiff, the plaintiff may collect all her damages from any one of them or from all of them in any combination whatsoever. For this reason one of the joint tortfeasors may be required to pay more than its fair share of the plaintiff's damages. After this happens, most jurisdictions allow the one who has paid to seek partial repayment from the others so that each ends up paying a fair share. The majority of jurisdictions apply the equal apportionment approach, determining fair shares by dividing the amount paid by the number of joint tortfeasors (treating an employee and employer who is vicariously liable for his tort as a single unit for this purpose.) In these jurisdictions, joint tortfeasors who pay more than their fair share are said to seek "contribution." Other jurisdictions apply the apportionment of fault approach, basing the determination of fair shares on the relative fault of the joint tortfeasors. In these jurisdictions, joint tortfeasors who pay more than their fair share are said to seek "partial indemnity." **B** and **C** are both incorrect, however, because all jurisdictions recognize that a party who pays only because he is vicariously liable for the tort committed by another person is entitled to complete indemnity from that person. (***Note:*** If Company succeeds in receiving full indemnity from Allen, the equitable concept of subrogation would enable Allen to stand in Company's shoes for the purpose of recovering contribution or partial indemnity from Boren. This is not relevant to the question asked, however.)

166. **C**   That joint tortfeasors are "jointly and severally liable" means that the plaintiff may collect all of her damages from either of them or from both of them in any combination. Obviously, however, the fact that there are multiple tortfeasors does not entitle a plaintiff to collect her damages more than once. Since Aspen and Botkin were jointly and severally liable to Peckham for $100,000, Peckham is entitled to collect $100,000 from either or both of them in any combination. Since Peckham has already received $10,000 from Aspen, she is entitled to collect the remaining $90,000 from Botkin.

A and B are incorrect because a statute basing contribution on apportionment of fault affects the rights which joint tortfeasors have against each other, but does not affect their joint and several liability to the plaintiff. **D** is incorrect because Peckham has already received $10,000 from Aspen, and to allow her to collect an additional $100,000 from Botkin would result in her collecting her damages more than once.

167. **D**   Until recently, most states which recognized a right of contribution between joint tortfeasors based their contributive shares on a system of equal apportionment. This meant that where there were two joint tortfeasors, each contributive share was 50 percent, regardless of their proportionate fault. Recently, statutes in several jurisdictions have provided that contribution shall be based on apportionment of fault. Although the plaintiff can still collect her judgment from either of them or from both of them in any combination, as between themselves, their contributive shares will be in proportion to their fault. Thus Peckham could collect $100,000 from Aspen. After paying this sum, how-

ever, Aspen is entitled to contribution from Botkin in a sum proportionate to Botkin's fault. Since Botkin was 60 percent at fault, Aspen is entitled to collect 60 percent of what he paid, or $60,000.

A is incorrect because the jurisdiction recognizes a right of contribution. **B** is incorrect because the court found that Botkin was 60 percent at fault. **C** is incorrect because the given statute based contribution on apportionment of fault.

168. **C**   One who is negligent is liable for all harm proximately caused by that negligence. Negligence is a proximate cause of harm if that negligence was a factual cause of the harm, and if the harm was a foreseeable consequence of (i.e., legally caused by) the negligence. Since Baker's right leg would not have been broken if Foy had not negligently knocked her off her bicycle into the roadway, Foy's negligence was a factual cause of Baker's broken right leg. Thus if it was foreseeable that Baker would by struck again while lying in the roadway, Foy's negligence was a proximate cause of the injury which she sustained in the second accident.

The principle that "a defendant takes the plaintiff as he finds her" is sometimes used to make a defendant whose negligence proximately caused harm to the plaintiff pay for complications which would not have occurred if the plaintiff had not been supersensitive. (e.g., a defendant who negligently puts out the good eye of a one-eyed plaintiff might have to pay for total blindness, even though the defendant's negligence would have left an ordinary person with one good eye.) This principle might help to determine the extent of Salmi's liability to Baker. Since Foy's liability does not depend on Salmi's, however, **A** is incorrect. If Baker's right leg would not have been broken but for Salmi's negligence, Salmi's negligence was a cause of it. Since an injury might have several causes, however, the fact that Salmi's negligence was one of them does not prevent Foy's negligence from being one of them also, or prevent Foy from being liable for it. **B** is, therefore, incorrect. Foy's negligence was a factual cause of Baker's broken right leg, because it would not have been broken if Foy hadn't knocked her off her bicycle and caused her to be lying in the roadway. **D** is incorrect, however, because a defendant is not liable for an injury which was factually caused by his negligence unless that injury was a foreseeable result of the negligence (i.e., the negligence was a legal cause of it).

169. **A**   One who is negligent is liable for all harm proximately caused by that negligence. Negligence is a proximate cause of harm if that negligence was a factual cause of the harm, and if the harm was a foreseeable consequence of the negligence. Since Baker's right leg would not have been broken without Salmi's negligence, and since a broken leg is a foreseeable consequence of being run over by a car, Salmi's negligence was a proximate cause of Baker's broken right leg. **II** is, therefore, correct. Since Baker's left leg would have been broken without Salmi's negligence, Salmi's negligence was not a factual cause of it, and Salmi cannot be held liable for it. **I** is, therefore, incorrect.

170. **B**   Self-defense is a privilege to use reasonable force to protect oneself against a threatened tortious contact or confinement. Some jurisdictions hold that it is never reasonable to use deadly force when it is reasonably safe to retreat. But even in those jurisdictions which do not *require* retreat, Darrell's privilege is likely to turn on whether he knew or should have known that he could safely retreat. In connection with the privilege of self-defense, "reasonable force" means the force which would have appeared necessary to

the reasonable person in the defendant's situation. If Darrell knew or should have known that he could safely and easily retreat without sustaining harm, the reasonable person in his situation would probably not have considered it necessary to use any force at all in self-defense. On the other hand, if Darrell could not have known that he could safely and easily retreat, the reasonable person in his situation might have considered the use of a knife necessary because of the extreme danger facing a person who has a pistol pointed at him.

Deadly force may be reasonable in self-defense if the person using it is being threatened by what reasonably appears to be deadly force. Since Pack was threatening Darrell with a pistol, the use of a knife — even if it was deadly force — may have been privileged in self-defense. For this reason, **A** is incorrect. If Darrell initiated the aggression by slapping Pack, then Pack was privileged to use reasonable force to defend himself against the possibility of further blows by Darrell. Thus, if the force with which Pack threatened Darrell was reasonable, it would have been privileged, and, therefore, not tortious. If that was so, then Darrell would not have been privileged to use force to defend himself against it. (This reasoning accounts for the rule that an initial aggressor is not privileged to use force to defend himself against a reasonable response to his aggression.) If, however, Pack's use of a pistol was unreasonable (i.e., excessive force), it was not privileged by self-defense. Then, the contact with which Pack threatened Darrell would have been tortious, and Darrell would have been privileged to defend himself against it by using reasonable force. Thus, even if Darrell was the initial aggressor, he might have been privileged to use a knife to defend himself against Pack's use of a gun. **C** is, therefore, incorrect. Since reasonable force depends on what the reasonable person in the defendant's situation would have considered necessary, Darrell's privilege depends on how *Darrell* perceived or should have perceived the threat with which he was confronted. Whether or not *Pack* knew that the pistol was loaded, Darrell's use of a knife might have been reasonable if *Darrell* believed that the pistol was loaded. **D** is, therefore, incorrect.

171. **D**   Negligence is the breach of a duty of reasonable care. In general, a defendant owes a plaintiff a duty of reasonable care if defendant's conduct creates a foreseeable risk to that plaintiff. Since it was obviously unreasonable for Castle to use steel which he knew to be of poor quality, he will probably be held liable to Page if he owed her a duty of reasonable care. He owed such a duty if his use of poor quality steel created an apparent danger (i.e., a foreseecable risk) to persons situated as Page.

If Castle was negligent, he is liable to Page if his negligence was a proximate cause of Page's injury. If Page's injury was brought about by a *superseding* (i.e., unforeseeable) intervening cause, Castle's negligence was not a proximate cause. On the other hand, if the injury resulted from a *concurring* (i.e., foreseeable) intervening cause, Castle's negligence was a proximate use. Thus, the fact that the presence of the gasoline truck was an intervening cause of harm is not, alone, sufficient to prevent Castle's conduct from being a proximate cause of that harm. **A** is, therefore, incorrect. Like any other intervening cause of harm, an intervening "act of God" may be a superseding cause if its occurrence was unforeseeable. Not every "act of God" is unforeseeable, however (e.g., April showers). Thus, the fact that the earthquake was an "act of God" is not, alone, sufficient to make it a superseding cause of harm. For this reason, **B** is incorrect. On the other hand, if the earthquake was unforeseeable — whether it was major or minor — its occurrence could be regarded as a superseding cause of harm, relieving Castle of liability. **C** is, therefore, incorrect.

172. **C** A defendant's conduct is a proximate cause of the plaintiff's harm if it was both a factual and legal cause of that harm. Conduct is a factual cause of harm if the harm would not have occurred without it. Since the truck would not have leaked gas if it had not been parked in front of Castle's construction site where it was struck by falling debris, Dacy's parking it there was a factual cause of Page's harm. Conduct is a legal cause of harm if the harm was a foreseeable result of it, and was not brought about by an unforeseeable intervention. Since the explosion would not have occurred if debris had not fallen onto the truck after Dacy parked it, the falling debris was an intervening cause of Page's harm. If that intervening cause was foreseeable, however, Dacy's conduct could still be regarded as a legal cause of the explosion. On the other hand, if the intervention of the falling debris was unforeseeable, Dacy's conduct would not be regarded as a legal cause of the explosion, and Dacy could not be held liable for the resulting damage. Whether Dacy could have anticipated that debris would fall and damage the truck cannot be determined from the facts, but **C** is the only argument listed which could possibly be effective in Dacy's defense.

A superseding cause of harm is an unforeseeable intervening cause. An intervening cause is something which happened after the defendant's conduct, and without which the accident would not have occurred. Although Castle's use of poor quality steel was a cause of Page's injury (because the injury would not have occurred without it), it preceded Dacy's conduct, and so was not an *intervening* cause. It could not, therefore, have been a superseding cause. For this reason, **A** is incorrect. The fact that the explosion would not have occurred if Hankin had not thrown a lit cigarette into the street proves that Hankin's conduct was a cause of Page's harm. The fact that Hankin's act occurred after Dacy's conduct makes Hankin's act an intervening cause. **B** is incorrect, however, because unless its occurrence was unforeseeable, the fact that there was an intervening cause is not sufficient to prevent Dacy's conduct from being a proximate cause of Page's injury. Since any result may have several proximate causes, it is never correct to conclude that one thing was not a proximate cause because another thing was. **D** is incorrect because Dacy's conduct and the earthquake could both have been proximate causes of Page's injury.

173. **A** Under the doctrine of respondeat superior, an employer is vicariously liable for torts committed by an employee acting within the scope of employment. At any given time, an employee is acting within the scope of employment if her conduct is likely to confer an economic benefit on her employer and if she is subject to the employer's right of control. Since Dacy's visit to her personal physician was not likely to confer an economic benefit on Gasco, she was not acting within the scope of her employment if she parked the truck for that purpose.

On the other hand, if she had been acting within the scope of employment, the fact that she violated a statute, or that she violated instructions from her employer, would not relieve Gasco of vicarious liability for her torts. **B**, **C**, and **D** are, therefore, incorrect.

174. **C** The law of torts knows only three possible bases of liability: intent, negligence, or strict liability. Since intent is desire or knowledge with substantial certainty that harm will occur, and since Mart did not desire or know that any person would be struck by the

door, no recovery is possible on an intent theory. Although strict liability is imposed on the sellers of defective products, strict liability is not available against Mart because Mart did not sell the product which injured Parker. The only remaining theory is negligence, which involves unreasonable conduct in the face of a duty of reasonable care. Since Parker entered the premises for the purpose of making a purchase, he is an invitee. The duty owed to an invitee is to keep the premises reasonably safe by making reasonable inspections and reasonable repairs. Thus, if a reasonable inspection would have disclosed the problem, then Mart was either negligent in not inspecting or negligent in failing to discover what a reasonable inspection would have disclosed.

A is incorrect because only a professional seller of products like the one which caused injury can be held strictly liable for defects in that product. The liability of a defendant does not depend upon the availability of remedies against others. Thus, even if the fact that Ingram was not negligent might leave Parker without a remedy, it would not affect the liability of Mart. **B** is, therefore, incorrect. A landholder owes an invitee a duty of reasonable care to keep the premises reasonably safe, while it owes a lesser duty to licensees and trespassers. For this reason, it might be relevant to determine whether Parker entered Mart's premises as an invitee. An invitee is one whose presence is likely to confer an economic benefit on the landholder, or one who has entered the premises in response to a public invitation. Supermarkets ordinarily invite the public (either expressly or impliedly) to enter their premises for the purpose of examining their wares. In addition, the courts usually hold that a person who is likely to buy confers an economic benefit by entering business premises, even if he does not actually make a purchase while there. For these two reasons, Parker was an invitee whether or not he made a purchase before leaving. **D** is, therefore, incorrect.

175. **A**   Although the manufacturer of a defective product may be held liable without fault to a person injured, it is necessary for the plaintiff to show that his injury was proximately caused by the product's defect. If there was a superseding intervening cause of the harm, the defect was not the proximate cause. An intervening cause of harm is a superseding cause if its occurrence was unforeseeable. Thus, if it was unforeseeable that the Ingram would disregard the warning, Ingram's conduct would be a superseding cause of Parker's injury. Although many cases have held that intervening negligence is foreseeable, many cases have held that when the intervention involves the disregard of a known risk, it is unforeseeable. For this reason, it is impossible to tell whether Ingram's intervening conduct would be found to be unforeseeable. Of all the arguments listed, however, **A** is the only one which could possibly be effective in Stepco's defense.

          B is incorrect because strict liability may be applied to make the manufacturer of a defective product liable without regard to whether it acted reasonably. **C** is incorrect because strict product liability may be imposed to benefit any injured person whose contract with the defective product was foreseeable, without regard to the existence of a business relationship between the defendant and plaintiff. **D** is incorrect for two reasons: first, there is no fact indicating that the reasonable person in Mart's position would not have selected Ingram to do the job; and, second, intervening negligence by a third party is not a superseding cause of harm unless it was unforeseeable.

176. **B**   Negligence is a breach of the duty to act reasonably. A defendant owes such a duty to a plaintiff when the defendant's conduct creates a foreseeable risk to the plaintiff. Since

the installation of an automatic door-opener creates obvious risks to future users of the device, the installer owes them a duty to install it in a reasonable manner. If Ingram failed to do so, he was negligent. Whether or not it was unreasonable to disregard the warning is probably a question of fact for the jury. The argument in **B** is the only one listed, however, which could possibly support Parker's claim.

When the defendant's conduct is unknown, the doctrine of res ipsa loquitur allows an inference that the defendant acted unreasonably to be established circumstantially by proof that the accident was one which would not ordinarily have occurred without negligence, and that the defendant was in exclusive control of the circumstances. It is inapplicable when the defendant's conduct was known and the question to be determined is whether that conduct was unreasonable. **A** is incorrect for this reason, and because there is no fact indicating that this kind of accident would not ordinarily occur without negligence by the installer. According to UCC section 2-314, every sale by a merchant implies a warranty that the product sold is fit for ordinary use (i.e., merchantable). **C** is incorrect, however, because Ingram did not sell the automatic door-opener, and, therefore did not impliedly warrant its fitness. The seller of a defective product may be held strictly liable for damage resulting from the product's defect. **D** is incorrect, however, because Ingram was not the seller of the automatic door-opener.

177. **C**   Battery is committed by intentionally causing harmful or offensive contact with the plaintiff. Since there was no contact with Pagan, he could not successfully maintain a battery claim.

A, **B**, and **D** are incorrect for the above reason. In addition, **A** is incorrect because the doctrine of transferred intent does not apply unless the defendant had a tortious intent, and there is no fact indicating that Cirque desired or knew (i.e., intended) any consequence which would be tortious. Use of the word "unless" is an additional reason why **D** is incorrect. As used in **D**, "unless" means that if Cirque knew that the lions would attack, Cirque would be liable to Pagan for battery. Since there was no contact with Pagan, however, this could not be correct.

178. **B**   False imprisonment is committed by intentionally confining plaintiff. For this purpose, "confining" means overcoming the plaintiff's will to leave. If Giles did not prevent Moira from leaving, he did not confine her and could not be liable to her for false imprisonment.

A is incorrect because damage is not an essential element of false imprisonment. Although Giles' conduct may have prevented Moira from obtaining physical custody of David, Moira cannot maintain an action for false imprisonment unless she herself was confined. **C** and **D** are, therefore, incorrect.

179. **C**   Intentional infliction of emotional distress requires an outrageous act by the defendant, committed with the intent to inflict mental suffering on the plaintiff, and which does inflict severe mental suffering. In this connection, "intent" means that the defendant was substantially certain that the plaintiff would experience suffering as a result of his act. If Giles was not certain that his conduct would cause Moira to experience mental suffering, he lacked the intent necessary to be liable for this tort.

A is incorrect because in the absence of the requisite intent, the fact that a plaintiff experienced mental suffering is not sufficient to result in liability. The fact that defendant's conduct was unreasonable, or that the reasonable person would have known that suffering would result from it, is not sufficient to result in liability, since intent is an essential element of this tort and since intent depends on what the defendant subjectively knew. **B** and **D** are, therefore, incorrect.

180.   **A**   Since the facts do not indicate that Daly intended contact with Chase or harm of any kind to Pagel, the only claim which could possibly succeed against him would be one founded on negligence. Negligence is a breach of the duty of reasonable care. Generally, a defendant owes a duty of reasonable care to a plaintiff only if his conduct created a risk to that plaintiff which was foreseeable to the reasonable person. Thus, if the reasonable person would not have expected (i.e., foreseen) harm to Pagel, Daly would have owed her no duty of reasonable care and could not be held liable to her for negligence. Many jurisdictions apply the "zone of danger" rule which holds that a plaintiff may not recover for mental suffering which she experienced upon seeing another person sustain a physical injury unless she was in the same zone of physical danger as the injured person. In those jurisdictions, Pagel could not succeed against Daly even if the harm to her was foreseeable. **A** is correct, however, because of all the additional facts listed it is the only one which could possibly result in a judgement for Pagel.

B is incorrect because the doctrine of transferred intent applies only when the defendant's intent was tortious to begin with. Since the facts do not indicate that Daly desired or knew with certainty that his car would strike Chase, he had no tortious intent. **C** is incorrect because there is no rule of tort law which transfers consequences or which is known as the "doctrine of transferred consequences." Liability for intentionally inflicting emotional distress requires outrageous conduct by the defendant. This tort also requires the intent to cause mental suffering, however. Since Daly lacked such intent, he could not be held liable for intentionally inflicting mental distress even if his conduct was outrageous. **D** is, therefore, incorrect.

181.   **C**   Negligence is the breach of a duty of reasonable care. In some jurisdictions, the duty which a landholder owes to a plaintiff who enters the land depends on the plaintiff's status as trespasser, licensee, or invitee. In other jurisdictions, the duty does not depend on the plaintiff's status. All jurisdictions agree, however, that a defendant does not owe a plaintiff anything more than reasonable care, no matter what the plaintiff's status. Since the lawn had recently been mowed and since the ladder was in plain view, it probably was reasonable for Owen to believe that Lewis saw it. If so, Owen's failure to warn Lewis about it probably was reasonable also, and, therefore, probably was not negligent. While it is not certain that a court would come to this conclusion, the argument in **C** is the only one listed which could possibly support Owen's defense.

The fact that Owen did not know with certainty that Lewis would be injured means that he did not intend her injury. **A** is incorrect, however, because negligence liability does not require intent or knowledge with certainty that harm will result. **B** is incorrect because a landholder's obligation to warn or protect others against dangerous conditions of his land may extend to conditions which he did not himself create. **D** is an incorrect statement of the law; in general a government employee entering on official business is at least a licensee, entitled to be warned of dangerous conditions known to the landholder and hidden from the licensee's view.

182. **A**   Under the "all-or-nothing" rule of contributory negligence, unreasonable conduct by a plaintiff is a complete bar to recovery. Since the ladder was in plain view, it was probably unreasonable (i.e., contributorily negligent) for Lewis not to see it. Although it is not certain that a jury would come to this conclusion, **A** is the only argument listed which could possibly provide Paynter with an effective defense.

B is incorrect because the special rules which limit the duty owed to trespassers protect only the landholder, and no one but he or a member of his household may successfully assert them in defense. **C** is incorrect because a defendant owes a duty of reasonable care to any person who may foreseeably be injured by his conduct, whether such persons are licensees of another or not. One whose negligence proximately causes an injury to another is liable for damages even though there were other causes of that injury. For this reason, **D** is incorrect.

183. **D**   Under the doctrine of *res ipsa loquitur*, an inference that the defendant acted unreasonably can be drawn from the facts that the injury involved was one which does not usually occur without unreasonable conduct and that the defendant was the only person whose conduct could have caused the injury (i.e., the defendant had exclusive control of the circumstances). If an expert witness testifies that surgeons do not usually leave instruments inside a patient unless they are acting unreasonably, Peck can rely on the inference established by *res ipsa loquitur* if she can show that Dr. Danh was the only person who could have left the instrument inside her. Since Danh was the only person who had ever performed surgery on Peck, Danh is the only person who could have left the instrument inside her.

A is incorrect because it is based on an inaccurate statement of law; there are many medical malpractice cases in which the plaintiff was permitted to rely on *res ipsa loquitur*. (Note: These frequently involve foreign objects which were left in the plaintiff's body during surgery). Ordinarily, in drawing an inference of negligence under the doctrine of *res ipsa loquitur*, a jury relies on what it knows about human experience to determine whether a particular accident is of a kind which does not usually occur without negligence. Because of its lack of specialized knowledge, a jury is not competent to decide whether the particular result of a professional's conduct is one which would not usually occur without negligence. Once a jury has heard testimony to that effect from an expert witness, however, it may base an inference of negligence on its decision about whether or not it believes that witness. This is a decision which a jury is uniquely competent to make. For this reason, **B** is incorrect. **C** is incorrect because *res ipsa loquitur* is not dependent on the existence of any "absolute duty," but rather on circumstantial evidence which justifies the inference that a particular defendant acted unreasonably.

184. **A**   In an "all-or-nothing" contributory negligence jurisdiction, a plaintiff whose own negligence contributed to the accident can not recover any damages for injuries which he sustained. Under pure comparative negligence statutes, a plaintiff's negligence does not bar his recovery, but results in a reduction of damages in proportion to his own fault. Since the jury found Walker's damage to be $100,000, and found Walker to be 20% at fault, Walker is entitled to collect $100,000 reduced by 20%. When two defendants are "jointly and severally" liable to the plaintiff, the plaintiff may collect the entire amount

of his judgment from either of them (several liability), or may collect it from both of them in any combination whatsoever (joint liability). Since the court found Ashby and Bloomfield to be jointly and severally liable to Walker, Walker can collect the full amount of his judgment from Ashby alone.

B is incorrect because of the "collateral source rule" which provides that money which a plaintiff receives from parties other than tortfeasors or their representatives is irrelevant in determining his damages. For this reason, the sum of $10,000 which Walker received from his own hospitalization insurer plays no part in determining the amount which he can collect from Ashby or Bloomfield. **C** is incorrect because the court found Ashby and Bloomfield to be jointly and severally liable to Walker as explained above. **D** is incorrect under the collateral source rule as explained above.

185. **D**   In general, there are only three potential bases for tort liability: intent, negligence, and liability without fault. Liability without fault is ordinarily imposed upon a person who knowingly engages in abnormally dangerous activities or who is a professional supplier of products. Since Darrin was neither, liability without fault cannot be imposed. Intentional tort liability is imposed upon a defendant who knew to a substantial degree of certainty that his act would harm the plaintiff. Unless Darrin *knew* that the stove would hurt someone, he cannot be liable for committing an intentional tort. Negligence is unreasonable conduct in the face of a risk about which the defendant should have known (i.e., a foreseeable risk). Unless Darrin *should have known* that his stove would injure someone, he cannot be liable for negligence.

Although liability without fault (i.e., strict liability) may be imposed upon a professional supplier who sells a defective product, **A** is incorrect because Darrin was neither a professional supplier of stoves nor did he sell the defective stove. If Darrin should have anticipated that a person would enter his cabin by mistake, he might have owed Perl a duty to act reasonably. **B** is incorrect, however, because there is no fact indicating that he breached that duty by acting unreasonably. It is often held that a landholder owes a trespasser no duty of reasonable care. Thus, if Perl was a trespasser at the time of the explosion, Darrin would probably not be liable to her for negligence. Even if she was not a trespasser, however, Darrin would not be liable unless he knew or should have known that the stove would injure someone. Perl's trespass is, therefore, not the *only* thing that would result in a judgment for Darrin. **C** is, therefore, incorrect.

186. **C**   Under the "but for" rule of causation, defendant's conduct is a cause of plaintiff's injury if the plaintiff's injury would not have occurred without it. Since Palco would not have been injured without Yeong's intoxication, and since Yeong would not have become intoxicated without Barney's conduct, Barney's conduct was a cause of Palco's injury.

A is incorrect for two reasons. First, given the facts it is uncertain whether Alfred's conduct was a substantial factor in making Yeong intoxicated. Second, even if Alfred's conduct was a cause of the harm (i.e., a substantial factor in producing it), Barney's conduct was also a cause of that harm. **B** is incorrect because the language of the statute ("... any person who sold said minor the alcohol which resulted in said minor's intoxication ...") indicates that liability depends on a causal relationship between the defendant's conduct and the minor's intoxication. Since Palco's injury would not have occurred without Yeong's intoxication, any cause of Yeong's intoxication must also have been a cause of

Palco's injury (see above explanation of "but for" rule). **D** is, therefore, incorrect.

187. **D**   Under the "substantial factor" rule of causation, defendant's conduct is a cause of a particular consequence if it was a substantial factor in bringing that consequence about. Conduct which would have produced a particular consequence all by itself was a substantial factor in producing that consequence even if other factors happened to combine with that conduct to bring the consequence about. Since either Alfred's conduct alone or Barney's conduct alone would have made Yeong intoxicated, each was a substantial factor in making Yeong intoxicated. Each was, therefore, a cause of Yeong's intoxication. Under the "but for" rule of causation, a condition is a cause of harm if the harm would not have occurred without that condition. Since Palco's injury would not have occurred had Yeong not been intoxicated, Yeong's intoxication was a cause of Palco's injury. Since the conduct of Alfred and Barney were causes of Yeong's intoxication, and since Yeong's intoxication was a cause of Palco's injury, the conduct of Alfred and Barney were causes of Palco's injury. For this reason, neither **I** nor **II** is correct.

188. **C**   Negligence is unreasonable conduct in the face of a foreseeable risk. If Brown acted reasonably in relying on Anderman's instructions, she could not have been negligent.

A plaintiff may be prevented from recovering for damages resulting from a defendant's negligence if the plaintiff "assumed the risk" by voluntarily encountering a risk of which he knew. **A** is incorrect because this concept applies only to the conduct of a plaintiff. **B** is incorrect because a defendant owes a duty of reasonable care to all persons who are placed at a foreseeable risk as a result of that defendant's conduct. Since it was foreseeable that Ocampo would hire a mover to bring furniture into the new house, Brown thus owed Myers a duty to act reasonably in building the house, and could be liable to Myers for breaching it. **D** is incorrect because a ritualistic protest is not sufficient to absolve a person of liability for the results of her conduct if that conduct is unreasonable.

189. **A**   The fact that an accident occurred is not enough to prove that Anderman was negligent, even if he could have avoided the accident by using two pillars. Negligence is unreasonable conduct. If Anderman's conduct was reasonable, it could not have been negligent. Since the facts are not sufficient to permit a conclusion as to whether or not Anderman's conduct was reasonable, it is not certain that a jury would be convinced by Anderman's contention. **A** is the only argument listed, however, which could possibly provide Anderman with an effective defense.

A defendant owes a duty of reasonable care to all persons who are placed at foreseeable risk as a result of that defendant's conduct. Since it was foreseeable that Ocampo would hire a mover to bring furniture into the new house, Anderman thus owed Myers a duty to act reasonably in designing the house, and could be liable to Myers for breaching it. **B** is, therefore, incorrect. The doctrine of "last clear chance" has become obsolete in most jurisdictions. All it ever did (and all it does in those jurisdictions in which it survives) is excuse a *plaintiff* from the consequences of his own contributory negligence. It was never an argument which a defendant would advance, because it never benefitted any party but a plaintiff. For these reasons, it is inapplicable to this problem, and **C** is incorrect. **D** is incorrect because the unreasonable exercise of professional judgement in making a decision is negligence (or malpractice) and may result in liability.

190.   **C**   The manufacturer of a product is strictly liable for damage which results from a defect in the product which existed at the time the manufacturer placed that product in the stream of commerce. In this connection, a product is defective if its condition would defeat the expectations of the reasonable consumer. Since a reasonable consumer would not expect liquor to contain poison, the liquor was defective. Since that defect existed when the liquor left Wheatstraw's factory, Wheatstraw is strictly liable for Prill's injuries.

        A is incorrect because strict liability is imposed regardless of the reason for the existence of the defect. **B** is incorrect because strict liability is applied for the benefit of any foreseeable plaintiff regardless of whether she was a purchaser, consumer or bystander. **D** is incorrect because strict liability (i.e., liability *without fault*) does not depend on the defendant's unreasonable conduct.

191.   **B**   Violation of a statute may establish the violator's negligence (or liability) in a particular case if the statute was designed to protect against the risk which led to the plaintiff's harm. Prill was not hurt because Drinker was drunk, but because Drinker had been poisoned. (Note that the facts indicate that Drinker was driving reasonably.) If the statute was not meant to protect against the risk of drinking poison, then its violation would not be relevant in the case of an injury which resulted from drinking poison. Since poison could as easily be drunk in non-alcoholic drinks, it is unlikely that the statute in this case was designed to protect against drinking poison.

        A is incorrect because the language of the statute appears to prohibit the sale of alcohol to a person who is already intoxicated, without regard to how he got intoxicated. **C** is based on an inaccurate statement. Conduct is a cause of harm if that harm would not have occurred without the conduct. Since Drinker's death and the resulting accident would not have occurred if Drinker had not drunk the poisoned Old Wheatstraw liquor, service of the liquor was a cause of Prill's injuries. **C** is, therefore, incorrect. If an intervening cause of harm was unforeseeable, it may be called a superseding cause and relieve a defendant of liability by resulting in the conclusion that his conduct was not a "legal" or "proximate" cause of the injury. Causes which existed or occurred prior to the defendant's conduct are not intervening causes, however, and, therefore, cannot be superseding causes of harm. **D** is incorrect because Fuller's conduct preceded Barr's service of liquor to Drinker.

192.   **A**   Strict liability (i.e., liability without fault) may be imposed on one who engages in an extremely hazardous activity. In this connection, an activity is sufficiently hazardous to result in strict liability if it is not a common activity and necessarily involves a serious risk of harm which risk cannot be eliminated by reasonable care. While it is not certain that a court would come to this conclusion, **A** is the only option which could possibly be correct.

        Although the doctrine of *res ipsa loquitur* may permit an inference of negligence to be drawn from circumstantial evidence, it does not impose negligence liability on a defendant who was not negligent. Since the facts indicate that Rocketcorp acted reasonably, negligence liability should not be imposed. **B** is, therefore, incorrect. Although tort liability is sometimes limited by the concept of foreseeability, the amount of damage need not be specifically foreseeable so long as the type of damage is. **C** is, therefore, incorrect. **D** is incorrect because a type of harm may be foreseeable even though it never happened before (e.g., It is foreseeable that a person will die even though she has never died before.) The fact that no such damage had ever occurred in the past is, therefore, not sufficient to make that damage unforeseeable.

193. **C**   A manufacturer is strictly liable for injuries which result from a defect in its product if the defect existed when the manufacturer placed the product in the stream of commerce. Beltco will thus be strictly liable if the absence of an acceleration suppressor was a defect. A defect is a condition which would defeat the expectations of the reasonable consumer. Unless the belt truck is equipped with an acceleration suppressor, it will lurch forward if the belt idle is adjusted improperly. The reasonable consumer probably does not expect a vehicle to lurch forward when it is being used for its intended purpose. Since persons who maintain belt trucks frequently adjust the belt idle improperly, belt trucks will frequently lurch in the absence of an acceleration suppressor. Its absence, therefore, is probably a defect.

The absence of an acceleration suppressor was a factual cause of Plum's injury because Plum would not have been injured if the truck had been equipped with one. The fact that the injury would not have occurred without the subsequent acts of others (i.e., intervening causes) would not prevent Beltco from being liable unless those subsequent acts (i.e., intervening causes) were unforeseeable (i.e., superseding causes). Since humans are frequently negligent, the unreasonable conduct of Treetop and McCann may have been foreseeable. For this reason, **A** and **B** are incorrect. **D** is incorrect because it is based on an inaccurate statement. Sometimes the relationship between two persons makes one of them responsible for conduct of the other (i.e., conduct of one is imputed to the other). There is no relationship between McCann and Beltco which would result in such an imputation, however.

194. **A**   Negligence is unreasonable conduct in the face of a foreseeable risk. Thus, unless the risk which McCann created was foreseeable, it was not negligent for McCann to create it. Adjusting the belt idle improperly does not cause a belt truck to lurch if it is equipped with an accelerator suppressor. Thus, if belt trucks are usually equipped with acceleration suppressors, it might not be foreseeable that adjusting the belt idle improperly would cause a belt truck to lurch. If this risk was not foreseeable, McCann was not negligent in creating it. Although it is not certain that a jury would come to this conclusion, the additional fact listed in **A** is the only one which could possibly result in a judgement for McCann.

Under the "all-or-nothing" rule, a plaintiff whose own negligence contributed to the accident is prevented from recovering. **B** is incorrect, however, because there is no fact indicating that it was negligent for Plum to attempt to activate the belt while standing on the ground. **C** and **D** are incorrect because a defendant is liable for damage which was proximately caused by his negligence even though there are other causes or other parties who may also be liable.

195. **D**   Private nuisance involves a tortious invasion of the plaintiff's right to use and enjoy realty. Although the fumes invaded Fox's right to use and enjoy his realty, their emission was not a nuisance unless it resulted from liability-forming (i.e., tortious) conduct by

Kemco. Since Fox has alleged that Kemco's conduct was liability-forming in that it was negligent, liability will depend on whether Kemco's conduct was unreasonable (i.e., negligent). Ordinarily, in determining whether conduct is unreasonable, it is necessary to weigh the risks resulting from such conduct against the burdens of eliminating those risks. If the cost (i.e., the burden) of eliminating the fumes would drive Kemco out of business, a court might find that the burden was so much heavier than the risk which it would eliminate that it was not unreasonable for Kemco to continue emitting the fumes, and that Kemco therefore, was not negligent. While it is not certain that a court would come to this conclusion, **D** is the only argument listed which could possibly provide Kemco with an effective defense.

A is incorrect because nuisance requires an invasion of plaintiff's rights in realty, but does not require a physical invasion of the realty itself. In order for an individual to prevail in a claim for public nuisance, he must show that the harm which he sustained was substantially different from that sustained by the general public. **B** is incorrect, however, because no such showing is required in a claim for private nuisance. If Fox's claim were based on intent, it would be necessary for him to show that Kemco knew that its activity was interfering with his right. Since his claim is based on negligence, however, it is sufficient for him to show that such interference was foreseeable. **C** is, therefore, incorrect.

196. **A**   Public nuisance is a tortious invasion of some right of the general public. Ordinarily, a public nuisance action is brought on behalf of the general public as an entity, and may result in a judgment for damage and/or an injunction. An individual may bring a public nuisance action on his own behalf, but only by showing that the public nuisance which the defendant created caused the individual plaintiff to sustain harm so different from that of the general public that his damages would not be included in a judgment on behalf of the general public. Most jurisdictions hold that in such an action, the plaintiff's only remedy is a judgment for those damages. Since Sal's claim is for an injunction rather than for Sal's special damage, public nuisance is not an appropriate vehicle for it.

An activity which does not disturb anyone but a super-sensitive plaintiff is probably not a public nuisance, since it does not interfere with a public right. If an activity does disturb the general public, however, and is, therefore, a public nuisance, the fact that the plaintiff's damage resulted from a special sensitivity will not prevent him from recovering for that damage. (Note: This is the essence of the famous "eggshell skull" hypo in which defendant accidentally drops an object which strikes the head of a plaintiff whose skull is as thin as an eggshell. If it was not foreseeable that dropping the object would injure the ordinary person, defendant was not negligent in dropping it. But if it was foreseeable that dropping it would injure the ordinary person, then defendant was negligent in dropping it and would be liable for the full extent of plaintiff's injury even though the ordinary person in the plaintiff's shoes would not have sustained an injury as serious as that of the plaintiff.) **B** is, therefore, incorrect. A plaintiff "assumes the risk" when he voluntarily encounters a risk of which he has knowledge. Although assumption of the risk is a complete defense in many jurisdictions, **C** is incorrect because the claim was asserted on behalf of Sal, and Fox could not "assume the risk" for Sal. **D** is incorrect, because, although violation of statute sometimes helps to establish tort liability, compliance with statute does not ordinarily prevent a defendant from being liable in tort.

QUESTIONS
PRACTICE MBE — A.M. EXAM

PRACTICE MBE — A.M. QUESTIONS

1. Deakin was looking out through the open window of his house when he saw Thead knock down Elder, who was an old and feeble woman, and snatch her handbag. As Thead ran off with Elder's purse, Deakin grabbed a wooden board and jumped through his window. After chasing Thead for two blocks, Deakin caught up with him and struck him on the head with the wooden board. Deakin retrieved the purse and returned it to Elder. Thead subsequently died as the result of being struck by Deakin.

If Deakin is prosecuted for criminal homicide, his most effective argument in defense would be that he used force which

(A) Elder would have been privileged to use to defend herself.

(B) the reasonable person in Deakin's position would have used to defend Elder.

(C) the reasonable person in Elder's position would have used to defend her property.

(D) the reasonable person in Deakin's position would have used to prevent Thead's escape from a crime.

2. At the trial of an action brought by Pelton against Donco for damages resulting from breach of contract, Pelton's attorney called Wayman as a witness on Pelton's direct case. After Wayman was sworn, Pelton's attorney asked only one question: "Are you employed by Donco, the defendant in this case?" Wayman answered, "Yes." Pelton's attorney then said, "I have no further questions."

On cross-examination, Donco's attorney asked Wayman, "Do you have any personal knowledge of the contract which is the basis of this lawsuit?"

If Pelton's attorney objects to the question, which of the following would be the most effective argument in support of that objection?

(A) Donco may not impeach its own witness.

(B) The question is leading.

(C) The question is argumentative.

(D) The question goes beyond the scope of cross examination.

Questions 3-4 are based on the following fact situation.

After being informed that members of a college fraternity were engaged in the unlawful sale of cocaine, police officers obtained a warrant to search the fraternity house. While searching, the officers discovered Gina, a guest of one of the fraternity's members, sitting on a bed in a room of the house. Under the bed was a locked trunk. Inside the trunk, the officers found a box of cocaine. They immediately placed Gina under arrest for possession of cocaine and, upon searching her, found a plastic bag in her pocket containing marijuana. Subsequently charged with the unlawful possession of marijuana, Gina moved to suppress use of the marijuana as evidence against her.

3. Which of the following would be the prosecution's most effective argument in response to Gina's motion?

(A) Marijuana found in Gina's possession could properly be seized as fruit of the poisonous tree.

(B) Gina's proximity to the trunk gave the officers probable cause to believe that she was guilty of possessing cocaine.

(C) The officers searching the fraternity house were entitled to frisk all persons present to protect themselves against the possibility of physical attack.

(D) A warrant authorizing the search of specified premises permits the arrest of all persons present at the time the warrant is executed.

4. If it was the only one true, which of the following additional facts or inferences would be most likely to result in a granting of Gina's motion?

   (A) The officer who searched Gina was male.

   (B) Gina was not guilty of possessing cocaine.

   (C) Gina's arrest for possession of cocaine was not lawful.

   (D) The warrant for the search of the fraternity house was issued solely on the basis of hearsay.

5. Upon inheriting her Aunt's ranch, Sadler subdivided it into 1,000 separate numbered parcels of realty and offered them for sale. After inspecting a parcel which had no building on it, Bain and his attorney Lawler went to see Sadler in her sales office. After negotiation, Sadler accepted Bain's offer to purchase the parcel for $15,000. At Bain's request, Lawler prepared a contract of sale, using a printed form which Lawler had brought with her. While doing so, Lawler asked Sadler how to identify the parcel involved. Although its correct identification was "Parcel 241," Sadler inadvertently referred to it as "Parcel 341." None of them was aware of Sadler's error. As soon as Lawler finished preparing it, Sadler and Bain signed a contract which described the realty as Parcel No. 341.

   Although Parcels No. 241 and No. 341 were the same size, Parcel No. 341 had a valuable building on it which made it worth $80,000. Prior to the date set for closing, Sadler realized her mistake. She immediately informed Bain of the error. If Bain sues Sadler for an order directing her to convey Parcel No. 341 to him for $15,000, which of the following would be Sadler's most effective argument in defense?

   (A) Bain should have known that realty with a building on it was more valuable than realty without a building on it.

   (B) Bain selected Lawler to prepare the contract.

   (C) Parcel No. 341 was substantially more valuable than Parcel No. 241.

   (D) Both Sadler and Bain were mistaken about the identity of the parcel described in the contract.

6. A state law provides that no person may hold elective state office while acting as a practicing member of the clergy of any religious organization. Causton, a practicing member of the clergy of a religious organization known as the Church of the Lord, asked the state commissioner of elections to enter his name as a candidate for the office of state legislator. The commissioner advised Causton that under the state law described above, she could do so only if Causton resigned his position within the Church of the Lord.

   If Causton challenges the constitutionality of the state law on the ground that it violates the free exercise clause of the First Amendment, which of the following arguments best supports the conclusion that the statute is unconstitutional?

   (A) A state may not set qualifications for elective state office which are different from those for elective federal office.

   (B) The state may not set qualifications for practicing members of the clergy of religious organizations.

   (C) The statute creates political divisiveness along religious lines.

   (D) The statute discriminates against persons because of their religious affiliations.

7. Semon owned a wooden pier which jutted out into the ocean, and a restaurant located on that pier. The structure was supported by wooden pilings driven into the ocean floor. Although the bottom ends of the pilings were under water, the top ends protruded several feet above the water's surface. Because he wished to sell the property, Semon painted the pier, the restaurant and the exposed parts of the pilings that supported the structure.

   Palen, who was interested in purchasing the property, inspected the building and pier. He did not ask Semon about the condition of the pilings or inspect the parts which were beneath the surface of the water because the fresh paint on the pilings made them look relatively new. After purchasing the property, Palen learned that portions of the pilings below the surface of the water were rotten, and would require expensive repairs.

If Palen asserts a claim for damages against Semon, alleging that Semon's failure to disclose the rotten condition of the pilings below the surface of the water was a misrepresentation, the court is most likely to find for

(A) Palen, if Semon knew or should have known that portions of the pilings which were located below the surface of the water were rotten.

(B) Palen, because Semon painted the portions of the pilings which were above the surface of the water.

(C) Semon, because Palen did not ask Semon about the condition of the pilings.

(D) Palen, if knowledge that the pilings were rotten below the surface of the water would have prevented Palen from purchasing the property.

8. Santana, who was employed as a security guard, was required to carry a loaded pistol on the job. While traveling to and from his job, however, he kept the pistol unloaded. Driving to work one day, Santana's car was struck from behind by a car operated by Reger. In the discussion which ensued, Reger used language which Santana found offensive. At that point, Santana turned his back on Reger and attempted to walk away. Angry, Reger ran after Santana and slapped him in the face. Although Santana did not intend to shoot Reger, he pulled his pistol from its holster and began loading it, hoping that Reger would become frightened and leave him alone. When Reger saw Santana loading the pistol, he thought of running away, but was afraid that Santana would shoot him if he tried to do so. Drawing a switchblade knife from his pocket, Reger stabbed Santana in the chest. Reger was subsequently arrested and charged with assaulting Santana

with a deadly weapon.

If Reger asserts the privilege of self defense, he should be found

(A) guilty, because as the initial aggressor Reger had no privilege to use deadly force.

(B) guilty, if Reger could have successfully escaped in his car without being shot by Santana.

(C) not guilty, if Reger's fear of being shot by Santana was reasonable.

(D) not guilty, because Santana should have known that by loading his pistol he was inviting the use of deadly force by Reger.

9. Palma was a passenger on a motorcycle operated by Causey when it collided with an car operated by Daniel. As a result of the collision, Palma sustained injuries which required her hospitalization. Although Palma's hospital bills were high, they were paid in full by the Mutual Insurance Company under a policy which Palma had purchased previously. In a litigation by Palma against Daniel for negligence, a jury found for Palma in the sum of $50,000. Prior to the entry of judgment, Daniel's attorney made an appropriate motion asking the court to reduce the damage award by the amount which Palma had already received from Mutual Insurance Company.

The motion to reduce Palma's damage award should be

(A) denied, because the Mutual Insurance Company was not acting for any person liable to Palma for negligence.

(B) denied, because payment by the Mutual Insurance Company was not the result of a judicial determination.

(C) granted, because Palma should not be permitted to receive a double recovery.

(D) granted, because Daniel is entitled to partial indemnity.

10. Morefield operated a computer repair business,

servicing the computers of several large organizations with the assistance of her daughter Danbury. When Morefield decided to retire, she sold the entire business to Danbury. As part of the sale, she assigned to Danbury a written contract to repair and service all of Execuco's computers for a period of three years in return for a fixed monthly payment.

The day after her assignment to Danbury, Morefield notified Execuco about it by telephone. Because Execuco knew that Danbury had worked on his computers in the past, he consented to the assignment and orally agreed to release Morefield from all further obligation or liability under their contract. Execuco subsequently became dissatisfied with Danbury's service, however, and asserted a claim against Morefield for breach of contract.

If Morefield's only defense is that Execuco agreed to release her from all further obligation or liability under their contract, which of the following would be Execuco's most effective argument in response to that defense?

(A) Morefield is attempting to use parol evidence to contradict or modify the terms of an unambiguous written agreement.

(B) There was no consideration for Execuco's agreement to release Morefield of further obligation or liability under the contract.

(C) The agreement to release Morefield of further obligation or liability under the contract was not in writing.

(D) Morefield's delegation to Danbury and Execuco's agreement to release Morefield constituted an accord and satisfaction.

11. Schilling and Barnes were collectors of antique automobiles. On April 15, Schilling told Barnes that she was thinking of selling an antique Arrowhead automobile which she owned. Barnes said that she might be interested in buying it. After discussion, Barnes paid Schilling $100 in cash, and on April 15 Schilling signed a document which contained the following language:

For $100 and other good and valuable consideration, I hereby offer to sell my antique Arrowhead automobile to Barnes at a price of $5,000. If Barnes decides to purchase the vehicle, the $100 which I have received from her shall be applied to the purchase price. If Barnes does not decide to purchase the vehicle, I will keep the $100. I promise to hold this offer open until October 1.

On May 15, Barnes informed Schilling that she had decided to purchase the Arrowhead, but Schilling said that she had already sold the car to someone else.

If Barnes asserts a claim against Schilling based on Schilling's promise to keep the offer open until October 1, the court should

(A) enforce the promise as an option contract.

(B) not enforce the promise.

(C) enforce the promise because it was a firm offer in writing.

(D) enforce the promise only if Barnes relied to her detriment on Schilling's promise to keep the offer open.

12. Congress passes a law providing that no one who has been a member of an organization which uses unlawful means to deprive any group of persons of their rights under the United States Constitution is eligible for employment by the federal government. If the constitutionality of that law is challenged, it should be held

(A) unconstitutional, because it is an ex post facto law.

(B) unconstitutional, because it prohibits members of certain organizations from holding public office without regard to whether those members knew the purpose of the organizations to which they belonged.

(C) constitutional, because employment by the federal government is not a right but a privilege.

(D) constitutional, because the federal government has the right to protect itself by not employing persons who hold views inconsistent with the United States Constitution.

13. The Ocalala river is located entirely within the State of Ocalala. Acting under authority granted by Congress, the Federal Transportation Commission awarded a contract to Bell Contracting Company for the construction of a bridge, to be known as the Ocalala Bridge, over the Ocalala river. The contract required that all materials used in constructing the bridge be purchased within the State of Ocalala.

A statute of the State of Ocalala imposes a 6 percent sales tax, to be paid by the buyer, on any purchases made within the state. Upon purchasing steel in the State of Ocalala for use in the construction of the Ocalala Bridge, Bell Contracting Company refused to pay sales tax. As a result, the State of Ocalala prosecuted Bell Contracting Company for violating the sales tax statute.

If Bell Contracting Company's only defense is that in fulfilling a contract with the federal government it was immune from the state sales tax statute, the court should find Bell Contracting Company

(A) not guilty, if the Ocalala Bridge was to be used in interstate commerce.

(B) not guilty, because the state lacks power to tax activities of the federal government.

(C) guilty, because independent contractors working for the federal government are subject to state taxes.

(D) guilty, unless Bell Contracting Company's contract with the Federal Transportation Commission was on a cost-plus-fixed-profit basis.

14. When Nelsen applied for a job as a nurse at Mercy Hospital, the hospital's personnel department sent questionnaires to doctors on its staff, requesting information about Nelsen. Dock, a doctor on staff, knew Nelson from when they had both been employed at Welby Clinic. Since Dock had heard another doctor at Welby Clinic accuse Nelsen of incompetence resulting in the death of a patient, Dock disliked Nelsen. In fact, however, the doctor who made the accusation had mistaken Nelson for another nurse, and Nelsen had been cleared of blame by a Welby Clinic board of inquiry.

Hoping that Nelsen's job application would be rejected, Dock wrote on the questionnaire, "I once heard that Nelsen's incompetence resulted in the death of a patient." Mercy Hospital did not hire Nelsen.

If Nelsen asserts a defamation claim against Dock for Dock's statement in the questionnaire, the court should find for

(A) Dock, if Dock reasonably believed that Nelsen's incompetence resulted in the death of a patient.

(B) Dock, because the statement clearly indicated that Dock had heard the accusation from another.

(C) Nelsen, because Dock's dislike of Nelsen and Dock's hope that Nelsen's job application would be rejected amounted to actual malice.

(D) Nelsen, if the statement resulted in Mercy Hospital not hiring Nelsen.

Questions 15-16 are based on the following fact situation.

In December 1984, Sada, a manufacturer of packaging materials, entered into a written agreement with Baldwin, a wholesaler of cazbah melons. The agreement provided that Baldwin would purchase from Sada all the boxes required by Baldwin for packaging cazbah melons in 1985, but that in no event would the number of boxes required be less than 2,000.

After the agreement was executed, the price of cazbah melons fell from $1.00 per melon to $.80 per melon. As a result, Baldwin notified Sada in January 1985 that he intended to package cazbah melons in bags instead of boxes, and that he would not order any boxes from Sada in 1985.

15. Assume for the purpose of this question only that in January 1985 Sada instituted an action against Baldwin for damages. If Baldwin asks the court to dismiss Sada's action, should the court do so?

(A) Yes, because Baldwin might still order 2,000 boxes by the end of 1985.

(B) Yes, because the provision which required Sada to furnish all the boxes required by Baldwin in 1985 makes it impossible for the court to determine Sada's damages.

(C) No, because damages are presumed to result from every breach of contract.

(D) No, because Baldwin has stated that he will not fulfill his obligations under the contract.

16. Assume for the purpose of this question only that Sada instituted an action for damages against Baldwin in January 1986. At the trial, Baldwin attempted to testify that in the cazbah melon industry it was generally understood that minimum requirements set forth in contracts for the supply of packaging materials were of no effect when the price of cazbah melons fell drastically. Should the court admit Baldwin's testimony over Sada's objection?

(A) Yes, because evidence of a regularly observed business practice may be offered to explain the terms of a written agreement.

(B) Yes, but only if the written agreement was not intended by the parties to be a final expression of their agreement.

(C) No, if the parties did not contemplate a decline in the price of cazbah melons.

(D) No, because the fact that the parties specified a minimum requirement of 2,000 boxes shows that they did not intend to be bound by any pre-existing industry standards.

Questions 17-18 are based on the following fact situation.

A riot broke out during a political rally in the town of Burg. Subsequently, *The Herald*, a daily newspaper, published an editorial about the rally and the ensuing disruption. The editorial stated that "Police present at the rally beat and kicked innocent bystanders and engaged in other acts of senseless and unnecessary brutality." Following publication of the editorial, four police officers who were present at the rally asserted a defamation claim against *The Herald*.

17. Assume for the purpose of this question only that the only argument raised by *The Herald* in defense is that the statements contained in the editorial did not identify the plaintiffs. The court should find for

(A) plaintiffs, if the number of police present at the rally was so small that readers who knew the plaintiffs would believe that the statement had been made about them.

(B) plaintiffs, but only if they were the only police present at the rally.

(C) *The Herald*, unless the statement is found to be slander per se.

(D) *The Herald*, because the statement did not specifically name the plaintiffs.

18. Assume for the purpose of this question only that all parties agree that *The Herald* lacked actual malice in making the statement, and that this is the only defense raised by *The Herald*. Which of the following arguments would be most likely to result in a judgment for *The Herald*?

(A) There is no such thing as a false idea.

(B) The plaintiffs were in a position of apparent control over public affairs.

(C) The editorial and resulting lawsuit made the public familiar with the plaintiffs.

(D) The plaintiffs were public employees.

Questions 19-20 are based on the following fact situation.

Vestco, a manufacturer of police equipment, obtained a

patent for a bullet-proof vest made entirely of recycled aluminum cans. On April 1, the Green City Police Department entered into a written contract with Vestco providing for the purchase and sale of thirty of Vestco's bullet-proof vests per month for the next year at a specified price. For the following three months, both parties performed as required by the agreement. On July 5, soon after the third delivery, Vestco's only factory burned completely to the ground without any fault on the part of Vestco. On July 10, officials of the Green City Police Department wrote to Vestco, asking whether Vestco would continue to deliver as agreed. When Vestco failed to respond within a reasonable time, the Green City Police Department entered into an agreement with another company for the purchase of thirty bullet-proof vests per month.

19. Assume for the purpose of this question only that Vestco failed to deliver any more bullet-proof vests, and that the Green City Police Department subsequently asserted a claim against Vestco for breach of contract. Which of the following would be Vestco's most effective argument in defense against that claim?

    (A) The destruction of Vestco's factory made delivery commercially impossible.

    (B) Vestco's failure to respond to the Green City Police Department's letter of July 10 resulted in a prospective inability to perform.

    (C) Vestco's contract with the Green City Police Department was divisible.

    (D) The Green City Police Department's contract to purchase bullet-proof vests from another company was a repudiation of its contract with Vestco.

20. Assume for the purpose of this question only that after the Green City Police Department contracted with another company for the purchase of bullet-proof vests, Vestco delivered 30 bullet-proof vests to the Green City Police Department, but the Green City Police Department refused to accept them. If Vestco asserts a claim against the Green City Police Department for breach of contract, which of the following would be the Green

City Police Department's most effective argument in defense against that claim?

    (A) The destruction of Vestco's factory reasonably appeared to frustrate the purpose of the contract between the Green City Police Department and Vestco.

    (B) Vestco's failure to respond to the Green City Police Department's letter of July 10 resulted in a prospective inability to perform.

    (C) Vestco's contract with the Green City Police Department was divisible.

    (D) The Green City Police Department's contract to purchase bullet-proof vests from another company was a repudiation of its contract with Vestco.

21. Pargas asserted a tort claim against Diaz for battery, but died of cancer before the trial. At the trial, Westall was called as a witness by the attorney for Pargas's estate. Westall testified that she was a police officer called to the scene of a shooting, and that when she arrived she found Pargas lying on the ground in a pool of blood. Westall stated that when she asked Pargas to tell her what happened, Pargas replied, "Tell my wife to meet me at the hospital and tell her that Diaz shot me."

    Diaz objected. If the court finds that Pargas's statement to Westall was not a dying declaration, it will probably be because

    (A) Pargas did not believe that he was dying when he made the statement.

    (B) Pargas did not die as a result of the shooting.

    (C) Westall's testimony was not being offered at the trial of a criminal prosecution.

    (D) Pargas's statement was not made spontaneously.

22. Partco manufactured airplane parts in a factory which it rented from Landis. Under a contract dated June 15, Partco sold three thousand coupling rods to Aerocorp, a manufacturer of airplanes. The contract of sale required payment by

Aerocorp on or before August 15. On June 30, because Partco was unable to pay the rent on its factory, its officials executed a document assigning to Landis the right to collect from Aerocorp under the June 15 contract, and sent a copy of the assignment to Aerocorp.

After a dispute developed between Partco and Landis, however, Partco officials told Partco's plant manager Martin that, as a bonus, he could collect and keep the money owed by Aerocorp under the June 15 contract. Partco officials then wrote to Aerocorp and Landis, notifying them that Partco had revoked its previous assignment to Landis and had assigned its rights to Martin. Martin thereafter demanded that Aerocorp make payment directly to him. Upon Aerocorp's refusal to do so, Martin asserted a claim against Aerocorp.

If Martin's claim against Aerocorp is UNSUC-CESSFUL, it will probably be because

(A) Partco's assignment to Martin was not in writing.

(B) Partco's assignment to Martin was not supported by consideration.

(C) Aerocorp did not consent to Partco's assignment to Martin.

(D) an assignee steps into the shoes of his assignor.

23. After serving a portion of his sentence in a state prison, Apollo applied for parole in accordance with state law. His application was denied following a State Parole Board hearing at which Apollo was not permitted to appear either in person or by counsel. Apollo subsequently instituted a proceeding in a state court in which he claimed that the hearing violated his right to due process under the federal and state constitutions. The state court found for Apollo. On appeal by the State Parole Board, the highest appellate court in the state affirmed. In its decision, the court refused to consider claims under the federal constitution, but concluded that the state constitution had been violated.

On application by the State Parole Board, is judicial review by the United States Supreme Court available?

(A) No.

(B) Yes, by certiorari only.

(C) Yes, by appeal only.

(D) Yes, by either certiorari or appeal.

24. Dakota was charged with violating a state law which made it a crime to knowingly issue a worthless check. On the presentation of its direct case at trial, the prosecution offered into evidence a properly authenticated judgment showing that Dakota had been convicted of violating the same law three years earlier. Dakota's counsel objected. Which of the following statements is correct about the judgment of conviction?

I. It is admissible as substantive evidence of M.O. (modus operandi).

II. It is admissible to impeach Dakota's credibility.

(A) I only.

(B) II only.

(C) I and II.

(D) Neither I nor II.

25. Ann and Bob met while serving abroad in the military. They lived together for more than fifteen years after their return to the United States although they never married. Ann's mother Marsh was a religious woman who did not believe that unmarried men and women should live together. For this reason, Ann told Marsh that she and Bob had married while living overseas.

Marsh was the owner of a parcel of realty known as Greenacre located in a jurisdiction which recognizes tenancy by the entirety. When Marsh died, she left Greenacre "to Ann and Bob." Shortly after Marsh's death, Ann and Bob separated. Upon Ann's death, she left a will devising her interest in Greenacre to Armstrong. Bob, who was alive at the time of Ann's death, then executed a quitclaim purporting to transfer all his interest in Greenacre to Boaz. Which of the following correctly states the relative interests of Boaz and Armstrong in Greenacre?

(A) Boaz and Armstrong are tenants in common, each holding a one-half interest.

(B) Boaz and Armstrong are tenants by the entirety, each holding an undivided one-half interest.

(C) Armstrong is the sole owner.

(D) Boaz is the sole owner.

26. Davin leased an automobile from Auto Rental for one year at $400 per month, by a valid written contract which gave Davin an option to purchase the vehicle for $9,000 at the end of the term. A clause of the contract provided that in the event Davin did not exercise the option, anything which had been added to the vehicle during the lease period would become the property of Auto Rental. Because this clause appeared in small print, Davin did not read it and was not aware of its existence.

At the end of the lease period, Davin offered to purchase the car for $8,500, but Auto Rental rejected her offer. Before returning the vehicle, Davin removed a radio which she had installed in it, damaging the car's dashboard in the process.

If Davin is charged with larceny as a result of her removal of the radio, she should be found

(A) guilty, because her removal of the radio resulted in damage to the property of Auto Rental.

(B) guilty, because a person who signs a contract is presumed to know its contents.

(C) not guilty, because a person cannot be convicted of stealing her own property.

(D) not guilty, because she did not know that the radio belonged to Auto Rental.

Questions 27-28 are based on the following fact situation.

Wells purchased a food and beverage processing machine as a gift for her husband Harris. The machine was manufactured by Blendco, and was purchased by Wells from Storr, a retailer. When Wells got home, she unpacked the machine, placed it on the kitchen counter, and plugged it into an electrical outlet. When she started the machine, however, she noticed a jarring vibration. She immediately switched the machine off and telephoned Storr. After she described the vibration to a Storr employee, the employee said, "If the processor vibrates like that, it is defective. Don't try to use it. It's inherently dangerous."

Because Wells was in a hurry to go bowling, she left the processing machine on the counter still plugged in and went out for the evening. Harris arrived home soon afterwards. With him was Nesbitt, a neighbor. When Harris saw the processing machine on the counter, he decided to use it to mix drinks for Nesbitt and himself. After placing the necessary ingredients in the machine's glass container, Harris switched it on. The machine immediately began to vibrate, causing the glass container to shatter. Nesbitt was seriously injured by flying glass.

27. Assume for the purpose of this question only that Nesbitt asserts a claim against Storr for damages resulting from a defect in the processing machine. Which of the following would be Storr's most effective argument in defense against that claim?

(A) Nesbitt was a bystander.

(B) Wells had assumed the risk by leaving the processing machine plugged into the electrical outlet.

(C) The processing machine was defective at the time it left Blendco's factory.

(D) Wells's conduct in leaving the processing machine plugged into the electrical outlet was a superseding cause of harm.

28. Assume for the purpose of this question only that Nesbitt asserts a claim against Wells, alleging that it was negligent for her to leave the processing machine plugged into an electrical outlet after learning that it was dangerous. In determining

Nesbitt's claim, a court should find for

(A) Nesbitt, under the doctrine of *res ipsa loqui-tur.*

(B) Nesbitt, unless Wells's conduct was foreseeable.

(C) Nesbitt, only if Wells's conduct was unreasonable.

(D) Wells, if the negligence of either Storr or Blendco was a proximate cause of Nesbitt's injury.

29. Hirsh challenges the constitutionality of a state law which provides that no contraceptive device which requires insertion into a cavity of the human body may be sold without a prescription. If the only argument used by Hirsh is that the statute violates the equal protection clause of the Fourteenth Amendment because only women use such devices, which of the following would be the most effective argument in opposition to Hirsh's claim?

(A) Gender is not a suspect classification.

(B) The statute has a rational basis because devices inserted into the human body are more likely to cause harm than devices manufactured solely for external use.

(C) The right to protect citizens against their own lack of judgment is included in the state's police powers.

(D) The statute bears a substantial relationship to an important government interest because devices inserted into the human body are more likely to cause harm than devices manufactured solely for external use.

30. On January 10, Berg, a builder, entered into a written contract with Orca to construct a building on Orca's realty. The contract required Berg to build to specifications furnished by Arch, an architect, and required Orca to make periodic payments to Berg during construction. A final payment of $30,000 was to be made when the building was complete. The contract provided, however, that "In no event shall said final pay-

ment be required unless Berg obtains and presents to Orca prior to July 30 a Certificate of Satisfactory Completion issued by Arch following final inspection by Arch."

On July 15, after making all periodic payments required by the contract, Orca asked Arch to delay issuing a Certificate of Satisfactory Completion until after July 30. Arch agreed to do so. On July 20, Berg notified Arch that the building was complete, and requested final inspection. Arch did not inspect the building or issue a Certificate of Satisfactory Completion until August 15. On August 16, Berg requested final payment from Orca, presenting the Certificate. Orca refused to make payment on the ground that Berg did not obtain the Certificate prior to July 30 as required by the contract.

In an action by Berg against Orca for breach of contract, which of the following would be Berg's most effective argument?

(A) The contract between Berg and Orca imposed upon Arch an obligation to act reasonably in issuing the Certificate of Satisfactory Completion.

(B) Berg substantially performed all conditions of the contract by completing the building prior to July 30.

(C) As a result of Orca's request that Arch delay issuing the Certificate of Satisfactory Completion, Berg was not required to obtain it prior to July 30.

(D) Applying an objective standard, satisfactory completion was achieved prior to July 30.

Question 31-33 are based on the following fact situation.

At Domino's trial on criminal charges, undisputed evidence established that Domino and Philip had planned to take a certain fur coat from Fleming's fur shop by threatening Fleming with a pistol carried by Philip; that when they did so Fleming began shooting at them; and that Philip shot back with his pistol, intentionally killing Fleming.

Testifying on behalf of the prosecution, Philip stated that Domino knew that Philip's pistol would be loaded. He also stated that Fleming had handed Domino the coat, that Philip had returned his own gun to his pocket, and that he and Domino were on their way out of Fleming's shop when Fleming began shooting at them.

Domino testified that the coat in question had previously been stolen from her by Fleming, and that she and Philip were trying to retrieve it.

Statutes in the jurisdiction define First Degree Murder as the intentional unlawful killing of a human being, and Second Degree Murder as the unintentional killing of a human being by defendant or an accomplice during the course of a burglary, robbery, rape, kidnapping, or arson committed by the defendant.

31. Assume for the purpose of this question only that Domino is charged with First Degree Murder on the ground that as a co-conspirator and accomplice she is vicariously liable for Philip's shooting of Fleming. If the jury does not believe the testimony of Philip or of Domino, Domino should be found

   (A) guilty, because she and Philip planned to take the coat by threatening Fleming with Philip's pistol.

   (B) guilty, because she was present when Philip shot Fleming.

   (C) not guilty, because Fleming shot first.

   (D) not guilty, because she did not aid or abet Philip in shooting Fleming.

32. Assume for the purpose of this question only that the jury believes the testimony of Domino, but does not believe the testimony of Philip. Which of the following would be Domino's most effective argument in defense against a charge of Second Degree Murder?

   (A) It was unforeseeable that Fleming would begin shooting.

   (B) Domino did not know that Philip's pistol would be loaded.

   (C) Fleming's death did not occur during the course of one of the crimes specified in the applicable statute.

   (D) The statute was not intended to impose criminal liability on one person for the acts of another.

33. Assume for the purpose of this question only that the jury believes the testimony of Philip and the testimony of Domino. On a charge of involuntary manslaughter, Domino should be found

   (A) guilty, because Fleming's conduct was in response to the initial act of aggression committed by Philip and Domino.

   (B) guilty, if Philip's use of a loaded pistol made it likely that death or serious injury would result from her conduct.

   (C) not guilty, if Domino's thoughts were inflamed by the heat of passion at the time she and Philip attempted to retrieve her coat.

   (D) not guilty, because Domino was privileged to retrieve her property by a threat of force.

Questions 34-35 are based on the following fact situation.

On February 1, Oakley conveyed a parcel of realty to Arnett as a gift. Oakley executed the deed in the presence of Carmody, a notary public, and Carmody affixed his seal as required by law. On March 1, after Oakley learned that Arnett had not recorded his title, Oakley purported to convey the same parcel of realty to Badel for value. Badel was unaware that Arnett held any interest in the realty. On March 15, Arnett recorded the deed which he had received from Oakley in February. In June, Badel executed a deed conveying the realty to Carmody. Carmody immediately recorded the deed.

34. Assume for the purpose of this question only that

a statute in the jurisdiction provides that "No transfer of an interest in real property shall be good against a subsequent purchaser for value without notice of such transfer unless it shall have been recorded." In litigation between Arnett and Carmody, who should be declared owner of the realty?

(A) Arnett, because Carmody had notice that the realty had first been conveyed to Arnett.

(B) Arnett, unless Badel recorded his deed before Arnett recorded his deed.

(C) Carmody, but only if Carmody purchased the realty for value.

(D) Carmody, because Badel purchased the realty from Oakley before Arnett recorded his deed.

35. Assume for the purpose of this question only that a statute in the jurisdiction provides that "Every conveyance of real estate which shall not be recorded is void as against any subsequent purchaser of the same real estate in good faith and for a valuable consideration whose conveyance shall be first duly recorded." In litigation between Arnett and Carmody, who should be declared owner of the realty?

(A) Carmody, because Arnett did not purchase the realty from Oakley for value.

(B) Carmody, if Badel recorded his deed prior to conveying the realty to Carmody.

(C) Arnett, unless Badel recorded his deed before Arnett recorded his deed.

(D) Arnett, because any recording by Badel was outside the chain of title.

Questions 36-37 are based on the following fact situation.

Adrian and Betty were 17-year-old girls. Charles and Dave were boys who attended the same high school as Adrian and Betty. At school one day the four of them agreed to have a party that night at Dave's house, knowing that Dave's parents would be out for the evening. Later that afternoon Charles and Dave agreed to encourage the girls to drink beer at the party in order to get them so drunk that they would allow the boys to have sexual intercourse with them.

When Charles got home from school, he began to regret agreeing to get the girls drunk, since he knew that Betty was only 17 years old. Without saying anything to Dave, Charles telephoned Adrian and told her about the plan. Adrian laughed, saying, "It doesn't sound like a bad idea to me. I've always wanted to be seduced." Adrian said nothing to Betty, but that night neither Adrian nor Charles went to Dave's house. Betty did, however, and drank a great deal of beer and permitted Dave to have sexual intercourse with her.

A statute in the jurisdiction provides that any male person who has sexual intercourse with a female whom he knows to be under the age of 18 shall be guilty of second degree rape.

36. If Dave is charged with second degree rape under the above statute, which of the following facts or inferences, if it was the only one true, would provide Dave with his most effective defense to that charge?

(A) Dave was 17 years of age at the time of the alleged crime.

(B) Dave did not know that Betty was below the age of 18 years when he had sexual intercourse with her.

(C) Dave was intoxicated at the time he had sexual intercourse with Betty.

(D) Betty was not intoxicated, and, in fact, consented to having sexual intercourse with Dave.

37. In a prosecution for conspiracy to commit second degree rape, which of the following persons is most likely to be properly convicted?

(A) Adrian, Betty, Charles, and Dave.

(B) Adrian, Charles, and Dave only.

(C) Betty and Dave only.

(D) Charles and Dave only.

38. At the trial of a negligence action, a jury found that the plaintiff's damage was valued at $10,000. The jury also found that the damage was caused 70% by the fault of the defendant and 30% by the fault of the plaintiff. A statute in the jurisdiction imposes a system of pure comparative negligence. Based on the jury's findings, the court should enter judgment for

(A) Defendant.

(B) Plaintiff in the sum of $4,000 (70% of $10,000 minus 30% of $10,000).

(C) Plaintiff in the sum of $7,000 ($10,000 minus 30% of $10,000).

(D) Plaintiff in the sum of $10,000 since Defendant's fault exceeded that of Plaintiff.

39. Terhune was driving her truck across the Mountain River Bridge when the bridge collapsed, causing a car driven by Pachos to fall into the river. Pachos subsequently asserted a negligence claim against Terhune for injuries which he sustained in the fall.

A statute in the jurisdiction prohibits the operation of a vehicle weighing more than 20,000 pounds at a speed in excess of 25 miles per hour on any bridge in the state. At the trial, it was proven that Terhune's truck weighed 30,000 pounds, and that Terhune was driving it at a speed of 40 miles per hour when the bridge collapsed. It was also proven that a truck weighing 30,000 pounds would have been more likely to cause the Mountain River Bridge to collapse if driven across it at a speed under 25 miles per hour than at a speed over 25 miles per hour.

In *Pachos v. Terhune* the court should find for

(A) Pachos, because Terhune's violation of the statute was negligence per se.

(B) Pachos, because Terhune's violation of the statute raises a presumption that Terhune's negligence was a proximate cause of Pachos's injuries.

(C) Terhune, because Terhune's violation of statute was not a factual cause of Pachos's injury.

(D) Terhune, because Terhune did not violate a statute which was designed to protect a class of persons to which Pachos belonged.

40. O'Brien conveyed a lakefront parcel of realty to Carmichael "unless the realty is used for non-residential purposes in which case grantor or his successors may reobtain possession." Two years later, by a properly executed document which was subsequently recorded, Carmichael granted Fuller a license to enter the realty for a period of five years to fish from the lake on which it fronted. If O'Brien commences an appropriate proceeding seeking possession of the realty, Carmichael's most effective argument in defense would be that

(A) the condition contained in O'Brien's deed to Carmichael violates the rule against perpetuities.

(B) fishing is a residential use of the realty.

(C) O'Brien's deed created a fee simple subject to a condition subsequent.

(D) the condition contained in O'Brien's deed to Carmichael is void as a restraint on alienation.

41. Adair was a well-known architect whose work was frequently featured in popular magazines. Slack was a well-known sculptress whose work was displayed in many museums throughout the United States. Slack decided to have a studio built which would artistically complement her sculpture and hired Adair to design it and to supervise its construction. Slack told Adair that she was hiring her because she had confidence in her artistic judgment, and that she intended to require the builder of her studio to obtain Adair's artistic approval at various stages of the construction. Slack and Adair entered into a written contract providing that "neither party shall assign or delegate this contract without the other party's written approval."

Slack subsequently hired a builder who began construction. As work progressed, Slack and Adair argued frequently. When the building was 85 percent complete, Adair refused to continue working for Slack and executed a document purporting to assign the contract to another architect. Slack immediately ordered the builder to stop construction and sued Adair for an order directing her to specifically perform her obligations under the contract.

Should the court grant the relief requested by Slack?

(A) Yes, if the architectural work which remained to be completed at the time of Adair's assignment involved personal services.

(B) Yes, because the agreement between Slack and Adair prohibited assignment.

(C) No, because an agreement not to assign destroys the power but not the right to make a valid assignment.

(D) No, if the architectural work which remained to be completed at the time of Adair's assignment involved personal services.

42. At the trial of a breach of contract action brought by Pacer against Dail, Pacer testified in her own behalf. Pacer stated that a man who called her on the telephone said that he was Dail and ordered goods from her at an agreed price. She said that when she tried to deliver the goods, Dail refused to accept them. Pacer stated further that she had never spoken to Dail before or after that telephone conversation, but that she had heard his voice in the judge's chambers immediately before the trial began and that she recognized it as the voice of the person to whom she had spoken on the telephone.

If Dail's attorney asks the court to exclude Pacer's testimony regarding the identification of the voice on the telephone, Pacer's statement should be

(A) admitted, because Pacer heard Dail's voice

in the judge's chambers before testifying.

(B) admitted, because the person to whom Pacer spoke on the telephone identified himself as Dail.

(C) excluded, because Pacer had never spoken to Dail prior to the telephone conversation.

(D) excluded, because Pacer had not dialed Dail's telephone number before speaking to him on the telephone.

43. A chemical known as green saltpeter which is used in the manufacture of munitions, is frequently found floating, as dust, in the air of munitions factories. Since prolonged inhalation of green saltpeter can cause lung disease, Congress passes the Green Saltpeter Control Act. Among other things, the Act prohibits the operation of any munitions factory in which airborne green saltpeter levels exceed specified standards. The Act establishes the Green Saltpeter Control Agency, authorizes it to inspect munitions factories, and empowers it to issue Closure Orders, enforceable by the Department of Justice, and directing the closing of any factory operating in violation of the Act. Section 34 of the Act provides that Closure Orders do not become effective until ten days after their approval by the National Defense Committee of the Senate.

After determining that airborne levels of green saltpeter exceed statutory standards in a munitions factory operated by General Explosives, the Green Saltpeter Control Agency issues a Closure Order, sending copies to the United States Department of Justice and to the Senate National Defense Committee as required by the Act. The Senate National Defense Committee refuses to approve the Closure Order.

If the Department of Justice challenges the constitutionality of § 34 of the Green Saltpeter Control Act in an appropriate proceeding, the court should find this section

(A) constitutional, because circumstances known only to the Senate National Defense Committee might make the continued operation of a particular munitions factory necessary to national security.

(B) constitutional, because after delegating its power to an administrative agency, Congress may continue to act in a supervisory capacity.

(C) unconstitutional, because Congress may not delegate to an administrative agency the power to impose criminal or quasi-criminal sanctions.

(D) unconstitutional, because Section 34 would allow the passage of legislation by a committee of Congress.

Questions 44-45. Each describes an offense. In each question, select from the choices below (A-D) the most serious offense of which the defendant is likely to be properly convicted.

(A) Robbery.

(B) Extortion.

(C) Larceny by trick.

(D) Embezzlement.

44. Robin, who lived alone, was a collector of antiques. One day, Defendant followed Robin to work. Knowing that Robin's valuable antique collection was stored in her home, Defendant phoned Robin at work and told her that he had placed a bomb in her home. He said that if she immediately paid him $1,000 in cash, he would give the police information necessary for them to defuse the bomb. If she did not pay him, he said would detonate the bomb, destroying her home and her collection of antiques. Robin paid Defendant as instructed. In reality, Defendant had not placed a bomb in Robin's home.

45. Air Lines was a commercial air transport company which carried passengers for hire in its airplanes. Defendant phoned Air Lines and stated that he had placed a bomb in one of its planes which was already in the air and carrying passengers. Defendant said that if Air Lines immediately paid him $20,000 in cash, he would tell them where the bomb had been hidden and how

to defuse it, but that if they did not, the bomb would explode when the plane landed. Air Lines paid Defendant as instructed. In reality, Defendant had not placed a bomb in any plane belonging to Air Lines.

46. A state law requires a permit for the use of certain recreational facilities in state parks, and fixes the annual fee for such permits at $25 for residents and $200 for non-residents. If a non-resident of the state challenges the law as unconstitutional, the LEAST effective argument in support of that claim would be that the law violates

(A) the Equal Protection clause of the Fourteenth Amendment.

(B) the Obligation of Contracts clause of Article I.

(C) the Privileges and Immunities clause of Article IV.

(D) the Commerce clause of Article I.

47. Seitz and Batista entered into a valid written contract for the sale of Seitz's home to Batista. Subsequently, Seitz's neighbor Darnell telephoned Seitz and said, "If you don't back out of your contract with Batista, there's going to be an accident and one of your children is going to be seriously hurt. Understand?" Before Seitz had a chance to answer, Darnell hung up. Seitz became so frightened by Darnell's threat that he suffered an immediate heart attack.

If Seitz asserts a claim against Darnell for assault, which of the following would be Darnell's LEAST effective argument in defense against that claim?

(A) Darnell's statement did not justify apprehension of immediate harm.

(B) Darnell told Seitz that he could avoid harm by complying with a specified condition.

(C) Darnell's threat was not directed against the person of Seitz.

(D) Darnell committed no physical act.

48. At his trial on a charge of arson committed in the city of Vicksville, Dague testified that on the day of the fire he was not in Vicksville, but was actually 1,000 miles away in another state. The prosecution subsequently called Walen who testified that on the day of the fire she was in a liquor store in the city of Vicksville when Dague came into the store with a gun and robbed its owner. Over timely objection by Dague's attorney, Walen's testimony should be

(A) admitted for impeachment only.

(B) admitted as substantive evidence only.

(C) admitted for impeachment and as substantive evidence.

(D) excluded.

Questions 49-50 are based on the following fact situation.

Odell was the owner of a parcel of realty on which there were several buildings and a gold mine. Odell lived in one of the buildings and personally worked the gold mine, earning a comfortable living by selling the gold which he removed. The other buildings were vacant. When Odell died, his will devised the realty "to Ambler, but if Ambler should die without issue from his wife Jane, to Borman." Soon after Odell's death, Ambler entered into a contract with Mineco. Pursuant to the contract, Mineco was to work the gold mine for ten years, and to pay Ambler 50% of the gross proceeds from the sale of gold removed from the mine. In addition, Ambler leased all the buildings on the realty to Mineco for ten years, for use by Mineco employees as living quarters. Ambler and Jane never had any children.

49. Which of the following statements is correct about Borman's interest in the realty?

   I. If Odell died before Jane, Odell's will gave Borman a shifting executory interest in the realty.

   II. If Odell died after Jane, Odell's will gave Borman a vested remainder in the realty.

(A) I only.

(B) II only.

(C) I and II.

(D) neither I nor II.

50. Assume for the purpose of this question only that Ambler's wife Jane died two years after Ambler contracted with Mineco, and that Borman then demanded that Ambler pay Borman all funds which Ambler would subsequently receive from Mineco as proceeds of Mineco's gold mining operation on the realty and as rent on the buildings. Borman is entitled to receive

(A) proceeds of the gold mining operation only.

(B) rent on the buildings only.

(C) proceeds of the gold mining operation and rent on the buildings.

(D) neither the proceeds of the gold mining operation nor rent on the buildings.

Questions 51-53 are based on the following fact situation.

Rider, a reporter for *The Daily Blade*, wrote an article about Peppard which contained several unflattering statements. After the article was published in *The Daily Blade*, Peppard threatened to sue Rider and *The Daily Blade* for libel. After negotiation, Peppard, Rider, and *The Daily Blade* entered into a written contract on March 5. According to its terms, *The Daily Blade* agreed to pay Peppard $20,000 in cash, Rider agreed to convey to Peppard some realty which she owned, and Peppard agreed not to sue either of them as a result of the article's publication. All parties were to draw up the necessary documents and exchange them on March 11 at an office in a bank where *The Daily Blade* maintained an account.

On March 11, Peppard and Rider appeared at the bank as agreed. While they were there, a representative of *The Daily Blade* telephoned to say that the officials of *The Daily Blade* had changed their minds and would not pay any money to Peppard.

51. Which of the following statements correctly describes Peppard's rights against *The Daily*

Blade?

(A) Peppard's only remedy is to sue *The Daily Blade* for libel.

(B) Peppard's only remedy is to recover $20,000 from *The Daily Blade.*

(C) Peppard may recover $20,000 from *The Daily Blade* and sue *The Daily Blade* for libel.

(D) Peppard may recover $20,000 from *The Daily Blade* or sue *The Daily Blade* for libel, but he may not do both.

52. Which of the following statements is most accurate about the agreement of March 5?

    I. Peppard's promise not to sue and *The Daily Blade's* promise of payment created concurrent conditions.

    II. Rider's conveyance of realty to Peppard was a condition precedent to Peppard's promise not to sue Rider.

(A) I only.

(B) II only.

(C) I and II.

(D) Neither I nor II.

53. Assume the following additional facts for the purpose of this question only: After Peppard and Rider were informed that *The Daily Blade* would not make payment, Rider tendered a conveyance of her realty to Peppard as agreed on March 5, but Peppard refused to accept it. Peppard subsequently sued Rider for libel. If Rider raises the March 5 agreement as a defense, and asserts a counterclaim based on Peppard's refusal to accept her conveyance on March 11, should the court enforce the agreement of March 5?

(A) No, if the contract of March 5 was divisible.

(B) No, because it would violate public policy to enforce a promise not to sue which was given in return for a conveyance of realty.

(C) No, if payment of $20,000 by *The Daily*

Blade was a condition precedent to Peppard's promise not to sue Rider.

(D) Yes.

Questions 54-55 are based on the following fact situation.

At Dalby's trial on a charge of rape, Vanna testified that on March 1, Dalby forced her to have sexual intercourse with him against her will. Testifying in his own defense, Dalby admitted that he had engaged in sexual intercourse with Vanna on that date, but claimed that Vanna had consented. Dalby stated further that Vanna had not accused him of rape until April 3, when she discovered that he was married and was living with his wife.

54. Assume for the purpose of this question only that the prosecutor subsequently offered a properly authenticated public record indicating that Dalby had been convicted of state income tax fraud in another jurisdiction two years earlier. On objection by Dalby's attorney, the record should be

(A) admitted.

(B) excluded, unless state income tax fraud is a felony in the jurisdiction where Dalby was convicted.

(C) excluded, unless state income tax fraud is a felony in the jurisdiction where Dalby was being tried for rape.

(D) excluded, unless the court finds that the probative value of the offered evidence outweighs its prejudicial effect.

55. Assume for the purpose of this question only that the prosecutor subsequently called Vanna's neighbor Willey to the stand. Willey testified that while she was conversing with Vanna on March 7, Vanna suddenly burst into tears and told her that she had been raped by Dalby a week before. Upon objection by Dalby's attorney, Willey's statement should be

(A) admitted, because Vanna's statement was an excited utterance.

(B) excluded, because it is hearsay not within any exception.

(C) admitted, because it contradicts Dalby's claim that Vanna did not accuse him of rape until she learned that he was married.

(D) admitted, because Vanna's statement was a sense impression.

56. Files had been convicted of fraud on three separate occasions and served three different prison sentences as a result. Soon after his most recent release, Files proclaimed himself to be the "Minister of St. Roquefort" and began conducting prayer meetings on Sunday nights. During these meetings, Files stated that his vows as the Minister of St. Roquefort prevented him from working for money, and asked the people present to make cash contributions to provide for his personal needs. After collecting several hundred dollars in this fashion, Files was arrested and charged with fraud under a state law which prohibits any person from making statements which he knows to be false for the purpose of obtaining money from others.

In defense, Files asserted that a court could not convict him without questioning the sincerity of his religious beliefs, and that the prosecution, therefore, violated his First Amendment rights to freedom of religion. He asked that the court dismiss the prosecution on that ground.

Should the prosecution be dismissed?

(A) Yes.

(B) No, because a court may determine the sincerity of a person's religious beliefs without violating First Amendment rights to freedom of religion.

(C) No, because First Amendment rights to freedom of religion cannot be used to justify what would otherwise be a criminal act.

(D) No, because First Amendment rights to freedom of religion protect beliefs, but not actions.

57. In which one of the following fact situations is the defendant most likely to be properly convicted of violating a state law which prohibits depriving any person of a right conferred by the Equal Protection Clause of the Fourteenth Amendment to the United States Constitution?

(A) Defendant, the president of a university operated by a religious organization, refused to admit certain students solely because of their religion.

(B) Defendant, a federal court official, prevented certain persons from serving on federal juries solely because of their race.

(C) Defendant, the principal of a public high school, expelled certain students solely because they were pregnant.

(D) Defendant, the vice president of a bank, refused to grant loans to certain applicants solely because of their place of national origin.

58. Kemco was the manufacturer of Woxibol, a chemical used by photo processors. Foto, a professional photographer, customarily used Woxibol in his processing laboratory. On August 15, 1986, while working in his laboratory, Foto read the label of a bottle of Woxibol which he had purchased several months earlier. The label said, "Woxibol. Best when used prior to June 1, 1986." Although Kemco knew that Woxibol fumes were extremely toxic, the label contained no other statements. Foto poured the contents of the bottle down a drain which emptied into a municipal sewer. Because the sewer was cracked, toxic Woxibol fumes entered the home of Pena causing Pena to become seriously ill. Pena's home was located one-half mile from Foto's laboratory.

Pena subsequently asserted a claim for damages against Kemco on the ground that the absence of a warning on the Woxibol bottle made the product defective and unreasonably dangerous.

Which of the following additional facts or inferences, if it was the only one true, would provide Kemco with its most effective defense to Pena's claim?

(A) The reasonable person would not have anticipated that Pena would come into contact with Woxibol or its fumes.

(B) Foto acted negligently in pouring Woxibol down the drain.

(C) Pena's damage would not have occurred but for the crack in the municipal sewer.

(D) Foto had purchased the Woxibol from a retail store which had purchased it from a wholesaler which had purchased it from Kemco.

59. In a medical malpractice action by Phoenix against Dr. Davis, Phoenix alleged that Davis, a physician, was negligent in treating a disease of Phoenix's pancreas. In order to establish that Davis was negligent, Phoenix must prove that Davis

(A) failed to act like the reasonable physician.

(B) failed to act like the reasonable physician who specializes in treating diseases of the pancreas.

(C) failed to act like the reasonable person of Davis's intelligence and experience.

(D) acted in a way which reasonable physicians would regard as negligent.

Questions 60-61 are based on the following fact situation.

Ward was the owner of a parcel of realty known as Wardacre on which she lived with her husband Hill. Ward was admitted to a hospital following a severe heart attack. While her husband Hill was visiting her in the hospital, Ward said, "I know I'm dying, and I want to be sure that you have Wardacre after I'm gone. Please have our lawyer take care of it." The following day, Hill asked the family attorney to prepare a quitclaim deed to Wardacre for execution by Ward. Hill brought the document to Ward in the hospital where she executed it according to the requirements of law. After signing the quitclaim, Ward handed the document to Hill and said, "Please put it in the safe deposit box at the bank." Hill did so, but never recorded the quitclaim.

Ward subsequently recovered from her heart attack and was moved from the hospital to a rest home where she resided until 30 years later when she died from other causes. At Ward's request, Hill continued to occupy, maintain, and pay taxes on Wardacre throughout that period of time. During the last nine years of her life in the rest home, Ward was attended by Norton, a nurse. When Ward died, her will purported to leave Wardacre "to my faithful nurse Norton." Hill and Norton subsequently asserted conflicting claims to Wardacre.

60. Which of the following additional facts or inferences, if it was the only one true, would be most likely to result in a judgment for Hill?

(A) Ward intended the quitclaim to be a testamentary substitute.

(B) The quitclaim to Hill was a gift causa mortis.

(C) The safe deposit box into which Ward asked Hill to put the quitclaim was held jointly by Ward and Hill.

(D) The statutory period for adverse possession is less than 30 years.

61. Which of the following arguments would be most likely to lead to a judgment for Norton?

(A) Hill did not record the quitclaim.

(B) A quitclaim is relevant only in disputes between grantor and grantee.

(C) No warranties of seisin or quiet enjoyment are created by a quitclaim.

(D) Ward did not intend for the quitclaim to be effective until after her death.

62. Assuming that the appropriate objection is made, in which of the following fact situations is the offered evidence LEAST likely to be excluded under the original document rule?

(A) In an action for breach of contract, plaintiff offers a photocopy of the contract, asserting that the original is kept at the plaintiff's branch office which is located in a foreign country.

(B) In a prosecution of defendant for forging a check, the prosecution — without producing the check or explaining its absence — offers to call a witness who will testify that the defendant paid the witness for merchandise with a check to which the defendant signed the name James Grant.

(C) In a personal injury action, the defendant — without producing the X-ray or explaining its absence — calls a medical expert who testifies that based solely on the examination of an X-ray, it is her opinion that the plaintiff did not sustain a fracture of the skull.

(D) In a lawsuit by plaintiff against the state tax collector, plaintiff offers to testify to the contents of her state income tax return, asserting that she sent the original to the state tax collector as required by law, and that she did not keep a copy.

63. Bale and Schmid entered into a valid written contract for the sale of Schmid's home. Prior to March 1, the date set for closing, Bale's employer transferred her to a company office in another state. On March 1, Bale informed Schmid that she would not go through with the purchase of the realty for that reason. Schmid made no further attempt to sell the realty, but asserted a claim against Bale one year later for breach of contract. In adjudicating Schmid's claim, the court should find for

(A) Schmid, in a sum equivalent to the difference between the price which Bale had agreed to pay and the fair market value of the realty on the date set for closing.

(B) Schmid, in a sum equivalent to any money which had already been paid by Bale in contemplation of the purchase.

(C) Bale, because Schmid made no further

attempt to sell the realty.

(D) Bale, under the doctrine of impossibility of performance.

64. Minx was employed by Bibb to clean his office and to sweep the parking lot every night. While sweeping one evening, Minx found Bibb's wallet where he had dropped it in the parking lot. The wallet contained $300. Planning to return it to Bibb the next morning, Minx took the wallet home for safekeeping. That night, however, realizing that nobody knew that she had it, Minx decided to keep Bibb's wallet. She went out and spent $4 of Bibb's money on ice cream. The following morning, Minx felt guilty about keeping Bibb's money. She replaced what she had spent and returned the wallet and cash to Bibb.

If Minx is prosecuted for crimes resulting from the above incident, she may properly be convicted of

(A) larceny only.

(B) embezzlement only.

(C) neither larceny nor embezzlement.

(D) larceny and embezzlement.

65. Resa purchased property in a popular resort area and constructed a restaurant on it. Resa's restaurant was equipped with a walk-up window, so that people who chose to do so could purchase food and soft drinks without entering the restaurant. Resa kept his restaurant and walk-up window open every night until 2 A.M. Soon, large noisy crowds of young people began congregating in front of Resa's restaurant, making occasional purchases at the walk-up window and remaining there until it closed. On many nights, members of the crowd openly smoked marijuana and used profane language in loud voices. Pahl, who resided in a house next to the restaurant, telephoned Resa. Pahl complained that the value of his home was being diminished by the walk-up window and by noise from the restaurant. He asked Resa to close the restaurant each night at 11 p.m., but Resa refused.

If Pahl subsequently asserts a claim against Resa for damages resulting from the reduction of his home's value, which of the following theories would be most likely to result in a judgment for Pahl?

(A) Trespass to land.

(B) Intentional infliction of emotional distress.

(C) Private nuisance.

(D) Invasion of privacy.

66. Because of severe economic recession, the State of Lenape has enacted a statute imposing a tax on corporations which have gross sales within the state in excess of one million dollars during a calendar year. The statute applies to all such corporations, whether incorporated inside or outside the State of Lenape. It establishes a sliding scale tax schedule with a maximum tax rate of ten percent of gross sales in excess of one million dollars.

Which of the following persons or entities is most likely to have standing to challenge the constitutionality of the statute on the ground that it violates the Commerce Clause of the United States Constitution?

(A) The governor of a neighboring state.

(B) The stockholders of a State of Lenape corporation with annual gross sales of one and one-half million dollars in the State of Lenape.

(C) The stockholders of an out of state corporation with annual gross sales of one-half million dollars in the State of Lenape.

(D) A taxpayer in the State of Lenape.

67. When Olson died she left a one-half interest in a parcel of realty to her niece Webb and Webb's husband Harris as joint-tenants, and a one-half interest in the realty to Susan, the 13 year-old unmarried daughter of Olson. One year later Webb, Harris, and Susan were killed simultaneously in an automobile accident.

Which of the following statements correctly describes ownership of the realty following their deaths?

(A) The heirs of Susan hold a one-half interest, the heirs of Webb hold a one-quarter interest, and the heirs of Harris hold a one-quarter interest.

(B) The entire property is held by the heirs of Susan.

(C) The heirs of Susan hold a one-third interest, the heirs of Webb hold a one-third interest, and the heirs of Harris hold a one-third interest.

(D) The heirs of Webb hold a one-half interest and the heirs of Harris hold a one-half interest.

68. Odden was the owner of a large tract of realty located in a heavily forested area. In January 1987, Odden leased the realty to Torres for a period of 20 years. In March 1987, Odden sold the realty to Arnold, executing a general warranty deed containing covenants of seisin, quiet enjoyment, the right to convey, and a covenant against encumbrances. In April 1987, Arnold conveyed the realty to Best by a deed containing covenants substantially identical to those contained in the deed which Arnold had received from Odden. In May 1987, Arnold became insolvent. In June 1987, Best attempted to move onto the realty, and was prevented from doing so by Torres, who claimed a superior right.

If Best subsequently asserts a claim for damages against Odden, Best's most effective theory would be that Odden breached the warranty

(A) of seisin.

(B) against encumbrances.

(C) of the right to convey.

(D) of quiet enjoyment.

Questions 69-70 are based on the following fact situation.

Carroll was the operator of a summer camp for children. Penny, was a nine-year-old child staying at the camp, her parents having paid Carroll a fee. Penny was playing softball with other children on a field which Carroll set aside for this purpose. When one of the children hit the ball, it rolled into a group of bushes alongside the field. Running into the bushes after the ball, Penny tripped on a tree-root which was covered by a pile of leaves.

69. Assume for the purpose of this question only that Penny asserted a claim against Carroll alleging that Carroll's negligence was a proximate cause of injuries which Penny sustained when she tripped on the tree root. The court should find for

(A) Carroll, if the tree root was a natural condition of the land.

(B) Carroll, because Penny assumed the risk by chasing the ball into the grove of bushes.

(C) Penny, because Carroll owed her an absolute duty to keep the premises safe.

(D) Penny, if the reasonable person in Carroll's position would have discovered and removed the tree root.

70. Assume for the purpose of this question only that Penny asserted a battery claim against Carroll for damages she sustained when she tripped over the tree root. The court should find for

(A) Penny, if the jurisdiction applies the theory of transferred intent.

(B) Penny, but only if Carroll knew that a child would trip over the tree root.

(C) Carroll, unless Carroll knew or should have known that a child might trip over the tree root.

(D) Carroll, because a danger which is not apparent to the reasonable person constitutes a trap.

71. Sackett owned a 10 acre parcel of realty known as Sackacre. On March 6, Sackett offered to sell Sackacre to Boland for $80,000. Boland said that he might be interested, but that he would not be in a position to make up his mind until July. Sackett said that she would hold the realty for Boland until then and signed a paper on which she wrote:

> "I hereby offer to sell Sackacre to Boland for $80,000 cash. In return for one dollar which I have on this date received, I promise to hold this offer open until July 15."

On July 1, Boland told Sackett that he was ready to purchase Sackacre, but Sackett told him that she had changed her mind and did not want to sell. Boland asserted a claim against Sackett based on her written promise to keep the offer open until July 15. At the trial, Sackett proved that she never actually received one dollar from Boland in return for her promise. In deciding Boland's claim, the court should find for

(A) Boland, because the parol evidence rule prevents Sackett from relying on oral evidence that she did not actually receive one dollar.

(B) Boland, because Boland detrimentally relied on Sackett's promise to keep the offer open until July 15.

(C) Sackett, because the realty is obviously worth more than one dollar.

(D) Sackett, because nothing was bargained for or given in exchange for Sackett's promise to keep the offer open until July 15.

Questions 72-73 are based on the following fact situation.

On March 1, Carlson, a well-known collector of antique automobiles, mailed to a newspaper an advertisement which read, in part: "I will pay $100 for information leading to purchase of 1927 Ford." On March 2, before the advertisement appeared in the newspaper and without knowing about it, Samsel phoned Carlson collect and offered to sell him a 1927 Ford.

On March 3, Wright saw Carlson's advertisement in the newspaper and remembered meeting someone who owned a 1927 Ford. After calling a few friends, Wright obtained the owner's name and address and mailed it to Carlson on March 3 with a request for the $100 reward.

On March 4, Carlson looked at Samsel's 1927 Ford and purchased it. Later that day, Carlson mailed to the newspaper for publication a second advertisement which in part read, "No reward for 1927 Ford. I hereby withdraw my previous request for information about 1927 Ford." The second advertisement did not appear in the newspaper until March 6.

On March 5, Carlson received Wright's letter, but discarded it because he had purchased Samsel's 1927 Ford.

72. If Samsel subsequently learned of the advertisement which was published on March 3 and asserted a claim against Carlson for $100, the court should find for

    (A) Samsel, because the advertisement was a general offer for a reward.

    (B) Samsel, because he contacted Carlson after Carlson mailed the reward offer to the newspaper.

    (C) Carlson, because Samsel was not aware of the advertisement when he contacted Carlson.

    (D) Carlson, because Samsel was, himself, the seller of the automobile.

73. If Wright asserts a claim against Carlson for $100, the court should find for

    (A) Carlson, because he mailed the second advertisement before receiving Wright's letter.

    (B) Carlson, because Wright's letter did not lead to the purchase of a 1927 Ford.

    (C) Wright, because he mailed the letter to Carlson before Carlson purchased a 1927 Ford.

    (D) Wright, because Carlson received Wright's letter before the second advertisement was published.

74. Paula, who was 4 years of age, was the plaintiff in a battery action against Davey, who was 7 years of age. At the trial of *Paula v. Davey*, Paula's attorney called Paula to testify on the plaintiff's direct case. After interviewing her, the trial judge ruled that because of Paula's youth, she was unable to appreciate her duty to testify truthfully, and therefore was not a competent witness. Paula's attorney subsequently called Wiseman, Paula's neighbor. Wiseman testified that immediately after the incident in question Paula had come running up to her on the street, crying and with her nose bleeding. Wiseman testified further that at that time Paula said, "Davey pushed me and gave me a bloody nose."

If Davey's attorney objects to Wiseman's statement about what Paula said to her, the court should rule that evidence

    (A) admissible as an excited utterance.

    (B) admissible because Paula's incompetence to testify made her a presently-unavailable declarant.

    (C) inadmissible because it is hearsay.

    (D) inadmissible because Paula was incompetent to testify.

75. Pursel asserted a claim against Diamond for injuries which Pursel received when she was struck by a truck owned by Diamond and driven by one of Diamond's employees. At trial, Pursel's attorney called Wren as a witness on the presentation of Pursel's direct case. In response to questions asked by Pursel's attorney, Wren stated that she was presently employed by Diamond, and that she had been driving Diamond's truck on the day of the accident. Pursel's attorney then asked, "You were going faster than 35 miles per hour, weren't you?" Diamond's attorney objected to the question on the ground that it was leading.

If the objection of Diamond's attorney is overruled, it will probably be because

    (A) Wren is employed by an adverse party.

    (B) Wren is a hostile witness.

    (C) leading questions are permitted on cross examination.

(D) the question was not leading.

Questions 76-77 are based on the following fact situation.

Gilroy, the owner of a gasoline delivery service, operated a tank truck for delivering gasoline. Gilroy's truck was thirty-five feet in length and had the words "DANGER — GASOLINE" printed on it. One day, while on the way to a gasoline delivery, Gilroy stopped at a bank on Baker Street. Although she saw an official sign which prohibited parking in that location, Gilroy parked her truck directly in front of the bank. A statute in the jurisdiction prohibited parking any vehicle longer than thirty feet on a city street. Another statute prohibited parking any vehicle directly in front of a bank. Gilroy was aware of both statutes.

While Gilroy was in the bank, Myatt, who was driving on Baker Street, lost control of her car and struck Gilroy's truck. As a result, a large quantity of gasoline in Gilroy's delivery tank exploded, injuring Myatt. Paige, a bank employee who was sitting at his desk inside the bank, was also injured in the explosion.

76. Assume that Paige asserts a claim against Gilroy for his injuries. If Paige's claim is successful, it will most likely be because

   (A) the statute which prohibited parking vehicles longer than thirty feet on a city street was a traffic safety statute.

   (B) Gilroy was aware that a statute prohibited parking any vehicle in front of a bank.

   (C) the reasonable person would not park a vehicle in violation of an official sign which prohibits parking.

   (D) transporting large quantities of gasoline is an unusually dangerous activity.

77. If Myatt asserts a negligence claim against Gilroy for her injuries, which of the following would be Gilroy's most effective argument in defense against that claim?

   (A) Myatt's injury did not result from Gilroy's

negligence.

   (B) Myatt assumed the risk of explosion, because Myatt knew or should have known that Gilroy's truck contained gasoline.

   (C) Gilroy was inside the bank at the time the accident occurred.

   (D) The collision was a superseding cause of the explosion.

Questions 78-79 are based on the following fact situation.

Mary Halsey, a seven-year-old girl, was admitted to a hospital unconscious. Doctors who examined her asked Mary's parents to consent to a blood transfusion for Mary, stating that Mary would probably die otherwise. Mary's parents refused, saying that they did not believe in blood transfusions.

A state statute provides that if a child is admitted to a hospital with a life-threatening disease or injury, and the parents of that child refuse to consent to treatment which in the opinion of hospital officials is necessary to save the child's life, the court shall designate the hospital administrator to act as the child's guardian for the purpose of consenting to such treatment. The hospital administrator immediately commenced a proceeding in a state court to have herself declared Mary Halsey's guardian under that statute. Mary's parents petitioned a federal court to enjoin the state court from granting the hospital administrator's application on the ground that the state law is unconstitutional on its face. Prior to the disposition of either proceeding, Mary died.

78. If the statute is found to be unconstitutional, it will most likely be because the statute

   (A) violates the Equal Protection clause of the Fourteenth Amendment.

   (B) is vague.

   (C) violates the Free Exercise clause of the First Amendment.

   (D) interferes with a fundamental right.

79. If the proceeding instituted by Mary's parents is

dismissed, it will most likely be because

(A) Mary's death has turned the controversy into a non-justiciable political question.

(B) Mary's death has made the proceeding moot.

(C) the court lacks jurisdiction under the Eleventh Amendment.

(D) the issues are not ripe since the highest state court has not yet ruled on the constitutionality of the statute.

80. After Isidore died without a will, the state treasurer instituted a proceeding for a declaration that Isidore's assets should escheat to the state, on the ground that there were no living persons eligible to inherit. Nancy opposed the proceeding, claiming that she was Isidore's niece, and therefore his heir under the state law of intestate distribution. In support of her claim, Nancy offered a Bible. She testified that the Bible had belonged to her deceased mother Marilyn, and that Marilyn had made notations in it indicating that her husband, Nancy's father, was Isidore's brother, and indicating the date of birth of her daughter, Nancy. The state treasurer objected to admission of the Bible.

If the notation in the Bible is admitted into evidence, it will probably be as

(A) an ancient document.

(B) a statement of Marilyn's personal history or pedigree.

(C) a transaction recorded under the "dead man's statute."

(D) a record of vital statistics.

81. Downing and Jensen agreed to rob a bank and planned the robbery for several weeks. According to their plan, Downing's car would be used as the getaway vehicle. Downing was to drive to and from the robbery, and was to wait in the car while Jensen went into the bank to hold it up. While driving to the bank with Jensen on the day the robbery was to take place, however, Downing began to have second thoughts. After a brief conversation with Jensen, Downing stopped the car

and went into a tobacco store where he telephoned the police and told them about the planned robbery. While Downing was in the store, Jensen left and robbed the bank himself. Because the police believed Downing's call to be a hoax, they took no steps to prevent the robbery. Later, Jensen was apprehended and convicted of robbing the bank.

If Downing is subsequently arrested and prosecuted for conspiracy to commit bank robbery, he should be found

(A) not guilty, if he removed his keys from the car when he got out to phone the police.

(B) not guilty, if he notified Jensen that he had changed his mind about going through with the plan.

(C) not guilty, if Downing's telephone call to the police led to the apprehension and conviction of Jensen.

(D) guilty.

82. Hicks was the owner and operator of a hotel. Because electrical wiring in the hotel was beginning to deteriorate, Hicks hired Lectric, a licensed electrician, to repair it. While doing so, Lectric negligently connected the wiring in room 201 to a dangerous high-voltage supply line instead of to a safe low-voltage supply line. The following day, when Greenleaf registered at the hotel, Hicks assigned him to room 201. That evening, while Greenleaf was attempting to adjust the electric heater in room 201, he received a severe electric shock as a result of the fact that the room had been connected to a high-voltage supply line.

If Greenleaf asserts a claim against Hicks for damage resulting from the electric shock, the court should find for

(A) Hicks, if Hicks hired Lectric as an independent contractor.

(B) Hicks, if reasonable inspection by Hicks would have failed to disclose Lectric's error.

(C) Greenleaf, if Hicks failed to use adequate care in hiring Lectric.

(D) Greenleaf, if Lectric's error made the wiring in room 201 ultra-hazardous.

83. When Oddo's mother died, she left him a 640 acre parcel of realty known as the Smith and Baker tract. Soon afterwards, Oddo executed a general warranty deed to his sister Silver conveying realty described as "the north 40 of the parcel of land known as the Smith and Baker tract." Oddo thereafter executed a quitclaim in favor of his wife Wiley to "all my right title and interest in a parcel of realty known as the Smith and Baker tract." If Wiley subsequently institutes a proceeding against Silver seeking to declare herself the owner of the entire Smith and Baker tract, should the court grant the relief requested by Wiley?

(A) No, because one who executes a quitclaim does not warrant that he holds any interest in the property described.

(B) No, if the description in Oddo's deed to Silver was reasonably sufficient to identify the property conveyed.

(C) Yes, if the jurisdiction is one in which reference to government survey markers is customarily used in describing realty in general warranty deeds.

(D) Yes, because a deed which conveys a portion of a parcel of realty must describe the portion conveyed in terms of "metes and bounds" or other survey terminology.

84. *The Daily*, a newspaper, published an article stating that Patton had once been convicted of armed robbery. In fact, Patton had never been convicted of any crime. If Patton asserts a defamation claim against *The Daily*, which one of the following additional facts or inferences, if it was the only one true, would be most likely to result in a judgment for *The Daily*?

(A) Official government records indicating that Patton had never been convicted of robbery were available for public inspection.

(B) Officials of *The Daily* responsible for publishing the article reasonably believed the statement to be true.

(C) Patton was a public figure.

(D) Patton failed to prove that damage resulted from the statement.

85. Moran was the owner of a house in which she lived with her 23 year old son David. After receiving a tip that David was involved in the unlawful sale of drugs, two police officers went to Moran's home for the purpose of questioning David. When they arrived, David was not in, but Moran admitted them to the house. The officers explained why they had come, and asked whether they could see David's room. Moran showed them to David's room and permitted them to enter, saying that David never locked his door. When the officers saw a footlocker in the room, they asked Moran whether they could look inside it. She told them that David was the only one who had a key to the footlocker, but said if they could find some way to open it, she had no objection to their looking inside. While Moran watched, one of the officers picked the lock and opened the footlocker. In it they found a plastic bag containing cocaine. The officers left the plastic bag there, and returned later with a search warrant which they obtained by swearing that they had seen cocaine in David's footlocker. After seizing the cocaine, they arrested David for unlawful possession of a dangerous drug. Prior to trial, David asked the court to suppress use of the cocaine as evidence.

David's motion should be

(A) denied, because Moran gave the police permission to open the footlocker.

(B) denied, but only if Moran had apparent authority to permit the search of David's room.

(C) granted.

(D) denied, if the officers had probable cause to believe that they would find cocaine in the footlocker.

86. After negotiation, Biddle and Sadick entered into a valid written contract for the sale to Biddle of Sadick's realty. The contract provided for closing of title "on or before June 15." On June 12, Sadick informed Biddle that she would not be able to close until June 16. On June 16 Sadick tendered a conveyance. Although Sadick complied with the requirements of the contract in all other respects, Biddle refused to accept the conveyance on the ground that the date for performance had passed.

   If Sadick asserts a claim against Biddle as a result of Biddle's refusal to accept Sadick's conveyance on June 16, the court should find for

   (A) Biddle, if circumstances contemplated by the parties at the time the contract was formed made it essential that the conveyance occur on or before June 15.

   (B) Biddle, only if the contract contained the phrase "time is of the essence" or language of similar import.

   (C) Sadick, only if a conveyance after June 15 would not cause Biddle to sustain damage.

   (D) Sadick, if she made a reasonable effort to comply with the terms of the contract.

87. Gascorp was the manufacturer of a gas known as Z-14, which it sold for commercial use. Gascorp produced the gas at its factory, and stored it in a large tank located behind the factory building. Although Gascorp made reasonable inspections of its storage tank at reasonable intervals, a leak in the tank allowed some Z-14 gas to escape. A wind carried the escaped gas to the home of Palmer, located one-half mile from the Gascorp factory. Palmer died as a result of his exposure to the Z-14 gas.

   In a strict liability claim against Gascorp for damages resulting from Palmer's exposure to Z-14 gas, which of the following must Palmer's personal representative prove in order to prevail?

   (A) The tank in which Gascorp stored the Z-14 gas was defective.

   (B) The Z-14 gas was defectively designed.

   (C) The Z-14 gas was defectively manufactured.

   (D) Z-14 gas is extremely deadly.

88. In 1968 Ford took a drug known as RST which, in the form of tablets, was routinely prescribed for increasing the fertility of males. At that time, only five pharmaceutical companies manufactured and marketed RST tablets, and these tablets were identical in every respect. Since, then, 95 percent of all the male children born to fathers who were taking RST at the time of conception have proved to be sterile.

   Ford's son Stewart was conceived in 1968 while Ford was taking RST. In 1986 Stewart, then eighteen years of age, learned that he was sterile. Medical experts agree that Stewart's sterility was caused by the RST which Ford was taking when Stewart was conceived. Because it was not possible to determine which company manufactured and marketed the particular RST tablets taken by Ford, Stewart asserted a claim against Drugstore, a retailer of drugs. In support of his claim, Stewart alleged that all RST tablets were defective, and that the tablets taken by Ford had been purchased from Drugstore. Drugstore admitted that all RST tablets were defective, but denied liability.

   The outcome of Stewart's claim against Drugstore will most likely turn on whether

   (A) the RST tablets taken by Ford were purchased from Drugstore.

   (B) the five manufacturers of RST were involved in a concert-of-action.

   (C) liability for damage resulting from defects in RST can be imposed on an industry-wide basis.

   (D) drugstore's sales of RST represented a substantial market share in 1968.

89. Pall asserted a negligence claim against Diner Restaurant for personal injuries sustained when Pall fell down a stairway while leaving the res-

taurant. Diner asserted a defense of contributory negligence. At the trial, Diner's attorney called Westbrook as a witness. After answering several preliminary questions, Westbrook testified that she observed Pall leaving the restaurant just before the accident, and that Pall appeared to be intoxicated. Upon timely objection by Pall's attorney, Westbrook's statement that Pall appeared to be intoxicated should be

(A) excluded, unless the judge decides that Westbrook's opinion is rationally based on her personal perceptions.

(B) excluded, unless the judge decides that Westbrook is an expert on intoxication.

(C) admitted, but the judge should instruct the jury to disregard it unless the jury decides that Westbrook is an expert on intoxication.

(D) admitted, but the judge should instruct the jury to disregard it unless the jury decides that Westbrook's opinion is rationally based on her personal perceptions.

90. The Department of Sanitation was established as an agency of the State of Caliope in the year 1860, for the purpose of providing free sanitation services to the people of the state. Since its inception, the Department's activities have included garbage collection and street cleaning. Ambriz, an alien residing within the State of Caliope, applied for a job as a Sanitary Street Engineer Class III with the state Department of Sanitation. Although he qualified in all other respects, the state Personnel Division rejected Ambriz's application on the sole ground that he was not a United States citizen. A statute of the State of Caliope provides in part that "no person shall be eligible for employment as a Sanitary Street Engineer Class III who is not a citizen of the United States." Ambriz challenged the constitutionality of that statute in a appropriate proceeding.

The statute should be found constitutional

(A) because street cleaning is a traditional government activity in the State of Caliope.

(B) if there is a rational basis for restricting employment by the State of Caliope to citizens of the United States.

(C) if a Sanitary Street Engineer Class III performs policy-making functions or has broad discretion in the execution of public policy.

(D) unless employment by the state is found to be a fundamental right.

91. So many pigeons and other birds gathered in the branches of trees in front of the Wave Crest Hotel that bird droppings frequently made the city sidewalk there slippery. For this reason, Wave Crest employees washed away the droppings on the sidewalk in front of the hotel with a hose every morning. One morning they failed to do so. While leaving the hotel later that day, Palko, a paying guest, slipped on the droppings and fell, fracturing his elbow. Palko subsequently instituted a claim against Wave Crest, alleging that his injury resulted from its negligent failure to wash bird droppings from the city sidewalk in front of the hotel.

If the only defense asserted by Wave Crest is that it has no duty to wash bird droppings from the city sidewalk, the court should find for

(A) Wave Crest, unless wave Crest was in possession and control of the trees in which the birds gathered.

(B) Wave Crest, because the city sidewalk on which the accident occurred was not the property of Wave Crest.

(C) Palko, because Wave Crest is strictly liable for injuries sustained by invitees while entering and leaving Wave Crest business premises.

(D) Palko, if the past conduct of Wave Crest employees led Palko to reasonably believe that the sidewalk would be free of bird droppings.

Questions 92-93 are based on the following fact situation.

Because of a deficit in the city transportation budget, the city council raised the fare on city buses from $.75 to $1.00. Although all members of the city council are well-to-do, 80 percent of the people who travel on city buses during peak hours have low incomes.

92. Which of the following is most likely to have standing to challenge the constitutionality of the fare increase?

    (A) The Drivers Union, an organization of city bus drivers which claims that without the fare increase many of its members will lose their jobs.

    (B) The Bus Riders Association, an organization dedicated to promoting low fares on public transportation systems throughout the state.

    (C) A person with a low income who does not normally travel on city buses, but who fears that the fare increase may prevent him from doing so in the future.

    (D) A wealthy stockbroker who travels on city buses to commute to and from her office.

93. Assuming that a person or organization with standing to do so institutes a proceeding to challenge its constitutionality, the fare increase should be found

    (A) constitutional, if it has a rational basis.

    (B) constitutional, only if it is necessary to serve a compelling interest of the state.

    (C) unconstitutional, only if it is found to interfere with a fundamental right.

    (D) unconstitutional, if it is found to discriminate against a discrete class of persons.

94. Down kept a pet cougar in a yard which was surrounded by a wire chain-link fence. Pierce, who lived in the vicinity, frequently walked on the public sidewalk adjacent to Down's yard. One day, while Pierce was standing on the public sidewalk looking at the cougar through Down's

fence, the cougar sprang toward Pierce. Because the fence was badly deteriorated, it collapsed under the cougar's weight and fell on Pierce, inflicting serious injuries.

If Pierce asserts a negligence claim against Down as a result of her injuries, the court should find for

    (A) Pierce, because the keeping of a wild animal is prima facie negligent.

    (B) Pierce, but only if the reasonable person in Down's position would have repaired the fence.

    (C) Down, because Pierce assumed the risk by standing by the fence and looking at the cougar.

    (D) Down, unless Down knew that the fence was in need of repair.

Questions 95-96 are based on the following fact situation.

On March 1, Grauer, a farmer, entered into a written contract with Trout. By its terms, Trout agreed to plow Grauer's fields by April 1, using Trout's own tractor. In return, Grauer promised to pay $2,000 upon completion of the work. On March 25, while Trout was plowing Grauer's field, her tractor broke down. Trout informed Grauer that because the tractor needed extensive repairs it would be impossible to finish the job by April 1 unless she rented another tractor. Trout said that she could rent one for $600, but would not do so unless Grauer agreed to add the rental charge to Trout's fee for preparing the field. Grauer agreed without complaint, afraid that the value of his crop would be reduced if the field was not plowed in time. Trout returned to work after renting a tractor for $600.

While plowing, Trout saw Grauer's prize bull fall into the creek. Knowing that the bull was worth $5,000 and that it was likely to drown in the creek, Trout rescued the bull, sustaining injury in the process. When Trout rescued the bull, she did not expect compensation, but when Grauer learned of Trout's injury, he promised to pay her an additional $1,000 for rescuing his bull. After Trout finished plowing Grauer's field, however, Grauer refused to pay her any more than $2,000.

95. If Trout asserts a claim against Grauer on account of Grauer's promise to pay an additional $600 for the rental of a tractor, which of the following would be Grauer's most effective argument in defense?

    (A) Grauer's promise to pay for the tractor rental was not in writing.

    (B) Grauer's promise to pay for the tractor rental was unsupported by consideration.

    (C) Grauer's promise to pay for the tractor rental was induced by economic duress.

    (D) Grauer detrimentally relied on Trout's original promise to complete plowing of the field by April 1 at a price of $2,000.

96. Assume for the purpose of this question only that Trout subsequently asserted a claim against Grauer on account of Grauer's promise to pay $1,000 to compensate her for rescuing the bull. If Grauer's only defense is lack of consideration, which of the following would be Trout's most effective argument in support of her claim?

    (A) Grauer's promise was given in exchange for Trout's rescue of the bull.

    (B) Grauer was morally obligated to compensate Trout for rescuing the bull.

    (C) Allowing Grauer to avoid compensating Trout for rescuing the bull would unjustly enrich Grauer.

    (D) Trout detrimentally relied on Grauer's promise by completing the plowing of Grauer's field.

97. After Daisy and Irvin met at a party, Daisy offered to give Irvin a ride home in her new car. When they got to the car, Irvin asked Daisy to let him drive it. Although Daisy knew that Irvin was intoxicated, she permitted him to drive the car while she sat in the passenger seat. While Irvin was driving, he collided with a car driven by Pachek. If Pachek asserts a claim against Daisy for injuries sustained in the accident, the court

should find for

(A) Pachek, because Daisy was present in the car at the time of the accident.

(B) Pachek, if Daisy consciously disregarded the fact that Irvin was intoxicated when she allowed Irvin to drive her car.

(C) Daisy, unless the accident resulted from Irvin's intoxication.

(D) Daisy, because Daisy was not driving the car at the time of the accident.

Questions 98-99 are based on the following fact situation.

Read the summaries of the decisions in the four cases (A-D) below. Then decide which is most applicable as a precedent to each of the cases in the questions that follow, and indicate each choice by marking the corresponding space on the answer sheet.

(A) *People v. Allison* — Believing that Vertin was attacking her, Allison swung a tennis racket at Vertin hoping to frighten Vertin away, but not meaning to strike Vertin with it. The tennis racket struck Vertin in the head, causing his death. At Allison's trial, over Allison's objection, the judge instructed the jury to find Allison guilty of involuntary manslaughter if the force used by Allison was excessive. Allison's conviction for involuntary manslaughter was affirmed.

(B) *Boddy v. State* — Boddy's wife was admitted to the intensive care unit of a hospital following an automobile accident. While visiting her, Boddy overheard doctors saying that there was no hope of saving the life of a certain patient who would be in intense pain and paralyzed for as long as she lived. Mistakenly believing that they were talking about his wife, Boddy subsequently smothered her to death with a pillow while she was asleep in the hospital bed. Boddy was convicted of murder after the court refused to charge the jury that if Boddy believed that his wife was hopelessly ill and in intense pain they could find him guilty of voluntary manslaughter. Boddy's conviction for murder was reversed.

(C) *Commonwealth v. Cain* — While Cain was robbing a tavern, the bartender attempted to grab Cain's gun. During the struggle, the gun accidentally went off, seriously injuring the bartender. At Cain's trial for attempted murder, the court instructed the jury to return a verdict of not guilty if they found that Cain did not intend to cause the bartender's death. Cain's acquittal was affirmed.

(D) *People v. Derby* — After Derby quarreled with her lover, she fired a gun at him while he was with his wife. The bullet missed Derby's lover, but struck and killed his wife. At Derby's trial, it was established that she fired with the intention of frightening both her lover and his wife, but that she did not mean to strike either of them. Derby was convicted of murder after the court refused to charge the jury on involuntary manslaughter. The conviction was affirmed.

98. At Elridge's trial for attempted murder, the prosecution proved that Elridge tried to strangle his wife while she was sleeping in bed beside him. Elridge testified that he had just awakened from a vivid dream in which he saw his wife having sexual intercourse with another man, and that when he tried to strangle her he believed that the dream was true. Elridge asked the court to charge the jury on attempted voluntary manslaughter.

99. At Fordham's trial for murder, the prosecution proved that Fordham was driving while intoxicated when his car struck another car, killing all its occupants. Fordham appealed from his conviction for voluntary manslaughter.

100. Van, who lived alone in the woods, frequently dressed in the skins of animals. One day during the deer hunting season, Van was crawling along on the ground, dressed in deerskin, looking for

edible mushrooms. Daisy, who was deer hunting, noticed movement in the bushes. Seeing Van's deerskin cloak, and believing him to be a deer, she shot at Van, wounding him severely. When she found that she had shot a human being instead of a deer, she was shocked. Van begged her to take him to a hospital, but she ran to her car and fled without making any attempt to secure aid for Van. Two hours later, having received no medical treatment, Van died of the bullet wound. If Daisy is charged with the murder of Van in a jurisdiction which applies the common law definition of murder, her most effective argument in defense would be that

(A) she did not intend to kill Van.

(B) Van would have died of his bullet wounds even if Daisy had gotten him to a hospital.

(C) Van's wearing of the deerskin during the deer hunting season was contributory negligence.

(D) Van's death was not the result of any affirmative act committed by Daisy.

QUESTIONS
PRACTICE MBE — P.M. EXAM

PRACTICE MBE — P.M. QUESTIONS

Questions 101-103 are based on the following fact situation.

Adam, who owned a home in a residential development, decided to have his driveway paved. He called Paver, a licensed contractor who specialized in residential driveways, and asked for an estimate on the job. Although the standard market price to pave a driveway the size of Adam's was $2,750, Paver was willing to do the job for $2,500 since business was slow. Adam agreed to hire him to do the job at that price and filled out and signed a detailed work order for Paver's work crew. Since Adam was planning to go on vacation for two weeks, he and Paver agreed that the job would be finished by the time Adam returned.

Three days later, Paver's work crew went out to do the job described in Adam's work order. By mistake they paved Bickley's driveway which was identical to Adam's except that it was on a different street. Bickley was out of town at the time. The job cost Paver $2,600 in labor and materials and increased the value of Bickley's realty by $2,100. Adam did not communicate with Paver while away on vacation. When he returned and discovered that his driveway had not yet been paved, he demanded that Paver perform as agreed, but Paver refused.

101. Assume for the purpose of this question only that Paver asserts a claim against Bickley on a quasi-contract theory. If Paver is successful, he is entitled to

   (A) $2,100 (the increase in the value of Bickley's realty).

   (B) $2,500 (the agreed price in the contract between Paver and Adam).

   (C) $2,600 (Paver's cost in paving Bickley's driveway).

   (D) $2,750 (the standard price of the paving job).

102. Assume for the purpose of this question only that

after the driveway was paved, Bickley promised to pay Paver $2,000 for the job. In a jurisdiction that adopts the view of the Restatement (2nd) of Contracts, if Bickley then refused to pay, and Paver sued him for breaching his promise, which of the following additional facts or inferences, if it was the only one true, would be most likely to result in a judgment for Paver?

   (A) When Bickley promised to pay, Bickley knew that Paver had already paved his driveway.

   (B) When Bickley promised to pay, Bickley did not know that Paver had already paved his driveway.

   (C) Bickley decided to have his driveway paved before speaking with Paver.

   (D) Bickley did not decide to have his driveway paved until speaking with Paver.

103. Assume that Adam asserts a breach of contract claim against Paver because of Paver's failure to pave Adam's driveway. Which of the following additional facts or inferences, if it was the only one true, would be most likely to result in a judgment for Paver?

   (A) Paver did not succeed in collecting from Bickley.

   (B) In filling out the work order, Adam accidentally wrote down Bickley's address instead of his own.

   (C) Paver could not pave Adam's driveway at the agreed price without sustaining a loss.

   (D) There is another contractor who is willing to pave Adam's driveway for $2,500.

104. Alonzo and Brookler, both residents of the State of DelMava, entered into an installment contract for the sale of goods. When a dispute arose between them under the contract, Alonzo asserted a claim for $52,000 against Brookler in a United

States District Court in the State of DelMava. Brookler moved to dismiss the claim on jurisdictional grounds.

Did the United States District Court have jurisdiction to adjudicate the claim?

(A) Yes, if a statute of the State of DelMava grants concurrent state and federal jurisdiction over contract disputes.

(B) Yes, if a federal statute grants jurisdiction to hear such a claim to the United States District Court.

(C) No, under Article III of the United States Constitution.

(D) No, under the Eleventh Amendment to the United States Constitution.

105. Oilcorp was a major corporation with shares of stock traded on several stock exchanges. When rumors began to circulate that Oilcorp was experiencing financial difficulties, the price of Oilcorp stock fell drastically. Dabbs was a journalist who wrote a financial news column for *The Bugle*, a daily newspaper.

One day, while Dabbs was discussing the Oilcorp rumor with her friend Frasier, Frasier said, "I wouldn't be surprised if the whole thing was some kind of stunt to manipulate the price of stock." Dabbs was aware that Frasier knew nothing about the stock market or about Oilcorp. The following day, based solely upon what she had heard from Frasier, Dabbs made the following statement in her column:

> "Don't be fooled by rumors that Oilcorp is in trouble. Insiders say that the whole thing is a stunt to manipulate the price of the stock. I say Oilcorp is still a good investment."

After reading *The Bugle*, Paba invested in Oilcorp stock in reliance on Dabbs's statement. Two days later, Oilcorp filed a petition in bankruptcy, and its stock became worthless. If Paba asserts a claim against Dabbs for misrepresentation, which one of the following facts or inferences, if it were the only one true, would be most likely to result in a judgment for Dabbs?

(A) At the time Paba purchased Oilcorp stock, Oilcorp's financial condition was a matter of public record.

(B) Dabbs's statement "I think Oilcorp is a good investment" was an expression of opinion.

(C) Paba did not purchase the edition of *The Bugle* which contained Dabb's statement, but read it after finding it on a bus.

(D) Dabbs did not know that any person would rely on her statement.

Questions 106-107 are based on the following fact situation.

Upon borrowing money from Ausler, Odish executed a note and a mortgage on her realty in favor of Ausler. Ausler immediately and properly recorded the mortgage. One month later, Odish borrowed money from Britt, executing a note and a mortgage on the realty in Britt's favor. Britt immediately and properly recorded the mortgage. Odish died soon afterwards, leaving a will which devised the realty to Lazarus for life, remainder to Richards. Lazarus subsequently moved onto the realty. Neither Ausler nor Britt received payment as required by the notes executed by Odish.

106. Assume for the purpose of this question only that without notifying or serving process on Lazarus and Richards, Ausler asks a court to order a foreclosure sale of the realty, the court should

(A) order the sale of a life estate only.

(B) order the sale of a remainder only.

(C) order the sale of a fee interest.

(D) deny Ausler's request.

107. Assume for the purpose of this question only that Ausler does not institute a judicial proceeding, but that Britt institutes a proceeding in which he joins Lazarus, Richards, and Ausler as parties, and in which Britt asks a court to order a foreclosure sale of the realty. Should the court order a sale?

(A) No, because Ausler's interest in realty is superior to Britt's.

(B) No, unless Ausler waives his prior right in writing.

(C) Yes, and the proceeds may be used to satisfy the debt owed to Britt because first in time is first in right.

(D) Yes, but proceeds of the sale must first be applied to satisfy the debt owed to Ausler because Ausler's right is superior to Britt's.

108. Dustin and Hodges, who resided in the City of Bronston, purchased rifles. Because neither of them had ever fired a rifle before, they decided to take them to the municipal dump to try them out. Although both believed that the dump was outside City of Bronston municipal limits, it was actually within municipal limits. At the dump, Dustin shot his rifle in Hodges's direction, aiming slightly to the right to miss Hodges. The bullet struck a rock and ricocheted, hitting Hodges in the back and causing his death.

A City of Bronston ordinance provides that "Any person who shall discharge a firearm knowing that he is within the municipal limits shall be guilty of a misdemeanor punishable by a maximum fine of $100." Which of the following is the most serious crime of which Dustin may properly be convicted?

(A) Murder.

(B) Voluntary Manslaughter.

(C) Attempted murder.

(D) Discharging a firearm within the municipal limits.

Questions 109-110 are based on the following fact situation.

Pailey asserted a personal injury claim against Dickman for injuries which she sustained when their cars collided at an intersection. At the trial, Westphal, an eyewitness to the accident testified that, when it occurred, the traffic light at the intersection was red

against Pailey. In a prior deposition given under oath, Westphal had stated that, at the time of the accident, the light was green in Pailey's favor.

109. Assume the following facts for the purpose of this question only: Westphal was called by Dickman and her testimony was given on direct examination by Dickman's attorney. On cross-examination Westphal authenticated the deposition described above, and Pailey's attorney offered it in evidence. Over Dickman's objection the deposition should be

(A) admitted for impeachment only.

(B) admitted as substantive evidence only.

(C) admitted for impeachment and as substantive evidence.

(D) excluded.

110. Assume the following facts for the purpose of this question only: Westphal had been called by Pailey and her testimony was given on direct examination by Pailey's attorney. After Westphal left the stand Pailey's attorney offered the above-described deposition, properly authenticated, into evidence. Over objection by Dickman's attorney, the court should rule that the deposition is

(A) not admissible, unless Westphal was asked about it before leaving the stand.

(B) not admissible, because Westphal was Pailey's own witness.

(C) admissible, because Westphal was a hostile witness.

(D) admissible, only if Westphal is given a subsequent opportunity to explain the inconsistency.

Questions 111-112 are based on the following fact situation.

By a valid written contract Brant and Sandler agreed to the purchase and sale of Sandler's 40 acre apple orchard. After the contract was executed but prior to the closing of title and while Sandler was still in possession of the property, a hurricane caused some of the apple trees to be uprooted and destroyed. Although both Brant and Sandler had an insurable interest in the realty at the time of the hurricane, neither had purchased insurance. On the day set for closing Sandler tendered a conveyance, but Brant refused to go through with the purchase.

111. If Sandler asserts a claim against Brant for breach of contract in a jurisdiction which applies the common law doctrine of equitable conversion, the court should find for

  (A) Brant, if the damaged trees were a material part of the realty.

  (B) Brant, because the trees became a personal property when the wind severed them from the realty.

  (C) Sandler, because the risk of loss passed to Brant upon execution of the contract of sale.

  (D) Sandler, but if the damaged tress were a material part of the realty the purchase price will be reduced in proportion to the value of the damage.

112. If Sandler asserts a claim against Brant for breach of contract in a jurisdiction which has adopted applicable provisions of the Uniform Vendor and Purchaser Risk Act, the court should find for

  (A) Brant, if the damaged trees were a material part of the realty.

  (B) Brant, because the storm changed the condition of the realty through no fault of Brant's.

  (C) Sandler, because the risk of loss passed to Brant upon execution of the contract of sale.

  (D) Sandler, but if the damaged trees were a material part of the realty the purchase price will be reduced in proportion to the value of the damage.

113. Which of the following constitutional provisions

is most likely to give Congress the power to pass a law making it a federal crime for persons or corporations in the construction industry to practice racial discrimination in their hiring practices?

  (A) The Due Process Clause of the Fifth Amendment.

  (B) The Involuntary Servitude Clause of the Thirteenth Amendment.

  (C) The Equal Protection Clause of the Fourteenth Amendment.

  (D) The Previous Condition of Servitude Clause of the Fifteenth Amendment.

Questions 114-115 are based on the following fact situation.

On March 1, Sack entered into a written agreement with Richmond, a licensed real estate broker. By its terms, Sack agreed to pay Richmond a commission equal to 6 percent of the price if, prior to April 15, Richmond procured a buyer ready, willing, and able to pay $50,000 for Sack's realty. In return, Richmond agreed to make reasonable efforts to sell it.

After the agreement was executed, Richmond advertised Sack's property and showed it to several prospective buyers. On April 10, Bader signed a document agreeing to purchase Sack's realty for $50,000 but stating that her agreement was contingent upon her success in obtaining the necessary financing. The same day, Richmond presented to Sack the document which Bader had signed. Sack read it, thought for a moment, and handed it back to Richmond, saying, "I won't even consider a deal built around a contingency." Although Richmond protested that the agreement between him and Sack did not specify a sale without contingencies, Sack refused to discuss the matter any further.

On April 11, Richmond informed Bader of Sack's response. Bader then obtained a cashier's check for $50,000 payable to Sack. She delivered the check to Richmond together with a signed document in which she agreed to purchase Sack's realty for that sum. On April 14, Richmond presented the second document to Sack with the cashier's check. Sack said, "I've changed my mind. I'm not interested in selling."

114. If Richmond asserts a claim against Sack for a commission, the court should find for

    (A) Sack, because he did not agree to sell the realty to Bader.

    (B) Sack, because his rejection of Bader's offer on April 10, terminated his agreement with Richmond.

    (C) Richmond, because Sack's oral rejection of Bader's written offer of April 10 was invalid under the Statute of Frauds.

    (D) Richmond, because on April 14 Bader was ready, willing, and able to purchase Sack's realty for $50,000.

115. If Bader institutes a proceeding against Sack for an order directing Sack to sell her the realty for $50,000 the court should find for

    (A) Sack, because he did not agree to sell the realty to Bader.

    (B) Sack, unless his attempt to orally modify his written agreement with Richmond was invalid.

    (C) Bader, but only if she can show that the realty is unique or that a judgment for damages would not be an adequate remedy.

    (D) Bader, because her written agreement to purchase was delivered with the cashier's check prior to April 15.

116. Darcy was driving her car on State Street when its steering mechanism failed, causing her to lose control of the vehicle. The vehicle spun approximately 250 degrees before skidding across Ponce's lawn and colliding with the side of Ponce's house, causing serious structural damage to the building.

    If Ponce asserts a claim against Darcy for damage to his realty, the court should find for

    (A) Ponce, because Darcy entered his realty without his permission.

    (B) Ponce, but only if Darcy negligently operated or maintained her car.

    (C) Ponce, if Darcy had the last clear chance to avoid damaging his realty.

    (D) Darcy, because she was privileged by necessity to enter Ponce's realty.

Questions 117-118 are based on the following fact situation.

In an action by Pinto against Dean, Pinto claimed that Dean breached a contract to market Pinto's products. At the trial Pinto testified that she and Dean had reached an agreement at a conference held in the office of Pinto's attorney Alvarado on October 15. She stated that she and Dean discussed five separate products on that occasion. On direct examination of Pinto, Alvarado asked her to name the products which had been discussed. Pinto named four of them, but said she could not remember the fifth. After having them properly marked for identification, Alvarado offered to show Pinto notes which Alvarado had made during the conference, asking whether looking at them would refresh Pinto's recollection.

117. Assume for the purpose of this question only that Dean's attorney objected to Pinto's looking at the notes. The objection should be

    (A) sustained, because the notes had not been made by Pinto.

    (B) sustained, because the notes were not in evidence.

    (C) sustained, because Alvarado's question was leading.

    (D) overruled.

118. Assume for the purpose of this question only that Dean's attorney did not object to Pinto's looking at the notes, and Pinto stated that looking at the notes refreshed her recollection. Assume further that after looking at the notes Pinto named the fifth product, and that Alvarado then offered the notes in evidence. If Dean's attorney objects to admission of the notes in evidence, the objection should be

(A) overruled, because the notes constitute a business record.

(B) overruled, because Pinto used the notes to refresh her recollection while testifying.

(C) sustained, because the notes are hearsay not within any exception.

(D) sustained, because the notes constitute an attorney's work product.

Questions 119-120 are based on the following fact situation.

A state law empowers any municipality within the state to collect a property tax from its landowners if a plan to do so is proposed by its governing body and approved by a majority of its eligible voters. The Township of Danvers is a municipality governed by a Township Council. Pursuant to the above law, the Danvers Township Council proposed a property tax plan and scheduled a special election for August 15 to submit the plan for voter approval. The Township Council declared that only persons owning land within the township were eligible to vote in the special election, and that eligible voters were required to register for that purpose at the Danvers Township Hall between the hours of 1 p.m. and 3 p.m. on Tuesday July 15. The constitutionality of the special election was challenged in an appropriate proceeding by a petitioner with standing.

119. If the special election is found to be unconstitutional, it will probably be because

(A) the eligibility requirements violated the Fifteenth Amendment by excluding a discrete class of persons.

(B) the registration requirement had the effect of imposing a residence qualification for voter eligibility.

(C) all persons who did not own land were excluded from the voting process.

(D) conducting the special election on an at-large basis could have the effect of diluting the political power of a particular interest group.

120. Assume the following facts for the purpose of this question only: The petitioner argued that the registration schedule was discriminatory, proving that a substantial percentage of persons who owned land in the township of Danvers were males who commuted to work in a city 45 miles away and were unable to register during the scheduled hours without missing a day's work and incurring a loss of income. In response, the Township Council argued that the registration schedule had a rational basis, proving that its timing allowed the process to be carried out with volunteer labor which would save the Township the cost of hiring special registration personnel. If these are the only arguments made, the court should declare the registration schedule invalid because

(A) it discriminates against commuters on the basis of their lifestyle.

(B) it discriminates on the basis of wealth by excluding those who cannot afford to lose a day's work.

(C) it results in benign sex discrimination.

(D) the right to vote is a fundamental right.

121. Charron was the manufacturer of the "Charron Reclining Basket Chair," which she usually sold only to furniture dealers. When Charron recently stopped making the product, she found that she had only 75 Reclining Basket Chairs left. As a result, Charron published the following advertisement in a popular magazine:

> "For Sale to the Public. Charron Reclining Basket Chairs at $100 each (or $80 each in orders of 10 or more). Act fast. There are only 75 left. When they're gone, don't ask for any more."

On February 12, Furness a furniture dealer saw the advertisement and wrote to Charron, "We will purchase all 75 Charron Reclining Basket Chairs at the wholesale price."

On February 15, Charron received Furness's letter and wrote to Furness saying, "This will confirm our agreement to the sale of 75 Charron Reclining Basket Chairs at $80 each. Shipment to follow immediately."

On February 20, Furness telephoned Charron to say that he had changed his mind and did not want the chairs after all. Within the next two weeks, Charron sold all the chairs for $80 each to individuals who purchased one chair each.

If Charron asserts a claim against Furness for damages resulting from breach of contract, the court should award Charron

(A) a sum equivalent to the profit which Charron would have made by selling all the chairs to Furness.

(B) a sum equivalent to the total of the difference between $100 per chair and the price which Charron actually received.

(C) a sum equivalent to the difference between the price which Furness had agreed to pay and the actual market value of the chairs.

(D) nothing because Charron sustained no loss as a result of Furness's failure to purchase the chairs.

122. Pabst brought an action against Discount for injuries which he sustained when a gas stove which he purchased from Discount exploded while he was attempting to use it. At the trial, Pabst produced a snapshot photograph which he said had been taken by him prior to the accident and which he said was an accurate representation of the stove. On behalf of Discount, a Discount employee named Weber testified that he had installed the stove. Weber produced a photograph from an advertising brochure and stated that it fairly and accurately represented the stove which Pabst had purchased from Discount and which Weber had installed. The stove in the photograph offered by Discount was clearly different from the stove in the photograph offered by Pabst.

Both photographs were offered into evidence, and each party's attorney objected to admission of the other party's photograph. In response to the objections, the court should

(A) admit both photographs and allow the jury to

decide whether either of them accurately represents the stove in question.

(B) admit only the photograph offered by Pabst.

(C) admit only the photograph offered by Discount.

(D) not admit either photograph.

Questions 123-124 are based on the following fact situation.

Luz, the owner of a seven-story office building, leased the entire sixth floor to Tuck, an attorney, for a period of five years by a written lease which fixed the rent at $2,000 per month. There were only two offices on the sixth floor, identified as Office 6A and Office 6B. A clause in the lease provided that in the event it ever became necessary to determine how the rent payments were apportioned, it was understood that $900 of each month's rent was to be applied to Office 6A, $900 was to be applied to Office 6B, and $200 to the hallways and other common areas. The lease prohibited assignment by Tuck without Luz's written permission, and provided that such permission would not be unreasonably withheld.

One year after executing the lease, Tuck entered into a written agreement with Seaver. Under its terms, Seaver was to occupy Office 6A for the balance of Tuck's term at a monthly rental of $1,500 payable to Tuck. Seaver was an attorney with a better reputation and a more lucrative practice than Tuck's.

123. Assume for the purpose of this question only that Luz refused to consent to Tuck's arrangement with Seaver, and that Luz subsequently asserted a claim against Tuck for breaching the lease provision prohibiting assignment. Which of the following would be Tuck's most effective argument in response to that claim?

(A) Tuck's agreement with Seaver was not an assignment because the rent paid by Seaver was not in the same sum as the rent paid by Tuck.

(B) Tuck's agreement with Seaver was not an assignment because it only gave Seaver the right to occupy part of the sixth floor.

(C) The clause prohibiting assignment was an invalid restraint on alienation.

(D) Luz's refusal to consent was not reasonable because Seaver's credit was as good as Tuck's.

124. Assume the following additional facts for the purpose of this question only: Luz consented to the arrangement between Tuck and Seaver, but one month before the term expired Seaver vacated the premises and made no further payments. After Seaver moved out, the office which Seaver had occupied remained vacant. For the final month of the lease term, Tuck paid only $1,100 to Luz, although Luz demanded an additional $900. In an appropriate proceeding, Luz can collect $900 from

(A) Tuck only.

(B) Seaver only.

(C) Tuck and/or Seaver.

(D) Neither Tuck nor Seaver.

125. Romero wrote a column about life in suburbia which appeared regularly in the *Daily Times*, a newspaper of general circulation. In one of his columns, Romero mentioned his neighbor Nadel by name, and referred to him as "a silly pig." If Nadel asserts a defamation claim against Romero as a result of this reference, which of the following would be Romero's most effective argument in defense?

(A) Romero did not have actual malice when he made the statement.

(B) Reasonable persons would not believe that the statement asserted a fact about Nadel.

(C) Reasonable persons would not believe the statement to be true.

(D) At the time Romero made the statement he was of the opinion that it was an accurate assertion of fact.

Questions 126-127 are based on the following fact situation.

WKKW was a public service radio station supported entirely by contributions from listeners. Every year, WKKW conducted a public auction at which it sold merchandise which had been donated by listeners. The auction was conducted over the radio, with announcers describing the goods which were on sale and identifying the persons who had donated them, and with listeners phoning in their bids.

Swiss, a cheese manufacturer, notified WKKW officials that he would donate 1,000 pounds of cheese to WKKW for sale at the fund-raising auction. At the request of WKKW, Swiss sent the radio station a certificate containing the following language:

> "For value received, WKKW hereby designates the following person to receive 1,000 pounds of cheese from Swiss. The cheese referred to herein is a gift from Swiss to radio station WKKW to enable the station to continue serving the public good."

During the radio auction, WKKW announcers stated that 1,000 pounds of cheese donated by Swiss was up for sale. Colby bid $120 for the cheese and was declared the highest bidder. Subsequently, Colby gave WKKW a check for that amount and WKKW officials signed the above certificate, writing Colby's name in the blank space provided. Swiss, who had heard the auction on the radio, was outraged that the cheese was sold for only $120. As a result, when Colby presented the certificate, Swiss refused to deliver the cheese.

126. If Colby asserts a claim against WKKW for breach of contract, the court should find for

(A) WKKW, because WKKW relied to its detriment on the promise made by Swiss.

(B) WKKW, if WKKW made all reasonable efforts to provide Colby with the cheese.

(C) Colby, but only if Colby is unsuccessful in recovering damages from Swiss.

(D) Colby, because Colby did not receive the cheese as promised by WKKW.

127. If Colby asserts a claim against Swiss on account

of Swiss's failure to deliver the cheese, the court should find for

(A) Swiss, because Swiss made no promise to Colby.

(B) Swiss, because Swiss received no consideration for his promise to deliver 1,000 pounds of cheese.

(C) Colby, as an assignee of WKKW's rights against Swiss.

(D) Colby, as an intended third-party creditor beneficiary of the contract between WKKW and Swiss.

Questions 128-129 are based on the following fact situation.

After inheriting a large tract of land, Odum subdivided it into 60 numbered lots pursuant to state law, filing a plat map and development scheme which indicated that all lots in the subdivision would be restricted to residential use. Odum thereafter conveyed lot 1 to Appel and lot 2 to Bishop by deeds containing a condition restricting the lots to residential use. Subsequently Columbus, who knew of the development scheme, bought lot 17 from Odum.

128. Assume for the purpose of this question only that Bishop announced his intention to erect a motorcycle repair shop on lot 2, and that Appel instituted a proceeding seeking to prevent Bishop from doing so. Which of the following additional facts or inferences, if it was the only one true, would be most likely to result in a decision in Appel's favor?

(A) Appel's deed to lot 1 was recorded prior to Bishop's purchase of lot 2.

(B) Appel purchased lot 1 before Bishop purchased lot 2.

(C) Appel was aware of Odum's development scheme when Appel purchased lot 1 from Odum.

(D) Bishop was aware of Odum's development

scheme when Bishop purchased lot 2 from Odum.

129. Assume for the purpose of this question only that Appel later sold lot 1 to Eubank, and that Columbus subsequently announced his intention to erect a motorcycle repair shop on lot 17. If Eubank instituted a proceeding seeking to prevent Columbus from doing so, the court should find for

(A) Eubank, if Odum's grants to Appel and Bishop resulted in an implied reciprocal servitude.

(B) Eubank, because permitting the construction of a motorcycle repair shop in a residential tract is likely to decrease the value of other real estate within the tract.

(C) Columbus, because Columbus was never in privity with Appel or Eubank.

(D) Columbus, if Columbus's deed did not contain language restricting lot 17 to residential use.

Questions 130-131 are based on the following fact situation.

Eno was hired as a probationary employee by the State Harbor Commission, an agency of the state, pursuant to a written contract. The contract provided that at the end of one year the parties could agree to renew the contract for an additional one year period, but that either party could, without cause, elect not to renew.

Eleven months after hiring him, the State Harbor Commission informed Eno in writing that his contract would not be renewed at the end of the year. Eno asked the State Harbor Commission for a hearing on his fitness to be rehired, but his request was denied. Eno subsequently instituted a proceeding to challenge the decision of the State Harbor Commission on the ground that its failure to hold a hearing before deciding not to rehire him violated his right to due process.

130. Which of the following would be the State Harbor Commission's most effective argument in

response to Eno's challenge?

(A) Due process was not required, since the decision not to rehire Eno did not deprive him of life, liberty, or property.

(B) State employment is a privilege rather than a right since no person is guaranteed employment by the state.

(C) There would be no point in holding a hearing in Eno's case, since the hearing officer would be an employee of the State Harbor Commission and the findings would necessarily support the decision already made by the Commission.

(D) Eno's constitutional rights could not have been violated by the decision not to renew his contract, since the contract provided that the decision could be made without cause.

131. If it was the only one true, which of the following additional facts or inferences would be most likely to lead to an order requiring the State Harbor Commission to hold a hearing before deciding not to rehire Eno?

(A) During the same year, the State Harbor Commission held hearings before deciding whether to rehire certain other probationary employees.

(B) The decision not to rehire Eno was based in part on the fact that while employed by the State Harbor Commission he had actively campaigned for a political candidate.

(C) The decision not to rehire Eno was likely to damage Eno's reputation.

(D) The job held by Eno was vital to the efficient operation of the State Harbor Commission.

132. Pinson purchased realty in the County of Durban in 1950 and has lived on it since then. The realty is located approximately one mile from a private airport owned and operated by De La Fuente. At the time of Pinson's purchase, County of Durban ordinances restricted the use of De La Fuente's airport to aircraft of a particular type. Noise from

the airport was not disturbing to Pinson. Recently, however, the Country of Durban adopted an ordinance allowing other kinds of aircraft to use the airport. Since then, noise levels from the airport have increased, disturbing the quiet atmosphere of Pinson's home.

If Pinson desires to assert a claim against De La Fuente on account of noise from the airport, which of the following would be his most effective theory of recovery?

(A) Private nuisance.

(B) Prescriptive aeronautical easement.

(C) Inverse condemnation.

(D) Continuing trespass.

Questions 133-134 are based on the following fact situation.

While Dangler and his wife Mary were standing in line outside a movie theater, Dangler whispered to Mary that he had committed a series of robberies the previous week. Dangler was subsequently arrested and charged with the robberies in a jurisdiction which holds that confidential marital communications are privileged.

133. Assume for the purpose of this question only that Lennon, a prosecution witness, attempted to testify that he overheard Dangler's whispered statement to Mary while standing behind them in the movie line. If Dangler objects to this testimony, his objection should be

(A) sustained, because communications made within a marriage are presumed to be confidential.

(B) sustained, because the statement is inadmissible hearsay.

(C) overruled, because the statement is admissible as an admission.

(D) overruled, because a communication concerning a crime is not subject to the marital privilege.

134. Assume for the purpose of this question only that Mary is called as a prosecution witness, and that the prosecutor attempts to question her about the statement which Dangler made to her while they were waiting in the movie line. Which of the following statements is most correct?

   I. The court should exclude this testimony if Mary is willing to testify but Dangler objects to her testimony.

   II. The court should exclude this testimony even if Dangler and Mary make no objection to it.

   (A) I only.

   (B) II only.

   (C) I and II.

   (D) Neither I nor II.

135. On Monday, Neal asked Landry to lend him $1,000 to buy a car. Landry said that she would have to think it over, since she knew that Neal did not have a steady job. Neal then asked his uncle Unger to help him. At Neal's request, Unger called Landry on Tuesday and said, "If you lend Neal the money he needs to buy a car, I promise to pay you back if Neal doesn't."

On Wednesday, Landry loaned Neal $1,000, requiring Neal to sign a document promising to repay the loan within one year. The same day, Landry made a photocopy of the document which Neal had signed, and sent it to Unger with a letter informing Unger that Landry had loaned the money to Neal as Unger requested. The photocopy and Landry's letter were delivered to Unger's home on Friday, but Unger had died on Thursday. Upon Neal's subsequent default in payment, Landry asserted a claim against Unger's estate on account of Unger's promise to pay if Neal did not.

Which of the following arguments would provide the administratrix of Unger's estate with the most effective argument in opposition to Landry's claim?

(A) There was no consideration for Unger's promise to repay Neal's debt.

(B) Unger died before Landry accepted his offer to guarantee payment.

(C) Unger's obligations under his suretyship agreement with Landry were terminated by Unger's death.

(D) There was no agreement in writing between Unger and Landry.

136. Dale was charged with assaulting Vollmer. At the trial, Vollmer testified that he accidentally bumped into Dale while walking on a crowded street, and that Dale responded by repeatedly hitting and punching him. As part of his defense, Dale denied that he had ever struck any person intentionally, and testified that any contact between Vollmer and him had been accidental.

The prosecutor subsequently called Whelan as a witness. Whelan testified that she and Dale were divorced, but that she had been married to him for ten years. She stated that during the period of their marriage, Dale had frequently struck her with his fists in public places. If Dale's attorney objects and asks the court to exclude Whelan's testimony, the testimony should be

(A) excluded, only if the jurisdiction recognizes a privilege for marital communications.

(B) excluded, because it is not relevant to a material issue.

(C) admitted, because it bears on Dale's reputation for truth and veracity.

(D) admitted, because Dale testified in his own defense.

Questions 137-138 are based on the following fact situation.

Coyne showed his silver coins to Fowler and asked whether Fowler would be interested in trading them for chickens. After inspecting the coins, Fowler and Coyne placed them in a bag which they sealed together and left with a banker whom they both knew. Then in a writing signed by both of them they agreed to the trade.

Pursuant to the terms of their agreement, Fowler was to deliver 6,000 fryer chickens to Coyne on July 1, at which time the bag of coins would be turned over to Fowler as payment in full. In May, weather conditions were such that the price of fryer chickens increased to three times what it had been when the agreement was signed.

137. Assume for the purpose of this question only that on July 1, Fowler refused to deliver 6,000 fryer chickens to Coyne. If Coyne asserts a claim against Fowler for breach of contract, the court should find for

    (A) Fowler, if in January neither party knew that the market price of fryer chickens would change.

    (B) Fowler, because the likelihood of fluctuation in the value of money makes this contract aleatory.

    (C) Coyne, if it was foreseeable that the market price of fryer chickens would change dramatically.

    (D) Coyne, because the transaction was not a sale as defined by the Uniform Commercial Code.

138. Assume the following facts for the purpose of this question only: In May Fowler notified Coyne that because of the increase in the price of chickens, Fowler would not be able to accept the bag of coins as payment for 6,000 fryer chickens in July. Coyne immediately sold the coins to a third person. On July 1, Fowler attempted to deliver 6,000 fryer chickens to Coyne, but Coyne refused to accept delivery. If Fowler asserts a claim against Coyne for breach of contract, the court should find for

    (A) Coyne, because Fowler said that he would not accept the coins as payment for the chickens.

    (B) Coyne, because Coyne's sale of the coins has resulted in Coyne's prospective inability to perform.

    (C) Fowler, because sale of the coins by Coyne

has made performance by Coyne impossible.

    (D) Fowler, because Fowler tendered the chickens as required by the contract.

139. Waterco, a water supply company, owned a well adjacent to O'Dowd's land. By a conveyance which properly described the size and location of the easement, O'Dowd granted Waterco an easement across his realty "for the installation of underground pipe or pipes for the transport of water to customers of Waterco." Pursuant to the easement, Waterco subsequently installed a single underground pipe across O'Dowd's land. After the installation, Waterco regularly entered O'Dowd's land to service its underground pipe, occasionally excavating for that purpose. Twenty years after the easement had been granted, construction of a nearby housing development caused the number of Waterco's customers to double, making it necessary for Waterco to transport more water than the single pipe could carry. Waterco notified O'Dowd that it planned to install a second underground pipe alongside the first within the area over which Waterco had an easement. O'Dowd objected and instituted an appropriate proceeding to stop Waterco from installing a second underground pipe.

Which of the following arguments would be most likely to result in a judgment for O'Dowd?

    (A) Twenty years of continuous use by Waterco established the scope of the easement.

    (B) The initial installation of a single pipe by Waterco established the scope of the easement.

    (C) When the easement was granted, neither party could have anticipated that the number of Waterco's customers would double.

    (D) O'Dowd's grant to Waterco did not specify the number of pipes which could be installed.

140. By a contract calling for the delivery of marketable title, Swinton agreed to sell Barney a parcel of realty consisting of 4 adjacent lots. On the date

set for closing, Swinton informed Barney that one of the 4 lots was encumbered by a utility company easement, Swinton said that it was unlikely that the utility company would ever attempt to exercise its easement, and offered to either execute a general warranty deed to the entire parcel including a covenant against encumbrances, or to convey the remaining three lots to Barney, deducting from the purchase price the reasonable value of the encumbered lot. Barney refused both offers.

In litigation between Swinton and Barney for breach of contract, a court should find for

(A) Swinton, because a covenant against encumbrances would have given Barney sufficient protection.

(B) Swinton, if title to the remaining three lots was marketable, and if abatement of the purchase price would assure Barney of receiving the value for which he had bargained.

(C) Barney, but only if Swinton knew of the easement at the time the contract of sale was formed.

(D) Barney, because Swinton failed to deliver marketable title.

141. At the trial of a personal injury action brought by Pacheco against Dagley and arising out of an automobile accident, Pacheco attempted to testify that immediately following the accident, Dagley offered to pay $500 to fix Pacheco's car. Over objection by Dagley's attorney, Pacheco's statement should be

(A) excluded, unless Dagley is given an opportunity to explain his offer.

(B) excluded, because to admit such evidence would violate public policy.

(C) admitted, as a declaration against Dagley's pecuniary interest.

(D) admitted, as an implied admission of a party.

Questions 142-144 are based on the following fact situation.

Richey was out walking when she saw Palermo, a seven-year-old child, suddenly chase a ball into the street in the path of a car driven by Driscoll. Afraid that Palermo would be hit by the car, Richey ran into the roadway and pushed Palermo out of the way. Driscoll's car struck Richey. Palermo was not hit by Driscoll's car, but hurt his knees when he fell to the ground as a result of being pushed by Richey. The jurisdiction applies the all-or-nothing rule of contributory negligence.

142. If Palermo asserts a negligence claim against Richey for the injuries to his knees, which one of the following additional facts or inferences, if it was the only one true, would be most likely to result in a judgment for Richey?

(A) Palermo's injury was proximately caused by the negligence of Driscoll.

(B) If Richey had not pushed him out of the way, Palermo would have been struck by Driscoll's car and killed.

(C) Richey was severely injured as a result of being struck by Driscoll's car.

(D) The situation confronted Richey with an emergency.

143. If Richey asserts a claim against Driscoll for injuries which she sustained as a result of being struck by Driscoll's car, the court should find for Driscoll

(A) because Richey assumed the risk by running into the path of Driscoll's car.

(B) unless Driscoll was driving the car in an unreasonable manner.

(C) if Palermo was contributorily negligent in running in front of Driscoll's car.

(D) if Richey had the last clear to avoid being injured.

144. If Palermo asserts a negligence claim against Driscoll for the injuries to his knees, which of the

following would be Driscoll's most effective argument in defense?

(A) It was unreasonable for Palermo to chase a ball into the street in the path of Driscoll's car.

(B) Palermo's injuries did not result from a physical impact with Driscoll's car.

(C) Richey removed Palermo from the zone of physical danger.

(D) Danger invites rescue.

145. At a jury trial Dahn was convicted of aggravated assault. On appeal Dahn's conviction was reversed on the ground that as a matter of law the evidence against her was insufficient to establish guilt beyond a reasonable doubt. Subsequently, the prosecutor attempted to try Dahn again on the same charge. If Dahn asserts that the subsequent prosecution violates the constitutional protection against double jeopardy and moves to dismiss it, her motion should be

(A) denied, because the reversal of her conviction ended any jeopardy which attached as a result of the initial prosecution.

(B) denied, because the reversal amounted to a declaration that the trial was a nullity and that she had, therefore, never been in jeopardy as a result of the initial prosecution.

(C) granted.

(D) denied, because Dahn waived the constitutional protection against double jeopardy by appealing her conviction.

Questions 146-147 are based on the following fact situation.

The telephone solicitation computer is a device which dials telephone numbers and plays a pre-recorded advertising announcement to anyone who answers. Although there are many federal statutes and regulations regarding telephone communication, none addresses the use of this kind of device. After many residents of the state of Champlain complained of being annoyed by calls received from telephone solici-

tation computers, the Champlain legislature enacted a statute which prohibited operating such a device from within the state.

Saleco, a manufacturing company doing business in the state of Champlain, planned to use the telephone solicitation computer to market its products within the state. After passage of the law, Saleco attempted to hire an out-of-state company to set up a telephone solicitation computer system connected to phone lines outside the state for the purpose of making calls to telephones within the state of Champlain. When Saleco learned that the cost of doing so would far exceed the cost of setting up such a system inside the state, Saleco challenged the constitutionality of the state law.

146. The most effective argument in support of Saleco's claim is that the statute is unconstitutional because

(A) federal statutes and regulations regarding telephone communications have pre-empted the field, making the statute invalid under the supremacy clause.

(B) regulation of communication is not one of the enumerated powers of the states under the Tenth Amendment.

(C) the statute discriminates against interstate commerce because the cost of using the telephone solicitation computer from locations outside the state of Champlain to communicate with telephones inside the state is higher than the cost of using it from locations inside the state for that purpose.

(D) the statute imposes an undue burden on interstate commerce by making the cost of marketing products to consumers in the state of Champlain higher than the cost of marketing those products to consumers outside the state of Champlain.

147. Assume for the purpose of this question only that Saleco's only claim is that the statute violates the First Amendment protection of freedom of expression. Saleco's most effective argument in support of that conclusion is that the statute is

(A) overbroad because it could interfere with non-commercial communications as well as with commercial communications.

(B) content-related because it is more likely that the telephone solicitation computer would be used for commercial communications than for non-commercial communications.

(C) likely to have a chilling effect on expression because of the increased cost of using the telephone solicitation computer from locations outside the state.

(D) not justified because prohibiting use of the telephone solicitation computer from locations within the states does not directly advance a substantial government interest.

148. The state Department of Transportation published an advertisement calling for bids "for a contract to be the exclusive supplier of fuel for Department of Transportation vehicles." Petrol submitted a bid and, after negotiation, entered into a written contract to supply at a specified price per gallon for a period of one year "all fuel ordered by the Department of Transportation." Several months after executing the contract, Petrol learned that the Department of Transportation was purchasing substantial amounts of fuel from other suppliers.

Petrol asserted a claim against the Department of Transportation for breach of contract. At the trial, Department of Transportation attorneys offered the written contract into evidence and pointed out that its language did not specifically state that Petrol was to be the exclusive supplier. When Petrol attempted to offer a copy of the advertisement calling for bids into evidence, Department of Transportation attorneys objected on the ground that the advertisement was inadmissible under the parol evidence rule. Petrol's most effective argument in response to the Department of Transportation's objections would be that the advertisement

(A) tends to show that the written contract was ambiguous.

(B) was in writing.

(C) was a communication which led to a written contract.

(D) was an invitation to negotiate.

149. In 1980, Ortiz conveyed a parcel of realty known as Greenacre to her oldest son Amaro in fee simple absolute as a gift. At Ortiz's request, Amaro did not record the conveyance. In 1982, Ortiz borrowed $10,000 from Marcus, executing a note purporting to be secured by a mortgage on Greenacre. Marcus did not record the mortgage. In 1984, Ortiz purported to convey Greenacre in fee simple to her youngest son Benedict as a gift. Benedict immediately recorded the deed. On default by Ortiz, Marcus now seeks to foreclose on Greenacre.

A statute in the jurisdiction provides that "No transfer of an interest in real property shall be good and effectual in law or equity against creditors or subsequent purchasers for value and without notice unless it shall be recorded."

Is Marcus entitled to foreclose on Greenacre?

(A) No, because his mortgage was not recorded.

(B) No, because Benedict recorded his deed in 1984.

(C) Yes.

(D) No, because Amaro owns Greenacre in fee simple absolute.

150. Pace bought from Dartmouth Motors, a car dealer, a new car manufactured by Gasden Auto Company. The vehicle was equipped with a seat belt warning indicator, although the law did not require such a device. The indicator was designed to cause a bright red light on the dashboard to begin glowing when the engine was started and to remain lit until the driver's seat belt was fastened. When the car was delivered to Pace, an employee of Dartmouth Motors explained to Pace that the seat belt warning indicator was not working, but that Dartmouth Motors would repair it without charge as soon as the necessary parts were received.

The following day, Pace was involved in an accident while driving the new car. As a result of the impact, she was thrown from the vehicle and sustained an injury when her head struck the pavement. If she had been wearing a seat belt at the time, she would not have been injured.

Pace subsequently asserted a claim against Dartmouth Motors for her injuries on the ground that the failure of the seat belt warning indicator made the vehicle defective. Which of the following would be Dartmouth Motors's most effective argument in response to that allegation?

(A) When Pace drove the vehicle, she was aware that the seat belt warning indicator was not working.

(B) The law did not require the vehicle to be equipped with a seat belt warning indicator.

(C) It is impossible to prove with certainty that Pace would have worn a seat belt if the seat belt warning indicator had been working.

(D) The failure of the seat belt warning indicator was the result of the negligence of Gasden Auto Company.

Questions 151-152 are based on the following fact situation.

Ortega was the owner of a small farm which had been in his family for many generations and which had become a well-known community landmark. Ortega had a son named Sander and a daughter named Dawn. Because Ortega was advanced in age, he was concerned about what would happen to the property after his death. He wanted to keep it in the family for as long as possible, and he wanted Sander to have the use of it throughout his lifetime. In addition, he wanted to be sure that the old family farmhouse would not be physically changed, and that it would always be painted white.

151. If Ortega consulted you for advice about how best to prevent physical change to the family farmhouse, you should advise him to convey the

realty by a deed containing the following language:

(A) … to Sander unless the family farmhouse is physically changed or painted any color other than white.

(B) … to Sander and his heirs, but if the family farmhouse is physically changed or painted any color other than white, to Dawn and her heirs.

(C) … to Sander and his heirs, but if within 40 years the family farmhouse is physically changed or painted any color other than white, to Dawn and her heirs.

(D) … to Sander for life, remainder to Dawn.

152. Assume for the purpose of this question only that Ortega died leaving a will which devised the property "to Sander for life, but if within 40 years Sander attempts to sell or mortgage his interest, to Dawn for life." If, in an appropriate proceeding, Sander challenges the validity of the restrictions on his estate his most effective argument would be that the restrictions

(A) constitute a disabling restraint on alienation.

(B) constitute a forfeiturial restraint on alienation.

(C) constitute a promissory restraint on alienation.

(D) violate the rule against perpetuities.

153. After PiCo instituted litigation against Dee Corp, Dee Corp's attorney demanded that PiCo furnish the answers to a list of interrogatories as provided by the state code of civil procedure. Interrogatory #4 was "List PiCo's gross sales receipts for each month during the four-year period in controversy." In response to this interrogatory, PiCo responded, "Gross receipts for the period in question are contained in an industry publication known as *The Commercial Journal*."

At trial, Dee Corp's attorney attempted to offer into evidence those portions of *The Commercial Journal* listing PiCo's gross receipts for the months in question. Upon objection by PiCo's attorney, the court should rule those portions of *The Commercial Journal*

(A) inadmissible, because the contents of *The Commercial Journal* have not been shown to be accurate.

(B) inadmissible as hearsay not within any exception.

(C) admissible as an admission of a party.

(D) admissible, only if *The Commercial Journal* is shown to be a reputable source which reasonably well-informed people regard as accurate.

Questions 154-155 are based on the following fact situation.

After Hamilton lost all his money to Danico in a dice game, the two men began to argue. During the course of the argument, Danico stabbed Hamilton in the leg with a knife. Hamilton staggered home and pounded on the door, begging his wife Wilma to let him in. Wilma realized that Hamilton needed medical attention because he was bleeding badly, but she was so angry at him for gambling that she refused to open the door or call a doctor. Hamilton collapsed on the doorstep and died an hour later from loss of blood. Wilma could have secured immediate medical attention for Hamilton, and if she had done so, Hamilton would not have died.

154. If Danico is prosecuted for the murder of Hamilton, which of the following would be his most effective argument in defense?

(A) Danico did not cause Hamilton's death because Hamilton would not have died if Wilma had secured prompt medical attention.

(B) Leg wounds do not usually result in death.

(C) It was unforeseeable that Wilma would refuse to secure medical attention for Hamilton when she knew that he needed it so badly.

(D) Wilma's omission to secure medical atten-

tion was a substantial factor in producing Hamilton's death.

155. If Wilma is prosecuted for the murder of Hamilton, she should be found

(A) not guilty, if Hamilton's death was proximately caused by the conduct of Danico.

(B) not guilty, unless the jurisdiction recognizes that she had a duty to secure medical attention for Hamilton.

(C) guilty, only if she knew that Hamilton was likely to die if he did not receive prompt medical attention.

(D) guilty, because she knew that Hamilton was in need of immediate medical attention.

Questions 156-157 are based on the following fact situation.

A statute of the state of DelMara grants state employees an annual 5% salary increase. Another statute provides that upon retirement a state employee shall receive an annual pension equivalent to 60% of the salary received during the year immediately prior to retirement. The state also maintains a group health insurance plan for state employees. After determining that the health insurance plan could be operated less expensively if it did not include persons over the age of 65, the state legislature passed a compulsory retirement law requiring state employees to retire at the age of 65.

Robello, who was employed by the state of DelMara as a station engineer, reached the age of 65 several years after the compulsory retirement law was passed. When he was informed that he was required to retire, Robello challenged the constitutionality of the mandatory retirement law. In support of his challenge, Robello proved that a federal law permits station engineers employed by the federal government to continue working until they are 70.

156. In deciding Robello's claim, the court should hold that the state's mandatory retirement law is

(A) invalid under the Supremacy Clause.

(B) invalid, if Robello's job did not require skills or abilities which were related to age.

(C) valid, if the state could operate its employee health insurance plan on a more economically efficient basis by mandating retirement at 65.

(D) valid, because the federal government may not impose economic burdens on the state.

157. Assume for the purpose of this question only that Robello's only argument was that the mandatory retirement law violated the obligation of contracts clause of Article I of the United States Constitution. If it was the only one true, which of the following additional facts or inferences would best support Robello's claim?

(A) Robello was a state employee prior to the time the mandatory retirement law was passed.

(B) Robello borrowed money for the purchase of a retirement home, planning to pay it back from his salary as a state employee.

(C) Robello is as physically fit as the average person 60 years of age.

(D) Robello's job as a state employee does not require any physical labor or strain.

Questions 158-159 are based on the following fact situation

Swiney, a farmer, was the owner of a prize-winning male hog known as Megahog. When Megahog was declared the American Champion at a national livestock show, Fair asked Swiney to exhibit the animal at an Agricultural Exposition which Fair was conducting. On May 1, Fair and Swiney entered into a written contract agreeing that Swiney would exhibit Megahog at Fair's Agricultural Exposition on June 30 in return for a fee to be paid at the conclusion of Megahog's appearance.

After executing the contract, Fair advertised the Agricultural Exposition extensively. All his advertising emphasized that Megahog, the American Champion, would be exhibited at the Exposition. On June 20,

Megahog contracted boarsitis, a highly contagious and frequently fatal disease of hogs. Swiney notified Fair on June 22 that because of the disease he could not exhibit Megahog as agreed. When Fair advised the public that Megahog would not be appearing at the Agricultural Exposition, many people who had planned to purchase tickets changed their minds and did not do so. Fair subsequently asserted a claim against Swiney for damages resulting from Swiney's refusal to exhibit Megahog as agreed.

158. Swiney's most effective defense to Fair's claim would be based on

(A) rescission.

(B) impossibility of performance.

(C) frustration of purpose.

(D) prospective inability to perform.

159. Which of the following additional facts, if it was the only one true, would be most likely to result in a judgment in favor of Fair?

(A) On May 1 Swiney was aware that many hogs in the area had contracted boarsitis.

(B) On June 21 the state Department of Livestock learned that Megahog had contracted boarsitis and issued an order prohibiting the exhibition of Megahog.

(C) On June 22 Swiney owned a hog with qualities equivalent to Megahog's.

(D) On the day of the trial Fair could prove exactly how much revenue Fair lost as a result of Swiney's failure to exhibit Megahog.

160. The Department of Highway Transportation is the agency of state government responsible for maintaining state highways. While driving on a state highway, Dain attempted to pass Parnell's vehicle on the right. As she did so, one of Dain's wheels struck a pothole, causing her car to go out of control and strike Parnell's car. The pothole existed because the Department of Highway Transportation was negligent in maintaining the road sur-

face. Dain would not have lost control of her car if she had not hit the pothole while driving at an unreasonably fast rate of speed. A statute in the jurisdiction prohibits passing on the right.

Parnell subsequently asserted a negligence claim against Dain for injuries sustained in the accident. If Dain's only argument in defense is that the pothole was a superseding cause of harm, the court should find for

(A) Parnell, because Dain's attempt to pass Parnell on the right was a violation of an automobile safety statute.

(B) Parnell, if potholes are often found on the road surfaces where the accident occurred.

(C) Dain, unless the concept of governmental immunity has been abolished in the jurisdiction.

(D) Dain, because the accident would not have happened but for the existence of the pothole.

161. Caswell had an exclusive five-year contract to sell products manufactured by Defcorp. When Defcorp canceled the contract in its third year, Caswell entered into a similar contract with another manufacturer. Caswell then asked Larkin, an attorney, to sue Defcorp for breach of contract. Because the compensation plans in Caswell's contracts with Defcorp and the other company were extremely complex, Larkin was unable to determine whether Defcorp's breach had damaged Caswell. Before agreeing to represent Caswell, Larkin therefore arranged for Caswell to meet with Ander, an accountant. At Larkin's request, Ander interviewed Caswell, obtained certain facts from her, and made mathematical calculations which she submitted to Larkin.

Larkin subsequently commenced a lawsuit against Defcorp on Caswell's behalf. At the trial, Defcorp's attorney called Ander as a witness and attempted to question her about her interview with Caswell. If Larkin objects to the examination of Ander, the most effective argument in support of her objection would be that statements made by Caswell to Ander are

(A) privileged as part of an attorney's work product.

(B) records kept in the course of business.

(C) inadmissible hearsay.

(D) confidential communications between client and attorney.

Questions 162-163 are based on the following fact situation.

Thies leased a parcel of real estate from Larsen for one year at a monthly rent of $2,000 with an option to buy it for a specified price at the termination of the lease. After moving onto the realty, Thies erected a storage building on it. The construction cost of the building was $6,000, but when it was completed, its value was $8,000. Thies's employer subsequently transferred him to a company office located in a different state. As a result, Thies vacated the realty four months before the expiration of the lease, advising Larsen that he would not exercise his purchase option. On the same day, Larsen conveyed the property to Barash.

162. Assume for the purpose of this question only that when Thies vacated the premises he left the storage building behind, and did not pay rent for the remaining four months of the lease term. Assume further that the premises remained vacant for the balance of the lease term. In a proceeding against Thies for unpaid rent, Thies should be required to pay

(A) nothing, since Larsen conveyed the realty to Barash on the day that Thies vacated it.

(B) $8,000 (4 months rent at $2,000 per month).

(C) nothing (4 months rent at $2,000 per month, minus $8,000), since the value of the building which Thies left behind was $8,000.

(D) $2,000 (4 months rent at $2,000 per month, minus $6,000), since the building which Thies left behind cost Thies $6,000 to build.

163. Assume for the purpose of this question only that Barash moved onto the realty on the day Thies vacated it, and that all parties agreed that, therefore, Thies would have no further obligation to pay rent. If Thies wishes to remove the storage building, but Larsen and Barash object, which of the following statements is correct?

     I.   Larsen and Barash may prevent removal of the building by declaring it to be realty and tendering its reasonable value to Thies.

     II.   If a court prevents Thies from removing the building, declaring that it has been annexed to the realty, Thies is entitled to receive its reasonable value from Larsen or Barash.

   (A)   I only

   (B)   II only

   (C)   I and II.

   (D)   Neither I nor II.

Questions 164-165 are based on the following fact situation.

Agriprod is the manufacturer of an agricultural insecticide known as Larvaway. Since Gold County is primarily devoted to farming, Agriprod has manufactured Larvaway at its factory there for the past 50 years. Although Larvaway is an important product commonly used by farmers for the control of an insect highly destructive to food crops, only three other companies have a similar product.

Due to the manufacture of Larvaway, fumes which issue from the Agriprod factory frequently have an unpleasant odor. These fumes cause no physical harm to persons, property, or crops, but residents of Gold County frequently complain about the foul smell. All of the factories which manufacture a product similar to Larvaway produce the same odor.

Tena, a farmer, began growing crops on a field near the Agriprod factory less than a year ago. Tena leases the field from its owner in return for a percentage of his crop. When he telephoned Agriprod to complain about the bad smell emanating from its factory, an Agriprod

official told him that nothing could be done about it.

164. Assume for the purpose of this question only that Tena asserts a claim based on public nuisance for injunctive relief against Agriprod for its emission of foul smelling fumes. Which of the following would be Agriprod's most effective argument in defense against that claim?

   (A)   Tena came to the nuisance.

   (B)   Tena's discomfort does not differ substantially from the discomfort experienced by other residents of Gold County.

   (C)   All factories which manufacture a similar product produce the same odor.

   (D)   The fumes cause no physical harm to persons, property, or crops.

165. Assume for the purpose of this question only that Tena asserts a claim against Agriprod based on private nuisance, seeking damages for discomfort which he experiences as a result of the bad smell produced by Agriprod's factory. Which one of the following additional facts or inferences, if it was the only one true, would be most likely to result in a judgment for Agriprod?

   (A)   There is no other factory within 1,000 miles which manufactures a product similar to Larvaway.

   (B)   Tena does not own realty in or reside in Gold County.

   (C)   It is impossible to manufacture a product similar to Larvaway without producing a bad smell.

   (D)   Tena's discomfort does not differ substantially from the discomfort experienced by other residents of Gold County.

Questions 166-167 are based on the following fact situation.

At the jury trial of an action by Bank against Dakin on a promissory note, Dakin testified that the signature on the note was not his. An employee of Bank testified that she recognized the signature as Dakin's.

166. If Bank's attorney offers the promissory note in evidence it should be

  (A) admitted, because any dispute regarding the genuineness of a signature should be decided by the jury.

  (B) admitted, only if the judge decides that the evidence is sufficient to support a finding that the signature on the note was Dakin's.

  (C) admitted, only if the jury is given an authenticated sample of Dakin's signature so that it can decide whether the signature on the promissory note is Dakin's.

  (D) admitted, only if the judge decides that the signature on the promissory note is Dakin's.

167. Assume for the purpose of this question only that Dakin's attorney asserts that the promissory note is hearsay. Bank's most effective response to that assertion would be that

  (A) the promissory note is a business record.

  (B) the promissory note is an original document.

  (C) the promissory note is not being offered to prove that any statement which it contains is true.

  (D) Dakin is in court.

168. National Boulevard is a public road located within the City of Haven. Churchill belongs to an ethnic minority which constitutes 10% of the general population of the City of Haven. Approximately 10% of the motorists driving on National Boulevard are members of Churchill's ethnic minority. One day, while Churchill was driving her automobile on National Boulevard, police officer Olander stopped her and issued a traffic summons charging her with driving in excess of the statutory speed limit. In her defense, Churchill asserted that the traffic statute was unconstitutional as applied.

Which one of the following additional facts or inferences, if it were the only one true, would best support Churchill's assertion?

  (A) In the past two years, Churchill has received three such summonses from Olander, but she has never received one from another officer.

  (B) In the past two years, Olander has issued a total of 300 summonses for driving in excess of the statutory speed limit on National Boulevard, all of which were issued to members of Churchill's ethnic group.

  (C) Properly compiled statistics indicate that members of Churchill's ethnic group do not customarily drive faster than members of any other ethnic group.

  (D) At the time Olander issued the summons to Churchill, many people who did not belong to Churchill's ethnic group were driving on National Boulevard at speeds in excess of Churchill's speed, and Olander did not issue summonses to any of them.

Questions 169-170 are based on the following fact situation.

Dafoe knew that he often became intoxicated upon drinking small quantities of alcoholic beverage. He frequently visited the neighborhood tavern because he liked the atmosphere, but he usually ordered orange juice or some other non-alcoholic beverage. While at the tavern one night, Dafoe drank half of a friend's glass of beer. Soon afterwards, he began shouting and throwing objects about the tavern. A chair which he hurled across the room struck the bartender, injuring her severely. As a result, Dafoe was subsequently arrested and prosecuted. At Dafoe's trial, the defense attorney called a psychiatrist to the witness stand to testify that Dafoe suffered from a mental illness which made him extremely susceptible to the effects of alcohol. The psychiatrist offered to testify further that even a small quantity of beer was likely to make Dafoe become physically violent, and that when this happened to him, he was not aware that his conduct would result in injury to others.

169. Assume for the purpose of this question only that Dafoe's prosecution was for criminal battery. If the prosecutor moves to exclude the psychiatrist's testimony, the motion should be

   (A) granted, because Dafoe knew that he often became intoxicated upon drinking small quantities of alcoholic beverage.

   (B) granted, because the sanity of a defendant is a question of fact to be determined by a jury.

   (C) denied, because a jury might find that Dafoe's intoxication prevented him from forming the intent to injure the bartender.

   (D) denied, because that testimony could establish that Dafoe's intoxication was involuntary.

170. Assume for the purpose of this question only that Dafoe's prosecution was for attempted murder. If the prosecutor moves to exclude the psychiatrist's testimony, the motion should be

   (A) granted, because Dafoe knew that he often became intoxicated upon drinking small quantities of alcoholic beverage.

   (B) granted, if Dafoe's intoxication was voluntary.

   (C) denied, only if Dafoe's intoxication was involuntary.

   (D) denied, because a jury might find that Dafoe's intoxication prevented him from forming an intent to kill.

171. Babcock and Sandag signed a written document agreeing to the sale of Sandag's realty to Babcock. The document adequately described the realty, required Sandag to deliver marketable title by a general warranty deed, and set the date for closing. It also stated that the price would be determined by agreement of the parties prior to the date of closing. Three weeks before the date set for closing, Babcock telephoned Sandag to discuss the price of the realty. At that time Sandag told Babcock that she had changed her mind and would not sell the realty to Babcock at any

price. If Babcock asserts a claim against Sandag for breach of contract, the court should find for

   (A) Sandag, because the Statute of Frauds requires a contract for the sale of realty to be in writing and to state the price.

   (B) Sandag, if the parties did not agree on a method for determining the price.

   (C) Babcock, if the value of real estate in the area can be objectively determined.

   (D) Babcock, because where a written contract omits the price term, the price is to be a reasonable price.

172. Dacon was a college student preparing to take an important exam. Before the exam, she sneaked into the professor's office hoping to steal a copy of the exam answer. The exam answer was, in fact, locked securely in the dean's safe, however, and Dacon was therefore unable to find it. While she was looking, the professor discovered her in his office, and Dacon told him her reason for being there. If Dacon is charged with attempting to violate a state statute which prohibits the theft of certain specifically defined "information," she should be found

   (A) not guilty, because the exam answers were, in fact, securely locked in the dean's safe and Dacon could not possibly have stolen them.

   (B) not guilty, if an exam answer is "information" as defined by the statute, but Dacon believed that it was not.

   (C) guilty, because the theft of an exam answer by one preparing to take the exam is "inherently immoral."

   (D) guilty, if an exam answer is "information" as defined by the statute, but Dacon believed that it was not.

Questions 173-174 are based on the following fact situation.

At the state nominating convention of a major political party, twelve persons who planned to make speeches on behalf of nominees for the office of governor were seated on a raised platform before an audience of more than 5,000 people. The speeches had been lengthy and the hour was late. When Platt stood up to make a speech, Dudley, who was seated beside him on the platform, decided it would be a good idea to introduce some humor into the proceedings by playing a joke on Platt. When Platt finished his speech and was about to sit down, Dudley quickly pulled Platt's chair away from where it had been. As a result, Platt fell to the floor. The audience howled with laughter for several minutes. Although Platt sustained no physical injury, he was embarrassed by the incident.

173. Assume for the purpose of this question only that Platt asserts a claim against Dudley for battery. The court should find for

    (A) Platt, if it was foreseeable that moving the chair would cause Platt to fall.

    (B) Platt, only if Dudley knew that moving the chair would cause Platt to fall.

    (C) Dudley, because Platt sustained no physical injury.

    (D) Dudley, unless Dudley was substantially certain that Platt would be embarrassed as a result of the incident.

174. Assume for the purpose of this question only that Platt asserts a claim against Dudley for the intentional infliction of emotional distress. Which of the following would be Dudley's most effective argument in defense?

    (A) Dudley's intent was to play a joke on Platt.

    (B) It was not Dudley's purpose to cause embarrassment to Platt.

    (C) Platt could not have experienced apprehension since he was unaware that he would fall.

    (D) Platt did not experience severe mental suffering as a result of the incident.

175. A will devised a parcel of real estate to Bert and his sister Sally as joint tenants. Bert died after

quitclaiming his interest in the realty to his wife Wilba. Subsequently Sally died, leaving a will which purported to devise her interest in the realty to her daughter Dot. Which of the following statements most accurately describes the rights of Wilba and Dot after the deaths of Bert and Sally?

    (A) Wilba is the sole owner of the realty.

    (B) Dot is the sole owner of the realty.

    (C) Wilba and Dot hold the realty as joint tenants.

    (D) Wilba and Dot hold the realty as tenants in common.

Question 176-177 are based on the following fact situation.

Congress authorizes the Tall Grasslands Bureau, a federal agency, to lease federally-owned land in an area known as Rolling Prairie to livestock ranchers for grazing purposes at specified rental rates. Realty Corporation also owns land in Rolling Prairie which it leases for grazing purposes. Realty Corporation complains that the rates charged by the Tall Grasslands Bureau are significantly lower than those charged by Realty Corporation, and that this has resulted in unfair competition which will cause Realty Corporation an immediate loss of revenue. In an appropriate proceeding, Realty Corporation challenges the constitutionality of the federal lease.

176. Which of the following arguments would be most effective IN OPPOSITION TO Realty Corporation's claim?

    (A) The Property Clause of Article IV of the Constitution empowers Congress to dispose of federal land as it sees fit.

    (B) The lease of federal land is valid under the Commerce Clause.

    (C) Realty Corporation lacks standing because the activities of the Tall Grasslands Bureau do not affect it directly.

    (D) The federal government is immune from

claims based on allegations of unfair competition.

177. Assume for the purpose of this question that after Realty Corporation institutes the proceeding, the Tall Grasslands Bureau raises the rental rate on federal lands in Rolling Prairie to match Realty Corporation's rate. If the Tall Grasslands Bureau moves to dismiss the proceeding on the ground that it is moot, the most effective argument IN OPPOSITION TO that motion would be that

   (A) the proceeding raises an important federal question.

   (B) a decision of the court is likely to have collateral consequences.

   (C) dismissal of the proceeding would leave the Tall Grasslands Bureau free to lower its rental rates again in the future.

   (D) once issues have become ripe they are not mooted by subsequent changes in circumstances.

Questions 178-179 are based on the following fact situation.

Stuart and Pattison are adults. During an argument, Stuart slammed a glass door against Pattison, causing Pattison to sustain serious cuts on her hand. After Pattison received medical treatment for her injuries, she spoke to Stuart's mother Milburn about it. Pattison told Milburn that she was thinking of suing Stuart for her medical expenses, but that if Milburn would agree to pay Pattison $250, Pattison would make no claim against Stuart for medical expenses. Milburn agreed in writing that she would do so.

Two weeks later, Stuart was prosecuted criminally as a result of the injuries which he had inflicted on Pattison. Pattison told Milburn that the prosecutor had asked Pattison to testify against Stuart at the proceeding. Milburn begged her not to. Finally, Pattison said that if Milburn gave her an additional $1,000 for her pain and suffering, she would not testify against Stuart. Milburn orally agreed to do so.

178. Assume for the purpose of this question only that Milburn refused to pay the $250 which she had promised Pattison, and that Pattison asserted a claim against Milburn for that amount. The court should find for Pattison

   (A) only if Pattison believed in good faith that Stuart was liable to her.

   (B) only if Milburn believed in good faith that Stuart was liable to Pattison.

   (C) only if both Milburn and Pattison believed in good faith that Stuart was liable to Pattison.

   (D) if either Milburn or Pattison believed in good faith that Stuart was liable to Pattison.

179. Assume for the purpose of this question only that Milburn paid $250 to Pattison, but refused to pay an additional $1,000. If Pattison asserts a claim against Milburn on account of Milburn's failure to pay the additional $1,000, which of the following would be Milburn's most effective argument in defense?

   (A) Milburn was not legally obligated to pay for damages done by her adult son Stuart.

   (B) Milburn's promise to pay an additional $1,000 to Pattison was not supported by consideration.

   (C) Milburn's payment of $250 to Pattison was an accord and satisfaction.

   (D) Milburn's promise to pay the debt of Stuart was not in writing.

180. At the trial of a robbery prosecution, a witness for the prosecution testified that the robber walked with a limp. While the witness was on the stand, the prosecutor asked the defendant to walk across the courtroom. If the defendant objects, asserting his Fifth Amendment privilege against self-incrimination, his objection should be

   (A) sustained, because the defendant has not waived the privilege by testifying in his own behalf.

(B) sustained, because the jury is likely to interpret a refusal by the defendant to walk across the courtroom as evidence that he is guilty.

(C) overruled, because the Fifth Amendment privilege applies only to testimony.

(D) overruled, because the defendant has waived the privilege by personally appearing in the courtroom.

Questions 181-182 are based on the following fact situation.

Following her indictment by a grand jury for bank robbery, Dahms voluntarily surrendered at police headquarters. After booking her, police officers advised Dahms that she had a right to remain silent, that anything she said might be used against her, that she was entitled to have an attorney present during questioning, and that if she could not afford an attorney one would be furnished without cost to her. Dahms said that she did not wish to answer any questions until her attorney arrived.

The officers went to lunch and returned to headquarters an hour later. Upon their return, they ordered Dahms to appear in a lineup for identification purposes in connection with the bank robbery. At first, Dahms refused. When the officer threatened to use force to compel her appearance, however Dahms appeared without resisting. Witnesses at the lineup identified her as the bank robber.

Following the lineup, the officers asked Dahms whether she knew anything about a series of residential burglaries. Although they did not think that she had committed the burglaries, they thought that she might know the people who had. Dahms admitted participating in the burglaries, however. She was subsequently prosecuted for bank robbery and the burglaries.

181. If Dahms objects to the admission of evidence of the lineup identification, which of the following would be her most effective argument in support of her objection?

(A) Dahms was deprived of her right to have an

attorney present during the lineup.

(B) The lineup deprived Dahms of the right to confront her accusers.

(C) The lineup violated her right against self-incrimination.

(D) Police officers coerced Dahms into appearing in the lineup.

182. If Dahms moves to exclude evidence that she admitted participating in the burglaries, her motion should be

(A) denied, because the police did not suspect her of being involved in the burglaries when they asked her about them.

(B) denied, because she received Miranda warnings before being questioned about the burglaries.

(C) granted, because she stated that she did not wish to answer any questions until her attorney arrived and did not in any other manner waive her Miranda rights.

(D) granted, because the police did not advise her that she was suspected of committing the burglaries before they questioned her about them.

183. *The Daily Tribune*, a newspaper published in the city of West, published a series of articles about unlawful drug-dealing at West High School. Roman, an employee of *The Daily Tribune*, wrote the articles, furnished the photographs used to illustrate them, and wrote captions for the photographs. One of the photographs furnished by Roman showed Pacifica, a student at West High School, in conversation with another student in the school yard. The caption which Roman provided with the photograph read, "Drug deal in progress at West High School." Although Pacifica was not involved in the use or sale of unlawful drugs, Roman sincerely believed that she was.

When the photograph and caption were published in *The Daily Tribune*, black squares were superimposed over the faces in the picture so that they could not be identified. Neither the caption nor the article named Pacifica as one of the people in the photograph. Because she wore a distinctive dress with an unusual floral design, however, many West High School students recognized Pacifica upon seeing the photograph.

If Pacifica asserts a claim against Roman and *The Daily Tribune* for invasion of privacy, under which of the following theories would she be most likely to succeed?

(A) Appropriation of identity, because the photograph which appeared in *The Daily Tribune* was a publication of her likeness without her permission.

(B) Intrusion, because the photograph which appeared in *The Daily Tribune* was taken without her permission.

(C) False light, because the photograph and caption which appeared in *The Daily Tribune* suggested that she unlawfully used or sold drugs.

(D) Public disclosure, because her identity was revealed by the publication of her photograph in a distinctive dress with an unusual floral design.

Questions 184-185 are based on the following fact situation.

By a properly executed and recorded deed, Olar conveyed a parcel of real estate with a building on it as follows:

> to God's Church for as long as the land is used by God's Church for church purposes; and when the land ceases to be so used, to Mercy Hospital for as long as the land shall be used by Mercy Hospital for hospital purposes; and when the land ceases to be so used, to Ulysses if Ulysses is then living.

God's Church moved onto the real estate, using the building as a house of worship.

184. If the validity of the interest held by Ulysses is challenged on the sole ground that it violates the

Rule Against Perpetuities, the interest of Ulysses should be declared

(A) void, unless God's Church and Mercy Hospital are charitable institutions.

(B) valid.

(C) void, because there is no assurance that the interest of Ulysses will vest during the period established by the Rule Against Perpetuities.

(D) void, if the interest of Mercy Hospital is void.

185. Assume that five years after Olar's conveyance, the size of the congregation of God's Church increased, creating the need for more space. As a result, church officials sold the realty, planning to use the proceeds to buy a bigger church, and executed a deed purporting to convey the realty to Real Estate Development Company. In subsequent litigation to determine the rights of God's Church, Mercy Hospital, and Real Estate Development Company, which of the parties should be found to have a present possessory interest in the realty?

(A) Real Estate Development Company, but only if God's Church uses the proceeds of the sale to purchase realty for church use.

(B) Real Estate Development Company, because Mercy Hospital's interest is void under the Rule Against Perpetuities.

(C) Mercy Hospital, because the conveyance to Real Estate Development Company terminated the estate of God's Church.

(D) God's Church, because its conveyance to Real Estate Development Company was invalid under the grant from Olar.

Questions 186-187 are based on the following fact situation.

After a nuclear power plant was built in the state of Aritoma, the state passed the Nuclear Waste Act. The Act regulates the storage of radioactive wastes, and authorizes the construction of radioactive waste storage facilities at specified locations within the state. Section 40 of the Act provides that "No radioactive waste storage facility in the state shall store or accept for storage any radioactive waste resulting from activities conducted more than 5 miles from said storage facility." All storage facilities within the state which are authorized by the Nuclear Waste Act are located more than 5 miles from the Aritoma state line.

186. If the constitutionality of Section 40 is challenged in an appropriate proceeding, it is LEAST likely to be declared unconstitutional under the

    (A) Privileges and Immunities Clause of Article IV.

    (B) Privileges and Immunities Clause of the Fourteenth Amendment.

    (C) Equal Protection Clause of the Fourteenth Amendment.

    (D) Due Process Clauses of the Fifth and Fourteenth Amendments.

187. Assume for the purpose of this question only that the constitutionality of Section 40 is challenged on the sole ground that it violates the Commerce Clause. Which of the following additional facts or inferences, if it was the only one true, would be most likely to result in a conclusion that Section 40 is constitutional?

    (A) Prohibiting the storage of radioactive wastes generated outside the state reduces the expense of operating nuclear power plants within the state.

    (B) The transportation of radioactive wastes within Aritoma over distances greater than 5 miles would pose a significant health and safety hazard to Aritoma residents.

    (C) There are only a few locations within the state where radioactive wastes can be stored safely.

    (D) There are many locations outside the state where radioactive wastes can be stored safely.

188. Barnett was a manufacturer of pine furniture. Sandifer was a lumber supplier who had sold pine lumber to Barnett on many occasions. On August 1, Barnett sent Sandifer a written order for "one unit of good quality white pine lumber" at a specified price to be delivered prior to August 30. On August 5, in a letter to Barnett, Sandifer wrote, "I hereby acknowledge your order dated August 1. I will deliver prior to August 30, but because of problems at the mill, I cannot assure you that the lumber will be of good quality." Barnett did not respond to Sandifer's letter. Subsequently, on August 28, Sandifer delivered one unit of white pine lumber to Barnett, but Barnett refused to accept it, claiming that the lumber delivered was not of good quality.

If Barnett subsequently asserts a claim against Sandifer for damages resulting from Sandifer's failure to deliver good quality lumber, which of the following would be Sandifer's most effective argument in opposition to that claim?

    (A) Sandifer's letter of August 5 was a rejection of Barnett's offer.

    (B) Barnett failed to respond to Sandifer's letter of August 5.

    (C) Barnett refused to accept the lumber shipped by Sandifer.

    (D) Sandifer's delivery of lumber on August 28 was not an acceptance of Barnett's offer because the lumber was not of good quality.

Questions 189-190 are based on the following fact situation.

The security guard of a warehouse was making his rounds after closing time one night when he found Dandy walking around inside the warehouse. When the guard asked him what he was doing there, Dandy replied that he had been driving past the warehouse when he noticed that its door was open, and that he had entered to report this to the guard. The guard called the police, and Dandy was arrested and charged with violating a statute providing that "any person entering the building of another for the purpose of committing a crime therein is guilty of burglary."

At Dandy's trial, the prosecutor tried to prove that Dandy's van, parked outside the warehouse at the time of Dandy's arrest, had license plates on it which had been stolen from an out-of-state vehicle the day before Dandy's arrest.

189. Over objection by Dandy's attorney, evidence that the license plates had been stolen should be

(A) inadmissible, because Dandy was not on trial for stealing license plates.

(B) inadmissible, because Dandy was not convicted of stealing license plates.

(C) admissible, because it tends to establish that Dandy was likely to engage in criminal behavior.

(D) admissible, because it tends to establish that Dandy made special preparations for the commission of a crime.

190. The prosecutor subsequently offered evidence that Dandy had previously been convicted of a crime other than burglary. Which of the following additional facts or inferences, if it was the only one true, would be most likely to result in the exclusion of that evidence?

(A) Dandy testified in his own behalf at the burglary trial and stated that he had never been convicted of a crime.

(B) Dandy did not testify in his own behalf at the burglary trial.

(C) Dandy's prior conviction was for involuntary manslaughter.

(D) Dandy's prior conviction was rendered in the court of another state.

191. Fuzz was the owner of a peach orchard known as Fuzzacre. On May 15, Elberta contracted in writing to sell Fuzzacre to Pitts for $200,000 under terms specified. The agreement called for the delivery of marketable title and set July 15 as the date for closing. Elberta did not own Fuzzacre on May 15, but planned to acquire title to it prior to

the closing. On June 1, Pitts assigned his rights under the contract to Aquino. On June 15, Elberta acquired title to Fuzzacre by purchasing it from Fuzz for $150,000. On July 15, Elberta tendered a general warranty deed, but Pitts and Aquino both refused to go through with the transaction.

If Elberta asserts breach of contract claim for damages against Pitts, the court should find for

(A) Elberta, because at the time of closing Elberta held marketable title to the realty.

(B) Elberta, under the doctrine of estoppel by deed.

(C) Pitts, because at the time of contracting, Elberta did not hold title to Fuzzacre.

(D) Pitts, because at the time of closing Elberta's interest was outside the chain of title.

Questions 192-193 are based on the following fact situation.

By a valid written contract, Ashe agreed to construct a house for Osman on Osman's realty at a price of $60,000, with work to begin on June 1, and to be completed by December 1. On May 15, however, Ashe wrote Osman that she did not believe it would be possible to complete the work for less than $90,000. As a result, Osman entered into a valid written contract by which he hired Bach to construct the house at a price of $75,000.

192. Assume the following additional facts for the purpose of this question only: On June 1, Ashe and Bach appeared at Osman's realty, both ready to begin construction. Osman did not permit Ashe to do so, advising her that he had hired Bach to do the job. If Ashe subsequently institutes an action against Osman for breach of contract, Osman's most effective defense would be based on the theory of

(A) anticipatory repudiation.

(B) frustration of purpose.

(C) novation.

(D) prospective inability to perform.

193. Assume the following additional facts for the purpose of this question only: Ashe never appeared at Osman's realty. On June 1, Bach commenced work. On July 1, Bach and Osman agreed that if Bach completed the work by October 1, Osman would pay Bach $90,000. Bach satisfactorily completed the work by October 1, and Osman paid $90,000 as agreed. If Osman subsequently sues Ashe for damages resulting from breach of contract, the court should award Osman

   (A) nothing, because Ashe offered to build the house for $90,000.

   (B) $15,000, because it is the difference between $60,000 and $75,000.

   (C) $15,000, because it is the difference between $75,000 and $90,000

   (D) $30,000, because it is the difference between $60,000 and $90,000.

194. Pursuant to a valid arrest warrant, police officers Hammet and Infeld stopped Daniels while he was driving his car and arrested him on a murder charge. Since Daniels was alone at the time of his arrest, Hammet drove Daniels' car to the police parking yard for safekeeping, while Infeld transported Daniels in the police car. Hammet examined the interior, trunk, and glove compartment of Daniels' car, listing the contents on a police department form.

   Later, Infeld told Hammet that in addition to the murder, he suspected Daniels of being involved in the robbery of a jewelry store near the murder scene. Hammet remembered seeing some jewelry in Daniels' glove compartment, so they decided to see whether any of it had been stolen from the jewelry store. In his car they found a watch in the glove box that matched a description on the list of stolen jewelry. While Daniels was never prosecuted for murder, he was later charged with robbing the jewelry store.

   If Daniels moves to suppress the introduction of the watch as evidence on the ground that it was obtained in violation of his constitutional rights,

his motion should be

   (A) granted, because evidence incidentally discovered during Hammet's inventory search could only have been used in the murder prosecution.

   (B) granted, because no warrant had been issued for a search of the glove compartment by Hammet and Infeld.

   (C) denied, because a search of the glove compartment by Hammet and Infeld was incidental to a valid arrest.

   (D) denied, because Hammet discovered the watch during the course of a valid inventory search.

Questions 195-196 are based on the following fact situation.

Dento, a dentist, owned an apparatus for putting patients to sleep while she operated on their teeth. The apparatus consisted of two canisters, one filled with oxygen and the other filled with anesthetic gas. By manipulating valves attached to the canisters, Dento used the apparatus to mix and administer a proper combination of gases to patients. Noticing that one of the valves was beginning to wear out, Dento sent the apparatus to its manufacturer MFR for repairs. After fixing the valve, MFR negligently filled the oxygen canister with anesthetic gas and the anesthetic gas canister with oxygen.

After MFR returned the apparatus to Dento, she attempted to use it on Paget, a patient. While treating Paget, Dento decided that it was necessary to administer pure oxygen and manipulated the valves accordingly. Because of MFR's error in refilling the oxygen canister with anesthetic gas, however, Dento administered pure anesthetic instead. As a result, Paget died in Dento's office.

195. If Paget's personal representative asserts an appropriate claim against Dento for damages resulting from the death of Paget, the court should find that Dento is

   (A) liable, only if Dento acted unreasonably in

treating Paget.

(B) liable, under the doctrine of *res ipsa loquitur.*

(C) not liable, because Paget's death resulted from negligence by MFR.

(D) not liable, unless the apparatus was defective when Dento attempted to use it on Paget.

196. If Dento asserts a claim against MFR for mental suffering which she experienced as a result of Paget's death in her office, which of the following would be Dento's most effective argument in support of her claim?

(A) MFR's error was outrageous because it created a high probability of serious harm.

(B) It was likely that MFR's error would lead Dento to experience mental suffering.

(C) Dento assumed all risks associated with using anesthetic gas.

(D) There was substantial certainty that Dento would use the apparatus on a patient.

Questions 197-198 are based on the following fact situation.

Hermes told his friend Pharma, a druggist, that he was planning to kill his wife Wanda and asked Pharma to help him by furnishing a poison. Although Pharma did not actually intend to help Hermes kill his wife, he said that he would because he did not want his friend to be angry at him. Pharma gave Hermes a commonly used antibiotic, telling him that it was a deadly and undetectable poison. Pharma knew that the antibiotic was not supposed to be dispensed without a prescription, and that about 2 percent of the people who received it developed an allergic reaction to it, but he did not believe that it would hurt Wanda. That night while Wanda was asleep, Hermes injected her with the antibiotic which Pharma had given him. Because she was allergic to the drug, Wanda became seriously ill and nearly died.

197. If Pharma is prosecuted for attempted murder he

should be found

(A) guilty, if giving Hermes the antibiotic without a prescription with knowledge that Hermes would give it to Wanda shows a reckless disregard for human life.

(B) guilty, because he did not attempt to stop Hermes from killing Wanda.

(C) guilty, because he furnished the drug knowing that Hermes would use it to attempt to kill Wanda.

(D) not guilty, because he did not believe that Wanda would die.

198. If Hermes is prosecuted for conspiracy to murder Wanda, which of the following would be his most effective argument in defense?

(A) Wanda did not die.

(B) Pharma did not believe that Wanda would die.

(C) The drug which Hermes gave Wanda was not likely to cause her death.

(D) The inchoate crime and the substantive crime merge when the defendant's overt act brings him substantially close to achieving his intended result.

Questions 199-200 are based on the following fact situation.

Delmar was arrested and charged in a state court with the unlawful possession of a dangerous drug. As his defense, Delmar asserted that he was an undercover officer employed by the Special Division of the State Police Department and that he had possessed the drug lawfully as part of an undercover assignment. During the presentation of its case, the prosecution called Waldron, an official of the State Police Department. Waldron testified that he was the custodian of a personnel file which contained the names of all undercover officers employed by the Special Division of the State Police Department and that he had studied the file before coming to court. He said that all entries in the file were made by the person who selected its personnel and issued their assignments when the Special

Division was formed and as new personnel were added.

199. Assume for the purpose of this question only that the prosecution then offers to have Waldron testify that the file contains no mention of Delmar, and that Delmar's attorney objects. Which of the following additional facts and inferences, if it was the only one true, would be most likely to result in the admission of Waldron's testimony?

 (A) The file itself is unavailable.

 (B) The person who makes the entries in the file is unavailable.

 (C) The person who made the entries in the file is dead.

 (D) The personnel file is available for inspection by the public.

200. Assume for the purpose of this question that the prosecution offers the file itself into evidence for the purpose of showing that it contains no mention whatsoever of Delmar. If Delmar's attorney objects, the personnel file should be

 (A) admitted as a business record.

 (B) admitted as past recollection recorded.

 (C) excluded, because government documents may only be used against the government.

 (D) excluded, because it calls for an inference to be drawn from negative evidence.

ANSWERS

PRACTICE MBE — A.M. EXAM

PRACTICE MBE — ANSWERS TO A.M. QUESTIONS

1. **D** A private citizen or police officer is privileged to use whatever non-deadly force he reasonably believes is necessary to prevent the escape of a criminal from a crime. Although there is some doubt whether the force used by Deakin against Thead was reasonable, or indeed whether it was non-deadly, **B** is the only argument listed which could possibly result in an acquittal.

   In some jurisdictions, a person defending another against a threat of immediate bodily harm is privileged to use whatever force the person being defended would have been privileged to use. In other jurisdictions, a person defending another against a threat of immediate bodily harm is privileged to use the force which reasonably appears necessary to the defendant himself. Both **A** and **B** are incorrect, however, because Thead was in the process of running away at the time of Deakin's blow, and Deakin, therefore, was not defending Elder against a threat of bodily harm. A person who owns or is in charge of property may use reasonable force to protect it. This may privilege the use of force to stop a person who is in the process of unlawfully carrying that property off. **C** is incorrect, however, because Deakin was not the owner or custodian of Elder's handbag, and, therefore, had no privilege to protect it.

2. **D.** Under FRE 611(b) (as well as the common law majority rule), cross-examination is limited to matters to which the witness testified on direct examination. Because Wayman did not testify about the contract, the question asked by Donco's attorney probably exceeds the scope of cross-examination. Since the trial court is given discretion in determining how far the scope of cross-examination extends, it is not certain that the court would sustain the objection on this ground. Of all the arguments listed, however, the one set forth in **D** is the only one which could possibly be effective in support of the objection.

   A is incorrect for two reasons: first, Wayman was called by Pelton and, therefore, is not Donco's witness; and, second, under FRE 607 a party may impeach its own witness. A leading question is one which contains a suggestion which would cause the ordinary person to believe that the questioner desires one answer instead of another. **B** is incorrect because the question asked by Donco's attorney contains no such suggestion and because leading questions are permitted on cross-examination. Argumentative questions are those which are used to emphasize some point to the jury rather than to elicit information. Although argumentative questions are improper, **C** is incorrect because the question asked by Donco's attorney did not seek to emphasize any particular point to the jury.

3. **B** For the purpose of discovering weapons or preventing the destruction of evidence, officers may make an incidental search of a person who has been lawfully arrested. Thus, if Gina's arrest was lawful, the search of her person was lawful as an incident to that arrest. An officer may make an arrest without a warrant if there is probable cause to believe that the person arrested has committed or is in the process of committing a felony. Thus, if Gina's proximity to the trunk gave the officers probable cause to believe that she was guilty of possessing cocaine, her arrest and incidental search were lawful.

Probable cause means a belief that the defendant is guilty supported by facts that would lead a reasonable person to entertain such a belief. While it is not certain that the officers had probable cause to believe Gina guilty, the argument set forth in **B** is the only one listed which might provide the prosecution with an effective argument in response to Gina's motion.

It is sometimes said that evidence discovered by violating a defendant's rights is inadmissible because it is "fruit of the poisonous tree." **A** is incorrect because evidence so classified is excluded, not admitted. Many states hold that officers executing a warrant to search premises are entitled to frisk all persons present for weapons. The frisk, however, consists of a patting down of the outside of the clothing and does not justify reaching into pockets unless the pat down has revealed something which feels like a weapon. Since there is no indication that the bag of marijuana felt like a weapon, **C** is incorrect. **D** is incorrect because, although a warrant to search premises might authorize a search of persons present, it does not justify their arrest unless there is probable cause to believe that they have committed or are committing a felony.

4. **C**   Officers may make an incidental search of a person who has been lawfully arrested, for the purpose of discovering weapons or to prevent the destruction of evidence. Thus, if Gina's arrest was lawful, the search of her person was also lawful as an incident to that arrest. On the other hand, if the arrest was unlawful, the search incident to it was also unlawful.

The purpose for permitting a search incidental to a lawful arrest is to protect against the dangers that the person arrested will attack the officers with a weapon or will destroy evidence which is hidden on her person. Since waiting for an officer of a particular gender might defeat both these purposes, the fact that the arresting officer is of a different gender than the defendant is not enough to invalidate the search. **A** is, therefore, incorrect. A search incidental to an arrest is valid if the arrest was lawful. Since even an innocent, person may be lawfully arrested (i.e., if there is probable cause to believe that she is guilty), the validity of an incidental search does not depend on whether the defendant was actually guilty of the crime for which she was arrested. **B** is, therefore, incorrect. **D** is incorrect because hearsay may be sufficient to support the issuance of a valid warrant.

5. **D**   To be enforceable, a contract requires mutuality of assent. If both parties are mistaken about a basic assumption of their agreement (i.e., there is a bilateral mistake), there is no mutuality of assent and no enforceable agreement can be formed. Both Sadler and Bain believed that they were contracting for the purchase and sale of one parcel of realty when in fact the written contract identified a different parcel of realty. Their bilateral mistake thus prevented the mutuality of assent necessary to make their "contract" enforceable.

If the mistake had been Sadler's alone (i.e., unilateral), it would not have prevented the formation of a contract unless Bain knew or should have known about it. For this reason, if Bain had known that the parcel described in the writing (#341) had a building on it while the parcel which he had inspected (#241) did not, Sadler's mistake would have prevented the formation of a contract. **A** is incorrect, however, because Bain did not know this at the time the writing was signed. If the only mistake in the formation of a contract is made by an intermediary chosen by one of the parties, that mistake is charged to the party who selected the intermediary. (If, for example, Lawler had said, "My client wants to buy #341," and Sadler and Bain had agreed on a price for #341, then Bain would have been obligated to buy #341 because his unilateral mistake would not have prevented the formation of a contract.) In this case, however, the error was bilateral — both Sadler and Bain believed that they were contracting for the purchase of a different parcel. For this reason, **B** is incorrect. **C** is incorrect for two reasons: first, if Sadler's mistake had been unilateral, the fact that she would suffer a substantial loss as a result would not be enough to free her of obligations under the contract; and, second, bilateral mistake regarding a basic assumption of the contract prevented the formation of an enforceable contract for the sale of #341 whether it was more valuable than #241 or not.

6.   **D**   The First Amendment prohibits laws which interfere with the free exercise of religion. A law which makes a benefit available to some people, but denies it to others because of their religious affiliations may violate this provision because it imposes a burden on the exercise of a religious belief. In 1978, the United States Supreme Court specifically held (*McDaniel v. Paty*) that a statute which prohibited members of the clergy from running for public office was invalid for this reason. Even without this decision, however, the argument set forth in **D** is the only one listed which could possibly support Causton's position.

Although a state may not set qualifications for state office which violate rights protected by the United States Constitution, there is no constitutional requirement that qualifications for state office be consistent with qualifications for federal office. **A** is, therefore, incorrect. **B** is incorrect because the statute in question does not attempt to set qualifications for practicing members of the clergy. **C** is incorrect for two reasons: first, although the creation of political divisiveness along religious lines may make a law invalid under the *establishment* clause, this is not relevant to rights protected by the free exercise clause; and, second, prohibiting members of the clergy from holding public office is not likely to have that effect.

7.   **A**   A defendant is liable for harm resulting from a plaintiff's justified reliance on a misrepresentation made by the defendant if the falsity of the defendant's representation was the result of fault (i.e., intent or negligence) by the defendant. A seller's failure to disclose a condition which would prevent the reasonable buyer from buying and about which the reasonable buyer would expect disclosure may be regarded as an implied representation that the condition does not exist. Thus, if Semon knew that the pilings were rotten (i.e., misrepresented *intentionally*) or should have known that the pilings were rotten (i.e., misrepresented *negligently*) he may be liable to Palen.

It is sometimes held that an affirmative act by a seller which hides a defect from the buyer is an implied representation that the condition does not exist. Thus, Semon's painting of the exposed portion of the pilings may be regarded as an implied statement that the pilings were in as good a condition as they appeared to be. **B** is incorrect, however, because unless Semon knew or should have known that the pilings were in rotten condition, he lacked the fault necessary to make him liable for this implied misrepresentation. On the other hand, if Semon knew or should have known the condition of the pilings, that knowledge (actual or constructive), coupled with the fact that painting the tops of the pilings disguised their condition, would have imposed upon him a duty to disclose their hidden condition whether or not Palen asked. **C** is, therefore, incorrect. A plaintiff has "relied" on a misrepresentation if it was a significant factor in his decision, even if it was not a determining factor. **D** is incorrect for this reason, and because even if Palen was damaged by justified reliance on Semon's implied representation, liability will not be imposed without proof of fault as described above.

8. **C**   The privilege of self-defense excuses a defendant from criminal liability when he is using reasonable force to protect himself against the commission of a crime. One is never justified in using deadly force in self-defense, however, unless he reasonably believes that he is in imminent danger of death or great bodily injury. Reger was not justified in slapping Santana's face; however, if Santana exceeded his privilege of self-defense when he began loading his pistol in apparent retaliation, this made him the aggressor. If Reger then had a reasonable (even though mistaken) belief that his life was in danger, he was justified in using deadly force to defend himself.

During the course of a fight, the role of aggressor may shift from one person to the other. Although a person is not privileged to defend himself against a privileged (i.e., reasonable) response to his own aggression, he is privileged to defend himself against an unprivileged attack. Although Reger was the initial aggressor, he may have been privileged to use force to defend himself against Santana's response to the slap if Santana's response was excessive (i.e., unprivileged). **A** is, therefore, incorrect. What force is reasonable in self-defense depends not so much on the facts, as upon the way the facts were perceived by the defendant and how they would have been perceived by the reasonable person in the defendant's position. Thus even in jurisdictions which require a defendant to make reasonable attempts to escape before using lethal force in self-defense, the fact that Reger could have escaped would not be relevant unless the reasonable person in his shoes would have realized that. **B** is, therefore, incorrect. **D** is incorrect because a determination of what force is reasonable in self-defense depends on the state of mind of the defendant, not on that of the victim.

9. **A**   Under the "collateral sources rule," sums which a plaintiff receives from anyone other than a tortfeasor or a tortfeasor's representative are not relevant in determining the amount of damages to which the plaintiff is entitled. This is because a benefit which is given to an injured person should not be used to the advantage of the person who injured him/her. Since the Mutual Insurance Company paid under a policy which Palma had purchased, Daniel should not derive a benefit from it by the reduction of damages which he is required to pay.

If a plaintiff has received payment from a tortfeasor (e.g., in settlement), the amount of such payment may be deducted from the plaintiff's damage to reduce the liability of other tortfeasors. **B** is incorrect since this is true whether or not such payment was made pursuant to a judicial determination. **C** is incorrect under the "collateral sources rule" for the reasons stated above. Ordinarily, when one joint tortfeasor pays more than his/her fair share of a judgment, s/he is entitled to recover part of it from other joint tortfeasors. Some jurisdictions base this recovery on equal apportionment, referring to it as "contribution" between joint tortfeasors. Other jurisdictions base this recovery on the relative fault of the joint tortfeasors, referring to it as "partial indemnity." Since Mutual Insurance Company was not a joint tortfeasor with Daniel, use of the term "partial indemnity" is not applicable. **D** is, therefore, incorrect.

10. **B**   Ordinarily, a promise is not enforceable unless it was supported by consideration. Consideration is something of value given in exchange for the promise. Since Morefield gave nothing of value in return for Execuco's agreement to release her, his agreement was unsupported by consideration and, therefore, unenforceable. A novation is an agreement to substitute the performance of a third party for that of a promisor coupled with the promisee's express agreement to release the original promisor from further obligation. In a novation, the third party's promise to perform for the promisee is consideration for the promisee's agreement to release the original promisor. (For example, X and Y have a contract requiring Y to perform. X, Y, and Z then agree that Z will perform instead of Y and Y is released from further obligation. Z's promise to perform is consideration for X's agreement to release Y.) A court could find that there was no novation in this case because Danbury's promise to perform had already been made, and, therefore, was not given in return for (i.e., as consideration for) Execuco's agreement to release Morefield. While it is not certain that a court would come to this conclusion, the argument given in **B** is the only one listed which might be effective in response to Morefield's claim.

The parol evidence rule prohibits evidence of a *prior or contemporaneous* oral agreement to contradict or modify the terms of certain writings. Since Execuco's oral agreement to release Morefield was made *after* their written contract, the parol evidence rule does not apply to it. **A** is, therefore, incorrect. The original contract between Execuco and Morefield was for a three year period (i.e., could not be performed within a year). For that reason, the statute of frauds required it to be in writing. Since Execuco's agreement to release Morefield had instant effect, however, the statute of frauds does not apply to it. **C** is, therefore, incorrect. Accord occurs when contracting parties agree to substitute a new obligation for an existing one; satisfaction occurs when that new obligation is fulfilled. Since Morefield's delegation to Danbury did not create any new obligation between Execuco and Morefield, it was not an accord; thus, there could have been no satisfaction. **D** is, therefore, incorrect.

11. **A**   Ordinarily, a promise to keep an offer open for a specified period of time is not enforceable unless supported by consideration. If such a promise is supported by consideration, it is called an option contract, and is enforceable as any other contract would be. Since Schilling's promise to keep her offer open until October 1 was given in return for Barnes's payment of $100 cash, it was supported by consideration and is enforceable as an option contract.

B is, therefore, incorrect. Under UCC § 2-205 a written and signed promise by a merchant to keep an offer open for a specified time not to exceed three months is called a firm offer and is enforceable without consideration. Since there is no indication that Schilling was a merchant, and since the period specified in the writing exceeds three months, it does not qualify as a firm offer. **C** is, therefore, incorrect. A promise which does not qualify as a firm offer and which was not supported by consideration may still be enforceable if the promisee justifiably relied upon it to her detriment. Since Schilling's promise was supported by consideration, **D** is incorrect because a promise supported by consideration is enforceable even if the promisee did not detrimentally rely on it.

12. **B**   Freedom of association is a corollary of the First Amendment freedoms of expression and assembly. For this reason, it has been held that neither the federal nor state government can impose a disability on a person as a result of membership in an organization unless the organization advocates illegal conduct, and the person is an active member who knows the organization's unlawful purposes and specifically intends to further them. Since the law in question would impose a disability (i.e., ineligibility for federal employment) solely because of membership in an organization without regard to knowledge of the organization's purposes or the intent to further those purposes, it is unconstitutional.

An ex post facto law is one which imposes a criminal penalty on the basis of something which occurred before the law was passed. Since the law in question does not impose a criminal penalty, it is not an ex post facto law. **A** is, therefore, incorrect. Whether government employment is a privilege or a right, ineligibility for it is a disability. Since the disability cannot be constitutionally imposed for mere membership in an organization, **C** is incorrect. **D** may be incorrect for several reasons, but at least because the law does not take into account the views held by the persons to which it applies.

13. **C**   The federal government is immune from taxation by the states. It is generally understood, however, that this immunity does not shield private parties from state tax liability, even though they have a contractual relationship with the federal government. Although Congress has the power to specifically exempt a particular contractor from state sales tax liability, there is no fact here indicating that Congress exercised that power.

A state attempt to regulate interstate commerce may violate the Commerce Clause of the U.S. Constitution. **A** is incorrect, however, because a sales tax imposed on the purchase of materials used to build a bridge does not regulate interstate commerce, even though interstate vehicles may eventually use the bridge. While the state lacks power to tax the federal government, **B** is incorrect because, so long as it does not discriminate against them, the state is free to tax persons doing business with the federal government. This has been held to be so even though the cost of such taxes may eventually be passed along to the federal government via cost-plus-fixed-profit contracts. **D** is, therefore, incorrect.

14. **A**   A person seeking to protect a legitimate interest is privileged to make defamatory statements which he reasonably believes to be true, under circumstances where the publication is reasonable in its scope. Clearly, a doctor has a legitimate interest in attempting to prevent the hiring of incompetent nurses by a hospital. Since Dock's response to the personnel department questionnaire was likely to reach only those people who could decide whether or not to hire Nelsen, it was probably reasonable in scope. Therefore, if Dock reasonably believed the statement, then it was privileged, and Dock would not be liable for defamation.

The publication of a false defamatory statement — unless privileged — ordinarily results in liability, even though the publisher heard the statement from another and so indicates when making the statement. **B** is, therefore, incorrect. The Supreme Court of the United States has held that a plaintiff who is a public person may prevail in a defamation action only by proving that the defendant had "actual malice." **C** is incorrect, however, because the Court has stated that in a defamation action, "actual malice" means that when publishing the statement the defendant either knew that it was false or entertained serious doubts about its truth. **C** is also incorrect because actual malice alone is not sufficient to result in defamation liability. In some defamation actions, the plaintiff must prove that the defendant's publication resulted in actual damage to the plaintiff. Proof of damage, however, is not sufficient to result in defamation liability where other elements of the plaintiff's case have not been established or where the defendant was privileged. **D** is, therefore, incorrect.

15. **D** A positive statement by the promisor to the promisee indicating that the promisor will not perform his contractual duty is a repudiation of the contract. Even though performance was not yet due at the time of repudiation, the non-repudiating party may usually sue on a theory of anticipatory breach as soon as the repudiation occurs. Therefore, Sada acquired an immediate right of action as soon as Baldwin communicated that he would not order any boxes in 1985.

A is, therefore, incorrect. **B** is incorrect for two reasons: first, UCC § 2-306 specifically recognizes the validity of "requirements" contracts and specifies the manner in which their terms should be construed; and, second, damages for failing to order the specified minimum requirement could be fixed with certainty. A party who seeks damages for breach of contract is required to prove those damages; they are not presumed. **C** is incorrect for this reason, and because — strictly speaking — a repudiation is not a "breach," but an "anticipatory breach."

16. **A** UCC § 1-205 defines usage of trade as a practice or method of dealing which is regularly observed in a particular industry. UCC § 2-202 permits evidence of usage of trade to explain the terms of a written contract, even when the contract was intended to be a final expression of the agreement of the parties.

B, therefore, is incorrect. Ordinarily, parties to a contract are understood to accept the economic risks resulting from subsequent events which were within their contemplation at the time the contract was formed. This means that if the parties *did* contemplate a decline in the price of cazbah melons, a strong argument could be made that Baldwin should be bound by the 2,000-box minimum set forth in the contract. The fact that they did *not* contemplate such a decline, if relevant at all, is thus more likely to support Baldwin's position than it is to support Sada's. In any event, although the contemplation of the parties might help determine the meaning of the terms which they used, it is not the only factor to be considered. In fact, the UCC specifically permits evidence of trade usage to be considered as well. **C** is, therefore, incorrect. Ordinarily, in construing contracts, courts consider the manifest intentions of the parties, and do so by examining the language of the written agreement between them. A problem may arise, however, since the words used may have meant different things to the different parties. Since trade usage may indicate the meaning that certain terms generally have for people in the industry involved, the UCC provision regarding trade usage is designed to help determine what the parties by the terms they used. If, for example, it was generally understood in the trade that minimum requirements were inapplicable in times of falling prices, the parties might have specified a minimum number meaning it to be applicable only if prices did not fall, even though this intention would not be apparent to persons not in the trade. The argument set forth in **D** however, is based on what the language means to people who are unaware of its special trade usage. For this reason, **D** is incor-

rect.

17. **A**   In order to prevail in an action for defamation, a plaintiff must prove that defendant published a defamatory statement about the plaintiff. A defamatory statement is about the plaintiff if the reasonable person who knows the plaintiff would recognize the plaintiff from the statement. For this reason, a defamatory statement made about a group to which the plaintiff belongs identifies the plaintiff so long as the group is small enough to lead the reasonable person who knows that the plaintiff is a member of the group to believe that the statement about the group is being made about the plaintiff.

A statement about such a group sufficiently identifies each of its members. Each might, therefore, have an action for defamation. It is, thus, unnecessary for all members of the group to join in the action. This makes **B** incorrect. A spoken defamation is called "slander per se" if it accuses the plaintiff of a crime of moral turpitude, of having a loathsome disease, of being an unchaste woman, or of being unfit for the plaintiff's occupation. In certain cases of slander per se, the plaintiff may be relieved of the need to prove actual damage. **C** is incorrect for two reasons: first, the statement cannot be called slander because it was in writing; and, second, calling a statement slander per se does not eliminate the need to prove that the statement was made about the plaintiff. If the group of police officers present at the rally was small enough, the statement about the group identifies the plaintiffs (for reasons given above) even though it does not name them. **D** is, therefore, incorrect.

18. **B**   The United States Supreme Court has held that the First Amendment of the United States Constitution require a public official or public figure suing for defamation to prove that the defendant had actual malice in making the defamatory statement. The Court defined a public official as a public employee who has or reasonably appears to have substantial control over the conduct of public affairs. The plaintiffs are clearly public employees. Whether they reasonably appear to have substantial control over the conduct of public affairs may be a question of fact, but **B** is the only argument listed which could possibly result in a judgment for *The Herald*.

The United States Supreme Court has said that there is no such thing as a false idea. Since defamation liability cannot be imposed for publication of the truth, this statement by the Supreme Court prevents defamation liability from being imposed for the publication of an opinion. **A** is incorrect, however, because — even though it was contained in an editorial — the statement that police beat and kicked bystanders is obviously an assertion of fact. The Supreme Court has defined a public figure as either one who has achieved such "pervasive fame and notoriety" that s/he is known to the great mass of humanity, or one who has voluntarily "mounted the rostrum" in an attempt to influence public opinion on a matter of public controversy. **C** is incorrect because there is no fact indicating that either definition applies to the plaintiffs. In addition, **C** is incorrect because the Supreme Court has held that a defendant may not successfully argue that the plaintiff has become a public figure as a result of the defamatory statements which the defendant published about the plaintiff. **D** is incorrect, since the Supreme Court's definition of public official makes it clear that not all public employees fit into this category.

19. **A**   When, after the formation of a contract, the happening of an unforeseeable event makes

performance by one of the parties impossible or vitally different from what was within their reasonable contemplation at the time of formation, the duties of both parties are discharged. Whether the destruction of a party's factory is unforeseeable at the time a sales contract is formed is uncertain. The argument set forth in **A** however, is the only one listed which could possibly provide Vestco with an effective defense.

A party's prospective inability to perform may excuse performance by the *other* party, but does not affect the obligations of the party who is prospectively unable to perform. **B** is, therefore, incorrect. An agreement calling for a series of performances by the parties may be regarded as a single contract or as a series of separate ones. Calling it "divisible" simply means that the court will treat it as a series of separate contracts. It is difficult to tell from the facts whether the contract between Vestco and the Green City Police Department is or is not "divisible." In either event, however, whether it is a breach of a single agreement calling for a series of performances, or of one of the separate agreements which result from calling the contract divisible, Vestco's failure to deliver bullet-proof vests might be a breach. For this reason, **C** would not furnish Vestco with an effective defense and is, therefore, incorrect. A repudiation occurs when a party to a contract unequivocally informs the other that he will not perform as required. **D** is incorrect for two reasons: first, the Green City Police Department did not inform Vestco of anything; and, second, the fact that the Green City Police Department contracted to purchase 30 vests per month from another company does not indicate that it will not also purchase 30 vests per month from Vestco.

20. **B**   Under UCC § 2-609, whenever it reasonably appears that a party to a sales contract will be unable to perform as required, the other party may demand an adequate assurance of performance. If the party on whom such demand is made fails to respond within a reasonable period of time, the party making that demand may treat the other party's prospective inability to perform as a repudiation. Since the destruction of Vestco's only factory raised reasonable questions about whether Vestco would be able to perform as required, the Green City Police Department was entitled to demand assurances as it did in its letter of July 10. When Vestco failed to respond within a reasonable time, the Green City Police Department was relieved of any further obligation to perform.

When unforeseen circumstances eliminate the underlying reasons for contracting, the doctrine of frustration of purpose may excuse performance by the parties. (If, for example, all the criminals in Green City stopped using guns so that there was no longer any reason for the Green City Police Department to need bullet-proof vests, the doctrine of frustration of purpose might relieve it of its obligation to continue purchasing vests from Vestco.) **A** is incorrect because the underlying reasons for the agreement between the Green City Police Department and Vestco (i.e., the Green City Police Department's need for bullet-proof vests) continued to exist even though the Vestco factory was destroyed. For reasons given in the explanation to the previous question, determining that the contract was divisible is not relevant in determining whether failure to perform constitutes a breach. **C** is, therefore, incorrect. Even before the time of performance, a party may treat the other party's repudiation as a breach. Thus, a repudiation by the Green City Police Department might provide Vestco with an argument in support of its position, but would not provide Green City with support for its position. **D** is, therefore, incorrect.

21.   **A**   Under FRE 804(b)(2) a statement is admissible as a dying declaration if it was made about the cause and circumstances of death by a presently unavailable declarant with a sense of impending death, was based upon the declarant's personal knowledge, and is offered at the trial of a criminal homicide prosecution or of any civil action. Since Pargas asked Westall to tell his wife to meet him at the hospital, it is possible that a court would find that he did not believe himself to be dying. This conclusion is, of course, not certain (since he may have been telling her where to claim his body), but **A** is the only reason listed which could possibly justify finding that Pargas' statement was not a dying declaration.

           B is incorrect because while the FRE requires the declarant to be unavailable, it does not require that he have died from the incident described in his statement or even that he is dead. Although some controversy exists at common law about whether a dying declaration is admissible in anything but a criminal homicide prosecution, the FRE specifically permits its use in a civil action. **C** is, therefore, incorrect. The common law provides that an excited utterance may be admissible under an exception to the hearsay rule, but only if the statement was spontaneous (e.g., not in response to a question). The FRE exception for excited utterance does not specifically mention spontaneity, but some cases indicate that excited utterances should be excluded under the FRE if they were made in response to a question. **D** is incorrect, however, because neither the common law nor the FRE requires that a *dying declaration* be made spontaneously.

22.   **D**   An assignment extinguishes the assignor's rights and vests them in the assignee. By its assignment to Landis, Partco thus extinguished its own rights against Aerocorp. Since an assignee receives only those rights which were held by his assignor (i.e., steps into the assignor's shoes), and since Partco's assignment to Landis had already extinguished any rights which Partco had against Aerocorp, Martin could receive no right against Aerocorp unless Partco effectively revoked its assignment to Landis. Most jurisdictions hold that assignments are not revocable if given for consideration. Since Partco assigned to Landis in writing and for consideration (i.e., in lieu of rent), the assignment to Landis could not be revoked. Martin, therefore, received no interest as a result of the assignment to him.

           A and **B** are incorrect because it is generally understood that an assignment may be valid although not in writing and given without consideration. **C** is incorrect because in the absence of an agreement to the contrary, the right to receive money is assignable without the debtor's consent.

23.   **A**   Although the United Supreme Court interprets the federal constitution, it does not have the power to interpret state constitutions. If it reviewed the decision of the state court, it, therefore, could not disturb the holding that the due process requirement of the state constitution was violated. Since that holding alone is sufficient to support the state court's finding on behalf of Apollo (i.e., the finding is based on an adequate and independent state ground), the United States Supreme Court lacks the power to overturn the state court decision. For this reason, review by the United States Supreme Court is not available. (**Note:** Recent legislation has largely eliminated appeal as of right, but questions like this may still be used to test the availability of review.)

24.   **D**   Under FRE 803(22), a judgment of conviction may be admissible as an exception to the

hearsay rule. For any evidence to be admissible, however, it must be logically and legally relevant. Whether a past conviction for passing bad checks is *logically* related to any material issues in Dakota's prosecution is uncertain, but there is little doubt about the *legal relevancy* of such evidence. Because of its capacity for arousing prejudice, evidence bearing on a person's character is not admissible as circumstantial evidence that his conduct on a particular occasion was consistent with that character. Thus, Dakota's conviction for passing worthless checks is inadmissible if offered to support an inference that because he passed bad checks that time it is likely that he did it again this time. If the crime charged had been committed in a highly distinctive way, evidence that Dakota previously used that same distinctive M.O. would tend to establish that he was familiar with it. It could be admissible since its purpose would not be to circumstantially establish conduct by showing character. **I** is incorrect, however, because there is no fact indicating that the crime with which Dakota is now charged and the crime of which he was previously convicted involved the same distinctive M.O. Since the fact that a person has committed a crime involving dishonesty suggests that his statements are not worthy of belief, evidence that a witness has been convicted of such a crime may be admissible for the purpose of impeaching that witness's credibility. Since Dakota has not testified, however, his credibility is not in question. **II** is, therefore, incorrect.

25. **A**   In states which recognize tenancy by the entirety, a conveyance to persons who are wife and husband may be presumed to create a tenancy by the entirety. Since only persons who are legally married may hold realty as tenants by the entirety, however, the rules regarding this form of co-ownership do not apply in this case. In general, in the absence of some specific language to the contrary, two or more persons who take real property by descent or conveyance are presumed to be tenants-in-common with equal interests. Tenants-in-common may freely sell or devise their interests, and those who receive them thereby become tenants-in-common with the remaining co-owners. Thus upon inheriting Ann's one-half interest, Armstrong became a tenant-in-common with Bob. Subsequently, upon Bob's quitclaim of his one-half interest to Boaz, Boaz became a tenant-in-common with Armstrong.

B is incorrect for several reasons, the most significant being that only persons who are married to each other may hold realty as tenants by the entirety. **C** is incorrect because Armstrong inherited a one-half interest from Ann. **D** is incorrect because Boaz received a one-half interest by quitclaim from Bob.

26. **D**   Larceny is the trespassory taking and carrying off of personal property known to be another's with the intent to permanently deprive that other of it. Since Davin had not read the fine print in the rental agreement, she did not know that its terms made the radio the property of another. For this reason, she should not be convicted of larceny.

Although a person who intentionally destroys property which she knows to be another's intending to deprive that other of it may thereby commit larceny, **A** is incorrect because there is no indication that Davin intended the damage to the dashboard of the car, and also because the "trespassory" requirement makes it impossible for a person to commit larceny as to property lawfully in her possession at the time of her act. A person who signs a contract may be bound by its terms even though she hasn't read it because of a presumption that she has done so. The presumption exists because of the objective theory of contracts combined with the fact that the reasonable person does not usually sign something which she knows to be a contract without first reading it. For this reason, Davin may be civilly liable for breach of contract or for the tort of conversion. **B** is incorrect, however, because guilt for larceny requires *subjective* knowledge that the property involved belongs to another. Thus, if Davin honestly believed that the radio was her own, even if her belief was unreasonable, she cannot be guilty of larceny for taking it. **C** is incorrect because a person can be convicted of stealing her own property if she took it from a person whose rights she knew were superior to her own. (For example, the owner of a chattel may commit larceny by taking it from one whom she knows to hold a valid mechanic's lien.)

27.   **D**   A professional seller who supplies a defective product is strictly liable for damage which proximately results from the product's defect. A defect is a proximate cause of harm if it was both a factual and a legal cause of it. A defect is a factual cause of harm if the harm would not have occurred without it. Assuming that the vibrations resulted from a defect, the defect was a factual cause of Nesbitt's injury, since the injury would not have occurred without it. A defect is a legal cause of harm if the harm was a foreseeable result of the defect, and not the result of unforeseeable interventions (i.e., superseding causes). Thus if the intervening conduct of Wells was a superseding cause of the harm, then the product defect — although a factual cause of the injury — was not a legal cause of it. Although it might take a jury to determine whether Wells's conduct was unforeseeable (i.e., a superseding cause), **D** is the only argument listed which might result in a judgment for Storr.

If all other requirements are satisfied, strict liability may be imposed to benefit any plaintiff whose contact with the product was foreseeable, regardless of whether the plaintiff is classified as a bystander. **A** is, therefore, incorrect. A plaintiff who voluntarily encounters a known risk assumes that risk. **B** is incorrect, however, because Wells was not the plaintiff, and only a plaintiff is said to assume a risk. If the processing machine was defective when it left Blendco's factory, Blendco might be strictly liable for Nesbitt's injuries which proximately resulted. **C** is incorrect, however, because if the product was defective when it left Blendco's factory, it must have been defective when it left Storr's premises, making Storr strictly liable as well.

28.   **C**   Negligence is unreasonable conduct in the face of a duty to act reasonably. If the defendant acted reasonably, she could not have been negligent. Unreasonable conduct by Wells is, therefore, the only thing which could result in a judgment for Nesbitt in a negligence action against Wells.

When the defendant's conduct is unknown, *res ipsa loquitur* may permit a plaintiff to establish an inference that the defendant acted unreasonably by relying on circumstantial evidence. This evidence must prove that the accident was one which would not ordinarily have occurred without negligence, under circumstances which eliminate all probabilities other than the negligence of the defendant (e.g., that defendant was in exclusive control of the instrumentality involved). **A** is incorrect because, by alleging the specific conduct of Wells and labeling it negligent, Nesbitt has made circumstantial evidence unnecessary and inadmissible. **A** is also incorrect because the circumstances do not exclude all probabilities other than negligence by Wells as a cause of the accident. If a defendant's conduct was negligent, she is liable for the harm which proximately resulted from that negligence. In determining whether a plaintiff's harm was proximately caused by a defendant's conduct, the operative question is not whether the defendant's conduct was foreseeable, but whether the plaintiff's harm was a foreseeable result of it. **B** is, therefore, incorrect. Since any injury might have several proximate causes, the argument that another person proximately caused the plaintiff's harm is never sufficient to shield a defendant from liability. **D** is incorrect because even if the negligence of Storr or Blendco was a proximate cause of Nesbitt's injury, the negligence of Wells might also have been a proximate cause of it.

29. **D**   A statutory system of classification which regulates social or economic interests is valid under the equal protection clause if it has a rational basis. On the other hand, if it discriminates against a suspect class of persons it is valid only if it is necessary to serve a compelling state interest. (**Note**: To withstand a constitutional challenge based on the claim that a statute interferes with a fundamental right, the statute must be necessary to serve a compelling state interest. Since Hirsh's challenge is not based on that claim, however, the compelling state interest standard does not apply.) Although it has been held that a statutory classification based on gender does not discriminate against a suspect class, the United States Supreme Court has developed a third, or middle, level of scrutiny (sometimes called "rational basis with a bite") for such classifications. It has been held that gender classifications are valid only if they are substantially related to an important governmental interest. Since Hirsh's sole claim is that the statute discriminates against women, the statute would be valid if it satisfied this middle level of scrutiny. Although it is not certain that the statute would satisfy the requirements of this test, the argument set forth in **D** is the only one listed which might possibly be effective in opposition to Hirsh's claim.

A is incorrect because the fact that a system of classification does or does not discriminate against a suspect class determines the standard to be applied, but does not itself determine whether the statute is constitutional. **B** is incorrect because a rational basis is not sufficient to make constitutional a statute which discriminates on the basis of gender. **C** is incorrect because the police powers, like all other powers of the state, may not be exercised in a way which is inconsistent with the United States Constitution.

30. **C**   The terms of a contract may provide that a party's performance is not required until the happening of a specified event (i.e., a condition precedent). If so, the duty to perform does not become absolute until that event has occurred (i.e., the condition precedent has been satisfied). In this contract, Orca's duty to make final payment was conditioned upon Berg's obtaining a Certificate of Satisfactory Completion from Arch prior to July 30. Thus, Orca's duty to pay would not become absolute until Berg satisfied the condition precedent by obtaining the certificate by that date. It is understood, however, that a party who wrongfully interferes with the other party's fulfillment of a condition may not rely on that unfulfilled condition to avoid performing. Sometimes this conclusion is based on what is referred to as a breach of the "implied promise to cooperate." Sometimes courts simply say that wrongful interference excuses performance of the condition precedent. Either way, since Orca's request caused Arch to delay issuing the certificate, Orca's duty to make final payment may become absolute in spite of Berg's failure to fulfill that condition of the contract.

A is incorrect because Arch was not a party to the contract between Orca and Berg, and that contract, therefore, could not have imposed duties on Arch. It is sometimes said that express conditions of a contract must be fully satisfied, but that "substantial performance" satisfies constructive conditions. Since the condition requiring Berg to obtain a Certificate of Satisfactory Completion by July 30 was express, substantial performance would not have been sufficient. **B** is, therefore, incorrect. Sometimes in a contract calling for performance to the satisfaction of the other party, a dispute arises as to whether that satisfaction is to be subjective or based on objective standards. Usually, in the absence of a clear agreement to the contrary, the standard is understood to be an objective one. In this case, however, the express condition required not only satisfactory completion, but the obtaining of a certificate by a particular date. For this reason, the application of an objective standard would not be sufficient to defeat Orca's claim. **D** is, therefore, incorrect.

31. **A**   One who intentionally aids, abets, or facilitates the commission of a crime is an accomplice, and is guilty not only of the crime which she aided, but is vicariously liable for all its reasonably foreseeable consequences. One who agrees with another to commit a crime is guilty of conspiracy, and is vicariously liable for any crimes committed by a co-conspirator in furtherance of the conspiracy. Since the jury did not believe Domino's testimony, Philip was committing a robbery when he used a threat of force to steal the coat from Fleming. Since Domino assisted him in doing so, she was an accomplice. Since she agreed to do so, she was a co-conspirator. As an accomplice, she is probably liable vicariously for Philip's intentional killing of Fleming, because her knowledge that Philip would be using a gun to coerce Fleming into handing over the coat probably made it foreseeable that he would shoot Fleming with the gun. As a co-conspirator she is clearly liable vicariously for the shooting, since it was clearly in furtherance of the robbery that she agreed to commit.

              B is incorrect because being present while a crime is committed is not sufficient to make a defendant an accomplice or a co-conspirator. Self-defense is a privilege to use reasonable force to defend oneself against the use of force. A person who is being shot at may, therefore, be privileged to defend himself by shooting back. **C** is incorrect, however, because self-defense does not privilege the use of force in response to force which itself was privileged by self-defense. Since Philip was menacing Fleming with a pistol, Fleming was privileged to use a pistol in self-defense. Since Fleming's use of force was privileged, Philip was not privileged to use any force in defense against it. **D** is incorrect because as a co-conspirator and accomplice to the crime of *robbery*, Domino is vicariously liable for the shooting which was a foreseeable consequence and done in furtherance of the robbery.

32. **C**   Under the statute Domino can be guilty of Second Degree Murder only if Fleming dies during the course of the commission of one of the enumerated felonies. Nothing in the facts suggests that Domino or Philip was committing a rape, kidnapping, burglary, or arson. Robbery is a larceny which is committed by force or a threat of force against a human being. Larceny is a trespassory taking and carrying off of personal property known to be another's with the intent to permanently deprive. Since the jury believed Domino's testimony, the coat which she was attempting to obtain from Fleming was her own. Her taking it could not, therefore, constitute a larceny. Her use of force to take it was thus not a robbery.

              A and **B** are incorrect because if a death occurs during the course of one of the felonies specified, the felony murder rule is frequently applied even though the death was unforeseeable. Since the statute provides that an unintentional killing is Second Degree Murder if perpetrated by the defendant *or an accomplice* during the course of a listed crime, **D** is obviously incorrect.

33. **B**   Involuntary manslaughter is an unintentional killing of a human being which results from conduct which is reckless (i.e., creates a high and unreasonable risk of death or great bodily harm). Since the jury believes Philip's testimony, Domino knew that Philip was going to use a loaded pistol. If this made it likely that death or serious injury would result, then her conduct was reckless, and the resulting death can be termed an involuntary manslaughter.

If Fleming's conduct was a *reasonable* response to Philip's threat with a pistol, it was privileged. If so, Philip's shot at Fleming was not privileged by self-defense. If, on the other hand, Fleming's response was excessive (as Philip's testimony suggests), then it was not privileged, and Philips return shot might have been privileged in self-defense. The fact, then, that Fleming's conduct was in response to Philip's act of aggression is not, alone, sufficient to deprive Philip or Domino of the privilege of self-defense. **A** is, therefore, incorrect. At common law, an intentional killing is murder, but may be reduced to voluntary manslaughter if committed in the "heat of passion." Since involuntary manslaughter involves an unintentional killing, however, passion does not provide a defense. **C** is, therefore, incorrect.

Depending on when Fleming stole Domino's coat (if he indeed did so), and depending on the substantive rules of the particular jurisdiction, it is possible that Domino was privileged to use *reasonable* force to reclaim her property. However, *deadly* force — force likely to cause death or serious bodily injury — is never permitted as a means of reclaiming property. Since Domino knew that Philip's gun was loaded, and since Domino was acting in concert with Philip in using the loaded gun to achieve the "reclamation" of property, Domino will be responsible for the use of deadly force and will forfeit any protection the right to use reasonable force to reclaim property might have given her. Therefore, **D** is incorrect.

34. **D**   Since Carmody received his interest from Badel, the validity of Carmody's title depends on the validity of Badel's title. For this reason, if Badel's title is superior to Arnett's, then Carmody's title is superior to Arnett's. The validity of Badel's title depends on the recording statute. The statute given is a typical "notice" statute. According to its provisions, the interest of a subsequent grantee for value and without notice is superior to that of a prior grantee unless the prior grantee's interest was recorded prior to the time the subsequent grantee received his interest. Since Arnett's deed was not recorded prior to Oakley's conveyance to Badel, Badel's interest is superior to Arnett's. Since Carmody derives his interest from Badel's grant, Carmody's interest is also superior to Arnett's.

As a result of this reasoning, it is correct to say that one who derives his interest from a bona fide purchaser for value (i.e., BFP) is protected by a recording statute even if he is not a BFP himself. Thus, Carmody's possible knowledge would not deprive him of the protection of the recording statute, and **A** is incorrect. **B** is incorrect because the language of the statute makes the interest of a subsequent grantee superior to that of a prior grantee unless the prior grantee's interest had been recorded prior to the subsequent *grant.* Since Badel purchased for value, without notice of Arnett's interest and before Arnett recorded, Badel's interest was superior to Arnett's. Since Carmody's title derives from Badel's, it too is superior to Arnett's. **C** is, therefore, incorrect.

35.   **C**   Since Carmody received his interest from Badel, the validity of Carmody's title depends on the validity of Badel's title. For this reason, if Badel's title is superior to Arnett's, then so is Carmody's. The validity of Badel's title (and therefore of Carmody's) depends on the recording statute. The statute given is a typical "race-notice" statute. According to its provisions, the interest of a subsequent grantee for value and without notice is superior to that of a prior grantee unless the prior grantee's interest is recorded before the subsequent grantee's interest is *recorded.* Thus, if Arnett's interest was recorded before Badel's, it was superior to Badel's (and therefore to Carmody's). If Badel recorded before Arnett, however, Badel's interest (and therefore Carmody's interest) was superior to Arnett's.

A is incorrect because although the statute makes the payment of value a condition for the superiority of a *subsequent* grantee's interest, it does not impose such a requirement on the prior grantee. Since the "race" aspect of the statute makes priority depend on who *recorded* first, the fact that Badel recorded before selling to Carmody would not defeat Arnett's interest since Badel may have recorded after Arnett did. **B** is, therefore, incorrect. Recording is "outside the chain of title" if it could not have been discovered by a reasonable title search. (For example, if Arnett recorded before Badel, a reasonable title search might not have disclosed a record of the deed from Oakley to Badel. This is because after finding a record of Oakley's grant to Arnett, the searcher would have expected that the next grant of an interest in the property was by Arnett and would have no reason to search for a subsequent grant by Oakley.) Most jurisdictions hold that a recording outside the chain of title is no recording at all since it does not give the reasonable searcher notice of the transaction. **D** is incorrect, however because if Badel recorded prior to Arnett, the recording of Oakley's grant to Badel would have been within the chain of title.

36.   **B**   Ordinarily, rape consists of sexual intercourse with a female not the wife of the defendant without that female's consent. Under most statutory rape laws, a female below a given age is determined to be incapable of consent, meaning that any male who has sexual intercourse with her does so without her consent. For this reason, knowledge of the victim's age is not ordinarily an element of statutory rape. Under the statute given in this question, however, knowledge of the female's age is specifically required. For this reason, Dave could not be convicted if he did not know that Betty was under the age of 18 years.

So long as a male defendant is old enough to be convicted of a crime, he may be convicted of statutory rape even though his age is the same as or younger than that of the female victim. **A** is, therefore, incorrect. Intoxication is a defense to a criminal charge only if it made the defendant incapable of possessing the necessary state of mind required. **C** is incorrect because there is no indication that Dave's intoxication affected his knowledge regarding Betty's age or prevented him from knowing that he was having sexual intercourse with her. Statutory rape, of which the crime charged is a form, is based on the concept that certain persons are incapable of consenting to sexual intercourse. For this reason, the victim's consent never furnishes a defense, and **D** is incor-

rect.

37. **D**   A criminal conspiracy is an agreement between two or more persons to commit a crime, and is completed when the agreement is made. Thus, when Charles and Dave agreed to get Adrian and Betty drunk so that they could have sexual intercourse with them they may have committed the crime of conspiracy to violate the statute (depending on whether Dave knew Adrian's or Betty's age). Although co-conspirators may be vicariously liable for certain crimes committed by other members of the conspiracy, many states hold that this vicarious liability terminates upon an effective withdrawal from the conspiracy. (**Note**: It is unlikely that a court would find that Charles effectively withdrew from the conspiracy, because he did not inform Dave of his change of intentions.) Even if he did effectively withdraw, however, his withdrawal would not prevent him from being found guilty of conspiracy to rape, which is a separate and distinct crime from rape.

Without an agreement to participate in the crime, mere knowledge that others plan to commit a crime is not enough to make a person guilty of conspiracy. Since Adrian did not agree to participate in the crime, she could not be convicted of conspiracy. **A** and **B** are therefore incorrect.

Where a crime necessarily requires two or more persons, but the legislature has imposed punishment on only one for the substantive crime, the immune party cannot be punished for conspiracy to commit that substantive crime. Since the legislature has chosen not to punish the underaged female (Betty) for rape, this rule means that Betty cannot be convicted of conspiracy to commit rape either. For this reason, **C** is incorrect.

38. **C**   Under pure comparative negligence statutes, plaintiff's recovery is not barred by plaintiff's fault, but is diminished in proportion to plaintiff's fault. Thus, if plaintiff's damage of $10,000 was caused 70% by the fault of defendant and 30% by the fault of plaintiff, plaintiff should recover $10,000 diminished by 30% (i.e., $7,000).

A is incorrect because under pure comparative negligence statutes plaintiff's recovery is not completely barred by plaintiff's negligence. **B** is incorrect because the formula on which it is based would result in diminishing plaintiff's recovery by a sum greater than the proportion of plaintiff's own fault. **D** is incorrect because it would not diminish plaintiff's recovery at all, even though a portion of the fault was plaintiff's.

39. **C**   Although a defendant's violation of a statute may help the plaintiff establish that the defendant was negligent, that negligence does not result in liability unless it was a factual and legal cause of the plaintiff's damage. Conduct is a factual cause of harm if the harm would not have occurred without it. Since obeying the speed limit was more likely to cause the collapse than exceeding it, the accident would have occurred if the statute had been obeyed. Since the collapse would have occurred without it, the violation was not a factual cause of the collapse.

In some jurisdictions, the violation of a statute may be negligence per se; in others it may raise a rebuttable presumption of negligence; in others it may merely raise an inference of negligence. **A** is incorrect, however, because negligence does not result in liability unless it was a factual cause of harm, and Terhune's violation of a statute — even if it establishes negligence — was not a cause of Pachos' harm. Although violation of a statute may raise a presumption of negligence, it does not result in any presumption as to causation and is usually not relevant to issues of causation. **B** is, therefore, incorrect. Unless the statute violated was designed to protect a class of persons which includes the plaintiff, its violation is not relevant to the question of negligence at all. **D** is incorrect, however, because it is generally understood that traffic laws are at least designed to protect other users of the roads.

40. **B**   Since the condition imposed by O'Brien's deed prohibited non-residential use, Carmichael's grant of a license to fish does not violate it if fishing is a residential use. Whether or not this is so is uncertain, but **B** is the only argument listed which could possibly provide Carmichael with an effective defense.

Under the rule against perpetuities no interest is good if it can vest after a particular period of time. The *creation* of an interest which might vest after the period is thus void under the rule, but the rule has no effect on the *termination* of an existing interest. **A** is incorrect for this reason, and because the rule against perpetuities is not applicable to future interests of a grantor. The fee simple determinable and the fee simple subject to a condition subsequent are possessory interests which may be terminated on the happening of a specified event. The most important difference between them is that the fee simple determinable terminates automatically on the happening of that event, and the fee simple subject to a condition subsequent does not terminate without some action being taken. The language of O'Brien's deed makes it difficult to determine which of those interests was conveyed to Carmichael, but the difference is insignificant to Carmichael since his interest is subject to termination in either event. For this reason, **C** is incorrect. A restraint on alienation is a condition which attempts to control the alienability (i.e., power to convey an interest) of realty. If the condition attempts to do so *directly* (e.g., the condition prohibits selling or mortgaging the realty) it may be declared void under certain circumstances. Although use restrictions are likely to affect the alienability of realty, policy does not require that they be declared void for this reason alone because their effect is *indirect*. **D** is, therefore, incorrect.

41. **D**   Ordinarily, specific performance is available as a remedy for breach of contract when damages would not be an adequate remedy. For several reasons, however, courts do not grant specific performance of contracts calling for personal service. These reasons include the constitutional protections against involuntary servitude and of freedom of association, as well as practical considerations which make it unwise for courts to become unduly involved in the supervision of performance. Thus, if the architectural work which remained to be completed involved personal services, specific performance would not be granted.

A is, therefore, incorrect. An agreement not to assign usually destroys the right but not the power to make an effective assignment. This means that an assignment made in the face of such an agreement is usually valid, although the assignor might be liable for damages resulting from the assignment and from her own failure to perform. For this reason, damages are usually the only remedy available for breach of a promise not to assign. **B** is, therefore, incorrect. **C** is a misstatement of the above rule. While an agreement not to assign may destroy the right to make a valid assignment (i.e., one who violates it may be liable for breach of contract) it does not ordinarily destroy the power to assign (i.e., an assignment made in violation of the assignor's promise may be valid). For this reason, **C** is incorrect. (**Note**: The obligation to perform personal services is not usually assignable or delegable. This rule is not relevant here, however, because the question asks not about the validity of the assignment, but about the availability of specific performance as a remedy.)

42. **A**   Under FRE 901(5) (and at common law), a voice may be identified by any person who testifies that she recognizes it based upon hearing the voice under circumstances connecting it with the alleged speaker. Although Pacer may not have known whose voice she was hearing when she had the telephone conversation, if she subsequently heard Dail's voice and recognized it as the same voice that she heard on the telephone, she is competent to testify that it was Dail's voice which she heard on the telephone. This is true even though her first real opportunity to connect Dail with the voice occurred on the morning of trial.

If a person's telephone number is listed in the telephone book, there is a presumption that one who properly dialed that number reached the premises of the person listed. Under FRE 901(6), this presumption combined with other circumstances, including self-identification of the speaker as the person listed, may justify the admission of voice-identification testimony by a witness who dialed the number. Since Pacer did not look up Dail's number in the telephone book or dial it, Dail's self-identification is insufficient to make Pacer's testimony admissible. **B** is, therefore, incorrect. **C** is incorrect because Pacer's subsequent hearing of Dail's voice is sufficient to make her voice-identification testimony admissible. The fact that Pacer had not dialed Dail's number before speaking to him would prevent her voice-identification testimony from being admissible under the special FRE provision discussed above regarding telephone identifications. **D** is incorrect, however, because the fact that she recognized the telephone voice as Dail's after hearing Dail's voice in the judge's chambers is sufficient to make her testimony admissible without that special provision.

43. **D**   Since the Green Saltpeter Control Act prohibits the operation of munitions factories in which airborne levels of green saltpeter exceed statutory standards, it would take a new law to permit the General Explosives factory to operate in violation of those standards. In effect, by giving the Senate National Defense Committee the power to permit such operation, § 34 purports to give it the power to make a law. Article I of the U.S. Constitution provides that federal legislation must be passed by both houses of Congress and then presented to the President for approval. An attempt to legislate without fulfilling these requirements violates the Constitution.

The committee system in Congress exists, in part, because it enables certain questions to be considered by bodies which have had an opportunity to develop expertise in certain areas. The principle of bicameralism established by Article I prevents those committees from legislating, however. For this reason, **A** is incorrect. Although Congress may supervise the activities of administrative agencies which it has created, the scope of such supervision is, of course, limited by the provisions of the Constitution. As indicated above, the system of supervision created by § 34 exceeds constitutional limitations because it purports to give a Senate committee the power to legislate. **B** is, therefore, incorrect. **C** is incorrect for two reasons: First, Congress *may* authorize an administrative body to impose quasi-criminal sanctions (although not to create them);

and, second, § 34 does not give an administrative agency the power to impose sanctions, but purports to limit that power.

44. **B**   Extortion consists of obtaining property from another by threatening future harm to persons, property, or economic interests. Since Defendant obtained money from Robin by threatening to blow up her real and personal property, he can be convicted of extortion.

Robbery consists of obtaining property from another by using or threatening force against a person. Since Defendant made no threat of harm to a person, **A** is incorrect. Larceny by trick is a larceny committed by making a misrepresentation which induces the victim to part with temporary possession of personal property. Since Robin did not expect her cash to be returned, she was not parting with temporary possession of it, and **C** is incorrect. Embezzlement is a criminal conversion of personal property by one in lawful custody of it. Since Defendant was not in lawful custody of Robin's money, **D** is incorrect.

45. **A**   Robbery consists of obtaining property from another by threatening force against a person. Since Defendant obtained $20,000 by threatening that a bomb would kill passengers if he was not paid, he is guilty of robbery.

Extortion consists of obtaining property from another by threatening future harm to persons, property, or economic interests. Although Defendant obtained $20,000 by threatening to destroy passengers and an airplane, **B** is incorrect because robbery, since it involves violence or a threat of immediate violence, is a more serious crime than extortion. Larceny by trick is a larceny committed by making a misrepresentation which induces the victim to part with temporary possession of personal property. Since Air Lines did not expect its cash to be returned, it was not parting with temporary possession of it, and **C** is incorrect. Embezzlement is a criminal conversion of personal property by one in lawful custody of it. Since Defendant was not in lawful custody of Air Lines' money, **D** is incorrect.

46. **B**   Article I, § 10 provides in part that no state shall pass any law impairing the obligation of contracts. This prevents states from repudiating their own contractual obligations or interfering with private contractual obligations except by regulations which are reasonable and appropriate to a significant state purpose. Since the statute in question does not result in a repudiation of the state's contractual obligations or interfere with private contractual obligations, it does not violate the Obligation of Contracts Clause.

The Equal Protection Clause prohibits states from invidiously discriminating. Since the statute requires higher fees from non-residents, it discriminates against them. Although some such discrimination has been held to be valid, it is possible that this statute is not. **A** therefore, could be an effective argument in support of the constitutional challenge, making **A** incorrect. The Privileges and Immunities Clause of Article IV of the United States Constitution provides that "The citizens of each state shall be entitled to all privileges and immunities of the citizens in the several states." Since this has been held to prohibit certain discrimination against out-of-staters, **C** also could be an effective argument in support of the constitutional challenge, and is, therefore, incorrect. The Commerce Clause prohibits the states from discriminating against or imposing undue burdens on interstate commerce. Violations have been found on both grounds in laws which denied to out-of-staters advantages which were available to state residents. For this reason, **D** also could be an effective argument and is, therefore, incorrect.

47. **B** An assault is committed by intentionally inducing plaintiff's reasonable apprehension of immediate harmful or offensive contact. It has been held that a threatening act is not an assault if accompanied by words which make clear that the threat will not be carried out, since any apprehension experienced by the plaintiff would not be reasonable. It is understood, however, that a defendant is not free to avoid assault liability by demanding compliance with a condition which he has no legal right to impose. Since Darnell had no legal right to require Seitz to back out of his contract with Batista, the fact that he told Seitz that he could avoid the threatened harm by doing so would not prevent Darnell from being liable for assault. **B** is, therefore, not an effective argument in Darnell's defense.

Since it was obvious from Darnell's statement that the threatened harm would not occur until some time in the future, **A** would be an effective defense. Since the threat was of harm to Seitz's children and not to Seitz, **C** would be an effective defense. Courts have generally argued (although this argument is not always credible) that apprehension induced by the defendant's mere use of words is not reasonable. This has led to a universally recognized rule that there can be no assault liability unless the defendant has performed some physical act. **D** is, therefore, an effective defense.

48. **C** Although extrinsic evidence of unconvicted bad acts is not usually admissible for the purpose of proving that a person has a bad character or was inclined to commit other bad acts, such evidence may be admissible for other purposes. Proof that a fact is not as stated by defendant may be admissible for the purpose of impeachment (i.e., to show that his testimony is not to be believed). If such proof is extrinsic (i.e., not from the defendant's own mouth) it may be used to impeach, but only if it relates to a material issue in the controversy. Since Dague claimed to be 1,000 miles away from where the crime of arson was committed, his whereabouts on the day of the crime are of consequence (i.e., material) in the arson prosecution. Walen's testimony is, therefore, admissible to impeach Dague. In general, evidence is admissible as substantive proof if it is relevant to some fact of consequence in the controversy. Since Dague's whereabouts on the day of the crime are material to the arson prosecution, Walen's testimony — which tends to establish that Dague was in Vicksville on the day of the fire — is admissible as substantive evidence.

49. **C** Since a will speaks upon the death of the testator, Borman's interest was created upon the death of Odell. An executory interest is a future interest in a grantee which will become possessory only upon the termination of a prior estate the termination of which is not inevitable. Since, according to the devise, Ambler's interest was to terminate only if he died without issue from Jane, and since prior to Jane's death it was not inevitable that this would happen, if Borman's interest was created prior to Jane's death, it was executory. A springing executory interest is one which will replace the interest of the grantor. A shifting executory interest is one which will replace the interest of another grantee. Since Borman's interest was to replace that of Ambler, it was a shifting interest. **I** is, therefore, an accurate statement. A remainder is a future interest in a grantee which will become possessory upon the termination of a prior estate the termination of which is inevitable. It was inevitable that Ambler would die. Since Ambler and Jane never had

any children, after Jane's death it was inevitable that Ambler would die without issue from Jane. The termination of Ambler's estate was thus inevitable. If Borman's interest was created after Jane's death, it was, therefore, a remainder. If, in addition to the inevitable termination of the prior estate, there are conditions precedent to the remainder's becoming possessory, it is a contingent remainder. If there are no conditions other than the inevitable termination of the prior estate, then the remainder is vested. After Jane's death without issue, the only thing necessary to make Borman's interest possessory was the death of Ambler, which was inevitable. Borman's interest was thus a vested remainder. **II** is, therefore, an accurate statement.

Since both **I** and **II** are accurate statements, **A**, **B**, and **D** are incorrect.

50. **D**   One who holds a present possessory interest in real estate is entitled to make all normal uses of the land and to keep the profits from those uses so long as he does not unreasonably decrease its value to the holders of future interests. This means, among other things, that the holder of a present possessory interest in realty is permitted to rent the realty and to keep the rent. For this reason, Borman has no right to the rents. On the other hand, since the permanent removal of minerals from the land will inevitably reduce the value of the realty, limitations on the removal of minerals are imposed on holders of certain present possessory interests. If, however, the grantor had been actively removing minerals from the realty, it is presumed that in granting a present possessory interest, the grantor intended to grant the right to continue removing minerals as well. Since Odell had been mining the gold on the land, it is presumed that he intended to grant Ambler the right to continue doing so, even though Ambler's interest in the realty was less than a fee. Thus, Borman is not entitled to proceeds from the mining operation either.

For the combination of reasons given above, **A**, **B**, and **C** are incorrect.

51. **D**   The standard remedy for breach of contract is a judgment for damages. In awarding damages for breach of contract, courts attempt to place the non-breaching party in the position which he would have held if the contract had not been breached. Since Peppard would have received $20,000 if *The Daily Blade* had performed as agreed, he is entitled to receive $20,000 as damages for breach. Where the breach is a major one, however, the non-breaching party may choose rescission as a remedy instead. Rescission is an equitable remedy which results in cancellation of the contract. Since *The Daily Blade* has not performed at all, its breach is obviously major, entitling Peppard to rescission and thus freeing him of his obligation under contract. Peppard may, thus, choose to sue for libel. Since the essence of rescission is a termination of the contract, a party who chooses it as a remedy may not enforce the rescinded contract by seeking damages for its breach. Peppard, therefore, may not sue for libel *and* for breach of contract.

A is incorrect because it would deprive Peppard of his right to damages. **B** is incorrect because it would deprive Peppard of his right to rescission. **C** is incorrect because it would enable Peppard to cancel (i.e., rescind) the contract, and then enforce it anyway.

52. **C**   A condition precedent is an event which must occur before a contractual obligation becomes due. When each party's performance is a condition for the other's there are "concurrent conditions." Since Peppard's promise not to sue required performance to

continue after payment by *The Daily Blade*, *The Daily Blade*'s payment was a condition for it. Since Peppard could have sued between March 5 and March 11, the part of Peppard's promise which required him to refrain from suit between those dates created a condition precedent to payment by *The Daily Blade*. The promise thus created concurrent conditions. **I** is, therefore, correct. When the language of a contract does not specify whether one party's performance is a condition for the other party's performance, the courts usually hold that if the parties obviously intended one performance to come before the other, it was a condition precedent to that other. Since Rider's conveyance was obviously intended to occur before Peppard's forbearance to sue, it was a condition precedent to Peppard's promise. **II** is, therefore, correct.

53. **C**   An obligation to perform contractual duties does not become absolute until all conditions precedent to it have been fulfilled. Thus, if *The Daily Blade*'s obligation to pay was a condition precedent to Peppard's promise not to sue Rider, the failure of that condition would prevent Peppard from being obliged to perform.

   D is therefore incorrect. If a contract consists of a pair of obligations each one of which can be regarded as a separate agreement, the contract may be "divisible." If this is so, the various obligations of a party do not depend upon each other, and a party's breach of one of his promises would not prevent him from recovering for his performance of the other promises. (For example, X agrees to sell Y a red widget and a green widget at a specified price. Ordinarily, X's failure to deliver the red widget would relieve Y of her duty to buy the green widget. If the contract is divisible, however, X may be able to enforce Y's promise to buy the green widget even though X failed to deliver the red widget.) If the contract between Peppard, Rider, and *The Daily Blade* was divisible, breach by *The Daily Blade* would not prevent Rider from enforcing the promise which Peppard made to her. **A** is, therefore, incorrect. An agreement not to sue in return for something of value (i.e., a conveyance of real estate) is called a settlement or a compromise. Such agreements promote public policy by reducing the need for litigation. **B** is, therefore, incorrect.

54. **A**   Under FRE 609, evidence that a witness has been convicted of a crime is admissible for the purpose of attacking his credibility under two distinct sets of circumstances. Such evidence is admissible if the crime was a felony *and* the court determines that the probative value outweighs the prejudicial effect to the defendant. Such evidence is also admissible, however, if the crime is one which involved dishonesty. Since tax fraud is a crime involving dishonesty, the evidence is admissible whether or not the crime was a felony, and without an affirmative finding that its probative value outweighs its prejudicial effect.

   B, **C** and **D** are, therefore, incorrect.

55   **C**   FRE 801(d)(1)(B) specifies that a prior consistent statement of a declarant is not hearsay if the declarant has testified and is available for cross-examination, and if the statement is offered to rebut a claim of recent fabrication. Since Vanna testified that Dalby raped her, and since Dalby claimed that Vanna's complaint was fabricated on April 3, evidence that Vanna made that same complaint to Willey on March 7 tends to rebut Dalby's claim. Willey's testimony is, therefore, admissible.

Under FRE 803(2), a statement is admissible as an excited utterance if it was made about a startling event while the declarant was under the stress of excitement caused by that event. Ordinarily, this requires the statement to have been made either during the event or immediately thereafter. Since a week passed between the alleged rape and Vanna's statement to Willey, it probably does not qualify as an excited utterance. **A** is, therefore, incorrect. Hearsay is defined as an out-of-court statement offered for the purpose of proving the truth of the matter asserted in that statement. If Vanna's out-of-court statement to Willey is not offered to prove the truth of what she asserted (i.e., that Dalby raped her), but is offered to prove that she did not fabricate her complaint after learning that Dalby was married, it is not hearsay. FRE 801(d)(1)(B) specifically provides that such a statement "is not hearsay." This means that in addition to being admissible for the purpose of rebutting Dalby's claim of recent fabrication, Vanna's statement may be admissible as substantive evidence as well. **B** is, therefore, incorrect. FRE 803(1) recognizes a hearsay exception for a statement of declarant's sense impressions. This exception applies, however, only when the declarant's statement describing an event is made during or immediately after the event. Since Vanna's statement to Willey was made a week after the incident which it purported to describe, **D** is incorrect.

56. **B**   In *Wisconsin v. Yoder* the United States Supreme Court specifically held that in determining whether a defendant's conduct is privileged by First Amendment rights to freedom of religion, it was proper to consider whether the defendant's religious beliefs were sincere.

A is, therefore, incorrect. Ordinarily, a state may prohibit specified activities whenever such prohibition serves a rational basis. Under the "free exercise" clause of the First Amendment, however, a state may not interfere with acts performed in the exercise of religious beliefs unless the interference bears a rational relationship to a compelling state interest. This means that there are some acts which the state may validly declare to be criminal and prohibit, because the prohibition has a rational basis, but which may still be performed by persons who are doing so in the exercise of their religious beliefs if the prohibition does not bear a rational relationship to a compelling state interest. Thus, First Amendment rights to freedom of religion might justify acts that would otherwise be criminal. For this reason, **C** and **D** are both incorrect.

57. **C**   The Equal Protection Clause provides that no state shall deny to any person within its jurisdiction the equal protection of the law. This means that any state agency which employs a system of classification granting rights or privileges to some persons while denying them to others may be violating rights conferred by the Equal Protection Clause. Some systems of classification are valid if they have a rational basis; other systems are valid only if they are necessary to serve a compelling state interest. It is uncertain whether the exclusion of pregnant students from a public high school system is valid. Of the fact situations given, however, **C** is the only one which could possibly involve a violation of rights granted by the Equal Protection Clause. This is because the Equal Protection Clause only regulates state action, and **C** is the only fact situation involving state action.

The defendant in **A** is employed by a religious organization. The defendant in **B** is a federal official. The defendant in **D** works in private enterprise. Since none of them is an agency of the state, **A**, **B** and **D** are, incorrect.

58. **A** Strict liability is imposed on the professional supplier of a product which is defective and unreasonably dangerous, if that defect proximately causes harm to a plaintiff whose contact with the product was foreseeable. If the reasonable person could not have anticipated Pena's contact with Woxibol (i.e., Pena's contact with it was unforeseeable), strict liability cannot be imposed to benefit Pena.

If the plaintiff's harm was produced by an unforeseeable intervening event, the product defect was not a proximate cause of it. **B** is incorrect, however, because intervening negligence may be (and usually is) regarded as foreseeable. If Pena's injury would not have occurred but for the crack in the sewer, the crack was also a cause of harm. The existence of an additional cause of harm is not sufficient to relieve any defendant of liability, however, unless that additional cause was unforeseeable. Since there is no indication that the crack in the sewer was unforeseeable, **C** is incorrect. **D** is incorrect because strict product liability does not depend on the existence of a commercial relationship (i.e., privity) between the defendant and any other person.

59. **A** In practicing medicine, a physician is required to act like the reasonable member of the medical profession. Failing to do so is negligence or malpractice.

A physician who holds himself out as a specialist in a particular field is required to act like the reasonable specialist in that field. **B** is incorrect, however, because there is no fact indicating that Davis held himself out as a specialist in treating diseases of the pancreas. The concept of negligence (and malpractice is nothing more than that) is based on an objective standard. Each person's conduct is judged by comparing it to that objective standard. In some jurisdictions, a physician, is expected to act as, and to have the skill and learning of, the reasonable physician. In others, a physician is expected to act as the reasonable physician from the same geographical area. **C** is incorrect because it would make negligence depend on the particular intelligence and experience of each particular defendant, rather than on an objective standard which could be applied to all. Although a plaintiff in a malpractice action must ordinarily offer the testimony of an expert who holds the opinion that the defendant failed to act as the reasonable member of the profession, it is the jury which decides whether the defendant's conduct was negligent. A plaintiff is neither required nor permitted to prove that reasonable members of the profession consider defendant's conduct negligent. **D** is, therefore, incorrect.

60. **C** An inter vivos conveyance of realty is not effective without delivery. Delivery occurs when the grantor, by some words or act, manifests an intent that the deed have a present operative effect. While Ward indicated that she wanted to be sure that Hill had the property after her death, she may have intended the quitclaim to transfer an interest immediately. If instead of handing the document to Hill she had locked it in a safe deposit box to which only she had access, it would be clear that she did not intend an immediate transfer. On the other hand, if she simply handed it to Hill, it would be clear that she did intend an immediate transfer. Here, because she was unable to leave the hospital, she could not personally place it in a safe deposit box. When she handed it to Hill with the request that he put it in the box, she may have intended to "deliver" it to him, or, without intending any present effect, she may have been asking him to lock it away for her since she was physically unable to do so herself. From the facts given it is impossible to determine with certainty what her intention was. If the safe deposit box was held jointly by

Ward and Hill, however, it is likely that she intended an immediate transfer since putting the quitclaim in the box would place it in Hill's immediate possession. **C** is correct since it is the only fact listed which could possibly result in a judgment for Hill.

Since the formal requirements for wills are usually more demanding than those for deeds, a deed which is intended to take effect only on the death of a grantor (i.e., a testamentary substitute) is invalid. **A** is, therefore, incorrect. **B** is incorrect because a gift causa mortis is revoked by operation of law if the donor recovers from the illness which threatened her life at the time the gift was made. **D** is incorrect because adverse possession requires possession inconsistent with the rights of the owner, and Hill's possession of Wardacre was at Ward's request.

61. **D**   Since the formal requirements for wills are more demanding then those for deeds, a deed which is intended to take effect only on the death of the grantor (i.e., a testamentary substitute) is invalid. Thus, if Ward intended for the quitclaim to have no effect until after her death, it is invalid. Although the facts make it impossible to determine with certainty what Ward's intention was, **D** is the only argument listed which could possibly result in a judgment for Norton.

A is incorrect because recording statutes protect only those who purchase for value. Since Norton received by will and without consideration, Hill's failure to record would not give Norton a priority. Although a quitclaim does not imply any warranties or covenants, it does serve to transfer whatever interest the grantor held at the time of its execution. **B** and **C** are, therefore, incorrect.

62. **A**   Under the best evidence rule (a/k/a the original document rule), secondary evidence of a writing is not admissible to prove the contents of the writing unless the original or a qualified duplicate is shown to be unavailable. If the writing involved is in the hands of a person located outside the jurisdiction of the court, it may be regarded as unavailable. This is not so, however, if the person who has it is the party offering secondary evidence. Since the original contract is in the hands of the plaintiff, it, therefore, cannot be regarded as unavailable. Nevertheless, the copy which the plaintiff offers in **A** will not be excluded under the best evidence rule, since the FRE treats all photocopies as originals.

In **B** the defendant is charged with forging a check. This obviously, places the contents of the check in issue. Since the check has not been shown to be unavailable, the best evidence rule will exclude oral testimony as to its contents. Ordinarily, an expert witness may base her opinion on things which are not in evidence. In **C** however, the expert has based her opinion solely on her examination of the X-ray. In effect, this means that all she is really doing is telling the court what the X-ray says. By doing so, she placed the contents of the X-ray in issue. Under the best evidence rule, her testimony is thus inadmissible unless the X-ray is produced or its absence explained. If the writing in question is in the control of an adverse party who has failed to produce the original after receiving notice to do so, the document may be regarded as unavailable. In **D** however, there is no indication that the state tax collector was asked to produce the plaintiff's original tax return, or refused to do so. Until the plaintiff establishes this, or otherwise establishes that the tax return is unavailable, the best evidence rule will prevent the admission of secondary evidence of its contents.

63. **A** The standard measure of damages for breach of a sales contract is the difference between the contract price and the fair market value on the date performance was required.

    B is incorrect because the amount of money already paid by Bale in contemplation of the purchase may bear no relation to the difference between the contract price and the fair market value. It is generally understood that a nonbreaching party has a duty to mitigate damages by acting reasonably following the other party's breach. This means that he may not sit idly by allowing those damages to increase when reasonable conduct would have prevented that from happening. Since the standard measure of damages is based on the difference between the contract price and the fair market value *at the time the contract was to be performed*, however, Schmid's failure to make an attempt to re-sell did nothing to increase his damages. **C** is therefore, incorrect. Unforeseeable circumstances which made performance of contractual duties impossible may excuse performance of those duties. **D** is incorrect, however, because although Bale's transfer may have made it inconvenient for her to purchase the realty, it did not make it impossible for her to do so.

64. **B** Embezzlement is criminal conversion of personal property known to be another's with intent to defraud, committed by one in lawful possession of that property. (**Note:** Some jurisdictions require that there be a fiduciary relationship between victim and defendant. Since Minx's possession of the wallet resulted from her employment relationship with Bibb, she may be found to have possessed it as his fiduciary.) When Minx spent some of Bibb's money on ice cream, she converted it. Since she planned to keep the money (i.e., use it as her own) she had the intent to defraud. At the time, she was in lawful possession of the wallet. Her use of Bibb's money for the purchase of ice cream was, therefore, an embezzlement. Once a crime has been committed, it cannot be un-committed. Thus, her returning the money to Bibb would not prevent her from being convicted.

    C is therefore incorrect. Larceny is a trespassory taking and carrying off of personal property known to be another's with the intent to permanently deprive. A taking is trespassory if it violates the rights of the owner. When Minx found Bibb's wallet in the parking lot and carried it off, she did not commit a trespassory taking since her purpose prevented the taking from violating the rights of Bibb. For this reason, and because she then lacked the intent to permanently deprive Bibb, she did not commit larceny by taking the wallet home. When she formed the intent to permanently deprive Bibb and when she acted on that intent by spending some of the money, the wallet was already in her possession, so she did not "take" or carry it off. For this reason, she did not commit larceny. **A** and **D** are, therefore, incorrect.

65. **C** Private nuisance involves liability-forming conduct by defendant which unreasonably interferes with the plaintiff's right to use and enjoy his realty. A defendant's conduct may be liability-forming if it involves an intentional invasion of the plaintiff's rights. A defendant "intends" a particular result if he acts with the desire or substantial certainty that it will occur. Here, as a result of his conversation with Pahl, Resa knew with substantial certainty that his conduct was interfering with Pahl's use and enjoyment of his realty — and, therefore, by definition intended the interference. Thus, if the interference was an unreasonable one, Resa is liable for nuisance. Although the (un)reasonableness

of the invasion depends on many factors not given, private nuisance is the only theory listed which could possibly result in a judgment for Pahl.

Trespass to land requires an intentional unauthorized entry onto plaintiff's realty by something tangible. Since there was no tangible entry onto Pahl's land, **A** is incorrect. Intentional infliction of emotional distress requires outrageous conduct by which defendant intentionally inflicts severe mental suffering upon the plaintiff. **B** is incorrect because Pahl does not seek damages for mental suffering, but for reduction in the value of his realty. Although an invasion of privacy may be committed by intentionally and offensively interfering with plaintiff's solitude, **D** is incorrect because this theory requires some physical intrusion into plaintiff's presence.

66.   **B**   The requirement of standing exists to assure that a person making a constitutional challenge will have incentive to fully and vigorously litigate the issues. For this reason, standing requires that a person challenging the constitutionality of a statute show some actual or immediately threatened concrete personal injury that will be avoided if the court grants the relief requested. Since the tax will reduce their profits, the stockholders of a corporation with sales in the State of Lenape in excess of one million dollars will suffer an actual injury under the statute. Since a finding that it violates the Commerce Clause would result in a declaration that the statute is invalid, and will therefore prevent the tax from being collected, the injury will be avoided if the court grants the relief requested. These stockholders, therefore, have standing to challenge the statute.

A is incorrect because there is no fact indicating that the people of the neighboring state face any injury under the statute, and additionally because a state government does not have standing as a representative of its residents. Since the corporation in option **C** does not have annual gross sales in excess of one million dollars within the state of Lenape, the statute imposes no tax on it. Thus, the corporation's stockholders lack standing because they face no actual or immediately threatened injury under the statute. **C** is, therefore, incorrect. Some cases have held that state taxpayers have standing to challenge certain expenditures of state funds. **D** is incorrect, however, because this statute provides for acquisition rather than expenditure of state funds.

67.   **A**   A transfer of realty to co-owners is presumed to convey equal interests unless its language specifies otherwise. Since Olson's will made Webb and Harris joint tenants as to a one-half interest, each is presumed to have received an equal interest in the one-half interest, or a one-quarter interest in the whole. Joint tenancy is a form of co-ownership best known for the right of survivorship. This means that upon the death of a joint tenant, her/his interest passes to the surviving joint tenant. Since a one-half interest was held by Webb and Harris as joint tenants, the death of either spouse would cause his/her one-quarter interest in the realty to pass to the surviving spouse. Since neither spouse survived the other, however, the interest of each passes to her/his heirs. A conveyance to co-owners which does not specify the form of co-ownership is presumed to create a tenancy in common. Since Olson's will did not specify the form of Susan's co-ownership, it made her a tenant-in-common with Webb and Harris. Co-owners do not have a right to survive to the interest of a tenant-in-common. For this reason, Susan's one-half interest passes to her heirs.

B is incorrect because Susan's tenancy-in-common with Webb and Harris gave her no right to their interest. **C** is incorrect because Olson's will did not make the shares of the co-owners equal, but specified that Susan held a one-half interest, and that the other one-half interest was held by Webb and Harris. **D** is incorrect because Olson's will gave Susan a one-half interest.

68. **D** The covenant of quiet enjoyment is a promise that the grantee shall peaceably and quietly enjoy possession without interference by the grantor or anyone with a lawful claim. This covenant is breached only when an actual eviction or other interference with possession occurs. For this reason, it flows from the covenantor to the grantee *and his successors.* Since Torres interfered with Best's possession under a lawful claim of right, the warranty was breached. Since it flowed from Odden to successors of Arnold, Odden may be liable to Best for damages resulting from the breach.

The covenant of seisin is a promise that the grantor has title to and possession of the realty. The covenant against encumbrances is a promise that no other person has encumbrances or liens against the realty. If the realty is not as covenanted, these covenants are breached the moment a deed containing them is delivered to a grantee. Since the covenants are breached upon delivery of the deed, however, they do not flow to successors of the covenantor's grantee. Since Odden did not have a right to possession (i.e., he had leased the realty to Torres) and since Torres held a lien on the realty (resulting from the lease) these covenants were breached by Odden when he conveyed the realty to Arnold in March. Since they do not flow to Arnold's successors, however, Best could not succeed against Odden on these theories. **A** and **B** are, therefore, incorrect. **C** is incorrect because a covenant of the right to convey does not include a promise that the grantor is entitled to possession, and this covenant was not breached by Odden at any time.

69. **D** Negligence is the breach of a duty of reasonable care owed to the plaintiff by the defendant. Ordinarily a defendant owes a plaintiff a duty of reasonable care if the defendant's conduct creates a foreseeable risk to the plaintiff. Most jurisdictions limit this duty if the plaintiff is a trespasser or licensee on defendant's land. Since Penny's parents had paid a fee for her to stay at Carroll's camp, however, she was an invitee to whom a duty of reasonable care was owed. Since Carroll set aside a particular area for use by children as a playing field, she owed the children who used it (i.e., her invitees) the duty of making reasonable inspections and taking reasonable steps to protect the children against dangerous conditions. Thus, if the reasonable person would have discovered and removed the tree root, Carroll's failure to do so was negligent (i.e., unreasonable).

Many jurisdictions have held that a landholder is not obligated to protect even invitees against dangers which result *solely* from natural conditions of the land. Since the way softball is played and the nature of children make it foreseeable that children using the field would run into the bushes, however, Carroll's designation of the field as a playing field for children resulted in a risk greater than that created by nature (i.e., the tree root's existence). Her creation of this risk imposed upon her a duty to act reasonably to protect the children against it. **A** is, therefore, incorrect. A plaintiff assumes the risk when she voluntarily encounters a danger of which she actually (i.e. subjectively) knows. Since the pile of leaves covering the tree root prevented Penny from knowing about it, she did not assume the risk by encountering it. **B** is, therefore, incorrect. Some writers have said that an invitee is owed "the highest duty of care." This is a much-misunderstood statement, however. All it really means is that the duty owed to invitees is generally higher than that owed to trespassers or licensees. Basically, it is a duty of reasonable care, not an absolute duty to keep invitees safe. It simply makes landholders liable if they fail to act reasonably. **C** is, therefore, incorrect.

70. **B**   Battery is intentional, harmful or offensive contact with the plaintiff. In a battery case, intent means that the defendant desired or knew with substantial certainty that harmful or offensive contact with the plaintiff would occur as the result of her act. There is no fact indicating that Carroll knew Penny would trip on the tree root. So, if she did not know that it would happen, she could not have intended it, and could not be liable for battery.

The doctrine of transferred intent may transfer a tortious intent to an unintended consequence. Since the facts do not indicate that Carrol desired or knew that harm would come to anyone, she did not have a tortious intent on which the doctrine could operate. **A** is, therefore, incorrect. Intent is a subjective matter — one who actually knows that a particular result will occur intends that result; one who does not actually know that it will occur does not intend it. This is so regardless of what anyone else in that person's position would have known or of what that person "should" have known. Thus, even if Carroll should have known that a child would trip, she did not intend it to happen unless she actually knew that it would happen. **C** is, therefore, incorrect. Similarly, even if the danger which led to Penny's injury could be called a "trap," Carroll could not be liable for battery unless she desired or knew that the trap would injure someone in Penny's situation. **D** is, therefore, incorrect.

71. **D**   Ordinarily a promise is not enforceable unless it is supported by consideration. Consideration is a bargained-for exchange of something of value for the promise. Because parties should be free to strike whatever bargains appeal to them, courts do not usually inquire into the relative values of the promise and the thing given in return for it. For this reason, the payment of one dollar could be consideration for a promise to hold open an offer to sell realty for $80,000. This is only true, however, if the payment of one dollar was bargained-for and given *in exchange* for that promise. Since Sackett did not ask for or receive anything in exchange for her promise, it was unsupported by consideration, and, therefore, unenforceable. In a few jurisdictions, a recital like Sackett's might be held to create a promise to pay one dollar, and that promise might be held to be consideration for Sackett's agreement to keep the offer open. **D** is correct, however, because it contains the only reason listed which could possibly support the conclusion which accompanies it.

The parol evidence rule prevents the use of extrinsic evidence of prior negotiations or agreements to modify the terms of an unambiguous written contract which the parties intended as a complete record of their agreement. Since the written statement that she had received one dollar was not a term of agreement but merely a recital of fact, the parol evidence rule does not prevent the use of extrinsic evidence to contradict it. **A** is, therefore, incorrect. When a promisee justifiably relies to his detriment on a promise, his detrimental reliance may make the promise enforceable without consideration. **B** is incorrect, however, because there are no facts indicating that Boland changed his position as a result of Sackett's promise (i.e., relied on the promise), that the reasonable person would have relied on it (i.e., that reliance was justified), or that Boland was damaged (i.e., suffered detriment) as a result of such reliance. **C** is incorrect for two reasons: first, courts do not ordinarily consider whether consideration was equal in value to a promise which it purports to support; and, second, the dollar was not recited to be consideration for the realty itself, but for an option to buy it.

72. **C**   A contract is formed upon the acceptance of an offer. Ordinarily, an offer can only be accepted by the person to whom it was made (i.e., the offeree). If an offer is made to the general public, as was Carlson's, it can be accepted by any member of the general public. Since acceptance of an offer involves assent to its terms, however, acceptance can occur only if the offeree is aware of the offer's terms. Since Samsel was unaware of Carlson's offer at the time that he telephoned Carlson, his communication with Carlson could not have been an acceptance of Carlson's offer. Since Samsel did not accept Carlson's offer, Carlson was never bound by its terms.

A and B are incorrect because a general offer can only be accepted by one who is aware of it. Although an offeror is free to restrict his offer to certain classes of people, Carlson did not. D is incorrect because the offer did not exclude sellers of automobiles.

73. **B**   It has been said that the offeror is monarch of the offer. This means, of course, that the person who institutes the contractual process by making an offer is in complete control of that offer's terms and, upon acceptance, is not bound to any terms other than those. Since Carlson's offer was to pay $100 for information "leading to purchase of 1927 Ford," he is not required to pay unless the information furnished actually leads to the purchase of a 1927 Ford. Since Wright's letter did not, it does not qualify Wright to receive the reward.

A is incorrect because an offer to the general public which is made by advertisement ordinarily is not revoked until a withdrawal is given approximately equal publicity. C and D are incorrect because Carlson only offered to pay for information leading to purchase, and Wright's did not.

74. **A**   Under FRE 803(2), a statement is admissible as an excited utterance if it was made about a startling event while the declarant was under the stress of excitement caused by that event. Since being pushed down and injured is a startling event, and since Paula's bleeding and crying indicate that she was under the stress of excitement which it produced, her statement qualifies as an excited utterance.

The fact that a declarant is presently unavailable is never, alone, sufficient to permit the admission of her out-of-court statements. B is incorrect for this reason, and because the excited utterance exception does not require that the declarant be unavailable. C is incorrect because although Paula's statement is hearsay, it is admissible under the excited utterance exception to the hearsay rule. The court found that Paula was incompetent to testify because she could not appreciate her duty to testify truthfully. The reason that hearsay is customarily excluded is that the fact that the hearsay declarant was under no duty to speak truthfully when making the out-of-court statement makes that statement inherently untrustworthy. The excited utterance exception to the hearsay rule, however, is based on the inherent trustworthiness of certain statements made even while the declarant was under no legal duty to tell the truth. For this reason, Paula's inability to appreciate her *duty* to tell the truth does not prevent her excited utterance from being inherently trustworthy. D is, therefore, incorrect.

75.   **A**   Leading questions are those which would give the ordinary person the impression that the questioner desires one answer rather than another, and are ordinarily improper if asked on direct examination. FRE 611 recognizes an exception to this rule, permitting leading questions to be asked in direct examination of a witness associated with an adverse party. Since Wren is employed by Pursel's adversary, Diamond, the objection should be overruled.

Leading questions may also be asked of hostile witnesses. **B** is incorrect, however, because a hostile witness is one who has manifested hostility or prejudice under examination, and there is no indication that Wren did so. While leading questions are permitted on cross-examination, **C** is incorrect because the question was asked on direct examination. (**Note:** The facts indicate that Wren was called by Pursel's attorney to testify on the presentation of Pursel's direct case.) Since the question made it clear that the examiner wanted an affirmative answer, it was a leading question. Thus, **D** is incorrect.

76.   **D**   One who engages in an abnormally dangerous activity is strictly liable for harm which proximately results from the dangerous nature of that activity. Most jurisdictions hold that transporting large quantities of any explosive substance is such an activity.

If a statute is designed to protect a class of persons to which plaintiff belongs against risks like the one which resulted in harm, its violation may raise an inference or a presumption of negligence, and may even be termed negligence per se. Since the statute prohibited parking without regard to a vehicle's contents, it was obviously not designed to protect against risks resulting from the explosion of a large quantity of gasoline. **A** and **B** are, therefore, incorrect. Since the "No Parking" sign was also not designed to protect against this risk, its violation is not relevant to determining whether Gilroy was negligent. For this reason, **C** is also incorrect.

77.   **A**   Since Myatt's claim is based on negligence, Gilroy cannot be liable unless Myatt's injuries resulted from Gilroy's negligence. **A** is, therefore, an argument which could result in a judgment for Gilroy.

A plaintiff assumes the risk when she voluntarily encounters a danger of which she is aware. Although the words printed on Gilroy's truck might have made Myatt aware of the danger of explosion, there is no fact indicating that her encounter with that risk (i.e., collision with the truck) was voluntary. **B** is, therefore, incorrect. If it was negligent for Gilroy to park her truck as she did, the fact that she did not happen to be on the scene when her negligence resulted in harm would not shield her from liability. **C** is, therefore, incorrect. A superseding cause of harm is an unforeseeable event which intervenes between a defendant's negligence and a plaintiff's harm, and without which the harm would not have occurred. Because the negligence of motorists is a common occurrence, automobile collisions on city streets are usually regarded as foreseeable events. **D** is, therefore, incorrect. (In addition, a plaintiff's conduct is not ordinarily referred to as an intervening or a superseding cause of her own harm.)

78.   **B**   The state statute could result in depriving Mary's parents of the liberty to decide what treatment their daughter should receive. The Due Process Clauses of the Fifth and Fourteenth Amendments require that a law which regulates a liberty interest must be clear

enough to be understandable by the person of ordinary intelligence. Otherwise, the law may be void for vagueness. The statutory use of the phrase "life-threatening" could violate this requirement, since the meaning of that phrase may depend on the opinion of the person using it. The statutory reference to "hospital officials" may also be vague since it is impossible to tell which officials the statute designates. Although the court might find that the statute is not vague, the argument set forth in **B** is the only one listed which could possibly result in the conclusion that it is unconstitutional.

The Equal Protection Clause prohibits invidious discrimination by the states. **A** is incorrect because there is no indication that the statute discriminates against any particular group. The Free Exercise Clause prohibits the government from interfering with the exercise of religious beliefs. **C** is incorrect because Mary's parents have not claimed that their refusal to consent to the blood transfusion was related to any religious belief which they held. (**Note**: Beware of reading into a question facts which the examiners did not write into it.) Determining whether a statute does or does not interfere with a fundamental right is relevant in selecting the standard which it must meet in order to be valid. **D** is incorrect, however, because the fact that a statute interferes with a fundamental right is never, alone, sufficient to justify the conclusion that it is unconstitutional.

79. **B**   A proceeding is moot when there are no contested material issues for the court to decide. Since Mary has died, the state court can no longer appoint the hospital administrator her guardian. Since the purpose of the federal proceeding was to stop the state proceeding, and since the state proceeding must terminate in any event, there is no longer any contested issue before the federal court. The issues have thus become moot. An exception to the mootness rule exists when a controversy is capable of repetition and evading judicial review. Under this exception, the federal court might decide to hear the case even though Mary's death has made it moot. Mootness, however, is the only argument listed which could possibly result in dismissal of the proceeding brought by Mary's parents.

A non-justiciable political controversy is a case in which a federal court is asked to interfere with the operation of a co-equal branch of the federal government. **A** is incorrect because the challenge raised by Mary's parents is to a state law, not to an action of the federal government. The Eleventh Amendment prohibits federal courts from hearing certain claims against state governments. **C** is incorrect, however, because the Eleventh Amendment does not prevent the federal courts from hearing claims that state action violates the United States Constitution. Where a pending state court proceeding might result in an interpretation of or a conclusion about a state statute which would resolve a federal challenge to it, federal courts are usually unwilling to enjoin enforcement of that statute. The reason given is sometimes said to be "equitable restraint." It is not related, however, to the question of ripeness. So long as there is someone who can actually benefit from a resolution of the issues, and so long as the issues are fully developed and clearly defined, those issues are ripe. Thus, although the issues in this case may no longer be "ripe," this is not because the highest state court has not decided, but because there is no longer any person who will actually benefit from a resolution of the issues. **D** is, therefore, incorrect.

80. **B**   Statements by a now-unavailable declarant concerning — among other things — the declarant's marriage, or relationship by blood or marriage, are admissible under the

FRE hearsay exception for statements of personal history, and under the common law exception for statements of pedigree. Since Marilyn was deceased at the time of trial, she was unavailable. Since the notations contained in the Bible were statements by Marilyn about her marriage to Isidore's brother, about her relationship by marriage to Isidore, and about her relationship by blood to Nancy, it qualifies for admission under both FRE 803(13) and the common law.

The FRE permit the admission, as an "ancient document", of a properly authenticated writing which is at least 20 years old. Common law usually requires 30 years. **A** is incorrect under both systems, however, because there is no fact indicating the age of Marilyn's notation in the Bible. In some jurisdictions, a law known as the "dead man's statute" prevents the admission of certain evidence regarding certain transactions with a person who is now deceased. Although the "dead man's statute" may *prevent* the admission of evidence, it never *justifies* the admission of evidence. **C** is, therefore, incorrect. Under FRE 803(9), "records of vital statistics" including birth, death, and marriage, may be admissible if such records were kept by a public office pursuant to the requirements of law. **D** is incorrect because the notation which Nancy offered into evidence was not reported to or kept by a public office pursuant to the requirements of law.

81. **D**   Criminal conspiracy consists of an agreement between two or more persons to commit a crime. When Downing and Jensen agreed to rob a bank, the crime of conspiracy was complete — whether or not they ever actually went through with the plan.

In most jurisdictions, once a defendant has become guilty of a conspiracy (by agreeing to commit a crime) he cannot avoid criminal responsibility for the crime of conspiracy by withdrawing from or renouncing their plan. In a few jurisdictions, a defense to the crime of conspiracy is available to a defendant who agreed to commit a crime but subsequently prevented its commission under circumstances which manifest a complete and voluntary renunciation of criminal purpose. Even in these jurisdictions, however, this defense would not be available to Downing since he did not prevent commission of the crime. **A**, **B** and **C** are therefore incorrect.

82. **C**   A defendant is liable for harm which proximately results from his breach of a duty of reasonable care. Since a hotel keeper obviously owes a duty of reasonable care to hotel guests, Hicks' failure to use adequate care in hiring Lectric would be a breach of that duty, making Hicks liable for injuries resulting from Lectric's error.

Although one who employs an independent contractor is not vicariously liable for torts committed by the contractor, the employer may be liable for his own negligence in failing to use adequate care in selecting the contractor. **A** is, therefore, incorrect. If reasonable inspection by Hicks would have failed to disclose Lectric's error, then Hicks' failure to discover Lectric's error would not be negligence. This alone would not be enough to result in a judgment for Hicks, however, because Hicks may have committed some other act of negligence (e.g., failing to use adequate care in selecting Lectric) for which liability can be imposed. **B** is, therefore, incorrect. Strict liability may be imposed upon one who engages in (or employs another to engage in) an ultra-hazardous activity. Strict liability does not apply, however, to an ordinary activity which has become ultra-hazardous because of a negligent error made by the person engaging in it. **D** is, therefore, incorrect.

83. **B**   A quitclaim conveys the interest held by the grantor at the time of its execution. Wiley could not own the entire Smith and Baker tract if Oddo had already conveyed part of it to Silver. Although certain methods of describing realty are popular or traditional, any description is adequate if it identifies the land conveyed with reasonable clarity. Thus, if the description contained in Oddo's deed to Silver was reasonably sufficient to identify the property conveyed, it effectively conveyed that property.

A conveyance by deed usually implies a warranty of title which, if breached, may give the grantee a right of action against the grantor. A quitclaim does not. But although one who receives a quitclaim has no right of action for breach of warranty against the grantor, the quitclaim may effectively convey whatever interest the grantor did possess. Thus, if Oddo's deed to Silver did not effectively convey part of the Smith and Baker tract, his conveyance to Wiley by quitclaim could have been sufficient to make her the owner of the entire Smith and Baker tract. **A** is, therefore, incorrect. **C** and **D** are incorrect because a description is sufficient if it identifies the realty conveyed with reasonable clarity.

84. **B**   The United States Supreme Court has held that a public person suing for defamation must prove "actual malice," and that a private person suing a media defendant for defamation must prove either "actual malice" or negligence. A defendant had "actual malice" if, at the time he made a defamatory statement, he knew the statement to be false or entertained serious doubts about its truth. A defendant was negligent if at the time he made a defamatory statement, he did not know that the statement was false, but would have known had he been acting reasonably. If officials of *The Daily* believed the statement was true, they lacked "actual malice." If their belief was reasonable, they were not acting negligently. Thus, if they had a reasonable belief in the truth of the statement, The Daily would not be liable for defamation.

Although some states recognize a privilege to publish false statements which are contained in public records, there is no privilege to misstate the contents of a public record. **A** is, therefore, incorrect. A defendant who defamed a public figure may be liable if he had "actual malice" as defined above. Thus, the fact that Patton was a public figure would not be sufficient alone to protect *The Daily* against liability for defaming him. **C** is, therefore, incorrect. A plaintiff asserting a claim for written defamation (i.e., libel) is not required to prove damage in order to make out a case if the written statement was defamatory on its face. Thus, Patton's failure to prove damage is not sufficient to prevent recovery. For this reason, **D** is incorrect.

85. **C**   The Fourth Amendment guarantee against unreasonable search and seizure is ordinarily violated when a search is conducted without a warrant. In order to enforce this guarantee, the United States Supreme Court has ruled that the fruits of an unlawful search should be excluded from evidence. A search occurs when there has been an invasion of an area as to which a defendant had a reasonable expectation of privacy. Since David was the only person who had a key to the footlocker, it was reasonable for him to expect that its contents would remain private. For this reason, the officers' first look into the footlocker was a search. Since the warrant was issued because of what the officers found, its issuance was one of the fruits of that first unlawful search. For this reason, David's motion to suppress the cocaine must be granted.

(**Note**: There are some special exceptions to the rule that a warrantless search is unlawful. The facts in this case do not satisfy the requirements of *any* of these exceptions, but the nature of the question only makes it necessary to eliminate those listed in the options.) Consent by a third party to search the property of the defendant makes a warrantless search lawful, but only if the person who consented had rights in the property which were equal to those of the defendant. Since David was the only person who had a key to the footlocker, Moran did not have rights to its contents which were equal to David's. Thus, her consent did not eliminate the need for a warrant to search it. **A** is, therefore, incorrect. Even the consent of a person who does not have an equal right to the premises might justify a warrantless search if the police officers reasonably believed that she had such a right (i.e., the person who consented had the "apparent authority" to do so). **B** is incorrect, however, because even if Moran had apparent authority to consent to a search of the *room*, the fact that David had the only key to the footlocker should have made it obvious to the officers that Moran's authority did not extend to its contents. Probable cause justifies an arrest without a warrant, but does not justify a search without a warrant. Thus, probable cause could not justify the first search. Although a search warrant may be issued upon a showing of probable cause, it is invalid if that probable cause was itself the fruit of an unlawful search. Thus, probable cause does not justify the issuance of the warrant, or the second search which was conducted pursuant to it. **D** is, therefore, incorrect.

86. **A**   Although a breach of contract may entitle the wronged party to suspend his own performance, it does not always give him the right to terminate the contract entirely. Fairness and the courts ordinarily require that the breaching party be allowed a reasonable period of time in which to cure the breach. If it is cured within that period, the breaching party may enforce the contract against the non-breaching party although she may be liable for damages resulting from her breach. In determining whether the breach was cured in a reasonable time, the courts consider the nature of the contract itself and the circumstances surrounding its formation. If the circumstances contemplated by the parties made it essential that the conveyance occur on or before June 15, the court is likely to determine that a conveyance on June 16 did not cure the breach.

Sometimes the phrase "time is of the essence" is inserted in a contract to make it clear that the circumstances contemplated by the parties did make it essential that performance occur by a certain date. Since those circumstances may be found to exist even without the insertion of specific language, however, its insertion is not the only thing which would result in a judgment for Biddle. **B** is, therefore, incorrect. Even if Sadick's breach resulted in damage to Biddle, a court could find that the breach was cured within a reasonable time, and that, therefore, Biddle's only remedy is damages. **C** is, therefore, incorrect. **D** is incorrect because contract liability does not depend on fault and may be imposed in spite of reasonable efforts to comply with the contract.

87. **D**   One who engages in an ultra-hazardous or abnormally dangerous activity is strictly liable for damage which proximately results therefrom. Since most jurisdictions agree that storing poisonous gases is an ultra-hazardous or abnormally dangerous activity, proof that Z-14 is an extremely deadly gas would be sufficient to result in the imposition of strict liability on Gascorp.

One who places a defective product — whether defective in design or in manufacture — in the stream of commerce may be held strictly liable for damage resulting from the product defect. **A** is incorrect, however, because Gascorp did not place the tank in the stream of commerce. **B** and **C** are incorrect because Gascorp did not place the gas which injured Palmer in the stream of commerce.

88. **A**   Strict product liability is applied to make a professional seller of a defective product liable without fault for damage resulting from the product's defect. Since Drugstore is a professional retail seller of drugs, and since Drugstore admits that all RST tablets were defective, and since the evidence indicates that Stewart's sterility was a result of that defect, the only remaining question is whether the RST tablets which caused Stewart's harm were purchased from Drugstore. If so, Drugstore will probably be liable to Stewart. If not, Drugstore will not be liable to Stewart. Although some jurisdictions refuse to hold a druggist strictly liable for the sale of defective drugs, **A** is the only issue which could possibly affect the outcome of Stewart's claim.

At least one jurisdiction has held that when manufacturers of a defective product are involved in a concert-of-action in the marketing of that product, any one of them may be held liable for damages resulting from a defect in the product regardless of whether the particular unit which injured plaintiff came from that manufacturer's factory. Since Drugstore was not a manufacturer of RST, however, it would not have been part of the concert-of-action described in B. **B** is, therefore, incorrect. At least one case has imposed liability on an industry-wide basis where (1) there were only a few manufacturers of a particular product, (2) all were named as defendants, (3) all complied with the product standards which were created by an industry-wide organization, (4) all belonged to the industry-wide organization, and (5) those standards resulted in the product's being defective. **C** is incorrect because Drugstore was not a manufacturer of RST (and because there are no facts indicating that requirements 2-5 of industry-wide liability are satisfied). At least one jurisdiction has held that where a large number of companies manufactured and marketed identical products with identical defects, and where plaintiff's injury resulted from the defect in one of those products under circumstances which make identification of its manufacturer impossible, a manufacturer or group of manufacturers which sold to a substantial share of the market might be held liable for the plaintiff's injuries regardless of whether the particular unit which injured plaintiff came from the manufacturer's factory. **D** is incorrect, however, because Drugstore was not a manufacturer of RST.

89. **A**   Lay witnesses are generally permitted to testify only to facts. When it would be helpful to a clear understanding of the witness's testimony, however, the opinion of a lay witness may be admissible if it is rationally based on the perceptions of the witness. The decision as to whether this is so and as to whether the lay opinion is admissible is made in the court's discretion. Therefore, if the judge decides that Westbrook's opinion is rationally based on her perceptions, it is admissible. Conversely, unless the judge so decides, Westbrook's opinion should be excluded.

So long as they do not go beyond matters in common knowledge, lay opinions about the physical and mental condition of another are usually admissible. For this reason, an opinion that another person was intoxicated is admissible (so long as it is rationally based on the witness' perceptions) even if the witness is not an expert on intoxication. **B** and **C** are, therefore, incorrect. The admissibility of opinion evidence is a question of law for the judge. This means that the judge cannot admit Westbrook's opinion testimony unless she finds it to be rationally based on Westbrook's perceptions, and cannot delegate that responsibility to the jury. **D** is, therefore, incorrect.

90. **C**   The Fourteenth Amendment to the U.S. Constitution prohibits a state from denying persons within its jurisdiction the equal protection of the law. A system of classification contained in social or economic legislation is usually presumed to comply with this requirement so long as it has some rational basis. When the classification is a "suspect" one, the presumption of constitutionality is inverted, and the statute is unconstitutional unless it is necessary to serve a compelling state interest. Since alienage is a "suspect classification," a statute which discriminates against aliens is ordinarily required to meet the compelling-state-interest test. Under the "political function" exception, however, a statute which prevents aliens from holding a particular state job may be constitutionally valid if the job is one which should be performed only by people familiar with and sympathetic to American traditions. The Supreme Court has held that the only jobs falling into this category are those which invest the public employee with the power to make policy, or with broad discretion in executing public policy.

A is incorrect because not all "traditional" government activities fall into this category. Since alienage is a suspect classification, **B** is incorrect because a rational basis is not sufficient to justify a classification based on alienage. Statutes which interfere with fundamental interests — like those based on "suspect classifications" — are also subject to the compelling-state-interest standard. **D** is incorrect, however, because a classification based on alienage is "suspect," making the compelling-state-interest standard applicable even if the right with which the statute interferes is not a fundamental one.

91. **D**   Negligence may consist of either an unreasonable act or an unreasonable omission (i.e., failure to act) in the face of duty of reasonable care. In order for an omission to be negligent, however, there must have been some duty to act. Generally, a defendant has a duty to act only when the defendant's conduct creates a need for action. This may happen when the defendant's conduct actually creates a risk which did not previously exist, or it may happen when the defendant's conduct causes a plaintiff to fail to protect himself against an already-existing risk because he has justifiably relied on the belief that the defendant would protect him. Thus, if the past conduct of Wave Crest employees led Palko to reasonably believe that the sidewalk would be free of pigeon droppings, Wave Crest had a duty to act reasonably to protect Palko against the risks resulting from that belief.

This would be so whether or not the initial danger (i.e., slippery sidewalk) was created by Wave Crest's conduct or was located on Wave Crest's property. **A** and **B** are, therefore, incorrect. Defendants owe their invitees a duty of reasonable care to keep the premises reasonably safe. If they are negligent (i.e., fail to act reasonably in the face of that duty), they may be liable for injuries sustained by their invitees — even while entering or leaving the premises. This is so only if the harm results from their negligence, however. Since **C** would make Wave Crest liable without regard to negligence, it is overinclusive, and, therefore, incorrect.

92. **D**   To assure that a person asserting a constitutional claim will litigate all issues fully and

vigorously, the concept of standing requires that she have a personal stake or direct interest in the outcome. Most of the time this means that a person challenging the constitutionality of a government action must be in danger of suffering some concrete injury which would be prevented or remedied if the court grants the requested relief. Since the stockbroker actually commutes on city buses, and since the action of the city council will increase her expense in doing so, she will sustain a concrete loss as a result. Since a decision that the increase is unconstitutional will prevent her from suffering that loss, she has standing to challenge the increase.

Members of the Drivers' Union claim that the fare increase is necessary to protect their jobs. A declaration that it is unconstitutional would, therefore, not prevent them from suffering harm, but would cause the very harm which they fear. The Union thus lacks standing to challenge the constitutionality of the increase. **A** is, therefore, incorrect. It has been held that a mere intellectual interest in the outcome of the proceeding is not sufficient to assure the complete and vigorous litigation of all issues. For this reason, unless the Bus Riders Association alleges that its members actually ride city buses, it lacks the personal stake necessary to confer standing. **B** is, therefore, incorrect. A person who fears that the increase will affect him in the future lacks a personal stake in the outcome unless he shows that the feared effect is likely to occur (i.e., that he will need to ride city buses in the future). **C** is, therefore, incorrect.

93. **A**   Economic regulation by the state is constitutionally valid if it has a rational basis. Regulation is held to the "compelling state interest" standard only if it discriminates against a suspect class or interferes with a fundamental right. The fare increase is an economic regulation, and, therefore, subject to the rational basis standard.

Obviously, any legal requirement of payment may have the effect of discriminating in favor of the wealthy and against the poor. The United States Supreme Court has rejected arguments that classifications based on wealth are "suspect," however. For this reason, **A** is correct, and **B** is incorrect. **C** is incorrect because even interference with a fundamental right may be constitutional if it is necessary to serve a compelling state interest. All laws discriminate against somebody. (e.g., Penal codes discriminate against criminals; vehicle and traffic codes discriminate against people who don't have driving licenses; etc.) Thus, unless a law has no rational basis (in the case of certain kinds of regulation) or is not necessary to serve a compelling interest of the state (in the case of certain other kinds of regulation) the fact that it discriminates against a discrete class of persons is not enough to make it unconstitutional. **D** is, therefore, incorrect.

94. **B**   Negligence is a breach of the duty of reasonable care. This duty is breached by a defendant's failure to act like the reasonable person. Thus, unless the reasonable person would have repaired the fence, Down's failure to do so was not negligent.

In most jurisdictions, a person who keeps a wild animal is strictly liable for damage which it causes. The jurisdictions which do not apply this rule generally hold that keeping a wild animal is prima facie negligent. Neither rule is applied, however, unless the injury sustained by plaintiff resulted from the wild and dangerous nature of the animal involved. Since even a domestic animal might knock over a fence which has become badly deteriorated, Pierce's injury did not result from the wild and dangerous nature of Down's cougar. For this reason, **A** is incorrect. A plaintiff assumes a risk when, knowing that it exists, she voluntarily encounters it. **C** is incorrect because there is no fact indicating that Pierce knew that the fence was deteriorated enough to create a risk that the cougar would injure her. In deciding whether a defendant's conduct was negligent, it is compared to that of the reasonable person. What matters is not what the defendant actually knew about the risks, but what the reasonable person in the defendant's position would have known about those risks. **D** is incorrect because Down's failure to know that the fence was in need of repair might itself have been negligent.

95.   **B**   Ordinarily, a promise is unenforceable unless it is supported by consideration. Consideration is a bargained-for exchange of something of value given in return for and to induce a promise. It usually consists of some benefit conferred upon the promisor, or of some detriment incurred by the promisee. Consistent with this definition is the rule that a promisee's undertaking to do something which she is already legally obligated to do (i.e., performance of a preexisting duty) is not consideration for a new promise by the promisor because it does not confer on the promisor any benefit which he was not already entitled to receive, and does not impose on the promisee any detriment which she had not already incurred. Since all that Trout gave Grauer in return for his promise to pay for the tractor rental was her promise that she would finish plowing by April 1, and since she was already legally obligated to do so, Grauer may successfully argue that his promise was unsupported by consideration. (**Note**: Although UCC §2-209(1) permits the modification of a sales contract between merchants to be enforced without consideration, it is inapplicable here because this was not a contract for sale.)

Although the Statute of Frauds makes an oral contract for the purchase of goods with a price of $500 or more unenforceable over objection, **A** is incorrect because the agreement between Grauer and Trout was not for the sale of goods. Duress is some compulsion or restraint which deprives a contracting party of the ability to exercise free will and usually involves some physical force or threat. A few cases have recognized the possibility of economic duress, but this defense is rarely applied, and, when it is, involves much more desperate economic threats than any indicated by the facts in this case. **C** is incorrect for this reason, and because a party to a contract is expected to show reasonable firmness in asserting his contract rights. Since Grauer failed to object to the additional charge, it is unlikely that a court would conclude that he did so under duress. When a promise would ordinarily be unenforceable because it is unsupported by consideration, or because it fails to satisfy the Statute of Frauds, justified detrimental reliance by the promisee may result in enforcement on a theory of promissory estoppel. **D** is incorrect, however, because Grauer's reliance on Trout's promise is not relevant to Trout's attempt to enforce Grauer's promise.

96.   **B**   Ordinarily, a promise is not enforceable unless there was consideration for it (i.e., something given in exchange for and to induce the promise). Since Trout had already rescued the bull without expectation of payment, the rescue was not given in exchange for or to induce Grauer's promise, and is, therefore, not consideration for it. Some cases have held, however, that a promise to do that which the promisor is morally obligated to do should be enforceable even without consideration. Although this is an infrequently applied exception to the requirement of consideration, the argument set forth in **B** is the only one listed which could possibly provide Trout with effective support for her claim.

Since Trout had already rescued the bull without expecting compensation, the rescue was not given in exchange for or to induce Grauer's promise. **A** is, therefore, incorrect. In determining whether to rescind a contract because of mutual mistake, fraud, duress, or undue influence, the court may attempt to decide whether its failure to rescind would unjustly enrich one of the parties. Ordinarily, however, the fact that a party will be unjustly enriched by something is not, alone, sufficient to result in the imposition of contractual duty on the party. **C** is incorrect for this reason, and because the fact that Trout rescued the bull without expectation of payment probably prevents Grauer's enrichment from being unjust. Sometimes a promise which is unsupported by consideration will be enforced under the doctrine of promissory estoppel if the promisee justifiably relied upon it to her detriment. **D** is incorrect, however, because there is no fact indicating that when Trout completed the plowing of Grauer's field she did so in reliance on his promise to compensate her for rescuing the bull, or, if so, that she has suffered some detriment as a result of that reliance.

97. **C**   A person is liable for damages which were proximately caused by her negligence. It was probably negligent for Daisy to permit Irvin to drive her car when she knew he was drunk. Unless her negligence was a proximate cause of Pachek's harm, however, Daisy is not liable for it. If the accident did not result from Irvin's intoxication, Daisy's negligence in allowing him to drive while intoxicated was not a factual (and therefore not a proximate) cause of the harm. Thus, Daisy is not liable for Pachek's injuries unless they resulted from Irvin's intoxication.

At one time, some jurisdictions applied a common-law rule which held the owner of a vehicle vicariously liable for the negligence of any person driving with the owner's permission and in the owner's presence. All jurisdictions have abolished that common-law rule. Some have replaced it with an "owner-consent" statute which makes the owner of an automobile vicariously liable for the negligence of anyone driving it with consent. **A** is incorrect for two reasons, however: first, liability under "owner-consent" statutes does not depend on the owner's presence in the vehicle; and, second, there is no indication that Irvin was driving negligently at the time the accident occurred. Although Daisy's conscious disregard of Irvin's intoxication was probably negligent, **B** is incorrect because there is no indication that it was causally related to the accident. **D** is incorrect because Daisy's negligence would have been a proximate cause of the accident if the accident resulted from Irvin's intoxication. Daisy, therefore, could be liable to Pachek even though she was not driving at the time.

98. **B**   Voluntary manslaughter is the unlawful killing of a human being with the intent to kill or inflict great bodily harm, but under circumstances of extreme emotional distress. A person is guilty of attempting voluntary manslaughter when he comes substantially close to unlawfully causing the death of another person with the intent to kill or inflict great bodily harm, but under circumstances of extreme emotional distress. The majority of jurisdictions apply an objective standard in deciding whether the defendant's emotional distress was sufficient to reduce an aborted homicide from attempted murder to attempted voluntary manslaughter. Thus, the defendant's emotional distress is usually sufficient to reduce the charge only if the reasonable person in his situation would have experienced similar distress to a similar extent. Under the Model Penal Code, however, it is proper to consider the circumstances which the defendant *believed* to exist, even if his belief was not reasonable. Thus, the disposition of Elridge's request for a charge on attempted voluntary manslaughter depends on whether the court accepts the traditional

view or that of the MPC. Since Boddy's conviction was reversed because of the court's failure to charge what is essentially the MPC view, the decision in *Boddy* is applicable as a precedent in Elridge's case.

Allison, on the other hand, was convicted of involuntary manslaughter. Since involuntary manslaughter is an *unintended* killing which results from recklessness, and since Elridge clearly intended his wife's death, the holding in Allison is inapplicable, and **A** is incorrect. **C** is incorrect for a similar reason. Like voluntary manslaughter, attempted murder cannot be committed without intent to kill. This explains why the court's charge in *Cain* was found to be valid. Since Elridge did intend to kill his wife, however, and since the holding in *Cain* depended on a finding that there was no intent to kill, the *Cain* case is inapplicable. In *Derby* the court held, in effect, that without the intent to kill there could be no conviction for voluntary manslaughter. Since Elridge did have the intent to kill, *Derby* is similarly inapplicable, and **D** is incorrect.

99. **D** Since there is no evidence that Fordham intended to cause death or great bodily harm, the issue in the Fordham case is whether a person who lacks such intent can be convicted of voluntary manslaughter. Although voluntary manslaughter requires such intent, murder does not. In *Derby*, the defendant was convicted of murder after bringing about the death of another person without the intent to kill or inflict injury. The affirmance of her murder conviction established that the trial court was correct in refusing to charge on voluntary manslaughter where the defendant lacked the intent to kill. Since this has a direct bearing on whether Fordham (who also lacked the intent to kill) can be convicted of voluntary manslaughter, *Derby* is applicable to the Fordham case.

The effect of *Allison* is to hold that one who acts unreasonably may be guilty of *involuntary* manslaughter. Since it does not say anything about what it would take to justify a conviction for *voluntary* manslaughter, it is inapplicable to Fordham's case. **A** is, therefore, incorrect. Since Boddy had the intent to kill and Fordham did not, the decision in *Boddy* that the court should have charged on voluntary manslaughter is inapplicable to Fordham's case. **B** is, therefore, incorrect. Like voluntary manslaughter, attempted murder requires the specific intent to cause death or great bodily harm. For this reason, **C** appears at first glance to raise an issue similar to that raised in the Fordham case. Since the crimes charged in the two cases were different, however, *Cain* is not really applicable as a precedent in Fordham's case. (i.e., A holding that the defendant cannot be guilty of *attempted murder* without specific intent does not logically relate to the question of whether a defendant can be guilty of *voluntary manslaughter* without specific intent.) **C** is, therefore, incorrect.

100. **None** It doesn't happen often, but the Bar Examiners sometimes goof and include a question which has no correct answer. This is an example of such a question. The common law definition of murder is the unlawful killing of a human being with malice aforethought. Since malice aforethought is satisfied not only by the intent to kill, but also the intent to resist a lawful arrest, the intent to commit any felony, and wanton disregard for human life, the lack of intent to kill is not a defense. **A** is, therefore, incorrect. Since **B** establishes that Daisy's conduct was a proximate cause of Van's death, it does not furnish her with a defense. **B** is, therefore, incorrect. **C** is incorrect because contributory negligence is not a defense to criminal liability. Since Van died of the wound inflicted by Daisy, **D** is clearly an inaccurate statement of fact, and is, therefore, incorrect. (The only thing to

do with a question like this is guess and move on. The chances are it will be invalidated by the Bar Examiners after early analysis of the Exam results.)

ANSWERS
PRACTICE MBE — P.M. EXAM

PRACTICE MBE — ANSWERS TO P.M. QUESTIONS

101. **A**   A person who renders a measurable benefit to another with the reasonable expectation of payment and not as an officious intermeddler may be entitled to recovery on a theory of quasi-contract (i.e., restitution for unjust enrichment). (**Note:** Since Bickley did not request Paver's performance, and since Bickley did not become aware of it until after it had occurred, it is not at all certain that a court would find in favor of Paver on this theory. But since the question calls for the assumption that Paver would be successful in his claim, it is necessary to consider the relief to which he would be entitled if successful.) Ordinarily, recovery on this theory is based on the benefit received by the person from whom payment is sought. This benefit may be measured in terms of net enrichment or cost avoided. If these amounts are unequal, the court will usually award the lowest of them. In this case, Bickley's net enrichment is the increase in his realty's value — $2,100. The cost avoided is what he would have had to pay another for the job (i.e., the standard market price) — $2,750. Since the net enrichment is the lesser of these two figures, Paver would be entitled to receive $2,100.

    B and **C** are incorrect because the benefit received by Bickley is unrelated to Paver's agreement with Adam or to Paver's cost. **D** is incorrect because it exceeds the net enrichment which Bickley received.

102. **A**   Ordinarily, a promise is not enforceable unless something of value (i.e., consideration) was given in return for it. Since Paver paved the driveway before Bickley promised to pay, he could not have done so in return for the promise. The paving job, therefore, could not have been consideration for Bickley's promise. Under the view of the Restatement (2nd) of Contracts, however, a promise made in recognition of a benefit previously received by the promisor from the promisee is binding to the extent necessary to prevent injustice. Thus, if Bickley knew that Paver had paved his driveway and made the promise to pay in recognition of this benefit, the promise would be enforceable.

    B is incorrect because Bickley's promise could not have been given in recognition of the paving job if Bickley did not know about it at the time he made the promise. Since the paving job done by Paver was not given in return for Bickley's promise, it would not be consideration for that promise no matter when Bickley decided to have the job done. **C** and **D** are therefore, incorrect.

103. **B**   A condition is an event which must occur before performance of a contractual obligation is due. Obviously, Paver could not be expected to pave Adam's driveway until Adam correctly identified the driveway to be paved. For this reason, correct identification of the driveway by Adam may be seen as a condition to Paver's obligation to pave it. An obligor is entitled to suspend performance until necessary conditions are fulfilled and his obligation is discharged when it is too late for the conditions to be fulfilled. Since the contract called for the job to be done before Adam returned from vacation, and since Adam did not furnish the correct address before returning, Paver's duty was discharged upon Adam's return.

    The law of contracts does not guarantee anyone a profit. If Paver's obligation was otherwise enforceable, the fact that he would lose money by performing or that he lost money by paving Bickley's driveway does not relieve him of the duty to do so. **A** and **C** are, therefore, incorrect. The standard measure of damage for breach of a contract for services is the difference between the contract price and the reasonable market price of the services. Since the standard market price was $2,750, the fact that there is a contractor willing to do the job for less would not be sufficient to prevent Adam from recovering the difference between the contract price and the market price. **D** is, therefore, incorrect. (**Note**: The situation would be different if Adam actually had the driveway paved by another contractor for $2,500. In that case, he would have sustained no damage and would not be entitled to recover from Paver.)

104.   **C**   Article III of the U.S. Constitution vests federal judicial power in the United States Supreme Court and in such inferior federal courts as Congress shall establish. In addition, by specifying what cases they may hear, Article III establishes limits on the jurisdiction which may be exercised by the federal courts. Although it gives federal courts the power (i.e., jurisdiction) to hear controversies between citizens of *different* states, or between citizens of the same state *claiming lands under grants of different states*, it does not give the federal courts any power to hear contract disputes between residents of the same state. Since the U.S. Constitution is the supreme law of the land, neither Congress nor a state legislature can confer this power on the United States District Courts.

        A and **B** are, therefore, incorrect. The Eleventh Amendment only prohibits the federal courts from hearing certain claims against a state and is inapplicable because Alonzo's claim is not against the State of DelMava. **D** is, therefore, incorrect.

105.   **D**   A misrepresentation is a false assertion of material fact intended to induce the plaintiff's reliance. A defendant intends to induce the plaintiff's reliance if she knows with substantial certainty that a class of persons to which the plaintiff belongs will rely on her statement. If Dabbs did not know that any person would rely on her statement, she could not have intended to induce any person's reliance. Her statement would, therefore, not be a misrepresentation.

        In addition, misrepresentation liability cannot be imposed unless the plaintiff was justified in relying (i.e., the reasonable person in plaintiff's situation would have relied) on the defendant's false statement. Since the reasonable person might believe a newspaper account instead of personally checking public records, however, **A** is incorrect. **B** is incorrect for two reasons: first, an expert's statement of opinion may be a misrepresentation because it asserts as a fact that the expert actually holds that opinion; and, second, Dabbs's statement that "Insiders say … (etc.)" is an assertion of fact on which misrepresentation liability could be based. In actions for negligent misrepresentation, it is frequently held that without privity the defendants owes the plaintiff no duty of reasonable care. In this case, however, since Dabbs knew that there was no basis for her statement, her misrepresentation was intentional. **C** is incorrect because privity is not a prerequisite to liability for intentional misrepresentation.

106.   **D**   One who inherits an interest in realty takes it subject to any existing prior interests. Since Ausler and Britt received interests prior to the death of Odish, and since both of those interests were immediately recorded, Lazarus and Richards took their interests in the realty subject to those of Ausler and Britt. Thus, Ausler is entitled to succeed in a

foreclosure proceeding. Because of the constitutional requirement of due process, however, persons who may be deprived of property as the result of a judicial proceeding must be given notice of an opportunity to be heard in that proceeding. For this reason, all persons with existing present or future interests in the realty are necessary parties who must be served with process in a foreclosure proceeding. Deciding who must be served thus requires nothing more than determining who holds a property interest — present or future — in the realty. Since Lazarus is the holder of a life estate (i.e., has a present interest), and Richards is the holder of a remainder (i.e., has a future interest), both are necessary parties. Since neither has been served or brought into the proceeding, Ausler's request for a foreclosure sale must be denied.

A, B and **C** are, therefore, incorrect.

107. **D** Since Britt's mortgage was recorded before either Lazarus or Richards received their interests, Britt's interest is superior to theirs, and he has the right to foreclose on the realty. Since Ausler's interest was created and recorded prior to Britt's, however, it is superior to Britt's. Thus, although Britt is entitled to foreclose, Ausler has a superior right to receive the proceeds of any foreclosure sale.

A and **B** are incorrect because any lienholder may institute a foreclosure proceeding so long as all other lienholders are joined as parties. **C** is incorrect because the prior creation and recording of his interest makes Ausler's right superior to Britt's.

108. **A** Murder is the unlawful killing of a human being with malice aforethought. Malice aforethought consists of a wanton disregard for human life, or of the intent to kill, or to inflict great bodily harm, resist a lawful arrest, escape from custody, or commit a dangerous felony. Because it was very likely to lead to death or serious injury, Dustin's firing slightly to the right of Hodges probably showed a wanton disregard for human life. This is particularly so in view of the fact that Dustin had never fired a rifle before, and therefore could not have been sure that he would miss Hodges. Thus, since Dustin caused the unjustified killing of Hodges with malice aforethought, he could properly be convicted of murder. While it is not certain that he would be convicted, murder is the only crime listed of which he could possibly be properly convicted.

Voluntary manslaughter is the intentional killing of a human being under mitigating circumstances. Since Dustin did not intend to hit Hodges with the bullet, he cannot be guilty of voluntary manslaughter. Thus, **B** is incorrect. A person is guilty of a criminal attempt when, with the intent of bringing about a criminally prohibited result, he comes largely close to achieving that result. Thus, while murder does not require the intent to kill or inflict great bodily harm, attempted murder does. Dustin did not intend to inflict harm upon Hodges, so he cannot be guilty of attempted murder. Thus, **C** is incorrect. **D** is incorrect because knowledge that the location is within the municipal limits is an essential element of guilt, and Dustin did not know the dump was within these limits.

109. **C** The fact that a witness has made prior statements which are inconsistent with her testimony suggests that her testimony is not worthy of belief. For this reason, such statements are admissible for purposes of impeachment. In general, substantive evidence is admissible if it tends to establish a fact in issue. Since the color of the traffic light is material to the determination of Pailey's rights against Dickman (i.e, is a fact in issue),

the deposition in which Westphal said that the light was green for Pailey is relevant evidence. Hearsay is ordinarily defined as an out-of-court statement offered to prove the truth of the matter which it asserts. FRE 801(d)(1)(A) specifically provides, however, that a deposition given under oath is not hearsay so long as the person who gave it is available for cross-examination. Thus, Westphal's deposition is not hearsay, although it was made-of-court and is offered to prove the truth of a matter asserted in it. For this reason, it is admissible as substantive evidence. **A**, **B** and **D** are, therefore, incorrect.

110. **D**   FRE 613(b) provides that extrinsic evidence of a prior inconsistent statement by a witness is not admissible unless the witness is afforded an opportunity to explain or deny making it and the opposing party is afforded an opportunity to interrogate her about it.

A is incorrect because the FRE does not require that this opportunity be given prior to the admission of the statement. Although some states prohibit a party from impeaching her own witness, **B** is incorrect because FRE 607 does not. A hostile witness is one who while testifying manifests hostility (i.e., anger or prejudice) against the attorney questioning her. Although Westphal did not give the answer which Pailey's attorney would have liked, there is no indication that she manifested hostility. **C** is, therefore, incorrect.

111. **C**   Under the doctrine of equitable conversion, the risk of loss occurring without fault of either party passes to the vendee of real estate as soon as a contract for sale is formed. Since the risk of loss has passed, the loss — even of a material part of the realty — is suffered by the buyer. As a result, the seller is entitled to enforce the agreement against the buyer even though the property no longer has the value that it did when the contract was made.

A, **B**, and **D** are, therefore, incorrect. **B** is also incorrect because the trees were part of the realty until uprooted by the storm.

112. **A**   Under the Uniform Vendor and Purchaser Risk Act, if neither title nor possession has passed to the purchaser and all or a material part of the realty is destroyed without fault of either party, neither party may enforce the contract of sale. Thus, if the damaged trees were a material part of the realty, Sandler cannot enforce the contract against Brant.

B is incorrect because if the damage to the realty was not material, Sandler would be entitled to enforce the contract with an appropriate abatement in the purchase price. **C** is incorrect because the effect of the Uniform Act is to prevent the risk of loss from passing until possession or title has been transferred to the purchaser. Although the Uniform Act permits enforcement with a reduction in the purchase price in the event of immaterial damage, the risk of loss continues to remain with the seller. Thus, if there has been material damage to the realty, the seller cannot enforce the contract at all. **D** is, therefore, incorrect.

113. **B**   The Thirteenth Amendment provides that, except as a punishment for crime, "Neither slavery nor involuntary servitude … shall exist within the United States," and grants Congress the power to enforce that provision. The United States Supreme Court has held that the prohibition against slavery was directed at individuals as well as at government action. This, the Court stated, gives Congress the power to define badges of servitude, and to eliminate them by enacting legislation regulating private conduct. The

Court further ruled that racial discrimination could constitute a badge of slavery.

The Due Process Clause of the Fifth Amendment has been held to protect certain substantive individual rights. Since the Fifth Amendment only protects against action by the federal government, however, it could not justify the regulation of private conduct. Thus, **A** is incorrect. Since the Equal Protection Clause only prohibits invidious discrimination by states, **C** is incorrect for the same reason. The Fifteenth Amendment provides that the right to vote shall not be denied on account of race or previous condition of servitude. Since the legislation in question does not protect the right to vote, it cannot be justified by the Fifteenth Amendment. **D** is, therefore, incorrect.

114. **D**   A contract may make the happening of a particular event a condition precedent to the performance of a contractual duty. If so, one party's strict compliance with the condition makes the other party's conditional duty absolute. The terms of the commission agreement made Richmond's delivery, prior to April 15, of a buyer ready, willing and able to pay $50,000 for the realty a condition precedent to Sack's duty to pay a commission. Since Richmond complied with that condition by presenting Bader's offer on April 14, Sack's duty to pay has become absolute.

A is incorrect because the commission agreement did not make completion of the sale a condition precedent to Sack's obligation to pay a commission. If an agreement specifies its own duration, then the obligations which it creates are understood to exist for the period specified. The commission agreement required Richmond to make reasonable efforts to sell the realty until April 15, and required Sack to pay a commission if Richmond procured a buyer prior to that date. Those obligations, therefore, continued to exist until April 15. Sack's rejection of Bader's offer of April 10 terminated Bader's offer, but did not affect the obligations created by Sack's contract with Richmond. **B** is, therefore, incorrect. The Statute of Frauds simply provides that certain agreements are unenforceable over objection unless they are in writing and signed by the party to be charged. The Statute of Frauds would thus prevent the enforcement of any contract which is claimed to have been formed as a result of Bader's April 10 offer. **C** is incorrect for this reason, and because while the Statute of Frauds may prevent an alleged oral contract from being enforced, it does not have any effect on the validity of the rejection of an offer.

115. **A**   Specific performance is a remedy available for breach of a contract for the sale of something unique. Since each parcel of realty is regarded as unique, specific performance is usually available as a buyer's remedy for a seller's breach of a contract for the sale of realty. Unless such a contract has been formed and breached, however, no remedy is available at all. A contract is formed by the acceptance of an offer. An offer is an expression of an unequivocal willingness to enter into a contract with another on specified terms. Since Sack never indicated a willingness to enter into a contract with Bader on any particular terms, he never made an offer to Bader. Bader twice made offers to Sack, but Sack did not accept either of them. Thus, no contract was ever formed between Sack and Bader, or breached by Sack. Bader is, therefore, without any remedy.

Whether Sack's statement to Richmond on April 10 was an attempt to modify an existing agreement is not at all certain under the facts regarding that agreement. **B** is incorrect in any event because the agreement between Sack and Richmond did not require

Sack to accept an offer procured by Richmond, and is not relevant to Bader's rights against Sack. Specific performance is not usually available as a remedy for the breach of a contract for sale unless the subject of the contract is unique or damages would be an inadequate remedy. **C** is incorrect, however, because — for the reasons given above — there has been no breach, and Bader, therefore, has no remedy at all. Since Sack made no offer to Bader, the document which was presented to Sack on April 14 was nothing more than an offer. Since Sack did not accept it, no contract between him and Bader was formed. **D** is, therefore, incorrect.

116. **B**   There are only three potential bases of liability in a tort action — intent, negligence, and liability without fault (i.e., strict liability). It is clear from the facts that Darcy's entry onto Ponce's realty was not intentional. Operating an automobile is not one of the activities for which strict liability is imposed. The only possible basis of liability is, therefore, negligence. Thus, Darcy can be liable only if she was negligent.

A is incorrect because an unauthorized entry onto realty is not a trespass unless it is intentional. The doctrine of "last clear chance" is practically obsolete, but where it is applicable, its only effect is to relieve a plaintiff of the consequences of her own contributory negligence. Since Darcy is not the plaintiff, whether or not she had the "last clear chance" to avoid an accident is irrelevant. **C** is, therefore, incorrect. The privilege of necessity permits the reasonable violation of property rights in the face of an emergency. **D** is incorrect, however, for two reasons: first, necessity is only available as a defense to intentional tort; and, second — even under the privilege of necessity — one who invades the property rights of another to protect her own interests must pay for any actual damage which results from that invasion.

117. **D**   It is generally understood that, even while testifying, a witness may look at any document (in fact, at anything at all) which serves to refresh her recollection about the matters to which she is testifying. Although there are dangers connected with this rule, it is thought that these can be averted by investing the judge with discretion to determine, while listening to the testimony, whether the witness' recollection has really been refreshed by consulting such a document, or whether the witness has no real present recollection but is simply reading from the document. Since Pinto had not yet looked at the notes or stated that looking at them would refresh her recollection, the judge is not yet in a position to exercise this discretion, and must overrule the objection.

A is incorrect because any material may be used to refresh the recollection of a witness, without regard to the origin of that material. **B** is incorrect because even material which has not been admitted or is not capable of being admitted may be used to refresh a witness' recollection. A leading question is one which suggests a particular answer. **C** is incorrect for two reasons: first, there are occasions when a direct examiner is permitted to stimulate a witness' memory through the use of leading questions; and, second, since Alvarado's question did not suggest a particular answer, it was not leading.

118. **C**   Hearsay is defined as an out-of-court statement offered for the purpose of proving the truth of the matter asserted in that statement. Since Alvarado's notes were made out of court, and since the only apparent reason to offer them is to establish the truth of their contents, they are hearsay.

FRE 803(6) recognizes a hearsay exception for properly authenticated business records recorded as part of the regular course of business, while the transaction recorded was fresh in the entrant's mind, regarding facts within the entrant's personal knowledge or from an inherently reliable source. Since the facts do not indicate what information was contained in Alvarado's notes, there is no way to determine whether all the information actually contained in them was within Alvarado's personal knowledge or from an inherently reliable source. An additional question exists as to whether an attorney's notes regarding a negotiation between a client and another party are kept in the regular course of business. No matter how these questions are resolved, however, Alvarado's notes cannot be admitted as a business record unless they are authenticated by a person who testifies to the record's identity and its mode of preparation. Since no one has testified as such, **A** is incorrect. Documents which have been used to refresh a witness' recollection while testifying may be consulted by an adverse party in cross-examining that witness. In addition, an *adverse* party may introduce into evidence those portions of the document which are relevant to the witness' testimony. **B** is incorrect, however, because the fact that a party used a document to refresh her recollection is not sufficient to justify its introduction by the party that used it. Under certain circumstances, an attorney may resist discovery of his own work product, and prevent it from being received in evidence. This privilege belongs to the attorney (and his client), however, not to his adversary. For this reason, Dean's attorney could not successfully object on the ground that the document was Alvarado's work product. **D** is, therefore, incorrect.

119. **C**   The United States Supreme Court has held that constitutional requirements of equality in the electoral process prohibit the use of property ownership as a qualification for voter eligibility in general elections. An exception to this rule has been recognized for special purpose elections on matters which relate only to the interests of landowners. The election in question does not fit this exception, however, since municipal revenues and their source are of interest to all residents of the municipality. For this reason, the land ownership requirement probably makes the special election invalid.

The Fifteenth Amendment only prohibits exclusion of persons from the electoral process on the basis of race, color, or previous condition of servitude. **A** is incorrect because there is no indication that any persons will be excluded from voting in the special election on this basis. **B** is incorrect because the United States Supreme Court has held that states can constitutionally limit the vote to residents and has specifically upheld residence requirements of up to 50 days and because persons owning land within the township are not necessarily residents of the township. **D** is incorrect for two reasons: first, unlike the election of representatives which may be conducted by district, this is an election which could not be conducted in any other way but at-large; and, second, in the absence of a specific intent to dilute the power of a particular interest group, at-large elections are valid even if they have that effect.

120. **D**   The Equal Protection Clause prohibits invidious discrimination by the state, but not all discrimination is invidious. Ordinarily, statutory systems of classification (i.e., discrimination) are valid so long as they have a rational basis. If the discrimination is based on a suspect classification or interferes with a fundamental right, however, it is presumed invalid unless it is proven to be necessary to achieve a compelling state interest. The Supreme Court has held that the right to vote is a fundamental right. For this reason, the Township Council's assertion that the registration schedule had a rational basis would

not be sufficient to prevent it from being declared unconstitutional.

Discrimination on the basis of lifestyle or wealth has been held not to involve a suspect classification. **A** and **B** are, therefore, incorrect. Some forms of sex discrimination, referred to as "benign" because they are aimed at compensating for the demonstrated economic disadvantages of women, have been found constitutional. Some forms of sex discrimination, called "benign" because they are based on old thought patterns about sex roles and the dependency of women, have been found unconstitutional. Thus, the term "benign sex discrimination" is not relevant in determining whether a statute is constitutional, and **C** is incorrect.

121. **D**   Upon breach by a buyer, UCC § 2-706 provides that the seller may resell the goods in a commercially reasonable manner and recover damages equivalent to the difference between the contract price and the price which the seller actually received upon the resale. Here, since Charron resold the chairs at the same price which she had agreed to accept from Furness, she has sustained no damage at all. (**Note:** If Charron incurred extra expense in making 75 individual sales of one chair each, rather than a single sale of 75 chairs as agreed by Furness, recovery for the extra expense might be available as incidental damages. **D** is correct, however, because the facts do not indicate that any extra expense was actually incurred, and because no other answer listed correctly describes damages which might be available.)

Where the goods which a breaching buyer contracted to buy are in unlimited supply, the seller may be entitled to recover the profit which the seller would have realized if not for the breach. Since there were a limited number of chairs, however, and since Charron succeeded in selling them all, she is not entitled to this remedy. **A** is therefore, incorrect. **B** is incorrect because Furness did not agree to pay $100 per chair. **C** is incorrect because when the seller resells under UCC § 2-706, the damages are measured by difference between the contract price and the price which she actually received.

122. **A**   Generally it is the judge's function to decide whether offered evidence may be considered by the jury (i.e., is admissible), and the jury's function to decide what weight to give evidence which the judge decides they may consider. In order to find them admissible, a judge must determine whether photographs offered into evidence have been properly authenticated. A party seeking to authenticate a photograph must establish that the photograph is an accurate representation of what it purports to picture. Pabst has authenticated his photo by testifying that he took it of the stove in question and that it accurately represents the stove. Weber has authenticated his photo by testifying that it accurately represents the stove in question. Both photos have thus been sufficiently authenticated to be admitted into evidence. It will then be the jury's job to decide which witness it believes — if any — and which photo it therefore believes to be an accurate representation of the stove in question.

B is incorrect because Weber's testimony that his photo fairly and accurately represents the stove sufficiently authenticates it even though he was not the photographer. **C** is incorrect because Pabst's testimony that he took the snapshot and that it accurately represents the stove sufficiently authenticates it. **D** is incorrect for a combination of the reasons that make **B** and **C** incorrect.

123. **B**   Restraints on the alienation of leasehold interests are generally regarded as valid but are strictly construed. For this reason, a restraint against assignment is held not to prohibit sub-lease. Assignment of a lease takes place when a lessee transfers to another his entire remaining interest in the premises. If any interest less than this is transferred, the transfer is a sub-lease rather than an assignment. Since Tuck retained a right to one of the offices, his transfer to Seaver was not an assignment and did not breach the lease provision prohibiting assignments.

   A is incorrect because if a transfer of the lessee's entire remaining interest occurs, the transfer is an assignment even though the terms in the agreement between assignor and assignee are not identical to the terms in the agreement between the landlord and assignor. Although courts generally disfavor restraints on the alienation of fee interests in realty, **C** is incorrect because clauses prohibiting the assignment of leasehold interests are generally regarded as valid. The financial status of a prospective tenant is only one of the factors which a landlord considers in deciding whether to rent to him. (For example, a landlord might be unwilling to rent to a person with a good credit rating if that person has a history of damaging leased premises or engages in an occupation inconsistent with other uses of the premises.) **D** is, therefore, incorrect.

124. **C**   Unless a landlord specifically agrees to release a tenant from further obligations under a lease, assignment or sub-lease does not relieve the original tenant from those obligations. For this reason, Luz can collect unpaid rent from Tuck. Since Luz was an intended third-party creditor beneficiary of the agreement between Tuck and Seaver, Luz can also collect from Seaver. **A**, **B** and **D** are, therefore, incorrect.

125. **B**   The United States Supreme Court has held that because defamation liability can only be imposed for a false statement, and because there is no such thing as a false opinion, defamation liability cannot be imposed for an assertion of opinion. The Supreme Court also ruled that a statement is an assertion of opinion if reasonable readers would recognize that it was an expression of the writer's feelings, and would not believe that it was intended to assert a fact. Thus, if reasonable readers would not believe that the statement asserted a fact, it was an expression of opinion, and, therefore, not subject to defamation liability.

   Although the Supreme Court has held that a public person suing for defamation must prove actual malice (i.e., knowledge of falsity or reckless disregard for truth) this requirement has not been imposed on private persons. For this reason, Romero could be liable for publishing a defamatory statement about Nadel which he negligently believed to be true even if he did not have actual malice when he made it. **A** is, therefore, incorrect. A statement, even if it is defamatory, will not subject its publisher to defamation liability unless it is false. But a defamatory statement is said to be false if it is not substantially true, without regard to whether or not the reasonable person would believe it. If damage results from the publication of a statement found to be defamatory (which *does* depend on what the reasonable person would think it means) and false (which does *not* depend at all on what the reasonable person would think) defamation liability is imposed. Although the amount of damage will probably be related to the number of people who believed the defamatory statement and held it against the plaintiff, it does not depend on whether or not those who did so were reasonable people. The argument in **C** would not, therefore, be an effective defense for Romero. Although (for reasons stated above) defamation liability is not imposed for stating an opinion, it may be imposed for a false assertion of fact even though the maker of that statement believed it to be true. Thus, if Romero's statement was defamatory, and if it was a false assertion of fact, Romero could not escape liability by proving that he believed it (i.e., in his opinion it was accurate) unless his belief was reasonable. **D** is, therefore, incorrect.

126. **D**   The law of contracts imposes liability without fault. Thus if a person makes an enforceable promise to deliver 1,000 pounds of cheese and fails to do so, that person is liable for damages to the promisee. Since WKKW promised Colby 1,000 pounds of cheese and received consideration for that promise in the form of Colby's payment of $120, WKKW's failure to deliver the cheese is a breach of contract for which Colby is entitled to damages.

WKKW's detrimental reliance on the promise of Swiss might take the place of consideration or of a writing (if one were required) in an action by WKKW against Swiss. It is not relevant to the enforceability of WKKW's promise to Colby, however, because contract liability is imposed without regard to fault. **A** and **B** are, therefore, incorrect. Since WKKW made a promise to Colby, WKKW is liable for breaching that promise without regard to the liability of any other person, and without regard to whether Colby attempts to collect from any other person. **C** is, therefore, incorrect.

127. **C**   An assignment is a transfer from an assignor to an assignee of the assignor's right to receive a benefit from a third person. Since Swiss promised to donate the cheese to WKKW, and since WKKW transferred this right to receive it to Colby, Colby is WKKW's assignee. An assignee stands in his assignor's shoes, receiving whatever right the assignor had at the time of the assignment. Swiss promised WKKW that it would donate cheese. Since that promise was either supported by consideration (in the form of free publicity) or by WKKW's detrimental reliance (in reselling the cheese), Swiss' promise to WKKW would be enforceable by WKKW, and is enforceable by Colby as WKKW's assignee.

A and **B** are incorrect for the reasons given above. An intended third-party creditor beneficiary of a contract is a third party to whom one of the contracting parties owed a pre-existing debt, and to whom the other party therefore agreed to render performance. Since WKKW owed no debt to Colby at the time of its agreement with Swiss, Colby could not have been an intended creditor beneficiary of that agreement. **D** is, therefore, incorrect.

128. **C**   Since the restriction to residential use was contained in the deed by which Bishop received his interest in lot 2, there is no question about whether the restriction is enforceable *against* him. But since Appel was not a party to the transaction in which the restriction on Bishop's use was created (i.e., the conveyance of lot 2), a question exists about whether that restriction is enforceable *by Appel*. The facts are unclear about who purchased first. (If Bishop purchased before Appel, the question would be an easier one. Then, the benefit which Odum received from the restriction in Bishop's deed probably ran with Odum's land and probably passed to Appel with the conveyance of lot 1. Unfortunately, this is not one of the options.) Even if Appel purchased first he may be able to enforce the restriction in Bishop's deed if at the time of his purchase he relied on a representation by Odum that lot 2 would be similarly restricted. In that event, Appel

might succeed on two theories: first, that he was an intended creditor beneficiary of Bishop's covenant; and, second, that there were implied reciprocal servitudes (see next explanation). One way of establishing reliance on such a representation would be to show that at the time of his purchase Appel was aware that the restriction was part of Odum's development scheme. The additional fact in **C** might thus result in a decision for Appel.

If Appel purchased before Bishop, the benefit which Odum received from the restriction in Appel's deed probably passed to Bishop with lot 2 because that benefit ran with the land. For this reason, the facts in **A** and **B** might be relevant if Bishop was trying to enforce the restriction contained in Appel's deed. They are irrelevant to Appel's attempt to enforce the restriction contained in Bishop's deed, however. For this reason, **A** and **B** are incorrect. If Bishop purchased before Appel, Bishop might be able to enforce the restriction in Appel's deed by showing that Bishop was aware of Odum's development scheme when he purchased. But since the question involves Appel's attempt to enforce the restriction in Bishop's deed, **D** is incorrect.

129. **A** An equitable servitude is a burden imposed on land. If a benefit which results from it runs with the land, the servitude is enforceable without privity by a person to whose land the benefit runs. Some cases hold that when a subdivider creates a restriction on the use of land which he grants, a resulting implied reciprocal servitude burdens the land which he retains with the same restriction. Other cases hold that an implied reciprocal servitude results only if the grantor promises grantees that subsequent grants will contain the same restriction. Other cases hold that no implied reciprocal servitude results unless at the time of the earlier grants there was a general plan of development which encompassed the restrictions involved. All agree, however, that *if* the grantor's land is burdened by an implied reciprocal servitude, it burdens subsequent grantees who take with notice of the restrictions in prior deeds, even though their own deeds contain no mention of the servitude. Thus, if Odum's land was burdened by an implied reciprocal servitude when Columbus bought it, Columbus' land would be burdened by it because Columbus was aware of the development scheme.

Ordinarily, people are free to use their realty for any lawful purpose, even if it should inconvenience neighbors or reduce the value of their land. For this reason, the fact that Columbus's intended use might diminish the value of Eubank's land is not, alone, sufficient to result in a finding for Eubank. **B** is, therefore, incorrect. **C** is incorrect because an equitable servitude may be enforced without privity. **D** is incorrect because an implied reciprocal servitude may burden subsequent takers even though not mentioned in their deeds.

130. **A** The Fifth and Fourteenth Amendments provide in part that no person shall be deprived of life, liberty, or property without due process of law. Since Eno's claim is that the State Harbor Commission's decision violated his right to due process, his claim must fail unless the decision deprived him of life, liberty, or property. If it did not, he was not entitled to due process in the decision-making process. Cases have held that if a state employee's contract provides that the state may decide not to rehire without cause, the employee's expectation of being rehired is not a sufficient property interest to require due process. Thus, the argument in **A** would probably be successful. Even without these cases, however, **A** would be the only argument listed which could possibly be an effec-

tive response to Eno's challenge.

Although no person has a right to state employment (i.e., no person is guaranteed employment by the state), the distinction between right and privilege is unimportant where the interest involved is an "entitlement" which is seen to be a property interest. **B** is, therefore, incorrect. **C** is incorrect because the hearing officer would presumably act properly in considering whatever evidence Eno might submit, and, therefore, might not come to the same conclusion as the Commission. **D** is incorrect because it is based on an overinclusive statement; even though the contract provided that the decision not to renew could be made without cause, it could still have been made for a reason (e.g., based on race) or in a manner inconsistent with the requirements of the constitution, thus violating Eno's constitutional rights.

131.   **B**   State action which imposes a penalty for the exercise of a constitutional right is a deprivation of liberty. If the decision not to renew Eno's contract was based on his speech (an exercise of First Amendment rights), it interfered with a liberty interest. Since the Fifth and Fourteenth Amendments protect against deprivation of liberty without due process, the additional fact set forth in **B** could result in a finding that a hearing (i.e., due process) was required.

A is incorrect because there is no indication that the contracts of the probationary employees who received hearings permitted non-renewal without cause as did Eno's. **C** is incorrect because the United States Supreme Court has specifically held that state action does not require a prior hearing merely because it interferes with reputation, particularly since a tort action for defamation is available to prevent abuse. Sometimes urgency plays a role in the court's decision about whether a prior hearing is required for particular action. For example, it has been held that because the denial of welfare benefits could leave a person in a desperate financial situation, a prior hearing is required. Similarly, if delaying governing action until after a hearing is held is likely to result in serious harm to the government, it might be appropriate to act without holding a prior hearing. The fact set forth in **D** might justify the conclusion that keeping Eno on the job until a hearing is held would result in serious harm to the state. In that case, it would hurt rather than help Eno's cause.

132.   **A**   Private nuisance is a tortious interference with the plaintiff's right to use and enjoy realty, and may be committed without any physical intrusion onto the realty. Although the County of Durban ordinance permitted use of the airport by certain aircraft, De La Fuente could still be liable for private nuisance if he was operating the airport in a manner other than that contemplated by the ordinance. While it is not certain that Pinson would recover on this theory, private nuisance is the only theory listed which could possibly result in a judgment in his favor.

It is sometimes held that repeated overflights for a given period of time result in a prescriptive aeronautical easement. **B** is incorrect, however, because this conclusion would privilege the continuing overflights, thus providing De La Fuente with a defense to an action brought by Pinson. The Fifth Amendment to the United States Constitution prohibits the taking by government of private property for public use without just compensation. If the County of Durban ordinance resulted in a reduction in the value of Pinson's realty, the Fifth Amendment might require that the County of Durban pay just compensation to Pinson. Although this right would be enforceable in an inverse condemnation proceeding, **C** is incorrect because this theory is available only against an agency of the government. Trespass to land and the variant known as continuing trespass require a physical or tangible entry onto the realty. **D** is incorrect because noise is not tangible.

133. **C**   An "admission" is a statement by a party offered against that party. Under the common law it is admissible as an exception to the hearsay rule; under FRE 801(d)(2), it is not hearsay. Since Dangler's statement to Mary is offered against Dangler it is an admission and, therefore, admissible.

The marital privilege is designed to protect the confidentiality of the marital relationship. For this reason, it prevents either spouse from testifying over objection by the other to a confidential communication made during the marriage. For the same reason, however, it does not prevent a stranger to the marriage from testifying to a communication which he overheard between the spouses. Thus, although communications made within the marriage are presumed to be confidential, **A** is incorrect because Lennon did not receive the communication within the marriage (i.e., as a marriage partner). **B** is incorrect because an admission is not hearsay under FRE 801(d)(2), and is admissible as an exception to the hearsay rule under common law. Communications which advance a crime are not protected by privilege. Dangler's statement did not advance a crime, however, because it was about a crime which had already been committed. The fact that it concerned a crime is not enough to take it out of the protection of the marital privilege, making **D** incorrect.

134. **A**   In jurisdictions which recognize the spousal privilege, a spouse is not permitted to testify to a confidential communication received during marriage if the spouse who made the communication objects to the testimony. For this reason, the court should exclude Mary's testimony if Dangler objects to it. **I** is, therefore, correct.

In general, all evidence which tends to establish a material fact is relevant and should be admitted unless excluded by some rule of law. Since Dangler's statement that he committed the crimes he is charged with tends to establish that he did so, it is relevant. Hearsay is an out of court statement offered to prove the truth of the matter asserted in that statement and is inadmissible unless it falls within an exception to the hearsay rule. A statement by a party offered against that party is an admission, however. An admission is admissible under common law as an exception to the hearsay rule and is not hearsay under FRE 801(d)(2). Thus Dangler's statement should be admitted unless excluded by the spousal privilege. A privilege may only be asserted by one who holds it. In some jurisdictions (and the FRE follow local state law as to privileges), the spousal privilege can be asserted only by the spouse who made the confidential communication. In other jurisdictions, the privilege may also be asserted by the spouse who received the communication. But all jurisdictions agree that the communication may be excluded only if a person holding it object. Therefore, if *neither* spouse asserts the privilege, it cannot be used to exclude Mary's testimony. Thus, II is incorrect.

135. **D**   The Statute of Frauds provides that a promise to discharge the debt of another is unenforceable over objection unless it is in writing and signed by the party to be charged. Since Unger never signed any writing in connection with his promise to Landry, the

promise is unenforceable under the Statute of Frauds.

Consideration is a bargained-for exchange of something of value given in return for and to induce a promise. It may consist of some benefit conferred upon the promisor in return for his promise, or some detriment incurred by the promisee in return for the promisor's promise. Here, in return for Unger's promise, Landry loaned money to Neal, thereby incurring a detriment, and thus giving consideration for Unger's promise. **A** is, therefore, incorrect. An offer to exchange the offeror's promise for the offeree's performance is an offer for a unilateral contract. Unless the offer specifies otherwise, an offer for a unilateral contract can only be accepted by performing the act which the offeror demanded in return for his promise. Thus, by loaning Neal money as requested by Unger, Landry accepted Unger's offer. While it is true that an unaccepted offer terminates upon the death of the offeror, **B** is incorrect because Unger's offer to Landry was accepted prior to Unger's death. **C** is incorrect because, once an agreement is formed, the death of a party does not terminate his obligations under it.

136. **B**   A basic principle of the law of evidence is that only evidence which is relevant to a material issue may be received in evidence. Evidence is logically relevant to a material issue if it has any tendency to prove or disprove a fact of consequence. Since Dale is charged with assaulting Vollmer, and not Whelan, his beating of Whelan could not tend to prove or disprove a fact of consequence in the prosecution. (It might *seem* logical to argue that Whelan's testimony tends to establish that Dale is the kind of person who is likely to have committed the crime with which he is charged. All jurisdictions agree, however, that evidence of a defendant's character is not admissible to create the inference that he engaged in particular conduct on a particular occasion.)

In some jurisdictions, confidential marital communications are privileged and cannot be revealed — even after the marriage has terminated — over the objection of the spouse against whom they are offered. There is some disagreement about whether this privilege applies to acts as well as communications. It is generally agreed, however, that communications or acts are privileged only if they were intended to be confidential. The fact that the acts to which Whelan testified occurred in public places indicates that they were not intended to be confidential, and the privilege, therefore, does not apply. **A** is incorrect for this reason and because, as explained above, the testimony may be excluded even if the jurisdiction does not recognize the marital privilege. The credibility of a witness may be impeached by evidence relating to his reputation for truth and veracity. **C** is incorrect, however, for two reasons: first, Whelan's testimony does not logically relate to Dale's *reputation* at all; and, second, FRE 608(b) specifically provides that extrinsic evidence (except for convictions) of specific conduct may not be used to impeach the credibility of a witness. Although a defendant who testifies in his own behalf may be impeached by cross-examination (i.e., intrinsically) regarding past conduct, FRE 608(b) prevents the use of extrinsic evidence of specific acts of unconvicted bad conduct. **D** is, therefore, incorrect.

137. **C**   Under the doctrine of impossibility of performance, a party may be excused from obligations under a contract if an unforeseeable change in circumstances has made performance vitally different than that which was contemplated by the parties at the time the contract was formed. On the other hand, if the change which occurred was foreseeable, the fact that it increases a party's burden of performance is not, alone, sufficient to

excuse that performance. Because contracts must remain stable even when the market does not, it is generally understood that, for this purpose, fluctuations in market price are foreseeable. In any event, *if* dramatic fluctuation in the price of chickens *was* foreseeable, then the increase in market price would not excuse Fowler's performance.

A is incorrect because if the change was foreseeable, it does not matter whether the parties actually knew that it would occur. In an "aleatory" contract, one party agrees to confer a benefit on the other upon the happening of a fortuitous event over which neither party has control (e.g., X agrees to pay Y if Y's roll of the dice comes up 7). Since the agreement between Coyne and Fowler was not conditioned upon the happening of any event over which neither had control, it was not aleatory. **B** is, therefore, incorrect. (**Note:** Under the reasoning of option B, all contracts for the future payment of money would be aleatory and invalid.) **D** is incorrect for two reasons: first, the rights of the parties would be the same under common law as under the UCC; and, second, the transaction is deemed a sale by the language of the UCC, which defines a sale as a passing of title from the seller to the buyer for a price.

138. **A**   A party's unequivocal statement that she will not perform is an anticipatory repudiation and entitles the other party to all rights resulting from a breach. Fowler's statement that she would not accept the coins in payment for the chickens was such a statement. Its result was to free Coyne from any further obligation under the contract and to give Coyne a right to an immediate action against Fowler for breach of contract.

A prospective inability to perform occurs when a party engages in some conduct which divests that party of the ability to perform. All jurisdictions agree that one party's prospective inability to perform excuses the other party's performance, and some jurisdictions hold that it gives him an immediate right to sue. **B** is incorrect, however, because *Coyne's* prospective inability to perform would not in any jurisdiction give *Coyne* a right of action. For the reason stated above, Coyne's refusal to accept delivery of the chickens was excused by Fowler's anticipatory repudiation, and was, therefore, not a breach. **C** is, therefore, incorrect. (**Note: C** may be confusing because of its use of the word "impossible." If an unforeseeable change in circumstances makes it impossible for a party to perform his obligation under a contract, his/her failure to perform might be excused under the doctrine of "impossibility of performance." Since Coyne's refusal to accept delivery did not result from an unforeseen change in circumstances, but rather from his decision to treat Fowler's repudiation as an immediate breach, the doctrine of "impossibility of performance" is not relevant to this case. If it were relevant, it would tend to defeat Fowler's claim, not to support it.) Since Coyne chose to treat Fowler's anticipatory repudiation as an immediate breach, Fowler cannot subsequently undo the breach by offering to perform. **D** is, therefore, incorrect.

139. **C**   When an easement is created by grant, the language of the grant determines the scope of the easement. When that language is unclear, the courts most often determine the scope of the easement on the basis of what could reasonably have been anticipated at the time the easement was created. Although there are insufficient facts to determine whether the argument in **C** would result in a judgment for O'Dowd, it is the only argument listed which could possibly support his position.

If an easement is created by adverse use over a specified period of time (i.e., by prescription), the use over that period determines the scope of the easement. If the easement is created by grant, however, its scope is determined by the language of the grant, construed in the light of what the parties contemplated at the time of its creation. **A** is, therefore, incorrect. The initial installment of a single pipe by Waterco might be evidence of what the parties contemplated at the time the easement was created. It is not conclusive, however, because the scope of an easement is usually understood to include those changes in the activities of the dominant estate which could reasonably have been foreseen. Thus, although Waterco only installed one pipe, it may be found that the parties anticipated that the installation of a second pipe might one day be necessary. If so, that anticipation would be relevant in determining the scope of the easement granted by the language given. **B** is, therefore, incorrect. **D** is incorrect because where the granting language is not sufficiently specific the scope of the easement is determined as explained above.

140. **D**   Since the sales contract called for delivery of marketable title to a parcel consisting of four lots, Barney could not be required to accept anything less. Outstanding encumbrances — including easements — make a title unmarketable. Since one of the four lots was encumbered by an easement, Swinton was unable to deliver marketable title, and was, therefore, in breach of contract.

A covenant against encumbrances is breached if an encumbrance exists at the time of conveyance, and gives rise to an action against the covenantor for any damage resulting from the existence of such an encumbrance. **A** is incorrect, however, because marketable title means a title which can be enjoyed without the likelihood of litigation, and title to encumbered realty is likely to lead to litigation. Since there may be reasons why Barney would want to purchase a parcel consisting of four lots but not a parcel consisting of three lots, he cannot be required to accept less than what he bargained for. Having bargained for a parcel consisting of four lots, he cannot, therefore, be compelled to accept a deed to only three of them. **B** is, therefore, incorrect. In a *tort* action for intentional misrepresentation, it would be necessary for Barney to show that Swinton knew that the easement existed when he promised to deliver marketable title. *Breach of contract* liability is not based on fault, however, and may be imposed simply because the promisor has failed to keep a promise which he made. Since Swinton promised to deliver marketable title (i.e., title free of encumbrances), he may be liable for breaching that contract without regard to whether he knew that it would be breached when he made it. For this reason, **C** is incorrect.

141. **B**   For various reasons, the law recognizes a policy to encourage settlements. Since a party might refrain from making a settlement offer if he believed that his offer could be used as circumstantial evidence of his liability, this policy prohibits the admission as evidence of the offeror's liability of an offer to settle or compromise a claim.

Since the offeror's explanation for his offer would not always prevent the offer from convincing a jury of his liability, policy would prevent the admission of evidence of the offer even if the offeror was given an opportunity to explain it. **A** is, therefore, incorrect. Although a declaration against pecuniary interest may be an exception to the hearsay rule, and although the admission of a party is an exception to the hearsay rule under common law, and not hearsay at all under FRE 801(d)(2), **C** and **D** are incorrect since the settlement offer is being excluded, not because it is hearsay, but because of the policy to encourage settlements.

142. **B**   The plaintiff in a negligence action must establish that the defendant breached a duty of reasonable care, and that the breach was a proximate cause of damage. In concept, a plaintiff has sustained *damage* as a result of a defendant's act if the plaintiff would have been better off without that act. If Palermo otherwise would have died, then Richey's act saved Palermo's life at the expense of his injured knees. Since Palermo's life was more important (i.e., valuable) than his knees, he would not have been better off without Richey's act, and, therefore, sustained no damage.

Since a result might have several proximate causes, any damage which Palermo did sustain could have been proximately caused by the negligence of Richey *and* by the negligence of Driscoll. This would make Richey and Driscoll joint tortfeasors — in most jurisdictions, jointly and severally liable for Palermo's damage. For this reason, the fact that Driscoll's negligence was a proximate cause of Palermo's injury is not likely to result in a judgment for Richey. **A** is, therefore, incorrect. If Palermo was damaged as a proximate result of the negligence of Richey, Richey would be liable for Palermo's damage. This is true regardless of any injuries which Richey might have sustained. **C** is, therefore, incorrect. Ordinarily a person who acts is required to act as the reasonable person would in the same circumstances. Since emergencies call for quick response without time for cool reflection, a person confronted with an emergency is not required to act as she would if not confronted by an emergency. She is, however, required to act like the reasonable person would if confronted with the same emergency. Thus, the fact that an emergency existed does not excuse a defendant from the obligation of acting reasonably. **D** is, therefore, incorrect.

143. **B**   The law of torts recognizes only three possible bases of liability. These are intent, strict liability, and negligence. Since intent means a desire or knowledge that a harmful result will occur, and since no fact indicates that Driscoll desired or knew that his car would hit Richey, he could not be liable to Richey on an intent theory. Strict liability is ordinarily imposed only on persons who engage in ultra-hazardous or abnormally-dangerous activities. Since operating a car is not one of these, Driscoll could not be liable on a strict liability theory. Negligence is unreasonable conduct in the face of a duty to act reasonably. Thus, if Driscoll did not act unreasonably, he could not be liable on a negligence theory either.

A plaintiff assumes a risk when he knows of the risk and voluntarily encounters it. It is generally understood, however, that a person who rushes into danger to rescue another person does not act voluntarily because she is impelled by the necessity of the moment. For this reason she does not thereby assume the risk. **A** is, therefore, incorrect. Although under the all-or-nothing rule, contributory negligence is a complete defense, **C** is incorrect because contributory negligence is unreasonable conduct *by the plaintiff*, and Palermo is not the plaintiff in this claim. In jurisdictions which apply it, the doctrine of "last clear chance" may permit a plaintiff to recover in spite of his contributory negligence. **D** is incorrect because the doctrine of last clear chance is never applied to *prevent* a plaintiff from recovering.

144. **A**   Under the all-or-nothing rule of contributory negligence unreasonable conduct by the plaintiff which contributes to the happening of an accident completely bars recovery by

the plaintiff. Thus, if it was unreasonable for Palermo to run into the street, his contributory negligence would serve as a defense for Driscoll. In deciding whether the conduct of a child was unreasonable, it is compared to that of the reasonable child of the same age, experience, and intelligence. Since this is usually a jury question, it is impossible to tell whether this argument would result in a judgment for Driscoll. It is the only argument listed, however, which could possibly lead to such a result.

Once popular, the impact rule provided that a plaintiff could not recover for mental suffering resulting from the defendant's negligence unless the suffering had been caused by some physical impact. Few jurisdictions continue to apply it. Even in this small minority, however, the impact rule would not apply to Palermo's claim since the claim is for *physical*, not mental, harm. **B** is, therefore, incorrect. Sometimes it is said that a defendant owes no duty of reasonable care to persons located outside the foreseeable zone of physical danger. If Driscoll was negligent, however, it was in the way he drove his car before Richey ran out from the street to rescue Palermo. Thus, the fact that Richey removed Palermo from the zone of physical danger would not prevent Driscoll from being liable for the proximate results of his negligence. **C** is, therefore, incorrect. A defendant owes a plaintiff a duty of reasonable care if the defendant's conduct creates a foreseeable risk to the plaintiff. Sometimes, in deciding whether a defendant whose conduct created a foreseeable risk to someone owed a duty of reasonable care to the plaintiff who was attempting to rescue that endangered person, courts have held that because "danger invites rescue" the coming of a rescuer is foreseeable. For this reason, it is said, if the defendant's conduct created the foreseeable risk that a person would need rescue, the defendant owes a duty of reasonable care to the rescuer. **D** is incorrect because, although this argument could be used to justify the conclusion that Driscoll owed Richey a duty of reasonable care, it cannot logically be used to justify the conclusion that Driscoll did not owe Palermo (or anyone else) such a duty.

145. **C**   The Fifth Amendment to the United States Constitution provides that no person shall for the same offense be placed twice in jeopardy of life or limb. In general, this prevents a person from being tried twice for the same crime. Since Dahn has already been tried, the subsequent prosecution violates this constitutional protection. **C** is correct for this reason, and because none of the reasons listed in the other options is sufficient to result in a denial of her motion.

In order for the protection against double jeopardy to be violated by prosecution for a crime, it must be found that the defendant has already been in danger (i.e., jeopardy) of losing her liberty as a result of a prosecution for the same crime and that the danger has ended. If the danger to Dahn which was created by the first prosecution has ended, subsequent prosecution would place her in danger again, thus violating the Double Jeopardy Clause. **A** is, therefore, incorrect. It is sometimes argued that a reversal based on a legal flaw in the trial results in the conclusion that the trial was a nullity, and that jeopardy, therefore, never attached in the first place. If this were so, subsequent prosecution would not violate the Double Jeopardy Clause because Dahn was never in danger as a result of the previous prosecution. **B** is incorrect, however, because the reversal by the appellate court was not based on a legal flaw, but on insufficiency of the evidence which is equivalent to an acquittal after trial. Usually a convicted defendant who appeals her conviction thereby waives the constitutional protection against double jeopardy. A reversal based on insufficiency of the evidence, however, indicates that the initial trial should have resulted in an acquittal which would have barred re-prosecution, and so in such a case the defendant does not waive her rights under the Double Jeopardy Clause. **D** is, therefore, incorrect.

146. **A**   Under the Supremacy Clause of Article VI of the United States Constitution, a state law is invalid if it is inconsistent with a valid federal law covering the same subject matter. It is easy to decide whether a state law which specifically contradicts a federal law is invalid under the Supremacy Clause. It becomes more difficult when, as here, the state law prohibits something which the federal law does not mention at all. The fact that the federal law is silent about use of the telephone solicitation computer might mean that Congress has permitted its use by not prohibiting it. It could also mean, however, that Congress deliberately left the matter to regulation by the states. In deciding which conclusion to draw, it is necessary to determine congressional intent. This can be done by examining the policy expressed in the existing federal regulations. Since the text of those regulations is not given, it is impossible to decide whether the argument set forth in **A** would lead to the conclusion suggested by Saleco. Of all the arguments listed, however, **A** is the only one which might possibly support Saleco's position.

The powers of the states are not *enumerated* by the United States Constitution, but are understood to include all governmental powers which are not exclusively those of Congress. The Tenth Amendment *reserves* these powers to the states, but does not *enumerate* them. Thus, **B** could not be correct. A state law which discriminates against interstate commerce by withholding from out-of-staters commercial benefits which are available to state residents may be unconstitutional because it violates the Commerce Clause. **C** is incorrect, however, because the Champlain law prohibits use of the telephone solicitation computer within the state by anyone. A state law may also be unconstitutional because it violates the Commerce Clause by imposing an undue burden on interstate commerce. If the state law made it more expensive to call from outside the state than from inside the state, it might be imposing such a burden. **D** is incorrect, however, because the state law does not regulate telephone rates. **C** and **D** are also incorrect because, although a state may not make the cost of doing business higher for non-residents than for residents, there is no reason why it cannot make the cost of doing business in the state higher than the cost of doing business in other states. (e.g., A state income tax law makes the cost of doing business in the state higher than the cost of doing business in a state which does not have such a law or which has a lower tax rate. A state law requiring the purchase of a business license or the filing of a business certificate also has such an effect.)

147. **D**   Expression with a primarily commercial purpose may be regulated so long as the regulation directly advances a substantial government interest by the least burdensome means necessary. Whether protecting the public against annoyance by computerized telephone calls is a substantial government interest, and whether the prohibition against the use of the telephone solicitation computer within the state directly advances that interest are two questions open to debate. If the answer to either question is "no," the statute violates the First Amendment. It is far from certain that a court would come to this conclusion, but the argument set forth in **D** is the only one listed which could possibly support Saleco's position.

Because of the importance of free expression, the rules of standing are ordinarily relaxed for First Amendment challenges based on a claim of overbreadth. Thus, a person whose speech can be constitutionally punished may challenge the constitutionality of a statute which punishes it on the ground that the statute is "overbroad" in that it also punishes speech which cannot be constitutionally punished. The purpose of this rule is to prevent the "chilling" of First Amendment rights by state regulations. Since it is believed that advertisers are unlikely to be chilled by such regulations, however, this rule does not apply in commercial speech cases. **A** is, therefore, incorrect. The selection of a standard to be applied in deciding the constitutional validity of a law regulating expression may depend on whether the regulation is content-related. This fact alone, however, is never sufficient to justify the conclusion that the regulation is invalid. **B** is, therefore, incorrect. A statute is said to have a "chilling" effect on freedom of expression if its terms are so unclear that the reasonable person could not tell what forms of expression are prohibited, and might, therefore, be afraid to engage in unprohibited forms of expression. Although the high cost of using telephone solicitation computers outside the state to call numbers inside the state might discourage people from doing so, this will not be because they are uncertain about what expression the law forbids. Thus, the law cannot be said to have a chilling effect for this reason, making **C** incorrect.

148. **A**   Under the parol evidence rule, extrinsic evidence of prior agreements or negotiations is not admissible to contradict or modify an unambiguous written contract which the parties intended as a complete expression of their agreement. The rule does not prevent the use of extrinsic evidence for other purposes, however. Virtually all jurisdictions permit its use to show that the written contract is ambiguous and to clear up the ambiguity. Since the phrase "all fuel ordered by the Department of Transportation" might mean all the fuel which the Department chooses to order from Petrol, or all the fuel which the Department orders at all during that period, the contract is probably ambiguous on its face. If it is not ambiguous on its face, the fact that the advertisement calling for bids indicated that the contract would be exclusive tends to show an ambiguity since it might mean that the parties intended Petrol to be the exclusive supplier even though the written contract does not specifically say so. The advertisement is probably admissible for this reason. Although it is not certain that a court would come to this conclusion, the argument set forth in **A** is the only one listed which might provide Petrol with an effective response to the Department of Transportation's objection.

         B is incorrect because the parol evidence rule may prevent the admission of extrinsic evidence, whether it is oral or written. **C** and **D** are incorrect because the parol evidence rule excludes extrinsic evidence of statements made prior to and during negotiations if offered to modify the terms of an unambiguous written contract.

149. **C**   At common law, priorities were determined by the dates of the transactions involved. The person who received his interest first had priority over all others. In all jurisdictions in the United States, recording statutes have modified the common law rule. Under the statute given (typical of the "notice" variety) an unrecorded interest does not defeat the rights of a subsequent taker for value and without notice. Since Benedict received the property as a gift (i.e., did not give value), however, he is not protected by the statute. For this reason, the interest of Marcus, since it was created before that of Benedict, has priority over it. Since Marcus did give value for his interest, and since the facts do not indicate that he was aware of Amaro's interest, Marcus is protected by the recording statute. Under the statute, Amaro's interest is not good against Marcus, since Amaro's

deed was not recorded. Thus, the interest of Marcus has priority, and Marcus is entitled to foreclose.

Although Marcus did not record his mortgage, it has priority over Benedict's interest because Benedict — not having given value — is not protected by the recording statute. Under the statute, the interest of Marcus — which is protected by the recording statute — has priority over the previously created interest of Amaro because Amaro's interest was unrecorded when Marcus received the mortgage. **A** is, therefore, incorrect. **B** is incorrect because Benedict is not protected by the recording statute for the reasons given above. Since Marcus's interest is superior to Amaro's under the recording statute, Amaro's interest is subject to the mortgage held by Marcus. **D** is, therefore, incorrect.

150. **A** Pace's allegation that the vehicle was defective means that her claim is based on the theory of strict liability in tort. Assumption of the risk may be raised as an effective defense to such a claim. Since a plaintiff assumes the risk when she voluntarily encounters a danger of which she knows, Pace may have assumed the risk by driving with the knowledge that the seat belt warning indicator light was not working.

B is incorrect because a product might be defective even though it does not violate a safety statute. If Pace would have ignored the seat belt warning indicator light, its failure to operate was not a factual cause of her harm, and Dartmouth Motors could not be liable for her injury. Factual cause is a question of fact for the jury, however, and a plaintiff only needs to prove it by a fair preponderance of the evidence. Thus, even if Pace cannot prove *with certainty* that she would have worn the seat belt had the indicator been working, she may still win her case if the jury finds it more likely than not that she would have. **C** is, therefore, incorrect. A professional seller who supplies a defective product is strictly liable for resulting harm whether or not the defect resulted from that seller's fault. **D** is, therefore, incorrect.

151. **A** The use of the word "unless" in this clause establishes a fee simple determinable on special limitation. An important characteristic of this estate is that it terminates automatically upon the happening of the event specified in the limitation. Unless the conveyance creates a future interest in another grantee, the termination of a fee simple determinable causes the estate to revert to the grantor or his successors. Thus, under the clause in option (A) the realty will revert to Ortega or to his heirs as soon as a possessor begins to make the physical changes which Ortega is trying to avoid. Since the rule against perpetuities does not apply to interests of the grantor, it does not operate to invalidate this reversion.

The phrase "but if" in options **B** and **C** creates a fee simple subject to a condition subsequent. It would give Dawn the power to terminate Sander's estate by taking action upon the happening of the specified event. Under the rule against perpetuities, no interest is good unless it must vest, if at all, within a period of time measured by a life or lives in being plus 21 years. Since it is possible that the event would occur outside that period (e.g., Sander and Dawn could die the day after the conveyance and the house could be painted green 22 years later), the interest of Dawn and her heirs might vest outside the prescribed period. Since Dawn's power to terminate is void, Sander's interest would not be subject to it, and would, therefore, be absolute. **B** and **C** are, therefore, incorrect. Since **D** would place no restrictions on Sander's use of the property, it would not prevent him from physically changing the house during his lifetime or painting it a color other than white. **D** is, therefore, incorrect.

152. **A**   A direct restraint on alienation is a covenant or condition which attempts to control the alienability of the estate granted. A disabling restraint purports to withhold the grantee's power to alienate. A promissory restraint consists of a covenant not to alienate. It does not withhold the covenantor's power to alienate, but subjects the covenantor to liability for damages for breaching the covenant by alienating. A forfeitural restraint terminates the estate upon an attempt to alienate it, causing the property to vest in someone else. Direct restraints on the alienation of *fee simple* estates are generally void and unenforceable, whether they are disabling, promissory, or forfeiturial. While disabling restraints on the alienation of life estates are similarly void, promissory or forfeiturial restraints on the alienation of *life estates* may be valid if reasonable. From the language of Ortega's will it is difficult to determine whether the restraint which it creates is disabling or forfeiturial. The argument presented in **A** is the only one listed, however, which might possibly support Sander's claim.

B and **C** are incorrect because promissory and forfeiturial restraints on the alienation of life estates may be enforceable. **D** is incorrect in spite of the 40-year period which it specifies, because Sander could not possibly alienate his interest except during his own lifetime. Thus, the vesting of Dawn's interest could not possibly occur beyond a period measured by a life in being (Sander's) plus 21 years, making the rule against perpetuities inapplicable to it.

153. **C**   An admission is a declaration by a party offered against that party. Under the common law, admissions are admissible as exceptions to the hearsay rule; under FRE 801(d)(2), admissions are not hearsay. Matters to which a party has stipulated on the record are known as "judicial admissions" and are conclusive in the proceeding in which they were made. Since PiCo specified that the information contained in *The Commercial Journal* was to be used as its response to Dee Corp's interrogatories, the appropriate portions of *The Commercial Journal* may be regarded as a judicial admission.

A is, therefore, incorrect. **B** is incorrect because an admission is either admissible hearsay (under common law) or not hearsay at all (under the FRE). A court may take judicial notice of facts contained in a reference work which is shown to be a reputable source beyond reasonable dispute. Since the portions of *The Commercial Journal* are admissible as admissions, however, judicial notice is not the *only* way that they would be admissible. **D** is, therefore, incorrect.

154. **C**   Murder is the unlawful killing of a human being with malice aforethought. Among other things, malice aforethought may consist of the intent to cause serious bodily harm or of a reckless disregard for human life. Stabbing with a knife is evidence of both these states of mind. Therefore, if Danico's stabbing of Hamilton proximately caused Hamilton's death, it was probably murder. An act is a proximate cause of death if it was a factual and legal cause of the death. Denico's act was a factual cause of Hamilton's death because Hamilton's death would not have occurred without it. Conduct is a legal cause of death if the death was a foreseeable result of it, and if there were no superseding intervening causes. Wilma's conduct was also a cause of Hamilton's death, since Hamilton's death would not have occurred if Wilma had secured medical attention. Further,

her failure to do so was an intervening cause of Hamilton's death because it came after Danico's act and before Hamilton's death. If Wilma's conduct was unforeseeable, it can be called a superseding intervening cause of death. Under the definition given above, this would prevent Danico's conduct from being a legal (or proximate) cause.

As indicated above, Danico's conduct was a factual cause of Hamilton's death, since the death would not have occurred if Danico had not stabbed Hamilton. Wilma's failure to secure prompt medical attention was also a factual cause of Hamilton's death, since it would not have occurred if she had secured prompt medical attention. Any result may have several causes; the fact that Wilma's conduct was a cause does not establish that Danico's was not. **A** is, therefore, incorrect. If Hamilton's death was an unforeseeable result of Danico's act, Danico's act was not a proximate cause of it. "Foreseeable," however, means that which the reasonable person would anticipate. Thus, even an unusual result may be foreseeable. For this reason, the fact that leg wounds do not usually cause death does not necessarily justify the conclusion that Hamilton's death was an unforeseeable result of Danico's act. **B** is, therefore, incorrect. If Wilma's conduct was a substantial factor in producing Hamilton's death, it was a factual cause of that death. Any result may have several proximate causes, however. **D** is incorrect because Danico's act was also a cause of Hamilton's death.

155. **B** Failing to perform a particular act cannot be a crime unless there existed some legal duty to perform that act. Ordinarily, no person owes to another a legal duty to protect him from harm or to secure medical attention when he needs it. Thus, unless the law in the jurisdiction imposed such a duty on Wilma, her failure to secure medical attention for Hamilton cannot be murder.

A is incorrect because any result may have several proximate causes; thus finding that Danico's conduct was a proximate cause does not establish that Wilma's was not. Malice aforethought may consist of an intent (i.e., desire or substantial certainty) that serious bodily harm will result from defendant's act, or a reckless disregard for human life. Since Wilma's conduct may evidence both these states of mind, the fact that she did not know that death would result is not, alone, sufficient to prevent her from being guilty of murder. **C** is, therefore, incorrect. **D** is incorrect because, even if she knew that Hamilton was in need of medical attention, Wilma's failure to secure it could not be murder unless she was under a legal duty to do so.

156. **C** Unless it involves a fundamental right (i.e., voting, or marriage and procreation) or discriminates on the basis of a suspect classification, state regulation of social or economic interests is valid if it has a rational basis. Since the United States Supreme Court has held that age is not a suspect classification, the state mandatory retirement law is valid if it has a rational basis. Under this test, if any state of facts can be imagined that would make the legislative choice a reasonable way to achieve a legitimate legislative purpose, the law will be upheld. Since providing state employees with the best insurance protection at the lowest cost is a legitimate legislative purpose, the mandatory retirement law probably has a rational basis which makes it valid. (**Note:** Although it is possible to conclude that the law does not have a rational basis because mandatory retirement is not a reasonable means of achieving this objective, **C** is the only answer which could possibly be correct.)

Under the Supremacy Clause a state law is invalid if it conflicts with a valid federal law covering the same subject matter. Since the federal law fixes the retirement age for federal employees, and the state of DelMara law fixes the retirement age for state employees, the two laws do not cover the same subject matter and are therefore not inconsistent with each other. **A** is, thus, incorrect. A law may have a rational basis even though its application to one particular person does not advance its objective. Thus, if many other state jobs require skills or abilities which are related to age, the fact that Robello's does not will not be sufficient to invalidate the law. **B** is, therefore, incorrect. **D** is too general a statement to be correct; the federal government may impose some economic burdens on the states (e.g., may tax certain state activities).

157. **A** Article I Section 10 of the United States Constitution prohibits the states from passing laws impairing the obligation of contracts. This prevents a state from unjustifiably repudiating its own contractual obligations or interfering with the contract rights of individuals. If Robello was a state employee prior to the time the mandatory retirement law was passed, the state of DelMara owed him certain obligations under the employment contract. Under the laws which then existed, these included the obligations to grant an annual salary increase and to pay a retirement pension based on the salary he earned the year immediately prior to this retirement. Accompanying all contract obligations is the implied warranty that the promisor will not willfully prevent the promisee from enjoying the benefits thereunder. By mandating retirement at 65, the state has prevented Robello from further increasing his annual salary and thus increasing the amount of his retirement pension. Since he had this right under the employment contract which existed prior to passage of the mandatory retirement law, the law may be held to impair an obligation of contracts.

On the other hand, unless Robello was a state employee prior to the passage of the mandatory retirement law, he has no contractual expectation of continued employment after 65. This is true even though he undertook financial obligations in contemplation of continued employment, because although he might have detrimentally relied on that expectation, such reliance was not justified. **B** is, therefore, incorrect. The fact that Robello was fit for continued employment after the age of 65 would not result in a finding that the mandatory retirement law impairs the obligation of contracts because his fitness did not create a contractual expectation unless he was employed prior to passage of the law. **C** and **D** are, therefore incorrect.

158. **B** When, after the formation of the contract and prior to the date of performance, an unforeseeable event occurs which makes performance of a contractual obligation impossible, the doctrine of impossibility discharges that obligation. Thus, if it was unforeseeable that Megahog would contract boarsitis, Swiney's contractual duty to exhibit him at the Agricultural Exposition would be discharged. While the facts do not indicate whether or not it was foreseeable that Megahog would contract the disease, impossibility of performance is the only concept listed which could possibly provide Swiney with an effective defense.

Rescission results when the contracting parties mutually agree to release each other from further obligations under the contract. Since Fair did not agree to release Swiney, there could not have been a rescission. **A** is, therefore, incorrect. Frustration of purpose is frequently confused with impossibility of performance, but differs from it substantially. When performance is possible but an unforeseeable change in circumstances destroys the underlying reasons for it, the doctrine of frustration may discharge the duty to perform. (For example, if Megahog did not become ill, but on the day of the Agricultural Exposition there was a rainstorm so severe that no one attended the Agricultural Exposition, the doctrine of frustration might relieve either or both parties from performing because although the performance was still possible, there was no longer any purpose for it.) Since the underlying purpose for Megahog's exhibition continued to exist, the doctrine of frustration of purpose does not apply, and **C** is incorrect. A prospective inability to perform occurs when a party divests himself of the power to perform. Its effect is to relieve *the other party* of obligations under the contract. The concept is not applicable here for two reasons: first, Swiney did not divest himself of the ability to perform; and, second, it is Swiney and not Fair who seeks to be excused from performance. **D** is, therefore, incorrect.

159. **A**   There are various theories which might exclude performance because of a change in circumstances, but all require that the change in circumstances be unforeseeable at the time the contract was formed. If Swiney knew on May 1 that many hogs in the area had contracted boarsitis, it was probably foreseeable to him that Megahog would contract it also. If Megahog's disease was foreseeable to Swiney, it would not excuse his performance under any theory.

There are various theories which might exclude performance because of a change in circumstances.

If performance required by a contract becomes illegal after the contract is formed, both parties are excused from further performance. Thus, if the state Department of Livestock issued an order prohibiting the exhibition of Megahog, Swiney would be excused from exhibiting him, and the court would find *against* Fair. **B** is, therefore, incorrect. **C** is incorrect because the contract called for the exhibition of Megahog, and not merely for the exhibition of a hog with Megahog's qualities. **D** is incorrect because if the change of circumstances which resulted in Fair's loss was unforeseeable, Fair cannot collect for that loss even if it can be established with particularity.

160. **B**   An intervening cause is an event without which the accident would not have occurred, and which took place after the defendant's negligence. Dain's encounter with the pothole was, thus, an intervening cause of the collision. A superseding cause is an unforeseeable intervening cause. In this context, the word "unforeseeable" may be used to mean either something which the reasonable person would not have anticipated, or something which in retrospect appears to have been extraordinary. If potholes are frequently found on road surfaces in the area, the presence of the pothole was foreseeable (in either sense of the word), and could not have been a superseding cause of harm.

A is incorrect because although violation of a statute may establish that the defendant was negligent, it does not establish that the defendant's conduct was causally related to the plaintiff's injury. A superseding cause may relieve a defendant of liability by justifying the conclusion that his conduct was not a legal cause of harm, whether or not the person responsible for the superseding cause can be required to compensate the plaintiff. Thus, Dain's liability does not depend on whether the Department of Highway Transportation is liable for its negligence or on whether governmental immunity has been abolished. **C** is, therefore, incorrect. The fact that the accident would not have occurred without the pothole proves that the pothole was one of its factual causes. Unless the presence of the pothole was an unforeseeable intervening cause, however, it was not a superseding cause of Parnell's harm, and would not relieve Parnell of liability.

161. **D**   The majority of jurisdictions recognize a client's privilege to prevent disclosure of a confidential communication which she made to her attorney while seeking legal advice even before retaining her. In addition, the privilege applies to confidences which the client communicates to an agent of the attorney in connection with the subject of the attorney-client relationship. Since Caswell's communication with Ander was at Larkin's request to enable Larkin to make decisions relative to her representation of Caswell, it is protected by the attorney-client privilege.

A document prepared by or for an attorney which contains the attorney's mental impressions may be privileged as an attorney's work product. **A** is incorrect, however, because the conversation between Caswell and Ander was not a document and did not contain Larkin's mental impressions. **B** is incorrect because there is no rule of privilege which protects records kept in the course of business simply because of that fact. (**Note:** Records kept in the course of business are sometimes *admissible* under an exception to the hearsay rule.) An admission is a declaration by a party which is offered against that party. Under common law, admissions are admissible hearsay; under FRE 801(d)(2), admissions are not hearsay at all. Since Defcorp seeks to offer Caswell's statements against Caswell, they cannot be classified as inadmissible hearsay. **C** is, therefore, incorrect.

162. **B**   A tenant who vacates leased premises is said to have abandoned them. Abandonment prior to the expiration of a lease does not terminate the tenant's obligation to pay rent unless the landlord relets on the tenant's account. A landlord is not obligated to do so, however. Thus, the continuing vacancy of the premises for the balance of the lease term results in a continuing obligation by Thies to pay rent — $2,000 per month for four months, or $8,000.

If Larsen had relet, Thies might argue that he is thus relieved of the obligation to pay for the balance of the term. Larsen's conveyance to Barash does not have that effect, however, since the premises remained vacant. (**Note:** It is common for the grantor of leased property to assign to the grantee the right to receive rents. Even without an express assignment, the grantee will probably acquire this benefit since it runs with the land. If, for any reason, the right to receive rent does not pass to the grantee, the tenant will be required to continue paying it to the original lessor.) **A** is, therefore, incorrect. Since the lease called for payment of the rent in money (i.e., $2,000 per month) the lessor is not required to accept payment in any other form. Thus, Thies cannot require his landlord to accept the storage building in lieu of rent. **C** and **D** are, therefore, incorrect.

163. **D**   Under the doctrine of accession, the owner of realty becomes the owner, as well, of anything which becomes part of it. Thus, if the storage building has become part of the realty, Thies may not remove it. Unless the parties agree, however, the decision as to whether the building has become part of (i.e., annexed to) the realty can only be made by a court. **I** is incorrect because the landlord does not have the power to decide it unilaterally. **II** is incorrect because if the building has become part of (i.e., annexed to) the realty, the landlord is already its owner by accession, and cannot be required to pay for it.

164. **B** Public nuisance is a tortious invasion of some right of the general public. Ordinarily, the public is the plaintiff, and the claim is asserted on its behalf by the public attorney. A private individual may assert a public nuisance claim on his own behalf only when a public nuisance has caused him to sustain harm which is different in kind from the harm sustained by the general public. Since Tena's harm did not differ from that sustained by the general public, his claim for public nuisance should fail. **B** would, therefore, be an effective argument in Agriprod's defense.

In determining whether a particular activity is appropriate to the location, courts sometimes consider how long it has been conducted there. However, the fact that a defendant was engaging in an offensive activity before the plaintiff arrived is not, by itself, sufficient to permit the defendant to continue engaging in that activity. For this reason, "coming to the nuisance" is not an effective defense, and **A** is incorrect. In the final analysis, the standards of proper behavior in a particular industry are determined by the courts, not by the members of that industry. Therefore, the fact that all members of the insecticide industry act in a particular way is not sufficient to prevent that conduct from being tortious. **C** is, therefore, incorrect. **D** is incorrect because a public nuisance may be committed by interfering with the public comfort or convenience, despite the fact that no physical damage occurs.

165. **C** Private nuisance is a tortious interference with the plaintiff's right to use and enjoy real property in which he has a present or future possessory interest. In effect, a plaintiff suing a defendant for private nuisance is claiming that the defendant's use of its realty unreasonably violates the plaintiff's right to use his realty. For this reason, in deciding a claim for private nuisance the courts must balance the rights of the plaintiff and defendant in an attempt to determine which right is more worthy of protection. In doing so courts consider many factors including the relative importance of the plaintiff's and the defendant's activity, the appropriateness of each to the location, and the ability of each to avoid the harm complained of. Because Larvaway is an important agricultural product, the fact that it cannot be manufactured without producing bad smells could lead a court to conclude that the production of bad smells is not a nuisance. It is by no means certain that a court would come to this conclusion, but of all the additional facts listed, **C** is the only one which might result in a judgment for Agriprod.

There was a time when a 1,000 mile distance might have made it impossible for farmers to obtain the insecticide from other manufacturers. Then, in balancing the rights of Agriprod against those of Tena, a court might have concluded that the importance of Agriprod's activity outweighed the importance of Tena's, and that the manufacture of Larvaway was, therefore, not a nuisance. Modern transportation makes that argument unpersuasive, however. **A** is, therefore, incorrect. **B** is incorrect because a tenant (i.e., the holder of a leasehold interest) has sufficient possessory interest in realty to maintain an action for private nuisance against one who interferes with his right to use or enjoy it. A private individual may not maintain an action for public nuisance unless his harm is substantially different from that sustained by the general public. No such requirement is imposed on the plaintiff in a private nuisance action, however. He must show only that the defendant tortiously interfered with his right to use and enjoy his realty. **D** is, therefore, incorrect.

166. **B** Ordinarily a relevant object is admissible into evidence if a witness testifies that she rec-

ognizes it. Because writings are particularly subject to fraud, however, special rules have developed regarding their admission. Where the legal significance of a writing depends upon its authorship, the writing cannot be admitted unless the court (i.e., judge) finds that there is sufficient evidence to warrant a finding regarding its authorship. Here, for example, the court may have to decide whether there was sufficient evidence that the witness knew Dakin's signature.

Unless the court determines that there has been sufficient authentication the jury should not be given an opportunity to see the document. **A** is, therefore, incorrect. FRE 901(b)(3) and the common law permit the jury to consider an authenticated exemplar of a party's signature in determining whether a document in question was signed by the party. **C** is incorrect, however, because this is not the *only* way of getting the promissory note before the jury. **D** is incorrect because once the court determines that there is sufficient evidence to justify a finding by the jury regarding the genuineness of a signature, the question of whether it actually is genuine is one of fact for the jury.

167. **C**   Hearsay is defined as an out-of-court statement offered for the purpose of proving the truth of the matter asserted in that statement. The language of a promissory note creates an indebtedness. It is offered into evidence for the purpose of establishing that indebtedness (i.e., for its independent legal significance), not for the purpose of establishing the truth of any facts which it incidentally communicates. For this reason, it is not hearsay.

A is incorrect because there is no indication that the note was prepared in the regular course of business, which is one of the requirements of a business record. Under the best evidence rule, secondary evidence to prove the terms of a writing is not admissible unless the writing itself is shown to be unavailable. This rule is thus a rule of exclusion. Although it may prevent the admission of a document which is not an original, it does not keep an original document from being hearsay, or permit the admission of an original document which is inadmissible for other reasons. **B** is, therefore, incorrect. If an out-of-court statement is offered to prove the truth of a matter which it asserts, it is hearsay. The fact that the declarant (i.e., the person who made the statement) is in court does not prevent it from being hearsay or permit its admission. **D** is, therefore, incorrect.

168. **B**   A statute which establishes a system of classification which discriminates against members of a particular ethnic group may violate the Equal Protection Clause of the Fourteenth Amendment to the U.S. Constitution. Even if a statute does not establish such a system of classification, however, it may be enforced in a way which makes it unconstitutional *as applied.* In determining whether the *application* of a statute violates the Equal Protection Clause, the United States Supreme Court has examined statistical evidence that the statute is being enforced in a discriminatory manner. Since the fact that 100 percent of Olander's speeding tickets were issued to members of an ethnic minority constituting only ten percent of the population suggests a discriminatory application of the speed limit statute, that fact furnishes effective support for Churchill's assertion.

On the other hand, the fact that Churchill has received such summonses only from Olander does not indicate a discriminatory application of the statute by Olander unless it is coupled with information about other summonses issued by Olander. **A** is incorrect for this reason, and because three incidents are probably not enough to justify any generalization. Coupled with the facts in option **B**, the facts in option **C** might support the conclusion that discrimination was behind the apparent inequity in Olander's issuing of speeding tickets. Standing alone, however, the fact that members of Churchill's minority do not drive any differently from members of other groups does nothing to show that the summons was issued to Churchill on a discriminatory basis. **C** is, therefore, incorrect. It is, of course, physically impossible for a police officer to apprehend all violators of a particular statute. This means that some will be apprehended while others will not. For this reason, the fact that one member of a particular ethnic group was apprehended while some persons who did not belong to that ethnic group were not apprehended is not, alone, sufficient to indicate that the apprehension of Churchill was the result of discrimination. **D** is, therefore, incorrect.

169. **A**   Criminal battery consists of the intentional, reckless, or criminally negligent application of force to the body of another person. One who knows that he often becomes intoxicated upon drinking small quantities of alcoholic beverage may be guilty of recklessness or criminal negligence by drinking half a glass of beer in the company of other people. Since this is all the mens rea required for a battery conviction, the fact that it was the alcohol which made Dafoe become violent would not be relevant to any material issue in the case. For this reason, the psychiatrist's testimony should be excluded.

The psychiatrist's testimony had no bearing on Dafoe's sanity under any definition of that term currently applied in the United States, but might be admissible for some other reason. **B** is, therefore, incorrect. **C** is incorrect because criminal battery may be committed recklessly or criminally negligently without the intent to injure (i.e., criminal battery is a general intent crime). A defendant's intoxication is involuntary if the intoxicant was taken against his will or without knowledge of its intoxicating properties. Since Dafoe was aware that even a small quantity of alcohol could intoxicate him, he cannot be said to have become intoxicated involuntarily. The psychiatrist's testimony would simply confirm what Dafoe already knew about himself when he drank the beer, and, therefore, could not establish that the intoxication was involuntary. **D** is, therefore, incorrect.

170. **D**   A person is guilty of a criminal attempt when with the specific intent to bring about a result which is criminally prohibited, he comes substantially close to achieving that result. Thus, although murder can be committed without the intent to kill, attempted murder cannot. If a defendant was unaware that his conduct could cause death, he cannot be guilty of attempted murder. This is true even though it was his voluntary intoxication which prevented him from being aware of the dangers which his conduct created. Since the psychiatrist's testimony indicates that Dafoe might not have been aware that his conduct could result in danger to the bartender, it is relevant to material issues in his trial and should be admitted.

A, B and **C** are incorrect because if intoxication (even voluntary intoxication) deprived a defendant of the ability to form the specific intent required for guilt, he cannot be convicted.

171. **B**   In order to be enforceable, a contract must be definite and certain in all its basic terms. One way of determining whether a purported agreement is sufficiently definite and certain is to ask whether its terms make it possible for a court to fashion a remedy for its breach. Most of the time, this requires that the agreement identify the parties, and show

that they have agreed to the subject matter, the time for performance, and the price. The writing between Babcock and Sandag leaves the price to be determined by a later agreement. But if the parties have not agreed as to how that subsequently-to-be-agreed-on price shall be determined, there is no way that a court could fashion a remedy for its breach. The writing would thus fail because it is not sufficiently definite and certain.

The Statute of Frauds requires that an agreement to transfer an interest in real estate be in writing. A writing might satisfy its requirements even though it does not specify a price, so long as it indicates the method which the parties have agreed to use in setting the price. For example, if the parties have agreed to set "a reasonable price" in the future, the writing might satisfy the Statute of Frauds even though it does not specify what the price will be. **A** is, therefore, incorrect. **C** is incorrect because the parties did not agree to be bound by the objective value of the property even if it could be determined. **D** is incorrect for two reasons: first, the UCC provision which deems an omitted price term to call for a reasonable price applies only to transactions in goods; and, second, this contract did not omit the price term, but provided that it would be set by mutual agreement in the future.

172. **D**   A person is guilty of an attempt when with the intent to bring about a result which is criminally prohibited, she commits some act which brings her substantially close to accomplishing that result. If the result which Dacon intended is criminally prohibited, and if Dacon came substantially close to accomplishing it, she is guilty of attempting it. If an exam answer is "information" as defined by the statute, its theft would be a crime whether Dacon knew it or not. Similarly, if she intended to steal it and came substantially close to doing so, she is guilty of an attempt to violate the statute even though she did not know that what she was attempting to do was a crime.

A person may be guilty of attempting to commit a crime, even though facts unknown to her would have made successful completion of the crime impossible. **A** is, therefore, incorrect. As a matter of policy, all persons are irrebuttably presumed to know the law. Thus a defense cannot be based on the defendant's ignorance of the statute which prohibits her conduct (i.e., ignorance of the law is no excuse). **B** is, therefore, incorrect. Since criminal attempt requires the intent to bring about a result which is criminally prohibited, a person cannot be guilty simply because the result which she intended to achieve was immoral. **C** is, therefore, incorrect.

173. **B**   Battery is intentional harmful or offensive contact with the plaintiff. An unauthorized contact is offensive. Since Platt's fall (i.e., contact with the floor) was unauthorized, the requirement of offensive contact is clearly satisfied. Dudley's liability therefore depends on whether he had the necessary intent. In a battery case, a defendant has the necessary intent if he knows to a substantial degree of certainty that harmful or offensive contact will result from his volitional act. Thus, unless Dudley knew that Platt would fall, he could not be liable for battery.

A is incorrect because intent requires knowledge to a substantial degree of certainty, and a risk which is merely foreseeable does not satisfy that requirement. **C** is incorrect because if there was an offensive contact, battery does not require that any physical injury result from it. If Dudley was substantially certain that an offensive (i.e., unauthorized) contact would occur, he will be liable for the results of that offensive contact, even though he was not substantially certain that those particular results would occur. **D** is incorrect because Dudley's knowledge that Platt would fall makes him liable for the embarrassment which resulted, even if he lacked knowledge that embarrassment would result.

174. **D**   Intentional infliction of emotional distress requires outrageous behavior which intentionally results in severe mental suffering. Some jurisdictions require that the mental suffering produce physical manifestations; some do not. All require, however, that the mental suffering be severe. Since the facts indicate that Platt was merely embarrassed, Dudley may argue that Platt's suffering was not sufficiently severe to result in liability.

If Dudley desired or knew that mental suffering would result from his volitional act, he had the necessary state of mind to satisfy the intent requirement for his tort, even if his motive was not a hostile one. **A** is incorrect because Dudley may have had the necessary intent, even though his motive was to play a joke. Since intent may consist of knowledge that mental suffering will result, the fact that Dudley did not desire to produce it is not sufficient to establish that he lacked the requisite intent. **B** is, therefore, incorrect. **C** is incorrect because, although apprehension is an essential element of assault, it is not an essential element of intentional infliction of emotional distress.

175. **D**   The right of survivorship is the best-known characteristic of a joint tenancy. It means that if one of the joint tenants dies, the survivor becomes the owner of the deceased tenant's share. Thus, if Bert died while he and Sally were joint tenants, Sally would have become the sole owner of the realty. When a joint tenant conveys his interest, however, the joint tenancy is severed, and his grantee becomes a tenant in common with the remaining co-owner. Tenants in common do not have a right of survivorship. Since a quitclaim conveys the grantor's interest, Bert's quitclaim to Wilba severed his joint tenancy with Sally, and made Wilma and Sally tenants in common. When Sally died, Dot inherited Sally's interest, thus becoming a tenant in common with Wilba.

A and **B** are incorrect for the reasons given above. **C** is incorrect because Bert's quitclaim to Wilba severed the joint tenancy.

176. **A**   Article IV, Section 2, paragraph 2 of the United States Constitution contains what is known as the Property Clause: "Congress shall have power to dispose of and make all needful rules and regulations respecting … property belonging to the United States." The United States Supreme Court has held that the Property Clause leaves the lease or other disposition of federal property within the discretion of Congress.

Although the Commerce Clause gives Congress the power to regulate interstate commerce, **B** is incorrect because there is no fact indicating that the lease of grazing land was for that purpose or would have that effect. A person has standing to assert a constitutional challenge if he is faced with some actual or immediately threatened concrete harm which the court could avoid by granting the relief requested. If the low rate will cause Realty Corporation to lose revenue, it faces an immediately threatened concrete harm. If the court declares the federal lease unconstitutional, the problems created by competition with the federal government will be solved, and the harm will be averted. **C** is, therefore, incorrect. This proceeding challenges the constitutionality of the action of Congress and the agency to which it delegated power. The authority of Congress and the federal government is limited by the Constitution. If the federal government were immune from such a challenge, constitutional limitations on its exercise of power would be meaningless. Whether the federal government is immune from tort claims based on allegations of unfair competition is irrelevant. **D** is, therefore, incorrect.

177. **C**   A claim has become moot when there are no longer any contested questions essential for the disposition of the controversy. This might make it possible for a litigant to temporarily change its behavior, removing the apparent need to litigate the issues involved, then have the proceeding dismissed on the ground of mootness only to return to its old behavior immediately afterward. For this reason, it is generally understood that when an issue appears to have become moot as the result of the voluntary conduct of the party moving for dismissal, that party must show that there is no reasonable expectation that the wrong will be repeated. Since the Tall Grasslands Bureau has not done so, a court could properly decide to hear the case. While it is not certain that a court would come to this conclusion, **C** is the only argument listed which could possibly result in denial of the motion to dismiss.

Because of the case or controversy requirement of Article III of the United States Constitution, the fact that a claim raises an important question is not alone sufficient to justify hearing it if the issues have become moot. **A** is, therefore, incorrect. Sometimes the disposition of a claim is likely to have an effect on one of the parties which is *indirectly* related to the relief sought by the claimant (i.e., collateral consequences). If this is so, the claim may be heard, even though all issues connected with the relief which the claimant seeks have become moot. [For example, a person may appeal a criminal conviction even after serving the entire sentence, because the conviction may have resulted collaterally in loss of the right to vote or to obtain a driving license.] Since there is no fact indicating that the disposition of Realty Corporation's claim will have collateral consequences, however, this rule would not provide Realty Corporation with an effective opposition to the assertion that the claim has become moot. For this reason, **B** is incorrect. If no concrete harm has occurred or is immediately threatened, a claim is said to be unripe. If a claim has become ripe, but because of a change in circumstances there are no contested issues left to resolve, it is said to be moot. A claim never really becomes moot until after it has become ripe. For this reason, **D** is an absurdity, and, therefore, incorrect.

178. **A**   Milburn's promise to pay $250 is enforceable only if it is supported by consideration. Consideration is something of value — either benefit to promisor or detriment to promisee — given in exchange for the promise. Since Pattison promised not to make a claim for medical expenses against Stuart in return for Milburn's promise to pay $250, it is necessary to determine whether, in doing so, Pattison was giving up anything of value. Generally, it is understood that even if there is doubt about whether a claim would be successful, a promise not to assert it is a thing of value (i.e., consideration) if the person making that promise believed in good faith that her claim was a good one. This is true whether or not the person promising to pay believed that the claim was a good one, since she might be willing to pay just to save the expense of litigation. Thus, if Pattison believed in good faith that Stuart was liable to her, her promise not to sue him was consideration for Milburn's promise to pay $250, whether or not Milburn believed that Stuart would be liable.

B and C are, therefore, incorrect. On the other hand, if Pattison did not believe that Stuart was liable to her, her promise not to sue him was not something of value (i.e., consideration) and Milburn's promise to pay would be unenforceable. **D** is, therefore, incorrect.

179.　**B**　Milburn's promise to pay $1,000 is enforceable only if it is supported by consideration. Consideration is something of value — either benefit to promisor or detriment to promisee — given in exchange for the promise. A promise to do something which the promisor has no legal right to do cannot be regarded as consideration because it has no value. Unless a privilege exists, no person has the right to refuse to testify in a criminal prosecution. Certainly, no person may do so in return for payment. Thus Pattison's promise not to testify was a promise to do something which she had no right to do. For this reason, it would not have been consideration for Milburn's promise to pay $1,000.

A is incorrect because although Milburn was not legally obligated to pay for damage caused by her adult son, she may have made an enforceable promise to do so. An accord is an agreement to substitute a new obligation for one which already existed. Satisfaction occurs when the accord is completely performed. Since Stuart may have had a duty to pay all of Pattison's medical expenses resulting from his act, and since Pattison agreed to accept $250 instead, there may have been an accord which was satisfied when Milburn paid as promised. But this accord existed only with respect to the obligation to pay medical expenses. Since the obligation to pay for pain and suffering is a separate obligation, it is not extinguished by satisfaction of the accord regarding medical expenses. **C** is, therefore, incorrect. A promise to pay the debt of another is unenforceable unless it is written. But a promise to pay in return for the promisee's forbearance to sue (even a third person) is not a promise to pay the debt of another but rather a personal obligation of the promisor. As such, it need not be in writing. **D** is, therefore, incorrect.

180.　**C**　The Fifth Amendment to the U.S. Constitution provides in part that "No person ... shall be compelled in any criminal case to be a witness against himself." The privilege only prohibits the government from requiring a testimonial communication, however. It does not protect a person against being required to participate in identification procedures which might lead to his conviction. For this reason, the Fifth Amendment privilege does not protect the defendant against being required to walk across the courtroom.

A defendant who testifies in his own behalf thereby waives the privilege and may even be required to utter testimonial communications which might tend to incriminate him. Since the Fifth Amendment privilege does not include non-testimonial communications, however, the question of waiver is irrelevant. **A** is, therefore, incorrect. A prosecutor may not comment on a defendant's assertion of the Fifth Amendment privilege; the jury may not draw inferences from it. **B** is incorrect, however, because the Fifth Amendment does not privilege the defendant to refuse to walk across the courtroom. Since no penalty can be imposed for the assertion of a constitutional right, and since a criminal defendant has a constitutional right to be present at his own trial, the defendant's presence in the courtroom cannot be a waiver of any other right. **D** is, therefore, incorrect.

181.　**A**　The United States Supreme Court has held that because manipulation of circumstances surrounding a lineup could create considerable likelihood of inaccuracy, and because it would be difficult at trial to fully develop evidence regarding such manipulation, the Sixth Amendment requires the presence of counsel at a post-indictment lineup. For this reason, Dahms' objection would probably be sustained for the reason given in **A**.

The constitutional right to confront witnesses requires that a defendant be given an opportunity to cross-examine such witnesses at a trial. It does not require, however, that the defendant be given an opportunity to question those witnesses at any other stage of the proceeding (i.e., at a lineup). **B** is, therefore incorrect. The Fifth Amendment protection against self-incrimination applies only to testimonial communication. For this reason, it does not prohibit compelling a defendant to show herself to witnesses for identification purposes. **C** is, therefore, incorrect. Since a defendant has no constitutional right to refuse to appear in a lineup, police may compel or coerce her to do so by the use or threat of reasonable force. **D** is, therefore, incorrect.

182. **C**   The Fifth Amendment right against self-incrimination protects a defendant against being coerced into answering questions asked by the police. Because police interrogation of a person in custody is inherently coercive, a person in custody is entitled to "Miranda" warnings like those given Dahms when she was first taken into custody. If, after receiving such warnings, the person in custody asserts her right to have an attorney present during questioning, all interrogation must stop and may not be continued without the presence of an attorney or a subsequent valid waiver. Because any further interrogation is regarded as coercive, a confession obtained in its course is not admissible in evidence. Although these rights were once held to apply only to a person who was a suspect, it is now clear that they apply to any person in custody.

A is, therefore, incorrect. **B** is incorrect because upon receiving the warnings. Dahms asserted her right to have an attorney present during questioning. Although the police are required to advise a defendant of her rights when she is in custody, they are not required to advise her of their suspicions or of their reasons for asking a particular question. **D** is, therefore, incorrect.

183. **C**   The invasion of privacy known as false light is committed by publishing false statements about the plaintiff which would tend to hold the plaintiff up to embarrassment. Since the use of and sale of unlawful drugs is generally frowned upon, and since the photograph which appears in *The Daily Tribune* suggested that Pacifica was involved in an unlawful drug deal, it probably invaded her privacy by casting her in a false light.

Appropriation of identity is committed by making unauthorized use of plaintiff's likeness for a commercial purpose. The United States Supreme Court has held, however, that liability may not be imposed for this tort if the use of the plaintiff's likeness was newsworthy. Since the photograph which appeared in *The Daily Tribune* was used to illustrate an article about drug dealing, it was newsworthy and not an appropriation of her identity. **A** is, therefore, incorrect. Intrusion (i.e., invasion of solitude) is committed when the defendant enters the plaintiff's private space in a way which would offend the reasonable person in the plaintiff's position. Since Pacifica was in the school yard, a relatively public place, when the photograph was taken, and since there is no indication that Roman came unnecessarily close to her in taking it, intrusion was probably not committed by the taking of her photograph. **B** is, therefore, incorrect. Public disclosure is committed by bringing private facts about the plaintiff to the attention of the public, when such disclosure would offend the reasonable person in the plaintiff's position. Since Pacifica's identity was not a private fact, public disclosure was not committed by publishing a photograph which identified her. **D** is, therefore, incorrect.

184. **B**   Under the Rule Against Perpetuities, no interest is good unless it must vest *if at all* within a period measured by a life or lives in being plus twenty-one years. Thus, a future interest which might never vest at all is valid under the rule so long as the language which created it will prevent it from vesting after the prescribed period (i.e., *if* it vests, it will do so during the prescribed period). Since God's Church might never cease using the land for church purposes, and since, even if it did, Mercy Hospital might never cease using the land for hospital purposes, it is possible that Ulysses's interest as created by Olar's deed will never vest at all. The language of Olar's deed provides, however, that in no event is the interest of Ulysses to vest unless Ulysses is alive when the conditions precedent are satisfied. Thus, since the interest of Ulysses must vest if at all during a period measured by a life in being (i.e., Ulysses's life), it does not violate the Rule Against Perpetuities.

Many jurisdictions recognize an exception to the Rule Against Perpetuities for the interest of a charitable organization which follows the interest of another charitable organization. Ulysses is not a charitable organization, however, so this exception would not prevent the Rule Against Perpetuities from applying to Ulysses's interest. **A** is, therefore, incorrect. **C** is incorrect because the Rule Against Perpetuities does not require that the interest in question will vest during the prescribed period, but that if it vests at all, it will be during that period. In a jurisdiction which does not recognize an exception for the interest of a charity which follows the interest of another charity, Mercy Hospital's interest would be void under the Rule Against Perpetuities. This is because the condition which would make its interest vest (i.e., cessation of use for church purposes) might occur after the period established by the rule. Since Olar's deed provides that the interest of Ulysses cannot vest unless it does so during the life of Ulysses, however, the interest of Ulysses would not violate the rule even if the interest of Mercy Hospital did. **D** is, therefore, incorrect.

185. **C**   The grant of an interest in realty "for so long as" a certain condition continues to exist or "until" a certain condition shall exist is traditionally held to create a fee simple determinable on special limitation. One of the characteristics of this particular interest is that it terminates automatically upon the happening of the specified event or condition. Since the conveyance to God's Church was "for as long as" the land is used for church purposes, it was a fee simple determinable on special limitation, and terminated automatically when God's Church conveyed the land. According to the language of the deed, the interest of Mercy Hospital was to become possessory at that time. Although the condition precedent might not have occurred within the period prescribed by the Rule Against Perpetuities, Mercy Hospital's interest is valid because in most jurisdictions the rule does not apply to the future interest of a charity which follows the interest of another charity. **C** is correct for this reason, and because it is the only option which could possibly be correct in any jurisdiction.

The estate system, and in particular the law of future interests, was developed so that a grantor could exercise some control over the subsequent use of the land conveyed. For that reason, restrictive language such as that contained in Olar's deed is understood to relate to the way the conveyed land itself is used. Although the sale by God's Church might serve to enable God's Church to continue operation elsewhere, it violates the special limitation contained in Olar's deed since it results in a cessation of the use of the land itself for the purpose stated in that limitation. For this reason, **A** is incorrect. **B** is incorrect for two reasons. First, as explained above, an exception prevents the interest of Mercy Hospital from being void under the Rule Against Perpetuities. Second, the Rule Against Perpetuities prevents the vesting of certain interests, but does not prevent the divesting of any interest. Thus, even if the interest of Mercy Hospital was void under the rule, the violation of the special limitation contained in Olar's grant would terminate the interest of God's Church no matter when it occurred. The language of Olar's grant limited the use for which the realty conveyed could be put. Restrictions of this kind are enforceable, even though they *indirectly* restrain alienation. The effect of the language used by Olar is to divest God's Church of its interest when God's Church ceases to use the land for church purposes. Since the sale would have that effect, God's Church is divested of its interest, and **D** is incorrect. (**Note:** Sometimes the language of a conveyance attempts to *directly* restrain subsequent alienation of the interest conveyed by prohibiting such alienation. Most of the time, courts hold that direct restraints on alienation are invalid. If a restraint on alienation is held to be valid, it might make the person who violated it liable for damages, but it does not void the alienation. Thus, even if the conveyance created a direct restraint on alienation, it would not make the subsequent conveyance by God's Church invalid.)

186. **D**   Although the Due Process Clause of the Fifth Amendment (applied to state action by the Fourteenth Amendment) prohibits the arbitrary regulation of economic interests, it is almost never used to justify the conclusion that an economic regulation is unconstitutional. In general, so long as such a regulation employs a means reasonably related to accomplishing a purpose within the scope of a state's general police power and does not amount to a "taking," it will be regarded as valid under the Due Process Clause. Since regulating the storage of radioactive wastes is reasonably related to the legitimate police power objective of protecting the public good, and since there is no indication that Section 40 drastically interferes with the operation of out-of-state power plants, the section does not violate the Due Process Clauses. Although it is not certain that Section 40 would be declared unconstitutional, due process is the only argument listed which could not possibly result in such a declaration.

The Privileges and Immunities Clause of Article IV prohibits a state from arbitrarily discriminating against out-of-staters. Since Section 40 effectively denies the use of Aritoma storage facilities to out-of-staters, it might violate this clause. **A** is, therefore, incorrect. The Privileges and Immunities Clause of the Fourteenth Amendment prohibits a state from interfering with any of the rights which go with United States citizenship. One of these is the right to travel freely from state to state. Since the section effectively prevents the importation of radioactive wastes from outside the state, it may be unconstitutional because it interferes with this freedom. For this reason, **B** is incorrect. The Equal Protection Clause prohibits invidious discrimination by a state. Since Section 40 effectively disqualifies out-of-state producers of radioactive waste from using facilities available to in-state producers it discriminates against them. If that discrimination is invidious, the section is unconstitutional. **C** is, therefore, incorrect.

187. **B**   Although the Commerce Clause gives Congress the power to regulate interstate com-

merce, some regulation by the states is permitted so long as the effect is not to discriminate against or impose an undue burden on interstate commerce. Even state regulations which do discriminate against interstate commerce or impose a burden on it may be constitutional, if they are aimed at a legitimate health or safety objective which cannot be achieved by less drastic means. It is possible that the additional fact set forth in **B** would result in a finding that Section 40 is valid because it protects the health and safety of the people of Aritoma in the least drastic way possible. It is far from certain that a court would come to this conclusion, but **B** is the only one of all the additional facts listed which could possibly result in a finding of constitutionality.

One of the purposes of the Commerce Clause is to ban artificial barriers to interstate competition. Since the fact in **A** would make creation of a business advantage for in-state nuclear power plants a purpose of the section, it would show that the statute is designed to create exactly the kind of artificial barrier which the Commerce Clause was designed to prevent. **A** is, therefore, incorrect. The shortage of storage facilities within the state underscores the competition for the use of such facilities. Thus, **C** would not justify finding Section 40 to be constitutional, since its terms effectively eliminate out-of-staters from that competition. Even if there are many safe storage locations outside the state, there may be sound business reasons why out-of-staters prefer to use Aritoma locations. The discrimination resulting from the provisions of Section 40 would, thus, not be justified by the existence of out-of-state locations. **D** is, therefore, incorrect.

188. **B**   UCC § 2-207 provides that, between merchants, unless the language of an offer expressly limits acceptance to the terms of that offer, additional terms contained in an expression of acceptance are to be construed as proposals for additions to the contract. The section further provides that unless those additional terms materially alter the contract they are to be deemed accepted if not objected to within a reasonable time. Since Barnett did not respond (i.e., object) to the additional term contained in Sandifer's letter, he is deemed to have accepted it unless it materially alters the terms of Barnett's offer. While it is not certain whether Sandifer's letter materially altered the terms of Barnett's offer, **B** is the only argument listed which could support Sandifer's position.

A is incorrect because UCC 2-207 provides that an expression of acceptance operates as an acceptance even though it contains terms different from those of the offer. **C** is incorrect because the UCC provides that a buyer who rightfully rejects non-conforming goods is entitled to damages for non-delivery. **D** is incorrect for two reasons: first, as explained above, Sandifer's letter of August 5 was probably an acceptance of Barnett's offer; and, second, the UCC provides that an offer calling for the offeree's shipment of goods is accepted by shipping conforming or non-conforming goods.

189. **D**   In general, all evidence is admissible if it is relevant to a fact of consequence in the litigation. The fact that there were stolen license plates on Dandy's van tends to establish that he was attempting to avoid recognition, and therefore that he was planning to commit some crime. Since the burglary statute requires an intent to commit a crime inside the entered premises, Dandy's plan is relevant to a fact of consequence. For this reason, evidence of the stolen license plates may be admissible in the burglary prosecution.

A is, therefore, incorrect. It is generally understood that evidence of unconvicted bad acts by a defendant is inadmissible for the purpose of establishing that he had a criminal disposition. Where such evidence is offered not merely to prove that defendant had a criminal disposition, however, but to establish an inference that he committed the act charged, it may be admissible. Here, evidence that Dandy made special preparations for a crime justifies the inference that he entered the warehouse to commit a crime therein. **B** is, therefore, incorrect. **C** is incorrect because evidence of unconvicted acts is inadmissible for the purpose of establishing a criminal disposition.

190. **B**   It is generally understood that evidence of a person's bad character is inadmissible for the purpose of proving that he acted in a particular way on a particular occasion. Since evidence of a criminal conviction is evidence of character, it is usually excluded by this rule. Under FRE 609, a judgment of conviction may be admitted for the purpose of impeaching the credibility of a witness, however, because it tends to establish that the person convicted is untrustworthy. If Dandy did not testify, there is no reason to impeach his credibility, and evidence of his prior conviction would be inadmissible.

On the other hand, if he did testify, evidence of his conviction would be admissible under the FRE. **A** is, therefore, incorrect. Under FRE 609 evidence of a conviction for a felony in any state or nation is admissible to impeach a witness without regard to the nature of the felony. Since involuntary manslaughter is a felony, **C** is incorrect. Since the FRE makes a conviction from any state or nation admissible, **D** is incorrect.

191. **A**   Generally, in the absence of an agreement by the promisee to release the promisor from his obligations under a contract, the promisor continues to be bound by his promise even after assigning his rights. Thus, any rights that Elberta had against Pitts under the contract of sale survived the assignment by Pitts to Aquino. Even in the absence of a specific provision requiring it, a contract for the sale of real property is understood to impose upon the seller an obligation to deliver marketable title. But the seller satisfies this obligation if his title is marketable at the time set for performance (i.e., the closing). Since Elberta acquired title to Fuzzacre prior to the closing, he is entitled to enforce the contract of sale against Pitts.

The doctrine of estoppel by deed provides that when a seller acquires title to realty which he has already purported to grant to another person, he acquires it on behalf of that grantee, and is estopped from denying the validity of his previous conveyance. It is inapplicable to this case because Elberta obtained title to Fuzzacre before attempting to convey it to Pitts. **B** is, therefore, incorrect. **C** is incorrect because the contract did not require Elberta to deliver marketable title until July 15, and on that date he did hold marketable title. An interest is said to be outside the chain of title if it could not have been discovered by a reasonable title searcher. Sometimes this occurs when a person claims to have received an interest from a grantor after a transfer of that same interest by the same grantor had previously been recorded. (e.g., O transfers to A. O then transfers to B. B records before A. A's interest may be outside the chain of title, because a reasonable title searcher finding O's transfer to B in the record would not look for any subsequent transfers of the same interest by O.) **D** is incorrect, however, for two reasons: first, this argument is normally relevant only in determining the priority of two different interests; and, second, there is no indication that Fuzz had previously conveyed Fuzzacre to another person or that such a conveyance had been recorded before Fuzz's conveyance to Elberta.

192. **A**   An anticipatory repudiation occurs when one party to a contract unequivocally informs the other party that she will not perform. Upon anticipatory repudiation, the non-repudiating party is excused from any further performance under the contract. Thus, if Ashe's statement that she did not believe it possible to complete the work for less than $90,000 was an unequivocal statement that she would not perform, it freed Osman of any further obligation. Although considerable question exists as to whether Ashe's statement should be so construed, the theory set forth in **A** is the only one listed which could possibly provide Osman with an effective defense.

     Under the doctrine of frustration of purpose, performance is excused if an unforeseen event destroys the underlying reason for performing the contract. **B** is incorrect because whatever reason Osman had for building a house on the realty continued to exist. Novation occurs when a promisee agrees to substitute the performance of a third person for that of the promisor. (In this case, for example, a novation might have taken place if Ashe agreed to build a house for Smith, with the understanding that Osman's obligations to her had been replaced by Smith's.) **C** is incorrect because no obligation was ever substituted for that of Osman. A prospective inability to perform occurs when, by her own action, a contracting party divests herself of the ability to perform as required. Since there is no fact indicating that Ashe had become unable to perform as agreed, **D** is incorrect.

193. **B**   The standard measure of damages for a builder's breach of a construction contract is the difference between the contract price and the owner's actual cost of completing the building *as agreed*. Since the contract price was $60,000, and Osman actually paid Bach $90,000, damages would — at first glance — appear to be $30,000. The agreement between Osman and Ashe called for completion by December 1, however. Since it would have cost Osman only $75,000 to have Bach complete the construction by that date, Osman's damages should be based on the difference between $60,000 (the price he had agreed to pay Ashe) and $75,000 (the price he would have had to pay Bach to complete the building by December 1).

     A and **C** are incorrect because the standard measures of damages is the difference between the contract price and the cost of completion. **D** is incorrect because the cost of completion *as agreed* would only have been $75,000.

194. **B**   The United States Supreme Court has noted that in general the Fourth Amendment requires that a warrant be obtained before a search may be carried out. Although there are exceptional circumstances under which a warrantless search may be valid, none applies here for reasons indicated below.

     A is incorrect because if the watch had been validly obtained during the course of an inventory search, it could be used in any prosecution to which it was relevant. Upon making a valid arrest, police may make a warrantless search incidental to that arrest. This incidental search is for the purpose of discovering weapons with which the prisoner might attack the officers and evidence which the prisoner might otherwise succeed in destroying or hiding. Thus, while an incidental search may extend to the defendant's person and anything within his immediate control including, perhaps, his glove compartment, the right to make such a search terminates when the need for it ends. Since Daniels had been removed from his car and was being transported in a separate vehicle, there was no longer any urgent need for an incidental search to discover weapons or evidence in his car, **C** is, therefore, incorrect. If a defendant's property is to remain in police custody for safekeeping, the police are entitled to inventory its contents to protect the defendant from theft and to protect the police from false claims. If an inventory search is valid, evidence incidentally discovered during its course may be used against the defendant. The watch was not evidence discovered during the course of Hammet's inventory search, however, because at the time, Hammet did not know that it was evidence. When Hammet returned with Infeld, they were not there to make an inventory but to search for evidence connecting Daniels with the jewel robbery. For such a search, a warrant was required. **D** is, therefore, incorrect.

195.   **A**   The law of torts recognizes only three potential bases of liability — intent, negligence, and strict liability. Since Dento did not desire or know (i.e., intend) that her conduct would result in harm to Paget, she could not be liable on an intent theory. Since the use of anesthetic by a professional has not been held to be an ultra-hazardous or abnormally-dangerous activity (i.e., the kind of activity for which strict liability is applied), and since Dento did not sell the defective apparatus to Paget, Dento could not be liable on a strict liability theory. The only remaining theory is negligence. Since negligence is unreasonable conduct, Dento can be liable only if she acted unreasonably in treating Paget.

Where there is no evidence as to what a defendant did, the doctrine of *res ipsa loquitur* might allow an inference that her conduct was unreasonable to be drawn from the circumstances. This doctrine applies when the accident is one which would not ordinarily have occurred without negligence, and when the defendant was in exclusive control of the circumstances surrounding the plaintiff's injury. **B** is incorrect for two reasons: first, since Dento's conduct is known, circumstantial evidence is unnecessary and *res ipsa loquitur* is inapplicable; and, second, the fact that the canisters had been filled by MFR prevented Dento from being in exclusive control. Since any harm may have several proximate causes, the fact that Paget's death resulted from the negligence of MFR does not establish that it did not also result from the negligence of Dento. For this reason, **C** is incorrect. A professional seller of products who sells a defective product may be strictly liable for harm which results from the product's defect. **D** is incorrect, however, because Dento was not a professional seller of anesthetic apparatuses and did not sell the apparatus to Paget.

196.   **B**   A plaintiff who experiences mental suffering as a result of witnessing the infliction of a physical injury on another may recover from a person who negligently inflicted that physical injury. Although the majority of jurisdictions permit such recovery only when the plaintiff is in the same zone of physical danger as the person who sustained physical injury, an important minority permits the plaintiff to recover if her mental suffering was a foreseeable result of the physical injury which she witnessed. In this minority of jurisdictions, Dento might recover from MFR for her mental suffering at witnessing Paget's death if it was likely (i.e., foreseeable) that MFR's negligence in causing Paget's death would lead to Dento's mental suffering. Because this is a minority rule, there is no guarantee that it would lead to a judgment for Dento. Of those listed, however, **B** is the only argument which could possibly be effective in support of Dento's claim.

A defendant who engages in outrageous conduct with the intent to cause the plaintiff to experience mental suffering may be liable for mental suffering which the plaintiff experiences as a result. **A** is incorrect, however, for two reasons: first outrageous conduct is conduct which exceeds bounds normally tolerated by decent society, not conduct which creates a high probability of harm; and, second, there is no fact indicating that MFR intended to cause Dento to experience mental suffering. When a plaintiff voluntarily encounters a risk of which she knows, she assumes that risk. Since Dento did not know that the oxygen tank contained anesthetic gas, she could not have assumed the risk resulting from that fact. **C** is incorrect for this reason, and because assumption of the risk would prevent Dento from recovering. A defendant who intends mental suffering to result from its outrageous conduct may be liable for the intentional infliction of mental harm. In this regard a substantial certainty that the suffering will occur is equivalent to an intent to bring it about. **D** is incorrect, however, because even if MFR was certain that the apparatus would be used on a patient, it did not intend Dento's suffering unless it was certain that the patient would die and that Dento would suffer as a result.

197. **D**   A person is guilty of a criminal attempt when, with the specific intent to bring about a criminally prohibited result, he does some significant act which brings him substantially close to accomplishing that result. Thus, although a person may be guilty of murder without actually intending to bring about a death, he cannot be guilty of attempted murder without the intent to bring about a death. Since Pharma did not really believe that Wanda would die, he could not have intended to bring about her death, and cannot be guilty of attempting to murder her.

Murder is the unlawful killing of a human being with malice aforethought. Malice aforethought includes a reckless disregard for human life. If Pharma's conduct showed a reckless disregard for human life, and if it resulted in the death of Wanda, then Pharma would be guilty of murder. **A** is incorrect, however, because no person can be guilty of attempted murder without the specific intent to bring about a death or to cause great bodily harm. **B** is incorrect for the same reason, and because ordinarily a person is under no duty to stop another from committing a crime. Since Pharma did not believe the drug which he furnished would harm Wanda, he lacked the specific intent necessary to make him guilty of attempting to kill her. **C** is, therefore, incorrect.

198. **B**   A conspiracy occurs when two or more persons with the specific intent to commit a crime agree to commit it. Since Pharma did not believe that Wanda would be hurt by the drug which he furnished, he did not have the requisite specific intent, and did not really agree to commit murder. For this reason, there was never an actual agreement between him and Hermes, and, therefore, no conspiracy.

Conspiracy, if it exists, is separate from the substantive crime, and is complete when the unlawful agreement is made. For this reason, a defendant may be guilty of conspiring to commit a particular crime even though he never succeeded and was not likely to succeed in committing it. **A** and **C** are, therefore, incorrect. **D** is incorrect because it is an inaccurate statement of law: the inchoate crime of conspiracy never merges with the substantive crime; a defendant can be convicted of both.

199. **A**   Under FRE 803(8) the file itself may be admissible as an official written statement, since it was made at or near the time of the matter recorded by a public official regarding matters in the declarant's personal knowledge in the course of the declarant's duties.

(**Note**: The file may also be admissible as a business record — see next explanation.) Even if the personnel file's contents are admissible, however, Waldron's testimony about its contents might not be. Under the common law and FRE 1002, the best evidence rule prohibits secondary evidence to prove the terms of a writing unless the writing itself is shown to be unavailable. Since the purpose of Waldron's testimony is to prove the contents of the file, he will not be permitted to do so unless the file is shown to be unavailable.

If the requirements of the best evidence rule are satisfied. Waldron's testimony would be as admissible as the file itself. Since the FRE makes business records and official written statements admissible without regard to the availability of the person who made entries in them, **B** and **C** are incorrect. **D** is incorrect because the official written statement exception, although it is sometimes called the "public document" exception, does not require that the record be one which is available for public inspection.

200.   **A**   Under FRE 803(6) a properly authenticated writing may be admitted under the business record exception to the hearsay rule if it was made in the regular course of business while fresh in the declarant's mind about facts which the declarant knew or learned from an inherently reliable source. Since Waldron's testimony satisfied all these requirements, the personnel file should be admitted as a business record. (**Note**: Do not be confused about a controversy which exists over whether police records *describing an accident* are kept in the "regular course of business." Police department personnel records clearly are.)

B is incorrect because to be admissible as "past recollection recorded" a writing must have been made by the witness himself, and because under FRE 803(5) and the common law the writing may be read aloud but not physically admitted into evidence. **C** is incorrect because business records and official written statements may be used by any party. Although negative evidence presents some special problems, FRE 803(7) specifically permits the absence of a business record to be admissible as evidence that an unrecorded transaction did not occur.